THE
INTERNATIONAL ENCYCLOPEDIA
OF
EDUCATION

THE
INTERNATIONAL ENCYCLOPEDIA
OF
EDUCATION
Research and Studies

Volume 3
D–E

Editors-in-Chief

TORSTEN HUSEN
University of Stockholm, Sweden

T. NEVILLE POSTLETHWAITE
University of Hamburg, FRG

PERGAMON PRESS

OXFORD · NEW YORK · TORONTO · SYDNEY · PARIS · FRANKFURT

U.K.	Pergamon Press Ltd., Headington Hill Hall, Oxford OX3 0BW, England
U.S.A.	Pergamon Press Inc., Maxwell House, Fairview Park, Elmsford, New York 10523, U.S.A.
CANADA	Pergamon Press Canada Ltd., Suite 104, 150 Consumers Rd., Willowdale, Ontario M2J 1P9, Canada
AUSTRALIA	Pergamon Press (Aust.) Pty. Ltd., P.O. Box 544, Potts Point, N.S.W. 2011, Australia
FRANCE	Pergamon Press SARL, 24 rue des Ecoles, 75240 Paris, Cedex 05, France
FEDERAL REPUBLIC OF GERMANY	Pergamon Press GmbH, Hammerweg 6, D-6242 Kronberg-Taunus, Federal Republic of Germany

First edition 1985

Library of Congress Cataloging in Publication Data
Main entry under title:
The International encyclopedia of education

    Includes bibliographies.
    Index: v. 10.
      1. Education—Dictionaries. 2. Education—Research—Dictionaries. I. Husén, Torsten, 1916–
II. Postlethwaite, T. Neville.
LB15.I569   1985   370'.3'21   84–20750

British Library Cataloguing in Publication Data
The International encyclopedia of education

    1. Education—Dictionaries

    I. Husén, Torsten   II. Postlethwaite, T. Neville
370'.3'21   LB15

ISBN 0–08–028119–2

Computer data file designed and computer typeset by Page Bros (Norwich) Ltd.
Printed in Great Britain by A. Wheaton & Co. Ltd., Exeter

CONTENTS

HONORARY EDITORIAL ADVISORY BOARD

EDITORIAL BOARD

D

Daily Living Skills

Daily living skills—sometimes called "survival skills" or "life skills"—include those competencies which are commonly used in day-to-day life. They are the capabilities which are necessary for functioning both at home and in society.

There are two worldwide educational trends which emphasize daily living skills. In countries where large portions of the population have had little or no formal education, educational programs are being expanded to provide more students with more instruction in the skills necessary for daily living. In countries where nearly everyone receives several years of schooling, educational programs are being changed by eliminating extraneous or very theoretical items from the compulsory curricula, to make room for a core of more practical or "relevant" competencies in a large number of subject areas.

There has been a tendency among curriculum planners in many countries (particularly since the emergence of competency-based education) to differentiate among three categories of core competencies: basic skills (providing a foundation for further education) (see *Basic Skills*), life skills, and job-preparation skills. There is, of course, a tremendous overlap between these categories, and most experts agree that numeracy and literacy are at the cognitive core of each.

1. Literacy

Literacy generally includes not only reading and writing, but also facility with the related language skills of speaking and listening. Even experts within individual countries disagree significantly about how developed these skills must be in order to achieve "minimal" competence. Nevertheless, they do recognize that literacy, at some level, is a prerequisite for normal, daily living in virtually every society. Furthermore, reading, writing, speaking, and listening skills are fundamental learning tools and are therefore essential for further education and continued intellectual growth beyond "minimal" or "survival" levels.

It is worth mentioning here that literacy has not always been recognized as a necessary skill for daily living. At the end of the eighteenth century, "literacy" was frequently judged by the capacity of a person to form the letters of their name. Furthermore, even that minimal level of competence was mastered by less than half of the population in the developed nations of Europe (Resnick and Resnick

1977). It is quite apparent that, over the last 200 years, there has been a substantial increase in societal expectations concerning literacy and a substantial increase in actual skill levels (by whatever definition of literacy used).

There seems to be general agreement that complex technological and/or bureaucratic societies demand higher levels of literacy. However, even in the rural areas of Asia, Africa, and Latin America, there is evidence of a growing determination to increase the level of literacy. The five-year readership promotion campaign in Malaysia (launched in 1980) and the earlier Brazilian literacy movement (MOBRAL) are just two examples of a worldwide trend.

2. Computer Literacy

An emerging "convenience" in a few highly technological societies, computer literacy may well become a necessity of survival in the not-so-distant future. Already, in the Federal Republic of Germany, for example, the Federal States, the *Gesellschaft fuer Informatik*, and various committees of the Ministry of Science have demanded that the basics of computers and informatics be taught in the schools. Similar suggestions can be heard from Scotland's Munn Committee (1977) and in the new curriculum (Lgr 80) implemented in Sweden in 1982.

In several countries computer literacy is regarded as a "daily living skill" for tomorrow's adults. It is therefore appropriately being identified as an area for emphasis in today's schools.

3. Mathematics

Curricular change in mathematics has been markedly tumultuous during the 1970s and early 1980s. There has been an almost worldwide shift in emphasis from the highly theoretical to the more practical—away from "new math" (see *New Mathematics*), and "back to basics" (see *Back to Basics Movement*). In other words, there has been an increasing educational focus on daily living skills, job-preparation skills, and basic skills needed for further education.

In the Federal Republic of Germany, a single term—*mathematische Allgemeinbildung*—is used to include all three of the above skill categories, and it is being given increased emphasis in the curriculum. In Sweden, Kenya, and South Australia, new mathematics curricula (implemented in the early 1980s) quite explicitly lay special stress on daily living skills. Each of these programs includes extensive testing to monitor the mastery of individual skills.

Numerous studies are being made to identify precise lists of necessary mathematical competencies. One of the most convenient sources of input is potential employers. In England, for example, the Shell Centre for Mathematical Education has been doing extensive research on the mathematical needs of school leavers entering employment. The Education for the Industrial Society Project has been performing similar investigations in Scotland, as has the University of Klagenfurt in Austria.

In some school systems, a focus on survival or daily living skills has been seen as a rationale for trimming down the curriculum and, concurrently, trimming down the budget. However, while serious inquiries are identifying some mathematical skills which do not have to be taught, they are identifying many more topics which are not being emphasized and should be. A 1979 survey by the Science Education Center of the University of the Philippines, and a slightly earlier study in the Federal Republic of Germany, are just two examples which support the growing realization that "trimming back" curricula to include basic, necessary, or relevant skills will result, in most societies, in an increase in the amount of mathematics instruction.

4. Multiple Subject Areas

While numeracy and literacy are widely thought of as the academic core of daily living skills, they are not generally considered the only skills necessary for survival in day-to-day life. Unfortunately, it would be quite impossible to construct a universally acceptable list of such skills. The individual items would vary significantly from country to country (depending on the level of technological development, the political system, cultural traditions, and even the climate). Nevertheless, in specific geographical areas, efforts have been made to identify (and implement in the school curriculum) a broad range of competencies used in daily living.

In British Columbia (Canada), for example, the Ministry of Education has introduced a core curriculum identifying the competencies which are generally accepted there as essential—competencies which should be mastered by all students throughout the province. This core curriculum focuses on basic skills in the areas of language, measurement and computation, scientific approach, cultural and physical heritage, analysis research, study and problem solving, and healthful living (Ministry of Education 1977).

The Maryland (USA) State Board of Education has outlined five areas in which students should develop at least minimum competencies (necessary for graduation after 1982): basic skills (numeracy and literacy), survival skills (consumer, parenting, interpersonal, mechanical, and financial), work skills, leisure skills, and citizenship skills (see *Basic Skills*; *Leisure-time Education*; *Civic Education*).

The important characteristic of the new curricula in both British Columbia and Maryland is the emphasis placed on learning skills which are needed for living, for working, and for learning. Similar movements toward educational relevance in multiple subject areas can be found at various stages of consideration or implementation throughout the world. In Scotland, the Munn Report (1977) provides one instance of curriculum change at the consideration stage. In Australia, the Northern Territory Department of Education reached the implementation stage in seven subject areas in 1981.

The relevance of education to daily living experiences has become a fundamental concern throughout the world. There is a clear understanding that, while in school, individuals must be given more knowledge and must develop more skills than they would have needed to survive a generation ago. Educational planning, then, has focused on providing the opportunities for more learning to more students, and on assuring that programs include the minimal competencies for daily living.

Bibliography

Avakov R M 1980 *The Future of Education and the Education of the Future*. UNESCO, Paris [also published in French]

Behrstock J 1981 Reaching the rural reader. *J. Read.* 24: 712–18

British Columbia Ministry of Education 1977 *Guide to the Core Curriculum*. Ministry of Education, Richmond, British Columbia

Resnick D P, Resnick L B 1977 The nature of literacy: An historical exploration. *Harvard Educ. Rev.* 47: 370–85

Riehs R J 1981 *An International Review of Minimal Competency Programs in Mathematics*. SMEAC Information Reference Center, Ohio State University, Columbus, Ohio

Scottish Education Department 1977 *The Structure of the Curriculum in the Third and Fourth Year of the Scottish Secondary School*. (Munn Report). Her Majesty's Stationery Office, Edinburgh

R. J. Riehs

Dalton Plan

The system of dividing the subjects of the curriculum into two parts and providing highly individualized contracts of work to students for the academic subjects, and class groups for the vocational, social, and physical activities developed by Helen Parkhurst was known as the "Dalton Plan". It was very popular and widely imitated throughout the United States, the Soviet Union, England and Wales, other English-speaking countries, and Europe from the early 1920s. Academic subjects were organized sequentially and students worked individually. The vocational subjects were grouped and students worked in classes in a nongraded way. The freedom allowed to individual children and the organization of teaching were said to increase the efficiency of schools when compared to the traditional forms of school organization and instruction, and to introduce into schools "community principles and practices". The Dalton plan offered procedures for organizing learning when changes were being contemplated, and appealed to the educational progressives' concern for freedom, individual expression, and social cooperation as an alternative to the formalism of the class lesson.

Helen Parkhurst developed the Dalton plan, known also as the "Dalton Laboratory Plan", to meet the criticisms of contemporary education and to provide a favourable environment in which children could prepare for life, freedom, and responsibility as "industrious, sincere, open-minded, and independent" individuals (Parkhurst 1923 p. 5). Learning had to be combined with experience to test character, to form judgment, and to develop self-discipline in social experience. She drew on her experience teaching in a rural school with 40 pupils over eight grades and in high school, primary school, normal training schools, and a training college. Her reading in 1908 of E. J. Swift's *Mind in the Making: A Study in Mental Development* (Scribners', New York) introduced the idea of an "educational laboratory" where student activity replaced the didactic method. A plan of work for children between 8 and 12 years of age which was finalized in 1913 "aimed at the entire reorganization of school life" (Parkhurst 1923 p. 11). Further work eliminated the restriction of the timetable through organizing pupils into groups with a free choice of the studies in laboratories with specialist instructors. Additional experience included working with Dr Maria Montessori in Italy and introducing the Montessori Method to California in 1915 (see *Montessori Method*), undertaking a practical test of the laboratory plan through the help of Dr F. Burk, and more work on the laboratory plan in 1918 with the support of Dr M. V. O'Shea of Wisconsin University. In 1919 the laboratory plan was applied in the ungraded Berkshire Cripple School for boys, and, after attracting much interest, it was introduced on a larger scale in 1920 at the Dalton High School, Massachusetts. One early visitor to the school was Belle Rennie, an English pioneer of educational change, whose account of the Dalton laboratory plan in the *Times Educational Supplement* in May 1920 led to Helen Parkhurst visiting England in July 1921. Her ideas were received enthusiastically.

The Dalton plan called for the reorganization of the school so that it functioned as a community where the individual was free to develop in culture and experience and prepare for life. The school both provided freedom for the students to work without interruption and at their own pace, and required cooperation in the social experience of the school community. Character and knowledge were determined by the experience of living and working as a member of society rather than upon the subjects of the curriculum. The Dalton plan was not advanced as a panacea for academic ailments. Rather it provided "a way through which the teacher can get at the problem of child psychology and the pupil at the problem of learning". School situations were diagnosed "in terms of boys and girls. Subject difficulties concern students, not teachers. The curriculum is but our technique, a means to an end" (Parkhurst 1923 p. 23).

Teaching and learning were reconciled in the educational reorganization involved in implementing the Dalton plan. Once the curriculum was agreed to, students were assigned to a class. The work for 12 months was presented to all students at the beginning of the year. Students accepted the tasks assigned for each month as contracts to be signed and returned to the teacher when the tasks were completed. The curriculum was arranged for convenience into major and minor subjects. The major subjects were: mathematics, history, science, English, geography, foreign languages, and so on. The minor subjects were: music, art, handiwork, domestic science, manual training, gymnastics, and so on. Students progressed at their own rate, organizing their methods of working as they thought best. This arrangement secured the understanding of the work and gave students a sense of purpose and responsibility.

One laboratory for each subject of the curriculum with a specialist teacher in each was an essential feature of the Dalton plan. The laboratories were places where the students were free to work on their contract tasks without the distraction of shifts from one task to another determined by a time-table. Group work was encouraged by the requirement that all members of any class in any laboratory at one time should work together as a stimulus to discussion and as part of the exercise of social influences. The progress of students was recorded on graphs and reviewed regularly by the teacher and the students as a vital means of assessing progress and providing support.

Written assignments were central to the contract system. These set out the work to be covered in each subject in as much detail as determined by the specialist teachers bearing in mind the books, equipment, and other teaching materials available in the relevant laboratory. Typically the school day was divided into free time for work on contract assignments in the morning from 8.45 a.m. to 12 noon, followed by a pupil assembly and faculty conference until 12.30 p.m., and group conferences for reviewing progress until lunch at 1.00 p.m. The afternoon session was devoted to work in class groups on vocational or recreational activities.

The widespread popularity of the Dalton plan lay,

in part, in the ease with which it could be varied and modified to suit particular circumstances such as limitations of space and the size of schools. Parkhurst encouraged this provided the spirit of the plan was preserved and schools for children under 9 years of age were excluded. Despite the emphasis on the suitability of the Dalton plan in catering for individual differences, the prescription of monthly work contracts in the case of slow or reluctant learners became a major limitation on the success of the plan as outlined by Parkhurst. It also lacked the detailed form and preoccupation with research and experimentation of the Winnetka scheme.

See also: Curriculum Integration; Winnetka Scheme; Individualized Instruction; Keller Plan: A Personalized System of Instruction; Teaching Methods, History of

Bibliography

Connell W F 1980 *A History of Education in the Twentieth Century World.* Curriculum Development Centre, Canberra
Dewey E 1922 *The Dalton Laboratory Plan.* Dent, London
Parkhurst H 1923 *Education and the Dalton Plan.* Bell, London
Selleck R J W 1972 *English Primary Education and the Progressives, 1914–1939.* Routledge and Kegan Paul, London

J. R. Lawry

Dance: Educational Programs

Within the American public school system, dance has been traditionally associated with physical education. This is reflected in the place of dance in the curriculum, the training and certification of dance teachers, and the content of learning experiences at the elementary and secondary levels. Currently, the field is marked by conflicting perceptions as to the meaning and function of dance as a separate discipline, from the conventional wisdom of society without, and from the educational community within. Available research while sparse and unstandardized, presents initial data on the status of dance in the schools and its attendant problems.

Dance in education has its origins in the expressive, improvisational forms developed by Isadora Duncan in the early part of the twentieth century. Her approach to movement and the use of the body, as a dramatic departure from ballet, was embraced by some educators as a unique contribution to the development of students. Its pertinence was viewed as evoking in students a consciousness of themselves as individual entities at a time of increasing mass education, allowing for their participation in an educational process based on their own personalities. This approach became a new current in dance education along with the prevailing folk dance and, on a more professional level, ballet. As most practitioners were involved in private schools, and dance (as folk dance) had become institutionalized into public schools, "modern" dance, as it was called, played a greater or lesser role in the ensuing years. Its entry into the public schools has been essentially through the efforts of individual teachers wishing to effect their own classes, or those few within the educational structure who recognized the arts as fundamental to education.

1. Definition

As an art form, dance may be defined as the expression of ideas, feelings, and sensory impressions in movement forms achieved through the unique use of the body. It is the language of movement which speaks through the vocabulary of space, time, and force, that is, a movement is shaped in relation to the space it occupies, the time it uses, and the energy which gives it power. These elements constitute the materials of dance and are essential in forming its kinesthetic–visual image (Dimondstein 1971).

Movement comes into being only through the combined use of these elements, but there is no objectively defined sequence. Yet, each achieves definition through an investigation of its formal properties: space, through direction, level, and range; time, expressed through the internal rhythms of the body (pulse, heartbeat, breath) and the external metrical rhythms (beat, accent, measure); force, through contrasts of sustained, swinging, percussive, vibratory movements.

2. Distinguishing Characteristics

Within the context of general education, the practice of making dance an adjunct to physical education has tended to equate it with recreation or physical skill, neglecting its characteristics as an art form. Although body control is the basis of all motor activity, control in dance differs from skills or techniques associated with sports or gymnastics. Dance is geared neither toward the refinement or skills in themselves nor toward competitive ends. Whether it is performed as an individual or group activity, its means are not rule bound as in a game, nor are its aims toward predetermined goals.

Dance involves kinesthetic perception, that is, an understanding and appreciation of movement developed through a "muscle sense." Evidence of such perception comes through a conscious awareness of the body: moving through space alone, in relation to others, and to the physical environment; responding to the dimensions of time, both metrical and created; resisting or acquiescing to gravity by restraining or expending energy. All of these function toward the controlled use of the body in expressing ideas and feelings. Thus, while work in dance techniques aids students in developing motor skills, technique alone is not sufficient in this process of discovering the qualities of expression that accompany each movement pattern.

The progression is one of transforming natural or basic movements (walking, running, leaping, swinging, turning) into improvisations (using basic movements to respond spontaneously to specific ideas intitiated by the student or teacher), into dance studies (arranging movements into more organized sequences), into choreography (structuring more complex dances using conventional or invented forms). In addition to the performing aspects, a well-balanced program helps students at all levels to develop critical judgments of their own work and that of others, and to communicate their ideas in appropriate verbal terms. The process may not be sequential and is not determined by age. It is one of presenting creative dance problems which move from simple to increasingly sophisticated solutions, to which students respond according to their sensibility and capacity at any given time.

3. Research

There was little research until the 1960s, a period of general curriculum assessment. Educators, aided by federal money, reconsidered the role of the arts in affecting general education. The perceived dichotomy between dance as a performing art and as an educational discipline led to innovative projects such as "Arts in General Education" (dance related to other subject matter) (Madeja 1973), "Aesthetic Education" (dance as a separate area), and "Artists in Schools" (professional dance residencies) (National Endowment for the Arts 1976). Most existed on a regional basis or were designed for particular school districts; some were initiated by dance educators within school systems through extra-curricular local agreements. Evaluations, while programmatic, revealed a range of student achievements from dance used as a unique mode of knowing and feeling, to incremental learnings in other subjects, to a heightened interest in schooling. Such implications, however, did not penetrate the mainstream of general education.

Limited research within the field reflects internal contradictions both theoretical and practical. A 1967 study conducted to determine the status of children's dance in elementary schools revealed fundamental misconceptions among practitioners as to the nature and function of dance (American Alliance for Health, Physical Education, and Recreation 1971). Although termed "dance," activities fell mostly into categories of rhythmic games, calesthenics, folk and square dance (with major emphasis on the latter). Curriculum leaders were found lacking a rationale as to the contribution of dance to the total development of young children, resulting in no clarity of purpose or coherent design. Problems were identified as inadequate college preparation, lack of inservice programs, and insufficient interest from sports-oriented personnel. Most pervasive is the conclusion that dance is relegated to the fringes of physical education programs and that even when taught in relation to other subjects, it retains a secondary character.

A survey on the status of dance in the secondary schools concerned the training and certification of teachers, and opportunities for students (American Alliance for Health, Physical Education, and Recreation 1971). The findings confirmed the previous study that college programs consisted primarily of physical education courses; some offered dance courses within physical education, a few included dance majors or minors, and almost none provided graduate degrees in dance education. In terms of opportunities for students, dance classes were offered in junior high (ages 12 to 14) with the number and frequency increasing in senior high (ages 15 to 18), with a maximum at age 15. Lacking specialization, most teachers had physical education backgrounds and were found inadequately trained in dance. Significantly, dance classes at this level are available only as "electives" for talented or interested students and do not qualify with other subjects for college entrance (see *Elective Subjects*).

Thus, available research suggests that dance is not regarded as a substantive area within general education, and is not given academic parity in terms of professional preparation, instruction, time, and facilities. Despite the successes of many experimental projects, most states still do not require dance as part of the curriculum and offerings are largely determined by the size of the school population and availability of competent staff. Contributing factors are school administrators unresponsive to granting dance a higher status, curriculum developers with insufficient training and experience to conceptualize programs, and lack of state certification to standardize requirements.

4. Issues and Concerns

Apart from empirical research, the controversies continue to generate literature around two central issues: the lack of consensus between physical education and dance education regarding the place of dance in the curriculum, and its function in the larger educational spectrum.

Among physical educators there are several currents, the dominant of which accepts no separation of dance from physical education, but projects a comprehensive program in which both would be complementary rather than competitive. The position taken by dance educators (and some generalists) is that dance is a form of educational development not available in other academic subjects. As such, it is a body of knowledge which requires study of its historical, aesthetic, and performing aspects, as well as its connections to other areas. Therefore, the important issues to be examined are the aims and content of dance as the theoretical framework for curriculum planning and research. These issues project a curriculum geared toward the development of aesthetic perception of dance as an art, that is, an ability to understand the formal, kinesthetic, and expressive elements found in various forms, and to interpret these meanings in relation to other knowledge. Such learnings would be acquired through direct participation, observation of performances, and reading and writing about dance.

To establish dance as a basic part of the school program would be to focus on its distinctive content and its relation to the broad aims of education. The concern is that dance should be separated from physical education and that its relation to other areas of subject matter be one of coexistence. Thus, the position within physical education is one of doing what is being done better; the other implies a fundamental philosophical and organizational change in conception, leadership, and instruction.

See also: Physical Education Programs

Bibliography

American Alliance for Health, Physical Education, and Recreation (AAHPER) 1971 Task force, children's dance, dance division. *JOHPER* (Journal of Health, Physical Education, Recreation) June 1971, Reston, Virginia

American Alliance for Health, Physical Education, and Recreation (AAHPER) 1971 The status of dance in the secondary schools. *JOHPER* October 1971, Reston, Virginia

American Alliance for Health, Physical Education, Recreation and Dance (AAHPERD) 1981 *Children's Dance*. Reston, Virginia

Dimondstein G 1970 Space-time-force: An aesthetic construct. In: Haberman M, Meisel T (eds.) 1970 *Dance: An Art in Academe*. Teachers College Press, New York

Dimondstein G 1971 *Children Dance in the Classroom*. Macmillan, New York

Gray V, Percival R 1962 *Music, Movement, and Mime for Children*. Oxford University Press, London

Madeja S S 1973 *All the Arts for Every Child*. Final Report on the Arts in General Education Project in the School District of University City, Missouri. The JDR III Fund, New York

National Endowment for the Arts, 1976 *Artists in Schools*. National Endowment for the Arts, Washington, DC

Russell J 1968 *Creative Dance in the Primary School*. Praeger, New York

G. Dimondstein

Data Analysis: Exploratory

Exploratory data analysis (EDA) is a collection of specialized tools and an approach to the analysis of numerical data which emphasizes the use of graphic displays and outlier resistant methods to detect and model patterns in data. Numerous researchers and statisticians have contributed to the development of EDA but the primary source of ideas is generally acknowledged to be John Tukey. Although many EDA tools have been known for some time, Tukey has created new procedures, improved older ones, and knitted them all together into a systematic method. Tukey's work, only partially described in his book, *Exploratory Data Analysis* (Tukey 1977), provides the data analyst with new capabilities for uncovering the information contained in numerical data and for constructing descriptive models.

Data exploration, as Tukey envisages it, is not simply an exercise in the application of novel tools. It is a phase of the empirical research activity, one which follows data collection (or acquisition) and precedes the application of confirmatory or "classical" inferential procedures (Tukey 1973). It is, thus, part of that twilight zone which experienced researchers find so exciting and challenging, novice researchers fear and misunderstand, and few researchers ever report. The excitement of this phase of research derives in large measure from the prospect of discovering unforeseen or unexpected patterns in the data and, consequently, gaining new insights and understanding of natural phenomena. The fear that novices feel is partly a response to this uncertainty, but it is also partly due to traditional teaching which holds that "playing around" with data is not "good" science, not replicable, and, perhaps, fraudulent. Many experienced researchers pay lip service to this view, while surreptitiously employing ad hoc exploratory procedures that they have learned are essential to research. Exploratory data analysis by making exploration routine and systematic, and by using theoretically justifiable procedures, opens the exploratory phase of research to public review, enhances its effectiveness, and allows for replicability.

Because Tukey's methods exploit the natural behavior of measurements, they allow researchers to rely on their intuitions. The simple logic of the methods helps clarify the process of modeling data and, consequently, makes it easier to detect errors in data or departures from underlying assumptions. Much of this is due to the graphical devices Tukey invented which are central to this approach because of their ability to portray a wide range of patterns that data can take. Well-designed graphics, such as those used in EDA, are useful for the guided searching that characterizes exploration and are also attractive mechanisms for communicating results to nontechnical audiences. As a consequence, EDA can serve in data analysis and for reporting the results of an analysis.

Many of the methods in EDA fall on the frontiers of applied statistics. Two important topics in statistics today are the robustness and resistance of methods, terms which refer to the ability of a procedure to give reasonable results in the face of empirical deviations from underlying theoretical assumptions. Clearly, robust and resistant methods are particularly advantageous in social science research because empirical social science data are so often obtained in an ad hoc fashion, frequently under nonreplicable circumstances, on opportunistically defined variables whose relation to substantive theoretical constructs are vague at best. Exploratory data analysis is especially important in educational research, where many of the variables studied and data collected are brought into analyses not because well-verified, substantive theory demands their inclusion, but rather because investigators "feel" they ought to be, because they are "convenient" to use, or because measurements have been recorded in some assumed "reasonable" manner. Nor are the data typically produced as a consequence of a scientifically designed experiment. It is precisely in such research that EDA can be used to its greatest advantage because it is here that an open mind is an absolute necessity: the analyst rarely has the support of theoretically based expectations, and the real task confronting the data analyst is to explore—to search for ideas that make sense of the data (Simon 1977).

In the following brief description of EDA, only a few of the more usable techniques and the philosophical essence behind EDA are presented. Mathematical details are avoided but references to more extensive treatments are provided. The general objective of the procedures presented can be easily summarized. The procedures are tools for achieving resistant estimates of parameters for traditional additive and linear models. In this respect, they speak to a common empirical problem, the presence of outliers in data and the sensitivity of traditional methods of parameter estimation to highly deviant observations. Resistant analogs to three cases are presented: (a) a set of observations on a single factor at one level, (b) a set of observations on a single factor with multiple levels, and (c) a set of observations on two factors. In each case, the traditional approach to parameter estimation is mentioned first and then the EDA approach is detailed.

1. Organizing and Summarizing Individual Batches of Data

One of the first tangible products of a quantitative research project is a set of numbers, "data" that might contain information about the phenomenon or process under investigation. In many cases, the sheer amount of data to be analyzed can be overwhelming, leading an investigator to rely on summaries rather than dealing with all the values obtained. In addition to the impact that quantity can have, computer routines often present data values and summary statistics in a printed format which obscures rather than

elucidates data properties. Automatically produced by routines designed to handle a wide variety of situations, output listings typically contain much that is distracting (e.g., decimal points, leading and trailing zeros, scientific notation) and little that is fundamental. In addition, such routines are usually designed to present values in what might be called an accounting framework, one that facilitates the location of identified values but provides little insight into the overall behavior of the data.

Even a small collection of data, for example, three variables for 50 cases, is extremely hard to visualize or to get a feel for. What is needed is a technique that preserves the detail of values but eliminates distracting noise and contributes to a first level of understanding. The stem-and-leaf display and the box plot are two such techniques.

2. Visual Organization: Stem-and-leaf Display

The stem-and-leaf display is an immensely useful and easily appreciated exploratory tool which can provide insightful first impressions. It combines the features of a sorting operation with those of a histogram. The basic procedure can be used to organize and provide information on a single batch of values in a wide variety of circumstances. (A batch is a collection of observations on a variable. The term is not meant to convey any notion of sampling from a population.)

Figure 1 presents a stem-and-leaf display of the

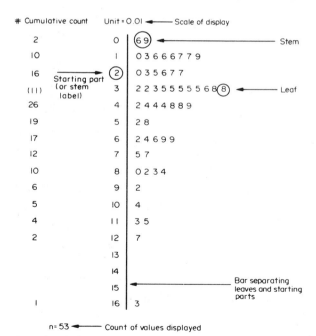

Figure 1
A stem-and-leaf display of direct silent

number of 5-minute segments out of 40 in which each of 53 children were observed to be reading silently and is referred to as direct silent in the figure (Leinhardt et al. 1981). The arrows, words, and circles are for explanation only. To construct a stem-and-leaf display, each number in a batch is partitioned into a starting part (to the left of the bar) and a leaf (to the right of the bar). When single digits are used in leaves each starting part will be an order of magnitude larger than each leaf. A set of leaves for a given starting part is a stem. The unit of display records the scaled value.

To reconstruct a data value, juxtapose a starting part with a leaf and multiply by the unit. For example, consider the two leaves that form the first stem of Fig. 1, 6 and 9. To reconstruct the two data values that these leaves represent, simply juxtapose each leaf with the common starting part, 0, and multiply by 0.01, that is, $06 \times 0.01 = 0.06$; $09 \times 0.01 = 0.09$. As another example, consider the bottom-most stem in Fig. 1. It has only one leaf, 3. Juxtaposing the 3 with its starting part, 16, and mulitplying by 0.01 yields 1.63. There are three starting parts 13, 14, and 15 that have no stems or leaves. This indicates that no observations have values between 1.27 and 1.63.

The display in Fig. 1 is actually the result of a two-step procedure (assuming the operation is carried out by hand). The first step normally yields a display in which the starting parts are ordered but the leaves on each stem are not. In the second step, each stem's leaves are ordered. This two-step procedure makes sorting a reasonably efficient operation.

Because all values in the display are represented by leaves occupying equal amounts of space, the length of a stem is proportional to the number of observations it contains. Thus, the display is like a histogram and provides information on shape and variation while also retaining information on individual values. This is true after the first step in construction. After the second step, the values are completely ordered and the display takes on the features of a sort. Because the display is like a histogram, anyone studying it can get the same kind of feeling for such elementary batch characteristics as overall pattern, bunching, hollows, outliers, and skewness that histograms provide. Those features that are akin to a sort allow the determination of maximum and minimum values quickly and, from them, the range of the values which can be used as a measure of overall variation.

Adding an inwardly cumulating count (depth) to the display greatly expands its utility. It facilitates finding other order statistics besides the maximum and minimum, such as the overall median and the medians of the upper and lower halves of the batch, which Tukey calls the "hinges." To form such a count, the number of leaves on a stem are cumulated from both ends in towards the middle. The median is located (not its value) at a depth halfway into the

batch from either end. The count of the number of leaves on the stem containing the median is given and put between parentheses because it is not cumulative.

To illustrate the use of this column of inwardly cumulating counts, the count column will be used to find the values of the median of the data in Fig. 1. The median will be located at depth $(n + 1)/2$. Since there are 53 values, the median is at depth 27, that is, it is the 27th value in from either the high or low end of the sorted values. Counting into the batch from the low-value end (which happens to be at the top of this display), it can be seen that the 27th value is represented by a leaf on the fourth stem. The value of the median could just as easily have been determined by counting into the batch from the high-value end (at the bottom of the display).

While the stem-and-leaf display is useful for describing data, it can also be an effective exploratory tool. For example, looking at Fig. 1 an asymmetry can be seen skewing the values toward the high end. The clustering between 0.1 and 0.4 is obvious, as are the two groups at 0.6 and 0.8 and the modal group at 0.3. The minimum value, 0.06, and the maximum value, 1.63, are easily determined. There is a gap apparent between 1.27 and 1.63. A researcher might be concerned, even at this point, with the question of why the maximum value seems to straggle out so much.

3. Numeric Summarization: Number Summaries and Letter-value Displays

While the stem-and-leaf display is a convenient and easily understood tool, it has its drawbacks. This is most evident when different batches of values are being compared. Although a simple comparison of the shapes of two batches can be achieved by placing the leaves of one batch on one side and the leaves of the second batch on the other side of a common set of starting parts, simultaneously comparing three or more batches using stem-and-leaf displays is obviously going to be difficult, possibly even confusing. While the visual quality of the stem-and-leaf display is a true asset in any first look at the behavior of a batch, it may be burdensome to continue to work with all the data values at once rather than a set of summary statistics.

The question is which summary statistics to use. The problem with choosing the mean and related statistics, such as the standard deviation, is their lack of resistance to the impact that one or a few deviant data values can have. Because the mean is a ratio of a sum to the number of values making up the sum, it can be equal to anything by simply changing a single value in the sum. This is not a problem, of course, if the data are reasonably well-behaved. Empirical data, however, often contain deviant values. Indeed, "weird" or "funny" values are rather commonplace occurrences (recall the value of 1.63

in Fig. 1) and, regardless of their source, they can cause traditional summary statistics to misinform.

Other statistics exist which are less sensitive to deviant values than is the mean, and, while they may not yet be fully supported by the inference procedures available for the mean, they may still be preferable at the exploratory stage of an analysis, where inference is not yet a focal issue. Some of the more useful and commonly known resistant measures of location and variation can be derived from the median and other order statistics. Most order statistics are little affected by the presence of a few outliers in a batch. One common resistant order-statistic-based measure of variation is the interquartile range.

Tukey exploits the resistance of order statistics, especially the median, in EDA. His first step in the numerical summarization of a batch for exploratory purposes involves computing five order statistics: the median, the extremes (or maximum and minimum), and the medians of the upper and lower quartiles (i.e., the hinges). When these five numbers are grouped together, they are called a "five-number summary" and can be arrayed conveniently as LE(LH, M, UH)UE, for lower extreme, lower hinge, median, upper hinge, and upper extreme, respectively. Tukey has introduced a truncation rule to avoid the inconvenience of small fractional ranks when finding medians of segments of a batch. The rule is

Depth of next median
$$= (1 + \lfloor \text{depth of prior median} \rfloor)/2 \quad (1)$$

The symbols $\lfloor$ and $\rfloor$ refer to the mathematical "floor" function which returns the largest integer not exceeding the number. That is, the fractional component of a value, in this case a fractional depth or rank, is discarded. This means that the only fractional depths used will be those that lie halfway between two consecutive values and, thus, will be easy to compute and understand. As a consequence of this truncation rule, exploratory summary statistics may not be exactly equal to analogous-order statistics whose computation is derived from more mathematically precise definitions.

The notion of a median is easily extended to provide a way of segmenting a batch resistantly. The hinges are themselves medians of segments, the upper and lower halves of the batch. Medians of the upper and lower quarters halve the quarter so that each segment bounds one-eighth of the values; medians of these segments bound 16ths, then 32nds, then 64ths, and so forth. In EDA, this process works outward from the center to the edges of a batch providing more and more detailed information on the behavior of the tails of an empirical distribution.

Although letter-value displays and five-number summaries (and extended number summaries in which medians of further foldings are recorded) provide useful, resistant information on location; their primary analytic use is in facilitating the computation of other features of batches. Differences of values provide information on spread or variation in a batch. For example, the range of silent reading data in Fig. 1 is computed by subtracting the lower extreme from the upper extreme: $1.63 - 0.06 = 1.57$. The range, however, is not a very resistant measure of spread. Obviously, it is very sensitive to deviant values when these appear as extremes, a common occurrence. A more reasonable measure of spread is the range between the hinges. Analogous to the interquartile range, it is called a "hingespread." The hingespread (which is symbolized as dH) of the silent reading data is $0.69 - 0.26 = 0.43$.

The hingespread is a statistic of central importance in elementary EDA. It is a useful tool in the search for values that deserve attention because they deviate from most values in a batch. This search can be started by computing another measure of spread, the "step," which is 1.5 times the hingespread. Using this quantity, one literally steps away from each hinge toward the extreme to establish another boundary around the central component of the data. These bounding values are called the "inner fences." Another step beyond these establishes the "outer fences." Note that the fences are not rank order statistics but are computed distances measured in the same scale as the values of the batch. Values that fall between the inner and outer fences are called "outside" values, and beyond these lie the "far outside" values. The two data values (or more if multiple observations occur at the same point) falling just inside the inner fences are called "adjacent values"; they are literally next to or adjacent to the inner fences.

It is useful to re-examine the stem-and-leaf display in Fig. 1 in light of the new information obtained on spread. In examining this display, it was noted that the data were evidently skewed out toward the high end. The numerical information on spread confirms this visual impression and suggests that one value at the high end deserves further attention. This value may be erroneous, or it may have been generated by a process different from that which generated the bulk of the values. Having identified a potential outlier, the problem of deciding what to do about it arises. If data are used which are made to appear highly asymmetric because of a few extreme observations, then it must be realized that many of the usual forms of inference, such as analysis of variance and least squares regression, will be strongly influenced by these few values. These procedures are not very resistant and, while removing values from empirical data should be done with utmost caution, the fact must be faced that unless omission of outliers is explored, fitted parameter values may describe the behavior of only a very small portion of the data. Replicability of findings in such situations is unlikely and generalizability is questionable.

The theoretical rationale underlying this approach to identifying outliers is not explicitly developed in Tukey's book on EDA. Some implicit support is available, however, by examining the properties of a normally distributed population in terms of EDA order-statistic-based measures. In a Gaussian or normal population, $\frac{3}{4}\, dH$ is approximately one standard deviation. Thus, $1.5\, dH$, a step, is approximately 2σ. Consequently, the inner fences, which are more than 2σ from the median, bound over 99 percent of the values of such populations. Observations drawn from a normal population that lie beyond the population's outer fences, which are an additional 2σ farther out, should indeed be rare.

4. Schematic Plots as Graphic Summaries

The quantities contained in number summaries and letter-value displays provide useful information on overall batch behavior. Most analysts, however, and certainly most nonspecialists, find that they can more easily appreciate the nuances of quantitative information when this information is displayed graphically. A schematic plot is an extremely useful graphic representation of the quantities contained in a number summary and, in fact, might well be considered a fundamental EDA summary device. It completely eliminates numbers (leaving them to a reference scale) and selectively obscures the data, drawing attention to some values and not others. Those values that are completely obscured are the values lying between the hinges, on the one hand, and those lying between the adjacent values and the hinges on the other. Attention is drawn by single marks to all values lying beyond the adjacent values. An example using the silent reading data appears in Fig. 2, which also shows the two other techniques that have been previously described.

Several points about schematic plots are worth noting. In the basic schematic plot, the width (or height, depending on orientation) of the box enclosing the central section of the data is arbitrary. However, this dimension can be used to represent information on other aspects of the data, such as batch size and significance of differences between medians (McGill et al. 1978). Whereas vertically oriented schematic plots are traditional and visually appealing, horizontal orientations are more effective for computerized printing operations because they permit a standard width to be used for any number of plots. Although the schematic plot is a visual device like the stem-and-leaf display, it is not as detailed and, indeed, is explicitly designed to reduce the amount of information being displayed. A related but even more elementary display, the box plot (so called because it consists of simply the box portion of a schematic plot and "whiskers" or lines extending to the extremes) obscures all except those in the five-number summary. Even though schematics speak to

Unit = 10^{-2}

Schematic plot

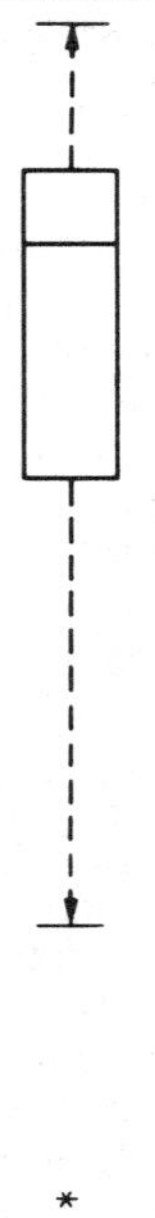

Number summary		Stem-and-leaf display	
LE	0.06	0	6 9
		1	0 3 6 6 6 7 7 9
LH	0.26	2	0 3 5 6 7 7
M	0.38	3	2 2 3 5 5 5 5 5 6 8 8
		4	2 4 4 4 8 8 9
		5	2 8
UH	0.69	6	2 4 6 9 9
		7	5 7
		8	0 2 3 4
		9	2
		10	4
		11	3 5
		12	7
		13	
		14	
		15	
UE	1.63	16	3

Figure 2
Schematic plot, five-number summary, and stem-and-leaf display for direct silent reading data

the issue of shape and spread, they can be somewhat misleading if gaps or multimodality occur between the adjacent values. Consequently, it is not advisable to use schematics as substitutes for stem-and-leaf displays, but rather as adjuncts.

5. Transformations

Frequently, naturally occurring data are modestly or extremely skewed, or exhibit some other property that make the data not normally distributed. Tukey emphasizes the need to consider the monotone transformation $y = kx^p$, where y is the transformed value, x is the original value, k is a constant set to -1 when p is less than zero and 1 otherwise. (The constant, k, retains order in the magnitude of the values when the transformation is a reciprocal.) The procedures for determining p are worked out and presented elsewhere and will not be described here (Leinhardt and Wasserman 1978). A summary of transformations is given in Table 1.

Thinking in terms of rescaled data values rather than raw data values is by no means straightforward and, given the central role that power transformations play in EDA, it is important that their rationale and validity is fully appreciated. There are several ways of thinking about transformations. One involves realizing that the well-grounded confirmatory tools of standard inferential statistics make specific assumptions concerning model structure and error properties. In many common procedures these include assumptions about normality of error distributions, additivity in parameters and variables, constancy of error variances, lack of functional dependence between error variance and variable location, and lack of interactions. When these assumptions are invalid, the procedures lose some of their appealing qualities. Their use in such problematic situations can be misleading. Unless procedures that deal directly with the known features of the data are used, one must resort to mathematical modification that adjusts the values so that their properties fit the assumptions of the model and/or estimation procedure. Transformations of scale can often provide the modifying mechanism.

6. Modeling Data

In EDA, models for data consist of two parts: a part that uses a mathematical statement to summarize a pattern in the data and a part that summarizes what is left over. Each observed value can be decomposed into a part that is typical of the pattern, the "fit," and a part that is not typical of the pattern, the "residual." Tukey constructs a verbal equation to represent a general class of models where the decomposition is additive:

$$\text{Data} = \text{Fit} + \text{Residual} \tag{2}$$

Other models are not ruled out, but Tukey emphasizes the use of simple models because they are easily understood, are easily estimated, help reveal more complex features, and often provide a good first approximation to these complexities. Additionally, many other forms can be rendered in terms of Eqn.

Table 1
Summary of transformations: roles, procedures, and failures

Data structure	Problem	Procedure	Failures
(a) Single batch	Asymmetry	Summary table (or equation)	Multimodality large gap
(b) One-way array	Spread heterogeneity	Diagnostic plot of $\log (dH_1)$ vs. $\log (x_1)$	Inconsistency in dH_1
(c) Two-way array	Interaction	Diagnostic plot of comparison values	Idiosyncratic interactions
(d) Paired observations	Curvature	Slope ratios or equation	Nonmonotonocity
	Spread heterogeneity	(b above)	(b above)

Note: Sometimes the "correct" transformation is not well-approximated by kx^p for any "reasonable" choice of p

An alternative view is more metatheoretical. In it the theoretical development of the social sciences is seen to trail that of the natural sciences in the sense of not yet having a well-developed, empirically verified, axiomatic and deductive body of theory from which the appropriate scale and dimension for representing a theoretical concept in terms of an empirical variable can be determined. Dimensional analysis in physics is an example of the power inherent in disciplines where such well-developed theory exists. In its absence, analysts must often use variables measured in arbitrary scales or variables defined in an ad hoc manner. Rarely is there any good reason to believe that such measures come in a form best suited to modeling relationships. In the absence of an a priori theory that could specify a model, EDA provides tools to determine whether rescaling a variable will lead to a better analysis.

(2) through an appropriately chosen transformation. Consequently, Eqn. (2) plays a fundamental role in EDA.

The computational procedure is straightforward. The median is subtracted from each observed value. This yields a batch of residuals, that is, a batch of adjusted values indicating the amount by which each raw value deviates from the fitted central value. In terms of a horizontally formatted schematic plot, the computation of residuals is analogous to centering the raw data around their median and relocating the zero point on the horizontal axis so that this origin rests exactly on the median.

7. A Model for Multiple Batches

Most research projects are not performed for the purpose of fitting single parameter models or obtaining a single summary statistic such as the mean or median. At the very least, the simplest objective involves comparing several batches in an attempt to determine whether one batch differs from another and by how much. A second-order question involves deciding whether an observed difference is important. These questions are traditionally approached through the analysis of variance (ANOVA) using ordinary least squares (OLS) estimation procedures (see *Analysis of Variance and Covariance*). While OLS has estimable properties when special conditions hold (i.e., the parameter estimates are unbiased, consistent, and have minimal variance), some of these properties are lost when the conditions fail to hold. Such losses can result from the presence of a single outlier. An EDA-based approach which exploits graphical displays to detect data inadequacies is presented here which employs resistant measures in determining effects and provides a useful guide in obtaining a transformation that facilitates the use of classical procedures.

In classical ANOVA, the errors, ε_{ij}, are assumed to be normally distributed random variables with zero mean and constant variance. Thus, the sum of squares for batch effects and the errors are multiples of χ^2 random variables. As a consequence, F ratios can be formed to test zero effect null hypotheses and symmetric confidence intervals can be constructed.

An analogous EDA procedure is presented here; one that is more resistant to outliers than ANOVA but lacking distributional assumptions and, consequently, lacking inferential tests. The purpose is to provide a resistant analysis that can be used in exploration. Furthermore, the EDA procedure provides a useful mechanism for studying the problem of inconsistency of variation in the errors, that is, heteroscedasticity.

The EDA modeling procedure is similar to that pursued in a classical analysis except that common effect and batch effect are estimated by medians and, consequently, involve different arithmetic computations. The model represented by the verbal Eqn. (2) yields a "fit" that is applicable to all batch values. For multiple batches, this model can be further elaborated so as to distinguish a general or common effect across all batches and a set of individual batch effects that are confined within their respective batches. Thus, the general model becomes:

$$\text{Data value}_{ij} = \overbrace{\text{Common effect} + \text{Batch}_j \text{ effect}}^{\text{Fit}} + \text{Residual}_{ij} \qquad (3)$$

Conceptually, the model represents each observed data value as a conditional response determined in part by imprecision, noise, or error. No specific assumptions are made about this last ingredient except that, taken as a batch, the residuals are devoid of an easily described pattern. The information they

contain relates solely to the overall quality of the model in terms of its ability to replicate the observed values.

The computational procedure is straightforward. First, consider the hypothetical multiple-batch data set represented by the box plots in Fig. 3. The median of the pooled batches is identified as the "common effect." Next, subtraction is used to "extract" this common effect from all data values. The result is simply a new centering of the adjusted batch values around a new grand median of zero. Second, the individual batch effects are obtained by subtracting the grand median from the individual batch medians.

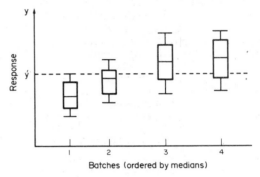

Figure 3
Box plots of multiple batches of hypothesis data

Finally, residuals are obtained by subtracting the batch effects from each adjusted value in the appropriate batch. The residuals are then examined as a whole and as batches. For the hypothetical example, the model is:

$$\text{Data value}_{ij} = \text{Common effect} + \begin{cases} \text{Batch effect}_1 \\ \text{Batch effect}_2 \\ \text{Batch effect}_3 \\ \text{Batch effect}_4 \end{cases}$$
$$+ \text{Residual}_{ij} \qquad (4)$$

The fitted value for the i,jth observation would simply be:

$$\text{Fit}_{ij} = \text{Common effect} + \begin{cases} \text{Batch effect}_1 \\ \text{Batch effect}_2 \\ \text{Batch effect}_3 \\ \text{Batch effect}_4 \end{cases} \qquad (5)$$

8. A Model for Two-way Classifications

A more complicated but quite common data structure arises when responses can be identified with the levels of two factors. The usual summary layout used to organize such data is the two-way table, an array of "responses" organized on the basis of row (r)

and column (c) factors. Such two-dimensional arrays consist of $r \times c$ cells or entries. Each row or column of a factor is referred to as a factor level or factor version. Factors are usually ordinally or nominally scaled but may be interval scaled. Responses are usually ratio scaled. The data are conceived of as triples of values: two classifying variables and a response variable.

The usual approach to such data involves an elaboration of the one-way model. A model, additive in factor-level effects, is posited. The array of responses is decomposed into an overall level or common effect, row effects, column effects, and interaction effects. A two-way ANOVA using least squares is the traditional method employed to estimate the model's parameters and to test for significance. In ANOVA, the grand mean is used to estimate the common term, and row and column means of the adjusted data estimate the row and column effects.

Once again, the EDA approach is analogous. The differences lie in the lack of distributional assumptions for the errors and the use of medians to estimate model parameters. Because no distributional assumptions are made, the hypothesis tests that are possible with least squares cannot be done. However, the use of medians ensures a result that is more resistant to the impact of deviant values. Furthermore, the EDA procedure provides a useful way to detect interactions even when there is only one observation per cell. When certain kinds of interactions are present, the EDA procedure can lead to a choice of a power transformation of the data that eliminates the interactions, that is, yields a scale in which the additive model provides a reasonable summarization of the data.

The model is in many respects an extension of the one-factor, multiple-level model proposed earlier for multiple batches. Indeed, a two-way table of responses can be thought of as two interwoven sets of multiple batches. Considering the column factor as the only dimension, there is a set of c multiple batches, each containing a maximum of r values. Considering the row factor as the only dimension yields a set of r multiple batches, each containing a maximum of c values.

Because the assumption is that each cell contains multiple observations, these data can be visualized as a two-way categorization of box plots as in Fig. 4. In the display, the vertical or y-axis is the scale on which the numeric response variable is measured. Factors R and C are categorical, so the distances between the levels, as well as their ordering, are arbitrary. The box plots of the multiply observed responses appear elevated above the origin plane by differing average positive amounts. The mathematical model represented involves a decomposition of the average elevation of each box plot into four parts: (a) an overall level; (b) a contribution from the column level (which occurs regardless of

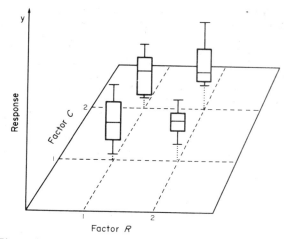

Figure 4
Graphical representation of hypothetical data for a two-way classification of responses (multiple unequal observations in each cell)

row level); (c) a contribution from the row level (which occurs regardless of column level); and (d) an error or residual. In verbal equation form this appears as:

$$\overbrace{\text{Data} = \text{Common effect} + \text{Row effect} + \text{Column}}^{\text{Fit}}$$
$$\text{effect} + \text{Residual} \qquad (6)$$

Whether the grand mean or grand median is used to estimate the common term, the result is conceptually identical. Its removal by subtraction effectively translates the origin plane so that the data are distributed around the origin rather than above it as in the hypothetical example. It is thus analogous to removing the grand median from a set of multiple batches, or the median from a single batch, and using the adjusted values, that is, the raw values with the grand median subtracted out, in constructing a new display.

By assuming that row and column effects are consistent, the model asserts that there will be only one effect for a row level regardless of the number of column levels, their size, and their effects and vice versa. In other words, the effect of row level 1 will be to elevate (or depress) the values in cells (1,1) and (1,2) the same amount, say a_1. Similarly, the effect of column level 2, according to the model, will be to elevate (or depress) the values in cells (1,2) and (2,2) the same amount, say b_2. Thus, any process of fitting this model to data must be constrained to finding these amounts according to a criterion that ensures an additive result. Given some estimate of these effects, the extent to which the data fail to conform can be studied by examining the residuals.

Thinking in terms of multiple observations in each

cell gives an opportunity to reflect on the occurrence of weird or deviant cell values in cases where there is only one observation per cell, a common situation. For example, analyses of previously reported data where access to raw values is not possible must usually proceed with cell values reported as averages. In many instances, even when raw values are available, only one observation per cell exists. Finally, in some cases it makes sense to think only in terms of single observations as in a longitudinal sampling frame, and, thus, the observed single cell entry, while drawn from a theoretical distribution of values, is the only observation that will ever be made.

In such cases, it is clear that when a single observation is drawn from the extremes of the cell distributions, a deviant cell results. Means of values, as was demonstrated earlier, provide little protection in such situations because they will be sensitive to any underlying asymmetries. The prospect of deviant observations in the cells as a consequence of poor initial measurement or erroneous data entry is obvious and remains a problem.

The traditional analytic procedure, using means and a least squares minimization criterion, will be highly sensitive to any instance of deviant cell values. As an alternative, Tukey suggests using "median polish." This procedure is relatively resistant and reasonably easy to perform. It involves the repeated (iterated) removal (subtraction) of medians. Several algorithms exist. The following procedure is relatively easy to perform by hand or to program for a computer.

First, the grand median is found and used to estimate the common effect. This term is removed (equivalent to a horizontal translation of the origin plane in Fig. 4) by subtracting the grand median from each cell value. The result of removing the common effect is a new array of positive and negative cell values centered around zero. Now a sweeping operation begins which alternately removes medians from the rows and then from the columns. There is no particular reason to start the steps on rows or on columns. However, because the solution provided by the algorithm is not exact, the results may differ slightly. The operation usually begins by sweeping rows.

In each sweep, each row or column median is found and subtracted out of its respective row and column of cell values. Usually, the process will quickly arrive at a point where row and column medians are zero or near zero. The values remaining in the table at this stage are the residuals. Row and column effects are calculated by adding the row and column medians obtained at each iteration. Individual fitted values can be found by using Eqn. (6) and the appropriate row and column effects. Row and column fits (i.e., estimated values) can be found by adding the common effect to the sum of each row effect and each column effect.

9. Summary and Discussion

The tools and approaches that have been described comprise as much a philosophy of data analysis as a set of specific answers to a number of common data analysis problems. The philosophy is one in which the analyst's first task is viewed as discovery of evidence, not evaluation, and consequently, the tools are designed to reveal unforeseen features rather than to create a decision-analytic framework for judging the importance of expected features. These evaluative tasks are left for another time and for different methods. Exploratory data analysis addresses the need for formulating models and developing hypotheses through the use of empirical data. Using data to test specific models and to determine the precision of parameter estimates remains the province of traditional inference.

There are many procedures associated with EDA which have not been discussed here. Some of these are considered in a number of recent articles and books. Several computer packages now contain EDA procedures. CMU-DAP is an especially versatile package of confirmatory and exploratory procedures. MINITAB, a system widely distributed by Pennsylvania State University, now also possesses some EDA capabilities.

Two features serve as continuous themes in the procedures that have been described. The first is the desire to use resistant procedures rather than to rely solely on traditional least square methods. The solution that Tukey provides in EDA is a set of fitting procedures that use medians instead of means. A good operational rule is to try both resistant and standard methods on a data set and to move cautiously when the two disagree. The second theme deals with deviations from simple models in the form of asymmetry, spread-by-level interaction, and curvilinearity. Tukey's solution here is a standard one, the use of transformations of scale so that in the new scale the data do not exhibit these patterns.

In conclusion, the belief should be reiterated that there is little in the philosophy of EDA that will be new to the experienced scientist. What is new, useful, and timely is the systematic and routine way in which Tukey's procedures allow this philosophy to be put into practice. Furthermore, while research scientists will appreciate these advantages, evidence indicates that EDA can be extremely helpful to students just commencing their education in statistical methods. Using EDA as an introduction to statistics and data analysis provides a refreshingly intuitive and intellectually appealing route to the development of quantitative analytic skills.

Bibliography

Duncan G T in press *Statistical Thinking*. Wiley, New York
Erickson B H, Nosanchuk T A 1977 *Understanding Data*. McGraw-Hill Ryerson, Toronto, Ontario

Hoaglin D C in press *A First Course in Data Analysis*. Addison-Wesley, Reading, Massachusetts

Leinhardt G, Leinhardt S 1980 Exploratory data analysis: New tools for the analysis of empirical data. *Rev. Res. Educ.* 8: 85–157

Leinhardt G, Zigmond N, Cooley W W 1981 Reading instruction and its effects. *Am. Educ. Res. J.* 18: 343–61

Leinhardt S in press *Exploratory Data Analysis: A Primer*. Duxbury, North Scituate, Massachusetts

Leinhardt S, Wasserman S S 1978 Quantitative methods of public management: An introductory course in statistics and data analysis. *Policy Analysis* Fall: 550–75

McGill R, Tukey J W, Larsen W A 1978 Variations of box plots. *Am. Stat.* 32: 12–16

McNeil D R 1977 *Interactive Data Analysis: A Practical Primer*. Wiley, New York

Mosteller F, Tukey J W 1977 *Data Analysis and Regression: A Second Course in Statistics*. Addison-Wesley, Reading, Massachusetts

Simon H S 1977 *Models of Discovery*. Reidel, Dordrecht

Tukey J W 1973 The zig-zagging climb from initial observation to successful improvement. In: Coffman W E (ed.) 1973 *Frontiers of Educational Measurement and Information Systems: 1973*. Houghton-Mifflin, Boston, Massachusetts

Tukey J W 1977 *Exploratory Data Analysis*. Addison-Wesley, Reading, Massachusetts

G. Leinhardt; S. Leinhardt

Data Analysis: Nonresponse

One of the problems with survey research is that no matter how carefully the survey is designed, the actual outcome is imperfect. Survey design is concerned with taking advantage of the population structure through techniques such as stratification and multistage sampling so as to yield a sample which will permit efficient estimation of the various population characteristics. Problems occur because responses are not obtained from all of the selected sample and the sample which is actually achieved is therefore deficient in comparison to what was intended. The reasons for this are complex and depend to some extent on the nature of the study, the survey procedures, and the relationship between the subjects and the researcher. How serious a problem this is and the effect on the survey objectives will depend on the level of nonresponse and how much respondents differ from nonrespondents in the variables of interest in the particular study.

In the simplest case, in schools for example, it may simply be the case that some selected subjects are unavailable on the day of the survey because of illness or absenteeism. Alternatively it may be the conscious choice of some selected individuals or their parents not to respond. A third situation, which can affect not just one subject but many, occurs when a third party, a headteacher for example, decides on behalf of a whole school, not to cooperate in a particular study. This creates a cluster of nonresponses from the selected subjects in that school. In the wider context of research studies which involve direct contact with individuals rather than via a school or other similar institution, the situation is much more like other social surveys. Nonresponse can now result from direct refusal to cooperate, failure to contact the chosen subject or, more rarely, failure to collect the required information because of communication, language, or other similar problems. Failure to make contact is a broad category which includes a variety of situations. This failure may be due to prolonged absence of, the subject or because the subject is simply unavailable on each occasion when contact is attempted. Alternatively, the subject may no longer be living at the last known address if the available information is out of date. This description relates to "unit nonresponse" where no information is obtained for some selected individuals. In other cases, answers to some questions are not given in an otherwise complete response. These may, for example, be more sensitive or personal questions which the respondent chooses not to answer. This is known as "item or question nonresponse".

Thus no matter how carefully the original sample design was made to achieve a sample properly representative of the population of interest, the final data yielded will represent a loss of some of the originally chosen subjects. How much effect this will have depends heavily on the type of study, the means of data collection, the nature of the data required and the purposes of the study, the quality and age of sampling frames used, and the level of cooperation achieved with the various levels of authority such as headteachers and administrators where appropriate. At one extreme a well-designed study with carefully executed methodology and the full support of education authorities may achieve almost complete response. Here nonresponse could be such a small problem that it is felt unlikely to significantly effect any of the conclusions drawn from the survey data. At the other extreme, poorly chosen methodology with poor follow-up using out-of-date information could result in a wholly inadequate response rate of 20 percent or less. It is the first responsibility of researchers to strive for as high a response rate as possible but it is nevertheless common for well-designed social surveys with good methodology to achieve response rates of only 75 percent–85 percent. Surveys based on schools or similar institutions are often carried out in favourable circumstances and might be expected to yield a higher response rate than this. It must be emphasized that the overall response rate, whilst important, is not a complete guide. It is quite possible that even when this is high, the level of response for particular subgroups may still be too low. Different ethnic groups, for example, may yield different response rates and if the research objectives call for separate statistical analyses for each ethnic group or a comparison between them, a low response rate in one group would still cause concern even though the response rate for all ethnic groups taken together was satisfactory.

Nonresponse may effect the survey results in two ways. First there is the effect of reducing the achieved sample below that intended. This alone will decrease the precision of estimates. If this were the only effect it could be overcome by enlarging the initial sample size and so allowing for a reduction in sample size due to nonresponse. The second and potentially more important, and more intransigent, effect is due to the fact that nonrespondents may differ systematically from respondents. The achieved sample is no longer fully representative of the original population and may result in biased population estimates. There is a substantial social survey literature showing that response rates differ with various factors such as social class and urban/rural location, in particular whether the population includes people in inner cities.

Consider the simple case of estimating the mean reading test score of a population of school children. Imagine that the population consists of two groups (a) potential respondents R who if they happen to be selected into the sample would be available on the survey day and (b) potential nonrespondents NR who if are selected would be unavailable on survey day perhaps through illness or absenteeism. It is assumed that the two groups have mean reading test scores of μ_R and μ_{NR} respectively and that in the whole population the proportion of potential respondents is P_R. The proportion of potential nonrespondents is $P_{NR} = 1 - P_R$.

The mean reading age for the whole population is μ,

$$\mu = P_R \mu_R + P_{NR} \mu_{NR} \tag{1}$$

but the achieved sample will contain only respondents and, subject to sampling fluctuation, will have a mean reading age of μ_R. The bias in using only the respondents is B,

$$B = P_R \mu_R + P_{NR} \mu_{NR} - \mu_R$$

$$= P_{NR}(\mu_{NR} - \mu_R) \tag{2}$$

Thus the bias is proportional to the difference in mean reading age between respondents and nonrespondents and to the proportion of the population who are potential nonrespondents. It should be noted that this bias is not reduced simply by increasing the sample size. The hopeful dictum that a large enough sample solves all problems does not apply to this situation. Researchers sometimes try to overcome the nonresponse problem by replacing nonrespondents with extra sampled individuals. This will overcome the reduction in overall sample size but the above analysis shows that nonresponse bias will remain. The basic difficulty has been illustrated above in the simplest of all cases when trying to

estimate the population mean. In more complex situations such as estimating a correlation coefficient the same principle applies although the systematic difference between respondents and nonrespondents is concerned with characteristics other than just the mean of each group. Under appropriate assumptions, the work of Pearson (1903) and Anderson (1957) on the effects of selection when estimating population characteristics is relevant.

1. Data Collection Methods to Reduce Nonresponse

It is generally held that the best way to attack the nonresponse problem is at source by achieving as high a response rate as possible. The methods used to do this are varied but all involve careful attention to procedures and a willingness to devote a disproportionate amount of the resources and effort available to potential nonrespondents. The basic data collection method may be crucial and it is usually the case that direct contact involving an interviewer will yield a higher response rate than a mail questionnaire although the latter is considerably cheaper in most situations. For interview surveys, refusals can be minimized by improved training for interviewers and sometimes a second contact by a more senior and experienced member of the field force. It is an obvious help if the objectives of the survey are clearly presented and may be seen to be of benefit. There is some evidence from social surveys that some refusals represent a situational response made by people for whom the particular moment of contact is inconvenient or who happen at that moment to be less responsive than they might otherwise be. For such people a second contact on another occasion will often meet with success. It is the interviewer's task to minimize the influence of factors which might lead to refusal and so promote the likelihood of a successful outcome. For mail surveys, response rates are typically lower but reminder cards, repeat mailing, or interview follow-up will often improve this although not so far as to compare with the response rate from interview surveys. In the usual situation in schools, the respondent is the student who is not approached directly. In this case the same principles apply to parents, administrators, and teachers who control access to the child. In other cases, such as higher education, it is more likely that the eventual respondent will be approached directly. Even in this case the active cooperation of authorities in providing address lists and other materials can minimize subsequent frame and response problems (see *Interviews in Sample Surveys*).

The question of noncontact is separate from refusal. Clearly people who are completely unavailable at the time of the survey through prolonged absence may be contacted later if this is practicable. People who are simply difficult to contact need to be sought at a variety of times on different days both in the daytime and evenings in order to maximize the possibility of successful contact. Call-backs and finding out from others when a person is likely to be available are both important parts of good fieldwork. Mail questionnaires and telephone interviews often overcome this initial contact problem although for mail surveys at least the motivation to respond is not as strong which more than offsets the gain.

The case of movers is sometimes a particularly difficult problem. If each mover is followed to a new address which is distant from the original, the field organization needs to be exceptionally well-controlled. The cost of such follow-ups can be very great. For wide-scale surveys, the sample is often designed using multistage sampling techniques so that the chosen samples cluster into locations saving considerably on travel costs. If this clustering relies on outdated information then movers will be located outside of the selected clusters and heavy costs will be incurred for each respondent who is followed to a new address. This problem is often overcome to a large degree by a conceptual change in the sampling unit so that it is not the individual but some other more stable unit, linked to individuals that is used. Thus the sampling unit might be addresses or schools which are located at fixed points and the final sample is taken from the de facto membership of each selected unit at the time of the study. In this way a sample is achieved which is still representative of the whole population (including recent movers for example) without having to trace specific individuals who have moved. Such a method may be suitable for school children or general population surveys but will have limited use if the target population is only associated with a small proportion of the general population of units to be sampled. For example, if the survey is concerned with graduates then a sample of all addresses will yield relatively few university graduates. A sampling frame provided by the university of the last known address of each graduate, however outdated, may be the best information available (see *Sampling*).

2. Other Fieldwork and Analytic Methods

However good the fieldwork procedures are, and however great the effort made, a residual nonresponse problem will remain. Good survey methods are the first line of attack and will reduce the problem but not eliminate it. The second line of attack is concerned with special data collection methods or statistical analysis techniques to correct for nonresponse bias. The essential difficulty is that nonrespondents by their very nature are unobserved and the proposed methods all depend to a greater or lesser extent on assumptions which are difficult to verify directly. All of the methods assume that in some way respondents and nonrespondents are alike

in the sense that data from respondents may be used in such a way as to make allowance for non-respondents. In some situations these essential assumptions are intuitively reasonable since the nonresponse mechanism is well-understood. In other situations this is not the case. In a survey of school children for example, nonresponse may be caused by absenteeism on survey day. In this case attendance records of all children may be available and so long as it is assumed that absenteeism on survey day is not abnormal (and in particular not related to the survey taking place), then some adjustment involving attendance records might be easily justified. The adjustment made can take various forms such as (a) duplicating the survey data from a child with a similar attendance record to the nonrespondent's, (b) giving greater weight in the analysis to children with similar attendance records to nonrespondents, or (c) some more sophisticated form of statistical adjustment using the attendance record as a covariate. The exact form of this will depend upon the type of statistical analysis required and assumptions about the relationship between the survey variables and attendance. The duplication of an individual data record as described in (a) is known as "hot-decking" (Madow 1979). This is more widely used in large-scale surveys.

Bartholomew (1961) proposed a simple form of adjustment which is primarily concerned with failure to make contact in social surveys and requires a single recall. He argued that successful first calls were clearly biased since they favoured people who spent much of their time at home. Bartholomew suggested that at the time of the first unsuccessful call, as much information as possible should be obtained from other members of the household, neighbours, and so on, so as to yield as good a chance of success at the first recall as possible. He then suggested that successful interviews at the first recall could be weighted to represent also the failures at the first recall stage. The essential assumption is that the additional information collected at the first call helps in the assumption that successes and failures at the first recall are similar and to provide the link between respondents and nonrespondents.

Politz and Simmons (1949) were also concerned with noncontact and suggested that data could be collected from respondents to allow adjustment for nonresponse without making any recalls. The essential idea is that contact is directly related to the availability of the subject during the survey period and people who are more often unavailable during the survey period will be underrepresented in the achieved survey data. Each respondent is asked about the periods when they were available for interview during the survey period and these data can be used to reweight the survey data. For example, someone who was at home on two days during the survey period is twice as likely to have been contacted as someone at home on only one day. The implicit assumption is that for any given level of availability, respondents can represent nonrespondents with whom no contact was made.

Algebraically, the Politz–Simmons method is a special case of the general situation when some auxiliary information is known which may be used to adjust estimation methods to allow for nonresponse. Suppose, for example, that it was known that response rate varied with age of subject and the proportions W_h in each age group (h) were known for the whole population. Then the population proportions W_h may be used to reweight the sample data for each age group in a form of poststratification to eliminate nonresponse bias. Thus the population mean would be estimated by $\Sigma W_h \bar{y}_h$ where $\bar{y}_h$ is the sample mean for the hth age group. The essential assumption being made is that whilst the response rate is known to vary with age, within any particular age group the respondents and nonrespondents are similar. Equation (2) is modified so that with the obvious extension to the notation, the nonresponse bias is given by

$$B = \sum_h P_{NR,h}(\mu_{NR,h} - \mu_{R,h}) \qquad (3)$$

Nonresponse bias now depends on the difference between the mean of respondents and nonrespondents within each age group and the implicit assumption is that this leads to smaller nonresponse bias when age is taken into account. Here it has been assumed that the auxiliary information, age group, is a categorical variable and this leads to adjustment through the population weights W_h by poststratification. Conceptually there is no further difficulty if the auxiliary information is not grouped but is treated as a continuous variable. If age is known for each respondent and the average age for the entire population is known then the adjustment could take the form of a ratio or regression estimate but the basic principle is the same.

This method depends on knowledge of the auxiliary information for the population as a whole to provide the link between the sample data and the population estimate required. If the auxiliary information was unknown for the population as a whole but was known for the sample including nonrespondents, then similar methods could be adopted. Now poststratification, ratio, or regression estimates as appropriate could be used to make "estimates" for the original selected sample including nonrespondents and the estimation procedure from this point to the whole population is that which would have been used had there been no nonresponse at all. In practice, of course, the two stages of estimation are combined. In the case of question nonresponse, the other responses on the questionnaire are available as auxiliary information. This provides a much

richer source of information for regression or poststratification adjustments for nonresponse.

The procedures have been described here in terms of estimating the simplest characteristic of the population, the overall mean. The same principles may be applied to more complex statistical procedures (Anderson 1957). Thus if auxiliary information is available as variable x and an estimate is required of the regression coefficient of variable y on variable z then a modification to the usual statistical formula would be

$$\beta_{yz} = \frac{s_{yz} + \dfrac{s_{yx}s_{zx}}{s_{xx}}\left(\dfrac{\sigma_{xx}}{s_{xx}} - 1\right)}{s_{zz} + \dfrac{s_{zx}^2}{s_{xx}}\left(\dfrac{\sigma_{xx}}{s_{xx}} - 1\right)} \qquad (4)$$

Here s_{yz} is the sample covariance between variables y and z based on the data achieved from respondents and similarly for s_{xx}, s_{zx} and so on. For the auxiliary variable x, σ_{xx} is the known population value of the variance. Thus if x were the attendance record for school children, s_{xx} would be the sample variance for respondent school children, and σ_{xx} would be the corresponding variance calculated from all the school children's attendance records whether they were in the sample or not.

The cases described here represent relatively simple situations. Little (1980) and Rubin (1976) and also both authors in Madow (1979) have developed a comprehensive framework describing the basis of statistical inference in the presence of nonresponse. In all the cases described here it has been assumed that the response mechanism is such that the distribution of data from respondents is the same as that for nonrespondents given the same value of the auxiliary variables. When this assumption cannot be made, the situation becomes much more complex. Heckman (1979) has considered this situation in the context of econometric models. Related work is reported by DeMets and Halperin (1977) in epidemiology, and Nathan and Holt (1980) in sample survey theory. Thomson and Siring (1979) have used the number of call-backs required for a successful interview to model the response mechanism in terms of an auxiliary variable (household size). By using Norwegian data where the true responses are obtainable from other sources, they are able to investigate the success of their methods and the extent to which call-backs are needed. For their empirical studies they show that their attempts to remove nonresponse bias are an improvement and secondly that a substantial number of call-backs are worthwhile.

This article has been focused on cross-sectional studies although many of the general principles apply to longitudinal studies where selected individuals are followed over time. In addition, such studies involve other methodological problems of nonresponse. Sample attrition over time and the increasing efforts which must be made to maintain contact are the most obvious. An account of these problems specifically related to longitudinal studies is given by Goldstein (1979).

See also: Survey Studies, Cross-sectional; Longitudinal Research Methods

Bibliography

Anderson T W 1957 Maximum likelihood estimates for a multivariate normal distribution when some observations are missing. *J. Am. Stat. Ass.* 52: 200–03
Bartholomew D J 1961 A method of allowing for "not-at-home" bias in sample surveys. *Appl. Stat.* 10: 52–59
Cochran W G 1977 *Sampling Techniques,* 3rd edn. Wiley, New York
DeMets D, Halperin M 1977 Estimation on a simple regression coefficient in samples arising from a sub-sampling procedure. *Biometrics* 33: 47–56
Goldstein H 1979 *The Design and Analysis of Longitudinal Studies: Their Role in the Measurement of Change.* Academic Press, New York
Heckman J 1979 Sample selection bias as a specification error. *Econometrica* 47: 153–61
Kalton G 1983 *Compensating for Missing Survey Data.* Survey Research Center, Institute for Social Research, University of Michigan, Ann Arbor, Michigan
Kish L 1965 *Survey Sampling.* Wiley, New York
Krewski D, Platek R, Rao J N K (eds.) 1980 *Current Topics in Survey Sampling.* Symp., Carleton University, May 7–9, 1980. Academic Press, New York
Little R J A 1980 Models for non-response in sample surveys. Invited paper, European Conference of Statisticians, Brighton
Madow W G (ed.) 1979 *Symposium on Incomplete Data: Preliminary Proceedings.* United States Department of Health, Education and Welfare, Washington, DC
Moser C A, Kalton G 1971 *Survey Methods in Social Investigation,* 2nd edn. Heinemann, London
Nathan G, Holt D 1980 The effect of survey design on regression analysis. *J. Roy. Stat. Soc. B* 42: 377–86
Pearson K 1903 On the influence of natural selection on the variability and correlation of organs. *Phil. Trans. Roy. Soc. A* 200: 1–66
Politz A, Simmons W 1949 I. An attempt to get the "not at homes" into the sample without callbacks. II. Further theoretical considerations regarding the plan for eliminating callbacks. *J. Am. Stat. Ass.* 44: 9–31
Rubin D B 1976 Inference and missing data. *Biometrika* 63: 581–92
Steeh C G 1981 Trends in non-response rates, 1952–79. *Public Opinion Q.* 45: 40–57
Thomson I, Siring E 1979 On the causes and effects of non-response: Norwegian experiences. In: Madow W G (ed.) 1979
Yates F 1981 *Sampling Methods for Census and Surveys,* 4th edn. Griffin, London

D. Holt

Data Banks and Data Archives

Research data are arranged in data sets, defined as organized collections of related data. The term data bank is commonly used to refer to a collection of related data sets, often associated with a single research project or survey. A data bank is thus conceptually similar to an item bank, containing a large collection of test items. The quantity of data in most data sets or data banks usually necessitates the use of computerized retrieval systems with data stored in machine-readable form. Data archives are places where machine-readable data, such as those contained in data sets, are stored, preserved, and catalogued for access and use by others. Many research workers today routinely make use of computerized storage and retrieval systems like the Educational Resources Information Center (ERIC) to locate published educational material. Increasingly, educational researchers are making use of data held in data archives to answer questions, for example, about the achievement, attitudes, or attributes of students and schools, or to compare their data with other data collected at a different time or in a different place.

1. Data Banks in the Social Sciences

Although the concept of an educational data bank may conjure up visions of vast amounts of information being kept on file about schools, teachers, and students and thus may be thought of as depersonalizing education, there are reasons that may be advanced for maintaining such data banks.

The collection of research data, particularly large longitudinal studies or studies conducted nationwide or across countries, is expensive. The possibility that such data may be used by other research workers, for secondary analysis or for providing benchmarks to enable comparisons at some time in the future, helps to justify the expenditure. There is too a certain obligation on the part of researchers to ensure that collections of data, especially if funded by public monies, are made available to colleagues in the wider research community. This represents an extension of the current practice of the evaluation of the quality of scientific work by means of peer review and thus may lead to better educational research. The analysis of a data set by secondary analysts asking different questions and using a variety of models and statistical techniques should lead to a more robust interpretation of the data, particularly where initial analyses were conducted under severe time constraints imposed by the sponsoring agencies.

The archiving of data and their use by others may also reduce the need to interrupt schools and other educational institutions, which may in turn enhance the response by institutions on occasions when data are collected in the future. This applies particularly to the use of archived data sets for the training of research workers who wish to concentrate their efforts on developing a repertoire of statistical techniques rather than on data collection. Part of the justification for establishing the Social Science

Research Council (SSRC) Survey Archive in the United Kingdom was that survey data are "a valuable resource in terms of both human effort and cash funds, and ought, therefore, to be protected and utilized so that the gain in knowledge that each individual effort represents is not needlessly dissipated, nor needlessly replicated".

One of the pioneering data banks in education was prepared for Project TALENT (Tiedeman 1972). Other well-known data banks have been associated with the cross-national studies conducted by the International Association for the Evaluation of Educational Achievement (IEA): the IEA Mathematics Data Bank (Wolf 1967) and the IEA Six-subject Data Bank (Schwille and Marshall 1975, Walker 1976). The IEA Six-subject Data Bank, for instance, holds data collected from approximately 250,000 students, 50,000 teachers, and 10,000 schools in 21 countries as part of six international surveys of achievement in science, reading comprehension, literature, civic education, and French and English as foreign languages. In each of the surveys, student achievement data, as well as information about students' home and socioeconomic backgrounds, attitudes, and interests, together with information from teachers and schools, were gathered by testing students age 10 years, 14 years, or in the last year or pre-university year of schooling. The data bank is lodged in data archives in Sweden (Institute of International Education, University of Stockholm) and in the United States (Inter-University Consortium for Political and Social Research, Ann Arbor, Michigan), as well as in other repositories at research centres and universities in Australia, the United Kingdom, Canada, Japan, and New Zealand. The rich IEA data banks have been accessed by research workers from many countries (Postlethwaite and Lewy 1979).

For preparing data for lodgment in a data bank as well as for accessing them once there, the computer is a vital research tool. However, even though physically smaller and ever more powerful computers are constantly being developed, not even today's largest computer could store in its central processing unit (CPU) more than a small fraction of, say, an IEA data bank. A data bank must usually be held in supplementary storage, such as on magnetic disc or tape. Data arranged in data files are stored as small magnetized dots on the iron oxide surface of the disc or tape. Reading heads, reading across the surfaces of a disc (random access) or sequentially through a tape (sequential access), are able to retrieve particular data as requested by users and return these to the CPU. In this way computers permit the storing of vast quantities of data in compact form for subsequent analysis by the research workers who gathered the data originally or by other researchers engaged in secondary analysis of the data.

The establishment of data banks in the social sciences has been paralleled by the development of refined statistical software packages which facilitate the researcher's task of accessing and analysing data. Most computer installations have integrated packages of programs for the management and analyses of social science data: for example, the Statistical Package for the Social Sciences, commonly known as SPSS (Nie et al. 1975), and OSIRIS (Institute for Social Research 1981). The major packages usually have the facility to access data sets prepared by the use of other packages.

2. Data Documentation

Before any use can be made of a particular data set, such as, say, the science survey data set for 10-year-olds in Italy held in the IEA Data Bank, it is necessary to have adequate documentation to enable the data to be interpreted.

The documentation requirements are of two kinds. First, there is general documentation providing information about the study for which the data were collected; and, second, there is specific documentation describing the format or layout of the machine-readable data. The central requirement is the adequacy of the documentation rather than the particular conventions adopted. The total documentation for any data set would normally contain:

(a) identifying information (e.g. title of study, investigator(s), abstract, related publications);

(b) background information (e.g. describing the context within which the study was conducted);

(c) details of design and sampling (of which greater detail may be included in a report cited in the bibliography);

(d) data gathering information (including test instruments and how these were administered); and

(e) information about data organization (e.g. coding of responses and how the response data are stored in the data set).

All or part of this documentation may be located with the data on the computer in machine-readable form. Again, the crucial issue is the availability of this information, rather than how it is stored.

3. Data Organization

In educational research a data set typically comprises measures obtained for a sample of cases. The case, which is the basic unit of analysis, may be some larger unit such as a class of students or a school. Measures might include, for instance, personal characteristics, demographic data, and achievement scores, in which event each case would contain these groups of variables, and the ordering of the variables would be exactly the same for all cases.

When data are being prepared in a form ready for analysis, all variables for each case are organized into a data file. Three steps are involved: coding, entering data, and file building. At the same time a codebook is usually prepared, containing information about the coding scheme adopted for all variables and their location on the data file.

3.1 Coding the Data

In entering data into the computer it is usual to code the information collected for each case by assigning symbols to each item on the completed instrument(s). Alphabetic and special characters are generally to be avoided in coding the data, since the computer is able to process numerical data more efficiently. The practice of using multiple codes for a single item, which would involve making several punches in a single column of a card, should also be avoided since many statistical software packages cannot handle this format.

To illustrate the assigning of symbols to items, respondents' names are often coded 001, 002, 003 . . . while sex might be coded as 1 (male), 2 (female). Coding is thus seen to result in compact storage and, in the case of personal data, helps to preserve confidentiality. Accompanying documentation must clearly indicate the meaning of all assigned codes (though names of respondents or schools are not usually displayed) and this information is commonly included in a codebook.

For open-ended questionnaire items coding must frequently follow the data collection. An example of an item involving both pre- and post-coding is illustrated in the following:

> Do you speak a language other than English? Yes? No?
> If so, which main one? ....

Upon examination of responses, a decision may be made to group the languages elicited in the second question: for example, as North European, South European, and Other. Consequently, a single digit could be used to code responses to both questions as follows:

1—English only
2—English and North European
3—English and South European
4—English and other

There are several good texts (e.g. Johnson 1977) that provide details of coding schemes.

Where possible, the coding of the data should preserve the information contained in the original responses, provided that the requirements of anonymity are observed. For example, a variable measuring school size should be coded in terms of the actual enrolments, allowing the investigator or secondary analyst to group the numbers as desired (e.g. less than 600, 601–800, 801–1,000, more than 1,000).

Similarly, if the study includes a test, the responses to each test item should be individually coded. Optionally, the data set may contain in addition certain derived scores, such as totals or subscores for groups of items, provided the accompanying documentation details how the derived scores were obtained.

Where respondents fail to answer, or respond "inapplicable" or "don't know", such responses should also be given specific code values. Many of the statistical software packages allow up to three values to be designated as missing and thus it is possible to distinguish between these particular instances of missing data and yet at the same time to process them similarly in any analysis (for example, by excluding all such cases in analyses). If, for instance, two digits have been used to code a given variable, then the following codes could be reserved as missing value codes:

97—Inapplicable
98—Don't know
99—Omitted (or not ascertained)

For some analysis packages, problems may occur if missing responses are represented by blanks or spaces on the data file, instead of by alphanumeric symbols.

3.2 Data Entry and File Building

Once the data are coded, they may then be entered into the computer. This is commonly accomplished by punching the data on to 80-column cards, or by using response formats that can be optically scanned by a computer-linked device, or by keying directly via a terminal (key-to-disc). Where there is more than one card per respondent (or case), it is usual to identify each record with the case and card number, a useful precaution with cards in the event of dropping them. Supposing each case extended over two cards, an arrangement such as that illustrated in Fig. 1 might be used.

The first stage in building a data file is to merge these cards into a single record, which means that

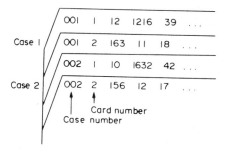

Figure 1
Arrangement for identifying records where each case extends over two cards

the identification data on each card need to be included once only on each record. As the cards are merged, a "sort-and-merge" check is usually made to ensure that the number of cases in the data file corresponds to the number of cases in the study and that for each case there is the same number of cards. Other kinds of checks attempt to identify the presence of "wild" code values (values outside the range specified for the variable), resulting from miskeying or mispunching.

When the originally coded data on the data file are assembled, and corrected as necessary, a common practice is to create a range of secondary variables from particular original or primary variables. For example, a variable to measure socioeconomic level may be a composite formed from variables measuring occupation, education, and income. The procedures adopted in forming such secondary variables always need to be fully documented.

3.3 Preparing the Codebook

The preparation of a codebook is an essential part of preparing the data file, since the codebook contains details about the characteristics of each variable and its location on the file. The following features are included for each variable in most codebooks:

(a) Variable identification: Each variable is identified by a number or a set of alphanumeric characters. For example, the SPSS system uses a set of alphanumeric characters with a maximum length of eight characters.

(b) Variable name: In general, the variable identification is linked to a variable name or label. Variables to be used in an analysis are usually selected by means of the variable identification, while the printout may give both the variable identification and the variable name in order to improve readability.

(c) Location: The location of each variable within a given record on a data file must be specified in terms of the numbers of the columns it spans, which is equivalent to giving the number of the first column of the entry for the variable and the width of the entry (the number of columns occupied by the entry).

(d) Format: The format of the variables should be specified in terms of the number of decimal places present or implicit in the data for the variable.

(e) Missing data code(s): Where code values have been assigned to missing responses, these should be specified.

(f) Item text: It is also useful to include with each item the actual text of the item used to solicit the data for each variable, even if such information is available in accompanying documentation.

(g) Code values: For each variable with a defined set of code values, the values should be given together with the responses to which they are assigned.

(h) Notes: It is often useful to add notes providing further information about a variable, especially for warnings about problems associated with the data for a given variable.

If the codebook is prepared in machine-readable form, access to data in a data file and statistical analyses of the data are greatly facilitated. Computer software is available for preparing and generating codebooks at most data archives. Software (written in FORTRAN) is also available (Anderson 1981) for reading machine-readable codebooks. This program extracts the information that defines and describes the full data set or any desired subset of the data, and then, in conjunction with SPSS, it generates SPSS data-definition control cards. Output from the program simply requires the insertion of SPSS task-definition or procedure cards and data analysis can immediately commence. Because the codebook is accessed directly, accuracy is ensured in locating all variables, variable labels, format specifications, missing data values, and value labels. This procedure avoids both the tediousness and susceptibility to error of the manual assembly of control cards.

4. Documenting Data Sets for Lodgment in Data Archives

The following description of a national study exemplifies the type of documentation necessary for a data set to be lodged in a data archive. The document was prepared under the kind of cost and time constraints which normally apply in research studies.

The Second IEA Mathematics Study (Rosier 1980a) collected information in Australia in 1978 from large samples of students in two target populations: 13-year-old students and Year 12 mathematics students. Information was also collected from mathematics teachers and school principals. The main report of the study made comparisons between the 1978 data and those collected in 1964 for the First IEA Mathematics Study (Husén 1967, Keeves 1968).

The data files from the IEA data bank for the First IEA Mathematics Study were reorganized to bring them into a form compatible with the files for the Second IEA Mathematics Study. Thus the second study included secondary analysis on the data from the first study. The data from the second study and the reorganized data from the first study were both set up using the OSIRIS system, which includes a machine-readable dictionary linked to the set of data. There were 12 data files altogether: separate files for students, teachers, and schools, for the two population levels, and for the two studies (1964 and 1978).

It was decided to present the documentation describing the data for the second study as a technical report in a microfiche format that could be reproduced by photocopying rather than in a machine-readable format (Rosier 1980b). The microfiche format was more economical in terms of the resources available for the study, and had the additional advantage that copies of administrative documents and the testing instruments could be included in the same volume. In particular, the mathematics test items for this study included diagrams, and so could not have been included in a normal machine-readable format.

The same technical document also included the codebooks for the reorganized data files from the first study, but excluded details of sampling and administration which had been reported earlier. The technical document contained the following sections:

(a) Section 1: Introduction, including reference to the main publications of the study and acknowledgment of the persons associated with its conduct.

(b) Section 2: Sampling of schools and students for each of the two populations.

(c) Section 3: Administrative procedures involved in liaison with education departments, and school coordinators, and in the conduct of the testing in schools.

(d) Section 4: Preparation of data for analysis including coding and punching procedures, and details of the stages following in building the data files for the second study and in reorganizing the data files from the first study.

(e) Appendix 1: Copies of the main administrative documents used in contacting schools and conducting the testing in schools.

(f) Appendix 2: Copies of the testing instruments, including the responses of the first case in each file and the code values assigned to these responses.

(g) Codebooks: The codebook for each of the 12 files contained:
   (i) description of variable types and names,
   (ii) variable list containing coding details for each variable,
   (iii) variable location, and
   (iv) sample data, giving the value for each variable for the first five cases on each file.

5. Access to Data Archives

Major data archives have already been established for the social sciences. The archives collect data sets, often reorganizing the data files and documentation before making them available to other users. The archives also provide a range of services to distribute information about the nature and availability of the data sets, and to assist researchers in accessing them.

Two major archives are the SSRC (Social Science Research Council) Survey Archive, and the Inter-university Consortium for Political and Social Research (ICPSR). The former is the national repository of social science data in the United Kingdom. Established in 1967, its brief is "to collect and preserve machine-readable data relating to social and economic affairs from academic, commercial, and governmental sources and to make that data available for secondary analysis". This archive is located at the University of Essex, Colchester, Essex C04 35Q, England.

The latter archive, the ICPSR, is based at the University of Michigan, and is a major source of archived data sets for universities and other institutions in the United States. The ICPSR also maintains links with universities and national bodies in other countries, such as the SSRC Survey Archive in the United Kingdom, and provides reciprocal borrowing rights. It is located at the Institute for Social Research, University of Michigan, Ann Arbor, Michigan 48106, United States.

The archives produce catalogues describing the data sets that may be borrowed. Researchers normally gain access to the data sets by using the formal channels that have been established between the archives and the institutions participating in the system. Data sets are usually supplied on magnetic tapes according to specified technical formats. Documentation in the form of codebooks and test instruments is usually supplied at a nominal cost.

Two international bodies have been established to promote the development and use of data archives. The International Association of Social Science Information Services and Technology (IASSIST) was established in 1976. The International Federation of Data Organizations (IFDO) was started in 1977.

6. Some Issues

Although much progress has been made in establishing good data archives, more work is needed before the level of data archiving can be regarded as satisfactory. Three issues affect future developments.

6.1 Obtaining Data Sets

One of the major problems faced by archives is the difficulty in obtaining data sets. Even where data sets are identified and located, there may be problems in obtaining them for inclusion in the archives. Some researchers are still wary of releasing their data for examination by other persons. Progress in this area will depend largely on a spirit of cooperation between the original researchers and the secondary analysts. One avenue is to encourage the joint authorship by the primary and secondary researchers of publications arising from secondary analysis. At the least, the original researchers should be offered the opportunity to make rejoinders in publications which include the results of secondary analysis.

Frequently, there are certain conditions governing access to particular data sets. The SSRC Survey Archive, for instance, has three access categories: (a) unconditional access, (b) access conditional on the depositor being informed of the request, and (c) access conditional on the prior consent of the depositor being obtained. The researcher requesting access to archived data is usually required to sign an undertaking to protect the anonymity of individuals and of institutions supplying the data, to acknowledge indebtedness to the original data collectors and to the archive, and to furnish to the archive any publications resulting from use of the data.

Some funding agencies are now making it a condition of their grants that any data collected under the grant should be lodged in appropriate data archives. However, the grants should also be large enough so that the researcher has sufficient resources to build good data sets supported by adequate documentation.

6.2 Adequate Documentation

The usefulness of a data set depends largely on the adequacy of the documentation which describes details of the collection of the data and characteristics of the data. Good documentation is necessary if for no other reason than that it reduces the costs of secondary analysis by increasing the efficiency with which data can be accessed.

For example, good documentation may include a listing of the data for the first few cases on each file. When the secondary analyst first reads an archived file, it is then possible to compare the results from the archived file with the documented listing to ensure that all the data are present, and that the data files correspond to those submitted by the original researcher. In the same way, the codebook entries for each variable should contain a statement about the number of cases (frequency) associated with each code value. The secondary analyst should be able to reproduce these frequencies from the archived data set. As further assistance to the secondary analyst, the set of data collection instruments could be reproduced with the original responses and the associated coding for one case—say, the first case.

6.3 Level of Aggregation of Data

Data are most useful to secondary analysts when they are stored at a minimal level of aggregation (the microlevel). This means that the original responses to questionnaire or test items are retained in a coded form on the data file. The secondary analyst then has the option of changing the level of aggregation, for example by deriving total test scores from a set of test items, or by deriving a mean school score from the data for students in a given school. If only the aggregated data (total or mean scores) are provided, the option of conducting analyses at the individual level is no longer available. Of course, steps must be taken to ensure that access to microlevel data does not enable conditions of anonymity or confidentiality to be breached.

Bibliography

Anderson J 1981 *Machine-readable Codebooks*. Flinders University of South Australia, Adelaide

Husén T (ed.) 1967 *International Study of Achievement in Mathematics: A Comparison of Twelve Countries*. Almqvist and Wiksell, Stockholm

Institute for Social Research 1981 OSIRIS *IV User's Manual*, 7th edn. Institute for Social Research, University of Michigan, Ann Arbor, Michigan

Johnson M C 1977 *A Review of Research Methods in Education*. Rand McNally, Chicago, Illinois

Keeves J P 1968 *Variation in Mathematics Education in Australia*. Australian Council for Educational Research, Hawthorn, Victoria

Nie N H, Hull C H, Jenkins J G, Steinbrenner K, Bent D H 1975 SPSS *Statistical Package for the Social Sciences*, 2nd edn. McGraw-Hill, New York

Postlethwaite T N, Lewy A 1979 *Annotated Bibliography of* IEA *Publications (1962–1978)*. International Association for the Evaluation of Educational Achievement (IEA), University of Stockholm, Stockholm, Sweden

Rosier M J 1980a *Changes in Secondary School Mathematics in Australia 1964 to 1978*. Australian Council for Educational Research, Hawthorn, Victoria

Rosier M J 1980b *Sampling, Administration and Data Preparation for the Second* IEA *Mathematics Study in Australia*. Australian Council for Educational Research, Hawthorn, Victoria

Schwille J, Marshall S 1975 *The* IEA *Six-subject Data Bank: A General Introduction*. University of Stockholm, Stockholm

Tiedeman D V 1972 *Project* TALENT *Data Bank: A Handbook*. American Institutes for Research, Project TALENT. Palo Alto, California

Walker D A 1976 *The* IEA *Six-subject Survey: An Empirical Study of Education in Twenty-one Countries*. Almqvist and Wiksell, Stockholm

Wolf R M 1967 *Data Bank Manual: International Project for the Evaluation of Educational Achievement, Phase I: International Study of Achievement in Mathematics: A Comparison of Twelve Countries*. Almqvist and Wiksell, Uppsala

J. Anderson; M. J. Rosier

Day Care

Day care is a term used to describe full-time public or private provision outside their own homes for children under compulsory school age; it usually caters for children of working mothers or from families in special need. The term also includes care out of school hours for school-age children. Facilities may be found in formal institutional settings as in a day nursery (crèche, day care centre), or more informally in a private home (childminding, family day care). The range of provision and practice is very wide, both between countries and within countries.

1. Historical Background

The need for day care grew from industrialization. In the West during the nineteenth century, wherever mothers were obliged to work all day in insalubrious mills and factories where infants could not be accommodated, solutions took two forms. Many women left their babies with relatives or neighbours, the latter being forerunners of today's childminders. Others took their children to day nurseries. These institutions were set up by philanthropic organizations and/or by individuals like Marbeau in Paris, Robert Owen in New Lanark, Margaret Macmillan in London, Maria Montessori in Rome, Charles Brace in New York and later, Yuli Tokunaga in Tokyo. A common aim was to support families and to keep slum children bathed, fed, and out of mischief.

In consequence, day nurseries came to be associated with needy families and to concentrate on hygiene, nutrition, and order under the eye of social welfare authorities. Many of the educational ideas of the pioneers were absorbed into kindergartens and nursery schools which developed separately under ministries of education. Day nurseries received early government recognition in Germany, France, and Belgium. Generally, official involvement in day care has increased from partial funding in the early 1900s, through legislation on health and safety, to regulations in the 1960s and 1970s aimed at improving quality of care. Simultaneously, recognition that the two systems should be integrated under one ministry has gained ground, and, in Sweden, has been achieved.

Expansion, worldwide, has been uneven, reflecting national needs in times of war and peace. For example, when immigrants flooded into the United States in the 1880s, after the 1918 Rice Riots in Japan, and during the two World Wars, governments stepped in to provide day nurseries. Once the crises passed, however, notably in the United States and the United Kingdom, facilities were run down. It is only where, on ideological grounds, women entered the labour force (USSR, People's Republic of China, Israel) or in some European and Scandinavian countries where smaller families, increased economic rewards, availability of part-time work, and improved education of women encouraged them to work outside the home, that day care is an accepted part of early childhood experience.

2. Theoretical Framework

Much professional opposition to day care, particularly in the United States and United Kingdom, has stemmed from the theory that separation damages the bond between a young child and its mother (Bowlby 1951). Yet more recent American and European research fails to support the view that day care necessarily has an adverse effect. Furthermore, cross-cultural studies of Israeli kibbutzim (collective settlements) and of children brought up in the Soviet Union and America (Bronfenbrenner 1971) indicate that children reared from an early age in a collective setting do not appear to suffer damage, providing their total environment is a stable, loving one. The issue is not clear cut, but current theory emphasizes the quality of care, the parents' happiness, and the child's relationship with its primary caretaker(s) for satisfactory child rearing (see *Mother–Child Relations*; *Soviet Theories of Human Development*).

Yet there is no worldwide consensus as to how to foster development. The communist East favours the collective experience for both children and parents. Soviet "upbringers" practice a "regime" in day nurseries which owes much to the learning theories of Pavlov, whereby a child's senses are methodically stimulated according to age. In contrast, Western theory centres on the individual child, encouraging free play and self-expression. following Piaget, the stages, rather than ages, of learning are emphasized. Above all, considerable prominence is accorded to the maternal role.

Where the mother–child relationship is poor and the quality of care questionable, the theory of compensatory education is relevant. A wide spectrum of experiments in the United States and Europe to improve cognitive, emotional, and social development in children from disadvantaged backgrounds suggests that help should be given as early as possible and in flexible and individual ways, with emphasis on parental involvement. The gap, however, between theory and practice is frequently considerable.

3. Provision and Practice

3.1 Auspices

Most commonly, municipalities, partly financed by central government, and partly financed through tax revenues and/or parent fees, are responsible for day care through their social welfare departments. Special projects may be sponsored by states, provinces, or central governments, but administered at local level [Project Head Start, USA (see *Head Start Program*); Integrated Child Development Scheme, India]. In the People's Republic of China and the Soviet Union, day nurseries are also run by rural communes or state farms, factories, and neighbourhood groups. In noncommunist countries, a variety of profit-making enterprises, voluntary agencies, employers, community, and other organizations operate in the private sector, especially where state run day care is deemed inadequate. Such bodies, sometimes aided by public funds, provide day nurseries in hospitals, universities, shrines, libraries, industrial and commercial enterprises, and military bases.

3.2 Aims and Objectives

These range from primary health care in emerging Third World countries, through purely custodial care characteristic of "traditional" day nurseries and some home day care (particularly in North America and the United Kingdom), to specific educational goals typified by highly structured compensatory programmes (USA, UK, GDR) and the scientifically devised scheme in the Soviet Union which aims to foster children's cognitive, emotional, and physical development.

Worldwide, most programmes aim to some degree to combine a caring service with educational objectives. Parental involvement, compulsory in some of the United States and in Israeli childminder projects, is increasingly aspired to. Parenthood education, training of paraprofessionals, and the use of the community and its resources are particularly featured in Peru, Venezuela, and Chile.

3.3 Types of Facility

Day care centres (day nursery, crèche, preschool, *vuggestue, krippe*) cater for between 5 and 60 children in small age-based or family groupings. Nurseries are open yearlong, 10–12 hours daily, at least 5 days a week. They accept children from a few months old up to the age of 3. In most east and west European countries, an age-related system operates whereby children of 2 years (France) or 3 may attend nursery school (kindergarten, *école maternelle*), and are thus absorbed into the country's education system. In the United Kingdom, Canada and the United States, however, children stay in day nurseries to compulsory school age (5). Some countries discourage use of day nurseries for very young babies.

Standards vary widely in both the public and private sectors, especially in the United States and the United Kingdom, as well as between states or provinces (Canada, India, FRG), and between rural and urban areas (USSR, People's Republic of China, Australia, Guatemala). Premises may conform to special architectural standards, notably in Scandinavia, the Soviet Union, Australia, and France, but many are in multipurpose and indifferent buildings. Very little hard, comparative data exist, but the adult:child ratio in most countries tends to be highest with babies, from 1:1 to 1:15 and reduces to between 1:8 and 1:30 by the age of 5. Staff training ranges from few or no formal qualifications, through nursery nurse preparation to comprehensive 2 or 3 year diploma courses.

Home day care (childminding, *crèche familiale*, family day care, public day care, *nourrice*, day foster mother) is when a childminder looks after other people's children on a regular basis for a fee. Parents usually bring the children to the minder's home and collect them after work. Hours are flexible and children are accepted from the age of a few weeks.

This is the most common form of day care, worldwide, (excluding the German Democratic Republic), and in much of Europe and Scandinavia is considered preferable for babies. Yet formal qualifications of caregivers, quality of care offered, standards of premises, safety, and equipment vary considerably, as do conditions of work, supervision, and enforcement of regulations. In Scandinavia, the Federal Republic of Germany, and France, childminders may be employed by the municipality and/or be carefully supervised and supported. Elsewhere, local authority supervision is often skeletal or, as in Yugoslavia, the service may be unregulated. Illegal childminding is said to be common and largely unchecked in many countries.

Leisure centres and family group care cater for school-age children of working parents, who would be otherwise "latchkey" children, out of school hours. Some countries run special centres (Netherlands, Scandinavia, and FGR) but more often the children are looked after by childminders. Care is mostly custodial.

4. Issues and Research Trends

The issue of day care highlights differences between cultures and political philosophies. In some Western countries, notably the United Kingdom and the United States, the recognition and extent of state provision raises fundamental issues for allocation of funding and for radical changes in society. In other countries where the rights of both men and women to work *and* to spend time rearing their children are widely accepted, attention can concentrate exclusively on what constitutes quality care and what forms family support should take.

Generally, availability of day care does not meet demand. A dilemma exists between what is theoretically desirable and what is economically and politically feasible. Most countries favour an extension of institutionalized provision and staff training. Certainly, the thrust of research in the Soviet Union and the German Democratic Republic is toward ways of raising the general levels of numeracy and literacy in that setting. In more pluralistic societies, there is greater variety. Concern over the consequences of poor quality care, of family versus day nursery provision, and the impact of different approaches for particular children and families, is reflected in the plethora of action research projects underway on these and related topics, notably in Scandinavia, United Kingdom, United States, Federal Republic of Germany, and Venezuela.

Other major issues are the balance between the needs of very young children and their parents, and between professionalism and parental involvement.

Some possibilities are to encourage parents to stay at home with very young children by providing realistic leave and allowances, as in Hungary; or, at least with the socially disadvantaged, to intervene with highly structured programmes from as early as six months. Another dilemma concerns cash incentives; do they encourage those most in need to benefit (as the French experience suggests), or may they, as some consider, erode parental responsibilities. A radical restructuring of employment to make more part-time jobs available and thus encourage shared parenting is another possible way forward, as in Sweden. Others prefer that parents and the community should run their own facilities, as in parts of the United Kingdom and Italy.

Overall, there is a marked trend for authorities to grapple with the problems of how to weld education- and welfare-oriented services into a flexible, comprehensive support network to meet the needs of all preschool children and their families. A major objective, reflected in comprehensive research projects (United Kingdom and Europe) is to find ways of ensuring continuity of children's good experience from the earliest years to entry into formal schooling and beyond, with increasing recognition of day care as a necessary and important part of the whole.

See also: Early Childhood Education

Bibliography

Bowlby E J M 1951 *Maternal Care and Mental Health,* WHO Monograph Series, 2. World Health Organization, Geneva

Bronfenbrenner U 1971 *Two Worlds of Childhood: US and USSR.* Allen and Unwin, London

Chazan M (ed.) 1978 *International Research in Early Childhood Education.* National Foundation for Educational Research Publishing Company, Slough

Early Childhood Education Association of Japan (eds.) 1979 *Early Childhood Education and Care in Japan.* Child Honsha, Tokyo

Educational Resources Information Center (ERIC) Clearinghouse on Elementary and Early Childhood Education, University of Illinois, College of Education, Urbana, Illinois 61801, USA

Kamerman S B, Kahn A J 1981 *Child Care, Family Benefits, and Working Parents, A Study in Comparative Policy.* Columbia University Press, New York

S. M. Shinman

Death Education and Counseling

Death education and counseling are social innovations that appeared in the twentieth century in response to changes in human modes of coping with death and dying. As scientific values, attitudes, and practices came to dominate Western societies, death moved from the world of familiar daily experience into segregated places, and control over dying shifted from the individual and family to the physician and hospital team. For many people religious belief lost much of its power to mediate fears of death. The rituals, direction, and support once provided by the extended family and the church to guide death-related transitions diminished in effectiveness (Benoliel 1978). Death became a "problem" instead of a normal part of human existence, and experiences with death became stressful life events without clear guidelines to assist people in coping with the intrapersonal and interpersonal changes produced by these experiences. Following the Second World War, death counseling and death education came into being as a multidisciplinary social movement to counter the death-denying practices of modern society.

1. Death Counseling

Death counseling is an interpersonal process through which one person helps another or group of others through a life crisis involving significant loss—most commonly the death or anticipated death of someone important. There are a number of death-related events and changes that create maturational crises for human beings. As a result, death counseling exists in several forms, for somewhat different purposes, and for different target populations. The recipients of these services include persons who are dying (Bowers et al. 1964), bereaved individuals and families (Schoenberg 1980), survivors of catastrophic experiences with loss (Ramsay and Noorbergen 1981), suicidal persons, and occupational groups engaged in offering care to the dying (Sobel 1981).

This form of counseling can be provided by psychiatrists, psychologists, nurses, social workers, ministers, and guidance counselors. It takes place in homes, clinics, hospitals, and other institutions. In recent years it has also been provided by lay people—usually through self-help groups and widow-to-widow programs. Lay counseling provides help in the form of assistance with concrete problems and support through shared experience with others in like circumstances. The broad goals of professional counseling are to provide support and to assist the individuals in clarifying goals, identifying problems, and seeking solutions in situations they are unable to manage on their own.

The methods used by the counselor vary from highly directive to nondirective depending on the theoretical model of intervention that guides the counselor's thinking. All theoretical paradigms underlying the concept of counseling have been influenced to some degree by Freud's ideas on unconscious beliefs about personal immortality and the death instinct as critical influences on human behavior (Feigenberg 1980 pp. 217–21). These ideas are central in the psychoanalytic model which emphasizes the importance of insight as an outcome of the therapeutic process. The goal of insight is also valued in client-centered and existential paradigms which, like psychoanalysis, rely heavily on nondirective counseling approaches (Sobel 1981 p. 4).

Another tradition in conseling comes from developmental psychology which relates models of intervention to the individual's capacity to cope with change in relation to stages of biopsychosocial development. This perspective has provided guidelines for identifying periods in the life cycle (such as childhood) when individuals are at high risk for maladaptive responses to significant loss (Benoliel 1981). Systems theory, family development, and crisis intervention have also made important contributions to theoretical perspectives underlying death counseling practices (Schoenberg 1980 pp. 98–105).

A more recent practice is behavior therapy which has origins in behavioral–cognitive and/or social-learning theories which stress the importance of social rewards and cognitive restructuring in bringing about behavioral change. Proponents of the behavioral modalities in death counseling use a variety of directive approaches including specific task assignments, role playing, training in coping skills, cognitive rehearsal, and problem-solving techniques. Insight is less important in these models of intervention than the achivement of behavioral change through desensitization to negative life stimuli and the learning of new coping skills (Sobel 1981 pp. 74–86). A powerful form of behavior therapy is guided confrontation therapy (GCT) developed in the Netherlands for the treatment of pathological bereavement problems through a forced confrontation with distressing emotions (Ramsay and Noorbergen 1981).

Regardless of the paradigm, however, the attitudes of the counselor are critical to the effectiveness of the counseling process. In practice, it is not unusual that counselors combine ideas from several theoretical paradigms. Increasingly common today is the counselor's use of specific goal-directed contracts that incorporate the values of the client with selected counseling practices (Sobel 1981, Feigenberg 1980). Evaluation of the results of death counseling to date is limited because of the relatively few studies that have had the benefit of control or comparison groups.

2. Death Education

Death education is a social transaction for making available valid death-related knowledge and opportunity to recognize how values and attitudes about death influence human behavior. The need for death education emerged in the 1960s out of growing professional and public awareness that the death-denying practices of modern society had a nonhumane influence on the dying, the bereaved, and people in general (Feifel 1977). Courses were created in a variety of disciplines by individuals with special interests in death. Variations in the courses are tied to six factors: target audience (children, adults, health professionals); target domain (cognitive, affective, behavioral); number of students; disciplinary focus (health education, nursing, art, sociology); methodology (lecture, films, direct experience); and goals (professional preparation, personal development, knowledge) (Feifel 1977 p. 263). Regardless of the variations, all levels of death education are concerned with information sharing, values clarification, and coping behaviors (Wass 1979 p. 389). The underlying rationale is human development across the life span. Based on learning theories, written guidelines for death education have been developed in relation to children of different ages (Mills et al 1976). Descriptions of courses for health professionals provide guidance to others with similar instructional interests (Benoliel 1982). The range of instructional approaches used in death education is well documented in *Death Education, Omega,* and *Essence* all of which are journals concerned with issues and research on death (thanatology). The evaluation of death education to date shows variable results in terms of changes in knowledge, attitudes, and behaviors—in great measure because of differences in evaluation methodologies in addition to variations in objectives, content, and teaching strategies (Feifel 1977 pp. 254–72).

Bibliography

Benoliel J Q 1978 The changing social context for life and death decisions. *Essence* 2(2): 5–14
Benoliel J Q 1981 Death counseling and human development: Issues and intricacies. *Death Education* 4(4): 337–53
Benoliel J Q 1982 *Death Education for the Health Professional.* Hemisphere, Washington, DC
Bowers M K, Jackson E, Knight J, LeShan L 1964 *Counseling the Dying.* Nelson, New York
Feifel H 1977 *New Meanings of Death.* McGraw-Hill, New York
Feigenberg L 1980 *Terminal Care: Friendship Contracts with Dying Cancer Patients.* Brunner/Mazel, New York
Mills G, Reisler R, Robinson A, Vermilye G 1976 *Discussing Death: A Guide to Death Education.* ETC Publications, Homewood, Illinois
Ramsay R W, Noorbergen R 1981 *Living with Loss: A Dramatic New Breakthrough in Grief Therapy.* Morrow, New York
Schoenberg B M 1980 *Bereavement Counselling: A Multidisciplinary Handbook.* Greenwood, London
Sobel H J 1981 *Behavior Therapy in Terminal Care: A Humanistic Approach.* Ballinger, Cambridge, Massachusetts
Wass H (ed.) 1979 *Dying: Facing the Facts.* Hemisphere, Washington, DC

J. Q. Benoliel

Decentralization and Education

Administration covers two orders of knowledge. The first is the understanding of the behavior of social organizations through a rational approach; the second refers to technical norms, designed according to the characteristics of the system in order to achieve self-direction. Thus, the study of administration acquires particular characteristics for each social context.

As a social phenomenon, administration is a set of techniques used to direct and coordinate resources, processes, and phenomena that interact within a given structure and within a historically determined set of social conditions. Public or private organizations operating in environments where socioeconomic insufficiencies predominate are thus faced with a set of administrative problems of a different nature than those which more developed societies face. At the same time the rapid economic growth of countries such as the United States, in conjunction with the technological development it has experienced, has allowed the development and utilization of rather sophisticated techniques of administration. As the example of the United States shows, industrial experience tends to be accompanied by advances in administrative sophistication. A country's political organization also affects the particular profile of public administration. In the United States, the relative economic and political independence of local government has permitted a good deal of administrative autonomy in terms of internal decision making and administrative and financial self-sufficiency. In these patterns, individual and collective ideologies are reflected in the emphasis on such values as material progress as a valid end to human activity; time, considered to be an expensive element over which men have control and one which, being scarce, must be well-directed; and the accumulation of wealth as a source of consumption and prestige.

In underdeveloped countries the condition of dependent peripheral economies has determined their social, political, and administrative structures. As a result of their recent industrialization and, in some cases, their recent political consolidation as independent states, they have had limited administrative experience. At the same time, in order to consolidate the state, governments have favored administrative structures based on centralization of functions and concentration of authority. In spite of these tendencies, however, most underdeveloped countries have pursued their development objectives not through an integrated plan for national development but rather through isolated, partial efforts that are temporary in nature and lack long-range perspective.

The progressive concentration of decision making in central structures has prevented the development of viable administrative practices at the regional and local level, this affecting the participation of the people involved as well as hampering administrative efficiency in public matters in different parts of the country.

1. The Concept and Meaning of Decentralization

Organizations have a specific mode of interconnection and interaction of their components from which specific forms of administration and communication are derived. One such form is decentralization, which involves a specific mode of structuring and managing a system. Its main principle is the delegation of authority and functions to all hierarchical levels, thus allowing the participation of all organizational components. Under decentralized forms of administration, it is the responsibility of the higher hierarchical levels to achieve harmony within the components in order to secure a dynamic equilibrium. The subordination of the parts reflects their special place and meaning within the overall process. Decentralization surpasses the concept of administrative control, typical of centralization, and adopts as its basic premise the participation of all components in order to guarantee and legitimate the decisions involved and to allow all decentralized groups relative independence.

2. Decentralization and Deconcentration

Decentralization and deconcentration are two related administrative principles. Both are conceived as efficient means to overcome limitations that originate in more centralized forms of administering public services, and that constitute obstacles in achieving development. Consequently, both alternatives have received considerable support in developing countries.

Administrative decentralization is a form of organization that attributes organic autonomy to certain institutional components. There are traditionally three forms of administrative decentralization: by technical services, by territorial function, and by cooperation.

Deconcentration consists of the delegation of authority by the central organization to internal or external groups. Deconcentration constitutes procedures that relieve higher powers of most of their tasks, allowing lower level authorities to make more rapid decisions. At the same time, deconcentration, through the creation of decision-making groups outside of the center of the organization, ensures a better and more efficient administration, allowing individuals and groups to settle their own matters without having to plead with the central organization. Deconcentration normally involves a legal process: the delegation of authority to the deconcentrated organ is accomplished through legal procedures.

3. Advantages of Decentralization

As is true of every administrative process, decentralization in any of its forms has advantages as well as disadvantages. Both are evident when compared with centralization, which is identified with political control and with numerous aspects related to a supreme and central authority. Some of the advantages of decentralization are:

(a) Participation: a greater degree of democracy is enjoyed by the participants in the decentralized administration process.

(b) Legitimacy: decisions which are adopted on a more participatory basis enjoy greater consensus.

(c) Proximity: decisions in decentralized systems pay closer attention to concrete needs.

(d) Creation and innovation: participation promotes the individual's creative processes for the benefit of the organization.

(e) Integration: the internal coherence of the organization is facilitated if coordination and direction function correctly and if efficient channels of communication are established.

(f) Efficiency: personnel and paperwork costs are reduced in central offices.

4. The Development of Decentralization

4.1 General

The Latin American countries have had similar experiences in administrative matters since they derive their traditions from centralist models. At the same time, there is more extensive background of self-determination and codetermination of workers in enterprises than in the decentralization of public administration.

There have been two interesting experiments, both set up in Mexico. The first is the decentralization of recently adopted "treasury" functions of the federal government, which refer to the collection of federal taxes through agreements made by the state governments and the fiscal administration, dividing the country into nine regions. The second deals with the deconcentration of public services in the federal district, the political capital of the country, which is accompanied by the responsible participation of people in different aspects of community life. Towards this end, the federal district was divided into 16 "delegations."

In general, the tendency observed in the developing countries is towards the creation of decentralized institutions with organic autonomy from the central offices of the state. Deconcentrated offices of the central sector have been established more slowly.

4.2 Deconcentration in Education

The administration of educational services is one of the areas that requires urgent administrative deconcentration. Since education is one of the most important areas for development, most countries have given it special priority. Therefore, educational systems have experienced a rapid growth in enrollment, in the establishment of educational centers, and in the administration of a great number of schools and financial resources. Traditionally, these services have been managed by the central government, but due to their growth it is necessary to take a different approach. The following steps might be taken to achieve greater deconcentration:

(a) General redesign of the system: a new administrative model could be designed, including the restructuring of the central levels from the beginning.

(b) Regionalization: a territorial division of the country could be determined, according to the most convenient geographical and political conditions. Central-office delegations and, if necessary, subdelegations and regional offices could be established in each region.

(c) Regional planning: following the general criteria of planning, each delegation could work out local plans, programs, and budgets; design manuals of policy and procedure; and train personnel.

(d) Deconcentration of technical and academic aspects: the delegations could organize, control, supervise, and evaluate educational services. The central offices could be responsible for designing curriculum, study plans and programs, and for the approval of textbooks. Technical and academic aspects, as well as services such as study accreditation and certification, registration of the professions, and cultural activities could be gradually deconcentrated, according to present educational levels and models.

(e) The elaboration, approval, and distribution of educational material and auxiliary textbooks could be deconcentrated to conform to local characteristics and needs.

(f) Resource management deconcentration: the last phase of deconcentration is related to the management of human, financial, and material resources for education by each delegation. Once the system has been perfected, this management must involve the elaboration, implementation, and control of annual educational budgets.

(g) Evaluation: the central powers, with direct participation of the deconcentrated powers, must implement the evaluation mechanisms of the system in order to adopt decisions that will permit its correction.

Educational deconcentration seeks to bring decision making to the place where the services are rendered, thus facilitating the participation of local officials, teachers, pupils, and the community. Another of its purposes is to identify educational needs at the local level and to make the appropriate decisions. Participation is the central point of educational deconcentration—the basic element to achieve national educational plans. The future looks promising for this process. Its goal is to acquire responsibilities at municipal and local levels and eventually at a school level, so that the form and content of education will be more relevant to each community, regardless of the administrative benefits achieved.

5. *Prospects for Decentralization*

It is evident that the growth of social organizations requires the introduction of more efficient administrative mechanisms, such as decentralization and deconcentration. Consequently, the states must resort to these processes for the administration of public services and the granting of justice, and will have to change their political schemes to support the decentralization of public functions. Theoretically, decentralization may have great advantages; however, it can not be judged in an abstract way. Its possibilities depend on the political and socioeconomic conditions of the population.

From this point of view, decentralization must be achieved within a global process of planning and programming which is capable of designing and controlling the actions of public administration. This planning process must transcend a merely indicative quality in order to assure the implementation of its results. It also must overcome the separation between political structures and administrative processes. Nevertheless, the implementation of decentralization is strongly limited for the following reasons:

(a) Particular characteristics of the socioeconomic system and the political power.

(b) The degree of evolution and complexity of public administration.

(c) The inequitable distribution of wealth between federal entities and the existence of different instruments for fiscal collection.

(d) A lack of specialized technical personnel.

(e) A low capacity to generate projects from the public and private sectors.

Deconcentration must employ formal and informal mechanisms to aid in the rationalization of resources of the developing countries in order to obtain the most favorable relation between means and ends. It will contribute to the consolidation of "democracy" by creating more efficient means of participation.

See also: Ministries and State Departments of Education; Participatory Planning in Education

Bibliography

Banco de Desarrollo Centroamericano 1979 *Entidades Públicas Descentralizadas del Istmo Centroamericano,* Banco de Desarrollo Centroamericano, San José, Costa Rica

Goehlert R U 1981 *The Planning and Implementation of Social Programs.* Vance Bibliographies, Monticello, Illinois

Jimenez Castro W 1978 *Problemática de la gestión en las instituciones descentralizadas del Istmo Centroamericano.* Instituto Nacional de Ciencias de la Administración, San José, Costa Rica

Mexico, Secretaría de la Presidencia 1976a *Advances de la desconcentración administrativa.* Dirección de Estudios Administrativos, Boletin de Estudios Administrativos No. 6. Secretaría de la Presidencia, Mexico City

Mexico, Secretaría de la Presidencia 1976b *Desconcentración administrativa.* Dirección General de Estudios Administrativos. Secretaría de la Presidencia, Mexico City

Prats Y 1973 *Décentralisation et développement* Cujas, Paris

J. A. Pescador

Decision-making Theory

Decision theory refers variously to prescriptive models for individuals to use in making decisions, to collections of techniques for overcoming barriers to these decisions, to descriptive models of the decision making which results from the imperfect application to these theories and techniques, and to the complications which arise when groups make decisions. Each of these four meanings of the term is important in education, though in different contexts. One aim of schooling, for example, is to improve individuals' decision-making ability, and to do so educators need a theory around which to build curriculum. Eventually large numbers of individual decisions become major policy issues: in most countries, for example, the structure and size of the higher-education system—or at least the demand for its services—depends on the patterns of decisions among recent and not-so-recent high-school graduates. In many cases educational institutions are relatively democratic and collaborative places, which means that collective decisions—and their complications—replace those of individuals.

1. *Prescriptive Individual Decision Theory*

Two concepts are particulary important—preference and option. Consider, by way of example, the problem facing a student during registration week. Assume that the student—Marion—has one elective class, and that the two courses she is considering are "Modern Detective Fiction" (henceforth referred to as "murder") and "Humor in American Literature" ("laughter"). These two courses are Marion's options. Each course has several attributes, and it is these which influence choice. Murder, for example, might be widely known as an easy course, while Laughter might be known as a hard course. On the other hand, Murder might meet at noon, while Laughter meets at 8 am. Murder might require a lot of reading, but that reading might be pleasurable; Laughter, on the other hand, might require reading that most tedious of literatures, research on the origins and meaning of humor. In any case, Marion's choice between the two courses will depend on the specific attributes she finds attractive (late meeting and hard course, for example) and on the values of those attributes for the two courses. The set of desirable values for specified attributes constitutes Marion's preference.

If she proceeds intuitively, Marion will think about the match between each course's attributes and her preferences. Something which comes closer to one's preferences than something else is said, in decision theory, to have more utility to the decision maker. The major contribution of decision theory to decision making is its formalization of the relationship between options' attributes and their utilities. Without decision-theory techniques, Marion will assign each option a utility and choose accordingly, but she will not make explicit her utility ratings. These intuitive assignments—and therefore her choice—might be different, given time and tools for careful analysis. In Marion's case the major obstacle to a simple decision is the required tradeoff between the two courses' difficulty and timing. The only late course is easy; the only hard course is early. If Marion's utility function weights difficulty and timing equivalently she should be indifferent between the two courses. The corollary is that if Marion prefers one of the two courses her utility function must not weight the two attributes equally. This observation is the basis for tradeoff analysis, whereby a decision maker considers hypothetical choices like Marion's and, on the basis of his or her preferences, develops a set of "indifference curves" which identify equivalent combinations of competing attributes. If Marion's set of curves suggest that she is more interested in timing than difficulty (since she will accept greatly reduced difficulty in return for slightly later time), then she could choose Murder as her elective class.

Another complication which might make someone's intuitive judgments unreliable is uncertainty. Say, by way of illustration, that the preferences of another student, Terry, were for a course which would maximize his grade-point average. Say, further, that Marion and Terry were enrolled in a very homogenous college, so that all their fellow students were equivalently intelligent and hard working. Grades in courses thus depend on the particular chemistry which develops among student, instructor, and subject matter. For the purposes of this discussion, the important observation is that Terry is unable to predict what grades he will get in Murder or Laughter. This is the only course attribute of any importance to Terry. To solve this problem, Terry looks up grade records for the two courses, and finds remarkable consistency. About half the students in Murder typically get As, 30 percent get Bs, and 20 percent get Cs. In Laughter, 40 percent of the students get As, and the rest get Bs. Terry thus must choose between two uncertain outcomes.

According to decision theory, Terry should choose individual courses on the basis of the average outcome each would yield if he were to make the same choice repeatedly. This is true so long as Terry is satisfied that three assumptions are met:

(a) the decision is part of a longer run set of decisions,

(b) the worst consequence, however unlikely, is tolerable, and

(c) the outcomes are close enough, and well-measured enough, to be averageable.

In this case these assumptions seem reasonable (the second might be questionable if Terry were on probation and not able to tolerate a C). Thus Terry must calculate measures of expected average outcomes for the two courses. Using the standard formula for grade-point averages (A = 4, B = 3, and so on), these averages, called "expected values," are for Murder $(4)(0.5) + (3)(0.3) + (2)(0.2) = 3.3$, and for Laughter $(4)(0.4) + (3)(0.6) = 3.4$. This makes Laughter the better choice, and according to decision theory Terry should choose accordingly.

But what if Terrry is not motivated solely by grade-point average? Suppose, for example, that he really values As, not his average. In this case the standard grade-point values for grades do not match Terry's utility function, the mathematical expression of his preferences for different attributes. A formula which did match A-seeking preferences would assign As a value of 10, and all other grades a value of 0. In this case Murder would be worth 5, Laughter would be worth 4, and the recommended choice would be the opposite of the first. If tradeoffs were involved a formula would be constructed which equally weighted grade-point values and A-likelihoods, but the point is clear: different preferences lead to different choices, even when the preferences appear similar on the surface. The value of decision theory is not that it makes decisions such as Terry's or Marion's better in some absolute sense; it is that decision analysis clarifies the relationship between the decision-maker's preferences and the relative attractiveness—utility—of the available options.

Decision theory proposes a similar approach to choices where the measurement of the outcomes, rather than (or, more usually, in addition to) their certainty is problematic. In this case the first step is to rank the possible outcomes. Next a series of hypothetical choices is considered in which one possible choice is a nonextreme option (that is, neither the highest nor the lowest ranked) and the other possible choice is a situation where the decision maker might get the first-ranked option and the last-ranked option with some given probabilities. Say, for example, that the decision maker is trying to assign utilities to an ice-cream cone, a new pen, an extra 15 minutes of lunch break, and two dollars. The ranking might be lunch break first, followed by money, ice cream, and finally pen. The first hypothetical choice would be between the ice cream, as one option, and an uncertain outcome of either the lunch break or the pen as the other. Presumably if the probability of the lunch break were high the second option would be the more attractive, while the opposite would be true if this probability were low. The question is, at what probability does the choice become difficult for the decision maker? If, for example, the decision maker had trouble with the hypothetical choice—this is called the "indifference point"—when the probability of the lunch break was about 20 percent, then decision theory suggests that the ice cream has a utility equal to 20 percent of the lunch break's utility. It is conventional to assign the most attractive item a utility of 1.0 or 100 and the least attractive a utility of 0; in this case the utility of the ice cream is 0.2 or 20. Repeating the hypothetical analysis for the money would yield a different utility somewhere between 0.2 (or 20) and 100 (or 1.0). These hypothetical utilities can then be used in more complex analysis, such as complex choices involving uncertainty in several of the items.

In an ideal rational world, decision makers would all behave like an idealized Marion or Terry: they would have clear senses of their own preferences, good information on the attributes of different options relevant to those preferences, and the time and skills necessary to analyze complex situations involving those preferences and attributes. Moreover, their preferences would not change unpredictably over time, and neither would the attributes of options. The real world is somewhat different, however: people have only general senses of their own preferences, limited information on the options available to them, and little ability or inclination to abandon intuitive judgment for formal analysis. Moreover, preferences and attributes change both predictably and randomly. The result is that individual decisions can be quite different from those prescribed by rational decision theory. Nevertheless, in a collection of individual decisions there may be a pattern which corresponds roughly to the preferences and option attributes which underlie them. Given appropriate techniques, it is possible to infer something about individual preferences for options' attributes from such a collection of data.

2. Descriptive Individual Decision Theory

A staff analyst in a school may be asked to analyze the elective-course choices of a particular cohort in order to find out whether the students' choices are motivated by particular attributes of the courses. If the school has collected data on each student and each elective course available to that student, the analyst must estimate the effects of different course and student attributes on choices from these data. Clearly the general model outlined in the preceding section is relevant here, but it does not provide a specific procedure for the analyst to follow. There are two complications: first, the analyst implicitly wants to estimate a single utility function for all students, but all students may not have the same utility function; and second, students' choices depart from those called for by their utility functions for the reasons outlined in the preceding section—imperfect information, insufficient analysis, and so on—and because they are to some extent motivated by whim. A more general problem, of course, is that the analyst does not know even the form of students' utility functions—linear, additive, discontinuous, or logistic—yet must assume the form in statistical work. It is tempting, in view of these complications, to simply say the analysis is impossible. But as the preceding section suggests this merely relegates judgment about the importance of course attributes to administrators' intuition. Surely it is possible to at least inform this intuitive judgment.

For simplicity, assume that the analysts' data include the student's aptitude (a test score, perhaps, or grade-point average to date) and interests (categories such as mathematics/science, humanities, or law/business) and each course's difficulty (on some scale), topic (in the same categories as student interests), and grade distribution (such as average grade). For the moment ignore the possibility of other variables being important. According to the preceding section, each student has a utility function which translates course attributes into an abstract quantity called "utility." Assume, for the moment, this function is, for student i and course j, $U_{ij} = f_i$ (difficulty$_j$, topic$_j$, grades$_j$). Different students presumably have different utility functions f_i, much as they have different attributes such as aptitude and interests. The major simplifying assumption which underlies descriptive theory is the assumption that attribute differences among choosers—students, in this case—affect utilities much the way attribute differences among options influence a given student's utilities. Specifically, if two students consider that same option *i*, then the difference between the utilities they assign that option is a function of their aptitudes and interests. This means that: $U_{ij} = f$ (aptitudes$_i$, interests$_i$, difficulty$_j$, topic$_j$, grades$_j$) where f is the general function which translates student and option attributes into utilities.

Given data on each combination of options and students, and on whether each combination resulted in "chosen" or "not chosen," the analyst's problem reduces to a classic (if difficult) statistical problem: estimating the relationship between a set of predictor variables and a dichotomous outcome. There are several ways to tackle this problem, the most prominent being ordinary least-squares discriminant analysis and conditional-logit analysis. The choice among these statistical techniques depends primarily on the number of options each student considers and the use to which the results are to be put. Whatever the estimating technique, the result is an equation which gives the probability a given option will be chosen by a given student as a function of the student's and the option's attributes. This corresponds roughly to the utility function students use to make their decisions in the first place, and can be used to predict the effects of changes in student or option attributes.

Two thorny issues arise in analysis of choices and other dichotomous outcomes. The first involves interpretation of results. If variables are scaled appropriately, discriminant techniques yield coefficients interpretable as the change in probability of a 1-outcome ("chosen" versus "not chosen", for example) for a unit change in an independent variable. Conditional-logit coefficients cannot be so interpreted. The two techniques have reversed benefits when the second issue, statistical validity, is considered. The distribution of errors in a discriminant analysis is far from the independent, normal ideal called for by least-squares techniques. In the case of choice analysis this means two key statistics—the standard errors of coefficients, and the coefficient of determination, or R^2—are not accurate. Conditional-logit analysis, on the other hand, is based on more accurate assumptions about misfits in dichotomous models, and its measures of standard errors and determination are more accurate. The result is a dilemma not unlike the uncertainty principle in physics: one can either know what the answer is or how accurate it is, but not both.

3. Applications

Part of the reason for introducing prescriptive decision theory using hypothetical choices was the dearth of documented, educational applications of the technique. In fact, although the noneducational (primarily business) literature on such techniques is substantial, documented applications are equally rare outside education. The major exception to this is the insurance industry, which regularly applies decision-analysis techniques for analyzing uncertainty (under the rubric "actuarial science") to the setting of premiums and the acceptance of risks.

Examples of descriptive decision theory in education and elsewhere are much easier to find. One long-term example involves United States students' decisions whether to enter college after high-school graduation. Early studies of this decision relied on the fact that summary statistics (such as average tuitions and participation rates) can be used to approximate utility functions. The findings were sensible, but insufficiently precise for the analysis of relevant policies, such as federal financial-aid policy or state college-expansion policy. More recent studies have relied on individual-level data sets like those outlined above. The data and statistical techniques have varied from study to study, but the general picture is remarkably stable: family-background factors are the most prominent influence on students' postsecondary decisions, followed by academic factors and then by college-related factors, such as location, tuition, and financial aid. Such consistency is also apparent in other research on educational choices, and this suggests that although individuals' utility functions are in fact different, they are similar enough for meaningful results to emerge from descriptive decision research.

These are brief introductions to the two major representations of decision theory, the making and the describing of individual decisions. The other two major representations of decision theory correspond to these, only they prescribe or describe group decisions rather than those of individuals. The major complication is the fact that the utility function for a group—that is, the groups' preferences for different attributes of options—is not simply the average of group members' preferences; the "average" utility function generally does not select the option most group members would choose, and thus is useless. Arriving at a group utility function requires group members either to discuss and negotiate preferences or to cede power to an individual, neither of which is easy to do. Decision theory for groups thus is essentially organizational theory—that is, organizational behavior, descriptively, and organizational development, prescriptively.

See also: Decision Theory in Educational Research and Testing; Decision Seminar Technique in Education; Organizational Development, Educational

Bibliography

Baird B F 1978 *Introduction to Decision Analysis*. Duxbury, Belmont, California
Brown R V, Kahr A S, Peterson C 1974 *Decision Analysis for the Manager*. Holt, Rinehart and Winston, New York
Cox D R 1970 *Analysis of Binary Data*. Chapman and Hall, London
Hanushek E A, Jackson J E 1977 *Statistical Methods for Social Scientists*. Academic Press, New York

Harrison E F 1981 *The Managerial Decision-Making Process*, 2nd edn. Houghton Mifflin, Boston, Massachusetts

Jackson G A 1980 The case of the dependent dichotomy. *Proceedings to the American Statistical Association, Social Statistics Section 1980* American Statistical Association, (ASA), Washington, DC

Jackson G A 1981 Linear analysis of logistic choices, and vice versa. In: Alvey W, Kilss B 1982. *Proceedings to the American Statistical Association Social Statistics Section 1981*. American Statistical Association (ASA), Washington, DC

Lave C A, March J G 1975 *An Introduction to Models in the Social Sciences*. Harper and Row, New York

Luce R 1959 *Individual Choice Behavior: A Theoretical Analysis*. Wiley, New York

McFadden D 1974 Conditional logit analysis of qualitative choice behavior. In: Zarembka P (ed.) 1974 *Frontiers of Econometrics*. Academic Press, New York, pp. 105–42

Manski C F 1977 The structure of random utility models. *Theory and Decision* 8: 229–54

Press S J, Wilson S 1978 Choosing between logistic regression and discriminant analysis. *J. Am. Statis. Assoc.* 73: 699–705

Raiffa H 1968 *Decision Analysis: Introductory Lectures on Making Choices under Uncertainty*. Addison-Wesley, Reading, Massachusetts

Stokey E, Zeckhauser R 1978 *A Primer for Policy Analysis*. Norton, New York

Theil H 1970 On the estimation of relationships involving qualitative variables. *Am. J. Sociol.* 76: 103–54

G. A. Jackson

Decision-oriented Evaluation

Decision-oriented evaluation is a process that produces information for selecting among alternative courses of action. An evaluation is decision oriented if it (a) services a decision, (b) implies a choice among alternatives, and (c) is used in committing resources for the next interval of time before another decision is to be made. Properly conceptualized, decision-oriented evaluation is a perspective for organizing and focusing the concepts of evaluation toward the broadly defined requirements of decision making rather than a specific method or technique by which decisions are made.

1. Some Decision-oriented Definitions and Concepts

The Phi Delta Kappa National Study Committee on Evaluation (Stufflebeam et al. 1971) represented one of the first attempts to consider evaluation from a decision-making perspective. They defined educational evaluation as "the process of delineating, obtaining, and providing useful information for judging decision alternatives" and divided evaluation into four distinct activities, each with its own decision-making purpose. Similarly, Hagedorn and co-

workers (1976), writing to mental-health professionals, defined evaluation as "a systematic set of data collection and analysis activities undertaken to determine the value of a program to aid management, program planning, staff training, public accountability, and promotion." This definition reflects the same view of evaluation as that which prevailed in education, that of an information feedback process to aid administrators and project management.

The primary impetus for the development of decision-oriented evaluation was a desire to maximize the utilization of evaluation results. For the Phi Delta Kappa National Study Committee on Evaluation utilization was to be fostered by having the evaluator serve "as an extension of the decision maker's mind." The Commission suggested that the evaluator must assume, in addition to a technical role, an interface role in which he/she interacts with the decision maker for the purpose of delineating decision alternatives and providing information for selecting among alternative courses of action. This role requires the evaluator to work with the decision maker in creating an awareness of the decisions to be made, spelling out the decision alternatives, and identifying the evaluative criteria to be utilized in the evaluation.

A similar decision-oriented view of evaluation can be found in the work of Alkin (1969). Alkin's definition of evaluation advanced the notion that evaluation is a process of ascertaining decision areas of concern, selecting appropriate information, and collecting and analyzing information in order to report summary data useful to decision makers. This definition, while affirming that evaluation should be an information-collection process used to make decisions about alternatives, goes further to suggest that "the manner in which the information is collected, as well as the analysis procedures, must be appropriate to the needs of the decision maker or a potential decision involved public." This definition laid the groundwork for a broad distinction between the decision-oriented evaluator whose role it was to delineate decision alternatives and to provide information for selecting among them, and the researcher whose role it was to discover or explain theoretical phenomena. Emphasized was the notion that the most important function that an evaluator can perform is to report summary data to the decision maker in the form of practical and unambiguous statements about what alternative course of action should be taken.

2. Decision-oriented Evaluation Paradigms

Given the diversity of evaluation contexts within any particular field, there is considerable diversity in the specific decision-oriented approaches and procedures utilized. Different decision makers have different values, priorities, and political presses on their activities. Other influences which may vary from setting to setting include administrative levels and leadership styles of decision makers, variety of organizational goals, and disparity in the communication networks that both form and inform decisions. Each context and information need places different constraints on the activity of evaluation. Some evaluation approaches and procedures will be inadequate or inappropriate in some contexts and perfectly matched with the decision-oriented information needs in others. From these practical considerations have emerged different procedural frameworks for conducting decision-oriented evaluations. Although varied in their explicit references to decisions, these frameworks—or models—are decision oriented in that they are devoted almost exclusively to the gathering and reporting of information relevant to the needs of decision makers for the purpose of selecting among alternative courses of action.

2.1 Educational Psychology Models

When applied in the context of a specific program or intervention, decision-oriented evaluation often takes the form of an evaluation of the objectives of that program or intervention. The decision is usually one of adopting or revising the program based on the degree to which the program did or did not meet its objectives. Generally these evaluation models employ the following steps: (a) identifying objectives, (b) stating objectives in measurable behavioral terms, (c) devising and administering measurement instruments, (d) comparing obtained results with the objectives prespecified in step (a), and (e) reporting to decision makers discrepancies between obtained results and objectives for the purpose of program revision or adoption. Common features of educational psychology models include (a) their almost exclusive application to the evaluation of curriculum and instruction, (b) the high priority they place on defining objectives, and (c) their limited focus on comparisions of "what is" with "what should be," with discrepancy information constituting the bulk of evaluation results. One educational psychology model commonly used for the purpose of gathering and reporting information relevant to the needs of decision makers was that developed by Provus (1971). Provus proposed a five-stage evaluation process: design, installation, process, product, and program comparison.

The design stage has as its objective a description of all intended program inputs, processes, and outcomes. The installation stage is concerned with field operations and the discrepancy between the intended and actual manner in which the program was installed. The process stage has as its objective the measurement of enabling or short-term outcomes. In the product stage the evaluator determines if terminal or long-term outcomes have been attained at the level specified by the objectives. In the final program comparison stage, the evaluator compares the experimental program with some competing program to show that benefit is commensurate with cost.

At each stage of this process there are three activities: (a) agreeing on program standards (usually program goals or objectives), (b) determining if a discrepancy exists between aspects of a program, and (c) using discrepancy information to identify program weaknesses. Discrepancy information at each stage is used to inform decision makers whether or not to proceed to the next stage or to revise program standards or operations.

Although the evaluator's role as an information provider is not as explicit in the educational psychology models as in the following set of models, these models identify the decision areas of concern, select appropriate information, and collect and analyze information in order to report summary data useful to decision makers. As is the case with other decision-oriented approaches, these models limit the evaluator's freedom in an evaluative context to activities that are congruent with the information needs of the decision maker.

2.2 Educational Decision Models

Some writers in the field of evaluation have explicitly put forth the notion that the role of evaluation is to provide decision makers with information. The following premises characterize this notion of evaluation: (a) the decision maker determines what is to be evaluated and may even choose the measures to be used, (b) the evaluator's role is that of an advisor to the decision maker, (c) the work of evaluation consists almost exclusively of information gathering and reporting, (d) the information gathered must be relevant to the decision maker's needs, and (e) the information that is important is dictated by the decision to be made.

The CIPP evaluation model (Stufflebeam et al. 1971) is particularly representative of this approach. This model divides evaluation into four distinct stages—context, input, process, and product evaluation, thus the acronym CIPP. Each of these stages are intended to represent a cluster of decisions to be served by the information provided within them. Context evaluation has as its objective to specify the operational context and to identify problems and underlying needs within the decision maker's domain. Input evaluation is concerned with identifying and assessing alternative means of achieving specified ends. Process evaluation has as its objective to inform decisions pertaining to procedural design or implementation and to make adjustments and refinements that seem to be called for from monitoring the program. The goal of product evaluation is to relate outcome information to objectives and to context, input and process data, eventually leading to a series of decisions (e.g. to terminate, revise, or recycle the program as is). At each stage outcomes are compared to stated objectives and differences between expected and actual results are reported to decision makers.

2.3 Educational Science Models

In this third view of the decision-oriented perspective, evaluative inquiry is conducted in much the same manner as in the previous models, except that the decisions to be made pertain almost exclusively to choices among alternative courses of action representing competing programs. The terms evaluative research and applied research reflect this attempt to use experimental design and the tools of classical research methodology for making practical choices among programs.

This evaluation process proposes a causal model consisting of three components: inputs (usually client or student characteristics or attributes), the programs (those experiences to which clients or students are exposed), and outcomes (certain targeted skills and abilities measured at program completion). The purpose of educational science models is to establish causal connections between these components. Regression or linear model techniques are used to compute predicted outcome scores on the basis of various input data. Then groups of students, subjected to various program alternatives, are tested to determine whether those in each program exceed, match, or fall short of what would be expected from input data alone. Program impact is inferred if outcome variance cannot be explained by input data alone and if the performance of clients or students in the experimental program represents a statistically significant improvement over the performance of those in a comparison program.

Although educational science models have not proliferated, a sorting through of evaluation studies reveals a strong reliance on the scientific method and an even heavier emphasis on the experimental designs and statistical tools of research. In this model statistical decision rules (e.g., $p < .05$) unequivocally determine program effectiveness and, hence, identify which alternative course of action (program) should be selected. Implicit in this paradigm is the translation of decisions about programs into notions of cause and effect.

Other quantitative approaches to decision-oriented evaluation can be found in the decision-theoretic work of Guttentag (1973) and the Bayesian statistics of Thompson, Schnelle, and Willemian (reviewed in Larson and Kaplan 1981). These highly quantitative procedures for informing decisions about programs attempt to bridge the gap between the complex multivariate world in which programs operate and unambiguous "go/no-go" decisions that are envisioned by decision makers who operate within it.

3. Other Perspectives

Some authors have taken exception to the decision-oriented perspective and, in particular, to the applied research model. The primary criticism of the decision-oriented definition of evaluation is that evaluator and decision maker share the function of evaluation unequally. The role of the evaluator is to provide the decision maker with meaningful information; the decision maker defines the information that is needed and makes the actual judgment of value or merit. The criticism of the applied research model is that all of the contextual and moderating factors that can affect a program's performance are covaried or randomized out of the evaluation, reducing the evaluation to a theoretical statement about program impact in a statistically sterilized environment. The role of the evaluator is to provide a "clean" interpretation of program effectiveness for the decision maker, sometimes at the expense of a more complex but more valid interpretation.

One approach to evaluation which is at variance with the decision-oriented notion is value-oriented evaluation. A value-oriented definition of evaluation stresses the value judgments made in evaluating programs and describes the act of judging merit or worth as central to the role of the evaluator. Scriven (1983) has argued that value judgments are a crucial part of all sciences, particularly methodological value judgments, and there appear to be no reasons to dismiss them in the evaluation of programs. He calls for goal-free evaluation, insisting that all aspects of a program should come under the scrutiny of an evaluator and that nothing should be taken as given, including the decisions to be made and the alternative courses of action to be taken.

A value-oriented definition of evaluation begins with the premise that evaluators or decision makers seldom know all of the decisions and alternative courses of action with which they or others will make a judgment of program merit. A value-oriented conception assumes that programs operate in environments characterized not by value consensus, but by value pluralism, and that different value positions should be objectively examined for the decisions and alternatives they hold. Thus, people gain from this definition the notion that evaluation includes not only the collection of data from which judgments of merit can be rendered, but also the objective determination of criteria upon which these judgements should be based. In essence, a value-oriented definition of evaluation implies that the program being evaluated ultimately must be justified in terms of the values of those it is to serve. These values should, but may not always, coincide with those values that are perceived to be important by the decision maker.

Another competing notion of evaluation is systems-oriented evaluation. The systems-oriented definition of evaluation assumes a view of programs as systems and reflects a theoretical/philosophical stance in the sciences called general systems theory. While traditional scientific inquiry attempts to understand humans within their environment by isolating the effects of single variables, holding everything else constant, the general systems paradigm posits that it is impossible to understand complex events by reducing them to their individual elements. Hence, a basic tenet of general systems theory is the often-heard exhortation of the Gestalt school of psychology that the whole is more than the sum of its parts; to understand the whole it is necessary to study the whole.

General systems theory holds that the complexity of any system, including programs, cannot be understood through analytical reduction and experimental control. Rather, programs are viewed as organismic entities that evolve and decay, depending on their relationship to other programs and the larger context to which they contribute. Furthermore, because all programs are ultimately seen as interrelated, changes in any program will have implications throughout the larger system of which the changed program is a part. This viewpoint differs from the decision-oriented perspective in which the immediate context is the focus of inquiry and the limits of the evaluation are bounded by the decision maker's information requirements and prescribed alternative courses of action.

Still other notions pertaining to the relevance of decision-oriented evaluation have emerged from the work of Cronbach et al. (1980) and from Guba and Lincoln (1981). Departing from an earlier distinction between decision-oriented and conclusion-oriented inquiry, Cronbach and co-workers question the appropriateness of an inquiry that focuses exclusively on decisions. Cronbach and co-workers point out that the theory of evaluation has been developed almost wholly around the image of command. By "image of command" these authors refer to a mistaken belief that there is a clearly identifiable decision maker on the horizon who makes decisions on the basis of informative input, including that provided by the evaluator. These writers point out that the actual context in which evaluation occurs is not consistent with the context of command assumed to exist in virtually all program settings. Their point is that only when a large confluence of data becomes available is a "decision" actually made, and even then, the decision is made interactively over a long period of time by a large number of persons (policy makers, bureaucrats, program monitors, project personnel, vested-interests, and others) who make up what constitute a "policy-shaping community." These authors advance the notion that the process of decision making does not terminate in a clearly defined decision but is a cumulative, never-ending process characterized by negotiation and accommodation among members of the policy shaping community (PSC) who

continually reassess and modify the decisions to be made and the alternative courses of action to be taken. Cronbach and his colleagues describe the evolution of decisions in the policy shaping community this way:

> Most action is determined by a pluralistic community, not by a lone decision maker. Parties having divergent perceptions and aims bear down on lawmakers and administrators. Information can change perceptions but is unlikely to bring all parties to agree on which facts are relevant or even on what the facts are. If the term *decision* is understood to mean formal choice at a particular time between discrete alternatives, decision making is rarely to be observed. When there are multiple participants with multiple views, it is meaningless to speak of one action as the rational or correct action. The active parties jockey toward a politically acceptable accommodation.

Hence, these authors suggest that the proper role of evaluation is not to service decisions but to participate in and contribute to the negotiation and accommodation process by raising new issues, stimulating new debate and illuminating the complexities of the problem at hand. For these reasons evaluations should focus on programs as implementations of policy and not on specific alternative courses of action to be taken in a particular context. Their reasoning is that by the time decisions are about to be made, the alternative courses of action to which they relate will have lost their significance, while the policy which underlies these alternative actions will have remained a relevant social issue.

Guba, one of the original founders of the CIPP decision-oriented model, also has recently voiced some changed views on the relevance of decision-oriented evaluation. Although acknowledging that the decision maker or client is entitled to issue directives to the evaluator, Guba and Lincoln (1981) warn that:

> . . . the evaluator need not be naive. He must recognize that the client may have many covert reasons for putting the charge in a particular way. He may, for example, select for evaluation only those program aspects that appear to be successful, cover up program failure by focusing on partisan testimonials, make evaluation gestures designed to promote a favorable public image, respond to government mandates that he does not take seriously but must be complied with overtly and the like. Sheer ignorance may also shape the client's directives.

Looking retrospectively at the CIPP model itself, Guba and Lincoln's views essentially echo those of Cronbach and co-workers ". . . it made what are probably unwarranted assumptions about the rationality of decisions, about the openness of the decision-making process (essentially political) and about the ease with which operational decision makers can be identified (in complex organizations or loosely coupled organizations decisions appear to 'bubble up' rather than be made explicitly at some particular time and place)."

The assumption of a context of command or the notion that evaluation is or should be decision-oriented has not been a result of accident or serendipity. Rather, the evolution of decision-oriented evaluation has resulted from the belief that evaluation's central role is to respond to the pragmatic needs of the decision maker and to the information requirements of those in most immediate control of the program. Hence, more complex decision making patterns involving negotiation and accommodation within a larger network of stake holders as well as more holistic and value-based criteria for program effectiveness, generally, are not assumed to be characteristic of the decision-oriented perspective.

See also: Evaluation Models: Development

Bibliography

Alkin M C 1969 Evaluation theory development. *Eval. Comment* 2(1): 2–7

Cronbach L, Ambron S, Dornbusch S, Hess R, Hornik R, Phillips D, Walker D, Weiner S 1980 *Toward Reform of Program Evaluation: Aims, Methods and Institutional Arrangements.* Jossey-Bass, San Francisco, California

Guba E G, Lincoln Y S 1981 *Effective Evaluation: Improving the Usefulness of Evaluation Results Through Responsive and Naturalistic Approaches.* Jossey-Bass, San Francisco, California

Guttentag M 1973 Subjectivity and its use in evaluation research. *Eval.* 1(2): 60–65

Hagedorn H J, Beck K J, Neubert S F, Werlin S H 1976 *A Working Manual of Simple Program Evaluation Techniques for Community Mental Health Centers.* National Institute of Mental Health, Rockville, Maryland

Larson R C, Kaplan E H 1981 Decision-oriented approaches to program evaluation. In: Wooldridge R (ed.) 1981 *New Directions for Program Evaluation: Evaluation of Complex Systems.* Jossey-Bass, San Francisco, California

Provus M M 1971 *Discrepancy Evaluation for Educational Program Improvement and Assessment.* McCutchan, Berkeley, California

Scriven M 1983 The evaluation taboo. In: House E (ed.) 1983 *New Directions for Program Evaluation: Philosophy of Evaluation.* Jossey-Bass, San Francisco, California

Stufflebeam D L, Foley W J, Gephart W J, Guba E G, Hammond H D, Merriman H O, Provus M M 1971 *Educational Evaluation and Decision Making.* Peacock, Itasca, Illinois

G. D. Borich

Decision Seminar Technique in Education

Harold Lasswell (1960) conceived the decision seminar as a policy sciences technique (Lerner and Lasswell 1951) for analyzing policy problems. The decision seminar technique uses four interacting models to establish a common problem-solving language, organize comprehensive analytical categories, and provide systematic, explicit procedures for collective problem solving. It also specifies support resources essential to any problem-solving group. This framework focuses the attention of problem solvers simultaneously on the parts and the whole of the problem, as well as its past, present, and future, thereby structuring an approach to problem solving designed to address modern complexities.

1. The Social Process Model

Of the four analytical models in the decision seminar technique, the social process model (SPM) is fundamental to portraying accurately the relevant social process. Without such a model to contextualize a problem adequately, the probability of problem-solving failure increases considerably, no matter how choices among alternatives are made. To build the context for problem analysis, the social process model asks seven critical questions about the decision environment: who are the participants (individuals, organizations, institutions, etc.); with what perspectives (experiences, beliefs, preferences, etc.); in what situations (locations, channels of communication, etc.); with what base values (assets, resources, capabilities, etc.); using what strategies (techniques, methods, tactics, etc.); toward what outcomes (immediate goals or objectives); and with what effects (long-term consequences). These data-collection categories facilitate the application of significant knowledge from various sources to problem solving.

2. The Eight Value Categories

Embedded within, but separable from, the social process model, the eight value categories (EVC) add another model for classifying actors in the social process; specifying their demands, indulgences, or deprivations; and evaluating projected policy outcomes. Organizations, for example, can be characterized by their attention to power values (legislatures or executive branches of government) or enlightenment values (media or universities). Some pursue wealth (banks, industries), while others collect or distribute well-being (hospitals or police). Similarly, the eight value categories can delineate the value demands of an individual who may seek skills at a vocational or technical school, affection through marriage or friendship, respect by joining a voluntary association, or rectitude by regularly attending religious services. The eight value categories are exhaustive, though not mutually exclusive, means of differentiating actors, their preferences, and policy outcomes.

3. The Decision Process Phases

Elements in the social process, particularly actual or potential policy outcomes, can be analyzed further through a seven-phase model: intelligence (who gathers, processes, or disseminates information); promotion (who recommends or agitates for particular policies); prescription (who develops which rules and sanctions to be applied); invocation (who identifies how and to whom prescriptions will be applied); application (how and by whom the rules and sanctions are actually applied); termination (how and when prescriptions are modified or ended); and appraisal (how and by whom each phase is evaluated). This analysis of the participants, the decision process phases (DPP) in which they operate, and the outcomes of these interactions help expand a problem solver's conceptual map of the social process.

4. The Five Intellectual Tasks

Although problem solving demands sufficient, useable, and reliable information to be effective, it also requires agreement about the criteria for selecting and using information. While the social process model, the eight value categories, and the decision process phases are used to analyze the context in which a problem occurs, detailing the actors, their locations, and their preferences, the five intellectual tasks direct the analysis of the actual policy problems. These tasks identify necessary steps for critical inquiry: goal clarification (determining preferred policy outcomes); trend description (comparing past and recent events with goals to discover discrepancies); analysis of conditions (identifying which factors have affected the trends); projection of developments (assessing future discrepancies between goals and outcomes); and selection of alternatives (selecting and assessing objectives and strategies designed to achieve preferred goals). Because details are difficult to understand apart from their context, these five tasks allow "the context to emerge as the focus of individual or group attention." Then, "the most productive procedure is to examine the whole problem by returning again and again to the separate tasks" (Lasswell 1971 p. 39).

5. Support Resources

The decision seminar technique also has several features which ensure continuity in the problem-solving process. These supporting elements include a permanent core group and physical location, systematic research and record keeping, and the use of audiovisual aids and outside experts. Regardless of the analytical procedures used, these six support resources can make any group problem-solving effort more effective.

6. Some Applications and Future Uses

The decision seminar technique has been used to restructure the social order of a Peruvian hacienda,

for high-level analyses of policies in Southeast Asia (Brewer 1975), to solve building-level problems in the San Francisco Public Schools, to develop upper-level staff in the Detroit Public Schools, to examine desegregation and student achievement in the St. Louis Public Schools, and for research projects, social action programs, classroom instruction, and doctoral theses in higher education (Cunningham 1981). Elements common to these experiences show that policy makers are willing to experiment and can quickly grasp and apply the technique's analytical categories to their problems.

A powerful tool for collective policy analysis and formulation, the technique will permit various sectors (commercial, governmental, educational) to share relevant data and to enhance the capabilities of each to act effectively on policy problems. Such networking may lead to a social planetarium, "a 'social commons' that allows citizens to address issues from increasingly shared conceptions of their origins and likely futures . . ." (Muth and Bolland 1981 p. 18). However manifested, Lasswell's policy sciences technique assists decision makers to gain increased control of the outcomes of their value preferences.

See also: Decision-making Theory

Bibliography

Brewer G D 1975 Dealing with complex social problems: The potential of the "Decision Seminar." In: Brewer G D, Brunner R D (eds.) 1975 *Political Development and Change*. Free Press, New York

Cunningham L L 1981 Applying Lasswell's concepts in field situations: Diagnostic and prescriptive values. *Educ. Admin. Q.* 17(2): 21–43

Lasswell H D 1960 Technique of decision seminars. *Midwest J. Polit. Sci.* 4: 213–36

Lasswell H D 1971 *A Pre-View of Policy Sciences*. Elsevier, New York

Lerner D, Lasswell H D (eds.) 1951 *The Policy Sciences: Recent Developments in Scope and Method*. Stanford University Press, Stanford, California

Muth R, Bolland J M 1981 The social planetarium: Toward a revitalized civic order. *Urban Interest* 3(2): 13–25

R. Muth

Decision Theory in Educational Research and Testing

In most educational situations, tests are used for decision making rather than measurement purposes. The ultimate purpose in these cases is to use test scores not as quantitative ability estimates but merely as data on which qualitative decisions can be based. Examples of such decisions are admissions to training programs, pass–fail decisions, certification, treatment assignment in individualized instructional systems, and the identification of optimal vocational alternatives in guidance situations. In all these examples, decisions are ordinarily based on cutting scores carefully selected with the aim to optimize the actions to be taken.

In spite of the fact that tests are used mostly for decision making, much psychometric research has been aimed at improving the use of educational and psychological tests as means for estimating ability scores from test performances. The first to recognize this paradox were Cronbach and Gleser (1965) in their classical monograph *Psychological Tests and Personnel Decisions*. Their plea for a more decision-theoretic approach to testing had more impact at first on (personnel) psychologists than on educators. During the 1970s, however, the situation changed dramatically, and now the use of decision theory in educational testing is one of the main research topics. The major impetus for this has come from the introduction of novel testing procedures in individualized instructional systems, and from politically controversial issues such as culture-fair selection for schools.

The application of decision theory to educational testing falls into two categories. First, decision theory can be used to optimize decisions based on tests. Typically, this takes the form of selecting one or more optimal cutting scores on the test. Second, it can be used for the evaluation of decision rules. Such evaluations show how much room there is for improving decisions by, for instance, redesigning the test.

1. A Typology of Educational Decisions

Decision problems in educational testing can be classified in many ways. A simple typology is the following one, using flowcharts consisting of three basic elements to define each type of decision. In each decision problem, minimally the following elements can be identified: (a) the test that provides the information the decision is based on, (b) the treatment with respect to which the decision is made, and (c) the criterion by which the success of the treatment is measured. "Treatment" is a generic term here, standing for any manipulation aimed at improving the condition of individuals. Examples include training programs, the use of special instructional materials, therapeutic measures, and the like. The criterion may be any type of success measure but is often a test itself. With the aid of these elements, four basic flowcharts can be formed, each defining a different type of decision problem.

1.1 Selection Decisions

In selection problems, the decision in general is whether or not to accept individuals for a treatment. The test is administered before the treatment takes place and only individuals promising satisfactory results on the criterion are accepted for the treat-

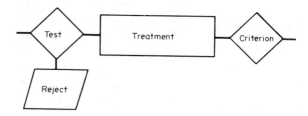

Figure 1
Flowchart of a selection decision

ment. Depending on the circumstances, selection decisions may imply that individuals who are rejected are not being admitted to the institute providing the treatment, or have to leave the institute if they were already in. Figure 1 shows the flowchart of a selection problem. Examples of selection decisions are admission examinations to schools (where grade-point averages are the usual criteria), hiring of personnel in industry, or the intake of students for a special remedial program.

The selection problem is the oldest decision problem recognized as such in the history of educational testing. Traditionally, the problem has been approached as a prediction problem in which regression lines or expectancy tables are employed to predict whether the criterion scores of individuals exceed a certain threshold value. Individuals whose criterion scores exceed the threshold value are accepted. Selection decisions with quota restrictions (see below) have long been evaluated with the aid of Taylor–Russell (1939) tables, which give success ratios for a number of parameters characterizing the selection situation (see *Regression Analysis*; *Expectancy Tables*).

1.2 Mastery Decisions

Mastery decisions are made for individuals who have already undergone some treatment. Unlike selection decisions, the question is not whether individuals are qualified enough to be admitted to the treatment under consideration, but whether they have profited enough from the treatment to be dismissed. Figure 2 shows the flowchart of a mastery decision. For this type of decision problem the test and the criterion coincide. The test is an unreliable representation of the criterion or, equivalently, the criterion is to be

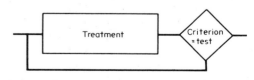

Figure 2
Flowchart of a mastery decision

considered the true score underlying the test. It is the unreliablity of the test that opens up the possibility of making wrong decisions and creates the mastery decision problem (see *Mastery Learning Model of Teaching and Learning*).

Mastery decisions usually imply that individuals may leave the institute providing the treatment or proceed with another treatment. Examples of mastery decisions are pass–fail, certification, and successfulness of therapies.

Concern for mastery decisions has grown because of the introduction of modern instructional systems such as individualized instruction, mastery learning, and computer-aided instruction. In the past the main concern has been for issues related to standard setting procedures; that is, to procedures for selecting threshold values on the (true-score) criterion separating "masters" from "nonmasters." The influence of measurement error on decision making was simply ignored. That this may lead to serious decision errors was clearly demonstrated by Hambleton and Novick (1973).

1.3 Placement Decisions

This type of decision problem differs from the preceding two in that alternative treatments are available. The success of each of these treatments is measured by the same criterion. All individuals are administered the same test, and the task is to assign them to the most promising treatment on the basis of their test scores. Unlike the selection problem, each individual is assigned to a treatment. The case of placement decisions with two treatments is represented in Fig. 3. Examples of placement decisions occur in individualized instruction where students are assigned to different routes through an instructional unit or are offered alternative instructional materials.

Interest in placement decisions has emanated from aptitude–treatment interaction (ATI) research which was motivated by the finding that individuals may react differentially to treatments and that treatments that are better on average may be worse in individual cases (see *Aptitude–Treatment Interaction Models of Teaching*). The placement decision problem has

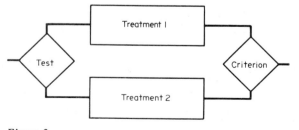

Figure 3
Flowchart of a placement decision (case of two treatments)

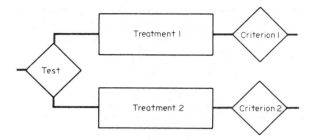

Figure 4
Flowchart of a classification decision (case of two treatments)

mostly been approached as a prediction problem to be tackled using linear-regression techniques. For each treatment, then, there is a regression line of the criterion on the test score, and individuals are assigned to the treatment with the largest predicted criterion score. The methodology needed for detecting ATIs is reviewed in Cronbach and Snow (1977).

1.4 Classification Decisions

In classification, the problem also consists of a choice among a number of different treatments. As opposed to placement decisions, however, each treatment has a qualitatively different criterion. The situation is as shown in Fig. 4. In order to be able to compare criterion performances, each criterion may have its own threshold value defining success or it may be clear for each criterion how to transform it on a common scale. Examples are vocational guidance situations in which most promising schools or careers must be identified, and testing for military service.

The most popular approach to classification decisions has been the use of linear-regression techniques again. For each treatment, the regression line of its utility (= transformed criterion) score on the test score is estimated and individuals are assigned to the treatment with the largest predicted utility score. Since more criteria are present, the test is often a whole battery covering relevant aspects of the various criteria. In that case, the use of multiple-regression techniques has been the traditional choice.

1.5 Conclusion

The above four types of problems involve elementary decisions which are not always met in their pure forms. For instance, in some situations, more than one treatment is available, but not all individuals are accepted for a treatment. This creates a combination of a selection and a placement problem. However, all such decisions can be mapped on flowcharts built up of Figs. 1–4 as elements.

Three further distinctions should be made to enable possible refinements to be considered within each type of decision.

(a) *Quota restrictions*. In some situations, the number of vacancies per treatment can be constrained by a quota. Such quotas usually simplify the selection decision (accept individuals with the highest test scores until the quota is filled), but complicate the placement decision.

(b) *Number of tests*. When the criterion is multifaceted or when two or more criteria are present, the single test can be replaced by a test battery. This means that decisions must be made on the basis of multivariate information, which may complicate the decision rule.

(c) *Subpopulations*. In some situations, subpopulations varying on a socially relevant attribute can be distinguished. If the test is biased against any of the subpopulations, the problem of culture-fair decision making arises.

2. Optimizing Decisions Based on Tests

Decision theory is a branch of statistics involving the use of data as an aid to decision making. More specifically, it is concerned with how random data on "true" or future states and utilities of outcomes can be combined into optimal decision rules. In the above decision problems, the data are provided by a test. Since a test may not be a perfectly reliable source of data, it should be considered a random indicator of an individual's criterion performance. For a population of individuals, test and criterion scores relate to each other in a way which is fully specified by their joint probability distribution. In some decision problems, a psychometric model would be needed to specify this distribution.

Several approaches to optimizing decisions can be taken, one of which is Bayesian decision theory. It is indicated below how (empirical) Bayesian theory tackles the four decision problems and provides optimal decision rules (called Bayes rules). First, the Bayesian solution to a classification problem is described. This, in a formal sense, is the most complicated type of decision problem. Then, solutions to the other decision problems are outlined. These problems impose certain restrictions and modifications on the classification model. In order to enhance understanding, some mathematical precision has been sacrificed (see *Bayesian Statistics*).

The classification problem is formalized as follows. Suppose a series of individuals, who can be considered as randomly drawn from some population, must be classified into $t + 1$ treatments indexed by $j = 0, \ldots, t$. The observed test scores are denoted by a random variable X with discrete values $x = 0, \ldots, n$. Each treatment leads to a certain performance on its corresponding criterion which is denoted by a continuous random variable Y_j with range R_j. It is assumed that the joint distributions of X and Y_j are given by probability functions $\eta_j(x, y_j)$.

Since all individuals are administered the same test, it holds for the marginal probability function $\lambda_j(x)$ of X that

$$\lambda_j(x) = \lambda(x) \tag{1}$$

for all values of j.

Generally, a decision rule is a function that indicates for each possible observation which of the possible actions is to be taken. In the present problem the observations take the form $X = x$, and the possible actions are the assignments to one of the treatments $0, \ldots, t$. It is assumed that the optimal rule takes a monotone form; that is, it can be defined using a series of cutting scores $0 = c_0 \leqslant c_1 \ldots \leqslant c_j \leqslant \ldots \leqslant c_{t+1} = n$ $(t \leqslant n)$, where treatment j is assigned to individuals whose scores satisfy $c_j \leqslant X < c_{j+1}$. For an optimal rule to be monotone, some conditions must be met which are, however, not unrealistic for the present problems (Ferguson 1967).

Suppose that the decision maker is able to express on a numerical scale his or her preferences for the outcomes $Y_j = y_j$ for individuals who were assigned to treatment j. Technically, such an evaluation is known as a utility function. If utility functions can be established for all treatment–criterion combinations, all possible outcomes of the decision have been made comparable on a common scale. To express its dependency on both the criterion and the chosen treatment, utility functions will be denoted as $u = u_j(y_j)$. Figure 5 shows some examples of utility functions that have received some interest in the literature. The threshold function represents the case where a critical value on the criterion discriminates between successful and unsuccessful performances. The other two functions increase more gradually with the criterion performance. The choice of a utility function may be facilitated by varying its form and studying the robustness of the optimal decision rule under these variations (e.g. Vijn and Molenaar 1981).

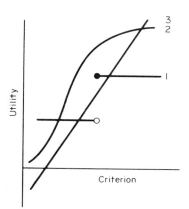

Figure 5
Examples of utility functions: (1) threshold; (2) normal ogive; (3) linear

For each possible series of cutting scores $(c_1, \ldots, c_t)$ the expected utility of the decision procedure can be calculated as

$$B(c_1, \ldots, c_t) \equiv \sum_{j=0}^{t} \sum_{x=c_j}^{c_{j+1}} \int_{R_j} u_j(y_j) \eta_j(x,y_j) dy_j \quad (2)$$

The set of optimal cutting scores in the Bayesian sense is the choice of values for $(c_1, \ldots, c_t)$ maximizing the expected utility. A simple procedure to find these values is as follows. Using Eqn. (1) the expected utility can be written

$$B(c_1, \ldots, c_t) = \sum_{j=0}^{t} \sum_{x=c_j}^{c_{j+1}-1} \lambda(x) \int_{R_j} u_j(y_j) \omega_j(y_j|x) dy_j \quad (3)$$

where $\omega_j(y_j|x)$ is the conditional probability function of y_j given $X = x$. For known utility and probability functions the integral in this expression only depends on x and j. Since $\lambda(x) \geq 0$, it is apparent that the double sum in Eqn. (3) is maximized if for each possible value of x the value of j is selected for which the integral is maximal. The dependency of the selected value of j on x provides a decision rule which is precisely the Bayes rule for the classification problem. The monotone character of the problem, assumed here, guarantees that the optimal value of j indeed changes at a series of cutting scores on x.

The Bayesian approach to classification problems in education testing still remains to be elaborated. This would amount to establishing classes of realistic utility and probability functions and studying the properties of their optimal rules.

The placement problem differs from the classification problem in that all treatments lead to the same criterion. Therefore,

$$Y_j = Y \quad (4)$$
$$\omega_j(y_j|x) = \omega_j(y|x) \quad (5)$$
$$u_j(y_j) = u_j(y) \quad (6)$$

for all values of j. These restrictions only simplify the expected utility expression in Eqn. (3), and Bayes rules for the placement problem are found in the same way as for the classification problem. The fact that the utility functions are defined on the same criterion implies that only one criterion needs to be scaled. Differences between the utility functions arise only from their treatment dependency. For instance, each treatment involves a certain amount of costs which may entail differences between the utility curves with respect to the lower asymptote, the intercept, or the location. Solutions to the placement problem for some intuitively appealing utility functions are given in Cronbach and Gleser (1965) and van der Linden (1981).

In the mastery decision problem the true score variable τ underlying the test score is considered as the criterion. Assuming the classical test model, the true score τ_i of a fixed individual i is defined as the observed test score X_i expected across replications: $\tau_i \equiv EX_i$. All individuals have followed the same treatment, so there is no treatment variable modifying the relation of test scores to criterion scores. Hence, the subscript j in $\omega_j(y \mid x)$ can be dropped. Usually two true states are defined, the mastery ($\tau \geq \tau_c$) and the nonmastery state ($\tau < \tau_c$), τ_c being a true cutting score set on educational grounds. Different utility functions for the mastery and the nonmastery decision are distinguished. In general, the former is a curve that increases in the criterion τ, such as the examples in Fig. 5; the latter usually is its decreasing counterpart (the larger the true test score, the lower the utility of a nonmastery decision). In these utility functions, the true cutting score τ_c is usually treated as a parameter; for example, to govern the location of the jump in the threshold utility function. Formally, the mastery decision model follows if, in addition to Eqns. (4), (5), and (6), the following restrictions are imposed:

$$y_i = \tau_i \equiv EX_i \quad (7)$$
$$\omega_j(y|x) = \omega(y|x) \quad (8)$$

with $u_0(y)$ decreasing in y, $u_1(y)$ increasing in y, and where $j = 0, 1$ now denotes the nonmastery and mastery decision, respectively. Cutting scores maximizing the expected utility under these restrictions have been examined for threshold (Huynh 1976), linear (van der Linden and Mellenbergh 1977), and normal-ogive utility functions (Novick and Lindley 1978, van der Linden 1980).

In selection decisions, only one treatment is available for which individuals are either accepted or rejected. Like the mastery testing problem, there is no treatment variable modifying the relation of test scores to criterion scores and the subscript j in $\omega_j(y|x)$ can be dropped. In the usual case, the utility function for the acceptance decision is an increasing function of the criterion, such as the examples in Fig. 5. When an individual is rejected, he or she is of no value to the institute making the selection decisions. This is formalized by putting the utility for the rejection decision equal to zero. In summary, optimal selection decisions follow from maximizing the expected utility in Eqn. (3) if in addition to the restrictions in Eqns. (4), (5), and (6) the following restrictions are imposed:

$$\omega_j(y|x) = \omega(y|x) \quad (9)$$
$$u_0(y) = 0 \quad (10)$$

where $j = 0, 1$ now denotes the rejection and acceptance decision, respectively.

3. Evaluating Decisions Based on Tests

The attractive feature about the expected utility defined in Eqn. (2) is that it can be used not only to find optimal decision rules but also to evaluate any decision rule. Equation (2) is positively related to the quality of the procedure—the larger the expected utility, the better the procedure. Hence, if two decision rules are compared, the one with the larger expected utility is better. Instead of comparing decision rules, it is also possible to evaluate individual rules on a scale defined by the maximum and minimum value of the expected utility possible for the given problem. Such evaluations have been worked out by Livingston and Wingersky (1979), Mellenbergh and van der Linden (1979), and Wilcox (1978).

4. Discussion

As indicated earlier, the four types of decisions discussed above are basic decisions that are not always met in their pure form. In some situations, mixed types of decision must be made. Moreover, within each type of decision further refinements can be made; for example, the presence of restricted numbers of vacancies per treatment, the use of more than one test, or the distinction between relevant subpopulations. The presence of restricted numbers of vacancies entails the necessity to maximize the expected utility under quota restrictions (e.g. Chuang et al. 1981). If more than one test is used, the decision is a function defined on the Cartesian product of their ranges of possible scores, and the probability functions $\omega_j(y_j|x)$ are conditional on points in this product. This leads to corresponding changes in Eqn. (3) which, however, complicate its maximization. If subpopulations must be distinguished, as is the case for instance when the requirement of culture-fair selection must be met, each subpopulation may entail its own utility and probability functions, and cutting scores must be selected for each population separately. Culture-fair decision rules are given in Gross and Su (1975), Mellenbergh and van der Linden (1981), and Petersen (1976). In principle, it is thus possible to deal with all these refinements within the framework of Bayesian decision theory.

Bibliography

Chuang D T, Chen J J, Novick M R 1981 Theory and practice for the use of cut-scores for personnel decisions. *J. Educ. Stat.* 6: 107–28

Cronbach L J, Gleser G C 1965 *Psychological Tests and Personnel Decisions*, 2nd edn. University of Illinois Press, Urbana, Illinois

Cronbach L J, Snow R F 1977 *Aptitudes and Instructional Methods: A Handbook for Research on Interactions*. Irvington, New York

Ferguson T S 1967 *Mathematical Statistics: A Decision Theoretic Approach*. Academic Press, New York

Gross A L, Su W H 1975 Defining a "fair" or "unbiased" selection model: A question of utilities. *J. Appl. Psychol.* 60: 345–51

Hambleton R K, Novick M R 1973 Toward an integration of theory and method for criterion-referenced tests. *J. Educ. Meas.* 10: 159–70

Huynh H 1976 Statistical considerations of mastery scores. *Psychometrika* 41: 65–79

Livingston S A, Wingersky M 1979 Assessing the reliability of tests used to make pass/fail decision. *J. Educ. Meas.* 16: 247–60

Mellenbergh G J, van der Linden W J 1979 The internal and external optimality of decisions based on tests. *Appl. Psychol. Meas.* 3: 257–73

Mellenbergh G J, van der Linden W J 1981 The linear utility model for optimal selection. *Psychometrika* 46: 283–93

Novick M R, Lindley D V 1978 The use of more realistic utility functions in educational applications. *J. Educ. Meas.* 15: 181–91

Petersen N S 1976 An expected utility model for "optimal" selection. *J. Educ. Stat.* 1: 333–58

Taylor H C, Russell J T 1939 The relationship of validity coefficients to the practical effectiveness of tests in selection: Discussion and tables. *J. Appl. Psychol.* 23: 565–78

van der Linden W J 1980 Decision models for use with criterion-referenced tests. *Appl. Psychol. Meas.* 4: 469–92

van der Linden W J 1981 Using aptitude measurements for the optimal assignment of subjects to treatments with and without mastery scores. *Psychometrika* 46: 257–74

van der Linden W J, Mellenbergh G J 1977 Optimal cutting scores using a linear loss function. *Appl. Psychol. Meas.* 1: 593–99

Vijn P, Molenaar I W 1981 Robustness regions for dichotomous decisions. *J. Educ. Stat.* 6: 205–35

Wilcox R R 1978 A note on decision theoretic coefficients for tests. *Appl. Psychol. Meas.* 2: 609–13

W. J. van der Linden

Decoding (Reading)

Decoding implies the analysis of spoken or written symbols of language with the purpose of extracting meaning. However, Harris and Hodges (1981 p. 80) claim that decoding in actual reading practice has come to mean word recognition. The implication is that while modern use of the term assumes a meaning emphasis, practice in a pedagogical sense has restricted the term to a small unit of language.

1. Alternative Views

Decoding in reading practice has traditionally required the oral realization of printed features of the language. This view of decoding requires the matching of each of the letters of an alphabet with a range of sounds. The assumption underlying decoding in this sense is that written language is an evolution of the oral form and is, in effect, a means of mapping oral language onto print. The corollary of the theory is that in order to read, it is first necessary to produce a matching of letters with their appropriate sounds. The logical development of the proposition is that "phonics instruction", or the method of teaching reading through the realization of matched symbols and sounds, or clusters of these, has dominated reading instruction over the years. The ultimate aim of this pedagogical practice is to achieve word recognition.

In more recent years there has been a questioning of the decoding assumptions. The alternative view is that decoding does occur in reading, but it is in reality a process that results in understanding, rather than letter/sound matching. In other words, readers decode to meaning, as occurs in the comprehension of morse code. The leading proponent of this view is Kenneth Goodman who suggests that all reading requires decoding to meaning, otherwise it is not reading. The capacity to match sounds and letters is therefore regarded as "recoding", or expressing the printed symbols in an oral form without paying attention to meaning. This view implies that not only is decoding from print to sound an impediment to reading, it is also an inappropriate use of the term "decoding", hence the term "recoding" used in its stead by its critics.

2. Applying the Two Theories—The Traditional

Historically, the pattern of traditional reading pedagogy has moved between phonics instruction to whole word instruction, the aim being to achieve decoding in the word recognition sense. Phonics assumes that the letters of the alphabet (graphemes) have a relationship with sound patterns (phonemes) that permit reasonably close mapping of one onto the other in a way that enables the learner to "sound out" new or unfamiliar words. In this practice it is necessary to teach clusters of sounds, represented by groups of realizable letters such as *ou*, *bl*, *ck*, *ch*, as well as individual sound/symbol relationships.

Whole word instruction entails the teaching of new words as a whole, as a result of which it is expected that children will deduce the sound/symbol relationships within or, if not, they will be taught them subsequent to word recognition. Very often the whole word approach is taught by the use of "flash cards" each of which contains a word. The cards are then "flashed" in turn before the child whose task it is to recognize the words. In some quarters the practice is termed "the look and say approach".

Both phonics and whole word methods are predicated on written language being a direct representation of oral language, which is primary (see *Literacy, Initial*). They also assume precise word knowledge as a prerequisite for reading success in a comprehension sense.

A major objection offered by critics of this traditional view of decoding is that the material written for young children is consequently artificial and uninteresting, particularly if phonics underlies the scheme. The need to write material with easily-sounded words, it is claimed, often results in such sequences as:

A fat man is in a can.

Similarly, whole word approaches are often criticized for their reliance on the memory of the child who, it is claimed, will guess wildly because of lack of insights into sound/symbol relationships.

3. Applying the Two Theories—The Nontraditional

Nontraditional theories of reading assume that decoding implies "decoding direct to meaning". Such theories discount the need to teach sound/symbol relationships or whole words in a formal sense. Proponents of the view claim that such traditional practices are not only unnecessary but they are also inefficient and stand in the way of the child becoming literate. The argument is based on the proposition that oral and written language are alternative elements and one is not derived from the other. The theory is, therefore, predicted on the belief that print is not a written representation of speech.

The application of the nontraditional theory assumes that children can be taught to read by focusing on the prime purpose, namely the meaning of the extract, and by using their intuitive knowledge of how language works, decode to meaning. The meaning focus is achieved by using natural language in experimental situations familiar to the child. The role of sound/symbol relationships, rather than being ignored, is seen as a further strategy available to the reader when predicted meaning is not realized and the reader is forced to refocus in a sharper manner upon the precise visual features.

Perhaps the distinguishing characteristic of the nontraditional theory is its focus on the whole rather than on the parts. In brief, this means emphasizing the total message and not the individual words.

The modern proponents of the theory are the psycholinguists, who argue that reading is not an exact, errorless activity, but rather one in which the reader interacts with print, with meaning uppermost in the mind. It is inevitable, according to theory, that deviations from the text will occur because the proficient reader uses the print only to the extent that meaning needs to be predicted. Naturally, because of this minimal use of graphic information, errors will occur from time to time. This should not be seen to be a problem but rather an indication that true decoding is occurring. Where it does become a problem, however, is when the predicted meaning is not met and the reader fails to regress to focus more carefully on the particular aspect of the print that caused the original confusion. This cycle of predicting, confirming, and regressing is seen as the inevitable behaviour of the proficient reader. Since this is regarded as desirable behaviour the implication is that beginning readers should be taught reading in a similar cyclical sense, and the practice of starting with sounds and letters should be discarded. The application of the nontraditional theory is stated to be "a psycholinguistic method". The psycholinguists claim, however, that this is a misnomer, and what they are really trying to inculcate in teachers and researchers is an understanding of the principles underlying the reading process, rather than mandate a particular pedagogical approach.

4. Summary

Decoding is, in practice, viewed from two conflicting perspectives. The traditional practice requires beginning readers to focus on the elements of language at the word level, while undertaking a range of tasks designed to build competence in subskills.

The alternative view is that decoding implies meaning gathering through a focus on the totality of language. Print is seen as an alternative mode to oral language and independent of it. Therefore it is unnecessary and illogical to process print by first passing through an oral rendition of it.

See also: Alphabetic Methods of Teaching Reading; Phonics: Reading Instruction; Literacy, Initial; Reading Methods, Initial

Bibliography

Bereiter C, Engelmann S 1966 *Teaching Disadvantaged Children in the Preschool.* Prentice Hall, Englewood Cliffs, New Jersey
Gollasch F V (ed.) 1982 *Language and Literacy: The Selected Writings of Kenneth S. Goodman.* Vol. 1: *Process, Theory, Research.* Routledge and Kegan Paul, London
Harris T L, Hodges R E 1981 *A Dictionary of Reading and Related Terms.* International Reading Association, Newark, Delaware
Smith F 1971 *Understanding Reading: A Psycholinguistic Analysis of Reading and Learning to Read.* Holt, Rinehart and Winston, New York

P. D. Rousch

Decroly Method

Physician, neuropsychiatrist, and psychologist, Decroly (1871–1931) is Belgium's best known educator. He put his principles and methods to permanent experimental test in several small teaching units in Brussels, which he created and used as psychopedagogical laboratories: *l'Institut du Vossegat* for abnormal children (1901), *l'Ecole de l'Ermitage* (1907), and the Home for Orphans (1915). Contrary to what usually occurs, these centres of education still pursue the aims of their founder; their vitality can be explained by the continuous interaction of theory and practice.

Decroly removed guidance and vocational orientation from the domain of classical tests by substituting nonverbal tests of practical intelligence (e.g., the "boxes", that are increasingly difficult to open) and precise monographs (e.g., the "Qualities of the Carpenter").

He was in daily, fatherly contact with a number of children whom he brought up, along with his own, in the "children's house" where he spent all his life. His theoretical work has its roots in this affective atmosphere; the first educational games, now widely commercialized, were developed there, as were the workshop–classroom and the nature–classroom characteristic of Decroly schools.

Decroly devoted himself to specific points (locomotion, imitation, etc.) in films of psychological observation; the first ("*Sur la Petite S . . .*", in 1907, a few months before Gesell) contains the material of "psychogenesis" (developmental psychology), which will later be called genetic epistemology. (The only copy of this film disappeared during the war.)

The many-sided work of Decroly finds its unity in a hypothesis largely confirmed by functional pedagogies: the spontaneous activity of the child constitutes the best dynamics for learning. Neither "a reduced-size adult", nor virgin wax, the child is vitally mobilized by his or her own development: "A growing living being, equipped with a highly developed cerebrospinal system, and possessing extended psychological and social virtualities" (Segers 1948). The basis is thus biopsychological; "Furthermore, it is dynamic, i.e. we are dealing with the active child, and must take into consideration what he is at each moment", without falling into a neo-Rousseau type of ideology of the so-called genius of childhood: "The best environment is one in which the child . . . is faced with real problems to solve . . . and where he sees adults occupied at the basic vocations". The educational theory thus derives from three basic sciences: biology, psychology, sociology; their respective contributions are integrated in a differential educational psychology.

Psychometrics cannot be reduced to measuring IQs only, for "the complexity of human nature is such that it is extremely difficult to describe the characteristics that can definitely identify different types" (Ecole Decroly 1973). Differential psychology has to refine criteria involving all the forms of nonverbal mental activity.

The constitutional factors of the personality seem to be partly inborn; others are more closely related to the diversity of the milieu. Decroly clarified this apparent contradiction: "There is no function without a preliminary structure, and only the structure is preliminary. . . . The most widely accepted formula seems to acknowledge both the hereditary nature of the structure starting in the egg itself, and the permanent interaction of the environment with the structure's integrity as well as with the development of the functional mechanisms."

Here the school finds its principal justification, in encouraging certain phylogenetic processes: if "The child . . . does not pass by all the stages where humanity has passed", it is still most important that "the environment offer him the opportunities for observation, reflection and adaptation that were available to mankind at the different stages of its evolution".

Thus it is important to locate schools in natural surroundings and to stimulate "rediscovery, personal experience, individual and collective activities and accomplishments—in brief, complex solutions for real problems". If the educator consents not to impose "immobility and silence upon beings who must learn to act and express themselves", he will be an artisan of a new education: "One goes to school to have a fore-taste of real life, less concerned with learning to read than with living." A political conception of education is thus essential; for Decroly, it must be democratic and "will not consider only intellectual verbal superiority, but will accord as much value, if not more, to social intelligence". In no longer according privilege to the verbal aspect, "an error which tends to confuse intelligence and language", Decroly's pedagogy is based on life, concrete reality, action, commitment. It is adapted to the critical developmental stages; for small children (from birth to 8 years of age), the function of globalization guarantees the apprehension of real, even highly complex situations, in response to their needs and interests; "It encourages the discovery, via the main sensory channels, of the true aspects of nature— those that most interest and are thus most likely to be retained and utilized as elements for reflection." Even more primitive than syncretism, globalization in fact "links matter to thought"; it transforms immediate sensations into perception and representation. Pedagogically, it implies that the child is truly self-taught—eliciting his or her desire to analyse global perceptions. For the very small child, the process englobes the surrounding world (parental images, time, space . . .) and reflexively constructs the self (body structure, affects, language). From 8 years on, the global approach structures cognitive curiosity around centres of interest; at school, an annual work plan, elaborated by the children, coordinates technical and conceptual acquisitions around a central axis chosen among the basic needs of living species (eating/reproduction; protection/adaptation; defense/fighting; working/recreation). Each school year is thus the fulfillment of a nine months project, realistically built to cover all the seasons' diversity, but wide enough to integrate also main current events. Globalization gradually becomes a scientific method: for older students, observation of phenomena induces association of direct sensorial data

with memories, hypotheses, cultural documents from other times and places, and the new acquisitions are expressed by making models, drawings, in speech, or in writing. Decroly's educational psychology insures the interaction of the abstract with the concrete, of analysis with synthesis, of experience with received knowledge. Its very principles keep it from establishing itself as a closed system; changes in economic, social, and cultural interests necessitate continuous renewal which is all the more welcome as it jeopardizes neither the coherence nor the permanence of its profound anthropological interests. The Decroly schools confirm this flexibility; beyond the diversity of their applications, the principles stand firm. Globalization goes hand in hand with active methods; they are the appropriate answer to the needs of growing children. As all of them are rooted in concrete reality, some approaches seem paradoxical for adult brains: volume spontaneously precedes surface, natural measurements prepare for the use of conventional units, observational sciences contribute complex content to the speculative sciences; the notions and techniques (global method of reading and writing, centres of interest, concrete activities, self-government, . . .) are used pragmatically and never fall into dogmatic or formalistic habits. The refusal to give privilege to verbal intelligence encourages manual activities in authentic artisan workshops, leading the child to produce useful objects, helping him or her to determine his or her own development by stimulating activity in the areas in which he or she feels most successful. Rejecting stereotypes and preestablished programmes implies direct contact with natural phenomena and original texts, without resorting to didactic materials or academic textbooks; the notebook, the talk on a given subject, the wall poster, are each child's personal creations—his or her book, the sum of his or her experiences.

Finally, social intelligence is acquired by rendering each individual increasingly responsible to put his or her freedom to good use: self-discipline, coeducation, coadministration; individual interests are confronted in many social activities, and solutions are sought together. The class plays, a collective creation, mirror these preoccupations, often related to the problematics of social life.

Respected as a person, the child has the benefit of continuous assessment of his or her progress, on a qualitative and noncompetitive basis; he or she is not judged by grades or class ratings, or examinations.

However, "no pedagogy can be adapted to every age and every mentality"; if the methods inspired by Decroly's work evolve, it is because they imply permanent and controlled experimentation. The primacy of reality runs counter to the reproducibility of teaching techniques; the principles must not be reduced to a system. "Children have a sense of observation; it suffices not to kill it. Children associate, abstract, generalize; one need only give them the opportunity to associate with elements of a higher order, to let them abstract and generalize on more elaborate data. Children act, create, imagine, express themselves; one need only give them materials and the opportunity to continue to develop their active tendencies." The main concern of a Decroly school is thus to insure a real bond between the spontaneous interests and the need for greater coherence and fruitfulness.

Bibliography

Decordes V 1973 *Docteur Decroly, Educational Principles.* The Learning Exchange, East Malvern, Australia and Ecole Decroly, Brussels
Decroly O 1979 *La Fonction de globalisation et l'enseignement.* Decroly, Brussels
Decroly O, Boon G 1974 *Vers l'école rénovée.* Ecole Decroly, Brussels
Ecole Decroly 1973 *Le Docteur Decroly et l'éducation.* Documents Pédagogiques de l'Ecole Decroly; no. 13–14, Brussels (Unless otherwise specified, all the quotations are borrowed from these documents).
Segers A 1948 *La Psychologie de l'enfant normal et anormal.* Stoops, Brussels

F. L. Dubreucq-Choprix

Delinquency

Delinquency may be defined as law-breaking behaviour on the part of those who, by virtue of their youth, are not yet seen as being fully responsible for their actions. The range of behaviour covered is often wide, including not only infractions of the criminal laws, which would apply equally to adults, but also failure to comply with rules pertaining specifically to them as nonadults. Because of the special position of children and adolescents, processing of delinquents is often strongly influenced by considerations of the child's welfare as well as justice. This further blurs the boundaries of "delinquency" in terms of a child's acts and introduces the notion of the child's needs in terms of assistance toward a nondelinquent future.

Despite the many papers which have been written about delinquents and delinquency, however, surprisingly little is known about it, its causes, and its prevention. One reason for this may lie in the extent to which attention has been concentrated on the attributes and activities of "officially recognized" offenders. The recognition that such people constitute only a small proportion of those actually committing delinquent acts has led to considerable speculation and controversy as to how far the "official" delinquents can be seen as representing the others. Such doubts have considerable methodological, theoretical, and practical implications and, in this article, some of the key issues are briefly discussed. For a more thorough coverage readers should consult specialist publications such as Gibbons' (1981) comprehensive survey; references covering specific aspects may be obtained by consulting abstracting journals.

1. Problems of Measuring Delinquency

Since the early 1950s juvenile delinquency has been presented as an increasing problem by the media in most parts of the world, and this picture is apparently supported by the official statistics. It is necessary, however, to proceed with extreme caution in trying to make assessments of changes in the incidence of delinquency over time in the same country, let alone comparisons between countries. Even within a single country, a change in policy with respect to law-breakers (or certain categories of them) might lead to an apparent rise or fall in the delinquency rate without any real change in the extent to which the relevant behaviour was occurring. The introduction of police warnings as an alternative to juvenile court proceedings (as happened in England in 1969) might, for example, reduce the number of juveniles appearing in court for minor offences. Conversely, a drive by authority against, say, truancy, could increase numbers of truants appearing in court without any accompanying increase in numbers actually truanting.

The figures that appear in official statistics reflect not only what young people are doing but also the legal provisions in force, the activity of law enforcement agencies, and the organization of the juvenile justice system. This makes it extremely difficult to compare the situation in different countries. Not only does the actual coverage, in terms of acts prohibited, differ from country to country (so that the Netherlands, for example, takes a much more lenient view of soft-drug use than most of her European neighbours), but so does the age range of offenders who are seen as juveniles. Thus, in Europe alone, the minimum age for processing as a juvenile delinquent and, hence, inclusion in the statistics, varies from 7 in Greece to 10 in France and England, 14 in Switzerland and the Federal Republic of Germany, and 15 in Finland and Sweden (most Swedes under 18 appear to be dealt with by child welfare boards rather than the courts).

Differences in law enforcement also assume considerable importance when comparing highly policed areas with those in which social control is mainly in the hands of family or community. In many countries this means that formal methods of processing juvenile delinquency—and hence the figures shown in the statistics—relate only, or mainly, to urban environments.

A major problem in basing a picture of delinquency in any area purely on official statistics is that one has no way of assessing how far these statistics reflect the actual amount of delinquency which is occurring. Self-report studies, where they have been carried out, indicate that official delinquents form only the tip of a much larger iceberg (see Hood and Sparks 1970 for a summary of relevant research in 1950s and 1960s) and that substantial proportions of "normal" adolescents admit to participation in illegal activities, such as theft. Moreover, all these studies agree that the vast majority of those making such admissions have remained undetected by the police. Nor does this picture hold only for the United States (where most studies were carried out): it has also been found in other parts of the Western world, including the United Kingdom and Scandinavia, and is probably worldwide.

2. Types of Delinquency

To speak of juvenile delinquency as a single entity is misleading. The range of behaviour covered can range from murder to defying one's parents, from armed robbery to petty pilfering. Most instances of delinquency, however, seem to fall into four main categories: theft, violence towards property, contravention of status laws (truanting, drinking) and behaviour, in groups, which has a high nuisance value for fellow citizens and which may appear menacing because of the noise and physical activity involved. The idea of violence towards other people as a major aspect of juvenile delinquency appears to owe more to the high publicity given to such happenings in the media than it does to the frequency with which they actually occur (Cohen 1980). The evidence of enquiries both by police and social scientists into football violence in the United Kindgom, for example, has indicated that, in the main, it is limited to remarks and gestures with remarkably little bloodshed. Furthermore, the increase in violent crime attributed to "young people" throughout Western Europe in recent years appears to relate much more to young adults, aged 17 to 21, than to juveniles.

The main cause of court appearances in younger age groups is undoubtedly theft. In Western Europe this accounts for 60–70 percent of officially recognized juvenile crime (European Committee on Crime Problems 1979) and in Japan 77 percent. The involvement of young people in thefts that do not result in a court appearance is even greater. Stealing from shops is widespread among children and adolescents in many countries, including Japan and the United Kingdom (where 70 percent of 13- to 16-year-old "nondelinquent" boys in a recent survey admitted to this). Evidence from self-report surveys and from the shop staff also indicates that girls are equally involved. In highly industrialized countries such escapades appear to be related to a search for "kicks" rather than material gain, and the same is true of the (usually temporary) removal of motor vehicles.

Most juvenile delinquency appears to occur in public places—on the street, in shops, sports stadiums, dance halls—but this may merely reflect the tendency for such public behaviour to come to official and media attention. There is little information available about antisocial or illegal behaviour carried out by children in their own homes, for example, so that while self-report studies have indicated that stealing within the home is not uncommon, parents seldom see this as delinquency and very rarely report it to the police. The extent of violence shown by young people within the home has been considered only in Japan where it has been identified as becoming a problem (Kazuhiko 1981), particularly in middle-class, education-oriented homes where the pressures to succeed in the highly competitive school system are extreme.

The issue of violence within schools is one which has had more publicity recently in various countries, including the United States, France, Japan, and the United Kingdom. Again, however, this is an area where it is difficult to assess the actual situation in any country or any school, as vandalism and physical violence towards teachers may be seen as matters to be dealt with by internal means (e.g., excluding the pupil from the school) rather than by referral to the police. Most of the evidence available is therefore impressionistic. The Safe School Study carried out in the 1970s by the United States Department of Health, Education and Welfare did, however, supply some factual data. This suggested that the problem was declining after reaching its peak in the 1960s and that, while vandalism was highest in suburban schools, interpersonal violence was concentrated in secondary schools in large cities. In those schools, however, the extent of violence, in terms of attacks on teachers, was considerable, with 1.8 percent of teachers reporting that pupils had made a physical attack on them within the period of one month and 1.3 percent that they had been robbed with force or threats (Rubel 1978).

3. Attributes of Delinquents

The picture emerging from the official statistics (and again this is found worldwide) is that the typical delinquent is male, comes from a low socioeconomic background and is resident in a materially, or socially deprived district in an urban area, usually a large city.

The data obtained from self-report studies, however, often show a different picture. Thus, while most self-report studies have tended to accept the nondelinquency of girls as given and, therefore, limit their coverage to "normal" boys, those that have included girls have found that the gap has been reduced considerably. Not only do the girls confess to more law-breaking behaviour than is indicated by their marked underrepresentation in official figures, it has also been found that both boys and girls show similar patterns of delinquency. The often accepted picture of girls as predominantly involved in sex offences and not in theft or vandalism was not supported.

The long-accepted link between juvenile delinquency and low socioeconomic status has also been challenged. Self-report studies have raised the important issue of middle-class delinquency and why, when differences have ceased to exist in some self-report studies, the official figures should still show such a marked relationship. This has stimulated sociological speculation, and empirical studies have been made into the phenomenon of bias in the processing of deviants. An alternative explanation, however, is that the delinquencies exposed in the general population are qualitatively different from those of official delinquents in terms of type of act and of frequency of participation (Hindelang et al, 1979). Many investigations have tried to map the attributes of delinquents more closely by looking within a social class or areal group and comparing the attributes of youths who had an officially recorded conviction with those that had none. Such studies have revealed that the official delinquent tends to suffer from a multiplicity of adverse factors. He (because such studies have concentrated on boys) is more likely to live in poor housing, to come from a family whose income is low and which relies on support from social agencies; his father is likely to be in unskilled manual work and to work erratically; his parents and/or siblings are more likely to have criminal records; marital disharmony is more likely, as is separation from one or both parents; discipline in the home is seen as unsatisfactory, inconsistent, too harsh, or too lax; and the parents themselves may suffer from mental or physical handicaps. Relationships between the delinquent and his parents may also be worse with less warmth and more rejection on both sides. At school, his measured intelligence is likely to be lower, as is his attainment level both in primary and secondary schools; he is more likely to be seen as troublesome by his teachers and his classmates. In temperament he is more likely to be impulsive and active, to like excitement and competition; to be more extrovert and/or neurotic; to plan less for the future and to have less realistic goals; and to have a different self-image. This is by no means a comprehensive list but details the relationships which have been found most often or most strongly established. The picture is a depressing one, showing the delinquent boy as subject to multiple problems. Girl delinquents are no more fortunate since, in addition to familial and educational problems, the few studies devoted to them have tended to emphasize their lack of feminine qualities. Such findings are, however, based on studies of officially processed delinquents. It is not known whether the attributes relate to the tendency to break the law or to an increased likelihood of being perceived by others as a lawbreaker.

The difference becomes crucial when we try to use such descriptive data to explain delinquency.

4. The Search for Causes

Much of the work which has been published on juvenile delinquency has concerned itself with causes—either the causes of delinquent acts ("What makes these people break the law?") or the determinants of official delinquency statistics ("What makes certain categories of people more likely to be arrested and tried?"). These two approaches should not be confused as they involve very different ideological perspectives. Those who are looking for the causes of delinquent behaviour concentrate on the social background and personal characteristics of the offender, taking the law-enforcement process as given. In other words, once the youngster has committed a delinquent act, the forces of law and order are seen as coming into operation with complete impartiality. If this is so, the explanations of delinquency can be based on the characteristics of officially recognized delinquents.

This assumption of the impartiality of the law-enforcement agencies is not shared by the second group of criminologists. Citing the results of self-report studies, they suggest that the groups featured in official statistics are there because their personal characteristics cause them to be seen as particularly "dangerous" by social-control and law-enforcement agencies. Thus the same adverse features (for example, living in a deprived area, belonging to a minority group, or being a migrant) which are seen by the first group as causing criminal activity may be seen by the second as making their major contribution in terms of producing differential outcomes in the interaction between juvenile and authority. The suggestion here, is that the picture of delinquency given in official statistics will be determined by the attitudes and actions/reactions of policemen, judges, and so on, as much as it will be by the actions of young people themselves. Looking first at the studies which have concentrated on the offender, it is possible to differentiate between those which try to explain delinquency in terms of the individual delinquent's psychological characteristics and primary experiences (in the family, school, and peer group) and those that see delinquency as the result of social forces operating differentially within the population.

The search for criminogenic attributes usually involves comparison of those with criminal records (representing delinquents) and those who have no official record (representing nondelinquents). This presents us with two problems. The first has already been mentioned. In the light of self-report studies, the nondelinquent status of the control group is open to doubt: it is not possible to know whether differences between the groups relate to a greater propensity to commit delinquent acts or merely to a greater propensity to be caught while doing so. Secondly, even if the control group is accepted as genuinely nondelinquent, it is still only possible to know that certain characteristics occur more, or less, often in the delinquent group. This does not prove that the relationship is a causal one. For example, the association between delinquency and broken families does not necessarily mean that lack of a parent is the direct cause of delinquency. It could be, for example, that broken families tend to live in areas or subareas where neighbourhood characteristics are particularly conducive to delinquency and/or where there is a strong police presence. Too often causal explanations are presented because they fit in with the preconceptions of the investigator and not because they have been properly established from the data. Another, perhaps more promising, approach at the individual level, sees delinquency as related to learning theory. Conformity is learned by conditioning, with the withdrawal of parental approval as the stimulus. Delinquency can occur when conditioning is unsuccessful either because the child has an inbuilt resistance (for example, Eysenck's cortical inhibition) or because the parents adopt ineffective techniques. Problems can also occur, of course, when the learning process is perfect but the content of the learning is not socially approved (see *Learning Theory: Historical Backgrounds*).

This idea that faulty learning underlies delinquency has been particularly influential in Eastern Europe. Since the classical Marxist–Leninist view is that crime is a by-product of the excesses of the capitalist system and the oppression of the masses, there should be no crime in a truly socialist society. As there demonstrably is a certain amount of delinquency in the countries of Eastern Europe, however, this must be explained in terms of relics of the capitalist system which have affected people's attitudes either because they are suffering from a time-lag in social consciousness or because they have been subjected to external (Western) values. Thus, writing from the German Democratic Republic, Buchholz and his co-workers (1974 p.48) say categorically that one of the main determinants of delinquency is "the lack of a fundamental political and ideological attitude" stemming from defects in "the education and upbringing of juveniles and children by parents, school, and social organizations, by groups in which individuals live wholly or temporarily, the negative influences of the West, etc."

Here two new themes are introduced: first, delinquency can involve learning just as much as conformity and, second, learning can take place outside the home. These themes have been developed also in Western criminology. Peer groups have been shown to play an important part not only in teaching delinquent skills and fostering appropriate attitudes but also through reinforcement by providing rewards, in terms of status or popularity, for delinquent activities. Much delinquency, particularly that carried out for fun, has been shown to involve group support. The most common types of juvenile theft—shoplifting and taking motor vehicles—are seldom solitary enterprises. Damage to property usually involves two or more people as does use of soft drugs and glue sniffing. Almost by definition, "rowdyism" is clearly a group activity. Such peer-group support is not limited to the working-class delinquent. The middle class also, according to self-report studies, may be supported in their delinquent acts by their friends. Whether or not more indirect influences, such as those of the West on East European youth or of television in the Western world, have any deleterious effects on those exposed to them is much more difficult to ascertain. The effects of television violence have been studied in various settings, in various ways, and with various age groups but, perhaps because of methodological differences, the results are not consistent. In general it appears that, in the very short term, violence on the screen may produce aggressive behaviour in the young viewer but that longer term effects have not been established.

At a more general level, some sociologists have suggested that delinquents are neither the victims of faulty socialization nor have they been seduced by alien influences. They say, rather, that delinquents are the well-socialized products of lower-class urban subgroups who have their own way of life. In other words, the delinquent is a conformist in terms of a minority subculture and only to be seen as a rule breaker by the standards of a different subgroup. In a hierarchically arranged society where some subgroups have more power than others to enforce their norms, this can lead to certain forms of minority subgroup behaviour becoming classified as illegal.

This type of reasoning has been applied in attempts to explain the concentration of officially recognized delinquency in "lower-class" areas in Western society. Its originator, William B. Miller (1958), for example, suggested that male adolescent groups in such areas displayed (perhaps in a rather overstressed form) the focal concerns of lower-class urban culture, such as trouble, toughness, excitement, smartness (ability to manipulate people and situations to your own advantage, not book-learning), fate, and autonomy. In the gang, then, the boy is learning the conventional lower-class male role, and it is the reactions of such "outsiders" as the police, which bring the attributions of delinquency.

This approach provides insights into some aspects of some kinds of delinquency in some areas, namely lower-class, urban, gang-based delinquency. It is arguable, however, whether the differences in values which exist between "lower-class milieus" and other areas are sufficiently marked to warrant their being viewed as subcultures.

The idea that the school might play a part in causing delinquency is a relatively new one. Officially the role of the school is to socialize children, compensating if necessary for defects in home training, and turning out good citizens at the end of the process. Recent studies in the United Kingdom, however, have shown that in the same or similar areas, different schools, ostensibly of the same type, have very different rates of official delinquency among their pupils and that these rates are stable over time (Rutter et al. 1979).

To some extent these differences appeared to reflect different attributes in the pupil intake. For the children considered as a whole, regardless of school, father's occupational status and the child's verbal-reasoning scores were found to be the best predictors of delinquency. Even allowing for this, however, differences between schools were such that a boy (girls were excluded from later analysis) with a favourable personal prediction and attending a high-delinquency school would have a higher likelihood of becoming delinquent than one with unfavourable characteristics attending a school with a low delinquency rate. The schools, themselves, must therefore play some part in generating or inhibiting delinquency among their pupils. How this happens is not yet clear. Variables found to be associated with low delinquency rates in school included a range of intellectual ability among pupils, a school ethos which stressed pupil responsibility, and teacher actions which provided a high level of pupil praise and reward. Why these factors should relate to delinquency outside school is not yet explained so that further research is clearly needed. Studies within schools have provided evidence that bad behaviour in the classroom relates to factors such as high staff turnover, ineffectual teaching, lax or overauthoritarian discipline, and adverse pupil perceptions of teachers; but as yet it is not known how, or if, such factors affect out-of-school activity.

One link which has been suggested is that some delinquency, particularly that of lower-class boys in groups, may be an attempt to compensate for the low status conferred on them in school. By setting up their own culture with values opposed to those of the school, participation in delinquent acts becomes a source of in-group prestige. Some empirical evidence in support of this idea has emerged from studies of schools which are divided rigidly on grounds of pupil ability and where the ethos overtly favours the most able groups. Under these circumstances it has been shown that the least able pupils, grouped together by the school and aware of their low status, develop an antiauthoritarian, antiestablishment and antiacademic way of life within the school.

Control theory is an attempt to write all these partial explanations of delinquency into one consistent whole. Instead of asking: "Why are some people delinquent?", the new question is: "Why do people conform?". Control theory suggests that deviance will occur when people have little to gain from conformity and little to lose or much to gain from deviation. Conformists are constrained by the bonds which link them to society; delinquents are freed from such restraints. Hirschi (1969) suggested that these bonds were of three types:

(a) Attachment in terms of one person being linked to others by affection. The more young people are linked by such bonds to conventional others—parents, other relatives, teachers, friends—the less likely they will be to commit delinquent acts.

(b) Commitment which refers to having a vested interest in conformity, seeing it as part of a master-plan for life, and making a rational assessment of what losses may be incurred by involvement in delinquency. Conformity will only be abandoned if expected rewards are seen as high enough to justify the risk.

(c) Involvement which describes the extent to which youths are caught up in conventional activities occupying their time and energy. As both time and energy are in limited supply, heavy involvement in legitimate activities will obviously militate against finding opportunities to indulge in the illegitimate, whereas long periods of "hanging around" lend themselves to delinquency.

In control theory, then, there is an explanation which has much more universal applicability than the others. It is not limited to the delinquent activities of lower-class males but can be applied equally well to girls, middle-class delinquents, and "good" adolescents in bad areas. It is sufficiently wide to include earlier partial explanations.

So far, in the search for causes, focus has been on the child's immediate environment of home, neighbourhood, and school since these make up the child's social world. It can be argued, however, that these little worlds cannot be viewed independently as they, in turn, are produced by wider social forces. War and civil unrest have been related to higher delinquency rates as have industrialization and migration to towns. All produce situations in which customary values become inapplicable and old bonds are attenuated or cease to exist. Poverty has been cited as a cause but in industrialized countries the delinquency rate has risen as poverty drops. Long-term unemployment is currently being cited as an impetus to crime in Europe, and, although this applies more directly to young adults, it may be that perceptions of an unemployed future are also affecting those in their last year at school. Implicit in much of what has already been said is also the assumption that delinquency and the adverse factors associated with it are all the products of an unequal social system.

Many sociologists would argue that in a society where economic opportunities, power, and prestige are unequally distributed, those who are at the bottom on some or all of these counts may find themselves also at a disadvantage in relation to the criminal law and its enforcement.

5. Creation of the "Official" Delinquent

So far the concern has been with factors seen as drawing individuals towards law-breaking or conformist behaviour. In recent years, however, more attention has been devoted to consideration of the processes by which certain people become officially identified as delinquents while other law breakers do not. This has been seen as involving interaction between the young people concerned and agents of social control.

Empirical studies have shown that officials tend to use considerable discretion in deciding how to classify and process individual law breakers. For example, while the police do not show much variation in the way they process juveniles involved in serious offences, their reactions toward minor offenders have been found to be influenced by their perceptions of the "kind of person" they were dealing with. Making quick decisions on the spot, they have been shown to be more lenient with girls, with younger children, and with boys who were conventionally dressed and who spoke to them respectfully. Detection of instances of juvenile law breaking can also reflect police discretion. Areas where trouble is expected may be policed more intensively, leading to more arrests, leading to confirmation that the area is a bad one. Certain categories of people may become more liable to be stopped, questioned, or searched.

The actions of the policemen on the street constitute only the first moves in the process which takes a young person from law-breaking act to officially certified delinquent. In the intermediate stages there usually lie several possibilities of diversion both formal and informal.

Formal methods of diversion occur when certain social-control agencies are given the right to take action to halt or to defer the child's progress towards the court. For example, the police might be given the power to dismiss certain categories of offenders after issuing them with a formal warning (as in the United Kingdom) or to refer them to specialized helping agencies such as the youth service bureau and university counselling schemes sponsored by the California police in the United States. Such diversionary decisions are usually made by special officers at police headquarters and do not rest on the discretion of the officer making the charge.

Diversionary programmes may also be implemented at court intake level. Thus, in Canada and some areas of the United States the probation officer acting as intake official can initiate short-term diversionary counselling programs with offenders and their families. If this is successful, the case will never go to court. The guidelines for selection for diversionary counselling are, however, such as to allow some discretion to the intake officer concerned. In general, severity of offence and recidivism would seem to be contra-indications, but in other cases choice appears to relate to the intake officer's views on the type of person the offender is and whether or not counselling would be successful (Needleman 1981). People with suspect personal qualities and/or perceivedly bad social backgrounds may therefore not only be more likely to be referred to the court by the police, but they are also less likely to be diverted once they reach there.

Diversion from court proceedings, however, does not always mean an escape from official processing. It may mean diversion to another type of agency, one concerned with welfare. In Norway, for example, all children were removed completely from the justice system as early as 1896, and young offenders became the concern of local child welfare boards set up in each area to deal with all children with problems whether they were law breakers or the victims of deprivation. This became the model for the other Scandinavian countries so that, though young people certainly continue to break the law, there are no delinquents in the sense of those found guilty in court. Sweden has moved even further from the conventional pattern so that the youth welfare boards have, since the 1970s, taken no action in the great majority of cases of delinquency referred to them, arguing that most children grow out of their delinquency and may do so more successfully if left to themselves and their families since most measures of compulsory intervention are ineffective and may even be counterproductive.

Even in countries where a juvenile court system is operative, it would be a mistake to see welfare considerations as necessarily subordinate to justice. The reverse often appears to have been the case. In the United States, for instance, decisions in the Supreme Court made in the late 1960s indicated that juvenile courts, in their determination to do what was best for young offenders, had succeeded in removing most of the legal rights of the accused which are taken for granted in adult courts. It has been argued that legal safeguards involve formality, legal representation, cross-examination of witnesses and a general atmosphere of learned argument and points of law which would be confusing and frightening for a child. On the other side it can be said that guilt has often been accepted by the court without adequate proof, that the accused were often ignorant of the evidence against them and therefore could not challenge it and that, even if the proceedings were informal, they were still confusing so that the accused and the accused's parents might be unable to correctly determine when, how, and to whom to put their case.

Such criticisms are not limited to American courts. They have been given force in the United States, however, because they have been made by the Supreme Court hearing appeals against specific judgments. The effect on juvenile justice has been considerable. Status offences, such as running away from home, have been removed from the statute books, and therefore from the courts, and are now seen as welfare problems. Legal representation of the accused has also led to more involvement of prosecution attorneys both in deciding which cases are to come to court and in presenting the case when it gets there.

Concern about the extent to which justice and welfare considerations can be observed within a single institution, combined with doubts about the suitability of legalistic court measures for all offenders, has led to considerable worldwide interest in the dual system set up in Scotland in the early 1980s (Martin et al. 1981). This centres on children's hearings staffed by lay members of the community who deal with all cases of children, including delinquents, who are seen as in need of compulsory care. The decision about the child's need is made by a local authority official, called the reporter, to whom all cases are referred, except those involving very serious crimes. Clearly this gives the reporter considerable powers of discretion, and investigations show that, like the intake officers in American courts (though perhaps with more justification in a tribunal concerned with "care"), they base their decisions not only on the nature of the act but, most strongly, on whether or not the child has family problems or a good report from school (Martin et al 1981). At the hearing, those who deny their involvement in the acts charged are sent to court for the facts to be judged, returning to the children's hearing for disposal. If the facts are admitted, there is discussion round the table between the three panel members conducting the hearing, the child, and the parents. The case is then disposed of in accord with the child's perceived needs by (a) sending the child home with no supervision order; (b) sending the child home but subject to a period of supervision by a social worker, or (c) sending the child away from home for residential supervision. These remedies differ little from the sanctions available to juvenile courts.

What factors influence the outcome? Here, again, courts and welfare tribunals do not appear to differ radically. The seriousness of the offence perhaps assumes more importance in court but, once guilt has been established, the decision on disposal appears to reflect the judge's view of the offender as an individual in the light of reports on family background, behaviour and attainment at school, and so on. In other words, the bases for decision are individualized in courts as well as in welfare tribunals. To obtain the relevant information on which to base the decision, judges must therefore rely on the reports of others (social workers, teachers) or must make snap judgments on the basis of clues available to them from the offender's appearance and demeanour. The same may be true of welfare tribunals, and in each case, concern has been expressed about the power given to those who supply information. Social workers, for example, can influence the outcome of cases by the way in which they present their social background reports. Instant judgments about type of person, on the other hand, can lead to stereotyping and possible racial, ethnic, or class bias. Decisions about disposal also involve beliefs about the efficacy of certain kinds of experience for certain kinds of children. As these views are intensely subjective, the results can be surprising, with relatively minor offenders on their first appearance being sent to residential establishments. These beliefs can also provide fuel for accusations of bias against certain groups who may be seen as being most at risk and hence in need of the most radical intervention.

6. Disposal and Outcome

Most delinquent children and adolescents who come before juvenile courts or other agencies do so only once. Relatively few return to court again, either as juveniles or as adults (if minor traffic offences are excluded). As a result, it has been argued that disposal of first offenders should involve minimum official intervention—a warning, a "conditional discharge", or a "no action" decision. Such a policy of nonintervention is well-illustrated in Sweden where the child welfare boards take action concerning only a relatively small proportion of juvenile offenders referred to them. This has now spread to the 15- to 18-year-old groups also. Even though older juveniles are officially dealt with by courts, the child welfare boards can intervene and, even though they take no action themselves, the intervention causes suspension of prosecution.

At the opposite extreme is the action which is seen as the most punitive by the child—sending him (or, less often, her) away from home. Such measures are expected to achieve two different goals. One is to protect society by incarcerating dangerous offenders. More often, however, the move is said to be for the children's own good—to provide an environment and experiences which will lead them away from delinquency. There is, however, little evidence that residential establishments achieve this aim. Indeed, the failure rate, in terms of reappearance in court within two to five years of release, has been found to be depressingly high. As a result, many attempts have been made to find alternatives which rather than segregating delinquents will attempt to integrate them more closely with the conventional community.

7. Practical Implications

For those involved in child rearing—as parents or as teachers—the crucial issue in juvenile delinquency is almost certainly prevention. Because the causes of delinquency are not yet understood, despite the efforts of many researchers and theorists, the best methods of prevention are also in dispute. Perhaps the best guideline at the individual level is provided by the very general precepts of control theory with its emphasis on bonds linking the young person to conventional life. Children living in a happy, united, conventional family where they have many activities and interests to occupy them are unlikely to become delinquent or, if they do become involved once, will not persist with a delinquent career. Some parents, however, cannot provide such an ideal environment, and this may well be for reasons beyond their control. Material assistance, provision of community facilities, and housing policy all have their part to play. A deliberate policy of housing all "problem families" in one area, for example, may contain the situation geographically but is unlikely to decrease the rate of delinquency among the children living there.

For teachers there is the suggestion that the pupil least likely to be delinquent is the one who is happy at school, has good relationships with teachers, feels that the curriculum is relevant and feels personally involved in school life. In other words, good classroom management and school administration can encourage conformity. Again, however, this can be of little comfort to teachers in schools where violence and alienation are already widespread. The provision of opportunities to use classroom skills to advantage may be determined by financial and political considerations outside the school itself.

One preventative measure is, however, within the reach of individual teachers—that of avoiding premature labelling and prediction. The attributes of delinquents which were outlined earlier relate to variables which are more likely to occur in relation to delinquents than to other children. This does not mean that all those who show the attributes will be delinquents nor that all delinquents will show them. To attempt prediction of delinquency potential in individual cases is risky. The literature on "self-fulfilling prophecies" in the classroom shows clearly how fast children can pick up clues to the teacher's view of them so that the child who feels he or she is expected to become delinquent may well act accordingly, having little to lose by it.

A similar message can be passed to those who have to identify lawbreakers in public places or to process them once identified. The police have the unenviable task of maintaining public order by prevention of crime as well as by dealing with lawbreakers. In each case, they may have to make decisions on little evidence as to whether to intercept some individual or not. Such intervention may result in the detection of delinquency or its prevention. It may also, if demonstrating systematic bias, be counter-productive, leading to increased delinquency and even to harassment of the police in return by those who see themselves discriminated against. Such reactions can stimulate further police action, so leading to a vicious spiral.

For those processing delinquents, however, perhaps the most important implication is that, in the present state of knowledge, there is no hard evidence about what kind of official action will provide the best outcome. Many children get better without any intervention; many get worse after a period of residential re-education or care. For the individual concerned, however, the choice of action clearly has important and far-reaching implications. In view of this, it is important that considerably more hard evidence should be gathered about the relative success rates, in terms of putting an end to delinquent activities, accruing to different types of treatment for different types of delinquent. This may not stop children and young people breaking the law, but might at least prevent young offenders from developing into adult criminals.

See also: Juvenile Delinquents: Counseling

Bibliography

Buchholz E, Hartmann J, Lekschas J, Stiller G 1974 *Socialist Criminology: Theoretical and Methodological Foundations*. Lexington Books, Lexington, Massachusetts
Cohen S 1980 *Folk Devils and Moral Panics*. Martin Robertson, Oxford
European Committee on Crime Problems 1979 *Social Change and Juvenile Delinquency*. Council of Europe, Strasbourg
Gibbons D J 1981 *Delinquent Behaviour*, 3rd edn. Prentice-Hall, Englewood Cliffs, New Jersey
Hindelang M J, Hirschi T, Weis J G 1979 Correlates of delinquency: The illusion of discrepancy between self-report and official measures. *Am. Sociol. Rev.* 44: 995–1014
Hirschi T 1969 *Causes of Delinquency*. University of California Press, Berkeley, California
Hood R G, Sparks R F 1970 *Key Issues in Criminology*. Weidenfeld and Nicolson, London
Kazuhiko T 1981 Changes in traditional society and "delinquencization". *Japan Q.* 28: 362–69
Martin F M, Fox S J, Murray K (eds.) 1981 *Children Out of Court*. Scottish Academic Press, Edinburgh
Miller W B 1958 Lower class culture as a generating milieu of gang delinquency. *J. Soc. Issues* 14: 5–19
Needleman C 1981 Discrepant assumptions in empirical research: The case of juvenile court screening. *Soc. Prob.* 28: 247–62
Rubel R J 1978 Analysis and critique of HEW safe school study report to the congress. *Crime Delinq.* 24: 257–65
Rutter M, Maughan B, Mortimore P, Ouston J, Smith A 1979 *Fifteen Thousand Hours: Secondary Schools and Their Effects on Children*. Open Books, London

S. Mitchell

Delphi Technique

The Delphi technique, named after the oracle at Delphi in ancient Greece, is a communications process which permits a group to achieve consensus in the solution of a complex problem without face-to-face interaction or confrontation by the individual members of the group. By eliminating face-to-face interaction, this process avoids such problems as the influence of dominant individuals on group decisions, the loss of time and energy on irrelevant or biased discussions, the distortion of individual judgment by group pressure, the inclination to reject novel ideas, and the tendency to defend a previous position. At the same time, it assures independent thought, anonymity, and the assessment without pressure of the ideas of others in the gradual formation of a considered opinion.

In general, the procedure is as follows: (a) participants are chosen and are asked to give anonymous opinions, suggestions, recommendations, or predictions (depending on the topic) to a series of questionnaire items; (b) each participant receives feedback, such as the median response of all participants, and a second round of responding begins in order to ascertain the intensity of agreement or disagreement with the group median response; (c) again feedback is given to the participants in terms of the group median and also the reasons why some participants do not agree with the median response; (d) after reviewing the reasons for the minority opinions, the participants again respond; (e) steps (c) and (d) can be repeated although convergence of opinion usually does not increase greatly after one round of these two steps. A detailed chronological description of how these five steps were employed in an actual study can be found in Uhl's (1971) investigation of institutional goals using the Delphi technique. It is interesting to note that while most studies incorporating the Delphi technique have used questionnaires, a few studies have adopted the technique for computer use which permits participants to respond through separate terminals. Linstone and Turoff (1975), in the most recent compendium of Delphi studies, describe such a study.

The Delphi technique was originally developed by the Rand Corporation in the 1950s to deal with complex defense problems and since the mid-1960s its use has expanded at a prolific rate. It is being used by business, government, industry, medicine, regional planning, and education in a wide variety of situations including futures forecasting, goal assessment, curriculum planning, establishment of budget priorities, estimates concerning the quality of life, policy formulation, as well as problem identification and formulation of solutions. While the Delphi technique was considered primarily a forecasting tool in its earlier uses, it is currently being utilized more and more as a process to improve communications and generate consensus in the solution to almost any type of complex problem.

The use of the Delphi may be warranted if any or all of the following conditions exist: (a) the resolution of a problem can be facilitated by the collective judgments of one or more groups; (b) those groups providing judgments are not likely to communicate adequately without an intervening process; (c) the solution is more likely to be accepted if more people are involved in its development than would be possible in a face-to-face meeting; (d) frequent group meetings are not practical because of time, distance, etc.; and (e) one or more groups of participants are more dominant than another.

It is surprising that of all the studies performed using the Delphi technique, very few are of a methodological nature. As a result, Delphi has a poor theoretical base and little is known about the variables that affect the process. This lack of a theoretical framework is its main weakness. A systematic research program is needed to determine how and why the method functions.

Bibliography

Linstone H, Turoff M (eds.) 1975 *The Delphi Method: Techniques and Applications.* Addison-Wesley, Reading, Massachusetts

Uhl N P 1971 *Identifying Institutional Goals: Encouraging Convergence of Opinion Through the Delphi Technique*, Research Monograph No. 2. National Laboratory for Higher Education, Durham, North Carolina

N. P. Uhl

Demand Elasticities for Educated Labor

The elasticity of demand for educated labor measures the percentage change in the number of workers with specified levels of education demanded by employers per percentage change in the wage of these workers, other wages and input prices assumed fixed. It is a central concept in the analysis of the market for labor skills, as it represents the responsiveness of employers to price incentives to employ workers of varying levels of education. When the elasticity of demand is relatively small (as in case a of Fig. 1) enormous changes in wages are needed to induce employers to alter the number of workers hired. In this case, one can practically ignore responses to wage changes and analyze demand for labor as if it did not depend on wages. When the elasticity of demand is moderate, by contrast, the concept is a critical element in understanding the effect of economic changes on demand for labor and wages (case b in Fig. 1). When the elasticity of demand is near infinite, it is probably not useful to think of educated labor as a distinct input in production at all, as it is

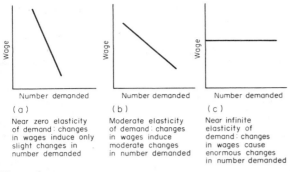

Figure 1
Elasticity of demand for educated labor

likely that other inputs are perfectly substitutable for it (case c in Fig. 1).

The magnitude of the elasticity of demand for educated labor depends critically on the extent to which educated labor is substitutable for other inputs in production. The ease of substitutability if generally measured by the *elasticity of substitution*, defined as the percentage change in the number of educated workers relative to the amount of other inputs (say, less educated workers) per percentage change in the wages of educated workers relative to the price of other inputs (say, the wages of less educated labor). Formally, if E_1 measures the number of educated workers and E_0 the number of other inputs and if w_1 and w_0 are the respective factor prices, the elasticity of substitution σ is

$$\sigma = -(\%\Delta E_1/E_0)/\%\Delta W_1/W_0)$$

where $\%\Delta$ measures percentage changes. In analyses which treat employer demand responses at a given level of output, the elasticity of demand is just a function of elasticities of substitution. When the level of output varies in response to changes in prices, the elasticity of demand for educated labor, like other inputs, depends on the elasticity of demand for the final product as well.

The elasticity of substitution between more and less educated workers (or other inputs) has been at the center of analyses of demand for educated labor for two reasons. First, because the validity of widely used "fixed coefficient" methods for forecasting educational demands or "needs" and the potential economic worth of educational planning to meet such demands or needs hinges critically on the size of the elasticity. Standard "fixed coefficient" forecast methods assume zero elasticities of substitution in order to focus on the impact of changes in the composition of industries on the demand for educated labor. The greater are actual elasticities, the less valuable are such forecasts. Similarly, planning education to meet future labor market demands is useful only if elasticities of substitution are small; if the

elasticities are large, employers can readily substitute less educated for more educated labor, so that even accurate planning will be of little economic value. Second, the elasticity of substitution between more and less educated labor is important in analyzing the impact of changes in relative supplies of workers on the distribution of earnings. When the elasticity is high, large increases in the supply of graduates relative to nongraduates will have little effect on their relative wages. When the elasticity of substitution is small, large increases in the relative supply of graduates will cause sizeable changes in relative wages and thus will alter the distribution of earnings.

Given these issues, it is not surprising that economists have undertaken empirical studies designed to measure the elasticity of substitution between more and less educated or skilled workers. Because the number of workers with varying levels of education is predetermined in any given year by supply decisions made years earlier due to the length of training, most analyses actually examine the inverse of the elasticity of substitution, the elasticity of complementarity, which measures the percentage change in relative wages due to percentage changes in relative supplies. While it is reasonable to assume that supplies are fixed in analyses that treat time series data, this assumption is less defensible in comparisons across geographic regions at a point in time: within a country, the supply of educated workers to an area can migrate in response to wage incentives and thus cannot be regarded as exogenous to wage determination; across countries, differences in supply may reflect responses to differences in the rewards to education that persist over time, weakening the assumption that supplies can be taken as independent of the wages. Accordingly, some studies have also used "simultaneous equations" techniques to estimate the relevant elasticities of substitution. In these studies demand and supply of educated labor are estimated conjointly in a system.

Table 1 summarizes the findings of the most important empirical studies on the elasticities of substitution between more and less educated labor. Initial work on elasticities of substitution focused on cross-sectional data, with most attention given to cross-country comparisons. While the early evidence on states of the United States supported relatively moderate elasticities (Johnson 1970, Welch 1970) the work of several analysts led many to believe that the elasticity was rather high, sufficiently so to yield practically horizontal demand curves. Bowles (1969) produced, in particular, an elasticity between workers with some college education and those with 8 to 11 years of school of 202, and smaller but still sizable elasticities (6 to 12) between other educational groups. With a sample of 28 states from the United States, Dougherty (1972) obtained a more moderate but still high estimate of over 8. Psacharopoulos and Hinchliffe (1972) divided the

Table 1

Estimates of the elasticity of substitution between highly educated and less educated workers

Study	Sample	Elasticity of substitution
Bowles (1969)	countries	202
Johnson (1970)	states, USA	1.3
Welch (1970) (Agriculture sector)	states, USA	1.4
Dougherty (1972)	states, USA	8.2
Psacharopoulos and Hinchliffe (1972) (countries)	developed	1000
	less developed	2.1–2.5
Tinbergen (1974)	countries	0.6–1.2
	states	0.4–2.1
Freeman (1975)	years, USA	1.0–2.6
Fallon and Layard (1975)	countries	0.6–3.5
Grant (1979)	Standard Metropolitan Areas (SMAs)	1.2

a Definitions of highly educated to less educated vary somewhat between samples. All except Fallon and Layard treat college relative to some other group. Fallon and Layard relate groups with 8 or more years to less than 8

international sample by degree of development, obtaining an essentially infinite elasticity (implying perfect substitutability at the relevant wage ratios) in the developed countries but a more modest value in the less developed countries. As the relative earnings of graduates remained constant or increased in the 1950s and 1960s, despite increased supplies of graduates from colleges and universities, these estimates were generally accepted as being in accord with reality. Some viewed them as casting serious doubt on the concept of educational bottlenecks as a barrier to economic growth and on the value of the fixed coefficient model of labor demand, then being used by the Organisation for Economic Co-operation and Development, among others, to analyze the graduate and skilled worker labor markets for the purpose of educational planning.

In the 1970s, concurrent with the observed decline in the relative earnings of college graduates throughout the developed world, analysts began to reexamine these results. New estimates based on better data and models provided a very different picture of the elasticity of substitution between educated and less educated labor. Nobel-laureate Jan Tinbergen amplified the country and state analyses to take account of the likely simultaneous determination of relative wages and relative supplies in cross sections and obtained quite different results from Bowles and Dougherty using their data sets. His elasticities ranged from 0.50 to 2.00, which were consistent with the earlier cross state work of Welch and Johnson in the United States. Freeman (1975) used time series

data for the United States to estimate the effect of the growth in the number of college graduates relative to high-school graduates on their relative earnings and obtained estimated elasticities of a similar magnitude, ranging from 1.0 to 2.6. Fallon and Layard (1975) examined a large cross section of countries, with the comparable results shown in Table 1. Grant (1979) developed estimates in a complete translogarithmic systems equation which included capital in the analysis and obtained a value of 1.2. All told, the current evidence suggests a value of the elasticity of substitution between more and less educated labor in the range of 1.0 to 2.0. This magnitude is consistent with changes in the supply of graduates altering their relative earnings and does not invalidate the potential economic worth of educational planning based on fixed coefficient models.

A large number of additional studies on substitution among groups of workers have used occupational disaggregation. While these results show a wider range than those given for educational groups in Table 1, the estimates are consistent with elasticities of substitution between highly educated and less educated workers of 1–2. In the Hamermesh and Grant (1979) review of 20 estimates of elasticities of substitution between production (blue collar) and nonproduction (white collar) workers, the mean estimate was 2.3, with half the studies yielding estimates below 1.0 and half above that value.

The relationship between capital and more educated or skilled labor and the relationship between capital and less educated or skilled labor have also been studied as important elements in the demand for labor of varying educational qualities. The key hypotheses in this work had been that capital is less substitutable (more complementary) for educated than for less educated labor (Griliches 1969). If this is the case increases in capital raise the demand for educated labor relative to less educated labor and changes in the price of capital cause employers to alter employment of the less educated more than employment of the more educated. The extant evidence appears to support this hypothesis. Of the 12 studies in the Hamermesh–Grant review article (Hamermesh and Grant 1979), eight show capital to be more easily substituted for blue-collar labor than for white-collar labor, and half indicate that white-collar labor is actually complementary with capital, so that changes in the price of capital raise demand for white-collar labor rather than reduce it. The only study to examine labor by education also shows lower substitutability between the more educated and capital than between the less educated and capital (Grant 1981).

With moderate elasticities of substitution between educated and less educated labor and with relatively small (or even oppositely signed) elasticities of substitution between more educated labor and capital, current evidence suggests that the elasticity of demand for educated labor is of a moderate magnitude. In terms of Fig. 1, the evidence suggests that case b represents actual labor markets. Hence, analyses of the impact of economic changes or policies on employment or wages of educated labor cannot ignore the employment response to changes in wages.

See also: Supply Elasticities for Educated Labor

Bibliography

Allen R G D 1938 *Mathematical Analysis for Economics.* Macmillan, London
Bowles S 1969 *Planning Educational Systems for Economic Growth.* Harvard University Press, Cambridge, Massachusetts
Dougherty C R S 1972 Estimates of labour aggregation functions. *J. Polit. Econ.* 80: 1101–19
Fallon P R, Layard P R G 1975 Capital–skill complementarity, income distribution, and output accounting. *J. Polit. Econ.* 83: 279–301
Freeman R B 1975 Overinvestment in college training? *J. Hum. Resour.* 10: 287–311
Grant J H 1979 Substitution among labor, labor and capital in United States manufacturing (Doctoral dissertation, Michigan State University) *Dissertation Abstracts International* 1980 40: 6356A (University Microfilms No. 80 13741)
Grant S 1981 Separability and substitution among labor aggregates and capital. Wellesley College Working Paper No. 40. Wellesley College, Wellesley, Massachusetts
Griliches Z 1969 Capital–skill complementarity. *Rev. Econ. Stat.* 51: 465–68
Hamermesh S, Grant J 1979 Econometric studies of labor–labor substitution and their implications for policy. *J. Hum. Resour.* 14: 518–42
Johnson G 1970 The demand for labor by educational category. *South. Econ. J.* October: 190–204
Psacharopoulos G, Hinchliffe K 1972 Further evidence on the elasticity of substitution among different types of educated labor. *J. Polit. Econ.* 80: 786–92
Sato R, Koizumi T 1973 On the elasticities of substitution and complementarity. *Oxf. Econ. Pap.* 25: 44–56
Tinbergen J 1974 Substitution of graduates by other labour. *Kylos* 27: 217–26
Welch F 1970 Education in production. *J. Polit. Econ.* 78: 35–59

R. B. Freeman

Demography in Educational Planning

The right to education has, in recent years, become a universally recognized notion. International organizations have made important efforts to promote this right. In the case of UNESCO, for instance, one of the most important programmes of the next Medium-Term Plan (1984–1989) is "Education for All". However, the way in which the right to education has been interpreted, and the extent to which it has become a reality, depend upon the country. In some countries only one child out of three or four gains access to primary education, and the rate of illiteracy among the adult population remains very high. In other countries, compulsory education of up to 12 years has been fully implemented with, at the same time, rather high enrolment rates at the post-compulsory levels.

The efforts required to translate the right to education into a reality, or for that matter, to implement any educational policy depend upon the amount of resources (human and material) which a country can mobilize for the development of its education, but they also depend, to a large extent, upon its population characteristics. It is quite obvious that the achievement of an objective such as universal primary education does not mean exactly the same thing for different countries. In a typical African country, the population is relatively young and the primary-school-age population (the 6 to 11 age group) is not only rather large as compared to the working-age population but is also growing at a rather high rate; by contrast, the population in a European country has a different age structure and the school-age population, in comparison with the working-age population, constitutes a much smaller group and is diminishing in size.

Population characteristics therefore play a significant role in the achievement of educational policies, objectives, and targets. This article will first discuss the role of population characteristics and then review some specific problems of educational planning linked to population characteristics and the change in populations over time.

One of the salient features of world population trends since the 1950s has been the decline in mortality in practically all countries and more significantly in developing countries, as a result of more generalized preventive medicine, epidemic control, better child care, and hygiene. The decline,

Table 1

Estimated infant mortality rates (per thousand) by region in the late 1970s[a]

Africa	140	*Asia*	103
Northern Africa	121	Southwest Asia	117
Western Africa	159	Middle South Asia	137
Eastern Africa	132	Southeast Asia	96
Middle Africa	167	East Africa	51
South Africa	101	*Europe*	19
Latin America	85	Northern Europe	13
Middle America	72	Western Europe	12
Caribbean	72	Eastern Europe	23
Tropical South America	98	Southern Europe	24
Temperate South America	44	*Oceania*	42
Northern America	13		
Soviet Union	31		

[a] Source: Haub C, Heisler D W 1980

Table 2
Life expectancy at birth, by major region, according to the medium variant of the United Nations population projection[a]

	1950–55	1965–70	1975–80	1985–90	1995–2000
Africa	37.4	44.4	48.7	53.3	57.9
Latin America	52.0	59.3	63.4	66.8	69.7
Northern America	69.0	70.6	73.2	73.8	74.3
East Asia	47.5	59.3	64.7	68.1	70.6
South Asia	39.4	47.3	51.8	56.4	61.0
Europe	65.4	70.5	71.9	73.2	74.2
Oceania	60.8	64.5	65.7	67.7	69.8
Soviet Union	61.7	70.0	69.6	70.5	71.4

[a] Source: United Nations, Population Division 1980

of course, has not been the same everywhere and large differences still exist particularly with regard to infant mortality, as can be seen from Table 1.

At the beginning of the 1980s, there were still a large number of countries where one child out of ten died before his first birthday. It remains nonetheless true that important progress has been made and this trend will continue. According to the medium variant of the population projections made by the United Nations, the life expectancy at birth in the different regions of the world will follow the trends shown in Table 2.

In every developing country, life expectancy at birth increased between 1950 and 1975, and the gap between developing countries and industrialized countries decreased. As an example, the difference between Africa and North America was 31.6 years in 1950–55, but it fell to 24.5 years in 1975–80 and will be only 16.4 in 1995–2000.

Along with this decline in mortality, a certain decline in fertility has also been observed. The rate of this decline, however, varies considerably from one region to the next. In 1975–80, the estimated total fertility rate (that is, the average number of children to be born to a woman during her child-bearing age, i.e. 15 to 49 years), according to the

Table 3
Estimated total fertility rates in 1975–80 according to the medium variant of the United Nations population projections[a]

Africa	6.4
Latin America	4.9
Northern America	1.8
East Asia	3.0
South Asia	5.5
Europe	2.0
Oceania	2.8
Soviet Union	2.4

[a] Source: United Nations, Population Division 1980

medium variant of the United Nations population projections, is shown in Table 3.

Although these figures are estimates only and in spite of the fact that information on fertility is fragmentary and not always accurate, it can be said that since the 1950s the decline in fertility has been rapid in the countries of East Asia (Japan, the People's Republic of China, Korea) but much less so in Africa,

Table 4
School-age population (5–14 years) as a percentage of the working age population (15–64 years), for various regions of the world[a]

	1975	1985
Africa	51.1	52.3
Eastern	52.5	54.5
Middle	48.4	49.9
Northern	48.8	48.3
Southern	47.5	47.5
Western	53.5	55.5
Latin America	46.0	44.1
Caribbean	43.6	34.7
Middle America	53.3	51.8
Temperate South America	30.2	29.3
Tropical South America	47.0	44.8
Northern America	23.0	22.4
East Asia	33.3	21.4
China	34.2	26.0
Japan	23.9	18.5
Other East Asia	38.2	33.3
South Asia	48.1	43.3
Eastern	48.1	43.3
Middle	47.5	44.6
Western	47.1	45.6
Europe	23.7	20.2
Eastern	23.5	23.9
Northern	23.4	18.5
Southern	25.6	21.6
Western	22.4	17.2

[a] Source: Computed from the absolute data given in United Nations, Population Division (1980). The classification of countries into regions is the one used by UNESCO. See UNESCO 1981

South Asia, and Latin America. The factors which may explain the high level of fertility are numerous (religion, marital traditions, social values, organization of the family, and distribution of responsibilities and work among its members, etc.). A vast amount of work and studies has been conducted on the determinants of fertility. Among the determinants which may lead to a reduction in family size, the most frequently mentioned in these studies are: the level of education of the mother, the awareness of the increasing needs and costs of children (as felt through housing problems, direct and indirect cost of education, earnings forgone by the mother, etc.), the policy measures taken by the government to penalize large families, and the availability of a family planning service.

As a result of the rapid decline in mortality, particularly in infant mortality, and of a slower decline in fertility, the population of developing countries is much younger than that of the more industrialized ones. If the school-age population (i.e., the population of 5–14 years) is related to the working-age population (i.e., the population aged 15 to 64 years), the dependency ratio obtained in developing countries is twice that of developed countries (see Table 4). The ratio is about 1 to 2 in Africa, Latin America (with the exception of temperate South America), and South Asia. In Northern America and in Europe the ratio is less than 1 to 4—East Asia and temperate Latin America occupy an intermediate position (1 to 3).

It may be said therefore that, ceteris paribus, the effort required of developing countries to achieve an objective such as universal primary education is twice as great as that required of more industrialized countries because of demographic characteristics, or more precisely, because of the distribution by age of the population.

In addition, as a result of past trends in the birth rate and its foreseeable level in the future, the growth of the school-age population will be quite different in the future. The different growth rates of the school-age population in the various regions of the world have been very well documented and illustrated by Zoltan Zsigmond and May Sue Devereaux (1980). Using United Nations data as their primary source (United Nations Population Division 1980), they have presented a series of graphs of the trends of the school-age population. The graph in Fig. 1 has been extracted from that report. It shows the growth of the 6–11 age group, which corresponds more or less to the children attending primary school. Index numbers have been computed for the growth of the 6–11 age group, for each region of the world, with a base equal to 100 in 1975. The curve shows the trends of these index numbers and provides a visual comparison of school-age population growth in the various regions.

As can be expected, the shapes of the curves are

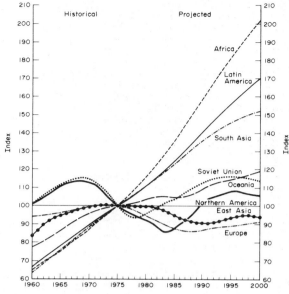

Figure 1
Extracted from: Zsigmond Z, and Devereaux M S 1981 Trends and projections of the world school-age population 1960–2000. In: UNESCO, Division of Statistics 1981 *World School-age Population until Year 2000: Some Implications for the Education Sector.* UNESCO, Paris. p. 77

quite different. In Africa, Latin America, and South Asia a steady growth is to be observed, but the rates of growth are not the same. Between 1975 and 2000, the school-age population will more than double in Africa; it will be multiplied by 1.7 in Latin America and by 1.5 in South Asia. Quite different are the trends in Europe and East Asia where, after a certain decline between 1975 and 1990, the primary-school-age population is projected to grow very slightly. Thus two quite opposing situations can be observed. On the one hand, there are regions such as Africa, South Asia, and, to a lesser extent, Latin America where not only the school-age population is extremely high as compared to the working-age population, but where also the growth of that school-age population is expected to be rather high throughout the period up to the year 2000. In addition, it is precisely in Africa and in South Asia that most countries have not yet achieved universal primary education. The resources required to gradually achieve universal primary education are substantial in a situation where the population is very young and where the young population is growing rapidly. In addition, the expansion also has to be monitored so as to ensure a satisfactory quality of the educational service offered and to reduce the extensive inequalities which continue to exist not only between the various parts of the country, but also between the rural and urban areas and between the different social groups. The problem is further complicated by the fact that, because of the expansion of primary education in order to reach the objective of education for all and because of the quantity of resources required for this task, a more severe selection becomes necessary at the postprimary stage, that is, at the entrance to secondary education. In these circumstances, the question is how to ensure that selection is equitable and how to ensure that the selection process is accepted as fair by all social groups. This issue is all the more difficult to solve since education continues to be the main mechanism by which position and status in society are allocated.

In Europe, the situation is quite the opposite with regard to both educational development and demographic trends. In most European countries, compulsory education of 10 to 12 years duration has already been achieved and the school-age population corresponding to compulsory education is declining. This means that enrolment in compulsory education in many European countries has decreased and will continue to do so in the years to come.

Planning the decrease of enrolment does raise difficult problems which, of course, are quite different from those faced in planning the expansion of the educational system. In the first instance, it is doubtful whether the decrease in enrolment will lessen the burden of education finance. Furthermore, decrease in total enrolment does not necessarily mean that enrolment will be reduced everywhere. Migration will continue towards more dynamic cities and to the centres of economic activities, and from the centre of cities to the suburban areas. New schools will have to be built whereas in other schools the roll will be decreasing rapidly. Moreover, it will be very difficult to close smaller schools, even if they have a decreasing roll, because of strong resistance of people who fear that school closure is the beginning of the end for small villages and communities.

It should also be emphasized that the stock of teachers is not going to decrease as quickly as enrolment. The result, of course, is a reduction in the number of students per teacher which is often considered an improvement of the educational service, but which is in fact the mere consequence of demographic trends. Indeed, the reduction of the pupil/teacher ratio, without a change in teaching methods, does not necessarily mean greater individual attention for the pupil, nor does it mean an improvement in the teaching process. What it does mean, however, is an increase in unit costs. An additional effect of decreasing enrolment is the ageing of the teaching force and the decline in recruitment of new teachers. This may have lasting consequences because it may make the introduction of innovations more difficult and changes in teaching methods more problematic. After all, it is through the training of new teachers that this process of change can normally be initiated. In addition, the reduced recruitment of new teachers will also create a series of problems in the planning of teacher-training institutions.

See also: Teacher Supply and Demand: Planning; School Mapping

Bibliography

Haub C, Heisler D W 1980 *1980 World Population Data Sheet.* Population Reference Bureau, Washington, DC

UNESCO 1981 *World School-age Population until Year 2000: Some Implications for the Education Sector.* UNESCO, Paris

United Nations Population Division 1980 *Selected Demographic Indicators by Country 1950–2000: Demographic Estimation and Projection as Assessed in 1978.* United Nations, New York

Zsigmond Z, Devereaux M S 1980 *World School-Age Population: Trends and Implications, 1960–2000.* Statistics, Ottawa, Ontario

Ta Ngoc Chau

Demonstration Methods of Teaching

Demonstration, that is, teaching by showing, has the advantage of communicating with the learner both visually and orally at the same time; language barriers can be overcome and rapport established between teacher and pupil.

Although demonstration is the "natural" method of teaching practised by many animal species and provides the foundation for the imitative behaviour so important in early childhood, the rapid development of educational technology in recent years has widened its scope in both training and education at all stages. Considerable progress too has been made in the *art* of demonstration.

When parents show children how to tie their shoe laces they are practising demonstration teaching. Throughout human history, teaching by demonstration has been a main method of preparation for adult life and the passing on of the cultural heritage. Demonstration, for example, provided the foundation of apprenticeship training in the medieval guilds and is firmly related to practical skills at the craft level but not restricted to them. Art and music are two areas in which demonstration by the master to the pupil has been particularly productive. Much of the progress in science after the Renaissance can be traced to the demonstrations performed at meetings of learned societies. Many of these societies continue to function in much the same way today and their public lectures to large audiences are examples of demonstration teaching on a sophisticated scale. Television and videorecording have encouraged the development of demonstration techniques.

An essential element in any learning situation in which demonstration is appropriate is the relationship between demonstration by the teacher and practice by the pupil. The educational requirement is to find the most effective balance between the two, which will depend upon local circumstances. These are so varied that, in order to avoid diffuseness, this article seeks to elucidate the general principles of demonstration teaching by special reference to science at secondary-school level, which lends itself to this purpose though craft teaching might also have served. Science is based upon sensory experience and, in learning science, observation and experimentation are essential ingredients; demonstration can contribute to both.

An obvious requirement in a demonstration is that every step should be clearly visible to every member of the class. Some schools and most higher education science departments have demonstration rooms with serviced demonstration benches and tiered seating, but these are not always as useful as more flexible furniture that can be adapted to a variety of circumstances.

In order to bring out important features of demonstration teaching, two kinds of demonstrations are now discussed in some detail.

1. Teacher Demonstration

This method may be selected for one or more of the following reasons:

(a) to demonstrate certain manipulative skills;

(b) because the processes involved are costly, dangerous, difficult, or time consuming;

(c) because the force of a logical argument might be lost if the pupils' attention is concentrated on the mastery of the practical skills involved.

Having decided upon the demonstration and its content and scope, the selection and arrangement of the equipment have to be settled. The materials should be set out in an orderly sequence so that the overall pattern is apparent.

The authenticity of observations, particularly measurements, made during the demonstration is crucial, so that, for example, the scales of meters should be large enough to be read by the audience, or projected on to a screen. Alternatively, members of the class can be employed as assistants to make the observations and relay them to the class. This last device also serves to engage attention and to break up the formality of the set lecture. This can also be achieved by skilled questioning, though a sensitive teacher will avoid the "patter" adopted by many television performers.

An effective demonstration requires attention to the smallest detail and meticulous rehearsal; judgment must be exercised and decisions made concerning every step, for example, whether anything is lost if reagents are measured out beforehand, or electrical connections made. Fumbling for switches or groping for a box of matches can be distracting. In general, a demonstration should set a high standard in preparation, manipulation, and logical presentation. The timing should allow for questions from the class, who should be encouraged to participate whenever possible, and for recapitulation and a summary at the end.

2. Collaborative Demonstration

This form of demonstration is much less of a set piece and requires a high degree of teaching skill for its success. It is particularly effective as a method of introducing pupils to the processes involved in scientific investigation. The demonstrator carries out operations suggested by members of the class. The skill lies in eliminating ideas that are obviously going to be unproductive while accepting those that can lead in the right direction or that attract support after thorough discussion. Part of the value lies in following promising but false trails, and the teacher cannot know for certain beforehand what these trails may be. Therefore, instead of a rehearsed flow of clearly defined stages along a predetermined path, the demonstration consists of a series of improvisations skilfully managed to achieve the double objectives of extending the pupils' knowledge while, at the same time, engaging their full cooperation and developing their powers of investigation. It follows that preparation lies in thinking out what kinds of materials and resources might be required and having them ready to hand but out of sight so that they do not predispose the pupils towards routes determined by the teacher. The demonstration therefore follows a course which is generally in the desired direction but to which the pupils' suggestions have substantially contributed after discussion, refinement, and acceptance by the class as a whole.

There is a place for many variations of these two kinds of demonstration depending upon whether didactic teaching or discovery learning are to be adopted for that particular situation. The secret lies in matching the method to the immediate circumstances and in holding a suitable balance between all the methods of learning that are available.

Bibliography

Comber L C, Keeves J P 1973 *Science Education in Nineteen Countries: An Empirical Study.* Wiley, New York

Ogborn J (ed.) 1977 *Practical Work in Undergraduate Science.* Heinemann Educational, London

Rowe M B (ed.) 1978 *What Research Says to the Science Teacher*, Vol. 1. National Science Teachers Association, Washington, DC

Shulman L S, Tamir P 1973 Research on teaching in the natural sciences. In: Travers R M W (ed.) 1973 *Second*

Handbook of Research on Teaching: A Project of the American Educational Research Association. Rand McNally, Chicago, Illinois, pp. 1098–148

L. C. Comber

Demonstration Programs

Demonstration programs involve the operation of an educational facility or the delivery of educational services in order to establish the characteristics and requirements of certain innovations in practice and to show their feasibility and value. Three elements distinguish demonstration programs from other forms of educational research: operation, scale, and purpose.

Demonstrations involve operation of an educational service, often throughout an entire school or group of schools, or through a common element such as a reading laboratory in several schools. Such operations may require installation of curricula, use of instructional materials and technologies, or application of administrative arrangements that were not available previously in the facility. Alternatively, demonstrations may be arranged through upgrading existing practices, such as expanding the use of microprocessors for instructional purposes from one classroom to the entire school. And, increasingly, operations involve selection of exemplary educational programs already functioning well to serve demonstration functions without changes in the existing program.

With regard to scale, demonstration programs are usually larger and more coherent than is required for testing curriculum elements or practices that eventually may be integrated into a demonstration. They are smaller, however, than would be required systematically to assess the consequences of an innovative approach. Most of the resources for demonstrations are invested in service delivery rather than in evaluation.

The primary purpose of demonstrations is to show in practice what an educational innovation looks like and to offer potential adopters a site where they can see for themselves how the innovation functions. Demonstrations can thus precede larger scale pilot or experimental programs, providing the opportunity to establish the feasibility and value of an innovation. They can also follow such programs and be used for the training and dissemination of the models of the innovation in operation.

Variants of this purpose have been fairly frequently used: convincing, developing, co-opting, and inspiring. In one form, demonstrations are intended to provide more convincing evidence than the written word for ideas which seem to work. Support for such exemplary programs is based on the notion that educators who come and see are more likely to return and do than those who merely read about the innovation. Demonstrations intended for convincing are often staffed with personnel trained to help visitors consider the advantages of the program for their own uses and are part of dissemination networks.

In a second form, demonstration programs are regarded more as living educational laboratories, whose lineage traces back to the early 1900s and the laboratory schools associated with teacher colleges (see *Laboratory Schools and Teacher Education*). Support for these projects is based on the notion that embedding development of new educational ideas in an operational facility staffed to integrate research and practice is a valuable, if not better, way to improve education than is relying only on shorter term, single purpose studies. Collaborative research programs and "contract schools" are contemporary variants on the principles of laboratory school-like demonstrations.

In a third form, demonstration programs are intended to lever changes which otherwise might be resisted. Funds and the technical assistance often associated with demonstration program status are offered in exchange for school adoptions of innovations planned elsewhere (see *Curriculum Adoption*). The assumption underlying such support is that providing some measure of local participation in shaping how new goals will be achieved or new practices established will ease adoption of changes.

And, in a fourth variant, some demonstration programs are intended to stimulate readiness for major shifts. They are established to exemplify what currently is far beyond the resources, practice, or philosophy of most educational programs, but what might be desirable in the future. The assumption underlying this variant is that the appetite for quite different and possibly more costly programs could be most sharply whetted by seeing an operational model.

Support for demonstration programs both within countries and through international agencies has been generous since the early 1960s. Demonstrations have included delivery of elementary-level schooling through satellite transmitted radio and television in countries as diverse as Guatemala and India (see *Distance Education*); operation of model technical secondary schools combining long-term economic planning with new instructional techniques merging literacy and vocational skill acquisition; programs aimed at adults as part of still more complex economic development schemes, such as the projects in the Philippines offering literacy training in improved boat construction and fishing techniques and changes in the distribution and marketing system for the catch; and the operation of demonstration bilingual education and compensatory education programs in countries with substantial numbers of children of immigrant workers or from very low-income families (see *Bilingual Education*; *Compensatory Education*).

Research on the effectiveness of demonstration programs has focused on two issues. The first is documenting the immediate effectiveness of the demonstration in reaching its goals; the second, on the longer term value of demonstrations. The first effort has led to a considerable body of publications based on the programs themselves (e.g., on the effectiveness of preschools), in which the results of the demonstrations are stand-ins for more experimental tests of the concepts themselves in optimum form. It has also yielded extensive analyses of the evaluation methodology appropriate for demonstrations. Expansion of qualitative and case study methods (see *Case Study Methods*) has been stimulated as evaluators have dealt with methodological problems of inference and contextualization of findings when true experimental studies are neither possible nor appropriate (see *Program Evaluation*).

The studies of the validity of the assumptions underlying the uses of demonstrations have been more abundant for the first and third than for the second and fourth purposes. Research suggests that support of demonstrations primarily for the purpose of levering changes that otherwise might be resisted works only when other local purposes happen to coincide with the ostensible purposes of the demonstration. These studies indicate that demonstrations are neither very subtle nor long-lasting instruments of that kind of social change.

In contrast, recent studies of educational change have generally shown that while the dissemination process is considerably more complex than simple availability of lighthouse programs, having operational facilities to visit does contribute significantly to dissemination. Both frequency of adoption and appropriate adaptations (see *Curriculum Adaptation*) seem fostered by demonstration sites, in combination with other elements of a dissemination system, and user satisfaction—including those who decide not to adopt the innovation—seems higher for those with the opportunity to observe the innovation in practice than those who do not.

Bibliography

Acheson K (ed.) 1977 *The Five Dimensions of Demonstration*. Teacher Corps Research Adaptation Cluster, Norman, Oklahoma. ERIC Document No. ED 183 558

May M J 1981 Demonstration project for handicapped young children: A review. *Young Child.* 36: 26–32

Vanecko J L 1978 ESEA *Title I Allocation Policy: Demonstration Study*. Abt, Cambridge, Massachusetts. ERIC Document No. ED 187–794

L-E. Datta

Denmark: System of Education

Denmark is a small lowland country covering 43,069 square kilometres (16,629 square miles). It has a population of 5.199 million with an average of 116 persons per square kilometre. The net population increase has for many years been decreasing and is now about 2.8 percent.

Until 1945, Denmark was an agricultural country, 37 percent of the population living in rural areas. Education was provided in many small rural schools as well as in the fewer but larger urban schools. At the beginning of the 1980s, only 8 percent of the workforce was engaged in agricultural work whereas the industrial sector engaged 32 percent and the tertiary sector comprised 57 percent. The number of schools for compulsory education had diminished to 2,265 by 1980.

The Danish mother tongue is spoken all over the country except in the border region next to Germany and in the Faroe Islands and Greenland, both of which have home rule.

In 1980, 9.2 percent of the workforce was unemployed and there was negligible economic growth. This has had an impact on the educational system. Many more pupils stay at school beyond the obligatory nine years, preferring this to unemployment. In 1980, parliament made a resolution in principle on youth education, the aim of which was to give each pupil a genuine opportunity for acquiring "relevant education".

Denmark is a kingdom ruled according to the principle of parliamentary democracy. Since the 1930s the Social Democrats have been in power most of the time. The Social Democratic ideal of equality has greatly influenced the school structure in bringing about a still more comprehensive educational system. In 1958, schools were allowed to have nondifferentiated classes. In 1975, schools, by legislation, became in principle comprehensive schools.

1. Goals of the Educational System

The goal of the Danish *Folkeskole* (elementary and lower-secondary school) is, in cooperation with parents, to offer pupils the opportunity to acquire knowledge, skills, working methods, and modes of expression that will contribute most effectively to the full development of the individual.

> The pupil's desire to learn and ability to make evaluations and decisions shall be developed through experience and self-activation, and the school shall prepare the pupil for responsible participation in a democratic society. (Ministry of Education 1979)

2. General Structure and Size of the Education Effort

2.1 Formal Education

Education in Denmark is free. Education is compulsory for nine years, from 7–17 years of age. There is no obligation to receive this education at school, but very few use any alternative. About 93 percent of pupils go to the *Folkeskolen*, and the rest go to

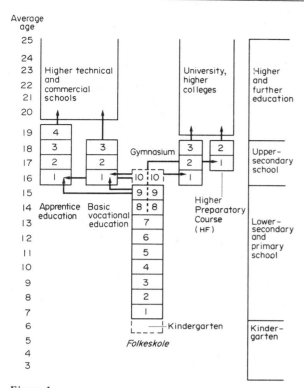

Figure 1
Structure of the educational system

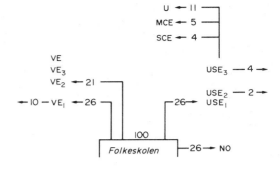

MCE = medium–length college education
NO = no further education
SCE = shorter college education
U = university, etc.
USE = upper–secondary education
VE = vocational training / education

Figure 2
Flow of the 1977 year group through the educational system (%)

private schools, supported by the state. The structure of the educational system is shown in Fig. 1.

Preschool education is voluntary. Some 40–45 percent of 3- to 6-year-olds go to kindergartens. About 60 percent of any year group attend an optional kindergarten class (for children aged 5–6 years).

For the first seven years, the *Folkeskole* is fully comprehensive. In grades 8 to 10 the school is comprehensive except in mathematics, English, German, and physics and chemistry. In these subjects, the pupils are differentiated into a basic course and an advanced course. However, the *Folkeskole* Act (1975) allows freedom in this differentiation, and in 1981–82 half the schools did not differentiate (Skov 1980 p. 14). Grade 10 in the *Folkeskole* is optional.

After the *Folkeskole*, pupils enter further schooling or leave school. As shown in Fig. 2, in 1977, 26 percent entered vocational education (compared with 30 percent in 1980), 26 percent entered a gymnasium or higher preparatory (HF) course (30 percent in 1980), and 26 percent left school; 21 percent continued to various other types of vocational education.

The school-enrolment ratios in 1977 were 100 percent for basic education, 83 percent for the secondary level, and 32 percent for the tertiary level. There

were almost no differences between the enrolment of males and females. In 1970, the enrolment at the tertiary level was, per 100,000 inhabitants, 1,542 students, and in 1977, 2,315 students.

Enrolment differs from one social group to another (Danmarks Statistik og Socialforskningsinstituttet 1981). Belonging to the highest of five social groups means a student has a high probability of entering higher education (Ørum and Hansen 1975 p. 32).

The increase in the number of pupils and teachers in primary and lower-secondary education from 1917 to 1977 can be seen in Fig. 3. In 1978–79, the total

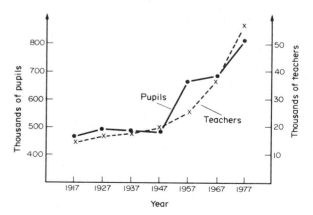

Figure 3
Numbers of pupils and teachers in primary and lower-secondary education 1917–1977[a]

a Source: Ministry of Education 1978 p. 66

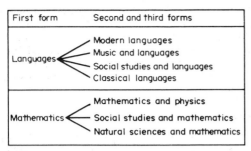

Figure 4
Structure of the gymnasium[a]

a Source: Ministry of Education 1979b p. 3

number of pupils enrolled in various levels of education was: preschool 59,390; primary and lower-secondary education 745,239; general upper-secondary education 64,171; vocational upper-secondary education 109,507; and further education 115,522. The overall percentage of female participation was 48. The pupil–teacher ratio was very low—18.8.

The gymnasium is structured into two tracks with subdivisions (see Fig. 4). The number of students in the gymnasium was 60,931 in 1980. There are more females than males in the languages track. The higher preparatory course (HF) is very popular, and students here are much more equally distributed among social groups than in the gymnasia. In 1980, 10,710 pupils were enrolled in HF courses.

2.2 Nonformal Education

Youth and adult education is nonobligatory and is based on a long tradition of freedom to study, as expressed in the Leisuretime Education (Consolidation) Act 1975. The following different types of youth and adult-education programmes are of note:

(a) The municipal youth schools work in close cooperation with the *Folkeskolen*, and approximately 60 percent of 14- to 18-year-olds take some subjects at a *Folkeskole* and some at a youth school.

(b) The 118 continuation schools are boarding schools for the same age groups. In 1978–79, they had an enrolment of just over 10,000 students.

(c) The 27 agricultural schools and 21 home economics schools are similar to the continuation schools but the students are slightly older.

(d) The 85 folk high schools accept students from the age of 18. About 10,000 persons attend their long courses (5–8 months), and about 32,000 their short courses (1–3 weeks).

(e) Evening schools for adults are very common. They cover a wide range of subjects, depending

on the interests of the students, who attend classes once or twice a week during the winter season (8 months).

Two-thirds of adult-education courses are arranged by private promotors (mostly large educational organizations). The annual attendance is about 600,000.

3. Administrative Structure

Responsibility for the education sector rests with the state, the counties, the local authorities, and private institutions. Preschool education is administered by the Ministry of Social Welfare. Primary and lower-secondary schools are run by the local authorities. The majority of upper-secondary schools are run by the counties. The universities are mainly run by the state. All county, municipal, and private schools are subsidized by the state.

The Ministry of Education is organized as shown in Fig. 5. The ministry controls and directs the educational system by, among other things, allocating public funds, issuing regulations, issuing guidelines, and general supervision such as approving curricula.

The ministry thus has an over-arching role. But, as Denmark has a tradition of extensive local government, responsibility for the functioning of the educational system and its results lies with the local authorities. The school system is very decentralized.

At the municipal level, responsibility for primary and lower-secondary schools lies with the municipal council, its education committee, and the joint teachers' council. At the school level, it lies with the school board (whose members are parents), the teachers' council, the headmaster, and the pupils' council.

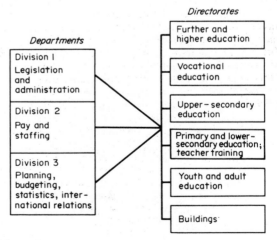

Figure 5
Organization of the Ministry of Education[a]

a Source: Ministry of Education 1980b p. 10

Table 1
Average per pupil/student expenditure by level 1977–78[a]

Level	Danish kroner
Primary and lower-secondary school	10,000
Upper-secondary school	18,000
Basic vocational education	5,000–21,000
Apprentice training	3,000–8,000
Independent boarding schools	17,000
Universities:	
humanities	11,000
natural science	46,000
medicine	48,400
Engineering college	50,000

a Source: Ministry of Education 1980b p. 77

Within the framework of general regulations, a single school has the power to determine its own curriculum. Hence, for primary and lower-secondary schools, there is some variation in curricula and timetables.

In general upper-secondary education, the gymnasia and HF schools are under the responsibility of the county councils. At each school, there is a school council. The school timetable must be approved by the school council whose opinions must also be heard on the distribution of the school budget.

The two main types of vocational education are apprentice training and basic vocational education. Both come under the Ministry of Education. However, the technical and commercial schools, where vocational education takes place, are self-governing institutions administered by their own boards whose members are appointed by employers' and employees' organizations. The boards also decide the curriculum.

Further and higher education is provided at the universities and a number of specialist technical colleges (e.g., in engineering). They all come under the Ministry of Education. A few institutions, such as the Royal Academy of Fine Arts, come under the Ministry of Cultural Affairs and some come under the Ministry of the Interior. The 1970 Act (revised in 1976) on the administration of the universities states that the minister of education decrees the regulations for access to studies and study programmes. Each institution is administered by a rector together with a number of collegial boards and committees which include representatives of the teaching staff, students, and technical–administrative personnel.

4. Finance

The overall state and municipal budgets for the fiscal year 1981 amounted to 216,000 million Danish kroner. Of this, health services received 10 percent, social welfare 11 percent, and education and research 12 percent. The total expenditure on education and educational research in 1977 was 15 percent of the state budget and 7.4 percent of the gross national product.

The state allocates money for primary and lower-secondary education by giving each municipality a block grant according to its number of inhabitants. Upper-secondary education and further and higher education are paid directly and almost fully by the state. The average per pupil/student costs per year are given in Table 1.

The state subsidizes all private schools irrespective of level from 51 to 78 percent of their total costs. The day nurseries and kindergartens are run by the local authorities or are private institutions; all are state subsidized. Youth schools, boarding schools, and folk high schools receive state grants covering up to 85 percent of their costs.

General adult education is financed partly by the state and partly by the local authorities. Adult education aiming at specific examinations or training is free and is paid jointly by the state and the local authorities.

Students in state-recognized courses of education and over 18 years of age may receive support from the state either as grants or as state-guaranteed loans. The grants are given according to the financial needs of applicants. Typical amounts for annual grants in 1981 ranged from 11,200 to 18,400 Danish kroner. State-guaranteed bank loans are given to all students wanting them, regardless of financial circumstances. The maximum loan is 16,700 kroner per year.

Table 2
Number of teachers at different levels 1977

Level	Full-time	Part-time	% Females
Preschool education	11,225	—	94
Primary and lower secondary	40,000	17,000	56
Upper secondary	4,300	1,400	51
Vocational training	3,700	2,700	—
Further education	7,000	8,000	41
Folk high schools, etc.	2,000	—	—
Leisure-time education	200	30,000	—

5. Teacher Training

There are 26 training colleges for preschool teachers. The training lasts three years. Students receive instruction in psychology, education, and social subjects and have 28 weeks of practical training. They must be 18 years of age, have completed 9 years of basic education, have passed the HF examination in Danish and one other subject, and have 2 years' vocational experience.

There are 31 colleges for training primary- and lower-secondary-school teachers. The training lasts from 3½ to 4 years. Students must have passed the upper-secondary-school leaving examination or its equivalent. The curriculum covers psychology, educational theory, social studies, teaching practice, Danish, arithmetic, religion, and optionally three creative/practical subjects. After training, the teachers are qualified to teach all classes from 1 to 10, and 61 percent of them in fact do this (Borg et al. 1981 p. 156). These teachers may receive further training at the Royal Danish School of Educational Studies, ranging from short courses to degree courses.

Upper-secondary-school teachers are normally university graduates who have completed a 6-month course in educational theory and practice. The state institute for the educational training of vocational teachers gives courses to permanent teachers at vocational schools. A course for technical-school teachers covers 400 lessons in educational theory and practice plus a practice-teaching period totalling 80 lessons. Corresponding figures for commercial-school teachers are 225 and 80.

University teachers and teachers at further and higher education institutions are graduates of these institutions. Emphasis is placed on their research qualifications.

Teachers in adult education have a diversified educational background. Most of them hold their position for a season or as overtime work. The number of teachers at different educational levels is given in Table 2.

6. Curriculum

The government acts for each school type state the subjects to be taught in those schools. The Ministry of Education sets the objectives for the subjects as well as the number of weekly lessons and the length of the school year (200 days). But the local educational authorities and the individual schools decide how the aims are to be achieved. Teachers are free to choose whatever teaching method they consider best and each individual school determines its own specific curriculum within the framework of the overall objectives mentioned above.

Learning materials are written on a private basis, mostly by highly experienced teachers, and published on a commercial basis. There is no control of the scope and content of textbooks. Individualized teaching and group work are used to some extent, but the traditional lecture is still much used in spite of the very low class ratio in Danish schools.

7. Examinations

In primary education, there are no end-of-year examinations, and no marks are given for the first seven years of compulsory education. In grades 8 to 10, marks are given twice a year on a 10-point scale. There is a leaving examination at the end of grade 9 and an advanced leaving examination at the end of grade 10. They may be taken on a single-subject basis, and the pupils themselves decide if they will sit for an examination. There is no pass mark.

Under these circumstances, promotion is no problem. Very few will not be promoted. Instead there is an extensive system of remedial teaching, mostly within the class. About 14 percent of the pupils in basic education receive remedial education (Jansen et al. 1976 p. 158).

The same marking scale is used throughout the educational system. In the gymnasia, marks are given regularly and students must pass an examination in each subject to get a leaving certificate. At the HF schools, no marks are given except in the leaving examination for which there is a pass mark.

Examinations at universities and higher education institutions are much the same as in other countries.

8. Educational Research

The first research work in education was undertaken in the 1920s, when a committee on school psychological investigations was formed. The committee's work concerned basic education and was centred upon constructing and standardizing attainment tests in Danish and mathematics. During the 1930s and 1940s, when the education sector grew fast, the problems arising from this growth brought about an interest in research. In 1944, the study of educational psychology was introduced at Copenhagen University in order to train people for school psychological services and educational research work. In 1955, the Danish Institute for Educational Research was established and, at the same time, the first two professors of education were appointed. At the beginning of 1980, education could be studied at four of Denmark's five universities. Governmental, municipal, and private organizations have research sections conducting educational research.

In 1977, the Research Council for the Humanities published a report on ongoing educational research (Forskningssekretariatet 1977). Some 206 projects were classified. Most were empirical studies related to basic education. Some concerned universities. Very few were related to youth or adult education.

The report's conclusion was that two education sectors are especially in need of research: youth education and that part of adult education which aims at giving both vocational and general education to those who have received relatively little education. This need for sector-aimed research work still exists, even if, by the end of the 1970s, some research work on university studies and on youth education had been carried out.

Most educational research is carried out by the Danish Institute for Educational Research and the Royal Danish School of Educational Studies. Typically, the bulk of research projects is concerned with basic education. However, from the beginning of the 1970s, there has been a trend to carry out research on the 16- to 19-year age group, at upper-secondary schools and youth education. Most research has focused on the question of comprehensive schooling and nondifferentiation and has had an impact on education legislation. The Danish National Institute of Social Research has made significant contributions to this research.

9. Major Problems

The Central Council of Education published in 1978 a report on educational planning and policy in a social context at the end of the twentieth century. This report dealt with future society and its expectations of education. It emphasized that the Danish society of the future must be based largely on education, education being a principal factor in the development of a rapidly changing society.

The aims and intentions of an educational policy of the 1990s should therefore be to qualify and to socialize. A person should be qualified not only for working and economic life, but also for family life, community life, and leisure life. If such qualifications are to be reached, it will be necessary to break down the traditional framework of a subject-based curriculum and provide instead a large number of general qualifications. Socialization is also an aspect of teaching, often in a rather unconscious way. Education should therefore not be neutral but take into consideration the fact that the individual must learn to be critical while, at the same time, accepting common moral concepts and having an attitude of social solidarity. The report pointed to the necessity of making education relevant to both society's and individuals' needs.

Denmark is about to go into the postcomprehensive era. This implies that compulsory education will not be prolonged beyond nine years, that youth education will be more adapted to vocation, that some form of recurrent education will emerge, and that content will be based to a great extent upon the student's interests.

The problems of education were for many years connected with the educational structure. The future problem will be to overcome the barriers of tradition so that the content of education can parallel the development of society.

Bibliography

Borg K et al. 1981 *Lærernes arbejdsmiljø i folkeskolen* [Working conditions of teachers in the *Folkeskole*]. Danmarks Lærerforening og Danmarks pædagogiske Institut, Copenhagen

Danish Institute 1981 *Schools and Education in Denmark*. Danish Institute, Copenhagen

Danmarks Statistik og Socialforskningsinstituttet 1981 *Levevilkår i Danmark. Statistisk oversigt 1980* [Living Conditions in Denmark: Compendium of Statistics 1980] *(English subtitles)*. Danmarks Statistik og Socialforskningsinstituttet, Copenhagen

Danmarks Statistik 1981 *Statistiske efterretninger: A 1981*, No. 43 [Statistical information]. Danmarks Statistik, Copenhagen

Denmark, Ministry of Education 1978 *U 90 Danish Educational Planning and Policy in a Social Context at the End of the 20th Century*. Central Council of Education, Copenhagen

Denmark, Ministry of Education 1979a *Act on the Folkeskole*. Ministry of Education, Copenhagen

Denmark, Ministry of Education 1979b *Curriculum Regulations for the Gymnasium in Denmark*. Ministry of Education, Copenhagen

Denmark, Ministry of Education 1980a *Parliamentary Resolution on Youth Education*. Ministry of Education, Copenhagen

Denmark, Ministry of Education 1980b *The Education System*. Ministry of Education, Copenhagen

Denmark, Ministry of Education 1981a *Curriculum Regulations for the Danish Higher Preparatory Examination*. Ministry of Education, Copenhagen

Denmark, Ministry of Education 1981b *Educational Statistics: Key Figures for the Educational Sector in the 1970s*. Ministry of Education, Copenhagen

Forskningssekretariatet 1977 *Om uddannelsesforskning* [On educational research]. Forskningssekretariatet, Copenhagen

Jansen M et al. 1976 Special education in Denmark. In: Tarnopol L, Tarnopol M (eds.) 1976 *Reading Disabilities. An International Perspective*. University Park Press, Baltimore, Maryland

Nordic Council and Nordic Statistical Secretariat 1981 *Yearbook of Nordic Statistics*. Nordic Council, Stockholm

Ørum B, Hansen E J 1975 *Illusioner om uddannelse: Temaer i Dansk Uddannelsespolitik* [Illusions about education]. Fremad, Copenhagen

Scharling W 1980 *Det nuværende uddannelsesmønster* [The present pattern of education], USP 126. Danmarks Statistik, Copenhagen

Skov P 1980 *Undladelse af kursusdeling på 8. og 9. klassetrin* [Omission of differentiation at classes 8 and 9]. Danmarks pædagogiske Institut og Folkeskolens Forsøgsråd, Copenhagen

Socialarbejdernes Fællesudvalg 1981 *Behovet for pædagoger 1980. En prognose for udbud og efterspørgsel 1980–90* [The Need of Pedagogs 1980. A Prognosis of Supply and Demand 1980–90]. Socialarbejdernes Fællesudvalg, Copenhagen

Undervisningsministeriet 1981 *Folkeskolen og fritidsundervisningen 1979–90* [The *Folkeskolen* and Leisure-time Education]. Undervisningsministeriet, Copenhagen
UNESCO 1980 *Statistical Yearbook*. UNESCO, Paris

J. Florander

Dependency Theory and Education

The concept of dependency has contributed significantly to efforts to explain the totality of the social structure of different societies. This importance derives principally from the concept's focus on the influence of international relations (economic, political, and cultural relations) on the internal social structure of the dependent countries. The concept attempts to provide a global perspective which few other social science concepts afford.

1. The Development of Dependency Theory

Developed and diffused during the 1960s, the notion of dependency was preceded by other concepts which attempted to explain issues such as the way societies with different levels of economic and social development relate to one another, the causes of backwardness of underdeveloped economies, and the reasons why the capitalist system of production has failed in the periphery countries.

Among these earlier concepts, the notion of imperialism stands out. In its earliest usage, by the Greeks, imperialism referred to the conquest of a territory, the imposition of taxes, and the establishment of a political authority through force. In a second usage, the concept described the colonial rule practiced by the European powers in Africa, America, and parts of Asia, beginning in the sixteenth century. By the nineteenth century, this European expansion was linked to the development of capitalism, which, in turn, generated the occupation of markets by force, and the conflict for control of raw materials. This process ameliorated internal social tensions within the imperialist powers, both because of the emigration of excess labor and because the benefits from the exploitation of the dominated countries favored, however unequally, all the social groups in the metropolitan countries.

The concept of imperialism has a special meaning in Marxist thought, beginning with the emergence of financial capital and the substitution of merchandise exports by the export of capital. Starting with the Stuttgart Congress of the Second International (1907) until the Russian Revolution of 1917, there was a broad and heated debate within socialist ranks about imperialism. In one camp were the theoreticians of revisionism (Van Kol, David, Bernstein), who undertook the open defense of imperialism. They perceived imperialism as revolutionary because of its impact in changing the mode of production, and considered it a necessary stage for the emergence of modern class structures. They argued that the existence of colonial possessions would provide some benefits for the workers in the metropolitan societies. By contrast, while recognizing that part of the wealth derived from colonial exploitation would go to the working class, Lenin believed this process would constitute a material base for contaminating the working class with bourgeois values. For his part, Kautsky denied that colonial possessions would enrich the dominant countries, except for Great Britain, and maintained that imperialist domination would not effectively develop the productive forces of the dominated countries because the benefits of the capital influx are offset by the growing weight of military expenditures and the external debt. Both Lenin and Kautsky saw imperialism as a new phase of capitalism which attempted to resolve the contradictions between production and distribution through the exploitation of the periphery. For them, the struggle against imperialism was a means of accelerating the crisis of capitalism, whose progressive function was historically superseded.

Until the end of the Second World War, the different schools of Marxian analysis studied imperialism from the perspective of the dominant countries (Marx 1967, Hilferding 1963, Luxemburg 1951, Lenin 1970, Mao 1965). They felt that the change in the world social system would be realized through crisis and revolution in the more developed countries. This perspective was manifested in the Third International's strategy until Lenin's death and in the theoretical discussion about the viability of constructing "socialism in one country"—the Soviet Union, which was part of the periphery of the world system. Only after the Second World War did Marxists begin to analyze the contradictions capable of generating liberation movements in the periphery and to consider the possibility of alternatives to social change different from those in the world centers of capitalism (Brown 1963, Alavi 1964, Baran 1957, Bettelheim 1965, Mandel 1971, Amin 1974).

In Latin America, the focus on imperialism from the perspective of the dominated countries developed some autonomy vis-à-vis the major lines of interpretation developed in the dominant countries. Within Marxist circles, Jose Carlos Mariategui (1972), writing in the late 1920s, linked the development of productive forces to the construction of a national identity. He argued that to achieve unity, the nation had to integrate the indigenous population and their cultural traditions. Another Peruvian, Victor Raul Haya de la Torre (1936), upon founding the Alliance for the American Revolution (APRA), developed the bases for a nationalist definition of the imperialist problem. He postulated that there was no possibility for changing social structures unless imperialist domination was destroyed. In his view, this domination prevented the emergence of a social class capable of leading a process of social change; as a result, Haya de la Torre proposed the formation of a multiclass, reformist alliance which would use the state to promote the transformation towards a more modern capitalism.

Another line of Latin American thought, the immediate precursor to the works on dependency, was based on the interpretation of international economic relations. Raul Prebisch (1951, 1976, 1978, 1980, 1981), first at the Economic Commission for Latin America (ECLA) and later at the United Nations Conference on Trade and Development (UNCTAD), leading a group of economists that included Anibal Pinto, Celso Furtado, and others, argued that the progressive deterioration of the terms of exchange in favor of the industrialized nations prevented the periphery from realizing a process of adequate capitalist accumulation. The presuppositions of classical economic theory, according to which technical progress and increases in productivity would cause a progressive decrease in the cost of industrial goods and a relative advantage for raw materials, were proven inaccurate by the functioning of international commerce. The real terms of exchange were exactly the opposite because, among other factors, power relations are a more important determinant of price than the so-called laws of the market. Consequently, the benefits resulting from increased industrial productivity were retained in the developed countries, leading to increased revenue for both capital and labor in those societies.

One of the direct corollaries of this analysis was to protect the economies of the periphery countries. The state would become the agent of change, acting as a direct producer and simultaneously promoting the development of a class of industrial entrepreneurs. This model implied the transformation of agrarian structures with low productivity, controlled by decaying oligarchies; the development of a process of import substitution of industrial goods; the expansion of the internal market; and the establishment of modern class relations which would give rise to a democratic society.

2. Dependency as a General Theory of Economic Relations

The work of Fernando Henrique Cardoso and Enzo Faletto (1979) provided the foundation of the concept of dependency. Their central hypothesis is that the type of economic relation established between the dominant and dominated countries conditions the social structure of the latter. In this interpretative framework, an "enclave" system would give rise in the dependent country to a society which could neither develop a system of communications nor a market which could form the basis for national integration and structuring of the state; the state

would be reduced to an agent of police control to make possible the functioning of the enclave. When the dependent country's relations to the international order were based on the production of primary goods for export, and there were some integration and communication across the national physical space, the dominant class would play a more central role in development. This class would have a subordinate position with respect to the elites of the leading economic powers, but it would assume a dynamic role in the development of the internal productive forces and the diffusion and internationalization of a set of norms and values around which the social system would function and the state would be consolidated. The relations of dependence, and the dominant mode of production to satisfy the demands of the external markets, would explain the emergence of an industrial bourgeoisie (whatever its degree of solidity and coherence as a class), the urban middle classes, and a proletariat inserted in forms of production ranging from manufacturing to industry. This perspective has the evident virtue of explaining the qualitative and quantitative differences among the Latin American countries, which range from the Rio de la Plata countries to those of Central America, to cite the extremes.

For Cardoso and Faletto, relationships of dependency do not necessarily function in an unequivocal way upon the development of the productive forces. The expansion or stagnation of the productive forces depends on the resources in the dependent country, the relationship the country has to the world market, and the society's ability to respond towards the market and other external attempts to establish the conditions of this relationship. The society's ability to respond to these external factors would, in turn, depend on the historical configuration and the interaction of the classes in the context of a social project.

The concept of dependency has a different meaning for authors who believe that capitalist development in dependent countries cannot reproduce the characteristics it had in the industrial societies of the North in the nineteenth century. For these authors, in the contemporary world, the penetration of capitalism leads to economic concentration, market monopolization, and the domination of the large multinational corporations achieved at the expense of the progressive impoverishment of the masses, inexorably culminating in a complete economic crisis.

For authors like Theotonio dos Santos (1969a), Ruy Mauro Marini (1969) and Gunder Frank (1972), dependency implies a process of continuous increases in the gap which separates the developed from the "backward" societies. The only means of overcoming this gap is the destruction of capitalist domination established through the multinational corporations. Not only does capitalist development prove nonviable in dependent societies, but these societies experience a process of disintegration, and the masses are progressively marginalized. The ever narrower sectors which benefit from this "perverse" capitalism manage to maintain their privileges only through means of pure force, so the new form of dependency and the internationalization of economies has as a corollary an increasingly repressive state and the destruction of civil society. International monopoly capital "produces the decapitalization of economies sorely in need of capital and tends to control the state and the economy to consecrate these stagnating, exploitative socioeconomic forms" (dos Santos et al. 1969 p. 73). "The industrial bourgeoisie in Latin America moves from the idea of an autonomous development towards an effective integration with the imperialist capitals, giving rise to a new kind of dependency, much more radical than the previous" (Marini 1969 p. 1). The political corollary is that the dependent countries have no possibility of capitalist development and that the only form of change is revolution, in which virtually the whole society would participate, against the multinational firms and their local representatives. The peasants and workers subject to a "salvage" extraction of relative and absolute surplus value, the subproletariats marginal to the productive system, and the political vanguard, "of whom many have already undertaken the supreme task of armed struggle" (Marini 1969 p. 24), would participate in this revolution. The progressive accentuation of the contradictions of a "lumpendevelopment" directed by a "lumpenbourgeoisie"—to use Gunder Frank's expression—would create conditions for a liberating revolution, not only of the dependent societies, but of the global structure of the capitalist system. It should be noted that this line of thought arose in the period immediately following the Cuban revolution, when many political groups attempted a violent confrontation with the system, negating all possibilities of political change except through armed struggle (Debray 1967).

The theme of dependence became central for about two decades, both in theoretical discussions in the social sciences and in political debates in Latin America, with different consequences in the domain of knowledge and in the relationship between knowledge and action. In the theoretical area, the historical–structural method for studying societies by means of analyzing the different stages of dependency in a region which had begun its colonial period almost five centuries earlier, became widespread. This method enriched the knowledge of these societies' peculiarities, despite the fact that most sociologists had limited knowledge of historical methodology and despite the limited information available, given the poverty of historical studies on economy and society. The concept of dependency was applied to new dimensions of social life, and the problems of education were studied within this new theoretical framework, as seen in the works of Martin Carnoy (1974), Tomas Vasconi (1977a, 1977b), and Guillermo Labarca (1977).

However, in attempting to demonstrate the nonviability of modern capitalism and the impossibility of economic development—notwithstanding concrete statistical evidence to the contrary in some countries—some sociological analyses overlooked significant changes in the social structure, especially the progressive differentiation and modifications in the relationship between classes and groups. These studies failed to address the issue of why some countries were able to develop while others remained stagnant or even regressed.

In other words, alongside the increasing usage of the notion of dependency as a means of explaining social reality, there was an impoverishment of studies about social class, the state, and the specific historical peculiarities of different societies. The studies which focused on dependency failed to perceive the specific historical differences between societies. The concept of dependency, used in a globalizing and universal way, gradually caused social interpretations to be forced into the framework of a political theory. Social phenomena and the interaction of social groups and classes were explained not so much in relation to the empirical information for each concrete national situation, but rather according to analogies to other situations of dependency. For example, the behavior of the middle classes was studied using classical Marxist analyses outside of historical context, and the penetration of capitalism in Latin American agriculture was explained according to the process which occurred in prerevolutionary Russia. This kind of analysis reduced the state to an instrument for transmitting the power of multinational corporations, greatly simplifying the state's complex function in societies in transition, in which the classes are defining and consolidating themselves. Another important oversight of this analysis was the role of the armed forces which, as the backbone of the state, have relative autonomy with respect to the social structure. The military can act in diverse ways, ranging from creating primitive authoritarian regimes incompatible with the development of a capitalist society, to creating the bases of social modernization, or implementing a transnational capitalism.

There were two principal effects of the theory's impact on the relationship between knowledge and action. First was a relative neglect of studies on the popular social forces which could forge alternative projects of development. These forces were implicitly considered passive actors, incapable of challenging the omnipotence of the dominant sectors except through armed struggle, which would raise consciousness and lead to action. Passive victims of the development process would suddenly be transformed through armed struggle into the creators and protagonists of an alternative process. Second, the usage of the concept of dependence as a globalizing category which determines other social variables led to a denial of the possibility for more limited changes (either sectoral changes or changes over time) unless the total destruction of conditions of dependence was effected.

These modifications in the initial usage of the concept of dependency were sharply criticized by the original dependency writers. Cardoso and Faletto (1979) questioned the following arguments:

(a) the insistence upon the nonviability of capitalist expansion in the periphery and the view that if this process occurred it would inevitably produce extreme deformations, including progressive marginalization of the masses, the "development of underdevelopment," and the generation of a "lumpenbourgeoisie";

(b) the view that armed revolution is the only path to change, arguing that most analyses failed to indicate what class or classes could lead the process of transforming the extant order and the path for arriving at the revolutionary moment;

(c) the adoption of a "typical" development as a model, although in favor of different classes, claiming that these analyses failed to consider new forms of social organization, different from those created by the advanced industrial—capitalist or socialist—societies.

3. Dependency Theory and Education

The development of dependency analysis had less impact in areas of cultural analysis, partially because the concept placed so much weight on economic variables. Culture was seen as an ideological expression, and its anthropological dimensions were relatively neglected. This perspective gave rise to studies on mass communication (Mattelart et al. 1971) which demystified cultural expressions, underscoring their ideological content.

3.1 Dependency Theory, Education, and Cultural Reproduction

As far as the education system as an instrument of cultural socialization was concerned, dependency analysis considered the phenomenon of domination, employing the works of Gramsci (1959), Bourdieu and Passeron (1977), and Baudelot and Establet (1971, 1975) as theoretical reference points. Using the dependent-class structure and the linkage between the local bourgeoisie and monopoly capitalism as a starting point, this line of analysis saw culture as a means of promoting consumption (needed to transnationalize the economies) and of diffusing values which would consolidate domination. In most cases, the reference to dependence was not direct since the theoretical framework was based on old and well-known postulates about the role the school plays in transmitting ideologies and in cultural reproduction.

Out of the crisis of the oligarchic order there emerged new dominant groups, including new bourgeois sectors, the remains of some *latifundia* groups, and an important role for the military establishment in economic institutions and civil administration, but the theme of the culture of these new dominant sectors remains relatively unexplored. The question of cultural differences between these groups and the dominant classes of the developed countries, which have a century-long tradition and provide their members with a solid education designed to confer a meritocratic legitimation of their social position, has also been overlooked. The linkage between the culture of the dominant classes and that generated by educational institutions in both kinds of societies constitutes another lacuna. Nobody has adequately explored the hypothesis that the formal education system is the principal means of cultural diffusion in Latin America. If this hypothesis were correct, intellectual elites rather than the direct representatives of the dominant classes would play the principal role in reproducing the ideological elements of domination. By contrast, the theme of a repressive ideology and the cultural proposals implicit in the concentration of power has been well-developed, especially in the work of Jose Joaquin Brunner (1981).

Studies which have focused specifically on education have underscored the education system's role as an ideological apparatus. These studies, following the line discussed for culture in general, have emphasized the dependence of the education system—particularly at the university level—on models from the developed countries, especially the United States. They have focused in particular on the influence of foundations and financial entities in imposing models of academic organization.

Clearly the North American pattern of academic organization had a significant impact in Latin America during the 1960s—the modernizing phase of the universities for many countries. Latin American universities were criticized as humanist, prescientific centers, oriented towards traditional careers, opposed to the implementation of new technologies, inefficient, and politicized. Some countries made efforts to adopt the model of a selective, politically "aseptic" university, with complete dedication from the professors and students, oriented towards science and technology. These universities were supposed to produce a rationalistic elite, bearer of the values of industrial society, prepared to undertake development as their enterprise. Success in implementing this model depended on the level of social and educational democratization, or on the degree of elitism. Generally speaking, this model prevailed in private universities closely linked to business and to some North American universities. Efforts to establish a university system with technocratic characteristics, which would accept and promote the values of the dominant classes and would legitimize their domination through the development of a technocratic formal rationality, do not seem to have succeeded at a national level, even though some private and state universities with these characteristics have emerged. In the process of segmentation of the university system, these more technocratic universities have assumed the specific function of forming certain elite groups.

Dependency theorists perceived the education system as a system for internalizing ideological values and controlling the social groups which were incorporated into the education process. In this perspective, education was an instrument for socializing people into their occupation and social position in the dependent bourgeois order. It was also seen as a tool for ameliorating certain contradictions in the development process by converting the middle classes to cultural consumption.

This analysis has several weaknesses. The first is the organic character of the cultural model, that is, its assumption that the state could control all aspects of socialization and prevent dissent. The second is the conceptualization of the education system as omnipotent in realizing the objectives which the elites supposedly assign to it. The model accepted the old pedagogical conception which saw the education system as determining an individual's values and added to this conception the notion of using the school system to implement an ideology for express political purposes. This scheme overlooks both the conflictual nature and the inherent contradictions of societies in transition and the weakness of the dominant classes in structuring a social project which would be coherent and have the appeal needed to obtain legitimation.

This approach postulated that the organizations considered revolutionary would be able to create in the masses a consciousness opposed to the forms of the new dependence. These masses would organize an education system parallel to that of the state. This implies the recognition of ideological and social conflict, but the model affirmed simultaneously the system's organic and omnipotent character. Thus, this perspective maintained that the dominant powers could control the whole education and cultural system, yet that it could not prevent the existence of a parallel system of popular education.

A third weakness of this analysis is that the characterization of the content of bourgeois culture imparted by the education system as ideology overlooks that the diffusion of science and technology requires that the education system serve as an instrument for producing knowledge. The notion of the bourgeoisie's "cultural capital," developed fundamentally by Bourdieu, was conceived with reference to the European societies, where the bour-

geoisie has controlled knowledge for centuries. The European bourgeoisie has affirmed its social superiority through its culture, and has organized elitist education systems in which the appropriation of knowledge is easier for people previously socialized in the bourgeois culture and in its forms of analysis and discourse. But following the crisis of oligarchical domination, it is difficult to locate a class in Latin America similar to the European bourgeoisie, capable of creating a cultural capital which would help ensure its position of domination in the society.

A fourth questionable element in this analysis is the capacity for cultural reproduction of the education system, including the state's capacity to control and direct education, in conditions such as those Latin America has faced since the Second World War. The dependency argument presupposes a highly efficient state, which exercises effective technical and political control over the education system. With rare exceptions, the Latin American reality has been otherwise.

Two fundamental questions must be posed regarding the reproductive capacity of the education system. The first is whether it is valid to speak of cultural reproduction in societies where education has undergone such profound changes. Since the early 1950s many countries have developed from a situation in which over half of the population was illiterate to one in which almost all the inhabitants are initially included in the education system, even though a significant number do not finish elementary education. At some levels—such as higher education—some Latin American countries have enrollments comparable to those of some European countries which have much higher levels of development and social differentiation.

The expansion of an education system which privileges intermediate and higher education to the detriment of basic education cannot be reduced to an express design of instrumentalizing the system for ideological control. In fact, the expansion of university enrollment has been accompanied by the development of student movements and of intellectual activity which challenges the model of domination. The dominant sectors have not been able to control these contestatory movements and activities and have repressed them in ways that hardly legitimize the system. The enormous demand for education by the excluded groups was the motor for expanding enrollment, while the more repressive regimes attempted to restrict access to, or exclude large sectors of the population, from cultural formation and the education system.

The way the original concept of dependency gave rise to problematic explanations for the development of peripheral capitalist societies, specifically the view that the nondominant social forces are objects and not subjects of their history, is manifest in discussions about education. Education was seen as an instrument of the dominant sectors for realizing their project, not as a result of a social struggle. The political corollary was to incite popular groups to abandon the formal education system and develop their own education, even though the analysis did not discuss the characteristics of this alternative system, the strategy to be followed, or the viability of the project.

3.2 The Linkage between Education and Dependency

The different writers who have linked education and dependency have different theoretical perspectives and conclusions, but some common points in their understanding of the system and of education policy may be indicated:

(a) *A devaluation of knowledge imparted through the education system.* For Guillermo Labarca, knowledge created and transmitted through the education system, "more than it generates a knowledge and control over reality, is separate from reality, producing the illusion of knowledge" (Labarca 1977 p. 79). Paulo Freire starts from the premise that all people have certain capacities, but the development of these capacities is blocked by the existence of oppression. As a result, conscientization and knowledge can come only through dialogue and liberation. "Nobody can educate anyone else, just as nobody can educate themselves; people educate each other, in communion, and the world is the mediator" (Freire 1978 p. 86—see Paiva 1980 for a critical analysis).

This perspective leads to positing the limited economic worth of the education system and the unscientific character of knowledge obtained through the education system: the dominant class has deformed the system for ideological purposes. These works do not specify whether these affirmations are valid for the totality of the education system or only for those parts dealing with the inferior social groups. Nor do they explain why inegalitarian economic systems which are characterized by industrial expansion and by technological change would encourage such rapid rates of growth of an education system which is supposedly of limited value.

(b) *Devaluation of education's productive function.* For Tomas Vasconi, education in Latin America has become "the purest form of the state's ideological apparatuses, that is, of apparatuses whose essential contribution to the system is ensuring its reproduction through the superstructure, as opposed to apparatuses whose principal purpose is linked to the development of the productive forces . . . . Having become separate from production, the bourgeois school hypertrophies incessantly and reproduces itself. . . As it loses its "functionality," the bourgeois school announces the need of its own extinction" (Vasconi 1977a p. 176, 1977b pp. 329–30).

In so far as the parameter of analysis is the relationship between cultural formation and positions which require education, these works seem to accept the values of the theory of human resources. At the same time, however, only those requirements related to the production of goods are considered socially useful education requirements, and occupation is disregarded. This perspective poses questions about the ideological framework which in practice values education for its adaptation to occupational demand and its ability to adjust according to the social hierarchies defined by the occupational demand. But above all, the negative view towards "relative overeducation" implies denying the aspect of social change which means an increasing capacity for the dominant social groups.

(c) *Assignment of an exclusively ideological role to education.* Education is said to be a social activity in which "the violence of the dominant class is exercised, although in this case it is symbolic rather than physical violence. For this reason education is an important element in the ideological struggle" (Vasconi 1977b pp. 322–3). Freire's starting point is the oppressive character of the society. He defines social action in terms of the dialectical relationship between oppressors and oppressed, generic categories which are not linked to or inserted in historical structures which define them. In education, these relationships are expressed in the categories of educators and students (*educandos*).

> The educator confronts the students as his/her necessary antinomy. He/she recognizes the reason of his/her being in the absolute character of the ignorance of the students. The students, alienated in the fashion of the slave in the Hegelian dialectic, recognize in their ignorance the educator's reason for being, but they do not reach the point, as the slave in the Hegelian scheme does, of discovering their own identity as educators of the educator. (Freire 1978 p. 73)

These authors imply that the oppressors constitute a homogeneous category and that the state does not reflect contradictions even though it forms part of and expresses societies divided by a capitalist system in transition. The elites would have the capability of choosing (or even, possibly, creating) the sum of societal values and of reproducing them without contradictions through the education system. This capacity means postulating the possibility of the existence of an organic control of the whole society, a control over the economic, political, and cultural systems which would be coordinated in such a way as to create a society with no history, because the society would reproduce itself in permanent fashion.

(d) *Devaluation of the education system and of alternative political projects.* The incorporation of the masses into the institutional educational apparatus would imply their submission to the ideological aspects of bourgeois domination. The reality of Latin America, however, has been otherwise. Fifty percent of the population, precisely the most exploited sectors, do not complete primary education. This means that the oppressors have not successfully integrated the potentially most revolutionary sectors into this ideological apparatus. This is not the only contradiction between this theoretical perspective and reality. Despite the continuous and growing middle-class demand for education, according to Vasconi (1977b p. 337),

> It is not only for the proletariat and the peasantry that the school is no longer a solution; vast sectors of the middle classes and the small bourgeoisie threatened by growing proletarization as a result of the increasingly monopolistic character of dependent capitalism, are giving up their hopes of climbing the social ladder through the school system.

The solution would be that the process of developing real knowledge "is carried out by the masses," although "the concrete manner by which to do this must still be discovered" (Labarca 1977 p. 89).

Given an education system characterized as pure ideological control, with no value for cognitive development, the answer is the creation of a system of political learning which has educative value. This explains the insistence on "the distinction which should be drawn between *the education system,* which can only be transformed by the political elites, and *educative work* which can be realized with the oppressed in the process of organizing" (Freire 1978 p. 47).

According to this reductionist perspective, education as a differentiated system with specific functions does not exist. This perspective also overlooks the fact that all humanity has collectively created a cultural capital which should be apprehended by all the different social groups, notwithstanding the barriers to realizing this goal. The negation of the existence of a specifically educational system amounts to downplaying all efforts to change that system and to postulating that the only alternative is the politicization of the masses through educational apparatuses led by revolutionary organizations. This rejection of the institutionalized education system brings this line of analysis close to those who propose eliminating the school system. The notion that education has a purely ideological function and that educational change is only a political process also leads to neglecting the consideration of education problems in their own right. Consequently, the theoretical current discussed in this article does not address questions such as the functional specificity of education, the conditions for the accumulation and transmission of scientific knowledge, the role of increasingly differentiated professional entities, or the problems of learning.

See also: Deschooling; Development and Education; Political Economy of Education; State and Education: Marxist Theories

Bibliography

Alavi H 1964 Imperialism old and new. *Socialist Register* pp. 104–26

Amin S 1974 *Accumulation on a World Scale: A Critique of the Theory of Underdevelopment.* Monthly Review Press, New York

Baran P A 1957 *The Political Economy of Growth.* Monthly Review Press, New York

Baudelot C, Establet R 1971 *L'École capitaliste en France.* Maspero, Paris

Baudelot C, Establet R 1975 *L'École primaire divisé: Un dossier.* Maspero, Paris

Bettelheim C 1965 *Problemas teoricos y practicos de la planificacion,* 2nd edn. Editorial Tecnos, Madrid

Bourdieu P, Passeron J-C 1977 *Reproduction in Education, Society and Culture.* Sage, Beverly Hills, California

Brown M B 1963 *After Imperialism.* Heinemann, London

Brunner J J 1981 *La cultura autoritaria en Chile.* Facultad Latinoamericana de Ciencias Sociales, Santiago

Cardoso F H, Faletto E 1979 *Dependency and Development in Latin America.* University of California Press, Berkeley, California

Carnoy M 1974 *Education as Cultural Imperialism.* Longman, New York

Debray R 1967 *Revolution in the Revolution? Armed Struggle and Political Struggle in Latin America.* Monthly Review Press, New York

dos Santos T 1969a *La Dependencia politico-economica de America Latina.* Siglo Veintiuno, Mexico City

dos Santos T 1969b El nuevo caracter de la dependencia. In: dos Santos T et al. 1969

dos Santos T et al. 1969 *La crisis del desarhollismo y la nueva dependencia.* Moncloa, Lima

Frank A G 1972 *Lumpenbourgeoisie: Lumpendevelopment; Dependency, Class and Politics in Latin America.* Monthly Review Press, New York

Freire P 1970 *Pedagogy of the Oppressed.* Herder and Herder, New York

Freire P 1978 *Pedagogy in Process: The Letters to Guinea-Bissau.* Seabury, New York

Gramsci A 1959 *The Modern Prince and Other Writings.* International, New York

Haya de la Torre V R 1936 *El anti-imperialismo y el* APRA. Ercilla, Santiago

Hilferding R 1963 *El capital financiero.* Editorial Tecnos, Madrid

Instituto Latinamericano de planificación económica y social–United Nations Children's Fund (ILPES–UNICEF) 1981 El desarolla en capilla. In: UNICEF 1981 *Planificacion social en America Latina y el Caribe* ILPES–UNICEF, Santiago, pp. 25–55

Labarca G 1977 El sistema educacional: Ideologia y superestructura. In: Labarca G et al. (eds.) 1977 *La Educación Burguesa.* Nueva Imagen, Mexico City, pp. 69–90

Lenin V I 1970 Imperialism, the highest stage of capitalism. In: *Selected Works of V. I. Lenin.* Progress Publishers, Moscow, pp. 667–768

Luxemburg R 1951 *The Accumulation of Capital.* Yale University Press, New Haven, Connecticut

Mandel E 1971 *Ensayos sobre neo-capitalismo.* Ediciones ERA, Mexico City

Mao T 1965 *Selected Works of Mao Tsetung.* Foreign Languages Press, Peking

Mariategui J C 1972 *Siete ensayos de interpretación de la realidad peruana.* Amauta, Lima

Marini R M 1969 *Subdesarollo y revolución.* Siglo Veintiuno, Mexico City

Marx K 1967 *Capital: A Critique of Political Economy.* International, New York

Mattelart A, Biedma P, Funes S 1971 *Comunicación masiva y revolución Socialista.* Ediciones Prensa Latinoamericana, Santiago

Paiva V P 1980 *Paulo Freire e o nacionalismo-desenvolvimentista.* Civilisaçao Brasileira, Rio de Janeiro

Prebisch R 1951 *Estudio económico de America Latina 1949.* United Nations, New York

Prebisch R. 1976 A critique of peripheral capitalism. *CEPAL Rev.* 1: 9–76

Prebisch R 1978 Socio-economic structure and the crisis of peripheral capitalism. *CEPAL Rev.* 6: 159–252

Prebisch R 1980 Toward a theory of change. *CEPAL Rev.* 10: 155–208

Prebisch R 1981 The Latin American periphery in the global system of capitalism. *CEPAL Rev.* 13: 143–50

Vasconi T 1977a Ideologia, lucha de clases y aparatos educativos en el desarrollo de America Latina. In: Labarca G et al. (eds.) 1977 pp. 173–236

Vasconi T 1977b Aportes para una teoria de la educación. In: Labarca G et al. (eds.) 1977 pp. 301–39

G. W. Rama

Deschooling

In recent years, some of the most interesting and challenging criticisms of established assumptions about education have concerned the idea that schooling should be abolished altogether. Such a thesis was based on two ideas which in principle date back to Rousseau: first, that education and schooling are not one and the same thing; and second, that the prescriptive and compulsory nature of schooling inherently discourages learning. To the extent that schools fail to educate and have an antieducational effect on society, modern deschoolers have argued that they should be dismantled. Indeed, it has been said that anything short of disestablishment and deschooling would be insufficient since schools, no matter how unstructured they may claim to be, remain in fact prescriptive and therefore place constraints on learning. Thus while "deschooling" has entered educational vocabulary as part of the rhetoric of educational reform, in terms of propositional content, it is fundamentally at odds with a number of reforms in the vein of "reschooling" or "free schooling" proposed in the general discussion of educational alternatives.

The first modern proponent of deschooling was the American social critic Paul Goodman, who in *Compulsory Mis-education* (1964) attacked the "mass superstition" of conventional belief in the social desirability of public schooling. He argued that while schooling is widely expected to promote literacy, creativity, social awareness, and expanded opportunities for the underprivileged, in reality there is very little evidence that schooling fulfills any of these objectives. Instead, schools were seen to produce conformist and regimented people who at best can only make a marginal contribution to society. Goodman believed that children's natural learning ability would allow them to make the most of "environmental education," learning from the city, from life itself, and by actually doing things as apprentices (see *Environmental Education Programs*). His faith in individuals and mistrust of institutions are themes shared with other deschoolers.

Although in the second half of the 1960s several other education critics joined Goodman in denouncing the authoritarian and repressive characteristics of schooling as part of their effort to explain the widespread phenomenon of student resentment, the term "deschooling" was not to be coined until 1971, when Ivan Illich's *Deschooling Society* was first published. As the most celebrated exponent of the deschooling thesis, Illich analyzed schooling within a more comprehensive framework and attempted a more rigorous explanation than can be found in Goodman's writings, placing the discussion of schooling problems within the broader context of institutionalization. He was joined in this endeavor by his colleague Everett Reimer, whose book *School is Dead* (1971) was based on the same set of ideas.

Whereas Goodman had been concerned with the general failure of schooling, Illich and Reimer saw that schools succeeded in doing a number of undesirable things. Thus they objected to the multiplicity of functions performed by the schools, including "custodial care, social role selection, indoctrination, and education as usually defined in terms of the development of skills and knowledge" (Reimer 1971 p. 33). On one hand, this combination of competing objectives contributes to the high unit cost and low student achievement found in most schools; on the other, it transforms the school into a "total institution" which is altogether too effective as an agent of social control. Moreover, Illich and Reimer argued that all institutions have an endemic tendency to ossify, with administrative expedience ultimately taking precedence over the provision of services. By substituting process for substance, schools in effect teach their students that all valuable learning is necessarily the result of schooling and that indeed no other educational alternative is conceivable. A schooled society thereby develops a contrived compulsion for schooling, creating a kind of consumer fetishism that leads to still more schooling expense, inefficiency and manipulation, while necessarily forestalling the development of new educational opportunities outside of school.

The inefficiencies and distortion-producing tendencies of modern school systems are such that Illich and Reimer admonished Third World countries to avoid the educational nemesis besetting developed countries by rejecting educational models based upon the school. They went on to propose nonschooling alternatives, essentially national systems of educational resource centers open to the public irrespective of age, where modern information networks would be used to match individuals according to their interests so that voluntary learning groups could be brought together. By maximizing free choice and eliminating compulsory and prescriptive requirements, education would become informal, incidental, lifelong, and "convivial."

The deschooling debate has raised a number of first-order theoretical questions about the role of schooling in society and has encouraged a far-reaching exploration of possible educational alternatives. The challenges that have been raised are serious and deserve further consideration. On the other hand, the principal protagonists in this debate have been altogether silent on central questions of political power. Some of the apparent deficiencies of state-regulated school systems intentionally serve a purpose by cutting down individual variations so as to create social conformity and respect for authority in the interest of preserving an existing social order. How the deschoolers would organize major, common human activities without central institutions still remains to be seen; however, at least potentially, the danger exists that education could become even more manipulative if defense ministries and multinational corporations decided to fill the void created by deschooling with new structures of legitimation.

See also: Planning Education, Politics of; Alternative Structures and Forms of Education; Nonformal Education

Bibliography

Barrow R 1978 *Radical Education: A Critique of Freeschooling and Deschooling.* Robertson, London

Goldberg G S 1971 Deschooling and the disadvantaged: Implications of the Illich proposals. *International Development Research Centre Bulletin* 7(5): 1–10

Goodman P 1964 *Compulsory Mis-education.* Horizon, New York

Illich I D 1971a After deschooling what? *Soc. Policy* 2(3): 5–13

Illich I D 1971b *Deschooling Society.* Harper and Row, New York

Lister I 1974 *Deschooling: A Reader.* Cambridge University Press, Cambridge

Reimer E 1971 *School is Dead: Alternatives in Education.* Doubleday, Garden City, New York

P. R. Fletcher

Desegregation in Schools

The term desegregation as used in this article will refer to attendance of racial or ethnic minority students at elementary and secondary schools with nonminority students. More specifically, most of the discussion will be concerned with assignment of black students to schools with non-Hispanic white students. School desegregation of racial or ethnic minority groups is of concern or importance throughout the world. However, most of the research on the effects and implementation of desegregation has involved black and white students in the United States. Therefore, this review is mostly based on research in the United States.

It should be noted that there are important issues and perspectives on school desegregation involving topics other than its effectiveness and implementation. For example, La Belle and White (1980) and others have been developing an international typology of intergroup relations which helps in understanding school desegregation within its larger societal context. Similarly, legal, moral, and philosophic issues are of unquestioned importance in understanding desegregation. Space does not permit treatment of these and other issues in this brief review.

1. Effectiveness of Desegregation

Most research on desegregation has been concerned with its effects on the academic achievement of minority students, or with its effects on interracial and intergroup attitudes and relationships. There has been considerable disagreement and confusion on both topics. Some researchers familiar with the literature firmly believe that desegregated schools improve the achievement of minority students and help develop positive interracial attitudes. Others confidently state that desegregation either has not had positive effects on achievement or attitudes or has not been shown to have positive effects. Conclusions differ according to selection and interpretation of the research and its meaning.

1.1 Achievement of Minority Students

Difficulties in assessing desegregation effects on achievement include problems in controlling for the effects of socioeconomic status, in measuring changes that may be relatively small but meaningful over a one- or two-year period, in comparing results for students who participate in different types of desegregation settings (e.g., voluntary transfer programs or mandatory assignment, urban or rural), and in assessing gains in different subject areas such as reading or mathematics. Among these and many other methodological problems, probably the most important involves the comparison of results in situations where desegregation has been well-implemented with results in situations—probably the vast majority—where it has meant merely racial–ethnic mixture with little real progress made in preparing teachers to work with students of diverse performance levels and backgrounds.

In this situation it is not surprising that scholars have reached differing conclusions regarding achievement effects of desegregation. St. John (1975) reviewed the major studies and concluded that due to methodological weaknesses and problems in data interpretation, it was not possible to say that desegregation had been either successful or unsuccessful. Weinberg (1977) also analyzed this research and concluded that overall, desegregation does have a positive effect on minority achievement. Bradley and Bradley (1977) analyzed studies which had been reported through 1976 and concluded that there are "well-designed" studies both supporting and disconfirming the use of school desegregation as an intervention strategy. Their general conclusion was that "the data collected since 1959 regarding school desegregation has (sic) been inconsistent and inadequate" (p. 444). Krol's (1980) review of 129 studies also raised questions about the effectiveness of desegregation. Krol concluded that even where desegregated minority students made greater achievement gains than comparable groups of segregated students, these gains generally were small and not statistically significant.

However, Crain and Mahard (1982) also assessed the research literature and came to somewhat different conclusions. After reviewing 93 studies reporting on 323 samples of black students, Crain and Mahard selected 45 which met their standards for adequate research design and analysis. They concluded that desegregation typically produces an achievement gain for minority students, and that desegregation is most effective when there is a minority—but not too small a minority—of minority students. The amount of gain attributable to desegregation in these studies is a matter of dispute among several researchers who have reviewed the data.

In addition, Crain and Mahard found that successful desegregated elementary schools apparently are effective in teaching reading and language to minority students. They also concluded that achievement gains probably were not due to racial desegregation per se, but to socioeconomic desegregation involving assignment of economically disadvantaged minority students to schools with higher status nonminority students. This latter conclusion is compatible with research indicating that low-status students benefit academically from attending mixed- or middle-status schools, that minority students attending segregated schools do not necessarily have low self-esteem or aspirations, and that schools with a predominance of poverty students generally do not function effectively (Levine and Havighurst 1984).

Other research indicates that desegregation does not result in improved achievement unless accompanied by major efforts to improve instruction. For example, this was the major conclusion of an intensive study of several elementary schools in Israel (Klein and Eshel 1980), and of a national study in the United States (Coulson 1976). Klein and Eshel found that socioeconomic desegregation when combined with improved instructional methods resulted in improved achievement of disadvantaged minority students, particularly in mathematics, and Coulson found that desegregation positively affected achievement when resources were focused on appropriate goals, there was assertive administrative leadership, parents were involved in the classroom, and teachers promoted positive interracial contact.

It should be emphasized that few if any scholars studying the effects of school desegregation believe that it can totally eliminate achievement differences that exist between low-status minority students and higher status nonminority students. A typical estimate of the potential effect of desegregation is that offered by Pettigrew (1973), who believes that desegregation by itself can close approximately only one-fourth of the achievement gap between minority and nonminority students. On the other hand, gains of this magnitude represent one or more years of achievement on standardized performance tests. For many students, such gains constitute the difference between functional literacy and illiteracy. It should also be kept in mind that desegregation combined with instructional improvements may well produce very large gains in academic achievement and related variables such as students' aspirations.

1.2 Interracial Attitudes and Relations

Research on group-relations effects of desegregation has not shown a consistent tendency for results to be positive. Some researchers have reported that desegregation tends to be associated with positive interracial attitudes (e.g., Scott and McPartland 1982), but others (e.g., Pascal 1977) have reported that desegregation rarely produces positive change in attitudes and friendships.

However, as is true with research on achievement effects, this conclusion understates the potential utility of desegregation in improving interracial attitudes and relationships. Desegregation typically has not been implemented very well, so it is not surprising that it has rarely been effective. In those cases where it has been well-implemented, it frequently appears to have some positive effects in terms of interracial relationships. For example, Forehand et al. (1977) conducted a national study and found that desegregation has positive effects on interracial attitudes and relations when there is strong and dedicated administrative leadership, teachers' attitudes are positive and supportive, and curriculum and instruction focus on the attainment of the goals of desegregation.

Social scientists have long recognized that interracial attitudes and relations are most likely to be improved when members of the interacting groups have equal-status contact and work together on common tasks to attain superordinate goals (Allport 1954). Unfortunately, desegregation generally has not involved systematic efforts to structure students' experience in accordance with this research. Based on experimental and demonstration projects, however, researchers have found that specific approaches to improving instruction can result in gains in interracial attitudes as well as academic achievement. In particular, Slavin (1980) and his colleagues have found that cooperative-learning techniques in which students are rewarded for academic work as part of heterogeneous teams have positive effects on interracial attitudes and achievement.

2. Implementation of Desegregation

As mentioned above, experimental research indicates that curriculum and instruction can be arranged so as to improve interracial relationships and minority students' achievement in desegregated schools and classrooms. In general, positive outcomes seem to be most likely when there is equal-status contact between members of differing racial or ethnic groups. Cooperative-learning approaches devised by Slavin (1980), Johnson (1981), and others are designed to bring about personal contact in which each student contributes in working toward a common goal. Efforts to improve the effectiveness of instruction, to focus on human relations, and to introduce multiethnic curricula are also intended in part to enhance contact and interaction on a relatively equal basis. For example, Cohen (1980) and her colleagues have been developing a "multi-ability classroom" approach which emphasizes cooperative learning, diverse channels and opportunities for success in learning, individualization, "private" evaluation, and reduction in competitive grading, in order to improve the participation and performance of low-achieving minority students in desegregated classrooms.

After reviewing available research on desegregation with reference to its implications for equal-status contact theory, Mercer et al. (1980) have identified some of the processes and practices that appear to minimize unproductive status-ranking processes in the school and classroom. Recommendations for enhancing constructive equal-status contact include the following: group evaluation and cooperation; racially mixed instructional grouping; multicultural programming; minimal use of norm-referenced standardized tests; equal power and participation for all groups of parents and staff members; treatment of all groups as "insiders"; equality of resource allocation; and equal student participation in school activities. Research suggests that these policies and practices can help generate a number of desirable outcomes for students, including high self-esteem, low school anxiety, high sense of personal efficacy, interracial or interethnic friendships, low ethnic stereotyping, and higher academic performance.

In addition to considerations described above, researchers have identified a number of policies and practices that appear to be associated with effective desegregation, that is, with desegregation that is relatively stable (comparatively little withdrawal of nonminority or middle-status students) and is effective in terms of improving academic achievement and/or interracial attitudes. Based on studies and research reviews such as those by Hawley and his associates (1982) and by Genova and Walberg (1980), the following recommendations and conclusions should be given attention in devising and implementing a desegregation plan:

(a) begin desegregation as early as possible;

(b) provide educational options within and among schools;

(c) magnet schools are most effective in the context of a mandatory plan for a district as a whole;

(d) enrich and improve instruction for all schools, not just magnet schools;

(e) take account of special needs of different racial and ethnic groups;

(f) provide a safe school environment;

(g) create schools and instructional groupings within schools of limited size that provide a supportive environment for students;

(h) maintain discipline through clear rules that are consistently and fairly enforced; and

(i) maximize participation in extracurricular activities that promote interracial interaction.

Emerging generalizations supported by research and analysis on effective implementation of desegregation include the following. First, teachers' behaviors are more important than their attitudes; teachers can work effectively to promote constructive desegregation despite negative personal attitudes (Crain et al. 1982). Related to this conclusion, teacher training that emphasizes improvement of curriculum and instruction appears to be more effective than training that concentrates mostly on attitude change (Mercer et al. 1980). Finally, effective desegregation is not a simple matter of bringing students from different groups into the same school or classroom. Unless vigorous efforts supported by adequate resources are made to improve academic achievement and interracial relationships, little or no progress can be expected toward accomplishing the goals of desegregated education.

See also: Multiculturalism and Education; Multicultural Education; Compensatory Education

Bibliography

Allport G W 1954 *The Nature of Prejudice*. Addison-Wesley, Cambridge, Massachusetts

Bradley L A, Bradley G W 1977 The academic achievement of black students in desegregated schools: A critical review. *Rev. Educ. Res.* 47: 399–449

Cohen E G 1980 Design and redesign of the desegregated school: Problems of status, power, and conflict. In: Stephan E G, Feagin J R (eds.) 1980 *School Desegregation: Past, Present and Future*. Plenum, New York

Coulson J E 1976 *National Evaluation of the Emergency School Aid Act (ESAA)*. System Development Corporation, Santa Monica, California

Crain R L, Mahard R E 1982 *Desegregation Plans that Raise Black Achievement: A Review of the Research*. Rand, Santa Monica, California

Crain R L, Mahard R E, Narot R E 1982 *Making Desegregation Work: How Schools Create Social Climate*. Ballinger, Cambridge, Massachusetts

Forehand G, Ragosta M, Rock D A 1977 *School Conditions and Race Relations*. Educational Testing Service, Princeton, New Jersey

Genova W J, Walberg H J 1980 *A Practitioner's Guide for Achieving Student Integration in City High Schools*. US Government Printing Office, Washington, DC

Hawley W D (ed.) 1982 *Strategies for Effective Desegregation: Lessons from Research*. Lexington Books, Lexington, Massachusetts

Johnson D W 1981 Student–student interaction: The neglected variable in education. *Educ. Res.* 10: 5–10

Klein Z, Eshel Y 1980 *Integrating Jerusalem Schools*. Academic Press, New York

Krol R A 1980 A meta analysis of the effects of desegregation on academic achievement. *Urban Rev.* 12: 211–24

La Belle T J, White P S 1980 Education and multiethnic integration. An intergroup-relations typology. *Comp. Educ. Rev.* 24: 155–73

Levine D U, Havighurst R J 1984 *Society and Education*, 6th edn. Allyn Bacon, Newton, Massachusetts

Mercer J R, Iadicola P, Moore H 1980 Building effective multiethnic schools: Evolving models and paradigms. In: Stephan W G, Feagin J R (eds.) 1980 *School Desegregation: Past, Present, and Future*. Plenum, New York

Pettigrew T F 1973 Busing: A review of the evidence. *Public Interest* (Winter) pp. 81–118

Scott R R, McPartland J M 1982 Desegregation as national policy: Correlates of racial attitudes. *Am. Educ. Res. J.* 19: 397–414

Slavin R E 1980 Cooperative learning. *Rev. Educ. Res.* 50: 315–42

St. John N H 1975 *School Desegregation: Outcomes for Children*. Wiley, New York

Weinberg M 1977 *Minority Students: A Research Appraisal*. US Government Printing Office, Washington, DC

D. U. Levine

Desensitization in Counseling

Desensitization is one type of behavior therapy, and is usually associated with the South African psychologist Joseph Wolpe. It is primarily used with people suffering from neurotic fears, particularly phobias, that is, irrational and exaggerated fears so intense that they interfere with the person's everyday functioning.

Behavior therapy is based on the view that an individual who experiences personal-adjustment difficulties has failed to learn appropriate behavior or else has developed faulty behavior patterns which can be altered by principles derived from learning theory. From the learning-theory perspective, such disorders as inordinate fears have derived from *conditioning*, meaning that patterns of behavior have been repeatedly reinforced by the individual's environment. Such inappropriate behavior can be unlearned through counterconditioning or eliminating the maladaptive response to a certain stimulus by associating the stimulus with new, more desirable reactions in the presence of the stimulus.

1. The Process of Systematic Desensitization

Wolpe first applied the name *reciprocal inhibition* to the method he developed to achieve the substitution of desirable for undesirable responses (Wolpe 1958). His technique is based on the assumption that a person cannot be relaxed and anxious at the same time, because these two reactions are involved with opposing functions of the autonomic nervous and hormonal systems. Such conflicting functions include lowering versus raising the blood pressure, facilitating versus inhibiting the digestive processes, and preparation of the muscles for action versus the dismantling of such preparations. Thus, Wolpe's treatment is designed to induce relaxation while the individual is in the presence of his real or imagined fear-producing situation or object (the stimulus). As a consequence, the bond between the stimulus and the habitual anxiety should be progressively weakened and eventually eliminated. The three steps involved in the process are comparatively simple:

First, the individual is given relaxation training. Wolpe has used a technique advocated by Edmund Jacobson in a 1938 book entitled *Progressive Relaxation* in which the person is taught to deeply relax all of the body muscles, usually starting by tensing the muscles in the toes so that the client is aware of the feelings engendered by such tension, then by relaxing the same muscles so as to experience the contrasting sensations. This procedure is repeated with other muscle groups progressing up the body. Sometimes the physical relaxation is accompanied by mental images, with clients picturing themselves in a pleasant peaceful environment, such as a quiet beach or mountain setting. Several visits to the counselor may be devoted to teaching this technique, in addition to the client's practicing the procedure at home.

Secondly, a hierarchy of anxieties is formed. The

therapist and client together work out a kind of rating scale of the fears that the client has been experiencing. At first the client is probably unaware that gradations of fear exist; he believes that he feels intensely anxious about the entire stimulus situation. However, invariably the feelings are stronger about what he sees as more threatening aspects of the stimulus setting. An objective scale called the SUDS scale is created, which breaks the anxiety down into specific steps representing progressively greater threats.

An example of this process is the case of a client who fears water (aquaphobia). He works out a scale that ranges from merely being on a beach and looking at the ocean, through wading up to his ankles near the shore, to standing with only his head above water, and eventually to swimming or floating face down, perhaps in the presence of high waves. In the process of creating the scale, the therapist elicits the client's specific feelings accompanying each step and perhaps draws out any associations or memories the client might have in conjunction with these sensations.

Thirdly, desensitizing procedures are implemented. The client first goes through his progressive relaxation routine. Then the therapist describes a series of scenes to him, beginning with the least anxiety-provoking (the first step on the client's hierarchy). The client next imagines himself involved in the described scene or activity, while maintaining his relaxed state. If at any point in the procedure the client becomes anxious and tense, it is necessary to go backwards in the scale until he is able to tolerate the imagined situation with equanimity. The process continues until the entire anxiety hierarchy is worked through. During the procedure, the counselor makes whatever alterations seem to be needed.

Underlying this approach is the assumption that the imagined behavior will be transferred to the real-life fear-provoking situation. If such transfer does not occur, the client may need to repeat at least some of the steps in the real-life setting. Some therapists accompany the client into the environment in order to help him transfer the newly acquired response. For example, the counselor might accompany a victim of claustrophobia (fear of enclosed places) in learning to ride up and down in an elevator until any remaining fear of enclosures is extinguished.

Typically each therapy session lasts from one-quarter to one-half hour, two or three times a week, for several weeks or months. Sometimes a client is given homework assignments to carry out between therapy sessions. An assignment for a person who fears crowds could be the task of standing in line at a market, or for one who fears thunderstorms the assignment could be listening to tape-recorded noise turned very low at first and gradually increasing in volume.

2. Applications

Systematic desensitization has become one of the most used forms of treatment in attempts to overcome phobias. These inordinate fears, most of which have been given rather intimidating Greek names, can become attached to almost any person or object, although some types of phobias are more common than others. Examples of the range of stimuli which can elicit fears are reflected in the names of the phobias—acrophobia (high places), hematophobia (blood), mysophobia (filth, germs), nyctophobia (the dark), xenophobia (strangers), belonephobia (sharp objects), and mellisophobia (bees).

In addition to treating phobias, Wolpe and others have reported success with combating obsessions and compulsions, reactive depressions, various sexual problems, behavior disorders and fears in children, and such psychosomatic or stress reactions as high blood pressure, asthma, and ulcers.

3. Problems and Criticisms

Wolpe himself notes three areas in which problems may arise with his method: (a) difficulties in the client's achieving sufficient relaxation, (b) incorrectly conceived hierarchies, and (c) the client's inability to visualize or create imagery, although some researchers do not believe this last to be very important.

A more basic criticism is directed at what many psychologists, particularly those with psychoanalytic training, contend is mere symptom removal which leaves an underlying psychological problem unchanged, since they see many phobias as representing the individual's defense against unacceptable and threatening impulses. Wolpe replies that in most, perhaps all, of the cases the client is disturbed by the symptom itself and its effect on his life. In any event, he holds, if an underlying condition exists at all, it is the result of faulty learning and can itself be erased through counterconditioning and relearning.

4. Rate of Success

Wolpe's original book (1958) reported a 91 percent success rate in an average of 11.2 sessions, which is a very brief period compared to other therapies and is an extremely high percentage of cure. Other experimenters have shown varying degrees of success with different kinds of phobia. Perhaps the type of phobia is an influence on success rate, or the opportunity to experience the exposure in real-life situations may be important.

At any rate, the advantages of this type of therapy from the standpoints of brevity of treatment, consequent savings in money and time, the specificity and relative simplicity of its methodology, amenability to evaluation, and reported high success rate suggest that systematic desensitization is an appropriate first alternative to attempt in instances of phobias. Then, in any cases with which desensitization does not succeed, other modes of therapy can be tried.

Bibliography

Lazarus A A 1971 *Behavior Therapy and Beyond.* McGraw-Hill, New York
Wolpe J 1958 *Psychotherapy by Reciprocal Inhibition.* Stanford University Press, Stanford, California
Wolpe J 1974 *The Practice of Behavior Therapy.* Pergamon, Oxford
Wolpe J, Wolpe D 1981 *Our Useless Fears.* Houghton Mifflin, New York

S. M. Thomas

Deutsches Institut für Internationale Pädagogische Forschung

The *Deutsches Institut für Internationale Pädagogische Forschung* [German Institute for International Educational Research] was established in 1951 at Frankfurt am Main as the *Hochschule für Internationale Pädagogische Forschung* [College of International Educational Research], whose main function was to introduce practising teachers to problems and methods of empirical educational research. Special consideration was given to international standards in educational research from which Germany had been separated for nearly two decades. The Institute was established on the initiative of Erwin Stein, at that time Minister of Education of the Land Hessen and for many years chairman of the *Stiftungsrat* [governing board] of the Institute. In 1964, the Institute was restructured into a pure research institution and was accordingly renamed. Its legal status is that of an independent foundation under public law. According to an agreement between the federal government and the Länder governments its regular budget has since 1977 been provided by both federal and Länder authorities in equal shares.

The organs of the foundation are:

(a) the governing board (*Stiftungsrat*), consisting of representatives of federal and Länder authorities as well as personally coopted scientists (predominantly university professors), which supervises all affairs of general and long-term importance;

(b) the managing committee (*Vorstand*), chaired by the chairman of the governing board, which is responsible for administration, including the planning and control of the budget;

(c) the research board (*Forschungskollegium*), consisting of directors of departments, past directors, and three elected research officers,

which coordinates research planning. One of the departmental directors holds the office of director of the research board (*Direktor des Forschungskollegiums*). He or she is elected by the research board for a two-year period and is in charge of all matters concerning day-to-day management and representation.

The main focuses of research conducted at the Institute are the following. First, since the establishment of the Institute, practice-oriented empirical research has been given specific preference, although not to the neglect of its theoretical foundations. Special attention is paid to interdisciplinary approaches as well as to the application of empirical methods and the testing and development of new procedures in the planning and realization of research projects.

Second, the Institute conducts its investigations with both national and international perspectives. Emphasis is laid on trends and predictions in the Federal Republic of Germany, with special regard to the historical dimension. The international orientation of the Institute has been deliberately widened and intensified in the course of the 1970s. This orientation is not restricted to comparative education as an academic discipline but is emphasized in varying degrees in the research activities of all departments. Consequently, the Institute is engaged in various forms of cooperation with foreign and international research institutions. While previous research had concentrated on Western Europe and North America, research into the educational systems of the Soviet Union and Eastern Europe were begun in the early 1970s when countries of the Third World also emerged as another new area of investigation.

Third, within the framework of its research activities the Institute fulfils a considerable number of advisory functions for policy-making bodies both within the Federal Republic of Germany and abroad, with special respect to international organizations (the Council of Europe, the European Community, UNESCO, the Organisation for Economic Co-operation and Development).

Research work is conducted in the seven departments, whose directors are formally responsible for the planning and realization of all projects. The operation of several scientific disciplines relevant to educational research under one roof proves advantageous for interdisciplinary approaches. As well as formal cooperation between departments, numerous informal contacts among members of the Institute (advisory talks and so on) take place and are particularly useful.

The following research areas are covered by departments: general and comparative education (including a subdepartment for historical studies); vocational education; educational psychology (including subdepartments for special education of physically and mentally handicapped children and test construction); sociology of education (with special emphasis on research on Third World problems); economics of education; law and administration of education; and educational and psychological statistics and research methodology (including data processing).

The library of the Institute comprises more than 110,000 volumes; about 600 periodicals and newspapers (of which 240 are foreign) are available. In 1981 the Institute had a staff of 86 people (48 researchers and 38 support staff) and a budget of approximately 6.4 million Deutschmarks, 15 percent of which is provided by sponsors such as the Volkswagen Foundation or the German *Stifterverband* [research community].

Research reports are published in several Institute series (commissioned by Böhlau Verlag in Cologne and Vienna, and other publishers), internal workshop papers and other reports, and the Institute journal (*Zeitschrift für Erziehungs und socialwissenschaftliche Forschung*), which appears twice a year. In addition, many studies have been published in books and articles outside the Institute. Completed and ongoing projects are recorded in biannual reports. The function of disseminating the research work done at the Institute is fulfilled by its members' participation in congresses, symposia, and workshops in the Federal Republic of Germany.

W. Mitter

Development and Education

The meaning of the term "development" has never been very well-defined and has been expanding constantly since its initial formulation. The relationships between development and education have therefore evolved with the meaning of the concept. Development initially referred to a stage reached by some national societies which were characterized by the ability to increase systematically the amount of goods and services available to its population through the application of science and technology to production. Education, and in particular schooling, was conceived as one of the necessary preconditions of development. The concept of development was enlarged later to include an equitable distribution of the wealth created among the different groups involved in the productive effort, and participation by the population in the process of deciding about the goals of, and the roads to, development and preservation of the cultural identity of the community. Education in general—both formal and informal, in the schools or in other institutions—was conceived at this stage as a means to ensure that development efforts did incorporate these dimensions. The latest revision of the concept maintains that the condition of development that some societies attain has been acquired at the expense of other societies which have, in turn, been underdeveloped by the same global historical process; development efforts therefore should aim at correcting the imbalance in the international distribution of the benefits of that process and should eventually change the world economic system. The implications for education of this definition are only beginning to be formulated.

1. The Changing Conception of Development and its Relationship to Education

1.1 First stage

The original conception of development was born out of the realization by some social scientists of the industrialized societies that a small group of national societies had acquired the ability to increase systematically, year by year, the total amount of goods and services produced and, therefore, were able to improve the living conditions of their populations in a sustained fashion, without changing the social structure. This ability was linked to the systematic recourse made to an ever-growing pool of scientific knowledge in order to derive from it new and more efficient ways of producing known goods and services, or to invent new ones, and to the institutionalization of such recourse in the public and private sectors of the economy. Since scientific knowledge is universal and institutions can be modeled after those in the developed societies, it was concluded that any underdeveloped society, having the necessary political will, could acquire the ability to grow economically in a systematic and ordered fashion, and in a reasonably short period of time. The process of development, however, would not be straightforward since it required (a) the transfer of social power from the traditional ruling group to new groups firmly committed to the goal of development; (b) the willingness to reorganize the institutional structure of the society along the lines suggested by the successful developed societies; (c) access to science, technology, and the capital of the developed societies; and (d) the acquisition by the population of the developing countries of a set of skills and abilities without which neither science can be mobilized for development nor modern institutions can function in a satisfactory way. In particular, the process of development required the ability to conduct systematic research on any aspect of reality, natural or social, before acting upon its findings (Hoselitz 1960).

The already developed societies could do little to bring about the first two conditions, but they could help with the remaining two, through the new concept of international development cooperation. Grants and loans at low interest rates were provided to those developing countries which had demonstrated their commitment to the goal of development by fulfilling the first two conditions and by enacting legislation encouraging and protecting private foreign investment. Since the existing educational institutions were not teaching the skills and abilities required for development, a long-term strategy was to be devised to reform them.

Particular attention was to be paid to the higher level of education. Internationally, the doors of the higher-education institutions of the developed countries were to be opened to the best talents of the developing countries, to enable them to learn how to conduct research and planning. Domestically, new modern institutions of higher education were to be set up, with international technical assistance, and existing institutions were to be overhauled to enable more people to gain access to higher education. Upon graduation from foreign institutions, the new generation of local intellectuals were to return home to replace the foreign experts in the modern institutions of higher education and to begin teaching their fellow countrymen and women their newly acquired skills and abilities. Gradually, the new mentality would reach the secondary schools and permeate the population of the country. Together with this effort to change the basic conception of knowledge production and utilization, a parallel drive was to be launched to increase the number and quality of technical and vocational schools that, with the assistance of experts from the developed countries, would produce a new generation of qualified workers for the modern productive organizations.

This initial conception of development considered education as a prerequisite for the attainment of the desired goal of becoming a developed society. The so-called traditional education of the underdeveloped countries, with its emphasis on rote learning, was to be replaced by an entirely new form of education that would emphasize the acquisition of practical skills and the abilities required to run complex modern organizations, and to conduct systematic research. In concrete terms, this notion of development led to a global reorganization of the educational institutions of the developing countries, with an emphasis on technical and vocational education, and on higher education. The vastness and complexity of the task of reforming the whole educational system of a society made it necessary to rely on the superior knowledge and experience of the already developed societies, which were asked to provide technical assistance (Harbison and Myers 1964).

Development at this stage became linked with concepts of political democracy, and it was argued that the former would lead to the latter, on the evidence of what had happened in Western Europe and the United States. Therefore, the outcome of the development effort was redefined as the ability of a society to grow economically at a sustained and predictable rate in the context of a democratic political regime. Such a conception of development, originally elaborated in the academic circles of the United States during the 1950s, was soon incorporated into the thinking and the actions of the international organizations of which that country was a member, and of the major United States foundations such as the Rockefeller and Ford Foundations. Throughout the presidency of John F. Kennedy in the early 1960s this conception of the relationship between development and democracy represented the cornerstone of this new foreign policy of the United States. A special agency, the United States Agency for International Development (USAID), was established to implement the development policy of the country. The developed countries of Western Europe subsequently adopted this policy and created their own institutions of development aid. As a consequence, during the 1960s, major educational reforms were launched in the majority of the developing countries, with the financial and technical support of the governments of the United States and other developed societies, either in bilateral or multilateral form, and of the private foundations (Millikan and Rostow 1957).

1.2 Second stage

Towards the end of the 1960s, however, doubts arose about the conception of development underlying development policies in general, and educational reforms in particular. The first line of criticism was raised against the assumption that economic growth would favor all sectors of the population equally. It was shown that the new wealth created by the implementation of these policies was benefiting a disproportionately small segment of the total population and did not reach the vast majority for whom it was intended, particularly in rural areas. Accordingly, it was deemed necessary to complement the initial conception of development as pure economic growth with the notion of a fair distribution of the new wealth among the different groups of the population. The situation of the developed societies was again used as a model of both economic growth and fair distribution among the different groups. It was argued that current development policies were not leading the developing countries towards that kind of society but rather to an extremely polarized one in which a small minority enjoyed a standard of living comparable to that of developed societies while the vast majority of the population barely managed to survive. As far as the outcomes of the educational reforms were concerned, it was argued that only a fraction of those with modern education could be absorbed by the productive activities of the country, due to the labor-saving technologies used by the mostly foreign-owned or foreign-controlled enterprises. Therefore it made little sense to continue producing substantial numbers of educated people. Instead, the emphasis should be put on the universal acquisition of a minimum of education that would allow citizens (a) to set up their own productive activities and to develop technologies appropriate to the local conditions, and (b) to organize themselves to put pressure on the political system to receive their fair share of the new wealth created by the economic growth policies. In other words, the new educative action should be directed to the adult population and should include not only the acquisition of new intellectual skills but also of organizational ones. Since this type of education could not be provided by the conventional schools, new approaches should be used, taking advantage of the progress made in the field of electronic communications technology (Adelman and Taft 1973).

A second line of criticism was directed at the lack of participation by the population at large in the decision-making process of development policy. It was argued that there were several roads to development, and that each route represented a different distribution of the burden to be carried among social groups. Therefore, it was necessary to consult the population before entering onto one of these roads. The implication of this line of thought for education was that the population at large should be educated to participate. The schools were then examined with respect to their ability to do this and were found inadequate. Furthermore, it was argued that the schools were preparing people to obey instructions from authority and not to participate in the process of decision making (Freire 1970, Illich 1971).

A third line of criticism was directed at the loss of cultural identity of the society concerned in the process of becoming a developed society. It was argued, on the one hand, that the cultural tradition of a society is a valuable asset that should not be lost in the attempt to reproduce the development of the societies of North America and Western Europe. The tradition may not have been as successful as the Western one in terms of increasing productivity on a permanent basis, but it certainly has other values that are as important for the well-being of its bearers. On the other hand, the cultural tradition contains elements that are easy to redefine in terms of the prerequisites of development and therefore is of positive value to the country. This line of argumentation normally contained also a critique of the cultural tradition of the developed societies and insisted on the point that every positive aspect of that cultural tradition was due to contributions made by other cultural traditions. The proponents of this line of thought about development are particularly unhappy about the curricula of the new educational institutions set up under the influence of the original notion of development, with their emphasis on scientific and technical subjects. They do not oppose the teaching of these subjects, but argue that they should be taught against the background of a humanistic education in the cultural tradition of the society.

Therefore, they argue for reform of the curricula to give more emphasis to the cultural achievements of the society and to their academic study (Mazrui 1976).

Following these criticisms, the notion of development came to include a just distribution of the new wealth created by the systematic application of science and technology to production, an appropriate participation in the decision-making process by the different groups involved in productive activities, and the preservation and enhancement of the cultural identity of the developing society. The ambitious educational reforms of the 1960s were put under close scrutiny and attempts were made at correcting what were perceived as biases in favor of a particular development strategy.

1.3 Third stage

A new kind of concern about development emerged in the 1970s, particularly in the most developed societies. The starting point was the realization that the unprecedented growth that had occurred after the Second World War had entailed the consumption of a considerable amount of nonrenewable natural resources and that the continuation of such a rate of growth would lead, in the not very distant future, to their exhaustion. It was argued that the systematic application of science and technology to productive purposes had brought, together with the increase in the total amount of goods and services available, an increase in the total amount of waste. The argument was made that development had brought an increase in the quantity, not the quality of life. Any future application of science and technology to production therefore had to be planned so that resources were used more carefully, bearing in mind not only the needs of the present generation but also those of future generations, and the preservation of the environment. To those formulating these ideas the situation seemed serious and urgent enough to warrant an effort to convince the population at large about the necessity of concerted political action to force both governments and enterprises to adopt the necessary policies. They typically brought their message directly to the people through books and pamphlets written in plain language rather than in the technical language of the social sciences. In a few cases this effort to educate the population at large about the dangers of unbridled growth was translated into courses and seminars for future scientists and technologists. The sudden realization by the developed countries at the beginning of the 1970s of the extent of their own dependence upon some of the developing countries for fossil fuels added a new dimension of urgency to this discussion. Social scientists and planners were persuaded to pay more attention to a line of thought about development that had been generated in the developing countries, particularly in Latin America (Meadows 1972).

Since the late 1960s, a group of Latin American social scientists had been arguing that the current conception of development lacked historical perspective. In the context of economic history since the sixteenth century, it was argued that underdeveloped countries had been forcibly incorporated into a worldwide division of labor, basically as suppliers of staples and raw materials. A succession of more powerful, imperialistic countries had benefited enormously from this division, while underdeveloped countries had been deprived of their resources and had seen their economic and social structure reorganized to serve the interests of developed societies. The developed countries owed their advanced development to a large degree to their favorable position in this international division of labor, and the underdeveloped countries had been reduced to such a condition because of their incorporation into it. The mobilization of science and technology for productive purposes had propelled the developed countries forward at an unprecedented speed, as a result of the historical accumulation of wealth derived from their position in the world economy. Reciprocally, the underdeveloped countries had seen their efforts at development thwarted by the constraints imposed on them by their position in the same world economy. Development could not be separated from underdevelopment: they were the two faces of the same process of historical social change. Development, therefore, could not be achieved by a developing society without changing the international division of labor, no matter how much capital and technical assistance was made available to it or how comprehensive the institutional and educational reforms which were implemented. On the contrary, it was argued that the development policies being implemented would have the effect of bringing the developing countries more deeply into a reorganized international division of labor which would maintain or even increase the gap between rich and poor, both internationally and internally (Villamil 1979).

According to this analysis, development is a process that happens at the level of the world economic system, not at the level of the individual national society; it implies the transformation of the world economic structure for the benefit of the developing countries. This interpretation of Latin American historical development became in the early 1970s an alternative theoretical interpretation of the process of development in general, as a consequence of contributions from social scientists of other regions of the developing world and from some social scientists of the developed world (Wallerstein 1979).

A loosely associated group of scholars, also from Latin America, questioned the assumptions of those studies that had predicted a dark future for mankind arising from the depletion of nonrenewable natural resources and the pollution of the environment by industrial waste. This group of scholars argued that these consequences were not inevitable but rather were products of an economic and social organization, and that a reasonable reorganization of the world economic system could provide a more civilized way of life for present and future generations (Herrera 1976).

As a consequence of the political and economic events of the early 1970s, there emerged a call for a new international economic order in which the developing countries would occupy a more advantageous position and would be able to improve the standard of living of their populations (Brandt 1980).

In the mid-1970s it was finally recognized—at least in the development literature—that development was a global process, and that both the developed and developing societies had to find ways to cooperate in order to balance benefits among themselves and to minimize negative effects. In other words, it was accepted that there was a need for a global development strategy.

2. The Current Conception of Development

Development is currently conceived as a global process of societal change that:

(a) is planned cooperatively by governments and international organizations with the full and informed participation of the inhabitants of the area to be developed;

(b) is implemented in different areas of the world system with variable contributions from private and public enterprises according to the political and economic systems of that area;

(c) generates in that area the capacity to constantly increase the total output of goods and services;

(d) preserves the cultural identity of the community affected;

(e) judiciously regulates the consumption of nonrenewable resources and assures that renewable ones will in fact reappear; and

(f) gives a fair share of the new wealth thus created to all the different participants in the process, but particularly to the poorest members of the community affected.

Development, then, has become a normative, not a descriptive, concept: it stipulates how things ought to be, not how they really are. These characteristics are intended to represent criteria for use in the evaluation of individual projects to decide if they deserve to be called development projects, or if they are just intended to increase the total amount of goods and services in a particular area of the world without consideration of the social and cultural implications of such actions.

3. Educational Implications of the Current Conception of Development

Any attempt to specify the consequences of the new conception of development for educational thinking and practice has to begin by recognizing that the educational development policies of the 1960s have been implemented throughout the world and have produced, together with a new generation of educated people, a complex web of educational institutions, both national and international, that constitute the transnational educational institution of the world economic system. From the higher education and research institutions down to the primary schools, this institution is working daily to reproduce and legitimize the present economic and social organization of the world system, by educating people to perform without question precisely defined occupational roles in the modern economic and political institutions. There is a remarkable similarity of purpose and method across countries and economic systems, with some very few exceptions.

It must also be recognized that the alternative view of development that emerged in the 1970s did not guide the foreign policy of any world power, as was the case with the initial conception of development and the United States. Rather, the opposite is true: small, recently decolonized countries are among the few that courageously attempt to organize their educational effort around the new conception of development (Nyerere 1968). The world powers have accepted this conception rather reluctantly due to the combined pressure of the world economic crisis and of the developing countries, led by the oil-rich states.

Therefore, in spite of its intellectual and moral merits, the new conception of development has very few realistic chances of superseding the established view as the basis of a new wave of vast educational reforms comparable to those of the 1960s. But, to recognize these rather obvious facts does not mean that this new conception of development has no important implications for educational theory and practice. Several guidelines may be derived from it, which can be implemented by taking advantage of some of the main characteristics of the contemporary educational institution.

One of these characteristics is the transnationality of the institution itself, particularly evident at the third and fourth levels of education. The objective behind this transnationalization process had been to increase the speed of elite modernization in the developing countries. An elite thoroughly familiar with the idea and the techniques of development planning would then make possible a rapid diffusion of modernity to the population at large. With this idea in mind, generations of young people of the developing countries have been trained in the institutions of higher education of the developed world,

have returned home to staff the new or renovated institutions of higher education of their countries, and have educated other generations in the modern notion of knowledge production and utilization.

The crisis of the world economic system and the emergence of a new notion of development have not interrupted this flow of students from the developing countries into the developed ones. The atmosphere has, however, changed since the 1960s. On the one hand, many professors and students share a skeptical view of the universal applicability of Western science and technology for development; on the other, both the new conception of development and the new importance of some of the developing countries in the world economy direct their attention to alternative development strategies.

Even if the second level of education is by no means as transnationalized as the third and fourth, it is a fact that the great wave of educational reforms during the 1960s had as a consequence a remarkable worldwide standardization of goals and curricula at this level, particularly in mathematics and science. It is also a fact that in spite of all the efforts, access to secondary schools is still a rare privilege in the developing countries, in great part due to a shortage of teachers. At the other extreme of the development continuum—in part due to the demographic cycle in the developed societies, in part due to the economic crisis—more and more secondary-school teachers are beginning to join the growing group of unemployed people.

In terms of the new conception of development as a global process, it would be perfectly appropriate to offer the opportunity to teachers of mathematics and science of the developed countries to go to the developing countries to teach in their secondary schools and help prepare new local teachers. The similarity of the curriculum and the universality of the subjects makes the move relatively easy, after an appropriate training in the language and culture of the host society. Once their temporary assignment is over, the teachers should find it much easier to reenter the labor market of their home country, equipped with an additional language and experience in the developing world.

The teaching of the reality of the developing countries at the secondary-school level is another aspect of education upon which the new conception of development as a global process may be applied. It is generally admitted that it is difficult to convey a foreign reality to pupils if the teacher is not familiar with it. A program by which secondary-school teachers of the developed countries have the opportunity to teach for a period of time in a school of a developing country would provide this familiarity with local conditions. In exchange for this opportunity, teachers of the developing countries should be invited to teach at schools of the developed ones, thereby increasing, with their presence and their teaching, the awareness of the commonality of development problems among the future citizens of these countries.

Adult education offers another area of application of the new conception of development. The developing countries have been experimenting with non-school approaches to education for a long time because of the nature of their educational problems and the limitations of their resources. In this process their educators have accumulated valuable experience and have developed sophisticated methodologies of education. Such experiences and methodologies have been considered for a long time peculiar to the developing countries and little systematic attention has been given to them by educators of the developed countries. With the crisis of unbridled development in the developed world and the realization of the need to exert more control on the agents of economic dynamism by the population affected by development, the notions and techniques of adult education generated by educators of the developing countries should be a valuable contribution to current efforts to alert, mobilize, and organize the population in defense of natural resources and the environment.

See also: Dependency Theory and Education; International Cooperation and Assistance in Education; Economic Development and Education; Modernization and Education; Reform Policies: Educational

Bibliography

Adelman I, Taft M C 1973 *Economic Growth and Social Equity in Developing Countries.* Stanford University Press, Stanford, California
Brandt W 1980 *North–South: A Program for Survival.* MIT Press, Cambridge, Massachusetts
Eisenstadt S N 1973 *Tradition, Change and Modernity.* Wiley, New York
Fägerlind I, Saha L 1983 *Education and National Development.* Pergamon, Oxford
Freire P 1970 *Pedagogy of the Oppressed.* Herder and Herder, New York
Germani G 1962 *Política y sociedad en una época de transición: de la sociedad tradicional a la sociedad de masas.* Paidós, Buenos Aires
Harbison F H, Myers C A 1964 *Education, Manpower and Economic Growth: Strategies of Human Resource Development.* McGraw Hill, New York
Herrera A O 1976 *Catastrophe or New Society?* International Development Research Centre, Ottawa, Ontario
Hoselitz B 1960 *Sociological Aspects of Economic Growth.* Free Press, Glencoe, Illinois
Illich I D 1971 *Deschooling Society.* Harper and Row, New York
Latapi P 1973 *Mitos y verdades de la educación mexicana, 1971–1972: una opinión independiente.* Centro de Estudios Educativos, Mexico City
Mazrui A A 1976 *A World Federation of Cultures: An African Perspective.* Free Press, New York
Meadows D H 1972 *The Limits to Growth: A Report for the Club of Rome's Project on the Predicament of Mankind,* 2nd edn. Universe Books, New York
Medina Echavarria J, Higgins B 1963 *Aspectos sociales del desarrollo economico en América Latina.* UNESCO, Paris
Millikan M, Rostow W W 1957 *A Proposal: Key to an Effective Foreign Policy.* Harpers, New York
Moreira R 1960 *Educacao e desenvolvimento no Brasil.* Centro Latino-americano de pesquisas em ciéncias sociais (CENTRO), Rio de Janeiro
Nyerere J K 1968 *Ujamaa: Essays on Socialism.* Oxford University Press, Dar es Salaam
Solari A 1977 Development and educational policy in Latin America. *CEPAL Rev.* 3: 59–91
Villamil J J (ed.) 1979 *Transnational Capitalism and National Development: New Perspectives on Development.* Humanities Press, Atlantic Highlands, New Jersey
Wallerstein I 1979 *The Capitalist World-Economy: Essays.* Cambridge University Press, Cambridge
Wolfe M 1979 Reinventing development: Utopias devised by committees and seeds of change in the real world. *CEPAL Rev.* 7: 7–39

E. Fuenzalida

Developmental Rate

A developmental process is a set of systematic, adaptive changes in the quantity and/or quality of a variable. Obviously, for such processes to occur and to be detected time must elapse. Simply, change is a time-bound concept and the detection of change requires at least two and, preferably, more measurement times. However, time may be used in at least two ways to appraise development. As an independent variable, a $time_1$–$time_2$ interval (or a $time_1$–$time_2$–$time_3$–$time_4$, etc., interval) is kept constant, and levels of some dependent variable (for instance a behavior) are measured at each time point. Alternatively, two (or more) different levels of development can be used as a standard, and the time taken to change from level 1 to level 2 (etc.) is then the dependent variable.

The concept of "rate of development" is most meaningfully represented by the second use of time. Thus, rate of development, as a feature of intraindividual development, refers to the magnitude of a $time_1$–$time_2$ interval associated with a fixed level 1–level 2 contrast. Rate of development, as a dimension of interindividual difference, refers to between-people differences in $time_1$–$time_2$ intervals associated with an interindividually fixed level 1–level 2 contrast. In turn, the presence of a particular level of development at a single time point cannot be unequivocally construed as revealing anything about rate of development. Interindividual differences in developmental level at a single time point are similarly equivocal as to their status as an index of interindividual differences in rate of development—a point often misunderstood or unrecognized in developmental research (Baltes 1968, Baltes et al. 1977, Schaie 1965).

1. Rate of Development in Evolutionary Theory

The concept of rate of development is not an organizing concept in major theories of ontogeny, although it is in theories of phylogeny (Gould 1977). Theories of ontogenetic development treat rate of development as a descriptive individual-difference concept; in evolutionary biology interspecies differences in rate of development (that is, heterochrony) is a central, explanatory concept (Gould 1977). That is, in evolutionary biology, heterochronic differences are presumed to account for species differences in plasticity and complexity of final developmental levels (Gould 1977, Schneirla 1957). One form of heterochrony is recapituation, which refers to the evolutionary compression of ancestral adult stages of development into the juvenile stages of descendants; such heterochronic changes have not been found, however, to be of general explanatory use in accounting for species differences in plasticity or complexity (Gould 1977). Another form of heterochrony—neoteny—has been seen to have such explanatory value. Neoteny refers to the retention of ancestral juvenile characteristics in the adult stages of descendants. Such retention, termed paedomorphosis, is produced by a slowing down of somatic development (Gould 1977). Such a retardation in rate of development allows greater lengths of time for learning and for the organization of the large brain, and especially the neocortex, that humans have evolved.

2. Rate of Development in Ontogenetic Theory

2.1 Organismic Theories

Organismic, stage theories of ontogenetic development see interindividual differences in rate of development as one of the two types of individual differences that can exist (Emmerich 1968, Lerner 1976), "final level of development" being the other. Explanations of interindividual differences in rate of development in such theories usually involve reference to: (a) individually distinct heredity, for example, different maturational "ground plans" (Erikson 1959); (b) facilitating or inhibiting experiences; or (c) some interaction between (a) and (b).

Structural models of cognitive development fare especially poorly with regard to the issue of rate of development. In general, organismic-stage models may conceptualize rate of intraindividual development in terms of the age at which qualitatively different stages of development are achieved, as well as the rate of consolidation (e.g., attainment of equilibrium) within a stage. Examination of the empirical literature on stage models of cognitive development reveals little if any interest in characterizing individual differences in the rate of stage acquisition. Thus, the typical paradigm in studying conservation behavior, for example, is a cross-sectional study spanning some childhood age range (for instance 5 to

9 years). Such studies show attainment of various conservation behaviors between ages 7 to 9 (see Elkind and Flavell 1969 for a review). It is as if individual differences in rate of stage attainment are irrelevant anomalies. For example, Liben (1981), in an essay describing a Piagetian perspective on children's contributions to their own development, emphasized the critical importance of the individual's internal representation of environmental forms. However, in this Piagetian perspective there is no discussion of whether there are individual differences in such representation and, if so, what implications there would be for individual differences in rate of development. Similar problems exist in other cognitive studies examining a variety of skills, even where new perspectives on cognitive development have emerged (Gelman 1979); in sum, interindividual differences in intraindividual development trajectories have not been a primary focus.

2.2 Mechanistic Theories

In mechanistically derived (e.g., behavioristic) approaches to ontogenetic development (Bijou 1976, Bijou and Baer 1961), interindividual differences in rate of development are explained by reference to contrasts in reinforcement history. Here differences in schedules of reinforcement (e.g., a fixed-interval versus a variable-interval schedule), and the types of reinforcing stimuli used therein, lead to interindividual variation in the rate of acquiring a given criterion behavior. In addition, some theoretical discussions have indicated that some organismic attributes (particularly those with evolutionary significance for the organism) potentially constrain the effects of some reinforcers on the acquisition of selected behaviors, that is, those that may interfere with the emitting of evolutionarily central behaviors (Breland and Breland 1961, Herrnstein 1977, Skinner 1966, 1977).

2.3 Contextual Theories

In approaches to ontogenetic development derived from a contextual perspective, interindividual differences in rate of development are universally expected. The person and context variables that interact to provide a basis for development do so in a temporally probabilistic manner (Lerner et al. 1983, Lerner et al. 1980, Schneirla 1957, Tobach and Schneirla 1968). Indeed, given the infinity of these variables, no two people are expected to have either isomorphic developmental profiles (at least insofar as the content of one's behavioral repertoire is concerned) or, therefore, identical rates of development. Indeed, since a contextual approach would, in the extreme, indicate that no interindividual isomorphism could exist between level 1–level 2 contrasts, precise interindividual comparisons of rate of development would be precluded.

However, as suggested elsewhere (Emmerich

1968, Lerner 1976), while such singularity of a developmental profile may require an ipsative analysis for complete description of an individual's development, general patterns of change are not logically excluded by the presence of idiographic phenomena. For example, comparable structural changes, for instance, as described by the orthogenetic principle, may occur despite distinct contents of an attribute repertoire. Such interindividual, structural comparability would permit level 1–level 2 contrasts in regard to developmental rate.

In sum, rate of development is a concept pertinent to all major approaches to developmental theory. Yet, the concept has not been a prominent one in any major instance of any type of theory.

3. Bases of the Lack of Attention to the Rate of Development Concept

For a variety of reasons, developmental psychologists have spent relatively little effort identifying interindividual differences in developmental trajectories—so it is not surprising that relatively little is known about individual differences in the rate of behavioral development. Consider the case of psychometric intelligence, which has been extensively studied over the adult life span (Bayley 1970, Horn and Donaldson 1979, McCall et al. 1977, Botwinick 1977, Schaie 1979). The psychometric model for intelligence derives primarily from a mechanistic perspective in which it is deemed reasonable to conceptualize intellectual development as a process of continuous development from young childhood to maturity. To be sure, longitudinal studies have suggested lability in the developmental trajectories of infants and of young children below the age of 3 years (McCall et al. 1973, 1977), but after age 6 the stability of individual differences in psychometric test performance increases markedly. Given, then, the relatively continuous nature of the development "growth" curves in psychometric intelligence from age 6 through adolescence, one might expect that developmental psychologists have attempted to identify the mathematical form of the average developmental function so as to estimate a rate parameter for the function. Certainly, developmental methodologists have provided the requisite mathematical tools (Cattell 1970, Goldstein 1979, Guire and Kowalski 1979).

However, efforts to characterize the mathematical form of the developmental function of intelligence are notably lacking in the literature. From a contextual perspective, this may not be at all bad, since it is unlikely that the averaged growth curve for intelligence would accurately reflect the intraindividual rates of development; the rate parameter of such functions would be representative of all individuals' rate parameters only if there were interindividual differences only in rate parameters, but

not in the form of the developmental function (Guire and Kowalski 1979). For instance, it is highly unlikely that an average developmental rate parameter for intelligence across the adult life span would be meaningful, since development during adulthood is critically dependent upon environmental contingencies, for instance, the impact of nonnormative life events and other nonorganismic influences on development (Baltes and Willis 1977, Hultsch and Plemons 1979).

The fact remains, however, that the psychometric literature has focused upon age norms for psychometric performance (Matarazzo 1972)—thereby indirectly measuring normative developmental functions—without addressing directly: (a) the issue of measuring the developmental function or (b) the examination of individual differences in either the focus of the function or the rate parameter of the function. Instead, individual differences are examined solely by comparison to age norms—the individual is characterized by the deviation from the age group's mean (or another measure of central tendency). As discussed above, this is hardly satisfactory, since interindividual differences at point in time—4, say, tell nothing about the rate of change leading up to status at time—4. It could be argued that adequate assessment of the likely educational implications of psychometric assessment of children can only be understood from the developmental context of intraindividual change leading to an antecedent–consequent model for the developmental processes producing the child's status at a fixed point in the developmental sequence (Baltes and Nesselroade 1979).

4. Towards Incorporating the "Rate of Development" Concept into Developmental Research and Intervention

What developmental psychology has to say about intervention or education in respect of the rate of development concept is limited. This omission is due to the fact that theory and research have not focused on the concept, at least in regard to interindividual differences in individual developmental trajectories. This lack of focus is in turn partially accounted for by the fact that developmental researchers have, by and large, not opted to do longitudinal research (Baltes and Nesselroade 1979, Livson and Peskin 1980). Since such research is necessary in order to have the database requisite for the study of rate of development, such "preferences" have precluded advances in understanding pertinent to the rate-of-development concept. For instance, developmental psychology has not progressed sufficiently to generate functional rate models, an outcome which would accrue if data relevant to "rate of development" had been generated in appropriately designed longitudinal research.

What information is needed to enhance knowledge? Why would this information be important? First, it would be necessary to know what constitutes formally equivalent points of development ("level 1" and "level 2") before rate of development can be studied. Simply put, it is necessary to understand, at least at a descriptive level, the target phenomena of interest before it is possible to begin to understand interindividual differences in developmental trajectories and rates. Perhaps it is the relative paucity of our knowledge about developmental phenomena which has precluded attention to individual differences in the rate of development. To achieve such knowledge about target phenomena, it is necessary to adopt ipsative methods (see *Ipsative Theory of Human Development*), along with nomothetic ones, in order to study rate of development between multiple levels of psychological structure. One obvious place to initiate such research is where the structures comprising each level are well-understood, as may be argued to be the case in regard to cognitive developmental stages (Piaget 1970).

Knowledge of rate parameters would have import for intervention and educational practice. It might be found that while children develop from one comparable level to another, they do so with lawfully different rates, that is, rates which might require different models of instruction if rate facilitation is desired. Attention to the issue of rates of development would logically lead educators away from global questions like: "Was Head Start effective?" to differentiated questions such as: "For whom was Head Start effective, and why?" (see *Head Start Program*). Developmental rate might well be a critical preintervention status variable which would predict successful intervention outcomes, and more importantly, might indicate qualitatively different intervention techniques for individuals differing in developmental profiles. In addition, there may exist multiple techniques for altering rates, but each rate involved might be associated with a different cost: benefit ratio. As such, intervenors and educators might have to begin to ask: "What technique is most feasible for altering the development rate of what type of child between what points in his or her life span?"

See also: Developmental Tasks

Bibliography

Baltes P B 1968 Longitudinal and cross-sectional sequences in the study of age and generation effects. *Hum. Dev.* 11: 145–71

Baltes P B, Nesselroade J R 1979 History and rationale of longitudinal research. In: Nesselroade J R, Baltes P B (eds.) 1979 *Longitudinal Research in the Study of Behavior and Development*. Academic Press, New York

Baltes P B, Willis S L 1977 Psychological theories of aging and development. In: Birren J E, Schaie K W (eds.) 1977 *Handbook of the Psychology of Aging*. Van Nostrand Rheinhold, New York

Baltes P B, Reese H W, Nesselroade J R 1977 *Life-span Developmental Psychology: Introduction to Research Methods*. Brooks/Cole, Monterey, California

Bayley N 1970 Development of mental abilities. In: Mussen P H (ed.) 1970 *Carmichael's Manual of Child Psychology*, Vol. 1. Wiley, New York

Bijou S J 1976 *Child Development: The Basic Stage of Early Childhood*. Prentice-Hall, Englewood Cliffs, New Jersey

Bijou S J, Baer D M 1961 *Child Development*, Vol. 1: *A Systematic and Empirical Theory*. Appleton-Century-Crofts, New York

Botwinick J 1977 Intellectual abilities. In: Birren J E, Schaie K W (eds.) 1977 *Handbook of the Psychology of Aging*. Van Nostrand Rheinhold, New York

Breland K, Breland M 1961 The misbehavior of organisms. *Am. Psychol.* 16: 681–84

Cattell R B 1970 Separating endogenous, exogenous, ecogenic, and epogenic component curves in developmental data. *Dev. Psychol.* 3: 151–62

Elkind D, Flavell J H (eds.) 1969 *Studies in Cognitive Development*. Oxford University Press, New York

Emmerich W 1968 Personality development and concepts of structure. *Child Dev.* 39: 671–90

Erikson E H 1959 Identity and the life cycle. *Psychol. Issues* 1: 18–164

Gelman R 1979 Preschool thought. *Am. Psychol.* 34: 900–05

Goldstein H 1979 *Longitudinal Studies*. Academic Press, New York

Gould S J 1977 *Ontogeny and Phylogeny*. Belknap, Harvard University Press, Cambridge, Massachusetts

Guire K E, Kowalski C J 1979 Mathematical description and representation of developmental change functions on the intra- and inter-individual levels. In: Nesselroade J R, Baltes P B (eds.) 1979 *Longitudinal Research in the Study of Behavior and Development*. Academic Press, New York

Herrnstein R J 1977 The evolution of behaviorism. *Am. Psychol.* 32: 593–603

Horn J L, Donaldson G 1979 Cognitive development in adulthood. In: Baltes P B, Brim O G (eds.) 1979 *Life Span Development and Behavior*, Vol. 2. Academic Press, New York

Hultsch D F, Plemons J K 1979 Life events and life-span development. In: Baltes P B, Brim O G (eds.) 1979 *Life Span Development and Behavior*, Vol. 2. Academic Press, New York

Lerner R M 1976 *Concepts and Theories of Human Development*. Addison-Wesley, Reading, Massachusetts

Lerner R M, Hultsch D F, Dixon R A 1983 Contextualism and the character of developmental psychology in the 1970s. *Annals of the New York Academy of Sciences*, 412: 101–28

Lerner R M, Skinner E A, Sorell G T 1980 Methodological implications of contextual/dialectic theories of development. *Hum. Dev.* 23: 225–35

Liben L S 1981 Individuals' contributions to their own development during childhood: A Piagetian perspective. In: Lerner R M, Busch-Rossnagel N A (eds.) 1981 *Individuals as Producers of Their Development: A Life-span Perspective*. Academic Press, New York

Livson N, Peskin H 1980 Perspectives on adolescence from longitudinal research. In: Adelson J (ed.) 1981 *Handbook of Adolescent Psychology*. Wiley, New York

McCall R B, Appelbaum M I, Hogarty P S 1973 Developmental changes in mental performance. *Monographs of the Society for Research in Child Development*, 38 (Serial No 150)

McCall R B, Eichorn D H, Hogarty P S 1977 Transitions in early mental development. *Monographs of the Society for Research in Child Development*, 42 (Serial No 171)

Matarazzo J D 1972 *Wechsler's Measurement and Appraisal of Adult Intelligence*, 5th edn. Williams and Wilkins, Baltimore

Schaie K W 1965 A general model for the study of developmental problems. *Psychol. Bull.* 64: 92–107

Schaie K W 1979 The primary mental abilities in adulthood: An exploration in the development of psychometric intelligence. In: Baltes P B, Brim O G (eds.) 1979 *Life Span Development and Behavior*, Vol. 2. Academic Press, New York

Schneirla T C 1957 The concept of development in comparative psychology. In: Harris D B (ed.) 1957 *The Concept of Development*. University of Minnesota Press, Minneapolis

Skinner B F 1966 The phylogeny and ontogeny of behavior. *Science* 153: 1205–13

Skinner B F 1977 Herrnstein and the evolution of behaviorism. *Am. Psychol.* 32: 1006–12

Tobach E, Schneirla T C 1968 The biopsychology of social behavior of animals. In: Cooke R E, Levin S (eds.) 1968 *Biologic Basis of Pediatric Practice*. McGraw-Hill, New York

C. Hertzog; R. M. Lerner

Developmental Tasks

One way to conceptualize the process of human development is as a succession of problems which the growing person must solve in order to progress from one stage of life to the next. These problems, faced by virtually everyone within a given social context, have been called developmental tasks.

Since the early 1930s, when the notion of developmental tasks was introduced in the United States by a group of progressive educators, several versions of tasks have been devised and applied to the fields of child rearing, education, and counseling. Perhaps the best-known version is Havighurst's (1953), which divides the life span into six stages and proposes between six and ten tasks for each growth period. For the period of infancy and early childhood, encompassing the first six years of life, Havighurst defined the nine tasks of learning to walk, to take solid foods, to talk, to control the elimination of body wastes, to recognize sex differences and sexual modesty, to achieve physiological stability, to form simple concepts of social and physical reality, to relate oneself to family members and other people, and to distinguish right from wrong and develop a conscience.

For middle childhood, covering ages 6 through 12, Havighurst identified the nine tasks of learning physical skills needed for ordinary games, building wholesome attitudes toward oneself as a growing organism, getting along with agemates, learning an appropriate masculine or feminine social role, developing literacy and numeracy, learning concepts needed in everyday living, developing a conscience and set of values, achieving personal independence, and building attitudes toward social groups and institutions.

Havighurst's 10 tasks of adolescence include achieving more mature relations with agemates of both sexes; adopting a masculine or feminine social role; accepting one's physique and using it effectively; achieving emotional independence of parents and other adults; attaining assurance of economic independence; selecting and preparing for a vocation; preparing for marriage and family life; developing intellectual skills needed for civic competence; achieving socially responsible behavior; and acquiring a set of values as a guide to behavior.

The stage of early adulthood was assigned the eight tasks of selecting a mate; learning to live with a marriage partner; starting a family; rearing children; managing a home; starting an occupation; assuming civic responsibility; and finding a congenial social group.

The seven tasks of middle age were those of achieving adult social responsibility; maintaining an economic standard of living; assisting teenage children to become responsible and happy adults; developing adult leisure-time activities; relating oneself to one's spouse as a person; accepting the physiological changes of middle age; and adjusting to ageing parents.

For old age Havighurst identified the six tasks of adjusting to decreased physical strength and health; adjusting to retirement; accepting the death of one's spouse; affiliating with one's age group; meeting social and civic obligations; and maintaining satisfactory physical living arrangements.

Developmental tasks are not identical for all societies. Because cultures differ in form and complexity, the list of tasks identified for one society can differ from the list identified for another. Furthermore, the items in a particular list are determined to some extent by the personal value system of the people who have prepared them. Havighurst (1953 p. 26) stated that the list he proposed was "based on American democratic values seen from a middle-class point of view, with some attempt at pointing out the variations for lower-class and upper-class Americans."

Some lists are brief, with relatively few tasks specified for each age level. A European author, Philippe Muller (1969), has cited four tasks for the period of infancy: coordination of eyes and movements; ingestion of solid food; acquisition of initial language skills; and achievement of toilet training. For the primary-school child, Muller has listed ten problems to be solved: those of growing self-awareness; achieving physiological stability; forming simple concepts about physical and social reality; developing concepts of good and evil while developing a conscience; communicating with agemates; assuming an appropriate sex role; mastering physical skills needed to play games; learning literacy and numeracy; achieving a positive attitude toward one's own development; and learning concepts needed for everyday living.

For adolescence Mulier has proposed the six tasks of recognizing one's limitations; developing new human relationships; attaining emotional independence from parents; selecting a life partner; choosing a career; and forming a personal philosophy of life.

Other theorists' lists of tasks are more detailed at each age level. Tryon and Lilienthal (1950 pp. 77–89) composed such a more complex scheme by proposing 10 categories of behavior, then specifying one or more developmental tasks at each of five stages of growth between infancy and late adolescence. The 10 categories are those of achieving appropriate dependence–independence relationships with other people; achieving a suitable pattern of giving and receiving affection; relating to changing social groups; developing a conscience; learning a suitable socio-biological sex role; adjusting to a changing body; learning new patterns of motor movement; understanding and controlling the physical world; developing a symbol system and conceptual abilities; and relating one's self to the cosmos.

The manner in which Tryon and Lilienthal defined specific tasks at each stage of growth for the 10 categories can be illustrated with their third category, that of the child's relating to changing social groups. At the first stage, the infant faces the task of becoming aware of the difference between things that are alive and things that are inanimate. At the next stage, the young child must adjust to the role within the family that the rest of the family members assign to the child. The older child must clarify the difference between the adult world and the child world and must also learn to get along with groups of agemates. The young adolescent needs to adjust to a changing peer code, and the older adolescent must begin adopting an adult set of social values.

Some writers have not attempted to encompass all major aspects of life in their lists of tasks. Instead, they have limited their attention to a particular facet. An example is Godin's (1971) succession of five developmental tasks in Christian education. The first task consists of the child's discovering Jesus at the center of God's plan in history, an accomplishment that becomes possible only when the child's historical consciousness is awakened at around age 12 or 13. Second is the task of comprehending that Jesus was not simply an historical figure but is a continuing symbol of God's present-day actions. Such comprehension first becomes possible when the adolescent at around age 13 has reached Piaget's formal-operations level of intelligence and thus can grasp the relationship between a material sign (the image of Jesus) and spiritual meanings (the relationship of humans to God).

Godin's third task is that of gradually abandoning a magical or superstitious view of religion during middle adolescence and replacing it with true faith in God's plan. Fourth is the task of progressively leaving behind the notion that moral behavior earns favors from God. This notion is replaced by a growing desire to do good works, because the works are an expression of humanism, without expecting God to provide gifts in proportion to the works performed. The fifth task, to be accomplished in later adolescence and early adulthood, is that of freeing one's Christian beliefs from the parental images of mother and father, images on which childhood beliefs have so depended. Godin has accompanied his five tasks with suggestions for Christian educational practices that depart markedly from the typical teaching strategies currently found in religious education programs.

For child-rearing and educational practice, an important assumption underlying the developmental-task perspective is that if a child is successful in achieving each task, he or she is happy and is approved by society. Furthermore, success builds a sound foundation for accomplishing later tasks. However, the individual who fails with a task can be expected to feel unhappy, will be disapproved by society, and will face difficulty with later tasks (Havighurst 1953 p. 2). As a consequence, parents and educators are expected to recognize the tasks at each age level and to help the growing child or adult accomplish the tasks.

While developmental-task schemes have stimulated relatively little research (Havighurst 1953 pp. 325–6), the schemes have been widely applied in certain curriculum-development projects and in books explaining child development for parents and educators (Bernard 1970, Muller 1969). The relatively popular acceptance of the developmental-task viewpoint is apparently due to the fact that advocates of a task approach have found this viewpoint to offer an easily understood way of describing to parents and educators why children and adults behave as they do at different stages of life.

See also: Human Development; Human Development Theories; Human Development, Stages of

Bibliography

Bernard H W 1970 *Human Development in Western Culture*, 3rd edn. Allyn and Bacon, Boston, Massachusetts
Godin A 1971 Some developmental tasks in Christian education. In: Strommen M P (ed.) 1971 *Research on Religious Development*. Hawthorn, New York, pp. 109–54

Havighurst R J 1953 *Human Development and Education.* Longman, Green, New York

Muller P H 1969 *The Tasks of Childhood.* McGraw-Hill, New York

Tryon C, Lilienthal J 1950 Developmental tasks: the concept and its importance. In: *Fostering Mental Health in Our Schools 1950.* Association for Supervision and Curriculum Development, Washington, DC

R. M. Thomas

Developmental Therapy

Developmental therapy (used synonymously with developmental counseling here) refers to therapy or counseling that focuses on two major issues. First, the therapist is concerned with the patient's/client's developmental age/stage along a variety of human development dimensions. Second, the therapist is concerned with the client's deficits in each of his or her developmental areas. Once the deficits (and sometimes also the client's strengths) are ascertained the therapist attempts to adapt the treatment/interventions to the age/stage level of the client.

Some individuals would make a fine discrimination between developmental therapy and developmental counseling, by referring to the process as therapy when a client's developmental deficits have led to serious personality problems (remediation) and as counseling when developmental deficits have not yet led to serious personality disorders (prevention and optimum development). Wood (1975 xi) defines her version of developmental therapy ". . . to include the rehabilitation of emotionally disturbed children by educators." The Division of Counseling Psychology of the American Psychological Association (1956 p. 283) implied a developmental rationale for counseling psychologists: "The counseling psychologist wants to help individuals toward overcoming obstacles to their personal growth . . and toward achieving optimum development of their personal resources."

Bockneck summarizes the developmental perspective quite well in the following:

> The developmental perspective is just that: a way of thinking about people and their concerns. It can encompass many theories and diverse methods. Wittenberg (1968), for example has modified classical psychoanalysis to the particular problems and needs of young adults. Actualization counseling (Brammer and Shostrom 1968) attempts to gear counseling objectives to hypothesized developmental crises. A more radical, and highly promising role for the developmental counselor is that of psychological educator (e.g., Mosher and Sprinthall 1972). In general, any counselor whose explicit goal is enhancing the self-potentiating capabilities of clients—whether through behavioral or client-centered techniques—can be arguably described as an applied developmental counselor. . . . (Bockneck 1976 pp. 39–40)

Table 1 provides a sampling and summarization of developmental therapy models.

1. Application of a Developmental Therapy Model

Gazda (1981) has presented the Life-skills Training model, which is the most efficient and comprehensive developmental treatment model available. This model emphasizes treatment/training of the whole person by focusing on seven areas of human development following a chosen expert's age/stage development theory: (a) the psychosocial stages of Havighurst and Erikson; (b) the vocational stages of Super; (c) the physical–sexual stages of Gesell; (d) the cognitive stages of Piaget; (e) the moral stages of Kohlberg; (f) the ego stages of Loevinger; and (g) the emotional stages of Dupont. From the coping skills found to be necessary for completion of a given developmental task, a series of generic life-skill areas are being developed by Gazda. These generic life-skill areas include (a) family relationship skills, (b) physical fitness/health maintenance skills, (c) career/vocational developmental skills, (d) interpersonal communication/relationship skills, (e) problem-solving skills, and (f) identity/purpose-in-life skills.

Since the model is based on the identification of coping skills for the successful mastery of a given developmental task (age and/or stage related), once these are located they can be placed by age-level into one of the generic families of life skills and then taught (in small groups or individually) just as any other content is taught. When life-skills content is taught at the optimum age for the learning of the given skill, the process is considered preventive and growth-enhancing (educational in the commonly accepted sense). When the life skills are taught to clients who are suffering problems because they lack the skills, the model is considered remedial or rehabilitative. By way of illustration, when generic areas of life skill are taught as part of the school curriculum at the optimum coping-skill level for a given age group of children, then Life-skills Training can be viewed as preventive since the children are learning these skills at the optimum time. However, if these same skills (for instance, interpersonal communication/relationship skills) are taught to a hospitalized group of psychiatric patients whose lack of such skills has led to their psychiatric disorder, the process is rehabilitative or remedial. Since hospitalized psychiatric patients rarely have a single life-skill deficit the patient is best helped if he or she receives training in two or more life-skill areas (Multiple-impact Life-skill Training).

A training model must by definition state its assumptions or hypotheses regarding the causes of personal disturbances. The position assumed in the Life-skills Training model is that most people become emotionally or mentally disturbed because they lack the basic life skills necessary to cope with the daily

Table 1
Summary of developmental therapy models

Author and title	Psychological theory base	Developmental concepts and mode(s) of therapy	Target population
Blocher, Don H. *Developmental Counseling* (1966)	Eclectic (a) Third force—Humanistic (i.e. Rogers) (b) Behavioral—Learning theory (i.e. Wolpe) (c) Cognitive (i.e. Ellis)	Chronological age/stages: Erikson's stages and developmental tasks Hierarchical framework: Maslow's actualization steps superimposed on Erikson's stages Emphasizes cognitive mode (i.e. Ellis)	Child to adult
Bockneck, Gene *A Developmental Approach to Counseling Adults* (1976)	Development psychology of adulthood Ego psychology perspective (author's preference) Also allows for other compatible theories	Chronological age/stages (a) Young adult (b) Established adult (c) Middle adult (d) Senescent adult Counseling objectives geared to hypothesized developmental crises Flexible therapeutic modes, i.e., catalyst, active interventionist, group leader, consultant Focus on present and future versus the past	Adult
Bordin, Edward S. *A Psychodynamic View of Counseling Psychology* (1979)	Psychodynamic theories (any theory which explains behavior in terms of drives and motives) (a) Psychoanalytic (i.e. Freud, Mann) (b) Self theory (i.e. Kohut) (c) Life/work theory (i.e. Super, Holland)	Suggests that the counseling psychologist's developmental counseling include all stages of the life cycle. Deals with ego development stages Uses J. Mann's Time Limited Psychotherapy as a model for psychotherapy Therapeutic issues include: (a) seeking ego identity (b) object relations (c) differentiation of self from others (d) activity vs. passivity (e) adequate vs. diminished self-esteem	Child to adult
Durand, Henry F. et al. *A Developmental Approach to Outreach Services for Counseling Centers* (1980)	Social learning theory Humanistic psychology	Five developmental growth phases (not age/stages) (a) Transition to college (b) Exploration of relationships	College

			Child to adult

		(c) Values clarification
		(d) Life/work planning
		(e) Transition from college
		Modes of therapy suggested
		  (a) Individual
		  (b) Groups
		  (c) Classroom presentations
		  (d) University events
		  (e) Community based field experiences	

Gazda, George M.
Multiple Impact Training: A Model for Teaching/Training in Life-skills (1981)
	Social learning theory used for overview
	Eclectic use of developmental psychology (developmental deficits, neuroses, and psychoses are seen as primarily resulting from failure to learn basic life skills)
		Seven age/stages each having developmental tasks
		(a) Psychosocial styles (i.e. Havighurst, Erikson)
		(b) Vocational stages (i.e. Super)
		(c) Cognitive stages (i.e. Piaget)
		(d) Moral stages (i.e. Kohlberg)
		(e) Ego stages (i.e. Loevinger)
		(f) Physical–sexual stages (i.e. Gesell)
		(g) Emotional stages (i.e. Dupont)
		Generic life skills are necessary to successfully master a given developmental task. Current research has identified generic life skills such as: (a) family relationship skills, (b) physical fitness/health maintenance skills, (c) career/vocational development skills, (d) interpersonal communication/relationship skills, (e) problem-solving skills, (f) identity/purpose-in-life skills
		Therapy is geared to the individual's age/stage development
		Modes of therapy
		(a) Preferred mode: small groups where generic life skills are taught, modeled, practiced. Applicable in schools, counseling centers, psychiatric hospitals
		(b) Acceptable modes:
		  (i) Individual counseling
		  (ii) Large group teaching/training	

Table 1—*continued*
Summary of developmental therapy models

Author and title	Psychological theory base	Developmental concepts and mode(s) of therapy	Target population
Swensen, Clifford H. *Ego Development and a General Model for Counseling and Psychotherapy* (1980)	Ego developmental theory provides overall view (i.e. Loevinger) For treatment purposes an eclectic approach includes: (a) Behavior therapy (b) Reality therapy (c) Rational emotive therapy (d) Client-centered therapy (e) Integrity therapy (f) Existential–humanistic therapy	Seven stages of ego development (a) Presocial stage (b) Impulsive stage (c) Self-protective stage (d) Conformist stage (e) Self-aware level (transition between stages) (f) Conscientious stage (g) Individualistic level (transition between stages) (h) Autonomous stage (i) Integrated stage Modes of therapy geared to stage of ego development, i.e., clients of lower stages generally respond better to tangible rewards and therefore contingency management may be therapy of choice	Child to adult
Widick, Carole "The Perry Scheme: A foundation for developmental practice" (1977)	Developmental psychology, cognitive and moral development (i.e. Perry)	Nine positions of Perry's Intellectual–ethical Development: (a) First three positions: the client deals with the polarized (right–wrong, good–bad) view of the world and moves from seeing the authority figure as all knowing to uncertain (b) Second three positions deal with relativism: Absolute right/wrong conceptions are changed. Abstract thought is more common (c) Third three positions deal with commitment in relativism. The	Late adolescent to adult

		client moves toward accepting responsibility of the pluralistic world and through commitment establishes identity. Therapy is geared to the developmental position of the client. Modes of therapy: Individual therapy, group therapy, consultation	
Wood, Mary M. (ed.) *Developmental Therapy: A Textbook for Teachers and Therapists for Emotionally Disturbed Young Children* (1975)	Learning theory Humanistic psychology Developmental psychology	Developmental Stages: (a) Responding to environment with pleasure (b) Responding to environment with success (c) Learning skills for successful group participation (d) Investing in group process (e) Applying individual and group skills in new situations Curriculum Areas (all four areas are addressed at each stage): (a) Behavior—physical development, awareness of environment, and physical adaptation to the environment (b) Communication—interpersonal processes—verbal and nonverbal communication (c) Socialization—processes which lead child into a group (d) Preacademics—processes used for cognitive functions. Therapy is geared to stage of development Mode of therapy—structured, individualized curriculum designed for the classroom. Specific objectives are given and progress is carefully measured and recorded	Emotionally disturbed children ages 3–8 (has been used successfully with disturbed children up to age 14)

requirements of living. These life-skill deficits occur because the individual has never really mastered the skills since appropriate models were not available and/or no systematic effort was made by institutions such as the school or church to teach them.

When the life-skills model is a part of the school curriculum, each of the generic areas is taught in much the same fashion as the 3 Rs (Reading, Writing, and Arithmetic), only more experientially, including practice in developmental application.

For example, if the topic is interpersonal communications/relationships then all of the coping-skill descriptors from the seven areas of human development that are related to the interpersonal communication/relationship areas for a given age group (say high school) are taken and grouped into subcategories for purposes of instruction, such as initiating a conversation, requesting information, expressing a compliment, listening for understanding. (Preferably a proven interpersonal communication/relationship model is taught so that the learner can perceive the relationship of the constituent parts.)

The assumptions of the Life-skills Training (prevention) model may be summarized as follows:

(a) In order to function effectively, all individuals must achieve a certain level of mastery of the seven areas of human development translated into generic life-skill areas.

(b) There are identifiable stages through which most individuals must progress if they are to function effectively.

(c) There are certain age ranges when specific coping skills are optimally learned.

(d) The capacity for learning is inherited. The degree to which individuals achieve their potential is closely related to their environment of life experiences.

(e) Life skills can be taught most efficiently and effectively in small groups of 6 to 12 people who are developmentally at the peak of readiness.

(f) Life skills will be learned best and transferred to everyday life situations when an entire life-skills curriculum is taught at the age/stage level appropriate to the learner's readiness.

Life-skills Training is equally appropriate for use in remediation. Essentially the treatment becomes training in the life skills which are lacking in the client/patient. Although remedial intervention can be done on a one-to-one basis, instruction is often more efficiently accomplished in small groups. Thus, clients are placed in groups with others suffering from similar deficits.

In the remedial application of the Life-skills Training paradigm, the authors have found that it can be most effective when the client simultaneously receives training in two or more areas of life-skill deficits.

The primary assumptions of the remedial (rehabilitative) applications of Life-skills Training (using multiple life skills) include the six assumptions of the preventive application plus the following four assumptions:

(a) Neuroses and functional psychoses are primarily the result of failure to learn basic life skills.

(b) Clients/patients with the help of counselors/therapists can determine which life skills need to be developed (and also which ones are adequate or even well developed).

(c) Clients/patients suffering from neuroses or functional psychoses typically have more than one life-skill deficit.

(d) Neuroses and functional psychoses can be most effectively overcome through the direct teaching of clients/patients in their generic life-skill deficits, especially when they receive training concurrently in two or more life-skill areas.

The Multiple-impact Life-skills Training model for remediation would proceed somewhat as follows. A group of patients with similar life-skill deficits would be selected and given intensive training in each of their major life-skill deficit areas. For example, chronic alcoholics often have severe problems in interpersonal relationships, physical fitness and health maintenance, as well as finding a purpose in life. A potent intervention, then, for the chronic alcoholic would be intensive, preferably concurrent, training in each of these three areas. Of course, concurrent medical intervention may be necessary for alcoholics who may have developed cardiac, liver, or other physical problems. But, the position assumed here is that the motives for escaping into alcoholism can best be treated by filling voids in needed skill areas, such as the three listed above.

The Life-skills Training (Developmental Therapy or Counseling) model is therefore a comprehensive intervention model for both primary prevention and remediation. It is appropriate for prevention, and in some cases remediation, in all levels of education from preschool to university level. It is also appropriate for use in community mental-health agencies and psychiatric hospitals.

See also: Counseling Theories

Bibliography

American Psychological Association Division of Counseling Psychology. Committee on Definition 1956 Counseling psychology as a speciality. *Am. Psychol.* 11: 282–85

Blocher D H 1966 *Developmental Counseling*. Ronald Press, New York

Bockneck G 1976 A developmental approach to counseling adults. *Couns. Psychol.* 6(1): 37–40

Bordin E S 1979 A psychodynamic view of counseling psychology. *Couns. Psychol.* 9(1): 62–70

Brammer L M, Shostrom E 1968 *Therapeutic Psychology: Fundamentals of Actualization Counseling and Psychotherapy*, 2nd edn. Prentice-Hall, Englewood Cliffs, New Jersey

Durand H F, Girton L G, Robinson B, Cox-Farmer J 1980 A developmental approach to outreach services for counseling centers. *Pers. Guid. J.* 59: 38–42

Gazda G M 1981 Multiple impact training: A model for teaching/training in life-skills. In: Gazda G M (ed.) 1981 *Innovations to Group Psychotherapy*, 2nd edn. Thomas, Springfield, Illinois

Mosher R L, Sprinthall N A 1972 Deliberate psychological education. *Couns. Psychol.* 2(4): 3–82

Swenson C H 1980 Ego development and a general model for counseling and psychotherapy. *Pers. Guid. J.* 58: 382–87

Widick C 1977 The Perry scheme: A foundation for developmental practice. *Couns. Psychol.* 6(4): 35–38

Wittenberg R M 1968 *Postadolescence: Theoretical and Clinical Aspects of Psychoanalytic Therapy*. Grune and Stratton, New York

Wood M M (ed.) 1975 *Developmental Therapy: A Textbook for Teachers and Therapists for Emotionally Disturbed Young Children*. University Park Press, Baltimore, Maryland

G. M. Gazda; J. A. Spalding

Diagnostic Assessment Procedures

A diagnostic assessment procedure is a means by which an individual profile is examined and compared against certain norms or criteria. Diagnostic assessment focuses on individuals whereas diagnostic evaluation is centered on schooling processes such as the curriculum, program, administration, and so on. In both cases the task is to determine the strengths and weaknesses of the individual or process under study. Testing is used for diagnostic assessment of student learning problems and focuses on the construction and utilization of tests as well as their interpretation. Mastery tests can also be used for diagnostic purposes since they describe the teaching/learning process and student performance. Finally, a distinction must be made between diagnostic procedures used for assessing specific learning disabilities and those used in the regular classroom for assessing learning difficulties. Only the latter will be discussed here.

Different explanatory mechanisms, or analogies, have been used in this field but their adequacy can be questioned. When the term "diagnosis" is used, it is often assumed that a medical model is implied. A set of objectives is to be reached; the student's actual performance is then measured and any pattern of discrepancies is examined and analyzed to find a "remedial treatment" or "prescription." Another analogy found in the literature is based on computer technology and refers to "procedural bugs" or "student bugs" when describing difficulties in learning. Not all researchers and educators accept the value of these analogies because most learning problems involve teaching problems as well. Hence, diagnosis should not focus on the student alone. There is nothing "pathologically" wrong with a student who has learning problems, as there is in the case of a diseased patient, but rather an incompatibility exists between a particular teaching method and the student's learning activity or cognitive style. These issues are important and need to be kept in mind when considering the uses of diagnostic testing and diagnostic evaluation in the classroom.

1. Diagnostic Assessment

Diagnostic assessment differs from summative types of assessment, such as minimum competency tests or final or certification examinations. The difference between summative, formative, and diagnostic assessment lies in the type of question each of them is addressing. Summative assessment is concerned with a final product whereas formative assessment provides a description of student progress. Diagnostic assessment draws a profile of student achievement, considering (a) the discrepancies between expected and actual achievement, (b) the cause for such discrepancies, and (c) appropriate "remedial treatment." This last type of assessment requires the definition of clear learning objectives and assessment techniques. A global approach to diagnostic assessment relies on teacher observations, analysis of student work, results obtained on achievement tests, and is not concerned with the construction of specific diagnostic instruments. From this perspective, diagnosis of student learning difficulties cannot be made through the examination of a single specific skill. Rather, student achievement on a broad range of objectives should be documented. Only after examining the entire student profile will it be possible to evaluate the possible causes of learning problems and make an accurate diagnosis. This "case study" approach is not intended to be used for each student in a classroom but only for those who experience persistent learning difficulties. Such a thorough examination is time consuming, and most students do not require this kind of assessment.

Effective diagnostic assessment relies on the right kind of data being collected and their correct interpretation. The danger exists that a diagnostician might define a limited set of learning-problem categories, label students according to these categories, and subsequently only prescribe familiar or readily available treatments. At each level of this process the validity of the diagnosis and the "treatment" is in question. Continuous evaluation of "prescribed treatments" is necessary. In addition, empirical data are needed to test the efficacy of the model as a whole (Thomas 1981).

2. Diagnostic Testing

If diagnostic testing is defined as providing feedback to teachers and students regarding their strengths and weaknesses, almost any test would be diagnostic. In effect, a score on any standardized test gives some indication of the student's performance and also informs the teacher as to how successful he or she was in teaching the material. But the total score does not give any real information concerning specific areas of difficulty or their causes. Examination of the individual items would tell us which answers are correct and which are wrong. However, most available tests have not been constructed for diagnostic purposes; they have too few items per objective and the analysis of the wrong answers cannot lead to a diagnosis of learning problems. Diagnostic testing is seen as one component of the ongoing teaching/learning process. In order to use tests for diagnosis, they should be specifically designed for that purpose.

Guidelines for constructing "good" multiple-choice tests for diagnostic purposes are needed. As with any other test, a clear definition of learning objectives is required; but each test addresses a very specific skill (e.g., addition, subtraction, etc.) and the items are designed to test a particular subskill from various perspectives. Each item provides information to the student and the teacher since each distractor has a precise meaning in terms of learning difficulties and possible remedial strategies. Here the emphasis is on the significance of each particular answer and the response patterns in general. The total score has no real importance or meaning, and guessing is not usually a concern in diagnostic testing since evidence that a student guesses does not provide the specific information needed for diagnosis and remediation.

A consensus does not exist concerning the use of distractors as sources of information for diagnosis. The three main approaches to this issue can be described as follows. One view maintains that the choice of a given distractor has a specific meaning in terms of learning difficulties (Baker and Herman in press). Working from open-ended questions, Tatsuoka and Tatsuoka (in press) analyze the responses to discover which rules are followed in finding the answers. And finally, in adaptive or sequential testing, the only information taken into consideration is whether or not the answer is correct. The last approach does not analyze or ascribe any meaning to the answers given by students.

In adaptive or sequential testing, the items are selected on the basis of the student's responses to previous items. More specifically, a correct response leads to a more difficult item, whereas an incorrect response leads to an easier one. Item selection does not depend on which distractor was chosen but in whether or not the answer was correct. This type of testing is usually administered by a computer which records the answers and selects the items. The pool of items used in one sequence is pretested for unidimensionality, and item difficulty is the basis for their selection. Finally, hypotheses about learning difficulties are formulated on the basis of the response pattern.

One problem with sequential or adaptive testing is that decisions are often made based upon the answer to a single item. However, certain diagnostic characteristics have been attributed to these tests. As they are currently designed, their main advantage is in improving the precision of measurement since each individual receives a different set of items corresponding to his or her level of performance. In order to effectively use adaptive testing for diagnostic purposes the number of items on which diagnostic decisions are made would need to be increased. Also, since adaptive testing has the flexibility to readily adjust to the subject's performance level, potential exists for its use in diagnostic assessment (see *Adaptive Testing*).

A final research perspective found in the literature attempts to explain why errors are made by identifying the "misconceptions" or "bugs" that produce them. The first task is to construct a "procedural network" for each skill under study by breaking down problems into the requisite subskills. What are the correct and incorrect procedures that can be followed in attempting to perform a task? Breaking the skill down into subskills is crucial because, in order to be efficient, a diagnostic model "must contain all of the knowledge that can possibly be misunderstood by the student or else some student misconceptions will be beyond the diagnostic capabilities of the system" (Brown and Burton 1978). Secondly, a set of items must be generated that provides opportunities for students to demonstrate all the identified subskills. Student answers are then examined to reveal those subskills which have not yet been answered. Based on these student "misconceptions" a second set of problems is administered to confirm the initial hypothesis. The information gained from this testing should suggest possible remedial strategies.

This approach has been implemented through the use of the "Buggy system" (Brown and Burton 1978), a computerized game used mostly for teacher training. The computer plays the role of the student, while the teacher has to recognize the source of student error (or bugs) and be able to replicate them. Hence, teachers become more sensitive to the causes of student learning problems. It seems evident that by following this model, single "bugs" can be easily diagnosed. However, when a student has "multiple bugs" or when different "bugs" interact, the diagnosis becomes more problematic. Also, if subskills or possible misconceptions have been omitted from the "procedural network" some of the response patterns may be interpreted as random error.

This research perspective is primarily concerned with developing a model to account for hundreds of "bugs" that can occur when skills being studied become more complex. A probabilistic model seems to be more appropriate for detecting aberrant response patterns when several hundred "bugs" are possible. Brown and Burton's model showed that it was possible to give the correct answer even when using "erroneous rules." Tatsuoka and Tatsuoka (in press) refined that aspect of the model by introducing the Individual Consistency Index (ICI). A low total score and a high Individual Consistency Index indicate that the student is using the wrong rules to solve the problems. This index can be used as a signal to point out students who need remediation and more refined diagnoses. Also, using item response theory (see *Item Response Theory*), they demonstrate that when the possibility exists to respond correctly by using the wrong rule, the data set obtained reveals multidimensionality. In other words, the test measures different dimensions depending on whether the student masters the skill or not. This finding has definite implications not only for diagnostic testing but for testing in general and points out the importance of checking for construct validity.

All "bugs" do not affect the learning process in the same way but a typology of "bugs" or misconceptions still has to be developed. Furthermore, teaching strategies to remediate these diagnosed learning problems are not always available. Before making any concluding comments, the testing techniques of mastery learning will be briefly examined to demonstrate how they may also be classified as diagnostic instruments.

3. The Mastery Learning Approach

This model uses testing in a way that is not always considered "diagnostic," but in fact does serve this function. It involves the use of "formative" or "mastery" tests at frequent intervals to test student performance on each item as compared to a "mastery standard." Examination of these answer patterns provides information on the level of learning and indicates whether a student needs more practice or another teaching method. Some theorists in the area of mastery learning contend that the construction of formative tests is based on a theory of learning. An underlying theory is useful in designing the test in such a way as to identify not only the learning problems but also the cause of the problems.

The difference between mastery and diagnostic testing is not always obvious. Since the term "diagnostic" is used in so many different ways, confusion regarding the application of this term persists. For example, the model of diagnostic assessment developed by the Scottish Council for Research in Education (Black and Dockrell 1980) differs little from a mastery learning model. The former model uses criterion-referenced tests constructed according to a taxonomy of objectives. These objectives, or intended outcomes, are directly linked to the curriculum. While the model is designed to assess mastery it does not necessarily provide information for detecting potential sources of learning difficulties. Therefore, although this has been labeled a diagnostic model, it does not contain many of the diagnostic features of some of the models presented here.

Formative or mastery tests have some of the same objectives as diagnostic tests. One difference may be with the way they are constructed. As indicated above, mastery tests seem to correspond to a theory of learning whereas most diagnostic instruments are constructed to test hypothesized erroneous rules that students follow in solving problems. Mastery tests are attached to a teaching method; they are used to assess student learning and provide students and teachers with feedback regarding skill mastery. This method may not be sufficient for all students, and more refined instruments with better interpretation techniques may be needed to diagnose skill mastery for some students. These are not necessarily included in mastery learning programs. Generally, the type of information sought determines the appropriate kind of test to be used. If the teacher wants to know who has mastered a particular skill and who has not, almost any testing instrument will suffice. However, if partial knowledge is considered important and if it is believed that knowing in detail what kind of error the student makes helps adjust teaching methods, then multiple testing and more refined instruments are necessary (see *Mastery Learning Model of Teaching and Learning*).

4. Conclusion

As has been seen, diagnostic assessment can be conducted in a variety of ways, ranging from global evaluation to more refined diagnosis of very specific skills. The particular demands of each situation will determine which type of assessment is most appropriate. Other factors such as time and cost effectiveness will influence the decision as well. For example, some learning difficulties are a function of developmental lag, therefore intensive diagnosis would be unnecessary and unproductive.

Diagnosis of temporary learning problems can also lead to persistent "labeling" that endures even after the learning problem has disappeared. Research has shown that teachers' expectation can influence their attitudes and behavior toward students.

A final point concerns the assumptions upon which diagnostic testing rests. The first is that learning can be "decomposed" into a set of discrete subunits or subskills. The second is that items can be generated to measure accurately and validly these subskills. All the diagnostic testing models described above are predicated on these assumptions. The practical or educational value of these models, therefore, depends on the validity of these assumptions, which in many areas of education remains to be established.

Bibliography

Baker E, Herman J in press Task structure design. *J. Educ. Meas.*

Black H D, Dockrell W B 1980 *Diagnostic Assessment in Secondary Schools: A Teacher's Handbook.* Scottish Council for Research in Education, Edinburgh

Brown J S, Burton R R 1978 Diagnostic models for procedural bugs in basic mathematics skills. *Cognit. Sci.* 2: 155–92

Tatsuoka K K, Tatsuoka M M in press Spotting erroneous rules of operation by the individual consistency index. *J. Educ. Meas.*

Thomas R M 1981 A model of diagnostic evaluation. In: Lewy A, Nevo D (eds.) 1981 *Evaluation Roles in Education.* Gordon and Breach, London

G. Delandshere

Differential Test Batteries and Omnibus Tests

A set of tests applied to produce information for prognostic or diagnostic purposes may be referred to as a battery of tests. An ad hoc battery may be composed of ability and attainment tests, personality questionnaires, interest inventories, attitude or motivation scales, and even physiological tests, such as reaction time. Each test should be chosen because it relates to a particular aspect of a criterion, such as selection for specialized occupational training. A test, in this context, may contribute relevant information (a) independently of any other test, and (b) in combination with results from other tests in the set.

1. Differential Test Batteries

An ad hoc assemblage of varied instruments would not be called a differential test battery. These are customarily more coherent in several ways and typically have been developed and produced by a publisher coordinating a team of authors working to a defined brief. The tests in a differential battery have a common structure; for example, a specified sequence of levels corresponding to age groups, and a unified scheme for expressing scores derived from the raw score (number of items correct) obtained by a person taking the tests. The derived score scheme is the key feature of differential testing because it enables the comparison of scores from the constituent tests to be made on scales with the same metric.

Whilst the administration of a battery of tests can be quite complicated, the interpretation of the differences between tests is undoubtedly complex. For this reason the supply and use of this type of battery is (customarily) restricted to people who have followed a recognized advanced course of training in psychometrics or the particular battery it is wished to use.

The tests in a battery each yield a raw score for every person tested; in turn, the raw scores are transformed to derived scale points. These scores express a person's actual performance as more or less accurate estimates of true performance on attributes represented by the items in the tests. Technically, test reliability governs the amount of error likely to inhere in an estimate. It is well-known that naive or badly trained testers accept obtained scores at face value. In differential interpretation, ignoring the likely errors inherent in scores which are compared could mislead those concerned and even result in tragic consequences.

2. Score Profiles and Differences

A common method for displaying scores is "the profile". An individual's profile considered in isolation from other pertinent data has little interpretive validity. For instance, someone's raw scores on three 50-item tests might be (A) 10, (B) 40, and (C) 15 respectively. If the tests represented (A)—mechanical, (B)—clerical, and (C)—mathematical aptitudes a naive interpretation would be that the person would succeed in clerical training but fail an engineering course. The difference between the extreme scores is (B) minus (A); i.e., $40 - 10 = 30$ points. But there would be errors of measurement for both tests. Assuming each test has a standard error of measurement (i.e., of obtained score) of 4, "confidence bands" of one standard error give a maximum likely difference of $(40 + 4)$ minus $(10 - 4)$; i.e. 38 points and a minimum of $(40 - 4)$ minus $(10 + 4)$, i.e. 22 points. Hence, over a range of 38 the error band takes up 16 points whilst the minimum difference between bands is 22 points. This oversimplified example illustrates that the error associated with a difference score is disproportionately higher than the error of the original scales.

Standardizing test score to the normal curve adds interpretive power to separate tests and differential batteries especially.

Thus normalized scales representative of defined populations allow subpopulation means to be compared with those for the parent population. Any individual's standardized scores can then be interpreted in relation to the means and differences for appropriate reference groups (and the appropriate standard errors). For example, a person may score near the average for adult males but lie only at the 10th percentile for computer operators.

Reputable publishers provide this type of data in manuals for differential test batteries. The technical data should, preferably, include tables of inter-correlations between the constituent tests for a variety of populations, e.g., school pupils, adults with college qualifications, migrant or ethnic minorities. The reliability of the difference between any pair of scores can then be estimated from the formula

$$r \text{ difference } (A - B) = \frac{r_A + r_B - 2r_{AB}}{2 - 2r_{AB}}$$

when r_A and r_B are the test reliability coefficients and r_{AB} is the correlation between tests A and B. Clearly, in a battery of, say, eight tests there are $7 + 6 + 5 + 4 + 3 + 2 + 1$ pairs of comparisons, or 28 in all. The complexity of profile interpretation is now apparent, as is the desirability of using constituent tests with only moderate to zero, or even negative, intercorrelations.

Score profiles are often plotted as points on a chart upon which the tests are listed in order. For some batteries, a division of the standardized score scale into categories is used (i.e. nine divisions, called "stanines"; 10 divisions "stens"; 100 divisions "percentiles"). The instructions should require that the standard error band is shown for each score recorded.

The common practice of joining successive profile score points with straight lines is potentially misleading in emphasizing differences between tests recorded adjacently whilst neglecting the more widely spaced results. Such profile charts are popular for matching individuals with criterion groups (e.g. computer programmers, vehicle mechanics).

Another matching technique utilizes prediction equations derived from the multiple correlation of several tests with a measure of the relevant criterion (e.g. job success as rated by superiors). The differential weights derived are applied subsequently to the scores obtained by a person taking the battery to indicate degree of match with criterion.

Standardized norm profiles for specific groups (such as successful system designers, ageing adults with dementia, or adolescent dyslexics, etc.) are sometimes given in the manual for a test battery. Users of differential batteries should (a) study critically the validation data given in publishers' manuals, (b) regard their own interpretations of results as conditional (i.e. probabilistic) rather than conclusive, and (c) seek salient evidence to complement test scores.

3. Omnibus Tests

Like differential test batteries, omnibus tests also aim at comprehensive coverage of a broad field. The items may be organized into subtests similar in structure to a test battery, but whereas battery subtests are generally scored so as to develop a profile of performance, all components of an omnibus test are combined together and a single total score is produced. Although the mixture of skills and content means that it is virtually impossible to give meaning to particular score values, the omnibus test may nevertheless be useful for ranking candidates or for relating overall performance to previously established norms.

In recent years, the increasing influence of technology on developing and scoring tests has led to the virtual disappearance of omnibus tests, and their replacement by test batteries, even when the statistical evidence for the viability of particular subscores is weak.

See also: Profiles, Educational; Norm-referenced Assessment; Tests, Sources of

R. Sumner

Direct Instruction

The term direct instruction has appeared in educational literature since at least 1920. Earlier authors have not given a specific, detailed definition of the term. In general, the term has been used to refer to explicit, step-by-step instruction directed by the teacher.

Because the term has been around so long, and because definitions can change from time to time, it would be inappropriate for anyone to provide an "official" definition of direct instruction. Instead, this article will describe the term as it exists in the United States in 1985. Direct instruction in 1985 is used interchangeably with other similar terms such as systematic teaching, explicit instruction, explicit teaching, and active teaching. All these terms refer to explicit, step-by-step instruction, in which there is an emphasis upon all students practicing successful responses and achieving academic success. Direct instruction and the similar terms can be summarized in the phrase: if you want students to learn something, teach it to them—directly.

Thus, if a teacher wants students to learn study skills, map skills, or critical reading skills, the advocates of direct instruction claim that such skills should be taught—directly. Simply asking comprehension questions or higher cognitive level questions is not enough; students need to be taught—directly—how to answer such questions.

Similarly, research on classroom management has found that effective managers (Evertson 1982, Emmer et al. 1980, Evertson et al. 1980) were those who directly taught classroom behavior skills—lining up, sitting down, moving from group to group. And these skills were taught in small steps, with active student practice, correction of student errors, and review and repetition when necessary.

1. An Overview of Direct Instruction

On the basis of correlational and experimental classroom studies conducted since 1974, it can be concluded that, in general, students taught with structured curricula do better than those taught with more individualized or discovery learning approaches, and those who receive their instruction directly from the teacher do better than those expected to learn new material or skills on their own or from each other (see *Individualized Instruction; Discovery- and Inquiry-based Programs*). In general, to the extent that students are younger, slower, and/or have little prior background, teachers are most effective when they:

(a) structure the learning experience;

(b) proceed in small steps but at a rapid pace;

(c) give detailed and more redundant instructions and explanations;

(d) have a high frequency of questions and overt, active practice;

(e) provide feedback and corrections, particularly in the initial stages of learning new material;

(f) have a success rate of 80 percent or higher in initial learning;

(g) divide seatwork assignments into smaller segments or devise ways to provide frequent monitoring;

(h) provide for continued student practice (overlearning) so that they have a success rate of 90–100 percent and become rapid, confident, and firm.

For younger students, the key concept is mastery to the point of overlearning. Basic skills—arithmetic and decoding—are taught in hierarchically organized strands, so that success at any given level requires application of knowledge and skills mastered at earlier levels. Typically, students are not able to retain and apply knowledge and skills unless they have been mastered to the point of overlearning—to the point where they are automatic (see *Mastery Learning Model of Teaching and Learning*). Thus, it is necessary to help students achieve this level so that they can proceed to the next step with success. The high success rates seen in the classrooms of highly effective teachers and programs is obtained because the initial instruction proceeds in small steps that are not too difficult and also because teachers see that students practice new knowledge and skills sufficiently to obtain this point of overlearning.

This overlearning and automaticity of skills is also necessary for higher processing. In discussing beginning reading, Beck (1978) noted that the data support the position that the brain is a limited capacity processor and that if a reader has to spend energy decoding a word (whether through phonics or context) then there is less energy available to comprehend the sentence.

2. Demonstration-guided Practice and Independent Practice

When teaching a class, or a group of students within a class, a three-step process appears to be most efficient: this three-step process might be called direct instruction. The first step is the demonstration of what is to be learned. This is followed by guided student practice in which the teacher leads the students in practice, checks for student understanding, provides prompts, and provides corrections and repetitions when necessary. When the students are firm in their initial learning, the teacher then moves them to independent practice where the students work with less guidance. The objective of the independent practice is to provide sufficient practice so that students demonstrate quickness and competence.

An example of these three steps would be teaching two-digit multiplication (e.g., 54 times 7). The first step would be teacher-led demonstration of the steps to be followed in solving these types of problems. This is followed by guided practice in which the students work two or three problems and the teacher circulates and checks on how well the students are doing. Those students who need additional instruction (or demonstration) receive it at this time. If necessary, the teacher repeats the demonstration or parts of the demonstration. When the students are firm in the guided practice, and are making few errors, they are moved to independent practice where they practice learning how to do the skill accurately and rapidly.

Sometimes demonstration and guided practice are combined. For example, when teaching a word list a teacher could demonstrate how to pronounce the first word, then conduct guided practice, then demonstrate the next word, then lead guided practice, and continue this mixture of demonstration and guided practice. Or, in teaching two-digit multiplication the demonstration could be broken into small steps where each step consists of student practice and repetition. Whether or not one mixes, the important points are the clarity of the demonstration of each step, and the adequacy of the guided practice.

Although the above three components—demonstration, guided practice, and independent practice—appear obvious and common sense, they are not always common practice. Frequently the time spent in demonstration is too short; the students do not receive enough guided practice; the teacher does not circulate, correct student errors, and reteach where necessary; and frequently, too much time is allocated to student independent practice and too little time to demonstration and guided practice.

There is evidence that these skills are not "obvious." In experimental studies (Anderson et al. 1979, Good and Grouws 1979, Evertson et al. 1982, Emmer et al. 1982, Becker 1977) where one group of teachers received training in direct instruction and another group did not receive training, each investigation found that (a) the trained teachers used more of the direct instruction skills in their classrooms and (b) the students of the trained teachers had higher achievement scores or had more time on task. Thus, although almost all teachers are using parts of direct instruction, experienced teachers who received specific training showed the results of this training in their own behavior and improved achievement (and/or engagement) of their students.

Now, the discussion will move to some specific items within demonstration, guided practice, and independent practice.

2.1 Demonstration

The first area—demonstration or presentation—unfortunately, has not received much attention in the classroom research literature. Current research is taking place under the general titles of task analysis and instructional design (see *Instructional Design: Task Analysis*). However, the following suggestions for effective demonstration have emerged from the experimental and correlational classroom literature:

(a) Stating lesson goals.

(b) Focusing on one thought (point, direction) at a time. Completing one point before beginning another.

(c) Giving step-by-step directions using small steps.

(d) Organizing material so that one point is mastered before the next point is given.

(e) Giving detailed and redundant explanations for difficult points.

(f) Having many and varied examples.

(g) Checking for student understanding on one point before proceeding to the next point.

When demonstrations are not clear the main problems appear to be giving directions too quickly, assuming everybody understands because there are no questions, and introducing more complex material before the students have mastered the early material.

2.2 Guided Practice

Teacher presentation is followed by guided practice. Because the presentation represents new material, the purpose of the guided practice is to help the students become firm in the new material. This is effectively done by:

(a) guiding students in practicing the new material;

(b) checking for student understanding and areas of hesitancy and/or confusion;

(c) correcting errors;

(d) providing for a large number of successful repetitions.

One common method for achieving these instructional functions is through teacher questions. Both correlational and experimental studies have shown that a high frequency of teacher-directed questions was important for acquisition of basic arithmetic and reading skills. Stallings and Kaskowitz (1974) identified a pattern of factual question–student response–teacher feedback as most functional for student achievement. Similar results favoring guided practice through teacher questions were also obtained by Stallings et al. (1977, 1979), Soar and Soar (1973), and Coker et al. (1980).

During successful guided practice two types of questions were usually asked by the teacher: questions which called for specific answers, and those which asked for an explanation of how an answer was found.

Two experimental studies (Anderson et al. 1979, Good and Grouws 1979) used controlled practice as part of the experimental treatment. In each study, the teachers who received the additional training were taught to follow the presentation of new material with guided practice. The practice consisted of students responding to teacher questions and doing exercises on their own. In each study, the teachers in the trained group asked more questions and had more guided practice than did the control teachers who continued their normal teaching. And, in each study, the students in the experimental groups had higher achievement than the students of teachers in the regular control groups. Furthermore, the Anderson et al. study found strong positive correlations for the amount of time spent in question–answer format and for the number of academic interactions per minute. Thus, it is not only useful to spend a lot of time in guided practice, it is also valuable to have a high frequency of questions and problems.

Of course, all teachers spend time in guided practice. However, the more effective teachers and their students spent more time in guided practice, more time asking questions, more time correcting errors, more time repeating the new material which was being taught, and more time working problems under teacher guidance and help.

(a) *The importance of frequency*. Note that in all of these studies, the consistently positive results are not being obtained merely by the type of teacher question being asked but by the frequency of direct convergent teacher questions and by the frequency of student responses. Elementary students, like adults, need a great deal of practice, and factual convergent questions provide a form of controlled practice whose frequency has consistently been correlated with student achievement.

Frequency is particularly important in primary grades because no matter how quick a learner is, it takes a large number of repetitions before she or he can recognize words rapidly. For example, Beck (1978) showed that among first grade children, words that were recognized in less than four seconds appeared more than 25 times in the instructional materials, whereas words which were recognized in five seconds or longer appeared less than 10 times.

(b) *High percentage of correct answers.* Not only is the frequency of teacher questions important, but the percentage of correct student responses is also important. One of the major findings of the Beginning Teacher Education Study (Fisher et al. 1980) was that a high percentage of correct answers (both during guided practice and when working alone) was positively correlated with achievement gain.

Similarly, Anderson et al. (1979) found that the percent of academic interactions where the student gave the correct answer was positively related (r = 0.49) to achievement gain. Gerstein et al. (1981) also found that teachers who obtained high reading achievement from their students had student accuracy rates near 90 percent, whereas those with lower class achievement had accuracy rates of less than 75 percent.

This principle, a high percentage of correct responses given rapidly and automatically, is a relatively new finding in research on classroom instruction. Specific answers on how high this percentage should be can probably never be given. As a reasonable benchmark for now, it is possible to recommend that the success rate be at least 80 percent during the instruction and at least 90 percent at the end of the new unit.

(c) *Checking for understanding.* With older students, guided student practice also includes teacher "checking for understanding." That is, the teacher attempts to determine whether all the students have mastered the major points in the presentation. Checking for understanding appears in the training manual developed by Good and Grouws (1979) and as part of the training manual developed by Emmer et al. (1980). The term has been in common use for a long time.

It is best that checking for understanding take place frequently so that the teacher can provide corrections and do reteaching when necessary. Because checking for understanding involves teachers asking questions, it is best that these questions be prepared beforehand. Some suggestions for conducting checking for understanding include:

(a) asking students to repeat directions, procedures, or main points;

(b) asking many brief questions on main points with oral responses;

(c) having everyone write the answer (on a small chalkboard or a piece of paper) while the teacher circulates and then having everyone show their answer to the teacher;

(d) having everyone write the answer and check the answer with a neighbor.

When working with younger students in small groups (i.e., 4 to 10) there are times when it is useful to have students respond in unison (see Becker 1977). Unison responses seem particularly appropriate when students are repeating word lists, word sounds, or number facts. Unison responses enable each student to make a larger number of responses. When doing unison responses in word lists (for example) the teacher should be sure that all students respond together, to a signal. Without a signal, the slower students tend to wait a fraction of a second and echo the faster students. When conducting unison responses, it is useful to give individual turns to the slower students to check whether they are firm and quick or whether they need additional repetitions.

The wrong way to do checking for understanding is to ask a few questions, call on volunteers to hear their (usually correct) answers, and then assume that all the class either understands or has now learned from hearing the volunteers. Another error is to ask "Are there any questions?" and, not hearing any, assume that everybody understands. The teacher's error, in the above cases, is in not having prepared enough questions (or problems) to use in checking for understanding.

(d) *Calling on students.* First in a correlation study (Brophy and Evertson 1976) and then in an experimental study (Anderson et al. 1979) it was found that in primary grade reading groups it was better for student achievement if the teacher called on students in ordered turns. Such ordered turns were for new words and when reading a story out loud. In explaining the results, the authors claimed that ordered turns insure that all students have opportunities to practice and participate, and ordered turns simplified group management by eliminating hand waving and other student attempts to be called on by the teacher.

Anderson et al. (1979) note that although the principle of ordered turns works well in small groups, it would be inappropriate to use this principle with whole class instruction in most situations. They suggest that when a teacher is working with a whole class it is usually more efficient to select certain students to respond to questions or to call on volunteers than to attempt systematic turns.

(e) *Feedback and correctives.* During guided practice, during checking for understanding, or during any recitation or drill part of a lesson, how should a teacher respond to a student's answer?

If a student is correct but hesitant, then it is important for the teacher to tell the student that the answer is correct. If the student is correct and firm then the research suggests that the teacher can simply ask a new question, maintaining the momentum of the practice. There is also value in short statements of praise (e.g., "very good") which do not disturb the momentum of the lesson.

There are two related schools of thought on handling an incorrect response. Some research (Stallings and Kaskowitz 1974, Anderson et al. 1979) suggests that the teacher should help the student arrive at the correct answer by asking simpler questions and providing hints. Other research (Good and Grouws 1979, Becker 1977) suggests that the teacher should reteach the material using small steps. Thus, one line of development suggests using hints and helps, and another suggests reteaching. The important point, in either approach, is that errors should not go uncorrected, and that there should be specific procedures to be sure that the student learns the new material. The wrong method is to give the student the answer and then move on.

2.3 Independent Practice

During the guided practice phase, students (a) have begun to work the new problems or apply the new skills, (b) receive additional process explanations, if necessary, and (c) receive corrections and reteaching when necessary. If the prompted practice is done successfully, the students can now move into the independent practice phase.

Providing time for students to independently practice new skills to the point of mastery is an important component of effective instruction. When doing this practice, students usually go through two phases. They begin with "unitization" (Samuels 1981) where the students are first putting the skills together. The early stages of reading or of mathematics computation are examples of unitization: the students are successful, but they are also quite slow. After a good deal of practice, students achieve the "automatic" stage where they are successful and rapid and no longer have to "think through" each step. When students are learning two-digit multiplication and are hesitantly working the first few problems, the students are in the unitization phase. When they have worked sufficient problems correctly so that they are confident, firm, and automatic in the skill, then the students are in the automaticity phase.

The advantage of automaticity is that students who reach it can now give their full attention to reading comprehension or mathematics problem solving. Thus, when learning new material, it is important that students continue their practice to the point of overlearning, where they are rapid, quick, and firm in their responses.

(a) *Managing independent practice.* Studies have shown that when students are working alone during seatwork they are less engaged than when they are being given instruction by the teacher. Therefore, the question of how to manage students during seatwork, in order to maintain their engagement, becomes of primary interest.

One consistent finding has been the importance of a teacher (or another adult) monitoring the students during seatwork. Fisher et al. (1980) found that the amount of substantive teacher interaction with the students during seatwork was positively related to achievement and that when students have contacts with the teacher during seatwork their engagement rate increases by about 10 percent. Thus it seems important that teachers not only monitor seatwork, but that they also provide academic feedback and explanation to students during their independent practice. However, the research suggests that these contacts should be relatively short, averaging 30 seconds or less. Longer contacts would appear to pose two difficulties: the need for a long contact suggests that the initial explanation was not complete and the more time a teacher spends with one student, the less time there is to monitor and help other students.

Another finding of Fisher et al. was that teachers who had more questions and answers during group work had more engagement during seatwork. That is, another way to increase engagement during seatwork was to have more teacher-led practice during group work so that the students could be more successful during the seatwork.

A third finding (Fisher et al. 1980) was that when teachers had to give a good deal of explanation during seatwork, then student error rates were higher. Having to give a good deal of explanation during seatwork suggests that the initial explanation was not sufficient or that there was not sufficient practice and corrections before seatwork.

Another effective procedure for increasing engagement during seatwork was to break the instruction into smaller segments and have two or three segments of instruction and seatwork during a single period. In this way, the teacher provides an explanation (as in two-digit multiplication), then supervises and helps the students as they work a problem, then provides an explanation of the next step, and then supervises the students as they work the next problem. This procedure seems particularly effective for difficult material and/or slower students.

(b) *Students helping students.* Researchers have also developed procedures for students to help each other during the seatwork. In some cases the students in the groups prepare a common product, such as the results of a drill sheet, and in other situations the students study cooperatively in order to prepare for the competition which will take place. Research using these procedures usually shows that students who do seatwork under these conditions achieve more than students who are in regular settings. Presumably, the advantages of these cooperative settings come from the social value of working in groups, and the cognitive value gained from explaining the material to someone and/or having the material explained to oneself. Another advantage of the common worksheet and the competition is that it keeps the group focused on the academic task and diminishes the possibility that there will be social conversation (see *Small-group Instruction*).

3. Summary

Direct instruction (or similar terms such as systematic teaching or explicit teaching) is not new. Examples of every one of the above points can be found which go back hundreds of years. But examples of the opposite points, also going back hundreds of years, can be found too.

What is new is that the above ideas have a research base. The research base comes from experimental studies conducted in regular classrooms with regular teachers teaching regular subject matter. The results have consistently shown that when teachers modify their instruction so that they do more systematic teaching, then student achievement improves with no loss in student attitudes toward school or self.

See also: Classroom Structuring; Teaching, Technical Skills of

Bibliography

Anderson L M, Evertson C M, Brophy J E 1979 An experimental study of effective teaching in first-grade reading groups. *Elem. Sch. J.* 79: 193–222

Beck I L 1978 *Instructional Ingredients for the Development of Beginning Reading Competence.* Learning Research and Development Center, University of Pittsburgh, Pittsburgh, Pennsylvania

Becker W C 1977 Teaching reading and language to the disadvantaged: What we have learned from field research. *Harvard Educ. Rev.* 47: 518–43

Brophy J E, Evertson C M 1974 *Process–Product Correlations in the Texas Teacher Effectiveness Study: Final Report.* University of Texas, Austin, Texas

Brophy J E, Evertson C M 1976 *Learning from Teaching: A Developmental Perspective.* Allyn and Bacon, Boston, Massachusetts

Coker H, Lorentz C W, Coker J 1980 Teacher behavior and student outcomes in the Georgia study. Paper presented to the American Educational Research Association Annual Meeting, Boston, Massachusetts

Emmer E T, Evertson C M 1981 *Teacher's Manual for the Junior High Classroom Management Improvement Study.* Research and Development Center for Teacher Education, University of Texas, Austin, Texas

Emmer E T, Evertson C M, Anderson L M 1980 Effective classroom management at the beginning of the school year. *Elem. Sch. J.* 80: 219–31

Emmer E T, Evertson C, Sanford J, Clements B S 1982 *Improving Classroom Management: An Experimental Study in Junior High Classrooms.* Research and Development Center for Teacher Education, University of Texas, Austin, Texas

Evertson C M 1982 Differences in instructional activities in higher and lower achieving junior high English and math classes. *Elem. Sch. J.* 82: 329–50

Evertson C M, Anderson C W, Anderson L M 1980 Relationship between classroom behaviors and student outcomes in junior high mathematics and English classes. *Am. Elem. Res. J.* 17: 43–60

Evertson C, Emmer E T, Sanford J, Clements B S 1982 *Improving Classroom Management: An Experimental Study in Elementary Classrooms.* Research and Development Center for Teacher Education, University of Texas, Austin, Texas

Fisher C W, Berliner D C, Filby N N, Marliave R, Cahen L S, Dishaw M M 1980 Teaching behaviors, academic learning time, and student achievement: An overview. In: Denham C, Lieberman A (eds.) 1980 *Time to Learn.* United States Government Printing Office, Washington, DC

Gerstein R M, Carnine D W, Williams P B 1981 Measuring implementation of a structured educational model in an urban school district. *Educ. Eval. Policy Analysis* 4: 56–63

Good T L, Grouws D A 1979 The Missouri mathematics effectiveness project: An experimental study in fourth-grade classrooms. *J. Educ. Psychol.* 71: 355–62

Good T L, Grouws D A, Beckerman T M 1978 Curriculum pacing: Some empirical data in mathematics. *J. Curric. Stud.* 10: 75–81

Samuels S J 1981 Some essentials of decoding. *Excep. Educ. Q.* 2: 11–25

Soar R S, Soar R M 1973 *Classroom Behavior, Pupil Characteristics, and Pupil Growth for the School Year and the Summer.* Institute for Development of Human Resources, College of Education, University of Florida, Gainesville, Florida

Stallings J A, Kaskowitz D 1974 *Follow Through Classroom Observation Evaluation, 1972–73.* Stanford Research Institute, Menlo Park, California

Stallings J A, Gory R, Fairweather J, Needles M 1977 *Early Childhood Education Classroom Evaluation.* Stanford Research Institute International, Menlo Park, California

Stallings J, Needles M, Stayrook N 1979 *How to Change the Process of Teaching Basic Reading Skills in Secondary Schools.* Stanford Research Institute International, Menlo Park, California

B. Rosenshine

Disabled Adults: Educational Provision

The World Health Organization (WHO) gives definitions of impairment, disability, and handicap. An impairment is any loss or abnormality of psychological, physiological, or anatomical structure or function. A disability is any restriction or lack (resulting from an impairment) of ability to perform an activity in the manner or within the range considered normal for a human being. A handicap is a disadvantage for a given individual, resulting from an impairment or a disability, that limits or prevents the fulfillment of a role that is normal (depending on age, sex, and social and cultural factors) for that individual. This article examines the educational needs, and the provision made for them, of disabled adults, that is, those who have physical or mental impairments which substantially limit their life functions. These include caring for themselves and others, fulfilling work and social roles, engaging in physical activities, and learning.

The definition and its implications suggest significant guidelines for public policy and the development of programs for disabled adults. The importance of such guidelines was acknowledged by the General Assembly of the United Nations when it proclaimed 1981 as the International Year of Disabled Persons (IYDP). The United Nations also specified objectives aimed at assisting disabled persons to overcome barriers, to adjust to society, and to obtain needed training and education; encouraging research designed to improve the physical environment for disabled persons; educating the public concerning the rights of disabled persons; and preventing disability and rehabilitating disabled persons.

Like everyone else, the disabled need social contacts. They also need to acquire new knowledge and new skills, and opportunities to use them, and to advance their personal development. They are, however, more frequently and more sharply aware of the obstacles in their environment than are other people.

Even with normally functioning adults, it is necessary to consider their specific characteristics and needs as learners. Planning for disabled adults must be based as well on an understanding of the difficulties they experience in society at large as a result of their condition.

1. Barriers in the Way of Disabled Adults

The following interrelated barriers in the way of disabled adults have been noted: architectural, attitudinal, occupational, legal, personal, and educational (Bowe 1978).

1.1 Architectural

These barriers refer to such obstacles as curbs, stairs, and narrow doorways. In recent years, in the United States, federal laws have been passed requiring removal of such barriers, or special provisions for the disabled, in present buildings and new buildings.

1.2 Attitudinal

Historically, attitudes toward the disabled have been shaped by a wide spectrum of beliefs. These include the Greek view that the physically disabled are inferior, the Hebraic view that the sick are being punished by God, the Christian view that moral virtue is served in helping the disabled, the Calvinistic assumption that failure in life attributable to a disability is visible evidence of lack of grace, Darwin's theory of the survival of the fittest, and faith in humankind's progress through science and technology (Gellman 1973 p. 6). In many countries, ignorant or negative attitudes toward disabled adults have changed for the better. The change is partly due to passage of legislation forbidding the exclusion of qualified handicapped persons from employment

by reason of their handicap; and partly due to strides toward their rehabilitation made by the medical profession.

1.3 Occupational

In many countries the occupational problems of the disabled relate to difficulties in obtaining employment, to underemployment, seasonal employment, part-time employment, and minimum wage jobs with little security and high turnover (Bowe 1978 pp. 27–30). Such job discrimination often occurs in countries that give the highest priority to maximum production. The reason is that organizations hiring disabled adults must make certain modifications to accommodate their needs, and these modifications increase costs and may slow production.

1.4 Legal

Although legislation has greatly helped the legal position of disabled adults with respect to access to buildings, transportation, civil rights, housing, and education, many laws are symbolic or not adequately enforced. Also, disabled adults are often poorly informed about the legal protection available to them, because of dissemination problems. For example, public service announcements frequently convey insufficient information, or the information is not specific enough. Moreover, disabled adults can be difficult to reach. Sometimes they resist being "found," because of their sensitivity about their condition.

1.5 Personal

Inferior education or training and low incomes pose restrictions for some disabled adults. Often these restrictions, combined with the disability, induce a low self-concept which further hinders them in their search for satisfying activity. Others compensate for disabilities by overachieving. Still others try to hide disabilities and suffer anxiety in the process, or they withdraw from society. Disabled adults are vulnerable to attacks by thieves, rapists, and the like (Bowe 1978).

1.6 Educational

A major educational problem with disabled adults arises from the fact that their early education was restricted or interrupted because of their disabilities. This circumstance has limited their ability to take advantage of later opportunities to continue learning.

2. Adult Education

Adult education for the disabled embraces rehabilitation, training, vocational education, and general education (see *Vocational and Industrial Education for Special Groups*). Its clientele include the physically disabled, the learning disabled, and the developmentally disabled. A fourth group, the socially disabled, is considered elsewhere (see *Adult Literacy: Developed Countries*). A fifth population, the psychologically disabled, is not included in this article because programs for the emotionally disturbed, for instance, require therapeutic assistance that does not come within the scope of adult education.

2.1 Physically Disabled

Many countries have legislation and regulations related to the education of the handicapped, much of it covering all the kinds of impairment treated in this article. In terms of implementation, however, it is the physically disabled who benefit most from the laws, partly because of the numbers requiring assistance. In the United States the number of physically disabled of all ages has been estimated as 11.4 million with visual impairment, 16.2 million having hearing disabilities, 1.2 million speech impaired, 1.5 million suffering partial paralysis, 358,000 with missing extremities, and 19.5 million with orthopedic disabilities (Feller 1981). Other countries have comparable populations.

The genesis of most educational programs for physically disabled adults can be traced to advances made during the First World War in orthopedic surgery and the advent of physical and occupational therapy. Initially rehabilitation was medically oriented, aimed at physical recovery, but later the concept embraced the social and work roles of the disabled and led to vocational rehabilitation programs that prepared them for the competitive labor market. For the severely disabled, however, competitive employment is an unrealistic goal, and so emphasis is placed on interpersonal and intrapsychic aspects of work through vocational rehabilitation programs offered in sheltered workshops or in homes.

In the United States, the initial success of vocational rehabilitation was achieved with First World War veterans, and led to the passage of a 1920 act designed to develop a similar program for civilians. The program for Second World War veterans was the most significant for the development of rehabilitation. It included education and rehabilitation counseling and job placement. The passage of the 1954 Vocational Rehabilitation Act Amendments extended the services to disabled civilians. Between 1954 and 1972, the composition of this group expanded from the physically disabled to persons separated from work for physical or psychosocial reasons (Gellman 1973 pp. 7–9).

The passage of the 1973 Rehabilitation Act extended affirmative action and antidiscrimination provisions to the disabled. These provisions applied to schools, colleges, and social service agencies in receipt of federal funds. In addition, the act recommended nondiscriminatory practices for colleges and other postsecondary institutions in the recruitment, admission, and treatment of the disabled.

These practices relate to testing, accessibility of programs by elimination of architectural barriers, and policies that support flexible programs for disabled adults. Finally, the act not only clarified their rights and responsibilities; it came closer to making rehabilitation programs an entitlement, rather than discretionary actions by agencies or counselors.

Other countries have legislation with similar aims. In the Federal Republic of Germany, for example, special provisions to facilitate the training of disabled persons for employment were introduced for the first time in the Vocational Education Act of 1969. The 1974 Law on the Integration of the Severely Handicapped in the World of Work and Society authorized the establishment of sheltered workshops in which those too severely disabled to find work in the open labor market may obtain work training and occupational therapy. The 1974 Law on Social Assistance contains further provisions to enable disabled persons to undertake occupational training (Sutter and Schulte 1981).

In the United Kingdom, the 1970 Chronically Sick and Disabled Persons Act lays upon local authorities a statutory duty to ascertain the number of disabled and chronically sick people living in their areas and to provide them with any help they need. Information is to be given concerning assistance in obtaining recreation and education services, and educational establishments are required to furnish physical facilities to meet the needs of the disabled (Groombridge 1981).

In Denmark the Act on Leisure-time Instruction 1968, lays down that special education must be available for both the physically and mentally handicapped. Other legislation decrees that rehabilitation centers must establish courses for retraining and vocational education. In Norway, responsibility for the education of physically and otherwise handicapped persons is laid upon the education and social welfare authorities (Nordic Council 1976).

There is a considerable gap, however, between the passage of legislation and its implementation. Of the 1970 law in the United Kingdom it has been written "This Act has not been consistently interpreted or vigorously enforced" (Groombridge 1981). Provision has grown, but unevenly and uncertainly.

In most countries the emphasis has been on rendering disabled persons capable of earning a living as far as possible. The Federal Republic of Germany has a network of vocational rehabilitation centers in which vocational training for the handicapped goes with intensive medical, social, and psychological care (Sutter and Schulte 1981). At vocational promotion institutions handicapped persons between the ages of 18 and 59 are trained for qualifications up to higher education level. In the United Kingdom the Manpower Services Commission also runs Employment Rehabilitation Centres, where both rehabilitation and assessment are carried out, after which disabled adults may proceed to sheltered work or to further training in Skill Centres or colleges of further education.

General education for the disabled tends to be more unevenly distributed. In the United Kingdom local authorities, which have considerable autonomy in educational provision, vary greatly in their attitude. Only a few have a coherent policy of education for disabled adults backed by the allocation of financial resources. On the whole, policy is directed towards making it possible for the disabled to be integrated into ordinary adult education programs. Also, a number of day centers for the physically handicapped exist throughout the country. Most offer occupational therapy, discussions, and lectures, and they are extending their formal adult education work. Local authorities also employ teachers to give courses in hospitals and residential homes.

Distance education has particular attractions for disabled adults (see *Distance Education*). Such institutions as the Federal German *Telekolleg* and *Télé-enseignement* in France offer multimedia educational programs based on television which enable the house-bound to participate. Concern for the disabled has perhaps been carried furthest by the United Kingdom Open University (see *Open University of the United Kingdom*) which has been very successful in attracting and retaining disabled students. It has a special department for them and its counseling service is geared to identifying special needs and giving practical assistance.

Those whose sight or hearing is impaired have particular problems in participating in education. In the Federal Republic of Germany the German Educational Institution for the Blind is engaged in the preparation of distance learning courses leading to state examinations in the general and vocational sectors. The Open University has taped most of its material for the visually handicapped, in many cases with tactual diagrams. For those with hearing difficulties, transcripts of radio and television programs are available on request.

2.2 Learning Disabled

The learning disabled are a more restricted and neglected group. The following is a comprehensive definition of the term "learning disabilities":

> . . . a disorder in one or more of the basic psychological processes involved in understanding or in using language, spoken or written, which may manifest itself in an imperfect ability to listen, think, speak, read, write, spell, or do mathematical computations. The term includes such conditions as perceptual handicaps, brain injury, minimal brain dysfunction, dyslexia, and developmental aphasia. (United States Office of Education 1977 p. 65083)

In North America where a number of programs began in 1963, the study of learning disabilities has focused primarily on children. Today it is difficult to locate those learning disabled adults who left school before 1963 or who have not been diagnosed as learning disabled. One reason why their problems continue to be ignored is that by the time people reach adulthood, they have acquired certain minimal coping behaviors which assist them in their jobs and their personal lives, but which do not allow adults to learn to their fullest potential. Many such persons enroll in adult basic education classes, but failure to fulfill their learning needs contributes to their high attrition rate. Work on adult illiteracy in developed countries has drawn attention to the plight of other disabled adults (see *Adult Literacy: Developed Countries*). However, in the United States, as in other countries, learning disabled adults have attracted little help, although the 1968 amendments to the Vocational Education Act and the 1973 Vocational Rehabilitation Act attempted to equip the learning disabled with marketable skills through specific job training. However, in both Canada and the United States, educators still need to recognize that the learning disabled constitute a special population and that their problems demand concerned joint efforts by adult educators and learning disability specialists.

2.3 Developmentally Disabled

The "developmentally disabled," more commonly known as the "mentally retarded," are those whose intellect functions at less than average efficiency. The condition, which may begin before birth, originates in genetic disorders, effects of disease and injury, or environmental factors. Three percent of the world's population is developmentally disabled. An estimated 6 million Americans, over half of them adults, are developmentally disabled. In the past, people in this group were usually institutionalized, in response to society's view of their condition. That view included the convictions that the developmentally disabled constituted a menace to society; that society had an obligation to provide care for them in an institutional setting; that the developmentally disabled are "eternal children" dependent on institutional care; and that they are unwell and need treatment or rehabilitation (Roos 1976).

Another problem relates to the schooling of the noninstitutionalized developmentally disabled. The child who left public school in the early grades usually failed to achieve social maturity or to obtain the training needed to cope with life.

In North America, in the late 1960s, a process of developmental growth was seen as attainable for the developmentally disabled; that is, the individual was considered capable of acquiring and maintaining acceptable personal behavior. Using a variety of delivery systems, programs have been designed around the learning capacities of adults whose degree of retardation has been classified from "profoundly retarded" to "mildly retarded." Facilities include sheltered workshops, which embrace a variety of services, including training, counseling, work experience, job placement, and follow up; community-supported centers offering purposeful activities for the developmentally disabled; and vocational rehabilitation programs that combine work study with counseling to train and place their clients. The curricula range from motor skill development and occupational training for individuals preparing for employment to recreational and socialization skills for those less able to achieve social relationships. Although the worth of these programs has been demonstrated in various countries, funding for them is still very limited.

It has been estimated that one person in every 100 in the United Kingdom is mentally retarded, therefore it is reasonable to assume that the total of mentally retarded/handicapped people is about half a million. Although some live with their families, the majority live in hospitals, hostels, or group homes. Consequently, the bulk of adult education provision for the mentally retarded over the years has taken the form of classes organized in the hospitals where they live. It is likely that most of those courses were in the category of arts and crafts. Some courses have been financed by local authorities and others by social services departments, but most have been organized by the hospitals and their management committees. The disadvantage of this "internal" system was that the students did not experience a change of environment when they attended a class, nor did they meet other people engaged in adult education activities. To overcome these disadvantages, experiments have been conducted whereby hospitalized mentally handicapped adults have attended courses in a local education center. Although initially they attended segregated classes, some were able later to attend general public classes and to benefit greatly from them.

3. Research

Most research into the education of the disabled has concentrated on children. There has been little study of disabled adults. In the United Kingdom the majority of studies have been local and lack a comparative or national dimension. They are concerned with the scale of provision, the nature of demand, and the problems of meeting it. For example, in 1970, it was found that 11 percent of local authorities made specific provision for blind students, 28 percent for the mentally handicapped, and there was no information available on the hard of hearing for lack of a national pattern of provision (Clyne 1972). A more recent study showed that in English and Welsh county boroughs there were 242 courses for the physically handicapped other than the blind and partially sighted (207) and the hearing handicapped (190) (Osborn et al. 1980). Disabled prefer to attend ordi-

nary classes rather than ones specifically designed for them. Researchers agree that the disabled have special problems of access, transport, special equipment, counseling, support, and financial assistance (Osborn et al. 1980).

In Sweden the long-term outreach program *Fövux* was aimed at adults with defective vision, hearing defects, and orthopedic handicaps among other categories (see *Outreach in Adult Education*). Experimental folk high school courses have been provided for similar groups. There has been evidence of substantial response to these offers of study opportunities.

A review of the literature in the United States shows that work on mentally handicapped adults was sparse and of recent origin (Long 1973). Provision was inadequate, but retarded adults could achieve fair levels of independence through vocational rehabilitation. This is confirmed by other work (Howard 1975). Evidence also shows that better results are achieved in open rather than segregated learning situations. Almost all aspects of education for disabled adults require further study—the numbers within different handicapped groups, the impact of courses on students' lives, organization of provision, the training of tutors, counseling, normalization programs. In particular, there is very little literature on instructional techniques for the disabled, yet there are grounds for believing that some disabled adults, at least, require teaching methods tailored to their situation and teachers trained in their use.

See also: Vocational and Industrial Education for Special Groups; Adult Literacy: Developed Countries

Bibliography

Anderson D, Niemi J A 1969 *Adult Education and the Disadvantaged Adult.* Syracuse University, Syracuse New York

Bowe F 1978 *Handicapping America: Barriers to Disabled People.* Harper and Row, New York

Brooks R B 1978 Adult education and the mentally handicapped student. *Adult Educ.* 51(4)

Brooks R B 1980 Adult education and the mentally handicapped. *Newsletter of the European Bureau of Adult Education* December

Carnes G D 1979 *European Rehabilitation Service Providers and Programs.* Michigan State University, East Lansing, Michigan

Clyne P 1972 *The Disadvantaged Adult: Educational and Social Needs of Minority Groups.* Longmans, London

Feller B A 1981 Prevalence of selected impairments. *Prevalence of Selected Impairments, United States 1977.* United States Department of Health and Human Services, Public Health Service, Office of Health Research, Statistics, and Technology, National Center for Health Statistics. Hyattsville, Maryland

Gellman W 1973 Fundamentals of rehabilitation. In: Garrett J F, Levine E S (eds.) 1973 *Rehabilitation Practices with the Physically Disabled.* Columbia University Press, New York

Groombridge B 1981 Education and disadvantaged adults in the United Kingdom 1970–1979. *Learning Opportunities for Adults*, Vol. 5: *Widening Access for the Disadvantaged*. Organisation for Economic Co-operation and Development, Paris

Howard M 1975 Adult training centres: The trainees and their instructors. *Adult Educ.* 48: 88–94

Long H B 1973 *The Education of the Mentally Retarded Adult: A Selective Review of Recent Literature.* ERIC Clearinghouse on Adult Education, Adult Education Association of the United States, Washington, DC

Nordic Council 1976 *Adult Education in the Nordic Countries: Nordic Co-operation in the Field of Education.* Nordic Council, Stockholm

Northcutt N 1975 *Adult Functional Competency: A Summary.* University of Texas, Austin, Texas

Osborn M, Withnall A W, Charnley A H 1980 *Review of Existing Research in Adult and Continuing Education,* Vol. 3: *The Disadvantaged.* National Institute of Adult Education (England and Wales), Leicester

Roos P 1976 *Trends in Residential Institutions for the Mentally Retarded.* Trends in Education Series. United Council for Educational Administration, Columbus, Ohio

Sutter H, Schulte E 1981 A German case study. *Learning Opportunities for Adults*, Vol. 5: *Widening Access for the Disadvantaged*. Organisation for Economic Co-operation and Development, Paris

United Nations General Assembly, December 20, 1971 *Declaration on the Rights of Mentally Retarded Persons.* A/RES/2856 (XXVI), New York

United States Office of Education 1977 *Assistance to States: Procedures for Evaluating Learning Disabilities.* Washington Federal Registrar, Washington, DC

J. A. Niemi; H. Dahlgren; R. B. Brooks

Discipline and Conduct in Schools

Discipline is integrally related to the culture of a social system, both national and communal. Norms and mores impact heavily upon educational systems and upon their students as well. The values which determine desirable conduct derive from cultural imperatives as do the means for educating youth (and others) into that behavior. Indeed, what is desired as disciplined behavior, and the methods used to attain such behavior, are perhaps better gauges of the link between schooling and social values than any other factor in the school (Montagu 1978).

Research into student conduct and school discipline has ignored those influences over human behavior which are subtle, tacit, and difficult to measure. Researchers schooled too narrowly in scientific methods in the Western traditions shun concepts which are inherently normative, such as discipline. So the topic has received more philosophical (metaphysical) attention than scientific investigation and its understanding has had to await less purist methods and observation from anthropologists and behavioral scientists who are not dismayed by the complexity of human interactions.

1. Sources of Recent Concern About Pupil Conduct

Discipline and pupil conduct have always been concerns for school personnel and, to a lesser extent, for parents and the general public. Since the early 1960s, however, discipline and conduct have become major issues for public discussion. The concern seems to be worldwide, though more is known about the situation in the United States and Western Europe.

Widespread concern emanates from several causes. Following the Second World War, social systems that seemed to be stable and unified began to disintegrate, revealing discrepant and conflicting values and norms. Industrialized, modernized nations began to experience conflicts which arose after high levels of economic and material wealth were achieved and became relatively widespread in populations which had gained sufficient time and energy to feel (if not to understand) the limitations of wealth and the dehumanizing effects of modernization. Less developed nations rushed to modernize by the shortest possible routes, forsaking ancient patterns of behavior that gave stability and meaning to individual and corporate behaviors. Wars, economic necessity, or other motivators caused individuals and families to migrate within nations or among nations, throwing them into circumstances requiring new behaviors for which few had capable tutors. Birth rates soared even in the developed nations. Communities as well as larger entities tried to accommodate youth in larger numbers than ever before, using methods still dependent upon the presumption of established family and community norms and structures. Technological advances came in larger numbers and at a faster pace, eliminating vocations and introducing new job requirements faster than preparation and retraining could proceed. All of those changes came together in a discoordinate manner, producing a bewildering array of demands upon institutions poorly designed for rapid and novel adaptation.

Concern about discipline has increased proportionately with the extension of schooling to populations which are new to the school system. The concern seems to reside as much in the school staff's fears as in students' behaviors. In the United States, concerns about disruptive behavior markedly increased after racially isolated schools were desegregated and high-school programs were extended to include students who would have dropped out (or been forced out) of school prior to 1960.

The United Kingdom seems to be experiencing similar problems as it incorporates excolonial minorities into its school system, though their attempts to democratize the school system have yielded valuable information about educating disadvantaged students. New nations, such as Israel, which are determined to bring diverse populations into full participation in their system, have also experimented with various ways to socialize students. Soviet and Chinese pedagogy, developed to support their respective ideologies, emphasizes responsibilities to the group and stresses active learning both in and out of the formal curriculum, a methodology which would appear to be effective for enculturating students in other nations as well.

2. Sources of Confusion About Maintaining Discipline in Schools

Discussions of discipline can become heated, pointless, and confusing if discussants do not differentiate among the various meanings given the term and the many influences upon behavior. More confusion is inherent in the etymology of the word in its English meaning. On the one hand discipline means to correct behavior by exerting external controls. On another, discipline means to develop internal controls over one's own behavior. The extreme interpretations of these two meanings often preclude explorations of the relationship between external environment and personality in the formulation of desirable behaviors.

Another source of confusion is the tendency to overgeneralize from a few cases. Misbehavior occurs among a small percentage of students at any given time in all but the most dreadful schools, but these are so few in number that they constitute an elusive sample for study.

Some of the Western nations have confounded the discussion of school discipline by including criminal behaviors and exaggerating their frequency. Research from the United States and the United Kingdom shows clearly that such criminal behavior comprises a very small part of the discipline problem in schools even in the worst situations. Most serious occurrences take place after school hours and are perpetrated by persons who are neither employed nor enrolled in the school.

Another source of confusion about discipline arises from disagreement about whether it can or should be taught in schools. Statements that discipline should be taught in the home, or the church, or that it is absorbed from the society at large often appear side by side with charges that schools have abdicated responsibility for turning out disciplined students.

In general, though not in all instances, in the United States socialization in schools is subtle and tacit. In the United Kingdom it appears to be somewhat more explicit, though still shunned by some educators as endangering "more appropriate" goals for schooling. In the Soviet Union and some of the Third World nations the process is more openly expressed as an outcome for schooling and more consciously pursued both in teacher preparation and in curriculum.

3. Concepts about How Behavior is Learned

Almost all studies of discipline and recommendations about discipline may be traced to one of three paradigms that govern conceptions about the causes of undesired behavior and the types of behavior that are desired from children. In one paradigm, the cause for misbehavior is assumed to reside within the individual and misconduct arises because of bad tendencies, innate qualities, or willful maladaptation. In a second paradigm, behavior is seen to be caused by external forces that impinge upon the individual in ways that elicit undesired behavior. In a third paradigm, behavior is seen as a result of transactions between individuals and environmental forces. Here, both individual characteristics and environmental ones are considered important determinants of behavior. The paradigm influences the actions taken to improve school discipline and it delimits what is studied in the attempt to understand, predict, and control discipline.

4. Studying Discipline and Conduct in Education

Studies of school discipline include status studies which attempt to describe discipline problems which exist in educational institutions; research on the use of techniques to help or to control individuals; research on classroom strategies and tactics; and studies of the effects of school characteristics.

4.1 Status Studies

Much of the literature on school discipline, in the United States at least, describes the current state of discipline problems in the schools. Such studies present statistics showing the number of suspensions, infractions of various kinds, teachers' opinions, or—if violence and crime are investigated—incidence of assault, vandalism, thefts, injuries, or cost of damage to property. They attempt to describe the situation in schools in ways that will indicate the nature and seriousness of the problem. For example, in London, Metropolitan Police figures indicate that a school or college is 38 times more likely to be burgled than a residential dwelling. Studies in the United States show that property there is similarly vulnerable. McKinna and Reynolds' (1978) status study of truancy in Australia indicates that truancy is a sizeable problem that is worsened by impersonal and overformalized treatments.

Most studies indicate that typical discipline problems are relatively minor. Thefts, for example, are usually petty, such as "taking" an eraser. A committee of the Australian Education Department suggested that the most frequently occurring disciplinary problems reported by teachers were failure to come to class equipped for lessons, noncompliance with school rules, failure to complete classroom work commensurate with ability, causing disturbance in class, and arriving late. The same problems appear in United States classrooms, and they have been reported since the early twentieth century; however, they occur more frequently now.

Policy makers and administrators in United States and former British Commonwealth nations have a tendency to react to status studies by imposing more stringent rule systems and codes of conduct with harsher punishments. Suspension and corporal punishment are frequently used, supposedly as deterrents to inappropriate behavior. American educators use corporal punishment frequently and for all degrees of infractions (Hyman and Wise 1980) despite a public misconception that the courts have outlawed the practice. Australian educators report much reliance on caning (McKinna and Reynolds 1978). The London *Times Educational Supplement* (May 3 1982 pp. 10–11) cites frequent corporal punishment in schools in English-speaking countries. The right to administer corporal punishment has been questioned in Europe at the Court of Human Rights, in response to complaints lodged by two Scottish mothers. The Court ruled that parents have the right to reject corporal punishment for their children. Many organizations in the United Kingdom such as the Society of Teachers Opposed to Physical Punishment and the National Confederation of Parent–Teacher Associations have welcomed the ruling. The Scottish Council for Research in Education conducted 600 hours of observation in 13 schools, five of which had abolished, or were about to abolish, the belt. Schools which had abolished corporal punishment seemed to have more coherent discipline policies and pupil–teacher relationships tended to improve. Heads (principals) tended to be the key figures in phasing out the belt successfully.

Most European countries have either never practiced corporal punishment or have abolished it, with Poland leading that movement in 1883. Alternatives to physical punishment vary. In Italy, teachers use a hierarchy of sanctions from private admonition to expulsion from all schools in the country. In the Federal Republic of Germany, offenses are recorded and parents are called. In France, poor conduct can result in the stopping of family allowances.

Student advocacy organizations such as the Children's Defense Fund (1974 and 1975) have shown that students are frequently suspended from schools in the United States, though rates vary widely among schools. More students are suspended when school systems desegregate; and black, poor, male, and low-achieving students are suspended in greater proportions than others. A small number of suspensions are given for serious offenses while nearly 25 percent of all suspensions are for truancy and tardiness. Suspension for truancy and class cutting seems to reward students by giving them the release from school that they seem to want but can ill afford. School administrators in the United States have responded to criticism against suspensions by adopting "in-school suspension programs" which allow students to remain in school in an alternative setting such as a study room. Alternatives to suspension must go beyond punishment to include activities aimed at changing the student's and the school's orientation to one another.

4.2 Individual Approaches

The common belief in the United States is that deviant behavior must be treated as a defect in the individual. Accordingly, it would be expected that much research on discipline and student conduct would focus upon treating the individual miscreant, either through direct interventions or group counseling. B. F. Skinner and his advocates have had profound effect upon school practices with students who are termed "exceptional" in the United States, and behavior modification has influenced some highly publicized approaches which have had mixed reaction from American educators. Interactive strategies developed by William Glasser, Rudolf Dreikurs, and Thomas Gordon have gained acceptance among some United States educators. Kurt Lewin and his students have influenced education in the United States (as they have international management systems) to look beyond assumed defects in individuals to see their interaction with the perceived world as the cause for behavior (including misbehavior).

Many Asian and European educators seem to approach their work with great regard for social impacts upon the individual. Parry-Jones and Gay (1980) sketch findings from several sources, including various United States scholars, as they describe a way for teachers to view disruptive interaction in classrooms. Their approaches could be emulated by other schools. Some characteristics common to all the studies were strong administrative leadership, high expectations, and belief that students could learn.

4.3 Classroom Management Strategies

A number of studies explore and test specific strategies and approaches used by teachers in classrooms to prevent or to deal with disruptive behavior. Kounin's work (1970) serves as a foundation for many such studies in the United States. Brophy and Evertson relate discipline to a number of instructional practices, such as planning, organization, and management.

Cummings' observations in Japanese schools (1980) suggest that such teacher behaviors as setting a fast classroom pace with many activities, announcing classroom rules, and monitoring students to be sure that they comply are associated with fewer discipline problems. Japanese teachers also use a complex set of subgrouping strategies to help students learn to work with each other.

Willower and others (Licata and Willower 1975) have related teachers' actions to basic ideology about the roles of students and teachers and the nature of control. Disciplining may be closely related to the educator's (and the culture's) beliefs about whether people, including students, are essentially good or bad, similar to the beliefs about workers set forth by McGregor's Theory X and Theory Y.

4.4 Studies of School Influences

A growing body of research suggests that student behavior may be affected more by the school climate or "ethos" than by individual characteristics. Research on "effective" schools suggests the wisdom of using systemic approaches to control and direct complex social patterns within schools so they will influence students and staff members toward disciplined production. Studies by Brookover and Lezotte, Edmonds and Frediriksen, and Phi Delta Kappa (D'Amico 1982) gathered descriptive data from schools where achievement and productivity were high. Each group of researchers attempted to distill the data into a list of characteristics that might reduce such problems. The Phi Delta Kappa Commission on Discipline (Wayson et al. 1982) found that United States and Canadian schools seemed to reduce discipline problems by improving operations in eight areas:

(a) the way people work together to solve problems and make decisions;

(b) the way authority and status are distributed;

(c) the degree to which students feel they belong in the school;

(d) the way rules are developed, understood, and enforced;

(e) the formal curriculum and the styles of instruction;

(f) the way personal problems are handled for both staff and students;

(g) relationships with parents and the community; and

(h) the appearance, organization, and utilization of the building and grounds.

Both the Safe Schools Study and "effective" schools literature indicated the importance of the principal or head teacher for fostering a school climate that supports positive behavior and self-discipline. Good schools do not adopt new practices or faddish panaceas; rather they effectively implement practices that have been advocated for bringing the student and the staff into deeper personal involvement with educative experiences.

See also: Behaviour Problems in the Classroom; Truancy; Punishment

Bibliography

Children's Defense Fund 1974 *Children Out of School in America: A Report.* Children's Defense Fund, Cambridge, Massachusetts
Children's Defense Fund 1975 *School Suspensions: Are They Helping Children? A Report.* Children's Defense Fund, Cambridge, Massachusetts
Cummings W K 1980 *Education and Equality in Japan.* Princeton University Press, Princeton, New Jersey
D'Amico J 1982 Each effective school may be one of a kind. *Educ. Leadership* 40(3): 61–62
Education Department of Western Australia 1972 Nature and extent of the discipline problem. In: D'urso S, Smith R A (eds.) 1978 *Changes, Issues and Prospects in Australian Education.* University of Queensland Press, St. Lucia, Queensland
Francis P 1975 *Beyond Control? A Study of Discipline in the Comprehensive School.* Allen and Unwin, London
Hyman I A, Wise J H (eds.) 1980 *Corporal Punishment in American Education: Readings in History, Practice, and Alternatives.* Temple University Press, Philadelphia, Pennsylvania
Kounin J S 1970 *Discipline and Group Management in Classrooms.* Holt, Rinehart and Winston, New York
Licata J, Willower D 1975 Student brinkmanship and the school as a social system. *Educ. Admin. Q.* 11(2): 1–15
Lunacharsky A V 1981 *On Education: Selected Articles and Speeches.* Progress Publishers, Moscow
McKinna C, Reynolds A 1978 Truancy: The size of the problem and some suggestions. In: D'urso S, Smith R A (eds.) 1978 *Changes, Issues and Prospects in Australian Education.* University of Queensland Press, St. Lucia, Queensland
Makarenko A S 1935 *The Road to Life: An Epic of Education.* Progress Publishers, Moscow
Montagu A (ed.) 1978 *Learning Non-aggression: The Experience of Non-literate Societies.* Oxford University Press, New York
Parry-Jones W L, Gay B M 1980 The anatomy of disruption: A preliminary consideration of interaction sequences within disruptive incidents. *Oxf. Rev. Educ.* 6(3): 213–20
Rutter M, Maughan B, Mortimore P, Ouston J, Smith A 1979 *Fifteen Thousand Hours: Secondary Schools and Their Effects on Children.* Open Books, London
United States Department of Health, Education, and Welfare 1978 *Violent Schools—Safe Schools: The Safe School Study Report to the Congress.* Report No. HE 19.202: Sch. 6/3/v.1. US Government Printing Office, Washington, DC
Wayson W, DeVoss G, Kaeser S, Lasley T, Pinnell G 1982 *Handbook for Developing Schools With Good Discipline.* Phi Delta Kappa, Bloomington, Indiana

W. W. Wayson; G. S. Pinnell

Discipline and Human Development

One of the major concerns of public education is managing student behavior. A series of studies (Cichon and Kloff 1978, NYSUT 1979, Bloch 1978) have found that teachers consistently rate "managing disruptive students" to be the leading stressor in their professional lives. According to O'Malley and Eisenberg (1973), for example, 5 to 10 percent of school-aged children are diagnosed as hyperactive. Fourteen consecutive Gallup polls have shown discipline to be the public's number one concern regarding its schools.

1. Causes of Misbehavior

Why do children misbehave? Many explanations have at one time or another been put forward as the primary causes of misbehavior: children wanting attention, being bored, feeling unfairly treated, not trusting adults or other children, experiencing school failure, being treated like spoiled brats, wanting power or control over others, having to prove something to friends, fearing, feeling rejected and/or frustrated, having poor nutritional habits and biochemical or neurological disorders. Probably some or all of these reasons are valid in certain cases.

The biochemical/neurological model postulates that misbehavior is related to neurologic or chemical imbalance problems, and treatment is often directed at altering the internal state of the child through diet and/or medication. The behavioral model suggests that all behavior is learned and that more appropriate behavior can be trained through the use of reinforcement. Cognitive theorists attend to faulty beliefs or self-statements and work at helping children to gain self-control by modifying their thinking. Affective approaches point to the necessity of an acceptant, nonjudgmental environment that encourages children to express their feelings. Misbehavior, according to this view, is caused by frustration when "significant others" fail to attend to the child's needs.

2. What is Discipline?

Curwin and Mendler (1980) define a classroom discipline problem as a situation in which the needs of the individual conflict with the needs of the group or authority who represents the group. When an individual behaves in a way that meets his or her needs, or at least that he or she perceives meets his or her needs, and these behaviors prevent the group from meeting group needs, then a discipline event occurs. In school, this typically means that a discipline event occurs when a student's behavior prevents other students from learning, or the teacher from teaching.

Self-discipline means that an individual is able to select which appropriate needs will be met at a given time, and is able to express those needs with regard to the social context in which they occur. Thus, a self-disciplined student is able to focus his or her attention on the task at hand, and reserve focusing his or her attention to other stimuli until a more appropriate time.

3. Theories of Discipline

The work of most theorists can be viewed as a continuum that ranges from those who favor an internal-control approach that tends to view the individual's needs as more important than those of the group or authority, to those who favor strict and complete control in which the needs of the group or authority are emphasized.

3.1 Internal Control

One set of theorists proposes that the more the school attempts to coerce, manipulate, control, and shape the behavior of students, the greater is the likelihood of discipline problems. The cause of discipline problems is seen as the result of the school's interference with the natural growth process of the child. The seeds for this position, which holds that there is a necessity to structure the learning environment so as to attend to the individual needs of each learner, can be traced to Plato. He discussed differences among individuals and recommended that steps be taken to discover each child's outstanding aptitude so that education and training along the lines of his or her particular talents might begin early. Rousseau suggested that no great harm to the child or to society will result if the child grows with little adult supervision and direction. Much later, John Dewey, a New England-born philosopher, said that children must have an opportunity to make their own choices, and then to try their choices for themselves so that they can give them the only final test—that of action. He thought this to be the only way to learn, which leads one to discover actions that lead to success and those which lead to failure. Snygg and Combs (1949) see learning as a natural and normal activity which is not dependent upon the stimulation of the teacher. It is their notion that adults actually interfere with much childhood learning through attempts to substitute their goals in place of those already possessed by the children.

All of these theorists would argue the virtues of approaches to education that minimize the role of the school as an agent for external control. Since learning is viewed as intrinsically rewarding, outside interference with this process might stimulate the child to resist the efforts of others to shape him or her in a way that is not natural. Discipline problems are therefore attributed to a poorness of fit between the natural growth processes of the child and the demands of the institution. One of the most widely known examples of this approach is A. S. Neill's Summerhill school in England (Neill 1960). Summerhill exemplifies the belief that the school should "fit the child," and Neill notes that in his school "lessons are optional. Children can go to them or stay away from them for years if they want to." He clearly places the needs of the individual above those of the group or authority and cautions against "imposed authority." Implicit in Neill's approach is that when children work joyfully and find happiness, they do not need to misbehave.

3.2 Strict External Control

A contrasting view of the purposes of school, and by implication the discipline methods to be employed, holds that the pleasantness of school is irrelevant and that schools should engage students in a mental toughening process which is of value in itself. The mind is strengthened through a series of difficult and frustrating experiences. John Locke (1934) was committed to the ultimate rationality of humans. He viewed education as a process to promote self-discipline, self-control, and the "power of denying ourselves the satisfaction of our own desires, where reason does not authorize them. From their very early cradles," he argued, "parents must begin instructing children in self-denial." Standards of achievement and behavior are therefore best left to "rational" institutions.

4. Methods of Discipline

Each behavioral school of thought has a set of methods of discipline based upon its theories. Some of these methods are also related to broader psychological principles.

4.1 Client-centered Therapy

This is a therapeutic method developed by Carl Rogers (1969) which involves listening in a reflective way to a person's thoughts and feelings, and then feeding back the message that was heard. The client (student) has the option of agreeing with the feedback if it "fits," or clarifying for himself or herself what it is he or she means. The key concept is that growth occurs in an acceptant, warm, empathic, nonjudgmental environment that allows students the freedom to explore their thoughts and feelings and to solve their own problems. Schools which lack these characteristics are breeding grounds for discipline problems.

Haim Ginott's work extended that of Rogers through the introduction of the concept of limits. Ginott (1972 pp. 147–48) stated that "the essence of discipline is finding effective alternatives to punishment. To punish a child is to enrage him and make him uneducable. He becomes a hostage of hostility, a captive of rancor, a prisoner of vengeance. Suffused with rage and absorbed in grudges, a child has no time or mind for studying. In discipline, whatever generates hate must be avoided. Whatever creates self-esteem is to be fostered." Ginott's model calls for firm limit setting on behavior but never on feelings.

Abraham Maslow constructed a hierarchy of human needs. This is a developmental model suggesting that growth occurs by having sufficient environmental support. The support gradually shifts in emphasis to an individual's ability to nourish and support himself or herself within his or her environment. Maslow (1954) constructed a pyramid that illustrates this shift. At the base of the pyramid are the basic human needs for food, clothing, and shelter. Survival comes first. A child who comes to school hungry will spend most of his or her time thinking and dreaming about food, not mathematics. In other words, this hierarchy of needs proposes that some needs must be met before others because they are more urgent and basic to our life function. People who have needs for security and safety must have these needs satisfied before they can move on to satisfy other needs. A child whose parents are frequently fighting and who threaten to divorce is often preoccupied with fantasies of abandonment. He or she is often motivated to seek security from others; if he or she becomes stuck in this pursuit, then much of his or her energy will be directed toward finding others to take care of him or her. The first two needs at the base of the pyramid are considered "outer needs" and are almost completely dependent upon being received from the environment outside. The next need is for love and belonging, and Bessel spells out four ways in which this need is met. They are (a) "attention" (young people must be aware that others know they exist); (b) "acceptance" (you have a right to be here); (c) "approval" (I like this about you); and (d) "affection" (I like you). Abidin (1976) has discussed the importance of a person's feeling worthwhile, lovable, competent, and responsible in order to develop a positive self-concept.

Factors that contribute to the needs for respect and self-esteem include recognition from others, accomplishments, having goals or a sense of worth, gaining influence, independence, and self-control. Knowledge and understanding are important in order to help children to make decisions which allow them to live their lives more effectively. The final human need is for beauty and self-actualization which is a need to experience the world directly and to be open to it. Maslow described self-actualized people as having their faults, but as perceiving reality more clearly. He viewed them as more creative, tolerant, and spontaneous. They accept themselves and others as they are.

Rudolph Dreikurs (Dreikurs and Soltz 1964) stated that misbehavior occurs because children have developed faulty beliefs about themselves which lead to their having goals which may lead to misbehavior. The goals for misbehavior include attention, power, revenge, and display of inadequacy. Children seek attention when they believe that they belong only when they are being noticed or recognized. Such children are often calling out answers in class, despite repeated admonitions, or cracking jokes which disturb the teacher or the other children. Parents sometimes say that their children will not do their homework unless they are right there. Students make their need for power felt through their faulty belief that they belong only when they are in control or are the boss, or when they are proving that no one else can boss them. Children who refuse to do their homework because it has been assigned by a teacher, or who are always in the middle of disputes and arguments with other students, are showing their need for power. Children want revenge when they believe that they belong only by hurting others as they feel hurt. Such students often see themselves as unworthy and unlovable. Unruly students who are angry with others who have repeatedly let them down may show their hurt through antisocial action. The delinquent population have often developed this belief about themselves. The final faulty belief discussed by Dreikurs is the child who believes that he/she belongs only by convincing others not to expect anything from him or her. This belief is frequently experienced by those who feel hopeless or helpless, by the student who is always at the teacher's desk asking for help and who is mostly pleading ignorance by convincing others that he or she is incapable or stupid. The goal here is the display of inadequacy.

Dreikurs suggests the use of natural or logical consequences for dealing with misbehavior and advises against engaging in power struggles with children. Simply stated, this amounts to making sure that the punishment fits the crime.

4.2 Values Clarification

This is a process that helps youngsters answer some of their questions and build their own value system. It is based on an approach formulated by Louis Raths (Raths et al. 1966). His focus was on how people come to hold certain beliefs and establish certain behavior patterns. He looked at specific behavior problems related to students with unclear values. He found that students with unclear values had one or more of the following characteristics: apathy, flight, uncertainty, inconsistency, drifting, overconforming, overdissenting, or role playing.

According to this model, discipline problems are caused by two factors. Students with unclear values are often experiencing considerable inner turmoil which leads them to engage in a variety of behaviors in an effort to restore themselves to more fluid functioning. In the process of restoration, they may "try on" behaviors that may lead them to conflict with the prevailing school system. The second cause of discipline problems, as viewed through the values-clarification model, occurs when both the identified misbehaving student and the school (teacher, administrator) have clear but different values and when either or both are unable to accept each other's differences.

The importance of values clarification is its emphasis on communication in a nonjudgmental, acceptant atmosphere. All participants, including the teacher, are to be free to share their thoughts, values, and feelings and to learn the values of recognizing and accepting their differences.

4.3 Transactional Analysis

This is concerned with analyzing transactions: analyzing, understanding, and paying attention to what goes on between two or more persons. According to this model, each person has three existing ego states. Even young children have each ego state, although the degree of functioning or voice that each is given is dependent upon one's age, past experiences, and current situation. There is the "parent ego state" which develops through the recordings of "all the admonitions and rules and laws that the child has heard and learned from his parents," parent surrogates, or other authority figures. The parent ego state is subdivided into the critical parent which is righteous, judgmental, and moral, and the nurturant parent, which is giving, loving, and caring. The "child ego state" relates to the feelings of the person and records the feelings of frustration, anger, and hurts in response to parental demands, as well as "creativity, curiosity, the desire to know and explore, and the urge to touch, feel, and experience." Both of these ego states begin at birth. The third ego state is the adult, which acts as a computer, making rational decisions after considering information from the parent, the child, and the data which the adult has accumulated. The adult begins to emerge as people begin to control and manipulate objects in their environment. As the adult develops, it begins to discard some of the messages from the parent that are experienced as inapplicable.

According to the view of transactional analysis (TA), discipline problems are to be viewed in terms of the transactions that occur between people. Discipline problems can be avoided by understanding how a teacher gets hooked into playing a game with a disruptive student, and by being sensitive to his or her own ego state and that of the student at any given moment. The TA model considers both the student and his or her environment as responsible for discipline problems, as well as the interaction of environmental factors.

4.4 Teacher-effectiveness Training

Thomas Gordon's approach to discipline places the focus upon communication as being of primary importance. Gordon (1974) considers his method to be democratic. He suggests that the primary reason that teachers spend so much classroom time with discipline is because of the emphasis on "repressive and power-based methods." These methods include "threats of punishment, actual punishment, and verbal shaming and blaming." He claims that these methods invite "resistance, retaliation, and rebellion" in students. His alternative is to provide teachers with a model of communication that includes "active listening," "I-messages," "problem ownership," and "negotiation."

Glasser (1969) believes that students misbehave as a result of a lack of involvement in the school process. School failure is the cornerstone of his theory of student misbehavior, which can be prevented through involvement, responsibility, and success experiences. He also stresses the importance of success experiences, believing that a child forms his or her self-concept of being a success or a failure between the ages of 5 and 10.

His plan for dealing with misbehavior includes an emphasis on behavior rather than on feelings. His approach is a rational, cognitive one which encourages problem solving by the student and elicits a plan for behavioral change that encourages a commitment from the student. He believes it necessary to reinforce appropriate behavior when the student is being successful. The teacher is advised to have clear rules which are firmly enforced and which are nonpunitive in that blaming and threatening are eliminated. Teachers need to provide students with a friendly greeting and classroom tasks that show the teacher's belief in the student's ability to be responsible.

4.5 Moral Reasoning

Lawrence Kohlberg has made a major contribution to the understanding of "moral development." His model is based on cognitive-developmental theory which suggests that moral reasoning progresses in stages. Kohlberg pays some attention to affective factors, such as guilt and sympathy in decision making, but emphasizes that moral decisions are cognitively developed by the judging individual. Consequently, intelligence and the individual's ability to reason abstractly are important factors in the attainment of an advanced morality.

Kohlberg (1968) defines moral development as occurring and progressing through six stages. Stage 1 is a morality based on an orientation to punishment or reward and to physical and material power. Stage 2 is defined as "social contract orientation" which involves an exchange of favors between people. Stage 3 is called the "good boy" orientation, in which the individual's actions are geared to pleasing others and thereby gaining acceptance from them. Stage 4 is a morality based upon the respect for those in authority. At stage 5, the individual is motivated through the recognition that all individuals have rights, and that each individual has a right to exist regardless of his or her social orientation, status, role, sex, race, or importance. Stage 6 is the "morality of individual principles of conscience" which have "logical comprehensiveness and universality." The highest value is placed on human life, equality, or dignity.

Kohlberg would probably argue that most school discipline problems can generally be viewed as a conflict between the school's stage 1, stage 3, and/or stage 4 morality and the student's stage 2 morality. Less frequently, the student's stages 5 and 6 morality can also lead to conflict for him or her.

4.6 Behavior Modification

This is among the most widely known and extensively researched approaches to classroom management. The basic tenet of behavior modification is that learning depends on events that occur after a certain behavior. E. L. Thorndike (1905), a pioneer learning theorist, developed his law of effect which states that "Any act which in a given situation produces satisfaction becomes associated with that situation, so that when the situation reoccurs, the act is more likely to reoccur. Conversely, any act which in a given situation produces discomfort becomes disassociated from the situation so that when the situation reoccurs, the act is less likely than before to reoccur."

Later on, B. F. Skinner (1968) developed extensive principles of operant conditioning which state that the events which follow a given behavior either strengthen or weaken that behavior. He used the term "reinforcement" to mean those events that follow a behavior and cause that behavior to increase in frequency. Skinner's theory suggests that all behavior is learned, and it is the outside environment that either strengthens or weakens a given behavior. In his paradigm, punishment describes a procedure in which a behavior is followed by an aversive or unpleasant event.

A classroom reinforcer can take several different forms, such as a concrete reward (pieces of candy, money, a small toy), an activity reward (10 minutes of free time for completed work), or a social reward (teacher praise, classroom monitor, etc.); or it can take a negative form, such as the removal of an unpleasant stimulus (the teacher who stops yelling, a loud interfering noise that stops, or the removal from the classroom of a child who hates the class).

Misbehavior occurs because it is reinforced by the environment. The antithesis is to change the child's behavior through a manipulation of his or her environment which reinforces or rewards "good" or socially appropriate behavior. This shaping process occurs through rewarding successive approximations (behaviors which gradually come closer to the desired outcome) of the target behavior. Reinforcement is contingent upon the student's emitting behaviors that are closer to those desired by the teacher. Reinforcement can be given continuously (for each and every appropriate student response) or periodically. Periodic reinforcement can be given on a fixed schedule (i.e. after every fifth appropriate response or after each 5-minute interval of appropriate behavior) or on a variable schedule (i.e. after approximately every fifth appropriate response or approximately 5-minute interval). Research indicates that in the initial phase of behavior shaping, continuous reinforcement is needed until the student gradually progresses to one of the intermittent schedules, which appears to ultimately have the strongest effect.

Proponents of behavior modification suggest the reinforcement of behavior that is incompatible with the student's misbehavior. A person cannot be behaving well and misbehaving at the same time, and by rewarding desired behavior, the probability of that behavior occurring again increases. Most behavior modification proponents advise against the use of punishment because of its well-documented deleterious side effects. If punishment is to be used, it should be done selectively and cautiously. Becker (1971) offers the following outlines:

(a) Effective punishment is given immediately.

(b) Effective punishment relies on taking away reinforcers and provides a clear-cut method for earning them back.

(c) Effective punishment makes use of a warning signal, usually words ("No," "Stop that") prior to punishment.

(d) Effective punishment is carried out in a calm matter-of-fact way.

(e) Effective punishment is given along with such reinforcement for behaviors incompatible with the punished behavior.

(f) Effective punishment is consistent. Reinforcement is not given for the punished behavior.

4.7 Drug Therapy

Proponents of drug therapy in the schools tend to see impulsive youngsters who do not fit any acceptable norm as lacking "self-discipline," "self-control," and the power of self-denial. Whether for biochemical, neurological, or environmental reasons, the goal of drug therapy is to have the child fit within the socially acceptable norm. Its use is designed to control misbehavior that the individual either cannot or will not control. The diagnosis that usually leads to drug therapy is based on parental or school complaints of distractibility, overactivity, inattentiveness, impulsivity, difficulty in disciplining, poor social controls, and academic problems in school. These complaints, coupled with the physician's clinical opinion, may lead to a prescription for psychoactive drugs.

The outcome of most studies indicates that stimulant drugs are generally effective in making the child less distractible, more attentive, less active, and better behaved. Research has generally failed to show positive scholastic results with children who are medicated. Despite numerous studies which have attempted to identify a target population for whom drugs are particularly effective, outcomes suggest that both drug responders and drug nonresponders come from a heterogeneous population that cuts across socioeconomic status and psychiatric or medical diagnoses.

4.8 Three-dimensional Discipline

Curwin and Mendler (1980) suggest a model for discipline which includes helping teachers to choose methods of behavior management based upon their philosophy of education and style of instruction. These authors emphasize the importance of discipline prevention which includes the teacher becoming aware of his behavior, values and attitudes; aware of his students' preferences; able to adequately identify and express feelings; able to participate with the students in formulating classroom rules and consequences; fully knowledgeable of the many theories of discipline and of methods based upon these theories. Prevention is highlighted, and methods of effective action to stop misbehavior when it occurs as well as techniques to help resolve conflict with children who chronically misbehave are offered.

Research with teachers in inner-city environments (Mendler 1981) has shown this program of discipline to be effective in reducing stress associated with disruptive student behavior.

5. Conclusion

Broadly speaking, discipline interventions are conceptualized as those which attempt primarily to alter either behavior (i.e., behavior modification, drug therapy, reality therapy), cognition (Kohlberg, transactional analysis), or affect (Ginott, Maslow, Gordon).

More recently, there have been efforts at integrating pieces of different theories (Meichenbaum and Goodman 1971, Homme et al. 1969, Curwin and Mendler 1980) in efforts to help teachers and students live more compatibly with each other. In each case, the intent is to provide the teacher with a set of skills that either define or facilitate ways to reduce disruptive student behavior so that more time is available for instruction.

See also: Management in the Classroom: Elementary Grades

Bibliography

Abidin R R 1976 *Parenting Skills: Trainer's Manual.* Human Science Press, New York
Becker W C 1971 *Parents are Teachers.* Research Press, Champaign, Illinois
Bloch A M 1978 Combat neurosis in inner-city schools. *Am. J. Psychiatry* 135: 1189–92
Cichon D J, Kloff R H 1978 The teaching events stress inventory. Paper presented at the annual meeting of the American Educational Research Association, Toronto, Ontario, March 27–31 1978
Curwin R L, Mendler A 1980 *The Discipline Book: A Complete Guide to School and Classroom Management.* Reston Publishing, Reston, Virginia

Dreikurs R, Soltz V 1964 *Children: The Challenge.* Duell, Sloane and Pearce, New York

Ginott H G 1972 *Teacher and Child: A Book for Parents and Teachers.* Macmillan, New York

Glasser W 1969 *Schools Without Failure.* Harper and Row, New York

Gordon T 1974 TET: *Teacher Effectiveness Training.* Wyden, New York

Holmes M, Holmes D, Field J 1974 *The Therapeutic Classroom.* Aronson, New York

Homme L, Csanyi A P, Gonzales M A, Rechs J R 1969 *How to Use Contingency Contracting in the Classroom.* Research Press, Champaign, Illinois

Kohlberg L 1968 The child as a moral philosopher. *Psychol. Today* 2(4): 25–30

Locke J 1934 *Some Thoughts Concerning Education.* Cambridge University Press, London

Maslow A H 1954 *Motivation and Personality.* Harper, New York

Meichenbaum D H, Goodman J 1971 Training impulsive children to talk to themselves: A means of developing self-control. *J. Abnorm. Psychol.* 77: 115–26

Mendler A N 1981 The effects of a combined behavioral skills/anxiety management program upon teacher stress and disruptive student behavior (Doctoral dissertation, Union for Experimenting Colleges and Universities). Dissertation Abstracts International, 1982, 42, 3917A. (University Microfilms No. 82-05171)

Neill A S 1960 *Summerhill: A Radical Approach to Child Rearing.* Hart, New York

New York State United Teachers Research and Educational Services (NYSUT) 1979 *New York State United Teachers Stress Survey Bulletin.* New York State United Teachers Research and Educational Services, Albany, New York

O'Malley J E, Eisenberg L 1973 The hyperkinetic syndrome. *Semin. Psychiatry* 5: 95–103

Raths L E, Harmin M, Simon S B 1966 *Values and Teaching: Working with Values in the Classroom.* Merrill, Columbus, Ohio

Rogers C R 1969 *Freedom to Learn: A View of What Education Might Become.* Merrill, Columbus, Ohio

Skinner B F 1968 *The Technology of Teaching.* Appleton Century Crofts, New York

Snygg D, Combs A 1949 *Individual Behavior.* Harper, New York

Thorndike E L 1905 *The Elements of Psychology.* Seiler, New York

R. L. Curwin; A. N. Mendler

Disciplines, Structure of

In curriculum practice, the term "structure" refers both to logical and psychological relationships between content elements. Logical structure establishes relations in terms of properties assumed to adhere to the content itself, for example, necessary relations between addition and subtraction. Psychological structure assigns relations in terms of properties assumed to adhere to the learner, for example, concept requirements based on Piagetian notions of cognitive development. There is a tendency to adopt logically structured content in the senior grades and psychologically structured content in the primary grades.

1. The Significance of Structure of the Disciplines in Education

The educational significance of the notion of the structure of the disciplines resides in the direct and practical effect it has upon planning and structuring curricula. Content sequence and integration, teaching method, and learning style are all related to the concept of structure adopted. Bruner (1963), has argued for the organization of curricula around the fundamental concepts and relationships which constitute, in his view, the structure of any given discipline. Every subject, he suggests, has a structure that provides the underlying simplicity of things, and it is by learning the nature of this structure that the intrinsic meaning of the subject can be appreciated. Such structure-based understanding aids comprehension by stressing fundamentals, makes knowledge gained usable beyond the learning situation, improves memory by organizing facts in terms of principles and ideas from which they may be inferred, and narrows the gap between elementary and advanced knowledge.

Any way of structuring a discipline reflects a theory of knowledge. Accordingly, the study of any curriculum carries with it implications for the learner's understanding of the nature of the world. Thus, for example, curriculum content structured in terms of a principle of induction implies a fixed phenomenal world with corresponding theories and facts. A curriculum structured in deductive terms may have the same implications for phenomena and knowledge. But the two have radically different implications for disciplinary enquiry and for the place of the human agent in enquiry. Another curriculum structure, based on the historical dynamics of enquiry, has other implications for enquiry, knowledge, and phenomena. Such a view would stress the interpretive act in enquiry, implying that all knowledge and, therefore, all phenomena are functions of mental acts. Such a view is usually labeled as a constructionist view.

2. Problems in the Structure of the Disciplines

2.1 Diversity in the Disciplines

Since disciplines, and terms for their structuring, are many, there are numerous plausible structures. Schwab (1964) has developed a typology of three kinds of structural questions that may be asked of the disciplines. The first type of question is one of classification: "What are the disciplines and how do they relate to one another?" For the curriculum designer this question becomes a problem in determining which of the disciplines are to be included in the school curriculum, and in what order. The second kind of question is one of syntax: "What methods are used to obtain warranted knowledge?" The curricular problem becomes one of determining how to reconstruct the history of enquiry in particular topics and of balancing instruction in method with instruction in content. The third type of question is one of substance, posing questions on the conceptual terms which define and bound the subject matter: "What conceptions of the discipline guide enquiry and how do they give rise to different structures?" For the teacher this question becomes one of determining which kinds of questions should be dealt with in the class.

2.2 Metastructure

A very generalized metastructure, which is at once interdisciplinary (see *Interdisciplinary Studies*) and intradisciplinary, has been identified independently by Kuhn (1970) and by Schwab (1964). Kuhn uses the terms paradigm and paradigm shift, with paradigmatic science generated by and succeeded by revolutionary science. Schwab uses the terms stable science and fluid science. The former identifies a series of discrete, relatively short, research programs, each of which is seen in terms of a definitive end and in each of which accuracy and thoroughness are considered a mark of excellence. The latter identifies an examination of principles carried out in research programs in which processes and ends are indeterminate and uncertainty is conspicuous. Both views present a definitive intradisciplinary structure, and a tool for the examination of structures common to the disciplines. Both describe the means by which established disciplines are extended and new disciplines developed. It is of interest that, despite the compatibility between the two views and despite their similarities, comparative discussion of the studies of Schwab and Kuhn has been limited, possibly because Kuhn addresses philosophers of science, whereas Schwab addresses philosophers of education.

2.3 Unification

The notion of unified knowledge, in which each of the disciplines is seen as part of a whole and in which all-embracing general statements are seen to apply to each of the disciplines, provides one way of answering Schwab's first kind of question on the organization of the disciplines. Some unified views are based upon broad themes such as "conservation of mass–energy," "generalized inquiry methods," and "unified field theory." Other unified views focus on topics at the interface of existing disciplines which have led to the creation of interrelated areas of research such as biophysics and biochemistry, or upon topics at the boundaries of established disciplines which have led to the development of new areas of research such as solid state physics.

There are curricular gains, or losses, in adopting either a unified or a categorized view of knowledge.

For instance, curriculum developers, wishing to present a unified world view, have generated integrated courses, such as "unified science," "general science," and "social studies." Some of these courses carry with them the risk that in stressing interconnectivity and unity they may omit knowledge derived from within the separate disciplines.

3. Curriculum Decisions and the Structure of the Disciplines

Considerations of the nature of knowledge, of the structures of the disciplines, and of structural differences apparent between one discipline and another are theoretical issues. They become practical when they are used to support decisions related to content selection, to curriculum organization, to the logical and practical relationship between content and experience, and so on. At the practical level, and within the framework of curriculum deliberation, the decision maker has to integrate considerations related to the concept "structure of the discipline" with those related to societal and to learners' needs, to views about the process of learning, and to the idiosyncrasies of the educational system.

See also: Curriculum Design; Curriculum Areas

Bibliography

Bruner J S 1963 Structures in learning. *Today's Educ.: J. Nat. Educ. Assoc.* 52(3)
Hirst P H 1970 Liberal education and the nature of knowledge. In: Martin J R (ed.) 1970 *Readings in the Philosophy of Education: A Study of Curriculum.* Allyn and Bacon, Boston, Massachusetts
Kuhn T S 1970 The structure of scientific revolutions. *Encyclopedia of Unified Science*, Vol. 2, No. 2. University of Chicago Press, Chicago, Illinois
Schwab J J 1964 Structure of the disciplines: Meanings and significances. In: Ford G W, Pugno L (eds.) 1964 *The Structure of Knowledge and the Curriculum.* 1st curriculum conf. San Jose, California, June 1963. Rand McNally, Chicago, Illinois
Steeves F L 1968 *The Subjects in the Curriculum: Selected Readings.* Odyssey Press, New York
Zais R S 1976 *Curriculum: Principles and Foundations.* Harper and Row, New York

M. Finegold; F. M. Connelly

Discovery- and Inquiry-based Programs

Discovery and inquiry processes can be described as methods of teaching and learning. This article will relate them to recent curriculum efforts, and specific models and classroom applications will be presented to further illustrate the dominant characteristics of the methods. Discovery refers to a process of self-learning whereby learners generate concepts and ideas with very little teacher intervention. Inquiry refers to stages beyond discovery where learners become systematically acquainted with scientific and logical rules used to verify those ideas. In a larger framework, discovery may be thought of as a psychological construct which is based on the concern to provide necessary motivation for students to participate in the generation of new ideas related to the subject of instruction. Inquiry, on the other hand, can be thought of primarily as an intellectual construct (or a construct dealing with Bruner's "analytic thinking") which is based on the concern of enabling students to move, step by step, from hypothesis, to data collection, verification, generalization, and so on. In the complete act of thought, discovery processes are used in the initial perplexing phases of thinking whereas inquiry processes are used in the more advanced formal verification phases. In this context, some may argue that discovery as contrasted to inquiry is more process oriented rather than product oriented (see *Process-oriented and Product-oriented Programs*).

1. What is Discovery?

Studies conducted by Bruner (1960), Thelen (1960), Massialas and Zevin (1967), and others have shown that children, regardless of their age, can fruitfully engage in discovering solutions to psychological or intellectual problems. Engaging in discovery involves the opportunity (a) to make a leap into that part of the world which is unknown to them personally; (b) to project and speculate intelligently, on the basis of limited clues, on underlying principles or generalizations explaining human interactions or physical phenomena; and (c) to develop and refine heuristic devices (conceptual schemes, documentary clues, measuring devices) which can then be used in future investigations. According to Bruner, the highest state of human autonomy and perfection is achieved when children begin to find out for themselves regularities or irregularities in their physical and sociopolitical environments (Bruner 1960).

Discovery-based programs focus on powerful classroom environments using springboards that prompt children and youth to participate in their own learning. These programs assume that children need to be highly motivated through an initial psychological perplexity to engage in meaningful (not memoriter) learning.

2. Applications of Discovery Processes

Bruner tried to recapture the kind of intellectual adventure 10-year-old students experienced when asked to locate Chicago on a physical map of the central states. The map contained all the conventional geographic information—rivers and other large bodies of water, mountains, natural resources,

agricultural products—but it did not include place names. A variety of suggestions and arguments were offered by the students in support of certain desirable locations for Chicago. One associated "big city" with waterways, transportation, and accessibility; another pointed to the fact that cities are large aggregates of people who require "lots of food." The discovery of each principle of urban location served as a clue which induced further learning.

In another situation, reported by Massialas and Zevin (1967), a group of students were asked to identify the country and the approximate year that the population count had been taken on the basis of an "age pyramid," which indicated the age structure in that country. The country's name was not given. A simple pyramid was drawn with five-year intervals (beginning with 0–5 up to 80+) marked on the vertical axis and the percentage of the total population in each group on the horizontal axis. In their search to find a justifiable answer the students explored a number of hunches dealing with birth and infant mortality rates, longevity rates, distribution of sexes, and the like. Virtually all class members participated in drawing further conjectures with regard to relationships between the composition of a population and personnel resources channeled to military, industrial, agricultural, or nonproductive activities. Had the experiences been extended, the students might have been given the opportunity to speculate intelligently and to anticipate the pattern of international politics and the complicated system of alliances in the years to come. Such speculation would have been based on the assumption that population growth, pressure, and structure are factors in estimating national power. Thus learning becomes a continuous interplay of intuitive and counterintuitive or analytic processes.

3. What is Inquiry?

One of the most important treatises on inquiry or "reflective thinking" is the work of John Dewey, published around the turn of the century. Although various authors since that time have referred to inquiry by using such terms as problem solving, inductive method, critical or reflective thinking, scientific method, or conceptual learning, the essential elements of the process in many studies or school programs are those identified and elaborated on by Dewey.

According to Dewey, inquiry is the "active, persistent, and careful consideration of any belief or supposed form of knowledge in the light of the grounds that support it and the further conclusions to which it tends" (Dewey 1933 p. 9). Inquiry generally aims at the grounding of belief through the use of reason, evidence, inference, and generalization. A person is prompted to engage in reflective inquiry when faced with a "forked-road situation" or a perplexing problem that causes some discomfiture. Thus thinking moves from a state of doubt or confusion (the prereflective state) to a situation characterized by satisfaction and mastery over the initial conditions that gave rise to doubt and perplexity (the post-reflective thought) which may be distinguished as follows: (a) suggestion, (b) intellectualization, (c) hypothesis, (d) reasoning, and (e) testing the hypothesis (Dewey 1933).

During the first phase (while the person is still under the immediate and direct influence of the felt difficulty) spontaneous suggestions (or wild guesses) are offered which may or may not lead to the solution of the problem. During this phase the mind leaps to possible solutions, and this may be thought of as being the phase of discovery. The second phase, which entails a more systematic and rational examination of the problem at hand, results in its location and definition. At this point the person begins to grasp the various aspects of the problem. A working hypothesis is formulated during the third phase of the thinking process (which may or may not derive from the original suggestion) that places subsequent intellectual operations under control and leads to the collection and selection of additional data. The working hypothesis, in other words, serves as a search model that guides the mind towards the solution of the problem. In the fourth phase the mind relates ideas to one another and traces the logical implications of hypotheses. Here the person tries to reason out what might happen if the proposed solution were acted on. The final phase brings about a confirmation, verification, or rejection of the idea or hypothesis based on direct observation or experimentation. If the hypothesis is confirmed, the individual may generalize about its applicability to a category of problems, one of which is the problem that initiated the thought process to begin with; if the hypothesis is not confirmed the individual may proceed to modify it in the light of the newly acquired experience. In sum, in inquiry, intellectual activity is always purposeful, moves from problem to solution, and entails a series of related but operationally distinguishable cognitive tasks (e.g., hypothesizing and testing the hypotheses).

4. Applications of Inquiry Processes

Several authors of programs of instruction have used or related to Dewey's framework in the development of their own instructional model based on inquiry. Joyce and Weil (1980) have identified six such models, all related closely to each other, based on John Dewey's initial conceptualization. These models are: "group investigation" (Thelen 1960, Dewey 1933); "social inquiry" (Massialas and Cox 1966); "laboratory method" (National Training Laboratory, NTL); "jurisprudential" (Oliver and Shaver 1966); and "social simulation" (Boocock and

Schild 1968). An example of these models applied to social studies inquiry is offered by Massialas and Cox and is presented in Fig. 1.

The classroom in which the model in Fig. 1 is applied is psychologically open and there is a definite sense of purpose to the discussion. Either the teacher or the student presents the problem or issue in the

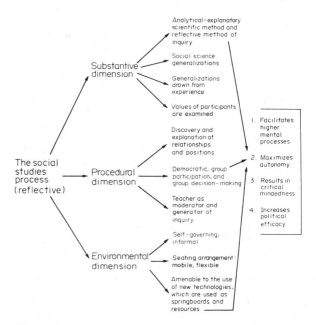

Figure 1
Social inquiry model

form of a "springboard." The goal of instruction is to clarify the problem or issue and to offer different hypotheses or positions related to it, and then to resolve conflicts that arise and to determine defensible solutions to them. The overall role of the teacher is to create conditions from which a problem may develop; to have materials and resources available that the students may tap to research the issue; and to encourage students through questions to identify additional issues, state hypotheses, and then clarify, probe, and resolve conflicting ideas and positions.

5. Summary

Discovery–inquiry learning processes, as illustrated by the forgoing examples, have been the basis for textbooks and materials developed in the United States and in many other parts of the world since the 1960s and 1970s. Due to this, the core subjects in the curriculum were radically transformed to what has become known as "new math," "new science," "new social studies," and "new English." Many of these programs were known by their initials: ISCS, Intermediate Science Curriculum Study; BSCS, Biological Science Curriculum Study; and so on. Beyond these subjects discovery–inquiry processes were used in the teaching of reading, art, home economics, music, and archeology, among others. Discovery–inquiry methods were also used with gifted students, adults, urban youth, handicapped, and preschool children, among others. The main characteristics of these programs were:

(a) a focus on ideas and concepts, rather than on conceptually unrelated pieces of information;

(b) a strong activity–participation component where students were motivated to "learn by doing";

(c) an emphasis on learning the methods of verifying and testing hypotheses in each field; and

(d) the idea that content and process are inseparable components of learning.

Unlike previously designed school programs, the major orientations of these programs were to explain the world rather than to merely describe it.

Bibliography

Boocock S S, Schild E O (eds.) 1968 *Simulation Games in Learning.* Sage, Beverly Hills, California
Bruner J S 1960 *The Process of Education.* Harvard University Press, Cambridge, Massachusetts
Dewey J 1933 *How We Think: A Restatement of the Relation of Reflective Thinking to the Education Process.* Heath, Boston, Massachusetts
Joyce B R, Weil M 1980 *Models of Teaching,* 2nd edn. Prentice-Hall, Englewood Cliffs, New Jersey
Massialas B G, Cox C B 1966 *Inquiry in Social Studies.* McGraw-Hill, New York
Massialas B G, Hurst J B 1978 *Social Studies in a New Era: The Elementary School as a Laboratory.* Longman, New York
Massialas B G, Zevin J 1967 *Creative Encounters in the Classroom: Teaching and Learning through Discovery.* Wiley, New York
Oliver D W, Shaver J P 1966 *Teaching Public Issues in the High School.* Houghton Mifflin, Boston, Massachusetts
Thelen H A 1960 *Education and the Human Quest.* Harper and Row, New York

B. G. Massialas

Discriminant Analysis

Discriminant analysis is the special case of regression analysis which is encountered when the dependent variable is nominal (i.e., a classification variable, sometimes called a taxonomic variable). In this case, either a single linear function of a set of measurements which best separates two groups is desired, or two or more linear functions which best separate three or more groups are desired. In the two-group application, the discriminant analysis is a special case of multiple regression, and in those applications where the criterion variable identifies memberships in three or more groups, the multiple discriminant analysis is a special case of canonical regression. However, because of its focus upon the parsimonious description of differences among groups in a measurement space, it is useful to develop the algebra of discriminant analysis separately from that of regression, and to have computer programs for discriminant analysis which are rather different in their printouts from general regression programs.

1. Aspects and History

Discriminant analysis has had its earliest and most widespread educational research applications in the areas of vocational and career development. Because education prepares people for a variety of positions in the occupational structures prevalent in their societies, an important class of educational research is concerned with the testing of theories about the causes of occupational placements and/or the estimation of prediction equations for allocating positions or anticipating such allocations. This research is characterized by criteria which are taxonomies of occupations or other placements, and predictors which are traits of the individuals who have been sampled from the cells of the taxonomy. Thus there are many independent variates which can be taken as approximately multivariate normal in distribution, and a dependent variable which is a nominal identifier of the cells of a taxonomy (or the populations in a universe). The resulting discriminant analysis design may be thought of as a reverse of the simple one-way MANOVA (multivariate analysis of variance) design.

Where MANOVA assumes a nominal independent variable and a multivariate normal dependent vector variable, discriminant analysis assumes a multivariate normal independent vector variable and a nominal dependent variable. Both methods share the assumption of equal measurement dispersions (variance–covariance structures) for the populations under study, so that much of the statistical inference theory of MANOVA is applicable to the discriminant design, especially the significance test provided by Wilks' Λ, Pillai's V, Roy's Θ, and the Lawley–Hotelling U statistics (Tatsuoka 1971 pp. 164–68, Timm 1975 pp. 369–82). There is also a formal equivalence of discriminant analysis to the canonical correlation design with dummy variates representing group memberships (Tatsuoka 1971 pp. 177–83). Discriminant analysis is also closely related to the statistical literature on the classification problem, since a discriminant space may be optimal for classification decisions in some situations (Rulon et al. 1967 299–319, 339–41). However, a good discriminant program will report interpretive results which will not be obtained from a canonical correlation program, and modern computers so easily compute classifications in original measurement spaces of very large dimensionality that the reduction in dimensionality provided by a discriminant space no longer has great utility when the emphasis is on classification.

Discriminant analysis serves primarily to provide insight into how groups differ in an elaborate measurement space. It is most useful when the number of measurement variates is so large that it is difficult for the human mind to comprehend the differentiation of the groups described by a table of means. Usually it will be found that the major differences can be captured by projecting the group means onto a small number of best discriminant functions, so that an economical model of group differences is constructed as an aid to understanding. Often the discriminant functions will be theoretically interpretable as latent dimensions of the manifest variates. It is even possible to make a rotation of the discriminant dimensions to more interpretable locations, once the best discriminant hyperplane has been located. Thus the goals and procedures are not unlike those of factor analysis (see *Factor Analysis*).

Barnard (1935) seems to have been the first to describe the discriminant problem clearly. She wanted to classify Egyptian skulls into four dynasties on the basis of four measurements, which was so definitely a discriminant problem that Rao (1952) and Williams (1959) presented her results in their texts. Barnard had the problem but not the optimal solution, as she regressed a single time-line comparison of the skulls on the four measurements, thus making a standard multiple regression. Rao commented, "Barnard maximized the ratio of the square of unweighted regression of the compound with time. It is doubtful whether such a linear compound can be used to specify an individual skull most effectively with respect to progressive changes, since linear regression with time does not adequately explain all the differences in the four series" (1952 p. 271). Fisher (1936) provided the appropriate criterion to be maximized by a discriminant function, as λ equal to the ratio of the between-groups sum of squares to the pooled within-groups sum of squares on the function. He treated only the two-group case, for which weights which maximize λ depend only on the inverse of the pooled within-group dispersion and can be found by regression. His example used four measurements on 50 flowers from each of two species of iris, and is reproduced in the text by Kendall (1957). Tatsuoka (1971 pp. 170–77) gives an outstanding treatment of the special two-groups case.

Bartlett was the first to develop the multiple groups generalization of discriminant analysis. "If the 'most predictable criterion' were to be used as a discriminant function" (1938 p.36) said Bartlett, it would be possible to maximize λ more than once when there were three or more criterion groups,

using dummy-coded variates to represent the group membership information. He stated with great clarity and elegance the application of Hotelling's 1935 invention of the canonical correlation method to the multiple discriminant problem. He showed that if there are g groups and p measurements, the number of nonzero λs must be the lesser of $g-1$ and p, and for each nonzero λ the corresponding canonical variable of the measurements is a discriminant function. He had no doubt that the desired discriminant functions should be uncorrelated and should span a hyperplane of minimum dimensionality to get the job done. Today when there is so much hard sell for modelling methods that encourage the use of correlated latent variables, it may be well to consider the motives of the great pioneers, including Pearson, Fisher, Hotelling, and Bartlett, who assumed that good constructed variables should be uncorrelated among themselves. Bartlett's 1938 paper deserves to be reprinted and read widely as a classic argument for parsimonious and mathematically disciplined modeling methods.

Hotelling's and Bartlett's inventions were destined to lie fallow for two decades for lack of computing machinery capable of evaluating the eigenstructures requiring numerical analysis in most practical applications of canonical and discriminant methods. In the interim there was one more major theoretical invention. Rao and Slater (1949) developed the algebra to generalize Fisher's λ criterion directly from the customary MANOVA accumulations matrices, rather than by using dummy variates in canonical regression (see *Canonical Analysis*). Since the Rao and Slater algebra is now accepted standard algebra for presenting the mathematics of discriminant analysis, it is reviewed in the next section of this article. Rao and Slater also originated the mapping of the group centroids in the best discriminant plane which has become the standard display of the model for the data, and is illustrated in the example provided later in this article, as Fig. 1. Strangely, Rao (1952) did not choose to incorporate these developments in his great pioneering textbook, but instead concentrated on the alternative device of using one classification discriminant function for each group, based only on the inverse of the pooled within-groups dispersion. He did reproduce the Rao and Slater (1949) demonstration of this approach (Rao 1952 pp. 307–29). Anderson (1958) also confined his treatment to classification discriminant functions, while Williams (1959) presented only the Barnard-type generalization to an arranged linear placement of the several groups which is then regressed upon the measurements. Rao's classification discriminant functions are mutually intercorrelated, and while they provide an efficient classification rule they do not provide an elegant and parsimonious descriptive model for the differences among the groups. Kendall seems to have provided the first textbook treatment of Rao and

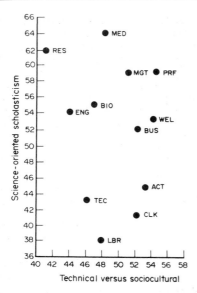

Figure 1
Group centroids in discriminant space

Slater's generalization of Fisher's λ to the multiple discriminants method. Kendall said vividly, "If [the means] are collinear, one discriminator is sufficient; if they are coplanar two are required, and so on" (1957 p. 169). Perhaps Rao and Anderson ignored the multiple discriminants method in their texts because it is not essentially a statistical method. The interesting statistical issues are subsumed under MANOVA and classification. Discriminant analysis is essentially mathematical and geometric modeling of data on group differences. The model provided is a spatial one. The researcher's decisions about the rank of the model (i.e., the number of discriminant dimensions) and the naming and interpretation of the dimensions, which are so critical to the meanings produced, are based more on theoretical or practical considerations than statistical ones. The special value of the discriminant analysis is heuristic, and as Kendall perceived, in this it "links up with component and canonical correlation analysis and our various topics are to be seen as different aspects of the same fundamental structure" (Kendall 1957 p. 169). The difference is that discriminant and canonical analyses involve regression structures which are not viewed by principal components.

2. Mathematics

Letting

$$\bar{x}_j = \bar{X}_j - \bar{X}(j = 1, 2, \ldots, g) \tag{1}$$

where g is the number of populations sampled (i.e., the number of groups), so that $\bar{x}_j$ is the vector of

deviations of the jth sample means from the grand means,

$$y_j = V' \bar{x}_j \tag{2}$$

is the desired discriminant model for the centroids, transforming the centroids into discriminant space. The necessary rank of y is the lesser of p (the number of variates in the measurement vector X) and $g - 1$, but often n (the rank of y) will be even smaller by choice of the analyst. Thus the desired transformation matrix V is a $p \times n$ matrix, each column of which contains the discriminant function weights for one of the functions v_r ($r = 1, 2, \ldots, n$). Fisher's (1956) criterion for v_r is

$$\lambda_r = (v_r' B v_r)/(v_r' W v_r)|_{max} \tag{3}$$

where

$$B = \sum_{j=1}^{g} N_j \bar{x}_j \bar{x}_j' \tag{4}$$

and

$$W = \sum_{j=1}^{g} \sum_{i=1}^{Nj} (X_{ji} - \bar{X}_j)(X_{ji} - \bar{X}_j)' \tag{5}$$

making B the between-groups matrix and W the within-groups matrix. This motivated by the assumption that the populations share a common dispersion Δ estimated by

$$D_w = W/(N - g) \tag{6}$$

where

$$N = \sum_{j=1}^{g} N_k \tag{7}$$

making N the total sample size. Thus by assumption information about population differences is concentrated in the centroids.

The required maxima are provided by the eigenvalues and eigenvectors of

$$(W^{-1} B - \lambda 1) = 0 \tag{8}$$

The resulting discriminant functions are uncorrelated among themselves, but when the column eigenvectors associated with the nonzero eigenvalues are placed in V, V is not column orthogonal. Tatsuoka (1971 p. 169) shows that the angle between two discriminant dimensions has cosine equal to $v_r'v_s$, and he remarks that the discriminants are an oblique rotation of the principal components of X (p. 163).

Since $W^{-1}B$ is nonsymmetric, the numerical analysis of its eigenstructure is complicated. In 1962 Cooley and Lohnes published a practical discriminant analysis program supported by a subroutine called DIRNM (diagonalize a real nonsymmetric matrix) which facilitated computation of the eigenstructure of $W^{-1}A$. The DIRNM subroutine lies at the heart of the improved programs for discriminant and canonical analyses they published later (Cooley and Lohnes 1971 pp. 192–98, 258–60).

The discriminant functions can be scaled to unit standard deviation for the total sample by creating the matrix $T = B + W$ and the matrix $D = T/(N-1)$, then defining the discriminant factors as

$$f_{ji} = (V' \, D \, V)^{-\frac{1}{2}} \, V' \, X_{ji}$$
$$= C' \, X_{ji} \tag{9}$$

Then

$$S = D \, C \tag{10}$$

is the very useful matrix of factor structure coefficients (i.e., correlations of the original variates with the discriminant functions). Users wishing to scale the functions to unit variance within groups may substitute D_w in Eqn. (9) and Eqn. (10).

Choice of scale for a discriminant function is arbitrary, since the weights are determined only with regard their proportionality to each other. Williams (1959 p. 177) suggested that it would be useful to set the variance for the total sample to unity, in order that the pooled within-groups variance on the discriminant function would decrease as further efficient predictors were added to the measurement vector. The complement of this pooled within variance provides a useful index of the discriminating power of the function which is both the correlation ratio for the function and the squared canonical correlation coefficient between the discriminant function and the implicit canonical function of the group-identifying dummy variates. This excellent statistic is calculable as

$$R_r^2 = \lambda_r/(1 + \lambda_r) \tag{11}$$

Cooley and Lohnes liked this argument and scaled the discriminant functions produced by their program this way, so that this convention is represented by the example of the next section, and by Fig. 1. Others have argued that the appropriate scaling would set the pooled within-groups variance to unity, so that the plot of the group centroids in a discriminant plane would display the distances among groups in units of within-groups standard deviation. Isofrequency contours could then be drawn around centroids as circles. Since the model is on the means and is a spatial model, the argument for facilitating the interpretation of distances among centroids is a good one. Bock (1975 p. 405) provides a strong statement of the case for scaling so that the within-groups variance is unity.

The Bock (1975) text is especially strong on interpretation of discriminant functions. It asserts that discriminants are most useful when the many measurements available are low in reliabilities and factorially complex in validities. "Working with linear combinations of these variables tends to reduce variation due to measurement error and to enhance the effect of latent sources of variation common to two or more variables" (p. 416). Bock distinguishes between the case where a new measurement increases the reliability of a discriminant function and the case where it sponsors an additional dimension of discrimination. His examples illustrate collinearity of centroids, bipolarity of functions, and suppressor variables. Bock asserts that discriminant functions may be difficult to interpret "until the results of a number of independent studies utilizing the same set of variables become available" (p. 416). This is so, but it would also be helpful if authors of reviews of research would be alert for the appearance of substantially the same discriminant functions in studies using different mixes of measurements. More research studies should also be looked at in which previously discovered discriminant functions are

Table 1
Career plan groups

Acronym	Group name	Sample size
MED	Medicine and Ph.D. biology	279
BIO	Medicine and biology below M.D. and Ph.D.	438
RES	Physical science and mathematics Ph.D.	221
ENG	Physical science and engineering M.S. and B.S.	939
TEC	Technical worker	1297
LBR	Laborer with no post H.S. training	706
CLK	Office worker with no post H.S. training	530
ACT	Accountants and other trained nontechnical	1430
BUS	Business B.A. and B.S.	1214
MGT	Management post baccalaureate training	270
WEL	Sociocultural M.A. and B.A.	1183
PRF	Sociocultural research degree	815

Table 2
Discriminant functions

MAP Measurement basis	Discriminant	
	Science-oriented scholasticism	Technical vs. sociocultural
Abilities	$R_c = 0.69$	$R_c = 0.37$
Verbal knowledges	0.62	0.20
Perceptual speed and accuracy	0.02	0.10
Mathematics	0.73	−0.49
Hunting–Fishing	−0.10	−0.26
English	0.28	0.23
Visual reasoning	−0.01	−0.43
Color and foods	0.08	0.10
Etiquette	0.05	0.07
Memory	0.00	0.01
Screening	−0.33	−0.25
Games	0.10	−0.05
Motives		
Business interests	−0.04	0.31
Conformity needs	0.21	0.12
Scholasticism	0.78	−0.19
Outdoors and shop interests	−0.41	−0.42
Cultural interests	0.25	0.47
Activity level	−0.22	−0.10
Impulsion	−0.01	0.08
Science interests	0.54	−0.36
Sociability	−0.19	0.47
Leadership	0.28	0.22
Introspection	−0.06	−0.03

moved intact to new samples. Many years ago Bartlett remarked about discriminants fitted by Hotelling's method to one sample, that "if a function suitable for discriminating species or groups were so devised, any subsequent use *on further data* would simply conform to orthodox analysis-of-variance lines" (1938 pp. 37–38).

3. *Example*

Cooley and Lohnes remark that the best discriminant plane is very often an adequate model for the data (1971 p. 244). The resulting reduction in rank, or simplification of the measurement basis, is perhaps the most attractive aspect of discriminant research strategy. In their Project TALENT researches, they found that approximately the same discriminant plane was discovered in a series of 14 researches using different samples and different taxonomic criteria but a common measurement basis (Cooley and Lohnes 1968 pp. 5–6 to 5–8). One of their studies can provide an example for this article.

The current career plan of 9,322 young men was collected by questionnaire five years after they left high school. These plans were classified into 12 categories of a careers taxonomy. Table 1 lists the 12 categories, with an acronym for each, and the subsample count. Six years earlier, when they were highschool seniors, these men had taken a battery of 60 ability tests and 38 typical performance scales. Lohnes (1966) created a factor analytic solution for these two batteries, and the measurement basis for the discriminant analysis was his 22 MAP factors. Table 2 lists these 22 factors and locates the two best discriminant functions by their correlations with the 22 scales of the measurement basis. The major discriminant function, called science-oriented scholasticism, is oriented toward mathematics and verbal abilities, and scholastic and science interests. The minor discriminant is bipolar, contrasting technical abilities and interests with sociocultural abilities and interests. Figure 1 maps the 12 group centroids on this plane. Note how it separates the laborer and office workers from the medical and research doctorates.

See also: Regression Analysis

Bibliography

Anderson T W 1958 *An Introduction to Multivariate Statistical Analysis*. Wiley, New York
Barnard M M 1935 The secular variations of skull charac-

ters in four series of Egyptian skulls. *Annals Eugenics* 6: 352–71

Bartlett M S 1938 Further aspects of the theory of multiple regression. *Proc. Cambridge Philos. Soc.* 34: 33–40

Bock R D 1975 *Multivariate Statistical Methods in Behavioral Research.* McGraw-Hill, New York

Cooley W W, Lohnes P R 1968 *Predicting Development of Young Adults*: Project TALENT *Five-year Follow-up Studies, Interim Report* 5. American Institutes for Research, Palo Alto, California

Cooley W W, Lohnes P R 1971 *Multivariate Data Analysis.* Wiley, New York

Fisher R A 1936 The use of multiple measurements in taxonomic problems. *Annals Eugenics* 7: 179–88

Kendall M G 1957 *A Course in Multivariate Analysis.* Griffin, London

Lohnes P R 1966 *Measuring Adolescent Personality*: Project TALENT *Five-year Follow-up Studies, Interim Report* 1. American Institutes for Research, Palo Alto, California

Rao C R 1952 *Advanced Statistical Methods in Biometric Research.* Wiley, New York

Rao C R, Slater P 1949 Multivariate analysis applied to differences between neurotic groups. *Br. J. Psychol. (Stat. Sect.)* 2: 17–29

Rulon P J, Tiedeman D V, Tatsuoka M M, Langmuir C R 1967 *Multivariate Statistics for Personnel Classification.* Wiley, New York

Tatsuoka M M 1971 *Multivariate Analysis*: *Techniques for Educational and Psychological Research.* Wiley, New York

Timm N H 1975 *Multivariate Analysis with Application in Education and Psychology.* Brooks/Cole, Monterey, California

Williams E J 1959 *Regression Analysis.* Wiley, New York

P. R. Lohnes

Discussion Methods of Teaching

The discussion method of teaching is a process in which a small group assembles to communicate with each other—using speaking, listening, and nonverbal processes—in order to achieve instructional objectives. The first part of this definition highlights the fact that discussion occurs in groups , usually involving six to ten persons (see *Small-group Instruction*). The group members perform one of two roles: leader–moderator (typically, the teacher), and participant (typically, the students). Because group members have reciprocal influence over one another, the learning of each student in a discussion group is affected by the behavior of other students in the group. Other teaching methods, such as lecture and computer-assisted instruction, are much less dependent on reciprocal influence among students to facilitate learning (see *Lectures*).

A limitation of the discussion method is that it requires students and teacher to assemble at a designated time and place. If this requirement cannot be met, other methods (for example, independent study and televised instruction) need to be used.

Another distinguishing feature of discussion is that participants use the available time to communicate with each other. The person who has the floor addresses his or her remarks to the entire group, and each group member has the right to speak. Discussions in a classroom setting should have many sequences in which one student remark is followed by another. By contrast, the prevailing method of classroom discourse is the recitation, in which the predominant pattern of interaction is teacher question–student response–teacher feedback–new teacher question.

A discussion member communicates to others in the group by speaking (utterances and intonation of voice) and by nonverbal signs, such as facial expressions, hand gestures, and bodily movement (see *Nonverbal Communication in Classrooms*). The other participants receive these communications by listening and by visually attending to the nonverbal signs. These processes of speaking, listening, and observing are critical attributes of the discussion method. Bridges (1979) noted that discussion has the advantage of encouraging young children and illiterate people to express their ideas and to learn new ones, despite the fact that they cannot read and write. Furthermore, the exercise of the basic communication processes involved in discussion may facilitate development of more abstract learning processes, such as are involved in reading and writing.

Discussion can easily degenerate into a superficial, disconnected exchange of opinion, unless it stays focused on explicit instructional objectives. Because the elements of discussion are flexible, it has been adapted to achieve these broad instructional objectives: subject matter mastery, attitude change, moral development, problem solving, and acquisition of communication skills. Additionally, a good discussion motivates students to engage in further inquiry and provides the teacher with feedback on student progress.

1. Effectiveness of the Discussion Method

Much evidence on the effectiveness of the discussion method in promoting instructional objectives has accumulated. Most of this research has involved college students, workers in business and industry, and adult volunteers for psychological experiments. A relatively small amount of discussion research has been done with elementary and secondary students. The sources of the research evidence cited in the following sections are available in several literature reviews (Gall and Gall 1976, Gage and Berliner 1979).

1.1 Subject Matter Mastery

Hill (1977), and many other educators, advocate the use of discussion (supplemented by textbook study or related instructional activity) for promoting critical thinking and other cognitive objectives. In Hill's model of discussion, the discussion agenda includes a review of key concepts and topics, integration of the subject matter with other knowledge, application of the subject matter, and evaluation of the author's presentation. McKeachie and Kulik (1975) reviewed the many studies evaluating the effectiveness of discussion for promoting subject matter mastery at the college level. They concluded that lecture is more effective for promoting acquisition of information, whereas discussion is more effective for promoting retention of information and higher level thinking. Discussion was also found to be more effective for stimulating students to have positive attitudes and motivation.

Bridges (1979) claimed that discussion contributes to participants' understanding of subject matter by: (a) supplementing each participant's information on a subject with the information that other participants have; (b) stimulating different perspectives on the subject; (c) allowing participants to put forth conjectures about the subject; (d) providing opportunity for other participants to criticize and refute a conjecture; and (e) encouraging mutual adjustments among participants' opinions to produce a group decision or solution. These processes may not facilitate subject matter mastery for all students, though. Dowaliby and Schumer (1973) found that in a college discussion class, low-anxiety students did better than high-anxiety students on course examinations. In a college lecture class, however, the high-anxiety students outperformed the low-anxiety students. Since discussion is less structured and certain than lecture, it may provoke anxiety in predisposed students and thereby interfere with their learning.

1.2 Attitude Change

Discussion provides a good forum for the expression of students' attitudes toward a topic or issue. Attitudes can be expressed at three levels: beliefs, feelings, and dispositions to act on the basis of one's beliefs and feelings. Discussion can simply aim to help students become aware of their own attitudes and the attitudes of other group members. More ambitious objectives are to use discussion to critically evaluate and change group members' attitudes. Oliver and Shaver (1966) developed the jurisprudential model of instruction, which makes use of discussion to achieve this type of learning outcome.

There is ample research evidence that discussion is effective in changing attitudes. This research has included such groups as parents, industrial workers, and students at all levels. Discussion may produce this effect through confronting group members with new data or through group coercion. Concerning the latter, educators have expressed concern about coercive forces—including the tendency to press for group consensus—in discussion groups. In the Humanities Curriculum Project in England, for example, the project directors (Bridges 1979) found

that pressure towards consensus inhibited open discussion among group members. Also, attitude change through discussion can fail if all the group members share a similar undesirable attitude, such as racial prejudice, at the outset.

1.3 Moral Development

Some educators advocate the use of discussion to advance students' capability for moral reasoning. This capability has been investigated using the six developmental stages of cognitive–moral reasoning identified by Lawrence Kohlberg and his colleagues. Reviewers of this line of research (Berkowitz 1981, Lockwood 1978) found that discussion generally develops students' moral reasoning by one-third to one full stage. Lockwood observed that discussion appears to be effective at moving students through the first three of Kohlberg's stages, but not through the next three stages.

Moral discussions focus on an issue with underlying value conflicts that the participants attempt to resolve. The most critical feature of a good moral discussion is the presence of arguments that exceed students' present moral reasoning stage. These arguments presumably create cognitive conflicts in students. In attempting to resolve the conflicts, students are stimulated to advance to the next stage of moral reasoning. Teachers can create such conflict by presenting advanced-stage arguments or by asking Socratic questions that note contradictions and problems in students' reasoning. Another approach is to form heterogeneous discussion groups that include students at different stages of cognitive–moral development.

The use of discussion to stimulate advances in cognitive–moral reasoning is still largely experimental. Procedures to be used by teachers in initiating and guiding discussions have been developed, but they have not been rigorously validated. Also, little is known about whether student gains in cognitive–moral reasoning are reflected in other important outcomes of education, such as good citizenship behavior.

1.4 Problem Solving

The discussion method is often advocated to help a group reach a solution to a problem. For example, brainstorming is a problem-solving procedure in which a discussion group first generates as many solutions as possible while withholding criticism (Osborn 1979). In the second stage the group critically discusses the solutions and converges on the one that best satisfies explicit criteria.

Researchers have found that problem-solving groups of a certain size are usually less effective than an equal number of individuals working alone. Maier (1967) suggested several explanations for this finding. Majority opinions in a discussion are more likely to be accepted than minority opinions, irrespective of their soundness. Also, once group consensus on a particular solution is reached, subsequent high-quality solutions tend to be rejected. Another adverse factor is that less capable individuals may dominate the discussion and thereby prevent more capable individuals from influencing the problem-solving process.

Despite the shortcomings of discussion group problem solving, it is probably more effective than individual effort in certain situations. For example, Maier (1967) suggested that when a solution will commit a group to a given course of action, the solution will be better accepted and implemented if it has been reached through the process of group discussion. Also, group discussion may be more effective than individual effort when working on problems that have multiple solutions or that require a variety of talents not likely to be present in a single individual.

1.5 Communication Skills

Discussion participants can choose to focus on their communication processes rather than on the outcomes of discussion described above. They might focus on such communication skills as: inviting silent group members to speak, avoiding monopolization of talk time, acknowledging and paraphrasing what other participants have said, and asking participants to clarify or elaborate on their remarks. Bridges (1979 pp. 29–32) classified these communication skills into three types: (a) intellectual rules of discourse (e.g., showing concern for reasons and evidence in one's remarks); (b) procedural rules and conventions (e.g., who speaks, when, in what order, and for how long); and (c) social conventions (e.g., whether the norm is to be abrasive or mild in criticizing another participant's ideas).

Systematic training has been demonstrated to improve these skills (Oliver and Shaver 1966, Gall et al. 1975). Few studies have been done, though, to determine whether training in communication skills improves the ability of group members to achieve the other outcomes of discussion—subject matter mastery, attitude change, moral development, and problem solving. Also, little is known about the effect of training in discussion communication skills on student's academic motivation.

2. Discussion Group Dynamics

How a teacher structures and leads a discussion will affect students' functioning within the group. The quality of group functioning in turn affects how much students learn from the discussion. Research on group dynamics has identified a number of structural and leadership factors that hinder or facilitate a discussion. Six of these factors are described below.

2.1 Group Size

Researchers have found consistently that small group size results in higher satisfaction, more participation from each discussion group member, and greater academic achievement. The optimal group size for discussion is between five and eight participants.

The reduced effectiveness of large discussion groups may be due to the fact that individual participants have less opportunity—given a constant amount of time—to contribute to the discussion. Another explanation is that more time in large discussion groups must be spent in regulating group processes, thus leaving less time for task-relevant talk.

2.2 Group Composition

Researchers have investigated the effects of discussion groups whose participants are similar (homogeneous) or diverse (heterogeneous) with respect to certain characteristics. The general finding of their research is that homogeneous groups are more cohesive than heterogeneous groups, but they are not always more effective in performance. In fact, under certain conditions discussion groups that are heterogeneous with respect to attitude or prior experience may be more effective than homogeneous groups. For example, Hoffman (1959) found that heterogeneous groups of college students showed superior performance on a problem that required multiple perceptions and cognitive reorganizations.

2.3 Group Cohesiveness

Discussion group cohesiveness is usually defined as the extent to which group members like each other. Research studies have demonstrated that high cohesiveness has several desirable effects on a group. Cohesiveness helps to maintain participants' membership in a group and leads to increased communication among participants. Members of a cohesive group also tend to experience heightened self-esteem and satisfaction with the group.

The effects of cohesiveness on group performance are less clear. A positive relationship between cohesiveness and group performance has been found in some research studies, but not in others. One explanation of these results is that group norms are more influential in high-cohesive groups than in low-cohesive groups. If norms in a high-cohesive group favor performance, its members will probably work harder than low-cohesive group members to achieve goals. If norms in a high-cohesive group denigrate such matters as academic learning or minority opinions, however, its members are likely to be less productive than members of a low-cohesive group.

2.4 Communication Patterns

Various aspects of communication in a discussion group affect its functioning and performance. One such aspect is the network of communication barriers and channels between the members of a discussion group. Decentralized communication networks, where communication channels between participants are open, have been compared with centralized networks, where messages must be channeled through a person who occupies a central position in the group. Student–student interaction is frequent in discussions with a decentralized network, whereas the teacher or a few assertive students control discussions with a centralized network. Researchers have found that participants in a decentralized communication network tend to be more satisfied with their groups, and they are likely to be more effective on complex tasks.

The spatial arrangement of participants in a discussion group has a pronounced effect on communication patterns. For example, researchers have confirmed the obvious principle that a group member is more likely to interact with other members if he or she can see as well as hear them. It is difficult to imagine, then, how discussion can occur in the usual classroom seating pattern, where students sit in rows facing the teacher. A circular seating pattern, such as may occur in a seminar, is preferable because all participants are in face-to-face contact.

2.5 Group Leadership

McKeachie (1978) identified six leadership functions in a discussion that a teacher should perform directly or should assign to students: (a) agenda setting; (b) calling the meeting to order and introducing the topic for discussion; (c) clarification of goals during the discussion; (d) summarization; (e) mediation and clarification of differences of opinion; and (f) evaluation of group progress.

Research on leadership styles suggests that these functions can be performed using an authoritarian, instructor-centered style or a democratic, student-centered style. Teachers characterized by the former style tend to determine all policies and procedures, to use personal praise and criticism, and to remain aloof. Democratic, student-centered teachers tend to submit policies and procedures for group discussion, to use objective praise and criticism, and to be involved in the group's work. Research findings generally favor a democratic, student-centered leadership style. The opposite leadership style may be more effective, though, if it is accepted or expected by group participants (see *Teacher-centred and Learner-centred Instruction*).

2.6 Group Norms

Students usually enter a discussion with a set of beliefs about the discussion process and about their fellow participants. As these beliefs become communicated (often, nonverbally), they form a set of group norms that determine discussion process and outcomes.

Bridges (1979 pp. 21–26) identified six group norms, which he calls "moral dispositions," that are necessary for good discussion: (a) willingness to be reasonable and to be influenced by others' evidence; (b) peaceableness and conformance to such rules as "only one person talks at a time"; (c) truthfulness in what one says; (d) giving each person the freedom to speak his or her mind; (e) the belief that participants are equal in that each one of them potentially has knowledge of relevance to the discussion; and (f) respect for all members of the discussion group. It is difficult to imagine that the objectives of discussion (e.g., subject matter mastery, moral development) can be achieved unless these norms are shared by all or most of the participants.

3. Educational Applications of the Discussion Method

The discussion method has been the subject of much experimental research, yet little is known about its prevalence and form under actual conditions of schooling. Discussion is probably rare at the precollege level, despite the fact that researchers have found it can be used to achieve instructional outcomes even with young children. Teachers may report that they use discussion when in fact they are using the recitation method, to which discussion is superficially similar. In a study of high-school discussion classes, Dillon (1981) found that teachers spoke at almost every turn of talk, for an average total time that was longer than the average talk time of all of the students.

Discussion may be used occasionally in college and university teaching, especially at the graduate level. University seminars, for example, are intended to promote discussion among participants. Discussion is probably more frequent in informal settings outside the classroom. Small groups of students can share perceptions about their coursework without worrying about the professor's reaction.

Discussion is included as a component of complex instructional methods, such as Herbert Thelen's group inquiry model and Oliver and Shaver's jurisprudential model. Because of the complexity of these methods and their radical departure from conventional instruction, it is unlikely that they are used with any frequency in teaching.

Discussion is generally considered most appropriate for instruction in the social sciences and the humanities, which are thought to be "low-consensus" fields (Gage and Berliner 1979 p. 479). Discussion is considered less appropriate for such "high-consensus" fields as mathematics, the physical sciences, and engineering. In fact, a careful analysis of most academic disciplines would reveal issues, problems, and subject matter that can be profitably approached through discussion. It is interesting to observe the absence of controversy in many textbooks, yet scholars and researchers in the disciplines represented by these textbooks find much to debate in their professional journals and conventions.

The explanation for the infrequent occurrence of classroom discussion is complex. Some teachers report that they do not use discussion because they tried it once and were discouraged by their lack of success. Because a good discussion requires highly skilled leadership, it is not surprising that teachers' initial experiences would be frustrating. For success to occur, both teachers and students need training in the rationale and techniques of discussion. Resources for such training range from brief textbooks (for example, Stanford and Stanford 1969) to extensive multimedia programs (for example, Gall et al. 1975).

Another reason why some teachers reject the discussion method is that it requires relinquishing part of their authority and control over the instructional process. Students can steer the discussion in directions unanticipated by the teacher, whereas other instructional methods (especially lecture) give the teacher continuous control of the pace and flow of instruction. Furthermore, teachers may be threatened by the occasional lack of control and discipline in discussion because they believe their effectiveness is judged by the ability to maintain quiet, orderly instruction.

A major use of discussion is to help students develop their attitudes and moral reasoning. Teachers, especially at the precollege level, may be reluctant to engage in this type of discussion because of concern about community reaction. Certain segments of the community are quite vocal in their belief that the school curriculum should not deal with issues, attitudes, and values.

Another obstacle to the use of discussion is that the school curriculum tends to emphasize acquisition of facts and skills. Discussion is less suited for these instructional objectives than such methods as lecture and mastery learning approaches.

Finally, teachers may avoid discussion because they feel their classes are too large to accommodate it. Groups of six to eight discussants are optimal, yet teachers usually have 20, 30, or more students in their classes. This problem can be solved by breaking a large class into small discussion groups, assigning a student leader for each group, and walking around to monitor each group's work. Another approach is to use the "fishbowl" technique in which the teacher and a small group conduct a discussion while the other students sit beyond the discussion circle. Following the small-group discussion, these other students may contribute additional ideas or complete a discussion-related assignment.

For the reasons described above, the discussion method is not easily incorporated into classroom instruction. Yet the classroom use of discussion should be promoted because of ample research evidence that it facilitates subject matter mastery, atti-tude change, moral development, problem solving, and communication skill. The discussion method is also important because it promotes the values and processes of democratic society.

See also: Grouping: Instructional Purposes; Group Teaching in Higher Education

Bibliography

Berkowitz M W 1981 A critical appraisal of the educational and psychological perspectives on moral discussion. *J. Educ. Thought* 15: 20–33

Bridges D 1979 *Education, Democracy and Discussion.* National Foundation for Educational Research, Slough

Dillon J T 1981 Duration of response to teacher questions and statements. *Contemp. Educ. Psychol.* 6: 1–11

Dowaliby F J, Schumer H 1973 Teacher-centered versus student-centered mode of college classroom instruction as related to manifest anxiety. *J. Educ. Psychol.* 64: 125–32

Gage N L, Berliner D C 1979 *Educational Psychology,* 2nd edn. Houghton Mifflin, Boston, Massachusetts

Gall M D, Gall J P 1976 The discussion method. In: Gage N L (ed.) 1976 *The Psychology of Teaching Methods.* 75th Yearbook of the National Society for the Study of Education, Pt. 1. University of Chicago Press, Chicago, Illinois

Gall M D, Weathersby R, Elder R A, Lai M K 1975 *Discussing Controversial Issues.* Agency for Instructional Television, Bloomington, Indiana

Hill W F 1977 *Learning Thru Discussion: Guide for Leaders and Members of Discussion Groups.* Sage, Beverly Hills

Hoffman L R 1959 Homogeneity of member personality and its effect on group problem solving. *J. Abnorm. Soc. Psychol.* 59: 27–32

Lockwood A L 1978 The effects of value clarification and moral development curricula on school-age subjects: A critical review of recent research. *Rev. Educ. Res.* 48: 325–64

McKeachie W J 1978 *Teaching Tips: A Guidebook for the Beginning College Teacher,* 7th edn. Heath, Lexington, Massachusetts

McKeachie W J, Kulik J A 1975 Effective college teaching. In: Kerlinger F N (ed.) 1975 *Review of Research in Education,* Vol. 3. Peacock, Itasca, Illinois

Maier N R F 1967 Assets and liabilities in group problem solving: The need for an integrative function. *Psychol. Rev.* 74: 239–49

Oliver D W, Shaver J P 1966 *Teaching Public Issues in the High School.* Houghton Mifflin, Boston, Massachusetts

Osborn A F 1979 *Applied Imagination,* 3rd edn. Scribner, New York

Stanford G, Stanford B D 1969 *Learning Discussion Skills Through Games.* Citation Press, New York

M. D. Gall

Dissemination of Educational Research

Dissemination will be considered here as the process whereby research results reach different audiences. In the case of educational research findings it is useful to think of at least three possible audiences that may be the objects of the dissemination process: (a) other researchers; (b) practitioners in the schools, colleges, and other parts of the education system; and (c) policy makers, including politicians, responsible for decisions about education at the national or local levels. It will also be valuable conceptually to look at dissemination in a North–South perspective, since there are many concerns about the present structures of dissemination, and the extent to which these are influenced by the relative power of Northern industrialized nations over the majority of less industrialized, developing countries of the South.

In both North and South, there are similarities between the relative difficulty of dissemination to the different audiences mentioned above. By far the easiest of the three is the dissemination of research results from the original researcher to other researchers; much more difficulty arises when trying to spread new educational findings to practitioners, whether school teachers, teacher trainers, or adult educators. Finally, the greatest difficulty is for new and important research to reach policy makers and politicians in Ministries of Education and regional or local councils. In part these differences are explained by the fact that for many researchers their preferred audience is other researchers. Their first inclination is the presentation of results in learned journals, or in specialist conferences of other researchers. The language of these communications is usually the technical language of their particular field. All this is to be expected, given that researchers seek recognition and eventual promotion in their professions by this first form of dissemination. The transfer of their findings to practitioners is normally left to the educational weekly newspapers, or if some research is particularly topical, it can be disseminated by the more serious daily papers. This question of topicality is equally important for dissemination into the policy process. Occasionally, independent research results are coincidentally to hand when a particular educational crisis sparks public and political attention, but there is little likelihood of the bulk of educational research being disseminated to the decision-making level. The principal obstacle to dissemination both with practitioners and policy makers is that the technical language of research is not accessible to those audiences and in addition, the task of "translating" research language into a commonsense summary is seldom undertaken. One way around this problem of poor dissemination from individual researchers to government bodies has been for the government agency itself to sponsor research on themes which it feels are important; as a corollary, an increasing amount of attention is given by some researchers to "policy research"—conducting research quite deliberately on issues upon which government can be expected to review policy options backed by research. It is possible to see three important dimensions in the dissemination of research in the North and in the South.

1. Research Dissemination in the North

In many ways this is the most active of the three dimensions. Researchers in the North are supported by the apparatus necessary to research communication. Journals both general and specialized are abundant and they appear with regularity. Copies of new research articles are readily available either from the original scholars or from data banks on educational research. Reprographic facilities are almost everywhere taken for granted and university and research libraries are committed to acquiring current books and periodicals. Despite this developed infrastructure for dissemination in the North, language remains a major barrier to the flow of information between industrialized countries. There is, for example, much more rapid diffusion amongst anglophone Canada, the United Kingdom, Ireland, and the United States than there is amongst Japan, the Soviet Union, France, the Federal Republic of Germany, Scandinavia, or Spain. To a limited extent, the language barrier can be overcome by multilingual data banks, and by the existence of small international networks of researchers in the North who meet on a disciplinary basis, and act as informal translators of research across language groups.

As far as dissemination to practitioners and policy makers in the North is concerned, it is again the case that many channels are available and open for the flow of research communication. Policy research centres and contracted research aid this process, as does the existence of research funding which frequently builds support to dissemination into the educational research grant itself.

2. Dissemination in the South

This covers dissemination of research within a particular developing country on the one hand, and from one country to another across the South. Both within and across countries of the South, there are major problems of research dissemination with all three types of audiences under discussion. In addition to many of the difficulties experienced in the North, notably language barriers, there are a series of dissemination obstacles which make the situation qualitatively different in many, but by no means all, of the developing countries of the South. Dissemination within the nation itself is often hindered by the absence or irregularity of scholarly journals, infrequent professional meetings, and the relatively small size and consequent isolation of some research communities. In some countries, the educational research community is extremely small, but this does not necessarily make it any more likely that research will be satisfactorily disseminated than where there are large numbers of competing research findings. It seems that some kind of critical mass is almost essential to afford researchers an audience to address in the first instance.

At the regional level or across continents, the situation is in general worse. Even within the same language group, there is not necessarily much research dissemination at all amongst anglophone East, West, Central, or Southern Africa, nor even much amongst neighbouring countries in East or West Africa. Indeed, without funding for regional meetings on a regular basis and the frequent interchange of national journals, the present very weak South–South dissemination cannot rapidly improve.

The very strength of the dissemination process in the North interferes with the improvement of dissemination in the South. Although scholars in the South may wish to have their findings read locally and regionally, their own local journals are frequently less regular, and less likely to be purchased by the national and university libraries than international journals in the field. Hence, many researchers prefer Northern journals for their findings and it is thus sometimes the case that research is disseminated from South to South via a journal of international standing in a Northern capital.

This seems certainly not to be the case as far as much of Spanish-speaking Latin America is concerned. Research is communicated through some journals across the continent and this is aided by an organization of Spanish language research summaries (*Resumenes Analiticos*). There is a widely based concern in the region with the dissemination of educational research, and an interest in exploring ways that researchers can communicate with both policy makers and practitioners.

The pattern is different again in South and Southeast Asia. In some countries, the existence of strongly centralized government research centres brings the research process much nearer to the decision-making process. There remains, however, a problem for university-based research to gain recognition in this situation.

Finally, on this South–South dimension, it has to be acknowledged that some countries, for example India, have a very large local research production, and many hundreds of educational journals. These may well have some direct policy impact within the country itself but there seems to be very little dissemination of Indian research findings in education to audiences outside India, either in the North, or to other anglophone countries in the South.

3. Dissemination between the North and the South

As a result of the long-standing patterns of communication between metropolis and colony during the colonial period, and their continuation after formal independence from the colonial empires, whole sections of the world look Northwards not only to disseminate their findings, but also to select the kind of research to undertake in the first place. Such is the influence of Northern university research centres,

their links to funding, and to the dissemination infrastructure, that new research themes and findings are disseminated rapidly and effectively. A powerful channel for their dissemination North–South has been the presence of very large numbers of developing country scholars in Northern universities since the early 1950s. Long-term doctoral training in the North has predisposed Southern scholars to work on topics and methodologies of interest in the North, and also to the reproduction (or dissemination) of these results in their own universities. The corollary of this has been very significant numbers of Northern scholars doing research in the Third World, often with more adequate funding than those they worked amongst. In many cases, the natural outlet for such Northern research upon the South has been Northern journals, or the bilateral and multilateral agencies concerned with education in developing countries. As a consequence both of the South–North movement of Third World scholars and the North–South movement of Northern scholars, the comparative advantage of dissemination via the industrialized countries has been strengthened. To some extent, therefore, the research dissemination situation is an analogue of the larger pattern of Northern dominance in information processing, storage, and communication.

It should be noted, however, that there have been some critical influences in research which have flowed from the South to the North. These would include insights into the conduct of participatory and action research, in which Latin America has been a particularly powerful disseminator Northwards of methodology and approaches. Another example would be methodologies for literacy, with Freire being only one of many sources of inspiration. Together, these do a little to correct the balance of Northern influence on the South. But although small in scope, some of these Southern successes in dissemination may also be instrumental in suggesting ways in which the research community can reach and involve practitioners, particularly teachers, in the research process. Collaborative research with teachers is of course by no means a Southern monopoly, but it does suggest some new ways of altering some aspects of educational research from being a specialist activity of the professional researcher to being also a part-time enthusiasm of the practising teacher. In this situation, the task of research dissemination is greatly altered, and collaborative research with teachers becomes the counterpart of the policy research mode with decision makers. Both, in different ways, reduce significantly the gap between the researchers and two of the principal audiences.

Bibliography

Husén T, Kogan M (eds.) 1984 *Education Research and Policy: How Do They Relate?* Pergamon, Oxford

Myers R 1981 *Connecting Worlds of Research.* International Development Research Centre, Ottawa, Ontario

Nisbet J, Broadfoot P 1980 *The Impact of Research on Policy and Practice in Education.* Aberdeen University Press, Aberdeen

K. King

Dissertations and their Supervision

Dissertations are extended essays written by postgraduate students to fulfil the requirements of a Ph.D. or other graduate research degree. Theses or dissertations are central to the current research tradition of most universities in the industrialized and developing world. Students registered by a university to undertake postgraduate research work have one or more members of the academic staff supervising the research work and the writing of a thesis. Such supervisors have a unique teaching relationship with graduate students.

A thesis may be more fully defined as a significant piece of research that makes a contribution to scholarly thinking. The work may be based on a scientific paradigm of inductive or deductive reasoning, or on an ethnomethodological approach to data collection and analysis. In all cases the thesis contains both a synthesis of existing knowledge and a significant contribution of new ideas. A thesis is the product of one scholar's work and is normally presented in a book form. It presents evidence in ways that facilitate verification of results and a disclosure of sources.

A similar definition of supervision would suggest a special form of individualized teaching involving an academic scholar and one or more students. Supervision implies an educational relationship that is loosely based on an apprenticeship model of training and learning. The exact nature of the relationship will depend on such factors as: the research topic, institutional requirements, (for example, the number of times the supervisor and student must meet), the stage of the research programme, and personal characteristics of the supervisor.

1. The Nature of the Supervisor's Role

It is unlikely that there can be any prescriptive role definition but there may be a wisdom in consensus. In some recent studies of the nature of teaching and learning at Aberdeen, McAleese asked both supervisors and students to identify their roles (McAleese and Welsh 1982). From the responses of 110 students and 298 staff it appeared that two main roles emerged. First, that of the knowledgeable expert; the person to provide answers to technical methodological problems and so on. The other was that of the caring, available, and helpful friend. The supervisor is seen as both guide and friend; "guide, mentor, and friend" as the role is often called. The evidence on such roles is elusive and even where it

exists it is erratic and does not take into account the dynamic nature of any pedagogic relationship. Consider the dynamic nature of supervision. Over a period of research training the way a supervisor approaches a student differs depending on the stage of the work. To begin with the relationship may be direct with a clear directive teaching role. As the research progresses then it is likely that the learning experience itself will place the student in a less dependent position with regard to the supervisor. Indeed there is a clear weaning effect with regard to the dependency that the student has on the supervisor. At the end of a research project the supervisor may take on a more judgmental role, particularly if he or she is involved in the evaluation of the thesis. This involvement is usually minimal, but it may be that students tend to see their supervisors in this moderating role whether it is de jure or not. A useful list of roles for supervisors is provided by Moses (1981). She reports on a questionnaire that asks respondents to say how essential a number of roles might be. The possible roles range from "selecting a topic for the student", through "training in research methods", to "assisting the student in general welfare matters".

Student problems with supervision have been well-documented in the United Kingdom by Rudd and Hatch (1968) and by Welsh (1979, 1981). Welsh (1979) and McAleese and Welsh (1982) list some of the reservations that one group of students had with their supervisors. These can be classified under two main headings; personal relationships and contact time. This study, which can be corroborated by colleagues in many other institutions, showed that there was a greater tendency for such nonsatisfied students to fail to submit their theses. In another research project based on a sample of 85 students in education departments, Delamont and Eggelston (1982) identify "isolation" as being the single biggest problem. This isolation is both physical, that is, working in small departments, and intellectual, that is, working with costudents who are nonsympathetic to the research work or with an unsympathetic supervisor. They quote one student as saying "I didn't realise before I started work what a *lonely* business research can be". Other problems that are frequently mentioned by authors and colleagues relate to part-time research students and overseas research students. It is argued that both these groups require special attention and their supervisors need special support to undertake the job.

2. Major Issues

Although the published literature on supervision of postgraduate theses is not extensive, four main issues emerge. First, is it possible and desirable to issue guidelines to minimize the risks of failure and to maximize the intellectual product of the work? Most institutions and many departments have developed such guidelines. They range in authority from "good advice if you like it" to "the letter of the law" often quoting departmental regulations.

Such advice is not only indicative of the degree of help that is provided for students but shows the explicitness of the contract between department and student. It is clear that the specificity, the nature of the help, and the points that are considered important differ considerably. There is nevertheless an emphasis on the technical as opposed to pedagogic or philosophical aspects of theses in these documents. Similar documents for supervisors are very rare (see the CNAA Handbook in the United Kingdom for some details).

Secondly, are there alternative formats for either the thesis or supervision that may alleviate some of the problems? It has long been suggested that team supervision has many advantages over the single supervisor. Indeed it seems that the one-to-one relationship is at last breaking down. Probably only in the United Kingdom university sector is there a predominance of this type of supervision. North American and European practice has for many years been based on the committee or team, with functional specialization and role differentiation. This has been true in the polytechnic sector in the United Kingdom. The regulations for the Council for National Academic Awards (CNAA) in the United Kingdom spell out this system in typical detail.

6. Supervision of Programme of Work
6.1 Normally two supervisors must be appointed.
6.2 One supervisor shall be the Director of Studies (first supervisor) with the responsibility to supervise the candidate on a regular and frequent basis . . .
6.3 The second supervisor may be appointed from the same institution . . .
6.4 In addition to supervisors an advisor or advisors . . . may be proposed to contribute specialised knowledge . . . (CNAA Handbook 1978)

However there have been fewer attempts to change the thesis format. The format is still traditionally the bound hard copy book. Examples of film and computer programs being allowed as part of the thesis and the inclusion of published papers has only changed the situation slightly. Different formats may not be the answer to many problems in the area of attrition but the inflexibility of the validating system has meant that not only are skills of researching tested in the thesis but skills in communication. Not all critics of the system agree with this emphasis. Why fail a student because of poor presentation of material? What is most important—intellectual contributions or neat presentation?

Thirdly, there is the question of style and relationship. Is there an ideal supervisory style? Supervisors have to steer an uncomfortable path between oppression and laissez-faire (McGuinness 1974). The "adaptive despot" (McAleese and Welsh 1982) is a term that some may wish to use for the supervisor's style. In other words how directive must the supervisor be to be effective? This focuses on the relationship that the supervisor has with his or her student. There is a concept of fairness in this relationship. Glasner and Mugford (1978) expanded on what they called the "taboo" subject of fairness in supervisory practice. Their typology of normal and deviant behaviour raises the question of the way supervisors treat their students. Are there proper standards of behaviour?

Finally, what training should there be for both supervisors and students, in particular the supervisors? Surely there must be a matching of the respective competencies and interests and a training programme for supervisors to help them achieve the most effective working relationships? There are very few instances of training within departments or with institutions. In Scotland the steering committee for staff development in Scottish universities has organized a number of workshops that provide an initial training for supervisors (McAleese 1980, Welsh 1981).

It is probable that with a more cost–effective approach taken by governments and research councils or other funding bodies who give grants for postgraduate study, the quality of the learning experience in writing theses will be brought under more critical scrutiny over the next few years. If this is the case then it is likely that more thought will have to go into the contract that the student and the supervisor have with regard to the production of the piece of scholarly communication called the thesis.

See also: Universities and Graduate Education, Research Role of; Project Work in Higher Education

Bibliography

Allen G R 1973 *The Graduate Students' Guide to Thesis and Dissertations: A Practical Manual for Writing and Research.* Jossey-Bass, New York
Avison D E 1980 *The Project Report.* Computer Centre, University of Aston, Birmingham
British Standards Institution 1972 *Recommendations for the Presentation of Theses.* BS 4821:1972. British Standards Institution, London
Cash P 1971 *How to Write a Research Paper: Step by Step.* Monarch Press, New York
Council for National Academic Awards (CNAA) 1978 *Regulations for the Award of the Council's Degrees of Master of Philosophy and Doctor of Philosophy.* CNAA, London
Delamont S, Eggleston J F 1982 *A Necessary Isolation.* Sociology Research Unit, University College, Cardiff
Glasner H G, Mugford S 1978 Of Kafka and Captain Kidd: The morphology of the supervisory role. *Aust. New Zealand J. Sociol.* 13: 216–21
James W 1903 The PhD octopus. *Harvard Monthly* 36: 1–9
McAleese R 1978 Staff development in the University of Aberdeen: A study of roles. Ph.D. thesis. University of Aberdeen, Aberdeen

McAleese R 1980 *Report of Workshops to the SCSDSU.* Steering Committee for Staff Development in Scottish Universities, University of Aberdeen, Aberdeen

McAleese R, Welsh J M 1982 *The Supervision of Postgraduate Students: A Review of Recent Research.* British Educational Research Association, University of Nottingham, Nottingham

McGuinness D 1974 The PhD's dilemma: A reply to Dr Watson. *Bull. Brit. Psychol. Soc.* 27: 452–54

Metzger B M 1950 *A Guide to the Preparation of a Thesis.* Princeton Theological Seminary, Princeton, New Jersey

Moses I 1981 *Postgraduate Study: Supervisors, Supervision and Information for Students.* Tertiary Education Unit, University of Queensland, St Lucia, Queensland

Parsons C J 1963 *Theses and Project Work.* Allen and Unwin, London

Phillips G R E, Hunt L J 1976 *Writing Essays and Dissertations.* University of Western Australia, Nedlands, Western Australia

Roth A J 1966 *The Research Paper: Form and Content.* Wadsworth, Belmont, California

Rudd E 1975 *The Highest Education: A Study of Graduate Education in Britain.* Routledge and Kegan Paul, London

Rudd E, Hatch S 1968 *Graduate Study and After.* Weidenfeld and Nicholson, London

Trott B 1966 *Report Writing.* Heinemann, London

Turabain K L 1978 *Students Guide for Writing College Papers.* University of Chicago, Chicago, Illinois

Walford G 1981 Classification and framing in postgraduate education. *Stud. Higher Educ.* 6: 147–58

Welsh J M 1979 *The First Year of Postgraduate Research Study.* Society for Research into Higher Education, Guildford

Welsh J M 1981 The PhD student. *Stud. Higher Educ.* 6: 159–62

Winkler A C, McCuen J R 1979 *Writing the Research Paper: A Handbook.* Harcourt, Brace and Jovanovich, New York

R. McAleese

Distance Education

Distance education, simply and somewhat broadly defined, is "education which either does not imply the physical presence of the teacher appointed to dispense it in the place where it is received, or in which the teacher is present only on occasions or for selected tasks". This French Government definition of the term *télé-enseignement* (Loi 71.556 du 12 juillet 1971) contains two basic elements: the physical separation of teacher and learner and the changed role of the teacher, who may meet students only for "selected tasks" such as counselling, giving tutorials or seminars, or solving study problems.

Distance education methods can be successfully used for catering to groups who, for geographical, economic, or social reasons, are unable or unwilling to make use of traditional (e.g., classroom-based) provision. In so doing, they can liberate the student from constraints of space, time, and age.

1. Principal Defining Features

In addition to the key element of physical separation of teacher and learner cited above, Holmberg identifies six main categories of description for the term (Holmberg 1981 pp. 11–13):

(a) the use of preproduced courses as the main basis for study;

(b) the existence of organized two-way communication between the student and a supporting organization, that is, the university, college, or school with its tutors and counsellors;

(c) the planned and explicit catering for individual study;

(d) the cost effectiveness of the educational use of mass communication methods when large numbers of students follow the same preproduced courses;

(e) the application of industrial work methods to the production of learning materials and to the administration of a distance education scheme (Peters 1973);

(f) the notion of distance study as a mediated form of guided didactic conversation.

The same characteristics will be found embedded in other definitions. For example, in discussing the planning and design of distance learning systems, Kaye and Rumble identify a number of key features, which, although not all found in every instance, contribute to the overall notion of a generalized distance learning system. Concerning students these are:

(a) an enlargement or "opening" of educational opportunity to new target populations, previously deprived either through geographical isolation, lack of formal academic requirements, or employment conditions;

(b) the identification of particular target groups and their key characteristics (needs, age, distribution, time available for study, local facilities, etc.) to enable appropriate courses, learning methods, and delivery systems to be designed on a systematic basis.

Concerning the learning materials and teaching methods which characterize the courses, notable features are:

(a) flexibility in the curriculum and content of the learning materials through, for example, modular structures or credit systems;

(b) the conscious and systematic design of learning material for independent study, incorporating, for example, clearly formulated learning objectives, self-assessment devices, student activities, and the provision of feedback from students to learning system staff and vice versa;

(c) the planned use of a wide range of media and other resources, selected from those available in the context of the system, and suited to the needs of the students; these media may include specially prepared correspondence texts, books, newspaper supplements, posters, radio and television broadcasts, audio- and video-cassettes, films, computer-assisted learning, kits, local tuition and counselling, student self-help groups, lending-library facilities, and so on.

Finally, the following logistical and economic features are characteristic of distance learning systems:

(a) great potential flexibility compared to conventional provision in implementation, in teaching methods, and in student groups covered;

(b) centralized, mass production of standardized learning materials (such as texts, broadcasts, kits, and so on) in an almost industrialized manner, implying clear division of labour in the creation and production procedures;

(c) a systematic search for, and use of, existing infrastructure and facilities as part of the system (e.g., libraries, postal and other distribution services, printers, publishers, broadcasting organizations, manufacturers, etc.);

(d) potentially a significantly lower recurrent unit cost per student than that obtainable through conventional (classroom or equivalent) teaching arrangements and also potentially a considerably lower capital cost per student (Kaye and Rumble 1981 pp. 18–19).

The development of distance education methods in the recent past owes a great deal to the pioneering work carried out in the field of correspondence education (see *Correspondence Study*). The print-based materials have remained but have been supplemented by modern communication media and personal contact. Thus distance education is often distinguished from correspondence study (Keegan 1980) by the notion of three-way teaching, combining ". . . the permanence of print, the reach of radio, and the intimacy of face-to-face study" (Young et al. 1980 p. 21). Slightly extending this definition, distance education can be equated with the combined, systematic, and flexible use of at least three major elements: print-based communication, broadcasting and/or other technologies, and face-to-face contact, in support of an independent learner. Distance education methods imply major differences to intramural or classroom-based provision on three main dimensions: the learning experiences

of the students, the nature of the teaching/learning materials, and the administrative and organizational structure of the providing institution. These three facets are briefly discussed below and are broadly relevant to the whole range of distance education provision, be it small, flexible, and localized, or large scale and highly centralized.

2. Learning at a Distance

Distance education methods cater *par excellence* for the individual learner studying independently. This entails, in most instances, high levels of motivation amongst the learners, and is a key reason for the fact that the great majority of distance education projects are aimed primarily at adults. Nevertheless, distance education provision does exist in some countries for school-age children unable (e.g., for geographical or health reasons) to attend classes. Examples, dating back for many years, can be found in Australia (radio plus correspondence tuition and personal contact), and in France, where the *Centre National d'Enseignement par Correspondance* was originally established during the Second World War to provide teaching, at a distance, to children unable to go to school. Most of its provision nowadays, however, is aimed at adults.

In general, then, distance students are adults. They also tend to form very heterogeneous groups, compared to those following more traditional educational channels, so it is difficult to characterize the "typical" distance student. In a review of student characteristics at distance teaching universities in 10 different countries, the following features were highlighted (Kaye and Rumble 1981 pp. 35–38):

(a) an age range of 20–40 years;

(b) majority studying on a part-time basis;

(c) men generally outnumber women;

(d) study is primarily carried out at home;

(e) high levels of motivation;

(f) the majority of students are from less privileged social groups;

(g) students studying voluntarily (as opposed to those in compulsory inservice courses) tend to be from urban areas.

Concerning reasons for study, it is evident that the obtaining of examinations, diplomas, and degrees, and the acquisition and/or updating of professional and career-related skills rank very highly amongst a large proportion of students enrolled on distance courses (see, for example, Holmberg 1981 pp. 21–24).

The skills needed for study at a distance have some features in common with those required in any learning environment. However, certain skills are of particular importance in the distance learning situation. These include:

(a) setting of personal study objectives;

(b) development of personal confidence in the ability to study primarily on one's own;

(c) planning and organizing study time and study strategies;

(d) developing study skills in learning from the reading and analysis of self-instructional and other print materials, and, where appropriate, from listening to and viewing broadcasts, using audio- and video-tape material, participating in group discussions, and undertaking practical work alone and/or in a group situation;

(e) making use of, and communicating with, a tutor—in writing, by telephone, or at face-to-face meetings. Tutors may play a range of different roles: counsellor, problem solver, provider of feedback, resource person, assessor.

The skills listed above are of particular importance because the distance learner does not benefit from the same levels and amounts of pacing, structure, and formal and informal contact with peers and teachers as a student in an intramural educational institution. However, distance students do have the advantage of being able to plan their study activities around a personal timetable in a relatively flexible manner, and this is one of the overwhelming reasons cited for enrolling on distance education courses, especially when employment and family obligations make other options impractical or inconvenient. Furthermore, it is evident that in well-planned and adequately financed distance education systems, the distance learner need not feel disadvantaged and may, in fact, be better served than many studying through more traditional channels.

The range of distance education situations and courses is now so diverse that it is impossible to make generalizations about study patterns and strategies adopted by learners. Even different students following the same course in the same institution will adopt and develop different approaches, according to their own tastes and interests. However, it is fair to say that in a large proportion of cases, the majority of the learner's time is taken up by individual study of specially prepared printed materials (which as the main "information channel" can be considered as analogous to a classroom presentation or lecture in a traditional context). Students may be provided with sets of learning objectives and related self-assessment questions and exercises, with model answers, against which they can check their understanding and progress. A much smaller proportion of time may be spent in viewing or listening to broadcasts or recorded audiovisual and audio material, often ideal for presenting real-life situations, or case-study or experimental material which cannot be clearly communicated in printed form. From time to time, either at the student's discretion, or by certain predetermined dates, the student will submit written work to a correspondence tutor in response to preset assignments. Assignment modes may consist of multiple-choice tests, short answer questions, essays on set topics, or more extensive self-chosen projects or dissertations. The correspondence tutor may grade and comment on this work, and may also be able to meet the student to discuss it at a regular tutorial. In many instances, tutorial sessions at local study centres also exist to enable students to discuss general study problems and clear up difficulties in understanding. For example, the Lesotho Distance Teaching Centre, because of difficulties experienced by students in studying at home, set up a network of local study centres where ". . . students could come once or twice a week, work in adequate comfort and good light by themselves at their courses and seek help from an 'elbow tutor' as they needed it" (Young et al. 1980 p. 71). Other opportunities for interpersonal contact also exist in many systems—ranging from informally organized "self-help" groups established by students living in the same neighbourhood, to week-long residential contact programmes (such as the British Open University's "summer schools") which can provide an opportunity for extended personal and group tuition and, for example, laboratory practicals and field work.

3. Distance Teaching Materials

Teaching materials designed for use in a classroom or other intramural learning environment are generally not suitable, and certainly not sufficient, for the distance learning situation. A standard school or college textbook, for example, is often designed to be used either as a source of reference, and/or as a basis for discussion and exposition by a teacher in a classroom situation. And it is assumed that the student will be able to refer to peers, teachers, or other information sources (e.g., a library) when experiencing difficulties in following the material in the textbook. Audiovisual material for classroom use is also generally designed for a group situation with a teacher's presence assumed. Some of these materials may be suitable for use in group tutorials in a distance education programme, but would probably not fit the situation of a distance learner viewing or listening to a broadcast in isolation, at home.

A number of criteria are of key importance in the design of materials for distance learning. Firstly, it is necessary to take a global approach to the range of media and materials that will be available within a given system, and decide on clear pedagogical functions and roles for each of them. For example, if radio is to be used only in a group situation at a local centre, say in the presence of an *animateur*, then the structure and objectives of the programme will be quite different from one made for individual listening in the home. And an audiotape for individual use will again have different functions to a radio programme for individual listening: a tape can be stopped, and replayed, or used in association with diagrams or experimental equipment.

Secondly, the organization of the materials needs to take into account the resources, capacities, and abilities, of both students and tutors. Prerequisite requirements for starting a course (i.e., knowledge and skills assumed by the course planners) need to be made explicit. Likely areas of difficulty need to be "signposted" to the tutors and perhaps covered by special guidance notes for tutorial and group work. And scheduling of course work should take into account realistic estimates of how much time a typical student is liable to be able to devote to study each week or month.

Materials designed for individual study—and in most cases these will be predominantly print materials—are prepared in a "self-instructional" format, namely: written and presented in a stimulating style (maybe a colloquial style in some cultures); easily "accessible" to the student through the use of aids such as lists of learning objectives, concept maps, indices, glossaries, self-tests, and reviews; attractively designed, making good use of illustrations and of different typographical styles; "student active", containing opportunities for the student to test and monitor progress through activities, questions, and self-assessment exercises embedded in the text; flexible, with some provision for alternative routes and bypasses through the material, (without necessarily resorting to the complexity of a traditional branching programmed text).

A final important criterion of good quality distance-teaching materials concerns the care with which the different media components are integrated with each other. Integration can be considered at two levels. Firstly, materials for tutors, *animateurs*, and other intermediaries in the system must complement and relate clearly to the materials provided for the students; this implies that items such as notes for tutors need to be developed in parallel with the students' course materials. Secondly, when the individual student may be required to use material in several different media (say print, radio, and television), then clear decisions need to be made as to how closely the different media are integrated within the segments of the course. Levels of integration may vary from occasional cross-references, to a very tight structure which obliges the student, for example, to view a specific television programme before being able to proceed with the next section of text.

An example of an extreme form of integration of broadcast and print material is that developed by Radio ECCA, in the Canary Islands, and subsequently adapted for use on the Spanish mainland and in distance education projects in several Latin American countries. In the ECCA system

> . . . every lesson is centred upon a "lesson master sheet". The teacher has a copy of the lesson master sheet in front of him while he broadcasts over the radio, and the student follows his own copy simultaneously in his own home. . . . The student is required to respond to the radio teacher by writing on the lesson master sheet during the course of the broadcast. . . . a full set of master sheets comprises a student's text book. Exercises are included on the back of each master sheet . . . to be completed after the student has listened to the radio broadcast. (Cepeda 1982 pp. 213–14)

This degree of integration of print and broadcast materials is perhaps unusual in the field of distance education, but experience shows that it can be successful in a range of contexts.

4. Institutional Structures

A great variety of institutional structures can be found amongst distance education organizations. In many cases, structures are derived from those of conventional teaching institutions such as universities or schools, which in themselves vary from country to country. In other cases, broadcasting organizations, commercial correspondence colleges, or voluntary organizations, may have provided the original structure on which a distance institution has been built. And more recently, there has been a growth in the number of projects which have involved collaboration between a number of institutions of different sorts, either on a long-term basis or for short-term campaigns.

However, regardless of the underlying institutional structure, a number of specific services to students need to be provided, organized, and administered:

(a) provision (acquisition, development, production), storage, and distribution of course materials;

(b) provision of educational support services (correspondence tuition, possibly telephone or other electronic communication, tutorial classes, study centres, counselling, etc.);

(c) maintenance of administrative and academic records and provision of administrative communication channels (e.g., for enrolment, fee payment, assignment data, etc.);

(d) in some instances, accreditation and the delivery of diplomas, certificates, and degrees.

The question of provision of course materials deserves particular attention in this context, because it is here that differences are perhaps greatest as compared to traditional educational methods, and where economies of scale are most noticeable (when large numbers of students use the same preproduced course materials). Some distance education projects use materials acquired elsewhere, that is, not produced in-house. However, even in this simplest model, the acquired materials may need adapting, translating, and reprinting or reproducing. The majority of projects develop their own teaching materials, both printed and audiovisual, either using their own full-time subject matter specialists and/or academic staff, and/or through the use of part-time consultants. Physical production of materials (printing, audiovisual production) may either be in-house, subcontracted, or carried out in collaboration with a production agency such as a publishing house, broadcasting organization, or a commercial audiovisual producer. Whatever the origin of the materials, they will require storage and distribution facilities, and the greater the variety or range of courses or materials on offer, the greater and more complex will these facilities need to be.

The overriding importance of these aspects of procurement, production, storage, and distribution calls for two comments which illustrate a clear-cut difference between distance and conventional educational provision. Firstly, it implies that distance education is " . . . an industrialized form of teaching and learning" (Peters 1973 p. 206). Rumble has pointed out that, in institutions such as distance teaching universities which " . . . have to undertake directly a number of quasi-industrial processes . . . there is a need for a clear definition of the interrelationships between two broad areas, one of which is more in the nature of a business enterprise . . . while the other is more in the nature of traditionally conceived academic areas" (Kaye and Rumble 1981 p. 179). The industrial, or quasi-industrial, nature of the materials development and production aspects of distance teaching is certainly a reality in many of the large-scale centralized systems. Course development planning may start five or six years before the finished product is "launched"; orders need to be placed with suppliers and sub-contractors; deadlines and production schedules drawn up and adhered to; personnel needs estimated; and contracts prepared. The constraints imposed by the production and distribution needs can lead to a situation of potential conflict between production demands and the working methods and values of the originators of the course materials—be they full-time academic staff employed by the institution, or outside consultants and lesson writers. This is related to a second main difference between traditional and distance education institutions: namely the changed role of the teacher in a mediated or distance learning system. A number of aspects contribute to this changed role:

(a) the need to develop skills in preparing mediated

materials (print, audiovisual, etc.) both for individual use, and for use by tutors and learners in group situations; these are not necessarily the same skills as those required of a good face-to-face or classroom teacher;

(b) the loss of direct personal control of the teaching/learning process and the lack of direct feedback from students characteristic of the classroom situation;

(c) the need to work with other professionals (designers, producers, editors) in the preparation and production of materials, and the resultant requirement to submit one's work to scrutiny and comment.

These aspects are present regardless of the course creation models adopted in any particular institution—which may vary from that of an author and editor working together, to that of a large-scale course team of academics, editors, educational technologists, producers, and designers.

When, in addition to course provision, the other three service areas (educational support, records, and accreditation) are provided by the same institution, and the number of students is large, then the need to adopt industrial working methods already referred to becomes even more imperative. For example, computerized systems for organizing despatch of course materials, and for maintenance of tutor and student records may become a necessity; industrial-style management and control methods may need to be introduced to ensure efficient integration of the work in a range of different specialized areas.

However, many distance learning projects and schemes are decentralized and even localized, with different organizations being responsible for each of the categories of services listed above. Such projects can maintain a flexibility of operation which is often more difficult to achieve in large-scale and centrally controlled institutions such as the British Open University.

Neil has presented an institutional analysis of distance learning systems on the basis of the locus and nature of the control of four key areas: finance, examination and accreditation, curriculum and materials, and delivery and student support systems (Neil 1981 pp. 140–41). He quotes five models or types of institution based on this analysis:

(a) the classic centre-periphery model, such as the British Open University, with high levels of control in all four areas;

(b) the associated centre model such as Spain's *Universidad Nacional de Educación a Distancia* which works with over 50 associated centres each responsible for their own delivery and student support services;

(c) the dispersed centre model (e.g., Coastline Community College, California) which cooperates with a whole range of organizations and bodies in the community but retains a fair measure of central control over accreditation for many courses;

(d) the switchboard organization model, exemplified by Norway's recently created distance education institute (*Norskfjernundervisning*) which has essentially enabling, coordinating, initiating, and approving roles in the further development of the country's existing educational resources for distance students;

(e) the service institution model, for example the *Deutsches Institut für Fernstudien* (DIFF) at Tubingen which provides services to a range of distance teaching organizations (e.g., materials development, consultancy, evaluation), and has little control over any areas except in the creation and production of course materials.

5. The Extent of Distance Education

With Perraton, the main early developments of distance education (as defined in this entry) would be traced to the mid-1960s when ". . . a series of projects began in which attempts were made to link the three components of broadcasting, correspondence, and face-to-face tuition" (Perraton 1979 p. 14). There were a few isolated earlier examples of broadcasts linked to correspondence tuition (e.g., using radio in New Zealand in 1937, and the programmes of the Chicago Television College, which started in 1956) but since the 1960s there has been a very significant quantitative and qualitative increase in the number and range of distance programmes throughout the world. Much of this development has built on earlier experiences of correspondence tuition (e.g., the United Kingdom, Scandinavia, and the United States), correspondence plus face-to-face tuition (e.g., the very extensive programmes in existence in the Soviet Union since the 1920s), and the combined use of broadcasting and study groups (e.g., farm radio forums in Canada, India, and a number of African countries).

It is not possible within the scope of this article to provide a complete coverage of distance education projects worldwide. Firstly, the number and range of projects is so large: in a small country like the United Kingdom alone, over 70 distance education projects have started since 1970—ranging from the national highly centralized Open University, to decentralized and community-based projects and campaigns. Secondly, developments in communications technology are likely to bring about qualitative and structural changes in the design of distance education systems in the near future in a number of

countries. These developments include applications of satellite communications (e.g., the University of the South Pacific, or the Open Learning Institute in British Columbia), of computers (e.g., the PLATO system in the United States), and of course the increasingly widespread availability of audio- and video-cassette/videodisc equipment. These developments are likely to bring about major changes in the roles of both broadcasting and print-based communication in distance education, at least in the industrially advanced countries.

At the present time, distance education projects exist in the majority of countries in the world at one level or another (see, for example, Daniel et al. 1982). The major part of this provision is concerned with adult education, which the Organisation for Economic Co-operation and Development defines as "organized programmes of education provided for the benefit of, and adapted to the needs of, persons not in the regular school or university system and generally older than 15". There appears to be no internationally recognized system for classifying adult education, but it is generally agreed that it covers both formal and nonformal curricula. Table 1 lists, purely for illustrative purposes, examples of the use of distance methods for a variety of adult education programmes. A number of the projects listed in the table emanate from institutions which also provide courses in other areas.

The examples listed form only a tiny fraction of existing provision, but detailed accounts of a wide range of projects can be found in a number of recent

Table 1
Examples of distance education provision

Programmes not equivalent to formal education levels:	
(a) Basic education	ACPO, Colombia
	Adult Literacy Project, United Kingdom
(b) Community education	Radio Learning Campaigns, Tanzania
(c) Agricultural extension	*Radio Educative*, Senegal
	Radio Farm Forums, Thailand
(d) Vocational	UNED, Costa Rica

Programmes equivalent to formal education levels:	
(a) Primary	Radio ECCA, Canary Islands
(b) General secondary	Air Correspondence High School, Korea
(c) Technical secondary	Open University of Sri Lanka
(d) Higher	Everyman's University, Israel
	Open University, United Kingdom
	Polytechnic Institutes, Soviet Union
(e) Teacher training	Allama Iqbal Open University, Pakistan
	Correspondence Course Unit, Kenya

publications. Young et al. (1980) list over 120 projects in developing countries, excluding those only operating at degree level. Rumble and Harry (1982) describe 9 institutions (from both developed and developing countries) which have been established in the 1970s to provide primarily degree-level programmes. MacKenzie et al. (1975) include case studies of postsecondary-level distance and open education projects drawn from 13 countries. And detailed accounts of eight basic education projects in Europe can be found in Kaye and Harry (1982). Finally, interesting samples of print materials taken from 30 or so distance education courses (from 10 different countries) can be found in the manual on writing for distance education prepared by the International Extension College (1979).

See also: Open University of the United Kingdom; Self-directed Learning in Distance Learning; Television: Distribution and Reception; Telephones in Education; Economics of Educational Technology

Bibliography

Cepeda L E 1982 Radio ECCA, Canary Islands. In: Kaye A R, Harry K (eds.) 1982
Daniel J F, Stroud M F, Thompson J (eds.) 1982 *Learning at a Distance: A World Perspective.* Athabasca University/ICDE, Edmonton
Holmberg B 1981 *Status and Trends of Distance Education.* Kogan Page, London
International Extension College (IEC) 1979 *Writing for Distance Education: A Manual for Writers of Distance Teaching Texts and Independent Study Materials.* IEC, Cambridge
Jenkins J 1981 *Materials for Learning: How to Teach Adults at a Distance.* Routledge and Kegan Paul, London
Kaye A R, Harry K (eds.) 1982 *Using the Media for Adult Basic Education.* Croom Helm, London
Kaye A R, Rumble G (eds.) 1981 *Distance Teaching for Higher and Adult Education.* Croom Helm, London
Keegan D J 1980 Defining distance education. *Distance Educ.* 1: 13–36
MacKenzie N I, Postgate R S, Scupham J, Bartram B (eds.) 1975 *Open Learning: Systems and Problems in Post-secondary Education.* UNESCO, Paris (also in French and Spanish versions)
Neil M W (ed.) 1981 *Education of Adults at a Distance.* Kogan Page, London
Perraton H D (ed.) 1979 *Alternative Routes to Formal Education: Distance Teaching for School Equivalency.* World Bank, Washington, DC
Perraton H D 1981 A theory for distance education. *Prospects* 11 (1)
Peters O 1973 *Die Didaktische Struktur des Fernunterrichts: Untersuchungen zu einer Industrialisierten Form des Lehrens und Lernens.* Tübingen Beiträge zum Fernstudium, 7. Weinheim, Beltz
Rumble G, Harry K (eds.) 1982 *The Distance Teaching Universities.* Croom Helm, London
Young M, Perraton H D, Jenkins J, Dodds T 1980 *Distance Teaching for the Third World: The Lion and the Clockwork Mouse.* Routledge and Kegan Paul, London

A. R. Kaye

Diversified Curriculum

Diversification of the curriculum refers to the introduction of more practical or vocational content into schools or stages of schooling which previously have been dominated by general education of an academic kind. In practice, the term refers to lower- and upper-secondary education and to schools in developing countries. There has, however, also been a strong interest in many industrialized countries in the 1970s and early 1980s in strengthening school-based vocational and prevocational education.

Curriculum diversification includes such changes as the introduction of "prevocational" subjects or streams, programmes aiming at complete vocational preparation, or work experience introduced as part of the general education that schools organize for all pupils. To establish or strengthen vocational schooling parallel to other schools is also to diversify provisions. But usually diversification policies aim at vocationalizing curricula in existing general education schools. A diversified curriculum is implied in the concepts of the comprehensive school and the multilateral school.

1. Aims

In its most radical form, curriculum diversification reflects a concept of general education that rejects the traditional Western academic idea of the educated person, also for those preparing for university entry, and which instead gives pride of place to vocational knowledge and skills, solidarity with manual workers, and ideological commitment. Socialist ideology, with its concepts of polytechnical education and of unity between theory and practice in education, provides strong support for radical curriculum diversification. It is those developing countries which have strongly pursued socialist policies in general, such as the People's Republic of China, Cuba, and Tanzania, which have tried to vocationalize secondary schooling most thoroughly, not only by stressing vocational education, but also participation in manual work as part of general education.

Curriculum diversification policies have often been pursued in order to enhance the economic value of schooling. In less developed countries and Western industrialized countries alike, vocationalization of general education to varying degrees was a typical policy response in the late 1970s and early 1980s to the employment problems facing school leavers. These problems have been especially severe in many developing countries where the growth in school enrolments has far outstripped the growth in opportunities for wage employment in the modern sector. By adapting curricula more directly to particular occupations, it was hoped to promote economic development and mitigate unemployment among school leavers. In some developing countries, vocationalization has also been accompanied by a shift in official development priorities away from the modern sector and towards improvement of peasant productivity. This idea of "adapting school curricula to rural development needs" and to the traditional local economy is not novel. It was promoted in many colonial territories in the 1920s and 1930s by influential administrators, notably in Sub-Saharan Africa. Such curricula failed to take hold then, because parents and pupils did not look to schools for useful skills in their traditional occupations, but for social promotion. "Adapted curricula" were also resented by leaders in the struggle for independence as a type of education that would bar indigenous people from ascent to position of influence.

2. A Sri Lankan Example

Events in Sri Lanka illustrate recent diversification policies and early unsuccessful attempts by the colonizers to vocationalize the curriculum. Recent attempts have been influenced by a blend of motives: socialist educational ideals, concerns about school leaver unemployment, and a "broadly based" development strategy (Wijemanne 1978). Developments there also illustrate another common experience: controversy about whether more vocationally biased curricula in fact serve their purpose. In Sri Lanka, the Handessa Rural Education Scheme in the 1930s sought to develop a curriculum to meet the needs of rural dwellers, but "it had to be abandoned as it came to be viewed as a ruse designed to keep the underprivileged away from the prestigious academic curriculum". In 1971, following political unrest among unemployed school leavers, prevocational studies were introduced for all pupils in junior secondary schools, geared towards agriculture and traditional crafts. Development-related projects were to be an important part of the senior secondary curricula. These policies were rooted in a development strategy that was both influenced by socialist ideals and stressed gradual improvement of productivity in the traditional rural economy. A new government came to power in 1977. It reaffirmed the importance of the modern sector and of a market economy. It reversed the policy of prevocational education, giving instead priority to general education on the grounds that it makes the school leaver more economically adaptable, and stressing the need for modern technical schools.

3. Critics and Advocates

There is a continuing controversy about vocationalization of general education. Critics, such as Foster (1965) and Blaug (1973), argue that vocational curricula will not be taken seriously by pupils and parents as long as the associated economic opportu-

nities remain very inferior compared to those provided by a general education. They also maintain that "academic" general education usually *is* a vocationally relevant training because of its adaptability, and that curriculum change would have negligible effects on school leaver unemployment, the drift to towns, or the superior esteem in which white-collar work is held. The cost per pupil is liable to be higher in vocational education. The most ambitious form of diversified secondary education—multilateral schools that provide vocational education in earnest for a range of occupations—is especially costly. Critics also question the effectiveness of school-based vocational education: competent teachers are scarce and hard to recruit and keep, and equipment is liable to be obsolete or too advanced for the local economy. Therefore, they argue, vocational education is generally better provided for on the job than in the school. Reportedly, employers often have a sceptical view of youth coming from the school-based vocational courses even in generously financed multilateral schools.

Compared to the critics, the advocates of diversified curriculum tend to have greater faith in manpower planning and in the role that schools can play in shaping attitudes, and in teaching needed occupational skills. President Nyerere of Tanzania stands out as an advocate (1967, 1977) for a vocational orientation, centred on community development problems, throughout the curriculum. His influential concept of *Education for Self-reliance* is, it should be noted, part of a socialist programme of societal transformation. This is increasingly stressed by advocates of diversified curricula in the face of the arguments of critics. They then concede that the prospects for successful curriculum diversification are bleak in the context of gradualist development strategies (Bacchus 1981). However, it is possible to speculate that school-based vocational education is more viable when "vocational" employment opportunities are already expanding in the modern sector of the economy.

4. Shifting World Bank Policy

In spite of the great many curriculum diversification projects which have been undertaken around the world, there is very little publicly available evaluation of such projects. Existing material is largely in the form of reports internal to ministries of education and international aid agencies, and the impression is that systematic evaluation of the effectiveness of projects is rare even in such internal documents. The World Bank has been a major source of finance for such projects: 79 in the 1963 to 1978 period. Curriculum diversification accorded well with the Bank's 1974 policy paper on education in which (1974 p. 21) it was claimed that school curricula were excessively theoretical and abstract, insufficiently orientated to local conditions, and insufficiently concerned with attitudes and with manual, social, and leadership skills. It was suggested (p. 22) that the content of education must be reorientated to relate skills taught to jobs, and vocationalization of the curricula of academic schools was mentioned approvingly along with separately provided vocational and technical schools.

The 1980 World Bank Sector Policy Paper on Education, on the other hand, written after an initial internal review of the Bank's experience with such projects, concludes that diversified secondary schools are in general inappropriate for "training large numbers in specific vocational skills" (1980 p. 45) and that there is no consistent empirical support for the hope that prevocational curricula would instil in students more favourable attitudes towards manual labour. However, it may be appropriate on a limited scale, as a basis for the training of technicians or as a preparation for higher education, especially in technical fields.

As of 1982, diversified curriculum remains a controversial concept. There appears to be mounting disillusionment in international aid agencies and some governments with that version of it which involves vocationalization of general secondary education. Comparative and more systematic evaluation of diversified curriculum projects is needed to illuminate the conditions which make different types of vocational education viable. Such research is now underway in Tanzania and Colombia in collaboration with the World Bank, and in Kenya with sponsorship from the Swedish International Development Authority.

Bibliography

Bacchus M K 1981 Education for development in underdeveloped countries. *Comp. Educ.* 17: 215–27

Blaug M 1973 *Education and the Employment Problem in Developing Countries*. International Labour Organization, Geneva

Foster P 1965 The vocational school fallacy in development planning. In: Anderson C A, Bowman M J (eds.) 1965 *Education and Economic Development*. Aldine, Chicago, Illinois

Lillis K, Hogan D 1983 Dilemmas of diversification: Problems associated with vocational education in developing countries. *Comp. Educ.* 19: 89–108

Nyerere J K 1967 *Education for Self-reliance*. Government Printer, Dar es Salaam

Nyerere J K 1977 *The Arusha Declaration Ten Years After*. Government Printer, Dar es Salaam

Wijemanne E L 1978 *Educational Reforms in Sri Lanka*. Report Studies C 70. Division of Educational Policy and Planning, UNESCO, Paris

World Bank 1974 *Education*. Sector Working Paper. World Bank, Washington, DC

World Bank 1981 *Education*. Sector Policy Paper. World Bank, Washington, DC

J. Lauglo

Divorce Counseling

Divorce counseling and its dynamics began to appear in the literature in the early 1970s, with the first *Journal of Divorce* appearing in 1977 (Kaslow 1981 p. 693). A review of the literature shows divorce counseling to be in a transitional stage in the emergence of this speciality (Kressel and Deutsch 1977 p. 443) which came about as an outgrowth of marriage counseling.

1. Definition

Although divorce counseling is expressed differently by different counselors, there are some commonly recognized goals which define the specialty at present. In general, it focuses on a couple's decision to get divorced and/or the negotiation of the terms of a divorce settlement. Within this definition, then, the goal of divorce counseling ". . . is to help a couple disengage from a marriage with a minimum of destructiveness to themselves and their children, and with the personal freedom to form new relationships" (Framo 1978 p. 77).

2. The Process of Psychic Divorce

To aid a separated couple in coping with their loss, in working through ambivalence and in fostering their autonomy and self-esteem as separate persons (Gurman and Kniskern 1978 p. 881) requires relating to a process of psychic separation, sometimes known as the mourning process, because it entails dynamics very similar to those involved in mourning a death (Lowenstein 1979 p. 196). The process of separating acquires this grieving quality because it is a disruptive psychosocial transition which involves multiple drastic changes that may include loss of significant others (such as children). This transition may also include changes in economic status, living routines, role as wife or husband, home, friends, and status in the community (Lowenstein 1979 p. 195). Since the individual's entire life-style may change, the grief and disorganization which emerge are often extreme.

The counselor's main responsibility becomes one of providing a time and space for the psychic divorce process which includes four commonly recognized stages: the predivorce decision stage; the decision stage; the mourning stage; and the reequilibration stage.

2.1 Predivorce Decision Stage

During this period there is an increased dissatisfaction and tension between the partners. There is a clear decline in intimacy, and eventually it becomes known publicly that the marriage is no longer viable. A physical separation may occur and lawyers may be contacted (Kressel and Deutsch 1977 pp. 417–18).

2.2 Decision Stage

In this period, at least one partner has made the decision to divorce. Anxiety over the prospect of living alone emerges, and sometimes partners try to return to their earlier intimacy, but renewed conflict usually occurs. This process is often repeated several times, but there is then a final acceptance of the reality of a divorce and conflict over the settlement emerges (Kressel and Deutsch 1977 p. 418).

2.3 Mourning Stage

This stage includes: (a) a feeling of numbness interrupted by outbursts of distress and/or anger; (b) the emergence, for a time, of yearning and searching for the lost person; (c) disorganization and despair; and finally (d) reorganization to a greater or lesser degree (Lowenstein 1979 pp. 196–97).

2.4 Reequilibration Stage

If the mourning process is completed, self-growth occurs along with lessened dwelling on the past and the former marriage. A balanced view of one another emerges in the former partners along with a sense of psychological closure (Kressel and Deutsch 1977 p. 419).

3. Interventions

To aid couples in reaching this sense of closure, divorce counselors use varied interventions which are contained in either reflexive, contextual, or substantive strategies (Kressel and Deutsch 1977 p. 425).

Reflexive strategies focus on building trust and confidence between therapist and separating parties. This is accomplished through explicit statements of reassurance and support, setting rules, and maintaining of confidentiality and impartiality. Impartiality is established by clarifying two points—the decision-making responsibility is the client's, not the counselor's, and the aim of treatment is the growth and well-being of each spouse as an individual (Kressel and Deutsch 1977 p. 430). During this time, an assessment must be made, including the gathering of information to determine whether or not the marriage is actually headed toward divorce (Kressel and Deutsch 1979 pp. 426–27).

Contextual interventions include those strategies by which the therapist tries to promote a climate conducive to decision making. Here the emphasis is on cognitive preparation for the individual's loss, through helping clients recognize the changes this loss entails and the accompanying grief process that occurs. The counseling task is one of reducing the level of hostility and tension while not denying or circumventing anger (Kressel and Deutsch p. 431). Full expression of intense feeling of blame, hatred, and guilt is encouraged to help the couple let go, ultimately, of the relationship (Lowenstein 1979 p. 210). Strategies for reducing destructive tension

include: education about the couple's patterns; negotiating physical separation; modifying the format of sessions by using cotherapy and/or couple groups; and baring the historical roots of the patterns by inviting members of the family of origin to counseling sessions to disentangle the past from the present (Kressel and Deutsch 1977 p. 433).

Substantive interventions are those tactics which produce resolution and settlement, including establishing a climate in which negotiations can take place. Educating spouses on the norms of equity and discouraging revenge seeking are essential; structuring negotiations so couples can operate to conduct joint bargaining is another aspect (Kressel and Deutsch 1977 p. 435). Some therapists also view the settlement phase as one where they mediate between lawyer and client, perhaps helping clients choose their attorneys and interpreting the client to the lawyer, as well as helping the client understand the lawyer's role.

Protecting the welfare of children is a widely acknowledged goal in the settlement phase. Tactics include: education of parents in understanding the overall effect of marital separation on their children; mediating terms for custody and visitation rights; and allowing space and time for expression of emotions between children and parents (Kressel and Deutsch 1977 p. 442). Joint sessions are encouraged so children can express their wishes regarding custody and visitation rights, and to allow parents time to explain their reasons for separation in hopes of preventing the children from taking on guilt and seeing themselves as the cause of the divorce (Lowenstein 1979 p. 313). In this way, the counselor becomes an advocate for the children.

4. Research on Divorce Counseling

At present there is no research which examines the comparative effectiveness of different divorce counseling techniques. While couples' group counseling has been shown to have measurable positive value, it has not been compared to the benefit derived from other counseling modalities. The research to date indicates no studies exist which examine the outcomes of divorce counseling when it is the modality in which the family unit is counseled (Kaslow 1981 p. 693).

See also: Marriage Counseling

Bibliography

Framo J L 1978 The friendly divorce. *Psychol. Today* 11(9): 76–102
Gurman A S, Kniskern D P 1978 Research on marital and family therapy: Progress, perspective and prospect. In: Garfield S L, Bergin A E (eds.) 1978 *Handbook of Psychotherapy and Behavior Change: An Empirical Analysis*, 2nd edn. Wiley, New York

Kaslow F W 1981 Divorce and divorce therapy. In: Gurman A S, Kniskern D F (eds.) 1981 *Handbook of Family Therapy*. Brunner/Mazel, New York

Kressel K, Deutsch M 1977 Divorce therapy: An in-depth survey of therapists' views. *Fam. Process* 16: 413–43

Lowenstein S F 1979 Helping family members cope with divorce. In: Eisenberg S, Patterson L E (eds.) 1979 *Helping Clients with Special Concerns*. Rand McNally, Chicago, Illinois

T. J. M. Cohen; M. Cohen

Djibouti: System of Education

The Republic of Djibouti in northeast Africa gained its independence in 1977, succeeding the former French territory of the Afars and the Issas. The nation is small, covering an area of 23,310 square kilometers (8,998 square miles) at the southern entrance to the Red Sea and bounded by the Gulf of Aden to the east, by Ethiopia to the north and west, and by Somalia to the south.

The population was estimated at 306,000 in 1982, with a high average annual growth rate of 4.1 percent (United States Central Intelligence Agency 1982 p. 57). The indigenous people are the Somali, mostly Issa, who make up the majority, and the Afar, of Ethiopian origin. In terms of religious affiliation, 94 percent of the populace are Moslem and 6 percent Christian. A small community of foreigners, mostly French or Arab, also reside in the country.

Djibouti is not well-favored in geographic resources. It is a hot, arid land of desert and volcanic soil. French involvement in the region began in 1859, centering on the port of Djibouti, whose strategic position invests the country with its economic potential. The colony was called French Somaliland until 1967.

Since independence, the nation has not enjoyed political peace. Political competition between the two major ethnic groups has led to terrorism, cabinet crises, and changes of prime minister. Such disturbances have affected the educational system by periodically distracting educators from their efforts. In the early 1980s, political power was shared by a Somali president and an Afar prime minister.

The nation's economic system is generally weak, based chiefly on services and commercial activities centered on Djibouti's seaport, airport, the Djibouti–Addis Ababa railway, and a growing banking sector. Thus, the government has had to depend on financial aid from such sources as the World Bank and the Arab states. Nearly all foodstuffs must be imported, as only 1 percent of the country's land is cultivated (Europa 1982 pp. 222–23).

1. Structure of the Educational System

Education in Djibouti has developed along the same lines as in other French dependencies—education by and for the *metropole* (see *France: System of Education*). Thus, in the limited number of schools maintained in the former colony, a goal of assimilating the indigenous peoples into French culture was pursued in disregard of their traditional culture. The lack of deep concern in the past for promoting education is reflected in the estimate that by the 1980s Djibouti's literacy rate was barely five percent (United States Central Intelligence Agency 1982 p. 57).

The first Western education in the area was offered by Roman Catholic missionaries, who, in 1884, opened embryonic schools in French Somaliland. Until the Second World War such mission schools, operating in parallel to the more popular Moslem Koranic schools, provided nearly all of the formal education in Djibouti. After the war, state schools forged rapidly ahead of the mission institutions in enrollment, so that by 1949 there were 463 pupils in state primary schools, 204 in mission schools, and 482 in Koranic schools (Thompson and Adloff 1968 pp. 147–48).

The objections of Moslem parents to sending their children to secular or mission schools were settled in 1964, when provision was made for Koranic instruction to be offered in such institutions but at different hours from the secular subjects. In this same year the first primary cycle of six years was extended to include courses leading to the higher elementary certificate (*brevet elementaire*).

The 1960s and 1970s saw rapid growth in primary-school attendance. The enrollment of 2,364 in 1958 had risen 2.4 times to 5,698 by 1967 (Thompson and Adloff 1968 pp. 143–44). Enrollment over these years was growing at 500 to 600 pupils annually until, by 1973, the yearly increase exceeded 1,000 children. In 1974, the government added 206 new classes, 123 of them in the city of Djibouti, with the rest spread over the rural areas. By 1975 primary-school attendance reached 11,000 (70 percent public, 30 percent Roman Catholic) and by 1979–80 was 13,740 in around 50 schools (Tholomier 1981 p. 113, Europa 1982 p. 223). An increasing willingness of parents to send girls to school was reflected in the tripling of female enrollment over the 1958–66 period.

The development of secondary education has been less spectacular (see Fig. 1). The first secondary school was instituted with the introduction of the *cours complémentaire* in 1949. Not until 1956 did this school become a lycée, a coeducational institution, which had a student body of 306 by 1963. By 1966, the school had 40 candidates prepared for the *baccalauréat* diploma (Thompson and Adloff 1968 p. 144). Secondary enrollment rose from 750 in 1970 to 1,400 in 1975. By 1980 the secondary system had grown to six *collèges d'enseignement secondaire* and two lycées enrolling 3,882 students (Europa 1982 p. 223).

There is no higher education in Djibouti, and so

students must travel abroad for further studies. Many Djiboutians are supported by grants to study in France. The lack of higher education opportunities in Djibouti has contributed to the nation's shortage of indigenous professional and technical personnel. For example, in 1973 there was only one native-born medical doctor in the country.

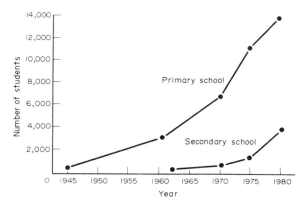

Figure 1
Primary- and secondary-school enrollments, 1945–80

Vocational opportunities in the country have increased significantly since the 1950s. Roman Catholic nuns were the pioneers in vocational education when they opened the *École Menagère*, a home-economics school for girls, and in 1950 the government followed by starting a similar school. In 1954, a two-year program in navigation was launched, and in 1956 commercial classes were offered. By 1966 there were 166 students enrolled in the government's *Centre de Formation Professionnelle* for boys over 14 years of age to train as mechanics, stenographers, and accountants (Thompson and Adloff 1968 p. 145).

The *Collège d'Enseignement Technique*, paralleling the liberal-arts curriculum of the lycées of Djibouti, offers industrial and commercial courses. Enrollment grew from 236 in 1970 to 800 by 1975 (Tholomier 1981 p. 114). A vocational-training center for adults and youths, created in 1968, offers courses in masonry, hotel operations, and automobile and refrigerator repair.

2. Administration and Finance

While Djibouti remained a French dependency, all final educational decisions—the curricula, budget, personnel—were made in France. However, the highest local authority, the territory's minister of education, did hold some power, such as that of appointing an educational advisory committee, con-

sisting of parents, government officials, and teachers (Thompson and Adloff 1968 p. 148). Since independence, the Djiboutian government has assumed overall responsibility for education under a minister of national education, youth, and sports.

The French government in 1964 agreed to pay all costs for secondary education, thus allowing the Djibouti government to allocate all available local funds (about 18 percent of local revenues) to primary education.

After independence, in 1979, slightly over five percent of the Djiboutian gross national product was reserved for public expenditure on education (UNESCO 1981). Educational funding is highly centralized, with the city of Djibouti continuing to be favored in the award of financial support at the expense of the rest of the country.

3. Curricula, Examinations, and Certification

During colonial times, curricula in both state and mission schools derived from France. Learning materials were provided by the *metropole*, and the main subjects were the same as those taught in France, except for the addition in Djibouti of home economics and the Islamic religion. Today, efforts are made to adapt curricula, both academic and vocational, to the needs of the new nation.

The *certificat d'études primaires* is the diploma awarded after the completion of six years of primary schooling. The *baccalauréat* is given after the three-year upper cycle in the lycées; and upon successful performance in the state examination a candidate can qualify for university entrance. The *certificat d'aptitude professionnelle* is awarded to graduates of the *Collège d'Enseignement Technique*. These diplomas are not equivalent to those conferred in France, for Djiboutian students' performance is generally below French standards.

4. Supply of Personnel

Before 1967, the training of local teachers was minimal, since public funds were sufficient to import most teaching personnel from France. In 1967, the primary school teaching corps consisted of 100 trained *instituteurs* and 36 monitors and locally trained teachers. By 1980, the total primary corps had risen to 260 (Tholomier 1981 p. 114, Europa 1982 p. 223).

The secondary level in 1967 had only 27 teachers, a number that rose to 57 in 1970, to 148 in 1975, and to 320 by 1980 (UNESCO 1981, Europa 1982 p. 223).

The significant increase in numbers of teachers began when the government started training teachers locally in 1970 and then opened the first normal school in the country in 1973. The earlier lack of such training facilities chiefly affected the upper-primary and secondary levels rather than the lower-primary grades (Tholomier 1981 p. 114).

5. *Future Prospects*

The structure of the educational system in Djibouti remains essentially the same as that of the French system, and it is expected that the French influence in education will remain strong for a long time to come. However, since independence, Djiboutians have gradually begun to liberate themselves culturally from the former *metropole* and to express their Arabism. The school system is becoming more productive than in the past, and efforts are being made to staff the schools locally so as to form stronger links with the local community. It seems clear that Djiboutian leaders consider an effective educational system a key element in their efforts to meet both the country's development needs and the aspirations of the people.

Bibliography

Deschamps H, Decary R, Ménard A 1948 *Côte des Somalis, Réunion, Inde*. Berger-Levrault, Paris
Europa 1982 *Europa Yearbook: A World Survey*, Vol. 2. Europa, London
Poinsot J P 1964 *Djibouti et la côte française des Somalis*. Hachette, Nancy
Tholomier R 1981 *Djibouti, Pawn of the Horn of Africa*. Scarecrow Press, London
Thompson V M, Adloff R 1968 *Djibouti and the Horn of Africa*. Stanford University Press, Stanford, California
UNESCO 1981 *Statistical Yearbook*. UNESCO, Paris
United States Department of State 1982 *Background Notes: Djibouti*. Department of State, Washington DC
United States Central Intelligence Agency 1982 *World Factbook*. Central Intelligence Agency, Washington, DC

C. M. Clermont

Documentation in Educational Research

Documentation is the collecting, classifying, retrieving, and distributing of all kinds of information. Documentation involves not only the analysis and utilization of information, but also the study of methods facilitating the search of information and the various ways of using documents.

The enormous flow of information makes it difficult for educational researchers to survey the existing relevant research material. Researchers must adopt "proper" methods and search strategies as well as identifying their own information needs when wishing to review the published research products as well as the so-called "grey literature"—mimeographed reports existing in many institutions. They must also prepare their own documentation.

The educational researcher has a special interest in documentation problems when starting an investigation or planning a project. It is particularly important to identify up-to-date research results published in scientific journals or research reports.

A distinction, on the basis of general availability, has to be made between conventional and non-conventional material. Conventional material covers:

(a) books, including encyclopedias, bibliographies, and abstract publications;

(b) printed articles in professional magazines and research journals;

(c) textbooks, including teacher guides and teaching aids and media;

(d) tests and other measurement instruments;

(e) governmental publications, committee reports, laws, parliamentary proceedings and reports, and official curricular outlines.

Nonconventional material includes:

(a) interim research reports and related material;

(b) innovation reports and papers;

(c) development plans;

(d) statistical compilations and data;

(e) school-building plans and descriptions;

(f) lectures, conferences, personal contacts;

(g) proceedings from congresses;

(h) newsletters.

Conventional material is to be found in the researchers' own bookshelves, the department library, the university library, and a special education library or documentation center (International Bureau of Education 1982). An increasing number of databases are available and many are in preparation. The university libraries, special libraries, and documentation centers often employ documentalists, who can help select among and within databases because they are familiar with the content and aims of the different databases as well as their terminology. Until now the database ERIC, from the Educational Resources Information Center in Washington, DC, has predominated, but European databases are increasing in number and importance (see *Data Banks and Data Archives*).

As a starting point in documenting research in a particular topic, it is important to know:

(a) aims and volume of the research;

(b) the audience—researchers, students, teachers, policymakers, or laymen;

(c) language barriers—important material can often be found in other languages in the form of abstracts or in the reference lists of journal articles. Journals in minor languages often have summaries in major languages or simply a translation of the title (as in the *Sovetskaja Pedagogika*). There are also journals with translation of articles, for instance *Chinese Education* and *Soviet Education*, published in New York by Sharpe.

In documenting educational research it is important to plan a systematic survey of search strategies and sources, and to evaluate the information collected. Certain handbooks (Burke and Burke 1967, Travers 1978) are helpful.

Libraries are, of course, useful information centers, but the user must learn how to use the library efficiently with its various catalogues and systems. In using a subject catalog one must know the meaning of basic terms. There are different library classification systems, such as the Dewey system and the Library of Congress system. Descriptions in detail are given in various handbooks and in library guides. The alphabetical catalogue provides information about authors and titles. If references are given to publications which are not available in the user's library it is often possible to obtain them through an interlibrary loan system.

Up-to-date handbooks and encyclopedias are important but there may be reasons for searching in older ones (Deighton 1971, Knowles 1977, Rombach 1970–1971, Mitzel 1982, Lenzen 1982).

The results from new research, the different educational systems of the world, new curricula, different educational methods and their problems, as well as political decisions and discussions are presented in professional and scholarly journals, some for teachers, and some for researchers. The following with a comparative orientation can be mentioned:

(a) *Comparative Education* (Carfax, Oxford);

(b) *Comparative Education Review* (University of Chicago Press, Chicago, Illinois);

(c) *International Review of Education* (UNESCO, Hamburg);

(d) *European Journal of Education* (Carfax, Oxford);

(e) *Prospects* (UNESCO, Paris);

(f) *International Journal of Educational Development* (Pergamon, Oxford).

Among national journals the following can be mentioned:

(a) *American Educational Research Journal* (American Educational Research Association, Washington, DC);

(b) *Educational Research* (National Foundation for Educational Research, Slough);

(c) *Educational Researcher* (American Educational Research Association, Washington, DC);

(d) *Nouvelle Revue de Pédagogie* (Nathan, Paris);

(e) *Pädagogik* (Volk and Wissen, Berlin, German Democratic Republic);

(f) *Review of Educational Research* (American Educational Research Association, Washington, DC);

(g) *Sovetskaja Pedagogika* (Akademiya Pedagogicheskikh Nauk SSSR);

(h) *Zeitschrift für Pädagogik* (Beltz, Weinheim).

Many research institutions produce newsletters, giving information on research and published reports, for example, the Scottish Council for Research in Education. The same is true of associations for educational research such as the International Association for the Evaluation of Educational Achievement (IEA) and the American Educational Research Association (AERA).

Bibliographies are also useful to researchers. In many countries there are national bibliographies, usually very complete, and with an alphabetical and classified section. The classification is often unsophisticated but the bibliographic references are given in detail. Examples are:

(a) *Education Index* (published in Australia, Brazil, the United Kingdom, and the United States);

(b) *Awareness List/Bulletin Signalétique*, P. 520: Sciences de l'Education (from UNESCO, International Bureau of Education);

(c) *Bulletin Signalétique*, P. 520: Sciences de l'Education (from Centre National de la Recherche Scientifique in Paris);

(d) *Bibliographie Pädagogik* (from Dokumentationsring Pädagogik);

(e) *Erziehungswissenschaftliche Dokumentation, Pädagogischer Jahresbericht* (from the Federal Republic of Germany);

(f) *Magyar Pedagóiai Információ* (from Hungary).

Special bibliographies are mostly published in book form and have special subjects (Altbach et al. 1981, Parker and Totter 1971–81). The journal *Educational Documentation and Information*, published by UNESCO, International Bureau of Education in Geneva has a special topic for every number and carries abstracts of the bibliographic items.

The borderline between bibliographies and abstract publications is often not quite clear. The most important abstract publications are periodicals. They cover international and national material. Books and journals are indexed and include: author, title, bibliographic reference, publication date, number of pages, abstract, and key words. The abstract must give essential information about content and character, problems, methods, and results. The key words are useful for a subject index in a printed publication or for computerized searches. The choice of keywords is important for retrieval purposes. Several thesauri are published, for example by ERIC, UNESCO, International Bureau of Education (IBE), and the Council of Europe (European Documentation and Information System for Education—EUDISED). The two last-mentioned present equivalents in several languages.

Important periodical abstract publications are:

(a) *Bulletin Signalétique*, P. 520: *Sciences de l'Education.* (Centre National de la Recherche Scientifique, Paris);

(b) *Current Index to Journals in Education.* ERIC. (Oryx Press, Phoenix, Arizona);

(c) *Exceptional Child Education Resources.* (Council for Exceptional Children, Reston, Virginia);

(d) EUDISED *R & D Bulletin* (Council of Europe). (National Foundation for Educational Research, Slough);

(e) LLBA (Language and Language Behavior Abstracts). (Sociological Abstracts, San Diego, California);

(f) *Psychological Abstracts.* (American Psychological Association, Washington, DC);

(g) *Resources in Education.* ERIC. (Oryx Press, Phoenix, Arizona);

(h) *Sociology of Education Abstracts.* (Carfax, Oxford).

Most of these periodicals are available as databases.

A special kind of abstract publication are the lists of projects of interest to the researcher who may wish to contact other researchers for discussion and actual information. The EUDISED *R & D Bulletin* is a very good example. Other publications of this type include *Research Bulletin, Journal for the South African Plan for Research in the Human Sciences* (SAPRHS) from the Human Science Research Council, Institute for Research and Development in Pretoria, South Africa, and *Permanent Inquiry into Educational Research* from the Swiss Coordination Centre for Research in Education in Aarau, Switzerland. The "grey literature," mostly mimeographed research reports, is often difficult to locate, but from lists of projects it is possible to identify the author or institution to be contacted.

See also: Comparative Education, Documentation in; International Bureau of Education (IBE); Information Storage and Retrieval; Educational Resources Information Center (ERIC)

Bibliography

Altbach P G, Kelly G P, Kelly D H 1981 *International Bibliography of Comparative Education*. Praeger, New York

Burke A J, Burke M A 1967 *Documentation in Education*. Teachers College Press, New York

Buros O K 1978 *The Eighth Mental Measurements Yearbook*. Gryphon Press, Highland Park, New Jersey

Centro Interamericano de Investigación y Documentación sobre Formación Profesional (CINTERFOR) 1976 *Catalogo de publicaciones didacticos Latinoamericanos de formación profesional*. CINTERFOR, Montevideo

Deighton L C (ed.) 1971 *The Encyclopedia of Education*. Macmillan, New York

De Landsheere G 1982 *Empirical Research in Education*. UNESCO, Paris

Desvals H 1975 *Comment organiser sa documentation scientifique*. Gauthier-Villars, Paris

Diccionario de las ciencias de la educación 1983 Santillana, Madrid

Dockrell W B, Hamilton D (eds.) 1980 *Rethinking Educational Research*. Hodder and Stoughton, London

Ebel R L (ed.) 1969 *Encyclopedia of Educational Research: A Project of the American Research Association*, 4th edn. Macmillan, New York

Foundation for Educational Research in the Netherlands 1983 *Directory of Educational Research Information Sources*, 2nd edn. Stichting voor Onderzoek van het Onderwijs (SVO), The Hague

Gage N L 1963 *Handbook of Research on Teaching: A Project of the American Educational Research Association*. Rand McNally, Chicago, Illinois

Hassenforder J, Lefort G 1977 *Une Nouvelle Manière d'enseigner pédagogie et documentation*. Cahiers de l'enfance, Paris

Holmes B 1979 *International Guide to Education Systems*. UNESCO, Paris

Idenburg J 1971 *Theorie van het onderwijsbeleid*. Wolters-Noordhoff, Groningen

International Bureau of Education 1982 *Educational Documentation and Information*. UNESCO, Paris

International Colloquium on Designing Educational Information Systems (EDICO) 1975 *Designing Information Systems in the Field of Education, Prague, 1974*. Institute of Educational Information, Prague

International Colloquium on Designing Educational Information Systems (EDICO) 1978 *Exchange of Educational Information as a Means for Further Advancement of European Cooperation in the Field of Education, Bratislava, 1977*. Institute of Educational Information, Bratislava

Johnson M C 1977 *A Review of Research Methods in Education*. Rand McNally, Chicago, Illinois

Kairov I A (ed.) 1964–1968 *Enciklopedija pedagogičeskaja*. Sovetskaja Enciklopedija, Moscow

Knowles A S (ed.) 1977 *International Encyclopedia of Higher Education*. Jossey-Bass, San Francisco, California

Lenzen D (ed.) 1982 *Enzyklopädie Erziehungswissenschaft: Ein Integriertes Hand- und Wörterbuch der Erziehung*. Klett-Cotta, Stuttgart

Mitzel H E (ed.) 1982 *Encyclopedia of Educational Research*, 5th edn. Macmillan, New York

Ness E (ed.) 1974 *Pedagogisk Oppslagsbok*. Gyldendal, Oslo

Parker F, Totter H L 1971–81 *American Dissertations on Foreign Education: A Bibliography of 356 Doctoral Dissertations.* Troy, New York

Peterson P L, Walberg H J (eds.) 1979 *Research on Teaching: Concepts, Findings and Implications.* McCutchan, Berkeley, California

Richmond W K 1972 *The Literature of Education: A Critical Bibliography, 1945–1970.* Methuen, London

Rombach H (ed.) 1970–1971 *Lexikon der Pädagogik.* Herder, Freiburg

Schmidt H 1968 *Erziehungswissenschaftliche Dokumentation.* Beltz, Weinheim

Schütz H 1975 *Function and Organization of a National Documentation Centre in a Developing Country.* UNESCO, Paris

Sciacca M F 1969–1971 *Enciclopedia Italiana della Pedagogia e della Scuola.* Curcio, Rome

Sekretariat der Ständingen Konferenz der Kultusminister der Länder in der Bundesrepublik Deutschland 1977 *Dokumentationsdienst Bildungswesen, 1977.* Luchterhand, Neuwied

Selltiz C, Wrightman L S, Cook S W, Balch G I, Hofstetter R, Bickman L 1981 *Research Methods in Social Relations,* 4th edn. Holt-Saunders, Tokyo

Sire M 1975 *Le Document et l'information: Leur rôle dans l'éducation.* Bourrelier, Paris

Skowronek H, Schmied D 1977 *Forschungstypen und Forschungsstrategien in der Erziehungswissenschaft.* Hoffmann und Campe, Hamburg

Travers R M W 1978 *An Introduction to Educational Research,* 4th edn. Macmillan, New York

Tuckman B W 1978 *Conducting Educational Research,* 2nd edn. Harcourt, Brace, Jovanovich, New York

UNESCO *World Survey of Education, 1955–1971.* UNESCO, Paris

UNESCO 1971 *International Guide to Educational Documentation, 1960–1965,* 2nd edn. UNESCO, Paris

Unwin D, McAleese R 1978 *The Encyclopaedia of Educational Media Communications and Technology.* Macmillan, London

Wilson J A R 1976 *Research Guide in Education.* General Learning Press, Morristown, New Jersey

Woodbury M 1976 *A Guide to Sources of Educational Information.* Information Resources Press, Washington, DC

E. Ekman

Domain-referenced Tests

A domain-referenced test attempts to provide clear specifications about the nature of the tested performance in order to clarify what is being measured and to provide a basis for assessing the representativeness of the items with regard to the competency in question.

Domain-referenced testing is a special case of criterion-referenced testing. Criterion-referenced testing focuses upon assessing the respondent's performance with respect to a well-defined level or body of knowledge. When the test designer wishes to describe well the content and skills sampled by the test, the use of domain-referenced testing is

suggested. The domain that is referred to in this context does not correspond to the term domain as used by Bloom et al. (1956) in describing broad areas of competency in their well-known taxonomies of objectives. Rather, domain refers to the specifically circumscribed universe from which performance is sampled and to which performance is expected to generalize. Thus, in domain-referenced testing, part of the problem is devising or describing the parameters of the domain and another is devising a rule of algorithm to permit sampling.

1. Specifications for Domains

All tests have certain specifications, describing the broad range of content and skills to be assessed. Domain-referenced tests present specifications that attempt to reduce successively the uncertainty first of the test item writer in creating comparable items, that is, items which represent the same universe of skills and content, and secondly, of the test user who is attempting to understand what a test score means. Because criterion-referenced testing emphasizes measuring what or how much the learner knows, the first problem is to describe that general area. Various writers have attacked this problem using their own special language. More generally, however, the problem consists of describing what content the respondent will be faced with under what conditions, in what form the response is expected, and what criteria will be used to judge the adequacy of performance. Because of the history of criterion-referenced testing in general and domain-referenced testing in particular, a common starting point is in the description of the objectives of the instructional program that the tests purport to measure. The point of entry derives from objectives because the entire movement of criterion-referenced tests and domain-referenced tests grew out of a preoccupation with assessing instruction (Glaser 1963). A common way for educators to think about domains is in terms of clarifying the objectives that they want to assess, [e.g., the "amplified objectives" of Popham (1981)].

At a practical level, it is necessary to assure that items used to assess a particular area conform in some regularized way to specifications. Although at the outset of this movement, in the late 1960s in the United States, much emphasis was given to the behavior that was to be elicited by the test, further effort pointed to the major problem of clarifying the content in the objective. The content limits of the domain are its most critical feature. How may content be circumscribed? One approach, taken by Hively et al (1973) depends upon the use of an item shell into which specific content may be inserted according to an algorithm, for example, $a + b = $ -----, where a equals any two-digit number and b equals any three-digit number. Given such a shell, and the rule "any," comparable items may be developed and an estimate may be made of the performance in respect to the entire universe of two-digit and three-digit sums. Because of the relative simplicity of using an algebraic form for a mathematical task, it is not surprising that the earliest efforts in domain-referenced testing came from mathematics and science problems that involved quantity (Hively et al. 1973). Naturally, the problem of content becomes unwieldly as a move is made from content that has a clear structure to content with arbitrary arrangements. For that reason, domain-referenced tests are easier to prepare in those fields where either there exists a complete list of content itself (e.g., English consonants), rather a vast set of information, or creative works that differ in more ways than they are similar, for example, French novels. Nonetheless, domain-referenced testing has developed some approaches to describing and limiting content for testing. One procedure involves describing features of the content thought to be critical to an assessment of competency. For example, in the assessment of reading comprehension, children may need to be presented with both fiction and nonfiction as stimuli, but because the cognitive processes for understanding may differ, such content domains might be separated and further specified in a domain-referenced test. Therefore, the content limits might specify not only the genre, (fiction or nonfiction,) but also the length of passage, the complexity of the writing, and the novelty of the information. Clearly such limits exclude certain passages from consideration, but permit enormous variation in those selected, raising the question of what is comparable content. Another approach to the problem of content limits in fields such as social studies or literature has been to enumerate the concepts or works to which students will be expected to generalize, for example, mercantilism, capitalism, economic socialism, or *The Duinio Elegies* by Rilke and *Four Quartets* by Eliot. In this approach, there is no attempt to equate the concepts or pieces to which the student is supposed to respond. Instead, the list is simply to assure that the test items (and, as well, the preceding instruction) take the enumerated content explicitly to heart.

Thus, content established by enumeration communicates content on a practical and concrete level rather than an abstract, rule level. Another type of enumeration occurs when all of a particular set of information represents the universe. The rule is simply "go to" a reference or resource and use it as a base for content. For example, to be able to read aloud any passage from the *London Times*. An effective universe of discourse has been circumscribed and clearly what is fair game for testing is any sort of article or advertising in the periodical named. Operationally, such a limit communicates a good deal to test writer, teacher, and perhaps to the learner (should the specifications be made available to students).

Another example is to refer to a particular text, for example, any anthropological concept from Beals and Hoijer, *Introduction to Anthropology*. The table of contents provides the functional content limits. However, the topics included in the book itself may be arbitrary and reflect the biases of the authors rather than some more generally applicable structure of the field. So in the same way that specifying particular concepts such as mercantilism is arbitrary, so is the reference to a particular work a weakened form of domain-referenced testing. Whereas the student may demonstrate competency with respect to the defined limits, the validity of those limits still needs demonstration.

A second feature of content limits relates to the determination of the adequacy of the students' responses. For constructed responses, the typical approach is to provide scoring criteria, and training regimens for their application. Thus, in the domain of expository writing, scoring criteria include (a) mechanical, (e.g., grammatical) errors, (b) topic-related criteria (e.g., correct information), and (c) stylistic criteria (e.g., support provided for assertions). When the explication of criteria is too complex, some examples of domain-referenced testing have used excellent, average, and poor samples of student effort to assist the scorer in classifying responses. To the extent such criteria can be identified into components, the domain-referenced test takes on more utility as a diagnostic or placement tool, for on the basis of poor performance on specific criteria, instruction can be developed or revised. The source of these performance criteria may be at best arbitrary, for example, no more than three spelling errors, thereby opening the test developer to the charge of casual curriculum design. It is probably best to include as criteria those features of performance that are expected to be subtasks of the major goal, for example, the inclusion of a thesis statement in an expository essay, or else those known to be prerequisites to a next course or unit in the same instructional sequence (e.g., past tense of Spanish verbs).

When the student is asked to make a selection from a set of options rather than to produce a response, the criteria of adequate performance are used as the basis for constructing the response options. For instance, if a student is to set the proper modifier for a given sentence, it may be critical that the test provide options that are modifiers but which differ according to semantic (does it make good sense?), and syntactic (adjective or adverb) features. Perhaps the greatest contribution of domain-referenced tests will be to regularize the manner in which response options are generated so that a right answer means some mastery over a comparable set of options, and a wrong answer has direct diagnostic value.

The next major feature of domain-referenced test specifications is the description specifically of the item format, the directions, and the conditions under which the response is observed. Although more properly the focus of the item writing article (see *Item Writing Techniques*), format decisions have strong implications for assessing the validity of the domains.

2. Problems in Domain-referenced Testing

A number of theoretical and practical problems remain in domain-referenced test generation and validation. One problem relates to the relative broadness and narrowness of the domain and whether it is practical to use specific domains in the large-scale assessment of a performance developed under a variety of conditions. Some efforts have been made to use domain-referenced testing in regional assessments and evaluations in the United States, but as yet no specific analysis of this problem has been undertaken. In addition, questions have been raised about the sampling rules, including the number of items necessary to get reasonable estimates of a domain. This problem has a tautological component since number of items, or test length, depends upon the cut score used, which may very well be a function of the quality of instruction. A third major question involves the addition of components explicitly addressed to the linguistic features of the test rather than to its content or response features. Of interest is the extent to which variation can be attributed to language rather than to more traditional characteristics of tests and instruction.

A fourth issue involves the match between items and the domain specifications to which they presumably relate. Present procedures are particularly weak, in that simple on–off judgments are usually made about a match. Clearly, the level of detail of the specifications will interact with the quality of judgment, for with very broad specifications almost any item will fit. However, some application of set theory appears promising.

See also: Criterion-referenced Tests

Bibliography

Baker E L 1974 Beyond objectives: Domain referenced achievement. In: Hively W (ed.) 1974 *Domain Referenced Testing.* Educational Technology Publications, Englewood Cliffs, New Jersey

Bloom B S (ed.) 1956 *Taxonomy of Educational Objectives: The Classification of Educational Goals: Handbook 1. Cognitive Domain.* McKay, New York

Glaser R 1963 Instructional technology and the measurement of learning outcomes: Some questions. *Am. Psychol.* 18: 515–21

Hively W, Maxwell G, Rabehl G, Sension D, Lundin S 1973 *Domain Referenced Curriculum Evaluation,* CSE Monograph Series No. 1. Center for the Study of Evaluation, University of California at Los Angeles, Los Angeles, California

Popham W J 1981 *Modern Educational Measurement.* Prentice Hall, New Jersey

E. L. Baker

Domain Scores

A type of achievement test, called a domain-referenced test (see *Domain-referenced Tests*), is based on a well-defined set of tasks known as a universe of items or domain. For many purposes, educators are interested in the proportion of tasks in the domain that a student can perform correctly. This proportion of tasks correctly mastered within a domain is the student's domain score.

Examples of domains include all items testing integer addition of the form, $i + j = ?$, or all possible items assessing pronunciation of the 5,000 most frequently occurring words in English-language textbooks. A student who is able to pronounce only simple words may have a domain score of less than 5 percent. Alternatively, a student that has nearly mastered the domain may have a score of 95 percent, in which case instruction may be redirected towards a new objective. Thus, domain scores can be used to assign instructional treatments as well as to assign a numerical value to the performance status of the student relative to the domain. In some cases, a standard or passing score such as 90 percent is set and the domain score is compared to this standard.

Domain scores cannot usually be measured directly because most domains are too large to be given in their entirety to students. Precise estimates of domain scores can be derived under two conditions: (a) where the domain is sufficiently specific such that all items can be generated or listed; and (b) items composing a test for the domain are selected by random or stratified-random sampling from the domain. In the absence of domain specification, an alternative test model such as classical or item-response theory would be needed. In the absence of random sampling of items from the domain, the clarity of test interpretation is reduced because it is not possible to generalize from the nonrandom sample to the domain.

When a relatively large number of items have been randomly sampled from the domain, the observed proportion of correct items on the sample test provides an unbiased estimate of the student's domain score. In statistical terms, the proportion correct score in this case is an unbiased maximum likelihood estimate and a sufficient statistic for estimating the student's ability in the specified domain.

Often, a small number of items are given for a particular domain and other procedures must be used to increase score reliability. Regression and Bayesian estimates have been proposed that add collateral or prior information to increase the precision of the estimate (Hambleton et al. 1978). Regression estimates use the collateral information that the student may belong to a definable group for which mean test scores are available. Bayesian estimates use prior information such as previous test scores or estimates of parameters such as the mean and variance of the test.

Bibliography

Hambleton R K, Swaminathan H, Algina J, Coulson D B 1978 Criterion-referenced testing and measurement: A review of technical issues and developments. *Rev. Educ. Res.* 48: 1–47

G. H. Roid

Dominican Republic: System of Education

The Dominican Republic is located on the eastern side of the island of Santo Domingo; in the west is the Republic of Haiti. It was formerly a Spanish colony and attained political independence in 1844. The island is in the Caribbean Sea, with Cuba to the west and Puerto Rico to the east.

The country has an area of 48,442 square kilometers (18,703 square miles) and a population of approximately 5.2 million people, giving a density of 103 people per square kilometer. The number of residents in urban areas was evenly divided at the beginning of the 1980s. The Dominican Republic has a very young population, of which more than 83 percent are under the age of 40 and about 75 percent are under 25.

The economy of the nation is basically a rural one, in which the output of agriculture and mining represents 23.6 percent of the gross national product. The traditional exports are sugar, tobacco, coffee, cocoa, gold, bauxite, and ferronickel. The main problem of the country is the lack of energy sources. Although some efforts have been made to develop new systems, there is still an almost total dependency on foreign oil for electricity and transportation. This, together with low prices for most local products, has helped to develop an increasing external debt and a negative balance of trade.

The economic differences between the population groups in the Dominican Republic are noticeable. The minority, in the higher strata (approximately 14 percent), receives 55 percent of total income while 29 percent of the population, at the bottom of the social pyramid, have only 6 percent of the total. The economy grew significantly during the 1960s and early 1970s, but not enough to be able to absorb the demand for jobs. The unemployment figures are already over 20 percent of the economically active population and they fail to reveal the extent of underemployment, which is considered to be a much more serious problem.

The Dominican Republic is a representative democracy with the traditional division of powers between the executive, legislature, and judiciary. The implementation of this political system shows all the limitations typical of a Third World country with a dependent economy and a history of dictatorships, which make political development slower and more painful.

In the 1976–86 national development plan, education is an important component of the drive toward better national conditions. Nevertheless, in spite of formal declarations, there has been a lack of coordination between the educational effort and socioeconomic requirements. Only in recent years has the government been able to link education to some of the specific regional development plans.

There are no great geographical obstacles impeding the education effort. Communications between the different regions are easy and there is a common language (Spanish). The two main problems are the scarcity of financial resources and the political struggles that have characterized the nation's history. The country has steadily increased its educational expenditures since 1968. Around 10 percent of the national budget is spent on education—a significant sum of money in the Dominican context but still insufficient to fulfill the growing demand. Public education is practically free at all levels and accounts for most of the system as a whole.

1. Structure of the Educational System and Enrollment

After the downfall of the dictator Rafael L. Trujillo in 1962 there was a new political openness and a desire for upward social mobility in all segments of society; in particular, the members of the middle sector wanted to improve their economic status. Since education was regarded as a prime factor of mobility, the demand for it increased greatly. From 1965 to 1975, primary school enrollment grew by 60.8 percent and secondary schools augmented their population by 219.6 percent (see Fig. 1). But the most astonishing process took place in higher education. In 1965, there were only two institutions, with a total enrollment of 6,963 students. Ten years later there were seven universities with 40,743 students. In 1982, there were at least 15 recognized universities with an approximate population of 100,000 students. Of the 15 universities established in 1982, the *Universidad Autonoma de Santo Domingo* is public, 5 are private with partial government support, and 9 are private without public funds. About 12 others are awaiting government approval. Since 1978 legislation has prevented other official recognitions.

All elementary and secondary schools, public and private, operate under the jurisdiction of the Ministry of Education (*Secretaria de Estado de Educación Bellas Artes y Cultos*). The state is required by law to give all citizens access to education up to sixth

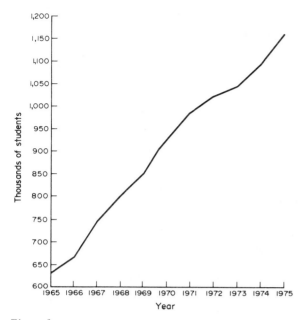

Figure 1
Educational growth 1965

at professionals and graduates of the universities and basic adult vocational programs. The former are mostly in the hands of the universities and private institutions and are mainly directed at keeping this population up to date with information and enhancing the possibility of their obtaining employment. The latter type of nonformal program is concerned primarily with elementary education for adults and the provision of vocational programs.

The role of the six-year primary school is to teach the basic skills of literacy and numeracy, basic knowledge of the social and physical world, and the patterns of behavior needed for a successful adaptation to the environment and to develop a clear consciousness of what it means to be a Dominican in the world today. There are two curricular plans used in the secondary schools. The first is traditional and is purely academic in orientation, designed to prepare students for university. The second is called the reform plan because it was introduced in 1970 as an ambitious scheme to change the curriculum of the secondary schools. It offers a variety of options to the students: academic, commercial, agricultural, industrial, and journalism studies and teacher education (for elementary-school teachers).

grade. However, by 1982 full attendance had not yet been achieved. Of the school-age population (ages 5–10), 10.8 percent attend private schools, 77.8 percent attend public schools, while 11.4 percent receive no schooling at all. Only around 22 percent finish this level in the public sector in the regular six years. The main problems are desertion, overage, and repetition.

Although education at other levels is not compulsory, there are major public efforts to provide services beyond the elementary-school level. The majority (90 percent) of those students who continue onto secondary-school level attend *liceos* (six-year secondary schools) obtaining *Bachillerato* certificates upon completion. Of the remaining 10 percent, 0.7 attend *escuelas normales* (teacher-training schools), and 9.3 percent polytechnics and vocational schools.

Higher education has its own laws and in practice all institutions are autonomous. There is no special supervisory or coordinating body at this level, and in 1978, a special commission was appointed by the president to study this situation and suggest possible solutions. The final report was delivered in January 1980 but no action has been taken on it.

Nursery education is largely an urban phenomenon. The majority of schools are private although the government is developing a new program to provide nursery education in the rural areas.

Although limited, there has been an increase in nonformal education in the Dominican Republic. It can be divided into two categories: programs directed

2. Curriculum Development

Curriculum development in the Dominican Republic is the responsibility of the Ministry of Education, which has a special unit for this purpose. Two major reforms have been started: the first, in 1970, for the secondary level was mentioned above; the other, at the elementary level, was introduced in 1977 and was not completed by 1982. Both reforms have experienced great difficulties in implementation. Lack of sufficient planning and the absence of the necessary support seem to have limited their scope and endangered their future development.

3. Administration

The educational system of the Dominican Republic is highly centralized, with very little participation at the local level. All decisions are made by central-government officials. The minister has regional representatives but their decision-making powers are very limited. A National Council of Education serves as an advisory body to the minister, but it meets very seldom and has been criticized for its lack of representativeness.

4. Promotion and Examination

Promotion is decided on the basis of teachers' evaluation of students' work. Usually, this consists of examinations given in the middle and end of the academic year. With the secondary-level reform, a new system of evaluation was introduced that aimed to use continuous assessment as the main basis for promotion. This has been very difficult to implement because of the lack of preparation of teachers.

5. Teacher Training

Elementary-school teachers are trained at the secondary level in six special institutions sponsored by the government. The universities are in charge of the preparation of secondary-school teachers. A unit in the Ministry of Education coordinates a variety of inservice programs to improve the quality of academic personnel. There have been some efforts to solve the problem of the shortage of qualified teachers and, though the results have been various, in general the number of certified teachers has increased. Nevertheless, because of the lack of financial resources and a not very well defined personnel policy, the problem still exists. In 1982, about 50 percent of teachers in the system did not have the required academic preparation.

6. Educational Research

Very little education research is carried out. Resources are limited, component researchers are few, and there is no tradition for such work. Most of what is done centers on an analysis of the performance of the educational system. Some studies involve an overall appreciation of the situation in the country (Fernandez 1980, SEEBAC 1979); others take a historical perspective (Nivar 1975); and one important set of studies was directed at examining how the education effort was serving the labor market (Schiefelbein 1976, Hernandez 1972). The bulk of research is undertaken by students in the universities and remains unpublished.

7. Major Problems

The Dominican Republic faces a great challenge in the development of its educational system in the next few years. Not only has the country to keep up with an increasing demand for educational services but it also has to confront the issue of quality. There has been much deterioration in the past few years (SEEBAC 1979). The efforts that need to be made could be summarized as follows:

(a) The system must be reorganized. There is too much centralization and inefficiency in the administrative structure. Changes must be made to improve communication, gain more flexibility, allow for more local responsibility, and foster participation at all levels.

(b) Curricula require reform. Clarification is needed so that the two unfinished reforms, especially

that at secondary level, can be more effectively implemented. The curriculum unit should start to do what it was created to do in order to ensure curricula relevance through a continuous process of evaluation and development of new programs.

(c) A great effort should be made to upgrade the training of both teachers and administrators. Ways of increasing their commitment and improving their performance should be sought. On the other hand, it is important to consider ways in which the social value given to this kind of work could be enhanced.

(d) The country must revise its funding policies. Most of the education budget is spent on wages and operational expenditures. There is a very limited amount left for investment and expansion. This makes the system too dependent on outside help. The Dominican Republic must find a way to produce high-quality education within the limits of the nation's reduced financial resources. This is the only way in which education can support the process of national development.

In higher education, the problems are basically the same as elsewhere in the system, with the additional difficulty of lack of central coordination and supervision. Each institution has complete autonomy whose legal framework is clearly insufficient (Fernandez 1979). Here the government faces a very delicate political problem. Nevertheless, something must be done if the tertiary level of education is to improve in the future.

To conclude, it must be emphasized that the problems of the Dominican Republic are not educational in nature but, rather, social and economic. The schools will not be effective unless they are part of an overall, more comprehensive, strategy of change for a more equitable society.

Bibliography

Centro de Investigaciones Pedagogicas 1977 *Educación, desarrollo e ideologia*. Taller, Santo Domingo

Fernandez J M 1980 *Sistema educativo dominicano: diagnostico y perspectivas*. Instituto Tecnologico, Santo Domingo

Fernandez P B 1979 Regimen Juricio general de las universidades Dominicanas. *Cuadernos Juridicos* 3(29): 11–31

Hernandez F M 1972 *Recursos humanos de nivel superior en la Republica Dominicana*. Sargazo, Santo Domingo

Instituto Tecnologico de Santo Domingo 1974 *Educación y cambio social en la Republica Dominicana*. Instituto Tecnologico, Santo Domingo

Nivar C 1975 *El Sistema educativo en la Republica Dominicana*, 2nd edn. Taller, Santo Domingo

Richardson F 1977 *Informe Richardson: Opiniones criticas sobre la UASD*. Taller, Santo Domingo

Schiefelbein E 1976 *Los Recursos humanos y el empleo en la Republica Dominicana*, Vols. 1–3. Editora Educativa, Santo Domingo

Secretaria de Estado de Educacion, Bellas Artes y Cultos (SEEBAC) 1979 *Diagonostico del sector educativo en la Republica Dominicana*. SEEBAC, Santo Domingo

J. M. Fernandez

Down Syndrome

Down Syndrome, formerly called mongolism, is a chromosome disorder which almost always results in mental retardation. It affects both sexes and all races. Incidence is approximately 1 in 800 live births. Mental retardation is not as apparent in the early years as later. The IQ is usually in the range of 20 to 80. Other manifestations are low birth weight, delayed development, small head, small nose with skin folds near the corner of the eyes, upslanting of outer corners of the eyes, deformed ears, protruding tongue, small hands, and short stature. Congenital heart defect, impaired hearing, increased susceptibility to infections, especially respiratory, and to leukemia are frequently associated with this disorder. Life expectancy is reduced with few surviving to the fifth decade.

Diagnosis is generally possible shortly after birth on clinical features alone but should be confirmed by chromosome analysis. Most affected individuals have three number 21 chromosomes instead of the usual pair. A small minority have a variation of this chromosome abnormality also involving the number 21 chromosome.

There is no cure for Down Syndrome. Formerly, such infants were often institutionalized following diagnosis. With recognition of the child's developmental potential, many now remain at home. Through special stimulation programs available in many communities, parents can learn to help these children attain their maximum potential. The children benefit from training in self-care skills and from vocational experience. As adults, many can be employed in tasks geared to their ability both in sheltered workshops and in private industry.

Down Syndrome is the most common chromosome disorder. Its incidence increases with increasing age of the mother. For most couples who have already given birth to a child with Down Syndrome, there is a 1 percent risk of it occurring in a future child. Chromosome studies of an affected individual permit identification of the small number of families with a higher risk of recurrence. Amniocentesis is available for detection of Down Syndrome in subsequent pregnancies of parents of an affected child, and in pregnancies of women of 35 years or older. Genetic counseling is important for all families of an affected child.

Bibliography

Fuchs F 1980 Genetic amniocentesis. *Sci. Am.* 242: 37–43

Pitt D 1974 *Your Down Syndrome Child*. National Association for Retarded Citizens, Arlington, Texas

Rynders J E, Spiker D, Horrobin J M 1978 Underestimating the educability of Down's Syndrome children. *Am. J. Ment. Defic.* 82: 440–48

Smith D W, Wilson A A 1973 *The Child with Down's Syndrome (Mongolism): Causes, Characteristics and Acceptance, for Parents, Physicians and Persons Connected with His Education and Care*. Saunders, Philadelphia, Pennsylvania

N. F. Bartnoff

Drama: Educational Programs

Modern educators use the term "educational drama" interchangeably with "creative dramatics," "drama in the classroom," "informal classroom drama," and "developmental drama," a term used widely in Canada. Earlier educators often used the term "playmaking" (Ward 1957 pp. 2–3) synonymously with the terms given below. Educational drama, as it is practiced in today's schools, encompasses all types and forms of improvised drama intended to have educational outcomes. Its foremost practitioners have been Winifred Ward (1884–1975) in the United States and Dorothy Heathcote (b. 1926) in the United Kingdom.

Ward's initial conception of educational drama was that it "comes from within, rather than [being] the imitative expression which so often characterizes the rehearsing of plays for public exhibition" (Ward 1930 p. 3). However, by 1957 she had broadened this conception to include "expression designating all forms of improvisation: dramatic play, story dramatization, impromptu work in pantomime, shadow and puppet plays, and all other extemporaneous drama" (Ward 1957 p. 2). Heathcote's conception of educational drama is "anything which involves persons in active role-taking situations in which attitudes, not characters, are the chief concern, lived at life-rate (i.e., discovery *at this moment*, not memory based) and obeying the natural laws of the medium" (Dodd and Hickson 1971 p. 43).

1. Role of the Teacher

Educational drama, which is used effectively with all age levels from preschool through elderly and which is used with success among the mentally retarded, the physically handicapped, the psychopathic and sociopathic, is centered more on the participants than on the teacher or director. Whereas in traditional school settings teachers are actors and students are audience, effective educational drama occurs when the teacher, aided by students, is inventor and the students, sometimes along with the teacher, are members of an ensemble. Discussing modes of teaching, Carroll writes of "the teacher becoming the inventor of differing modes of expression by using the whole range of teaching registers available. The pupils in this situation become members of an ensemble, both as participants in the activity, and spectators of their own understanding of it" (Carroll 1980 p. 40). Some contend that "the teaching of creative drama is essentially charismatic. Creative teachers develop creativity in their pupils" (Fone 1973 p. 3). However, training in the technique, such as that offered by Dorothy Heathcote, appears to help teachers find their own charismas.

2. Mime

Few students can be plunged directly into successful playmaking by any but the most exceptional teacher. Mime is one step towards bringing students to the point of losing their self-consciousness and of becoming aware of the dramatic possibilities of their own bodies and gestures. Katherine Sorley Walker identifies mime as "the accomplishment of conveying sense without speech, by imitating action, or by using gesture which someone else understands" (Walker 1969 p. 12). Many of those who trained with Ward, depend heavily upon mime as a warming-up device which precedes the actual making of a drama and recommend this activity as a starting point for drama in the classroom. Some contemporary Australian practitioners of educational drama also depend considerably on such techniques: "The key point . . . is the kind of exercises that the teacher introduces to precede the improvisation" (Fone 1973 p. 24).

Mime requires participants to communicate solely through body gesture, movement, and facial expression. It may be spontaneous with each participant or it may be done in response to suggestions from teachers or classmates. It cannot be accompanied by words.

3. Role Playing

Some teachers use role playing as the step between mime and independent playmaking. Role playing is often quite similar to mime in that each participant needs to convey to an audience a convincing portrayal of a type of person in a given situation—a drunk walking on ice, a woman who has just learned that her husband has been killed, a beauty queen who has come in second in the beauty pageant. Words accompany role playing, although gestures are of exceeding importance if the role is to be presented convincingly.

Through role playing, students gain the ability to experience a broad range of emotions and to project these emotions to those watching them—in the classroom setting, their fellow students. They learn how to merge words and actions into credible portrayals of character and situation.

4. Student-generated Improvisation

The highest level of educational drama is reached when students devise dramatic situations, assume roles, and proceed spontaneously with the development of their own drama. The creative flow in such situations is pronounced, particularly among young children (ages 6 to 9), most of whom have been similarly inventive in their childhood play.

Heathcote is much concerned with getting students to see and understand implications that underlie ideas and actions and to use their insights and understandings in playmaking, which is, for her, "about how children can read implications, transform them into meaning for themselves, and then [through playmaking] teach someone else" (Heathcote 1980 p. 4). Heathcote does not give students any firm ideas about what they should enact in their plays. She guides them into considering what their interests are by asking them such questions as, "Do you wish your play to be in the here and now or in the past?" "Do you want to have both men and women in your play?" "Do you want your play set in a city or in the country?" However, the situations must come from the students and are acted out solely by the students unless, as frequently happens, they request the teacher to take a role.

5. Educational Outcomes

Educational drama forces students to invent and to be aware of implications and nuance. However, it has sometimes been attacked as a frill, as a technique without a substance easily quantifiable in terms of students' educational needs and the development of their skills of literacy. In answer to this criticism, Wolfe detailed 16 basic academic and behavioral skills that he observed during a single session by Heathcote:

> (a) Newspaper reading and reporting; (b) values clarification; (c) intercultural exploration; (d) vocabulary development; (e) self-awareness and self-expression; (f) creative and critical thinking; (g) importance of cooperative effort; (h) self-discipline; (i) perceiving implications and drawing inferences; (j) following directions; (k) decision making; (l) importance of making commitments and accepting responsibility; (m) developing community concern; (n) [engaging in] clear and effective articulation; (o) listening; [and] (p) conceptualizing. (Wolfe 1975 p. 15)

Educational drama has been used successfully to help students understand texts (Carroll 1978) and to develop their language skills, particularly when their normal speech is nonstandard (McLeod 1980, Moffett 1967). Moffett notes that "drama is the matrix of discourse. As information, it is the inner speech of the observer at the moment of coding raw phenomena. The corresponding educational activity is recording" (Moffett 1967 p. 25). Classroom drama has a distinct advantage to students: "Drama is not theatre and so the pressure of showing a finished product does not intrude into the learning situation" (Carroll 1978 p. 22). The influential Bullock Report presses for more emphasis on drama, as did the Anglo–American Seminar in the Teaching of English (1966). The Bullock Report stresses the connection between drama and language learning.

Bibliography

Bullock Report 1975 *A Language for Life.* Her Majesty's Stationery Office, London
Carroll J 1978 Drama as code-cracking: Focus on a text. *The Teaching of English* 35: 21–27
Carroll J 1980 Language: The role of the teacher and drama in education. *English in Australia* 53: 35–43
Dodd N, Hickson W 1971 *Drama and Theatre in Education.* Heinemann, London
Duke C R 1974 *Creative Dramatic and English Teaching.* National Council of Teachers of English, Urbana, Illinois
Fone B 1973 Some techniques in teaching creative drama. *The Teaching of English* 26: 3–26
Heathcote D 1980 *Drama as Context.* National Association for the Teaching of English, Huddersfield
McCaslin N 1980 *Creative Dramatics in the Classroom*, 3rd edn. McKay, New York
McLeod J 1980 The role of drama in language development. *English in Australia* 54: 59–67
Moffett J 1967 *Drama: What Is Happening?* National Council of Teachers of English, Champaign, Illinois
Shuman R B 1978 *Educational Drama for Today's Schools.* Scarecrow, Metuchen, New Jersey
Walker K S 1969 *Eyes on Mime: Language Without Speech.* John Day, New York
Ward W L 1930 *Creative Dramatics for the Upper Grades and Junior High School.* Appleton–Century, New York
Ward W L 1957 *Playmaking with Children from Kindergarten through Junior High School*, 2nd edn. Appleton–Century–Crofts, New York
Way B 1967 *Development through Drama.* Longman, London
Wolfe D 1975 Creative dramatics as a tool for learning. *North Carolina Educ.* 6: 15

R. B. Shuman

Drug-abuse Counseling

Drug abuse is one of the major problems affecting individuals throughout the world today, with much of the drug use beginning in the school-age years, so the problem has become of serious concern for educators. Drug counseling is the term used to describe the many methods for treating drug abusers.

While certain drugs can be constructively used to treat a number of physiological and psychological disorders, in many cases people misuse drugs as devices to cope with other difficulties in their lives. An example of such misuse is the dependence on alcohol or marijuana to improve one's social skills, when there is nothing in the chemical makeup of either of these drugs which can make a person socially adept. Continuous misuse of drugs is termed drug abuse, a practice that can lead to socially deviant behavior and often to psychological or physiological dependence, causing the user to feel compelled to take the drug.

Counseling drug abusers typically takes place in three types of settings—detoxification centers, outpatient drug-free clinics, and therapeutic communities.

1. Detoxification Centers

Detoxification programs are usually provided in a hospital setting and involve the gradual withdrawal of the drug of abuse, a process that often includes the use of a less harmful drug to alleviate the painful symptoms of withdrawal. The rationale behind this method is that the sudden withdrawal from many drugs of abuse results in severe physiological and psychological discomfort which discourages certain addicts from attempting withdrawal. The desire to avoid the withdrawal symptoms often reinforces the use of illicit drugs. Thus, the principal aim of the drug-substitution approach is the elimination of a physiological dependency through a medically safe and relatively inexpensive procedure.

Research shows that detoxification programs have resulted in a high rate of relapse into drug abuse when detoxification is used as an independent treatment. For some participants in such programs, the comfortable withdrawal through use of a different drug may reinforce recurrent cycles of addiction, of withdrawal, and of new addiction, thus lessening the user's motivation to abstain or to seek entry into a more demanding treatment regime. When detoxification is combined with other modes of treatment that seek to alleviate the problems and motivations underlying the drug use, the chances for success are improved.

Probably the best known detoxification agent is methadone, employed in treating users of opiates, especially heroin. Methadone-maintenance clinics generally operate on an outpatient basis, although some hospitals and community-based residential centers incorporate methadone as part of a multimodality treatment approach. Such programs have been founded on the idea that opiate addiction is a recurring disease which may relate to physiological or metabolic abnormalities and that addiction to illicit substances almost always includes involvement in a criminal life-style. The principal aim of methadone maintenance is to permit the addict to sustain or acquire a positive social life-style without the illegal pursuit of narcotics. Abstinence from chemical dependency is not a primary goal of such treatment, although some clients do eventually give up drugs entirely.

2. Outpatient Drug-free Clinics

The term *outpatient drug-free treatment* is a broad designation for a multitude of day-care services that have little in common except that they do not regularly employ drugs and they are not residential. Clients for these programs include: (a) those undergoing their first treatment experience; (b) those who have completed other treatment programs, such as detoxification, and they need aftercare; (c) those referred by the court for drug-diversion treatment; (d) people sent by their families; and (e) people who require counseling after a stay in prison or in a hospital. Such clients vary widely in terms of social class and ethnic status and in the length and severity of their problems (Nahas 1981).

The fundamental services provided by outpatient drug-free programs are individual, group, and family counseling. The individual counseling services encompass a great variety of approaches, such as client-centered or nondirective counseling, reflective therapy, humanistic–existential counseling, reality therapy, environmental manipulation, authoritative–persuasive techniques, gestalt therapy, role playing and psychodrama, and such behavioral counseling as aversion therapy and covert sensitization (see *Client-centered Counseling; Humanistic Counseling; Reality Therapy; Gestalt Therapy; Psychodrama; Behavioral Counseling*).

Group counseling has been a highly successful type of therapy for drug users, with several features of the group approach suiting it particularly well to a drug-free clinic setting. One feature is the nature of the group's leadership. Since drug addicts often distrust conventional therapists who represent the very authority structure the drug user has rebelled against or that sent the addict for treatment, some clinic counseling groups are run by former drug users to whom clients can more readily relate. Furthermore, in groups that stress openness and honesty, peers can feel more comfortable sharing common interests, establishing relationships. learning communication skills, and discovering how to deal more constructively with their families, authority figures, and society in general. In groups counseling, not only do individuals receive support and guidance but they also give such aid and thereby improve their own self-image (see *Group Counseling*).

Self-help organizations, such as Narcotics Anonymous and Alcoholics Anonymous, are larger and more structured groups of reform—or reforming—drug abusers whose priority is that of adapting members to society, often from the viewpoint that the deviant persons are worthwhile but their deviance

(abuse of drugs or alcohol) is immoral. Many such groups function as religious or quasireligious organizations, emphasizing strict nondeviance from group norms. They commonly use a group-discussion format for sharing experiences about their drug-use problem and their techniques for conquering it (Goldstein 1980).

Family therapists contend that the deviant behavior of one member of the family reflects problems in the family as a whole. Often when the client is addicted to a drug, detoxification in a hospital or clinic is necessary. However, without follow-up counseling that involves other family members, the user relapses because he or she has returned to an environment conducive to drug use. The advantage of successful family therapy is that it rearranges the environment of the newly detoxicated individual by teaching the family new methods of behaving toward one another and of coping with their problems (Jaffe 1980).

3. Therapeutic Communities

The therapeutic community is a drug-free residential center, frequently operated by former addicts. It is often effective for treating the more serious drug abuser who has no stable friendships or social support in the community. The center aims at restructuring the client's life by attempting to help him adapt to a totally drug-free existence through playing a more responsible, active, and positive role in life (Farmer 1978). The counseling techniques employed include the individual and group approaches mentioned earlier.

4. The Success of Drug-abuse Counseling

The overall record of effectiveness of drug-abuse treatment is not very promising. Studies show a very high relapse rate, as high as 99 percent under some circumstances (Goldstein 1980 p. 467). There appear to be several reasons for this low success rate. One is that therapists lack sufficient knowledge about how various drugs lead to inappropriate use and about which treatments are best suited to different sorts of cases. Another major reason is that drug abusers are often forced into treatment by the family, public agencies, or the criminal justice system, so that these clients do not willingly participate in the treatment process. Furthermore, individuals are frequently assigned to treatment programs without the assignment being based on an adequate evaluation of the individuals' unique problems and needs.

There appear to be several factors leading to the effective treatment of drug abusers. First, the individual's specific needs and personality characteristics require careful assessment so that he or she can be placed in a proper treatment setting. Second, a decision needs to be made about whether detoxification is required before the client is placed in a counseling program where therapy can be conducted in a drug-free environment. Third, treatment appears to be most effective when an alternative to drug use is offered to the client, with such alternatives including relaxation exercises, yoga, hypnotism, recreation, or transcendental meditation. It is appropriate as well to provide clients with new skills for coping with life's problems and to furnish them vocational and educational guidance.

Bibliography

Farmer R H 1978 Drug abuse problems. In: Goldenson R M (ed.) 1978 *Disability and Rehabilitation Handbook.* McGraw-Hill, New York, pp. 363–80

Girdano D D, Girdano D A 1976 *Drugs: A Factual Account,* 2nd edn. Addison-Wesley, Reading, Massachusetts

Goldstein M J, Baker B L, Jamison K R 1980 *Abnormal Psychology: Experiences, Origins, and Interventions.* Little, Brown, Boston, Massachusetts

Jaffe J, Petersen R, Hodgson R 1980 *Addictions: Issues and Answers.* Harper and Row, New York

Nahas G G 1981 A pharmacological classification of drugs of abuse. In: Nahas G G, Frick H C (ed.) 1981 *Drug Abuse in the Modern World: A Perspective for the Eighties: An International Symposium held at the College of Physicians and Surgeons of Columbia University.* Pergamon, New York, pp. 111–21

K. E. Thomas

Drug Education Programs

Drug education takes many forms involving varying permutations of objectives, targets, teaching personnel, and contents and methods. Objectives typically call for either the prevention/elimination of all unacceptable drug use or for the maintenance/reduction of use to levels that minimize negative consequences. The targets are potential users, experimental users, regular users, or the friends, relatives, or associates of any of these groups. The teaching personnel include classroom teachers and personnel drawn from the ranks of the professional and lay communities, from drug users and exusers, and from among the target group themselves. The content of programs ranges from unbiased presentations of drug facts to discussion of the legal, personal, and social ramifications of drug use, to the use of materials with a strong antidrug orientation. Methods include the use of scare tactics, logical arguments (one-sided or two-sided), authorities or experts, self-examination and values clarification, peer approaches, alternative approaches, and others.

1. Background

There exists extensive evidence that the use of alcohol and other drugs has occurred in most societies throughout the world and has probably been known since the Paleolithic Age and certainly since the Neolithic Age. Accounts of alcohol or drug use are found on ancient Egyptian carvings, Hebrew script, and Babylonian tablets. The Code of Hammurabi (c. 2225 BC) devoted several sections to problems created by the abuse of alcohol and in China, laws that forbade making wine were enacted and repealed 41 times between 1100 BC and AD 1400. These and other sources of evidence indicate that concern over alcohol and drug use and abuse are not unique to present societies.

Although drug education can be traced back for many decades, minimal attention was directed to it before the mid-1960s. At that time, recognition of drug abuse as a major problem emerged throughout much of the world. The common reaction was to call for the rapid establishment or expansion of drug prevention education programs. In response to the perceived crisis, numerous educational programs were quickly developed during the late 1960s and early 1970s. Faith in education as the primary preventative agent of undesirable conditions receives widespread support, yet it is important to evaluate the effectiveness of educational programs. By analyzing the effects of various components of drug education, educators may have a more secure foundation on which to design or choose their programs.

2. Curriculum

Basic issues faced in developing a drug education program include objectives, target group, teaching personnel, and content and method.

2.1 Objectives

Objectives of drug prevention education are typically categorized as cognitive, affective, and behavioral. They can also be long or short range and simple or complex. However, in all cases they should be explicit, consistent with other objectives of the larger educational framework, and understood by those charged with achieving them.

A major problem in drug education lies in determining objectives. Among the objectives of such education, the following are often identified: (a) to increase accurate knowledge about drugs; (b) to change attitudes about drugs; (c) to bring about values clarification so as to assist students in making their own decisions regarding drugs; (d) to assist students' emotional maturity and stability so as to reduce motivation for drug use; (e) to deter experimentation with illicit drugs; (f) to prevent chronic use of illicit drugs; and (g) to teach responsible use of legal drugs.

Implicitly, these objectives are all directed toward the larger goal of drug abuse reduction. However, it should be recognized that increasing accurate knowledge about drugs does not necessarily lead to that larger goal. The same has been demonstrated to be true for values clarification and increased emotional security.

Clearly, specifying the objectives of drug education is especially important when evaluations of its effectiveness are to be conducted.

2.2 Target Group

The potential target groups of a drug education program are typically categorized as either the general public or as subgroups of the general public. The latter are sometimes identified on the basis of social role, such as parents, physicians, police, students, politicians, the clergy, and so on. Subgroups can also be identified according to stage of intervention. Such stages are usually categorized as primary, secondary, and tertiary. Primary prevention occurs when the target group is not involved with inappropriate or illicit drug use. Secondary prevention occurs when the group is experimenting with drug use, while tertiary prevention occurs when the group is regularly involved in drug use.

There is increasing evidence that preventative drug education should be introduced in early childhood while beliefs, attitudes, and behavior patterns are in their formative period. Most drug education programs exist in schools, and while school students can be viewed as a single target population, they clearly are not a homogeneous group. The educational needs of nonusers, experimenters, and users/abusers may differ greatly.

Evidence also suggests that the school program should be part of a total community effort since students are affected by the environment outside the school as well as in it. What is learned in school can then be reinforced outside it.

The fact that most drug education programs occur in schools is understandable. Students in school constitute "captive audiences" of relatively young and impressionable individuals. On the other hand, attendance by most nonschool groups is voluntary. Programs for such groups also typically require physical facilities, trained staff, promotional activities, and money. The cost of programs for mass media use tends to be very high. As a consequence of these problems there are relatively few drug education programs for nonschool populations.

2.3 Teaching Personnel

While classroom teachers usually present drug education programs, health professionals, law enforcement officers, exusers (typically young), and student volunteers are frequently used.

There is some disagreement over whether or not exusers should be utilized in prevention programs.

Credibility is important in attitude change and research has demonstrated that people tend to like and believe communicators who are similar to themselves. They also tend to be more likely to believe those who speak with the voice of experience. Recognizing that traditionally trained teachers usually do not possess either the ability or the inclination to relate well with drug-using students, many programs have utilized exusers who "know the scene." While students generally report favorable reaction to the use of such individuals, some authorities have suggested that students might idealize their life-style and seek to emulate them.

It is frequently asserted that whoever presents a drug program should ideally be someone students like and trust, someone who knows and will present relevant facts and materials accurately, and someone who is relaxed and comfortable teaching the subject.

2.4 Content and Method

There is general agreement today that drug education should be comprehensive and should focus not only on the physiological and pharmacological aspects of drug use and abuse, but also upon the psychological and emotional, the legal, the social, the economic, the political, and the moral implications of drug use and abuse. While drug education has traditionally been located in health and physical education courses, some authorities argue that it should also be infused into other parts of the curriculum.

An area of major concern to drug educators involves the methods to be used in achieving their objectives. Possible methods include the following:

(a) Negative reinforcement—the negative reinforcement or "scare tactic" approach asserts that undesirable consequences (illness, emotional disturbance, death, etc.) can result from the use or misuse of various drugs. The basic assumption is that fear of consequences will prevent use or misuse of drugs.

(b) Logic—the logical argument approach utilizes the presentation of facts which students can use in making personal decisions regarding drug use. The presentation can be either one-sided or two-sided. If one-sided, it may resemble the scare approach. The logical argument approach tends to assume that individuals are logical and rational decision makers regarding their own behavior.

(c) Authority—the authoritative source approach uses traditional experts (medical personnel, law enforcement officers, scholars, etc.) and experiential experts (drug users, exusers, etc.) to present facts and/or opinions on drug abuse. It is assumed that such authorities enjoy a higher level of credibility than the classroom teacher. This approach may or may not utilize scare tactics.

(d) Self-examination and values clarification—self-examination and values clarification attempts to involve students in examining their values, beliefs, and feelings regarding themselves, their lives, and the role of drugs. This approach assumes that students must come to know themselves and their values in order to make informed decisions regarding drugs.

(e) Peers—the peer approach utilizes students to lead (or aid in) discussions or other instructional activities with other students. With training, student leaders can assume the role of teacher. Alternatively, the group may act as a team in exploring the subject. It is assumed that students are strongly influenced by peer pressure and expectation; that students feel more comfortable in discussing and learning about this sensitive topic within their own group; and that, by increasing students' responsibility for their own learning, the approach may increase their motivation to learn.

(f) Alternatives—the alternatives approach seeks to introduce students to alternative activities in order to reduce or eliminate their desire either to become involved, or to maintain their involvement with drugs. It is assumed that individuals crave "highs" and that "natural highs" found in sports or other activities will be perceived as acceptable substitutes for drug highs.

(g) Coping skills—the psychological and social coping skills development approach attempts to achieve its objective through role-playing exercises or any of a diversity of other techniques. It assumes that people who have a broad repertoire of acceptable ways for coping with stressful personal feelings and social situations are less likely to turn to drugs in times of stress.

3. Evaluation

Unfortunately, the vast majority of drug education programs reported in the literature lack any evaluation. Those that do are typically flawed by inadequacies of either research design and/or analysis. Thus, the literature provides little data for guidance in the development or modification of programs. Because some program components can be expected to be more effective with certain types of student or in certain settings, careful evaluation should make it possible to specify the optimal conditions for maximum effectiveness.

Just as early abolitionists assumed that teaching the "evils of alcohol" in schools would lead to abstinence, so too it was believed that if youth were taught the facts about drugs they would tend to abstain. However, it has frequently been argued that drug education has failed to prevent or even reduce the consumption or abuse of drugs and might actually stimulate interest in such substances. The National (US) Commission on Marihuana and Drug Abuse recognized the lack of knowledge regarding the impact of drug education and recommended a moratorium on all drug education programs in the schools, at least until existing programs could be evaluated. It asserted that no drug education program anywhere in the world had proven sufficiently successful to warrant recommendation and speculated that the avalanche of drug education may have been counterproductive.

A review of existing research demonstrates that while most programs evaluated are successful in increasing drug knowledge, far fewer are successful in changing attitudes. A number of studies have reported greater changes in knowledge than in attitude, or have reported changes in knowledge unaccompanied by change in attitude. Clearly the most rigorous test of educational effectiveness involves study of subsequent drug usage. By far the largest number of studies have found no effects of drug education upon use. A few have found drug use to be reduced while others have found it to be increased following drug education.

While there is much correlational evidence that drug users possess greater drug knowledge than do nonusers, there is no evidence that increases in such knowledge actually stimulate use. It is possible that drug education might stimulate use by (a) providing students with facts that overcome beliefs which inhibit use; (b) providing students with facts that overcome the prejudices that had been inhibiting use; (c) desensitizing students about drugs through repeated discussion of drug concepts in environments such as schools, which have traditionally been disassociated from drug use; (d) leading students to think of themselves as potential drug users merely by virtue of their having been included in drug education programs; (e) changing attitudes that were the bastion of defense against drug use; or (f) occasionally including inaccurate or biased information, which undermines the credibility of the basic educational message. On the other hand, it is also plausible that greater knowledge results from use rather than vice versa.

A massive expenditure of funds and energy is being used in numerous countries to deploy a diversity of theories, personnel, techniques, and materials in attempts to influence drug beliefs, attitudes, and behaviors. The generally nonsupportive results of summative evaluation (i.e., evaluation which occurs at the end of a course) in drug education suggest the desirability of conducting formative evaluation (see *Formative and Summative Evaluation*). The latter, by occurring during the progress of a program, permits educators to modify the program so as to improve its effectiveness.

The research to date suggests that drug prevention

education is most effective when (a) it is planned according to clearly defined objectives, (b) it utilizes personnel, content, and methods appropriate to the target group and for the achievement of its objectives, and (c) it incorporates carefully designed evaluation based upon sound research principles.

See also: Drugs and Human Development; Drug-abuse Counseling; Drug Therapy

Bibliography

Blum R H 1976 *Drug Education: Results and Recommendations.* Heath, Lexington, Massachusetts

Corder B W, Smith R A, Swisher J D 1975 *Drug Abuse Prevention: Perspectives and Approaches for Education.* Brown, Dubuque, Iowa

Cornacchia H J, Smith D E, Bentel D J 1978 *Drugs in the Classroom: A Conceptual Model for School Programs,* 2nd edn. Mosby, St. Louis, Missouri

Engs R C 1979 *Responsible Drug and Alcohol Use.* Macmillan, New York

Girdano D A, Dusek D 1980 *Drug Education, Content and Methods,* 3rd edn. Addison-Wesley, Reading, Massachusetts

Goodstadt M S (ed.) 1974 *Research on Methods and Programs of Drug Education.* Addiction Research Foundation of Ontario, Toronto, Ontario

Goodstadt M S (ed.) 1981 Planning and evaluation of alcohol education programmes. *J. Alcoh. Drug Educ.* 26: 1–10

Hanson D J 1980 Drug education: Does it work? In: Scarpitti F R, Datesman S K (eds.) 1980 *Drugs and the Youth Culture.* Sage, Beverley Hills, California

National Institute on Drug Abuse 1975 *Doing Drug Education: The Role of the School Teacher.* United States Public Health Service, Rockville, Maryland

Ostman R E (ed.) 1976 *Communication Research and Drug Education.* Sage, Beverley Hills, California

Smart R G, Fejer D 1974 *Drug Education: Current Issues, Future Directions.* Addiction Research Foundation of Ontario, Toronto, Ontario

D. J. Hanson

Drug Therapy

Drug therapy, as the term implies, is the treatment of psychological or behavior disorders through the use of chemical substances. Such therapy is based on the belief that psychopathology is the result of biochemical imbalances affecting the manner in which nerve impulses are transmitted in the brain. Drug therapy is important for the field of education because the behavior and learning disabilities of students (both adults and children) are sometimes treated with drugs. Thus, it is useful for teachers, special-education personnel, and counselors not only to recognize the sorts of disorders that can be improved with drugs but also to be aware of undesirable side effects of drug treatment that may be observed in students under medication.

1. Brain-function Chemistry

The biological model on which drug therapy operates proposes that messages, in the form of electrical impulses, travel through the brain via individual nerve cells called neurons. For an impulse to pass from one neuron to another, the first cell must release a chemical neurotransmitting substance into the space separating the two neurons, a space called the *synaptic cleft*. The neurotransmitting substance activates receptor sites on the receiving neuron, causing the receptor cell to electrically "fire" and carry the message to other neurons (Goldstein 1980).

Malfunctions in the production, release, or reclamation of neurotransmitters are proposed as the cause, in part, of several types of abnormal behavior. First of all, only certain neurotransmitting substances activate specific areas of the brain. Consequently, any deviation in the amount of specific substances can affect specific brain areas and, in turn, lead to particular alterations in mood or behavior. In addition, the amount of neurotransmitting substance available in the space between the two neurons determines whether the neural transmission occurs correctly. Either too much or too little of a substance will alter perception, mood, thinking, and overt behavior (Goldstein 1980).

Since different neurotransmitting substances affect different behaviors, it takes specific drugs to change their effects. Some drugs, such as LSD (lysergic acid diethylamide), cause neurotransmitters to imitate psychopathological symptoms, producing such psychomimetic effects as hallucinations, distortion of perception, delusions, and severe anxiety. In the past, people willing to participate in research programs were given these drugs so their simulated mental illnesses could be studied. However, because the drugs were found to exert serious side effects— in some cases creating permanent states of abnormal behavior—they are no longer used in the study of mental illness (Hollister 1973).

The drugs used legitimately today to treat psychiatric illnesses are called *psychotropic* drugs. Usually they are classified according to the illness being treated, thus producing groupings of antipsychotic, antidepressant, antimanic, and antianxiety drugs. A further class is composed of drugs used to treat various disorders of children.

2. Antipsychotic Drugs

The antipsychotic drugs, which are also known as the major tranquilizers or neuroleptics, have a specific capacity to diminish or reverse the disordered thought processes and other symptoms of psychotic patients, particularly schizophrenics. It is not certain what part of the brain antipsychotics affect, but theory proposes that the drugs decrease neurotransmission by blocking the dopamine (a neurotransmitter) receptors in the brain. The explanation is that patients with schizophrenia are responding to excessive amounts of dopamine, which causes them to be bombarded with so many internal and external stimuli that they are unable to select out the most important ones at any given time. Since the antipsychotic drugs decrease neurotransmission, the patient is able to be more selective and appropriate in her response to stimuli.

Antipsychotic drugs produce calmness without loss of consciousness or loss of brain-cortex functioning. Consequently, they are used to control acute and chronic symptoms of schizophrenia, manic excitement (until administered lithium has time to work), panic, agitation, delusions, hallucinations, hostility, tension, insomnia, and hyperactivity (Hollister 1973, Heath 1979). Antipsychotic drugs are not considered proper treatments for depression, anxiety states, and such personality disorders as hysteria or obsessive-compulsive neurosis.

Since the antipsychotics can produce disturbing side effects, their dosage must be carefully monitored. Among the common side effects are:

(a) Anticholinergic effects (dry mouth, blurred vision, constipation, urine retention).

(b) Extrapyramidal symptoms (EPI), of which there are four general types: (i) pseudoparkinsonism (resembles Parkinson's disease, with tremors, mask-like facial expressions, rigidity, drooling, and shuffling gait); (ii) akinesia (weakness in the arms and legs, fatigue); (iii) akathisia (inability to sit still, constantly moving the hands, mouth, or body); and (iv) dyskinesia (stiff neck, protruding tongue, difficulty swallowing, and often a feeling of panic).

(c) Such a variety of results as sedation, hypotension, weight gain, allergic reactions, impotence, menstrual irregularity, liver dysfunction, photosensitivity (sensitivity to the sun), or mental depression.

(d) Tardive dyskinesia, which physically resembles Huntington's chorea and involves symptoms of brain damage that are apparently irreversible.

Despite the dangers of side effects, antipsychotic drugs have proven effective in 65 to 75 percent of the cases in which they have been used (Hollister 1973).

3. Antidepressant Drugs

At present the two types of antidepressant medications prescribed for individuals suffering from bipolar (manic-depressive) and unipolar (solely depressive) disorders are monoamine oxidase (MAO) inhibitors and the tricyclic antidepressants (TCA). Research shows that these two groups of drugs work differently in different types of depression. Consequently, those people who respond to monoamine oxidase inhibitors are unlikely to respond to tricyclic antidepressants and vice-versa (Hollister 1973). People's reactions to the drugs appear to bear a genetic link, since some families respond better to one type of drug while other families respond better to the other type (Goldstein 1980).

Tricyclic antidepressants are the most commonly prescribed medications for depression in the United States. They are most appropriate for persons suffering a major unipolar or bipolar disorder. It usually takes from 2 to 3 weeks before improvement is seen in the patient, but the results are very positive. Studies show the drugs to be effective in 75 to 80 percent of cases (Hollister 1973). While the exact action of tricyclic antidepressants is unknown, it is hypothesized that they increase neurotransmitter activity in the brain.

As with the antipsychotics, these drugs may also yield undesirable side effects, including anticholinergic symptoms, cardiac arrhythmias (heart problems), sedation, hypotension, tremors, fatigue, convulsions, excessive perspiring, headaches, numbness of the extremities, insomnia, or impotence. They can also prove toxic, with as little as a one-week supply of tricyclic antidepressant being fatal if taken as an overdose (Heath 1979).

Although the tricyclic antidepressants are more often used for the major depressive disorders, the monoamine oxidase inhibitors are used in cases of less common depressive disorders. These include: (a) phobic-anxiety states, which are often characterized by anxiety; (b) somatic (physical-health related) or hypochondriacal concerns; (c) obsessive-compulsive symptoms; and (d) increased sleep (rather than decreased sleep, which is more common in depressive disorders).

Monoamine oxidase inhibitors achieve their effect by preventing nerve impulses from being metabolized following transmission of a nerve impulse.

Possible side effects of monoamine oxidase inhibitors include hypotension, liver damage, cardiovascular disease, headaches, renal damage, and an intensive reaction to certain other drugs, such as cold and sinus drugs, analgesics, amphetamines, cocaine, barbiturates, hypnotics, and insulin, with such reaction possibly leading to hypertensive crisis and stroke.

4. An Antimanic Drug: Lithium Carbonate

Lithium was used as early as the second century AD to treat mental illness, but it was not until 1949 that it was found to be helpful in treating both mania and depression (Goldstein 1980). Lithium thereafter practically revolutionized the diagnosis of psychotic disorders, since before its widespread use almost any psychotic patient was diagnosed as schizophrenic and treated with antipsychotic drugs.

Lithium has proven to be the treatment of choice

for acute mania, being effective in 80 percent of the cases of this type. It is also used to prevent recurring manic-depressive episodes. Exactly how lithium operates within the body is still not clearly understood, but it is believed to inhibit the release of the neurotransmitting substances norepinephrine and dopamine. It usually takes 5 to 10 days after its initial administration for the drug to display its effects.

Because lithium is highly toxic, its dosage requires close monitoring. And since it takes so long to show effect, often a faster working antipsychotic drug must be taken concurrently with lithium for the first 5 to 10 days of its use. Undesired side effects range from nausea, vomiting, diarrhea, a dazed or tired feeling, muscular weakness, hand tremor, increased thirst and urination (with these early symptoms usually subsiding spontaneously in a few days) to slurred speech, muscle twitching, lethargy, drowsiness, confusion, convulsions, coma, and, at highly toxic levels, even death.

5. Antianxiety Drugs

The antianxiety drugs, or minor tranquilizers, are used to relieve anxiety, irritability, tension, and insomnia. They are also applied along with psychotherapy to reduce anxiety associated with the process of treating psychological disorders (Heath 1979). Among the depressant drugs most commonly used for medical treatment are chloral hydrate, various barbiturates, meprobamate, benzodiazepines, glutethimide, and methaqualone.

Low doses of such drugs produce mild sedation. High doses may produce mood depression and apathy and may result in impaired judgment, slurred speech, and loss of motor coordination similar to the intoxication caused by alcohol. While large doses are effective in controlling the psychomotor agitation of an acute psychotic episode, they are not recommended for the long-term treatment of psychotic conditions (Hollister 1973).

The depressant drugs vary with respect to the effects an overdose may produce. Moderate overdose symptoms resemble those of alcohol intoxication, while severe overdose symptoms are those of cold and clammy skin, weak and rapid pulse, and slow or rapid breathing. Coma and death can follow if such symptoms are not counteracted by proper medical treatment. More specifically, the nature and effects of the main types of depressants are as follows:

(a) *Chloral hydrate* was first synthesized in 1862 and soon replaced alcohol, opium, and cannabis preparations for inducing sedation and sleep. Its popularity has declined since the introduction of barbiturates. Chloral hydrate's depressant effect, as well as its withdrawal symptoms, are quite like those of alcohol. Ingesting it along with alcohol can cause death.

(b) *Barbiturates* are among the drugs most frequently prescribed for sleep and sedation. Although there are many types, only about 15 are now in medical use. They are classified as ultrashort-, short-, intermediate-, and long-acting. The ultrashort barbiturates produce anesthesia within 1 minute of administration. The short-acting and intermediate-acting barbiturates take 15 to 20 minutes to show their effect, and they last up to about 6 hours. These two types are often prescribed by physicians to induce sleep and sedation. Long-acting barbiturates have onset times up to 1 hour, and their duration of action is up to 16 hours. They are used as sedatives, hypnotics, and anticonvulsants (Heath 1979). An overdose of barbiturates or sudden withdrawal from them can be fatal.

(c) *Meprobamate* was first synthesized in the 1950s. It introduced the era of mild or minor tranquilizers. It is prescribed mainly for the relief of anxiety, tension, and associated muscle spasms. Its onset and duration of action are much like those of the intermediate-acting barbiturates, but it differs in that it is a muscle relaxant and does not produce sleep at therapeutic doses. It is also less toxic.

(d) *Benzodiazepines* relieve anxiety, tension, and muscle spasm. They have a relatively slow onset but long duration of effect, usually losing their effectiveness after 3 to 4 weeks. Addictive risk is minimal at therapeutic doses. Side effects include drowsiness, headache, and muscular incoordination.

(e) *Glutethimide* (Doriden) is a central nervous system depressant that causes sedation. Originally it was said to be a safe substitute for barbiturates, but recent experience has shown it can be quite dangerous. The effects begin about 30 minutes after administration and last from 4 to 8 hours. Because the effects are of such long duration, it is difficult to reverse overdoses, which often result in death.

(f) *Methaqualone* (Quaaludes) is a sedative chemically unrelated to the drugs discussed above. Originally methaqualone was thought not to be addictive, an impression that since has proven quite in error. Tolerance occurs rapidly, and the increasing dosages necessary for the desired effect rise quickly to a toxic level, resulting in many cases of serious poisoning.

6. Drug Therapy for Children

The major tranquilizers and antidepressants, so important in treating adults, seem to have limited effect in treating children. They not only impair cognitive functioning and learning, but also have severe side effects (Goldstein 1980). The drugs that do appear effective in treating children are the central nervous system stimulants. Interestingly enough, they have the effect of sedating hyperactive children and helping them focus their attention, enabling them to concentrate on assignments in school that ordinarily they would be unable to complete.

The most widely used stimulants are methylphenidate (Ritalin) and dextroamphetamine (Dexedrine). Such drugs do not actually decrease activity in the child but, rather, help him increase his control over motor behavior. Usually children begin taking the drug between ages 7 and 9, then cease treatment around the age of puberty when the drug no longer appears very effective. These stimulants appear to be helpful in 65 to 76 percent of cases of hyperactive school-age children (Goldstein 1980). Side effects include loss of appetite, sleeplessness, suppression of growth in both height and weight, and a sunken-cheeked, sallow appearance, with dark shadows under the eyes.

Although such drugs have some beneficial effect on impulsiveness and attention span, too often the dosages are unduly high and the monitoring of the drugs' use is inadequate. In addition, frequent misdiagnosis of the child's disorder results in children taking a drug unnecessarily.

7. Conclusion

Drug therapy for all ages is most beneficial when carefully monitored and combined with psychotherapy or counseling. The drugs alleviate symptoms, and psychotherapy equips the client to deal with problems of daily living and social interactions. Drug therapy is probably the most effective way to treat severe depression, an outcome which appears to support the theory that there is a biological predisposition for some forms of mental illness.

See also: Drugs and Human Development

Bibliography

Girdano D D, Girdano D A 1976 *Drugs: A Factual Account*, 2nd edn. Addison-Wesley, Reading, Massachusetts
Goldstein M J, Baker B L, Jamison K R 1980 *Abnormal Psychology: Experiences, Origins, and Interventions.* Little, Brown, Boston, Massachusetts
Heath H 1979 Drugs of Abuse. *Drug Enforcement* 6: 2–41. Drug Enforcement Administration, U.S. Department of Justice, Washington, DC
Hollister L E 1973 *Clinical Use of Psychotherapeutic Drugs.* Thomas, Springfield, Illinois
McLellan A T, Woody G E, O'Brien C O 1980 Drug abuse and psychiatric disorders: Examination of some specific relationships. In: Nahas G G, Frick H C (eds.) 1981 *Drug Abuse in the Modern World: A Perspective for the Eighties.* Pergamon, New York, pp. 27–46

K. E. Thomas

Drugs and Human Development

While it is widely recognized that drugs can exert a significant influence on human development, it has been difficult to specify the nature of this influence because (a) the term drug has not been defined in a consistent manner over the centuries, (b) a variety of conditions determine how a given drug will affect a particular individual's development, and (c) the influence of drugs can differ from one period of a person's lifespan to another. These three matters of definition, influential conditions, and stage of life of the individual are the central concerns of the following review.

1. Definitions and Backgrounds

The term drug can be defined as any substance other than food for use in diagnosing, curing, relieving, or preventing disease. Additionally, a drug can be defined as any narcotic or chemical agent other than food that is taken for other than medical reasons to produce a special physiological effect or to satisfy a craving.

Drug use is not simply a present-day phenomenon but, rather, it has a long history. In China, marijuana was used 20 centuries ago as an anesthetic in surgery, while even earlier, in Egypt, opium was used to hush crying babies.

In ancient times the purpose of a drug or potion was usually to cure people's physical illness, to help them bear pain, or to poison them. But over the past 200 years, with the rapid growth of scientific knowledge, new drugs and new properties of old ones have been discovered, radically altering people's ideas of drug use. The most dramatic modern-day change occurred around the 1950s with the discovery of tranquilizers to help the mentally ill become a functioning part of society again. This development was important for two reasons. First, psychiatric medicine was greatly improved by the fact that the mentally ill could be treated with drugs. Second, drugs were now going beyond assisting with physical disorders and were entering the realm of intentional alteration of mental states. As a consequence, the role of drugs has been extended from the ancient meaning of treating physical problems to that of using them in an attempt to cure social and psychological problems as well (Girdano and Girdano 1976).

As a consequence of these developments, people have begun taking drugs to fulfill needs which the drugs cannot pharmacologically fulfill, a function that has been called drug misuse. An endless cycle of misuse can be termed drug abuse. As Farmer (1978 p. 364) has defined it, abuse is "persistent or sporadic excessive drug use inconsistent with medical practice where a drug is taken to such a degree as to impair the ability of the individual to adequately function or cope."

The recently discovered capacity for drugs to alter the mind has caused experts to reevaluate drug definitions. Originally, the World Health Organization (WHO) defined drug addiction as "a condition in which the addict was committed to his or her drug physically and mentally, had progressed steadily along the tolerance ladder, and was a societal problem" (Farmer 1978 p. 365). However, many of the new drugs were found not to cause physical dependence, but rather to create a strong mental drive. Consequently, the World Health Organization had to create a new definition for all conditions that were formerly called drug addiction or habituation: "Drug dependence is a state, psychic and sometimes also physical, resulting from the interaction between a living organism and a drug, characterized by behavioral and other responses that always include a compulsion to take the drug(s) on a continuous or periodic basis in order to experience its psychic effects, and sometimes to avoid the discomfort of its absence. Tolerance may or may not be present, and a person may be dependent on more than one drug" (Farmer 1978 p. 365).

Drugs may cause psychological dependence, physical dependence, or both. Physical dependence occurs when the drug has altered the biological state of the body so that continuous use of the drug is necessary for the person to avoid withdrawal or abstinence symptoms specific to that drug. If there are no withdrawal symptoms, there is no physical dependence. Withdrawal symptoms are defined as those physical effects resulting from the discontinuation of a drug that are relieved either by time or by using the drug again (Girdano and Girdano 1976).

Tolerance often occurs with the chronic use of a drug. This means that repeated equivalent dosages of the drug have less and less effect, so that the individual needs to take increasingly larger amounts in order to produce the desired euphoria. Eventually the dosage required to attain the euphoric effect becomes an overdose, that is, it is sufficiently toxic to cause coma or even death. Tolerance develops relatively quickly for such drugs as opiates and amphetamines, but it is also lost quickly so that a person might take a dose formerly tolerable for him or her but which, after a period of abstention, serves as an overdose.

Psychological dependence occurs when a person feels a compelling desire to use a drug and cannot reduce either the frequency or the dosage. Such people feel they need the drug in order to continue functioning in life or to maintain a feeling of well-being. Dependence can be located any place along a continuum from mild desire to an all-consuming craving for the substance.

2. Conditions Affecting Drug Influence

There appear to be three main sets of factors leading to the use or abuse of drugs: the social setting, the personality or attributes of the individual, and the attributes of the drug itself.

2.1 Social Setting or Environment

The environment which influences how drugs may affect development can be analyzed according to several factors. One is the community in which a person lives. For instance, in some ghetto areas in the United States, exposure to drugs and the pressure to try them are so constant that drug use is almost inescapable for the child or youth.

A second factor—and one of the most powerful— is the peer culture. If a young person's agemates encourage drug use, the youth will likely try drugs. Rebellion against the established adult social system is often part of the motivation for the peer group's turning to drugs, although this rebelliousness may be short lived and more in the spirit of adventure than of breaking with the adult culture. Lettieri (1980) reported that the majority of Americans between ages 16 and 25 had tried drugs at least once or twice, though most did not repeat the experience further.

The child's family is a further important influence. A study by Dunette (Lettieri 1980) showed that parents of drug abusers were frequently people who abused alcohol, fought often, and were divorced or separated. The family's ethnic and social-class values can also be significant. Kandel (Lettieri 1980) reported that white adolescents were more likely than blacks in America to have tried alcoholic beverages, marijuana, various pills, psychedelics, and inhalants, and less likely to have tried cocaine or heroin. Hispanic secondary-school students were less likely than either whites or blacks to have tried alcohol, cigarettes, or marijuana and more likely to have tried cocaine. Youths of Oriental heritage showed dramatically lower rates of drug use than all other ethnic groups.

2.2 Individuals' Personality Attributes

Drugs affect all people somewhat differently, as determined by individual biological disposition, psychosocial characteristics, and skills for coping with problems.

In regard to biological differences, some theorists hold that drug addiction involves a "deficiency disease" in brain function, and that those suffering this deficiency turn to drugs as a form of self-medication (Farmer 1978). Thus, one issue which has long plagued researchers is whether the psychopathological behavior of drug addicts develops because of a biological predisposition for the disorder before the drug's use. Studies show that adolescents who use drugs manifest more psychopathology than nonusers. The users' symptoms often include depression, immaturity, self-alienation, poor relations with others, major deficiences in ego structure and functioning, poor impulse control, and feelings of inadequacy, of frustration, and of helplessness. But whether biological composition has contributed to such characteristics and thus has encouraged overuse of drugs is not yet known (Breschner and Friedman 1979).

Social characteristics that contribute to personality and are related to drug use include gender, social class, sexual behavior, and delinquency. Studies have shown that more males than females use drugs and that drug users are more likely to be from upper-income families than from lower socioeconomic levels. Furthermore, drug use is higher among adolescents who engage in more sexual behavior and who are involved in delinquency and school misbehavior (Chitwood et al. 1981).

Individuals who have poor skills for coping with life's problems and who display a lack of self-esteem use drugs to excess as an escape from either daily stresses or from boredom. Among regular users, "getting high" on drugs is a primary coping mechanism that begins to dominate the individual's life as he or she turns to drugs with increasing frequency. Then the person's energies may be almost completely consumed by the drug life. At this point there is a noticeable decrease in overall functioning of the individual and a high risk of overdoses. Many rehabilitation programs are aimed at the formation of a positive identity within the individual so he need not seek to escape reality through drugs (Hundleby et al. 1982).

2.3 Properties of Drugs

Each drug has properties that produce particular psychobiological effects. Thus, reasons for a person's turning to certain drugs are directly related to the specific effects those drugs offer. For example, alcohol, marijuana, or heroin may be used to produce feelings of pleasure. Barbiturates, amphetamines, or sedative-hypnotics are used to help a person cope with moods he or she wishes to escape, such as depression, tension, or anxiety. Psychodelic drugs are usually taken in an attempt to expand awareness or to achieve a personal identity. Drugs also differ from each other in their potential for overdose, dependency, withdrawal symptoms, and tolerance. (See Table 1 for particular effects of specific drugs.)

3. Drugs and Age Levels

In addition to the factors related to drug use reviewed above, the influence of drugs on development can be viewed from the standpoint of four stages of the lifespan: (a) prenatal life, (b) infancy and childhood, (c) adolescence, and (d) adulthood.

3.1 From Conception to Birth

When a pregnant woman takes a drug, it circulates not only through her body but also through that of the fetus. And since the fetus develops very rapidly, drug use by a mother can have severe consequences for the unborn child's growth.

Some drugs are teratogenic, meaning they cause malformations in the fetus. One such drug is thalidomide, a tranquilizer, which can cause flipper-like appendages rather than arms and legs to develop on the baby. Long-term use of antibiotics can cause abnormalities ranging from stained teeth to jaundice and bone deformities.

Alcoholic women can give birth to infants who go through withdrawal symptoms in the first few days after birth, and such women can bear babies who display vitamin depletion, biochemical imbalances, and low birth weight. A further danger is that excessive use of alcohol may produce premature birth and even intrauterine death of the fetus. Heroin and morphine addiction can lead to similar results, with the babies going through withdrawal symptoms following birth (Heath 1979).

Other drugs create specific effects. For instance, a mother's smoking cigarettes can retard growth of the fetus, causing low birth weight and premature birth. Steroids can cause birth defects, synthetic hormones can cause masculinization of female fetuses and feminization of male fetuses. Diethylstilbestrol (DES), which was often given to mothers in the 1950s to prevent miscarriage, has since been seen as a possible cause of cancer in young daughters whose mothers were injected with the drug. Corticosteroids can produce jaundice, low birth weight, cleft palate, and stillbirth. Alexania (1982) reports recent studies showing that marijuana may cause birth defects, and there is evidence that lysergic acid diethylamide (LSD) can cause chromosome changes that result in malformed infants.

Even such common medications as aspirin and antihistamines have been cited as causing malformations.

These discoveries about the influence of drugs on the unborn child suggest that by avoiding such substances during pregnancy, women enhance the chances of producing a healthy baby.

3.2 Infancy to Puberty

Newborn infants are particularly susceptible to the effects of drugs because they have not yet developed the enzymes necessary to metabolize the drugs (Alexania 1982). Thus, special caution is warranted in prescribing drugs for babies. After infancy and throughout the years of childhood, the likelihood that a boy or girl will begin to use drugs is strongly influenced by the model of drug use offered by members of the family. The child who sees his father drinking beer each night to relax from the day's labors, or the girl who sees her mother constantly taking diet pills in order to lose weight, is apt to follow the parental model and be more susceptible to accepting drugs offered by peers.

Childhood is pictured by developmentalists as a

Table 1

Uses and effects of common drugs

Drug type	Trade or street names	Used to produce:	Physical dependence	Psychological dependence	Tolerance developed?	Effect duration	Typical mode of use	Possible immediate effects	Possible later effects	Withdrawal symptoms	Overdose effects	Physiological dangers
Alcohol Wine, beer, whiskey, gin, vodka, rum	Booze, hootch, sauce, juice	Euphoria, sedation, hypnotic state, pain relief	High	High	Yes	4 to 12 hours	Swallowed	Distorted judgment, perception, coordination, reflexes, speech, numbness, inhibition loss	Headache, nausea, depression, fatigue, dehydration, yearning for alcohol	Chills, tremor, appetite loss, seizures, hallucinations, paranoia, delirium	Chills, tremor, coma, seizures, perhaps death	Damage to liver, kidneys, heart, pancreas, stomach
Cannabis Hashish, hash oil	Hash, goma de mota, soles	Euphoria, escape from life's problems, no medical uses	Degree unknown	Moderate	Yes	2 to 4 hours	Swallowed, smoked	Inhibition loss, euphoria, short-term memory loss, disoriented thought and action, passivity, distorted sensations, panic, heightened appetite	Sleeplessness, restlessness	Undetermined	Possible but rare, cannabis psychosis: paranoia, depression, hallucinations	In constant users, lung and bronchial disorders, altered endocrine functions
Marijuana	Pot, weed, grass, jay, hemp, joint, smoke, acapulco gold, herb, sativa, colombian, yerba, cannabis, stick, sinsemilla, panama red, reefer	Euphoria, mental-pain relief, medical uses under study	Degree unknown	High to moderate	Yes	2 to 4 hours						
Tetrahydro-cannabinol	THC	Euphoria, medical uses unknown	Degree unknown	High to moderate	Yes	2 to 4 hours						
Depressants Barbiturates	Amytal, Seconal, Amobarbital, Butisol, Phenobarbital, Tuinal, Nembutal, Secobarbital, barbs, downers, pinks, reds and blues, rainbows, yellows	Euphoria, sedation, hypnotic state, relief	High to moderate	High to moderate	Yes	1 to 16 hours	Swallowed	Sedation, drowsiness, slurred speech, distorted judgment and coordination, loss of sensation and inhibitions, depression, loss of consciousness	Depression, slowed movement, weariness, yearning for drug	Weakness, fever, tremor, anxiety, disturbed sleep, rapid pulse, seizures that can be fatal	Confusion, staggering, rage, coma, cold skin, dilated pupils, weak and rapid pulse	Slowed body functions, damage to central nervous system, breathing and heart may stop
Benzo-diazepines	Ativan, Azene, Valium, Clonopin, Librium, Serax, Tranxene, Diazepam	Sedation, hypnotic state, euphoria, less anxiety, anticonvulsive condition	Low	High to low	Yes	4 to 8 hours						

Drug	Trade or Other Names	Medical Uses	Physical Dependence	Psychological Dependence	Tolerance	Duration (Hours)	Usual Method	Possible Effects	Effects of Overdose	Withdrawal Syndrome
Chloral hydrate	Noctec, Somnos	Sedation, hypnotic state, relief from anxiety or insomnia	Moderate	Moderate	Possibly	5 to 8 hours	Swallowed or injected			
Glutethimide	Doriden, doors	Sedation, hypnotic state, euphoria	High	High	Yes	4 to 8 hours	Swallowed			
Methaqualone	Optimil, Parest, Sopor, Somnafac, Quaalude, soapers, quads, sopes, ludes	Sedation, hypnotic state, euphoria	High	High	Yes	4 to 8 hours				
Other depressants	Equanil, Miltown, Noludar, Placidyl, Valmid	Sedation, hypnotic state, euphoria, reduced anxiety	Moderate	Moderate	Yes	4 to 8 hours				
Hallucinogens										
Amphetamine variants	DMA, DOB, DOM, MDA, MMDA, PMA, STP, TMA	Euphoria, altered mental state, no known medical use	No	Unknown extent	Yes	8 to 12 hours	Swallowed or injected	Distortions in visual, auditory, kinesthetic perception, panic, loss of inhibitions and coordination, illusions, hallucinations	Under investigation	Sleeplessness, acute anxiety, yearning for drug
Lysergic acid diethylamide (LSD)	Acid, big D, cube, microdot, mike, trip	Euphoria, altered mental state, no known medical use	No	Unknown extent	Yes	8 to 12 hours	Swallowed		Fright, acute emotional pain, loss of physical control, possible death	Under investigation
Mescaline peyote	Mes, mesc, mescal, buttons, cactus	Euphoria, altered mental state, no known medical use	No	Unknown extent	Yes	8 to 12 hours	Swallowed or injected			
Phencyclidine	Angel dust, PCP, fuel, crystal, herms, hog, shermans, supergrass, killerweed, "embalming fluid"	Euphoria, altered mental state, anesthesia for animals in veterinary practice	Unknown extent	High	Yes	Hours to days	Swallowed, injected, or smoked	Loss of hold on reality, distorted thought and speech, anger, violence		
Phencyclidine analogs	PCE, PCPy, TCP	Euphoria, altered mental state	Unknown extent	Unknown extent	Unknown extent	Varies	Swallowed			
Other hallucinogens	Bufotenine, DMT, Ibogaine, Psilocybin (mushrooms), psilocyn	Euphoria, altered mental state, no known medical use	No	Unknown extent	Perhaps	Varies	Swallowed, injected, smoked, or sniffed			
Inhalants										
Aerosol products, benzene, gasoline, lead-base paint, lighter fluid, nail-polish remover, nitrous oxide		Euphoria, altered mental state, no known medical use	High to moderate	High to moderate	Yes	Moments to hours	Sniffed (inhaled)	Appetite loss, irritated eyes and nose, chest pain, double vision	Seizures, nausea, chest pain, coma, death. Many brain cells destroyed, pulmonary bleeding	Anxiety, depression, headache, vomiting, muscle pain, diarrhea, cramps

Table 1 (*continued*)

Drug type	Trade or street names	Used to produce:	Physical dependence	Psychological dependence	Tolerance developed?	Effect duration	Typical mode of use	Possible immediate effects	Possible later effects	Withdrawal symptoms	Overdose effects	Physiological dangers
Narcotics												
Codeine	Codeine. Empirin Compound with codeine. Robitussin AC	Euphoria. pain relief	Moderate	Moderate	Yes	3 to 6 hours	Swallowed or injected	Pain relief. euphoria. drowsiness. nausea. itching. loss of appetite. constricted pupils. poor vision. infected sores and needle scars	Depression. constipation. yearning for drug	Nausea. irritability. itching. nasal discharge. cramps. chills. sweats. tremor. intense anxiety	Nausea. seizures. slow breathing vomiting. coma. death	Convulsions. coma. death
Heroin	Big H. boy. brown. H. heroina. horse. junk. smack. stuff. Diacetyl-morphine	Euphoria. pain relief	High	High	Yes	3 to 6 hours	Injected. smoked. or sniffed					
Hydro-morphone	Dilaudid	Euphoria. pain relief	High	High	Yes	3 to 6 hours	Swallowed or injected					
Meperidine. Pethidine	Demoral. Pethadol	Euphoria. pain relief	High	High	Yes	3 to 6 hours						
Methadone	Dolophine. Methadone. Methadose	Pain relief (substitute for heroin)	High	High	Yes	3 to 6 hours						
Morphine	Cube. firstline. morfina. morfo. muo. pectoral syrup	Euphoria. pain relief. cough relief	High	High	Yes	3 to 6 hours	Swallowed. smoked. or injected					
Opium	Dover's Powder. Paregoric. Parepectolin	Euphoria. pain relief. diarrhea relief	High	High	Yes	3 to 6 hours	Swallowed or smoked					
Other narcotics	Darvon. Dromoran. LAAM. leritine. Lomotil. Numorphan. Pentanyl. Percodan. Tussionex	Euphoria. pain relief. cough relief	High to low	High to low	Yes	Varies	Swallowed or injected					
Stimulants												
Ampheta-mines	Benzedrine. Biphetamine. Desoxyn. Dexedrine. beans, bennies, black mollies, copilots, crank, crystal, Christmas trees, dexies, doxies, hearts, meth, mollies, pep, pills, roses, speed, truck drivers, uppers	Heightened mood. reduced fatigue. reduced appetite. counteraction to depressant drugs. reduced hyperactivity in children. reduced sleepiness. weight control. reduced bedwetting	Perhaps	High	Yes	2 to 4 hours	Swallowed or injected	Sense of clarity energy. euphoria. insomnia. loss of appetite and memory. raised blood pressure. dilated pupils. Heavy use over long period may cause temporary psychosis and schizophrenia symptoms	Depression. fatigue. irritability. cramps. yearning for drug	Depression. anxiety. fatigue. loss of hold on reality. suicidal tendency	Headache. dizziness. tremor. hostility. chest pain. delusions. convulsions. heart failure	Undue stress on heart and body endurance. When alternated with depressants can cause nervous-system. liver, and heart damage

Name	Other/Slang Names	Medical Uses				Duration	How Taken	Effects		Withdrawal		Long-term Effects
Caffeine (in aspirin, coffee, cola drinks, tea)	No-Doz, Tirend	Reduced fatigue, headache relief	No	Moderate	Yes	2 to 4 hours	Swallowed	Reduced feeling of fatigue, sense of clarity	Similar to amphetamines	Irritability, anxiety, yearning for drug	Rapid heart, trembling, ringing in ears	Heart and blood vessel damage, digestive disorders
Cocaine	Blow, C, coca, coke, dust, flake, heaven, lady, nose candy, paradise, perico, rock, snow	Euphoria, reduced coughing, local anesthesia	Perhaps	High	Yes	1 to 2 hours	Sniffed or injected	Similar to amphetamines	Similar to amphetamines	Like amphetamines	Like amphetamines	Like amphetamines
Methyl-phenidate	Ritalin	Reduced hyperactivity in children, weight control	Perhaps	High	Yes	2 to 4 hours	Swallowed or injected	Similar to amphetamines	Similar to amphetamines	Like amphetamines	Like amphetamines	Like amphetamines
Nicotine (in tobacco)	Various trade names, smokes, weeds, fags	Reduced tension and uneasiness	Perhaps	Unknown	Yes	Varies	Smoked or chewed	Constricted blood vessels, greater bowel activity	Similar to amphetamines	Like caffeine	Nausea, stomach pains, dizziness	High blood pressure, cardiovascular damage
Phenmet-razine	Preludin	Reduction of appetite, fatigue, hyperactivity	Perhaps	High	Yes	2 to 4 hours	Swallowed or injected	Similar to amphetamines	Similar to amphetamines	Like amphetamines	Like amphetamines	Like amphetamines
Other stimulants	Adipex, Bacarate, Cylert, Didrex, Ionamin, Pondimin, Pre-Sate, Sanorex, Tepanil	Reduced appetite and fatigue, reduced hyperactivity in children	Perhaps	High	Yes	2 to 4 hours	Swallowed	Similar to amphetamines	Similar to amphetamines	Like amphetamines	Like amphetamines	Like amphetamines

time of industry, of striving for mastery of skills, or learning society's rules, and of developing peer relationships. Introducing drugs during this period can disrupt the need to develop skills and can upset the emotional equilibrium and intellectual striving needed for the achievements expected by late childhood. While the effects of drugs vary with different children, in general they produce apathy, listlessness, and impairment of memory and of the processing and retrieval functions of the brain. The child influenced by drugs may fail to succeed normally during this goal-oriented stage of life because of a lack of will and a resultant lowered sense of self-esteem.

At this period of life certain drugs can influence children differently from adults. An example is the effect of Ritalin when used as a medication for hyperactive children (see *Drug Therapy*).

3.3 Early Adolescence to Later Youth

Adolescence has been seen as an important time for developing a person's sense of self-identity, a process that involves separating from parental attachments and values and establishing new social ties, values, and ideals. In separating from parents, the youth needs to form other meaningful relationships. Sometimes the peers with whom the growing youth associates influence him or her to adopt drugs as an important part of their social behavior. However, the effect of drugs may not be to enhance social relationships and self-identity. Rather, the drugs may cause the growing girl or boy to become apathetic and emotionally detached and, consequently, to face problems of establishing social bonds, with the result that the youth becomes increasingly isolated emotionally and socially.

Drugs can decrease cognitive operations, making it difficult for the youth to develop a functional set of values and ideals. Reduced cognitive efficiency also leads to poor academic performance and a resultant decrease in self-esteem, contributing to instability of the individual's sense of identity.

Besides such psychological effects, normal hormonal changes at the time of puberty, combined with drug use, can result in drastic chemical imbalances that negatively affect the youth's physical and psychological well-being.

3.4 Adulthood

Frequently adults who become heavily involved with drugs find that their main interest in life becomes that of drug procurement and use. The self-absorption and emotional detachment resulting from drug use frequently makes it impossible for the individual to form adequate intimate relationships with others. Soon the only friends the drug user has are others using drugs themselves, and the friendship often dissipates once the drugs are gone. Since drugs are expensive and the drug abuser usually cannot hold

down a job due to the drug habit, the individual frequently turns to crime, either stealing objects to sell or else selling drugs to support the drug habit.

In conclusion, the general effect of different drugs as reviewed in Table 1 is usually much the same across all age levels. but as noted earlier, drugs affect different people in somewhat individualistic ways. An amphetamine which animates one person may depress another, depending upon their individual biological and psychological composition. While certain drugs can have a salutary effect on development when properly administered as medications, they exert such deleterious effects as those reviewed above when they are abused.

See also: Drug Education Programs

Bibliography

Alexania K 1982 *Workbook and Readings for Health and Safety No. 456.* California State University, Los Angeles, California

Breschner G M, Friedman A S (eds.) 1979 *Youth Drug Abuse: Problems, Issues, and Treatment.* Heath, Lexington, Massachusetts

Chitwood D D, Wells K, Russe B 1981 Medical and treatment definitions of drug use: The case of the adolescent user. *Adolescence* 16: 817–30

Farmer R H 1978 Drug-abuse problems. In: Goldenson R M (ed.) 1978 *Disability and Rehabilitation Handbook.* McGraw-Hill, New York, pp. 363–80

Girdano D D, Girdano D A 1976 *Drugs: A Factual Account.* Addison-Wesley, Reading, Massachusetts

Goldstein M J, Baker B L, Jamison K R 1980 *Abnormal Psychology: Experiences, Origins, and Interventions.* Little, Brown, Boston, Massachusetts

Heath H 1979 Drugs of abuse. *Drug Enforcement* 6(2): 2–41. Drug Enforcement Administration, United States Department of Justice, Washington DC

Hundleby J D, Carpenter R A, Ross R A, Mercer G W 1982 Adolescent drug use and other behaviors. *J. Child Psychol. Psychiatry Allied Discip.* 23: 61–68

Lettieri D J (ed.) 1980 *Predicting Adolescent Drug Abuse: A Review of Issues, Methods, and Correlates.* National Institute on Drug Abuse, Rockville, Maryland

Parish P 1977 *The Doctors and Patients Handbook of Medicines and Drugs.* Knopf, New York

K. E. Thomas

Dyslexia

Dyslexia, a condition affecting reading, is one easily recognized by teachers, tutors, and clinicians. Unfortunately, definitions have ordinarily included symptoms of other information processing disorders. While these other symptoms are correlates of dyslexia, they are actually independent dysfunctions and not part of the processes that constitute it.

Since the early 1970s, two government committees in the United Kingdom have reviewed the scientific evidence and instructional procedures pertaining to dyslexia and concluded that the term was not operationally definable and served little purpose. In the United States, the Office of Education Advisory Committee on Dyslexia and Related Reading Disorders, after a year of study, stated that dyslexia clearly existed but agreed that there was no prospect of defining the disorder at that time. (The government subsequently listed dyslexia as one of the learning disabilities within a broader set of disorders, which presented even greater difficulties with definitions.) Many researchers, clinicians, and theorists have pointed out that the definitions suggested by the World Federation of Neurology, and by various theoreticians, were so ambiguous that they were of little operational value. Such a summary of symptoms can indicate a relation to the problem but is not satisfactory as a definition.

Fortunately, a clearer view of the disorder has been made possible by developments in research and neuropsychological theory. The following definition is based on a process orientation which highlights the basic dysfunctions, provides a base for operational measurement, and gives new insight into treatment. The elaboration following the definition is aimed at clarifying the elements and limitations of the disorder and tracing the difficulty dyslexics have in learning four different ways of reading.

1. Definition of Dyslexia

Dyslexia is a disorder in learning to read and spell words resulting from specific brain dysfunctions in the processing of written language.

In the definition there is no specification of amount of reading or spelling difficulty. Dyslexic dysfunctions are distributed along a continuum of severity. The distribution of reading achievement scores of young children with normal IQ shows a tail that extends from the lowest point on a normal bell-shaped curve, to the even lower point of total nonreading. While there are many reasons for reading failure, most of the 10 to 15 percent in the long tail that falls entirely below the normal curve show some dyslexic processing deficits, including tendency to overload in learning words or language sounds and difficulty in remembering letter sounds or nonmeaningful syllables. Many of these children will also display correlated symptoms, including aphasoid-like language difficulty; confusion of left and right, telling time, months and seasons; poor handwriting; problems with numerical computation; short attention span; perceptual–motor difficulties; motor incoordination; and early hyperactivity. These correlates, however, should not be confused with the basic disorder. While gross neurological measures seldom identify dyslexics, the correlated problems suggest that these children have broad areas of brain dysfunctions which overlap the major reading center and adjacent parts of the brain.

The phrase in the definition, "learning to read and spell words," refers to getting meaning from words in consecutive reading or in isolation. It also refers to the ability to spell words alone or in a sentence. This terminology is used because, if there are not correlated speech or broader language difficulties, the processing dysfunctions of dyslexia appear to end at the point where word reading finally enters the speech system. This point of the reading process, which is just prior to the generation of inner speech and the first conscious step in reading, is the basis for subsequent comprehension.

Dyslexics often, but not always, have continuing difficulties in comprehension. Some comprehension problems result from dyslexic processes such as less automatic and less rapid processing of words. For example, errors in processing related to assigning meaning may produce erroneous words, but in the correct semantic category (dysnomia). However, most comprehension problems are due to broader language and intellectual dysfunctions.

Retarded children can have dyslexia, or hyperlexia (where complex material is read aloud with correct pronunciation far beyond the child's years—this indicates effective processing in the primary reading area except for meaning). The designation "specific" dysfunctions is important. For example, mentally retarded youngsters may have so many processing dysfunctions that reading is a minor, or even incidental, part of the overall intellectual disorder. "Specific" in the definition indicates that the dyslexic process dysfunctions can be differentiated from other impairments.

Reference to the brain, in the definition, is also important, since it is in the brain that the processes of reading and spelling are located. It is not possible to process language, spatial relations, or other intellectual functions except in the brain. The use of the phrase "brain dysfunction" does not imply damage. Head injuries, metallic poisons (particularly cadmium which damages the association areas to the rear of the brain where reading is primarily processed), extensive use of drugs or alcohol by the mother during pregnancy, prematurity, convulsions, lengthy high fever—all can contribute to dyslexia by causing actual brain damage. However, dyslexia is more likely to be due to abnormal development. Genetic defects, biochemical disorders, or other developmental factors may cause the brain to have areas of structural abnormality. All five severe dyslexics who have been autopsied showed a similar structural abnormality in and around the area of the brain that most specifically relates to reading, spelling, and language processing.

Severe spelling difficulty often occurs without reading problems, but severe reading difficulty is always accompanied by a spelling disorder which is usually more severe than the reading problem. Spelling is included in the definition because some of the processes involved in reading are also used in processing spelling, for example, sound association, sound memory, sequencing, segmenting.

2. Processing Sequences and Disorders

Depending on the structure of the reader's particular language, written symbols may be processed in one of four different sequences. Chinese writing can use only two processes (whole characters and syllable sounds). In alphabetic languages all four sequences are used but only two (whole words and letter sounds) are usually taught. Dysfunctions are greatest for letter–sound decoding, less for syllable–sound decoding, and common visual word-part sorting (including structural analysis), and least for whole word recognition. In addition, specific dysfunctions occur at particular steps (e.g., memory for sounds, blending, sequencing). The sequence in all four reading processes will be given in the sections below.

2.1 Eye Movements and Visual Functioning

While visual skills could certainly affect reading (blindness is an extreme example), the differences between dyslexics and normal learners, as a group, are not significant when single words are presented. Eye movements of dyslexics are often inefficient, in both reading and nonreading tasks, but this could be a result or a correlate of reading difficulties. There is evidence that no significant difference exists between dyslexics and normal readers for visual input. Since visual input involves processing of individual words, and dyslexia is evident in single word as well as consecutive word reading, normal performance at the visual coding level indicates that visual factors are not likely to be causative for dyslexia.

2.2 Visual Processing of Letter Sequences

There is generally no difference between dyslexics and normal learners in form learning. This applies to simple paired association of visual form with constructed production or recognition of other forms.

2.3 Coding the Visual Sequence into a Word

The visual sequence of forms arriving from both hemispheres enters the primary reading area, the angular gyrus. This area is nearly always located on the left side of the brain just behind and above the left ear, higher than the auditory language areas. The relationship of right and left hemispheres is more important in dyslexics than in normal readers, since the localization of language in the left hemisphere seems to occur later and less completely than in normal readers. This area, from birth, has a selective advantage in dealing with language sounds and sequences.

Immediately upon entering the primary reading area, the visual input is coded as a word and the processing rate of dyslexics appears to become slower than normal. In addition, there is limited processing capacity, vulnerability to interference, memory difficulties, as well as trouble abstracting, generalizing, and applying skills. These dysfunctions are the basis of dyslexia.

2.4 Working Memory and Word Part Analysis

The coded word is held in working memory and an analysis is made of word parts. Since the original visual letter sequence (or characters in some languages) was lost when it was coded as a word, this process represents a new analysis. Errors are often made by dyslexics in identifying and sequencing the letters in the word. In this stage, word length is very important in increasing difficulty. The perceptual errors of dyslexics tend to occur here and not at a visual reception stage.

2.5 Whole Word Learning

At this point, processes for different types of reading totally separate for a while. Whole words are processed in a small number of steps and with greater speed and accuracy than any other process. Whole word recognition is the technique all adequate readers use in alphabetic or character languages, but it is ineffective for unfamiliar words.

Next, the sequence of letters (or the details of the character in other languages) that were analyzed are coded into a visual representation of the word and transmitted to a processing stage that recognizes the patterns of words. The pattern generates word associations as well as projecting to the speech process in case sounds can help read the word. (All four reading sequences go through this word association and the subsequent stages.) The word associations are now tested against word context. Eye fixation can be maintained longer if the word does not fit the content.

Then, semantic meaning is assigned and transmitted to the speech system. This step is preparatory for reading orally or in inner language. Outside the primary reading area, general comprehension processing begins. Here, before speech or inner language occurs, the rate of processing for dyslexics appears to become normal, unless there are associated dysfunctions in the language and comprehension areas. With inner language, the individual for the first time becomes conscious of the word. This step occurs about a second after fixating on the word that is to be read. During this time three to five subsequent words may have been partially processed. Dyslexics have little difficulty with this whole word processing if they are not overloaded by the instructional demands.

2.6 Letter–Sound Decoding

It is in this type of processing that the greatest disabilities occur for dyslexics. There are many steps, and errors can occur at any point. In addition, specific dysfunctions contribute to difficulty in this sequence. Letter–sound decoding of a word is seldom used by adequate readers; instead, whole words and syllable sounds are the essential processes. Letter–sound reading is limited by maximum processing boundaries to about 10 words per minute, instead of the 150 words per minute of spoken language and the 300–400 words per minute of silent reading.

The process for letter–sound decoding begins with the association of letter sounds to match the visual analysis of letters. Because of memory-for-sound deficiencies, this is a step filled with errors for the dyslexic and can only be mastered by learning each minor step automatically. The sounds must also be sequenced and blended into a syllable. In polysyllabic words, while one syllable is being processed, the others are often forgotten or distorted by the dyslexic. A subprogram, prior to blending of a consonant and a vowel, must be used to eliminate the isolated vowel sound which changes after many consonants. This subprogram is often in error for dyslexics. Some other sound may be substituted instead of the vowel sound. The letters must be maintained in correct sequence and the dyslexic may lose this sequence and decode "animal" as "aminal." Blending of separate letters, or ending vowel-consonant bigrams with an initial letter, is often difficult for dyslexics. If initial bigrams are blended with a final consonant, it is less difficult. However, if syllables, rather than individual sounds, are remembered, they are blended much more easily.

After being sequenced and blended, the sounds are temporarily transmitted out of the primary reading area into speech areas, where they are coded as speech sounds. Pattern recognition for a spoken word is transmitted back into the primary reading area and finally converges with whole-words processing at the point of word associations. These word associations, such as "purr sent" for an unfamiliar word "percent" might include: "cat sound," "satisfied," "made to go," "smell," "perfume," and, only infrequently, the numerical value "part of one hundred." As in whole words, word context is tested and meanings are then assigned. Dyslexic children may make a seemingly psychotic response such as "smell of cat sound." This does not indicate psychotic thinking, only poor testing of context for the correct association meanings of the word. After assigning meaning, all reading sequences go back to the speech area and prepare a word for oral reading or inner language.

2.7 Two Seldom-taught Processes

Reading of unfamiliar words can also be accomplished by skipping many steps in the decoding of individual letter–sound associations and, instead, learning the entire syllable as one unit. Adults decode by syllable sound. It is a useful technique, in itself, and facilitates learning of letter–sound decoding.

The other seldom-taught process of decoding unfamiliar words is by sorting of whole words that are known, to find word parts that are the same as in a new word. Word sorting is an effective approach and most readers do it incidentally. Nonreading kindergarten children, when taught a few whole words, incidentally learn word parts. Dyslexics a year or two older, who learn the same words, are not aware of word parts. Because dyslexics are poor incidental learners, these skills must be specifically taught if they are to be used.

3. Incidence

Incidence within and between countries cannot be compared until there are operational measures. If there are dissimilarities between countries, it may reflect genetic differences, but may also result from the characteristics of the language as well as from the instruction given to children. Where countries report no dyslexia, it is usually a function of the criteria used. For example, in Japan the promotional policies in schools often prevent a poor reader from going to the next grade, so that children in a given grade all seem to read approximately the same. However, studies of Japanese dyslexics show that they exist in substantial numbers and that their primary problem is more with the phonetic characters rather than word characters.

An estimate of incidence can be made by using United States figures. Research suggests that teachers rate 3 to 5 percent of children in a given class as severely disabled in reading, and another 3 to 5 percent as moderately disabled. Other studies indicate a higher incidence: 10–15 percent of school children reportedly display dyslexic processing difficulties, but only 5 percent or less are considered to have severe problems.

4. Relationship of Sex, Socioeconomic Status/Race, and IQ with Dyslexia

The ratio of the number of boys to girls increases with severity of dyslexia. For the broad group of 15 percent of poor readers, the ratio is about two boys for every girl. There is no appreciable relationship between IQ and reading ability for young dyslexic boys. Only 15 to 20 percent of poor reading boys are below 90 on verbal and performance IQ. For the smaller number of girls, over half are below 90 IQ. It is clear that girls are less likely to have reading problems, but if they do, the impairment is usually broader, so that intelligence is also affected. The difference could be a genetic one of sex relatedness.

Girls localize language functions in the primary language hemisphere earlier, by a year or more, than boys. Thus, boys may not be as efficient in language processing, and, for them, minor dysfunctions are probably more handicapping. Dyslexics also lateralize language later than most children, and may never become as fully lateralized as nondyslexics. Therefore, they cannot benefit as much from the "wired in" ability to handle language in the primary language area of the left hemisphere. While the right hemisphere can read words, it generally cannot pronounce them and cannot deal with sequences of words or with sounds. Left hemisphere sound processing advantages have been demonstrated even with infants.

There are more low socioeconomic status (SES) children with reading difficulties. In America, this means more blacks and other minorities. There is probably greater prevalence of brain injury due to environmental factors, for example, lead and cadmium consumption, and a higher frequency of premature births. Additionally, less adequate instruction may result from overcrowded, chaotic schools and the variation of school language from the child's spoken language or dialect. Reading-disabled children of average or above average intelligence show little or no apparent difference in characteristics due to sex, SES, or nationality. However, these same children differ from normal readers due to slower processing, vulnerability to interference, poor memory for sound, and the other symptoms associated with dyslexia. They often show additional disabilities, suggesting dysfunctioning of broader areas of the brain.

5. Relations of Dyslexia to Developmental Disorders and to Alexia

5.1 Learning Disabilities

Dyslexia is only one of a variety of disorders of oral and written language. Like dyslexia, other learning disabilities are based upon dysfunctions in basic psychological processes, but are poorly defined because of symptom debates. Also, like dyslexia, they are influenced by instructional procedures and are associated with other correlated problems. About two-thirds of identified learning-disabled children are reading disabled, and their disorders are basically those of dyslexia. Most of the dyslexics have correlated problems in mathematics and other language skills which are mediated near the primary reading area in the brain. Certain perceptual errors are aspects of dyslexia which occur within the primary reading area at the stage of word meaning.

5.2 Associated Symptoms

Left–right confusion; concept confusion of months, weeks, seasons and telling time; motor difficulty; limited memory for sounds; history of hyperactivity, speech, and language disorder; and poor writing ability are among the other frequent correlates of dyslexia. These functions are also processed in areas near the primary reading area. While relatively pure dyslexia does occur, it is uncommon. The disorder is usually associated with several or most of the correlated disorders.

5.3 Emotional/Behavior Consequences

Emotional disturbances, poor self-concepts, behavior difficulties, and social problems often result from failure in school. Emotional disorders, whatever the cause, can often interfere with attention, concentration, and effort, making it harder for the dyslexic to learn to read and spell. This vicious circle does not produce dyslexia; it only accentuates the problems.

5.4 Alexia

If there is damage to the primary reading area, or to the connections bringing visual information to the primary reading area from both left and right hemispheres, normal reading adults will develop an inability, or very reduced ability, to read. This condition, termed *alexia*, is part of a broader language disorder, one of the aphasias, just as dyslexia tends to be. Also, as in dyslexia, alexia may involve perceptual problems in visual word-part analysis, semantic errors associated with word meaning (correct semantic category but wrong word), and the inability to use sound associations in reading words. In addition, alexics often have spelling and writing problems (with one exception: alexia without agraphia, which cannot occur in the process of learning to read). Alexics have many correlated processing disorders. There are differences between an acquired reading disorder, after reading has been mastered, and a developmental disability, which interferes with learning to read. However, since alexia is similar in location and process dysfunctions to dyslexia, it gives insight into processes involved in the developmental reading disorders.

6. History of Dyslexia

Specific disorder in learning to read as a result of brain dysfunction has been recognized for almost 2,000 years. More recently, in 1895, a Scottish physician, James Hinshelwood, wrote of a case of acquired "visual word blindness." An English school physician, Pringle Morgan, suggested that a similar congenital condition might exist, an idea that Hinshelwood developed into a book. An American pathologist and neurologist, Samuel T. Orton, proposed a theory of delayed hemispheric lateralization which has since been partially confirmed. Orton postulated a simple interference between the two hemispheres during processing, a theory which is probably more complex than he suggested. He identified this interference as strephosymbolia, or "twisted symbols." He suggested the teaching of phonic decoding as the method of remediation and stressed the use of multisensory input: visual, auditory, kinesthetic, and tactile—or VAKT. A remedial technique involving VAKT was also initiated by Grace Fernald, who used it for the rather tedious learning of whole words. The technique proved to be more appropriate in aiding recovery of alexics than in helping beginning readers. Anna Gillingham and Bessie Stillman developed a remedial method based more specifically on Orton's suggestions. Since then, dozens of remedial programs have been produced along the same lines, making multisensory instruction with phonic decoding the main remedial approach in this and other countries. However, neither Orton's emphasis upon phonic decoding, nor the advantages of multisensory over comparable learning without writing or tracing, has been supported by research.

7. Educational Intervention

Treatment can be given to minimize the effects of processing dysfunctions. If the instruction does not overload the processing capacities and slow speed of the dyslexic child, learning can be accomplished quite easily. Whole words and their application, if taught, are readily learned. However, overloading must be avoided, since it will prevent learning. Most current teaching programs overload the child and produce reading failure.

Phonic decoding must not only be free from overloading, but must also overcome specific disabilities in memory for letter and syllable sounds, and sequencing and blending problems. Whole word learning produces immediate reading success, while phonic decoding requires many steps before it can contribute to reading. Once mastered, however, decoding is a major way of converting previously unread words to sight words.

Overloading occurs if too many items are to be learned, if two tasks are done at the same time, or if the teacher adds tasks through incidental "teacher talk," (e.g., "can you find the little word in the big word"). Even response competition can overload a dyslexic. When several items are being learned it is important to temporarily remove any that have been

correctly identified two or three times, so that the child can concentrate on responses not yet learned. After all items have been correctly identified two or three times, they can be recombined for additional practice. This reduction in response competition usually cuts errors of dyslexics in half and often aids retention.

Wherever there is a problem, such as confusion of similar words, there needs to be discrimination training to resolve the confusions. Dyslexics do not generalize well; therefore, it is important to specifically teach application, for example, reading a mastered word in phrases, then in sentences, and finally in paragraphs. When a memory problem exists, there must be more frequent review. If each step in learning is mastered to an automatic level (where responses occur immediately and without thinking about them), the processing load is considerably lessened.

Dyslexics can be taught successfully by using appropriate, nonoverloading learning principles. In addition, there is usually improved ability to learn skills as a result of maturation. Thus, dyslexia is a handicapping condition affecting many processing steps and compounded by correlated difficulties. However, with use of instructional principles to circumvent the many areas of dysfunctions, the effects of the disorder can be minimized

Bibliography

Benton A, Pearl D (ed.) 1978 *Dyslexia: An Appraisal of Current Knowledge.* Oxford University Press, New York

Doehring D, Trites R, Patel P, Christina A 1981 *Reading Disabilities: The Interaction of Reading, Leading, and Neuropsychological Defects.* Academic Press, New York

Pavlidis G, Miles T R (ed.) 1981 *Dyslexia Research and its Applications to Education.* Wiley, New York

Tzeng O, Singer H (eds.) 1981 *Perception of Print: Reading Research in Experimental Psychology.* Erlbaum, Hillsdale, New Jersey

N. D. Bryant

E

Early Childhood Education

The term early childhood education refers to a variety of types of provisions for young children in different countries, regions, and provinces. In this article the term is used to refer to group settings for children between approximately 3 and 6 years old which are deliberately designed to support and stimulate their intellectual development. Group settings for children under 3 years old, usually referred to as "child care" institutions, are dedicated to the total care of children of a wide age range (see *Day Care*). In child care institutions the promotion of intellectual growth is just one among many functions. Group settings for children above the age of 6 (or 7 in a few countries) are typically called elementary and primary schools. The main function of elementary and primary schools is academic instruction.

Although the settings in which early childhood education is provided are known by a variety of names [e.g., nursery school, kindergarten (see *Kindergarten*), playgroup, day nursery, *école maternelle*, *jardin d'enfants*, etc.] they may provide the same services. For the sake of simplicity they are called preschools in this review.

While it is difficult to estimate the magnitude of early childhood education, worldwide reports from a variety of countries indicate that there is great variability from country to country in the proportion of young children enrolled in early childhood programs. In many nations the exact number of children involved cannot readily be determined because early childhood care and education is conducted by a variety of public and private agencies. Public agencies include health organizations, social welfare agencies, labor groups, and their enrollment data are typically not reported to a central agency. However some impression of the range of enrollment can be gained from data in selected nations. For example, out of 43 nations, five indicated less than 10 percent enrollment, six between 10 and 50 percent, three between 50 and 70 percent, and six over 70 percent.

World interest in early childhood education has grown steadily since the early 1960s, as reflected in the documents produced in observance of the International Year of the Child in 1979, as well as in numerous reports issued by the Organisation for Economic Co-operation and Development (OECD), the Council of Europe, and UNESCO. This interest stems in part from the increasing number of mothers of young children employed outside the home, more often than ever in industrial or quasi-industrial settings in which the child's presence is neither feasible nor desirable. Although at one time grandparents or older siblings might have taken care of the young, the former are now frequently employed themselves, and the latter are staying in school longer. Another stimulus for interest and expansion in early childhood education in many parts of the world is the slow but steady improvement in basic child health which has been accompanied by greater attention to the social and intellectual development of the child.

Converging upon these trends is the spreading conviction among professionals as well as the wider community, that experience during the early years may have significant, if not irreversible, effects upon all subsequent development—particularly on later responsiveness to schooling. Together these trends have resulted in a high rate of expansion, research, innovation, and development which can only be sketched in brief here.

Descriptions of the educational systems of some 70 countries indicate that 43 of them include the provision of some type of early childhood education program. It is most likely that this number seriously underestimates the actual worldwide provision of early childhood education programs. Because many such programs fall outside of the purview of educational agencies and are overseen by health, social welfare, or labor agencies (e.g., Bahrain, Bolivia, Denmark, Finland, etc.) provision and enrollment data are often omitted from national statistical reports of education. In addition, much early childhood provision is either privately or municipally supported and is, therefore, unmonitored by national data-gathering agencies.

Of those 43 countries reporting the availability of early childhood programs, 20 do not indicate what proportion of eligible children is served. Among the remaining countries, five indicate that less than 10 percent of children are enrolled, six serve between 10 and 50 percent of those eligible, three countries between 50 percent and 70 percent, and six countries more than 70 percent of the age group. In some countries the age group includes only 5- to 6-year-olds; in others, the age spread is wider. For example, Finland reports that 18 percent of 4-year-olds, 27 percent of 5-year-olds, and 43 percent of 6-year-olds are enrolled in day care centers provided under the supervision of the Ministry of Social Affairs.

Enrollments in nursery schools and kindergartens are not included in the report. Thus it is difficult to know the overall pattern of provision for that country. Similarly, these data are difficult to compare or summarize alongside those for countries in which early childhood programs are provided by governmental agencies primarily for migrants or for the economically disadvantaged (e.g., Israel) and the private institutions are not counted in the data reports. Where detailed data are available, many countries report increasing enrollments and plans for further expansion (e.g., Albania, Costa Rica, Finland, Greece, Spain, Venezuela, etc.).

It has been suggested that at least eight major categories or groups of variables both determine and constrain the activities and events constituting the day-to-day experiences provided to children in preschools. These categories are: contextual factors, characteristics of clients, characteristics of teachers, curriculum, parent influence, administrative factors, length of program, and physical facilities and climate. Each is considered in turn below. It is difficult, of course, to disentangle the separate contributions of each category to the total quality and impact of preschool education.

1. Contextual Factors

At least three subcategories falling under the general heading of contextual factors seem to influence the daily events in the preschool program, typically indirectly. These include historical, philosophical, and cultural factors.

1.1 Historical Factors

Data concerning the historical factors, including the social, political, economic, religious, and other antecedent events that give rise to the development of preschool education around the world, have not yet been compiled, nor does such a compilation appear to be a feasible project. While events fostering the expansion of preschool education have varied at different times in different countries, some general factors seem to emerge across countries.

One such common factor has been change in the employment status of women, sometimes due to the exigencies of war, and sometimes related to rapid industrialization. Another common factor has been recurring waves of moral and ethical zeal directed to the rescue of young children from hazards variously associated with urban life, poverty, disease, and other types of neglect (Lazerson 1972). It is interesting to note that in several cases, the history of preschool education is not a record of steady development and expansion, but is marked by fluctuations in support and size associated with the internal changes suffered by the society in which it exists. For example, Pringle and Naidoo (1975) point out that "a greater proportion of 3- and 4-year-olds in England received schooling in 1900 than in 1972" (p. 7). Similarly, in the United States the Second World War was accompanied by dramatic increases in the employment of women that stimulated the provision of child care institutions, most of which were dismantled at the close of the crisis.

1.2 Philosophical Factors

Philosophical factors include such variables as the "school of thought" governing decisions about the goals and methods used in the preschool, linked to a variety of values, goals, and objectives all of which may be embedded in an educational or social ideology. Revolutionaries, reformers, and Utopianists frequently set out to strengthen their achievements by means of intervention with the very young. In some countries preschools are designed primarily to serve the purposes of "citizenship education" as in the People's Republic of China (Gilliom 1978). However, in many others the recent expansion and interest in preschools has been guided by efforts to minimize the ill-effects of poverty and to increase the ultimate chances for equality of opportunity. Educational philosophers have a more direct influence on the goals, curriculum organization, and content of education offered, than on the methods used. Early philosophers and innovators who continue to have some impact on contemporary preschool education are Pestalozzi, Froebel, Montessori, Freinet (in Europe), and Dewey (in the United States), although their ideas have been modernized in many ways.

Preschool education continues to be marked by sharp ideological disputes concerning such issues as the appropriateness of formal instruction—sometimes called "structure"—for preschoolers, the value of play, and the relative emphases on academic versus emotional and social goals. To some extent these disputes line up alongside various "schools of thought" in psychology such behaviorism, psychoanalysis, Piaget's genetic epistemology (see *Genetic Epistemology: Piaget's Theory*), and so forth.

1.3 Cultural Factors

The number of potentially significant cultural factors that affect preschool education is too large to be dealt with in detail here. These factors constitute a pervasive aspect of the context in which all education occurs, but seem especially salient in considerations of preschool practices for several reasons. One reason is that the younger the child served, the closer the institution's link to the home has to be, and the stronger and more intense the feelings of all involved are likely to be. Another reason is that the younger the child served, the greater the malleability of the child, and the less certain anyone can be about the ultimate long-range effects of the events and activities provided, even though immediate effects are easily visible.

Two features of cultural factors that are of particular interest are complexity and modernity. Complexity refers to the extent to which a given society is marked by differentiation of roles, technical specialization, density of population, use of money in exchange, and so forth. Indices of modernity include openness to new experiences, dispositions to form opinions about matters not of direct or immediate concern, trust in unknown people, independence from parental authority, concerns about the passage of time, and so on (Triandis 1980). All of these subcategories of contextual variables affect attitudes and practices in preschool education and the importance it is accorded in a given society. For example, familism, and a narrow time perspective, both aspects of traditional (vs. modern) cultures, affect the importance given to preschool education within a specific culture. Familism implies a tight network of kin with a distinct, age-related authority structure in which young children are at the bottom suggesting a low emphasis on development-over-time as a basis for preschool planning. Thus both the complexity and the modernity of a culture would be related to goals and practices in preschools. In as much as many societies vary on several levels, being modern on some levels and traditional on others, it is not always possible to distinguish specific practices along these dimensions. No studies have been found which report the potential effects of participation in two divergent cultures (e.g., home/school) upon children's development at the preschool level.

Much of the available literature, by virtue of its constant pleading for cooperation and coordination between home and school, implies that the divergence of cultures in which young children may have to function simultaneously is a source of stress (CERI 1981). The proportion of children for whom divergent cultural patterns are stress-producing has apparently not been empirically established. Finally, in some countries a major objective of the preschool is to ease the assimilation of immigrant children and their families into the host country or mainstream (e.g., Federal Republic of Germany, Israel).

2. Characteristics of Clients

This category of factors affecting preschool education includes the variable characteristics of both the children and their parents (in their child-rearing roles) served by a given preschool program.

One important variable is the age of the children. Not surprisingly, age appears to be one of the least precise criteria by which to describe a population of preschoolers within countries, as well as among them. While Scandinavian countries (Denmark, Finland, Iceland, Norway, Sweden) consider the "under 7s" to be preschoolers, in the United States, Cyprus, Hong Kong, Jordan, and Czechoslovakia, among others, "under 5s" attend preschool programs. Most European countries (other than those mentioned above)—Austria, Belgium, France, Yugoslavia, Federal Republic of Germany—as well as the United

States, India, and the People's Republic of China set the upper limit for preschool at 6 years. Just as the upper age limit varies, there is also no consensus about entrance age. In many countries (Ghana, Japan, the Soviet Union, Chile, the United States) children under 2 years old can attend some preschool institutions. In others, for example, Argentina, Belgium, and Thailand, the entrance age is 3 years and above (Mialaret 1976). For younger children, the institution is more likely to be a crèche or day care center, not primarily educational in function. The common thread in all institutions that conform to this definition of preschool is that they are not compulsory (Woodhead 1979), and that they are available to children for about three years before the age at which schooling becomes compulsory.

The age group composition of a preschool class remains a subject of some controversy among specialists and practitioners. In those locations where a choice of age group exists, the evidence—though not without ambiguity—suggests that a number of logistical as well as pedagogical purposes can be served by mixing the ages within classes so that the oldest and youngest age groups represent about 15 percent each of the total enrollment.

In such classes, the youngest have more mature linguistic as well as social models to emulate; the eldest have opportunities for "teaching and leadership/responsibility," and the middle age group might be in the best position to consolidate gains on many developmental fronts. Special benefits may accrue to the teachers of such age-mixed groups in that the wider range of maturity thereby available decreases the proportion of pupils who are highly dependent, increases the number of "helpers" available to the youngest members, and minimizes the temptation teachers often have to under- or overestimate children's abilities.

Another important variable is the socioeconomic status of the children and their families. Evidence suggests that much socioeconomic segregation occurs in preschool enrollments, in part due to the initial purposes to be served by the preschools provided (Mialaret 1976). In many countries, publicly supported preschools are attended by the children of lower income families and private or even charitably supported preschools serve children from higher income families. Associated with socioeconomic differences are differences in attitudes towards child rearing in general, and education and preschool education in particular (Clark and Cheyne 1979, Shinman 1981, Delhaye and Pourtois 1979) (see *Preschool Children: Characteristics*).

LeVine (1980) offers a perspective on parental goals across cultures using the concept of parental "investment" strategies, and what parents want from their children immediately as well as ultimately. For example, while the African parents he studied seemed to pursue a strategy aimed at linking the child's welfare to that of the parent and the family, American parents pursue investment strategies which involve the allocation of large amounts of resources (e.g., time and attention) to a small number of children aimed at producing an independent, self-reliant person capable (among other things) of maintaining or enhancing the parents' social and economic position. In many other ways, background characteristics of the children and their families influence what "lessons" are emphasized, what indices of good adjustment to school are used (e.g., obedience), the extent of sex differences in what behaviors and activities are encouraged, and so forth.

It may be that children of the higher socioeconomic groups in preschools in different countries are more like each other than they are like the children of lower socioeconomic groups within their own countries. It seems reasonable to assume that greater wealth increases the young child's experiences with making choices (from among such things as foods, toys, activities, etc.). In an environment in which choices are relatively few, emphasis on self-determination, self-efficacy, and/or on autonomy and reflectivity may not be pertinent. In a study of the differences between preschool experts and Head Start parents, Lewis (1978) found that parents gave greater importance to "interpersonal–affective" goals (e.g., learning to share, cooperativeness, respect for others, etc.) than did the 26 preschool experts surveyed. The latter group assigned greater importance to "intrapersonal–affective" goals (e.g., self-confidence, independence, self-reliance, love of learning, etc.). It is reasonable to hypothesize that teachers in preschool fall somewhere between the parents and the experts in the degree to which they emphasize these two sets of goals by virtue of their contact and/ or sensitivity to both groups. Differences between the experts, teachers, and parents in what goals they emphasize can affect the preschool program in many ways. The experts are likely to have greatest impact on the development and selection of the curriculum to be implemented in the classroom. Teachers' goals have greatest impact on the actual experiences of the children as well as in the ways they interact with the parents. Parents' goals are likely to be related to the extent to which they participate in the programs, with greater participation bringing them closer to the views of the teachers. In many programs for low-income and/or minority group children, efforts have been made to encourage parents to set their own goals and curricula. [Compare this with the Aboriginal Family Education Centers described in Teasdale and Whitelaw (1981) and the enabler model described in Katz (1973)].

Bernstein's formulation of the concept of "invisible pedagogies" (Bernstein 1975) addresses some of these issues in that he suggests that the informal child-centered and play-oriented curricula may be invisible to the parents of low-income children, leaving these parents puzzled and feeling unable to assist their children or to support their children's intellectual striving, as well as uncertain of the educational value of the program being offered to the child. On the other hand, he suggests that the parents of high-income children seem to find the informal and child-centered curriculum visible, understandable, and usually desirable. In as much as many preschool programs have been developed by the experts for the low-income child and his or her family, potential sources of miscommunication due to goal and visibility differences are important to consider. Preschool programs designed to assist rural, village, or culturally different groups require special sensitivity to their goals, values, and beliefs concerning the nature of childhood and family relations. Helping the families to change in the direction thought by experts to be most beneficial, but in conflict with local values, can cause acute dissension and dissatisfaction with the program and its implementors. In addressing the ethical conflicts inherent in such cultural and goal differences, Triandis (1980) points out that when one of the values within a cultural group is in conflict with another of its own values (for whatever reason), "a change in culture which maximizes a cultural group's most important values, even if it is inconsistent with other values, or one that attempts to modify a behavioral pattern that is no longer functional, or one that brings accurate information into a situation where magical beliefs, or inaccurate information, are widely used, can be ethically defensible."

There are other characteristics of the clients—both children and their parents—that require consideration in program planning and evaluation. They constitute variables in a major category of determinants of the ultimate qualities as well as outcomes of preschool education.

3. Characteristics of Teachers and Other Assisting Adults

While virtually all specialists in preschool education agree that the teacher's role is a central determinant of the ultimate effectiveness of the program offered, little systematic research is available from which to extract the teacher variables associated with given effects. In a review of research, Phyfe-Perkins (1981) reports that teachers observed to have a high ratio of encouragement to discouragement behavior had children who persisted in activities longer, and who demonstrated more independent behavior than the children of teachers with low ratios. It appears that these ratios are not independent of such other teacher competencies as the ability to arrange play space, to offer appropriate materials and activities, and to manage the children's transitions from one activity to another smoothly.

There is some evidence to indicate that, in a given classroom of young children, teachers tend to engage in greater amounts of interaction with those children who have greatest verbal fluency and ability (Crahay 1980). This phenomenon is one of a class of interaction patterns that can be characterized as a recursive cycle, a concept which refers to the fact that having a given characteristic or behavior such as verbal ability stimulates responses from others which leads to strengthening it or acquiring more of it. Thus the more verbally able a child is, the more verbal input he or she gets from adults, and the more verbally able the child becomes. If the child's verbal abilities are weak, teachers and other adults tend to see the child as wanting to be left alone. In the light of how busy teachers are, they tend to avoid interactions in which the child can be expected to hesitate or stammer; this causes such a child to fail to progress as fast as others. The recursive cycle deals with a behavior and/or characteristic that tends to "feed on itself." One of the issues suggested by the concept of the recursive cycle is that the child cannot break the cycle alone; the intervention of an adult is required to break and thus change the cycle a child is caught in.

One of the issues of central concern to program developers and planners is the ratio of adults to children in preschool classes, especially since salaries and wages constitute the largest costs for most educational institutions. A comprehensive study of the quality of child centers in the United States (Smith 1979), included staff–child ratio as an index of quality and showed that it was related to measures of cognitive outcome taken of the children. The investigators recommended that the best impact on children is obtained when the group size is less than 14 children, and the staff–child ratio is equal to or exceeds 1:7 (Smith 1979 p. 24).

In an extensive study of provisions for children under 5 years old in Oxfordshire, England, Bruner (1980) reports that the content of the relationships between teachers and children in various kinds of preschool settings was heavily centered on "petty management—housekeeping, talk about meal time—instructions about picking up, washing, and the like" (p. 61). In addition, Bruner reports that only 20 percent of all interactions observed consisted of sustained conversations and two-thirds of those were between children. Given the importance of sustained and sequentially contingent interaction to both intellectual and social development these proportions suggest that the preschools from which they come may not be supplying adequate patterns of adult–child interaction.

One unique approach to the adult–child ratio problem adopted in preschool classes (*Vorschulklassen*) in Hamburg, in the Federal Republic of Germany, provides for half of the children in the class to attend the first two hours of the three-hour morning session, and the other half to attend the last two hours of the morning. In this way the staff has only half the total number of children enrolled for two of the three hours of the daily session. This arrangement maximizes the advantages of small- and large-group activities and experiences, though it may be inconvenient for parents.

4. Curriculum

Included under this heading are such variables as the extent to which activities are provided for the children as a whole group, in small groups, or on an individual basis; the temporal sequence of activities; the extent to which the children or adults initiate activities; the quantity and variety of stimulation offered; the variety and types of materials; the substantive content of activities and lessons; the formality–informality of instruction; and the extent of didactics, spontaneous play, and structured projects.

The organization of preschool curricula depends to some extent on the ideological and theoretical perspectives on young children held in particular countries and their cultural subgroups. In addition, the availability of instructional or learning materials offered in classrooms may affect their potential stimulus value as well. In countries or regions within which households have relatively few materials, a small stock of them in the preschool class may be highly stimulating; conversely, children surrounded by many materials at home and then also at preschool may have difficulty achieving sufficient focus or involvement for intellectual development to be fostered (Phyfe-Perkins 1981). Thus there may be an optimum ratio of amount and types of materials available at home to those available in the preschool in order to foster intellectual and other development.

Preschools in different countries utilize different types of materials and equipment, so that some are of the readymade variety, others are found naturally in the surroundings (e.g., leaves, stones, sand, and water, etc.), and some are specifically made by teachers or parents, and even by the children themselves.

A great variety of teaching methods are used, probably stemming largely from traditions within cultural groups with regard to children in general. In some countries guidelines are offered on teaching methods to help individuals choose from among alternatives (e.g., Italy, Iran). While the influence of Montessori (India, Colombia, the United States), Froebel (Australia, Greece, Peru, the United Kingdom), and Decroly (Belgium, El Salvador, Mauritania, Singapore) appear to be quite marked in the methods chosen, many other methods are also encouraged. Curriculum and teaching methods vary between countries as well as within them. The discussion below is drawn primarily from the United States since the bulk of the recent research on curriculum methods has been conducted and reported there.

4.1 Curriculum Models

Several classifications of programs and curricula have appeared since the early 1960s (Miller 1979), none of which seems to capture completely the dimensions on which some 200 of them appear to vary (see Maccoby and Zellner 1970). Some classifications focus on the intentions and goals of the originators of curriculum models, some on the observed activities and interactions, some on so-called philosophy or ideology, and still others on content or context emphasis. In as much as the available research points to no clear curriculum determinants of effectiveness of the models, no single classification scheme seems more useful than any other.

For the purposes of this article, three groups of curricula classified in terms of their main goals as follows are used: (a) academic models, (b) intellectual models, and (c) parental effectiveness models. Obviously many curriculum models do not clearly fall into either of these three rubrics, but represent mixtures of each as well as sometimes placing strong emphasis on psychosocial developmental goals. For example, it would be difficult to classify the typical playgroup curriculum of the United Kingdom or New Zealand into either of the three categories since their emphasis on intellectual development is at least as strong as the emphasis on social development and/or parent education. The typical curriculum of nursery schools in the Soviet Union and the Eastern European countries appears also to emphasize physical, perceptual, social, or character development. Much emphasis is also given to learning how to participate in a group or collective society as well as to preparation for the next level of schooling (Jacoby 1975). However, research on the effects of these curricula is not available.

Curriculum models classified as having "academic" goals are those oriented toward the preparation of preschool children for later school-type tasks, and the development of those skills expected to be demanded in later school experiences. In the United States, the United Kingdom, and Australia such academic curriculum models received much of their impetus from the assumption that children from either low-income families and/or from given subcultures come to school with linguistic and other cognitive deficiencies that can be made up by specially designed lessons related to anticipated school requirements (De Lacey 1979, Chazan 1973). Many such academic curricula have been studied, especially in the United States and the results are discussed below. Among the best known United States examples are Bereiter–Engelmann, DARCEE, and Behavior Analysis (see Maccoby and Zellner 1970).

Preschool curriculum models having "intellectual" goals are those oriented toward what are sometimes called "discovery" methods, Piagetian-type tasks, direct experience with a variety of materials in play situations, and the provision of so-called enriched environments characterized by frequent verbal interaction between the adults and children as well as among the children themselves. The Montessori curriculum comes under this heading although it is somewhat more restrictive in terms of the materials offered and in the extent to which the teachers intervene in the children's activities and encourage them in interaction (see *Montessori Method*). Some well-known examples of this curriculum model also include High/Scope, and Bank Street (see Maccoby and Zellner 1970).

Curriculum models focusing directly on the enhancement of parental effectiveness are not really models of preschool curricula. Rather they are focused on helping the parent—usually mother—to interact and to stimulate the child in ways assumed to be more effective and appropriate at home. Examples of these include the Florida Model (Maccoby and Zellner 1970), the Mother–Child Home Program (Levenstein 1972), and the HIPPY Program (Lombard 1980). Curriculum models in the other two categories have often included parent training components as well. Many preschool classes can be thought of as mixtures of two types: of the preschool curriculum plus home intervention. The term "traditional" is also often applied to those preschool classes in which strong emphasis is placed on social development, emotional expression, creativity, and basic cognitive and physical skill development.

The best known preschool intervention project in recent years is Project Head Start (see *Head Start Program*), launched in the United States in 1965. Since the beginning it has served more than 8,000,000 children of low-income families. Project Head Start is national in scope and comprehensive in services. While its main objectives have been to give the children a "head start" on later schooling, that task was approached on many fronts at once, including parent involvement, health, nutrition, social and psychological services, as well as the educational enrichment provided by classroom experiences based on a fairly traditional view of the needs of preschool children and of teaching methods.

The results of the evaluations of Head Start (as one type of preschool program for poor children) have shifted at least three times since the program's inception. During the first three years the results of evaluations indicated that the educational component of Head Start achieved the positive educational benefits it was originally designed to produce. During the subsequent five-year period, disillusionment set in as more data cast doubts upon the original positive findings. By the late 1970s, however the general climate of opinion had changed into an optimistic one as a result of increasingly favorable results reported from longitudinal studies of preschool graduates.

4.2 Immediate Effects of Preschool Education

In a review of studies of the comparative effectiveness of different curriculum models, Miller (1979) analyzed and summarized the findings of three separate studies in which at least four different curriculum models were implemented and evaluated. According to Miller, no one of the various curriculum models tested was superior to any of the others when all of the immediate child outcomes were considered. It appears that all well-developed models had beneficial effects on the children when the children were compared to those who had no preschool education. However, in terms of specific measures, those models with strong academic emphases yielded greater gains on academic tests than did other models. Two factors may account for the immediate positive outcomes associated with the academic curriculum models. One is that the more closely the curriculum materials and lessons approximate the items on the tests used for evaluation, the more likely the children are to score well on them. A second one suggested by Miller is that it may be easier to train teachers to implement the academic models than the more child-centered or "discovery"-oriented models; the academic goals and teaching techniques are easier to specify and to learn to use. Indeed, in some respects the more highly didactic ones are said to be "teacher proof."

4.3 Long-term Effects of Different Curricula

The pattern of outcomes of longitudinal studies of preschool education is complex as well as somewhat controversial. Miller (1979) examined data on the long-term effects of different curriculum models and reported that the early favorable results produced by the academic curriculum models do not endure much beyond the second year of primary school, although children with preschool education generally are better off than those children who had none. One study was conducted by Miller and colleagues in which four distinctly different models were compared and long-term follow-up data were gathered on the children's school performance two and three years following their preschool and kindergarten years. Of the four curriculum models studied, two were of the academic type, one Montessori (see *Montessori Method*), and another generally called "traditional," implying an emphasis on social development as well as environmental enrichment, provision of opportunities and encouragement to explore the environment, support for creative expression and for spontaneous verbal interaction with adults and other children.

In general the stable effects shown in measures taken four years after the program, as well as seven and eight years later, indicated that the Montessori curriculum produced "superiority in a number of areas, notably reading" (Miller 1979 p. 214). The follow-up data produced by the comparative studies suggest that while the skill-learning emphasized in academic curriculum models during the preschool period yields good effects when tested immediately after the program, these effects fade because motivational and dispositional factors play a greater role than skill factors in children's school performance as they get older. Thus, children in the sixth or seventh year of schooling may have the skills that are required for optimum functioning in school, but may lack the motivational and dispositional characteristics required for sustained effort in the school situation This dispositional deficit may lead to a decline in use of skills which ultimately shows up on the tests during the later grades, but is not noticeable immediately following the preschool experience. Thus, the notion of "fade out" or "cumulative deficit" used to describe the pattern often associated with early gains resulting from preschool experience and subsequent decline in achievement, may need to be understood in terms of the relative shift in the importance of skills versus motivational dispositions to use them at the different age levels. The data suggest the hypothesis that the academic models succeed in obtaining early skill acquisition at the expense of dispositions (such as interest, persistence, curiosity, verbal–social participation, etc.) and that these dispositions are more susceptible to negative influences associated with poverty, poor teaching, and to other threats in the educational environment, thus contributing greater proportions of the variance in achievement as the children progress through the elementary grades (Miller 1979). In the absence of confirmatory data, preschool planners may maximize benefits by offering curricula that optimize the acquisition of both relevant skills *and* motivational dispositions at the same time. That is tempering the academic models with sufficient opportunities for self-direction and social interaction and some degree of informality.

4.4 Lasting Effects of Preschool Education in General

In 1975 investigators in the United States who had offered special preschool programs to the children of low-income families in the 1960s began coordinated studies of the graduates of their various programs in order to ascertain whether any long-term effects could be detected. Under the title of the Consortium on Developmental Continuity, the investigators applied a variety of measures to the graduates of their preschool programs who ranged in age from 9 to 19. The following results emerged:

(a) Preschool education significantly reduced the number of low-income children assigned to special education classes.

(b) Preschool education had an "average" effect of reducing the incidence of grade failure among low-income children.

(c) Children who had preschool education more

often met the grade level expectations of their schools.

(d) Preschool education positively affected later school performance independently of the effects of the early background measures.

(e) Preschool graduates gave achievement-related reasons for feeling proud of themselves more often than control group children.

(f) When 10 program characteristics were tested for their contribution to the effects (e.g., length of program, degree of parental influence, program location, professional versus paraprofessional staff, and so forth) none appeared more influential than others.

A more recent report of follow-up data on graduates of the Perry Preschool Project (Schweinhart and Weikart 1980) confirms the same pattern of positive outcomes. In addition, Schweinhart and Weikart present an analysis of the economic implications of the long-term effects showing that the investment in preschool education can yield substantial savings in terms of the costs of special education, subsequent employment, and other categories of social and economic difficulties associated with the effects of poverty on young children and their later life chances.

In summary, all of the available follow-up data on the lasting effects of preschool education indicate general positive effects. No one curriculum model seems to show overall greater effectiveness than any other, although within some comparative studies, different models produce differentiated effects in the short and the long term. It should be noted that all of the long-term data available thus far were generated by specially and carefully operated preschool programs, often in laboratory-type environments, with funds for staff training, testing, and other program amenities. Their outcomes give a picture of the potential benefits of preschool education when careful planning, operation, and monitoring of the programs are possible.

5. Parental Influence

Preschool programs vary widely in the extent to which parents have power over the staffing, curriculum, and other aspects of the program, whether or not they pay for the service, as well as how much they pay. In most countries a full range of patterns of parental power and influence can be found. In some countries (e.g., the United Kingdom, New Zealand, Canada, and the United States) programs in which parents make all major decisions as well as staff the daily programs are found under the title "playgroups" or "cooperative nursery schools" (Somerset 1976, Bruner 1980). Generally these kinds of preschools have served middle-income families.

One variant of this kind of program is that in which the preschool program is located in a factory or on a college campus (for students' children) having one paid and qualified worker in each class of 15 or 20 children. The remainder of the staffing is made up of parents who each voluntarily take a turn to "work" in the classroom a few hours per week thus improving the adult–child ratio. Arrangements like these may have multiple benefits in that they increase the adult–child ratio, expose parents to professional attitudes and techniques of working with children, and alleviate some of the potential tedium experienced by many preschool teachers when working with very young children every day; the presence of the parents can increase teachers' feelings that their work is significant and appreciated by relevant other adults.

6. Administrative and Sponsorship Factors

Variations in program administration include the size of the preschool, the distribution of authority and decision making, and staff coordination/cooperation. Sponsorship refers to the source of funding, authorizing body, and official regulating agency. Subcategories within each of these two factors tend to be interrelated. Small preschool units tend to be supported through private funds, charities, service organizations, or from fees paid by parents. Larger institutions may be parts of larger municipal, regional, or national networks, supported by public funds and subjected to centralized authority and decision-making processes.

In general, preschool institutions fall into four broad categories of sponsorship: (a) state supported, (b) private, (c) local or provincial authorities, and (d) semiprivate institutions under partial state supervision (Mialaret 1976). Preschool institutions representing all four types are typically found within each country although their distribution varies across countries. The French system, for example, offers unified, centrally planned preschool education with very little private provision and few programs offered by voluntary agencies. Some all-day nurseries are sponsored by the Ministry of Education and operated by local authorities or corporations. But the largest segment of preschool institutions is under the administration and sponsorship of the Ministry of Education and modeled on primary schools (CERI 1981).

Preschool education in diverse countries falls under the purview of a variety of agencies, a phenomenon that gives rise to interagency tension, and "territorial" disputes concerning which governmental agency has the most appropriate expertise and the best interests of children and families at heart. The list of agencies includes ministries of education, public health, youth, welfare, social welfare, mental health, population, labor, etc. It also includes semipublic agencies (e.g., Mining Corporation of Bolivia) or specially created bodies attached to the Department of the President of the Republic. In Norway, for example, one centralized body—the Department of Family Affairs and Equal Status—has total responsibility for policies related to children. In Japan, the two types of institutions for preschoolers are both centrally administered with the kindergartens coming under School Education Law, and the day nurseries or crèches under the Child Welfare Law.

Private preschool institutions constitute a heterogeneous group and can be categorized as follows: (a) preschools organized by a private individual or small group unsupervised by an official body, (b) private schools operated by a private but well-known agency, for example, a group of voluntary agencies providing preschool education for low-income children in Hong Kong. In Greece, preschools/kindergartens are provided by industrial companies; in Trinidad and Tobago some preschools are supported by the Bernard Van Leer Foundation, and in Czechoslovakia some are attached to factories and cooperatives, (c) religious organizations such as the Roman Catholic Church, Islamic (Khalwa in Sudan), or Protestant institutions. Parochial preschools are found in most countries around the world.

In countries like Belgium, Canada, and Switzerland, where education in general is a provincial responsibility and, in addition, where provincial differences in language usage sometimes creates tension, preschool education is the responsibility of the provincial or canton government. Semiprivate schools under official state government supervision operated by certified private individuals, groups, or associations exist widely in almost all countries. In Cyprus, preschool education (called kindergartens) occurs under five types of sponsorship and is supervised by diverse ministries.

The variety of official supervising agencies and funding sources affect the qualifications of the staff, the amount of autonomy available to the staff, the responsiveness of the curriculum and teaching methods to local preferences, values, and purposes served by the institution. Ultimately these can be expected to be associated with differences in effectiveness and impact on developmental outcomes.

7. Length of Program

Variables within this category of factors include the length of the preschool day and the number of days per week. Some preschools provide service for two or three hours per day, some twice weekly. Other preschools provide all-day programs, every weekday morning, and others the whole variety of possible lengths of the day and frequencies of the week, as well as length of the year. Most countries offer a variety of time schedules at the preschool level. In the People's Republic of China, some community-operated preschools (translated as "kindergartens")

offer a 24-hour service for seven days a week, with both full day care and boarding facilities. Denmark has two types of preschool institutions: all day and part day. Japanese preschools are typically four hours per day while Norwegian preschools are available as both four hours per day (short time kindergartens) and four to six hours per day (half day kindergartens). Thus there is great variation in total time available to children for preschool education. However, little is known about the relative benefits to the children of the number of hours in total, the number of hours per day, or the frequency per week of attendance, or the problems the time variations create or solve for the teaching staff and for the parents.

One of the unresolved issues in the field is the potential benefit or harm of multiple versus single caregivers or teachers which in turn is related to the total number of hours per day and per week that the preschool service is available. Furthermore it is not clear whether children's relationships with a number of different adults whose behavior patterns are very similar to each other (e.g., in expectations, demands, responses to children, etc.) create different effects from a relationship with one adult whose own individual behavior varies greatly.

8. Physical Facilities and Climate

The variables within these factors include the amount and type of space, outdoor and indoor facilities, accessibility to open spaces, neighborhood location, number of rooms per site, as well as a range of climate variables.

The physical environment of a preschool is likely to have a large impact on the program in terms of the ease or difficulty with which activities can be managed, the variety of activities offered, frequency of indoor versus outdoor activity, and the ease with which the safety of the children can be maintained.

In as much as the uses of open and closed spaces may be culture bound, it is difficult to draw generalizations that might apply from one country or region to another. For example, one study of Head Start classes in the United States indicated that the amount of controlling behavior of teachers varied with the number of square feet per child (Phyfe-Perkins 1981). However, it is not known whether such space-related behavior patterns would occur in other contexts.

On balance, the available evidence suggests that preschool education can have significant beneficial effects on young children's subsequent schooling and life adjustment, especially for children growing up in economically disadvantaged, or in cognitively understimulating environments. Most of the data available, however, are generated in industrialized countries or urbanized segments of societies.

Several important issues remain to be studied more fully. One is that the most positive long-term effects come from those "intervention programs" which were developed by highly trained specialists and implemented under nontypical circumstances including special funding and extra technical support such as are rarely available to the average or typical early childhood program in most countries. Thus the generalizability to other settings of the positive long-term effects thus far reported remains to be tested.

A second issue stems from the fact that the data do not make clear which aspects of these atypical "intervention programs" account for the long-term benefits observed. It seems reasonable to infer, however, that the traditional controversy in the field over emphasis on play versus pre-academic curricula should give way to the mutual inclusion of both; the available data imply that the optimal preschool environment is one that balances emphases on intellectual, pre-academic, as well as socialization goals. Such combinations should optimize both short- and long-term effects.

Another persistent set of issues surround the measurement of long-term effects. The topological differences in behavior at age 3 or 4, at age 6, and at 7 or 10 are so great as to make the study of the development of the "deep structure" underlying trait or competence very uncertain. In as much as almost all country documents concerning preschool education indicate great concern over the potential role of preschool education in enhancing language development, the conceptual and psychometric issues concerning appropriate sampling, reliable measurement and prediction of language development should occupy a high priority on the research agenda for the future. Progress on these issues should facilitate the testing of innovative approaches to stimulating and strengthening language development through various preschool teaching strategies.

Finally, another issue to be resolved and clarified by further research concerns the potential contribution of various types of parent involvement and education to the effects of preschool education. It is not clear which kinds of parental involvement are most congenial and effective with which kinds of parents, or what content and type of parent education are most helpful in which social and cultural contexts. Experimental variations in types of both involvement and education should be studied with a view to formulating policies concerning their inclusion in preschool programs in various settings.

See also: Nursery Schools

Bibliography

Bernstein B 1975 Class and pedagogies: Visible and invisible. *Educ. Stud.* 1: 23–41
Bruner J S 1980 *Under Five in Britain*, Vol. 1. Oxford Preschool Research Project. High/Scope Press, Ypsilanti, Michigan
Centre for Educational Research and Innovation (CERI) 1979 *Early Childhood Education in Yugoslav Society*. Organisation for Economic Co-operation and Development, Paris
Centre for Educational Research and Innovation (CERI) 1981 *Children and Society: Issues for Preschool Reforms*. Organisation for Economic Co-operation and Development, Paris
Chazan M (ed.) 1973 *Compensatory Education*. Butterworths, London
Clarke M M, Cheyne W M (eds.) 1979 *Studies in Preschool Education*. Scottish Council for Research in Education. Hodder and Stoughton, London
Crahay M 1980 *Characteristics socio-culturelles de la population scolaire et curriculum realise dans quatre classes maternelles*. Document de travail. Laboratoire de Pedagogie Experimentale, Université de Liège, Liège
De Lacey P R 1979 Compensatory education: A basis for more equal opportunity. *Aust. J. Early Childhood* 4: 4–9
Delhaye G, Pourtois J P 1979 *La Perception differentielle de signifiants scolaire en milieu parental socialement contraste*. Université de l'Etat, Faculté des Sciences Psycho-Pedagogiques, Mons
Gilliom M E 1978 Citizenship education in the People's Republic of China. *Theory Pract.* 17: 389–95
Jacoby S 1975 *Inside Soviet Schools*. Schocken, New York
Katz L G 1973 Helping local Head Start staff and parents plan their own program: The Enabler model. *Children Today* 1: 20–23
Lazar I 1979 *Lasting Effects After Preschool: Summary Report*. Department of Health, Education and Welfare, Pub. no. (OHDS) 79-30179, Washington DC. ERIC Document No. ED175 523
Lazerson M 1972 The historical antecedents of early childhood education. In: Gordon I (ed.) 1972 *Early Childhood Education*. Seventy-first Yearbook of the National Society for the Study of Education, Part 2. University of Chicago Press, Chicago, Illinois
Levenstein P 1972 *Verbal Interaction Project*. Family Service Association of Nassau County, Mineola, New York
LeVine R 1980 A cross-cultural perspective on parenting. In: Fantini M D, Cardenas R (eds.) 1980 *Parenting in a Multicultural Society: Practice and Policy*. Longman, New York
Lewis M S 1978 *Congruence of Goals for Early Childhood Between Head Start Parents and Experts*. Unpublished Doctoral Dissertation, University of California. ERIC Document No. ED 171 368
Lombard A D 1980 *HIPPY, A Home Instruction Program for Preschool Youngsters*. Paper presented at the meeting of the International Congress on Early Childhood Education, Tel Aviv, Israel, January 6–10, 1980. ERIC Document No. ED 190 251
Maccoby E E, Zellner M 1970 *Experiments in Primary Education: Aspects of Project Follow-Through*. Harcourt Brace Jovanovich, New York
Mialaret G 1976 *World Survey of Preschool Education*. UNESCO, Paris
Miller L B 1979 Development of curriculum models in Head Start. In: Zigler E F, Valentine J (eds.) 1979 *Project Head Start: A Legacy of War on Poverty*. Free Press, New York
Moore S 1978 The persistence of preschool effects: A national collaborative study. *Young Children* 33(3): 65–71

Phyfe-Perkins E 1981 *Effects of Teacher Behavior on Preschool Children: A Review of Research.* ERIC/EECE, University of Illinois, Urbana, Illinois

Pringle M K, Naidoo S 1975 *Early Child Care in Britain.* Gordon and Breach, London

Schweinhart L J, Weikart D P 1980 *Young Children Grow Up: The Effects of the Perry Preschool Program on Youths Through Age 15.* High/Scope Educational Research Foundation, Ypsilanti, Michigan

Shinman S M 1981 *A Chance for Every Child? Access and Response to Preschool Provision.* Tavistock, London

Smith A N 1979 *Children at the Center: Final Report of the National Day Care Study.* Executive Summary. Office of Human Development Services, Dept. of Health, Education and Welfare, Washington, DC. ERIC Document No. ED 168 706

Somerset G 1976 *Parent Involvement in Early Childhood Education.* Wellington Playcentre Association, Wellington. ERIC Document No. ED 156 317

Teasdale G R, Whitelaw A J 1981 *The Early Childhood Education of Aboriginal Australians.* Australian Council for Educational Research, Hawthorne, Victoria

Triandis H C 1980 Values, attitudes and interpersonal behavior. In: Page M M (ed.) 1980 *Nebraska Symposium on Motivation, 1979.* University of Nebraska Press, Lincoln, Nebraska, pp. 195–259

Woodhead M 1979 *Pre-school Education in Western Europe; Issues, Policies and Trends: A Report of the Council of Europe's Project on Pre-school Education.* Longman, London

L. G. Katz; C. T. Mohanty

Early Childhood Education, Teacher Education for

The term "early childhood education" is used here to refer to group settings for children between the ages of approximately 3 and 6 years old. These settings are specifically designed to provide care, supervision, and education for them outside of their homes. The settings included under the general term "early childhood education" are quite varied, but have in common the fact that they serve children before entry into primary school. Thus the term "preprimary" education is also often used in discussions of education for this age group, and for the sake of simplicity is used throughout the material presented here.

Although specialists in the field differ on many aspects of goals and methods, there is general agreement among them that teachers' competence and attitudes are major determinants of program effectiveness. In spite of such agreement, few empirical studies of teachers themselves have been reported, and virtually no research on the preparation and education of teachers has been accumulated, even though a few projects designed to improve teacher performance have been reported.

From the general literature on preprimary education it appears that around the world, the majority of people teaching children under 5 or 6 years old have had no preservice training at all, and only sporadic inservice courses or workshops. The proportion of trained to untrained personnel is not simply related to the level of industrialization of a given country, to per capita income, or to average educational attainment, but to complex historical, political, and economical forces (Goodnow in press). One of the few fairly reliable generalizations about the field and its teachers is that the younger the child being taught, the less training the teacher has, the lower the status and prestige attached to the job, the fewer qualifications are required, the lower the pay, and the longer the hours of work.

In many respects, the education of preprimary teachers has some of the same problems as primary and secondary teacher education, but in other respects, it has some unique ones stemming from special characteristics of the field.

1. Teacher Education and the Unique Characteristics of the Field

In countries and regions where preservice education is available for preprimary personnel, it is offered in a wide variety of institutions and departmental units, reflecting the equally wide variety of settings in which such personnel are employed. Indeed, in many settings the personnel are not called teachers, but go under a variety of other titles. Some training is available in social work or social welfare departments, or in institutions sponsored by social work agencies, for example, in Finland, Denmark, Bahrain, and the Federal Republic of Germany. Other training is offered in nursing or medical agencies, for example, in the German Democratic Republic; others in highly specialized institutions, for example, Montessori institutes (see *Montessori Method*), teacher-training colleges, nursery nurses' colleges, home economics or domestic science departments of colleges or secondary schools, vocational or technical-secondary schools, as well as in human development or child development divisions of psychology departments in colleges and universities.

Thus while the majority of teachers in preprimary settings have little or no training, some have a year of special secondary school instruction, for example, in Hungary and Chile; some have three-year diploma courses (Australia, and the United Kingdom), and some have diplomas or baccalaureate degrees. Such diversity exists not only across countries, but within some of the larger countries as well (Canada, Chile, India, and the United States).

The diversity of training arrangements as well as employment settings (e.g., nursery schools, crèches, kindergartens, day care centers, playgroups) operating for different lengths of the day and serving a variety of age groups, exacerbates a long-standing problem in the field of role boundaries and role ambiguity, which in turn leads to ambiguity and confusion about appropriate content for whatever training and education courses are available. Questions concerning what proportion of time available for training should be allocated to educational or health issues, and within these, how much emphasis should be given to theoretical versus pedagogical studies, as well as to the development of techniques for working with and educating parents, are constant sources of discussion in the field (Katz 1977). Almost all reports and proposals concerning the education of preprimary teachers emphasize the acquisition of skills and knowledge for building strong ties with parents and for helping parents to improve their child rearing as well as for working closely with professionals in such related fields as medicine, social work, nutrition, and primary schools (Indian Council of Child Welfare). As stated in a report on early childhood care and education prepared by the Organisation for Economic Co-operation and Development (OECD) ". . . the whole question of professional and sub-professional training in the Early Childhood Care and Education field is overdue for reconsideration against the background of recent developments, both within individual countries and across the international scene. As in any such considerations, this should start with a detailed analysis of the work likely to be carried out by one or more categories of ECCE staff" (CERI 1977 p. 51). In the case of developing countries, many teachers are also expected to recruit the mothers and children into the program, as well as to teach them about child rearing, hygiene, crafts, home management, and environmental sanitation (Pakjam 1978).

Another special characteristic of the field is the extent to which educational programs are staffed by volunteers, in some cases because of the lack of funds for paid staff, but in others to create a "family-like" atmosphere, and, in others to strengthen relations between the home and the preschool (Singer 1979, Preschool Playgroups Association n.d.). The volunteer groups tend to undermine the arguments put forward by professional associations that teachers of young children need special skills and knowledge, and advanced training by which to acquire both. Aside from the relatively large role played by volunteers at this level of schooling, preprimary education seems to be caught in a vicious cycle such that, in the absence of training and qualifications, many preprimary teachers have few skills and are therefore very poorly paid, and because of the poor pay, people with skills will not seek employment in this field. Because employees lack sophisticated skills or training, clients as well as sponsoring agencies are unwilling to increase their pay. Added to the poor skills–poor pay cycle is the fact that the younger the child in the setting, the lower the child–adult ratio. This means that when wages are increased, the costs of a program increase relatively dramatically without corresponding increases in the number of children assigned to an individual teacher (Woodhead 1979). Rigorous or lengthy training is unlikely to attract candidates when the ultimate pay scale is so low. Nevertheless, some attempts to break this cycle with new training initiatives and with the introduction of "professional" standards and qualifications have been reported (e.g., in the United Kingdom and the United States) and are discussed below.

2. General Issues in Preprimary Teacher Education

Like teacher education for other levels of schooling, the education of preprimary teachers suffers from the absence of agreed upon criteria of effectiveness, or definitions of "good teaching" (Medley 1982). The field is so diverse in terms of "philosophy," curriculum styles, ages of children served, length of the teaching day, scope of functions of teachers and so forth, that such consensus is unlikely to be achieved on a fieldwide basis. However, within particular types of settings (e.g., crèches), or curriculum styles, (e.g., Montessori), criteria or outcome measures against which to evaluate the effectiveness of teacher education might be more easily attained. Since academic achievement of children in preprimary settings is rarely of concern to the staff, standardized achievement test scores are unlikely to be accepted as appropriate or meaningful measures of teachers' effectiveness from which to make inferences about the effectiveness of their training.

Another problem shared by preprimary teacher education with all other levels of schooling is that in those countries and regions where training is available, doubts about its impact on ultimate teacher performance are widespread (Raths and Katz 1983). Some of these doubts are cast in terms of the relatively greater impact of the ultimate work place on teacher performance compared to the impact of the experiences provided during the preservice training. Other doubts are expressed by both trainees themselves and the practitioners who receive them when training has been completed. The latter critics assert that from their "objective" view, training offered in preservice programs is too theoretical and idealistic. The candidates themselves, from their "subjective" view of the training they receive also claim that it is not sufficiently relevant or useful, and reject it as too theoretical as well. It is possible that both the "objective" and "subjective" views are justified and appropriate. However, in the absence of agreed upon criteria of teacher effectiveness, competing views concerning the best types of training cannot be empirically tested.

Along similar lines, one of the major difficulties in designing and assessing the impact of preservice training programs is the so-called "feed forward" problem (Katz et al. 1981), that is, preservice training involves giving students answers to questions they have not yet asked, or giving students training experiences which provide methods of dealing with eventualities rather than actualities. This "feed forward" problem, no doubt generic to all anticipatory professional training in all professions, becomes a problem mainly when the training staff expects trainees to appreciate and perceive the relevance and usefulness of the training exercises and components provided for them. If the hypothesized "feed forward" problem really exists, it suggests that it is the nature of things that trainees cannot know how they will feel about a given experience once it has passed and in the light of experience not yet obtained. The concept also implies that training programs cannot be designed on the basis of the current responses of trainees, since at a later point in time, looking at those responses retrospectively, the graduate may change the meaning and value assigned to them quite substantially. One type of research of potential use in illuminating various dimensions of this problem would be a longitudinal study of candidates' perceptions of their experiences at selected points in time during their preservice training, and again at several subsequent points in time when they are employed, that is, a longitudinal study of the changes in perceptions of given past events as time passes.

During the posttraining period, graduates could be asked for their preconceptions of various elements of the training program they had, and be asked to compare how they said they perceived them while undergoing them, with how they perceive them at "time n" later. It may be that the very components of their training they rejected while undergoing them are the ones they subsequently wish they had had more of. The hypothesis is that though the experiences obtained during training never change, in the light of on-the-job experience, graduates change the value of meaning ascribed to them in retrospect. Another question is whether such retrospective changes are systematic, and if so, what is the "system"? If the "feed forward" construct is empirically confirmed, it could imply that teacher education must be designed and rationalized on bases other than whether the trainees "like" or see the relevance of its components. Ideal bases for rationalizing the design of teacher education should be theories of adult learning and of professional or occupational socialization. However, it appears that the pattern and structure of training programs are determined more by tradition, economic exigencies, and common sense than by such theoretical formulations.

Another problem shared by early childhood and other teacher training, is that concerning appropriate and sufficient content of the training course. Invariably course revisions concern additions of new specialities and experiences giving rise to steady increases of the length of the training required. Questions arise constantly such as: What proportion of the required work should be theoretical, historical, methodological, or practical? What subjects should be studied and with how much depth? What criteria, theories, or decision rules should be used to answer these questions?

Considerable interest has been shown in addressing such questions as these in terms of developmental stages that trainees and teachers are thought to go through. Katz (1972) proposed that in the case of preschool teachers, most of whom have had little or no preservice training, the aspects and components of teaching with which they need assistance change as experience accrues. Four stages of preschool teacher development were hypothesized, although the length of time in each stage was not indicated, and was thought to vary among individuals even if the sequence in which stages occur does not.

The first of the four hypothesized stages was called "survival," characterized by the trainee or teacher being preoccupied with management and control of the group of children, keeping them reasonably busy and content, having the children accept their authority and accede to their demands, and being liked by them. A second stage, called "consolidation," was defined as a period that begins when the trainee or teacher has mastered control and management of the whole group, the provision of suitable activities to which the children respond favorably, and now becomes concerned about individual children whose behavior is different to that of most of the others, who appear to be atypical, or are seen not to be learning or responding as the teacher would like. A third stage, called "renewal," beginning perhaps after four or five years of teaching, was defined as characterized by a subjective feeling of becoming stale or weary of the same routines, tired of reading the same stories, singing the same songs, celebrating the same festivals, and possibly finding that work with very young children can become intellectually understimulating. Teachers in this stage typically ask for fresh ideas and techniques, new materials and methods, and enjoy and welcome opportunities to exchange ideas and materials with colleagues in workshops. A fourth stage, called "maturity," reached earlier by some than others, includes the teacher's acquisition of self-renewal strategies, but is marked further by the tendency to ask deeper and broader questions about the nature of education and its relationship to society, about historical philosophical, or ethical issues in their work, and so forth. The latter stage was difficult to validate since many preschool personnel move up into directorships or other supportive and administrative positions if they stay in the field as long as five years.

The application of developmental stage constructs to preprimary teacher education can have three kinds of benefits. First, trainees and teachers can be helped to accept their own "survival" struggles at the beginning of their careers as "in the nature of things," and can thus put their lack of assurance and occasional fumbling into perspective, achieving greater patience with their own learning processes. Secondly, teacher education courses could be designed in such a way as to concentrate on providing at least minimal "survival skills" for trainees, but can do so in such a way as to strengthen trainees' dispositions to be resourceful and to go on learning after the basic survival stage is over. That is to say, trainees could be offered very clear simple practical "how to" exercises, equip them with activities to carry out during their initial teaching experiences (perhaps enough for the first two or three months of teaching), and indicate to them that such activities and projects are to help get started, and as soon as they feel comfortable with these activities in the real-life setting with the children, they can begin to develop their own activities and style, and make class plans over a longer period. The third and related value of looking at teacher education with a developmental perspective is that courses could begin with the very practical "how to" aspects of teaching, and end with the theoretical subjects (e.g., history and philosophy)—just the reverse of the typical sequence.

Most preservice programs require some classes involving the observation of children. In many institutions this is a highly valued part of training; it is frequently included in the list of ideal training activities, no doubt a heritage of Montessori's ideas. If there is any validity at all to the application of developmental stages, and the four stages proposed above, the exercises in observation should come after some real work in the classroom, rather than before, as is the custom. Inexperienced young students generally find observation of children unrewarding, if not boring. Studies of the extent to which exercises in the observation of children affect subsequent teaching skills have not been found. Yet it remains an almost sacred component of many teaching courses.

Of all of the components of a preservice education course most strongly recommended for teacher education, teaching practice or "field experience" appears to have top priority, though the amount of practice provided in preservice teacher education courses varies widely. Some courses require practical or field experiences in a suitable or approved setting before admission to a formal certificate or diploma course, as found in Sweden. Others feature practical experience similar to an internship throughout the period of training (e.g., nursery nurses' training in England and Wales), and still others provide as many as three years of academic work prior to field practice, for example, courses for social pedagogues in the Federal Republic of Germany (Austin 1976). Empirical studies of the effects of different amounts of practice are few and inconclusive (Davis 1975).

Another problem in need of empirical investigation is the relative effectiveness of imposing the practical or field experience requirement early rather than later in the training course. Early field experience is assumed to have the advantage of giving trainees better opportunities to try on the future training role and therefore to be able to make a more informed career choice earlier rather than later in the training sequence. Early field experience is also assumed to make theoretical studies more meaningful and useful, since the practical and theoretical components occur simultaneously. However, one study of students in training for elementary teaching indicates that the early field experience overwhelmed the students and that their more theoretical courses, rather than assuming greater relevance, became distractions from the urgent and salient realities of coping with the field setting (Luttrell et al. 1981). The results of another study failed to confirm the assumed benefits of early experience (Shorter 1975).

Another major issue in need of empirical investigation is the frequent complaint of insufficient opportunities for students to observe or to practice "good" practices. Questions concerning both the timing and amount of practice become virtually irrelevant if the community lacks settings in which trainees can observe "good" practices. In such conditions the truism that "practice makes perfect" leads to a situation in which "bad practice makes perfectly bad." It can be argued that trainees do learn from imperfect or "bad" practices in field placements. However, just what is learned is not clear. At the other extreme, some training courses provide practice only in idealized laboratory settings which may be different from typical extracampus settings in ways that make the graduates' skills maladaptive to the field.

Helping trainees to become aware of a range of alternative practices and field conditions by using films, slides, videotapes and so on may minimize the distorting effects of constant exposure to "bad" practices, or to highly idealized settings. In addition, simulation exercises, role playing, microteaching, and the use of specially prepared slides or videotaped incidents together with solicitation of students' responses to specially prepared questions about the incidents may help them to transcend local practices (Medley 1982).

In an interesting series of studies of selected characteristics of students and the field placements to which they were assigned for practice teaching, Becher and Ade (1982) reported data suggesting that students relatively low in self-confidence perform better in practice teaching when matched with a cooperating teacher who is relatively weak or "underwhelming." Apparently, such students' self-confidence is further eroded when matched with a cooperating teacher who appears to be full of assurance and one who makes the teaching task "look easy." Becher and Ade's research suggests that attempts to "match" students' characteristics such as self-assurance with those of the personnel in the field placement could increase the effectiveness of the practice teaching or field experiences provided in training.

Students in preservice education programs are known to complain often that the field settings in which they practice require them to engage in pedagogical practices that their trainers and supervisors deplore or reject. The "bad field setting" predicament implies that the supervisors or tutors have special responsibilities to help trainees interpret and understand the realities of the field setting as well as to cultivate their capacities to adjust to those realities while they are becoming prepared to ultimately progress beyond them. The apparent gulf between educators of teachers and practitioners in field settings has apparently not been studied empirically, but is reflected in much comment in the general literature in the field (Katz 1977). Such discrepancies between the idealized practices advocated by the staff of teacher education institutions and the actual professional practices in the field are no doubt generic to professional education in all professions.

From the scattered reports available concerning the preservice education of preprimary teachers it appears to be following the trend noted in education for teaching at the upper levels, namely toward longer periods of training and greater proportions of the training being allocated to theoretical or "foundation" subjects. One of the best-known specialized training programs for those who work with young children—nursery nurses' training—has undergone great changes. In 1974, the two-year course was changed so that instead of its traditional three-fifths time allocated to practice and two-fifths to theoretical or academic work, the proportions are now reversed. In addition, the required age at entry was raised from 16 to 18 years. Many of the specialized nursery nurse training institutions and programs upgraded their general academic entrance requirements as well, and the certifying examinations have been upgraded substantially. These changes reflect increases in the knowledge base, particularly in the area of child development and parent–child relations, increasing complexity of child rearing and education in general, and strong pressures within the field for greater "professionalization" (Batten 1981).

3. Recent Developments in Inservice Education

Inasmuch as most preprimary personnel have little or no preservice education, various approaches to the education of those already employed merit particular attention. Two particular forms of inservice education provided to preprimary personnel are outlined below. The first known as the "advisory approach" (Katz et al. 1974) employed in the United Kingdom, parts of Australia, and sporadically in the United States and elsewhere, grew from the earlier role of school inspectors (Bolam 1982). In the early 1970s,

Queensland became the first Australian state to adopt a policy of universal access to preschool education. This very large state was divided into nine regions, and preschool advisors were assigned to provide technical assistance to preschool classes within the regions, some of which are geographically extremely isolated. Many of the preschool teachers in country schools are very young, fresh from their training college courses taken in the larger cities of the state, and are assigned to "county service" for at least two years of their teaching careers. Preschool advisors are appointed by the Department of Education of the state of Queensland. They are selected from among practicing preschool teachers and serve as advisors for three years after which they return to preschool classroom teaching. These advisors are expected to make regular visits to all preschool classes within their regions, to provide moral as well as technical support, to conduct workshops on particular teaching or curriculum issues, and many of them also provide services through resource or teachers' centers in the region. The preschool advisors have no inspection or sanctioning authority; their roles are limited to providing support, encouragement, and stimulation to practitioners.

A variant of the advisory approach was the enabler model of inservice training (Katz 1972) developed especially for the inservice education of Head Start teachers in the United States and subsequently adapted for the support of day care staff (Holt n.d.) (see *Head Start Program*). This variant of the advisory approach may be useful in regions and countries just beginning to develop their preprimary resources. The objectives of the model were to help the local communities served by the Head Start program to define and achieve their own goals and purposes, to offer help and advice in such a way as to enable local leaders and participants of the Head Start programs to discover and develop their own strengths and talents, to solve problems on their own, and to help local staff and participants to build and strengthen relationships with their own local resources and agencies. Qualifications of the consultants engaged to perform the enabler model included extensive experience in early childhood education and related fields, special skills in working with parents of diverse backgrounds, and demonstrated ability to be sensitive to the community's strengths and resources (Holt n.d.). The model was conceived in terms of two phases: "initiation" and "maintenance." During the "initiation" phase the enabler was expected to meet with all community groups involved in the program, for example, staff, volunteers, parents, social, medical and nutritional workers, primary school liaison persons, and so forth. During formal and informal discussion with each group and among the groups, the enabler encouraged and facilitated the expression of the preferences, goals, and purposes the community members themselves wanted to achieve.

During the second phase of the model, "maintenance," the enabler's role was to provide support for smooth operation of the program. During this phase the enabler's functions included supplying information, serving as a link between all segments of the wider community involved in the welfare of the preschool children in the program, interpreting the program in terms of its own agreed-upon goals, serving as a source of support and encouragement, appreciating staff strengths, demonstrating skills or techniques occasionally, and serving as a neutralizer of conflict (Katz 1982). Although no controlled empirical studies of the application of this model or other variants of the advisory approach to preprimary inservice education have been reported, the following points emerged from years of experience with the enabler model. Advisors had to struggle to resist the temptation to give advice too early in the development of their relationships with the program or community to be served. This is not a matter of the rightness of their advice, but of allowing enough trust between advisor and advisees to be developed so that the advice could be interpreted in the context of offering help rather than of criticism from an outside expert. Advisors who live in the community being advised have the advantage of greater understanding of local concerns and preferences, but they have the great disadvantage of being in too close and continuous contact with the participants to be able to have a detached, respectful, and realistic overview of the participants' contribution to the day-to-day quality of the program offered to the children. It appears that, depending on the distances between preprimary settings to be served, a maximum number of settings served by any one advisor or enabler might be between six and ten. This makes the advisory approach to inservice education very expensive, since the qualifications for advisors are those at the highest level available in the educational system, and their salaries should reflect the high educational qualifications. In addition, their work by definition is itinerant and incurs costs of travel and accommodation in most regions. Studies of the relative cost–benefit ratios of the advisory approach compared to other forms of inservice training (e.g., mounting courses, workshops, secondments of selected staff, etc.) which take into account the ultimate long-term benefits to the preprimary field in a given location are greatly needed.

By far the single largest and most radical inservice program for preprimary personnel was launched in the United States in 1972 and called the Child Development Associate (CDA) project and was a deliberate attempt to upgrade the quality of teaching in Head Start classes. A Child Development Associate (CDA) is defined as a person able to meet the specific needs of children in a preprimary setting by addressing their physical, social, emotional, and intellectual growth, and by establishing and maintaining an appropriate child care and learning environment, and by promoting good relations with the parents they serve.

At the time the CDA program was conceived in the early 1970s, competency- or performance-based teacher education (see *Competency-based Teacher Education*) and certification was enjoying great popularity and credibility in the United States, especially among state and federal education agencies, and the CDA project was heavily influenced by it. To date, the United States federal government has invested more than US$50 million in its development, testing, and application, indicating the importance given to strengthening the competence of Head Start personnel especially, and other preprimary personnel, generally. In the 10 years of its existence approximately 11,000 individuals have been credentialed, virtually all of whom were already employed in Head Start or similar programs at the time they undertook the training and completed the credentialing process.

The CDA system consists of several interrelated segments. The fundamental segment is the set of teaching competencies on which all candidates are assessed. Another is CDA training, and the third is the Credential Award System.

Among its unique features are the specification of teaching competencies for preprimary staff, the separation of the training from the credentialing processes, and the participation of clients in the credentialing process. The competencies required for the CDA cover six broad goals of preprimary teaching emphasizing such areas of teacher responsibility as health, safety, stimulation of physical and intellectual development, strengthening self-concept, group participation skills, cooperation between home and school, and other supplementary responsibilities. Each competency goal is further subdivided to yield a total of 13 so-called "functional areas." In addition, nine "personal capacities" are listed as essential features of the CDA requirements. These include such capacities as sensitivity to children's feelings, listening and adapting language to suit the children and families, being protective of childrens' individuality, and so forth. The competencies, functional areas, and personal capacities form the basis upon which CDA training programs are designed. Though no restrictions are placed on how the training should address these competencies, functional areas, or personal capacities, the system does require that no less than 50 percent of the training be field or practice based. Inasmuch as most candidates are already employed, the field-based requirement has not been problematic. Another unique feature of the guidelines for CDA training is that no set length of training is imposed on all candidates (Office of Child Development 1973), although to be eligible for candidacy for a CDA credential, applicants must have had at least 600 hours of experience working with children aged 3 to 5 years in a group setting within the five years preceding application (Human Development Services 1982). The training guidelines for the CDA credential were also designed so that any institution with relevant personnel and experience may provide training for CDA credential candidates, and may adapt their own training in any way they wish to ensure the candidate's acquisition of the prescribed competencies. Since the training and credentialing parts of the CDA system are completely separate, no institutions are specifically or officially "entitled" by the government to offer training, and no institutions or organizations are excluded from the same.

The original planners of the CDA training and credentialing system specifically wished to make training and the subsequent credential available to those candidates traditionally excluded from or denied admission to tertiary institutions in many parts of the United States. Thus CDA training is available in a wide variety of institutions at various levels of postsecondary education.

By far the most unique aspect of the CDA system is its Credential Award program or process (Ward et al. 1976) which continues to undergo development, extension, testing, and refinement. The process begins when an applicant for candidacy has been accepted "into the credential award system." As indicated above, the applicant must be at least 18 years old and have had some 600 hours of experience. Once the applicant formally becomes a CDA credential candidate he/she must select a field trainer/advisor (often an experienced member of the staff with whom he or she is working) and a parent/community representative. Trainers/advisors must be approved by the national CDA office and have appropriate experience.

The candidate, with the help of the trainer/advisor, begins the work of preparing a portfolio. He/she collects exhibits and materials to enter into this portfolio which is to serve as a repository of evidence that the work has successfully been carried out on all the competencies required. The portfolio thus composed is used by the local assessment team, described as follows: a local assessment team (LAT) consists of the candidate, the trainer/advisor, a parent/community representative selected by the candidate, and a CDA representative representing the national headquarters of the CDA National Credentialing Program in Washington, DC.

This group of four people becomes the local assessment team that makes the final decision as to whether or not the candidate meets the standards for the award of the credential. The next step leading to assessment is to gather information and materials indicative of the candidate's competence in each of the 13 fundamental areas for the portfolio. In this way, the system by which competence is assessed and the credential that is awarded are completely separate from the training institution—a real departure from conventional training and certification practices.

The trainer/advisor member of the LAT makes three separate observations in each of the functional areas and reports his/her findings in specially prepared formats. The parent/community representative distributes a parent opinion questionnaire to the parents of each of the children served by the candidate, and summarizes the information yielded by the questionnaire for admission into the LAT discussion. In addition, the parent/community representative makes direct observations of the candidate's performance in each functional area specified in the CDA competency standards. Once all the information is collected, the candidate and her trainer/advisor call for an LAT meeting lasting usually about four hours, though sometimes much longer. At this meeting all the information and evidence gathered concerning the candidate's competence is reviewed and discussed with the candidate present and participating. This four-member team votes on the candidate's competence in each of the 13 functional areas separately and then takes a final over-all vote on global competence. Though the four votes may be split in each of the functional areas, in order for a candidate to be awarded a credential, the final overall vote must be unanimously in favor of the award.

The processes involved in assessment and ultimate receipt of the CDA credential are fairly complex, time and energy consuming, and heavily dependent upon the willingness of various participants to contribute many hours voluntarily to help the candidate whilst training, and in participation in the local assessment team's required observations and meetings. However, a number of aspects of the CDA training and credentialing process could be adopted by others without taking on the whole system. The competencies and functional areas constituting the "standards" are both basic and reasonably universal and can serve as guidelines for the training or pre-primary personnel in a variety of cultures and settings; competencies deemed locally inappropriate could certainly be discarded. Another aspect of the training system of potential value in various settings is that it is flexible and individualized so that no single cohort of candidates must engage in all of the same exercises in the same sequence or at the same time; many candidates will be able to demonstrate competence in some of the functional areas at the outset of their training and thus can move on to others for which they do need training and practice.

From the information available to date, it appears that the actual training provided to CDA candidates improves upon conventional training primarily in terms of the explicitness of its goals and objectives, and in its clear commitment to the acquisition of demonstrable skills in working with children and their families. Unfortunately no studies of the validity of the credential have been reported yet. Thus while the functional areas nominated as representing essential competencies for effective teaching of young children appear to have face validity, it is not yet known whether those awarded the CDA credential and those who fail the credentialing process would be judged different from each other by "blind" observers. Since the pass/fail decision is made by the LAT, three of the four members of which are selected by the candidates themselves, the possibility of highly biased evaluation is very great. It is certainly likely that the votes are "stacked" in the candidate's favor in advance. Similarly, the extent to which the pass/fail standards applied by one LAT in one setting or community are like the standards applied by another LAT is not known. The potential for a "rubber yardstick" is very high indeed. Whether universalistic standards of competence are important enough to forgo opportunities for local input into staff quality is not a research issue, but lies in the realm of educational policy.

Given the present state of the art of teacher education in the preprimary field, elements of the CDA training and credentialing system deserve exploration and empirical study. For example, the composition of the LAT provides for genuine participation of the representatives of the local community served by the candidate and gives the candidate a role in his or her own assessment. What are some of the important dynamics of this process? What happens when the LAT member representing the CDA national headquarters differs with the local judgments of the candidate's competence? How can the overall competence of the "profession" be upgraded or modernized to incorporate innovations and new ways of thinking about children if the local (and often remote) community has such a large voice in the credentialing process? On the other hand, the extent of local participation in the process may facilitate dissemination of new ideas to the community in a way that formal meetings and lectures might not.

Some informal and anecdotal reports of the experiences of candidates who have progressed successfully through the CDA credentialing process itself suggest that its various elements (e.g., creating a portfolio, appointing an LAT, being observed by the LAT members, and receiving their feedback in the LAT meeting) create a type of "Hawthorne Effect" (see *Hawthorne Effect*). All the details involved in bringing together the assessment team, knowing that the parent/community representative will solicit the views of parents, and so forth, seem to emit a strong signal that the job for which one is trying to become credentialed is a very important one, one in which many have a real stake and a genuine interest. While so many people who work with young children, particularly in day care centers, feel undervalued and often depressed (Whitebook et al. 1982), the activity surrounding CDA training and credentialing may play a powerful role in improving morale and commitment. The kinds of potential side benefits of the system should be studied with naturalistic methods; questions of the validity of the credential should be addressed with formal experimental methods, and both of these types of studies should be undertaken before others are urged to adopt the rather cumbersome system. Research confirming its validity and other positive effects would then make the CDA system a potentially valuable one, particularly in regions and countries in the early stages of developing training methods for preprimary teachers.

4. Summary

Information concerning the education of preprimary personnel is scattered, and is primarily descriptive in nature. Virtually no research concerning the relative effectiveness of alternative approaches to training and education have been found. In developed countries in which preservice training and education are available, it appears to be quite varied and to be caught in the general trend toward increasing its length as well as its academic components. Research testing the relative impact of various types of content, the early versus late teaching practice, the value of training in "child observation" skills, and the application of "developmental stage" concepts to the design of preservice training would be useful.

In the less developed countries, few teacher-training resources seem to be available at the preprimary level. One of the major issues in need of empirical testing for the developing countries and regions concerns the question of what is the optimum proportion of preservice to inservice training, given that financial resources are limited. In order to produce information suitable for policy formulation, the relative benefits (versus costs) of preservice training (in terms of teacher performance) can be compared with long-term benefits. The hypothesis to be tested is that preservice training programs show strong immediate effects on teacher performance, which subsequently fade, and that certain types of inservice training show few immediate effects on teacher performance, but strong long-term effects on the same. The hypothesis assumes that the types of inservice training approaches to be studied are like those described above under the general heading of the advisory or enabler model.

See also: Evaluating Teaching: Criteria; Inservice Teacher Education; Microteaching: Conceptual and Theoretical Bases; Student (Practice) Teaching in Teacher Education; Supervision of the Practicum in Teacher Education; Teaching Effectiveness Research, Synthesis of; Adult Education, Training Teachers for; Special Education: Personnel Training

Bibliography

Austin G R 1976 *Early Childhood Education: An International Perspective.* Academic Press, New York

Batten A 1981 Nursery nursing: Past and present (2). *Early Childhood* 1(5): 14–19

Becher R M, Ade W 1982 The relationship of field placement characteristics and students' potential field performance abilities to clinical experience performance ratings. *J. Teach. Educ.* 33(2): 24–30

Bolam R 1982 Innovations adopted. In: Thompson A R (ed.) 1982 *Inservice Education of Teachers.* Commonwealth Secretariat, London

Centre for Educational Research and Innovation (CERI) 1977 *Early Childhood Care and Education: Objectives and Issues.* Organisation for Economic Co-operation and Development, Paris

Centre for Educational Research and Innovation (CERI) 1981 *Children and Society: Issues for Pre-school Reform.* Organisation for Economic Co-operation and Development, Paris

Davis M D 1975 A comparison of the development of teaching sophistication and estimates of professional enhancement between eight week and sixteen week elementary student teachers at the University of Illinois (Unpublished Doctoral Dissertation, University of Illinois at Urbana-Champaign, 1975) *Dissertation Abstracts International* 1976 36: 6012A (University Microfilms No. 76-6744)

Goodnow J, Burns A 1982 The relationship between research and the development of child care educational policy relating to young children: Some implications from the Australian experience. In: Katz L G, Steiner K, Wagemaker P J, Spencer M S (eds.) 1982 *Current Topics in Early Childhood Education*, Vol. 5. Ablex, Norwood, New Jersey

Holt B no date The enabler model of early childhood training and program development. Unpublished paper

Human Development Services (United States Department of Health and Human Services) 1982 *The Child Development Associate Credential.* DHS Publication No. (OHDS) 82-31162-A. Office of Human Development Services, Washington, DC

Indian Council of Child Welfare 1978 *National Seminar on Education of the Teacher for the Pre-school Child.* New Delhi

Katz L G 1972 Developmental stages of preschool teachers. *Elem. Sch. J.* 73: 50–54

Katz L G 1977 Socialization of teachers for early childhood programs. In: Spodek B, Walberg H J (eds.) 1977 *Early Childhood Education: Issues and Insights.* McCutchan, Berkeley, California

Katz L G 1982 *Helping Others Learn to Teach.* ERIC Clearinghouse on Elementary and Early Childhood Education, Urbana, Illinois

Katz L G, Morpurgo J, Wolf R L, Asper L 1974 The advisory approach to inservice training. *J. Teach. Educ.* 34: 267–71

Katz L G, Raths J D, Mohanty C, Kurachi A, Irving J 1981 Follow-up studies: Are they worth the trouble? *J. Teach. Educ.* 32(2): 18–24

Luttrell H D, Bane R K, Mason B 1981 Early elementary field-based experience: A university and public school approach. Unpublished paper

Medley D M 1982 *Teacher Competency Testing and the Teacher Educator.* Bureau of Educational Research, University of Virginia, Charlottesville, Virginia

Office of Child Development 1973 *The Child Development Associate: A Guide for Training.* D 74-1065. United States Department of Health, Education, and Welfare, Washington, DC

Pakjam G 1978 Pre basic education. In: Indian Council of Child Welfare 1978

Peters D L (ed.) 1981 New methods for educating and credentialing professionals in child care: The child development associate program. *Child Care Q.* 10: 3–83

Preschool Playgroups Association (in press) *Playgroups in the Eighties.*

Raths J D, Katz L G 1983 The best of intentions for the education of teachers. *J. Educ. Teach.* 8: 275–83

Shorter C A 1975 Early field experiences of sophomore students in two preservice teacher education programs (Unpublished Doctoral Dissertation. University of Illinois, Urbana-Champaign, 1975) *Dissertation Abstracts International* 36: 6026A–6027A (University Microfilms No. 76-6960)

Singer E 1979 Women, children and child-care centers. In: Centre for Educational Research and Innovation (CERI) 1981

Ward E H et al. 1976 The Child Development Associate consortium's assessment system. *Young Children* 31: 244–54

Whitebook M, Howes C, Darrah R, Friedman J 1982 Caring for the caregivers: Staff burnout in child care. In: Katz L G, Steiner K, Wagemaker P J, Spencer M S (eds.) 1982 *Current Topics in Early Childhood Education*, Vol. 4. Ablex, Norwood, New Jersey

Woodhead M 1979 *Pre-school Education in Western Europe; Issues, Policies and Trends.* Council of Europe. Longman, London

L. G. Katz; J. Cain

Earnings and Education

It is a well-established fact that educated workers earn higher wages or salaries than those who are illiterate or those who have completed less education, or have lower educational qualifications. In both developed and less developed economies, in capitalist and socialist countries alike, there is a relationship between education and earnings. This relationship has been extensively analysed in order to throw light on the relationship between education and economic growth, to measure the social and private returns to education, to evaluate education as a form of investment in human capital, and to examine the links between education and the distribution of income.

The relationship between education and earnings is important on distributional grounds because the distribution of educational opportunities will have an impact on the future distribution of income, so that governments committed to long-term redistribution of income must consider the role of education. However this is still a matter of considerable controversy, with some economists arguing that there are strong links between education and earning capacity, while others point to the importance of inherited characteristics, family background, and pure luck in determining an individual's earning power.

The links between education and earnings are also of crucial importance in decisions about the efficient allocation of resources, since it is argued that the higher earnings of the educated reflect their superior productivity. However, the pattern of wages and salaries reflects many other factors, apart from the education of workers. Not only the individual's natural ability, family background, and other personal characteristics, but also historical and institutional factors and trade union bargaining all help to determine the pattern of earnings differentials. Thus, there is considerable disagreement between economists who argue that education is a form of investment in human capital, and that techniques such as cost–benefit analysis should be used as a guide to resource allocation, and those who argue that education simply acts as a screening device, allowing employers to identify the most productive workers. An alternative objection to the notion of human capital is put forward by those who point to the existence of dual or segmented labour markets, with educated workers tending to concentrate in the primary sectors, and other workers, including the less educated, but also including women and workers who are likely to be discriminated against on grounds of race or background, confined to secondary labour markets, where different factors determine earnings.

For a variety of reasons, therefore, the relationship between education and earnings is important but controversial, and disagreement centres around the question of what determines an individual's earning capacity, whether the existence of earnings differentials reflects differences in the productivity of workers, and how information about earnings differentials should be used to guide educational planning decisions. The one point of general agreement is that education and earnings are closely related. Blaug sums up the evidence as follows:

> We begin by noting a remarkable fact of life: between any two groups of individuals of the same age and sex, the one with more education will have higher average earnings than the one with less, even if the two groups are employed in the same occupational category in the same industry. The universality of this positive association between education and earnings is one of the most striking findings of modern social science. It is indeed one of the few safe generalizations that one can make about labour markets in all countries, whether capitalist or communist. (Blaug 1972 p. 54)

Data on average earnings and level of educational attainment of samples of workers exist now for at least 40 countries, and there is no doubt that it is the workers with higher levels of education who enjoy high earnings. Data on earnings can be collected on a time-series basis, which shows how the pattern of wages and salaries changes over time, or on a cross-section basis, which shows how earnings vary with the age, educational level, and other personal characteristics of workers, at a single point in time.

The relationship between the costs of acquiring education and the extra lifetime income that can be expected as a result of investing in education forms the basis of cost–benefit analysis of education, which usually relies on cross-section data on earnings. The question of how much education contributes to economic growth through improvements in the quality of the labour force requires time-series data. A third type of analysis, the study of earnings functions, attempts to explain what determines earnings and variations in earning power, and compares the relative importance of education and other factors, such as race, sex, family background, ability, and occupation, in determining wages and salaries. All three types of analysis use data on the average annual earnings of workers with different levels of education to construct age–earnings profiles, which show the expected lifetime earnings associated with different amounts or types of education. These age–earnings profiles show that the average earnings of samples of workers are closely correlated with both the age and educational attainment of the workers, even though for the individual the relationship may be less close.

1. Age–Earnings Profiles

Information on earnings and level of education has been collected regularly in the United States census since the 1940s, but most countries have to rely on sample surveys for data on the average earnings of workers, classified by educational level. Such data now exist in abundance, but for some countries the samples are small, and include only urban workers, or workers in particular industries or occupations, although other countries have extremely detailed information on earnings and education of large samples of workers. Certain clear patterns can be identified from these data. The age–earnings profiles of workers with different levels of education or length of schooling share three general characteristics:

(a) The average earnings of all workers, both highly educated and illiterate, increase with age up to a maximum in mid-career and then the curve either flattens or starts to decline.

(b) The higher the level of educational attainment, the steeper the rate of increase of earnings, and, in most cases, the higher the initial earnings of workers at the start of their working life.

(c) Workers with higher levels of education reach their maximum earning capacity later than the less educated, and their level of earnings at retirement is also higher.

These three characteristics mean that over a lifetime the total earnings of educated workers are considerably higher than the lifetime earnings of those with very little or no education, but they also mean that it is important to look at total lifetime earnings of workers, rather than earnings differentials at one point in time, since these may seriously underestimate the total financial benefits of education. The age–earnings profiles of two groups of workers with different levels of education, for example university graduates compared with those who left school after completing secondary education, show the earnings differential of the graduates throughout their working lives, and this provides a measure of the extra lifetime income associated with higher education. Early attempts to analyse the relationship between education and earnings in the United States, in order to discover whether education was a profitable form of investment, calculated the additional lifetime income of college graduates, compared with those who had only secondary schooling (i.e., who had completed high school) and concluded, on the basis of 1949 census data on age, education, and earnings that, over a lifetime, a college education in the United States is worth $100,000. This finding has been extensively reported, and helped to foster the belief that education is a profitable form of investment, both for the individual and for society. It is, however, a very crude estimate of the economic value of higher education, since it takes no account of the other factors that determine earnings, nor does it allow for the fact that the present value of expected future income is lower than the monetary value of such a sum received today. In other words, no discounting factor was applied in calculating the value of the lifetime income of college graduates.

Far more sophisticated examples of cost–benefit analysis are now available which do calculate the present discounted value of future income streams, which adjust age–earnings profiles to allow for the influence of ability and other factors in determining earnings and which therefore provide more accurate assessments of the economic value of education, even though this remains a controversial issue.

Figure 1 shows the age–earnings profiles that were calculated from the 1949 census data for the United States and Fig. 2 shows the age–earnings profiles for a sample of workers in urban India in 1960. Both sets of age–earnings profiles show the close relationship between age, education, and average earnings. Similar data now exist for at least 30 countries, revealing a near-universal relationship between education and earnings, and also revealing the importance of age in determining the average income of workers. The following sections will examine the significance of these relationships for the concept of human capital and for alternative theories of the determination of wages and salaries, and will show how the information contained in age–earnings profiles has been

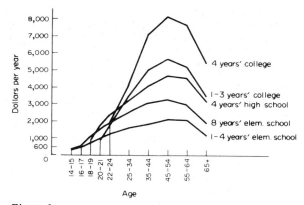

Figure 1
Age–earnings profiles by level of education in the United States, 1949[a]

a Source: Blaug (1970 p. 24)

used to estimate the profitability of education as a private or social investment.

2. The Determination of Earnings Differentials

The age–earnings profiles shown in Figs. 1 and 2 demonstrate that both age and educational level determine a worker's earning capacity. The average earnings of workers rise as they grow older until they reach their peak earning capacity between the ages of about 40 and 55; thereafter the average level of earnings declines, even though the earnings of individuals may continue to increase until retirement. The average earnings of all workers decline steeply after retirement, around the age of 60 or 65. Similarly, the level of education or educational qualifications of workers influence their average

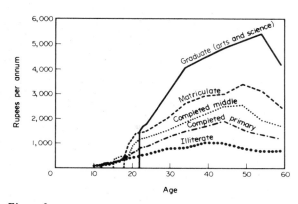

Figure 2
Age–earnings profiles by level of education in urban India, 1960[a]

a Source: Woodhall (1970 p. 20)

earnings, and university graduates have consistently higher average earnings than workers with only secondary schooling; these in turn earn more than those with only primary, middle, or elementary schooling, or illiterates with no schooling at all. If age and education were the only factors that differentiated workers, then the age–earnings profiles shown in Figs. 1 and 2 would prove conclusively that education was a profitable investment for the individual, even though they would not necessarily prove that education confers economic benefits on society as a whole, unless it could also be proved that the higher earnings of educated workers were a direct result of their superior productivity, and hence a measure of their contribution to output.

However, even though age and education are important in determining the earning capacity of workers, they are clearly not the only factors that influence relative earnings. Race and sex also play a part in determining an individual's earning potential, since in many countries and in many industries or occupations within countries, discrimination may exist which artificially distorts earnings patterns. In order to isolate the effect of these variables it is necessary to compare the earnings of men and women separately, or of blacks and whites separately, and this has been done in many countries, showing that age and education are still important, but that sex and race are also important determinants of earning power.

Data for the United Kingdom and for the United States show that women consistently earn less than men, and blacks have lower average earnings than white workers, but nevertheless, the more highly educated earn more than less educated workers, when race and sex are held constant. For example, in the United States in 1966 the median income of women with only elementary schooling was $1,404, while women who had completed high school earned $2,673, female college graduates earned $4,165, and women who had completed five or more years of college education earned an average of $6,114 (Woodhall 1973a). In the United Kingdom the relationship between education and earnings is equally obvious. The absolute earnings differential of male graduates compared with all male employees was greater than the female differential, but female graduates enjoyed a greater relative advantage; the ratio between the earnings of graduates and all workers was 2.6 in the case of women, compared with 2.3 for men (Woodhall 1973a p. 280). Similarly, in the United States the higher a woman's educational level, the closer her income to that of similarly educated men. In 1966 the average earnings of women with only elementary schooling was only about a third of the average for men of the same educational level, but women who had some higher education earned over 40 percent of the male average and women with at least five years of college education

came closest to the income level of similarly qualified men, with over 60 percent of the male average. This shows that though women have lower average earnings than men for a variety of reasons, including shorter working hours and a concentration of women workers in low-paid occupations, nevertheless education still confers financial benefits in the form of higher lifetime earnings (see *Sex Earnings Differentials*).

When the earnings of white and nonwhite workers in the United States and the United Kingdom are compared, this also shows that though race is important in determining earning capacity, whether as a result of discrimination, or as a result of differences in other personal characteristics and the tendency for coloured workers to be concentrated in a few occupations and industries where low rates of pay are the norm, nevertheless, education does make a difference. Coloured workers with higher levels of education do earn more than coloured workers with lower educational qualifications, but one recent study in the United Kingdom suggests that the type of school attended is more important for coloured workers than the amount of schooling, whereas for white workers the level of educational qualifications has a substantial impact on earnings (McNabb and Psacharopoulos 1981) (see *Race Earnings Differentials*).

Apart from race and sex, hours of work, and occupation, which have all been mentioned as factors which help to explain differences in the average earnings of different workers, there are many other variables that play a part in determining the pattern of wages and salaries. It may well be, for example, that the higher earnings of educated workers reflect superior natural ability and family background, as well as their extra education, and in fact some critics of the idea of human capital and the attempt to measure the rate of return to investment in education have gone so far as to deny that education, by itself, has any influence on earnings. Instead they attribute all the extra income of educated workers to such factors as natural ability, motivation, social class, access to well-paid jobs (by virtue of urban residence or other factors), and even pure luck. However, this extreme view ignores the attempts that have been made, over many years, to identify the effects of age and education on earnings by comparing the influence of many other variables on average earnings, and isolating the effects of age and education.

One very early example of such research was an attempt by Gorseline (1932) "to separate the effect that schooling has upon income from the combined effects that schooling, inheritance, health, good luck, bad luck and other factors have upon income". The method was to compare the incomes of a sample of brothers, in the hope of standardizing incomes, in this way, for the effects of family background and other environmental factors. Their incomes were analysed in terms of age, level of schooling, grades attained in school, and scores on standardized tests (as a measure of natural ability), occupation, place of residence, size of family, and windfall income and medical expenses (as measures of good or bad luck). This showed that, at every age, brothers with more schooling in 1927 earned significantly more than their less educated brothers.

From this early attempt to identify the contribution of education to earnings, there has been a considerable improvement in the sophistication of techniques of analysis, and in the availability of data. Multivariate regression analysis and earnings functions have been used to analyse the determinants of earnings. The results of this research will be summarized in the following section, but for the moment it is enough to point out that even when a wide variety of factors are taken into account, age and education remain the most powerful determinants of earnings. In other words, sex, race, occupation, natural ability, and even luck may be important in determining earning capacity but these factors together cannot explain earnings differences.

3. The Influence of Ability

Although research has established that there are a wide variety of characteristics that determine earnings apart from age and education, attention has focused particularly on the influence of ability, and the literature on cost–benefit analysis and the rate of return to educational investment often refers to the calculation of the proportion of earnings differentials that are attributable to factors other than age or education as the "ability adjustment" or "alpha coefficient" [see *Alpha Coefficient (Economics); Ability: Effect on Earnings*]. However, the adjustment of earnings differentials by means of the alpha coefficient in fact reflects the influence of many other factors, apart from ability, including social class and family background.

The alpha coefficient is an adjustment factor which shows the proportion of earnings differentials that are attributed to education alone. Thus, an alpha coefficient of 0.5 or 50 percent means that half the observed earnings differentials calculated from the age–earnings profiles of workers of different educational levels is attributed to education, and half to other factors, including ability and social class background. There are two ways in which such alpha coefficient adjustments have been used in research in the economics of education. One of the first examples of research which used earnings differentials adjusted by an alpha coefficient was the attempt by Edward Denison (1962) to measure the contribution of education to economic growth in the United States. He used the earnings differentials of workers as a measure of the quality of the labour

force, and he assumed, in this calculation, that 60 percent of the observed earnings differentials of educated workers was due to their education and 40 percent to other factors such as ability. This assumption was not based on empirical assessment of the actual proportion of earnings differentials due to education, but Denison later justified his assumption by reference to cross tabulations of the earnings of a sample of workers classified by age, education, scores in intelligence tests (IQ), rank in high-school class, and father's socioeconomic status, which suggested that about two-thirds (0.67) of the actual earnings differentials of this sample of American workers was due to their education.

The same data was used by Becker (1975) in his early estimates of the rate of return to education, and Becker also referred to several other examples of multiple regression analysis which suggested values for the alpha coefficient of about 0.8 when ability was considered alone, and about 0.65 when ability and socioeconomic background were considered together.

As a result of these early studies the value of the alpha coefficient has been widely assumed to be about 0.6 or 0.67, but Psacharopoulos has reviewed over 20 American studies which have attempted to calculate the value of the alpha coefficient, or the proportion of earnings attributable to education, on the basis of cross tabulations or multiple regression. He concludes that the value of alpha varies according to the level of education, but the overall average value of the alpha coefficient is 0.77.

In other words, regardless of the level of education or the ability—plus other factors distinction, education is responsible for over three-quarters of observed earnings differentials. This is a considerably higher value than Denison's "three-fifths" ($\alpha = 0.60$) used almost universally thus far. When we concentrate on the ability adjustment only, then the value of alpha rises to 0.86. . . . The greatest part of observed earnings differentials by educational level is due to education. (Psacharopoulos 1975 pp. 54–58)

3.1 Earnings Functions

The evidence cited by Psacharopoulos, in his review of the influence of ability and other factors on earnings, relies heavily on the concept of an earnings function, which can be fitted to multivariate data to show the influence of variables such as age, education, and ability on the independent variable, earnings. A simple form of an earnings function is

$$Y = f(S, A, F, \text{ Age } \ldots)$$

where Y is the level of income, or earnings, S indicates the number of years of schooling, A indicates ability, as measured by IQ test scores or some similar measure, and F indicates father's occupation or socioeconomic status.

If data exist showing the earnings, age, education,

and other characteristics of a sample of workers, then it is possible to calculate regression coefficients for each of the variables and to fit an earnings function which relates the earnings of the individual to his or her personal characteristics. Earnings functions have been calculated for workers in the United States, the United Kingdom, Sweden, and some other developed countries; few such studies exist for developing countries, although Mexico is one example of a less developed country for which such data exist (see *Earnings Functions*). For the moment the main conclusion of research on earnings functions can be summarized quite simply as showing that age and education are the two most powerful determinants of earnings. The following sections now turn to the question of the significance of this conclusion.

4. *The Influence of Age on Earnings*

A number of different explanations have been put forward for the relationship between average earnings and age. One explanation is that the rising trend of earnings, followed by a levelling-off and then a decline, simply reflects the process of physical and intellectual maturation and decline. However, Becker argues that the shape of age–earnings profiles reflects investment in human capital (Becker 1975). The fact that earnings in the early years of working life tend to rise steadily reflects the fact that individuals are investing in themselves not only by means of formal schooling and on-the-job training but also by acquiring information about the labour market by means of job search and geographical mobility. Later in their working lives these individuals reap the returns to these investments in the form of higher earnings, but as retirement approaches depreciation of skills and abilities occurs, leading to a decline in earnings.

Mincer (1974, 1976) has gone further than Becker in analysing the effect of age on earnings in terms of the acquisition of experience. He summarizes his results thus:

> There is evidence to indicate that the inherent age factor affects earnings to only a minor degree during the usual working life. In data where age and work experience are statistically separable, the earnings curve is found to be mainly a function of experience, rather than of age. (Mincer 1976 p. 140).

This means that it would be better to collect information on the years of work experience and educational qualifications of workers, rather than simply use age as a proxy for work experience. It would then be possible to construct experience–education profiles, rather than the age–education profiles that are normally used to analyse the relationship between education and earnings. For workers with a continuous history of employment throughout their working lives it makes little difference whether age

or experience is used, but for those whose working lives are interrupted, for example, women who leave the labour market for child bearing and child care, or those who are unemployed for a period, information on age is not a good proxy for work experience. However, most data on earnings of workers are not classified in terms of work experience, and it is very much easier to collect information on age. Therefore most research on the relationship between education and earnings relies on age–earnings profiles, as a proxy for information on experience.

5. *Human Capital*

The reason why work experience determines earnings is explained by Mincer quite simply: "Years of labour market experience represent cumulated investments in job training and job mobility" (Mincer 1976 p. 148). By "job training" Mincer means not only formal training programmes, but informal on-the-job training and "learning by doing". In fact Becker and Mincer both explain the relationship between earnings and education and age (or experience) in terms of investment in human capital which includes not only formal schooling and postschool investments such as training and learning experience but also preschool investments which may include environmental influences normally classified as "socioeconomic background", but which Mincer describes as "parental investments in preschool children". He argues that "the quality and quantity of time that parents spend with their children may be viewed as inputs in child quality (human capital)" (Mincer 1976 p. 172).

Of course, the input of time during preschool years, as Mincer points out, is mainly that of the mothers who take the major responsibility for child care, and reduce their labour market earnings as a result. The earnings forgone by mothers who are looking after young children instead of taking paid employment thus represent the cost of this preschool investment.

The time spent by women in child care may, therefore, increase the future earnings of their children, if it increases their stock of human capital by making them more receptive to formal schooling, or improving their educational opportunities in some way. It is likely to reduce the lifetime earnings of the women themselves, however, both during the period the women are out of the labour market, because of the need to look after young children, and because of the effect on work experience. Mincer sums up the conclusions of his analysis of women's work experience and its effect on earnings as follows:

(a) The smaller the expected lifetime participation in the labour market, the less are the investment aspects of women's formal education, and the less is the acquisition of job training at work compared to men with comparable education.

(b) During the period of child bearing and child care, prolonged nonparticipation may cause the skills acquired at school and work to depreciate.

(c) Women who return to work after their children reach school age have strong incentives to resume investment in job-related skills.

(d) This implies that the investment profile of married women is likely to show negative values (net depreciation) during the child-bearing age, whereas the investment profile of unmarried women, with greater continuity of work experience is closer to that of men.

(e) The implications for earnings profiles are clear. Earnings profiles of men are the steepest and concave; those of childless women are less so; and those of mothers are double peaked with least overall growth (Mincer 1976 pp. 162–63).

However, one of the effects of education on women's earnings is that higher levels of education enable a woman to regain her former level of earnings after a number of years and again to enjoy the benefit of rising income associated with increased work experience. Women with less education, on the other hand, may never overcome the loss of earning capacity due to interruptions in their working life and loss of work experience. This can be seen clearly in Fig. 3, which shows the average weekly earnings in 1965 of a sample of British women, classified by age of completion of schooling. The average earnings of those who continued their education to the age of 19 or over decline between the ages of 30 and 40, but then increase, with age, until the age of 60. Women who left school at the minimum leaving age of 15, however, reach their peak earnings in their early

twenties and their average earnings decline steadily until retirement.

This shows that for women one of the ways in which formal education brings economic benefits is through its effect on postschool investments in job training and work experience. Training and work experience are both examples of investment in human capital by means of learning, in just the same way as formal education. Becker emphasizes this point strongly when he writes of learning by experience:

> The conclusion must be that learning is a way to invest in human capital that is formally no different from education, on-the-job training, or other recognised investments. So it is a virtue rather than a defect of our formulation of costs and returns that learning is treated symmetrically with other investments. And there is no conflict between interpretations of the shape of earnings profiles based on learning theory and those based on investment in human capital because the former is a special case of the latter. (Becker 1975 p. 46).

Those who accept the idea that education is a form of investment in human capital argue that it is possible to measure the rate of return to that investment by comparing the present value of the additional lifetime earnings stream associated with education, suitably adjusted by means of the alpha coefficient for the influence of other factors on earnings, with the costs of the investment. The relationship between education and earnings is doubly important for this type of cost–benefit analysis. On the one hand earnings forgone represent a major cost of investment in education. On the other hand, it is the extra earnings of the educated that constitute the main benefit of education, but to accept this as a measure of the benefit means that it is necessary to make a crucial assumption about earnings and productivity.

6. Earnings Forgone

The costs of investing in education should be measured not in terms of money expenditure but in terms of opportunity cost, that is the value of the alternative opportunities for using resources that are given up when resources are devoted to education, rather than some other activity. In other words, the cost, either to the individual or to society, must be measured in terms of all the real resources that are involved in the education process, rather than simply what is bought and sold. One of the most important resources is the time of students and pupils which has an economic value, an opportunity cost, even though it does not have a monetary value.

The imputed value of student time, which is normally used to measure opportunity cost, is the earnings forgone by students when they choose to enrol in secondary or higher education, rather than to join the labour market. Data on earnings forgone are

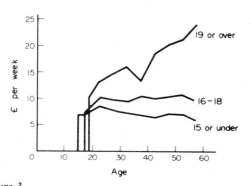

Figure 3
Average weekly earnings of women workers, by age of completing education, United Kingdom, 1965[a]

a Source: Woodhall (1973b p. 16)

collected in exactly the same way as data on the extra lifetime earnings of educated workers, that is from age–earnings profiles calculated for a sample of workers classified by age and by educational level.

A comparison between the earnings of university graduates and secondary-school leavers, for example, shows the additional lifetime earnings of the graduates, measured by their cumulated earnings differentials, and the earnings of the secondary-school leavers during the three or four years in which the graduates were enrolled in higher education provide a measure of earnings forgone.

For the individual these earnings forgone represent a major cost of higher education. In many countries the opportunity cost of higher education is reduced by student aid, either in the form of grants, scholarships, or subsidized loans. However, student aid normally does not cover the whole of the loss of earnings during higher education, so that students must bear the burden either through a lower standard of living than their contemporaries in employment or through contributions from their families, in which case the burden falls on parents or other relatives who finance the living expenses of the students.

This argument presupposes that the alternative to education is paid employment. In many cases, of course, students would be unemployed if they were not enrolled in higher education, and for younger pupils employment may not be a realistic alternative, either because compulsory schooling legislation makes it impossible for children to seek paid employment, or because there are few jobs open to children. Even in these cases, however, the concept of earnings forgone has some relevance.

In the case where unemployment among school leavers is widespread this reduces, but does not eliminate, earnings forgone. Here the actual earnings of young workers aged 16 to 18 or 18 to 20 must be adjusted to allow for the probability of unemployment. If half the age group is unemployed, then the observed earnings of young workers must be reduced by 50 percent in order to estimate the earnings forgone by students in higher education. Even when unemployment rates are high the opportunity cost of student time is not zero, but for pupils in school, who would not be able to find employment, the opportunity cost of the time spent in school may be very close to zero. However, in many developing countries even very young children may be able to find paid employment, or may contribute to subsistence farming, or may engage in other activities that have an economic value. For such children the concept of earnings forgone is perfectly meaningful, and many studies of the causes of educational wastage have shown that dropout among primary-school children is often due to the fact that their families cannot afford the financial burden of earnings forgone. Instead, the children leave school to seek paid or unpaid employment.

So far, the argument has been solely in terms of the private costs of education, that is the cost to the individual of choosing to continue education rather than to seek a job. However, there is also a cost to society as a whole: the earnings forgone by the student represent output forgone by the economy. If the time of students were available to the labour market, instead of the education system, then the output of goods and services could be higher.

Thus, earnings forgone are an important element of both the private and social costs of education, and research into the costs of education show that earnings forgone represent a higher proportion of the total opportunity cost of education in developed countries, where earnings forgone constitute over half the total social costs of secondary and higher education. Table 1 shows the summary by Psacharopoulos (1973) of the proportion of costs

Table 1
Forgone earnings as percentage of total social cost per student year by educational level and country[a]

Country	Secondary	Higher
United States	62.4	63.4
New Zealand	65.0	50.4
United Kingdom	72.4	44.3
Average	67	53
Israel	75.3	34.7
Mexico	62.0	64.9
Chile	66.4	48.6
Colombia	61.0	52.7
Average	66	50
Malaysia	38.5	19.5
Ghana	62.6	24.3
Korea, Republic of	69.5	62.0
Kenya	43.6	23.0
Uganda	42.6	34.3
Nigeria	59.4	27.7
India	56.2	47.1
Average	53	34

a Source: Psacharopoulos (1973 p. 126)

of education represented by earnings forgone in 14 developed and less developed countries. Even in developing countries, about half the total cost of secondary education and a third of the cost of higher education consists of the value of student and pupil time, as measured by earnings forgone.

This information is important for debates about student aid policy and the question of private contributions to the finance of education. If the costs of education are measured solely in terms of money expenditure, this seriously underestimates the true costs of education, both to the individual and to society as a whole. It is true that earnings forgone are not a perfect measure of the economic value of student time, but it is now widely accepted that it is better to use earnings forgone as the imputed value of student time, rather than to ignore this important element of opportunity cost.

However, the use of earnings forgone in estimates of the social cost of education presupposes that earnings are a satisfactory measure of the value of output produced by workers, and hence the value of the output that is sacrificed when students enrol in education rather than take a job. This is disputed by those economists who deny that earnings reflect the marginal productivity of workers. The question of the relationship between earnings and productivity is therefore crucial to the whole issue of the links between education and earnings (see *Earnings Forgone*).

7. Earnings and Productivity

The basic assumption of the notion that education is a form of investment in human capital is that education raises the productivity of workers and that the higher earnings of the educated reflect the value of their product. The most obvious way in which education raises productivity is by imparting knowledge and skills which make a worker more efficient, and hence more valuable in the labour market, than less educated workers. If earnings reflect differences in marginal productivity, then the extra earnings of the educated measure their contribution to output. The marginal productivity of a worker is the addition to total output which is achieved by employing one additional (marginal) worker, and a considerable body of classical and neoclassical economic theory rests on the assumption that relative prices of goods and services and the relative wages and salaries of workers reflect their relative scarcity and hence, in the case of workers, their productivity.

If this assumption is accepted, the relationship between earnings and education has two implications. In the first place, the fact that educated workers earn more than the uneducated means that their earnings can be used as a measure of the contribution of education to the growth of national income, over time. This was the approach adopted by Denison (1962, 1967), who analysed the rate of economic growth in the United States and later in various European countries, in terms of an aggregate production function, and he used relative earnings as a measure of the marginal productivity of different groups of workers. In the case of the United States Denison concluded that between 1930 and 1960 about 23 percent of the rate of growth of national income was due to the increased education of the labour force, which raised its productivity (see *Economic Growth: Contribution of Education*).

The other important corollary of the link between education and earnings, if it is accepted that relative earnings reflect productivity differences, is that earnings differentials can be used as a measure of the economic benefits of education in calculations of the social rate of return to educational investment. However, this basic assumption that earnings reflect productivity rests in its turn on the assumption that markets, including labour markets, are basically competitive, so that prices reflect relative scarcities. If markets are perfectly competitive, then earnings provide a completely satisfactory measure of productivity; but even if there are some imperfections in the degree of competition, earnings will still reflect differences in productivity provided the forces of demand and supply ensure that scarce factors command a higher price than plentiful factors of production. Since highly educated workers are scarcer than unskilled and uneducated workers, this is enough to ensure that they are paid more, in terms of average wages and salaries.

Those who oppose the idea of measuring the returns to education in terms of the extra earnings of the educated point to imperfections in the labour market, particularly in developing countries, and argue that this demonstrates that earnings reflect historical, administrative, and other noneconomic factors, and cannot possibly be used as a measure of productivity. As Blaug (1972 p. 73) explains, "Provided labour markets function competitively, earnings are a satisfactory measure of productivity . . . but this is precisely the point at which the misgivings begin." There have been some attempts to measure the productivity of educated workers in physical terms, rather than in terms of relative earnings. Mincer sums up this research as follows: "Actually research on production functions by Griliches (1963, 1967) and others has shown that not only differences in wage rates but also differences in productivity are related to differences in the education of the labour force across states, regions, or enterprises. The potential contribution of education to aggregate economic growth is not merely a conjecture. But these findings tend to be ignored by critics" (Mincer 1980 p. 125). The reason is probably that it is difficult to measure productivity in physical terms, so that it is impossible to prove conclusively that earnings differentials measure differences in physical productivity.

However, it is not necessary to accept that earnings are a perfect measure of productivity to believe that earnings differentials reflect the scarcity, and hence the economic value, of resources. If market forces operate, even imperfectly, so that scarcity is reflected in price, then the fact that educated workers command higher salaries than the uneducated can be taken as evidence of superior productivity. However, an alternative explanation is often put forward, namely that employers pay educated workers more because they simply use education as a "screening device".

8. Education as a Screening Device or Filter

Some critics of the notion of human capital believe that education does not impart vocationally useful knowledge or skills, but simply acts as a means of socialization (Gintis 1971). Others argue that it simply serves as a screening device, enabling employers to identify individuals who have superior natural ability or attitudes or personal qualities that make them more efficient or more able to benefit from on-the-job training. In this case, the higher earnings of the educated simply demonstrate that education acts as a filter or screening mechanism, not that education makes workers more productive. A considerable controversy has developed over what is called "the screening hypothesis", because if it is true that education simply serves to identify individuals with superior natural ability, then it involves a huge waste of resources, since more productive individuals could, presumably, be identified far more cheaply than by means of years of socially costly, subsidized education.

The fact that employers have not been able to develop quicker and cheaper methods of identifying able workers is in fact one powerful argument against the screening hypothesis. The whole controversy has been reviewed by Layard and Psacharopoulos (1974), who conclude that a number of observed facts run counter to the screening hypothesis. For example, the fact that age–earnings profiles by level of education diverge, rather than converge over time, demonstrates that employers continue to pay educated workers more, throughout their working lives, when they have direct evidence about their productivity, and are not forced to rely on education as a screening device. As Blaug argues:

> We cannot have it both ways: either the educational system is a superb discriminant of the sort of abilities industry demands, in which case we must conclude that this is the economic role of education until such a time that a better screening device is invented, or it is only a crude way of selecting people that misinforms as frequently as it informs, in which case it is not clear why employers do not correct their initial hiring mistakes . . . We come back full circle to the question of competition in labour markets. Thus, the much publicised idea that education contributes directly to economic growth by the formation of human capital . . . rests ultimately on the belief that competition is at work in labour markets. (Blaug 1972 pp. 73–4)

In fact, it is now recognized that the screening hypothesis has been of some value in emphasizing that education not only imparts vocationally useful knowledge and skills, but also affects attitudes, motivation, and values, all of which help to determine a worker's productivity and employability. Mincer sums up the debate:

> The productivity and screening functions of schooling are not mutually exclusive in a world of imperfect information, given that ability is an input in the educational process. The controversy, if any, concerns the *relative* importance of the productivity and screening functions of schooling in affecting earnings. (Mincer 1980 p. 125)

It is therefore perfectly possible to believe that education raises the productivity of workers while at the same time recognizing that many employers use it as a convenient screening device, because they do not need the skills directly imparted by education but they do value the attitudes and abilities normally associated with education, including social and communication skills which are indirectly fostered by education. The view that employers value the certificates or diplomas provided by the education system, rather than the knowledge and skills that are actually taught in schools or universities, is called by some writers "credentialism". Some critics go further, and argue that in developing countries it has become a "diploma disease" (Dore 1976).

However, a more common view is that, in the words of Mincer, "Education is neither a panacea nor a conspiracy" (Mincer 1980 p. 127). It does raise the productivity of workers, and hence their earnings, and though the precise way in which education influences productivity may not be perfectly understood, there is now a widespread view that education affects productivity both directly, by imparting vocationally useful knowledge and skills, and also indirectly, through its effect on attitudes. It also works in conjunction with other forms of investment in human capital, including on-the-job training and learning by experience. Thus, the earnings of educated workers reflect a variety of pre- and post-school investments, as well as the effect of pure education.

Bibliography

Becker G S 1975 *Human Capital: A Theoretical and Empirical Analysis*, 2nd edn. Columbia University Press, New York

Blaug M 1970 *An Introduction to the Economics of Education*. Allen Lane, London

Blaug M 1972 The correlation between education and earnings: What does it signify? *Higher Educ.* 1(1): 53–76

Denison E F 1962 *The Sources of Economic Growth in the United States and the Alternatives Before Us*. Committee for Economic Development, New York

Denison E F 1967 *Why Growth Rates Differ: Post-War Experience in Nine Western Countries*. Brookings Institution, Washington, DC

Dore R P 1976 *The Diploma Disease: Education, Qualification, and Development*. Allen and Unwin, London

Gintis H 1971 Education, technology, and the characteristics of worker productivity. *Am. Econ. Rev. Pap. Proc.* 266–79

Gorseline D E 1932 *The Effect of Schooling Upon Income*. Indiana University, Bloomington, Indiana

Griliches Z 1963 The sources of measured productivity

growth: United States agriculture, 1940–60. *J. Polit. Econ.* 71: 331–46

Griliches Z 1967 Production functions in manufacturing. In: Brown M (ed.) 1967 *Theory and Empirical Analysis of Production.* Conf. on research in income and wealth, 1965. Columbia University Press, New York

Layard R, Psacharopoulos G 1974 The screening hypothesis and the returns to education. *J. Polit. Econ.* 82: 985–98

McNabb R, Psacharopoulos G 1981 Racial earnings differentials in the UK. *Oxf. Econ. Pap.* 33(3): 413–25

Mincer J 1974 *Schooling, Experience and Earnings.* Columbia University Press, New York

Mincer J 1976 Progress in human capital analyses of the distribution of earnings. In: Atkinson A B (ed.) 1976 *The Personal Distribution of Incomes.* Allen and Unwin, London, pp. 136–92

Mincer J 1980 Human capital and earnings. In: Atkinson A B (ed.) 1980 *Wealth, Income and Inequality: Selected Readings.* Oxford University Press, Oxford

Psacharopoulos G 1973 *Returns to Education: An International Comparison.* Elsevier, Amsterdam

Psacharopoulos G 1975 *Earnings and Education in OECD Countries.* Organisation for Economic Co-operation and Development, Paris

Woodhall M 1970 *Cost–Benefit Analysis in Educational Planning.* UNESCO-11EP, Paris

Woodhall M 1973a The economic returns to investment in women's education. *Higher Educ.* 2: 275–99

Woodhall M 1973b Investment in women: A reappraisal of the concept of human capital. *Int. Rev. Educ.* 19: 9–29

M. Woodhall

Earnings Forgone

Forgone earnings are a major cost component of educational provision that came to the surface in the wave of the economics of education literature since the late 1950s. This cost component is also known as the opportunity cost, indirect cost, or hidden cost of education.

The visible direct costs of education are the budgetary outlays for school facilities, teacher salaries, classroom maintenance, and equipment. However, the fact that a student is studying in school instead of participating in the labor market means that there is some lost production for the economy as a whole. It also means a lost income for the person who is studying. Hence, a fully inclusive resource cost of education should include the lost production component. As a first approximation this is measured by the earnings of those in the labor force with a level of educational attainment one step lower than the one for which the student is currently studying. For example, the indirect cost of college education is what a person with a secondary-school certificate of the same age is earning in the economy.

The opportunity cost of education is substantial and it varies with the level of education, the type of country where it is measured, and the business cycle.

Thus, the opportunity cost of studying for a doctorate is enormous because the individual could have been working with his or her master's or bachelor's degree. The forgone earnings of primary-school children in advanced countries is trivial because of minimum working-age laws. However, in a poor developing country, for instance, the opportunity cost of attending primary school is substantial because of the lost agricultural help (and thus, lost agricultural output) provided by children of young ages. Furthermore, during a period of economic recession in any country the opportunity cost of schooling falls as the number of employment possibilities are reduced.

It is estimated that earnings forgone roughly represent one-half of the total resource cost of educational provision.

See also: Earnings and Education

Bibliography

Psacharopoulos G 1973 *Returns to Education: An International Comparison.* Elsevier, Amsterdam

Psacharopoulos G 1980 Spending on education in an era of economic stress: An optimist's view. *J. Educ. Finance* 6: 160–75

G. Psacharopoulos

Earnings Functions

One question which has puzzled economists, sociologists, and laypersons alike for a very long time is the determinants of personal earnings. Why should A earn so much while B earns only half that much? Is it because A is more astute, or better educated, or was born to a richer family, or somehow secured a better position in a more affluent sector of the economy, or for some other reason?

The recent availability of data on personal earnings along with information on other characteristics of the individual has resulted in a flood of empirical studies attempting to test alternative hypotheses about the determinants of personal earnings. This kind of research activity is known in the literature under the heading "earnings functions." Such functions attempt to answer a number of questions regarding the relationship between earnings and variables such as education, ability, age, and experience.

1. Why do Earnings Differentials Exist?

The theory behind the existence of personal earnings differentials goes back to the foundations of economics as a discipline and it has not changed much since.

As a first step, wages can be thought of as prices and thus determined by supply and demand. To add a degree of realism, institutional factors interfering with competitive equilibrium can be introduced. The following four headings are broad enough to include many old and modern theories put forward to explain earnings differentials.

(a) *Equalizing wage differentials*. Adam Smith wrote about equalizing (or compensating) wage differentials between jobs. Since some occupations are more dangerous than others or involve dissatisfaction of some sort, it is natural for the employee to expect a compensating premium. Moreover, since some occupations require additional training relative to others, the extra earnings could be seen as a compensation for the costs incurred during the training period.

(b) *Noncompeting groups*. Cairnes and Mill later introduced the concept of noncompeting groups to explain earnings differentials. Whereas Adam Smith mostly referred to differences between jobs, this concept refers to differences between people. If more able people are scarcer than less able people, then the extra earnings of the more able are due to restrictions on the supply side of labor classified into different watertight and therefore noncompetitive groups.

(c) *Institutional factors*. Both of the above explanations assume the existence of a competitive labor market. In the absence of perfect competition, institutional factors have been introduced to explain wage differentials, for example, the degree of unionization, the existence of civil-service pay scales, social custom, and the degree of industrial concentration.

(d) *Luck*. Lastly, the intuitive reason of differential luck between individuals in explaining earnings has always been considered (Jencks et al. 1972).

2. From Theory to Earnings Functions

Initially, empirical tests of the above theories were conducted mainly by means of cross tabulation of the earnings of employees by the different explanatory variables (Reder 1962). However, the recent availability of data on earnings (Y) and other characteristics (X) of the individual (i) has made possible the fitting of the following earnings function:

$$Y_i = f(X_{1i}, X_{2i}, X_{3i}, \ldots.) \tag{1}$$

where the X's stand for factors such as ability, occupation, costs of training, and so on, any residual arising from the actual specification and fitting of Eqn. 1 being attributed to unspecified factors, such as luck.

It should be noted that there is a great leap between the theories listed in the previous section and Eqn. 1. Earnings differentials theories are based on a wage determination at the intersection of supply and demand schedules for labor of different kinds. Equation (1), however, cannot be easily interpreted as supply and demand or even as a reduced form of a multiequation system.

Once the veil of theory is removed, all one can analyze via Eqn. (1) is associations between different

characteristics of the individual and his or her earnings. Causation cannot be established without a theory of some sort, no matter how intuitive some of the variables appear on the right-hand side. Given this theoretical caveat one should be cautious in using the terms "effects of" or "determinants of" in an earnings function framework.

3. Uses of Earnings Functions

The following list gives an overview of the different uses to which earnings functions results can be put. The list is definitely not exhaustive and some items on the list overlap, but they have been listed separately so as to make explicit a variety of possible uses of earnings functions.

3.1 Isolation of the Effect of One Individual Variable on Earnings

This is achieved by controlling a set of other characteristics, for example, what is the effect of race on earnings, given family background, schooling, and urban residence?

3.2 Rate-of-return Analysis

Historically, this has been the use par excellence of earnings functions. In cost–benefit analysis, education benefits are measured as the difference between the earnings of a graduate of school level S and a graduate of the lower school level $S - 1$. Of course it would be naive to assume that the whole differential ($Y_S - Y_{S-1}$) is due to education. A part of it should be due to differences in other factors between individuals of different educational attainment such as ability, socioeconomic background, and the like.

When cost–benefit analysis was first applied to education, the correction of the earnings differentials for factors other than education was done by applying the so-called alpha (α) adjustment coefficient (Blaug 1965). The part of the earnings (B) strictly due to the completion of school level S over school level $S - 1$ was found by the following expression:

$$B = \alpha(Y_S - Y_{S-1}) \tag{2}$$

The alpha coefficient was a catch-all factor, including not only ability but all determinants of earnings other than education. The value of alpha assumed in empirical analysis was around 0.60.

In fitting an earnings function one can perform a more accurate adjustment by setting all variables other than education equal to their sample mean and predicting the expected earnings of individuals with different levels of schooling. In this way, one does not have to rely on a catch-all factor, the effects of particular variables being made explicit. What may be more important is that through earnings function analysis one can derive different values of the alpha coefficient specific to different educational levels or different levels of economic development. Earnings adjustments until now have proceeded with unique values of alpha (usually equal to 0.6), regardless of the educational level the earnings refer to or the country's per capita income.

3.3 Income Growth Accounting

This is a use closely related to Sect. 3.2 above. In accounting for the sources of past economic growth it is necessary to construct a measure of aggregate labor services. In order to arrive at this index the number of persons employed are augmented for quality via a set of earnings weights classified by educational level. Once again, a "factors other than education" adjustment of the earnings weights is necessary and this can be done by utilizing the results of an earnings function.

3.4 Income Distribution Analysis

Old "theories" of income distribution have been descriptive rather than analytical in respect of the causes that underlie its particular shape. Now earnings functions make it possible to study the factors associated with income inequality. If the earnings function is fitted in a semilog form and variances of both sides taken,

$$\text{Var}(\log Y_i) = \text{Var} \, f[(X_{1i}, X_{2i} \ldots .)] \quad (3)$$

then the left-hand side of Eqn. (2) represents a direct measure of income inequality and this can be associated to the variability of the different characteristics of the individuals in the right-hand side.

3.5 Study of Interaction Effects

Formerly the interaction between different independent variables in determining earnings has been studied via finer and finer subtabulations. However, the sample size is rapidly reduced in this way; and moreover, one cannot easily assess the statistical significance of the results. By fitting an earnings function one can answer such questions as whether education and ability are complementary or substitutes in determining earnings. If they are substitutes, increased emphasis should be given to educating the less mentally gifted students. The opposite conclusion would hold if education and ability were complementing each other.

Another related controversial issue in the United States is the interaction between the effects of schooling and race. Positive or negative correlations between these variables would have diametrically opposite implications on what racial group should receive more education.

3.6 Testing of the Screening Hypothesis

A recent attack on the economic value of education comes from the "screenist" who challenges the fact that school certificates per se have a productive value other than filtering the more able for employment in high-paying jobs (Berg 1971, Wiles 1974, Taubman and Wales 1973).

Since this hypothesis involves the interrelationships of earnings, schooling, and ability, earnings functions could be potentially useful for testing it (on why they might not, see Layard and Psacharopoulos 1974).

3.7 Educational Planning

Isolating the effects of different types of education has obvious implications for educational planning or policy in general. For example, it may be that on-the-job training has a greater effect on earnings than certain forms of formal schooling.

Moreover, instead of relying on past wage data by age and education, educational planning could use the wages of recent graduates of different schools. The advantages of using wages of new graduates rather than wages for all ages would be the following: firstly, starting salaries are least contaminated by the effects of social conventions and other usual caveats concerning the relationship between market wages and the social value marginal product of labor; secondly, they give the most recent indication as to the relative benefits of a given educational level. This could not be detected by looking at average wages by educational level referring to all ages. Through earnings function analysis one can arrive at an idealized age–earnings profile for each educational level, controlling for effects other than education. Once this profile is constructed, starting salaries would provide the intercept of an expected age–earnings profile to be used for planning purposes.

3.8 Testing of Some Major Political Issues

Is it education or social class that determines earnings? If social class is more important than education, then one should find an alternative way (other than education) to redistribute earnings (Gintis 1971, Bowles 1972, Jencks et al. 1972). Is it native ability or social background that determines earnings? The predominance of native ability would support a Right-wing view. But if social background is more important, a Left-wing view would be supported; for example, the low-earnings, adverse-background B did not have the same opportunity to acquire human capital as A who belongs to the upper class.

Since earnings functions are geared to isolate the effects of education, ability, and social class they could be useful in answering questions such as the ones listed above.

4. Variables and Specification

The independent variables used by the different authors to explain earnings range from the conventional ones such as age and education to whether the individual has a Spanish surname (Rees and Shultz 1970), whether his or her state voted Republican, or whether he belongs to the Kalenjin-speaking tribe (Thias and Carnoy 1972).

Figure 1 gives the most common variables found in most studies, classified into two groups: personal and environmental. Another possible distinction is between variables that are subject to the individual's choice and those beyond his or her control. Whether earnings are determined mostly by choice or nonchoice factors leads to different policy implications.

```
┌─────────────────────────────────────────────────────────┐
│ Personal characteristics                                │
│                                                         │
│ Mostly not subject to choice   Sex                      │
│                                 Age                     │
│                                 Race                    │
│                                 Genetic ability         │
│                                 Family background       │
│                                   (social class)        │
│                                 Motivation              │
│                                                         │
│ Mostly subject to choice       Occupation               │
│                                 Marital status          │
│                                 Number of children      │
│                                 Weeks worked             │
│                                 Human capital  Years of schooling │
│                                          Quality of schooling     │
│                                          Achievement              │
│                                          Experience and on-the-job training │
│                                          Rate of return to schooling │
│                                          Migration               │
│                                          (Health)                │
│                                                         │
│ Environmental and institutional                         │
│                                                         │
│    Geographic locality                                  │
│    Economic sector                                      │
│    Unionization                                         │
│    Monopoly, monopsony                                  │
│    Discrimination                                       │
└─────────────────────────────────────────────────────────┘
```

Figure 1
The determinants of earnings

The majority of earnings functions have used labor income as the dependent variable. Labor earnings represent about three-quarters of total income in advanced countries and about one-half of total income in poor countries. Therefore, whatever explains labor earnings would explain a large component of income. Also, the investigation of what determines earnings is a much more difficult task than finding what determines nonlabor income. The latter is a direct function of inheritance: previously accumulated wealth and the rate of return on it. It is a greater challenge to find what makes A earn more than B. Further, on policy grounds, it is politically easier to enact a policy affecting earnings rather than redistributing wealth.

Many authors, however, have used total income as the dependent variable in the absence of data on earnings (Chiswick and Mincer 1972). Others have included income from self-employment.

The dependent variable is often the logarithm of earnings rather than absolute earnings. This is either for easier interpretation of the effect of individual variables (in terms of percent increment of earnings) or for theoretical reasons following the human capital school (Mincer 1974).

One important distinction in earnings functions analyses is whether the data refer to individuals (i.e., the dependent variable ranges over the earnings of A to the earnings of Z) or to groups of individuals. In the latter case, the average earnings of a group of people is treated as one observation in the earnings function. The classic example of averaging across states is found in the works of Becker and Chiswick (1966), Chiswick (1968), Chiswick (1970), and Chiswick and Mincer (1972). Averaging has also taken place across the provinces of Canada (Chiswick 1970), across seven countries (Chiswick 1971), across earnings by level of schooling and IQ in Sweden, and across age groups in Iran (Psacharopoulos and Williams 1973). Most earnings functions, however, have used individual earnings as the dependent variable.

The reason why the distinction between average and individual data is important is that in the case of averages a major part of the variation of earnings is removed before the dependent variable enters the regression. Hence, the higher R^2's of studies using average earnings.

5. Sample Size and Coverage

The reference sample or population varies widely between different studies. It ranges from 45 observations in the case of Carroll and Ihnen (1967) to 200,000 in Tolles and Melichar (1968). However, the average operating sample size is around the 3,000 mark, with the exception of those studies that have used 1/1,000 samples of the United States census and therefore included 40,000 to 60,000 observations (Mincer 1974). Very few earnings functions refer to the representative sample of the population as a whole. The usual early triple restriction in the United States was white urban males only (Chiswick and Mincer 1972). But there exist also studies exclusively on blacks, on farmers, and some that have paid particular attention to female workers. Samples in developing countries are typically limited to employees in the modern sector of the economy.

6. Years of Schooling

According to the human capital school (Mincer 1974), the relationship between earnings (Y) and years of schooling (S) is specified in the semilogarithmic form

$$\mathrm{Ln}\, Y = a + bS \qquad (4)$$

where a and b are the regression estimated parameters. The theoretical reasoning of the semilogarithmic specification is as follows (Becker 1971, lecture 36). Assuming zero direct costs of schooling, the total cost of schooling in investment period 1 is $C_1 = Y_0 + 0$, where Y_0 represents forgone earnings during the previous period 0. Then the income-generating function takes the form

$$Y_1 = Y_0 + r_1 Y_0 \qquad (5)$$

If investment continues for S periods (or S schooling years),

$$Y_2 = Y_1 + r_2 Y_1 \qquad (6)$$

$$\cdots\cdots\cdots$$

$$Y_s = Y_{s-1} + r_s Y_{s-1} \qquad (7)$$

Assuming secondly that $r_1 = r_2 \ldots = r$ is the eventual earnings of an individual with S years of schooling,

$$Y_s = Y_0(1 + r)^S \qquad (8)$$

or, in log-linear form,

$$\text{Ln } Y_s = \log Y_0 + \bar{r}S \qquad (9)$$

Hence, by regressing earnings data by level of schooling on the number of years of schooling,

$$\text{Ln } Y_s = \text{const.} + bS \qquad (10)$$

the b coefficient can be interpreted as an approximation to the average private rate of return to schooling. It is an approximation only because it uses the assumption of direct costs equal to part-time student earnings and constant age–earnings profiles.

The human capital specification of the earnings function has been fitted in a large number of countries and the b coefficient gave results similar to those obtained by the "elaborate method" of estimating the rate of return to investment in education (for a review of such studies see Psacharopoulos 1982). Other independent variables present in the regression are years of work experience and its square (to take into account the parabolic relationship between earnings and age) and, perhaps, weeks worked if the earnings data refer to an annual basis. The inclusion of other variables (such as occupation or rural–urban residence) is not appropriate on the grounds that their inclusion gives a downwards bias to the estimated rate of return, as they restrict the mobility (occupational or geographic) by means of which the returns to education are realized.

Earnings functions have been used extensively to study the relationship between education and income distribution. This is typically done in two ways: first, by taking variances of both sides of the human capital specification (equations above) and thus relating the dispersion of years of schooling (var. S) to the dispersion of logarithmic earnings (Marin and Psacharopoulos 1976). Second, by econometric simulation of increasing the number of years of schooling of a particular population group and predicting the change in the dispersion of earnings (Blaug et al. 1982). Although the relationship between education and income distribution is still a highly debated issue in the literature, studies using the earnings functions

as an analytical tool have found that the provision of education is generally associated with less income inequality.

See also: Alpha Coefficient (Economics); Cost–Benefit Analysis in Education; Earnings and Education

Bibliography

Becker G S 1971 *Economic Theory*. Knopf, New York

Becker G S, Chiswick B R 1966 Education and the distribution of earnings. *Am. Econ. Rev.* 56(2): 358–69

Berg I 1971 *Education and Jobs: The Great Training Robbery*. Beacon Press, Boston, Massachusetts

Blaug M 1965 The rate of return on investment in education in Great Britain. *Manchester School* 33: 205–61

Blaug M, Dougherty C, Psacharopoulos G 1982 The distribution of schooling and the distribution of earnings: Raising the school leaving age in 1972. *Manchester School* 50: 24–40

Bowles S 1972 Schooling and inequality from generation to generation. *J. Polit. Econ.* S219–51

Carroll A B, Ihnen L A 1967 Costs and returns for two years of post-secondary technical schooling: A pilot study. *J. Polit. Econ.* 85: 862–73

Chiswick B R 1968 The average level of schooling and the intra-regional inequality of income: A clarification. *Am. Econ. Rev.* 58: 495–500

Chiswick B R 1969 Minimum schooling legislation and the cross-sectional distribution of income. *Econ. J.* 79: 495–507

Chiswick B R 1970 An inter-regional analysis of schooling and the skewness of income. In: Hansen W L (ed.) 1970 *Education, Income and Human Capital*. National Bureau of Economic Research, New York.

Chiswick B R 1971 Earnings, inequality and economic development. *Q. J. Econ.* 85: 21–39

Chiswick B R, Mincer J 1972 Time-series changes in personal income inequality in the United States from 1939, with projections to 1985. *J. Polit. Econ.* 80(3): 534–66

Gintis H 1971 Education, technology and the characteristics of workers productivity. *Am. Econ. Rev.* 61(2): 266–79

Jencks C S, Smith M, Acland H, Bane M J, Cohen D, Gintis H, Heyns B, Michelson S 1972 *Inequality: A Reassessment of the Effect of Family and Schooling in America*. Basic Books, New York

Layard R, Psacharopoulos G 1974 The screening hypothesis and the returns to education. *J. Polit. Econ.* 82: 985–98

Marin A, Psacharopoulos G 1976 Schooling and income distribution. *Rev. Econ. Stat.* 58: 832–38

Mincer J 1974 *Schooling, Experience and Earnings*. National Bureau of Economic Research, New York

Psacharopoulos G 1982 Returns to education: An updated international comparison. *Comp. Educ.* 17: 321–41

Psacharopoulos G, Williams G 1973 Public sector earnings and educational planning. *Int. Labor Rev.* 108: 43–57

Reder M W 1962 Wage differentials. In: National Bureau of Economic Research 1962 *Aspects of Labor Economics*. Princeton University Press, Princeton, New Jersey

Rees A, Shultz G P 1970 *Workers and Wages in the Urban Labor Market*. University of Chicago Press, Chicago, Illinois

Taubman P J, Wales T J 1973 Higher education, mental ability and screening. *J. Polit. Econ.* 81: 28–55

Thias H H, Carnoy M 1972 *Cost–Benefit Analysis in Education: A Case Study of Kenya*. Johns Hopkins University Press, Baltimore, Maryland

Tolles N, Melichar E 1968 Studies of the structure of economists' salaries and income. *Am. Econ. Rev.* 58(5): whole issue

Wiles P 1974 The correlation between education and earnings: The external-test-not-content hypothesis. *Higher Educ.* February: 43–58

G. Psacharopoulos

Earth Sciences: Educational Programs

Earth science offers a convenient vehicle for the integration of the sciences. For this reason it has recently become a popular curriculum subject in many countries, at the middle- and junior-high-school level. The conceptual revolution of the 1960s (plate tectonics) also gives it a unique advantage with respect to new developments and a growing body of knowledge. Different countries have used different approaches to the question of how to bring these developments into the classroom.

Earth science is an umbrella term for the study of different aspects of the earth. The major part of earth science is drawn from the more defined discipline of geology: the study of the earth. This core is complimented by the hybrid fields which bridge between geology and other sciences: geophysics, geochemistry, meteorology, oceanography, pedology, and so on.

The earth sciences currently occupy a unique position in the natural sciences, having recently undergone a major conceptual revolution. Until the early 1960s, the earth sciences were a conglomeration of piecemeal theories, each attempting to explain a small part of the physical world. The introduction and establishment of the theory of plate tectonics (the movement and interaction of vast crustal plates across the face of the earth) revolutionized all previous concepts about the earth and provided a unified framework upon which to hang all previous knowledge and partial theories.

1. Curricula Around the World

This rebirth and conceptual revolution which only began in the early 1960s, and the continued thrust in earth science research, has kept it in the world headlines. Earth science attempts to explain natural phenomenon on a macroscopic level which can be readily understood by a layperson, an advantage which it has over the physical sciences (the microscopic level) and the space sciences (the super-macro-level). By virtue of the nonesoteric nature of this revolution, many countries have adopted earth science as a convenient vehicle for fulfilling the main objectives of teaching science. In these countries, earth science plays various roles according to the philosophical approach of the curriculum planners. In the United States, earth science has traditionally been seen in the main as a preparatory science course for the junior-high-school level. A number of courses have been developed, mainly for the eighth and ninth grades, to provide an overview of the place of science in the natural world. It is thus perceived as providing a good general knowledge for nonscience majors as well as a strong conceptual base upon which to relate the pure science disciplines to be studied in subsequent years by science majors.

In England and Wales and in Australia, earth science topics have tended to be incorporated into integrated science curriculum materials. The Australian Science Education Project (ASEP) developed modular units from many areas of science which were moulded into an overall curriculum design (see *Module Approach*). Some of the units had clear earth science associations. In England and Wales, several of the celebrated Nuffield programs (Nuffield Secondary Science, Nuffield, Combined Science) incorporated units on earth science, although many schools in England and Wales teach geology as an independent curriculum subject. This may be due to the United Kingdom's significant contributions to the development of the science of geology, from the eighteenth century until the present day. In Israel, two projects have been developed to introduce geological topics into the existing school curriculum. A "floating" module based on the identification of the common local rocks was developed (Mazor 1976) and an optional course for 10th grade chemistry students based on the chemistry of minerals and rocks was recently completed (Pezaro and Mazor 1979). In the above examples, earth science is considered as an ancillary subject, supporting, illustrating, and extending existing disciplines. This results from the dilemma which has faced the most enthusiastic attempts to introduce earth science as a fully fledged curriculum topic in many countries. Earth science is usually squeezed out in the struggle for curriculum hours, where it must compete with the traditional "giants" of science curricula (biology, physics, chemistry).

2. Some Major Curriculum Projects

2.1 Earth Science Curriculum Projects

The most comprehensive attempts to build a complete curriculum in earth science in the Western world was the Earth Science Curriculum Project (ESCP) in the United States. ESCP was one of the later of the federally funded projects of the 1960s, being developed jointly by the American Geological Institute (AGI) and the National Science Foundation. It culminated with the publication of *Investigating the Earth* (AGI 1967), the most integrative of all the junior-high-school science curricula in the United States. The dissemination stage of the project was very successful and quickly produced a shortage of teachers. Teacher preparation became a major problem as soon as the enrollments in earth science began to rise dramatically [850,000 students (26.2 percent of total enrollments) in 1969: over 3,000,000 students in 1977]. Consequently, two additional projects were initiated, "Environmental Studies" and the "Earth Science Teacher Preparation Project." The teacher shortage was particularly acute because the integrated nature of the subject matter intimidated teachers who had majored in just one of the major science disciplines.

2.2 Crustal Evolution Education Project

Following the era of the 1960s, the 1970s saw new curriculum concepts replace earlier ideas. In the earth sciences, one of the most significant developments in the United States was the Crustal Evolution Education Project (CEEP). This project was established under the auspices of the American Geological Institute and was a direct result of the desire to involve the school student population in the nascent revolution of the earth sciences which had begun with the publication of the notions of seafloor spreading and plate tectonics. The desire to circumvent the lengthy process of textbook production spawned a new concept in curriculum development: "the articulation of a system of development which brings the latest scientific developments into the classroom whilst research into these developments is still ongoing and far from complete" (Thompson 1980). The involvement of a professional subject association in providing the whole of the project staff for the initiation, planning, and execution of the project constituted another innovation in science curriculum development.

Modules were developed in six centers spread throughout the United States. Individual module themes were chosen according to the areas of interest, expertise, and inspiration of the particular development team. In all, 64 modules were involved. After conventional stages of writing, formative evaluation, revising, and peer review, 32 modules were ultimately published. A wealth of curriculum materials were therefore available to teachers within two to three years, a period considerably less than for "conventional" curriculum materials.

The CEEP project underwent extensive curriculum evaluation, mainly at the formative stage of preparation of the materials. Three types of data were gathered; student background characteristics, student performance variables, and process or climate variables. Initially the modules were tested on a restricted basis, using one of the teachers who had been involved in the module's development. The second stage involved a more systematic collection of data. Between one and four teachers (who had not been involved with the module's development) with at least 100 students each, were monitored with

an evaluation package provided by the project evaluation center at Ohio State University. All data were analyzed and used to revise the modules before publication. A final stage of evaluation was on a much larger scale, involving some 12,000 students constituting broadly representative student and teacher populations.

3. Research

Compared to other branches of science education, little systematic educational research has been carried out in earth science. Review of the science education literature in general indicates a paucity of articles in earth science research. Even in the earth science education literature [*Journal of Geological Education* (USA), *Geology Teaching* (UK)] the majority of contributions relate to descriptions of innovative courses or approaches to conventional subject matter, reports on recent geological events of developments in the discipline, or didactic hints and comments.

Considerable educational research has been continued at Ohio State University using the CEEP materials. The materials have been used to explore the feasibility of adapting a novel evaluation technique to science education. Interrupted time series analysis had been virtually unused in educational research until it was applied to the teaching of an instructional unit based on the CEEP modules, in Ohio. This method allowed the sophisticated modeling of the instructional and learning process, and was used to monitor the development of concrete and formal geological concepts in adolescent students over time. It was based on the daily collection of evaluation data, a task which was possible in the research framework but not practical for the average classroom teacher. The tremendous growth in the availability of computers in schools could soon bring this evaluation tool within the easy reach of all teachers. This approach enabled the construction of learning curves for plate tectonics concepts, which indicated clear differences for students at different cognitive levels of development. This result has ramifications for teachers who want to adapt their teaching practices to their students' cognitive levels (Mayer and Kozlow 1980).

4. Summary

Earth science education seems to be still on the upswing around the world. Most curricula tend to be locally orientated, using local examples as much as possible. This makes direct adoption difficult, but lends itself to easy adaptation. The possibility of presenting many earth science concepts in concrete terms makes earth science an attractive first science course and, in fact, it is commonly introduced as such at the middle- or junior-high-school level.

See also: Geography: Educational Programs; Science Education: Secondary-school Programmes; Science Education: Primary-school Programmes

Bibliography

American Geological Institute 1978 *Investigating the Earth*, 3rd edn. Houghton Mifflin, Boston, Massachusetts

Mayer V J, Kozlow M J 1980 An evaluation of a time-series single-subject design used in an intensive study of concept understanding. *J. Res. Sci. Teach* 17: 455–61

Mazor E 1976 *The World of Rocks*. Weizmann Institute of Science, Rehovot

Pezaro P E, Mazor E 1979 *Chemistry of Minerals and Rocks in Israel*. Weizmann Institute of Science, Rehovot

Thompson D B 1980 Plate tectonics for the people: The Crustal Evolution Education Project (1976–79). *Geol. Teach.* 5: 21–25

P. E. Pezaro

Eclectic Approaches in Counseling

According to Thorne, eclectic counseling "involves the selective application of basic science methods using the most valid current knowledge available for specific clinical situations according to indications and contraindications" (1973 p. 445). The Greek root of the word eclectic means to "pick out," and in modern counseling usage it suggests selecting the best elements from various counseling theories and strategies to meet the needs of specific client problems. The eclectic counselor finds a single theoretical orientation limiting and, rather than mold the client's problem to fit a particular theory, prefers to draw upon a number of strategies across various theories to fit the client's need.

1. Assumptions and Principles Underlying Eclectic Approaches to Counseling

Basic to the differences between counseling theories are the differing assumptions they make about the development of human behavior. Eclectic counselors are less concerned with how human behavior develops than how it can be changed most efficaciously. An underlying principle of eclectic counseling is that of experimentalism; that is, the pragmatic utility of a technique is more important than the theory behind it (Barclay 1971). A major assumption of eclectic counseling is that in order to be optimally effective, each counselor must develop a personal counseling style that fits the counselor's unique personality and stylistic characteristics (Brammer 1969).

Brammer (1969) has identified three prerequisites to the development of a personalized counseling style. First, the counselor must learn the skills associated with experimentalism, principally the skills associated with observation, experimentation, and evaluation. Next, the counselor needs to become familiar with a variety of counseling theories and strategies. Finally, the counselor must know his or her own personal strengths that may relate to counseling.

2. Models of Eclecticism

The leading proponent of eclectic counseling and psychotherapy has been Thorne (1950, 1961, 1973). Thorne's approach to eclectic counseling involves the selection and orderly combination of compatible elements from diverse sources (Thorne 1973 p. 451). The counselor's task is to follow a rational plan for selecting out from all the strategies available to him or her, the techniques that are most likely to benefit the client. The choice of counseling techniques is guided by the following factors (Thorne 1950):

(a) Specificity of action: which strategy is known to result in the specific change desired (p. 105)?

(b) Economy of action: brief therapy is preferred to extended therapy if it can be assumed both will produce similar results (pp. 105–06).

(c) Natural history of the disorder: some counseling strategies are more effective in certain stages of the problem development than in others (p. 106).

(d) Distributive principle: treatment approach is flexible and can be easily adjusted to fit changes in client response (pp. 106–07).

(e) Total push: every resource available to the counselor is brought to bear on the problem if needed (p. 107).

(f) Failure of progress: as a last resort, experimentation with any method available (pp. 107–08).

Delaney and Eisenberg (1972) have also described an eclectic approach to counseling as one that incorporates features of phenomenological, cognitive, and behavioral counseling theories. They define counseling as a time-oriented process consisting of five stages: (a) the initial session, (b) the facilitative relationship, (c) goal identification and determination of counseling procedures, (d) counseling strategies, and (e) termination and follow-up. During the fourth stage, Delaney and Eisenberg suggest that six basic principles can be used to guide the selection of strategies by counselors. These principles are:

(a) People learn new behaviors by receiving verbal instructions from significant others (p. 105).

(b) People learn to behave in new ways by imitating the behaviors, beliefs, values, and attitudes of significant others (p. 126).

(c) The reinforcement contingencies in a person's environment influence the way he or she behaves in that environment. Changing the reinforcement contingencies can be expected to influence a change in behavior (p. 131).

(d) Some people learn to function more effectively by becoming aware of certain characteristics about themselves or their environments (p. 137).

(e) Some people learn to function more effectively by acquiring a specific method for decision making (p. 142).

(f) Some people learn to function more effectively by acquiring a more favorable sense of self-esteem (p. 156).

3. Criticisms and Contributions

Perhaps the most serious criticism of eclectic counseling is that eclectic counselors have nothing to guide them given novel client problems. Counselors who subscribe to a particular theory have the precepts of the theory to direct their action in such cases. Eclectic counseling has also been criticized because: (a) the superiority of various techniques has yet to be firmly established, (b) few counselors can master the variety of techniques required, and (c) changing techniques during the process of counseling may actually be counterproductive for the client.

Proponents of eclectic counseling argue that it is superior to any approach based on a single counseling theory because it uses only those techniques that work. Further, they argue that an eclectic approach deals with a greater variety of etiological factors than does any other counseling approach and therefore has greater depth than any approach based on a single theory. Finally, proponents point out that eclectic counselors are less emotional and dogmatic about their counseling strategies than are single-theory counselors, making them more objective in their treatment of client problems (Shertzer and Stone 1980).

See also: Counseling Theories

Bibliography

Barclay J R 1971 *Foundations of Counseling Strategies.* Wiley, New York
Brammer L M 1969 Eclecticism revisited. *Pers. Guid. J.* 48: 192–200
Delaney D J, Eisenberg S 1972 *The Counseling Process.* Rand McNally, Chicago, Illinois
Shertzer B, Stone S C 1980 *Fundamentals of Counseling,* 3rd edn. Houghton Mifflin, Boston, Massachusetts
Thorne F C 1950 *Principles of Personality Counseling: An Eclectic Viewpoint.* Journal of Clinical Psychology, Brandon, Vermont
Thorne F C 1961 *Personality: A Clinical Eclectic Viewpoint.* Journal of Clinical Psychology, Brandon, Vermont
Thorne F C 1973 Eclectic psychotherapy. In: Corsini R J (ed.) 1973 *Current Psychotherapies.* Peacock, Itasca, Illinois

D. R. Atkinson

Ecological Theory of Human Development

. . . much of developmental psychology, as it now exists, is *the science of the strange behavior of children in strange situations with strange adults for the briefest possible periods of time.* (Bronfenbrenner 1979 p. 19)

Ecological research contrasts sharply with more traditional psychology research. Proponents of the ecological study of behavior have typically avoided the use of experimental methods involving controlled manipulation of isolated variables in the laboratory. Ecological psychologists have generally laid great stress on the importance of using naturalistic methods, of studying behavior in its situational context, and as a corollary, of careful description of the environment.

In the 1940s, two psychologists working at the University of Kansas, Roger Barker and Herbert Wright, started the Midwest Psychological Field Station as a center for the ecological study of human behavior. Two major strands of ecological research were conducted at the field station. One strand focused on the behavior of individual children in their everyday environments. The other strand examined the influence of the ecological environment on behavior. Methods of identifying, unitizing, and describing the settings of behavior were the focus of this aspect of the research conducted at the field station. In this article, both of these strands will be briefly reviewed.

1. Specimen Record Research

An important part of the early work conducted at the field station was the preparation of a set of records documenting the behavior of individual children in their everyday environments. The records which were collected are known in the literature as specimen records of behavior. These records were termed "specimen records" since they preserve for later study actual specimens of behavior with minimal disturbance to the behavior in the process of observation. One specimen record, consisting of 435 pages, was published commercially as the book *One Boy's Day* (Barker and Wright 1951). This book and other specimen records are stored in an archive at the University of Kansas, and many researchers both from this university as well as from other universities have utilize' it to answer a variety of psychological questions.

Two kin of specimen records have been developed. The first, called a day record extends through an entire day, from the time of waking to the bedtime of a subject. In this type of specimen record, the subject is held constant, but the settings in which he or she participates vary. The second kind of specimen record is called a setting record. Here observers record the behavior and context of an individual for the entire time that he or she is in one particular behavior setting. Subsequent individuals are observed in the same setting. Here, the setting is held constant, but the subjects vary.

Both the day record and the setting record are detailed, sequential, and narrative accounts of behavior and its immediate environmental context. To make a specimen record, a trained observer watches a target individual and records in ordinary, nontechnical language the behavior of the individual and his or her environmental context in concrete, specific terms (see *Observation Techniques*).The Stenomask is a recording device that is often used by observers. This mechanical aid permits oral note taking without the observer's voice being audible to others. Complete details on how to collect and analyze specimen records, as well as information on the reliability of this method of observation, have been provided by Wright (1967).

As part of the specimen record research, Barker and Wright identified a unit of behavior which they termed the behavior episode. A behavior episode is the smallest ecological unit of an individual's stream of behavior. The basic criterion used to identify episodes is that they have a constancy in the direction of behavior exhibited throughout the unit. Two other defining characteristics of episodes are that they occur within the normal behavior perspective, and that the whole episode has greater potency than any of its parts. Examples of behavior episodes include, "rejecting lemonade," "recollecting pancakes eaten for breakfast," "cutting tomatoes," and "helping self to noodles."

The first major quantitative study conducted at the Midwest Psychological Field Station was based on a set of day records of 12 children between the ages of 2 and 10, and four physically disabled children within this age range. The 12 normal children lived in a small Midwest community in the United States. The four disabled children lived in a private institution for disabled children. Results of this investigation are published in a book called *Midwest and Its Children* (Barker and Wright 1955).

The results of the Midwest study provide important information regarding the structure of children's stream of behavior. Surprisingly, there were not any clear-cut differences between the episode structure of normal and physically disabled children. On a typical day, the Midwest children engaged in between 500 and 1,300 episodes. These episodes ranged in duration from a few seconds to 121 minutes, with more than 70 percent of the episodes lasting less than 2 minutes.

One of the most interesting findings of Barker and Wright's analysis of the structure of the children's behavior episodes was that it changed as a function of age. Younger children did more things in a day and their episodes were generally shorter than those of the older children. Not only did the older children engage more often in episodes of longer duration, but they tended to carry on more than one action at a given time. Conversely, the younger children tended to shift from one action to another, to do things sequentially, one at a time. While about three-quarters of all episodes were carried through to full completion, the younger children stopped short of the goal more frequently than the older children. Age was not related to the frequency of success, failure, or frustration in the episodes. Further, the spontaneity of episode initiation and termination was not related to age.

Although specimen sets have generally been used to record the behavior of children, obviously there is nothing inherent about the methodology which restricts its use to this age group. In fact, in recent years, researchers have used the specimen approach to record the behavior of adults. Scott (1977) used specimen records to investigate the episode structures of "effective" and "ineffective" preschool teachers during two contrasting school activities: morning greeting and large-group instruction. Scott discovered that in both settings the more effective teachers could be differentiated from the less effective teachers by at least three factors. First, effective teachers had fewer episodes which, reciprocally, lasted a longer period of time. Second, effective teachers had more episodes ending in attainment of their goals than did ineffective teachers. Finally, effective teachers had more positive and less negative emotional feeling tone in their contacts with the children. Further, during morning greeting, effective teachers had more episodes lasting at least a minute and had more enclosing episodes than the less effective teachers. In contrast, the ineffective teachers showed more isolated, single episodes than the effective teachers. Kounin (1970) similarly found that the ability to manage overlapping activities was characteristic of effective teachers.

Barker and Wright's (1955) finding that the episodes of young children tend to be sequential rather than overlapping, coupled with the finding that ineffective teachers also tend to have sequential rather than overlapping episodes, suggests that it is the less competent and less experienced individual who is less likely to be able to engage in overlapping activities.

2. The Same Child in Different Milieus

One of the most robust and perhaps most important findings of the specimen record studies is that children's behavior predictably changes as they enter different settings. One study which clearly demonstrated this finding was conducted by Gump et al. (1963). The researchers observed one boy, Wally O'Neill, for one full day at home and for one full day at a summer camp. They found that the settings which Wally entered on these two days were quite different. On the camp day, Wally entered 17 different settings including a craft shop, a swimming area, and a cookout. At home, this same child entered only six different settings, and few of them were specifically designed for children's play. The researchers also found that Wally's behavior differed in these contrasting environments. At camp, Wally engaged in a significantly more active, exploratory, constructive, and dramatic play, while at home, he spent more time in passive recreation (including several hours of television viewing), dallying, and formally competitive play.

Wally's associates and social interactions also differed in these two environments. His camp associates included many adults, many peers, and few nonpeer children. The number of different peer and adult associates was twice as great at camp as at home, as was the number of episodes devoted to adults and peers. On the other hand, the number of different nonpeer children and the number of episodes with them was much greater at home than at camp. Wally's associates were more aggressive, resistant, and appealing at home than his camp associates. His camp associates were more nurturant and sharing than his home and neighborhood associates. Camp adults, as compared to those at home, extended more interest-centered, less aggressive, and less resistant social behaviors to Wally. At home, Wally was more dominant, aggressive, and tended to be less submissive than he was at camp. At camp, Wally was more nurturant. The fact that most child associates at camp were peers probably contributed to the more egalitarian social relationships that developed in that setting. Differences in the settings were also related to aspects of Wally's emotionality on the two days. He more often demonstrated strongly positive emotions and more ambivalent emotions at camp than at home.

Ecological psychologists have found that the behavior of children can be predicted more accurately from knowing the situation children are in than from knowing individual characteristics of the children. The specimen record studies revealed that over the course of a day, each child's behavior varied with the immediate surroundings and that in similar surroundings, different children behaved quite similarly. For example, when children were eating dinner with their families, they behaved differently than when they were playing outdoors with their friends. Further, the way different children behaved while playing outdoors was more similar than the behavior of the same child in contrasting situations. Barker and his colleagues concluded from observing children

in their natural environments that it was important to learn more about the contexts in which behavior occurs.

3. Behavior Setting Research

The second major strand of research and theory conducted by ecological psychologists involved examination of the ecological environment. Methods of identifying, unitizing, and describing the settings of behavior were the focus of this aspect of the research conducted at the field station. As part of this line of research, a series of behavior setting surveys were conducted in several small towns in the United States, England, Norway, and Africa, in institutions such as high schools, churches and hospitals, and in special environments such as military bases and a mining town in Canada's far north. Procedures for conducting behavior setting surveys have been described by Barker (1968).

A behavior setting is an ecological unit consisting of both a physical milieu (spatial enclosure, facilities) and a behavioral program (a standing pattern of behavior, a regime, a set of procedures). Examples of behavior settings are basketball games, Easter parades, and Sunday church services. Once an individual enters a behavior setting, his or her behavior is markedly influenced by the milieu and program.

In the most extensive study of behavior settings, Barker and Schoggen (1973) measured the environments and the environmental usage of two towns—Midwest in Kansas in the United States and Yoredale in England. Both towns were described with identical methods, at two points in time, a decade apart. These researchers enquired as to what proportion of a community's environment children are free to choose entry or nonentry. Communities have a range of settings with various entrance requirements and obligations. Children discover that they are often restricted from entering certain settings like hospitals, factories, office buildings, banks, or bars. Some restaurants do not encourage families with children to patronize them. Some films may not be viewed by children. In contrast, there are other settings that encourage the participation of children. Zoos, children's rooms in the library, children's museums, child-oriented restaurants, schools, and parks can generally be entered freely by children. Barker and Schoggen's results showed that Midwest allowed children more freedom to choose which of the town's public behavior settings to enter than did Yoredale. In Midwest only 21 percent of all settings required that children enter (e.g., school settings) or stay out (e.g., taverns) whereas in Yoredale the comparable figure was 34 percent. In both communities, the territorial range of the residents (i.e., the actual number of settings entered during the year) increased steadily from the youngest age group (the infants) up to the adult age group. For example, in Midwest, the infants entered only 60 percent of the town's settings, while the adults entered nearly all the settings in the town. However, the elderly (age 65 and up) were found in only 80 percent of the town's settings, a figure which closely matched that for the adolescent age group.

Behavior settings are highly dependent upon people for their operation and maintenance. Behavior settings specify human components for certain positions within them. These are termed the habitat claims for human components. For example, the instructor's position in an academic class is a habitat claim; this position requires an appropriate human component—one with the necessary knowledge and skills—in order for the behavior setting to become operational. The number of habitat claims of a behavior setting is the number of positions of responsibility that must be filled for the normal occurrence of the setting. In settings, persons may be assigned relatively low power (guests, audience persons), moderate power (members, customers), or high power (functionaries, leaders). The leadership range is a measure of the amount of habitat within which members of the age subgroup are very important and responsible persons; for a town's behavior setting the leadership range is the extent to which members of an age subgroup serve as single or joint leaders.

On average Midwest residents spent more time and occupied more positions of leadership in their behavior settings than was true for their Yoredale counterparts. Not surprisingly, infants and small children served in positions of responsibility or leadership in only a very small part of the town's habitats. However, young people in Midwest were more often found in relatively high-power positions than children and adolescents in Yoredale. Midwest's behavior settings produced leaders at a younger age (older elementary-school subgroup) than Yoredale's (adolescent). The towns differed most in the leadership range of adolescents; Midwest's adolescents exceeded Yoredale's adolescents in the number of behavior settings where they were joint or single leaders. Thus, in the ecological sense, children and adolescents were more needed in the American than in the English community. The elderly were also leaders in the behavior settings of Midwest more often than they were in the Yoredale behavior settings.

The English system tended to reserve significant participation in community life for adults. Midwest, on the other hand, used young people in some of the significant action. While this can be expressed as a contrast in values, it is important to consider the accompanying ecological conditions. Compared to Yoredale, Midwest had a substantially larger number of behavior settings but a smaller number of persons to staff and operate them. Thus in Midwest, there were many more positions of responsibility to be filled than there were in Yoredale and there were fewer residents in Midwest to fill these positions. In fact, there were more than twice as many positions per resident in Midwest than in Yoredale. Midwest, relative to Yoredale, appeared to be short-handed; the behavior settings of Midwest were undermanned. To maintain its settings Midwest had to accept—even instigate—significant contributions from children and adolescents.

As an environment for behavior development, Midwest differed from Yoredale in that the Midwest system required the responsible participation of other than its most able class of human components. In Midwest, the elderly as well as children and adolescents were expected to perform difficult and important functions more frequently than in Yoredale.

This finding and similar ones in other investigations led Barker to develop a behavior setting theory with special reference to the consequences of undermanning on the behavior and experience of the inhabitants (Barker 1968). The main thesis of this theory is that undermanned settings exert more pressure than adequately manned or overmanned settings on potential participants to enter and take part in the operation and maintenance of the setting. If, for example, the high school junior class play has parts for 12 actors and there are only 25 members of the junior class, no member of the class is likely to be exempt from pressure to take a part or at least to help backstage. But if there are 250 juniors, only the more talented and highly motivated are likely to become involved.

The theory of undermanning has been tested in a number of other investigations. The relation of school size to student behavior and experience has been carefully investigated by Barker and Gump (1964). They found that students in small high schools experienced more invitations and more pressures to assume setting work than students in large schools. As a result, students in small schools worked harder and assumed more responsible and difficult setting positions in extracurricular affairs. Students in small high schools who were more active in central positions in an activity had different experiences from those who were merely audience members. Not surprisingly, small-school students also reported different attitudes and feelings regarding their settings than large-school students.

The fact that undermanned schools must utilize all students in order to maintain extracurricular operations has important implications for academically marginal students. Barker and Gump found that in small schools, academically marginal students were very likely to become a part of the enterprise. In large schools, academically marginal students were also marginal in their extracurricular participation and in their feelings of being responsible for their school's settings.

An important finding of the studies reviewed is that the behavior of children depends on the particular environments they enter and on how much these environments need their contributions. While the data collected by Barker and Wright and other ecological psychologists have made important contributions to the developmental literature, the most important contribution of this line of research has been the creation of methods for studying behavior in natural situations and the provision of new units of measurement for analyzing both behavior and the settings in which behavior occurs.

Bibliography

Barker R G (ed.) 1963 *The Stream of Behavior: Explorations of its Structure and Content.* Appleton-Century-Crofts, New York

Barker R G 1968 *Ecological Psychology: Concepts and Methods for Studying the Environment of Human Behavior.* Stanford University Press, Stanford, California

Barker R G et al 1978 *Habitats, Environments, and Human Behavior.* Jossey-Bass, San Francisco, California

Barker R G, Gump P V 1964 *Big School, Small School: High School Size and Student Behavior.* Stanford University Press, Stanford, California

Barker R G, Schoggen P 1973 *Qualities of Community Life.* Jossey-Bass, San Francisco, California

Barker R G, Wright H F 1951 *One Boy's Day: A Specimen Record of Behavior.* Harper and Row, New York

Barker R G, Wright H F 1955 *Midwest and Its Children: The Psychological Ecology of an American Town.* Row and Peterson, Evanston, Illinois

Bronfenbrenner U 1979 *The Ecology of Human Development: Experiments by Nature and Design.* Harvard University Press, Cambridge, Massachusetts

Gump P V 1975 Ecological psychology and children. In: Hetherington E M (ed.) 1975 *Review of Child Development Research,* Vol. 5. University of Chicago Press, Chicago, Illinois

Gump P V, Schoggen P, Redl F 1963 The behavior of the same child in different milieus. In: Barker R G (ed.) 1963 *The Stream of Behavior: Explorations of its Structure and Content.* Appleton-Century-Crofts, New York, pp. 169–202

Kounin J S 1970 *Discipline and Group Management in Classrooms.* Holt, Rinehart and Winston, New York

Kounin J S, Sherman L W 1979 School environments as behavior settings. *Theory Pract.* 18: 145–51

McGurk H 1977 *Ecological Factors in Human Development.* North-Holland, New York

Schoggen P 1964 Mechanical aids for making specimen records of behavior. *Child Dev.* 35: 985–88

Schoggen M, Barker L S, Barker R G 1963 Structure of the behavior of American and English children. In: Barker R G (ed.) 1963 *The Stream of Behavior: Explorations of its Structure and Content.* Appleton-Century-Crofts, New York, pp. 160–68

Scott M 1977 Some parameters of teacher effectiveness as assessed by an ecological approach. *J. Educ. Psychol.* 69: 217–26

Wicker A W 1979 *An Introduction to Ecological Psychology.* Brooks/Cole, Monterey, California

Wright H F 1967 *Recording and Analyzing Child Behavior with Ecological Data from an American Town.* Harper and Row, New York

R. P. Ross

Economic and Career Impacts of Education: Assessment by Means of Kin Studies

The analysis of kin data can provide valuable insights into at least four questions about education that are important but difficult to investigate. First, to what extent is there mobility in educational attainment across generations within family lines? Second, what role does family background in general, and of genetic endowments and family-determined environment in particular, play in determining individuals' differences in educational attainment? Third, what determines the expenditures on the education of each child within a family? How important is pure maximization of expected return versus parental aversion to inequality? Fourth, to what extent are estimates of the impact of education on various socioeconomic outcomes biased by the failure to control for factors such as ability, tastes, and motivations?

While there are a number of data sets of kin which permit exploration of the first and of some aspects of the second and third questions, there are relatively few data sets with later life-cycle outcomes included that permit the full investigation of the last three questions (Sect. 1). Also, much of the analysis to date has been on samples which might not be representative because of peculiar criteria for selection. Moreover, in most such studies education is represented empirically by grades of schooling completed, with only minor adjustments—if any—for the quality of that schooling. Furthermore, some possibly important statistical issues affect the estimates based on kin samples (Sects. 4, 5, 8).

Despite these limitations, kin studies have provided valuable insights. First, intergenerational variability has been less for schooling than for other observed measures of social or economic welfare, such as socioeconomic status (SES) (Sect. 2). Schooling has been a brake on socioeconomic mobility rather than a facilitator. Second, sibling studies suggest that in the United States the variance in family background accounts for about three-quarters of the intragenerational variance in schooling for white males born in the early twentieth century. Twin data indicate that this family background contribution can be decomposed further into genetic and family-determined environmental factors which are about equal (Sect. 6). Third, sibling studies indicate that the pattern of intrafamily expenditures on children's education reflects a mixture of expected returns and inequality aversion, and not just one or the other of these (Sect. 7). Thus intrafamilial allocations of schooling expenditures are not consistent with pure investment models of education (Sect. 3). Fourth, analyses of sibling data suggest that standard estimates of the returns to education in the form of increased earnings may overstate such returns considerably—perhaps by a factor of two to three—because of the failure to control for partially unobserved family background related to abilities and motivations (Sect. 8).

Thus, analysis of kin data has led to important insights into the determinants and the impact of education. Such data generally imply considerably less optimism than do standard analyses about the extent to which education has affected socioeconomic outcomes and has led to greater equality of opportunity.

1. Siblings, Twins, and Other Kin Data for Studies of Education

A basic problem of many studies is how to define education. Education can be conceived of as the process through which individuals learn about their environment, how it functions, and how it can be altered. On-the-job training, reading, exposure to communication media, verbal interchange, and many other experiences may make important contributions to education. Also different individuals have different aptitudes for learning because of differing genetic endowments and nonschooling environments. Thus individuals with identical grades of formal schooling may have a highly varying amount of education. Nevertheless, because of a general lack of better measures of education, most kin studies define education to be grades of formal schooling completed.

Of course schooling is a better representation of education the more it is associated with the capacity for learning from other experiences. Also schooling is widely thought to be an important dimension (or correlate) of education, and is of particular interest because it is perceived to be relatively amenable to policy action.

In many sample surveys respondents provide information on their parents' and their own schooling. These data can be used to study intergenerational mobility. Although some of these data sets are for special populations (examples are given below), others are representative of large populations and have sufficient numbers of observations to permit the statistical testing of alternative hypotheses. Contemporaneously collected (as opposed to recalled) data and information on more than two generations are relatively rare (though the second and seventh examples given below have these characteristics).

There are also large numbers of data sets which have childhood data on siblings (and fewer, but still many, on child twins) together with some measure

of schooling prior to the date of the data collection. For example, many censuses contain such data, which can be used to explore questions about the impact of birth order, sex, and family size on schooling.

However, most such data sets do not have sufficient information to permit the exploration of most of the dimensions of the last three questions raised in the introductory paragraph. To explore such questions, information on socioeconomic career is also required (Sect. 5). The number of data sets with such information available on siblings is not large. Brief descriptions of most of the major relevant data sets follow [more details or further references concerning the first five and item (k) can be found in Taubman (1977); more details regarding items (b), (d), and (h)–(j) can be found in Jencks and Bartlett (1979)].

(a) 156 pairs of brothers from Indianapolis, Indiana, United States, born in the nineteenth and twentieth centuries with income in 1927 (Gorseline data, analyzed by Chamberlain and Griliches 1975).

(b) 2,478 pairs of white male twins (about half monozygotic) born in the United States between 1917 and 1927, both of whom served in the military, with health and some socioeconomic data from military records and repeated surveys from 1967 onwards, detailed socioeconomic data from a 1974 survey, detailed socioeconomic data on offspring from a survey in 1981 (National Academy of Science—National Research Council Twin Registry, analyzed by Behrman et al. 1977 and Behrman et al. 1980).

(c) 292 pairs of brothers from the United States surveyed in 1966–71 and biannually thereafter with measures of early socioeconomic career and expectations regarding later outcomes (National Longitudinal Survey of Young Men, analyzed by Chamberlain and Griliches 1975).

(d) 346 pairs of brothers in sixth grade between 1928 and 1950 in Kalamazoo, Michigan, United States, with socioeconomic data collected in 1973-74 (analyzed by Olneck 1977).

(e) 2,000 sibling pairs of both sexes, one member of which was a randomly selected senior in secondary school in Wisconsin, United States, in 1957 with socioeconomic data from school records, parental income tax data, and surveys over the next two decades (Wisconsin Data, analyzed by Sewell and Hauser 1977).

(f) About 500 pairs of sisters with original respondents selected in a random area-stratified sample in Nicaragua in 1977–78 with socioeconomic data (Behrman and Wolfe 1981).

(g) A sample of about 80,000 people who can be

grouped into some 270 "families" of 270 people, who between 1900 and 1918 were institutionalized in Minnesota because of mental retardation. The grandparents of these people were ascertained. A family contains all the descendants and spouses of each set of grandparents. The data set includes information on education, occupation, and IQ test scores which were gathered by personal interviews in the early 1900s, by mail surveys in the 1950s, and from school records. The sample covers the period 1800 to 1960. There are thousands of siblings (Reed and Reed 1965).

(h) 150 pairs of brothers in the United States age 25–64 in 1973 (National Opinion Research Center sample analyzed by Eagersfield 1979).

(i) 50 pairs of brothers enrolled in grades 11 and 12 in 1960 in the United States and interviewed in 1971–72 (analyzed by Jencks and Brown 1977).

(j) 151 individuals from 66 families in which one of the parents died in Cleveland, United States, in 1964–65 (Cleveland sample analyzed by Brittain 1977).

(k) 312 New Jersey 55–61-year-old male employees of a New Jersey utility company who gave information on their own and siblings' age, sex, education, and most recent occupation (New Jersey sample analyzed by Lindert 1977).

This list suggests that sibling data sets with information on adult outcomes are relatively few in number, largely from the United States, often relatively small, and often based on sample designs that may not lead to data sets representative of larger populations. Moreover, the sibling samples cannot be completely random since they do not include representatives of single-child households. Most of the relevant studies attempt to address the question of representativeness by comparing sample characteristics or regression coefficients with those from censuses or other random samples. Such comparisons lead to some confidence that analysis of most of these data sets probably has more general validity.

2. Kin Data and Intergenerational Mobility Regarding Education

Intergenerational mobility refers to how well the relative position of a family in one generation measured by some index (e.g., schooling) predicts the relative position of the family's children by the same index. If the absolute value of the correlation of the index between generations is close to one, there is almost no intergenerational mobility. If the correlation is close to zero, there is considerable intergenerational mobility. Social mobility is usually regarded as a desirable characteristic of a society,

since the greater such mobility, the less parentage can be said to determine social position.

Intergenerational kin data are obviously needed to calculate the degree of mobility with regard to education. As noted in Sect. 1, the necessary schooling data for two generations are often available. Intergenerational correlations for schooling from a number of quite different samples [including (b), (d), (f), (h), and (i) in Sect. 1 and several others in Jencks and Bartlett (1979)] are in the 0.3 to 0.5 range. The same samples' intergenerational correlations for socioeconomic status are never larger, and generally somewhat less, and in the 0.2 to 0.4 range. Thus there is considerable but incomplete intergenerational mobility for schooling. But schooling mobility is, if anything, somewhat less than that for socioeconomic status, another widely available indicator. Unfortunately, few data are available to make comparisons for income or earnings measured at the same point in the life cycle. However, Dwyer and Phelan (1976), using a sophisticated model and estimating technique, estimate the intergenerational coefficient for earnings in the fifth sample at about 0.33. Behrman and Taubman (1984) estimate this R as no more than 0.2 using the twin sample augmented with children's data.

3. Investment Model of Education and Role of Family

Before turning to the other questions raised in the introductory paragraph, the investment model of education, measures of heritability with twins (Sect. 4), and extended latent variable-variance decomposition models (Sect. 5) will be examined (Behrman et al. 1980, Chamberlain and Griliches 1975).

The economic analysis of education generally focuses on the investment dimension (but see Sect. 7). There is an expected return to education, which depends on motivation and abilities that vary with genetic endowments and nonfamily environment. The downward sloping demand curve (DD) in Fig. 1 gives the locus of such expected returns for an individual. An individual with greater (less) capabilities would have a demand curve above (below) the indicated one. The horizontal supply curve (SS) in Fig. 1 gives the marginal cost of investment in education for this individual. The maximizing investment in education for this individual is E_0, at which point the expected marginal return is equal to the marginal costs; to the left of E_0 the marginal returns exceed the marginal costs so it pays to expand education. For another individual facing the same marginal cost curves but with a higher demand curve, the optimal education is greater than E_0. This framework has been refined to explore more complex issues (Becker 1967, Rosen 1976), but Fig. 1 captures the essence of the model for the present purposes.

An implication of this model is that family back-

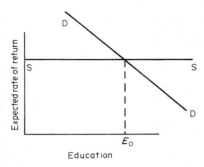

Figure 1
Determinants of education within investment model
with horizontal marginal costs

ground may be very important in determining optimal levels of education. Across families there may be differences in capabilities that imply systematic differences in average family demand curves for education and (given the capital market imperfections) differences in the marginal costs of educational investments.

Moreover such differences may be important within families. Siblings may have different expected returns because of different capabilities or because of imperfections in labor markets (for example, if there is sexual discrimination against women, the expected returns for a girl may be less than those for her equally or even less capable brother). Without sibling data the importance of these types of differences can be explored only marginally.

4. Twins and Heritability Estimates

The simplest form of heritability analysis assumes that the optimal grade of schooling for a given individual reflects his or her genetic endowments (G), family-determined environment (N), and other random environmental determinants (U) in an additive relation:

$$S = G + N + U \qquad (1)$$

Taubman (1981) argues that variation in N is an important component of inequality of opportunity whose elimination will improve economic efficiency.

Generally, it is not possible to determine how important are each of the right-side components in determining schooling levels because these variables are not observed. Usually at best there are some proxies for overall family background, which reflect the combined effects of genetic endowments and environment.

Data on twins make possible one somewhat controversial approach to at least a partial decomposition of each of the right-side variables to the variance. To understand this procedure one has first to rewrite

Eqn. (1) with the environmental variables combined into one (i.e., $N + U = V$).

$$S = G + V \qquad (2)$$

Schooling is an example of an observed phenotype which equals the sum of an unobserved genotype (G) and an unmeasured environment (V). The two right-side components are assumed to be uncorrelated in the simplest model so the total phenotypic variance is

$$\sigma_s^2 = \sigma_G^2 + \sigma_V^2 \qquad (3)$$

First names are used to decide who is to be designated twin 1 and twin 2. Arrange all twin 1's by family number and separately arrange all twin 2's by family number. It is then possible to calculate a cross-twin covariance and correlation by treating the data for schooling for twin 1 and twin 2 as two separate variables.

This covariance can be calculated separately for monozygotic and dizygotic (fraternal) twins. Each of the two twin covariances can be expressed in terms of σ^2 and σ_V^2 and other unknown parameters. In the most general model, there are seven unknown parameters. The observed variance and covariances can be used to estimate no more than three unknowns; therefore, a much simpler model must be employed.

Heritability is defined as the proportion of the observed variance that comes from genotypic variation:

$$h^2 \equiv \sigma_G^2 / \sigma_S^2 \qquad (4)$$

In the simplest model, h^2 is estimated as twice the difference in the two twin correlations.

The calculation and interpretation of heritability estimates has generated considerable controversy (Goldberger 1977, 1979, Taubman 1978, 1981). The three major issues are as follows.

First, critical to the estimation of heritability measures is the assumption that the expected covariance in environments does not vary between types of twins. There is some direct evidence that monozygotic twins are more likely to be treated alike in some respects than are dizygotic twins (for example, identical clothing on a given day), but there may not be a difference in parental determination of environments for the two types of twins in more basic respects (for example, general quality of clothing, etc.).

Second, the difference in the environment may be in response to differences in genetic endowments and not just a desire to treat identical twins more alike. Scarr-Salapatck (1965) has examined cases in which parents have been mistaken regarding the zygosity of their twins and has concluded that the parental environments are responsive to genetic factors whether or not parents correctly know the type of twin. Taubman (1981) argues that it is legitimate to count that part of the environment that is a response to genetic difference as due to genetic differences. While some have been comfortable with this assumption, others have been very critical on these grounds and have argued that heritability is overestimated since more similar environments for monozygotic twins are wrongly attributed as genetic effects.

Third, some have interpreted high heritability estimates to mean that the phenotypic outcome could not be changed by variations in the environment. Such an inference is clearly wrong. Figure 2 provides an illustrative hypothetical example. The horizontal axis measures the environment (V), the vertical axis measures a phenotypic outcome such as schooling,

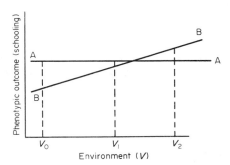

Figure 2
Reaction functions for genetic groups A and B with environment to determine schooling

and the curves A and B give the reaction of schooling to different environments for the only two genetic groups that are assumed to exist in the relevant population. Assuming that environment is identical for everyone, say at V_0, in this case a calculation of heritability indicates that all of the variance in schooling is due to genetic differences between group A and group B. But that does not imply that environmental changes are ineffective since these are measured by the slope of the curves A and B. One could almost eliminate schooling inequality, for example, by changing everyone's environment to V_1 or one could reverse the inequality by changing only group B's environment to V_2. Heritability, like any variance decomposition measure, refers to a given distribution of the other factors. As such it describes a particular situation, but does not indicate what phenotypic changes would occur were there environmental changes.

5. Extended Latent Variable-variance Decomposition Models

Recently heritability studies have been extended to a multiequation context which allows better control

for and estimation of the effects of unobserved or "latent" variables, such as family background, genetic endowments, and environment. This extension provides better estimates both of the determinants of schooling (Sect. 6) and of possible biases in the estimation of the impact of schooling (Sect. 8).

The essence of the latent variable model is that if such a variable is associated with enough observed variables, its variance may be estimated. For example, in Eqn. (3) above there are two unobserved variances which cannot be calculated since the only observable datum is the variance of schooling. But suppose that in addition to Eqn. (2) there was a series of other outcomes (Y_i) that depend on the same genetic endowments (G), schooling (S), and independently distributed environmental factors (V_i) in an additive manner:

$$Y_i = a_i S + b_i G + V_i \qquad (5)$$

Then for each additional relation three unknowns are added (i.e., a_i, b_i, and $\sigma_{V_i}^2$). But the observable data also increase: there are variances of the new variables, ($\sigma_{Y_i}^2$), and their covariances with all other observed variables ($\sigma_{Y_i T_\kappa}$ for all $i \neq w\,k$, $\sigma_{Y_i S}$ for all i). These covariances increase relatively rapidly as one adds more relations of the form of Eqn. (5). With enough relations there are enough data points to estimate all of the unknown parameters. For example, with Eqn. (2) and four additional indicators determined as in Eqn. (5) there are 15 observed variances or covariances and 14 unobserved variances to be estimated (i.e., 4 a_i's, 4 b_i's, 4 $\sigma_{V_i}^2$'s, σ_G^2, and σ_V^2).

In this illustration the latent variable methodology requires a relatively large number of observed variables to identify a fairly simple model (for example, schooling only affects subsequent outcomes and not other Y_i, the genetic and environmental factors are not correlated, and the environmental factors are assumed to be independent across relations). However, data on siblings increase substantially the observed covariances for a given number of Y_i because of the additional covariances among siblings. Such models have been developed by Chamberlain and Griliches (1975) for siblings and by Behrman et al. (1977) for the special case of twins. In the siblings models the researchers identify the latent variables as family factors (common to all siblings) and individual factors, both of which affect a number of outcomes. In the twin models the researchers identify them as genetic endowments (i.e., latent variables that are perfectly correlated across monozygotic but not dizygotic twins) and family-determined environmental factors which are not perfectly correlated across either type of twins but are correlated across Y_i. For more details see Behrman et al. (1980), Chamberlain and Griliches (1975), and articles by these authors in Taubman (1977).

The advantage of these models is that they permit control for the latent factors in the estimation of the determinants of schooling (Sect. 6) and in the estimation of the impact of schooling (Sect. 8). They also permit variance decomposition.

The latent variable twins model is a more satisfactory framework for obtaining heritability estimates than the procedures reviewed in Sect. 5 because it requires weaker assumptions. However, the controversial assumption regarding identical expected environmental correlations for the two types of twins cannot be tested within latent variable twin models.

6. The Role of the Family in the Intragenerational Variance of Schooling

While there are available a large number of estimates of heritability of IQ scores based on the model in Sect. 4 (Jencks et al. 1972), estimates for schooling are much less common. The siblings correlations for schooling for monozygotic and dizygotic twins are 0.78 and 0.53 in the National Academy of Science-National Research Council sample used by Behrman et al. [1980, item (b) in Sect. 1]. Using the simplest model, we obtain an estimate of heritability of schooling of about 0.50. Conditional on the validity of the assumptions in this model, about half of the intragenerational variance in schooling for white males born in the United States between 1917 and 1927 could be traced to variance in the genetic components and the other half to variance in the whole environment.

With the latent variable extended-twin model sketched in Sect. 5 and a distinction in the schooling relation between family-determined environment and other environment as in Eqn. (1), Behrman et al. (1980) decompose this same schooling variance into 32 percent from genetic variance, 45 percent from family-determined environmental variance, and 23 percent from other environmental variance. For the environment in which this generation was raised, family background is very important in determining relative schooling, with the family-determined environment being somewhat more important than the genetic component.

7. Pure Investment versus Inequality Aversion

The investment model of education in Sect. 3 assumes pure maximization of expected returns from education without any consideration of allocation within the family. However, the accumulating evidence of the importance of the family in determining education (Jencks et al. 1972, Jencks and Bartlett 1979, Taubman 1977) has increased interest in the question of how schooling (and other) allocations within the family offset or reinforce variations in genetic endowments among children.

Behrman et al. (1982) have developed a model which permits the testing of whether allocation of schooling among children within a family reflects pure maximization of expected returns, pure inequality aversion, or some combination. In essence the model posits that the distribution of schooling among children in a family is the outcome of the maximization of parental utility which depends upon each child's earnings capacity. The utility function is maximized subject to both a budget constraint and the earnings capacity production function which depends on schooling, other parental investments, and genetic endowments.

Figure 3 illustrates this model. The axes refer to expected returns of the ith and j^{th} children in a family.

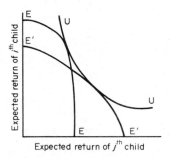

Figure 3
Parental preferences (UU) and two alternative expected returns frontiers (EE, E'E') reflecting differential relative genetic endowments

The curve UU is a parental indifference curve based on the distribution of expected returns between these children. The case drawn reflects a balance between pure investment and pure inequality aversion concerns. If the parents were concerned only with the child who had the lowest expected return, this curve would be square cornered along the 45° line from the origin. If the parents were indifferent about the distribution of expected returns between the two children, this curve would be a straight line from a given expected return level for one child to an identical level for the other.

Becker and Tomes (1976) have proposed a similar model with one major difference. In their model, parents' utility derived from each child depends on the sum of that child's expected earnings and returns from financial bequests. Since it is assumed that there are no diminishing returns to financial investments but diminishing returns to investments in schooling, parents who plan to leave positive bequests should only spend for schooling on each child to a point where its return equals the return earned on financial investments. Thus parents should invest efficiently in each child's education and then compensate the less able with larger financial bequests. Behrman et al.

(1982) evaluate the available empirical evidence regarding patterns of bequest in order to discriminate between these models. They conclude that the evidence is inconclusive.

The curve EE is the expected returns frontier between these two children, given the budget and earnings capacity production function constraints and the relative genetic endowments of the two children. This curve is drawn to reflect the relatively better genetic endowment of the ith child. Curve E'E' is for a different family in which the relative genetic endowment of the jth child is better. The variance in such relative genetic endowments across families enables one to trace out the curvature of the parental indifference curve, and thus estimate the parental weight on inequality aversion versus pure investment maximization in their allocation of schooling among their children.

The extent of parental inequality aversion in allocating schooling among their children can be estimated with data on siblings' education and a measure of the expected earnings. Behrman et al. (1982) estimate this model using adult earnings as a proxy for expected earnings for the adult male United States dizygotic twins in item (b) in Sect. 1. Behrman and Wolfe (1981) estimate an extended version of it with a multidimension representation of returns for adult women siblings in Nicaragua in item (f) in Sect. 1. Both estimates are substantially and significantly different from the extremes of complete inequality aversion on the one hand (Rawls 1971) and of pure returns maximization on the other. Such estimates imply that parental allocation of resources to their children's schooling mitigates substantially the intrafamilial inequality of genetic endowments as compared with the pure investment model outcome.

8. Biases of Standard Estimates of the Impact of Schooling on Various Outcomes

There are many estimates of the impact of schooling on earnings, socioeconomic status, health, and many other outcomes. However, such estimates may be biased because of the failure to control for unobserved variables, such as ability and motivation. This can be illustrated by considering the estimation of Eqn. (5). With ordinary estimation techniques the estimates of the coefficient of schooling are biased upwards if significant genetic and environmental variables, which are positively correlated with schooling, are omitted. Therefore in multivariate estimates of the impact of schooling on various socioeconomic outcomes an attempt has been made to include available measures of ability and of family background. Generally, the inclusion of these variables has resulted in lower estimates of the effects of schooling than those obtained in large random samples, such as the census. Findings suggest important variables which are positively correlated with schooling (Jencks and Bartlett 1979).

Sibling data permit controlling for certain dimensions of family background that usually are unobserved and that may cause biases. For the special case of monozygotic twins, Eqn. (6) controls for genetic background and common environment [where ΔU_i is assumed to be noncommon environment, as in Eqn. (1)].

$$\Delta Y_i = a_i \Delta S + \Delta U_i \tag{6}$$

For fraternal twins and other siblings the differenced version controls for common environment, but not for genetic background:

$$\Delta Y_i = a_i \Delta S + b_i \Delta G + \Delta U_i \tag{7}$$

The latent variable models of Sect. 5 provide a somewhat more satisfying control for unobserved variables, the exclusion of which may cause biases in the estimated impact of schooling.

Measurement error also leads to biased estimates. When sibling differences are the unit of observation, measurement error may be more prominent and biases from this source may be increased. Such "noise" in independent variables tends to bias their estimated coefficients towards zero (Griliches 1979). However, measurement error does not seem to account for most of the difference between the differenced siblings estimates and the non-differenced estimates (Behrman et al. 1980, Jencks and Bartlett 1979). Moreover, if measurement error is correlated between the siblings (because it is due to quality of schooling, for example), the bias is much smaller.

The estimated results from sibling data do not suggest large omitted variable bias if applied to samples (a) and (c) in Sect. 1 (Chamberlain and Griliches 1975 and their article in Taubman 1977). However, one can hardly generalize from these samples since the former is a regionally localized sample with overrepresentation of occupations in which nonpecuniary returns are relatively important (e.g., teaching, ministry) and the latter is of men at very early stages of their life cycle (in fact much of the analysis is of expected, not actual outcomes).

In contrast other siblings studies suggest the possibility that standard methods overestimate considerably the impact of education on later socioeconomic outcomes [Olneck (1977) and Behrman et al. (1977), Olneck in Jencks and Bartlett (1979), Behrman et al. (1980)]. For sample (d) in Sect. 1 controlling for common background of brothers reduces the estimated impact of schooling on early occupational status by 11 percent, on mature occupational status by 20 percent, and on earnings by 33 percent. For sample (b) controlling for common environment reduces the estimated impact of schooling on early occupational status by about 33 percent and on earnings by about 25 percent. In the same sample controlling for both genetic endowments and common environment reduces the estimated effect of schooling on early occupational status by 50 percent, on mature occupational status by 12 percent, and on ln earnings by 70 percent.

Such evidence is not conclusive because of the special nature of existing sibling samples (Sect. 1) and possible measurement bias and contradictory results. But it does suggest the possibility that standard estimates substantially overestimate the impact of education in the form of schooling on important socioeconomic outcomes.

9. Conclusion

Samples of twins and siblings have been used to study a number of issues related to the determinants of schooling and subsequent labor market success. There is considerable but incomplete intergenerational mobility when years of schooling is the mobility metric. The family plays a major role in determining intragenerational inequality in schooling and in earnings. There is some evidence, which is not accepted by all researchers, that much of this inequality is attributable to differences in genetic endowments. There is also some evidence that parents care about inequality of earnings capacity among their offspring and provide more schooling to the less able than they would if parents were only concerned about the total earnings of their offspring.

Finally, these kin-related samples have been used to eliminate or reduce the bias on schooling coefficients in earnings equations. While the evidence is mixed, these studies suggest the possibility that studies of the effects of schooling on earnings that are based on individuals may be strongly biased upward. The next generation of kin samples may be able to refine and resolve many of the current uncertainties.

See also: Twin Studies; Expected Rates of Return

Bibliography

Becker G S 1967 *Human Capital and the Personal Distribution of Income: An Analytical Approach.* Woytinski Lecture No. 1. Institute of Public Administration, Ann Arbor, Michigan

Becker G S, Tomes N 1976 Child endowments and the quantity and quality of children. *J. Polit. Econ.* 84: S143–62

Behrman J R, Hrubec Z, Taubman P, Wales T J 1980 *Socioeconomics Success: A Study of the Effects of Genetic Endowments, Family Environment, and Schooling.* North-Holland, Amsterdam

Behrman J R, Taubman P 1984 Intergenerational mobility in earnings in the US: Some estimates and a test of Becker's intergeneration endowments model. Mimeo. University of Pennsylvania, Philadelphia, Pennsylvania

Behrman J R, Wolfe B L 1981 A multi-target parental preference analysis of the allocation of schooling between sisters in a developing country. Mimeo. University of Pennsylvania, Philadelphia, Pennsylvania

Behrman J R, Pollack R A, Taubman P 1982 Parental preferences and provision for progeny. *J. Polit. Econ.* 90: 52–73

Behrman J R, Taubman P, Wales T J 1977 Controlling for and measuring the effects of genetics and family environment in equations for schooling and socioeconomic success. In: Taubman P (ed.) 1977

Brittain J 1977 *The Inheritance of Economic Status.* Brookings Institution, Washington, DC

Chamberlain G, Griliches Z 1975 Unobservables with a variance-component structure: Ability, schooling and the economic success of brothers. *Int. Econ. Rev.* 16: 422–49

Dwyer J, Phelan T 1976 Education in America and the reproduction of social inequality: A method divergent model of indicator error. Mimeo. State University of New York, Stony Brook, New York

Eagersfield D 1979 The NORC brothers sample. In: Jencks C S, Bartlett S (eds.) 1979

Goldberger A 1977 Twin methods: A skeptical view. In: Taubman P (ed.) 1977

Goldberger A 1979 Heritability. *Economica* 44: 327–47

Griliches Z 1979 Sibling models and data in economics: Beginnings of a survey. *J. Polit. Econ.* 87: S37–64

Jencks C S, Bartlett S 1979 *Who Gets Ahead? The Determinants of Economic Success in America.* Basic Books, New York

Jencks C S, Brown M 1977 Genes and social stratification: A methodological exploration with illustrative data. In: Taubman P (ed.) 1977

Jencks C S, Smith M, Acland H, Bane M J, Cohen D, Gintis H, Heyns B, Michelson S 1972 *Inequality: A Reassessment of the Effect of Family and Schooling in America.* Basic Books, New York

Lindert P 1977 Sibling position and achievement. *J. Hum. Resources* 12(2): 198–219

Olneck M 1977 On the use of sibling data to estimate the effects of family background, cognitive skills and schooling: Results from the Kalamazoo study. In Taubman P (ed.) 1977, Chap. 5

Rawls J 1971 *A Theory of Justice.* Belknap Press, Cambridge, Massachusetts

Reed E, Reed S 1965 *Mental Retardation: A Family Study.* Saunders, Philadelphia, Pennsylvania

Rosen S 1976 A theory of life earnings. *J. Polit. Econ.* 84: 545–67

Scarr-Salapatck S 1965 Twin method: Defense of a critical assumption. Mimeo. University of Minnesota, Minneapolis, Minnesota

Sewell W, Hauser R 1977 On the effects of families and family structure on achievement. In: Taubman P (ed.) 1977, Chap. 8

Taubman P (ed.) 1977 *Kinometrics: Determinants of Socioeconomic Success Within and Between Families.* North-Holland, Amsterdam

Taubman P 1978 What we learn from estimating the genetic contribution to inequality in earnings: Reply. *Am. Econ. Rev.* 68: 970–76

Taubman P 1981 On heritability. *Economica* 48(192): 417–20

J. R. Behrman; P. Taubman

Economic Aspects of Educational Planning

The subject matter of economics as a science is the allocation of scarce resources among alternative uses. Since economics deals with supply and demand, economic considerations are increasingly used in many stages of the educational planning process. In recent years the title "educational planner" has been assigned to someone who by formal training is an economist, econometrician, or statistician, rather than an educator. There are several reasons for this tendency. In the first place, the majority of contemporary crisis symptoms in education are economic or financial in nature. Second, schools are immediately affected by the economic environment within which they operate: for example, a booming economy generates more revenue that can be allocated to the education system than does a period of recession. Third, taking a long-term perspective, schools can affect the economic environment itself, for example, by providing qualified personnel and by contributing to the growth of national income. Conversely, a depressed labor market might appear to create graduate unemployment, hence obliging schools to revise their curricula for "relevance," or particular segments of a booming labor market might give "signals" to students and their families as to what types of schools or faculties they ought to apply for admission.

A further important reason for the current dominance of economics in the necessarily interdisciplinary field of educational planning is that it offers a systematic framework for the analysis of many components of the planning process. This article is organized in terms of these components.

1. Definition

One operational definition of planning in general, which can also be used in education, is: (a) the examination of many feasible alternatives, and (b) the choice among them according to an objective.

This definition has the advantage of analytically splitting the problem into two separate components. Component (a) is "positive" in the sense of examining, for example, technological alternatives and finance possibilities. Component (b), on the other hand, is "normative" in the sense of bringing into the planning process subjective values as to what alternative to choose among the many that are feasible.

Another important advantage of this definition is that it corresponds to the problem of constrained optimization in mathematics. Hence, the relationship implicit in (a) and (b) can be formulated in a system of equations and an optimal "solution" arrived at by using well-known techniques such as linear programming (see *Linear Programming Models in Educational Planning*).

2. Formulating Criteria

This is known in economics as specifying the objective or welfare function. There are several distinct objectives the educational planner might stipulate, such as to increase the level of achievement of secondary-school students, to equalize opportunities for school attendance in various parts of the country, to accelerate the rate of economic growth, to provide increased employment opportunities among graduates, to make income distribution more equitable, or to provide the necessary skills needed by the expanding sectors of the economy. Such criteria then become arguments on the right-hand side of the welfare (or objective) function the planner wishes to maximize. For example, if economic efficiency and distributive equity are the only two arguments adopted by the planner, the function could be generally expressed as $SW = (GNP, EQ)$, where SW is social welfare, GNP is the country's gross national product and EQ is a measure of equality of income distribution.

Removal of the comma in the equation in order to algebraically specify the function involves major normative assumptions on the way efficiency and equity considerations determine social welfare. For example, the additive specification $SW = GNP + EQ$ assumes infinite possibilities of substitution between the two arguments, namely, a high level of welfare could be achieved by increasing the country's gross national product, even if the equity measure were equal to zero. However, such a possibility would be excluded if the objective function were specified in a multiplicative form, as $SW = (GNP) . (EQ)$. In such a case, a zero equality measure would also reduce social welfare to zero, no matter what the size of gross national product is.

3. The Weights

Another major normative assumption that has to be made in order to specify the social welfare function is what weights to assign to its arguments. For example, having opted for a multiplicative specification, efficiency and equity can be given explicit differential weights, α and β, respectively, in the welfare generating process, for example:

$$SW = (GNP)^{\alpha} . (EQ)^{\beta}$$

Such weights are usually derived from the country's political system, for example, a conservative government might assign a higher value to α relative to a socialist one, which might assign a higher value to β.

4. Links with Policy Variables in the Education System

The right-hand side of the objective function must be expanded in order to be explicitly expressed in terms of policy (alterable) variables in the educational system. Such a set of variables might be the enrollment in the different levels of schooling in the country, say, S_1, S_2, and S_3 for primary, secondary, and tertiary education, respectively. In this case, further weights are needed on how much each level of education contributes to the respective argument of the function. For example, if such weights are labeled c_1, c_2, and c_3, the efficiency argument of the social welfare function might look as follows:

$$SW = (c_1 S_1 + c_2 S_2 + c_3 S_3)^\alpha \cdot (EQ)^\beta$$

It should be noted that the c weights do not need to be normatively assigned as in the case of α and β. Instead, the former can be empirically derived on the basis of the actual contribution of the different levels of education to the country's gross national product. Similar weights can be derived on the contribution of each level of education to income distribution.

Once the objective function is fully specified in such a way, constraints are introduced in the form of equations using S_1, S_2, and S_3 as policy variables. The solution to the constrained maximization problem can yield the optimal level of enrollments by level of schooling in order to maximize social welfare (see *Bowles Model*).

5. Modeling in Educational Planning

Even if they are not blended in a social welfare function framework or used in constrained optimization, the modeling and derivation of the c-type weights mentioned above is instructive on its own in educational planning. Such weights or equivalent ones, applied to the equity component of the function, document the intricate links between the educational system and the country's economy. As such, they provide important signals to the policy maker for action on different fronts in order to satisfy the adopted objectives. The rest of this article elaborates on such economic links in the educational planning process.

6. Efficiency

The traditional involvement of economists in educational planning has been for the purpose of introducing an element of efficiency. Narrowly defined, the efficiency argument might refer to the improvement of input–output relationships within the school system in producing graduates and minimizing dropouts. This is often known as the internal efficiency of the educational system, linking to the literature on educational production functions (see *Production Functions in Education*). In the 1970s, however, much emphasis was put on the external efficiency of the school system, that is, its links with the world of work. This type of efficiency is in turn interpreted

differently by different schools of thought in the educational planning literature.

According to the manpower requirements approach (see *Manpower Requirements Approach*), the social "benefit" associated with the provision of education is achievement of a given level of production. The educational system produces the labor skills without which the level of production would be lower or even halted for some goods and services that require highly specialized workers. Hence, the planning of education should be geared to providing the kinds of qualifications key personnel should have in the future for the efficient operation of the economy.

According to the cost–benefit (or rate of return) model (see *Cost–Benefit Analysis in Education*), efficiency takes the form of comparing the social costs and benefits of providing at the margin more of a particular type or level of education. If the discounted benefits exceed the costs, or if the social rate of return is higher than a criterion rate, this is interpreted by the educational planner as a "signal" for expansion. If the rate of return is low, the signal is read as an indication against the expansion of the particular level or type of education.

These two models are based on diametrically opposite assumptions regarding the links between education and the economy. The manpower requirements model assumes a rigid relationship between output and the proportions of each type of educated labor used in production. At its extreme, it assumes that the elasticity of substitution (see *Substitution Elasticities Between Educated Labour*) between types of educated labor is zero. The rate of return model, on the other hand, assumes the existence of a flexible world in which there exist high possibilities of substitution between different kinds of labor. Therefore, less emphasis is put on predicting and producing the exact number of graduates necessary for achieving sectoral production targets. Instead, the model recommends the expansion of those levels and types of schooling that exhibit the highest cost–benefit ratio or that yield the highest social rate of return.

Historically, the manpower requirements approach has been used more often than cost–benefit analysis in the actual planning of educational systems. The main reasons for its popularity are its intuitive appeal and the relative availability of data for its application. The rate of return model has been more data demanding (e.g., it requires age–earnings profiles by level of education) and hence it has not been used as often in actual planning exercises. This trend, however, has tended to be reversed in recent years following the generation of microdata sets by means of labor surveys.

The difference between the two approaches in planning for external efficiency of the school system is far from academic. The application of the two models often yields different policy prescriptions for the same country. Typically, the manpower requirements model results in a recommendation for the expansion of the higher levels of education and technical schools, as this type of manpower is usually "required" for meeting production targets. By contrast, the rate of return model typically favors the expansion of primary schools and general education because they are least costly and exhibit a higher cost–benefit ratio relative to the upper levels and other types of education.

The type of country also is an important consideration in the choice between the two models. Therefore, it could be argued that the manpower approach is more appropriate for a small, low per-capita-income country where, because of recent independence, the educational planner may wish to replace expatriates and to indigenize the labor force. However, in a big and rich country there exist more possibilities of substitution between labor skills, and hence manpower shortages are unlikely to develop or, in any case, to impair the level of production.

In view of the above controversy several attempts have been made to develop synthetic models (see *Synthetic Educational Planning Models*) by using selected features of the cost–benefit and manpower requirements model.

7. Cost–Effectiveness Analysis

This is a special type of cost–benefit analysis, borrowed from military operations, in which the "benefit" is axiomatically given and no attempt is made to measure it. The analyst focuses instead on minimizing the cost to achieve the given objective. In education, for example, a case can be made for the provision of primary education in rural areas on the grounds of literacy with no attempt to evaluate the benefits via the creation of a more educated manpower to work in agriculture or the rate of return to investment in primary schooling. Rather, it concentrates on what architectural type of school, teaching load, etc. would fulfill the objective of providing primary education at a minimum cost (see *Cost–Effectiveness Analysis in Education*).

8. Equity

Equity considerations in education have been traditionally treated in sociology, as have the differential access to various schools by social class or family background, and the role of education in determining "life chances" or "who gets ahead." In economics, two separate, although highly linked, streams of analyses have developed in treating equity issues in educational planning: first, the "who pays–who benefits" argument and, second, the role of education in equalizing income distribution.

The first topic was started by a public finance-subsidy study of the California higher education system by Hansen and Weisbrod (1969). It was found that because of public subsidization of higher education by the average taxpayer, in effect lower income families were paying for the education of the children of better-to-do families, since the latter had a greater tendency to send their children to higher education. Several similar studies conducted in other states or other countries have produced mixed results on the alleged inequitable effects of higher education.

The second topic relates to a comparison between the distribution of educational attainment in the population to the distribution of incomes. One of the most documented effects in the economics of education is the increasing level of earnings with the length of education. Hence, the provision of education has the effect of moving some groups of the population from a given income class to a higher one and so it affects income distribution. For example, the provision of primary education, beyond being economically efficient, is also equitable in the sense of moving a group of persons (those who would otherwise be unschooled) from a low-income class towards the mean income of the population, hence it reduces the dispersion of earnings.

Still another way to calculate the effect of educational provision on income distribution is by means of wage ratios of labor with different educational qualifications. Thus, as the supply of the more educated relative to the less educated increases over time, the corresponding wage ratio is depressed, contributing to a more equal income distribution. The extent of the relative decline of the wages of the more educated depends not only on the rate of increase of their supply, but also on the relative strength of the demand for their services and the elasticity of substitution between different types of labor in the economy. Thus it has been found that the strength of demand for college labor in the United States between the 1940s and 1960s was such that the substantial increase in the supply of college graduates has not appreciably altered the relative salary structure. Similarly, if the elasticity of substitution between different types of educated labor is high, an increased supply of college graduates, for example, could be absorbed, causing only a small reduction in their salary advantage. According to Freeman (1976), in recent years this relative advantage has started to deteriorate as the demand for their services has not kept up with the increase in their supply.

Of special interest in educational planning is the effect of minimum-schooling legislation on income distribution. Studies in several countries (like England and Wales and Greece) have shown that raising the school-leaving age has a substantial effect on reducing the dispersion of earnings in the population.

9. Social Demand

Another criterion for planning an educational system is for the policy maker to try to conform to what students and their families wish to study. This is known in the literature as satisfying the "social" demand for education, although it is often referred to more accurately as "private" or "individual" demand.

The planning of an educational system based on social demand starts from a projection of the school age population which is followed through the system (and, of course, over time) by means of "transition proportions." These are probabilities established from historical data on the number of students advancing from one level of education to the next. A famous case study in this respect has been the provision of higher education in England and Wales, which was based on the criterion of social demand (Robbins 1963). It should be noted again that the choice of the overall criterion for planning an educational system is a function of the type of country where planning is applied. Thus, it is more likely that the social demand model is adopted by advanced industrial, rather than low per-capita income, developing countries, since a rich country can afford to satisfy the people's study wishes without much concern for the external efficiency of the expenditure. In these countries there exists a big overlap between what individuals want to study and the skills needed by the economy, hence manpower-oriented planning is relegated to a residual role. This is in contrast to the situation in a developing country where the overlap between the spontaneous supply (by means of social demand) and the demand for certain types of educated labor is much smaller. Finally, an additional source of skill creation in advanced countries relative to developing ones is the existence of more on-the-job training possibilities because of the longer tradition of an industrial base.

See also: Social Demand Models; Social Demand Approach; Manpower Requirements Forecasting

Bibliography

Adelman I 1966 A linear programming model of educational planning: A case study of Argentina. In: Adelman I, Throbecke E (eds.) 1966 *The Theory and Design of Economic Development.* Johns Hopkins University Press, Baltimore, Maryland

Ahamad B, Blaug M 1973 *The Practice of Manpower Forecasting: A Collection of Case Studies.* Jossey-Bass, San Francisco, California

Anderson C A, Bowman M J 1967 Theoretical considerations in education planning. In: Adams D K (ed.) 1967 *Educational Planning.* Syracuse University Press, Syracuse, New York

Blaug M 1967 Approaches to educational planning. *Econ. J.* 77: 262–87

Blaug M 1970 *An Introduction to the Economics of Education.* Penguin, Harmondsworth

Blaug M, Dougherty C, Psacharopoulos G 1982 Distribution of schooling and the distribution of earnings: Some British evidence. *Manchester School* 1: 24–40

Bowles S 1969 *Planning Educational Systems for Economic Growth.* Harvard University Press, Cambridge, Massachusetts

Chiswick B R 1969 Minimum schooling legislation and the cross-sectional distribution of income. *Econ. J.* 79: 495–507

Dorfman R (ed.) 1965 *Measuring Benefits of Government Investments.* Papers presented at a Conference of Experts held 7–9 Nov. 1963. Brookings Institution, Washington, DC

Dougherty C 1971 The optimal allocation of investment in education. In: Chenery H B (ed.) 1971 *Studies in Development Planning.* Harvard University Press, Cambridge, Massachusetts

Freeman R B 1971 *The Market for College-Trained Manpower: A Study in the Economics of Career Choice.* Harvard University Press, Cambridge, Massachusetts

Freeman R B 1976 *The Overeducated American.* Academic Press, New York

Hansen W L, Weisbrod B A 1969 *Benefits, Costs and Finance of Public Higher Education.* Markham, Chicago, Illinois

Jolly R, Colclough C 1972 African manpower plans: An evaluation. *Int. Labour Rev.* 106 (2–3): 207–64

Layard P R G 1972 Economic theories of educational planning. In: Peston M H, Corry B (eds.) 1972 *Essays in Honor of Lionel Robbins.* Weidenfeld and Nicolson, London

Organisation for Economic Co-operation and Development (OECD) 1965 *The Mediterranean Regional Project: An Experiment in Planning by Six Countries.* OECD, Paris

Psacharopoulos G 1975 The macro-planning of education: A clarification of issues and a look into the future. *Comp. Educ. Rev.* 19(2): 214–24

Psacharopoulos G 1978 Educational planning: Past and present. *Prospects* 8(2): 135–42

Psacharopoulos G 1979 Synthetic approaches in manpower planning. *De Economist* 127(2): 289–97

Psacharopoulos G 1980a Questionnaire surveys in educational planning. *Comp. Educ.* 16(2): 159–69

Psacharopoulos G 1980b Educational planning and the labor market. *Eur. J. Educ.* 15: 201–20

Psacharopoulos G (ed.) 1980c *Information: An Essential Factor in Educational Planning and Policy.* UNESCO, Paris

Psacharopoulos G 1982 A social welfare analysis of educational reform in Greece. *Compare* 12: 5–18

Robbins L C 1963 *Higher Education: Report of the Committee appointed by the Prime Minister under the Chairmanship of Lord Robbins, 1961–63.* Her Majesty's Stationery Office, London

G. Psacharopoulos

Economic Development and Education

Although economic development is conventionally defined in terms of a rise in real gross national product (GNP) per capita, a distinction can usefully be made between development and growth. Growth may involve no major changes in factor inputs nor any transformations in existing institutions. By contrast, development presupposes a process of innovation in which new technologies will be generated and new input and output mixes will emerge (Flammang 1979). In sociological terms, it implies that major social and structural change will occur involving a process of institutional transformation in sectors that are only peripherally linked to the core of the economy.

Historically in the developed world and currently in the less developed countries (LDCs) development has involved the monetization of local economies and the progressive substitution of subsistence by exchange activities; a growth in the proportion of populations living in urban centers with the associated phenomenon of enhanced migration rates; the emergence of new systems of social differentiation based on occupation and income in contradistinction to those based primarily on lineage and descent; and, finally, the creation of new forms of polity based on the nation–state.

These transformations have not been uniform in all societies and for this reason the term "modernization" has less currency in the literature than formerly, conveying as it does the idea of unilineal evolution or societal convergence toward some general stage of "modernity." However, the broader notion of the institutional transformations that are associated with development suggests that patterns of change are uneven: development is neither a smooth nor a continuous process and tension emerges as between institutional sectors that are undergoing differential rates of change. Indeed, much of the more specifically economic literature concerned with development has ignored the sociological dimension and remained somewhat insensitive to the institutional and normative constraints within which the process takes place.

As development proceeds, educational institutions, both formal and informal, undergo a corresponding shift in function. Within so-called "traditional" societies education is concerned with the transmission of received knowledge, the maintenance of broad societal consensus, and the perpetuation of existing patterns of social differentiation. These functions do not disappear as development continues but the balance shifts towards the utilization of educational institutions as agencies in the selection and allocation of individuals and groups to various economic roles and positions within the social structure. Thus education becomes an independent variable in the process of social change and as structural differentiation increases it emerges as a quasi-autonomous institution that can both facilitate or even impede the development process. The whole literature on education and development is ultimately concerned with this issue: the specific problem of measuring the effect of enhanced educational inputs upon economic outputs must be seen within a broader historical and sociological perspective which attempts to examine the problematic relationship between education and development in the widest sense.

1. A Historical Review

Research confirms that by 1800 literacy had been acquired by the vast majority of males and about one-third of adult females in the countries of North America and northwestern Europe. The evidence suggests that a substantial literacy base was a necessary if not a sufficient prerequisite for the massive economic transformation that occurred in the northern hemisphere during the eighteenth and nineteenth centuries. However, inter- and particularly intranational variations in the diffusion of schooling and literacy were substantial and continue to persist in more muted form. Further, the literature shows that substantial differences in levels of educational development cannot be explained primarily in terms of state intiatives but are to be seen largely as a result of a rise in public demand stemming from changes in the economic environment and the emergence of more complex and interrelated national occupational structures (Craig 1981).

While not ignoring the significance of local historical and cultural circumstances, it is fair to say that the expansion of formal education in the contemporary less developed world has followed a similar pattern. Quantitative educational growth appears to have a definite ecology and it has been closely associated with the monetization of local economies, the growth of urban centers, the development of transport networks, and the appearance of new occupational opportunities, access to which becomes increasingly dependent on formal schooling. In many less developed communities these developments were initially associated with colonial rule but, as in the developed world, rates of intranational educational development were and remain very uneven. Likewise, the role of colonial regimes in stimulating educational development was often limited: indeed the dynamics of educational expansion were often such that they ran counter to colonial and currently postcolonial educational policies.

Thus, while the specifically economic literature concerns itself with the measurable individual and social returns to educational investment and uses these as an indicator of the contribution of education to economic development, a historical or sociological perspective emphasizes the essentially interactive relationship between the economic and educational dimensions. Educational expansion is initially consequent upon a degree of structural economic change having already occurred in local economies, though it may, in turn, become a catalyst for further economic development. For example, although a broad literacy base may be a prerequisite for sustained growth (some have suggested a threshold of 30 to 40 percent) it is apparent that a demand for literacy and schooling will not emerge unless traditional social and economic structures have already been partly integrated into a broader exchange economy. If economic development is an objective the diffusion of schooling among desert nomads or subsistence farmers and cattle herders can hardly be considered a policy priority.

This suggests that the role of schooling as an instrument of economic development will be highly variable over time. In colloquial terms, the expansion of formal education (classified by sector and type and not in gross terms) may have a substantial "payoff" at some stages in the development process while at others its impact may be negligible in terms of other development options that may be available. Thus in spite of the spate of literature on the role of schooling in development that has appeared since 1955, failure to recognize this caveat has led to overly simplistic educational policy prescriptions. In fact, rather than constituting the key to economic and social development, education might be properly regarded as a component in a jigsaw puzzle whose linkage with other pieces is as yet obscure.

2. Research and Policy Issues since the Second World War

The principal strands of what Bowman first termed the "Human Investment Revolution in Economic Thought" (Bowman 1966) have been delineated and commented upon by her and subsequently by Sobel (1978) and do not require extensive treatment. Some brief comments are, however, appropriate. As noted, the human capital approach is a largely post-Second World War phenomenon whose roots can in part be traced to the productive outcomes of aid programs to the war-devastated regions of Western Europe and Japan as contrasted with the more equivocal consequences of the transfer of physical capital and technology to the less developed world. The effectiveness of such transfers, it was suggested, depended on the existence of educated populations who could effectively utilize them. Concurrently, research in the United States had led to the conclusion that historically just over 40 percent of the growth of per capita income in that country could be inferentially attributed to educational investment in people. It must be recognized, however, that commentary or research of this nature had virtually no implications for educational policy. Its general effect was rather to create a climate of opinion that was favorable to enhanced educational investment in both the developed and less developed nations, without at the same time providing any meaningful guidelines as to the optimal form of such investments or any suggestion as to how education actually contributed to the development process.

The same reservations can be attached to the various exercises in national correlation comparisons that reached their apogee in the widely published work of Harbison and Myers (1964) on human resource indicators. Although a contemporaneous correlation analysis using similar measures of educational development had suggested that primary schooling and literacy were more highly correlated with level of economic development than the provision of secondary or tertiary education (Anderson and Bowman 1963), the human resource indicators developed by Harbison and Myers were weighted in such a manner as to emphasize the greater contribution of postprimary and particularly tertiary-level technical and scientific education to economic development.

Unfortunately, although the creation of indicators of educational development requires a degree of technical expertise, the assumptions underlying the whole correlation approach were simplistic in the extreme. Governments bent upon educational provision inferred that simple correlations had causal significance and reached the erroneous conclusion that rates of economic development were largely determined by the supply of high-level manpower, particularly in the technical and scientific fields. The equally plausible assumption that developed nations had larger pools of such skills because they were developed received little attention.

Retrospectively, it could be argued that the human resource indicator approach had deleterious effects on the developmental efforts of some nations. It led to a distortion of resource allocation toward higher levels of the educational system while primary schooling was viewed largely in terms of its feeder role to the secondary sector. Indeed, educational systems as a whole were seen as passive suppliers of skills to the occupational structure with no independent role, as it were, in the development process. Finally, the belief that scientific and technical training would make a greater contribution to development than general education was without foundation.

Similar strictures can be applied to the whole practice of manpower forecasting, whose rationale was closely linked to the intellectual assumptions of the resource indicator approach. Besides overemphasizing the contribution of tertiary training, manpower planning was based on a set of largely untenable assumptions, viz: zero price elasticity for skills, low levels of substitutability between factor inputs, and above all a more pervasive belief in a unilineal pattern of structural economic change. The latter assumption had particularly unfortunate consequences where less developed countries based their estimates of manpower "needs" on "labor coefficients" that were presumably based on means derived from manpower distributions prevailing in developed nations.

By the early 1970s both the assumptions and consequences of manpower forecasting activities had become increasingly unacceptable. Indeed, it is roughly from this date that a decline can be noted in the belief in the efficacy of macroeducational planning as an instrument of economic development. Thereafter, planning for development took on a far more pragmatic emphasis and based itself on increasingly limited and short-range sets of objectives (Windham 1975).

This new trend was not only a result of the demonstrable failures of macroplanning but stemmed from a substantial literature based on cost–benefit (rate of return) analysis, whose assumptions concerning the role of education in development were totally at variance with those of the manpower and macroplanning traditions. The historical origins and assumptions of cost–benefit analysis, its major empirical findings, and its principal policy implications have been treated by Psacharopoulos in two major cross-national studies (Psacharopoulos 1973, 1981). The results have been to question both the premises and major conclusions of the manpower planning approach. Briefly, the findings are that in all countries private and social rates of return are highest at the primary level; all rates of return to investment in education are above the 10 percent common yardstick of the opportunity cost of capital; returns to education in less developed countries are higher than the corresponding returns in developed countries, and rates of return to general education are, in general, higher than those for technical, scientific, and more specifically vocational types of training.

The policy implications of these findings are clear. Both developing and developed nations would do well to pay particular attention to the quality and provision of schooling at lower levels while at the same time adopting a more skeptical attitude to the development of highly specific (and high-cost) forms of technical and vocational training. In particular they should be conscious of the dangers of expansion and massive public subsidization of tertiary education where the individual rates of return may be substantial but the social benefits far more problematic.

In recent years the cost–benefit approach has itself come in for criticism (Blaug 1976). Basically, most objections stem from a degree of skepticism concerning the nature of the relation between productivity and observable income–education profiles. Some of these criticisms are, in fact, not incompatible with the assumptions of cost–benefit analysis but others have a greater measure of cogency, particularly in the context of less developed countries characterized by a relatively small "modern" exchange sector but with a far greater proportion of the population involved in subsistence or semisubsistence activities. In these nations analytic problems of specification and measurement are formidable and the calculation of rates of return thus more hazardous. Moreover, although the approach works well in terms of explaining individual investment behavior, in terms of explaining individual investment behavior, its definition of social rates of return is perhaps more questionable and intuitively less convincing.

Despite these reservations it is fair to say that the positive contributions of the cost–benefit approach (in contrast to those of the manpower tradition) have far outweighed its limitations. Its initial assumptions are more flexible and provide a means by which a crude and partial estimate of the economic consequences of educational expansion can be made. More pragmatically its findings concerning the relatively greater importance of basic and primary education in the development process are more consonant with the demands for social equity that are salient in many less developed nations.

3. Equity and Opportunity

In the two decades after the Second World War a climate of optimism concerning the putative economic benefits of educational investment led to a massive expansion in educational provision in both the developed and less developed nations. In the former, growth occurred at the secondary and particularly tertiary levels but in the less developed countries absolute enrollments in primary schools rose massively. Everywhere, however, rates of expansion were greatest at higher levels. Integral to most expansionary policies was the notion that development not only involved rises in GNP per capita but that increased educational provision would be associated with the equalization of educational opportunities (defined at that period largely in terms of access and continuance in schooling).

In the event, growth was associated with a series of unanticipated consequences that were not predicted in the conventional economic literature and which in the less developed countries stemmed largely from uneven rates of structural change. Although it was recognized that early educational development had been associated with major inequalities in access to schooling in terms of the region or the ethnic and social provenance of students, it was believed that these disparities would largely disappear as development proceeded.

In terms of intermediate stages of educational expansion this view was erroneous: while absolute levels of enrollment everywhere rose, regional differentials in access also increased, with the gap between "leading" and "backward" areas becoming more pronounced. This was the result of a "piling up" of resources in more advanced regions, which social geographers termed the "backwash effect." In themselves, such inequalities were not incompatible with policies designed to maximize the short-term contribution of education to economic development, but in the long run the political and economic consequences of these disparities could be serious, particularly where regional inequalities were conjoined with ethnic differences in plural societies. Although

1531

political decisions concerning the allocation of resources invariably have economic consequences it is equally true that policies dominated by economic criteria have political effects which, in turn, influence future rates of economic development.

Thus, almost uniformly, economically oriented strategies had to be tempered by policies designed to minimize the most salient inequalities resulting from development. These took the form of special educational aid to "backward" regions or, in some cases, the de facto imposition of "ethnic quotas" in educational recruitment. The long-term consequences of such policies are, as yet, obscure but in the short term they seem to have had no radical effect on the distribution of educational life chances: once patterns of inequality emerge their eradication is less a matter of decades but generations. However, the issue remains even more salient in the less developed countries as a result of the limited resources at their disposal and the fact that rates of return to education are higher than in the developed world.

Although regional or ethnic inequalities persist in muted form in developed nations the inequality of opportunity issue in them tended to focus on the relation between educational achievement and social background. (The term "social class" must be used with reservation in many less developed countries.) However, in all societies it was anticipated that educational expansion would eradicate disparities ultimately stemming from the social background of students. This issue has little to do with the degree of aggregate mobility in a society for this is overwhelmingly determined by the rate of structural and economic change, but rather concerns the extent to which educational achievement is influenced by social origins and how far final social or occupational position is predicted by achievement level independent of social background.

Institutional or structural studies, of course, show that throughout the developed and less developed world educational access and continuance is correlated with social background. However, in many less developed coutries a substantial minority (or even majority) of students at the more selective levels of education come from lower status families. This is partly a result of the heavy weighting of most of the population toward the lower end of the occupational spectrum, but it implies that substantial inequalities in life chances can be associated with considerable "openness" in educational access. The issue is whether such openness will continue as development proceeds. Status transmission studies in a variety of societies are suggestive in this regard.

Everywhere, social background is the strongest single predictor of educational achievement but, of equal importance, it is rather less significant in the less developed countries than in the developed nations, particularly in the least developed areas, for example sub-Saharan Africa. Moreover, in all societies the final social (or occupational) status achieved by an individual is only weakly predicted by his social background and mainly in an indirect fashion through educational achievement. Of equal importance, however, is the fact that the direct influence of educational achievement on final status is rather stronger in the less developed countries than the developed nations.

What are the implications of these findings in macrodevelopmental terms? If it is assumed that economic development requires a degree of "openness" in status hierarchies it is fair to say that educational systems have served this function reasonably well. They have everywhere mediated the effects of ascribed social status and even where aggregate mobility rates are low (as in most less developed countries) there is a degree of fluidity in social structures consequent, in large measure, upon educational expansion. This is not to suggest, however, that the latter radically reduces inequalities in the pattern of life chances of individuals or groups insofar as these are determined by social background. Indeed, the influence of social background on level of educational achievement is if anything higher in more developed countries. In the less developed countries it is possible that as development proceeds processes of incipient "class formation" may increase the influence of social background on achievement and if this phenomenon is, in turn, associated with low levels of structural mobility, development might result in an increasing degree of rigidity in social structures and a decreasing amount of circulation of individuals and groups within the social structure.

Such a development is not inevitable but it suggests that as with regional, ethnic, or even income differentials the development process does not in itself reduce social inequalities—it may frequently increase them. In sociological terms development does not imply a simple unilineal movement from "ascription" to "achievement" or from "particularism" to "universalism."

4. "Overeducation" and Urbanization

In developed nations postwar educational expansion was associated with rapid economic development and burgeoning occupational opportunities. The demand for educated manpower tended to keep pace with increasing supply and thus in cost–benefit terms private and social rates of return remained constant or fell only marginally. However, given a current diminution in development rates there is evidence that average rates of return are falling (particularly at the tertiary level) though they may still vary significantly by type of education.

It has, therefore, been contended that the current labor force is "overeducated" and a growing skepticism has emerged concerning the profitability of continued educational investment. It should be noted that the term "overeducation" is ambiguous in meaning. It may suggest that there is an appropriate level of education for every occupation, which is a form of argument derived ultimately from manpower planning assumptions. Alternatively, it can imply that private and social rates of return to education are lower than could be obtained through alternative forms of investment. Current data would suggest that this is probably not the case but sharp dips in rates of return must not be excluded as a future possibility.

Ironically, current concerns about educational overexpansion in the developed nations were foreshadowed in the literature on the less developed countries by almost a decade. Here it was contended that three sets of interrelated and problematic consequences had emerged from educational growth.

4.1 The Ratchet Effect

In many societies limited mobility opportunities, combined with the domination of the modern employment sector by government agencies, had placed an immense premium on the possession of educational qualifications for job access. Concurrently, the effect of massive public subsidization of education (particularly at secondary and tertiary levels) had enhanced private rates of return and stimulated increasing demand. However, in societies characterized by the presence of a large subsistence or semisubsistence sector the rate of growth in full-time wage employment opportunities in the small "modern sector" was never commensurate with the increase in supply of educated manpower. This led to a rapid escalation in the minimal levels of education required for job access which, in turn, generated further demand for higher levels of schooling. This ratchet effect has been referred to as "credentialism" or the "diploma disease" in some literature. Its consequence was the displacement of the less educated from their jobs by the more educated, mass unemployment among primary-school leavers, and increasing employment problems for secondary- and even tertiary-level graduates.

That the ratchet effect exists is incontrovertible and ensuing problems of labor market adjustment may be exacerbated by continuing government subsidization of education or relatively inflexible labor-pricing policies. However, the negative consequences of the phenomenon may have been exaggerated so far as the unemployment issue is concerned. First, its incidence is extremely difficult to measure in societies with large semisubsistence sectors. Individuals reporting themselves as unemployed in fact often mean that they have not been able to obtain employment commensurate with their initial expectations given their level of education. A substantial proportion, in fact, may be employed or self-employed within the more informal sectors of the exchange economy while waiting for full-time employment in the formal sector. While this is the

case the research literature would suggest that the widespread belief that the educated will only accept employment in white-collar jobs is quite without foundation. Though they may, in fact, wait for opportunities (while often utilizing family support) their expectations are realistic and adjust downwards to market conditions. The literature indicates that unemployment is, in fact, heavily concentrated among younger age groups and first-job applicants while gross unemployment statistics mask considerable internal circulation: the permanently unemployed constitute but a small proportion of these figures. This is not to underestimate current problems of labor market adjustment but the evidence does not suggest a negative return to educational investment and the concept of overeducation is subject to the same caveats as in developed nations.

4.2 Effect on the Rural Economy

In countries where the bulk of the labor force is concentrated in subsistence or semisubsistence agriculture, it is contended that educational expansion has had a deleterious effect on rural economic development. The educated migrate to urban centers thus denuding the countryside of its potentially more productive and innovative cohorts while, concurrently, massive in-migration to the town exacerbates problems of urban unemployment with the attendant "pathological" phenomenon of rising urban crime rates.

A conventional educational solution to the rural problem (short of the politically disastrous policy of limiting schooling in rural areas) has been to suggest curricular reform: the replacement of an ostensibly academic and bookish education by rurally biased curricula which would engender a commitment to life on the land, lower out-migration rates, and impart a degree of agricultural knowledge that would facilitate rural economic development. At the same time, urban unemployment would be reduced through the introduction of vocational education in the schools matched to the needs of the urban labor market.

Research suggests that this analysis is misleading. While the propensity of rural individuals to migrate to the towns undoubtedly increases with level of formal education, the educated may only form a tiny proportion of the total group of migrants. Moreover, the argument of rural denudation is not sustained: in view of population distributions as between town and countryside a very low rate of overall rural out-migration can be associated with massive increases in urban populations. Indeed there is now some evidence that the propensity of the educated to migrate actually diminishes if the imbalance between urban and rural opportunities becomes less pronounced. In the urban context there is little evidence, however, that employment opportunities have in fact deteriorated while the contention that urban unemployment is associated with in-migration is, in some cases, refuted by the data: migrants often fill positions that nonmigrants are unable or unwilling to occupy, while recent migrants may be better qualified than nonmigrants to fill many positions (Hawley et al. 1979). Moreover, field studies of school leavers would suggest that, although they may visit urban centers for variable periods to seek employment, a substantial proportion return to the villages if disappointed.

The analysis rests, indeed, upon the creation of a false dichotomy between town and countryside that ignores the symbiotic relationship between urban and rural development. Capital resources, both human and physical, flow back and forth between the two: income derived from urban employment is ploughed back to stimulate rural development while this, in turn, diminishes the propensity to migrate. Migration and urbanization thus make a positive contribution to the overall development process and attempts to artificially restrict their incidence are both counterproductive and ineffective. In particular, attempts to control "urban drift" through curricular reform have everywhere been unsuccessful, although such notions still have some vogue in less developed nations. The propensity to migrate is a function of perceived alternative occupational opportunities and has nothing to do with what is taught in schools. Moreover, the thesis that an agriculturally oriented vocational curriculum in the schools will contribute in any substantial manner to rural development rests on a fundamental misconception as to the role that formal education plays in the development process. The same can be said regarding the provision of specifically vocational education to counteract urban unemployment (Foster 1965).

4.3 The Dual Labor Economy

It has been contended that another dysfunctional consequence of educational development in the less developed countries has been the emergence of a "dual labor economy." This implies the existence of a very small, highly paid modern employment sector manned by an educated minority alongside a massive informal sector wherein the bulk of the labor force enjoys, at best, marginal rates of subsistence. In its extreme form the thesis may assert that rising standards for the small minority are associated with an increasing "immiseration" of the masses: a contention refuted by the demonstrable fact of universally rising life expectancies among all strata. In order to be empirically acceptable the dual labor market thesis would have to show that income distribution is indeed bimodal, with the peaks concentrated at the extremes and nothing much in between. Research suggests that this is not the case: earnings in the informal sector overlap with those in the highly paid formal sector (though the mean is lower) and they are significantly higher than in agriculture (Gregory 1980). All this suggests that the

range in income is considerable (far greater, as is well-known, than in developed countries) while the bulk of the labor force is concentrated at lower levels: an unequal distribution of income, however, is hardly the same thing as a dual distribution.

In summary, the problems discussed above do not suggest that the expansion of formal education has had negative consequences for development in both developed and less developed countries. In some cases, they lack empirical support while in others they simply draw attention to issues stemming from uneven rates of change as between institutional sectors: these are an inevitable consequence of the development process. However, the problems that have emerged might in some cases have been mitigated by more informed market-oriented educational policies. Finally, although the economic literature indicates that thus far both private and social rates of return to educational investment have been high this is no reason to suggest that they may remain so. To assume this would be to make an extrapolation of existing data as unwarranted as that of the earlier generation of manpower planners.

5. How Does Education Contribute to Development?

Although the economic literature presents a convincing argument concerning the role of education in development, it remains relatively silent concerning what it is that schooling actually does to people that makes them more productive, nor has it been so concerned with those putative "spillover" effects of education which may contribute indirectly to development. Discussion on spillover effects has tended to focus on the relations between education and political development and schooling and population growth (see *Spillovers in Education*).

It has been asserted that insofar as economic development is facilitated by a political framework that provides an orderly process of transfer of power and low levels of political violence, the expansion of schooling should indirectly stimulate development. This inference is based on survey data (mainly collected in more developed nations) pointing to a relationship between level of education and democratic political attitudes and also to cross-national studies which indicate that the political stability associated with an orderly transfer of authority and low levels of violence is confined to those relatively few countries whose populations exhibit high levels of literacy and general education.

These data must be treated with extreme caution as must all forms of simple correlation analysis, for it is demonstrable that the process of development is linked not only with rising levels of education but with an increased incidence of violence and political instability. Moreover, in less developed nations education is neither associated with increased personal commitment to the nation–state nor to the existing political order (however stable). Basically, the evidence concerning education and political development is so unsatisfactory (and perhaps ethnocentric) that the nexus between education and political and economic development is problematic in the extreme. If in the long run educational development is shown to be plausibly (and causally) linked to stable and democratic polities then so much the better. Currently, the data do not establish a basis for pursuing educational policies based on this assumption.

Likewise the literature on education and population growth is ambiguous in its implications. In spite of the literature concerning the negative effects of rapid population expansion there is evidence that a growth in population based on increased life expectancies is associated with an increasing rate of savings and capital formation and an enhancement of productivity. Generally there seems to be an inverse relation between education and fertility acting indirectly through deferred marriage and knowledge of birth control but there is a rise in fertility among women with up to three or four years of schooling which declines thereafter. Unquestionably education is associated with increased life expectancies due to improved nutrition and illness diagnosis and also with an income effect involving higher expenditures on food and housing. Basically, however, the relationships between education, population growth, and economic development are so complex that population control cannot be considered as a rationale for educational expansion. Once again, if a positive spillover effect occurs then this is desirable but it cannot, at present, enter into major policy considerations.

Research on what education actually does to people to make them more productive has centered principally upon the social–psychological research of McClelland and Inkeles (McClelland and Winter 1969, Inkeles and Holsinger 1974) which suggests that education may operate through a transformation of values and attitudes that have direct implications for development. McClelland has attempted to show that historically periods of development have been associated with a rise in the "need for achievement" among populations. He has argued, on the basis of limited evidence, that a rise in the need for achievement can be obtained through educational means thereby stimulating economic development. In a closely related tradition, Inkeles and others have suggested on the basis of substantial cross-national evidence that the emergence of "structural modernity" is associated with an individual attitudinal correlate, viz the "modernity syndrome." Individual modernity scores are raised through experience in modern work situations but level of formal education is everywhere the strongest predictor of such scores. Although Inkeles himself stresses the "correspond-

ence" between structural and attitudinal modernity, his work would imply that a principal contribution of education to development lies in its ability to transform individual attitudes and values from the "traditional" toward the "modern," thereby enhancing the rate of structural modernization in a society and plausibly rates of economic development.

Other traditions have placed particular emphasis on the role of literacy and enhanced communication in development. Some have argued that a literate tradition is essential for the emergence of "formal rationality" in any society (Goody and Watt 1968). Others have suggested that insofar as development depends on the effective transmission of new information in complex social systems the role of education lies particularly in its effect on the costs of such informational transfers. In the context of the less developed countries the recognition of the importance of literacy and education in facilitating communication processes essential to development stem directly or indirectly from Lerner's early research (Lerner 1958).

It must be recognized, however, that although research in the social sciences has provided a series of plausible hypotheses concerning the "intervening variables" that explain the relationship between education and economic development, the direct policy implications of such research are by no means self-evident. Indeed, one of the weaknesses of earlier developmental planning was that tentative research findings were used selectively to justify educational policies that had been decided upon for very different (often political) reasons.

6. Some General Developmental Strategies

Notwithstanding the limitations of current knowledge it is possible to delineate a few broad lines of policy that stem from the more robust findings of economic and social research. Such policies designed to maximize the contribution of education to development will be necessarily tempered by the exigencies of politics and alternative or conflicting educational objectives in both the less developed countries and the developed nations.

Most of the literature tends to emphasize the greater importance of general education and the significance of literacy and numeracy in the development process. It is questionable whether highly specific forms of vocational and technical training represent an efficient form of investment unless they are closely geared to on-the-job experience and actual labor market conditions. Earlier manpower planners tended to see the role of education as lying essentially in the provision of specific skills, but it is manifest that most formal systems of education do not and cannot function in this manner. Formal schooling is essentially complementary in nature to less formal systems that impart such vocational skills and the weakness of many earlier educational strategies lay in their disregard of the existence of highly efficient informal educational structures. Perhaps formal schooling largely through the provision of literacy, numeracy, and general education generates a basic "ability to learn" that is vital in the innovatory development process.

This, in turn, implies the greater importance of basic and primary education in development, particularly in the less developed countries. In the latter, the issue has become increasingly one of upgrading quality as much as expanding quantity. Correspondingly, greater caution needs to be exercised in the less developed countries and elsewhere over the expansion of tertiary education, particularly where this is heavily publicly subsidized. Considerations of both equity and efficiency would, in this case, suggest a greater devolution of costs towards the consumers of tertiary education though in all societies such proposals have met strong political opposition.

In general, it is likely that the efficiency of educational systems could be improved by a greater decentralization of decision-making processes thereby effecting a greater responsiveness to market signals and forces at both local and national levels. This type of policy orientation results from a greater understanding of the ecology of educational development and a recognition of uneven rates of structural and economic change within national boundaries. The manifest failures of macroeducational planning suggest the need for new micro- and pragmatically-oriented policies that can be rapidly adjusted to meet changing circumstances.

Finally, in the case of the less developed countries greater emphasis must be placed on the development of rural areas so long neglected in earlier educational planning. The evidence now seems overwhelming that education is associated with substantial gains in the efficiency and productivity of farmers (Lockheed et al. 1980). However, it is equally clear that such gains are maximized in environments that are already changing rather than in static traditional circumstances. The effect of education seems to depend upon the existence of literacy and numeracy (rather than the provision of agricultural education in the schools) but schooling must be regarded as an accelerator in the rural development process: its role will be limited without the existence of other modernizing elements. Once again this points to the interactive relation between schooling and other aspects of change in the development process.

See also: Economic Growth: Contribution of Education; Migration (Internal) and Education

Bibliography

Anderson C A, Bowman M J 1963 Concerning the role of education in development. In: Geertz C (ed.) 1963 *Old Societies and New States: The Quest for Modernity in Asia and Africa.* Collier Macmillan, London, pp. 247–79

Blaug M 1976 The empirical status of human capital theory: A slightly jaundiced view. *J. Econ. Lit.* 14: 827–55

Bowman M J 1966 The human investment revolution in economic thought. *Sociol. Educ.* 39: 111–37

Craig J E 1981 The expansion of education. In: Berliner D C (ed.) 1981 *Review of Research in Education*, Vol. 9. American Educational Research Association, Washington, DC, pp. 151–213

Flammang R A 1979 Economic growth and economic development: Counterpart or competitors? *Econ. Dev. Cult. Change* 28: 47–61

Foster P 1965 The vocational school fallacy in development planning. In: Anderson C A, Bowman M J (eds.) 1965 *Education and Economic Development.* Aldine, Chicago, Illinois pp. 142–63

Goody J R, Watt I 1968 The consequences of literacy. In: Goody J R (ed.) 1968 *Literacy in Traditional Societies.* Cambridge University Press, Cambridge, pp. 27–68

Gregory P 1980 An assessment of changes in employment conditions in less developed countries. *Econ. Dev. Cult. Change* 28: 673–700

Harbison F H, Myers C A 1964 *Education, Manpower, and Economic Growth: Strategies of Human Resource Development.* McGraw-Hill, New York

Hawley A H, Fernandez D, Singh H 1979 Migration and employment in Peninsular Malaysia, 1970. *Econ. Dev. Cult. Change* 27: 491–504

Inkeles A, Holsinger D B (eds.) 1974 *Education and Individual Modernity in Developing Countries.* Brill, Leiden

Lerner D 1958 *The Passing of Traditional Society: Modernizing the Middle East.* Free Press, Glencoe, Illinois

Lockheed M E, Jamison D T, Lau L J 1980 Farmer education and farm efficiency: A survey. *Econ. Dev. Cult. Change* 29: 37–76

McClelland D C, Winter D G 1969 *Motivating Economic Achievement.* Free Press, New York

Psacharopoulos G 1973 *Returns to Education: An International Comparison.* Jossey-Bass, San Francisco, California

Psacharopoulos G 1981 Returns to education: An updated international comparison. *Comp. Educ.* 17: 321–41

Sobel I 1978 The human capital revolution in economic development: Its current history and status. *Comp. Educ. Rev.* 22: 278–308

Windham D 1975 The macro-planning of education: Why it fails, why it survives, and the alternatives. *Comp. Educ. Rev.* 19: 187–201

P. Foster

Economic Growth: Contribution of Education

Economic growth of a steady and positive nature has been a consistent goal of most countries since the Second World War. For developed countries, economic growth means reduced unemployment as well as real increases in the social welfare of the population. For developing countries, there has been the added goal of trying to raise their standard of living to a level commensurate with that of the advanced countries, and to reduce widespread poverty and deprivation. But the attainment of high, steady rates of economic growth, measured by the growth rate of gross national product (GNP), has been an elusive goal for many countries. In attempting to understand the growth process, economists have examined the relative importance of investment in capital stocks, technical progress, changes in the size and quality of the labor force, and other factors.

The contribution of education to growth is presumed to occur through its ability to increase the productivity of an existing labor force in various ways, including both technical training and general education. But exactly how education increases productivity, how important it is, and in what ways it is important, are difficult questions which remain unsettled.

In primitive societies, basic education of known techniques of production was generally handed down through oral teaching, often associated with some form of apprenticeship system. A modern growing economy requires more people who can read and write in order to keep financial records, read plans and blueprints, and carry out similar functions related to the production and distribution of goods and services. Higher levels of per capita income are also based on a higher level of scientific and technological attainment, requiring a larger number of scientists, technicians, and engineers to conduct research and oversee the technological adaptation of research. However, while a shortage of educated people might limit growth, it is not clear that promoting education will foster more rapid growth. Furthermore, it is not clear what kinds of education are best at assisting growth—general formal education, technical training, or informal education related to specific jobs.

In general, countries that have higher levels of income also have higher levels of educational attainment (see Table 1), but this cannot be interpreted to mean that education is a necessary cause of higher levels of output and income. Education is both an investment good and a consumption good. As income grows people demand more education, and can afford more education, both for themselves and more importantly for their children. Whether this education contributes to raising productivity is a debatable point. Education may become a kind of screening device used by employers to make hiring decisions. Faced with a large number of applicants for a given job, an employer tends to narrow his or her options by looking seriously only at those with the highest levels of education. As a result the education level required to gain entry to certain jobs tends to move upward over time with little or no change in basic productivity (see *Screening Models and Education*).

1. Growth Accounting

In order to understand education's contribution to growth, one first must understand the causes of growth and the growth process itself. Traditionally, economists have identified three factors of production: land, labor, and capital. In the growth process land will presumably not change, so that the key

Table 1
Education data: Selected countries[a]

	Per capita income US$ 1980	Adult literacy rate % 1977	Enrollment rates % 1979		
			Primary	Secondary	Higher[b]
Sweden	13,520	99	98	86	37
France	11,730	99	112	84	24
United States	11,360	99	98	97	56
Japan	9,890	99	101	90	29
United Kingdom	7,920	99	105	83	20
Spain	5,400	n.a.	109	78	24
Soviet Union	4,550	100	101	104	21
Romania	2,340	98	98	83	11
Brazil	2,050	76	89	32	11
Korea, Republic of	1,520	93	111	76	12
Tunisia	1,310	62	102	25	5
Philippines	690	75	98	63	27
Sudan	410	20	51	16	2
India	240	36	78	27	8
Bangladesh	144	26	65	25	2

a Source: World Bank 1982   b 1978

factors are the growth of labor and capital. If the growth rates of labor and capital are weighted by their shares in total output, one can derive an index of the growth of factor inputs. The growth of total factor productivity can be measured by the growth rate of total output less the growth of total factor inputs.

More formally, output (Q) is assumed to be a function of the stock of capital (K), the labor force (L), and the level of technical progress (A), which is also a measure of total factor productivity. Hence, $Q = f(K,L,A_t)$ where A is assumed to be a function of time, t. Recasting in terms of growth rates and transposing results in a production function of the type:

$$\frac{dA}{A} = \frac{dQ}{Q} - \frac{dL}{L} + \frac{dK}{K}$$

Thus the term dA/A is a residual between the growth of output and the growth of factor inputs, and is susceptible to errors in the measurement of output, labor, and capital. Changes in the quality of the labor force can also affect the results in a misleading direction. The major work on growth accounting has been done by Denison (1967, 1979). In this work, he makes adjustments for the changes in the age and sex composition of the labor force, changes in hours worked, and most importantly for changes in education. The differentials in earnings at different education levels are assumed to reflect the added productivity of education. Dension acknowledges, however, that earnings differentials can also reflect unmeasurable factors such as ability and family background, and reduces these differentials by 60 percent to allow for these factors. This reduction factor, while somewhat arbitrary, is generally accepted by practitioners of growth accounting as a reasonable estimate, although it indicates that growth accounting itself is somewhat a combination of an art and a science.

For the period 1948 to 1973, Denison estimates that total United States potential national income grew at an annual rate of 3.87 percent per year (Denison 1979 p. 105), while total factor input grew at a rate of 2.2 percent. The growth rate of labor inputs, making allowance for hours worked and so on, but excluding education, accounted for 28 percent of total growth. Education of the labor force accounted for 11 percent. This is somewhat lower than Denison's earlier estimates for the period 1950 to 1962, when education accounted for 15 percent of total growth, and other labor inputs only 18 percent. Overall, however, both labor and capital inputs explain about 60 percent of total growth; the remaining 40 percent is accounted for by changes in factor productivity or output per unit of input. A certain part of this productivity growth Denison explains by improvements in resource allocation, changes in the legal and human environment, and economies of scale. There is a large residual, however, labeled "advances in knowledge and miscellaneous determinants," which accounts for about 29 percent of total growth. In Denison's words, "The advance in knowledge is the biggest and most basic reason for the persistent long-term growth of output per unit of input." Broadly speaking, it can be said to constitute nonformal education, and technical and managerial knowledge, obtained in a variety of ways ranging from organized research to simple observation and experience. But the residual also includes other factors which are not advances in knowledge and which are not otherwise incorporated in the estimates, including statistical discrepancies and measurement errors.

If one combines the direct influence of education (11 percent) and the indirect influence of advances in knowledge (29 percent), a very large proportion of growth (about 40 percent) can be attributed to improvements in human capital or education broadly conceived. This proportion furthermore has not shifted dramatically since Denison's earlier work in 1967 (which gave a 15 percent share for direct education and 23 percent for advances in knowledge). However, estimates for the period 1973 to 1976 show a decline in the residual, indicating declining productivity. With total output growing more slowly than total factor inputs, "advances in knowledge" have had a negative contribution of -0.56 percentage points. While a number of alternatives are examined by Denison (higher energy prices, more government regulation, less research and development) no clear explanation of the negative residual can be clearly identified. Thus, it raises the question whether or not "advances in knowledge" have been overstated as an explanation of growth in the past, and suggests that there are other factors at work which are yet to be uncovered in both periods. It is also possible that the shorter period (1973 to 1976) is too brief to capture the lags inherent to a period when the world economy has been undergoing some fundamental restructuring. Furthermore, a review of growth accounting exercises of various countries compiled by Bowman (1980) shows much lower contributions for education in other countries. In 22 countries having estimates for about the 1950 to 1962 period, only in four did the direct contribution of education exceed 10 percent (Argentina, Belgium, United Kingdom, and the United States). For most countries, education seems to be a minor factor, and to be a smaller factor in countries having rapid growth rates. Furthermore, the unexplained residual seems to be larger the higher the growth rate, that is, productivity itself grows faster when total output grows faster. For instance, Japan's growth averaged 10 percent per year during the period 1955 to 1968, of which only 39 percent could be attributed to the growth of factor inputs. Education explained only 1.4 percent of total growth.

Finally, it should be again noted that the size of the residual is a function of the methodology and its assumptions. Jorgensen and Griliches (1967) argue that if the inputs and outputs were correctly measured, the residual would be reduced or eliminated. Using different methods for measuring the capital stock, Christensen and Jorgensen (1969) found, for the period 1948 to 1967 in the United States, a growth of total factor productivity of about 0.3 percent per annum, versus Denison's estimate of 1.7 percent.

2. Returns on Human Capital

Another approach which attempts to measure the impact of education on productivity consists of recasting education as an investment in human capital (see *Human Capital and Education*). In theories developed by Becker (1964), Schultz (1961), and a host of others, it is assumed that rational people will attempt to invest in education up to the point where returns to them in terms of extra income are equal to the costs of undertaking education, including the income forgone while education is being undertaken (see *Earnings Forgone*). Social returns to education will differ from private returns to the extent that recipients of education do not pay the full costs of this education. On the other hand, the social gains from education will be measured as pretax income, while the private gains will be net of taxes.

Table 2
Social returns to investment in education (%)[a]

Country group	Primary	Secondary	Higher
Developing	27	16	13
Intermediate	16	14	10
Advanced	n.a.	10	9

a Source: Psacharopoulos 1981

Decisions on investment in human capital generally relate to the amount of education to give children; income earners usually cannot afford to resume education on a full-time basis or may be barred from doing so. Parents must decide how much of present consumption to forgo in investing in the education or human capital of their children, which is counterbalanced by the real and expected income earned by more educated offspring. Expected returns from education can vary in perception and in fact, and financial markets do not permit sufficient borrowing to allow parents to equate marginal benefits to marginal costs. Thus, it could be expected that rates of return would be higher in less developed countries.

Returns to education have been calculated for many countries, and have been summarized by Psacharopoulos (1981). Basically he finds that:

(a) returns to primary school are higher than those to other levels of education;

(b) private returns exceed social returns, particularly at the university level;

(c) all rates of return are above 10 percent (a commonly accepted estimate of the opportunity cost of capital);

(d) returns to education were higher in the poorer countries, reflecting the greater scarcities of trained manpower in these countries.

For developing countries, the high social returns found for primary education (27 percent) contrast sharply with the more modest returns for higher education (13 percent) (see Table 2). This suggests that these countries may have overinvested in higher level education, and neglected primary education. For the more advanced countries, the social rates of return for higher education averaged only 9 percent, suggesting that further rapid expansion of higher education would not be warranted. The fact that private returns still averaged 12 percent, however, indicates that there may still be popular pressure to expand higher education beyond the point where it has a net social benefit, or any real impact on growth. Thus primary education in developing countries could still make significant contributions to growth assuming that other investments could not match the average rate of return of 27 percent. Further investments in higher education in developed countries could actually slow growth, if more productive investments elsewhere are forgone. Thus education's impact on growth depends on the level of development of both the economy and the labor force, and will be country and time specific. The whole process becomes self-equilibrating: an oversupply of a certain class of educated people will drive down salaries and lower prospective rates of return, which in turn will discourage entrants. Where systems of public education are well-developed, and financial markets permit borrowing against future earnings, rates of return on education will, in the long run, equal the rates of return on other productive assets. Thus, higher than normal rates of return reflect some sort of market imperfection, such as in developing countries where neither public nor private education is available, and people are unable, because of their low incomes, to sacrifice present consumption levels to finance education. In short, education is likely to be more important to economic growth in situations marked by underinvestment in human capital, limited supplies of skilled and educated workers, and relatively undeveloped education systems. Many would agree with Schultz (1975) that education is more likely to be important in modernizing environments than in traditional ones.

In developing countries, there seems to be a clear bias against, and resulting underinvestment in, primary education, as reflected in relatively higher rates of return compared to secondary and higher education. Recent evidence and work, in addition to the rates-of-return evidence, has increased the stress on investing in primary education. A survey of studies on farmer productivity by Lockheed et al. (1980) suggests that the microlevel evidence supports this view. A summary of 31 individual studies covering various developing countries found that four years of education increased farmer productivity on average by 7.4 percent. This average centers around a fairly wide range, however, with several studies showing a negative correlation between education and productivity. The authors explain this by dividing the sample into modernizing/nonmodernizing subsamples. In nonmodernizing societies, marked by traditional and primitive farming methods and little exposure to innovation and new methods, four years

of education was found to increase production by only 1.3 percent, compared with 9.5 percent under modernizing conditions.

3. Cross-country Comparisons

Other cross-country evidence also supports the idea that human capital development in general, and education in particular, is an important element in explaining variations in growth rates and levels of per capita income. Krueger's study (1968) made a pioneering attempt to compare differences in per capita income between the United States and a wide range of other countries. Her technique consisted of breaking down the labor force by age, education, and rural–urban areas for each country. If each of these categories had the same productivity as that of the United States, an estimate of "attainable income" can be derived. In most cases, even if countries had the same factor endowment as the United States, Krueger finds that they would attain a per capita income only half that of the United States level (see

Table 3
Education and gaps in per capita incomes between the United States and other countries[a]

Country	Per capita GDP as percentage of US value	Per capita attainable income with present human resources[b]	Percentage by which attainable income is reduced by gap in education[c]
United States	100.0	n.a.	n.a.
Canada	72.6	100.5	8.1
Israel	38.3	83.8	13.6
Japan	14.4	93.2	3.7
Puerto Rico	23.2	59.8	12.6
Jamaica	16.2	56.7	16.0
Panama	15.0	51.5	16.0
Mexico	14.2	45.6	22.9
Greece	12.5	71.2	28.6
Portugal	11.6	67.1	29.9
El Salvador	7.5	45.5	24.1
Honduras	7.5	36.6	23.9
Peru	7.3	51.0	18.3
Iran	7.2	39.8	33.2
Jordan	6.9	38.7	23.3
Malaysia	7.9	44.2	25.0
Indonesia	3.1	37.3	32.2
Korea, Republic of	4.7	44.3	24.8
China, Republic of (Taiwan)	3.9	48.5	21.6
Thailand	3.6	46.5	21.4
India	3.0	34.1	32.6
Ghana	7.7	38.0	30.3

a Source: Krueger (1968)   b Per capita income attainable with present human resources if the country has US per capita nonhuman resources   c Controlling for age and sector

Table 3), with the balance being attributed to the different levels of development of human capital. Mexico, whose 1960 per capita income was 14 percent of that of the United States, serves as useful illustration. If Mexico had the United States' endowment of land, capital, and other resources, it would have had a per capita income of 46 percent of the United States' level. Explained another way, 63 percent of the gap in per capita incomes must be explained by other factors, namely differences in human capital stocks.

It is worth noting, however, that Krueger does not equate human capital entirely to education. Other important differences include the age structure of the population, and the split between rural and urban areas. In most countries, attainable income is reduced by about 15 to 30 percent due to education deficiencies, or about half of the total gap explained by human capital differences. In the case of Mexico, education lowers attainable income by about 23 percent, compared to a total reduction attributable to human capital of 54 percent.

Despite the work of Krueger (1968), Selowsky (1969), and others, education and human capital factors were often ignored in studies of growth in developing countries until recently. This deficiency has been overcome in recent years, however, as economists have been increasingly concerned with such issues as reducing poverty and increasing employment, in addition to promoting growth.

Improving the basic health and education of the poor is now seen as an important mechanism for increasing their welfare directly, and their productivity indirectly. This has led to a renewed interest in the "social sectors" consisting not only of education, but also of health services, water supply and sanitation, nutrition, and housing. The question arises whether these are investments or a form of consumption; in much of the development literature before 1970 investments in social sectors were considered to have little or no effect on output growth.

In a recent cross-country study, Hicks (1980) found that the rapidly growing developing countries were those that had above average performance in both literacy and life expectancy. Growth, of course, can add to the resources available for making improvements in health and education. In order to circumvent this cause and effect problem, he examined the growth of a sample of 75 developing countries for the period 1960 to 1977 and their respective levels of achievement in 1960 for life expectancy (an assumed health measure) and literacy. He finds that literacy levels and growth are related. The top 12 countries (see Table 4) had an average per capita growth rate of 5.7 percent during the period, compared to 2.4 percent for all countries. These fast-growing countries started the period with above-average literacy levels: 65 percent compared to an average of 38 percent. However, the fast-growing countries also have above-average income levels,

Table 4
Economic growth and life expectancy: Selected countries[a]

Country	Growth rate 1960–77[b] %	Life expectancy 1960	Deviations from expected levels of life expectancy[c]	Adult literacy 1960	Deviations from expected levels of literacy 1960[c]
Singapore	7.7	64.0	3.1	n.a.	n.a.
Korea, Republic of	7.6	54.0	11.1	71.0	43.6
Taiwan	6.5	64.0	15.5	54.0	14.2
Hong Kong	6.3	65.0	6.5	70.0	6.4
Greece	6.1	68.0	5.7	81.0	7.5
Portugal	5.7	62.0	4.7	62.0	1.7
Spain	5.3	68.0	1.8	87.0	1.2
Yugoslavia	5.2	62.0	4.7	77.0	16.7
Brazil	4.9	57.0	3.0	61.0	8.6
Israel	4.6	69.0	2.0	n.a.	n.a.
Thailand	4.5	51.0	9.5	68.0	43.5
Tunisia	4.3	48.0	−0.5	16.0	−23.8
Average: Top 12	5.7	61.0	5.6	64.7	12.0
Average: All countries	2.4	48.0	−0.0	37.6	−0.0

a Source: Hicks 1980   b Growth rate of real per capita GNP   c Deviations from estimated values and derived from an equation where life expectancy in 1960 (LIEX) and adult literacy in 1960 (LIT) are related to per capita income in 1960 (Y) in the following way:

$$\text{LIEX} = 34.29 + 0.07679Y - 0.0000430Y^2 \quad R^2 = 0.66;$$
$$\text{LIT} = 9.23 + 0.1595Y - 0.0000658Y^2 \quad R^2 = 0.44$$

and one would expect higher than average levels of literacy. But even if one adjusts for differences in income, these countries had literacy rates 12 percentage points higher than would have been expected at their income levels.

Correlation analysis such as this suffers from many deficiencies, and the problem of cause and effect identification remains. In addition, Hicks points out the strong correlation between literacy levels and life expectancy, suggesting that literacy may have an important influence on health and hygiene. In a more extensive study, Wheeler (1980) attempted to overcome the causality problems by using a system of simultaneous equations. While more rigorous, this approach reduces the number of countries that can be included in the analysis, since data must exist for all countries for all variables. His findings contradict Hicks's somewhat in that he does not find a strong association between the life expectancy or nutrition variables and growth. Rather, he supports the strong influence of changes in literacy on changes in output, and finds an important influence for literacy in reducing fertility. This finding supports the work of Cochrane (1980) and others who generally find that education and fertility reductions work together, but the evidence here is not always clear. Cochrane's work, for example, also suggests that in some instances, increased education at lower levels increases fertility, probably because of the effects of improved health and hygienic practices that come with increased education.

Wheeler's work has been extended by Marris (1982). Using data from 66 developing countries for the period 1965 to 1979, he estimated a model that confirms the previous findings on the importance of education for growth in developing countries. Furthermore, he found a relatively weak role for investment, as normally measured in terms of the construction of fixed tangible assets. The estimated cost–benefit ratios for education (measured by primary enrollment rate) ranged in his model between 3.4 and 7.4, depending on one's assumptions on costs. By contrast, the cost–benefit ratios for investments in nonhuman capital ranged between 0.4 and 1.0.

Finally, some mention needs to be made of some of the microlevel work on the influence of education. These studies are important, because they can more directly associate education differences at the worker level with variations in worker productivity. The study by Lockheed et al. (1980) has already been mentioned. Similar studies for more advanced countries also come to similar conclusions. In the United States, for instance, agriculture, studies by Griliches (1964) and Welch (1970) suggest that a 10 percent increase in farmer education raises productivity by 3 to 5 percent, compared to only a 1 to 2 percent increase to be gained from a 10 percent increase in either land, fertilizer, or machinery. In a classic study of the Japanese textile industry, Saxon-

house (1977) found that in the period between 1891 and 1935 improvements in productivity occurred almost entirely because of modest changes in labor force characteristics and working conditions. He concluded that the standard production function which examines only the conventional inputs of capital and labor, and the rate of substitution between them, is deficient to the extent it ignores the nonconventional inputs of worker education, training, and experience.

4. Conclusion

The overall conclusion from the literature surveyed here suggests a strong positive relation between education and growth. But it must be immediately qualified by stating that education is broadly defined to include worker training and experience. Human capital, not merely education, is a critical element in the production function, and a major element in explaining differences in productivity and productivity growth between countries.

Furthermore, it is possible to have too much investment in education, just as it is possible to have too much investment in plant and machinery. The higher rates of return to education in developing countries attest to the thesis that investment in education makes most sense where the supply of educated manpower is relatively scarce, as it is in most developing countries. Furthermore, there appears to be even in these countries too much investment in higher education and too little in primary education, which appears to be clearly related to farmer productivity in these countries. Overinvestment in education also appears a potential problem in some of the developed countries, such as the United States, whose current enrollment rates for higher education (56 percent) are almost double those of Europe (see Table 1). Overinvestment of this type is a particular problem in countries which subsidize higher education, and where, as a consequence, the private returns to education are substantially higher than the social returns.

See also: Economic Development and Education

Bibliography

Becker G S 1964 *Human Capital: A Theoretical and Empirical Analysis with Special Reference to Education.* National Bureau of Economic Research, New York

Bowman M J 1980 Education and economic growth: An overview. In: King T (ed.) 1980 *Education and Income: A Background Study for World Development Report, 1980.* World Bank Staff Working Paper No. 402. World Bank, Washington, DC, pp. 1–71

Christensen L R, Jorgensen D W 1969 The measurement of US real capital input, 1929–1967. *Rev. Income Wealth* 15: 293–320

Cochrane S H 1980 *Fertility and Education: What do we Really Know?* Johns Hopkins University Press for the World Bank, Baltimore, Maryland

Denison E F 1967 *Why Growth Rates Differ: Post-War Experience in Nine Western Countries.* Brookings Institution, Washington, DC

Denison E F 1979 *Accounting for Slower Economic Growth: The United States in the 1970s.* Brookings Institution, Washington, DC

Griliches Z 1964 Research expenditures, education, and the aggregate agricultural production function. *Am. Econ. Rev.* 54: 9r !-74

Hicks N 1980 Is there a trade-off between growth and basic needs? *Finance and Dev.* 17(2): 17–20

Jorgensen D W, Griliches Z 1967 The explanation of productivity change. *Revised Econ. Stud.* 34: 249–83

Krueger A O 1968 Factor endowments and per capita income differences among countries. *Econ. J.* 78: 641–59

Lockheed M, Jamison D, Lau L 1980 Farmer calculation and farm efficiency: A survey. In: King T (ed.) 1980 *Education and Income: A Background Study for World Development Report, 1980.* World Bank Staff Working Paper, No. 402. World Bank, Washington, DC

Marris R 1982 Economic growth in cross-section. Mimeo, Department of Economics, Birkbeck College, London

Nadiri M I 1972 International studies of factor inputs and total factor productivity: A brief survey. *Rev. Income Wealth* 18: 129–54

Psacharopoulos G 1981 Returns to education: An updated international comparison. *Comp. Educ.* 17: 321-41

Saxonhouse G R 1977 Productivity change and labor absorption in Japanese cotton spinning, 1891–1935. *Q. J. Econ.* 91(2): 195–219

Schultz T W 1961 Investment in human capital. *Am. Econ. Rev.* 51: 1–17

Schultz T W 1975 The value of the ability to deal with disequilibria. *J. Econ. Lit.* 13(3): 872–76

Selowsky M 1969 On the measurement of education's contribution to growth. *Q. J. Econ.* 83: 449–63

Welch F 1970 Education in production. *J. Polit. Econ.* 78: 35–59

Wheeler D 1980 *Human Resource Development and Economic Growth in Developing Countries: A Simultaneous Model.* World Bank Staff Working Paper, No. 407. World Bank, Washington, DC

World Bank 1982 *World Development Report 1982.* World Bank, Washington, DC

N. L. Hicks

Economics: Educational Programs

Every research discipline has three categories of expertise: (a) that which adds to the theory of the discipline; (b) that which applies the tools of the discipline; and (c) that which studies systematic ways of communicating the theory and application. There are economic theorists, economic application experts, and economic educators. It is this third category of expertise which is the focus of this article. Economic education for children aged 5–18 will be discussed from an historical perspective to the current state of the art with an emphasis on prototype programs and new research directions in the field. Economic education programs exist in the United Kingdom and Canada, and there is some isolated activity in other parts of the world including Scandinavia and Australia. However, the major research activity in this area is currently centered in the United States.

Chief among the goals of economic education is economic literacy. This is the ability of citizens to operate effectively in the economic areas of their lives as workers, voters, and consumers. It is not merely common sense nor intuition. Economic literacy is rational economic decision making utilizing a process of economic analysis and the skills of economic reasoning. Economic literacy, gained through economic education, both elementary and secondary, remains relevant throughout adulthood as people apply logical economic principles, not myths, to the economic realities of their lives. If students are not given economic training before college, it is much more difficult to develop both the conceptual understanding and the analytical skills needed for economic literacy. The attainment of economic literacy hinges upon combining the elements of economic reasoning in a variety of real-world decision-making situations as students and adults.

The field of economic education for kindergarten through 12th grades (K–12), appears to progress in predictable stages within a given country: (a) the recognition and adoption of economic education as an educational priority; (b) the relatively unstructured development and implementation of economic curricula; (c) the recognition of the relationship of child development and learning theory to curricular decision making (in economic education); and (d) the systematic research endeavors necessary to integrate curricular development and decision making (in economic education) with the principles of child development and learning theory.

Until the middle of the 1960s, most of the literature on economic education dealt with the question of whether there was a need for economic education in the curriculum prior to college. That question was answered in the affirmative in the United States as revealed by the United States Task Force Report of 1961. Subsequently similar affirmative answers were obtained in other parts of the world including the Scandinavian countries, the United Kingdom, Australia, and Canada. By the end of the 1960s a strong realization of the desirability of economic education and a commitment to implementing programs was manifested in many countries, but most visibly within the United States. The challenge to economic education in the 1970s expanded to include precisely how to bring about an effective (K–12) curriculum in economics and how to train implementors and disseminators.

The research in the 1970s addressed two major issues with respect to economic education in kindergarten through high school: (a) what facets of economics *can* actually be taught prior to college;

and (b) which of those concepts are important to teach. However, the end results of this research were primarily ad hoc curricula. Economic concepts were sometimes ranked on a continuum of easiest to most difficult and introduced accordingly; more often they were assigned arbitrarily to grade levels on the rationale that with proper instructional intervention any concept could be taught at any grade level. There was a deluge of curricula in which scarcity was taught in kindergarten, opportunity cost in the first grade, and so on. Although these curricula reflected some sequencing of ideas, they tended to disregard the developmental stages of learners as well as the depth of inquiry and critical thinking skills necessary to master the concepts. Similar approaches were tried and discarded in the teaching of history. For example, in the United States the Revolutionary War was taught in the third grade, the Civil War in the fourth, and the First World War in the fifth. Economic educators also began to realize that sequencing of concepts alone would not result in learning at desirable levels of cognition (Hansen et al. 1977, Highsmith and Little 1981, Kourilsky 1981).

In the late 1970s and early 1980s economic education experienced significant advancement in its state of the art. Attempts were initiated to broaden the scope of curricula to reflect the developmental/ heuristic hierarchy of the learners. Questions addressed in the research literature expanded to include what *should* be taught from a developmental point of view, at what grade level, and to what degree. It was discovered that children as young as kindergarten age could understand a concept like opportunity cost when applying it in choosing a recess game. At the high-school level some learners were developmentally ready to apply the same concept at a much more complex level such as assessing the time value of money (Larkins and Shaver 1969, Kourilsky 1977). Thus it became apparent that concepts could and should be repeated in the curriculum at different grade levels to obtain ascending levels of cognition. This realization is reflected to varying degrees in programs which represent the major models in use today for teaching economics.

1. Current Models for Teaching Economics

The principal current models for teaching economics can be characterized as: (a) media based; (b) experience based; and (c) textbook/materials based. Some contemporary programs that are prototypes of these models and whose effectiveness have been empirically verified and reported in the research literature are described below.

Media-based education places major emphasis on the use of films. In most cases the films are not utilized as a total instructional system but rather are employed as instructional aids. The rationale for using media in teaching economics is to increase cognition through multisensory stimulus and to enhance motivation by depicting concepts in the context of interesting and/or familiar environments.

Trade-offs (Joint Council on Economic Education 1978) and *The People on Market Street* (Disney Corp. 1978) are two widely used media programs. *Trade-offs* is a television/film series consisting of 15 programs designed to improve and expand economics instruction in grades 5–8. Each program is 15–20 minutes long and focuses on a specific economic principle, for example, "demand." The programs are used as motivators for economic lessons, class discussions, and follow-up activities. *The People on Market Street* is a seven-part film series geared to the cognitive sophistication of secondary students. As with *Trade-offs*, each film focuses on one economic concept, but at a higher level of analysis. Series of this type usually include question sets, explanations of economic principles and their current applications, and student activities.

Studies on each of these programs have indicated significant improvement in student knowledge of and attitude toward economics. It is also interesting to note that students of teachers specifically trained in the use of these series significantly outscored those viewing the same with untrained teachers (Walstad 1980) (see *Film Use in the Classroom*).

Experience-based models are based on the premises of active versus passive learner roles, personal as opposed to vicarious involvement, and the importance of decision making in which learners actually bear the consequences of their decisions (see *Experience-based Curriculum*).

The most extensively implemented experience-based program is Mini-Society (grades 3–6), with Kinder-Economy (grades K–2), and Maxi-Economy I and II (middle- and senior-high school) being offshoots of the original program (Kourilsky 1977, 1983). Although all three programs concentrate on economics and the experience-based approach, each of the three program designs was carefully tailored for the specific intellectual development stage of the program's intended student users.

Mini-Society is designed as a 10–20 week unit in which the students actually experience and then resolve various economic problems through the creation and development of their own classroom society. The program utilizes two complementary components: the economic experiences themselves and a formal postexperience debriefing procedure for the concepts and ideas derived from these experiences. The formal debriefing paradigm is the key to integrating into the students' formal knowledge base the concepts which emerge from the experience-based activities. The Mini-Society participants are the decision makers as they design and print their own currency, buy and sell student-conceived and student-produced goods and services, and resolve the economic dilemmas they are certain to encounter.

Teachers are specifically trained in the 25 predictable economic dilemmas which arise in most economic systems, and in the facilitation of the Mini-Society.

Studies on the effectiveness of the Mini-Society programs have revealed significant gains in economic understanding as well as increases in learner self-concept, autonomy, personal responsibility, and favorable attitudes toward school and learning (Kourilsky and Hirshleifer 1976, Kourilsky 1979b, Cassuto 1980).

The materials-based model usually combines textbook reading with teacher exposition and class discussion. One of the principal rationales for a materials-based model to teach economics is that a written text allows both the student and the teacher to access repeatedly specific text materials without regard to order of appearance in the text. It is assumed that because of the perceived difficulty of digesting economic concepts, learners will benefit from the capability of individualized, repeated, and random access to presented material. A typical learning sequence involves assignment of a chapter to read, teacher presentation of the content of the chapter, and classroom discussion/activities that are often suggested in the teacher's guide.

Our Working World (Senesh 1973), *Our Economy: How It Works* (Clawson 1979), and *Managing Your Money* (Wolf 1977) are examples of texts widely used in the United States at the grade-school, middle-school, and high-school levels respectively. Although these texts are geared to different grade levels, they can be characterized by a tendency to introduce economic concepts in the context of everyday life applications. All three books have been shown to enhance economic knowledge (Yankelovich et al. 1981).

2. Research in Economic Education

The key research in economic education appears to be moving in new directions with its focus guided by the following premises:

(a) *Children are not miniature adults*. Attempts are being made to systematically integrate economic concepts into curricula according to psychological criteria. Investigations are concerned with whether learners are developmentally ready to learn a particular concept and at what level of abstraction. Economic educators are taking into account in their research that the learners they are addressing, regardless of their intelligence, progress through different stages of cognitive development ranging from preoperational to formal operations (Fox 1978, Kourilsky 1981) (see *Cognitive Development*).

(b) *Research in economic education is more than "show and tell" activities*. The preponderance of papers and articles on "What I did in my class" and "Method A versus method B," is slowly giving way to studies on the underlying principles of learning which are common to large classes of successful programs in economics as well as investigations of models of teaching excellence (Saunders et al. 1978, Kourilsky 1981, Lima 1981).

(c) *The students of the K–12 classroom teachers must be viewed as the ultimate consumers of economic education*. In the past, inservice training, staff development, and economic education workshops were geared toward enriching the teacher's knowledge of economics with little or no systematic assessment of whether such knowledge was transferred to their students. The newest trend is to view the teachers as intermediaries and to conduct research on the acquisition of concepts, skills, and attitudes of their learners—the ultimate consumers of economic education (Kourilsky 1980, Walstad 1980).

See also: Social Studies: Elementary-school Programs; Social Studies: Secondary-school Programs

Bibliography

Cassuto A 1980 The effectiveness of the elementary school Mini-Society Program. *J. Econ. Educ.* 11: 59–61
Clawson M 1979 *Our Economy: How It Works*. Addison-Wesley, Menlo Park, California
Fox K F A 1978 What children bring to school: The beginnings of economic education. *Soc. Educ.* 42: 478–81
Hansen L et al. 1977 *Master Curriculum Guide in Economics for the Nation's Schools. Part I, A Framework for Teaching Economics: Basic Concepts*. Joint Council on Economic Education, New York
Highsmith R, Little L 1981 *A Scope and Sequence Outline for Teaching Economics K–12*. Economic Literacy Council of California, Long Beach, California
Joyce L 1979 Understanding productivity. *Understanding Economics*, Series No. 2. Canadian Foundation for Economic Education, Toronto, Ontario, ERIC Document No. ED 173 188
Kourilsky M 1977 The Kinder-Economy: A case study of kindergarten pupils' acquisition of economic concepts. *Elem. Sch. J.* 77: 182-91
Kourilsky M 1979a Rx for economic illiteracy. *TELemetry* 7(2): 1–9
Kourilsky M 1979b Optimal intervention: An empirical investigation of the role of teacher in experience-based instruction. *J. Exp. Educ.* 47: 339–45
Kourilsky M 1980 Predictors of entrepreneurship in a simulated economy. *J. Creat. Behav.* 14: 175–98
Kourilsky M 1981 Economic socialization of children: Attitude toward the distribution of rewards. *J. Soc. Psychol.* 115: 45–57
Kourilsky M 1983 *Mini-Society: Experiencing Real-world Economics in the Elementary School Classroom*. Addison-Wesley, Menlo Park, California
Kourilsky M, Hirshleifer J 1976 Mini-Society vs. token economy: An experimental comparison of the effects on learning and autonomy of socially emergent and imposed behavior modification. *J. Educ. Res.* 69: 376–81
Larkins A G, Shaver J P 1969 Economics learning in grade one: The USU assessment studies. *Soc. Educ.* 33: 958–63
Lima A 1981 An economic model of teaching effectiveness. *Am. Econ. Rev.* 71: 1056–59

National Task Force on Economic Education 1961 *Economic Education in the Schools: Summary of the Report*. Committee for Economic Development, New York

Ryba R, Robinson B (eds.) 1980 Aspects of upper secondary economics education in EEC countries. Economics Association of London, ERIC Document No. ED 187 636

Saunders P, Welsh A, Hansen L (eds.) 1978 *Resource for Teacher Training Programs in Economics*, No. 271. Joint Council on Economic Education, New York

Senesh L 1973 *Our Working World*. Science Research Associates, Chicago Illinois

Walstad W B 1979 Effectiveness of a USMES in-service economic education program for elementary school teachers. *J. Econ. Educ.* 11(1): 1–12

Walstad W B 1980 The impact of trade-offs and teacher training on economic understanding and attitudes. *J. Econ. Educ.* 12(1): 41–48

Wolf H A 1977 *Managing Your Money*. Allyn and Bacon, Boston, Massachusetts

Yankelovich S Kelley, White, Inc. 1981 *National Survey of Economic Education 1981—Grades 6–12*. Playback Associates, New York

The People on Market Street. A filmstrip produced by the Disney Corporation, Burbank, California (released 1978)

Trade-offs. A movie series produced by the Joint Council on Economic Education, New York (released 1978)

M. Kourilsky

Economics of Education

The economics of education is a branch of economic theory and investigation which has developed rapidly since the 1960s but has a much longer history. Several of the classical economists writing in the eighteenth and nineteenth century, including Adam Smith, Alfred Marshall, and John Stuart Mill, drew attention to the importance of education as a form of national investment and considered the question of how education should be financed. In the Soviet Union the Russian economist Strumilin examined "the economic significance of national education" in 1924. However, it was a revival of interest in the concept of investment in human capital which developed in the United States and the United Kingdom in the late 1950s and early 1960s that stimulated new interest in the question of the relationships between education and the economy. Since that time there has been a tremendous growth of research and publications in the area of the economics of education, including such topics as the contribution of education to economic growth, the profitability of investment in education (including estimates of the social and private returns to education), the role of educated manpower in economic development (including attempts to forecast manpower requirements), the costs of education (including questions of cost effectiveness and productivity), the finance of education, and more recently studies of the effects of education on the distribution of income and wealth.

More detailed information on all these topics is given in other entries in the Encyclopedia (see *Human Capital and Education*; *Cost Analysis in Education*; *Finance in Education*; *Manpower Requirements Forecasting*; *Income Distribution and Education*). This section provides a brief summary of the main areas of research in the economics of education and shows how this relates to other branches of economic theory.

1. Human Capital

The concept of human capital is central to much of the research in the economics of education, and is also important in other branches of economics which at times overlap with the economics of education, particularly analysis of the labour market and employment policy, the determinants of earnings, and the distribution of income. An important distinction in economics is between investment and consumption. All expenditure can be classified as either investment or consumption, although the borderline is not always clear cut. Consumption refers to the purchase or use of goods and services which bring immediate but short-lived benefits. Investment, on the other hand, refers to the acquisition of assets which yield benefits over a long period of time. Expenditure on food, for example, must obviously be classified as consumption, whereas expenditure on buildings or equipment which will provide benefits over many years is a form of investment, and the stock of assets which will yield benefits in the future is called capital.

Economic theories of capital and investment tended to concentrate on investment in physical capital, such as buildings, factories, and machines which generate income in the form of production of goods and services. However, many economists have pointed out that education and training create assets in the form of knowledge and skills which increase the productive capacity of manpower in just the same way as investment in new machinery raises the productive capacity of the stock of physical capital. Adam Smith pointed out in 1776 in *The Wealth of Nations* that "a man educated at the expense of much labour and time. . . may be compared to one of those expensive machines", and other classical economists observed that expenditure on education could be regarded as a form of investment that promised future benefits. In the early years of the twentieth century the Russian economist Strumilin (1924) and economists in the United Kingdom and Europe drew analogies between investment in education and investment in physical capital. However, it was in the period 1955 to the present day when there was such a growth of interest in the idea that expenditure on education represented investment in human capital that one writer, reviewing the theoretical and empirical work on the subject, has described it as "the human investment revolution in economic thought" (Bowman 1966). Economists such as Schultz (1961, 1971) and Becker (1975) have developed and analysed the concept of human capital, treating education and training as a form of investment, producing future benefits in the form of higher income for both educated individuals and for society as a whole.

The concept of human capital can be applied not only to education and training, but to any activity which increases the quality and productivity of the labour force and thus raises future income levels. Thus expenditures on health and migration can also be regarded as investment in human capital and the question is then raised of how profitable it is for individuals or for society to invest resources in education or training, rather than in physical capital or in other forms of human capital.

Techniques of cost–benefit analysis have therefore been applied to education, in order to compare the total costs of education, either to the individual or to society, with the expected returns from investment in schooling or on-the-job training. This provides a measure of the private or social rate of return to investment in education, which shows the relative profitability of education and other forms of investment for the individual (in the case of the private rate of return) or for society as a whole.

The costs of education are measured in terms of the total resources devoted to education, which economists call the opportunity cost, rather than simply the money spent on education by governments or by individuals. The opportunity cost includes the value of all the goods and services used in the education process, not only the time of teachers and other staff, the use of books, equipment, furniture, heat, light, materials, and school or college buildings, but also the time of students and pupils, which does not form part of the money costs of education, but is part of the real resource cost. The usual way of measuring the economic value of student or pupil time is in terms of earnings forgone, which represent the opportunity cost of their time. The loss of the opportunity to earn wages or salaries in the labour market is the true cost, to the individual student, of his or her decision to enrol in a full-time or part-time course of education. For the economy as a whole, the loss of the output that the student could have produced, if in employment, is part of the resource costs of education.

The benefits of education are measured in terms of the extra lifetime incomes or earnings enjoyed by educated manpower, compared with workers with lower levels of education, or illiterate workers (see *Earnings and Education*).

Analysis of the costs and benefits of education show that not only do educated workers receive higher wages and salaries than the less educated in a huge number of cases, but when compared with the direct and indirect costs of education, these benefits mean that education is a profitable form of investment offering returns as high or even higher than the average rate of return to physical capital. A review of cost–benefit analysis of education in 32 countries (Psacharopoulos 1973) showed that not only is education profitable but that in many cases, particularly in developing countries, the rate of return to education exceeds the rate of return to physical capital, the social rate of return is consistently higher than the private rate of return, and the rate of return to primary education is generally higher than the rate of return to secondary or higher education.

This means that, from a purely economic point of view, it is more profitable to invest additional resources in the lower levels of education than to expand higher education, although the social and private demand for higher education has expanded rapidly in recent years, particularly in less developed countries. Thus, the concept of human capital, and in particular the concept of the rate of return to investment in education, is relevant to the question of how society's resources should be allocated between different types of investment. Comparisons between the rate of return to human capital and the returns to investment in physical capital are relevant to the question of how many resources should be devoted to education or to other forms of investment in human capital such as vocational and industrial training or health care. Comparisons between the rate of return to different levels or types of education can be used as a guide to resource allocation within the educational system.

Since education is not a purely economic activity, but has many other objectives, concepts such as human capital and cost–benefit analysis can never provide a complete answer to the question of how resources should be allocated. However, the analysis of the returns to investment in education can throw some light on the question of how to allocate resources most efficiently or profitably, in other words how to maximize the returns or benefits derived from those resources. A great deal of economic theory is concerned with the vital issue of resource allocation, since society's resources are scarce and therefore choices must be made between alternative ways of allocating resources between competing ends.

2. Economic Efficiency

The question of how resources should be allocated in order to produce different goods and services raises the question of economic efficiency. The term efficiency can be used in many different ways, but in economics resources are said to be allocated efficiently if it is not possible to reallocate resources, that is to say increase the quantity of some goods or services at the expense of other goods or services, without reducing welfare. A whole branch of economics, known as welfare economics, has developed around the crucial question of how welfare should be defined and measured and how resources should be allocated in order to maximize welfare. The criterion of efficiency that is used as a basis for much of welfare economics is called Pareto efficiency, after the nineteenth-century Italian economist Pareto, who proposed that welfare should be defined as a condition where it is not possible to increase total utility by reallocating resources, if any reallocation which makes one group of individuals better off would make another group worse off. If it is possible to make all groups better off by changing the balance between different goods and services, then resources are not being used as efficiently as possible. If, however, any changes which benefit one group would be at the expense of another group, then welfare is already maximized, and this condition is described as Pareto optimal.

This concept is relevant to the economics of education since a large part of recent research is concerned with the question of how society's resources should be allocated between education and other forms of investment, or between different types or levels of education, in order to maximize the economic returns. The criterion of Pareto efficiency or optimality suggests that cost–benefit analysis should be used as a guide to resource allocation, in order to show which types of investment are most profitable, and offer the highest rate of return. However, this is still a controversial question in the economics of education, since cost–benefit analysis has not succeeded in measuring all the indirect benefits of education, or of other types of social investment, so that it is not possible to identify optimality.

Nor is economic efficiency the only criterion for decisions about resource allocation. The question of equity is also important, although techniques for measuring efficiency, such as cost–benefit analysis, are not concerned with equity issues. Much recent research in the economics of education has centred on questions of equity, for example how the burden of financing education should be shared between different groups in society. This research will be summarized later in this entry, but first there are other aspects of efficiency which have been extensively explored, and which will now be summarized.

3. The Contribution of Education to Economic Growth

The question of how efficiently society's resources are allocated is crucially linked with the concept of economic growth, usually defined as an increase in the total national income or product. Economists have tried to answer the question of how much education has contributed to economic growth (see *Economic Growth: Contribution of Education*). One of the first was an American economist, Edward

Denison, who used the concept of a production function in order to identify the contribution of different factors of production to the increase in the national income or gross national product (GNP) of the United States between 1910 and 1960 (Denison 1962). Preliminary analysis showed that increases in the quantity of labour and physical capital in the United States did not explain the increase in GNP. There was a large "residual factor" and Denison set out to analyse the components of this residual. He suggested that improvements in the quality of the labour force, including increased education, were important, together with other factors such as technological progress and economies of scale. His analysis then led to the much publicized conclusion that increases in the level of education of the labour force accounted for as much as 23 percent of the annual rate of growth of GNP in the United States between 1930 and 1960 (Denison 1962).

Denison then went on to apply similar techniques to various European countries but his results were less clear cut. Nevertheless the results of his research have been much quoted as demonstrating the link between investment in education and economic growth, and led to a conference organized by the Organisation for Economic Co-operation and Development (OECD) on "the residual factor and economic growth" (Organisation for Economic Co-operation and Development 1964). However, the findings have also been extensively criticized, and it has been suggested that the residual factor is simply a measure of ignorance about the causes of economic growth.

It is now generally recognized that education does contribute to economic growth but that it is very difficult to identify and measure the precise contribution of education relative to other factors. Research has now tended to shift away from attempts to quantify this towards other questions about the efficiency of resource allocation.

4. The Internal Efficiency of Education

The term "efficiency" also refers to the relationship between the inputs and outputs of a process, and can be applied to education in the same way as economists analyse the relationship between inputs and outputs in any productive process, such as manufacturing. The difference between analysing the efficiency of a factory or an industrial process and the efficiency of a school, university, or a country's educational system is simply that it is very much more difficult to define and measure the output of education.

Nevertheless, a considerable amount of research in the economics of education has been concerned with the relationship between inputs and outputs in educational institutions, or in the education system as a whole. This is normally called internal efficiency, in order to distinguish this concept of efficiency from the external efficiency of the allocation of resources within society.

A number of different economic techniques have been used to analyse the relationship between inputs and outputs in education. One of these is cost–effectiveness analysis, which is used to compare the efficiency of alternative ways of achieving the same objective. For example, comparisons between different schools, different types of institution, or different teaching methods may be concerned to show which of the alternatives achieves a stated objective, or level of output, at least cost. Output may be measured in terms of pupil scores in achievement tests or examination results, or simply in terms of pupil-hours, or number of school-leavers, although such measures of output are unsatisfactory because they ignore the quality of education.

An alternative approach to cost–effectiveness analysis is to compare two or more schools or other institutions with similar levels of cost in order to identify which achieves the highest level of output from a given quantity of inputs. Once again, however, the main problem is to find ways of measuring the quality as well as the quantity of both inputs and outputs. Examples of cost–effectiveness analysis, for instance comparisons between full-time and part-time study, or studies of the effects of educational television, computers, or other new media on inputs and outputs (Wagner 1982) are discussed more fully in the article on cost–effectiveness analysis (see *Cost–Effectiveness Analysis in Education*).

Another technique which is concerned with the relationship between inputs and outputs in education is productivity measurement. This also is an economic technique more usually applied to manufacturing or industrial processes, but equally relevant to education. Productivity is the relationship between inputs and outputs and is measured in terms of output per unit of input. The term labour productivity is used to refer to output per person employed, while total factor productivity refers to the relationship between output and all factors of production, including labour, physical capital (such as buildings or equipment), and raw materials.

Attempts have been made to compare the productivity of education at different periods of time, in order to analyse trends in productivity. This requires information on trends in inputs and outputs, which once again raises the problem of measurement of quality, as well as quantity, of education. Because of the difficulties of measuring the quality of educational inputs and outputs, it is sometimes argued that it is impossible to measure the productivity of education. Other writers go further and suggest that "if education falls into that part of the nation's life where productivity is not a relevant criterion, then it serves little purpose to measure it" (Vaizey et al. 1972 p. 221).

On the other hand, attempts have been made to measure productivity trends in education, despite the difficulties. As one study emphasized:

> Educationists must recognise that if they deny the possibility of measuring educational output or quality this is tantamount to admitting that schools have no way of judging how successful they are in achieving whatever they set out to do. (Woodhall and Blaug 1968 p.4)

It is recognized that it is difficult to define and measure the success of schools "in achieving whatever they set out to do", for the simple reason that education has many different aims and is trying to achieve many different objectives, or outputs, at the same time. In economic jargon the process of transforming inputs into outputs is known as the "production function", and research on the causes of economic growth makes use of the concept of an aggregate production function, for the economy as a whole (Denison 1962). However, there is the difficulty that education represents both an input and an output, since educated manpower is one of the most important inputs of the economy, but at the same time the output of the education system is a significant part of the total national product.

There have been attempts to analyse the production function of education, by examining the outputs of education compared with the inputs (for example, Alexander and Simmons 1975) but one problem is the measurement of one of the most important inputs, namely the time of pupils or students in the educational process. One solution to this problem is to measure the input of pupil time in terms of the earnings forgone by students or pupils, as a measure of the opportunity cost of their time, but once again it is difficult to make adequate allowance for variations in the quality of inputs.

The problems of relating trends in inputs to trends in the output of education are considerable, and this remains a controversial issue in the economics of education. A fuller discussion of this research is given in separate entries in the Encyclopedia (see *Input–Output Analysis in Education*; *Production Functions in Education*).

5. The Demand for Educated Manpower

Educated manpower is one of the most crucial inputs in the economy of any country, and in developing countries, where there is frequently a shortage of physical capital, the availability of skilled manpower may be particularly crucial. Recognition of the fact that education makes workers more productive, and the belief that shortages of skilled manpower represent one of the major constraints to economic growth in developing countries, has resulted in a great deal of research effort being devoted to the problems of forecasting demand for educated manpower.

The idea that it is possible to forecast or project a country's manpower structure and then to use the result as a basis for planning the scale of education in order to satisfy the economic needs of the country is not only appealing, at first sight, since it appears to offer the hope of unambiguous guidance to educational planners and policy makers; it has also exerted a powerful influence over educational planning in many countries, over a number of years. Economists such as Herbert Parnes advocated educational planning based on what is usually called the manpower requirements approach. He described this in 1962 in an influential report by the OECD in the following terms:

An attempt is made to foresee the future occupational structure of the economy and to plan the educational system so as to provide the requisite numbers of personnel with the qualifications which that structure demands. (Parnes 1962 p. 15)

This approach, called variously manpower forecasting, estimating future manpower demand, or manpower requirements or needs, dominated educational planning in a number of countries for some years, and still exerts a powerful influence. One of the earliest and most comprehensive attempts to base educational planning on manpower forecasting techniques was the Mediterranean Regional Project (see *Mediterranean Regional Project*) which was established by the OECD in the early 1960s in six Mediterranean countries: Greece, Italy, Portugal, Spain, Turkey, and Yugoslavia. Detailed forecasts of the manpower requirements of these countries over a 15-year period were drawn up and these forecasts were used as a basis for estimating the number of places to be provided at each level of education, together with the number of teachers and the capital expenditure that would be necessary to produce the desired rate of increase in the supply of qualified manpower.

However, many economists challenged the validity of manpower forecasting, on the grounds that the assumptions of this approach were mistaken. The underlying assumptions of any forecast of manpower demand or requirements are that:

(a) there is a fixed and stable relationship between the level of educational qualifications of workers and the level of output of an industry or sector of the economy;

(b) there is also a rigid relationship between the occupational structure and the educational qualifications of workers; and

(c) it is therefore possible, and desirable, to make long-term forecasts of future levels of output and the occupational structure and educational qualifications of the labour force that will be needed to produce that output.

Economists who challenge these assumptions argue that it is possible to produce the same level of output with different combinations of inputs, that there are no fixed educational requirements for the majority of jobs, and it is impossible to make accurate long-term forecasts because of the problem of predicting technical change. Many who oppose the manpower forecasting approach advocate cost–benefit or rate-of-return analysis of education, on the grounds that this takes account of the possibility of varying the proportions of different inputs, including labour or capital, or qualified and less qualified manpower (i.e., the elasticity of substitution), and takes explicit account of the costs of education, which tend to be disregarded by an approach which emphasizes "requirements" or "needs".

The controversy between the manpower forecasting approach and cost–benefit analysis attracted considerable attention during the 1970s. One attempt to evaluate manpower forecasts in eight countries concluded that:

The manpower forecasting methods in current use certainly can lead to erroneous policy decisions . . . there are important weaknesses in the methods that have been used to make manpower forecasts . . . (which are) subject to large errors . . . We are, therefore, driven to the central conclusion that manpower forecasting has not so far proved to be particularly useful for educational decision-making; we may even go so far as to say that it has on occasion been positively misleading. (Ahamad and Blaug 1973 pp. 313–33)

On the other hand, other economists are equally sceptical about the validity and accuracy of techniques of cost–benefit analysis. Blaug has summarized the controversy between advocates of a manpower forecasting approach and a cost–benefit approach to planning in terms of "two views of the state of the world" (Blaug 1970). The disagreement is, fundamentally, one about the degree of flexibility in the economy and the labour market. Manpower forecasting rests on assumptions of a set of fixed or rigid relationships between inputs and outputs and between educational qualifications and jobs. Cost–benefit analysis, on the other hand, assumes flexibility and substitutability between different factors of production, not only between different types of manpower but also between labour and capital.

Research in this area now suggests that economic systems are in fact more flexible than manpower forecasters usually assume, but subject to more rigidities and market imperfections than is assumed by cost–benefit analysis. Blaug characterizes the dispute in terms of two views of the state of the world, but admits "Needless to say, the real world lies somewhere in between" (Blaug 1970 p. 216).

A technical evaluation of the Mediterranean Regional Project exercise (Hollister 1967) suggested that there were greater possibilities for flexibility and substitution than were assumed in the manpower forecasts, pointed out that "the problems raised by uncertainties about productivity change (technological change) loom quite large", and concluded that ignorance about the relationships between education and occupation is "the weakest link in the manpower requirements estimating procedures" (Hollister 1967 p. 72). Nevertheless, this evaluation did not reject manpower forecasting, but argued that instead of providing single-valued forecasts, on the basis of rigid assumptions, planners should use sensitivity analysis to test the implications of alternative assumptions and should attempt to integrate the various approaches to educational planning. Hollister concludes:

> In reviewing the arguments over which "approach" to educational planning is the "right" one, it becomes clear that when one views the educational system as a whole, and, more generally, the educational complex as an element within the overall social and economic system, all of these "approaches" fit together within the logic of the total system. (Hollister 1967 p. 76).

Similarly, Blaug (1967 p.287) argues that "social demand projections, manpower forecasting and rate of return analysis are reconcilable and in fact complementary techniques of educational planning". In fact, the literature on the economics of education is no longer dominated by the disagreements between advocates and critics of manpower forecasting, but the dispute remains, mainly as a matter of differences in emphasis and ideology, as another review of the controversy makes clear:

> Evidently both manpower planning and rate-of-return approaches have severe limitations. The contrasts between them have roots deep in the ways men look at political–economic systems and in the controls over those systems that are attempted in practice. (Anderson and Bowman 1967 p. 374)

6. The Finance of Education

Another issue in the economics of education on which there are ideological differences is the question of how education should be financed, in particular how the financial burden should be shared between the government, employers, and individuals, and what should be the balance between public and private sources of finance.

This is a question which has both efficiency and equity implications. The question of how the financial burden should be distributed raises the question of the extent of the public and private benefits of education which has already been discussed. Measures of the rate of return to educational investment relate the public or private benefits to the costs of education, and the social rate of return measures the benefits that are enjoyed by society as a whole, compared with the total resource costs of education, whereas the private rate of return includes the direct benefits that are enjoyed by the individual, compared with the costs which are borne by the individual or his or her family.

The difference between the social and the private rate of return thus reflects the degree of public subsidy of education, and since education is, in general, highly subsidized, there is usually a wide gap between social and private rates of return. If individuals were expected to contribute a greater share of the costs of education themselves, by means of fees or some other form of payment, then the gap between the social and the private rate of return would be reduced. However, there are very few cases where individual students are expected to pay the whole of the costs of their education themselves, and thus private rates of return exceed social rates of return.

In most countries a significant part of the costs of education, particularly at the primary and secondary level, are met out of general taxation or other government revenue, and pupils receive free schooling or pay low fees. In the case of private schools, fees may be a substantial or even the only source of revenue, but even in the case of private schools there is often some degree of public subsidy, either by means of tax concessions for institutions, or direct subventions for teacher salaries. In many countries fees are charged in institutions of higher education, but these are often well below the true resource costs (and therefore the social cost) of higher education. In addition many students receive financial aid in the form of scholarships, bursaries, grants, or subsidized loans, which help to reduce the financial burden of fees or of the students' living expenses. In either case, student aid reduces the private costs of education and therefore increases the private rate of return.

Economic theory cannot answer the question of who should pay for education, but it can throw light on both the efficiency and equity implications of alternative methods of financing education. The question of how society's resources are allocated between competing ends and whether this is efficient in terms of maximizing social welfare is, as Sect. 2 has already made clear, a crucial part of economic theory and the principle of Pareto optimality suggests one criterion for judging efficiency. However, this is not the only criterion that is relevant to the question of how education should be financed.

Since education confers financial benefits on the individual, in the form of higher lifetime earnings, the question of who pays for the education raises important questions of equity, as well as efficiency. If educational opportunities are unequally distributed, because of inequalities in the distribution of income, and hence the capacity of individuals to finance investment in education, then this will perpetuate inequalities of income in the future, since earning power is related to a worker's education. Thus, the question of who should pay for education is closely linked to the question of equality of educational opportunity, as well as the question of equity. The title of one American book sums up the dilemma: *Higher Education: Who Pays? Who Benefits? Who Should Pay?* (Carnegie Commission on Higher Education 1973).

This issue has provoked considerable controversy, particularly in the United States, since one widely publicized study of the benefits, costs, and finance of public higher education in California (Hansen and Weisbrod 1969) concluded that the general effect of public subsidies for higher education in California is to promote rather than to discourage inequalities of income. The reason is that those who are most likely to benefit from higher education are the children of upper-income families, so that the authors concluded, after analysing data on lifetime earnings differentials and relative tax burdens, that subsidies for higher education involve a transfer of income from the average taxpayer to those who come from higher than average income families and who may expect to earn higher than average incomes in the future.

This research has been extensively debated in the United States and has aroused considerable controversy, as other writers have analysed similar data for California or for other states, and have come to different conclusions (Pechman 1970, Hight and Pollock 1973). More recently there has been research on the effects of education subsidies in developing countries, which also throws doubt on the assumption that providing free or subsidized higher education will benefit low-income families, since it is the sons and daughters of upper-income families who are most likely to benefit from higher education (Psacharopoulos 1977a). However, when subsidies for lower levels of education are also taken into account, it is possible that subsidies for education may contribute to a redistribution of income in developing countries (Jallade 1974) although it is not necessarily so.

Apart from studies of the distribution effects of public subsidies for education there have been a number of studies of the effects of alternative methods of financing education. The two topics that have attracted most attention are student loans and the idea of financing education by means of vouchers.

The question of whether students should receive financial aid by means of grants, loans, subsidized work–study opportunities, or a combination of different forms of aid has provoked some controversy in Europe and the United States, although the majority of countries now provide aid for students by means of a combination of grants and subsidized loans. Japan is one of the few countries where loans are used almost exclusively, and the United Kingdom is one of the few Western countries which provides only grants. Canada, the majority of European countries, and the United States provide a mixture of grants and loans, and loans are also extensively used

in South America to provide financial support for students. There has been research on the effects of student loans and comparisons of different types of student support schemes in developed countries (Woodhall 1978, 1982) and the question of student aid policy in developing countries is now attracting increasing attention (see *Student Loans*).

The idea of financing education by means of vouchers, however, has not been widely put into practice, although it has been the subject of considerable discussion. The idea, put forward in both the United States and the United Kingdom, is that parents should be given a voucher which could be used to purchase education for their children, at the school of their choice. Schools would charge fees and the vouchers would be used to meet all or part of this cost. The role of the government would be confined to the financing of schools, rather than the actual provision of schooling, and it is argued that this would encourage competition between schools or other institutions, and would increase parental choice.

In the United Kingdom advocates of vouchers have argued that while there are strong arguments in favour of state intervention in education this need not imply state provision, and they suggest that a system of vouchers would make schools more responsive to the wishes of parents, or students, and thus increase efficiency (West 1965). In the United States there have been proposals to provide vouchers of varying value for different population groups, so that children from low-income or deprived families could be given the advantage of a compensatory voucher of higher than average value. One attempt to experiment with vouchers in the district of Alum Rock, California, was widely reported and investigated, but produced fairly ambiguous results. There is very little empirical evidence on the effects of financing education in this way.

7. Equity and Efficiency

The two criteria of equity and efficiency, which are of crucial importance in debates about educational finance, are also relevant to studies of resource allocation. There has been a striking change in emphasis in recent years in many of the studies in the economics of education. One review of "recent methodological advances and empirical results" suggested that the main shift in emphasis in the economics of education was a shift of concern from efficiency to income distribution.

No one would disagree that this is the number one shift that has taken place in the economics of education. When the concept of investment in education was first discovered, in the late fifties, it was natural for researchers to try to assess the profitability of this new kind of investment. Once this curiosity had been satisfied, the next question was: what has education to do with income distribution in our society? Does schooling act as an equaliser or as a transmitter of the status quo from generation to generation? One big question . . . is if there exist any trade-offs between the efficiency and equity effects of education. (Psacharopoulos 1977b)

Although this question has not yet been answered, the two concerns of equity and efficiency continue to dominate the economics of education.

8. Reviews of the Literature

This article can do no more than summarize the main areas and topics which have been studied in the economics of education in recent years. The literature is now vast, and has grown rapidly. A bibliography of the subject by Mark Blaug was first published in 1966, with nearly 800 items, but the third edition, published in 1978, contained over 2,000 annotated entries (Blaug 1978). Blaug has also written an introduction to the economics of education (Blaug 1970) which reviews research in both developed and developing countries and there are a number of American textbooks on the subject (for example, Cohn 1972) and a number of books of readings, which provide useful compendia of significant studies and research (UNESCO 1968, Blaug 1968, Baxter et al 1977). More detailed summaries of research will be found in the individual entries in this Encyclopedia to which references have been made in this entry.

Bibliography

Ahamad B, Blaug M (eds.) 1973 *The Practice of Manpower Forecasting: A Collection of Case Studies*. Elsevier, Amsterdam

Alexander L, Simmons J 1975 *The Determinants of School Achievement in Developing Countries: The Educational Production Function*. World Bank Staff Working Paper, No. 201. World Bank, Washington, DC

Anderson C A, Bowman M J 1967 Theoretical considerations in educational planning. In: Bereday G Z et al. (eds.) 1967 *World Yearbook of Education 1967: Educational Planning*. Evans, London

Baxter C, O'Leary P J, Westoby A 1977 *Economics and Education Policy: A Reader*. Longman, London

Blaug M 1967 Approaches to educational planning. *Econ. J.* 77: 262–87

Blaug M 1968 *Economics of Education: Selected Readings*. Penguin, Harmondsworth

Blaug M 1970 *An Introduction to the Economics of Education*. Allen Lane, London

Blaug M 1978 *Economics of Education: A Selected Annotated Bibliography*, 3rd edn. Pergamon, Oxford

Becker G S 1975 *Human Capital: A Theoretical and Empirical Analysis, with Special Reference to Education,* 2nd edn. Princeton University Press, Princeton, New Jersey

Bowman M J 1966 The human investment revolution in economic thought. *Sociol. Educ.* Spring: 111–37

Carnegie Commission on Higher Education 1973 *Higher Education: Who Pays? Who Benefits? Who Should Pay? A Report and Recommendations*. McGraw-Hill, New York

Cohn E 1972 *The Economics of Education*. Heath, Lexington, Massachusetts

Denison E F 1962 *The Sources of Economic Growth in the United States and the Alternatives Before Us*. Committee for Economic Development, New York

Hansen W L, Weisbrod B A 1969 *Benefits, Costs, and Finance of Public Higher Education*. Markham, Chicago, Illinois

Hight J E, Pollock R 1973 Income distribution effects of higher education expenditures in California, Florida, and Hawaii. *J. Hum. Resour.* 8: 318–30

Hollister R G 1967 *A Technical Evaluation of the First Stage of the Mediterranean Regional Project*. Organisation for Economic Co-operation and Development, Paris

Jallade J P 1974 *Public Expenditures on Education and Income Distribution in Colombia*. Johns Hopkins University Press, Baltimore, Maryland

Organisation for Economic Co-operation and Development (OECD) 1964 *The Residual Factor and Economic Growth*. OECD, Paris

Parnes H S 1962 *Forecasting Educational Needs for Economic and Social Development*. Organisation for Economic Co-operation and Development, Paris

Pechman J A 1970 The distributional effects of public higher education in California. *J. Hum. Resour.* 5: 361–70

Psacharopoulos G 1973 *Returns to Education: An International Comparison*. Elsevier, Amsterdam

Psacharopoulos G 1977a The perverse effects of public subsidization of education, or how equal is free education? *Comp. Educ. Rev.* 21: 69–90

Psacharopoulos G 1977b Economics of education: An assessment of recent methodological advances and empirical results. *Soc. Sci. Inf.* 16: 351–71

Schultz T W 1961 Investment in human capital. *Am. Econ. Rev.* 51: 1–17

Schultz T W 1971 *Investment in Human Capital: The Role of Education and of Research*. Free Press, New York

Strumlin S G 1924 The economic significance of national education. In: UNESCO 1968

UNESCO 1968 *Readings in the Economics of Education: A Selection of Articles, Essays and Texts from the Works of Economists, Past and Present, on the Relationships between Economics and Education*. UNESCO, Paris, pp. 413–50

Vaizey J E, Norris K, Sheehan J, Lynch P, Ferreira Leite M 1972 *The Political Economy of Education*. Duckworth, London

Wagner L 1982 *The Economics of Educational Media*. Macmillan, London

West E G 1965 *Education and the State: A Study in Political Economy*. Institute of Economic Affairs, London

Woodhall M 1978 *Review of Student Support Schemes in Selected OECD Countries*. Organisation for Economic Co-operation and Development, Paris

Woodhall M 1982 *Student Loans: Lessons From Recent International Experience*. Policy Studies Institute, London

Woodhall M, Blaug M 1968 Productivity trends in British secondary education. *Sociol. Educ.* 41(1): 1–35

M. Woodhall

Economics of Educational Technology

The production of educational services is a sector where the relationship between inputs and outcomes is much less clearly identifiable than in most other sectors of production of goods or services. What is the effect on educational results of a better qualified teacher, a lower pupil–teacher ratio, or educational media such as audiovisual aids, television programs, or computers? There is some evidence on these questions, but it is very often contradictory or inconclusive. These uncertainties are due to the variety of educational outcomes (cognitive and affective, internal and external, immediate and long term), and to the difficulty of measurement of most of them, in spite of some significant progress, at least in the measurement of cognitive achievements.

Most educational systems or educational institutions do not consider as a major and central objective the optimal use of inputs to maximize their outcomes, not only in public educational systems, but even in supposedly competitive private institutions. The survey carried out by Bowen (1980) among American colleges and universities leads to the conclusion that in higher education institutions, both private and public, unit costs are determined quite simply by the amount of money that can be raised from diverse sources: it is the "revenue theory of cost." The analysis of the relationship between expenditures (or costs) and outcomes (quantitative and qualitative) is basically inconclusive. It seems that the variance of costs is much higher than the variance of outcomes, which would mean that a certain number of institutions could have the same results with less resources. But on the other hand, the author argues that in its present trend, American higher education tends to be underfinanced and that the quality is declining.

These apparently contradictory results mean two things: there is a likely relation between available resources and academic excellency, but the right inputs remain to be specified. The provision of better educational services, leading to better educational results, requires more resources, and is therefore more expensive. But more expensive educational services are not necessarily better ones if the right inputs have not been clearly identified.

Traditional teaching takes place in classrooms with a teacher facing students. The teacher has the main role, and the basic additional input is the use of textbooks. The concept of new educational technologies is applied to systems where the traditional system is either enriched, or completely redesigned, in order to provide a substitute for the traditional system. Such a substitute is essentially covered by the concept of distance education.

An important aspect of both enrichment in traditional schools and distance education is that they were not originally introduced to improve the cost–effectiveness ratio of educational systems. Enrichment is aimed at improving school performances, fighting against failures, dropouts, repetition rates, and so on. Distance education objectives are mainly to provide access to education to excluded segments of the population: sick or handicapped people, mothers raising children, working people, adults who did not have the opportunity of studying while they were children, people living in remote areas, etc. The introduction of distance education for such target audiences was motivated principally by equity rather than economic considerations.

The situation in the early 1980s is entirely different. Most countries, especially the poorest, are facing dramatic budgetary difficulties which have stopped the expansion of public resources allocated to education (Eicher and Orivel 1979). This shrinking of resources for education accelerated in the second half of the 1970s and raised serious problems in satisfying a growing demand for educational services. More generally, after a quarter century of rapid expansion of public resources allocated to education (1950–75), public authorities and public opinion are increasingly concerned with the idea of a "good" use of these resources, which explains the growing popularity of the concept of a "cost–effectiveness ratio" applied to educational services. This concept may be used for traditional teaching as well as for the so-called new educational technologies. Up to 1970, studies and data on the costs of these new educational technologies were very scanty, and usually based on inadequate or noncomparable methodologies. Rapid progress has been made during the 1970s, both methodologically and empirically, especially through the pioneering work of D. T. Jamison. The results of these efforts to measure costs are such that one tends to have more evidence on cost comparisons (between traditional teaching and new educational technologies) than on results and outcomes.

In the first section of this entry, a description of the field of educational technology is provided, along with some tentative taxonomies; in the second and third sections, the economics of the two main uses of this technology, namely within and out of school, are examined; and finally, in the fourth section, some additional information is given on a medium-by-medium basis.

1. Taxonomies of Educational Technology

As shown above, the two great objectives of new educational technologies were the improvement of school performances and the expansion of access to education of excluded groups. For an economist, the emphasis is rather on the potential changes in the productivity of educational services, namely to provide more or better services for a given budget, or to provide similar services at a lower cost.

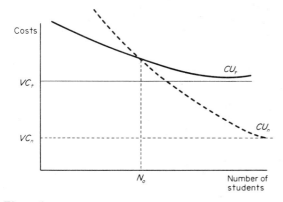

Figure 1
Unit costs in traditional teaching (CU_t) compared to distance education (CU_n)[a]

a Note: $FC_t < FC_n$

Fortunately, this first dichotomy between new educational technologies is particularly adequate to fit with economic analysis. The introduction of new media within schools does not significantly modify the labor input (teaching staff) that exists in traditional teaching. One cannot expect, as a consequence, dramatic changes in terms of cost reductions. The typical case is characterized by a slight increase in costs, and potential changes in results, which are more likely when the former level was low than when it was already high or satisfactory.

The second objective, however, opens large possibilities of changing the share of the labor input. The costs of a centralized production of didactic materials, printed or broadcasted, may be shared by a large number of users, and as the fixed part of costs tends to be higher than in traditional systems, a large audience may substantially reduce the unit costs, as shown in Fig. 1, where FC is the total fixed cost, VC the per student variable cost (or marginal cost), and where the index t refers to traditional teaching and n to new educational technology. It appears clearly from Fig. 1 that above a certain number of students in the system (N_o), the unit costs in distance education are lower than in traditional teaching.

This cost behavior suggests the taxonomy of new educational technologies given in Fig. 2. From an economic perspective, the differences between the two basic models are significant. The pupil–teacher ratio (it would be more correct to say pupil–labor ratio) in distance education is much larger, and that means that the cost of labor is lower than in traditional teaching; as a result, it usually more than compensates the additional costs of supplementary teaching inputs. (Distance education systems may be followed by working adults, and therefore have a reduction effect on forgone earnings, i.e., on private costs.) Finally, most of the study time is spent at home, and that reduces transportation and boarding costs.

2. Within-school Applications of New Educational Technologies

Two main objectives have pushed the introduction of new educational inputs in the context of schools. The first is to improve school performances in a context of relatively qualified teachers, in order to help at least a certain number of students who tend to fail through lack of motivation, family support, or adequate cultural background (language mastering, etc.). This model appears mostly in developed countries, where thousands of such projects have been implemented in the twentieth century. Tons of evaluation literature, poor and good, have been produced, but most are inconclusive on the effectiveness of such programs. The economic analysis of these projects has been dramatically neglected. In spite of the fact that the most costly programs, with motivated teachers, reinforced pedagogical teams, and access to a great variety of didactic supports, are likely to have measurable positive impact on school performances, there has not been a serious attempt either to relate these effects to costs, or to measure productivity changes. One of the pioneering countries in this field, Sweden, is experiencing a rapid decline in such use of educational technologies, as shown by Brusling (1982). This may be due, as Brusling argues, to new approaches in pedagogical ideologies, the use of technological devices being associated with an outdated Skinnerian and behaviorist theory, and to the development of more "participation-group-animation" types of pedagogical approach, in which hardware-type didactic inputs are used minimally. But another interpretation could be linked with the economic failure of these technologies, unable to demonstrate adequately any productivity increase. As a consequence, the tightening and shrinking of educational budgets in most countries, developed countries included, is rapidly killing these innovations.

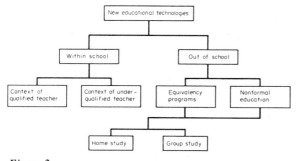

Figure 2
Taxonomy of educational technologies

Table 1
Cost effectiveness of some within-school educational projects

Project	Units for measuring N[b]	Value of N at time of study	Cost function in 1978 US$ at 7.5 percent discount rate	Average cost for given N in 1978 US$	Project impacts on		
					Pedagogical quality	Access	Cost per enrollment
Brazil Maranhão FMTVE[a]	Number of students reached per year	1976 N = 13,000	TC(N) = 1,551,000 + 116N	235.3	Improvement	Improves access to disadvantaged groups	Between traditional public schools and private
Brazil Ceára Educational tele. project[a]	Number of students reached per year	1978 N = 19,800	TC(N) = 971,000 + 87N	136.6	No effect	No effect	Slight decrease
Mexico Radioprimaria[b]	Number of students reached per year	1972 N = 2,800	TC(N) = 57,500 + 139.2N	160.0	No effect	Improves geographical access	38 percent decrease
Mexico Telesecundaria[c]	Number of students reached per year	1972 N = 29,000	TC(N) = 842,700 + 204.1N	235.7	Slight improvement	Improves geographical access	40 percent decrease
Ivory Coast PETV[d]	Number of students reached per year	1980 N = 700,000	TC(N) = 4,500,000 + 200N	206.4	Slight improvement	No effect	10 percent increase
Senegal PTS[e]	Number of students reached per year	1980 pilot project N = 400 Possible extension 140,000	TC(N) = 2,100,000 + 120N	135.0	Slight improvement	No effect	8 percent increase

a Arena A, Jamison D T, Oliveira J, Orivel F 1977 Economic analysis of educational television in Maranhão, Brazil. Mimeo (French and English). UNESCO, Paris. Also available in Portuguese (ABT–Av Erasmo Braga 255 grupo 401, Rio de Janeiro) and in Spanish in the *Revista de Centro de Estudios Educativos* 1978 8(1): 121–40. An updated version by Oliveira and Orivel (1980) has been published in two languages (English and French), with a comparison of a similar system. the Ceára Education Television system   b Jamison et al. 1978, Chap. 6 (on Mexico's *Radioprimaria*)   c Jamison et al. 1978, Chap. 11 (on Mexico's *Telesecundaria*). See also Mayo et al. 1975   d Eicher and Orivel 1980   e Orivel 1981

The second objective is to improve school performances in a context of underqualified teachers, either underqualified in general, or underqualified in specific fields. This case is more common in developing countries, where shortages in qualified teachers have been, and sometimes still are, particularly acute. From an economic point of view, the introduction of one or several audiovisual aids is supposed to compensate for the lack of teacher qualification, but in turn, such teachers ought to be paid less than regularly qualified ones. Unfortunately, this last assumption has been rarely verified, except in a couple of Brazilian projects (Maranhâo, at least in the beginning of the project, and Ceâra—see Table 1).

The two main media used in this context are television and radio. The focus was first placed on television (as in projects in the Samoa Islands, El Salvador, Mexico, Brazil, Ivory Coast, Niger, and Senegal) and later on radio (Nicaragua, the Philippines, and Thailand). As can be expected, radio is much cheaper than television and the risk of a negative productivity effect is much lower. The majority of these projects have shown a positive impact on school performances and on access to education of previously excluded children. The question of cost effectiveness is less clear, except that it is more likely to be positive with radio than with television.

Several of the above projects have already been closed (Tele-Niger, Samoa Islands, Ivory Coast). The Senegal pilot project will probably not be expanded, and the future of the Nicaraguan Radio Math is uncertain. In most cases, these closures are not due to a negative cost–effectiveness ratio, but to various sociopolitical factors. Even when financial difficulties have been emphasized, as in the case of Ivory Coast, they were actually minor compared with sociopolitical issues.

Table 1 summarizes some of the cost studies carried out on these systems and provides some evidence, mostly on within-school projects, where the basic auxiliary medium is television (except for Mexico's *Radioprimaria*). The cost–effectiveness performances of these projects is not clearly demonstrated. Except in Mexico, where the costs are lower for similar results, the four other cases do not bring decisive improvements: a slight gain in school performances is obtained at the expense of a slight increase in unit costs. The results are somewhat better in Latin America than in Africa for two reasons: (a) supplementary costs of television are lower than in Africa because this technology is entirely mastered by local resources, while in Africa costly expatriate specialists have to be hired; (b) the labor qualification substitution is better obtained in Latin America, while in Africa such a substitution has not taken place.

Subsequent similar projects, based on radio instead of television, have been tried in Nicaragua (Radio Math), in the Philippines, and in Thailand. Radio is much cheaper than television (Jamison and McAnany 1978, Perraton, Jamison, and Orivel 1982), and above a rapidly reached audience threshold, unit costs tend to be negligible. As a consequence, when significantly positive performances appear, as is clearly the case in these three projects, one can reasonably assume that one has a positive cost–effectiveness ratio (Suppes, Searle, and Friend 1980).

The main conclusions we can draw from these economic evaluations are the following:

(a) Within-school educational technology has not dramatically improved the cost–effectiveness ratio of educational services compared with traditional teaching.

(b) Radio is more likely to be cost effective than television, especially when carefully designed curricula are implemented.

(c) The labor qualification/media substitution, which assumes that underqualified teachers supported by media will be paid less to compensate media costs, is in most contexts unrealistic. Sometimes the opposite occurs: in the Ivory Coast, PETV's teachers have been promoted to higher salaries.

(d) The high death rate of within-school media projects is often due to teachers' rejection. This rejection may be explained by the rigidity of broadcast systems, and also by the fact that after some years of implementation, the underqualified teachers have assimilated the content of broadcast programs, and feel able to teach by themselves, without this now useless and constraining tool. Such an evolution may be seen as an unexpected result of this system, i.e., a successful inservice training of teaching staff.

(e) From an economic and organizational perspective, such a result implies that such projects should be conceived of as temporary institutions, using part-time external consultants (media specialists or curricula designers) instead of a full-time permanent staff.

3. Out-of-school Applications of New Educational Technologies

This field is the most promising area of the economically successful introduction of technology in education. While within-school technology is tending to decline, there is a rapid expansion of out-of-school systems, both formal and nonformal. There is a large variety of such systems, from simple and long-established correspondence courses to sophisticated multimedia projects, such as the now-famous Open University (UK), and in between, numerous nonformal educational projects in the field of hygiene

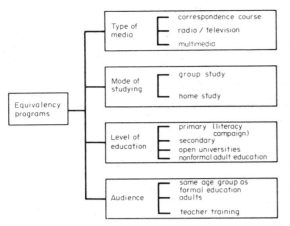

Figure 3
Classification of out-of-school use of educational technology

and health habits, agricultural information, family planning, literacy and numeracy campaigns, etc. Several classifications of these systems are possible, according to the type of media used, the audience, the mode of studying, and the level of education, as shown in Fig. 3.

3.1 Type of Media

From an economic point of view, the differences in costs between the simplest correspondence course and a sophisticated multimedia system are larger than the differences in effectiveness. The marginal productivity of each additional medium is therefore decreasing. But many authors argue that even if the additional impact of the last medium is lower than its costs, it may have significant external effects. For instance, in most open universities, the broadcasting of television programs is frequently considered by students as less important than printed material, in spite of the fact that it is substantially more expensive. But the broadcasting of these television programs generates useful external effects: large audiences, respectability, advertising possibilities, international recognition, and exports of didactic material and pedagogical expertise.

3.2 Mode of Studying

In contexts where the majority of the target audience owns a receiver for the broadcasted programs at home, the reception may take place on an individual basis (home study) but when this is not the case, the project has to organize a group study system, and to provide the receivers and the space. Very often the broadcasting is done early in the morning or late in the afternoon, when regular classrooms are available. But there are many alternatives to classrooms, such as a church or under a tree. Group study generally requires the presence of a monitor or "animateur,"

and is therefore more expensive than home study. On the other hand, group study provides more assistance, both from the monitors and from the peers (peer tutoring), and stimulates the motivation of students more efficiently. There is relatively little evidence on the respective cost effectiveness of both systems, and the choice is very often dictated by contextual constraints (for example, finances, distance, existence of qualified monitors).

3.3 Level of Education

Since it radically reduces the face-to-face component of traditional teaching, distance education is more likely to succeed with students able to show some autonomy in the learning process. As a consequence, young children are less able to follow these types of courses than older children and adults. In practice it is difficult to enroll in such systems children below the age of 15. From an economic perspective, this is approximately the age from which forgone earnings can be estimated as private costs. (This limit is actually lower in rural areas, and higher in developed countries, where the working age may begin at 16 or 18.) Furthermore, for young children, the formal school system plays an additional role, which one could call a "child care" role, provided at no cost by the formal system as a by-product. This service would no longer be free under a home-study distance education system, and the economic advantage of a larger pupil–teacher ratio in distance education would be lost for children who still need the permanent presence of an adult, teacher or nonteacher.

Nevertheless, in developed countries the rapid development of microcomputers and the fact that many households possess these microcomputers as well as video recorders will increase the possibilities of individual instruction, young children included. However, the most appropriate level of education for distance education is clearly the university level, at which students have a solid basic background and can study by themselves. The second clear field of distance education is in nonformal education aimed at adults (permanent education, lifelong education, etc.). Secondary education, especially at the senior level, and literacy programs for illiterate adults may be provided through distance education, but more easily with a system of group study than with a system of home study, in order to provide some minimal supervision and assistance (from the peers and/or from the monitor).

3.4 Audience

The audience of distance education systems may theoretically be composed of the same age groups as formal systems for equivalent programs, as they were originally considered as equivalency programs, aimed at pupils who have missed the formal system for reasons such as sickness, social background, excessive private costs, distance, motherhood, etc.

Distance education is a substitution system, some sort of second best to give a second chance to people excluded for nonacademic reasons. It is still exceptional to have a distance education system considered as a normal, regular, and fully competitive alternative to traditional schools or universities. Primary-school teachers are another common audience for distance education projects, especially in developing countries where they are often underqualified. Such systems allow the retraining of these teachers without formal meetings in a single place, thus avoiding potentially high transportation costs.

Table 2 provides cost information on 10 distance education projects. It does not include several other available case studies, such as the Open University, the French *Télé-Enseignement* or the Brazilian Logos II for inservice teacher training. In these three cases, as in 8 out of 10 cases in Table 2, costs per student and per graduate are lower than in equivalent formal systems, with similar results. The proportion of fixed costs within the total cost is important, often exceeding 50 percent and reaching 90 percent in the case of Everyman University in Israel. The importance of fixed costs in the projects reviewed here should be seen in conjunction with what is to be observed in traditional education where, for the most part, fixed costs and administration costs are the same thing, the latter, however, being less "fixed" on the whole than production costs in media-based projects. The administration component is only slightly sensitive to marginal changes in system size (the same administrative unit being able to cope with an increase of up to, for example, 20 percent in system size without having to increase its staff, and probably not needing to reduce its staff if system size is marginally reduced by, for example, up to 20 percent). On the other hand, a significant change in size necessarily involves a strengthening (or paring down) of the administration. Not only are the fixed costs of traditional education systems fixed only within a certain range, but they are also proportionally very low, administration costs rarely exceeding 10 percent of the total. This statement must however be corrected for certain institutional contexts. When teacher legislation does not allow the employing authority to relocate or dismiss teachers when reductions in staff are called for, labor costs tend to become almost a fixed item, which is possible only when it is the taxpayer who bears the bulk of education system costs (a private school without pupils would be obliged to dismiss its teachers).

Going back to the case of media systems, fixed production costs are real fixed costs. If a film costing $100,000 is seen by 1,000 pupils, the fixed production cost per pupil is $100; it if is seen by 10,000, the cost falls to $10 per head; if it is shown to 100,000 the cost is as low as $1; and if the number of viewers rises to 1,000,000 the cost per head falls to a negligible 10 cents.

This cost structure means that enrollment levels are of particular importance. For an equivalency program to succeed it must be assured of an appropriate minimum number of students over a long enough period. To take one clear example, the Kenyan project has probably reached a stage where it no longer has enough students to justify its continuation; the Bahia project probably never will, if we take into account the alternatives in Brazil, such as Minerva or *Telecurso*. It is, of course, impossible to set a precise figure for the minimum number of students as this varies from project to project. But at the level of secondary education, projects with fewer than 10,000 students per year are generally at risk, and this figure may be a good enough estimate for general postsecondary education. Specialized vocationally oriented projects whose audience is dispersed and working may sometimes be justified with far fewer students. In this type of project, seen quite often in teacher retraining, the closest conventional alternative would show particularly high unit costs, due mainly to:

(a) the need to assemble the participants in a single place, necessarily at a distance from where some of them reside;

(b) the need for participants to abandon their usual employment temporarily, and therefore to receive payment equal to their normal salaries;

(c) the additional cost of accommodation for nonresidents;

(d) possible cost of family accommodation, if the training course is a prolonged one, or the alternative psychological cost produced by the separation.

Under these circumstances the cost of the closest alternative is likely to be very high. In Kenya, for example, it was shown that the system could be economically justified if there were 2,000 enrollments for certificates.

In any event, the general figure of 10,000 should not be regarded as a magic threshold. The threshold will actually depend on four factors:

(a) the level of study (primary, secondary, higher, adult);

(b) the choice between radio and television;

(c) the cost of the closest alternative;

(d) the degree to which the capital–labor substitution is extended.

These factors are linked. It is in adult education that the costs of the closest alternative are likely to be highest and where it is easiest to go much further ahead with capital–labor substitution, since adults

1559

Table 2
Cost effectiveness of 10 out-of-school educational projects

Project	Units for measuring N	Value of N at time of study	Cost function in 1978 US$ at 7.5 percent discount rate	Average cost for given N in 1978 US$	Project impacts on			Cost per enrollment
					Pedagogical quality	Access		
South Korea Air Correspondence High School (ACHS)	Student enrollments	20,000	$TC(N) = 51,500 + 42.8N$	68.4	ACHS students do less well on tests but evidence suggests that this is because they start at a much lower level than regular high-school students	Improves access for students who must work to support themselves		The ACHS cost per enrollee is about 24% of the $250 annual cost of the regular high schools
Kenya inservice teacher training	Subject equivalent per year	1977 N = 790	$TC(N) = 165,850 + 114.8N$	324.7	Improvement	Improves access in rural areas		Though comparisons are difficult, can be considered high
Israel Everyman's University	Course enrollments (18 courses required for bachelor's degree)	8,000 in 1978 (26,000 in projected steady state)	$TC(N) = 5,286,500 + 81.7N$ (fixed costs are long-term steady state operation)	324.0 (284.0)	No evidence	Improves access for geographically and other disadvantaged groups		n.a.
Dominican Republic *Radio Escuela* Santa Maria	Student enrollments	20,000	$TC(N) = 187,000 + 10.7N$	20.0	Test results suggest that Radio Santa Maria students score as well as students in traditional adult schools even though they start further behind	Improves access in rural areas		Costs are about half those of traditional adult education for equivalency

Project	Output measure	Enrollment (N)	Cost function	Cost per unit	Quality	Access	Cost relative to alternatives
Brazil *Telecurso Secundo Grau*	Student enrollments	40,000	TC(N) = 5,632,100 + 53.4N	194.2	Improvement	Improvement	Between 25 and 67% of alternatives
Chinese Television University	Student full-time equivalent	186,000	Not available	Not available	No evidence	Strong improvement in urban areas	Clear indication of reduced cost
Brazil Minerva project	Number of subject equivalence a year	1977 N = 177,000	TC(N) = 907,120 + 19.7N	24.8	No evidence	Slight improvement from both geographical and social point of view	Between 0 and 50% decrease, according to the alternatives
Brazil Bahia *Madureza* project	Number of subject equivalence a year	1977 N = 8,000	TC(N) = 437,900 + 12.6N	67.4	Rather lower than other systems of preparation to *Madureza* exams	No effect	Between 50% and 1150% increase, according to the alternatives
Malawi Correspondence College	Number of students reached per year	1978 N = 2,800	TC(N) = 132,000 + 117N	160.0	Pass rates lower than in traditional schools, but students enter much less well prepared	Increases fractions of cohort enrolled; improves access in rural areas	The cost is 62% that of day secondary schools and 23% that of boarding schools
Mauritius College of the Air	Number of course enrollments	1976 N = 12,000	TC(N) = 143,800 + 1.98N	14.0	Probably improved quality in remote schools	No effect	Project costs are in addition to the sum of $77 per student per year which was given to the schools in which it was used

a Source: Jamison and Orivel 1982

are more capable than young children of studying alone with the media, unassisted by a teacher. In this type of situation, a relatively modest number of students, say in the vicinity of 2,000, will justify a well-defined radio or radio-correspondence project economically. On the other hand, at the primary and secondary levels, where the teacher is crucial, many more pupils are necessary (several tens of thousands, usually) before a positive cost–effectiveness ratio can be obtained, especially when television is the medium used. For these reasons it is important to look closely at the pupil target groups in a media project. Since many projects are experimental, or quasi-experimental, they involve small numbers of pupils, by definition, so that unit costs prove relatively high, since fixed costs must be spread over a small number of users.

Projects that use television have higher unit costs. But television makes only a small difference to total costs where, despite the use of media, projects still rely to a great extent on teachers (as in the two Mexican examples). An additional factor is that television costs vary greatly depending on whether the system utilizes an existing network at its marginal cost during off-peak times, or whether it operates its own transmitter and its own network of ground relay transmitters. For out-of-school distance teaching projects it is impossible to use television unless numbers of the intended audience already own receivers.

Most of the projects studied here are less expensive than equivalent traditional methods of education, especially if we take into account the fact that many of them are aimed at adults in employment who, by studying part time at a distance, avoid a loss of earnings while they study. This cost in salary would either be borne by the individual, who agrees to undergo training or retraining on a nonsalary basis (rare), or, as is more often the case, by the employer, who continues to pay the trainee's salary but must find a replacement and therefore disburse two salaries on a single occupied work slot. For many such students these equivalency program systems are the only available way of studying. There was, however, substantial variation among projects in the extent to which they were cost saving, as compared with traditional education. Since the costs of both electronic and printed media are declining relative to the cost of teacher time, cost advantages for distance teaching can be expected to increase in the future.

Equivalency program projects seem to have a clear and positive impact on educational equity, in terms of making quality education more widely available and of making access to any education at all possible for previously excluded groups.

The majority of projects in developing countries are relatively unsophisticated if one compares them to certain multimedia systems used in the developed countries (the Open University, for instance). This simplicity has proved a sound choice. It is clear that a systematic quest for programs of high artistic quality would have swung the cost–effectiveness ratio to the negative side, something particularly true of television-based systems. All the school television projects described here, except *Telecurso*, are the work of absolutely minimal production teams, perhaps 10 times smaller than similar professional groups in the high-income countries. The achievement of professional standards while maintaining a good cost–effectiveness ratio would be possible only if enrollments were far more numerous. In most cases, television personnel have gained their experience on the job, so that a certain amateurism is a feature of the production studios. If, instead of making do with modest local talent, reliance had been placed on a large complement of technicians from high-income countries, it is likely that, in the absence of a significant increase in enrollments, the cost–effectiveness ratio would again have been an inverse one.

4. Further Comments on the Economics of Some Specific Media

Several means have been introduced in conventional schools to improve the quality of teaching services. A common belief among educators is that the reduction of the number of pupils per teacher is the most appropriate solution to improve the quality of their teaching. From an empirical point of view, this point remains today highly controversial. Most studies do not show significant changes in student performances associated with class size. Some others tend to show that some slight improvements can be reached when the average number of students goes from 40 to 20, and more substantial improvements below, especially around 10, but this solution is clearly impractical in most developing countries because of its cost implications.

One word should be said concerning the provision of textbooks. It is not a new medium, but its cost–effectiveness ratio remains remarkable. In a school context where a substantial proportion of pupils have no access to textbooks (essentially for economic reasons), the free provision of textbooks has a relative small effect on the per student cost (in the range of 1 percent) and a significant impact on cognitive performances (a 10–20 percent improvement in test scores is not exceptional). A review is given below of the potential impact of the newer media used in classes, that is, radio, television, language, laboratories, and computers.

4.1 Radio

Radio is by far the cheapest means to reach a wide audience. A study on Malawi (Perraton, Jamison, and Orivel 1982) has shown that to provide relevant information and training to farmers, an hour of contact by radio is 3,000 times cheaper than face-to-face communication. When radio sets are widespread, the use of radio for informal educational programs is certainly appropriate. But it can also be used for in-class direct teaching in some fields, such as mathematics, when primary teachers are unsufficiently qualified, or for the retraining of teachers themselves. Finally, radio can be used for distance teaching systems, especially for equivalency programs (late secondary and postsecondary levels). This last point will be expanded below.

4.2 Language Laboratories

The introduction of language laboratories in school institutions in most developed countries has produced rather disappointing results. Their pedagogical impact is usually not statistically significant and the per student costs tend to be high. The hourly student cost is, for instance in the case of France, around US$4 (Orivel in press), of which half is due to the language laboratory itself, and half due to additional teaching staff, because the class has to be divided into two groups (the majority of classes being between 20 and 40 students). Furthermore, the utilization of these language laboratories follows the traditional school rhythm, instead of intensive periods of learning during a short period of time. This means usually 1 hour every 2 weeks, which tends to be too long an interval between two sessions to produce significant results. Very likely, the utilization of language laboratories will tend to encourage free access by students and a more intensive rate of utilization. It is also possible that language-teaching computers will be developed for autonomous learning (see the paragraph below on computer-assisted instruction).

4.3 Television

Great expectations were placed on the introduction of television programs in education. A wide range of experience has been gained around the world with uneven success. Today, the feelings of decision makers in educational systems concerning the advantages of using television in formal education are rather mixed. It is therefore necessary to try to clarify what we have learned from these experiences and what we can predict for the future.

(a) *The question of the costs and quality of television programs.* Table 3 shows, for 12 educational projects using television programs, the yearly number of program hours produced and the average cost of production of a one-hour program. Of course, some of these figures are out of date, but the most surprising overall result is the very large variability of the cost of a unit of output.

The nature of the programs produced in these different projects may vary considerably. In the case of Stanford University, it is a live production of a professor giving a lecture; while in the case of the Open University, one has sophisticated programs with professional standards similar to the British Broadcasting Corporation (BBC) programs (the television unit in the Open University is part of the BBC staff). In between, there are a variety of television productions, managed either by nonprofessional television people, mainly retrained teachers, or by semiprofessional or professional television specialists. Using professional television criteria, it is possible to find a close relation between the unit costs of these different television programs and their technical quality. But the relation between the cost and/or the

Table 3
Quantity and costs of different television programs[a]

Project	Number of hours of programs produced per year	Cost of a 1-hour program (US$ 1980)
El Salvador	333	5,665
Hagerstown (USA)	1,440	1,450
Telesecundaria (Mexico)	1,080	925
Korea, Republic of	n.a.	3,220
Stanford (USA)	6,290	175
Open University (UK)	288	18,150
Ivory Coast (formal)	201	25,900
Ivory Coast (nonformal)	17	51,200
Telecurso (Brazil)	75	53,800
Ceâra (Brazil)	300	2,750
Maranhâo (Brazil)	525	1,815
Senegal (TSS)	49	16,600

a Source: Evans and Klees 1976, formal Ivory Coast; Klees 1977, nonformal Ivory Coast; Klees 1980, *Telecurso*; Oliveira and Orivel 1980, Maranhâo and Ceâra; Orivel 1981, Senegal; Jamison et al. 1978 all others quality of educational television programs and their pedagogical impact is much less close. In any case, even if it were possible to show that technically good programs have a better pedagogical impact, there is no chance that the differences of impact may have the same range as of costs (1 to 300). This means that with a given budget constraint, it is rational to sacrifice some technical quality in favor of other educational material (especially books).

(b) *Computer-assisted instruction*. The recent development of microcomputing systems has raised great expectations. Nevertheless, their introduction in the educational systems has to be carefully evaluated. In spite of a rapid decline of the costs of the hardware, the costs per student remain relative high: most projects show hourly per student costs around US$4, and as long as the software costs cannot be shared by a great number of students, it is unlikely to have a positive cost–effectiveness ratio in the context of most developing countries in the near future, except for some specific reasons, namely: (a) the teaching of computer science should rapidly be undertaken, to avoid the building of a new gap between developed and developing countries in a strategic field; and (b) the teaching of foreign languages may very soon become cost effective with computers. That does not mean that developing countries themselves should invest in the development of this material, but they should be ready to use, at a relatively low marginal cost, what is implemented in this field in richer countries.

5. Conclusion

The economics of educational technology is a new field within educational sciences, but has already produced significant results which will probably affect the design of innovative educational projects. The shrinking of educational budgets, especially from public sources, makes the need for a better use of educational resources more urgent. The cost–effective allocation of educational resources means that one of the clear objectives of educational technology is the improvement of the productivity of the educational sector, and not only the improvement of school performances, regardless of its costs.

Within-school introduction of educational technology, to enrich traditional teaching, has been and still is the most common area of educational media. Nevertheless, this type of use has not produced dramatic changes in educational productivity (either negative or positive). In a context where the teaching staff is underqualified, especially in certain fields such as mathematics or foreign languages, the support of broadcast media may have a positive cost–effective impact, relatively often with radio, and sometimes with television.

But the main area where educational technology has been successful from a cost–effectiveness point of view is in the framework of out-of-school projects, for both equivalency programs and nonformal education, where the labor/media substitution has significantly taken place. In such projects, fixed costs are higher than in traditional teaching but variable costs, thanks to a larger pupil–teacher ratio, are lower, and when a large enough number of students are registered in the system to share the fixed costs, total unit costs are lower than in traditional teaching. Case studies on such systems have shown that most are indeed cost effective, in spite of the fact that this was not their original objective. This often unexpected result could therefore be achieved more demonstratively if this objective became more explicit, as will probably be the case with growing budgetary constraints. Optimization of media combination remains to be assessed, but after centuries of face-to-face teaching without any significant productivity change, education is now entering a new age, in which technology will play a growing role.

See also: Educational Technology: Conceptual Frameworks and Historical Development; Educational Technology: Personnel; Educational Technology: Training; Distance Education; Higher Education: Curriculum

Bibliography

Bowen H R 1980 *The Costs of Higher Education: How Much do Colleges and Universities Spend per Student and How Much Should They Spend?* Jossey-Bass, San Francisco, California

Brusling G 1982 Essor et déclin de la technologie de l'éducation en Suède. *Perspectives* 12(3): 7

Eicher J-C, Orivel F 1979 *L'Allocation des ressources à l'éducation dans le monde*. Office des Statistiques, UNESCO, Paris

Eicher J-C, Orivel F 1980 Cost analysis of primary education by television in the Ivory Coast. *The Economics of New Educational Media*, Vol. 2. UNESCO, Paris

Evans S, Klees S 1976 *ETV Program Production in the Ivory Coast*. Academy for Educational Development, Washington, DC

Jamison D T, McAnany E 1978 *Radio for Education and Development*. Sage, Beverly Hills, California

Jamison D T, Orivel F 1982 The cost effectiveness of distance teaching for school equivalency. In: Perraton H (ed.) 1982 *Alternative Routes to Formal Education*. Johns Hopkins University Press, Baltimore, Maryland

Jamison D T, Klees S, Wells S 1978 *The Costs of Educational Media: Guidelines for Planning and Evaluation*. Sage, Beverly Hills, California

Klees S 1977 *Cost Analysis of Non-formal ETV Systems: A Case Study of the Extra-scolaire System in the Ivory Coast*. Academy for Educational Development, Washington, DC

Klees S 1980 Cost analysis of Telecurso. In: Araujo J G, Oliveira J B (eds.) 1980 *Telecurso Ilè Grau*. ABT, Rio de Janeiro

Mayo J, McAnany E, Klees S J 1975 The Mexican Telesecundaria: A cost effectiveness analysis. *Instruc. Sci.* 4: 193–236

Oliveira J B, Orivel F 1980 Socio-economic analysis of two systems of educational television in Brazil in the States of Maranhâo and Ceâra. *The Economics of New Educational Media*, Vol. 2. UNESCO, Paris

Orivel F 1981 *La Télévision scolaire du Sénégal: Evaluation économique et perspectives*. DEDPH Discussion Paper No. 81–50. World Bank, Washington, DC

Orivel F in press *Critères technico-économiques pour la mise en oeuvre des média dans les institutions d'éducation*. UNESCO, Paris

Perraton H, Jamison D T, Orivel F 1982 *Mass Media for Agricultural Extension in Malawi*. International Extension College, Cambridge

Suppes P C, Searle B, Friend J 1980 *The Radio Mathematics Project in Nicaragua 1976–77*. Stanford University Press, Stanford, California

F. Orivel

Ecuador: System of Education

The Republic of Ecuador was founded in 1830, when the department of Southern Colombia separated from the Greater Colombia confederation, which also included Venezuela. Its name derives from its geographic location below the equator; this South American country borders on Colombia to the north and Peru to the south and east. The total land area is 272,258 square kilometers (105,120 square miles). The Galapagos Islands, one of Ecuador's 20 provinces, are located 1,200 kilometers off the northwest coast, in the Pacific Ocean. The country is crossed from north to south by the Andean ranges, which divide the continental territory into three regions: the coast, the highland or sierra, and the Amazon basin or oriental region.

The 1982 census put the population figure at 8,072,702: 3,944,172 located on the coast, 3,799,578 in the highland, 322,833 in the oriental region, and some 6,119 in the Galapagos Islands. Approximately 20 percent of the population is of white descent, 25 percent are Indians who live largely in the highland and the oriental region, 51 percent are *mestizo* groups of Spanish and Indian descent; blacks account for 4 percent. The population growth rate in 1982 was 2.6 percent.

Ecuador's history of human settlement goes back from AD 600 to 4,000 BC, to the establishment of the indigenous cultures of La Tolita, Chorrera, and Valdivia which achieved advanced levels of social and economic organization. During precolonial times, until the Spanish landings and conquests beginning in the mid-1520s, Ecuador became a part of the Inca empire or Tahuantinsuyo.

The social organization of the country has maintained an upper class made up of landowners and, more recently, financiers and industrialists. Middle-class growth became a phenomenon in the 1970s with an acceleration of social mobility brought about by the expansion and modernization of the economy.

However, it is estimated that approximately 40 percent of the population is located outside the mainstream of economic activity, living at subsistence levels.

The economy experienced a very rapid rate of growth during the 1970s, when the country became a net oil exporter. As a result, the gross national product (GNP) in 1981 stood at US$10.4 billion and per capita GNP was in the order of US$1,200. The gross national product composition reflects the decline of agriculture. Whereas in the mid-1960s agricultural activities made up 28 percent of GNP, by 1980 they represented 17 percent. Industry's share has remained steady at around 16 percent since the early 1970s. Petroleum production represents close to 15 percent of GNP. In 1982–83, economic activity declined sharply as a result of the widespread foreign debt crisis which caused a major decline in the country's foreign exchange reserves. Economic performance was also affected as a result of widespread flooding during the onset of the rainy season.

Ecuador's political life has been characterized by the alternative exercise of power by civilians and the military. A total of 18 constitutions have been written, the last one having been approved by the Ecuadorean people in a plebiscite in 1978. Government is divided into executive, legislative, and judicial powers. The form of government is unitary and the country is divided for administrative purposes into provinces and cantons.

1. Structure of the Educational System

The educational system (see Fig. 1) is made up of a primary level of six year's duration (ages 6–11); a secondary level also of six years, divided into a three-year basic cycle (ages 12–14) and a three-year upper level (ages 15–17). Primary-school attendance is compulsory, while public instruction is free at all levels. School entrants must be at least 6 years old.

Institutional strengthening has been a priority concern. In 1974, a major process of ministerial reorganization was put into effect, promoting the centralization of educational planning, control, and evaluation and decentralization in the execution of plans and programs which became the responsibility of the provincial directorates of education.

In 1981, 20 percent of primary schools were located in the urban areas and 80 percent in the rural areas. About 49 percent of enrollment was in urban schools and 51 percent in rural schools. On average, 3.5 teachers work in each school. In urban schools, the number is 8.7, whereas in the smaller rural schools it is 2.3. Average enrollment is 155 per school, with 311 students enrolled in each urban school and 83 in rural schools. The national student/teacher ratio stands at 36:1.

Enrollment is not universal. According to the most recent data, 25 percent of the 6 to 12 age group is

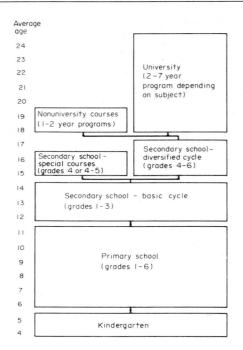

Figure 1
Structure of the educational system

not enrolled in school: 40 percent of rural school-age children do not attend school, whereas in the urban areas the proportion is 10 percent. The dropout rate is 57 percent from grades 1–6, but the differential between urban and rural areas is highly significant: 33 percent in the urban schools and 75 percent in the rural schools.

In the three-year basic cycle the program of studies is an extension of the primary level, whereas in the diversified cycle a number of specialization possibilities are offered to students in the liberal arts or in technical areas such as agricultural sciences, accounting, and vocational skills. Students who complete the program are awarded a *bachillerato*.

In 1982 there were 1,341 secondary schools in the country. Of these 49 percent were located in the highland area, 48 percent on the coast, and 4 percent in the oriental region. School enrollment stood at 535,445 in 1980. Of these 345,569 (64 percent) were in the basic cycle and 189,876 were in the diversified cycle; in this cycle 68 percent were enrolled in the liberal arts programs and 32 percent in the vocational tracks.

Approximately 72 percent of students who finish the primary level go on to the basic cycle. Retention is highest between the basic and diversified cycle, being 93 percent and overall secondary-level retention is 45 percent. From grade 1 to graduation from secondary school the retention rate is 14 percent.

Higher education is financed largely by the central government through corresponding appropriations in the Ministry of Education. However, by law, universities are autonomous in their management and administration, and they are free to set up their own self-governing mechanisms. Coordination is the responsibility of the National Council for Higher Education which, however, has no administrative or control powers.

University entry requirements include a *bachillerato*. There are 12 state universities (six on the coast and six in the highland) and five private ones (two on the coast and three in the highland). Enrollment stands at 263,000. Of these, 44 percent attend the state universities of Quito and Guayaquil, 12 percent are enrolled in the polytechnic schools of the above-named cities, and 12 percent in private institutions. Figure 2 presents the enrollment trends from 1960 to 1981 for each level of education.

The number of teachers stands at 11,186, giving a student/teacher ratio of 19:1. In state schools, the ratio is 23, in private schools 14. However, these figures hide the fact that practically all teaching is done part-time, and due to the pyramidal structure of enrollment, which is heavily concentrated in the first two years, there is crowding in the most sought-after fields: teaching and business administration.

Adult education and literacy education are integrated into the national system of education and include three programs: primary with three cycles of nine months' duration each, the middle level with basic and diversified cycles, each of three years' duration, and apprenticeship training which varies in accordance with the specialization.

There is a School of Higher Military Studies as well as other educational institutions in each of the branches of the armed services. These function apart from the rest of the educational system and have

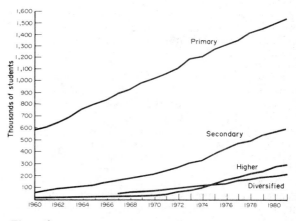

Figure 2
Primary, secondary, and higher enrollment trends, 1960–81

their own structure of supervision and control. Apprenticeship training is carried out by the Ecuadorean Apprenticeship Service (SECAP).

2. Finance

Education's share of the national budget has increased from 16 percent in 1963 to 21 percent in 1971 and to a constitutionally mandated 30 percent in 1984. As a proportion of GNP, education expenditures make up 6 percent. Education is financed largely with public funds. Investment outlays, mostly for construction, are channeled through the National Directorate of School Construction (DINACE). The allocation of public funds by level is 21 percent for higher education, 31.5 percent for the secondary level, and 39.2 percent for primary.

Approximately 90 percent of resources are used in current expenditure, largely for payment of teachers' salaries. School materials and transportation expenses are financed by the students, and schools often charge nominal fees. Private education constitutes an important component of the overall education effort, particularly in the coast region, where the public system is unable to meet the ever–increasing demand for schooling. Thus, private instruction is not solely a phenomenon of elitism and by and large private schools have second-rate facilities or teaching staffs.

It has been estimated that Ecuador's overall financial effort in education is about one and a half times that revealed by the allocations in the government budget. Educational expenditures have a slight regressive tendency in the middle to upper income range.

3. Teacher Training, Curriculum Development, and Certification Procedures

Primary-teacher training is carried out in the so-called higher normal schools, which are two-year postsecondary teacher-training programs. Secondary-level teachers are trained in the schools of education, where they go through a full-fledged university curriculum leading to the degree of *licenciado* and then Doctor of Education. There are no comparable programs for training university faculty since all training is professional with no academic specialization.

Although curricula for primary and secondary levels are unified, textbooks differ from place to place. Normally, textbooks are written by the most able and qualified teachers, but these are largely freelance efforts as there is no official sponsorship of textbook writing. Distribution of texts is carried out through local bookstores and through the system of bookstores of the Ministry of Education and the National Association of University Bookstores.

Program control is exercised through a network of supervisors in the Ministry of Education. Control is also maintained through the approval of the "questionnaires" for final examinations. No national achievement test is administered to students.

Ecuadorean education is bereft of an adequate base of support for the research and development of innovative teaching techniques. Teaching methods are traditional, with little interaction of teacher and students in the classroom. Dictation and memorization are preferred teaching techniques. Teaching aids such as audiovisual materials are scarce.

At the university level, the swelling of enrollment due to an open-door admissions policy has compounded the problems of organization and achievement of recognized academic standards in the institutions of higher education. Except for the polytechnic schools in Quito and Guayaquil which are making a serious effort in the quest for academic excellence, university instruction is weak in analysis and scientific inquiry and strong in memorization and political content.

Evaluation of student performance and promotion to the next higher grade is based on examination results. At the primary level, the rules for grading and promotion are not set on a uniform basis, but at the secondary level the final grade is based on the combined results of the final exam and the quarterly examinations. The same system, with variations, is adopted in higher education.

The system of examinations in Ecuador is judged by a number of local experts as a highly conventional and traditional structure for promotion. Emphasis is put on rote learning and memorization as measures of learning rather than on the acquisition of analytical skills. The evaluation procedures are therefore not integrated and do not reflect the overall learning capacity and individual formation of the student.

4. Educational Research

Most of the effort of educational research has been geared to the collection of primary information and statistics. In the 1970s, however, there was a significant surge in the number of qualitative and quantitative research studies undertaken by independent researchers, sometimes in association with the Ministry of Education, and usually sponsored by international organizations.

The following topics were the focus of educational research at the beginning of the 1980s: teacher training and upgrading; evaluation of the educational system; school-learning determinants; human-resources development for education; evaluation of the educational plan; sector analysis of education; and costs, financing, and efficiency of education. New areas of research include curriculum development, teaching methodology, teaching aids, biculturalism and education, and certain areas of educational psychology.

5. Major Problems

The main current and future problems of Ecuadorean education can be summarized as follows:

(a) the maintenance of an adequate and improving educational effort with a population growing at the rate of 2.6 percent per annum;

(b) the adoption and implementation of new guidelines to renovate the educational system and to make it forward looking;

(c) the coordination and planning of higher education in accordance with the requirements for high-level human resources. Overcoming the current notion of university autonomy remains a major stumbling block;

(d) the adoption and execution of a wide-ranging teacher-training scheme;

(e) the upgrading and equipping of school facilities;

(f) the improvement of rural education and its assimilation to a modernizing society.

Bibliography

Ecuador, Ministerio de Educación y Cultura 1975 *Analisis sectorial de la educación ecuatoriana.* Ministerio de Educación y Culturo, Quito

Ecuador, Ministerio de Educación y Cultura 1980 *Bases para la reestructuración del sistema ecuatoriano de educación.* Ministerio de Educación y Cultura, Quito

Swett F X 1979 *Los factores determinantes de la escolarización y aprovechamiento en la educación ecuatoriana.* National Planning Board of Ecuador, Quito

Swett F X 1979 *El financiamiento y los costes de la educación ecuatoriana en los niveles primario y secundario.* National Planning Board of Ecuador, Quito

F. X. Swett; S. Carrasco Toral

Education Through Service

Service and helping others as a voluntary activity have long been a familiar social phenomenon in many countries. But service *as* education—or even credits obtained through service—is a comparatively recent development. Its integration with the curriculum is even newer. Perhaps for that reason outstanding examples can be drawn equally well from developing as from industrialized countries.

This article will not attempt to review the full variety of patterns which service can take, primarily by youth but involving people of all ages, but will concentrate on those aspects of service that have an educative effect, not only in regard to awareness of what the concept means and responding to actual situations of need, but particularly in regard to its impact on attitudes and feelings. Typical terms for these programmes are study service and service learning.

1. The Mix—Serve and Learn

People engage in service for a variety of reasons—the influence of example, indignation, companionship, religious conviction, career exploration, enlightened self-interest, fulfilment of an inner need to feel wanted—or for a mixture of motives. But if education is to be a stimulus for, and consequence of service, its undertaking cannot be left to chance: it has to be consciously planned.

The nature of the "mix" may be crucial. In Tuscany, for example, ambulances are manned by a nongovernmental agency, with its members, unpaid, being available day and night on a rota basis. The ambulance stations become in effect social centres; but recreation is incidental: rescue is the pivot.

The same criterion may apply to businessperson's organizations which include service amongst their aims. If their approach becomes overritualized, if geniality and mutually beneficial contacts result in token grants to charitable causes rather than in a more profound penetration of the problems which beset their neighbourhood, then not only is their impact on needs reduced, but there may even be a loss of sensitivity to those needs. Both service to others and its educational effect on the givers may actually stagnate.

Many youth organizations provide for some form of service in their programmes, but in order that exposure to the problems of others should not be unduly disturbing, service is combined with the acquisition of skills, self-reliance, and adventure. Insofar as feelings are enriched if they include responding to the joys as well as the sorrows of others, their hopes as well as their frustrations, this view of service commands respect. But if the element of service is so diluted that it becomes peripheral then methods and priorities should be reviewed.

2. Full-time Service

There are circumstances when it becomes important for people to break away from a reasonably comfortable, self-centred existence to plunge full time into the problems of others. Sometimes, in fact, the needs of the disadvantaged can be met in no other way than by a period of total commitment. The United States Peace Corps, Volunteers in Service to America (VISTA), Frontier College, CUSO, and the Katimavik programmes in Canada, Community Service Volunteers and Voluntary Service Overseas in the United Kingdom, and Australian Volunteers Abroad are examples of this pattern. Full-time service often coincides with a bridging gap in young people's lives, between high school and college, or after graduation from university. In these situations what is educationally advisable and what is useful for those needing help interlock so that both volunteers and those with whom they work benefit equally.

Curiosity about conditions in other situations, a desire to test abilities to cope with exacting demands, and a hope that the experience will be challenging are contributory factors for people offering service. One observer notes, "volunteers come to learn as well as to teach". The fullest value is attained when participants neither keep this experience to themselves, as something intensely personal, nor see themselves just as agents of technical assistance—but rather act as *animateurs*, spreading the ethos of service amongst those whom they are teaching or training, so that they establish a chain-reaction of helping. Then education and service become not only reciprocal but on-giving processes.

These young people might be regarded as advantaged in having the opportunity to serve full-time. But availability is not solely a matter of good fortune: employers can create availability as a planned policy of training or career development. The period may not be so long: the impact of service, however, should be measured, like other seminal experiences, not by its chronological duration but by its intensity. Police cadets in the United Kingdom have been attached for three to four months, as an integral part of their training, to reformatories and remand homes: by accepting responsibility for the welfare of the youngsters in their charge they learn that rehabilitation may be more demanding than making arrests; that delinquents do not belong to a separate subspecies of the human race; and that in the 1980s, in order to operate effectively, the police have to win the confidence of the public—which includes the young.

Central government departments in London are beginning to release promising civil servants in their late 20s for six-month assignments to battered wives' refuges, to hostels for the homeless, to beleaguered inner-city schools, in order to deal with people rather than paper, to discover the impact of legislation on real-life problems, and to apply their administrative skills to tackling community needs. IBM, Xerox, the Bank of America, and other corporations, in releasing staff for comparable attachments, have recognized that no amount of role-playing or simulations during company-organized training courses can compare with the influence of this kind of experience on personal attitudes and values. They loan, gratis, the managerial or technical skills of their personnel to perform a service: they receive back staff who have a deeply enhanced understanding of human relations and social issues.

3. New Sources of Service

Of greater significance still, perhaps, has been the number of young offenders, many from maximum security institutions administered by the Prison Department in the United Kingdom, released towards the end of their sentence to engage in a period of community service. They learn of others in trouble worse than theirs and of their ability to give help and gain the gratitude and respect of staff and patients. It has generally been assumed that a samaritan conscience is a precondition for altruistic action: now it is evident that it may in fact be a consequence of immersion in help to others. The implications are far reaching (Dickson 1980).

4. When Service is Obligatory

Mere exposure to situations of need does not automatically arouse an enduring sense of empathy. Experience has shown, for example, that it is important to allow police cadets, who must give service as part of their training, to express a preference for a particular field of action—for with choice comes commitment.

Many people find unacceptable the idea that service undertaken as a requirement or duty can have educational value. But commonly held expectations influence attitudes. In the United States young Mennonites and Mormons grow up expecting to be involved in a period of service. Young people in the Federal Republic of Germany who look after the sick, old, and handicapped in the Alternative Service (which is mandatory for conscientious objectors) show that they care genuinely for those whom they tend. Since all young people are obliged by law to attend school until the age of 16 in many countries, perhaps involvement in service could become an intrinsic (and attractive) part of their educational experience.

5. Service Approaches Through Schools

In school settings, for students of all ages, several approaches have proved their worth in stimulating service and creating awareness of human needs. Teachers use newspapers to develop a "seeing eye" amongst students, so that they quickly discern, especially in local items of news, situations where they might intervene to ameliorate distress. "Exercise Empathy" is one where, for example, students experience the difficulties which handicapped people face in addition to their physical disability, such as, using a public telephone, boarding public transport, or entering a library; and then begin persuading the authorities to improve access. This exercise is most effective when undertaken alongside the genuinely disabled. Another activity enables students to identify "ordinary" citizens who endure daunting experiences—a wife caring for a paralysed husband, or a parent bringing up a child with Down Syndrome, or a miner who years ago risked his life in rescue work. They discover thereby that heroes are not just historical figures, but can be living yet unacknowledged in their own community. Reciprocity—where, for example, recently arrived immigrant students visit local elderly people living alone, the one practising conversation in the language of the host country, the other enjoying companionship—enables each party to receive and give service.

Civil and other emergencies—certain to increase in frequency and intensity everywhere—can be used to educate through service. A sudden influx of refugees, floods, or other crises have frequently offered teachers and students a chance to cope with the unexpected as a team.

Some of the examples quoted earlier—though valid responses to needs which both stimulate awareness and an ability to cope with problems—have borne little connection with the formal school syllabus. Dangers then arise. Abler students may be excused from participation lest it may impair their academic hopes. In no time service work is reduced to a subject in its own right, reserved often for early leavers, devoid of any intellectual challenge. In comprehensive schools in the United Kingdom there is a tendency for sports and community service to be timetabled for the same afternoon, the boys opting for the former, the girls for the latter, thus perpetuating the stereotype of males demonstrating their virility in physical competitiveness whilst caring is left to the women.

But when helping and service are linked with learning, when what is being studied is related to problems of significance to the community, the way is open for one of the most effective of all approaches to education through service—"the humane application of knowledge" (Thelen 1970). Thus in Salford, near Manchester, secondary schools have—as an integral part of woodwork, home economics, handicrafts, technical drawing, and so on—invented and made over 300 different pieces of equipment for the disabled, each custom-built for an individual adult or child, each involving a face-to-face encounter which often develops into personal friendship (Whitley 1980). The greatest lesson for educators is, of course, that humanitarian concern and intellectual challenge are not necessarily in mutual conflict: service can, indeed, stimulate study and bring understanding born of personal experience. That most forms of knowledge have a commercial relevance and/or military significance is a commonplace: however, it has scarcely begun to be perceived that virtually every subject in the curriculum is capable of a humane application and linkage with service projects.

6. Service while Learning

Hitherto the view has been held, professionally and academically, that it is only *after* graduation, *after* completing a required course, that a person becomes qualified to assist others. But in the oldest form of training (one that still flourishes in many countries)

apprentices have created or contributed even as they have acquired their skills. The new interpretation of social apprenticeship now gaining credence is that it is possible for people to serve as they learn, and learn from their serving.

At the level of higher education this approach assumes even greater importance. What in the United States has become known as Service Learning—UNESCO prefers the phrase Study Service—has much in common with experiential education (see *Experiential Learning for Adults*). Both provide a bridge between the worlds of study and work; both help to develop more practical graduates; both enable students to relate their subjects to real life, to communicate with people of different backgrounds, to exercise personal initiative, and to cope with situational problems. In experiential education, however, students are the chief beneficiaries; Service Learning, on the other hand, is concerned additionally with what students have given, with the kind of contribution they have made to those in need. Study Service, at its best, is a happy fusion of clients' practical needs and students' learning needs.

Study Service activities are found in many countries (Fussell and Quarmby 1974). The approach of Hong Kong Polytechnic entails the commitment of a whole institution to developing technology to help the community; for example, electronics students adapted a scanning system to illumine a number of Chinese characters, thus enabling children with cerebral palsy to communicate. Several developing countries (e.g. Tanzania and Nigeria)—disillusioned with their graduates' reluctance to work where they are most needed—now require them to serve for a year in rural areas. These mandatory programmes stem generally from decisions reached by frustrated governments rather than through action initiated by the academic authorities.

More recent tendencies may be less visibly dramatic but more intrinsically radical. One, noticeable in India (e.g. Mysore and Aligarh Muslim University), is recognizing how far the problems of the surrounding area should determine the focus of university courses and research, with students and staff working in the field alongside villagers and slum dwellers to find solutions.

Institutions of higher education are beginning to accept additional responsibility in acting as resource centres for their neighbourhood or nation. Whilst many prestigious ones are apt to claim that the pursuit of excellence in teaching and research represents their contribution to society, others believe that they should pursue three integrated goals—teaching, research, and service. This last role, of outreach, is often left to students of extramural, continuing education, and extension service departments, thereby reducing the effectiveness of the whole institution to serve the community, and gain strength from the experience. Nevertheless new trends may bring education and service closer together. When institutions perform two functions—for example, university college hospitals combine the training of medical students with the treatment of patients—then the distinctions between learning and helping, between service and work, are less important.

7. Service as a Unifying Experience

When governmentally funded service programmes are set up to help the unemployed, two things are vital: first, that human energies are matched against urgent, genuine needs (as with the American Civilian Conservation Corps in the 1930s); second, that the educationally and socially advantaged should also participate, joining in common endeavours and sharing talents and experience with those in less favourable circumstances. Service should not be left to the losers.

Learning outcomes from service work may not necessarily advance careers or personal well-being. To go to the help of those in need, or to identify oneself with the oppressed, is to incur danger. Education through service, and for service, calls for high-risk educators.

8. Requirements for Promoting Education Through Service

(a) Current problems such as drugs, violence, loneliness, racial tension, which are yielding neither to expert advice not costly programmes, require new inputs of imaginative activity.

(b) Comparable insight into the potential for service is needed by individuals and groups hitherto seldom used—for example, pupils as partners, clients as colleagues, the handicapped as helpers, the retired as resource persons.

(c) Existing institutions of education/training should be utilized as untapped sources of service to the community, no less than companies, constabularies, and so on.

(d) Provision should be made for growth in the patterns of service, so that students are progressively challenged as they develop in age and maturity.

(e) There should be an inclusion in the preparation of educators, social workers, government administrators, and others not only of an element of service but, still more importantly, experience of how to involve others in service.

(f) The child to child movement has shown how in developing countries the very young can care for infants. Tutoring—where an older pupil or student in a "cross-age" relationship individually helps another having learning difficulties—not only benefits both parties, it embodies the heart of education through service. It could enrich every school in the world.

See also: Experiential Learning for Adults

Bibliography

Chickering A W 1977 Experience and learning. *Change Magazine Press*, New Rochelle
Community Service Volunteers 1975 *The Experience of Giving: Borstal Boys*. Community Service Volunteers, London
Dickson A 1980 *Study Service: Problems and Opportunities*. UNESCO, Paris
Eberly D, Sherraden M 1982 *National Service: Social, Economic, and Military Impacts*. Pergamon, Oxford
Fussell D, Quarmby A 1974 *Study-service, a Survey*. International Development Research Centre, Ottawa, Ontario
Goodlad S 1975 *Education and Social Action: Community Service and the Curriculum in Higher Education*. Allen and Unwin, London
Goodlad S 1979 *Learning by Teaching*. Community Service Volunteers, London
Thelen H A 1970 Comments on "What it means to become humane". In: Scobey M M (ed.) 1970 *To Nurture Humaneness: Commitment for the 70s*. Association for Supervision and Curriculum Development Yearbook. Association for Supervision and Curriculum Development, Washington, DC
Thomas D 1978 *The Competitive Ethic and the Pacific Way*. University of Waikato Press, New Zealand
White R 1981 Humanitarian concern. In: Chickering A W (ed.) 1981 *The Modern American College*. Jossey-Bass, San Francisco, California
Whitley P 1980 *Enquiry into Study Service in Higher Education in the* UK. Community Service Volunteers, London

A. Dickson

Educational Facilities

It has been known for a long time that human beings are both consciously and subconsciously affected by their environments. Winston Churchill phrased this interrelationship aptly when he said, "We shape our buildings and then they shape us." The physiological and, to some extent, psychological effects of the built environment in terms of heat, light, sound, and space have been explored and documented. However, research has not yet supplied complete answers about the effects of the built environment on human attitudes and behavior. Although most designers demonstrate an awareness of the ways people are "shaped" by spaces they occupy, their work is based largely on personal preference, imagination, and intuition rather than on the results of systematic research.

Space as a design factor in learning environments has assumed new meaning. Those concerned with programming, planning, and designing educational facilities can no longer assume a set of fixed conditions. Due to program variables and differences of setting, educational practice now requires new forms and new geometry in the design of contemporary school buildings. The techniques for controlling an environment of fluid dimension and changing character, an environment that incorporates a variety of sizes, shapes, and ambient qualities, are considerably different from those used in controlling a fixed and uniform condition.

Planning a school building is becoming more and more complicated due to such factors as (a) technological developments, (b) changing populations, (c) cost control needs, (d) the integration and complexity of engineering factors, and (e) energy conservation needs. In addition, landscape architecture and site planning are also becoming more important as traffic, transportation, and parking needs increase, and as outdoor activity areas are becoming more specialized and complex.

The composition of the planning team is becoming more complicated too. In addition to administrators and policy makers in the educational system, specialized consultants, committees of educators and teachers, special interest groups, and citizen groups need to be involved. These groups combined with governmental reviewing and regulatory agencies that deal with health, safety, sanitation, traffic, insurance, space, and functional adequacy must be a part of the school building planning team.

The planning process has become more and more complex. This is not due to significant changes in the process itself, but is related more to the application of the process. The involvement and participation of a multitude of actors add to this complexity. Coordination of the various groups by the planning team complicates the task and extends the amount of time necessary to achieve the final product.

Generally, school facility planners are striving to do a better job of planning, designing, and constructing buildings to accommodate educational programs. But there is a danger of overdesign. Care should be taken to guard against tailoring a facility too closely to a program without allowing for the changes that may result from changing goals, emphases, programs, communities, personnel, or for changes stemming from the inventiveness and imagination of competent educators.

1. Environmental and Functional Characteristics

There is an increased awareness about the environmental and functional aspects of school buildings. All too often school buildings have been planned, designed, and constructed without due regard to the quality of the physical environment. This is due partially to a limited amount of research in this area.

In one study 10 functional characteristics were identified (Landes and Sumption 1951) that have a profound impact upon the quality of school buildings. These characteristics have been extensively used as guides throughout the world by planners and designers of learning spaces. These 10 characteristics are:

(a) Adequacy—the relationship between the size of site and the overall housing space and the number of students to be served.

(b) Suitability—includes those features, such as type of plant and facilities available, that enable the school to satisfactorily house a specified educational program.

(c) Safety—those features that make the building structurally sound and protect its occupants from hazards of traffic, fire, and accidents.

(d) Healthfulness—the degree to which pupils are ensured freedom from dirt and excessive noise and are provided with satisfactory facilities for lighting, heating, ventilation, and sanitation, and a plentiful and convenient supply of water.

(e) Accessibility—the proximity of the school to the pupil population center, the character of approaching roads and streets, and general access features to the building.

(f) Flexibility—the possibility of change, as incorporated in the construction of the building and the development of the site, to meet new demands as the program changes.

(g) Efficiency—the amount of pupil travel, convenience of custodial facilities, isolation of noise, and location of facilities to obtain maximum utilization.

(h) Economy—the achievement of proper plant operation at minimum cost by fully utilizing natural light and conserving heat, electrical energy, and water.

(i) Expansibility—the possibility for enlargement of the building and site to meet educational needs.

(j) Appearance—the landscaping, color harmony, appropriateness of furnishing, and use of decoration to serve the aesthetic needs of occupants.

To improve the environmental condition of school buildings, techniques have been employed to enhance the contribution of space to educational program needs. A design of space that provides for change, modification, and adaptation must use flexibility as an organizational concept. Flexibility requires attention to the potential alterations of mechanical services, that is, heating, ventilating, lighting, and plumbing systems. Care should be taken, when applying the flexibility concept, not to carry it to the extreme. Too much flexibility can lead to a lack of commitment which, in turn, can result in structures that are without character, indistinguishable, and undistinguished.

Ugliness can become a pervasive element to users of the physical environment. Hence, it becomes important that individuals develop an ability to recognize and appreciate beauty in both the built and natural environments. School buildings can become hallmark examples for aesthetic aspects of learning and living. It is essential that schools are planned, designed, and constructed to contribute to the aesthetic development of the user and to respond to an elemental need for and appreciation of what is pleasing and beautiful. Attention must be given to color, texture, line, and form in the structure of the building itself, and to the incorporation of many art forms and decor.

A good visual environment permits fast, accurate, and comfortable vision—an essential condition in the communication of knowledge. Level of illumination is not the only factor that produces good lighting. Balanced brightness in the environment and the elimination of glare contribute to visual accuracy and comfort too. When designing a good visual environment, illuminating engineers take into consideration size, configuration, contrast of object and background, and the distance from the viewer.

A primary consideration in planning the visual setting is to encourage the use of effective and efficient illuminating systems. Not all lighting systems use energy efficiently. Not all designs of space maximize the use of natural illumination. It is possible to overlight an environment and to create inadequate levels of glare-free illumination relative to energy consumed.

Lighting should create a mood as well as make objects visible. It should create an ambience whereby the users are warm, comfortable, and pleased, yet it should be effective, economical, and energy conserving. If human needs are not met, the users either suffer under poor illumination conditions or devise ways of combating and overcoming unpleasant aesthetic situations.

Since contemporary education programs often require multiple uses of space, acoustical problems have increased in complexity and magnitude. A good acoustical environment responds to two needs: (a) the control of sound within a specified space so that what is to be transmitted can be heard and (b) the prevention of intrusive and unwanted sounds from outside the space. Acoustics are affected by the use of space, its size and shape, its relationship to other spaces and activities, its location within the school building, and the proximity to sound-producing objects on, or adjacent to, the school site. Through the improved knowledge about the science of acoustics, it has become possible to determine, within reasonable limits, what materials and shapes will enhance good acoustical qualities. Prevention of unwanted noise and control of undesirable sounds

has been possible through a variety of techniques and materials. Zoning, for example, for both the site and the building, has been employed on the premise that prevention is better than correction. Acoustical materials for noise reduction and reverberation control have been successfully applied by planners and designers. Research and development in the field of acoustical materials was stimulated by the popularity and application of the open space design concept.

The thermal environment is currently receiving widespread attention throughout the world. Variations in climate and the need to conserve energy have encouraged research and development aimed at solving some of these severe and compelling problems. Hence, the planner's objective is to provide an economical, energy-conserving, healthful, comfortable, controlled environment. This often involves balancing one need or priority against another and selecting the most advantageous alternative.

The goal in creating a thermal environment that does not create excessive energy demands is to maximize uncontrolled or unwanted heat transfer through the building shell. Successful efforts have been realized through the use of effective thermal materials and through design that gives full consideration to natural environmental conditions.

2. Emerging Concepts of Planning

Historically, educational systems were planned principally for the purpose of "schooling" or "teaching" children. Often planning occurred in isolation from the communities the schools were meant to serve. Evolving today is a new emphasis on planning as a dynamic process to better serve clients.

School-building planning is in a state of change in response to many factors. There are changes in goals and values, technology, knowledge about the human race, population numbers and their distribution, and emphases in education. Hence, there is a need to address the sources and content of such changes while planning an educational environment.

3. Design Considerations

Care should be taken to allow for differences between primary- and secondary-school students. Architecture should reflect differing needs. A relaxed, homelike situation should be available which compares with that from which primary-school students come. The environment should encourage the children to live, work, and play together with materials and equipment. The design of facilities for the very young should emphasize use by this age group, permitting every object to be child oriented and child sized. The secondary school on the other hand is a much more complex institution. It is generally much larger than the primary school in both size and enrollment and must accommodate a broader range of learning needs.

If space is to motivate, inspire, and satisfy all learners, it must be accessible, versatile, and adaptable. Well-organized and well-designed spaces allow for maximum participation in total group activities with a minimum of distraction and frustration, and encourage self-directed and self-selected experiences.

A school building must meet the needs of each student as an individual and must exist not simply as an administrative or organizational convenience. It should permit individuals to be organized into groups of appropriate size for learning purposes. Likewise, specialized facilities for program areas such as the arts, physical education, vocational training, and special education must allow for good communication, display, performance, and movement as well as for joy, edification, and appreciation.

The school building should not be at its best when it is new, but it should mature, change, and improve with use. It need not be perfect at all times; obsession for spotlessness may inhibit initiative and kill creativity. The school building should be a place of freedom, freedom without license, freedom to be oneself under proper discipline, freedom to experiment within limits, and freedom to do things poorly on occasion.

Safety in the school building is critical and must extend beyond basic protection from fire, smoke, and fumes, and protection from hazards caused by vehicles, machines, equipment, and other hazards. Special consideration should be given to the safety requirements of the physically handicapped.

School buildings ought to be hallmarks of excellent architecture in the community. They should reflect the best examples of what can be built based upon superior planning with an eye to function and effectiveness. The emphasis should not be on luxury, but on good quality.

School buildings are places of many moods. There should be spaces for play and for contemplation, for groups and for individual privacy. There should be spaces of many shapes and sizes—tall, low, large, and small. They should contain a variety of finishes and materials, not all hard, durable, antiseptic, sterile, and unyielding. Some space should have softness and be pleasant to touch, feel, and see.

People are the most important factor to be considered in school design and planning. The relationships and interactions among people—teachers, pupils, parents, administrators, staff, and public—are the most essential aspects of the environment of a school. The facilities (site, building, and equipment) should not get in the way of the learner, nor deter, discourage, or prevent high achievement. School facilities must enhance the relationships among people and provide them with the proper setting and necessary tools and equipment to help them develop.

4. Trends for the Future

While no-one can precisely predict what education in the future will be like, it is possible to distinguish some clear trends that will have effects on the architecture of educational buildings and the design of facilities. Since the early 1970s, the Council of Educational Facility Planners, International commissioned a group of planning and design experts to formulate a set of predictions about the future of school buildings. The following discussion is based upon the commission's report which appeared in the *CEFP Journal* (Burr 1970).

Perhaps the major trend educationally will be an emphasis on individualized learning. To plan and design school buildings to meet the needs of individualized learning, architects will need to translate and interpret this educational philosophy into brick and mortar. No longer will a school building be designed with a certain number of cubicles—classrooms—to handle a given number of students. In the past, classrooms implied boxes, both visually and mentally. Buildings of this design became commonplace in most parts of the world during the twentieth century. If change is to take place, moving away from standardized settings to those which deal genuinely with individual differences, then the design of the physical environment for education will be dramatically altered.

A second major trend will be the changing role of the teacher and its impact on school buildings. The commission suggested that the teacher will:

(a) become a manager of the education program and learning process;

(b) provide counseling and motivational support;

(c) listen to small group discussion;

(d) develop and manage instructional materials;

(e) seek out and organize learning experiences in the community; and

(f) manage assistants.

In addition, the teacher will orchestrate the use of new forms of high technology such as microcomputers. Obviously, these functions imply flexible settings where learning takes place in group sizes unlike those considered normal during most of the twentieth century. School facilities will have to offer a vast assortment of learning situations and adapt to frequently changing technologies as well as to diverse schedules of individual students. In these schools, new concepts of time and space will emerge.

It is possible that many learning experiences currently housed in school buildings may be moved into the community. The learning process for students will be organized around places and events under the control of teachers functioning in managerial roles. If this third trend is carried to the extreme, schools of the future will be places for brokering and managing instruction as well as centers of learning.

Educational facilities may not need to include shops or other trade-related learning opportunities. Education will not be contained within the walls of a school building but be based upon and involved with the entire community. Schools will become a base of operations, with constant movement to and from the building.

Future trends in education may have a profound effect upon the functional relationship of most traditional learning activities to the school building and, thus, affect the facilities design. The learning path (flow of physical movement) of a student through time will change. It is possible that classes will not change en masse from one situation to another at a designated time. The concept of quiet, flowing situations—with students coming and going individually and in small groups—will evolve. This change is extremely significant in architecture, for it ushers in a variety of new choices regarding shapes, spaces, and facility usage. It will, for example, increase the efficiency of school buildings because it will no longer be necessary to commit 15 percent or more of the building for halls and student passageways. Likewise, student transportation needs will be dramatically changed, suggesting major shifts in the design and operation of school sites to accommodate modifications in transportation.

These trends may result in an entirely different setting for housing and managing educational programs. Regardless of the scope and form of school buildings, the need for flexible and adaptable space will continue. The speed with which such trends develop will vary across the nations of the world consistent with cultural changes and economic and political conditions. The rates of adoption of new educational philosophies and methods have historically been uneven among countries as well as within individual nations. It is likely to be so in the future as far as school buildings and facilities are concerned.

See also: Learning Environments; Physical Plant: Planning for Educational Use

Bibliography

Burr D F 1970 New trends in education. *CEFP Journal* 8(5): 7–14
Council of Educational Facility Planners, International 1982 *Guide for Planning Educational Facilities*. Council of Educational Facility Planners, International, Columbus, Ohio
Landes J L, Sumption M R 1951 *Citizens Workbook for Evaluating School Buildings*. Brown, Dubuque, Iowa

D. Gardner

Educational Organizations: Micropolitics[1]

Both practitioners and theorists tend to regard administration as an essentially rational process. Although the current emphasis on contingency theory recognizes that effective patterns of administration are relative to the contexts in which they are to operate, there remains the fundamental assumption that if plans are well-conceived, clearly set out, and adequately communicated, then systems can be improved. Yet everyone working in organizations is all too well-aware of their often idiosyncratic, adventitious, unpredictable, and intractable nature when every day brings a new organizational "pathology" to disrupt well-laid plans. This uncertainty occurs at the highest levels of policy making and implementation. In his much cited work on the Cuban missile crisis Allison (1971) showed that what had been interpreted as the outcome of carefully considered and rationally enacted policies could be viewed as the result of actors within a highly uncertain situation bargaining within their own camps as well as across national boundaries. Policy makers and administrators in the less lethal field of education will recognize the aleatory dimension of the institution—described by Kogan (1975) as "pluralistic, incremental, unsystematic, and reactive"—as they attempt to improve the service in conditions which appear to be perennially turbulent.

The question to be considered is whether social scientists have explored sufficiently all dimensions of institutions as a source of explanation of what, within the prevailing paradigms of social science research, appears to be irrational, adventitious, and peculiar to a unique setting at one point in time. It is the purpose of this article to suggest that there is one dimension of organizations which has been largely ignored in administration and organization theory. This can be referred to as the "micropolitics of organizations". It is an organizational underworld which everyone recognizes and in which everyone participates. It is acknowledged when one speaks of "organizational mafias", "hidden agendas", "playing politics", and "Machiavellianism". Micropolitical activity is engaged in by the very administrators who profess a rational theory of administration. Yet it is very rarely made the focus of academic study.

There may be good reason for the academic neglect of micropolitics. It is perhaps considered slightly unrespectable, or too self-indulgent, or a threat to conventional administrative theory—which it is—or as having no practical application—which it may not. Or it may be that it simply is not a single dimension of organizations at all but a range of different processes

1 This article originally appeared in *Educational Management and Administration*, Vol. 10, 1982. It is reproduced by permission of the British Management and Administration Society.

each best handled separately through existing bodies of theory and research.

The sections which follow deal with the hypothesized domain of micropolitics, reasons for its omission from the major approaches to the study of organizations and their administration, the approaches to organization and administrative theory which deal to some degree with micropolitics, and implications of micropolitics for the training of administrators.

1. The Domain of Micropolitics

Micropolitics embraces those strategies by which individuals and groups in organizational contexts seek to use their resources of power and influence to further their interests. This might seem to be simply a definition of administration. It is true that the relationship between administration and micropolitics is symbiotic in that in practice they are inextricably linked, but it can be hypothesized that there is some measure of independence. Administrative theory focuses on structures and the associated processes of power, decision making, communication, and so on. But the space between structures is occupied by something other than individuals and their motives. This "other" consists of micropolitical structures and processes. It is characterized more by coalitions than by departments, by strategies rather than by enacted rules, by influence rather than by power, and by knowledge rather than by status. The micropolitical dimension may be largely shaped by the formal structure—which may well be the dimension which best accounts for organizational activity—but it is nevertheless worthwhile reversing the traditional approach by perceiving the micropolitical as the "figure" and the administration as the "ground" to explore whether this throws a different light on the operation of organizations. Such a procedure would lead to a focus on the major elements of micropolitics: interests, interest sets, power, and strategies.

Politics are inevitably concerned with interests. Administrative theory often underestimates the plurality of interests in organizations because it tends to be attuned to organizational goals as determined by the leadership. That there are interests other than those of organizational effectiveness has of course long been taken into account by most administrative theories, but they nevertheless tend to be treated as recalcitrant, a suitable case for leadership, or socialization or coercion. It is beyond the scope of this article to offer a taxonomy of interests, but any classification would at least include personal, professional, and political interests. Personal interests would include autonomy, status, territory, and rewards. Professional interests involve commitments to particular forms of practice: curriculum, pedagogy, organization, and so forth. Political interests

involve a commitment to certain macro- or party-political policies. It is easily seen that, taking these three areas of interest alone, it is difficult to disentangle the personal, the professional, and the political at a substantive level. The tendency is perhaps for personal or political interests to be presented in terms of the professional, since normatively this is the most "respectable" form of interest in education. Thus a proposed innovation which threatened the territorial interests of a teacher might well be resisted by mobilizing "professional" arguments against it. Similarly, political interests can be presented as professional interests. However, it can be seen that here even the conceptual distinction is very difficult to sustain. In institutions other than education the distinction between personal and political interests is blurred. The conceptual difficulties are particularly acute when "the micropolitics of macropolitics" is considered, where the question is whether X is espousing a political interest per se or as a means of pursuing a personal interest in a political career.

Interests are pursued by individuals but frequently they are most effectively pursued in collaboration with others who share a common concern. Some of these may have the qualities of a group in that they are relatively enduring and have a degree of cohesion, but others—which are perhaps best referred to as interest sets—will be looser associations of individuals who collaborate only infrequently when a common interest comes to the fore. Some interest groups will be coterminous with formal organizational groupings, for example departments or teams. These will be particularly strong. Others will transcend formal boundaries and will form when a common interest has to be pursued. The basis of group or set association may be age, sex, professional interests, politics, union activity, etc. Burns (1955) distinguished between cliques which are committed to sustaining the status quo and cabals which are committed to organizational change.

Coalitions have been the focus of attention of a number of writers. Selznick (1957) has made a sociological contribution to their study. Bacharach and Lawler (1980) review the major sociopsychological theories of coalitions before offering their own theory which is essentially a sociopsychological approach to the political dimension of organizations. They define a coalition as "a grouping of interest groups who are committed to achieving a common goal". In turn, interest groups are defined as "groups of actors who are aware of the commonality of their goals, and the commonality of their fate beyond simply their interdependence with regard to the conduct of work".

Some interest groups will be permanently mobilized; interest sets will mobilize as and when their interest becomes salient. Components of the formal structure will remain the most powerful set of groupings in an organization, but there is at least a case for viewing an organization in terms of the alternative structure of shifting interest sets which, in fact, interpenetrate with the formal organization at many points.

Power is one of those social science concepts which refer to an important social phenomenon but about which there are theoretical and empirical disputes which are likely to remain unresolved. Given the libraries of works on power produced by political scientists, philosophers, sociologists, and social psychologists, it would be impossible to review the complex theoretical and methodological issues involved in this article. Thus the remarks made will be those of particular relevance to micropolitics.

The distinction between two major aspects of power are important. Authority is the legally supported form of power which involves the right to make the decisions and is supported by a set of sanctions which is ultimately coercive. Influence is the capacity to affect the actions of others without legal sanctions. The distinction is conceptually important but difficult to sustain empirically because, since authority can be latent, it is difficult to establish when control is exercised through influence or through latent power. However, the distinction between authority and influence remains potentially useful since the power deployed in micropolitics frequently takes the form of influence in which interest sets will draw on resources other than those of authority to achieve their ends.

Administrative theory tends to focus on authority which has its source in the hierarchical structure of the organization. Micropolitical theory would give greater prominence to influence. Influence is derived from a number of sources, for example personality (charisma), expertise, access (especially to information), and resources (material or symbolic). Influence differs from authority in having a number of sources in the organization, in being embedded in the actual relationships between groups rather than located in an abstract legal source, and is not "fixed" but is variable and operates through bargaining, manipulation, exchange, and so forth.

The headteacher in England and Wales has a high degree of authority; but his or her exercise of this authority is increasingly modified as teachers' sources of influence through expertise, access to symbolic resources, and so on, increase and thus involve the head in a greater degree of exchange and bargaining behaviour (Hoyle 1981). These are the aspects of power which are the appropriate focus of micropolitics.

Micropolitics takes account of the strategies used by interest sets to attain their ends and gives these greater attention than formal procedures. Organizational politics have been insufficiently studied to yield a systematic taxonomy of such strategies although there are good individual studies. For example, Pettigrew (1973) identified four strategies used

by a group of programmers to protect their interests: norms which denied the outsider's competence, protective myths, secrecy, and control over recruitment and training. Handy (1976) discusses a number of protective strategies such as the distortion of information, the imposition of rules and procedures, and the control of rewards. There is little discussion of micropolitical strategies in educational organizations. As an example: a college may have a "collegial" structure, but the principal, caught in the dilemma of all who would manage pluralistic organizations, that is, the reconciliation of legal authority and the expectation of participation, may indulge in micropolitics in order to cope with this dilemma. Thus he or she may attempt to handle situations by "losing" recommendations from working parties by referring them to other groups in the hope that they will disappear or become transformed, "rigging" agendas, "massaging" the minutes of meetings, "nobbling" individuals before meetings ("I'm glad you see it my way, I hope you'll make your views known at the meeting"), "inventing" consensus ("Well, we all seem to be agreed on that") when consensus has not been tested, "interpreting" the opinions of outside groups ("The governors would never accept it"), and so forth. As Noble and Pym (1970) discovered, "collegial" organizations are characterized by a "receding locus of power". The course of power is difficult to identify in a collegial organization. The principal can draw on his or her resources of legal power, but other members of staff have their own resources.

Thus micropolitics involves a study of interests, interest sets, power, and strategies. These are intimately related to the more formal aspects of an organization which is the main focus of much administrative theory, but the political dimension of an organization constitutes an alternative focus for understanding organizational processes. However, from the brief discussions of these four components in this section it can be seen that it is likely to be a conceptually and methodologically complex area of enquiry.

2. The Neglect of Micropolitics

Theories of organizations and administration are relative (that is, products of their place and time), partial (that is, in adopting one theoretical perspective others are excluded since a total perspective is not a possibility), and normative (that is, to a greater or lesser degree they are infused with values).

The dominant paradigm in organizational and administrative theory is one in which political aspects do not easily fit. Although it is a great oversimplification to group all prevailing theories within one paradigm, and although it is impossible to do justice to the diversity of existing theories, some broad points can be made in order to illustrate the reason for the neglect of micropolitics.

Current organization theory has two origins: Weber's theory of bureaucracy and early theories of management. These two strands converge and diverge at many points in the development of theory. Sociological theory in the Weberian tradition is potentially concerned with understanding organizations; management theory is potentially concerned with improving them. However, theories of management need to be based on understanding if they are not to be merely recipe theories, and organization theory has not retained a detached purity since its protagonists have also been concerned with improving organizations in various ways: their efficiency and the quality of life of participants. Hence they share a common paradigm which can be termed the maintenance paradigm. The major lineaments of this paradigm are its metatheory which assumes that the social world is, to a greater or lesser degree, rational, amenable to scientific study, and predictable. Its perspective on organizations follows from this in emphasizing the centrality of structure, the legal authority inherent in that structure, a relatively high degree of integration and systemness, participants who will continue to be committed given an appropriate mix of rewards, and conflicts which are either "creative" or arise from some malfunction of the structure or leadership. The associated management theory is concerned with the effective use of resources, maximizing the fit between organizational goals and personal needs, and an organizational responsiveness to contingent conditions in the environment. The theory of change inherent in the model is essentially that of planned change whereby adaptation to a changing environment is handled by structural changes and the retraining and resocialization of participants. Overall the paradigm views organizations in a top-down manner.

The operation of the maintenance paradigm in education can in a gross oversimplification be summarized as follows: educational organizations—schools, colleges, universities—have to cope with changes in their environment: cultural, technological, economic, and political changes of various kinds. Political changes are initiated at the macropolitical level and tend to focus on the allocation of resources, legal enactments, and overall structure with rather less focus on matters of curriculum and pedagogy. It is assumed that practitioners will interpret these external changes in an attempt to keep in balance the interests of society and the interests of clients. Hence the expectation is that innovation will be professionalized rather than politicized. In order to equip institutions and practitioners to cope with the professional demands of innovation, programmes of professional development, organizational development, and the development of interpersonal skills have emerged. The appropriate strategy of change,

within the coercive strategies of national and local government, is considered to be a mixture of rational and re-educative approaches.

A major alternative is the action paradigm which again has a complex history and embraces a wide range of perspectives so that to bring them together under one heading is to oversimplify. The lineaments of the action paradigm are as follows: its metatheory holds that the social world is nothing other than the construction of the minds of people and hence has no objective reality "out there". Social life is sustained because people through their daily interaction and their language, create intersubjectively shared meanings. These meanings may be relatively persistent and perhaps come to have the appearance of objectivity but, in fact, as people continue to solve the problems of their daily lives, they can voluntarily construct new meanings. It follows then in strict terms there can be no action theory of organizations since organizations are not "objects" but social constructs, and the meanings attached to them will differ according to one's perspective. The action theorist is interested in activities within what are conventionally termed organizations because he or she is interested in how participants construe organizations and their processes. He or she treats as "problematic" the organizational structure and administrative processes which organizational theorists take for granted. As there can strictly be no organization theory, there can likewise be no theory of management since management is only a constructed label for a group of organizational processes dominated by those who have resources of power which tend to become problematic only if treated phenomenologically. It should follow that an action perspective is neutral in relation to change since it is a paradigm more concerned with understanding the world—or, more precisely, understanding others' understanding of the world—than with initiating change. Its active contribution to the change process is the assumption that social theorists of this persuasion should work with practitioners at any level of the organization helping them to clarify their own perspectives, helping them to question what had previously been taken for granted which then becomes potentially amenable to change. Thus it generally encourages an "active" stance on the part of participants. Whoever the process consultant is, however, independent of management he or she may profess to be, ultimately he or she is concerned with improving organizational functioning in relation to the goals of management. The action theorist tends to be orientated towards enabling the lower participants to perceive the possibility of reconstructing the organization in ways alternative to that perceived as "effective" by management. In short, action theory, like maintenance theory is relative, partial, and normative. Yet there is more potential within the action perspective for focusing on microplitical activities since these are actions which can be made the strict focus of enquiries and not treated as pathological or deviant activities.

What can be termed the radical change paradigm has political activity at its centre. It is concerned with understanding the social world in order to change it in accordance with a set of political beliefs. This perspective is strongly Marxist in orientation. Again, at the risk of great oversimplification, the following are some of the main characteristics of this approach: the metatheory may, according to the particular view of Marx taken, share the same view of the world as the maintenance theorists, in that it is taken that there is an objective world out there which is amenable to scientific understanding and control via the manipulation of structures and the socialization of individuals, or the action theorists. Essentially it is not an organization theory but a broad sociopolitical theory in which organizations are seen as arenas in which occur the clashes between the prevailing ideology and the alternative radical ideology. Thus the political transformation of organizations is a necessary step towards transforming society. This is captured in the phrase about "the long march through the institutions" which became prevalent in the late 1960s. Thus there is no management theory as such, only a theory-in-waiting. Current theories of management are held to be simply theories supportive of the capitalist hegemony. There are theories about using "the organizational weapon" in the period of transformation but only when the transformation occurs can a radical, egalitarian, and democratic theory of organization—"management" is perhaps a tainted word—emerge. Although this perspective certainly has political concerns, organizational politics are subsumed within macropolitics, with micropolitical activities which do not obviously contribute to the political transformation of the organization being regarded as pathological.

3. Approaches to Micropolitics

The chief elements of micropolitics: power, coalitions, strategies, and interests have been the focus of studies in a number of social science disciplines. In social psychology there has been considerable study of interpersonal power particularly in group settings. However, the sociopsychological study of organizations has been largely concerned with problems of leadership and communication and is clearly located within the maintenance model. Weick (1979) is an exception to this trend in that he has concerned himself with the "negotiation" of organizational order, but the focus has not been directly upon the micropolitical. The concern of political theorists has been games, choice, and coalitions (Brams 1975, Laver 1981). They have tended to be concerned with establishing formal theories rather than with understanding political activity in vivo.

There are a number of sociological approaches which, though not focusing directly on micropolitics, are nevertheless concerned with relevant issues. Of particular significance is exchange theory which is predicated on the assumption that many aspects of social life are explained in terms of the implicit and explicit bargains struck between groups which, though they may be different in relation to the degree of relative power which each has, necessarily needs to reach an accommodation with the other in order to serve their mutual interests (Homans 1958, Blau 1964). Other sociological theorists of organizations, particularly Selznick (1966) and Gouldner (1954a, 1954b) attended to the "dysfunctional" elements in organizations which were often the outcome of the pursuits of group interests rather than organizational interests via what are here being termed as micropolitics. However, neither has pursued the implications of this in the direction of making micropolitics central to his analysis. Selznick resorted to classical functionalism and although Gouldner was to come to adopt a radical view of social institutions, this was developed within a Marxist rather than a micropolitical framework.

In decision-making approaches to organization, Simon's (1964) notion of "bounded rationality" is concerned with the boundary between rational and nonrational aspects of social behavior. The "nonrational"—which would now, in these postphenomenological days, be referred to as "alternative rationality"—relates to the activities which have been referred to as micropolitical. However, in the theories of March and Simon (1958) organizational analysis remains well within the maintenance framework in noting these aberrant behaviours as evidence that organizations do not in fact function according to the rational model.

Three organizational theories which are more directly concerned with micropolitics can be noted.

The first is that the later work of March who now appears to have brought what was earlier considered to be "nonrational behavior" in the decision process, that is, micropolitics, to the centre of the stage. In *Ambiguity and Choice in Organizations* (March and Olsen 1976) he and his colleagues concentrate less on how decisions ought to be made if they are to conform to canons of rationality, than on how in fact they are made. What is described is how decisions, which are rarely the clear-cut events usually described, emerge out of a complexity of micropolitical activities. They advance what is now their well-known "garbage can" model of decision making:

Although choice opportunities may lead first to the generation of decision alternatives, then to an examination of the consequences of those alternatives, then to an examination of the consequences in terms of objectives, and finally to a decision, such a model is often a poor description of what actually happens. In a garbage can situation, a decision is an outcome or an interpretation of several relatively independent "streams" within an organization.

They consider four streams which might go into the "garbage can" model:

(a) Problems—these are the personal problems of participants as they relate to such matters as pay, status, promotion, personal relationships, families, and even the problems of humankind.

(b) Solutions—they reverse the normal view of solutions and see them as sometimes preceding problems. They cite the installation of a computer in an organization which may represent a solution to problems not yet conceived. In the educational context one could conceive a new curriculum or a plan for school-focused inservice training generating new problems rather than solving existing ones.

(c) Choice opportunities—these are occasions such as those when a new member of staff is to be appointed or where a responsibility allowance is to be allocated which generate behaviour which can be called a decision.

(d) Participants—individuals come and go and their different attributes will shape the outcomes which are termed "decisions".

The rates, patterns of flow, and confluence between these four streams shape certain organizational events which come to be labelled as "decisions". March and Olsen write of organizations "running backwards" in the sense that organizational events are the outcome of bargaining, negotiating, and exchange and only after they have occurred is their history "rewritten" by managers to give them the appearance of having been the outcome of a rational decision-making process.

Crozier (1964) has long been interested in how power and influence operate in organizations and has developed the view that organizational processes are best understood by focusing not on formal organization and power as a commodity but on the games which individuals and groups play in order to solve problems and in which power is treated as a bargaining relationship. He argues for a change in paradigm. Thus the research problem is to explore how different systems of games can solve the problems which organizations face. He believes that the way forward is to learn more about current games in all forms of organization and the forms of regulation inherent in these games. This will be best approached by case and comparative studies at the present time with the prospect of formalization and measurement left until the future. Crozier has written (1975 p. 186):

> The dominant paradigm revolved around the basic question concerning the structure: how contextual variables

determine the basic structural features of an organization and how these features command the behaviour of the members and the performances of the organization. The new paradigm emerges first around the idea that the contextual features of the organization should not be considered as variables determining the structure of the organization, but as problems to be solved, and second around the idea that structure is not the necessary nodal point of the organization, but that the games with their rational mathematical features as well as their human parameters will be a much more concrete and rich focal point.

Bacharach and Lawler (1980 p. x) set out their concerns as follows:

> An understanding of organizational politics requires an analysis of power, coalitions, and bargaining. The power relationship is the context for political action and encompasses the most basic issues underlying organizational politics. As the primary mechanism through which individuals and subgroups acquire, maintain, and use power, coalitions crystallize and bring to the foreground the conflicting interests of organizational subgroups. Through bargaining, distinct coalitions attempt to achieve their political objectives and protect themselves from encroachments by opposing coalitions. Power, coalitions, and bargaining, therefore, constitute the three basic themes in our theoretical treatise on organizational politics.

They review the existing literature and argue that in sociological studies there has been too great an emphasis on formal structure and power and that the traditional social psychology of oganizations has tended to focus on motivation, leadership, and so forth and has thus ignored the political nature of organizations. They therefore focus on the activities of work groups, such as departments and interest groups (i.e., groups of actors with common goals which are not necessarily coterminous with work groups), and coalitions (i.e., groups of interest groups which engage in joint actions against other interest groups). On the basis of a detailed analysis of power, authority, group formation, and bargaining, they develop a formal theory incorporating over 100 hypotheses.

In sum, there have been a number of approaches to the study of micropolitics but at the present time they cannot be said to constitute a coherent body of theory. The question is whether such a coherence is likely to be achieved and, if so, what its contribution to the study of educational administration might be.

Empirical studies of micropolitics are extremely rare. Some exceptions are Thompson (1967), Pettigrew (1973), and Mangham (1979) but none of these studies were conducted in educational organizations.

4. The Prospects for Micropolitical Studies

This article is based on the assumption that a considerable gap exists between the organizational world which is presented in theory and research and the organizational world which everyone experiences. This gap is acknowledged by administrators who gain little help from administrative theory because it is not of their world, or at least it relates to a rather sanitized version of the world in which they function. The gap is also increasingly recognized by theoreticians and researchers who have become somewhat disenchanted with the prevailing paradigm but are not wholly happy with the action and radical change alternatives. Thus the importance of the micropolitical world is existentially acknowledged. The question is: can it be captured by the theories and methods of the social sciences and, if so, will what is learnt be of value to practising administrators?

The answer to the first of these questions must remain tentative. There are two basic levels of answer. One relates to the fundamental problem of the social sciences of whether in principle a knowledge of the social world can be attained by the methods of objective enquiry. There are three broad positions: a knowledge of the social world is in principle impossible, that it is possible only through an understanding of the meaning which actors ascribe to situations, and that the social world is, in fact, knowable by the procedures of the natural sciences. If the assumption is made that it is, in principle, knowable, then it has to be asked how it might be knowable. It could be argued that the micropolitical world is so ideographic, idiosyncratic, contingent, and volatile that in practice it cannot be grasped. It could be further argued that it is indeed of this character but it can be grasped in its particular concrete setting via a detailed case study, although generalizations are very difficult to achieve in practice. Or it can be argued that the micropolitical world is amenable to study by the methods of the social sciences which permit generalization.

If the latter position is taken, then two things have to be said. One is that "the real stuff" of micropolitics is particularly elusive. As it has been shown, different approaches focus on different components of micropolitics, so the interactive nature of power, coalitions, interests, and strategies is unclear. However, if studies that concentrate on one or other aspects are carried out in an effort to clear the way towards formal, testable theory, then the configuration disintegrates. Thus there is a choice between case studies proving rich data and formal studies providing generalizable findings. The inevitable conclusion is that both approaches should proceed, if, indeed, it is worthwhile pursuing at all the study of micropolitics in education.

If it is concluded that it is worthwhile to conduct research into the micropolitics of educational organizations, by whatever method, it has to be asked whether the outcome is likely to improve the practice of educational administration. Would it, in fact, provide theory-for-understanding or theory-for-improving? It would appear more likely to provide theory-for-understanding. Studies of micropolitics could well bring the area much more into the arena of open discussion, but it is not easy to see in what ways this might improve the quality of administration or the quality of life in educational organizations for participants. It is even more difficult to see how the outcome of the study of micropolitics would feature in courses for practising administrators other than as a general mirror-raising component and as theory-for-understanding. In what sense could it contribute to improvement of skills? It could form the basis of various forms of simulation and games, but the degree of transfer from gaming to practical decision-making contexts must be somewhat dubious. And even if it were possible to teach micropolitical skills to practising administrators, this would, to say the least, generate some obvious moral issues.

Micropolitics are, therefore, difficult to embrace within the conventional theory, research, and training patterns of educational administration since administrative theory is normatively oriented to rationalizing order and control and eliminating the alternative world of micropolitics.

See also: Theories of Educational Organization: Classical; Theories of Educational Organization: Modern; Organizational Climate in Schools; Management Theory: Reconciling Professional and Administrative Concerns in Education

Bibliography

Allison G T 1971 *Essence of Decision: Explaining the Cuban Missile Crisis.* Little, Brown, Boston, Massachusetts
Bacharach S B, Lawler E J 1980 *Power and Politics in Organisations.* Jossey Bass, San Francisco, California
Blau P M 1964 *Exchange and Power in Social Life.* Basic Books, New York
Brams S J 1975 *Game Theory and Politics.* Free Press, New York
Burns T 1955 The reference of conduct in small groups: Cliques and cabals in occupational milieux. *Human Relations* 8: 467–86
Burrell G, Morgan G 1979 *Sociological Paradigms and Organisational Analysis: Elements of the Sociology of Corporate Life.* Heinemann, London
Crossman R 1975 *The Diaries of a Cabinet Minister,* Vol. 1: *Minister of Housing 1964–66.* Hamilton, London
Crossman R 1977 *The Diaries of a Cabinet Minister,* Vol. 2: *Lord President of the Council and Leader of the House of Commons, 1966–68.* Hamilton, London
Crozier M 1964 *The Bureaucratic Phenomenon.* Tavistock, London
Crozier M 1975 Comparing structures and comparing games. In: Hotstede G, Kassem N S (eds.) 1975 *European Contributions to Organisation Theory.* Van Gorcum, Assen, pp. 193–207
Goffman E 1969 *Strategic Interaction.* University of Pennsylvania Press, Philadelphia, Pennsylvania

Goffman E 1971 *Relations in Public: Microstudies of the Public Order*. Basic Books, New York

Goffman E 1974 *Frame Analysis: An Essay on the Organization of Experience*. Harper and Row, New York

Gouldner A W 1954a *Patterns of Industrial Bureaucracy*. Free Press, Glencoe, Illinois

Gouldner A W 1954b *Wildcat Strike*. Antioch Press, New York

Greenfield T B 1975 Theory about organization: A new perspective and its implications for schools. In: Hughes M (ed.) 1975 *Administering Education: International Challenge*. Athlone Press, London, pp. 71–99

Greenfield T B 1980 The man who comes back through the door in the wall: Discovering truth, discovering self, discovering organisations. *Educ. Admin. Q.* 16(3): 26–59

Handy C B 1976 *Understanding Organisations*. Penguin, Harmondsworth

Homans G C 1958 Social behavior as exchange. *Am. J. Sociol.* 63: 597–606

Hoyle E 1981 The process of management. *Management and the School*: Block 3: *Managerial Processes in Schools*. Open University Press, Milton Keynes

Kogan M 1975 *Educational Policy-Making: A Study of Interest Groups and Parliament*. Allen and Unwin, London

Laver M 1981 *The Politics of Private Desires*. Penguin, Harmondsworth

Mangham I L 1979 *The Politics of Organizational Change*. Associated Business Press, London

March J G, Olsen J P 1976 *Ambiguity and Choice in Organizations*. Universitetsforlaget, Bergen

March J G, Simon H A 1958 *Organizations*. Wiley, New York

Noble T, Pym B 1970 Collegial authority and the receding locus of power. *Br. J. Sociol.* 21(4): 431–45

Ouchi W G 1981 Markets, bureaucracies and class. *Admin. Sci. Q.* 25: 129–41

Pettigrew A M 1973 *The Politics of Organizational Decision-making*. Tavistock, London

Selznick P 1957 *Leadership in Administration: A Sociological Interpretation*. Harper and Row, New York

Selznick P 1966 TVA *and the Grass Roots: A Study in the Sociology of Formal Organization*. University of California Press, Berkeley, California

Silverman D 1970 *The Theory of Organisations: A Sociological Framework*. Heinemann, London

Silverman D, Jones J 1976 *Organisational Work: The Language of Grading, the Grading of Language*. Collier Macmillan, London

Simon H 1964 *Administrative Behavior: A Study of Decision Making Processes in Administrative Organization*, 2nd edn. Collier Macmillan, New York

Thompson J D 1967 *Organizations in Action: Social Science Bases of Administrative Theory*. McGraw-Hill, New York

Urban G 1981 The perils of foreign policy: A long conversation with Dr Zbigniew Brzezinski. *Encounter* pp. 13–30

Weick K E 1979 *The Social Psychology of Organizing*, 2nd edn. Addison-Wesley, Reading, Massachusetts

Willower D 1980 Contemporary issues in theory in educational administration. *Educ. Admin. Q.* 16(3): 1–25

E. Hoyle

Educational Research and Policy Making

Educational research has two constituencies of practitioners: (a) teachers and school administrators, and (b) policy makers in education. Classroom practitioners expect educational research to help them improve the planning and execution of teaching. At the turn of the century the emerging psychology with its empirical and experimental methods was expected to provide guidelines for educational practice by identifying the facts and laws of learning, and by providing an understanding of individual development, and individual differences. In his *Talks to Teachers on Psychology* (1899) William James underlined that education being an art and not a science could not deduce schemes and methods of teaching for direct classroom application out of psychology. "An intermediary inventive mind must make the application, by using its originality." In order to bridge the gap between theory and practice, James tried over and over again to make his presentation of psychology less technical. In the preface to his book which appeared several years after the lectures were given for the first time he says: "I have found by experience that what my hearers seem least to relish is analytical technicality, and what they most care for is concrete practical application. So I have gradually weeded out the former, and left the latter reduced; and now, that I have at least written out the lectures, they contain a minimum of what is deemed 'scientific' psychology and are practical and popular in the extreme."

In general, there is a similar relationship between research and practice in policy making. For a long time this relationship was, by both partners involved, conceived of in a rather simplistic way. Policy makers wanted research that primarily addressed their pressing problems within the framework of their perceptions of the world of education. They wanted findings that could be more or less directly applied to issues and problems under their consideration. Researchers conceived of their role as expert problem solvers who advised policy makers what to do.

The problem of how research in education is related to policy making was hardly studied before the 1960s. However, after this date, resources given to educational research grew markedly. Governments and private foundations within a period of a decade massively increased the funds for research in education, most of which was conducted by behavioral scientists. Hopes grew correspondingly high about what research might achieve in broadening the knowledge base for educational practice. Research was expected to provide recipes for the successful solution to classroom problems. Policy makers expected educational research to help them in the planning and execution of reforms that would improve the quality of a nation's schools. Typically, the enormous increase of funds for educational research under the provisions of the Elementary and Secondary Education Act passed by the United States Congress in 1965 was part of a big package of legislation on compensatory education being in its turn part of the Great Society program (Husén 1979).

In the 1960s the research and development (R & D) model which had been developed in science and technology was extended to the fields of education and social welfare. The model assumes a linear relationship between fundamental research, applied research, development of a prototype, its mass production, and dissemination in the field (see *Knowledge Diffusion in Education*). The high hopes easily led to frustrations. Researchers began to be accused of coming up with "findings" which were "useless" to practitioners, be they school teachers or administrators, in schools or governments. There was a growing demand for "relevance."

The simplistic model of "linear" or "direct" application does not work in education for two main reasons. In the first place, education is, like other areas in the social realm, imbued with values. Educational research deals with a reality which is perceived differently depending upon ideological convictions and values held by both practitioner and researcher. The way a problem is conceptualized, how it is empirically studied and analyzed, and how the findings from studies are interpreted often depends very much on tacit or overt value assumptions. One typical example is research on bilingual education, the extent to which a minority child in a country with a main language should have an opportunity to be instructed in his or her mother tongue. Secondly, and often overlooked, are the widely different conditions under which researchers and policy makers operate. Studies of these conditions began in the 1970s.

The value problem in educational research has begun to be analyzed by educational philosophers. It is highlighted by the controversy between logical positivism or neopositivism which has dominated the social science scene since the 1940s and critical philosophies of various brands. The former takes the social reality educational research deals with as a fact and takes for granted that research can advance "objectively" valid statements about that reality. The role of the researcher vis-à-vis the policy maker is that of a technician: he or she provides the instrument or the expertise that policy makers and practitioners "use" in framing and implementing their plans and policies. The latter type of philosophy sees critical studies as a means of changing society and thereby more or less explicitly allows value premises to enter into the research process.

In the following, the different conditions under which policy makers and researchers operate will be analyzed and the differences in ethos which guide endeavors in the respective categories will be described. After that, various research utilization models will be dealt with.

1. The Setting for Policy Making

Tensions between researchers and policy makers depend on certain constraints under which policy is shaped and implemented. Some of these have been discussed by Levin (1978).

Policy makers are primarily or even exclusively only interested in research that addresses problems which are on their agenda. This means that what researchers conceive as fundamental research which bears no or only a very remote relationship to the issues of the day is of little or no interest, if change in political regime or administration can mean a rearrangement of issues. For instance, the issues of private schools, educational vouchers, and busing have taken on quite a different importance under the Reagan than under the Carter administration in the United States. In Europe after the Second World War the central issue in many countries was to what extent the structure of the mandatory school should be comprehensive with regard to intake of students and programs. In countries like Sweden, England and Wales, and the Federal Republic of Germany many studies pertaining to the pedagogical and social aspects of comprehensiveness have been conducted and have been referred to extensively in the policy debate. In England the 1944 Education Act with its provisions for tripartite, secondary education in grammar, technical, and modern schools, and the selection for grammar school (the so-called 11+ examination) became an issue of the first order and gave rise to a large body of research on methods of selection and their effects. The issue of equality of educational opportunity has been a major one in Europe and the United States since the 1950s and recently in many developing countries as well. It has consequently inspired a large volume of research (Husén 1975).

Politicians have party allegiances which influence not only what they regard as relevant, innocuous, or even dangerous research but also their willingness to take research findings into account. Research, even if it addresses itself to a major issue on the political agenda, can be discarded or even rejected by one side in a political controversy if it does not support its views. Politicians, in the same way as court advocates, tend to select the evidence which they interpret as supporting their views.

Policy makers have their particular time horizon which in a parliamentary democracy tends to be rather narrow and determined not only by regular general elections but also by the flow of policy decisions. Research which takes years to complete cannot be considered if the policy maker's timetable requires the outcomes of a research project or program to be available "here and now." Research findings have to be made available in time for the decisions that by necessity have to be taken, irrespective of the nature of the "knowledge base" on which the decision maker stands. He or she needs immediate access to findings. This is a dilemma which planners and policy makers in a government agency continuously have to face. On the one hand, strategic planning with a relatively broad time perspective goes on. On the other hand, operational decision making is a continuous process which cannot wait for specially commissioned research to produce "relevant facts" of a rather simple, straightforward nature. This had led many administrators involved in policy making to demand that research should be strictly decision or policy oriented and address problems "in the field" only.

Policy makers are concerned only with policies in a particular area of their own experience as politicians or administrators. They therefore tend to disregard the connections with other areas. Educational policies have been advanced in order to solve what basically are problems in the larger social context. For example, in the United States in the mid-1960s compensatory education programs with enormous federal funds were made available to local schools. The intention was to "break the poverty cycle" by providing better education and thereby enhancing the employability of the economically disadvantaged (Husén 1979).

Policy makers are in most cases not familiar with educational research or social science research in general. In particular, they are not familiar with the language researchers use in communicating with each other, a language that ideally serves precision in presenting theories and methods, but by laypersons is often perceived as empty jargon. The problem then is to disseminate research findings in such a way that they can be understood by "ordinary people."

2. The Setting for Research

Researchers operate under conditions that in several respects differ from those under which people of practical affairs in politics and administration operate under. There are differences of background, social values, and institutional settings.

Researchers in education have traditionally been performing their tasks at teacher-training institutions, most frequently at universities. As a result of growing government involvement, research units have more recently been established by public agencies as instruments of planning and evaluation. Researchers conduct their work according to paradigms (see *Research Paradigms in Education*) to which they have become socialized during their graduate studies. They are in the first place anxious to preserve their autonomy as researchers from interferences by politicians or administrators. Secondly, their allegiance is more to fundamental or conclusion-oriented research than to applied or decision-oriented research. Thirdly, and as a consequence of this orientation, they pay much more attention to how their research is received by their peers in the national or international community of scholars in their field of specialization than by their customers in public agencies. This means among other things that once a technical report has been submitted, the researcher tends to lose interest in what happens to his or her findings.

Researchers are much less constrained than policy makers with regard to what problems they can tackle, what kind of critical language they can employ, and, not least, how much time they can use in completing a study. An investigation by the Dutch Foundation for Educational Research (Kallen et al. 1982) found that the great majority of projects financed by the Foundation lagged behind the timetable agreed upon for their completion. In order to conduct an empirical field study properly several years are required. The relevant literature on the "state of the art" has to be reviewed, methods have to be developed, data have to be collected in the field, data have to be processed and analyzed, sufficient time has to be allowed for writing the report, and finally, it takes some time for critical reviews in scholarly journals to appear. This is a process which typically takes about four to six years. Thus, the researcher has a different time horizon to that of the policy maker, both in terms of how much time he or she can allow for a study but also in terms of how his or her study fits into the ongoing research in the field. He or she perceives the study as an often humble contribution to an increasingly growing body of knowledge in a particular problem area.

Status in the research system depends upon the reputation that crystallizes from the continuously ongoing review of a researcher's work by colleagues inside or outside his or her own institution. Whereas in an administrative agency status depends on seniority and position in the organizational hierarchy, it is in the long run the quality of a person's research and the recognition of this that determines the reputation in the scholarly community to which the researcher relates himself or herself.

3. Disjunctions between Researchers and Policy Makers

The differences in settings and in value orientation between policy makers and educational researchers constitute what could be referred to as different kinds of ethos. It is even possible to speak of "two cultures." The research customers, the politicians, and/or the administrators/planners in a public agency, are by necessity pragmatists. They regard research almost entirely as an instrument for achieving a certain policy or for use in planning or implementing certain administrative goals. They want research to be focused on priority areas of current politics.

University-based researchers are brought up in the tradition of "imperial, authoritative, and independent" Research with a capital R. In order to discharge properly what they regard as their task, academics tend to take an independent and critical attitude, not least toward government. They tend to guard anxiously their academic autonomy.

These differences in value orientation and outlook tend to influence the relationship between the policy maker and the researcher all the way from the initiation of a research project to the interpretation of its findings. The "researchworthiness" of a proposed study is assessed differently. The policy maker looks at its relevance for the issues on the agenda, whereas the researcher in the first place tends to assess it on the basis of "research-immanent" criteria, to what extent the proposed research can contribute to fundamental knowledge. The researcher wants to initiate studies without any particular considerations to the applicability of the findings and with the purpose of extending the frontiers of fundamental knowledge.

The fact that education by necessity deals with values anchored in various ideologies easily brings educational research into the turmoil of political controversy. Most regimes and administrations in power tend to perceive social science research with suspicion because of its critical nature. Those who want to preserve the status quo often tend to regard research as subversive radicalism. It is, however, in the nature of research to be in a literal sense "radical," that is to say, to go to the root (Latin *radix*).

The close relationship between education and certain political and social philosophies has made it tempting for social scientists to become ideological evangelists. This has had an adverse effect on their credibility. The common denominator of what is understood by "academic ethos" is critical inquiry that does not spare partisan doctrines, not even the ones of the party to which the researcher belongs.

In the 1960s, social science and behavioral research on an unprecedented scale began to be supported by the government in countries such as the United States, Sweden, the United Kingdom, and the Federal Republic of Germany. Social scientists began to have a strong appeal and provided the arguments liberal politicians needed in favor of programs in education and social welfare. The liberals had a strong confidence in what social science could achieve. This meant that economists, sociologists, and psychologists were commissioned to conduct research that was part of the implementation of various programs in education (Aaron 1978). At the same time there was a quest for evaluation of these programs and increasingly a component of evaluation was included in planning them.

Soon discrepancies between expectations and actual research performances began to be aired and led to demands for accountability (see *Accountability in Education*). There have since the early 1970s been indications of a decreasing credibility on the part of policy makers vis-à-vis researchers. Expert testimonies on major policy issues have been seen as inconclusive and inconsistent. James Coleman's 1966 survey of equality of educational opportunity was interpreted to support desegregation in the public schools of the United States (Coleman 1966). His subsequent studies of busing were interpreted as providing counterevidence. Policy makers want, as President Truman once expressed it in talking about his economic advisors, "one-handed" advice and are not happy with "on the one hand—on the other hand." Furthermore, the credibility gap has been widened by allegations of ideologically imbued professional advice. In some countries social scientists working in education have been accused of "Leftist leanings" and subversive intentions. Political preferences among social scientists have even led to the establishment of research institutions with different political orientations, such as Brookings Institution and the American Enterprise Institute in the United States.

There are some inherent difficulties for educational research to prove its usefulness. The committee which at the end of the 1970s evaluated the National Institute of Education pointed out that improvements in the learning and the behavior of students as a result of research endeavors are difficult to demonstrate. The committee gave three main reasons for this: (a) a low level of sophistication in the social sciences in comparison with the physical sciences does not allow it "the luxury of predictable results"; (b) problems of bringing about and measuring changes in human learning and behavior are "vastly more complex" than those in the field of technological change; (c) the need for improvement in education is so great that expectations on educational R & D have been set much higher than is possible to achieve.

The crucial problem behind many of the frustrations felt by customers of educational research is that research cannot provide answers to the value questions with which social issues, including those in education, are imbued. This means that research even of the highest quality and "relevance" can only provide partial information that has to be integrated with experience and human judgment. The Australian Minister of Education (Shellard 1979) quoted Gene Glass as saying that there is more knowledge stored in the nervous systems of 10 excellent teachers about how to manage classroom learning than what an average teacher could distill from all existing educational research journals.

Implied in what has been said so far are three major reasons for a "disjunction" between policy making and research.

Research does not "fit" a particular situation. It might not at a given point in time be related to any political issue. Women's equal rights were for a long time a dead issue. But when they became an issue, they rapidly began to spur an enormous amount of research. But research addresssing itself to issues on the agenda might come up with evidence that is out of phase with the policy-making process. As pointed out above, policy makers, like advocates, want to use research in order to support or legitimize a "prefabricated position." Often the situation occurs whereby research findings are in contradiction with or at least do not support the policy that a decision-making body or an agency wants to take or has already taken.

Research findings are from the policy maker's point of view not particularly conclusive. Furthermore, it is in the nature of the research process that in order to make a public issue "researchable" the overall problem has to be broken down into parts that more readily lend themselves to focused investigations.

A third major reason for the disjunctions between researchers and policy makers is ineffective dissemination (see *Knowledge Diffusion in Education*). Research findings do not by themselves reach decision makers and practitioners. Researchers seek recognition in the first place among their peers. They place high premium on reports that can enhance their academic reputation and tend to look with skepticism upon popularization. It has been suggested that this problem can be dealt with by middlepersons who can serve in the role of "research brokers" or policy analysts and can communicate to practitioners what appears to be relevant to them. A particular type of research broker is the one who conducts meta-analyses of research, that is to say, reviews critically the existing research in a particular field in order to come up with relatively valid conclusions from the entire body of research (see *Meta-Analysis*).

4. Models of Research Utilization

The way research, in particular social science research, is "utilized" in educational policy making, in general has been studied in the first place by political scientists. Important contributions to the conceptualization have been made by Weiss (1979, 1980) and to the empirical study of the problem by both her and Caplan (1976).

In the first place, Weiss points out that "decisions" on policies or policy actions are not taken in the orderly and rational way that many think, namely that individuals authorized to decide sit down and ponder various options, consider relevant facts, and choose one of the options. Policies are decided upon in a much more diffuse way. What occurs is a complicated dynamic interaction between various interest groups, where by means of arguments advanced by them, administrative considerations, and, not least, the inertia in the system, guidelines for action begin to emerge. The best way to characterize this process is to talk about "decision accretion."

Not least researchers have been caught in rational and "knowledge-driven" models of how research findings relate to policy making. Research findings rather "percolate" through public opinion to policy makers. Instead of the latter taking into consideration particular studies, they tend to be influenced by the total body of research in a particular field. Findings usually do not reach those in positions of influence via scientific and technical reports but to a large extent via the popular press and other mass media. A body of notions that forms a *commune bonum* of "what research has to say" is built up via diverse channels of popularization. Theoretical conceptions and specific findings are "trickling" or "percolating" down and begin to influence enlightened public opinion and, in the last run, public policy (see *Knowledge Diffusion in Education*).

Weiss (1979) distinguishes between seven different "models" or concepts of research utilization in the social sciences. The first model is the research and development (R & D) model which has dominated the picture of how research in the physical sciences is utilized. It is a "linear" process from basic research via applied research and development to application of new technology. There was a time in the 1960s and early 1970s when the R & D model was expected to apply in education by the development of programmed instruction and material for individualized teaching. Weiss points out that its applicability in the social sciences is heavily limited, since knowledge in this field does not readily lend itself to "conversion into replicable technologies, either material or social."

The second model is the problem-solving one, where results from a particular research project are expected to be used directly in a pending decision-making situation. The process can schematically be described as follows: identification of missing knowledge → acquisition of research information either by conducting a specific study or by reviewing the existing body of research → interpretation of research findings in the context given policy options → decision about policy to pursue.

This is the classical "philosopher-king" conception. Researchers are supposed to provide the knowledge and wisdom from which policy makers can derive guidelines for action. Researchers, not least in Continental Europe, for a long time liked to think of themselves as the ones who communicated to policy makers what "research has to say" about various issues. The problem-solving model often tacitly assumes consensus about goals. But social scientists often do not agree among themselves about the goals of certain actions, nor are they in agreement with the policy makers.

The third model is the interactive model which assumes "a disorderly set of interconnections and back-and-forthness" and an ongoing dialogue between researchers and policy makers.

The fourth model is the political one. Research findings are used as ammunition to defend a standpoint. An issue, after having been debated for quite some time in a controversial climate, leads to entrenched positions that will not be changed by new evidence. A frequent case is that policy makers in power have already made their decision before they commission research that will legitimize the policy for which they have opted.

The fifth model is the tactical one, whereby a controversial problem is "buried" in research as a defense against taking a decision at the present moment.

The sixth model is the "enlightenment" one, which according to Weiss is the one through which "social science research most frequently enters the policy arena." Research tends to influence policy in a much more subtle way than is suggested by the word "utilization," which implies more or less direct use according to the first model. In the enlightenment model, research "permeates" the policy process, not by specific projects but by its "generalizations and orientations percolating through informed publics and coming to shape the way in which people think about social issues." Furthermore, without reference to any specific piece of evidence, research can sensitize policy makers to new issues, help to redefine old ones, and turn "nonproblems into policy problems." Empirical evidence appears to support this model. In a study where she was interviewing 155 policy makers in Washington, DC, Weiss found that 57 percent of them felt that they "used" research but only 7 percent could point to a specific project or study that had had an influence.

The seventh model in Weiss's taxonomy, finally, is referred to as "research-as-part-of-the-intellectual-enterprise-of-society" (research-oriented) model. Social science research together with other intellectual inputs, such as philosophy, history, journalism, and so on, contribute to widening the horizon for the debate on certain issues and to reformulating the problems.

5. Overcoming Disjunctions

The conclusion from analyses and studies of the relationships between research and educational policy making is that the former has an influence in the long run but not usually in the short term following specific projects at specific points in time. The impact of research is exercised by the total body of information and the conceptualization of issues that research produces. It does not yield "products" in the same way as research in the physical sciences. In spite of misgivings about research as "useless" to practitioners and allegations that it contributes little or nothing to policies and practice, research in the social sciences tends to "creep" into policy deliberations. The "linear" R & D model of research utilization derived from science and technology does not apply in the field of social sciences relevant to educational issues. Nor does the problem-solving model which presupposes either value-free issues or consensus about the values implied.

Research "percolates" into the policy-making process and the notion that research can contribute is integrated into the overall perspective that policy makers apply on a particular issue. Research contributes to the enlightenment of those who prepare decisions which usually are not "taken" at a given point in time but are rather accretions (Husén and Kogan 1984).

See also: Knowledge Utilization; Educational Research, Politics of; Policy-oriented Research; Educational Research, History of

Bibliography

Aaron J H 1978 *Politics and the Professors: The Great Society in Perspective.* Brookings Institution, Washington, DC

Caplan N 1976 Social research and national policy: What gets used by whom, for what purposes, and with what effects? *Int. Soc. Sci. J.* 28: 187–94

Coleman J S et al. 1966 *Equality of Educational Opportunity.* United States Department of Health, Education and Welfare, Washington, DC

Cronbach L J, Suppes P (eds.) 1969 *Research for Tomorrow's Schools: Disciplined Inquiry for Education: Report.* Macmillan, New York

Dutch Foundation for Educational Research 1978 *Programming Educational Research: A Framework for the Programming of Research Within the Context of the Objectives of the Foundation for Educational Research in the Netherlands.* Stichting voor Onderzoek van het Onderwijs (SVO), Dutch Foundation for Educational Research, Staatsuitgeverij, 's-Gravenhage

Her Majesty's Stationery Office (HMSO) 1971 *The Organisation and Management of Government R and D* (The Rothschild Report). Her Majesty's Stationery Office, London

Husén T 1968 Educational research and the state. In: Wall W D, Husén T (eds.) 1968 *Educational Research and Policy-making.* National Foundation for Educational Research, Slough

Husén T 1975 *Social Influences on Educational Attainment: Research Perspectives on Educational Equality.* Organisation for Economic Co-operation and Development (OECD), Paris

Husén T 1979 Evaluating compensatory education. *Proceedings of the National Academy of Education*, Vol. 6. National Academy of Education, Washington, DC

Husén T, Boalt G 1968 *Educational Research and Educational Change: The Case of Sweden.* Almqvist and Wiksell, Stockholm

Husén T, Kogan M (eds.) 1984 *Educational Research and Policy: How Do They Relate?* Pergamon, Oxford

James W 1899 *Talks to Teachers on Psychology: And to Students on Some of the Life's Ideals.* Longmans, Green, London

Kallen D, Kosse G B, Wagenar H C (eds.) 1982 *Social Science Research and Public Policy Making: A Reappraisal.* National Foundation for Educational Research–Nelson, London

Kogan M (ed.) 1974 *The Politics of Education: Edward Boyle and Anthony Crosland in Conversation with Maurice Kogan.* Penguin, Harmondsworth

Kogan M, Korman N, Henkel M 1980 *Government's Commissioning of Research: A Case Study.* Department of Government, Brunel University, Uxbridge

Levin H M 1978 Why isn't educational research more useful? *Prospects* 8(2)

Lindblom C E, Cohen D K 1979 *Usable Knowledge: Social Science and Social Problem Solving.* Yale University Press, New Haven, Connecticut

Rein M 1980 Methodology for the study of the interplay between social science and social policy. *Int. Soc. Sci. J.* 32: 361–68

Rule J B 1978 *Insight and Social Betterment: A Preface to Applied School Science.* Oxford University Press, London

Shellard J S (ed.) 1979 *Educational Research for Policy Making in Australia.* Australian Council for Educational Research, Hawthorn, Victoria

Suppes P (ed.) 1978 *Impact of Research on Education: Some Case Studies: Summaries.* National Academy of Education, Washington, DC

United States Office of Education 1969 *Educational Research and Development in the United States.* United States Government Printing Office, Washington, DC

Weiss C H 1979 The many meanings of research utilization. *Public Admin. Rev.* Sept.–Oct.

Weiss C H 1980 Knowledge creep and decision accretion. *Knowledge: Creation, Diffusion, Utilization* 1: 381–404

T. Husén

Educational Research, History of

Educational research as disciplined inquiry with an empirical basis was first known as "experimental pedagogy". This term was analogous to that of "experimental psychology", an expression coined by Wundt in Leipzig around 1880. Experimental pedagogy was founded around 1900 by Lay and Meumann in Germany; Binet and Simon in France; Rice, Thorndike, and Judd in the United States; Claparède in Switzerland; Mercante in Argentina; Schuyten in Belgium; Winch in England; and Sikorsky and Netschajeff in Russia. Some years earlier, three publications—*The Mind of the Child* by Preyer, a German psychologist, in 1882; *The Study of Children* by Stanley Hall from America in 1883; and articles by an English psychologist, Sully, in 1884 concerned with children's language and imagination—marked the beginning of the child study movement. Although progress was slow during the 1880s the foundations were laid through this movement for research into related educational problems. From 1900 onwards,

the study of educational questions developed rapidly and three movements can be identified: (a) the child study movement, where educational research was associated with applied child psychology; (b) the New Education or progressive movement where philosophy took precedence over science, and life experience over experimentation; and (c) the scientific research movement with a positivist approach. This article is primarily concerned with the third movement which involves empirical research.

In the first major identifiable period (1900–1930), Cronbach and Suppes (1969) speak of a "heyday of empiricism", empirical educational research focused on rational management of instruction, challenging the concept of transfer of training, psychology of school subjects, development of new curricula, psychological testing, administrative surveys (school attendance, failure rates, etc.), and normative achievement surveys. Descriptive statistics were already well-established and in the 1920s and 1930s inferential statistics and multivariate data analysis developed rapidly (see *Statistical Analysis in Educational Research*).

In the second period (1930 to the late 1950s), however, the strict scientific approach to education lost impetus to make room, practically all over the developed world, for the more philosophically oriented and innovative progressivism. Behind this shift were three factors: (a) the atomistic character of most educational research; (b) a questioning of the scientific approach to the management of education at a time when there was an economic crisis soon to be followed by war; and (c) the charisma of the progressive movement with its combination of empirical research and a social and political philosophy merging the free enterprise, liberal spirit with humanistic socialism.

Nevertheless, during this period interest in cognitive development and language studies continued with the work of Piaget in Switzerland, and Vygotsky, who died in 1934, and his associates Luria and Leontief in the Soviet Union. In addition, a new strand of enquiry was opened up in the field of the sociology of education with the publication in 1944 of *Who Shall be Educated* by Warner, Havighurst, and Loeb in the United States. These authors brought together a substantial body of research to establish that schooling in the United States favoured white children from an urban middle-class background. Other studies into adolescence and adolescent development soon followed.

In the third period (1960s and 1970s) the knowledge "explosion" took place and its applications to technology really began (see *Knowledge Explosion*). Educational research was soon influenced by this dynamic development. Challenged by the Soviet technological advance (e.g., Sputnik) and being economically affluent, United States governmental and private agencies supported educational research to an unprecedented extent. A similar development, although not so spectacular, occurred in other highly industrialized countries. During the 1960s the computer added a new dimension to educational research leading to the introduction of sophisticated experimental design since data processing and data analysis were no longer limited by calculation time as in the precomputer era. From this, new ways of thinking about educational issues developed, which were concerned with assessing probabilities, the interaction of the influences of many factors on educational outcomes, and the introduction of mathematical and causal modelling to predict and explain educational phenomena (see *Models and Model Building*).

The Anglo–Saxon world led the field in educational research followed by the Scandinavian countries, while West European countries tended to move more slowly. The profound impact of the Anglo–Saxon research methodology has been felt all over the world since the 1960s. But the 1960s were also marked by the beginning of an epistemological debate in the social sciences, perhaps a reaction to the strident empiricism which had developed. It is now fully realized that the rigid scientific ideal, embodied in the neopositivist approach, cannot take into account the multifaceted aspects of human behaviour and all its environment-bound subtle nuances (see *Research Paradigms in Education*).

Confrontation took place. Just as the student movement and revolt can now be considered as part of an emerging, new human culture, the positivistic versus the anthropological or hermeneutic debate can be conceived as a new era in the social sciences. The answer of educational researchers of the 1980s is not either–or, but both. The research community has come to realize that sound inquiry develops in a spiral way combining methods or approaches that some would earlier have considered as incompatible: the scientific or hard data approach is seen to be complementary to the anthropological, historical, phenomenological, or soft data approaches.

Thus, it took empirical educational research approximately a century to reach its present status of maturity. For the first time in the history of humankind, the art of education can rely upon a sound and increasingly comprehensive basis.

In tracing the development of educational research this article will examine the successive periods: pre-1900 era, 1900 to 1930s, 1930s to late 1950s, the 1960s and 1970s, and developments in the 1980s.

1. Pre-1900

It is certainly not incidental that within a period of about 25 years empirical educational research was born and began to tackle most of the pervasive educational problems which are today still under study throughout the Western world. The foundations for this sudden rise were laid during centuries of educational experience and philosophical thinking, and were inspired by the explosion of the natural sciences during the nineteenth century. More specifically, longitudinal observations of individual children were recorded during the nineteenth century and attained a high-quality level with the pioneering study, in 1882, by Preyer, *Die Seele des Kindes* [The Mind of the Child]. This was the first textbook on developmental psychology. The idea of an experimental school and of experimentation in education is present in the writings of Kant, Herbart, and Pestalozzi, but this idea implied field experiences and not experimentation according to an elaborated design.

In the second part of the nineteenth century, several signs show that developments in the natural sciences slowly began to influence psychology and education. In 1859, in *The Emotions and the Will*, Bain considered the construction of aptitude tests. Five years later, G. Fisher proposed, in his *Scalebook*, a set of scales for the rating of ability and knowledge in major school subjects including handwriting. Fisher also introduced statistics into educational research by using the arithmetic mean as an index of achievement of a group of students. In 1870, Bartholomaî administered a questionnaire to 2,000 children entering primary school in order to know the "content of their mind" at that moment. Three years later, the first experimental study of attention was published by Miller in Göttingen. In 1875, James opened the first psychological laboratory of the United States at Harvard in order to carry out systematic observation, but not experimentation. The year 1879, saw the publication of Bain's *Education as a Science*.

It is clear that the immediate origin of modern educational research (and of experimental psychology) is not to be found in the emerging social sciences, but in the natural sciences. With his *Origin of Species* (1859), Darwin linked research on humans with physics, biology, zoology, and geography. Six years later, Bernard published his *Introduction to the Study of Experimental Medicine*, the guide to modern scientific research. In 1869, Galton suggested, in *Hereditary Genius*, applying statistics to the study of human phenomena and began work on the concepts of standardization, correlation, and operational definition. Carroll (1978) saw in Galton's *Inquiry into Human Faculty and its Development* (1883) the invention of the concept of mental testing.

Experimental psychology—soon to be followed by experimental pedagogy—was created in German physics laboratories by scholars with a strong philosophical background. Wundt, a student of one of these scholars, Helmholtz, founded the first laboratory of experimental psychology in 1879. Wundt's laboratory had a considerable impact, and the scientific leadership of the German universities at the end of the 1800s must be recognized in order to understand what happened between 1880 and 1900.

At that time, many students, particularly from the United States, completed their advanced education at the universities of Berlin, Leipzig, Heidelberg, or Jena. This explains the extraordinarily rapid dissemination of Wundt's ideas: Cattell, Hall, Judd, Rice, and Valentine were among his students. His work was immediately known in France by Ribot and Binet, in Russia by Netschajeff, in Japan by Matsumoto, in Santiago, Chile by Mann, and in Argentina by Mercante. Psychological laboratories were soon opened on both sides of the Atlantic.

In the meantime, certain key events were associated with the birth of modern educational research:

1885 Ebbinghaus's study on memory drew the attention of the education world to the importance of associations in the learning process.

1888 Binet published his *Études de Psychologie Experimentales*; at that time he was already working in schools.

1890 The term mental test was coined by Cattell.

1891 Stanley Hall launched the review *Pedagogical Seminary*.

1894 Rice developed a spelling test to be administered to 16,000 pupils. He published the results of his testing in his *Scientific Management of Education* in 1913.

1895 In the United States, the *National Society for the Scientific Study of Education* was founded (initially called the National Herbart Society for the Scientific Study of Teaching).

1896 In Belgium, Schuyten published a report of his first educational research study on the influence of temperature on school children's attention. Dewey, a student of Stanley Hall, opened a laboratory school at the University of Chicago.

1897 Thorndike studied under James at Harvard and there discovered the works of Galton and Binet.
Ebbinghaus published his so-called completion test to measure the effect of fatigue on school performance. This can be considered to be the first operational group test.
In the same year Binet began to work on his intelligence scale.

1898 Lay suggested distinguishing experimental education from experimental psychology.
Binet and Henri condemned traditional education in their book *La Fatigue Intellectuelle* and indicated the need for experimental education.

1899 Schuyten opened a pedological laboratory in Antwerp (Belgium) to study experimentally, among other things, group teaching methods.

Who is the father of "experimental pedagogy"? The answer to this question differs whether the activity covered by the term or the term itself is considered. Empirical research in education definitely existed before 1900. Many American authors regard Rice as the founder because of his research on the effect of spelling drills (1895–1897), but other names: Binet, Lay, Mercante, or Schuyten, could also qualify. As for the term itself, it was coined by Meumann (Wundt's former student) in 1900, in the German *Zeitschrift für Pädogogik* where he dealt with the scientific study of schooling. In 1903, Lay published his *Experimentelle Didaktik* where he made his famous statement about ". . . experimental education will become all education". In 1905, Lay and Meumann together published the review *Die Experimentelle Pädagogik*. Subsequently, Meumann's three-volume work *Einführung in die Experimentelle Pädogogik* (1910, 1913, 1914) emphasized both the strict scientific and quantitative side of the laboratory, while Lay continued to emphasize both quantitative and qualitative approaches (empathy, intention) in classroom research.

When did modern educational research appear in France? There is no doubt that Binet inspired it. In his introduction to his book *La Fatigue Intellectuelle* (1898), he wrote:

> Education must rely on observation and experimentation. By experience, we do not mean vague impressions collected by persons who have seen many things. An experimental study includes all methodically collected documents with enough detail and precise information to enable the reader to replicate the study, to verify it and to draw conclusions that the first author had not identified. (Simon 1924 p. 5)

It is obvious throughout the whole psychological work of Binet that he had a strong interest in education. In 1905, he founded the School Laboratory in rue Grande-aux-Bettes in Paris. With him were Vaney, who in 1907 published the first French reading scale and Simon, the coauthor of the *Intelligence Scale* (1905) and later author of the *Pédagogie Expérimentale*. Binet and Simon's *Intelligence Scale* presented in Rome at the 1905 International Conference of Psychology was the first truly operational mental test covering higher cognitive processes. Like Wundt's ideas, Binet's test became known throughout the world within a very few years. But beyond its intrinsic value, this test had a far greater historical significance. It was now acknowledged that a test could be a valid measurement instrument both in psychology and education.

In 1904, Claparède, a medical doctor, founded the Laboratory for Experimental Psychology at the University of Geneva with his uncle Flournoy. In 1892, Claparède had visited Binet in Paris and in the following year was, for a short time, Wundt's student in Leipzig. In 1905, he published the first version of his *Psychologie de l'enfant et pédagogie expérimentale* that was the only French educational research methods handbook until 1935 when Buyse published his *Expérimentation en Pédagogie*. In 1912, Claparède established the J. J. Rousseau Institute in Geneva which over the next 50 years was to make a marked contribution to child study and education through the work of Jean Piaget. However, Claparede remained mostly psychologically and philosophically oriented. With his theory of functional education, he was the European counterpart of John Dewey. Together they were seen as the two main leaders of progressive education.

Among many interesting features in the work of Claparède (following Dilthey's work in 1892 on *Verstehen* vs. *Erklären*) is his analysis, in 1903, of the explaining (positivist, nomothetic approach) versus the understanding (hermeneutic) approach. This elicited a debate which still lasts today.

At the end of *Les Idées modernes sur les enfants*, Binet (1924 p. 300) mentioned that "it is specially in the United States that the remodelling of education has been undertaken on a new, scientific basis". In fact, at the beginning of the century, education research advanced at an extraordinarily quick pace in the United States.

At Columbia University, Cattell, who had obtained his Ph.D. under Wundt and had known Galton in Cambridge, had, in 1890, as mentioned above, coined the term mental test in the philosophical journal *Mind*. In 1891, he established his psychological laboratory just above the laboratory for electricity. Under his supervision Thorndike completed his Ph.D. in 1898 on animal intelligence. Like many psychologists of the time he soon developed a keen interest in education. In this period, so much attention was focused on objective measurement that the experimental education movement was sometimes called "the measurement movement" (Joncich 1962).

Thorndike can be considered as the most characteristic representative of the scientific orientation in education. During the following decades, he dealt with all aspects of educational research. He was the first person to conceive of teaching methods in terms of an explicitly formulated and experimentally tested learning theory. In so doing, he opened a new teaching era. The influence of Thorndike in the field of educational research can probably be compared with the influence of Wundt in experimental psychology.

2. The Flourishing of Quantitative Research, from 1900 to 1930

During this period, most educational research was quantitatively oriented and geared to the study of effectiveness. For a while, Taylorism and the study of efficiency, became a component of educational thinking. The behaviouristic and antimentalist study of human behaviour was regarded as the best weapon against the formalism of the past.

The following aspects of research activities, although not comprehensive, are representative illustrations of the era.

2.1 Statistical Theory

It has sometimes been said that there is an inconsistency between the limitations of measurement in the social sciences and the rapidly increasing sophistication of the statistical techniques resorted to. However, it can be argued that many statistical advances were achieved by researchers in education precisely because they were aware of the complexity and the instability of most phenomena they had under study and had to look for increasingly sophisticated methods to obtain sufficient validity of measurement or else indicate the limitations of their conclusions.

The applicability of the Gaussian probability curve to biological and social phenomena was suggested at the beginning of the 1800s by Quetelet, who coined the term statistics. Galton was the first to make extensive use of the normal curve to study psychological problems. He sometimes preferred to express the same distributions with his ogive because this representation gave a better picture of the hierarchy of characteristics. Galton also suggested percentile norms. In 1875, he drew the first regression line, and developed the concept of correlation in 1877. In 1896, Pearson, who worked under Galton, published the formula for the product–moment correlation coefficient. In the first decade of the 1900s, the essentials of the correlational method, including the theory of regression, were well-developed, especially by British statisticians, Pearson and Yule. In the same period, Pearson developed the chi-square technique and the multiple correlation coefficient. Reliability was measured with the Spearman–Brown Formula. In 1904, Spearman published his analysis of a correlation matrix to sustain his two-factor theory and factor analysis began to emerge.

Researchers were also aware of the statistical significance of differences. They used rather crude methods indeed, but did not take many chances. Carroll has written:

> Fortunately, American psychologists in the early days, tended to employ such a conservative standard in testing statistical differences (a "critical ratio" of four times the probable error, corresponding to $p < .007$) that at least it can be said that they only infrequently made "Type 1 errors." (Carroll 1978 p. 20)

In 1908, under the name of Student, Gossett showed how to measure the standard error of the mean and the principle of the t-test was formulated.

Experimental design was also used. In 1903, Schuyten used experimental and control groups. In 1916, McCall, a student of Thorndike and probably the first comprehensive theorist of experimentation in education, recommended the setting up of random experimental and control groups. In a research study with Thorndike and Chapman (Thorndike et al. 1916), he applied 2×2 and 5×5 latin square designs. This was 10 years before the work of R. A. Fisher in England.

The contribution of Sir Ronald Fisher was critical. With the publication of his *Statistical Methods for Research Workers* in 1925, small-sample inferential statistics became known, but were not immediately utilized. In the same work, Fisher reinforced Pearson's chi-square by adding the concept of degrees of freedom, demonstrated the *t*-test, and explained the technique of analysis of variance. In 1935, Fisher crowned his scientific career with his famous *The Design of Experiments*, originally conceived for agriculture, and not widely applied in educational research before the late 1940s.

A look at some of the statistical texts available in the 1920s is often a surprise for today's students: Thorndike (1913), McCall (1922), Otis (1925), Thurstone (1925) in the United States: Yule (1911), Brown and Thomson (1921) in the United Kingdom; Claparède (1911) in Switzerland; Decroly and Buyse (1929) in Belgium had a surprisingly good command of descriptive parametric statistics and also a keen awareness of the need for testing the significance of differences.

2.2 Testing and Assessment

It has been shown that both mental and achievement tests already existed at the turn of the century. Between 1895 and 1905 tests were administered in schools in the United States, Germany, France, Belgium, and many other countries. Perhaps the critical moment was the appearance in 1905 of Binet and Simon's test, the first valid and operational mental measurement instrument. Group testing began in England in Galton's laboratory in 1905, and Burt and Spearman assisted him. In 1911, the United States National Education Association approved the use of tests for school admission and final examinations. A breakthrough occurred with the development and wide-scale, efficient use of tests by the United States Army, which were quickly constructed in 1917 mostly by drawing upon existing mental tests. Soon after the war, these tests were modified for school use (Carroll 1978).

The 1918 *Yearbook* of the National Society for the Study of Education was entirely devoted to the measurement of educational products. In 1928, about 1,300 standard tests were available in the United States. By the 1930s, normative-test construction techniques could be considered to be fully developed: item formats, order of items, parallel forms, scoring stencils and machine scoring, norms, reliability, and validity. The psychometric advance of the United States, at that time, was such that standardized tests were often referred to as "American tests".

Mental tests were soon used in all industrialized countries. In particular, Binet's scale was used in Europe, North and South America, and Australia, and was tried out in some African countries. This was far from being the case with achievement tests. Some fairly crude tests were used as research instruments but frequently remained unknown to the classroom teacher. It is, for instance, surprising to observe the lack of sophistication of the achievement tests developed in France after Binet and Simon. This continued until the 1940s, and the situation is particularly well-illustrated in the book by Ferré, *Les Tests a l'école*, a fifth edition of which appeared in 1961. It is all the more surprising since in the 1930s traditional examinations (essay and oral tests) were sharply criticized in England and in France where Piéron coined the French word *docimologie*, meaning "science of examinations". Lack of validity, of reliability, and sociocultural bias were denounced with documented evidence. In Continental Europe, standardized achievement tests were not extensively used in schools.

2.3 Administrative and Normative Surveys

Among educational research endeavours, surveys are the oldest. In 1817, Marc Antoine Jullien de Paris became the founder of comparative education by designing a 34-page national and international questionnaire covering all aspects of national systems of education. The questions were posed, but unfortunately not answered, at that time.

The modern questionnaire technique was developed by Stanley Hall at the end of the 1800s to show, among other things, that what is obvious for an adult is not necessarily so for a child. This observation has, of course, direct educational implications.

In 1892, Rice visited 36 towns in the United States and interviewed some 1,200 teachers about curriculum content and teaching methods. Subsequently he carried out a spelling survey (1895–1897) on 16,000 pupils and found a low correlation between achievement and time invested in drill. This survey was repeated in 1908 and in 1911 (Rice 1913). Thorndike's 1907 survey of dropouts was followed by a series of other surveys of school characteristics: differences in curricula, failure rate, teaching staff qualifications, school equipment and the like. The most comprehensive survey of the period was the Cleveland Schools Survey undertaken in 1915–16 by L. P. Ayres and a large team of assistants. The study was reported in 25 volumes each dealing with different aspects of urban life and education.

In Germany, France, Switzerland, and Belgium, similar but smaller surveys were carried out by "pedotechnical" offices such as that opened in 1906 in the Decroly School in Brussels.

Several large-scale psychological surveys were undertaken: the Berkeley Growth Study (1928), the Fell's Study of Human Development (1929), and the

Fourth Harvard Study (1929). In 1932, the Scottish Council for Research in Education carried out its first *Mental Survey* on a whole school population which provided a baseline for later surveys and for determining the representativeness of samples of the population of the same age.

A landmark in the history of experimental education was the *Eight-year Study* (1933–1941) conducted in the United States by the Progressive Education Association (see *Eight-year Study*). The initial purpose of the study, which was carried out using survey research methodology, was to examine to what extent the college entrance requirements hampered the reform of the high-school curriculum and to demonstrate the relevance and effectiveness of progressive ideas at the high-school level. In this study students from 30 experimental schools were admitted to college irrespective of subjects they had studied in high school. The by-products of this project were probably more important than the project itself. Tests covering higher cognitive processes and effective outcomes were developed by an evaluation team directed by Ralph Tyler. The careful definition of educational objectives was advanced. In 1950, influenced by the *Eight-year Study*, Tyler wrote *Basic Principles of Curriculum and Instruction*, in which he presented his model for the definition of objectives. It was followed by Bloom's first taxonomy in 1956 (see *Objectives, Educational, Taxonomies of*), and this marked the beginning of the contemporary thinking on the definition of objectives and on curriculum development and evaluation (see *Curriculum Evaluation*).

2.4 Curriculum Development and Evaluation

Curriculum was one focus of attention of empirical educational research from its very beginning. The article, in 1900, in which Meumann used the term "*experimentelle Pädagogik*" for the first time dealt with the scientific study of school subjects. Shortly afterwards, Thorndike introduced a radical change in curriculum development by conceptualizing teaching methods in terms of a "psychology of school branches", and by demonstrating through his work on the transfer of learning the lack of validity of the prevailing theories of formal education, and how it ignored the needs of contemporary society. This psychological approach was perfectly compatible with the new pragmatic philosophy and the attempts to rationalize work and labour. Some years later, Decroly and Buyse hoped to "taylorize instruction to save time for education". The psychology of school subjects was also dealt with by other leading scholars such as Judd. But, as far as research on curriculum, in the broad sense of the word is concerned, the work of Thorndike on content, teaching methods, and evaluation of material is second to none (see *Curriculum Development*; *Curriculum Evaluation*).

During the same period, the progressive movement, partly inspired by Dewey, remained in close contact with these specific developments, although it soon rejected—as William James had done earlier—a strictly quantitative experimental approach to educational phenomena. According to Thorndike's scientific approach, there could only be one standard curriculum at a given time, the best one that scientific research could produce. Most important to the movement was the rejection of formalism for functionality. The main criteria for curriculum content became individual needs in a new society, as conceived by liberal, middle-class educators of the time.

In 1918, Bobbitt published *Curriculum*, soon to be followed by Charters' *Curriculum Construction* (1923). This led to a series of studies with increasingly strong emphasis on a systematic and operational definition of educational objectives. On the European side, the Belgian *Plan d'études* (1936), written by Jeunehomme, can be considered as a curricular masterpiece, built on contributions of both strict empirical research and the progressive philosophy.

3. From the 1930s to the late 1950s

The economic crisis of the 1930s made research funds scarce. The need for a new social order was interpreted differently: fascism in some countries (Germany, Italy, Japan); socialism in others (the *Front Populaire* in France and Spain). Progressivism, advocated by the New Education movement outside the United States, seemed to be an obvious educational solution in most democratic countries and a guarantee for the future of democracy.

The Second World War and the years immediately following froze most educational research activities in European countries. Freedom of research was (and still is) not acceptable to dictators. In the Soviet Union, the utilization of tests (as incompatible with political decisions) and more generally the "pedological movement" were officially banned in 1936 by a resolution of the Communist Party, and this situation lasted until Stalin's death. However, other forms of research continued, arising from the publication in 1938 of *Thought and Language* by L. S. Vygotsky four years after his death in 1934, and the subsequent work of his associates such as Luria and Leontief in the development of Pavlov's ideas. In occupied countries, school reorganization was planned by underground movements which tried to draw conclusions from previous experiments and to design educational systems for peace and democracy. The *Plan Langevin–Wallon*, for the introduction of comprehensive secondary education in France is an example.

Conditions were different in the United States, Australia, and in Sweden. Even if no spectacular advances occurred in educational research in those countries, the maturation of ideas went on and prepared the way for the postwar developments. Warfare had again raised problems of recruitment and placement and the role of military psychology and the development of selection tests is exemplified by the work of Guilford in the United States and Husén and Boalt (1968) in Sweden.

The strong field of interest in the 1940s and 1950s was without doubt in sociological studies. The seminal investigations were those concerned with social status and its impact on educational opportunity. A series of studies in the United States showed the pervasive existence of the school's role in maintaining social distinctions and discriminatory practices. From this research it was argued that schools and teachers were the purveyors of middle-class attitudes and habits. These effects of schooling were particularly evident at the high-school stage, and this trend of research became closely linked to the study of adolescent development. This work spread to England in the mid-1950s and subsequently to other parts of the world and led to challenging the maintenance of selective schools and to establishing comprehensive high schools. This research emphasis on issues associated with educational disadvantage has continued subsequently, with concern for disparities in the educational opportunities provided for different racial and ethnic groups, for inner urban and rural groups and, in particular, for girls.

4. The 1960s and 1970s

During the first part of the 1960s in affluent countries educational research enjoyed for the first time in its history the massive support necessary for it to have a significant impact. This development was particularly marked in the United States. At that time money for research and curriculum development, particularly in mathematics and science, was readily available in the United States. In 1954, federal funds were first devoted through the Cooperative Research Act to a programme of research and development in education (Holtzman 1978). The big, private foundations also began to sponsor educational research on a large scale. The civil rights movement, Kennedy's New Frontier, and Johnson's Great Society continued the trend.

In 1965, the Elementary and Secondary Education Act was passed which authorized funding over a five-year period for constructing and equipping regional research and development (R & D) centres and laboratories. President Johnson implemented developments that had been planned under Kennedy and in 1968, federal support for educational research reached its peak: 21 R & D centres, 20 regional laboratories, 100 graduate training programmes in educational research, and thousands of demonstration projects, represented a total federal investment of close to 200 million dollars per year.

On a much smaller scale, a similar development took place in England. Wall (1968 p. 16) wrote:

In 1958, it was possible to demonstrate that expenditure of all kinds on research relating to education represented no more than 0.1 per cent of all expenditure on education: in 1967 the proportion may well be thirty times as much and will probably grow over the next decade.

A similar expansion took place in the Soviet Union. Between 1960 and 1970 the professional staff engaged in educational research increased considerably. In 1966, the Soviet Academy of Pedagogical Sciences took on its present status. Initially under the name of the Academy of the Russian Republic it was founded in 1943. In 1967, the *Institut Pédagogique Nationale* of France, for the first time, received significant funding for educational research. Girod de l'Ain (1967) considered 1967 as the Year 1 of educational research in France.

By the late 1960s, all highly industrialized countries were in the midst of a cultural crisis which had a deep impact on scientific epistemology and thus affected the research world. There was also talk about a "world crisis" (Coombs 1968) in education which applied in the first place to the imbalance between demand and supply of education, particularly in Third World countries. Deeply disappointed in their hope for general peace, wealth, and happiness, people realized that neither science and technology nor traditional—mostly middle-class—values had solved their problems. An anti-intellectualist counterculture developed, emphasizing freedom in all respects, rejecting strict rationality, glorifying community life. The value of "traditional" education was questioned. "Deschooling", nondirectivity, group experience, and participation seemed to many the alpha and omega of all pedagogy. This trend did not leave socialist countries unaffected. In May 1976, a group of researchers in the Soviet Union regretted a too rationalistic approach in educational research (Novikov 1977).

At the same time, scholars also began to question science, some with great caution and strong argumentation, others superficially in the line of the Zeitgeist. Kerlinger (1977) condemned the latter with ferocity: "mostly bizarre nonsense, bandwaggon climbing, and guruism, little related to what research is and should be".

This was not the case in the crucial epistemological debate inspired by scholars like Polanyi, Popper, Kuhn, and Piaget. Fundamentally, the world of learning acknowledged both the contemporary "explosion" of knowledge and the still, very superficial, comprehension of natural, human phenomena.

While Piaget (1972) showed in his *Epistémologie des sciences de l'homme,* that nomothetic and historical (anthropological) approaches are not mutually exclusive but complementary, in 1974, two of the best-known American educational researchers Cronbach (1974) and Campbell (1974), without previous mutual consultation, chose the annual meeting of the American Psychological Association to react against the traditional positivist emphasis on quantitative methods and stressed the critical importance of alternative methods of inquiry.

Since the 1960s, the computer has become the daily companion of the researcher. For the first time in the history of humankind, the amount and complexity of calculation are no longer a problem. Already existing statistical techniques, like multiple regression analysis, factor analysis, multivariate analysis of variance, that previously were too onerous for desk calculation suddenly became accessible in a few moments. Large-scale research projects became feasible. Simultaneously, new statistical methods and techniques were developed (see *Statistical Analysis in Educational Research*).

Huge surveys, such as Project Talent in the United States and the mathematics and six subject surveys of the International Association for the Evaluation of Educational Achievement (IEA) would have been unthinkable without powerful data-processing units. Campbell and Stanley's (1963) presentation of experimental and quasiexperimental design for educational research can be considered to be a landmark.

Scientific developments in the field of educational research were not only stimulated by access to funds and to powerful technology, but also by the "explosion" of knowledge in the physical and social sciences, especially in psychology, linguistics, economics, and sociology (see *Instructional Psychology*; *Economics of Education*; *Sociology of Education*).

Many scientific achievements in the field of education can be mentioned for the 1960s: the new ideas on educational objectives (see *Objectives, Educational, Taxonomies of*), the new concepts of criterion-referenced testing (see *Criterion-referenced Tests*) (the most important advance in test theory since Galton's invention of normative testing), formative and summative evaluation (see *Formative and Summative Evaluation*), teacher–pupil interaction analysis, research on teacher effectiveness, compensatory education for socioculturally handicapped children (see *Compensatory Education*), the study of cognitive and affective handicaps, research into the importance and methods of early education, social aspects of learning aptitudes, deschooling experiments, adult education (see *Adult Education: An Overview*), the development of new curricula and of an empirical methodology of curriculum development and evaluation, and developments in research methodology.

5. Developments in the 1980s

With the advent of the last quarter of the twentieth century, the scientific status of educational research has attained a level of quality comparable to that of other disciplines. The epistemological debate of the previous decade clarified considerably the respective strengths and weaknesses of the qualitative and the quantitative approaches. It is now widely acknowledged that no one research paradigm can answer all the questions which arise in educational research.

A clear impact of this scientific maturity can also be spotted in educational practice. Both the scientific quest for the most efficient standard teaching method and the progressivist improvisation (for a while replaced by nondirectivity) have been succeeded by subtle classroom management including careful definition and negotiation of objectives, consideration of student and teacher's characteristics, of cognitive and affective styles, and of economic and social needs. Thanks to the advancement of developmental and educational psychology it is now understood, for instance, how the Piagetian constructivist theory implies that many crucial educational objectives can only be defined by or with the learner, while interacting with his or her environment. The naive concept of individualized teaching (see *Individualized Instruction*) and the dogma of group work is replaced by flexible group structuring and flexible scheduling. Beyond the original model of mastery learning (see *Mastery Learning Model of Teaching and Learning*) now appears the more general concept of a school making sensible use of time and of all human and technological resources available. Opportunities to learn are multiplied. The future appears to belong to a more modular system of education. The new perspectives opened by the computer technology are also more clearly perceived and are probably best illustrated by the "Logo environment" (Papert 1972), which is a challenge to intellectual creativity and development. These new developments, given as examples among many others, still have to be disseminated to the majority of schools, their validity and feasibility in terms of daily practice having been established.

6. Conclusion

Like medicine, education is an art. That is why advances in research do not produce a science of education, in the positivist meaning of the term, but yield increasingly powerful scientific foundations for practice and decision making. In this perspective, it can be said that from 1900 to 1980, educational research has gathered a surprisingly large body of knowledge containing valuable observations and conclusions.

See also: Educational Research and Policy Making; Historiography of Education

Bibliography

Binet A 1924 *Les Idées modernes sur les enfants*. Flammarion, Paris
Brown W, Thomson G H 1921 *The Essentials of Mental Measurement*. Cambridge University Press, Cambridge

Campbell D T 1974 Qualitative knowing in action research. Paper, American Psychological Association, Los Angeles, California

Campbell D T, Stanley J C 1963 Experimental and quasi-experimental designs for research on teaching. In: Gage N L (ed.) 1963 *Handbook of Research on Teaching*. Rand McNally, Chicago, Illinois, pp. 171–246

Carroll J B 1978 On the theory–practice interface in the measurement of intellectual abilities. In: Suppes P (ed.) 1978 *Impact of Research of Education*. National Academy of Education, Washington, DC

Claparède E 1911 *Psychologie de l'enfant et pédagogie expérimentale*, Vol. 2: *Les Méthodes*. Delachaux and Niestlé, Neuchâtel

Connell W F 1980 *A History of Education in the Twentieth Century World*. Teachers College Press, New York

Coombs P H 1968 *The World Educational Crisis: A Systems Analysis*. Oxford University Press, London

Cronbach L J 1974 Beyond the two disciplines of scientific psychology. Paper, American Psychological Association, Los Angeles, California

Cronbach L, Suppes P (eds.) 1969 *Research for Tomorrow's Schools: Disciplined Inquiry for Education: Report*. Macmillan, New York

Decroly O, Buyse R 1929 *Introduction à la pédagogie quantitative: Éléments de statistiques appliqués aux problèmes pédagogiques*. Lamertin, Brussels

De Landsheere G 1982 *La Recherche expérimentale en éducation*. International Bureau of Education, UNESCO, Geneva

de l'Ain G 1967 L'an I de la recherche pédagogique. *Le Monde* 5th Sept. 1967

Holtzman W H 1978 Social change and the research and development movement. In: Glaser R (ed.) 1978 *Research and Development and School Change*. Erlbaum, Hillsdale, New Jersey, pp. 7–18

Husén T, Boalt G 1968 *Educational Research and Educational Change: The Case of Sweden*. Wiley, New York

Husén T, Kogan M 1983 *Researchers and Policy-makers in Education*. Pergamon, Oxford

Joncich G 1962 Wither thou, educational scientist? *Teach. Coll. Rec.* 64: 1–12

Kerlinger F N 1977 *The Influence of Research on Educational Practice*. University of Amsterdam, Amsterdam

McCall W A 1922 *How to Measure in Education*. Macmillan, New York

Novikov L 1977 Probleme der Planung und Organisation der pädagogischen Forschung in der Sowjetunion. In: Mitter W, Novikov L (eds.) 1977 *Pädagogische Forschung und Bildungspolitik in der Sowjetunion: Organisation, Gegenstand, Methoden*. Deutsches Institut für Internationale Pädagogische Forschung, Frankfurt/Main

Otis A S 1925 *Statistical Method in Educational Measurement*. World Book, Yonkers-on-Hudson, New York

Papert S 1972 Teaching children thinking. *Program. Learn. Educ. Technol.* 9: 245-55

Piaget J 1972 *Epistémologie des sciences de l'homme*. Gallimard, Paris

Rice J M 1913 *Scientific Management in Education*. Hinds, Noble and Eldredge, New York

Simon T 1924 *Pédagogie expérimentale: Ecriture, lecture, orthographe*. Colin, Paris

Thorndike E L 1913 *An Introduction to the Theory of Mental and Social Measurements*, 2nd edn. Teachers College Press, New York

Thorndike E L, McCall W A, Chapman J C 1916 *Ventilation in Relation to Mental Work*. Teachers College Press, New York

Thurstone L L 1925 *The Fundamentals of Statistics*. Macmillan, New York

Wall W D 1968 The work of the National Foundation for Educational Research in England and Wales. In: Butcher H J (ed.) 1968 *Educational Research in Britain*. University of London Press, London, pp. 15–32

Yule G U 1911 *An Introduction to the Theory of Statistics*. Griffin, London

G. De Landsheere

Educational Research, Information for

Information is a valuable resource which is essential to the progress of research and development. In order for information to be effectively utilized, it should be identified, managed, and disseminated in a systematic and efficient manner. Information systems have been devised to store and provide access to data. Modern computer technology together with developments in the telecommunications field have resulted in storage and retrieval services from which the user can obtain information from the computer at low cost with almost negligible delays. In this article, the transfer of education information from source to user will be discussed. Special emphasis will be given to bibliographic information services or systems which have been developed to manage the vast range of information in the field of education together with information exchange arrangements which have been established both internationally and nationally.

1. Information Transfer

Educational information or knowledge is presented in a variety of forms which can be categorized into five groups, namely "facts" which are small but true pieces of knowledge; "ideas" or perceptions of existing systems or innovations which can be creative or original as well as developmental and relevant; "methods" by which facts are collected and ideas are implemented; "frameworks" which are complex packages of ideas and methods merged together logically; and "combinations" of other knowledge types which are derived from various groupings of facts, ideas, methods, or frameworks. Information is obtainable from a variety of sources and can also be classified according to these sources. Havelock and Huberman (1977) suggest at least five generic categories of sources, which include "settings", "institutions", "vendors", "knowledge storage centres", and "personal networks". Information storage is assuming greater importance with the need to control the vast quantities of available information. The 1,000 databases in the United States, 600 of which are available online (i.e., by direct interaction with the computer), are evidence of the quantity of current information in all fields of knowledge and its control by modern technology. Furthermore, in Europe there are now 1,400 databases of which 500 are accessible online. The role of the storage centre or information service is to act as an interface between the user and the range of information resources in printed or other forms and to manage the channels of communication by which information is retrieved and disseminated. These mainly autonomous services have the advantages of being unbiased, of covering a range of needs and situations, and of affording the user freedom of access and freedom to choose his or her own information selectively according to his or her own pattern of needs. Finally, information must take form in a certain medium before transfer to its destination for assimilation by the receiver for further utilization and development. Table 1 summarizes the transfer of information.

The *Directory of Educational Research Information Sources* (Foundation for Educational Research in the Netherlands 1979) provides an overview of the main bibliographical publications and databases in the field of educational research and related areas in the social sciences in as many countries as possible. This first edition of the directory lists 293 data files and includes registers of educational and social science research, theses and dissertations listings, abstracting and indexing journals, bibliographies and directories of documentation, and research institutions. A second edition is planned for publication in 1983.

2. Information Services

The ERIC (Educational Resources Information Center) is the largest and most diversified information system in education in the world. The United States Office of Education established the ERIC programme in 1966 to acquire, select, abstract, index, and disseminate the rapidly increasing fugitive literature in the field of education—research findings, conference proceedings, papers presented at professional meetings, and so on—and to accelerate widespread adoption of research-based educational programmes. The utilization of high-speed computer technology has enabled the bibliographical citations to be produced, sorted, and disseminated in a variety of forms for searching both manually and by computer. Documents are gathered and processed in 16 decentralized clearinghouses connected to organizations and institutions throughout the United States. The ERIC clearinghouses are subject oriented and contracts for clearinghouse operations are granted on the basis of subject-specialist capabilities. The clearinghouses have responsibility within the network for acquiring the significant educational literature within their particular scope, selecting the highest quality and most relevant material, and processing the selected items for input to the database. In addition, the ERIC clearinghouses provide reference and retrieval services, develop information analysis products, conduct workshops and make presentations, and generate other types of communication links with the educational community. As well as the computer database consisting of all ERIC files, which is available on the major online network services, two monthly publications, *Resources in Education* and *Current Index to Journals in Education*, are produced. By June 1982, the computer database of the ERIC file contained half a million records of documents and journal articles and is available on the major online network services. All noncopyrighted documents and any others for which reproduction permission is obtained are reproduced on microfiche and are available either on demand or on a subscription basis. There are currently over 700 organizations throughout the world that subscribe to the entire ERIC collection on a continuing basis.

Table 1
Model of information or knowledge transfer[a]

| Sources | Information or knowledge transfer | | |
	Knowledge types	Forms—media	Uses
Settings	Facts	Observation	Diagnosis
Institutions	Ideas	Oral expression	Awareness Goal setting
Vendors	Methods	Print	Management Construction–fabrication
Knowledge storage centres	Frameworks	Electronic	Installation Evaluation
Personal networks	Combinations	Training (combination)	Diffusion Adaptation

a Source: Havelock and Huberman 1977 p. 182

The diversity of information retrieval systems reflects the individuality and differences of databases available in the field of education. There is no coordination of accessible files and researchers must familiarize themselves with the files, including the scope of subject or geographic coverage and time period, the format of presentation (whether hard copy or machine readable), and methods of accessing machine-readable files. There are at least eight online services, each offering a variety of databases and with differing accessibility and restrictions of use, in addition to utilizing differing software and search languages. These services include:

(a) AUSINET—Australian Information Network.

(b) BLAISE—British Library Automated Information Service.

(c) BRS—Bibliographic Retrieval Service.

(d) DIALOG—Lockheed Information Systems (US).

(e) DIMDI—Deutsches Institut für Medizinische Dokumentation und Information.

(f) EISO—Educational Information Systems for Ontario.

(g) IRS—Information Retrieval Service ESRIN (Italy).

(h) ORBIT—System Development Corporation (US).

Many countries support national educational indexes and databases as well as research registers. A selection from the *Directory of Educational Research Information Sources* includes:

(a) African Source Research (Institute of African Studies, Zambia).

(b) Australian Education Index (Australian Council for Educational Research). Database online through AUSINET.

(c) BIB Report; Bibliographischer Index Bildungswissenschaften und Schulwirklichkeit (Verlag für Pädagogische Dokumentation).

(d) British Education Index (British Library). Database online through BLAISE.

(e) Canadian Education Index (Canadian Education Association).

(f) Indian Education Abstracts (India, Ministry of Education and Social Welfare).

In addition, the Ontario Ministry of Education in Canada maintains a computer-developed file of research and reports from school board research units across the province, and from the Ontario Educational Communications Authority (OECA), the Ontario Institute for Studies in Education (OISE), and the Ontario Educational Research Council (OERC). This file is available as *ONTERIS Abstracts* from 1978

and as machine-readable file through the Educational Information Systems for Ontario (EISO) network.

Other specific subject-oriented databases together with related subject files offer further access to educational documentation. Major files are:

(a) Comprehensive Dissertation Index (University Microfilms International, US). Database online through BRS, Dialog, Orbit.

(b) Exceptional Child Education Resources (Council for Exceptional Children, US). Database online through Dialog.

(c) Labour Documentation (International Labour Organization, Switzerland). Database online through Orbit.

(d) Language and Language Behavior Abstracts (Sociological Abstracts, US). Database online through Dialog.

(e) National Center for Child Abuse and Neglect (US). Database online through Dialog.

(f) Programs Applique à la Selection et à la Compilation Automatique de la Literature (Centre National de la Recherche Scientifique, France). Database online through IRS.

(g) PsychInfo (Psychological Abstracts, US). Database online through Dialog, Orbit.

(h) Social SciSearch (Institute for Scientific Information, US). Database online through Dialog, Orbit.

(i) Sociological Abstracts (Sociological Abstracts, US). Database online through Dialog.

A unique service is offered to social science researchers by the Institute of Scientific Information in addition to its database Social SciSearch. The weekly issues of *Current Contents: Social and Behavioral Sciences* present the titles of papers and all other substantive material from more than 1,300 journals reporting worldwide research and practice in the social and behavioural sciences. Copies of the issues are airmailed to subscribers throughout the world ensuring the rapid dissemination of information. The selection of journals scanned is determined by an editorial advisory board with representatives from seven countries.

3. International Exchange

Between 1971 and 1976, the activities undertaken by the UNESCO International Bureau of Education (IBE) in the field of educational documentation and information established the bases for the development of the International Network for Educational Information (INED) which began to take form as a result of decisions made during the 36th session of the International Conference on Education and expressed in Recommendation No. 71 adopted at that conference. The recommendation sets forth the underlying principles of recognition of the importance of educational information to the policy-making process and to the improvement of educational systems and practices, and confirms as further underlying principles the concepts of cooperative networking, standardization, professionalization, and international cooperation. Practical measures at the national level are then recommended in the fields of policy and legislative provisions, services and programmes, and status and training of educational information personnel. All relevant national, regional, and international authorities, organizations, and agencies were requested to cooperate in improving regional and international exchanges of information so as to establish a world information network in education (International Conference on Education, 36th Session, 1977). Seventy countries have agreed to participate in the exchange and in coordinating the activities of regional and national networks. The fourth edition of the *Directory of Educational Documentation and Information Services* (UNESCO/IBE 1982) reflects the development of INED and lists 102 national services, seven regional services, and five international services in operation. A quarterly publication, *IBEDOC Information* reporting worldwide activities, is also issued.

The International Educational Reporting Service (IERS) Awareness List includes abstracts of recent documents of educational innovations, particularly those taking place in developing countries and is published quarterly by UNESCO/IBE. A select bibliography series under the title of *Educational Documentation and Information* is also compiled and published quarterly by UNESCO/IBE. Number 221 of the series on educational research was prepared for the international colloquium on "Research and practice in education: How to strengthen links between research and practice in order to strengthen general education" which was organized by UNESCO in 1980 in Bucharest, Romania. In 1980, UNESCO/IBE adapted the computer system CDS/ISIS (Computerized Documentation System/Integrated Scientific Information) for its information activities, coordinating the bureau's activities with the UNESCO's integrated documentation network through the UNESCO computer system. The sectoral documentation centres within the network reflect the discipline-oriented (education, social sciences, documentation, etc.) nature of UNESCO. The following databases at UNESCO are currently operated under CDS/ISIS:

(a) CDS—UNESCO Bibliographic Database, UNESCO Publications and Documents, UNESCO Library Acquisitions.

(b) CDTHES—UNESCO Thesaurus.

(c) DARE—Experts, institutions, research projects, documents, and journals in the field of the social sciences.

(d) ISORID—Research projects and reports in the field of libraries, documentation, and archives.

(e) EDFAC—Basic references on educational facilities.

(f) IEEN—Experts and institutions in the field of environmental education.

(g) UNED—Industry and environment (operated by the Paris office of UNEP).

(h) DESDATA—Project descriptive data.

(i) PEDPROF—Personnel roster.

Member countries of the Council for Cultural Cooperation support the European Documentation and Information System in Education which was established following a survey of the educational documentation and information systems in Europe by the Documentation Centre for Education in Europe in 1967. An experimental programme for a European network for educational documentation and information, which involved the collection of information on research in progress and completed research, and on national pilot projects of educational reform in various member countries was initiated and the first listing of projects and abstracts, EUDISED *R & D Bulletin* appeared in 1975 and continues to be the only access to the computer-originated files (Davies 1978, 1980).

Also in Europe, a programme was been developed within the framework of the CMEA scientific and technical information system to coordinate activities between educational documentation and information centres. Seminars are held every three years with the support of UNESCO/IBE to consider the exchange of educational information and the means of further advancement of European cooperation. The third seminar, EDICO-3 was held in Prague in October 1980 and attended by experts from 14 European countries. The Institute of Educational Sciences at the University of La Laguna, Tenerife, Spain has initiated a project concerned with bibliographic control of books in the field of education published in English, French, German, Italian, Portuguese, and Spanish. Support has been received from UNESCO to publish the first edition in 1982.

As one of its functions, the UNESCO Regional Office for Education in Asia and Oceania provides clearinghouse services to member states through the Asian Centre of Educational Innovation for Development in Bangkok, Thailand. The centre supports the activities of the Asian Programme of Educational Innovation for Development (APEID) and collects and disseminates information on innovative projects and programmes through a variety of publications and services: *Inventory of Educational Innovations in Asia and Oceania*; *Experiences in Educational Innovation in Asia*; ACEID *Newsletter*. A Regional Educational Media Resource Exchange Service (REMRES) has been established to disseminate information on media materials.

The Department of Education of the Arab Educational Cultural and Scientific Organization (ALECSO) is responsible for projects of cooperation in the development of education in all Arab countries. The Department of Documentation and Information provides services by gathering and processing documents, preparing material for basic research, supplying institutions in the Arab world with journals, documents, and statistical and bibliographical bulletins, and assisting Arab countries in developing library and documentation services.

In conclusion, the rapid expansion of educational research in recent decades has been accompanied by an effective control of the flow of information. There is continued advancement in the mechanics for the efficient management and low-cost access to information. Utilization of computer-based videotex systems such as PRESTEL in the United Kingdom and TELDON in Canada is well-advanced and provides access to information through telephone and television systems. Furthermore, cooperation at the international and national levels by information centres and systems benefits all researchers by providing access to the world's rich information resources, improving communication between the researcher and practitioner, and improving educational research and development.

See also: Knowledge Diffusion in Education; Documentation in Educational Research

Bibliography

Bina J V 1978 *Databases and Clearinghouses: Information Resources for Education.* National Center for Research in Vocational Education, Columbus, Ohio. ERIC Document No. ED 162 634

Davies J 1978 The educational policy information centre: An introduction and a review of the background of European co-operation. *Educ. Libr. Bull.* 21(2): 19–29

Davies J 1980 EUDISED: Image and reality: A crisis of identity. *Educ. Libr. Bull.* 23(3): 1–15

Foundation for Educational Research in the Netherlands 1979 *Directory of Educational Research Information Sources.* Foundation for Educational Research, The Hague

Havelock R G 1969 *Planning for Innovation through Dissemination and Utilization of Knowledge.* Institute for Social Research, Ann Arbor, Michigan

Havelock R G, Huberman A M 1977 *Solving Educational Problems: The Theory and Reality of Innovation in Developing Countries.* UNESCO, Paris

Hudson B M, Davis R E 1980 *Knowledge Networks for Educational Planning: Issues and Strategies.* International Institute for Educational Planning, Paris

Institute of Educational Information 1977 *Exchange of Educational Information: A Means of Further Advancement of European Co-operation in the Field of Education.* Proc. of the European colloquium: EDICO-2. Bratislava

International Bureau of Education 1981 *Education Research.* Educational Documentation and Information No. 221. UNESCO, Paris

International Conference on Education (36th Session) 1977a *Final report, Geneva, 30 August–8 September 1977.* UNESCO, Paris

International Conference on Education (36th Session) 1977b *International Information Networks and their role in the Transfer of Educational Experience.* UNESCO, Paris

Lancaster F W 1979 *Information Retrieval Systems: Characteristics, Testing and Evaluation,* 2nd edn. Wiley, New York

Mellor W L 1982 Information storage and retrieval systems. In: Rao B A, Ravishankar S (eds.) 1982 *Readings in Educational Technology.* Himalaya, Bombay, pp. 176-96

Schmittroth J, Kruzas A T (eds.) 1980 *Encyclopedia of Information Systems and Services,* 4th edn. Gale Research, Detroit, Michigan

UNESCO/International Bureau of Education 1977 *Current Bibliographical Sources in Education.* UNESCO, Paris

UNESCO/International Bureau of Education 1978 International information networks and their role in the transfer of educational experience. UNESCO *Bull. Libr.* 32: 232–51

UNESCO/International Bureau of Education 1982 *Directory of Educational Documentation and Information Services,* 4th edn. UNESCO, Paris

United Nations 1980 *Directory of United Nations Information Systems.* Inter-organization Board for Information Systems, Geneva

Williams M E (ed.) 1981 *Computer-readable Data Bases: A Directory of Data Sourcebook.* American Society for Information Science, Urbana, Illinois

M. A. Findlay

Educational Research, Politics of

A distinct politics of educational research was created worldwide during the 1960s and 1970s, as the support of such inquiry became established government policy in many developed and developing nations (Myers 1981, King 1981). This spread is part—usually a modest part—of the broad development of government support for research in many areas of national significance, ranging from defense and space to physical science, health, agriculture, economics, and other social-policy concerns.

Modern governments support research on education and other social services for a variety of reasons. Policy makers today are more likely to seek and absorb information from research in considering new policies and programs; they understand that information from research can raise important new questions about policies, help improve program performance, and help control program activities; more cynically, they also understand that research results can be used to legitimate policies, and vindicate choices—including the choice to delay (Weiler 1983).

At the same time, policy makers have placed only modest confidence in the saving power of educational research. Educational research has been considered a "soft science," unpersuasive either in prospect or product. There were extremely limited numbers of first-rate research scholars or institutions to be enlisted in the enterprise. Equally limited was the political support that educational research enjoyed from the politically more powerful educational associations, such as teachers' unions, associations of administrators, and regional, state, and local educational policy makers (Timpane 1982).

Within this general setting, the politics of educational research operate at three levels: in the establishment of government research institutions and agendas of study; in the selection and conduct of specific research studies; and in the utilization of the results of research. The most visible of these is the first.

1. Establishing Institutions and Agendas

As public institutions and research agendas have emerged in educational research, so has a complicated and fragile politics. A series of related questions are always under political consideration: from what source shall goals and priorities be derived; to whom shall the available resources be allocated; what type of research will best accomplish the agenda? These questions range from the mostly political to the substantially scientific, but politics is absent from none of them.

There is, to start with, no obvious single source from which goals and priorities for educational research may be derived. Goals and priorities may be suggested by government policy makers themselves, but these are multiple in all national political systems. In the United States these include, at least, federal, state, and local officials and officials in the executive, legislative, and judicial branches—and probably more than one agency in each instance. Moreover, the individual researchers and the institutes and universities in which they work have obvious standing to help determine what research is important and possible. So, too, do the field practitioners, such as teachers and local officials, and the concerned publics, for example, parents, taxpayers, and the representatives of special educational interest groups such as the disadvantaged, the handicapped, and the victims of discrimination.

No national government has allocated sufficient resources to carry out any substantial part of the research agenda that these parties of interest might establish in a negotiated political process. Even in the United States, with by far the most ambitious educational research program, funding for the National Institute of Education (NIE) has never been more than a fraction of that suggested in the initial studies proposing its agenda (Levien 1971). In consequence, the politics of educational research are, at this level, typically a desperate attempt to spread resources too thinly over some representative set of research projects, punctuated by the more or less arbitrary selection of one or two politically and substantively important topics—be they reading or vocational preparation, school finance or organization, bilingual or science education—for concentrated attention and support. The choices made typically disappoint more constituents than they encourage. They also leave government research agencies such as the NIE exposed to continual political attack: for not being "useful to the field" or for "doing bad science"; for being a "tool of the Right" (as Democrats charged during and after the Nixon Administration) or for inveterate "funding of the Left" (as the supporters of President Reagan have claimed); for neglecting local realities or for ignoring emerging national problems. The most consistent (and predictable) criticism of the choices that has been made across time and nations is that the research supported is too much applied in character and thereby of too little value with respect to fundamental policy change and to intellectual progress (Nisbet 1982, Kiesler and Turner 1977). Some critics have gone further, to note inherent conflicts between the requirements of politics for timeliness, relevance, and self-protection and the requirements of research for elegance, parsimony, and objectivity, concluding that the research enterprise requires strong protection from the diurnal incursions of public and governmental interest (Coleman 1972, 1978).

2. Selecting and Conducting Studies

The actual conduct of educational research is infested with a similar swarm of political dilemmas. Once governmental research agencies or offices and their priorities are established, there remain a host of questions having no completely "rational" or "scientific" answers. An important set of methodological questions turn out to be political. For the most important areas of educational research, there are no a priori grounds for choosing a disciplinary approach; historians, ethnographers, sociologists, and several varieties of psychologists, for example, have important contributions to make in solving education's most vexing riddles. Inter- and multi-disciplinary approaches can bridge some, but only some, of the chasms in perspective amongst these disciplines. More often, choices must be made among them, and representatives of the disciplines must enter bureaucratic politics to secure consideration of their proposed inquiries. Similarly, proponents of the several functional forms of research must promote their longitudinal and cross-sectional case studies, surveys, experiments, evaluations, ethnomethodologies, data reanalyses, meta-analyses, development activities, or other qualitative and quantitative designs in a context where many arguments are plausible but only a few will be successful. Finally, in many cases, individuals qualified to perform or assist in the research may operate in diverse settings—in colleges and universities, in research institutes, in regional and local agencies, in professional associations, and at the very site of schooling or education. Each institution will provide technical assistance and political support for their candidates seeking to participate in the supported research.

The government research agency has a few strategies available to deal with these political dilemmas: it may adhere to a "free grant" process that distributes resources to traditional places in research, in accordance with the procedures and canons of the disciplines (study groups, peer review, etc.); it may sharply define and manage its research requirements through in-house or contract research; or it may establish a process for negotiation with all or some of the prospective recipients seeking to establish some mix of research activities serving various educational agendas. The selection of any such strategy places the research policy makers and program directors at risk. Each has the goal of sustaining effective research programs, but must do so through the development of successively more imaginative bureaucratic processes involving service to higher political authority, the continual taking of outside advice, the extension of selection and review processes to include all pertinent perspectives, and the creation and administration of justificatory documents—in a context where political support for the entire enterprise is at best unreliable. The result, in the United States at least, has been the segmentation of the research agenda into an array of topically significant programs (reading, teaching bilingual education, desegregation, educational organization, finance, and so forth) within which are nested continuing grant programs for individuals and small groups of investigators and selected directed studies performed mostly by institutions—all undergirded by published research plans and broad field participation in project review and selection. There is important emphasis at every stage on the ultimate significance that the research may have for the national educational enterprise: the basic political objective is to create a balanced portfolio of basic and applied studies of sufficient significance, quality, and utility to satisfy, if not delight, all important constituencies.

3. Utilizing Results

Political perspectives concerning the use of educational research have developed swiftly since the early 1960s. Two developments which precipitated this change were: (a) the collapse of linear models of research, development, testing, demonstration, and evaluation as explanations of the progress of educational research results into program operations (Cronbach and Suppes 1969); and (b) the parallel collapse of systematic planning models as explanations of the progress of educational research results into new educational policy (Cohen and Garet 1975).

Each of these two models has been replaced by a more political view. The delivery of new knowledge to classroom teachers and other educators is now usually understood as part of an extended process of synthesis (where bodies of related research results are gathered and made interpretable) and of introduction into an actual process of classroom or school improvement. The program improvements suggested by the research are considered along with the insights of artful practice and the opinion of respected peers, with the entire process dependent upon consistent administrative encouragement and community support (Mann 1978). The emphasis has shifted from "design" of educational innovation to the "mobilization" of a receptive staff. The process is fundamentally political, and only secondarily technical.

Similarly, new research knowledge enters policy deliberations by the compatible processes of "knowledge creep" and "decision accretion" (Weiss 1980). That is to say, research results from many studies are absorbed irregularly as part, but only part of the information environment of decision makers, who arrive at their conclusions on given policy issues over an extended period of time, not at one decisive moment. Careful policy analysis may sometimes have a significant impact at an opportune time, but the decision is most often substantially formed by the more gradual process of "accretion" and "creep." In such a view, there is wide play for political forces. The value of research information becomes bound up with the credibility, political influence, and interpretive skill of its bearer.

These new understandings spotlight one of the most important weaknesses in the political system of educational research—the lack of authoritative interpreters who can speak both objectively and practically about both policy and practice from positions grounded in the state of current knowledge (e.g., Wildavsky 1979). These commentators are especially missed because they can simultaneously perform two additional functions essential to the political survival of educational research: to translate many of the significant issues of educational policy and practice into appropriate questions for fundamental and applied research; and to be witness, by their own effectiveness, to the contribution educational research can make to the public interest which supports it.

See also: Educational Research and Policy Making; Policy-oriented Research; Educational Organizations: Micropolitics; Knowledge Utilization

Bibliography

Cohen D K, Garet M S 1975 Reforming educational policy with applied social research. *Harvard Educ. Rev.* 45: 17–43

Coleman J S 1972 *Policy Research in the Social Sciences.* General Learning Press, Morristown, New Jersey

Coleman J S 1978 The use of social science research in the development of public policy. *Urban Rev.* 10: 197–202

Cronbach L J, Suppes P (eds.) 1969 *Research for Tomorrow's Schools: Disciplined Inquiry for Education: Report.* Macmillan, New York

Kiesler S B, Turner C F (eds.) 1977 *Fundamental Research and the Process of Education.* National Academy of Sciences, Washington, DC

King K 1981 Dilemmas of research aid to education in developing countries. *Prospects* 11: 343–51

Levien R E 1971 *National Institute of Education: Preliminary Plan for the Proposed Institute.* A Report Proposed for the Department of Health, Education, and Welfare. Rand, Santa Monica, California

Mann D (ed.) 1978 *Making Change Happen?* Teachers College Press, New York

Myers R G 1981 *Connecting Worlds: A Survey of Development in Educational Research in Latin America.* International Development Research Centre, Ottawa, Ontario

Nisbet J 1982 The impact of research: A crisis of confidence. *Aust. Educ. Res.* 9(1): 5–22

Timpane P M 1982 Federal progress in educational research. *Harvard Educ. Rev.* 52: 540–48

Weiler H N 1983 West Germany: Educational policy as compensatory legitimation. In: Thomas R M (ed.) 1983 *Politics and Education: Cases from Eleven Nations.* Pergamon, Oxford, pp. 35–54

Weiss C H 1980 Knowledge creep and decision accretion. *Knowledge: Creation, Diffusion, Utilization* 1(3): 381–404

Wildavsky A B 1979 *Speaking Truth to Power: The Art and Craft of Policy Analysis.* Little, Brown, Boston, Massachusetts

M. Timpane

Educational Resources Information Center (ERIC)

The Educational Resources Information Center (ERIC), an information system established in 1966, is sponsored by the National Institute of Education, within the United States Department of Education. Through a network of 16 subject-specialized clearinghouses, educational documents are acquired, reviewed, and processed into the database. Journal articles are selected and indexed as well. Access to documents is through *Resources in Education* (RIE), a monthly abstract journal, and microfiche. Citations for journal articles appear monthly in the *Current Index to Journals in Education*, but ERIC does not make the text of these copyrighted materials available through the database. The *Thesaurus of ERIC Descriptors* facilitates access to the printed abstract journals and the database, which can be searched online by computer.

1. Information Available

The Educational Resources Information Center (ERIC) collects primarily English-language documents which are not published or made available through normal channels, that is, publishers. Almost all the information is directly relevant to some aspect of education: counseling; management; elementary, early childhood, handicapped, gifted, and higher education; library and information science; educational technology; junior colleges; languages and linguistics; reading; rural education; science, mathematics, and environmental studies; social studies; teacher education; testing and evaluation; and urban education.

Types of material include such items as: research reports, project descriptions, position papers, speeches, evaluation studies, instructional materials, syllabi, curriculum guides, conference papers, bibliographies, tests, glossaries, statistical compilations, and taxonomies. At the end of the first 15 years, there were 198,624 documents in ERIC.

The Educational Resources Information Center (ERIC) selects and indexes articles from about 700 English language journals in the content fields noted above. At the beginning of 1982, there were 250,663 citations in ERIC.

2. Access to Information

Documents in the ERIC system are listed in the monthly abstract journal, *Resources in Education*, published for ERIC by the United States Government Printing Office. There are approximately 2,700 locations worldwide which subscribe to RIE. Documents are listed by subject, title, author, and institution, and an abstract is provided for each title. The *Thesaurus of ERIC Descriptors* is a basic tool for locating specific information by using key words.

The Educational Resources Information Center (ERIC) obtains permission from authors to reproduce approximately 95 percent of the documents announced in RIE. These items are available in microfiche or paper copy. For those items not available in this form, sources are always given. The microfiche and paper copies may be purchased directly from the Educational Document Reproduction Service (P.O. Box 190, Arlington, Virginia 22210, USA) or they may be found and used at any of the more than 700 depositories, mostly libraries, worldwide. The biannual *Directory of ERIC Microfiche Collections* is a geographically arranged reference tool which includes address, telephone number, contact person, collection status, services provided, and access hours. There are 79 collections in 17 countries in addition to the 663 in the United States. The directory is available from the ERIC Processing and Reference Facility, 4833 Rugby Road, Suite 301, Bethesda, Maryland 20814, USA.

The periodical literature from journals is indexed by subject and author in *Current Index to Journals in Education* and is published by Oryx Press (2214 North Central Avenue, Phoenix, Arizona 85004, USA). The articles can be found in the designated journal or copies from about 65 percent of the journals may be obtained from University Microfilms International, Article Reprint Service, 300 N. Zeeb Road, Ann Arbor, Michigan 48106, USA.

Both *Resources in Education* and *Current Index to Journals in Education* can be searched online by computer through online retrieval services or by purchasing ERIC tapes from the ERIC Facility. Searching requires a computer terminal which can be linked by telephone to a central computer source. Arrangements for use must be made with the organization which handles the central computer. Computer searching provides responses in real time, permitting users to make complex logical demands and obtain immediate responses. It is possible to interact with the computer so that search requirements can be adjusted. The increased efficiency of computer searching is usually at some cost to the user. More than 500 locations in eight countries which provide computer search services are listed in the *Directory of ERIC Search Services*, a biannual compilation which gives address, telephone number, contact person, population served, price, turnaround time, services provided, files accessed, how to submit an inquiry, and the search system used. It is available from the ERIC Facility.

The *Thesaurus of ERIC Descriptors* is the master list of approved terms used by the ERIC system, with a complete cross-reference structure and rotated and hierarchical displays. It is available from Oryx Press.

3. Special Information Sources

Beyond access to information in the system, there are two major services provided by ERIC: question answering and information analysis.

(a) Within the ERIC system, subject expertise resides primarily within the various specialized ERIC clearinghouses. Questions that involve substantive matters can be directed to the appropriate clearinghouse. Such requests may be for a specific document or for matters closely associated with the specialty of the clearinghouse.

(b) In addition to collecting the literature of education for announcement in RIE and CIJE, the ERIC clearinghouses analyze and synthesize the literature into research reviews, state-of-the-art reports, interpretative essays on topics of high current interest and similar publications. These publications are designed to compress the vast amounts of information available and to make it more easily accessible for users.

4. Submitting Documents to ERIC

The Educational Resources Information Center (ERIC) actively solicits documents concerned with any aspect of education. The user audience is broad and therefore all information which can be placed in the public domain is considered. Each document is reviewed by a specialist in the content area and selected (or rejected) on the basis of its utility to educators.

See also: Educational Research, Information for; Documentation in Educational Research

Bibliography

Educational Resources Information Center (ERIC) 1981 *Pocket Guide to ERIC*. ERIC Processing and Reference Facility, Bethesda, Maryland

D. P. Ely

Educational Technology: Conceptual Frameworks and Historical Development

Educational technology came into existence as an occupational category during the course of the 1960s. Prior to that time people were engaged in jobs and activities, which are now regarded as pertaining to educational technology, without being labelled as educational technologists, and to some extent this situation still persists in the early 1980s. The occupational history is so short that an account of how various occupations and patterns of thinking were brought together to create the field of educational technology is essential for understanding the contemporary situation. Indeed the conceptual frameworks evolved during the 1960s still provide the basis of what is taught as educational technology today, even though they have undergone considerable modification.

In order to establish a boundary for discussion, this article will confine itself to conceptual frameworks used or advocated by people describing themselves as educational technologists. Most of these frameworks are often treated as occupationally specific, although this is rarely the case. Many have been imported and adapted, and some are still shared with other occupations. There is also a more philosophical line of thinking which examines the idea of educational technology in the context of knowledge claims in general, the impact of the social and natural sciences, and the nature and historical significance of technology. This proceeds with only token attention to the occupational niches taken up by people calling themselves "educational technologists". However, this apparently disinterested pursuit of philosophical argument may also serve important political purposes. Educational technologists can be viewed as an interest group whose conceptual frameworks are intended not only to guide and describe practice but also to gain political or academic credibility. Thus claims about the effectiveness and utility of educational technology serve an important political purpose in attracting resources and sponsorship, and claims about the theoretical foundations of educational technology play an important part in justifying its academic status, for which criteria related to disciplined and research-based study usually count for more than those related to utility.

1. Early Developments

Entrants to educational technology during the 1960s usually came by one of two routes—audiovisual education or programmed learning (see *Programmed Learning*). Each was associated with a number of possible conceptual frameworks, which practitioners adopted according to the nature of their job, their training, and their personal preference. However, whilst programmed learning could be viewed as theory driven in its initial stages, audiovisual education found it difficult to formulate any theoretical basis for its practice. In contrast, audiovisual educators could easily link their expertise to the accumulated professional experience of classroom teachers while programmed learning specialists tended to criticize teachers with a detachment that did little to promote mutual understanding.

Most audiovisual specialists saw themselves solely as practitioners: advisers to teachers, trainers of teachers, and providers of learning resources for use by teachers. In so far as they had a theoretical base it consisted of two assumptions: (a) that stimulus richness and variety would enhance attention and motivation, and (b) that degree of abstraction was a critical variable in learning. Dale's *Cone of Experience,* with "direct purposeful experience" at the base and "verbal symbols" at the apex (see *Instructional Design: Media Selection*), was probably the most frequently cited conceptual model. Although there were always provisos about appropriateness, quality, and effectiveness, it was generally believed that the more audiovisual materials used the better, and that students needed to spend a significant amount of time in contact with "the real world" or with lively mediated representations of it, for example motion pictures. Neither of these assumptions is theoretically tenable today, but they are not without merit as "rules of thumb".

Communication theorists have shown that there is a limit to the amount of information that can be received and processed at any one time, and that multiple-channel communication can be disadvantageous (Travers 1970). But the average classroom remains a long way from media saturation. The conclusion seems to be that, in using audiovisual materials to enhance richness and variety, basic principles of message design such as simplicity, clarity, and logical organization need to be carefully observed.

Similarly, the notion of "authentic reality" inherent in Dale's cone of experience has been undermined by perception theorists' demonstration that much of what is seen and heard is framed by preexisting cognitive/perceptual schemas. It is not just experience but its interpretation that is crucial. Nevertheless, the problem of abstraction is still recognized by developmental psychologists who stress the role of concrete–operational experience for young children and distinguish between concrete, iconic, and symbolic modes of representation (Bruner 1966). The audiovisual specialists' concern with "real experience" can also be reformulated in terms of the sociology of knowledge, with attention being focused on the tensions and barriers to learning which arise from the gap between school knowledge and knowledge that has currency in the students' lives outside school.

How then did the move towards educational technology begin? One of the key individuals was Dr. James Finn who became president of the Division of Audiovisual Instruction, the United States media specialists' professional association, in 1960. His seminal paper "Technology and the Instructional Process" (Finn 1960) examined the possible relations of technology with education but set this in the context of a general discussion of the role of technology in society. His main argument was that many areas of society in the United States were being transformed by technology, and that it was inevitable that education would eventually undergo a similar transformation. Moreover, although technological change might be led by changes in instrumentation, it was never limited to that. The transformation would involve organizational and cultural changes so radical that it was impossible to predict them. At that time two major trends were discernible but they led in opposite directions: one was the trend towards mass instructional technology as exemplified by the new prominence of television; the other was a trend towards individualization of which programmed learning provided a new example. The concept of programming was central to both these trends.

Underneath Finn's mantle of social prophet was some hard political advice. Recent highly publicized experiments in instructional television had by-passed the audiovisual specialists, and this could happen again with teaching machines. "How many of us", he asked "will go overboard and sink with the old concepts that will be absorbed or outmoded and tossed to the sharks by the new technology?" The concept of audiovisual education may go "down the drain, or it may not, depending on whether or not it can be redefined acceptably". Referring to teaching machines, he then added:

It is my position that the audio-visual field is in the easiest position to help integrate these mechanisms properly into the instructional process. They are not primarily audio-visual; they are primarily technological. The audio-visual field, I think must now suddenly grow up. The audio-visual specialists, are, of all educational personnel, the closest to technology now; we have, I think, to become specialists in *learning technology*—and that's how I would redefine audio-visual education. (pp. 393–94)

Significantly, the Department of Audiovisual Instruction (DAVI), published a major sourcebook *Teaching Machines and Programmed Learning*, edited by Lumsdaine and Glaser, that very same year. It was the second major book in the field and, apart from a shortened version of Finn's paper, was written entirely by psychologists. Finn explained the reasons for DAVI sponsorship in a foreword:

> the audiovisual professional, as a technologist of the teaching profession, must relate to fields like psychology exactly as the medical doctor relates to his basic sciences.

The editors' concluding remarks suggested that psychologists were now ready to play their part:

> It seems to us that the numerous contributors whose writings have produced this volume have reflected one dominant idea. This is the concept that the processes of teaching and learning can be made an explicit subject matter for scientific study, on the basis of which a technology of instruction can be developed. . . . As we learn more about learning, teaching can become more and more an explicit technology which can itself be definitively taught. (pp. 563–64)

> The basis for consistent improvement in educational methods is a systematic translation of the techniques and findings of the experimental science of human learning into the practical development of an instructional technology. To achieve the full benefits inherent in this concept, instructional materials and practices must be designed with careful attention to the attainment of explicitly stated, behaviorally defined educational goals. Programmed learning sequences must be developed through procedures that include systematic tryout and progressive revision based on analysis of student behavior. (p. 572)

This introduces two new concepts, which were to be of seminal importance. First, there is the concept of instructional technology as applied learning theory. Then secondly, there is the idea of product development through the systematic testing and revision of learning materials. Though familiar in industry it appears that the idea of product development was rediscovered in education almost by accident:

> An unexpected advantage of machine instruction has proved to be the feedback to the programme. (Skinner 1968 p. 49)

Linking the two concepts gives the idea of scientific research leading to technological development which gradually evolved among psychologists between 1954

and 1964. Indeed, associations between science and technology, research and development, and psychology and education provided an attractive platform for expanding psychological research during the 1960s, without the precise nature of the linkages and dependencies needing to be agreed.

At least three different perspectives on this issue can be discerned in the psychological writings of the period.

(a) Technology is seen as the direct application of the findings of instructional scientific research. Laboratory-derived procedures need only minor modification to fit them for general use in education. The psychologists' expertise is paramount (Skinner 1958).

(b) Technological research and development is needed to combine findings from learning research with other forms of knowledge. Research and development centres are needed to accomplish the often major modifications that are required to put theory into practice (see *Curriculum Development Centers*). These should be run by a partnership of psychologists and educators (Hilgard 1964, Glaser 1965).

(c) Science and technology proceed in parallel. Each is capable of contributing to the other, especially if mutual communication is improved. Education is not just the straightforward application of learning theory, and psychological research has generated no more than "islands of knowledge and understanding within the science of learning" (Melton 1959).

The third perspective uses the term technology descriptively, much as social anthropologists would use it, but the first two perspectives use the term prescriptively with an aspirational futurist connotation. Thus Melton would describe current educational practice as technologically primitive, while Skinner and Hilgard describe it as nontechnological.

On the whole, these psychologists saw educational technology being developed within the educational sector, though very closely linked to training technology in the industrial and military sectors. But Finn et al. (1962) saw it coming mainly from the outside:

> . . . Education, as a sector of national life, has, for the most part, been cut off from technological advances enjoyed by industry, business, military establishments, etc. The American educational enterprise exists out of technological balance with great sectors of the society. As such, it can be viewed as a relatively primitive or under-developed culture existing between and among highly sophisticated technological cultures.

He was overtly sceptical about the psychologists' claims that a science of learning was almost developed (Finn 1968).

Many writers confuse these different meanings of the term educational technology or simply choose

		Imported into education and adapted	Developed within the educational sector
Description of: Dissemination of:	Good current practice	(a) Use of existing devices, mainly developed outside educaton (Audiovisual education)	(c) Currently used teaching techniques and educational practices (Teacher as educational technologist)
Prescription for: Prediction of:	Future practice	(b) Wholesale use of post-industrial instruments, techniques and organizational patterns (Educational futures)	(d) Results of massive investment in research and development (Technological research, applied science)

Figure 1
Conceptions of educational technology

the one that best suits their argument. So, for easy reference, they have been depicted in Fig. 1.

The descriptive categories (a) and (c) have been expanded to include educators' common concerns with disseminating practices developed in one place and thought to be improvements on tradition. Box (d) includes both the psychological perspectives described above, the "strong" applied science of Skinner and Lumsdaine, and the weaker "technological research and development" perspectives of Hilgard. Box (c) could also have been subdivided between those who extrapolate from existing trends (the prophets) and those who have advocated redesigning the educational system from a new set of "first principles" (the utopians), but this is probably too fine a distinction for our current purposes.

Lumsdaine (1964) made a widely quoted distinction between educational technology 1, the application of physical science and engineering technology to the design of instructional devices [corresponding with Box (a) in Fig. 1], and educational technology 2, the application of the behavioural sciences to create a technology of learning [corresponding with Box (d) in Fig. 1]. However, he somewhat marred the discussion with the implication that a technology was dependent upon rather than interdependent with its "underlying" sciences—an unfortunate misapprehension when technological developments such as paper, ink, and movable type are discussed which preceded scientific understanding of the phenomena by several centuries. More significant for the future, perhaps, was Lumsdaine's generic definition of a programme:

An instructional program is a vehicle which generates an essentially reproducible sequence of instructional events

and accepts responsibility for efficiently accomplishing a specified change from a given range of initial competences or behavioral tendencies to a specified terminal range of competences or behavioral tendencies. (p. 385)

This goes beyond the idea of a programme as a reproducible presentation to the idea of a programme as guaranteed learning, with the programmer accepting responsibility for student learning whenever the conditions meet the original specifications. This concept of a validated learning package neatly combined the scientists' need for reproducibility with the technologists' practice of empirical development to meet specified criteria, and provided the cornerstone for several important future developments.

Finn also identified programming as a central concept, but for a different reason. In noting that programming was common to several new technological developments—both in mass communication and in individualized learning—he perceptively added:

The heartland is programming. He who controls the programming heartland controls the educational system. (Finn 1960 p. 393)

Moreover, the economics of programme production demanded thinking about learning resources on a larger scale, for only then could the high production costs of television or the high development costs of programmed learning be justified. At the same time, however, people began to be aware that utilization of programmes might be an even greater problem than design (Miles 1964). The concept of "systems" became increasingly dominant during the mid-1960s and assumed a central role in the emergent field of educational technology (see *Programmed Learning*).

2. The Systems Approach

The term "system" appeared fairly regularly in the early writings on educational technology referred to above, but did not immediately become part of people's central conceptual frameworks. The Oxford English Dictionary gives it two main types of meaning:

> An organized or connected group of objects; a set or assemblage of things connected, associated, or interdependent, so as to form a complex unity; a whole composed of parts in orderly arrangement according to some scheme or plan.

> A set of principles, etc.; a scheme, method.

The physical, biological, and social sciences used it only in the first sense, but the influential new field of systems engineering began to use it in the second sense as well. The fields having the most immediate impact on the thinking of educational technologists were those of man–machine systems, management, and systems engineering.

The central concept of thinking about man–machine systems was that it made little sense to design machines without also thinking about their human operators or to design human jobs without considering whether some tasks were more appropriately delegated to machines than others. It was the system as a whole which needed to be optimized. These ideas were developed in military and industrial contexts where the use of machines was taken for granted, and resulted in the coordination of the previously separate fields of personnel selection, training, and equipment design. Its attractiveness to educational technologists was that it addressed one of their most pressing problems, the respective roles of classroom teacher and mediated instruction. This recurrent issue was raised in dramatic form by early experiments with closed-circuit television and programmed instruction. The consequence, as Heinich (1968) persuasively argued, was the need for media specialists to reconceptualize their role. Decisions about the use of machines and materials needed to be made at the curriculum planning stage rather than the classroom implementation stage, according to Paradigm 2 rather than Paradigm 1 in Fig. 2.

Hoban (1965) added a further strand to the reconceptualization process when he emphasized the need for a management of learning perspective:

> When we consider the part machines play in education, we are forced into a consideration of man/machine systems. When we consider man/machine systems, we are forced into a consideration of technology . . . . technology is *not* just machines and men. It is a complex, integrated organization of men and machines, of ideas, of procedures, and of management. (p. 242)

> The central problem of education is not learning but the management of learning. . . . . No matter which of the new educational media is introduced, the situation into which it is introduced is transformed by the introduction. Acceptance of management of learning as a central problem of organized and institutional education would, at least, permit the admission of a wider range of alternative procedures, techniques, and methods in teaching—without threatening or substantially altering the critical functions of education, teaching, or learning. (p. 244)

By this time systems thinking had become an important aspect of the field of management. The initial influence came not from engineering but from biology, where Bertalanffy (1950) first formulated his theory of open systems. The theory was taken up and further developed by organization theorists during the 1950s and early 1960s (Griffiths 1964), and their prime concern was not with designing new systems but with analysing and improving existing systems, not with man–machine systems but with social systems. In particular, the systems concept drew attention (a) to an organization's interaction with its environment, and (b) to the interplay between and coordination of its various subsystems. For educational technologists intimately concerned with the problem of change, this kind of understanding was crucial, and so was the growing body of

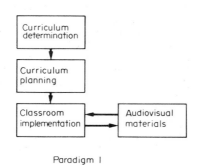

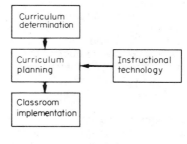

Paradigm 1   Paradigm 2

Figure 2
Two paradigms for educational technology[a]
a Source: Heinich R 1968

research on innovation which followed it. But this particular strand of systems thinking had relatively little influence for some considerable time, because it was overshadowed by the impact of the systems engineers.

Systems engineering (sometimes described as operations research) evolved during the Second World War as a field concerned with the design of large-scale technical systems. Its reputation was based on successes in the military and aerospace sectors but it also found increasing application in sections of industry. Ramo (1973) defined it as follows:

> The systems approach is a technique for the application of a scientific approach to complex problems. It concentrates on the analysis and design of the *whole,* as distinct from the components or the parts. It insists upon looking at a problem *in its entirety*, taking into account all the facets and all the variables, and relating the social to the technological aspects. (p. 15)

Ramo illustrated his argument with a telling comparison between telephones and automobiles. The telephone system was designed as a system from the outset and provided a closely integrated network of people and equipment that handled a wide range of demands with considerable efficiency. The automobile system was never designed as an integrated system, its subsystems (e.g., roads, repair, manufacture, insurance, parking, etc.) were uncoordinated and it was extremely inefficient. Media specialists had no difficulty in identifying the "audiovisual system" with the latter, for it suffered from an equally frustrating lack of coordination between such aspects as hardware manufacture, building design, teacher training, and software production and distribution. The message was to "think big" and throughout the 1960s it was felt that systems engineers were waiting in the wings, itching to redesign the United States educational system from scratch.

Ramo's use of the term "technique" was significant because what began as an approach to the design of systems rapidly evolved in the educational context (and indeed many other contexts) into a system of design, thus transforming the meaning of the word "system" from its first dictionary definition to its second, from a mode of conceptualizing an organization to a set of design principles (see *Instructional Design: Systems Approach*). The first definition led to what Andrews and Goodson (1980) later described as integrated models of instructional design, while the second led to task-oriented models.

Integrated models derived also from general systems theory and continued to stress communication feedback, large-scale planning, and interaction between subsystems. They advocated a problem-solving approach with exploration of many alternatives and a design team with a diverse range of talents. Their most obvious disadvantage was that it

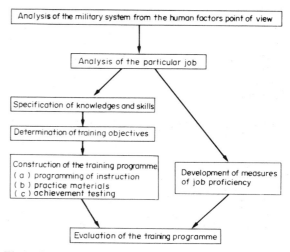

Figure 3
Steps in the development of training[a]

a Source: Crawford M P 1962 p. 314

was only rarely possible to mobilize the necessary finance, political support, and human talent. A series of experimental institutions and projects—Oakland Community College, Oklahoma Christian College, Project PLAN, Oakleaf School, the Open University, Televised Primary Education in the Ivory Coast, IMU Mathematics in Sweden, and many others—captured the imagination of educational technologists and nurtured their ambitions. But most of them had no opportunity to work on this scale, and could only use systems analysis to choose innovation strategies for smaller scale efforts.

Task-oriented models attempted to list all the design tasks that had to be performed and tended to stress specific steps and linear progression through them with only occasional feedback. An early example from the United States Army is given in Fig. 3. The similarity with Tyler's model of curriculum development is immediately apparent, and it requires only slight modification to incorporate the models for designing programmed instruction which were also evolving in the early 1960s (see *Curriculum Development*). Variations on this theme mushroomed throughout the 1960s and 1970s and models of this kind soon became a central part of the conceptual frameworks of educational technologists. They had three main advantages.

(a) Although insisting on detailed specification of objectives and preordinate evaluation, these models still allowed considerable flexibility of interpretation.

(b) The tightly coupled objectives–evaluation framework gave sufficient sense of a scientific approach to remain attractive both to psychologists and to politicians concerned with accountability.

(c) The product orientation and often implicit promise of a multimedia approach gained the allegiance of media specialists.

3. Consolidation

The period between 1967 and 1972 can be regarded as a period of consolidation. Educational technology became a recognized term and people began to accept it as an occupational definition which covered a range of jobs in all sectors of education. The early conceptual frameworks were tried, developed, and modified according to three main types of criteria. (a) Did they provide a credible rationale for a newly emerging field? (b) Did they define a distinguishable set of activities as being primarily the concern of educational technologists? (c) Did they create a boundary for the occupation that was politically defensible?

The first official endorsement of a field called educational technology may well have been the establishment in the United Kingdom of a National Council for Educational Technology in 1967. This followed the report of a committee on Audiovisual Aids in Higher Scientific Education, which only used the term educational technology in its concluding section. The United Kingdom Association for Programmed Learning promptly added Educational Technology to its title in 1968, while in the United States it was the Department of Audiovisual Instruction of the National Education Association which changed its name to Association for Educational Communications and Technology in 1970. This coincided with the publication of a major report by a Commission on Instructional Technology appointed by Congress, and anticipated the creation of a National Center for Educational Technology within the National Institute of Education in Washington, DC. UNESCO held a conference on Training Programmes for Educational Technologists in June 1970, and the International Bureau of Education published an important bibliography of educational technology later that year (Huberman 1970). Though the first periodical, *Educational Technology*, had been founded in the United States as early as 1960, it was some time before the second journal, *Programmed Learning and Educational Technology*, added the term in 1967.

As official recognition grew, the problem of defining educational technology became even more acute and is still the subject of lengthy debate (Mitchell 1978). The definition produced by the National Council for Educational Technology (NCET) in the United Kingdom when it first met in 1967 was:

> Educational technology is the development, application, and evaluation of systems, techniques, and aids to improve the process of human learning. (NCET 1969)

This shrewd compromise has stood the test of time because it allowed all the appropriate interest groups to identify with it without appearing too threatening to the others. The United States Commission on Instructional Technology showed a similar concern for reconciling the aspirations of educational technologists with the beliefs and expectations of educators and politicians:

> Instructional technology can be defined in two ways. In its more familiar sense, it means the media born of the communications revolution which can be used for instructional purposes alongside the teacher, textbook, and blackboard. In general, the Commission's report follows this usage. In order to reflect present-day reality, the Commission has had to look at the pieces that make up instructional technology: television, films, overhead projectors, computers, and the other items of "hardware" and "software" (to use the convenient jargon that distinguishes machines from programs). In nearly every case, these media have entered education independently and still operate more in isolation than in combination.
>
> The second and less familiar definition of instructional technology is more than the sum of its parts. It is a systematic way of designing, carrying out, and evaluating the total process of learning and teaching in terms of specific objectives, based on research in human learning and communication, and employing a combination of human and nonhuman resources to bring about more effective instruction. The widespread acceptance and application of this broad definition belongs to the future. Though only a limited number of institutions have attempted to design instruction using such a systematic, comprehensive approach, there is reason to believe that this approach holds the key to the contribution technology can make to the advancement of education. It became clear, in fact, as we pursued our study, that a major obstacle to instructional technology's fulfillment has been its application by bits and pieces. (Tickton 1970 pp. 21–22)

More useful perhaps for current purposes is the much longer definition statement produced by the Association for Educational Communications and Technology (AECT) in 1972, which included a rationale for the field of educational technology, a description of what people in the field do, and a discussion of its social and professional context (Ely 1972). The rationale section identified the uniqueness of the field with three major concepts and their synthesis into a total approach. These were "the use of a broad range of resources for learning, the emphasis on individualized and personalized learning, and the use of the systems approach". The development of each of these concepts during the consolidation period is discussed below.

The concept of resources for learning was a useful expansion of the earlier term, audiovisual materials, because it incorporated printed resources and could also be interpreted as including environmental resources (school trips and visits) and resource people (visitors). Although some resource production was integrated with curriculum development in the manner envisaged by Heinich's Paradigm 2 (see Fig. 2), most of it remained only loosely coordinated with the curriculum. Hence the teacher retained a major role in the selection of learning resources, and considerable attention was given to resource management, distribution, and utilization. Indeed the teacher was often referred to as a manager of learning resources (Taylor 1970), an idea suggesting that every teacher was an educational technologist (Fig. 1 Box 3) and that teacher education, therefore, was the highest priority (Witt 1968). Resource production was assumed to be a shared responsibility. Some would be produced by commercial firms, some would be produced by locally based educational technologists, and some would be produced by the teachers themselves, preferably with technical and advisory support from educational technologists.

The associated term resource centre also came into common currency, combining a number of functions now considered essential for the teacher's role as a manager of resources. Thus a teachers' resource centre was a place where teachers could select from a collection of existing resources, make multiple copies of a resource, produce their own resources, or even commission others to produce resources for them (see *Teachers' Centres*). Similar facilities could also be envisaged for pupils, for whom the term learning centre or pupils' resource centre was sometimes used.

The resources concept raises the issue of the respective roles of educational technologists and librarians, and in most countries there is now a long history of interprofessional discussion and mutual accommodation. It has become increasingly common for simple audiovisial materials to be stored in libraries and for pupils to have access to them there, while production facilities are usually found in educational technology units. Arrangements for storing complex software such as film or videotape and for managing the audiovisual equipment used in classrooms are much more varied, with reprographic equipment often being lodged with the administration [see *Libraries: School (Resource Centers)*].

Attention to individualized learning was not a new concept, but the idea was given a considerable boost by the advent of programmed learning. Earlier initiatives such as the Dalton and Winnetka plans were revived and redeveloped under the influence of behavioural psychologists to incorporate tightly specified student assignments, programmed learning sequences, and criterion-referenced tests (see *Dalton Plan*; *Winnetka Scheme*). Most of these systems individualized only the pace at which students could learn but some such as the IMU in Sweden or Project PLAN in the United States introduced assignments of different levels of difficulty, the latter backed by a computer-based record-keeping and advisory system. Later, terms such as mastery learning, modular instruction, audiotutorial systems, and personalized systems of instruction (PSI) came to be

associated with this line of development, and these are discussed elsewhere in this Encyclopedia (see *Mastery Learning Model of Teaching and Learning*; *Module Approach*; *Keller Plan: A Personalized System of Instruction*). On the whole, mastery learning and PSI came to be associated with extremely specific objectives and repetition of units by students who failed to get high scores on criterion-referenced tests (see *Criterion-referenced Tests*), while modular instruction and audiotutorial systems allowed a looser interpretation of the systems approach and put more emphasis on the use of nonprint media. Some systems incorporated short tutorials and even some group teaching into what remained basically individualized systems (see *Individualized Instruction in Higher Education*).

Another approach to individualization was the introduction of Dial Access Information Retrieval Systems (DAIRS), which allowed students to dial up audiotapes from remote learning carrels or even from their dormitories. This can be seen both as an extension of the library and as an extension of the language laboratory for private study. Some installations have incorporated a video facility, but most institutions found even audio facilities too expensive. Very little is heard of DAIRS today but the concept remains attractive and it awaits further technological development before its potential can be more fully realized.

Computers have proved to be more powerful and flexible devices than DAIRS for delivering individualized learning. During the period under discussion, 1967–72, computer-assisted learning (CAL) was also confined to a few experimental facilities, but the technology has developed much faster and the advent of microcomputers has greatly enhanced the chance that the average child in the average school will gain access to such a facility. Moreover, while DAIRS is only an improved delivery system for existing types of programme, CAL demands radical changes in programming techniques if its potential is to be properly exploited (see *Computer-managed Learning*).

The third key concept in this first AECT definition statement was the systems approach, whose origins have already been discussed. By this time some of the more flagrantly overambitious claims on its behalf had been dispersed by the criticisms of, among others, Travers (1968) and Oettinger and Mark (1969), and its main area of application was instructional design (see *Instructional Design: Systems Approach*). However, the boundary between instructional design and curriculum development was not at all clear, particularly in higher education where there was no established professional group of curriculum specialists and in those school systems where curriculum development was already associated with the production of learning materials, for example, in the United Kingdom. The situation was usually resolved by subject specialists retaining control and using

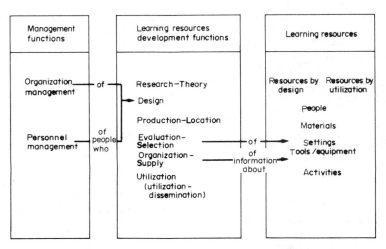

Figure 4
The domain of educational technology[a]

a Source: Ely 1972

whatever kind of consultancy assistance was available, or, in the case of large projects, by whoever was able to acquire the necessary support and finance.

Ely's description of what educational technologists do in practice was organized round the concept of learning resources, and it is important to recognize that neither of the other two concepts, individualized learning and systems approach, could have served this purpose because significant numbers of practitioners would then have been excluded. However, the term "resources" is used in a very broad sense that includes both people (human resources) and settings (the resources of the organization and its environment). This usage is similar to that of economists and planners, but wider than the educators' meaning which generally refers only to materials and equipment. Thus educational technologists could negotiate local meanings in their own work settings, according to what they felt was feasible and appropriate.

A slightly modified form of Fig. 4 (with the first two boxes headed educational management functions and educational development functions) provides the basis for AECT's (1977) current definition (see *Educational Technology: Personnel*).

4. Educational Technology and Mass Communications

The field of mass communications has grown up in parallel with that of educational technology with contributions from an equally wide range of perspectives. As with educational technology, three distinct types of knowledge are involved: social science knowledge (psychology, sociology, and linguistics), engineering knowledge, and production/design knowledge from practising broadcasters, journalists, advertisers, and publishers.

The main area of overlap with educational technology has been educational broadcasting and closed-circuit television, where work has usually been undertaken by mixed groups of educators and broadcasters. The broadcasters have usually been trained outside education and neither they nor the associated educators often describe themselves as educational technologists. This is not surprising when educational broadcasters are employed by broadcasting organizations whose main interest lies outside education, and whose criteria for success derive (a) from the aesthetic criticism of their peers, and (b) from their ability to attract and hold audiences (not to instruct captive audiences). Thus it is only when instruction is seen as the main purpose of a broadcast that a television or radio producer is likely to identify with the field of educational technology. This occurs most often with closed-circuit television systems, with certain adult education programmes, and with large educational broadcasting systems that are specifically designed to make a major contribution to the delivery of instruction (as in the Ivory Coast). This more integrated perspective on mass communication and educational technology has been promoted in many Third World countries by international organizations such as UNESCO and the World Bank which have sponsored a large number of important initiatives.

Many of the concepts employed by producers of motion pictures, still pictures, sound, and graphics are common to those working inside and outside education (see *Graphic Production: Educational*

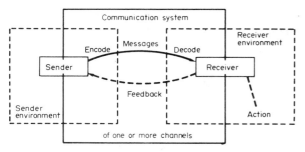

Figure 5
A composite communication model

Materials; *Television and Film Production; Photographic Production and Photographic Services*), and the same is true for engineers. But the social scientists' contributions to mass communication have been less widely used in education. Although communication models were frequently cited by media specialists during the formative period of educational technology, they were discussed only in the most general terms. However, the development of research in related fields suggests that communication theory concepts could have more direct application today. Since communication theory models have as many variants as systems models, a composite model is presented in Fig. 5 to show the main features of this approach.

Traditional educational technology research focused primarily on the interaction between message characteristics and subsequent receiver action, and was thus dependent on the constructs available for describing them. Receiver characteristics were also considered, first in terms of prior learning alone, then later (but not too successfully) in terms of "learner attributes". Neither simple media distinctions nor the simple "types of learning" classifications of the behavioural psychologists have provided adequate descriptions of messages, and this is now recognized as a much more complex problem to which linguistics, visual communication semiotics, cognitive psychology, and the relevant content specializations also have to contribute. Similarly, the "decoding" of messages is now seen as dependent on the receiver's idiosyncratic cognitive structure and cognitive strategies, which are only beginning to be adequately portrayed by cognitive psychologists (and then only in certain limited content areas). Receiver actions have also to be understood as part of their ongoing interaction within their environment in which some messages and some actions are given greater priority than others. So receiver behaviour cannot be interpreted in terms of the communication system alone.

Even in culturally familiar settings the sender often lacks appreciation of the receiver's environment and encodes the message in some inappropriate way or misinterprets the feedback he or she receives, and this problem is magnified as the cultural gap between senders' and receivers' environments widens. The often unconscious influence of the senders' attitudes and beliefs is being increasingly researched, as also is the influence of the politics of the senders' environment on message selection. Then, finally, there is the question of control over the communication system as a whole. Whose interests does it serve and to what extent can any of the available channels be described as responsive or interactive?

This enormous range of research that is now relevant to the work of educational technologists is likely to remain a major problem for a field with a strong commitment to improving professional practice (Hawkridge 1981), especially since the links between such theories and the practices of message or system design are so very complicated. Yet there is an equal danger that if such research is ignored, the impact of existing practice will become too strong and "educational technology will only confer a *rational cover* for already existing conventions" (Ahlström et al. 1975). The opposite danger, that of "scientism", is rapidly receding as the monolithic early influence of behavioural psychology diminishes, but it could arise again if some other branch of social science were to begin to exaggerate its knowledge claims.

5. The Interactionist Concept of Educational Technology

Flechsig (1975) defines a fourth, interactionist, concept of educational technology as a necessary addition to three which have already been discussed—the teacher's tool concept, the mass communication concept, and the systems concept:

> This fourth concept is characterised by the principle that learners take over the control over their learning processes, whereas the three other concepts—explicitly or implicitly—locate the control functions within the teacher or the teaching system. (p. 8)

Thus unlike the systems concept, which he identifies with values such as "achievement" and "efficiency", the interactionist concept could be associated with "emancipatory education" and the "democratization of society".

Ten years earlier, Lewis and Pask (1965) had argued that "although learning can be approximated as goal-directed adaptation . . . a complete specification must entail the possibility of *creating*, as well as satisfying, goals" (p. 217). But it was Moore's conception of an educational environment with which Flechsig most readily identified. Moore began by using the term "autotelic responsive environment" to describe his computer-controlled "talking typewriter". An autotelic activity is defined as something one engages in for its own sake and not for obtaining some external reward (an explicitly anti-Skinnerian concept) and a responsive environment is one which satisfies the following conditions:

(a) It permits the learner to explore freely.

(b) It informs the learner immediately about the consequences of his actions.

(c) It is self-pacing, i.e., events happen within the environment at a rate determined by the learner.

(d) It permits the learner to make full use of his capacity for discovering relations of various kinds.

(e) Its structure is such that the learner is likely to make a series of interconnected discoveries about the physical, cultural, or social world. (Moore 1968 p. 419)

The much admired work of Seymour Papert (1980) clearly belongs in this same direction.

Later, Moore expanded his ideas still further when he added a "perspectives principle" to the autotelic principle and the productive principle [implied in condition (e) above] for the design of what he now called "clarifying environments". The perspectives principle, which he derived from the symbolic interactionist theory of Mead, stated that learners should have a chance to take at least four roles in each learning situation: agent, patient, significant other, and generalized other. For example they might create a goal (agent), achieve a goal defined for them by someone else (patient), advise another learner (significant other), or become part of an audience for another learner's presentation (generalized other). This principle can be considered as reinterpreting the principle of learner control for a democratically oriented social context. It suggests giving special attention to the social organization of groups of children engaged in group projects or working with computers, and it also assigns an important role to simulations and games (see *Simulation and Gaming in Education*).

The interactionist concept is also fundamental to new developments in information technology. It is now relatively easy to store knowledge and make it available to possible users, but difficult to make much of it accessible, in the sense of finding it, understanding it, and appreciating its significance. Thus the physics section of a library is available for inspection by all who enter, but little of it will be accessible to someone without any scientific background. Then there is the additional question of how to find knowledge of whose existence one is not even aware. Hence the problem of how different users can interact with stored knowledge is a major concern of cognitive scientists, information scientists, and educational technologists alike. Travers (1973) argued along similar lines when he wrote:

Educational technology needs to become preoccupied with the development of rich and interesting environments in which children can make real decisions about what to explore. It needs to bring out the importance of significant intellectual relationships between people and the significance of intellectual interaction. It needs to encourage self-initiated exploration. (p. 990)

Returning to the political aspect of Flechsig's conception, Boguslaw (1973) has noted that the systems approach was originally developed for use with nonsocial systems where the goals were formulated by people outside the system itself. But in any social system there are people within the system who may wish to participate in defining the system's objectives, or at least their own personal objectives, and their concerns cannot easily be ignored. The implications for educational technology are twofold. Concerning personal objectives, Azuma has argued as follows:

An important problem we have to recurrently rethink during this coming decade is the proper balance of the two approaches which we have seen in technological development over the two preceding decades. One is the effort to improve the effectiveness of mastering externally defined learning tasks, the other is an orientation towards providing a learning environment wherein learning is intrinsically motivated and self-directed. (Azuma 1977 p. 3)

Concerning wider participation in defining the system's objectives, there will be value issues which cannot be resolved by arguments concerned only with efficiency or effectiveness. Under these conditions, Boguslaw suggests:

It may be possible to define one task of the systems designer as essentially similar to the task of a labor arbitrator in industry—that of working out acceptable tradeoffs and compromises; of dealing with the realities and prospects of power; and defining objectives acceptable, if not completely satisfactory, to all parties involved. (Boguslaw 1973 pp. 182–83)

This broker role is inherently attractive to those with little power who wish to stimulate the process of educational change. But compromises based on the realities of power will not always be compatible with one's personal values, and reluctant agreements do not always get implemented. Educational technology necessarily involves social and political processes which cannot be understood in purely technical terms, and like other professionals, educational technologists need to clarify and attend to their own and other interested parties' values (Greene 1968, Hoban 1977, Travers 1973).

See also: Economics of Educational Technology; Educational Technology: Field of Study; Educational Technology: Local Centers; Educational Technology: Personnel; Educational Technology: Training; Instructional Design: Media Selection; Instructional Design: Systems Approach; Instructional Design: Media Attributes; Media Program Administration; Programmed Learning; Television: Classroom Use

Bibliography

Ahlström K G, Lindblad S, Wallin E 1975 *Notes on Educational Technology*. Steering Group on Educational Technology, Council for Cultural Cooperation, Council of Europe, Strasbourg

Andrews D H, Goodson L A 1980 A comparative analysis of models of instructional design. *J. Instruct. Dev.* 3(4)

Association for Educational Communications and Technology (AECT) 1977 *Educational Technology; Definition and Glossary of Terms*. AECT, Washington, DC

Azuma H 1977 The third decade of educational technology. *Educ. Technol. Res.* 1: 1–4

Bertalanffy L von 1950 The theory of open systems in physics and biology. *Science* 111: 23–29

Boguslaw R 1973 Systems concepts in social systems. In: Miles R F (ed.) 1973 *Systems Concepts*. Wiley, New York, pp. 177–90

Bruner J R 1966 *Toward a Theory of Instruction*. Harvard University Press, Cambridge, Massachusetts

Crawford M P 1962 Concepts of training. In: Gagné R M 1962 *Psychological Principles in System Development*. Holt, Rinehart and Winston, New York, pp. 301–42

Ely D P (ed.) 1972 The field of educational technology: A statement of definition. Report of AECT Committee *Audiovis. Instr.* 17(8): 36–43

Eraut M, Squires G (eds.) 1971 *An Annotated Select Bibliography of Educational Technology*. National Council for Educational Technology, London

Finn J D 1960 Technology and the instructional process. In: Lumsdaine A A, Glaser R (eds.) 1960

Finn J D 1968 The emerging technology of education. In: Weisgerber R A (ed.) 1968

Finn J D, Perrin D G, Campion L E 1962 *Studies in the Growth of Instructional Technology I: Audiovisual Instrumentation for Instruction in the Public Schools, 1930–1960: A Basis for Take-off*. Department of Audiovisual Instruction, National Education Association, Washington, DC

Flechsig K-H 1975 *Towards a Critical Appraisal of Educational Technology Theory and Practice*. Steering Group on Educational Technology, Council for Cultural Cooperation, Council of Europe, Strasbourg

Glaser R 1965 Toward a behavioral science base for instructional design. In: Glaser R (ed.) 1965 *Teaching Machines and Programmed Learning: A Source Book*, Vol. 2: *Data and Directions*. Department of Audiovisual Instruction, National Education Association, Washington, DC

Greene M 1968 Technology and the human person. In: Witt P W F (ed.) 1968 *Technology and the Curriculum*. Curriculum Conf., Columbia University, 1967. Teachers College Press, Columbia University, New York

Griffiths D E 1964 Administrative change in organizations. In: Miles M B (ed.) 1964

Hawkridge D 1981 The telesis of educational technology. *Br. J. Educ. Technol.* 12: 4–18

Heinich R 1968 The teacher in an instructional system. In: Knirk F G, Childs J W (eds.) 1968 *Instructional Technology: A Book of Readings*. Holt, Rinehart and Winston, New York

Hilgard E R 1964 A perspective on the relationship between learning theory and educational practices. In: Hilgard E R (ed.) 1964 *Theories of Learning and Instruction*. 63rd National Society for the Study of Education (NSSE) Yearbook Part 1. University of Chicago Press, Chicago, Illinois

Hoban C F 1965 From theory to policy decisions. *Audiovis. Commun. Rev.* 13(2): 121–39

Hoban C F 1977 Educational technology and human values. *Audiovis. Commun. Rev.* 25(3): 221–41

Huberman M 1970 Educational technology: A bibliography. *Bull. Int. Bur. Educ.* 177: 263–309

Lewis B N, Pask G 1965 The theory and practice of adaptive teaching systems. In: Glaser R (ed.) 1965 *Teaching Machines and Programmed Learning: A Source Book*. Department of Audiovisual Instruction, National Education Association, Washington, DC

Lumsdaine A A 1964 Educational technology, programmed learning and instructional science. In: Hilgard E R (ed.) 1964 *Theories of Learning and Instruction*. 63rd National Society for the Study of Education (NSSE) Yearbook Part 1. University of Chicago Press, Chicago, Illinois

Lumsdaine A A, Glaser R (eds.) 1960 *Teaching Machines and Programmed Learning: A Source Book*. Department of Audiovisual Instruction, National Education Association, Washington, DC

Melton A W 1959 The science of learning and the technology of educational methods. *Harvard Educ. Rev.* 29: 96–106

Miles M B (ed.) 1964 *Innovation in Education*. Teachers College Press, Columbia University, New York

Mitchell P D 1978 Educational technology. In: Unwin D, McAleese R (eds.) 1978 *The Encyclopedia of Educational Media Communications and Technology*. Macmillan, London, pp. 307–32

Moore O K 1968 Autotelic responsive environments and exceptional children. In: Weisgerber R A (ed.) 1968

Moore O K 1969 Some principles for the design of clarifying educational environments. In: Goslin D A (ed.) 1969 *Handbook of Socialization Theory and Research*. Rand McNally, Chicago, Illinois

National Council for Educational Technology (NCET) 1969 *Towards More Effective Learning*. The Report of the National Council for Educational Technology 1967–1968. Councils and Education Press, London

Oettinger A G, Mark S S 1969 *Run, Computer Run: The Mythology of Educational Innovation*. Harvard University Press, Cambridge, Massachusetts

Papert S 1980 *Mindstorms: Children, Computers and Powerful Ideas*. Basic Books, New York

Ramo S 1973 The systems approach. In: Miles R F (ed.) 1973 *Systems Concepts: Lectures on Contemporary Approaches to Systems*. Wiley, New York, pp. 13–32

Skinner B F 1958 Teaching machines. *Science* 128: 969-77

Skinner B F 1968 *The Technology of Teaching*. Appleton–Century–Crofts, New York

Taylor G (ed.) 1970 *The Teacher as Manager: A Symposium*. Councils and Education Press, London

Tickton S G (ed.) 1970 *To Improve Learning: An Evaluation of Instructional Technology*. Bowker, New York

Travers R M W 1968 Directions for the development of an educational technology. In: Witt P W F (ed.) 1968 *Technology and the Curriculum*. Curriculum Conf., Columbia University, 1967. Teachers College Press, Columbia University, New York

Travers R M W 1970 *Man's Information System: A Primer for Media Specialists and Educational Technologists*. Chandler, Scranton, Pennsylvania

Travers R M W 1973 Educational technology and related research viewed as a political force. In: Travers R M W (ed.) 1973 *Second Handbook of Research on Teaching:*

A Project of the American Educational Research Association. Rand McNally, Chicago, Illinois, pp. 979–96

Weisgerber R A (ed.) 1968 *Instructional Process and Media Innovation.* Rand McNally, Chicago, Illinois

Weisgerber R A (ed.) 1971 *Developmental Efforts in Individualized Learning.* Peacock, Itasca, Illinois

Witt P W F 1968 Educational technology: The education of teachers and the development of instructional materials specialists. In: Witt P W F (ed.) 1968 *Technology and the Curriculum.* Curriculum Conf., Columbia University, 1967. Teachers College Press, Columbia University, New York

M. Eraut

Educational Technology: Field of Study

Educational technology is firmly established as a field of study. Institutions which offer training programs in, for example, instructional development, educational communications, and educational resources use many labels to describe the field. Current efforts to describe the field are reflected in position papers of professional organizations and curricula of training programs. Beyond these sources, interpretations of the field are largely inferential and based on the performance of individuals in the field and published accounts about various aspects of the field. Such sources often lead to conclusions based on earlier definitions of the field which focused on the mass media rather than on the processes of instruction and learning, the current emphasis. As new technologies and learning strategies have appeared, educational technology has added and integrated them to bring about new dimensions to an ever-changing field. This article traces the evolution of educational technology as a field of study by highlighting the contributing disciplines and changing content which constitute the field.

1. A Brief History

In North America, educational technology was first recognized as a field of study with the establishment of the audiovisual education curriculum at Indiana University in 1946. Separate courses had been offered in the 1930s but no comprehensive program had been organized until L. C. Larson inaugurated the Indiana graduate program. An emphasis on the selection, use, production, evaluation, and management of audiovisual media provided the substance of courses at Indiana and other North American universities which used the Indiana curriculum as a model. The 1960s saw the introduction of communication concepts thus giving the field a process orientation with concerns for the "sender–message–channel–receiver" aspects of communication being grafted onto the audiovisual roots. Academic programs called "audiovisual communications" and "instructional communications" began to appear.

About the same time, the results of B. F. Skinner's research in operant conditioning were manifest in the programmed instruction movement which was embraced by the budding field of educational technology. Learning psychology was incorporated into many educational technology curricula. James D. Finn was probably the first person to label the field "instructional technology" when, in 1961, he organized a department at the University of Southern California.

In the United Kingdom, programmed instruction marked the inauguration of educational technology as a field of study. The audiovisual movement had been growing through the National Committee for Audio Visual Aids in Education and the Educational Foundation for Visual Aids but did not embrace the communication or learning psychology developments as did the North American practitioners. The Association for Programmed Learning (and Educational Technology) was organized in 1962 and became the focal point for educators and trainers who espoused the tenets of the new behavioral psychology applied to the instructional process.

The changing nature of the field was confirmed in 1970 when the Department of Audiovisual Instruction (of the National Education Association) in the United States became the Association for Educational Communications and Technology. The Council for Educational Technology in the United Kingdom was started in 1968, then established in its present form in 1973.

The expanding use of computers in education during the 1970s was compatible with most of the new technologies and procedures which had characterized the growth of the field since the Second World War. Thus instructional applications (computer-based education)(see *Computer-assisted Learning*), management applications (computer-managed instruction)(see *Computer-managed Learning*), and information applications (database retrieval systems) came naturally into educational technology.

Even as educational technologists are insisting that their major concern is with the design, development, and evaluation of instruction, there are practitioners contemplating ways in which videodiscs (see *Videodiscs: Instructional Uses*), videotex (see *Videotex*), and new computer systems can find their place in the field.

2. The Nature of a Field

A field of study is much less rigorous than a discipline. A discipline is usually defined as an organized body of knowledge which is constantly tested and changed by research. Disciplines are more often found in the sciences although the term covers the social sciences and humanities as well. Fields are usually found in areas of applied study—the professions. Fields often draw on disciplines for basic substance as engineering draws on physics and mathematics, and medicine on biology and chemistry. A field, such as educational technology, is an amalgam of several fields and disciplines. It uses those concepts, theories, procedures, and tools which help it to accomplish its basic purpose: the design and implementation of learning systems.

There are signs that a field has become a legitimate entity. Formal programs of study with curricula which are substantially congruent from institution to institution is one such sign. Another is the creation of associations where individuals who are engaged in common practice can share ideas and explore new research findings. An outgrowth of the associations is usually a journal through which information can be shared among practitioners in diverse locations. Continuing demand for personnel who are being trained in the academic programs is another indicator that a field exists and is performing a valuable societal function.

For a field to become a profession, additional criteria need to be met (Finn 1953). Quality control of graduates through certification of individuals or accreditation of academic programs by agreed-upon standards; establishment and enforcement of a code of ethics; and an organized body of intellectual theory constantly expanding by research all constitute some of the requirements for a profession. In some parts of the world, educational technology may be called a profession (see *Educational Technology: Professional Associations*).

3. Contributing Fields

Educational technology is a field made up of elements of other fields. There is very little content which is unique. It has taken elements of cognitive psychology, perception psychology, measurement, evaluation, communications, management, media, and systems engineering and arranged these elements synergistically to a point where the whole is greater than the sum of its parts.

Stakenas and Kaufman (1981) have graphically shown how scientific knowledge is used and transformed by educational technology into tools for instruction and learning. They have grouped the contributing fields into the "behavioral sciences," "management sciences," and "physical sciences." The "techniques" derived from the "principles" become curricular topics in academic programs (except for the engineering area). The "artifacts" are the tangible outcomes created by practitioners in the field. Table 1 shows how contributing fields are used in educational technology as a field of study. Educational technology, in its broadest sense, is concerned with all these elements as they contribute to the design and use of effective learning systems.

Short's (1981) study of graduate educational tech-

Table 1
Development sequence and scientific areas that contribute to educational technology[a]

Development sequence	Behavioral sciences	Management sciences	Physical sciences
Principles	Learning Perception Cognition Motivation Measurement	Systems approach Management Cybernetics Macroeconomics Microeconomics	Optics Mechanics Electricity Circuits Chemistry
Techniques based on scientific principles	Programmed learning Learner analysis Task analysis Reinforcement scheduling Message design Test construction	Needs assessment Systems analysis Systems design Cost–effectiveness analysis	Optical engineering Communications engineering Chemical engineering Electrical engineering
Artifacts produced by applying scientific principles	Learning materials and activities that satisfy the conditions of learning	Management by objectives Systematically designed learning systems	Devices for transmitting, e.g., television, radio, telephone Devices for storing and retrieving, e.g., computers

a Source: Stakenas R G, Kaufman R 1981 *Technology in Education: Its Human Potential.* © Phi Delta Kappa Foundation nology programs in the United States indicated emphasis on materials production and utilization/application, at the master's level; on management/administration at the post-master's level; and on research, instructional development, theory, evaluation, and instructional systems design at the doctoral level. Each of these content areas draws from the behavioral, management, or physical sciences.

4. Preparation for Career

Educational technology as a field of study appears to lead to placement within the field. Sink's (1980) study of about 1,000 1979 graduates of educational technology programs in the United States indicates about 90 percent placement with the greatest numbers being placed in management/administrative, instructional development, and media production positions. These three major categories represent distinct categories in which educational technologists often seek employment (AECT 1977). The Association for Educational Communications and Technology (AECT) has published a list of competencies required for instructional development specialists and material design and production specialists (*Instructional Innovator* 1980). These competencies have been used by many educational technology academic programs to plan courses and curricula. The composite list is a fairly good representation of the content in the field of educational technology. Another view eschews the body of knowledge approach to the field (McCormick 1976) and opts for description of the educational technologist's role as a more valid statement of its content.

5. Beyond Content

The field of educational technology has established its credibility in the academic community and in the marketplace. The field will continue its identity struggle in the fashion described by Hawkridge (1976): "The time is now coming when educational technology should take its place as a specialized branch of educational research and development, retaining its identity but cementing ties with other fields instead of rivalling them."

The critics will no doubt continue to raise their voices. Lewis (1980) suggests how to handle the criticism. He suggests making "a preliminary statement of what educational technology is seeking to do, and why society (a) needs such a profession now, and (b) is likely to go on needing it in the future. The statement should also make a preliminary attempt (i) to justify any assertions made about societal needs, and (ii) to say why such needs cannot (for the present time at least) be satisfactorily met in ways *other than* the establishing of a new profession."

The field may show signs of ambivalence in its many settings but there appears to be more uni-formity of opinion now than ever before as to the content and approach of educational technology. It is a field which has come of age and will find its place among the twentieth-century movements in education.

See also: Educational Technology: Conceptual Frameworks and Historical Development; Educational Technology: Personnel; Educational Technology: Training

Bibliography

Association for Educational Communications and Technology (AECT) 1977 *Definition of Educational Technology*. AECT, Washington, DC

Finn J D 1953 Professionalizing the audio-visual field. *Audio-Vis. Commun. Rev.* 1(1): 6–17

Hawkridge D G 1976 Next year, Jerusalem! The rise of educational technology. *Br. J. Educ. Technol.* 7: 7–30

Instructional Innovator 1980 Competencies for instructional development specialists. Competencies for materials design and production specialists. 25(9): 27–31

Lewis B N 1980 The professional standing of educational technology. *International Yearbook of Educational and Instructional Technology 1980/81*. Kogan Page, London, pp. 20–36

McCormick R 1976 Educational technologists: Knowledge retention and role change. *Br. J. Educ. Technol.* 7: 75–84

Short R 1981 *An Analysis of Instructional Technology Graduate Degree Programs in US Colleges and Universities*. Farmland Industries, Kansas City, Missouri

Sink D L 1980 Employment trends for media graduates. *Instr. Innovator* 25: 36–37

Stakenas R G, Kaufman R 1981 *Technology in Education: Its Human Potential*. Phi Delta Kappa, Bloomington, Indiana

D. P. Ely

Educational Technology: Local Centers

Local centers for educational technology are considered as units below the level of the national, regional, or state level and above the level of the individual school. In North America, local centers have a variety of titles—learning resource center, district media center, media/library services—and are usually located in the system's administrative offices. In Europe, some of the functions of such centers may be found in other units. The various states in Australia set standards for resources and educational technology but do not mandate local centers. The functions and activities described herein are more typical for local centers in North America than for other parts of the world, because in North America local centers are more abundant, tend to be discrete administrative units, and have a clearer mission.

The purpose of these centers for educational technology is to promote learning through the systematic identification, development, and utilization of a full range of human, material, and physical resources.

To fulfill this mission the center usually establishes a division of labor that brings to bear knowledge about the nature of the learner, the teacher, the system, the media, and people's perceptual systems, as well as methodological problems such as sequencing of instruction. Such centers employ an eclectic, pragmatic philosophy to accomplish their purposes.

1. Functions and Activities

Four functions are generally visible in well-developed local centers—management and administration, instructional design and development, information services, and media production.

1.1 Management and Administration

Management tasks include developing a philosophy of service, setting goals and priorities, developing a long-range plan, and evaluating programs and personnel. Most local centers have advisory committees that assist in these activities. These committees are usually composed of persons who represent the user population—students, teachers, principals, administrators, and members of the community.

Administration includes duties that ensure that plans and services developed by management are implemented. Typical tasks include supervising production, circulation of machines and materials, and maintaining work flow.

An important activity associated with management and administration involves working with the individual schools and the community since they provide both resources and support for local centers for educational technology. These activities point to the leadership role expected of management and administrative personnel (see *Media Program Administration*).

1.2 Instructional Design and Development

The close relationships between educational technology and instructional design are discussed in other articles (see *Educational Technology: Conceptual Frameworks and Historical Development*; *Instructional Design: An Overview*; *Instructional Design: Systems Approach*). Here it may be noted that many local educational technology centers engage in at least some instructional design activities, especially those located in the affluent suburbs of large cities. Typically they will stress the systems approach to instructional design, rather than cognitive approaches.

1.3 Information Services

Local centers for educational technology have a broad view of the critical nature of information, and are intimately concerned with making it more widely available in the most appropriate and useful form. This concern, allied to rapid changes in information technology, has led to the merging in many districts of what had previously been two distinct forms of activity: media services and library services [see *Libraries: School (Resource Centers)*]. In districts where these services are still separate, it is usual for the media center to handle the more complex nonprint materials such as 16mm motion pictures and videocassettes, and to provide technical assistance with the associated equipment. This responsibility may extend to reprographic equipment and even to word processors.

Local centers are likely to be the agency for district participation in television distribution systems and information networks, and for maintaining links with regional centers, where they exist.

Still another important aspect of information services is machine distribution and maintenance. Media equipment includes 35mm slide, overhead, 8mm and 16mm film, and video projectors. Also common are microform readers, record players, public address systems, audio and video recorders and players, cameras, and speech compressors. Local centers usually maintain records on such equipment so that they can estimate maintenance costs and project costs for needed replacements as machines are retired.

Professionals working in information services of local centers also play a consultative role, helping teachers and students utilize the various pieces of communication equipment and the accompanying software. These professionals frequently conduct workshops and assist individuals to use media in the most appropriate and effective way. These services usually include alerting teachers and other educational professionals to new materials on the market and recently acquired materials. Local centers encourage other school personnel to preview materials before use as well as to preview materials for purchase.

1.4 Media Productions

Local centers usually have much more sophisticated production facilities than the individual schools. For example, many have both television and radio production capabilities.

Many educational systems use their local centers to print, duplicate, and distribute curriculum materials in many formats. These centers frequently have the capability of typesetting, editing, mimeo and spirit duplicating, visualizing, offset and letterpress printing, and binding. Word processing is also common in preparation of printed materials in local centers. Some centers have the ability to create covers for books and to make posters and other items through processes like silkscreen reproductions.

Most local centers have the capacity to produce a variety of photographic materials. These usually include producing black and white and color negatives and prints, color 35mm slides, overhead transparencies, 8mm and 16mm motion pictures, microforms, and filmstrips.

Original artwork is rarely produced in the individual schools; however, such work is common in local centers. Graphic artists create original illustrations, design graphs and charts, make posters and signs, design and layout materials for reproduction, and create computer graphics.

Production of audio materials includes creating masters for reel to reel and cassette tape playback units, audiotape duplication, and programming for single and multiple screen programs.

2. Types of Local Centers

A full range of centers exist from those having developed all functions to those engaging in only a few activities under a single function. Some systems perform functions normally associated with local centers in different administrative units. For example, the printing of educational materials is sometimes carried out in a department of curriculum development within the system. Other centers provide little if any material support yet maintain a professional staff to work with schools in developing functions associated with local centers. In centers with limited functions, the most frequently promoted services include: circulation and maintenance of a film library, a professional collection of books and periodicals for use by central-office staff and teachers of the system, a production facility, and a circulation and maintenance system for media and machines not commonly found in schools. In addition, local centers with limited services usually provide technicians who can make repairs on communication equipment for schools.

Coordinators or directors of fully developed local centers frequently hold the position of assistant or associate superintendent of schools and function in the highest governing bodies of the educational system. Such coordinators manage all functions of local centers while other administrators are responsible for specific functions commonly grouped in divisions. The staff may include a wide array of personnel such as instructional designers, test and measurement experts, writers, editors, graphic artists, photographers, and computer programmers. Well-developed centers usually have budgets which permit hiring consultants and purchasing services that are not provided for in the local center. For example, a college specialist in social studies might be employed to help produce a series of units for the high-school curriculum.

At the opposite extreme, the most minimal center might have a clerk who is responsible for a few activities, such as acquiring and circulating a collection of books for use by the professional staff of the school system. This individual's immediate supervisor might be a secretary. In somewhat more developed local centers the coordinator operates at the level of a subject supervisor or consultant which is considered a level between building-level principals and assistant and associate superintendents.

The separation of activities associated with print media from those activities associated with nonprint media is becoming less and less common in North America. National and international associations have recommended the merger of both functions into local centers under one administrative unit as have state, province, and national legislations. Under these more comprehensive units the personnel, material, and physical resources can develop the broad functions that describe information and educational technology.

3. Problems in Local Center Development

In North America, the pattern has been to merge separate departments within the system. For example, an audiovisual distribution system, a systemwide professional library, and a department for media production would be combined into a local center for educational technology. These mergers obviously resulted in power struggles in many instances and a shift in policy by the governing body of the educational system.

Another problem that local centers face is the lack of understanding of center operations by teachers and school administrators. "The greatest misfortune . . . is the lack of acceptance, understanding, and respect on the part of teachers and administrators" (Shapiro 1979 p. 26). Similar findings were reported in studies made in Houston, Texas, and in a study conducted by the Massachusetts Institute of Technology (Mugnier 1979 p. 19–23).

Perhaps an even greater problem is a lack of general understanding of the concept of educational technology on the part of most school personnel. Various centers tended to define educational technology in a way that reflected their restricted view. Time has helped correct this problem with the assistance of over 300 colleges and universities in North America preparing professionals in educational technology.

More recently, funding has become a major problem. As inflation raises the costs of machines and materials, and as wages go higher and higher, less and less money is available to support local centers. This tends to be less of a problem in well-developed centers that have carefully articulated their services with the educational programs of their constituent schools, the reason being that such centers are considered a critical rather than an auxiliary service that teachers could do without.

4. Issues in Local Centers

Many issues exist, some of which may be resolved by professional organizations while others may be resolved by forces outside the educational system.

Some may never be resolved. Issues involve terminology used in the field, role and training of personnel in local centers, cooperation and networking among information services agencies, censorship, role of national and international organizations, high technology, and school organization.

4.1 Terminology

At least two basic issues exist with regard to terminology: the use of certain terms and the number of synonyms that exist. For example, professionals trained in educational technology think first of technology as a process or technique for accomplishing some task. On the other hand, educators and the public at large think of hardware—satellites, telephones, assembly lines, and so on. Another example is use of the term media. The profession defines media as "all of the forms and channels used in the transmittal process" (AASL/AECT 1975 p. 109). However, other education professionals as well as members of the community think of newspapers and television when they think of media; they see mass media and media as one and the same.

4.2 Role of Personnel in Local Centers

Most personnel managing local centers are educated in departments of educational technology in colleges of education. These personnel tend to view themselves as specialized educators. On the other hand, library schools also produce personnel serving in local centers. They tend to think of themselves as specialized librarians. Compounding the issues raised by these two points of view is the school administrator's lack of understanding of the role and technical operations of local centers. The academic preparation of administrators makes little mention of principles of management as they are applied in the operation of local centers.

These different views create a basic issue. What constitutes legitimate activity in local centers for educational technology?

In the United States the personnel situation is further complicated by the uncoordinated nature of accreditation and certification procedures. The National Council for the Accreditation of Teacher Education (NCATE) accredits college of education programs preparing professionals to work in local centers. Programs found in library schools are accredited by the American Library Association (ALA). To complicate matters, both programs in colleges of education and in library schools must undergo approval by the individual states where the programs exist. Each of these three groups—NCATE, ALA, and state departments of education—exist for somewhat different purposes and have different expectations. This situation creates a number of issues that tend to block efforts to bring into clear focus the role of local centers.

The fact that each of the states requires the professionals working in local centers to have state certificates in order to practice also creates several issues. The first relates to the great variation in the requirements among the states. These variations create difficulties with the reciprocity of certificates when a professional moves from one state to another or when local center personnel are trained in an out-of-state institution. Also, contributing to the problems created is the slowness of changing state legislation needed to keep abreast of the rapidly changing role of local centers.

4.3 Cooperation and Networking

Local centers are expected to cooperate with other information agencies such as public libraries and to participate in information networks. Issues that surround cooperation and networking include overcoming psychological and legal barriers, funding, and planning.

Psychological barriers are directly tied to attitudes of local center staff as well as personnel in other information agencies. Too many reasons for not cooperating seem to overpower perceived benefits. In addition, making available vast databases poses copyright and royalty problems. Funding and planning also raise numerous issues as to who should do what and who should pay for what. Center personnel agree that cooperating and networking have enormous benefits yet most are individually afraid to become involved.

4.4 Censorship

When selection, circulation, and withdrawal of material in local centers is influenced by political, religious, or other groups, the centers are being censored. Extreme examples exist. Groups have requested that the Bible be placed on an adult reading list, and some dictionaries have been banned in Texas because they contained "bad words." Because most material has the potential of being offensive to someone, objections frequently come unexpectedly and quickly bring out differences within the community at the expense of local centers.

Local centers should have a written policy statement on procedures for selecting, circulating, and withdrawing materials. When censors come, they should put their concerns in writing, and the local center should follow an established procedure in each case. Unfortunately, the basic issue may never be resolved. What are the ultimate criteria for determining content of materials found in local centers and who should be responsible for applying these criteria?

4.5 High Technology

Developing technology will change many basic routines for everyone in increasingly dramatic ways. The use of computers to access information from the growing number of databases and the capacity of videodiscs to store information are changing basic concepts of information storage and retrieval. Personal computers are bringing these resources directly into the home and changing the way people shop, compose, copy, scan newspapers, and conduct research. Using videodiscs and microcomputers can reduce the proliferation of formats, access enormous collections of still and moving images, reduce costs, and increase flexibility in using educational materials. When this technology is in place, it may change the role of local centers in dramatic ways. Implications for collections development and for storage and retrieval are a case in point. In the future any student, teacher, or administrator may have easy access to most films, telecasts, filmstrips, records, tapes, books, magazines, or other media.

When this occurs, local centers may no longer need to maintain collections of materials and machines for circulation. Will these centers become expert in programming computers to access materials from videodiscs for individual schools? Will local centers expand their instructional design and curriculum production efforts? Will personnel in local centers play a leadership role in conceptualizing what schools will ultimately develop? Will they become "resource thinkers" rather than "resource warehouses"? Or, will they be eliminated since the new technology is available to everyone?

4.6 School Organization

Largely because schools are organized around the concept of a class directed by a teacher, more cost-effective educational systems have failed to develop. Theoretically, as local centers produce more and more autotutorial materials, a greater number of the programs associated with the traditional classroom should be replaced. This would mean that local centers would receive increased budgets and savings accrued from expenditures in local schools. This trade-off is common in business and industry and is one reason why educational technology is increasingly more popular in those sectors.

The issues that develop from these concepts relate to how traditional structures can be replaced to allow for development. This is where power, control, and school organization become critical to realizing the potential of both local centers and high technology.

5. Research and Local Centers

What research is produced or utilized in local centers for educational technology depends upon the operation of the center. If a large part of a particular center's activity is devoted to creating educational programs, then much of the research discussed becomes important. In addition, research in the area of management becomes more and more useful as local centers expand into complex organizations.

Research that is concerned with the program of a local center for educational technology tends to draw broadly from more general educational research. The reason for this is that any research that assesses the effect of the school and district environment on learning has implications for the local center. Several studies have demonstrated that the presence of a local center improved the instructional program. Some research shows that an important function of local centers is the integration and articulation of center services and the local curriculum. The way media are introduced in teaching and learning activities appears critical.

Another body of research concerns user services and how they impact on clients of local centers. This research studies policies and procedures that improve or hamper user satisfaction. They also analyze statistical data for the purpose of making local center operations more cost effective and for justifying their existence.

The quality of research conducted by local centers tends to be uneven and sometimes misleading. For example, countless studies have tried to demonstrate that one media is better than another—programmed instruction is better than a lecture, television is better than printed messages. Again, the various media have different capacities which probably make all media better for some messages and worse for others (see *Instructional Design: Media Selection*).

The widespread use of instruments for planning and evaluation constitutes another body of research. Several schemes are used nationwide, and many states have produced procedures and instruments for evaluating centers for educational technology on several levels. Some states require specific procedures and services from schools and districts for accreditation.

Although the research is not as abundant as everyone would like, it does provide a useful body of information for helping centers to improve their contributions to the educational program. One critical need is to improve the quality of research in and about local centers. The development of doctoral programs in educational technology has greatly contributed to reaching this goal. Also needed is research that concentrates on the effect of the presence or absence of services offered by local centers.

6. Literature on Local Centers

The literature that details operations of local centers generally falls into one of three categories—management and administration, production, and instructional design and development. Materials devoted to center administration tend to provide guidelines for particular operations such as planning, acquisitioning, budgeting, production, reference, storage and retrieval, evaluation, research and development, and maintenance. Materials on production tend to provide references for various production techniques, such as all of the ways to produce overhead transparencies. Materials on instructional design tend to be a set of prescriptive procedures for creating and validating an instructional sequence.

Media Programs: District and School (ALA/AECT 1975) provides guidelines for functions and operations of local centers for educational technology. This book presents a set of national guidelines useful to states developing standards of their own. As a result of this work, many states have publications that present guidelines or set standards for local centers. Many books are currently on the market that provide assistance in the details of center operations— *Administering Educational Media: Instructional Technology and Library Services* (Brown et al. 1972), *Administering Instructional Media Programs* (Erickson 1968), *AV Instruction Technology Media and Methods* (Brown et al. 1982), and *Media Personnel in Education* (Chisholm and Ely 1976). However, some tend to be oriented toward school libraries while others are oriented toward audiovisual materials.

The literature dealing with production is vast since it deals with all aspects of all media. The most useful general reference is *Planning and Producing Audiovisual Material* (Kemp 1975). This work presents a philosophy and techniques for using media, summarizes research in the design of material, and provides easy-to-follow, well-illustrated guides for producing most media appropriate for local centers. More detailed advice on production and instructional design can be found in the more specialist articles (see *Graphic Production: Educational Materials*; *Photographic Production and Photographic Services*; *Instructional Design: An Overview*)

Bibliography

American Association of School Librarians (AASL)/Association for Educational Communications and Technology (AECT) 1975 *Media Programs: District and School.* AASL/AECT, Chicago, Illinois

Brown J W, Lewis R B, Harcleroad F F 1982 *AV Instruction: Technology Media and Methods*, 6th edn. McGraw-Hill, New York

Brown J W, Norberg K D, Srygley S K 1972 *Administering Educational Media: Instructional Technology and Library Services*, 2nd edn. McGraw-Hill, New York

Chisholm M E, Ely D P 1976 *Media Personnel in Education: A Competency Approach.* Prentice-Hall, Englewood Cliffs, New Jersey

Erickson C W H 1968 *Administering Instructional Media Programs.* Macmillan, New York

Hug W E 1975 *Instructional Design and the Media Program.* American Library Association (ALA)/Association for Educational Communications and Technology (AECT), Chicago, Illinois

Kemp J E 1975 *Planning and Producing Audiovisual Materials*, 3rd edn. Crowell, New York

Mugnier C 1979 Views on school librarianship and library education. *Sch. Libr. J.* 26: 19–23

Shapiro L L 1979 Celebrations and condolences: A time of reckoning for the school library. *Sch. Libr. J.* 26: 13–18

W. E. Hug

Educational Technology: National and International Centers

The *International Yearbook of Educational and Instructional Technology* for 1982/83 lists nearly 1,000 centers which promote and offer services in educational technology. This list is undoubtedly incomplete but it does indicate an extremely wide dispersal of activity. Practically every country has at least one center, and more than 20 countries have more than 10 such centers. Most but not all of these centers can be considered as having some influence at the national level, and many are primarily national rather than local in the audiences they serve.

Centers of activity with a national impact can be grouped into five main types: (a) research and teaching units in colleges and universities; (b) governmental centers, units, and agencies; (c) professional associations and nongovernmental organizations; (d) units located within business or industry; and (e) proprietary corporations whose major purpose is the sale of educational technology services. Some centers have a wide range of activities while others tend to be more specialized, providing services such as television and film production, development of computer courses, or general support of institutional instruction. The more highly developed centers deploy people with a variety of specialized skills, including instructional designers, subject matter experts, educational psychologists, script writers, graphic artists, and editors.

1. College and University Units

Most colleges and universities have centers of educational technology or media service centers to support their instructional programs (see *Higher Education: Teaching Consultancy Services*).

A second function assumed by some such centers is the training of educational technology personnel (see *Educational Technology: Training*). Major training centers have an important national role, and several of them have international reputations. Such centers will also have a significant research and development role and obtain funding from a range of governmental agencies, charitable foundations, industry, and business. Some centers, particularly in the United States, may contract for projects that frequently have little bearing on the instructional programs. Colleges and universities producing research in the new educational technologies, like videodiscs programmed with computers, may be producing training programs for industry or the military. Others have outside support for the applications of educational technology directly related to the educational programs of the institution. For example, in the United Kingdom, the University of Bath was supported by the British Petroleum Company, in the design of an instruction program for business studies. In this respect centers for educational technology resemble many other university-based research units. Their research role enhances the quality of their advanced teaching, and probably also their reputation with colleagues in other fields.

Universities also house a significant number of more specialized research and development centers, which have no formal training or consultancy function. These will usually focus on a specific area within educational technology such as information science, television, or computer-based learning. The PLATO laboratory at the University of Illinois and the Centre for Mass Communications Research at the University of Leicester are well-known examples.

2. Governmental Centers, Units, and Agencies

The first distinction to be made under this heading is between centers which provide services within the governmental sector and agencies which the government has set up to coordinate, promote, provide, or even regulate educational technology activities in the nation as a whole. The most prominent centers in exploiting the use of educational technology within government have tended to be those concerned with the dissemination of government information and those concerned with the training of military personnel. The latter, in particular, have been prominent in the development of educational technology in the United States and the United Kingdom.

The organizational mechanisms devised by governments to coordinate, promote, or provide educational technology services are remarkably varied. National production facilities are most common in the area of broadcasting, with the United States being a significant exception (see *Broadcasting in North America*). Film, however, is supported in a variety of ways. Only some nations have national film production agencies, the National Film Board of Canada being one of the best-known examples. The Federal Republic of Germany and the Netherlands have central scientific film institutes to produce and distribute research films and films for higher education. New Zealand has a national film library, while the British Film Institute is best known for its archival and educational functions.

Many governments, for example, in the Federal Republic of Germany, the Netherlands, and the People's Republic of China, also support national audiovisual centers which may or may not include any responsibility for film or broadcasting. Singapore has moved its Division of Educational Technology into its Curriculum Development Institute, while India has a Center for Educational Technology within the National Council for Educational Research and Training. Japan has an office for audiovisual education within the Ministry of Education, and Israel has a National Center, supporting pedagogic centers at the regional level, located within the Ministry of Education and Culture.

National institutions are most prominent in the United States in the area of libraries and information science. In addition to the famous Library of Congress, there is an associated National Information Center for Educational Media (NICEM), a National Commission on Libraries and Information Science to provide policy advice to government, and a nationally coordinated network of 16 Educational Resources Information Centers (ERIC) [see *Educational Resources Information Center (ERIC)*].

The most all-embracing national center for educational technology is probably the Institute for School Equipment and Educational Technology of the Soviet Union Academy of Pedagogical Services (Kerr 1982) which undertakes basic research, media production, and instructional design on a substantial scale. This contrasts with the very small Council for Educational Technology in the United Kingdom, where, in keeping with the decentralized character of the school system, a government-financed but independent council with a core of administrative staff provides leadership in the field, advises central and local government, and gets additional finance for special separately approved projects (Hubbard 1981).

3. Professional Associations and Nongovernmental Organizations

Professional associations play a particularly important role in the dissemination of knowledge about educational technology (see *Educational Technology: Professional Associations*). The majority of journals in the field are published by such associations. Their membership also comprises a larger number of professionals working outside higher education than many comparable organizations. Membership is largely confined to a single country with the exception of strong Canadian participation in organizations in the United States and European and Commonwealth participation in the United Kingdom-based Association for Educational and Training Technology.

Nongovernmental organizations range from a quasigovernmental consortium, such as the Agency for Instructional Television (AIT) which serves the United States and Canada, through trade associations like the Canadian Book Publishers Council, to special interest groups like Action for Children's Television. Charitable foundations such as Ford in the United States and Nuffield in the United Kingdom have also played a particularly significant part in the development of educational technology.

4. Units Located within Business or Industry

Educational technology is being applied in business and industry in ever-increasing ways. In fact, many training programs in business and industry use a higher degree of educational technology than do schools, colleges, and universities. Sometimes the degree of specialization is also highly advanced, especially where complicated simulations or computer-based training are involved. Several units located within business or industry have national reputations outside their parent companies and contribute to conferences and journals on a significant scale.

5. Corporations Selling Educational Technology Services

Apart from the educational equipment and publishing industries and the more commercially oriented higher education centers, there are several firms which develop educational technology programs for business, industry, education, and government. The largest of these firms employ a wide range of technologists—instructional designers, writers, editors, graphic artists, test and measurement specialists, and printers. These proprietory companies generally use consultants as subject matter experts because of the wide variety of their clients. A significant proportion of the training in the United States military is designed by proprietory corporations, but few other countries have a similar degree of private sector involvement. However, it is common for such firms to design training or assist in its development within the industrial and commercial sectors of a number of countries. Other services frequently provided by proprietory corporations include cost–effectiveness studies of training; evaluation of techniques like testing procedures, analyzing jobs and duties, producing training manuals, and evaluating trainers; and serving as consultants to personnel producing training materials.

6. International Centers

International centers of activity include the various United Nations agencies, several nongovernmental organizations, an increasing number of regional organizations and national institutions whose prime purpose is to provide aid and develop international links. Within the United Nations, UNESCO's Division of Structures, Content, Methods, and Techniques of Education has a major responsibility for educational technology; but significant units also exist within the International Labour Organization (ILO), the Food and Agriculture Organization (FAO), the World Health Organization (WHO), and a number of smaller United Nations agencies (Dieuzeide 1976). A number of nongovernmental and regional organizations

are linked to UNESCO through membership of the International Film and Television Council. This council of about 40 organizations includes among its members the regional broadcasting organizations for Asia (ABU) and Europe (EBU) and the International Council for Educational Media (ICEM). ICEM promotes worldwide contacts among media professionals and has also assisted UNESCO in a series of comparative studies on the administration of audio-visual services in advanced and developing countries.

Other nonregional centers of international activity include professional associations such as the International Association for the Study and Promotion of Audio-visual Methods and confederations of associations such as the International Federation of Library Associations and Institutions (IFLA). The Center for Educational Research and Innovation (CERI) of the Organisation for Economic Co-operation and Development (OECD) also has an important educational technology program.

At the regional level, the UNESCO regional centers at Bangkok and Dakar have strong educational technology programs. The Arab League Educational, Cultural, and Scientific Organization (ALECSO) established an Arab States Educational Media Center in Kuwait in 1976, and the South East Asian Ministers of Education Organization (SEAMEO) established a Regional Centre for Educational Innovation and Technology (INNOTECH) in 1970.

National Agencies with an international brief include both those specifically concerned with educational technology, such as the Japanese Council of Educational Technology Centers which provides consulting assistance throughout Asia, and educational technology divisions within larger organizations such as the United States Agency for International Development (AID) and the British Council.

See also: Educational Resources Information Center (ERIC); Centre for Educational Research and Innovation (CERI)

Bibliography

Dieuzeide H 1976 Education and training for development: Towards united technologies in the UN? *International Yearbook of Educational and Instructional Technology 1976/77.* Kogan Page, London

Educational Media Yearbook. Association for Educational Communications and Technology (AECT)/Libraries Unlimited, Littleton, Colorado

Hubbard G 1981 Educational technology in the United Kingdom. *Educational Media Yearbook 1981.* Libraries Unlimited, Littleton, Colorado

International Yearbook of Educational and Instructional Technology. Kogan Page, London

Kerr S T 1982 Innovation on command: Instructional development and educational technology in the Soviet Union. *Educ. Comm. Technol. J.* 30: 98–116

W. E. Hug

Educational Technology: Personnel

Increased use of the concepts of educational technology in education and training programs worldwide has led to the creation of a new genre of personnel. New methods and techniques of educational practice, often derived from adoption of new media and technologies, have brought about new specialists who are not teachers, supervisors, or administrators but educational technology professionals. These new professionals do not always work in the classroom, on the university campus, or in the training department of an organization. They may be concerned with production of instructional media, the dissemination and distribution of learning resources, or with the design, development, and evaluation of courses and curricula. To understand the scope of personnel who are within the domain of educational technology, it is helpful to know the functions they perform, the levels of service, the locus of employment, and the nature of the positions they fill.

1. Functions

The job responsibilities of educational technologists are as wide and varied as the number of titles which are used to identify individuals serving in this field: television producer, instructional developer, film librarian, evaluator, curriculum developer, learning resource center director, and audiovisual specialist—to name just a few. To bring order out of this jumble, the concept of function is useful. Function is used to refer to a group of interrelated activities engaged in by an educational technologist to achieve a particular outcome or purpose. These outcomes or purposes may involve data, people, things, or combinations thereof. Seldom, if ever, is a job composed entirely of one function.

The functions of educational technology personnel were studied extensively in the United States by the Jobs in Media Study (Wallington et al. 1971). Detailed task analyses were made of personnel who were employed in a variety of positions related to the field of educational technology. By clustering the tasks in logical groupings, nine functions were established. Later modification of these functions by the Definition and Terminology Committee of the Association for Educational Communications and Technology (AECT) yielded more comprehensive descriptions of each function which now serve as the basis for planning training curricula, establishing certification requirements, and preparing job descriptions. The functions are (AECT 1977, Chisholm and Ely 1975):

(a) Organization management—to plan, establish, and maintain policies and procedures for operating a program or agency related to educational technology.

(b) Personnel management—to hire, interact with, supervise, and terminate personnel.

(c) Research—to generate and test theory related to educational technology.

(d) Design—to translate theoretical knowledge into instructional specifications.

(e) Production—to create instructional products based on specifications.

(f) Evaluation/selection—to examine and judge the worth, quality, and significance of instructional products and programs.

(g) Logistics—to acquire, store, retrieve, distribute, and maintain information in all formats.

(h) Utilization—to bring learners into contact with instructional products and programs.

(i) Utilization/dissemination—to bring learners and others into contact with information about educational technology.

Each function includes a cluster of competencies and each competency, in turn, is composed of many tasks (Chisholm and Ely 1975 p. 166). For example, the design function can be divided into six competencies, one of which is analyzing learner characteristics. Tasks associated with this competency then include diagnostic testing, learner interviews, reviewing student records, and meeting with parents.

It is unlikely that one professional person would perform all functions and all the competencies and tasks within each function. Some people may specialize in one function; others may acquire a few competencies in all functions.

2. Levels of Training and Responsibility

Many of the tasks within each function are performed at various levels of sophistication. There are three basic levels of responsibility: (a) aide, (b) technician, and (c) specialist and/or generalist. Each level is determined by the amount of instruction required to fulfill the tasks. For example, an aide would perform relatively low-level tasks in which the procedures are completely specified. Almost everything the person needs to know is part of the job assignment and can be learned on-the-job. The technician has received training in a specialty, such as photography or electronics, but not necessarily at the tertiary level. The specialist or generalist is usually professionally prepared and has completed graduate work in the field of specialization, such as television or computers, or in a broader aspect of educational technology, such as instructional design and development or management of media programs. The concept of differentiated staffing is evident in many multistaff educational media and technology programs. Each level serves a distinct purpose and personnel who fill the positions have different types of preparation and experience.

2.1 Aide Level

Aides usually have no specific training in educational technology. They learn on-the-job. They may serve in such positions as clerks, secretaries, and delivery people. They perform according to standards set by a supervisor.

2.2 Technician Level

Technicians usually provide services or create materials according to specifications established by others. The technician is responsible for a product or service as long as all the tools are made available. Technicians can have such titles as graphic artist, television camera operator, or electronics maintenance repair person. Training usually comes from formal study in a technical or vocational curriculum and from on-the-job experience.

2.3 Specialist or Generalist Level

Specialists, as the label implies, emphasize one aspect of educational technology and usually complete advanced study beyond the baccalaureate degree. Typical specialists are television producers/directors, computer-based education personnel, and audiovisual media designers.

Generalists choose to prepare themselves broadly so that they might manage or coordinate the work of an educational technology organization. They tend to study at the graduate level to gain competencies in most of the functional areas of the field. They usually do not specialize in one aspect of the field but may possess more competencies in management than other functions.

It is important to note that aides, technicians, specialists, and generalists can be employed in all of the nine functional areas. There are tasks at each level. The combined performance of staff at all levels provides the output of any educational technology program. Not all tasks are performed by people at each level; sometimes one person tries to handle all functions at several levels. The success of such an effort depends upon individual competencies and time available.

3. Locus of Employment

Educational technology is a young field. Its practitioners carry a wide array of job titles. There are three categories of positions which include most of the personnel who operate within the field: (a) instructional program development, (b) media product development, and (c) media management. Some educational technologists teach in academic programs preparing people for the field.

3.1 Instructional Program Development

Positions in this category primarily emphasize the functions of design, research, evaluation/selection, and utilization. They include such generic positions as curriculum supervisor, media consultant, instructional developer, and staff developer. Employers who seek instructional program development personnel are school systems; colleges and universities; training departments in business, industry, military, and health organizations; and other agencies which use instruction as a vehicle for education and training.

3.2 Media Product Development

The production function is the major focus of personnel who work in this area. Some minor aspects of research, evaluation/selection, and utilization are usually included. Individuals who are employed in this area have such job titles as graphic artist, photographer, cinematographer, computer programmer, and television director. People who work in media product development are often employed in the same settings as individuals who perform instructional program development and media management functions. In such cases they usually work as a member of an instructional development team or a media support services staff. In some cases, media product development competence is acquired through short-term contracts with freelance personnel or with organizations and agencies that specialize in media production.

3.3 Media Management

Positions in this category fall primarily within the functions of organization and personnel management, logistics, and utilization dissemination. Some aspects of research, evaluation/selection, and utilization are also included. Some of the titles of persons who serve in this category are: director of learning resource center, film librarian, audiovisual director, and instructional materials manager. Sink (1980) reports that 40 percent of the 1979 graduates of educational technology programs in the United States were employed in management positions.

The settings for media management personnel are largely in the schools, colleges and universities, libraries, and training departments of companies and governmental agencies. There are some aspects (tasks) of management that are required for the successful operation of instructional program development and media product development projects.

3.4 Trainers of Educational Technologists

The growth of educational technology has brought about more formal training programs. These programs offer new career opportunities for people who have had experience in the field and want to help prepare others. The study of Sink (1980 p. 37) indicated that 12 percent of 1979 educational technology graduates entered programs as trainers or professors of future educational technology personnel.

4. The Nature of Positions

There still remains some confusion regarding educational technology personnel. Some organizations require personnel possessing the competencies in one or more of the functional areas noted earlier but often they do not know that such people are being trained. Other employers may hire educational technology personnel to handle specific media production tasks and discover that the new employees have instructional program development competencies. The broad nature of educational technology calls for specificity in job description and professional training which will ensure an appropriate match of the people and jobs. A case study analysis of educational technology job profiles as seen through roles and competencies was made by Leedham and Berruer (1979) for UNESCO.

Another problem stems from the misperception of employers regarding the level of personnel needed. Some organizations who seek personnel with technical competencies but hire more highly trained specialists or generalists are often disappointed because the more highly trained person feels the need for a technical level person to handle routine matters. On the other hand, a person who is engaged at a technician level and is expected to perform as a specialist does not have the requisite competencies to achieve the higher level tasks within a functional area.

Leedham and Berruer (1979) mention the problem of status among educational technology professionals. They note the "lack of identity between vocational roles and the public service sector" (p. 21). The misperception of what educational technologists do, and the assumption that communication media are the major products, lead some employers and the general public to think that the people who serve in this field do not play a significant role in the instructional process.

As the field grows and matures, so will the understanding of those who employ educational technologists.

See also: Educational Technology: Training; Media Program Administration

Bibliography

Association for Educational Communications and Technology (AECT) 1977 *The Definition of Educational Technology.* AECT, Washington, DC
Chisholm M E, Ely D P 1975 *Media Personnel in Education: A Competency Approach.* Prentice-Hall, Englewood Cliffs, New Jersey
Leedham J, Berruer A 1979 *Status of Staff Employing Modern Educational Techniques.* UNESCO, Paris
Sink D L 1980 Employment trends for media graduates. *Instructional Innovator* 25(9): 36–37
Wallington J et al. 1971 *Jobs in Instructional Media.* Association for Educational Communications and Technology, Washington, DC

D. P. Ely

Educational Technology: Professional Associations

A professional association is an organization of individuals with a common background in a subject—medicine, law, engineering, and so on, whose chief purpose is to expand knowledge in their professional field or to establish professional standards which will improve the way in which individuals practice their profession. There are an increasing number of professional associations involved in the development of educational technology and the introduction of the products of today's technological society into education, and they have a set of functions that are held in common with all professional associations. They have grown up mostly in the industrialized countries, but there are emerging groups in most regions of the world who find it useful to band together in order to accomplish more by associating themselves than they can accomplish as individual professionals.

1. Defining a Profession

A profession can be simply defined as a person's occupation, if it is not commercial, mechanical, agricultural, or the like. The traditional professions have been the law, medicine, and clergy. There is a substantial literature on the characteristics of a profession which was first linked to the emergence of educational technology by Finn (1953). The definition later adopted by a committee of the Association for Educational Communications and Technology comprised ten characteristics:

(a) *An organized body of intellectual theory, constantly expanding by research.* This is a fundamental and very important characteristic. A systematic theory must constantly be expanded by research and thinking within any profession. Alfred North Whitehead said, " . . . the practice of a profession cannot be disjoined from its theoretical understanding or vice versa . . . The antithesis to a profession is an avocation based on customary activities and modified by the trial and error of individual practice. Such an avocation is a Craft . . . (Price 1954).

(b) *An intellectual technique.* This is the manner in which an individual searches for solutions to problems. Intellectual technique serves as a bridge between theory and practical application.

(c) *An application of that technique to practical affairs.* Practical application involves making ideas and processes result in tangible products. For example, a person actually performing a scientific experiment is making a practical application of intellectual technique.

(d) *A long period of training and certification.* Specialists and technicians in the profession have undergone long periods of training. Training issues include the nature and content of professional education, certification standards, admissions standards and practices, and job placement.

(e) *A series of standards and a statement of ethics which is enforced.* Codes of ethics indicate how members of a profession should behave. Sets of standards specify guidelines for the tools and the facilities used by people in a profession. Merely stating standards and publishing codes of ethics do not guarantee anything—professionalization requires that the standards and the code of ethics be universally followed.

(f) *The ability to provide its own leadership.* Enough leadership must be present to ensure that the present status of the profession is attended to and that the members of the profession are looking to the future.

(g) *An association of members of the profession into a closely knit group with a high quality of communications among the members.* A strong organization for the people in the profession is needed to help implement and develop the other characteristics—standard setting, a code of ethics, leadership, and training. A strong association is needed to achieve vigorous enforcement of practices, standards, and ethics.

(h) *Acknowledgement as a profession.* The members of the profession must believe in it and be conscious of their membership of it: they must form an association and must make public statements that ensure they achieve some recognition as a professional group.

(i) *Professional concern for responsible use of its work.* Using the intellectual technique for practical application is not enough; the members of the profession must exercise a responsibility for the practical work they do. As a group they must be concerned about the uses to which their work is put in society. They must examine the values for which their profession stands and take positions on societal issues that are affected by its work.

(j) *An established relationship with other professions.* Since there is probably more than one profession operating within the general field of educational technology, the professional group must acknowledge its relationship with those other professional groups.

2. The Origins of Professional Associations

Professional associations and learned societies have manifested themselves primarily in the industrialized countries. Tocqueville (1969) observed this phenomenon in the United States in the nineteenth century.

> Americans of all ages, all conditions, and all dispositions constantly form associations. They have not only commercial and manufacturing companies, in which all take part, but associations of a thousand other kinds, religious, moral, serious, futile, general or restricted, enormous or diminutive. The Americans make associations to give entertainments, to found seminaries, to build inns, to construct churches, to diffuse books, to send missionaries to the antipodes; in this manner they found hospitals, prisons, and schools. If it is proposed to inculcate some truth or to foster some feeling by the encouragement of a great example, they form a society. Wherever at the head of some new undertaking you see the government in France, or a man of rank in England, in the United States you will be sure to find an association.

Professional associations are nonprofit-making, cooperative, voluntary organizations. Academic credentials, an accrediting examination, or a license may be a prerequisite for membership, but not always. Membership is usually composed of individuals who seek an exchange of ideas and discussion of common problems within the profession.

Today's professional associations were preceded by scientific or learned societies. Such scientific societies have always been preeminent agencies for collecting and diffusing knowledge. They originated in Europe during the Renaissance. The first known scientific society seems to have been the Academia Secretorum Naturae in Naples in 1560. In the next century the Royal Society was founded in London (1662). This was the leading scientific society serving the American Colonies before 1776. The oldest American scientific society, in continuous existence since its founding in 1743 in Philadelphia by Benjamin Franklin, is the American Philosophical Society. In the middle of the nineteenth century in America, many of the leading professional groups still in existence today were founded: the American Statistical Association in 1839, the American Psychiatric Association, 1844, the American Society of Civil Engineers, 1852, and the National Education Association, 1857.

Before the mid-1800s most American scientists were generalists whose interests ranged over the whole field of human knowledge. From the latter half of that century, science became increasingly specialized and men devoted more and more time to particular aspects of a broader subject. This lead to a demand for scientific and technical societies of a specialized character.

Educational technology was one of several specialized groups which developed under the auspices of the National Education Association between the First and Second World Wars. The Association for Educational Communications and Technology of the United States grew as a part of the National Education Association into an autonomous organization in the last quarter of this century.

Though professional associations stress their roots in the learned societies, their functions also include the pursuit of their members' interests in ways that sometimes resemble the trade associations. A trade association can be defined as a nonprofit-making, cooperative, voluntary organization of business competitors designed to assist its members and its industry in dealing with mutual business problems in several of the following areas: accounting practice, business ethics, commercial and industrial research, standardization, statistics, trade promotion, and relations with government, employees, and the general public.

The history of the trade associations demonstrates their antiquity. The ancient empires of China, Egypt, Japan, and India contained trade groups operating for the benefit of their members, as did Rome, whose groups set wages and prices and fostered apprentice training. During the Middle Ages, European craft and merchant guilds increased in number and power and developed strict regulations and many member services. Merchant guilds were associations of merchants and traders formed originally for protection and increased profit. Craft guilds were made up of artisans and craftsmen producing consumer goods who set quality standards for their work. Both groups set up monopolies with severe entrance requirements and limited the training of apprentices.

In the eighteenth century the rising tide of invention with the Industrial Revolution doomed the efforts of the old guilds to oppose economic and social change and they gradually declined. However, in America, trade associations were found to be necessary as early as the mid-eighteenth century. The New York Chamber of Commerce, the oldest trade association still in existence in North America, was formed by 20 merchants in 1768. The New York Stock Exchange was formed in 1792. National trade associations were not formed, however, until the second half of the nineteenth century.

3. Functions of Professional Associations: A Case Study of the Association for Educational Communications and Technology (AECT)

A description of the above association serves as a good example of the development of the functions of a professional association. The AECT had its origins in the National Education Association's Division of Visual Education, which began in 1923 in the United States. Until recently, the AECT was called the Department of Audiovisual Instruction (DAVI); and the change in name reflects the development of the field from visual education to educational technology. The following account is organized under headings that characterize the major functions of most professional associations.

3.1 Communications with Members and the Field

The association's *Journal of Educational Communications and Technology* (formerly *AV Communication Review*) is more than 20 years old and highly regarded in the field. *Instructional Innovator*, the association's journal of practical applications of media and technology to instruction, is widely read by both members and nonmembers. In addition, the AECT maintains communications with its members through other, nonperiodic publications and through an annual convention and regional meetings.

3.2 Ethics

The AECT has a code of ethics along with procedures for the review of the behavior of its members. This is considered a hallmark of professional responsibility.

3.3 Standards

The AECT has devised standards for school (kindergarten through grade 12) media programs; newly revised standards for the cataloging of nonprint materials; standards for learning resource programs in two-year colleges; technical standards for audiocassettes; and standards for media training in teacher education programs and advanced programs in educational media.

3.4 Leadership

Leadership is evident through the standards of the association as well as through participation in joint groups such as the Educational Media Council and the Joint Council on Educational Telecommunications. The AECT was chosen by the National Center for Education Statistics to develop a handbook of definitions and terminology for educational technology. In 1977, the AECT, as the representative of the United States, hosted the International Council on Educational Media. The association develops the leadership capabilities and responsibilities of individual members through national and regional leadership seminars. Leadership is also a goal of the association's special foundation, the Educational Communications and Technology Foundation.

3.5 Training

Training is performed mostly through colleges and universities for which the association has developed standards for training programs. Additionally, some training seminars are conducted at the association's annual convention and at regional meetings and workshops. It is currently developing continuing education programs for its members by offering courses and certification. Task competencies for media management, instructional program development, and media product development have been identified and will serve as the basis for training and certification programs.

3.6 Cooperation with Other Associations

Cooperation with other associations pervades the forgoing activities. Most standards (such as the standards for school media programs) have been developed in conjunction with other associations. Some of the workshop and seminar activities are developed with other associations. The AECT assists states in the formation of certification programs. The development of a Handbook of Definitions and Terminology for Educational Technology directly involved 19 other education and media organizations. Finally, the participation of the AECT in consortia and joint councils shows its commitment to interdependence with other associations related to education and technology. As technology plays an increasing role in education and instruction, the interaction between the AECT and other associations will inevitably increase and lead to a concerted attempt to improve education through the application of technology.

4. Professional Associations of Educational Technology Worldwide

Around the world, the professional associations with a primary focus on the field of educational technology number approximately 60. The 40 associations in the United States with a clearly identified relationship to educational technology range from a concern with student development in media, such as the American Student Media Association, through organizations that focus on particular media of communication, such as the Association for Educational Data Systems and the Biological Photographic Association, to organizations that are primarily concerned with behavioral change, such as the National Society for Performance and Instruction and the International Visual Literacy Association.

In Canada, there is a national Association for Media and Technology in Education in Canada (AMTEC). The United Kingdom numbers at least seven organizations which are readily identifiable, preeminent among them being the Association for Educational and Training Technology. India also has several. Australia has the Australian Society for Educational Technology (ASET); Japan has the Japan Audio-Visual Education Association (JAVEA); Brazil has the Brazilian Association of Educational Technology; Uruguay has the Inter-American Association

of Broadcasters. Finally, Spain formed a new national Association of Educational Technology in 1982.

The field of educational technology is growing worldwide, with thousands of active professionals organized loosely in professional associations which are sometimes national and sometimes international in scope. The history of the professions demonstrates that working cooperatively in associations ensures regular growth of the academic and intellectual field at the same time as it provides professional people with an opportunity to develop their roles and improve their contribution to society.

See also: Educational Technology: Field of Study; Educational Technology: Personnel; Certification and Licensing of Teachers

Bibliography

Association for Educational Communications and Technology 1977 *Educational Technology: Definition and Glossary of Terms*. Association for Educational Communications and Technology, Washington, DC

Brown J W, Brown S (eds.) 1981 *Educational Media Yearbook*. Libraries Unlimited, Littleton, Colorado

Finn J D 1953 Professionalizing the audio-visual field. *Audiovis. Commun. Rev.* 1(1):6–17.

Howe A (ed.) 1980–81 *International Yearbook of Educational and Instructional Technology*. Kogan Page, London

Lieberman J K 1970 *The Tyranny of the Experts: How Professionals are Closing the Open Society*. Walker, New York

Price L (ed.) 1954 *Dialogues of Alfred North Whitehead. Recorded by Lucien Price*. Little, Brown, Boston, Massachusetts

Tocqueville A C H M de 1969 *Democracy in America*. Doubleday, Garden City, New York

H. B. Hitchens

Educational Technology: Training

Professional preparation of educational technologists began in the late 1940s, partly stimulated by the successful use of audiovisual training aids during the Second World War. Colleges and universities in the United States offered the first formal graduate programs leading to master's degrees and later, doctoral degrees. Other countries followed, but about 20 years later. The formal training of educational technologists occurs at two levels: generalist/specialist, and technician (see *Educational Technology: Personnel*). This article discusses the preparation of generalists and specialists. Technicians are usually trained in specific vocational areas such as graphic arts, photography, television production, and computer programming. They later apply these skills to education-on-the-job. The location of training programs worldwide, the content of the curricula, and issues pertaining to professional education of educational technologists are discussed.

1. Training for What?

As educational technology has become a more integral part of teaching and learning at all levels of education and in other settings, the demand for specialized personnel has accelerated. Schools, universities, industrial training programs, open universities, medical education, international educational planning programs, and educational broadcasting are representative types of organizations which seek educational technology personnel. The general functions of such personnel include management, instructional development, media production, evaluation, and research.

Some positions seek generalists who are competent in many functions and move freely from one responsibility to another. Many of the educational technology managers are generalists. In some cases specialists are required to handle specific functions in depth such as instructional design, product development, or evaluation. Most educational technologists are prepared to serve a wide range of responsibilities pertaining to systematic instruction.

There appears to be a continuing need for educational technology personnel as new technologies enter the education and training arena. Professional education programs preparing such people currently exist and are growing throughout the world.

2. The Location of Educational Technology Training Programs

Virtually all programs are located within higher education institutions. They are not uniform in designation. A sample reveals such program titles as: educational media, instructional systems technology, educational communications, instructional technology, and learning systems. Some departments are located within faculties of education, others are independent. Some offer special emphasis within departments of educational psychology or communications. Some are aligned with library and information science. Still others use an educational technology label to cover one specialization such as computer-based education. There is little order among professional training programs. An extensive search is often required to find them.

The greatest number of programs is in the United States. From 1955, when there were 50 programs, the number increased to 193 programs in 1980 (Short 1981). In 1981, Harvard University and Stanford University announced new programs in the field. The largest enrollment is at the master's level. There are more part-time students than full-time students. Short (1981) determined that there were 788 full-time and 469 part-time faculty in 1980 with the largest

percent of full-time faculty holding the professor's rank and a doctoral degree. Moore (1981) studied the most influential educational technology programs in the United States and determined that the top five were at Indiana University, Syracuse University, Michigan State University, the University of Southern California, and Florida State University. A complete list of United States graduate programs appears in the annual edition of the *Educational Media Yearbook*.

Professional training programs in the United Kingdom are found in 24 institutions. The nature of these programs varies. Some are diploma programs, some are postgraduate programs approved by the Council for National Academic Awards (CNAA), others grant bachelor's, master's, and doctoral degrees. Programs of study are described in *Courses Leading to Qualification in Educational Technology*, which is updated and published annually by the Council for Educational Technology for the United Kingdom. Some of the innovative professional training programs have come from Scotland. The CNAA Diploma in Educational Technology at Jordanhill College of Education and the Diploma in Educational Technology at Dundee College of Education were the first professional training programs to be offered to part-time students at a distance. Each institution has made the modules available through local sources.

Beyond the programs in educational technology in the United States and the United Kingdom are several in the commonwealth countries: Australia and Canada. Major programs in Australia are located at Macquarie University in Sydney, the University of Melbourne, Salisbury College of Advanced Education in Adelaide, South Australia, and the Western Australia Institute of Technology in Perth. Canada's major programs are located at Concordia University in Montreal, the Ontario Institute for the Study of Education, Toronto, the University of Alberta at Edmonton, and the University of British Columbia. In South Africa, Rand Afrikaans University offers a substantial program in the field.

Europe has pockets of interest in training for educational technology, but the programs are not generally self-contained. They are associated with departments of pedagogy, computer science, or other cognate areas. An exception is the program in Applied Instructional Science at the Twente University of Technology in the Netherlands which began an undergraduate program in 1981. There are programs at the *Ecole Normale Supérieure* at St. Cloud in France, the University of Tübingen in Germany, and the Department of Education of the *Eötvös Lorand Tudomanyegyetem* in Budapest.

Various countries in Latin America have made efforts to build academic programs in educational technology but there appear to be only a few in operation. The University of Trujillo in Peru has a department of educational technology, the *Uni-*

versidad Nacional de Lujan in Argentina offers courses, and several Brazilian universities have basic programs. The *Universidad Nacional Experimental Simon Rodriguez* in Venezuela has a program in the planning stage.

It is more difficult to determine the existence of programs in Asia. In Japan, several universities offer courses and programs to prepare educational technologists. A graduate program in educational technology has been established at the State Teacher Training Institute (IKIP) Jakarta, Indonesia with the assistance of United States institutions of higher education. An educational technology diploma is available through the Tokyo Institute of Technology. In India, South Gujarat University, Department of Education in Surat, has an educational technology concentration. There is no doubt that other universities in Asian countries offer courses and programs but there is no comprehensive listing of such information.

3. Content of Training Programs

Since most of the training programs in educational technology are on the graduate level, they tend to build on undergraduate studies, most frequently teacher education. The trend is shifting away from the teacher education base as more educational technology personnel are being employed in nonschool settings. Most academic programs provide new content which is not dependent upon previous studies. Persons who have good preparation in mathematics and psychology seem to have a head start.

The content of academic programs changes as one goes further into a training program and seeks advanced degrees. Most of the individuals who enter the field spend most of their time acquiring the basic vocabulary, concepts, and procedures of practitioners. There is some formal way of acquiring competencies in each of the nine functional areas stated by the Association for Educational Communications and Technology (AECT) in the United States (1977). Thus, courses, experience, and independent study in organization management, personnel management, research and theory, design, evaluation, logistics, utilization, research, and utilization/dissemination constitute the bulk of most curricula. Short (1981) found that the major emphases of master's programs in the United States were materials production and utilization/application. All programs included in his survey offered at least one course each in management, production, and utilization. Curricula in other countries appear to follow the same pattern. Other high frequency offerings include management, selection, instructional development, instructional systems design, and evaluation. Cognate areas most frequently used by educational technology are educational psychology (learning, instructional, and developmental), statistics, communications (theory and applied areas—radio, television, and film), computer science, and library and information science.

In the United States there has been a strong movement to prepare educational technology personnel for elementary and secondary schools through library science programs. The term "school media specialist" has been frequently used rather than educational technologist. The programs, largely at the graduate level, merge competencies of school library (resource center) management and some of the nonprint media competencies such as production, utilization and, to some extent, evaluation. Many of the programs are competency based and require demonstrated minimal performance before degrees are awarded (see *Competency-based Teacher Education*). This American trend has not spread widely to other countries, but several programs in Canada and Australia appear to be moving in that direction.

In an attempt to bring about some uniformity of the training programs, national efforts have been initiated in the United States and the United Kingdom to develop standards for professional training programs. In the United States the Association for Educational Communications and Technology has developed a list of competencies for: (a) instructional development specialists; (b) material design and production specialists; and (c) media management specialists. In the United Kingdom, the Council for Educational Technology explored core competencies for educational technology personnel. These documents have become basic planning tools for determining the content of new curricula in educational technology in many institutions (see *Educational Technology: Field of Study*).

4. Issues in Professional Training

As any field grows and matures, fundamental questions are raised regarding the training of future professionals. Finn (1953) insisted that one major criterion for a profession is "a period of long training . . . before entering into the profession." As today's professionals consider that criterion, certain issues seem to be paramount. They center on (a) the definition of the field; (b) recruitment of personnel; (c) core competencies; (d) theory/practice balance; and (e) certification of personnel and accreditation of academic programs.

4.1 Definition of the Field

As the field rapidly evolved from audiovisual education through educational communications to educational technology, there has been no consistency in its definition. A series of statements regarding the definition were published by AECT in 1963 and 1972. The most recent and comprehensive (1977) seems to have taken hold in North America but there is not wide agreement on it from all concerned parties. Until there is conceptual agreement, professional training programs will vary according to the definition they value. If it is oriented toward media and their application, one type of curriculum will emerge; if the systems design definition is accepted, then another type of curriculum will be developed. The issue has not been resolved.

4.2 Recruitment of Personnel

Many educational technologists stumble into the field through participation in innovative teaching and learning activities. There is no natural and logical route from one undergraduate program to a graduate program in educational technology. There is not much active recruiting of new personnel into training programs. Most people are steered by individuals who are already practitioners or by circumstances which lead to a career change such as from teaching to educational technology. The lack of knowledge regarding professional training programs and the technical image often turn potential practitioners away. There appears to be sufficient demand for personnel worldwide, so more active recruiting of candidates should be considered.

4.3 Core Competencies

There is probably no other question which can create such disparate answers and feelings as, "What essential knowledge must all educational technologists possess?" Translated to academic training programs, this question means identification of those core competencies which all individuals who enter professional training programs must acquire. There is no agreement among programs or official statements of professional associations which provide guidance. Short (1981) reports courses in management, production, and utilization at all 193 master's programs in the United States. The content of these courses would have to be examined to determine consistency from institution to institution. The list of competencies compiled by the AECT (*Instructional Innovator* Dec. 1980) provides some agreement among professionals in the United States. There may be more agreement than is realized, but the basic question still goes unanswered.

4.4 Theory/Practice Balance

The field of educational technology began with a practical orientation. The early emphasis on the media of communication in a teaching/learning environment and the continuing acceptance of new technologies tends to perpetuate the image of practice. However, with the establishment of academic programs came the need for theoretical bases. Individuals were asking, "What medium should be used and why?" The psychology of learning was obviously closely related to the use of communication media. Theories were borrowed or adapted from psychology, communication, and psychometrics programs and found their way into educational technology curricula. Graduates of programs were expected to perform practical tasks in the real world of education and training and they wondered about the value of theory. There seems to be more agreement among academics about theory for advanced graduate studies. The basic conflict has not been resolved in any widespread fashion. Some institutions are known to have programs which are more practical in curricular offerings while others are more theoretical. Each program will probably continue to determine its own balance.

4.5 Certification of Personnel and Accreditation of Programs

Another criterion for a profession is the standards established for entry into the profession (Finn 1953). Each country has control mechanisms at the national or state levels to ensure that academic programs prepare people according to specific standards. These standards have not yet touched the field of educational technology to any great degree. Some exceptions are the Council for National Academic Awards (CNAA) validations in the United Kingdom. In the United States, about 30 states have established certification requirements for educational technology personnel working in the public schools. The Association for Educational Communications and Technology (AECT) has attempted to implement an association-oriented certification program but has not been successful. Accreditation of academic programs in educational technology is usually covered by institution-wide approval by regional academic accrediting associations or sometimes by the National Council for the Accreditation of Teacher Education if the program is housed within a faculty of education which prepares teachers. Without published standards for academic programs it is possible for any institution to claim a legitimate academic program in the field and for an individual to declare himself/herself as an educational technologist. The approach of benign self-regulation may be sufficient until there are abuses of current procedures.

See also: Educational Technology: Conceptual Frameworks and Historical Development

Bibliography

Association for Educational Communications and Technology (AECT) 1977 *The Definition of Educational Technology.* AECT, Washington, DC
Courses Leading to Qualification in Educational Technology. Council for Educational Technology, London
Educational Media Yearbook. Libraries Unlimited, Littleton, Colorado
Finn J D 1953 Professionalizing the audio-visual field. *Audio-vis. Commun. Rev.* pp. 6–17
Howe A 1980 *International Yearbook of Educational and Instructional Technology, 1980–81.* Nichols, New York

Instructional Innovator 1980 Competencies for instructional development specialists, and competencies for materials design and production specialists. 25(9): 27-31

Moore D M 1981 Educational media professional's perceptions of influence and prestige in the field of instructional technology: A national survey. *Educ. Technol.* 21: 15–23

Short R 1981 *An Analysis of Instructional Technology Graduates Degree Programs in United States Colleges and Universities.* Farmland Industries, Kansas City, Missouri

D. P. Ely

Ego Psychology Theory of Human Development

Ego psychology deals with the development, organization, and functioning, both normal and aberrant, of those core aspects of human personality that account for psychological growth, adaptation, adjustment, and disorder. It is not concerned with the nature of such psychological processes as perception, learning, memory, cognition, problem solving, or creativity in their own right, but only insofar as they are directly implicated in the mechanisms of ego development and functioning. Thus, ego psychology and cognitive psychology constitute two fundamentally independent bodies of knowledge in terms of their respective basic science thrusts and major applications, even though they are obviously related and interdependent at numerous points of intersection, as will become abundantly clear throughout this article. Contrary to the broader implications of its title, however, this article will be restricted to an ego psychology interpretation of only the personality (ego) aspects of human development and will not consider as such either cognitive development or contemporaneous (nondevelopmental) aspects of personality structure and functioning.

To avoid later confusion, the reader should be aware at the outset that there are two completely different major versions of ego psychology in terms of their historical antecedents and theoretical orientation, namely, psychoanalytic ego psychology and naturalistic ego psychology, that have very little in common with respect to philosophy of science orientation, underlying psychological theory, empirical methodology, and accepted database.

Psychoanalytic ego psychology is basically a derivative and extension of orthodox psychoanalytic psychology to problems of ego development and functioning that accepts all of the major tenets of psychoanalysis, although positing some "conflict free" or "autonomous" areas. As a separately identifiable movement within the larger psychoanalytic framework, it was first identified with the work of Hartmann (1958) and Anna Freud (1937), later with such figures as Mahler (1968) and Erikson (1950), and more recently with Kernberg (1967) and Kohut (1971).

Naturalistic ego psychology, on the other hand, is not only nonpsychoanalytic in its theoretical orientation but is also based on a theoretically opposite set of psychological and developmental propositions and on a naturalistic, rather than a largely speculative and impressionistic, approach to theory building and verification. Its principal protagonist, the American psychiatrist and psychologist Ausubel formulated between 1946 and 1952 the first comprehensive and unified nonpsychoanalytic theory of ego development and of its relation to mental disorder. This theory was derived both from his own diverse clinical experience with narcotic addicts and from a broad range of other mentally ill persons (children, adolescents, and adults in both inpatient and outpatient settings), and from the then available naturalistic data in personality and ego development. Much of the initial impetus for the elaboration of Ausubel's ego psychology theory came from his postulated identification of the motivationally inadequate personality as pathognomonic of the predisposing premorbid personality structure of both narcotic addicts and of so-called process schizophrenics, thereby establishing the first significant etiological and psychopathological linkage between narcotic addiction and other major forms of mental disorder.

In this article only the naturalistic version of ego psychology will be considered (except for a brief comparison between the two versions) because (a) it is based on a currently more tenable and generally accepted theoretical approach to personality and developmental psychology; (b) it is related to, and consonant with, findings from methodologically rigorous studies of ego development rather than being derived uncritically from a combination of orthodox psychoanalytic theory and new speculative assertions about the nature and stages of human development which are buttressed only by impressionistic and anecdotal clinical material; and (c) it is more compatible with modern biological and ethnological conceptions of human development and of the interaction between heredity and environment as expressed in such fields as behavioral genetics, embryology, and cultural anthropology.

1. Historical Antecedents of Naturalistic Ego Psychology

Although the modern version of naturalistic ego psychology evolved contemporaneously with psychoanalytic ego psychology, and also antedated it in many significant respects, this fact has tended to be obscured by the dominant position of psychoanalysis in the middle third of the twentieth century (particularly in the United States) in psychiatry; in other mental health professions such as social work, child guidance, and counseling; in other social sciences (e.g., cultural anthropology); and in the social science aspects of more distantly related fields such as pediatrics, education, art, literature, law, religion, history, and philosophy. As a result, it is hardly surprising that psychoanalytic ego psychology came to be perceived in North America as coextensive with ego psychology generally, both by its protagonists and by other mental health professionals, social scientists, and informed laymen.

Paradoxically enough therefore, even though naturalistic ego psychology was rooted both empirically in the longitudinal studies of personality and ego development conducted at American child development institutes [particularly by Gesell and his associates (1946) at Yale University] as well as theoretically in the pre- and non-psychoanalytic speculative mini-self-psychologies developed by such American philosphers and psychologists as Baldwin, Cooley, Dewey, G. H. Mead, G. W. Allport, and Maslow, it tended to flourish more in Europe. This was largely the case because of the less dominant influence of psychoanalysis on European social and behavioral science than on their American counterparts. These latter nonpsychoanalytic trends in American ego psychology, both speculative and empirical, reinforced by several influential critiques of psychoanalytic predeterminism and of psychoanalytically oriented views on sexuality and on the impact of child-rearing practices on personality development in American and primitive cultures (e.g., Kinsey et al. 1948, Orlansky 1949, Sherif and Cantril 1947), set the stage for Ausubel's more definitive, naturalistically grounded ego psychology theory of ego development over the life span and of its relation to mental disorder. Ausubel's stages of ego development were organized around his key concepts of satellization and desatellization and his key distinctions between satellizers and nonsatellizers, on the one hand, and between executive and volitional independence, on the other. These concepts and stages will be delineated below in greater detail.

2. Principal Differences between Naturalistic and Psychoanalytic Ego Psychology

Gernerally speaking, naturalistic ego psychology differs from the psychoanalytic variety in the following ways (see *Psychoanalytic Theory of Human Development*).

(a) In accordance with modern trends in genetics, embryology, comparative psychology, primate behavior, and cultural anthropology, naturalistic ego psychology is devoid of any taint of preformationism or predeterminism, eschewing all prestructured and predetermined drives and "stages of psychosexual development," instincts, or innate identifications.

(b) It repudiates the notion of innate, "original" and finite sources of psychic energy (libido) from

which all socially acceptable drives are said to be derived, largely through such mechanisms as sublimation, symbolic equivalence, and reaction formation. All drives are held to be acquired, completely undifferentiated at birth, and "functionally autonomous."

(c) All components and functions of the ego are conceptualized as acquired from interaction between relevant genetically determined potentialities, predispositions, and preferences on the one hand, and corresponding interpersonal experience on the other. Neither ego nor character structure is regarded as a precipitate of id or "pleasure principle" drives that are modified by corrective contact with the "reality principle" or with particular child-rearing practices impinging on erogenous activity during successive stages of psychosexual development and resulting in over- or under-gratification with subsequent fixation of libido.

(d) The responsiveness of infants and children to various affective and attitudinal cues is held to be limited by their relative perceptual, cognitive, and social immaturity and also by the primitiveness of their prevailing ego structures. Thus, for example, the alleged qualitative comparability of infant and adult sexuality and the alleged psychoanalytical sensitivity of infants to subtle attitudinal cues of parental rejection, emotional distancing, or guilt are categorically denied.

(e) Armchair speculation about stages of ego development is abandoned in favor of naturalistic longitudinal observation and testing of children, adolescents, and adults for purposes of designating stages of ego development of the life span. Little essential scientific difference, for example, is seen between Shakespeare's poetic characterization of successive stages in the life cycle and Erikson's corresponding developmental stages of personality development (see *Eriksonian Theory of Human Development*).

(f) Naturalistic ego psychology rejects all impressionistic clinical and anecdotal "evidence" as scientifically inappropriate for confirming or disconfirming hypotheses regarding ego development or functioning, insisting on methodologically rigorous data for these purposes.

(g) Emphasis is placed on relating all aspects and dimensions of ego structure and functioning to each other at each stage of development. It does not reduce all of ego development to progress along a single linearly progressive dimension as Mahler (1968), for example, does in describing movement from a symbiotic relationship between mother and infant to a later stage in which ego boundaries are sharpened and a sense of self is individuated out of an undifferentiated and amorphous mother–infant mass.

(h) Naturalistic ego psychology makes no arbitrary distinctions or divisions between aspects of ego that refer to ego functioning generally and aspects having to do with expressions of conscience or sexuality. The ego as an entitiy is regarded as functioning as a whole. Sexual self-expression or moral self-expression, for example, is not considered to be categorically or qualitatively separate from problems of self-esteem, independence–dependence, or deferred versus immediate gratification of hedonistic needs. Hence, separate personality substructures such as id or superego are not postulated but, rather, are incorporated within the general framework of ego structure.

(i) Finally, unlike psychoanalytic ego psychology, naturalistic ego psychology does not place the role and significance of repression completely out of perspective as a defence mechanism and, hence, elevate it as the principal source of psychopathological symptomatology and/or concomitantly, perceive insight as the cornerstone of psychotherapy. On the contrary, most significant motives and attitudes are generally perceived as being functionally accessible to awareness, at least in their broad outlines, and with respect to their basic essentials.

3. Definition of Ego and Related Terms

The terms self, self-concept, ego, and personality constitute, in the order given, an ascending hierarchy of complexity and inclusiveness. The self is a constellation of generally tangible individual perceptions and memories that have self-reference. It consists of the visual image of the appearance of one's body, the auditory image of the sound of one's name, more amorphous images of kinesthetic sensations and visceral tensions, memories of personal events, and so forth. The self-concept, on the other hand, is an abstraction of the essential and distinguishing characteristics of the self at each stage of development that differentiate an individual's selfhood from the environment and other selves. In the course of development, various evaluative attitudes, values, aspirations, motives, and obligations become associated with the self-concept. This system of interrelated self-attitudes, self-motives, self-esteem, self-values, self-obligations, self-ideals, and self-aspirations organized around the self-concept may be conceptualized as the ego.

Personality is a still more inclusive term than ego. It includes all of the psychological and behavioral predispositions characteristic of individuals at a given point in their life history. Thus it embraces the peripheral, transitory, and trivial, as well as the central ego aspects of their behavioral propensities and their cognitive as well as their motivational, moral, and affective traits.

4. Stages of Naturalistic Ego Development

In Ausubel's naturalistic schema of ego development, three main normative stages are delineated: (a) ego omnipotence during infancy (roughly 6 months to $2\frac{1}{2}$ years); (b) satellization during a childhood (roughly age 3 to puberty); and (c) desatellization during adolescence and early adult life. The key new concept here is that of satellization which will, therefore, first be described briefly before the three stages are examined more closely.

Much conceptual confusion has resulted in the past, and still prevails today, because of failure to distinguish between two essentially different kinds of identification, each of which involves a reciprocal relationship between a relatively dominant and independent individual (or group) and a relatively dependent and subordinate individual. In a satellizing relationship, the subordinate party acknowledges and accepts a subservient and deferential role, and the superordinate in turn accepts the subordinate as an intrinsically valuable "retainer" in his or her personal orbit. As an outcome of this type of dependent process and relationship, satellizers acquire a derived (vicarious, attributed) biosocial status that is wholly a function of the dependent relationship and independent of their own competence or performance ability, and that is bestowed upon them through the fiat of simple intrinsic valuation by a superordinate individual whose authority and power to do so are regarded as unchallengeable.

On the other hand, the two parties to the same "transaction" could relate to each other in quite a different way. The subordinate party could acknowledge dependency as a temporary, regrettable, and much-to-be remedied fact of life requiring, as a matter of expediency, various acts of conformity and deference but, at the same time, not accept a dependent and subservient status as a person. In turn, he or she could either be rejected outright or accorded qualified acceptance, that is, not for intrinsic reasons (as a person for his or her own sake) but in terms of current or potential competence and usefulness to the superordinate party. The act of identification, if it occurs at all, consists solely in using the latter (superordinate) individual as an emulatory model so that the subordinate can learn the superordinate's skills and methods of operation and thus eventually succeed to his or her enviable status. Accordingly, the nonsatellizing child acquires no derived (vicarious, attributed) status. The only type of biosocial status that can be engendered in this situation is the earned status that reflects the subordinate's actual functional competence, power, or control.

This nonsatellizing type of identification occurs for one of two reasons: either the superordinate party will not extend unqualified intrinsic acceptance (as in the case of rejecting parents or those who value their children for ulterior self-enhancing purposes) or, much more rarely, because the subordinate party is unwilling to undergo satellization or is incapable of satellizing.

4.1 Stage 1: Omnipotent Ego Structure (about Age 6 Months to Age 2½ Years)

Paradoxical as it may seem at first glance, the omnipotent phase of ego development coexists with the period of the child's greatest degree of objective helplessness and dependence on parents. Yet this apparent paradox is easily resolved if the nonunitary concept of dependence is divided into its easily discriminable executive and volitional components. When this is done, concomitant self-perceptions of volitional independence and executive dependence are not mutually contradictory at all, but are, on the contrary, very compatible with each other under the pancultural biosocial conditions of infancy. Unlike the psychoanalytic doctrine of infantile omnipotence—which unparsimoniously assumes the existence, in part, of a preformed ego and of a sense of volition even before birth—the present theory conceives of omnipotent feelings in infants as a naturalistic product of both actual interpersonal experience (i.e., experienced parental deference) and of their perceptual cognitive immaturity.

At the same time that infants are developing a functional concept of executive dependence from their gradual appreciation of their own inability to gratify their most elemental needs, and of their consequent absolute dependence on familiar competent caretakers to do so, concomitant notions of volitional independence and omnipotence gradually begin to emerge. This is the case because it is precisely when children are most helpless that, almost invariably in all cultures, they are accorded more indulgence and deference by parents than at any other period of childhood. At this time, parents tend to be most solicitous and eager to gratify the child's expressed needs. In general they make few demands upon infants and usually accede to their legitimate requests. If training is instituted, it tends to be delayed, gradual, and gentle. In this benevolent environment, therefore, much support is provided in external interpersonal conditions for a perception of parental subservience to the child's will.

Furthermore, it is unlikely that infants are sufficiently mature, perceptually and cognitively speaking, to appreciate the relatively subtle motivations (love, duty, altruism) underlying this deference. As a result they quite understandably acquire the developmentally autistic misperception that, because of their volitional power, parents are obliged to serve them rather than the correct perception that the superservience is altruistic and practiced in deference to their extreme helplessness. Hence, their appreciation of their executive dependence does not conflict with, or detract essentially from, their self-concept of relative volitional omnipotence and independence inasmuch as volitionally powerful persons do not have to be executively competent and independent as long as they have an executively competent person at their beck and call.

4.2 Stage 2: Satellization (Age 3 to Puberty)

Devaluation of the omnipotent ego structure begins when the infant loses his or her extreme helplessness and acquires sufficient cognitive, motor, and language competence to help in his or her own care, to become responsive to parental direction and to conform to parentally transmitted cultural norms. The imposition of these new demands and expectations (e.g., for sphincter control and control of aggression), coupled with markedly decreased parental deference and reciprocally increased parental dominance and assertiveness in the relationship, tends to undermine environmental supports for infantile self-perceptions of omnipotence and volitional independence. At the same time, greatly increased cognitive and perceptual sophistication contribute to ego devaluation by enabling children to perceive their actual impotence in the household power structure and to appreciate that they are just as dependent on their parents volitionally as executively. Thus, ego devaluation is characterized by increased executive independence and decreased volitional independence.

Under these circumstances, given a minimal degree of acceptance and intrinsic valuation, most children elect to undergo satellization. Since in no culture can children compete with adults on better than marginal terms, and since they can no longer be omnipotent themselves, the next best thing in terms of their self-esteem needs is to be satellites of persons who apparently are. By so doing they not only acquire a guaranteed derived status which they enjoy solely by the fiat of being accepted and valued for themselves irrespective of their competence and performance ability, but also, by perceiving themselves as allied with their parents—albeit in a subordinate role—they share vicariously in the latter's omnipotence.

In all cultures, however, a variable number of parents are psychologically unable, unwilling, or negatively disposed by circumstances to extend acceptance and intrinsic valuation to their offspring. Under these conditions genuine and thorough-going devaluation of the omnipotent ego structure does not occur; and deprived of intrinsic feelings of security and adequacy on a derived basis, the children have no alternative but to strive compensatorily for their extrinsic counterparts by seeking an earned status based on their own competence, hierarchical position, and power to influence and control their environment. Unlike satellizers who assimilate parental training goals and standards uncritically and unselectively on the basis of personal loyalty, these children merely acknowledge parents as suitable emulatory models for acquiring power and prestige and internalize their values selectively in terms of the expediential criterion of potential usefulness for ego enchancement.

4.3 Stage 3: Desatellization (Adolescence and Early Adult Life)

Before ego development can be completed by the attainment of adult personality status, one more important maturational step is obviously necessary: emancipation from emotionally dependent attitudes towards parents. This essentially involves a process of desatellization that includes not only assuming the role of a volitionally independent adult in society, but also seeking the major source of one's biosocial status and self-esteem from earned rather than derived sources, that is, from one's own competence and achievement. These new ego-status goals of desatellization are self-evidently the opposite of those prevailing during the satellizing period; but the ego-maturity goals necessary for implementing these new adult drives and ego characteristics are identical and continuous with those operative throughout childhood, namely, increased executive independence, frustration, tolerance, responsibility, self-critical ability, and deferral of hedonistic gratification. However, the motivation for assimilating these same trait values, and for acquiring the traits themselves, shifts from the expression of uncritical personal loyalty to parents and desire for parental approval to perceived necessity for, and compatibility with, the acquisition of increased earned status and volitional independence.

Desatellization is precipitated by cultural, parental, and internal individual needs for attaining adult personality status and is supported by corresponding shifts in demands and expectations that are triggered by the onset of pubescence. In Western cultures it is effected through three main mechanisms: (a) resatellization—the replacement of parents by peers as the essential socializing agents of children and as the individuals in relation to whom residual satellizing trends are maintained; (b) the displacement of derived by earned status as the principal source of self-esteem; and (c) the displacement of uncritical personal loyalty to parents by considerations of expediency, ego enhancement, and abstract ideals of equity, virtue, and morality as the basis on which values are assimilated.

Inasmuch as the nonsatellizing child has never undergone satellization, the basic aspects of desatellization are unnecessary and its objectives may be considered as largely accomplished in advance.

5. Implications of Naturalistic Ego Psychology for Child Rearing, Counseling, and Educational Practice

The major implication of naturalistic ego psychology for child rearing, counseling, and educational practice follows naturally from the logical plausibility of the proposition, supported by clinical findings, that the most tenable and felicitous course of ego development—from the standpoint of mature, stable and productive personality functioning and the avoidance of disabling personality distortions and mental disorders—is the modal type prevailing panculturally, namely. satellization during childhood followed by desatellization during adolescence and early adulthood. Failure to satellize typically results in compensatorily and unrealistically high and tenacious needs for achievement, severe impairment of self-esteem, neurotic anxiety and its various distortive defences, and susceptibility both to conduct and antisocial personality disorders and to such psychotic complications as affective, reactive schizophrenic, and paranoid disorders (Ausubel and Kirk 1977). Failure to desatillize, on the other hand, is associated with a motivationally immature and inadequate personality structure predisposed to chronic academic and vocational underachievement, the amotivational syndrome, substance abuse, and process schizophrenia (Ausubel and Kirk 1977).

Nonsatellization is preventable, at least in part, by educating parents about the causes and consequences of the rejecting and extrinsically valuing parent attitudes that beget it. To some extent it is reversible by treatment of such parents when nonsatellizing children are identified in early childhood education and treatment centers. When parent attitudes are resistive to change (and also in the case of nonsatellizing older children and adolescents, and adults with clinical symptoms), then compensatory satellization to counselors, teachers, spouses, and older relatives can be encouraged, as well as the formulation of more realistic ego aspirations.

Failure to desatellize can be similarly prevented and counteracted, in part, by parent and teacher education regarding the child-rearing and teacher attitudes (overprotecting, overpermissive, overdominating) that promote it, by providing corrective identification with teachers, counselors, and surrogate parents, and, in more serious cases, by appropriate character re-education in residential centers.

Bibliography

Ausubel D P 1952 *Ego Development and the Personality Disorders: A Developmental Approach to Psychopathology.* Grune and Stratton, New York

Ausubel D P, Kirk D 1977 *Ego Psychology and Mental Disorder: A Developmental Approach to Psychopathology*. Grune and Stratton, New York

Erikson E 1950 *Childhood and Society*. Norton, New York

Freud A 1937 *The Ego and the Mechanisms of Defence*. The International Psycho-analytical Library, No. 30. Hogarth, London

Gesell A L, Ilg F L 1946 *The Child from Five to Ten*. Harper, New York

Hartmann H 1958 Ego psychology and the problem of adaptation. *J. Am. Psychoanal. Assoc.*, Monograph Series No. 1. International Universities Press, New York

Kernberg O F 1967 Boderline personality organization. *J. Am. Psychoanal. Assoc.* 15: 641–85

Kinsey A C, Pomeroy W B, Martin C E 1948 *Sexual Behavior in the Human Male*. Saunders, Philadelphia

Kohut H 1971 *The Analysis of the Self: A Systematic Approach to the Psychoanalytic Treatment of Narcissistic Personality Disorders*. The Psychoanalytic Study of the Child, Monograph No. 4. International Universities Press, New York

Mahler M S 1968 *On Human Symbiosis and the Vicissitudes of Individuation*. The International Psycho-analytical Library, No. 82. International Universities Press, New York

Orlansky H 1949 Infant care and personality. *Psychol. Bull.* 46: 1–48

Sherif M, Cantril H 1947 *The Psychology of Ego-involvements, Social Attitudes and Identifications*. Wiley, New York

D. P. Ausubel

Egypt: System of Education

Egypt is situated in the northeastern corner of Africa. It is bordered on the west by Libya and in the south by the Sudan, while the Mediterranean and the Red Seas form the frontiers to the north and the east. The Red Sea and the Mediterranean are joined by the Suez Canal. Part of Egypt, the Sinai peninsula, is in Asia. Because Egypt is centrally located it is also a focal point in the worldwide network of water and air transport. This may be why, throughout its history, it has been a mediator in the spread of culture and civilization from one part of the world to another.

The total area of Egypt is 1,001,400 square kilometres, only one-thirtieth of which is inhabited and cultivated. Most of the population is concentrated in the strip of fertile land on both sides of the River Nile. The total population was 46.2 million in mid-1983, with a population growth rate of 2.4 percent annually. The population is expected to be 70 million around the year 2000. Research in Egypt has shown that the increase in women's education and employment is an effective factor in the control of population increase.

Family planning is now being attempted as part of the education policy. Migration is on the increase to adjacent oil-rich countries and within Egypt from rural to urban areas. The percentage distribution of rural and urban population was 81 and 19 percent

respectively in 1907 and 56 and 44 percent in 1976. Greater Cairo and greater Alexandria together have one-quarter of the total population. All this is not without its adverse effect on the equitable distribution of education and other services.

Illiterates comprised 70.8 percent of all persons over 10 years of age in 1960, 56.3 percent in 1976, and 52.9 in 1982, the numbers of illiterate women being always 70 percent more than those of illiterate men. In spite of the marked improvement in percentages, the absolute number of illiterates is on the increase.

Due to the relative youth of the population and the rate of population increase, internal migration, and limited resources, the dependency burden is extremely high. There are 8 million children of pre-school age and 9 million of compulsory school age (6–14). This is much more than the available resources can cope with and much more than the number of children actually enrolled.

Due to the high population density and the scarcity of space, people have to move outside the Nile valley to reclaim land for habitation, cultivation, and industry. This movement is planned and it is not without important educational implications.

Since 1950, Egypt has transformed its economic structure from a primarily agricultural economy to a more diversified structure with the industrial sector making an increasing contribution to the gross domestic product (GDP). Although agriculture suffered a decrease in its share of GDP from 34 percent in 1955–56 to 23 percent in 1976, production has increased at an average annual rate of approximately 3 percent, which is too small to cope with the increasing demand for food and other agricultural products. The cultivable land is so intensively utilized that the crop area is twice the cultivable area. Land reclamation is also encouraged and yet the demand for food is increasing at a rate above what current efforts can cope with. From 1955 to 1975, the industrial sector increased its contribution to GDP from 20 percent to 30 percent, and the tertiary sector increased its share from 46 to 47 percent. The per capita income in 1980 was estmated at US$580 (World Bank 1982).

The total number of employed persons was 10 million in 1977, over 12.5 million in 1980, and 14 million in 1982. The percentage distribution among the government, public, and private sectors was 19.10, 10.26, and 70.64 percent respectively. Government employment increased from 1965 to 1979 by 137 percent, while the population increased in the same period by 35 percent. Services other than education increased in the same period by not more than 40 percent. This overemployment and disguised employment may be partly due to the policy, adopted since 1961, whereby every university or intermediate graduate is guaranteed employment.

Employment in agriculture decreased from 58.4

percent in 1947 to 43.9 percent in 1976 and increased from 10.1 to 17.6 percent in industry and electricity and from 31.4 to 38.5 percent in services. An examination of the educational level of the labour force reveals that illiterates and semi-illiterates together formed 88 percent of the total in 1968 and 79 percent in 1977, indicating an obstacle against progress in a technological age. There is a shortage of ancillary staff (as compared with professional staff) which is detrimental to productivity. It is officially reported that unemployment is around 2.5 percent, and analysis has shown that unemployment is more prevalent among the educated than among the uneducated. Given the extent of migration and unemployment, it would appear that education is in need of reform to make it relevant to current needs.

In 1952, when the revolution overthrew the monarchy, Egypt was, by charter, declared a sovereign Arab state, a democratic republic, and an integral part of the Arab nation. Sovereignty belonged to the people. Islam was the religion of the state, and Arabic was its official language. The democratic ideal was pursued with a number of measures against feudalism, monopoly, and exploitation. According to the charter, education is compulsory for six years at the primary level, and this can be extended to higher levels. Education is free at any of the state institutions. The state supervises all educational activities and guarantees the independence of universities and research centres on condition that they direct their efforts to societal needs and to productivity. Abolition of illiteracy is a national duty, and religion is a basic subject in the curriculum. There are a number of other articles relating to freedom, human dignity, equality of opportunity, security, etc.

The Arab Republic of Egypt has a people's assembly consisting of 382 elected members of whom 10 are appointed by the president. Some 50 percent of the elected members are peasants and workers. Egypt also has a so-called consultative council and a body named the "National Specialized Councils" whose function is to assist the president. The country is administratively divided into 26 governorates each headed by a governor appointed by the president. By law (43 of 1979), the governorates have important administrative functions in the fields of education, health, housing, agriculture, irrigation, transport, etc. The central Ministry of Education is responsible for policies and overall plans, and for following them up, while the governorates are responsible for their implementation and administration.

1. Goals of the Educational System

The president declared in 1974 that an overall revolution must take place in education, and must review the concept, structure, function, and management of education. The community must be literate and educated, benefit from progress in science and tech-

nology, and be more productive. Education should also be more flexible, more diversified, and more relevant to societal needs.

The Ministry of Education stated (1980) the main goals of education as follows:

(a) education is intended for the reinforcement of democracy and equality of opportunity and for the formation of democratic individuals;

(b) it is also intended for the country's overall development, that is, to create a functional relationship between education and work;

(c) it should also be directed towards strengthening the individual's sense of belonging towards the country and to the reinforcement of the Arab cultural identity; and

(d) it should lead to further and lifelong learning through self-renewal and self-education.

These are general state objectives. Naturally, educational aims vary according to level of education, region, program, and the individual. Many Moslem villagers, for example, give as the main reason for wishing to become literate that they want to understand Islam better. Many parents send their children to school to help them avoid manual or physical labour in their future lives. With most people, education leads to a diploma, which brings a position with a regular income and security and ensures a respectable social status. However, this motive is losing weight because of the recent increase in the number of well-paid jobs in the private sector.

The different sex roles have also given rise to differences in educational objectives, but this gap is quickly disappearing. Finally, it should be mentioned that, in general, an academic emphasis of a verbal nature is gradually giving way to a more practical pattern of education.

2. Size and Structure of the Educational System

The formal school system, as it was established in 1957, is shown in Fig. 1. At the age of 6, the pupil joins a Ministry of Education primary school or an al-Azhar primary school, the latter being under the auspices of the Ministry of Islamic Affairs and oriented towards the religion of Islam. Preprimary facilities are restricted and are provided by the private sector or by the Ministry of Social Affairs. The total primary school enrolment (age group 6–11) was 1.5 million in 1951, with an enrolment ratio of 47 percent. In 1981–82, the total enrolment was 5 million with an enrolment ratio of 72 percent, while the grade 1 ratio was 85 percent. This is a rough indicator of a rather high wastage in primary school. The causes for such wastage, which arises from dropping out and repetition, can be found in conditions at

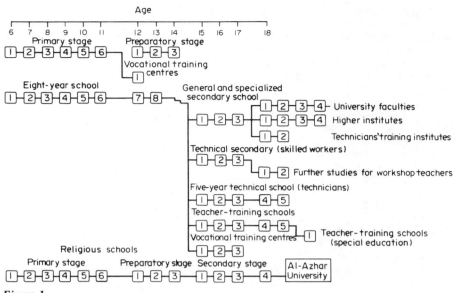

Figure 1
Structure of the educational system

school and in the socioeconomic conditions of the family.

Enrolment ratios in 1981–82 were 47.3 percent for the preparatory level (age group 12–14) and 44.5 percent for the secondary level (age group 15–17). Taking the age bracket 6–17, the enrolment ratio was about 58.5 percent. For the university level, it was 39,630 in 1951–52, 199,074 in 1971–72, and 580,000 in 1983–84 including Al-Azhar and the American University. According to official plans, enrolment in technical education should be more than in the academic stream. At present (1982), it is 56:44, while the target is 60:40.

Between 1956 and 1981, the percentage of females in total enrolment rose from 37 to 41 percent at the primary level, from 23 to 38 percent at the preparatory level, from 16.0 to 37.0 percent at the senior-secondary level, and from 14 to 33 percent at the university level.

The total student population reached 8.5 million in 1983–84, but the higher the level of education the higher the rate of increase, with the result that the education pyramid is narrower at the base and broader at the higher levels.

There are vast nonformal educational activities covered by various ministries, institutions, and organizations. A number of associations run schools for nurses and centres for training in various arts and crafts. The Ministry of Communications has post-office and telecommunication schools. Arab Contractors has a well-developed programme for training in architectural industries and many other practical areas. The Ministry of Health has schools for nurses,

for those learning first-aid, and for x-ray and laboratory assistants. These are but a few examples of the many agencies training more than 250,000 persons in more than 100 vocations and professions. It is estimated, however, that much more provision is needed, and the present strategy is to have a nation-wide machinery for cultural, vocational, and professional development through nonformal programmes.

3. Administration and Finance

Egypt's educational system is the responsibility of the Ministries of Education and of Higher Education. There is a state minister responsible for both ministries and for the Academy of Scientific Research. The central Ministry of Education is responsible for preuniversity education with regard to planning, policy formulation, quality control, coordination, and follow-up. The education offices in the governorates are responsible for all implementation. They chose the sites of the schools, construct and equip the schools, and see that they are well-run. They encourage local contributions and citizen participation. In short, they are responsible for everything that guarantees the efficient operation of schools.

Figure 2 presents the organizational structure of the Ministry of Education. The minister meets at regular intervals with the council of undersecretaries and a number of other councils. He presides over the meetings of the Supreme Council of Universities which is responsible for planning and policy making. The organizational structure of the governorates is

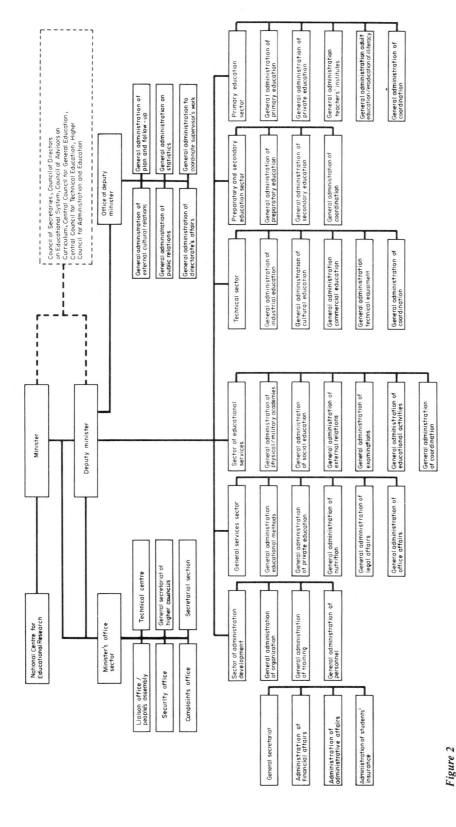

Figure 2
Organizational structure of the Ministry of Education (March 1979)

1643

similar in principle to that of the central ministry, but it is rather smaller and simpler. The country is also divided into 140 separate education districts with a network of supervisors and administrators.

The Ministry of Islamic affairs looks after the educational policy and plans of the Al-Azhar University, colleges, and schools. Government expenditure on formal education in 1981 was 6 percent of the gross national product and 18.5 percent of total public expenditure. Salaries absorbed more than 80 percent, while current expenses and investment accounted for the remaining 20 percent. Investment in school buildings increased at the beginning of the 1980s from 7 to 13 percent. There are still not enough school buildings and, if demand is to be met, more than 3 billion Egyptian pounds must be spent on construction in the next 10 years, according to estimates. From 1964 to 1978, expenditure on preuniversity education increased fourfold while expenditure on higher education increased more than fivefold. Higher education in 1970 used 20.4 percent of the country's total expenditure on education, and in 1978 it used 31.4 percent. Of the ministry's total budget, primary education received 44 percent. Some maintain that this should be appreciably increased.

Egypt receives aid from the World Bank, UNICEF, UNESCO, and friendly countries like the United States, the German Democratic Republic, the United Kingdom, and other Arab states. Although the aid received is substantial, there is a great deal yet to be done in education, particularly in the rationalization of management and of expenditure.

4. Personnel

The central Ministry of Education has somewhat fewer than 2,000 professional and ancillary officials. They are usually very carefully selected. The planners, for example, are usually university graduates with an additional year of training at the Cairo Institute of Planning. Preference is given usually to those who have demonstrated superior teaching skills. Suitable courses of training are given to those who will become inspectors, consultants, supervisors, technical assistants, senior masters, headmasters, directors, etc. Elaborate evaluation methods are used for allocation and promotion. Between officials in the ministry and those in the governorates there is a continuing exchange of information through regular meetings and through other channels of communication.

The Ministry of Higher Education is much smaller than the Ministry of Education because most of its responsibilities are invested in the universities and in the Supreme Council of Universities.

The estimated total number of teachers (nearly 250,000) may be somewhat imprecise. The definition of a teacher in practice and as used for statistical purposes is not well-defined. If planning assumptions, school requirements, and the country's expectations are to be met, 13,000 new teachers are needed every year in order to reach a 95 percent enrolment ratio in grade 1 by 1990. This means an intake to teachers' institutes and colleges of 13,500 in the first year. The universities are at present establishing primary-education departments which will ultimately raise the level of the compulsory basic education of teachers.

There are severe shortages in teachers of Arabic language and Islamic religion—a strange phenomenon. There are also shortages of teachers of art, agriculture, music, home economics, and the various branches of technical education. This may be because in Egypt teaching seems to be one of the least attractive professions. The status of teachers in general and teachers of Arabic in particular needs to be seriously reconsidered.

5. Curriculum Development and Teaching Methodology

In Egypt, curriculum construction is the result of teamwork. Committees are formed which include consultants, supervisors, experts, professors of education, and experienced teachers. There is usually one committee for each subject or group of subjects. The chairpersons of the various committees are invited to meet so that decisions may be coordinated. When a curriculum has been produced by a committee, it is referred to the Supreme Council of Preuniversity Education which formally issues it for implementation. By law, curricula may sometimes be adjusted to local conditions or specific events.

The National Centre for Educational Research is responsible for collecting information about curricula, teaching materials, and implementation in the field. The results of such studies are channelled to the council of undersecretaries and if change is needed a committee is formed and charged with the task. There are various ways to ensure relevance and to help in the dissemination of new programmes. A large number of supervisors and consultants at all levels meet regularly with teachers for guidance and for collecting information. There are various training centres, experimental schools, and demonstration schools, all aiming at curriculum reform and the improvement of methods.

Once a curriculum outline is set, a small team similar to the ones described above is asked to write the textbooks. The curriculum text is not always identical to the curriculum implemented. The gap is due to a large number of factors such as classroom conditions, lack of aids and equipment, and teacher quality. Contrary to curriculum instructions, most teaching is verbally oriented.

In higher and university education, there is a great deal of freedom in curriculum construction and textbook usage. The progressively increasing class or course size, the scarcity of aids and resources, and other factors tend to lower the standards achieved by students. Dependence on one textbook and on the lecture method is prevalent.

It is charged that curricula in Egypt are geared more to subject matter than to the learner. The teacher's role can be characterized as that of a knowledge transmitter and the student's as that of a passive recipient. Also, relevance to the environment tends to be absent.

6. Examinations

The examination system in Egypt has a strong hold on the minds of pupils, parents, and education authorities. The reasons lie in the importance attached to the results. Promotion examinations are given at the end of grades 2, 4, and 6. The first public examination is held at the end of grade 9. The successful student obtains the Basic Education Certificate and can then proceed to further education. The aggregate score determines the type of school a student enters and is critical, for only the highest scoring students go to the preferred option of the academic-secondary school, leading to the university. Otherwise, students register in technical schools or in teacher-training institutes. A youngster's future is thus determined by the aggregate score in the Basic Education Certificate examination, which makes it exceedingly important and creates a high degree of competitiveness and anxiety throughout the country. Similarly, the secondary-school-leaving examination determines on the basis of the aggregate score which faculty and even which university the student can enrol in. Highly competitive examinations held at the end of the year are responsible for the trade in cram or crib books and for the demand for private coaching.

There have been attempts at reform, such as increasing the weight of the year's work in final assessments and using objective tests. The main solution would of course be to make examinations part of the process of effective learning.

7. Educational Research

Educational research began in Egypt with the establishment of the Institute for Teaching Education in 1929. It grew slowly but steadily until Ain Shams University incorporated the institute as one of its colleges in 1951. In 1955, a strong department of research was established in the ministry and was replaced in 1972 by the National Centre for Educational Research (NCER). Apart from the prolific work going on at the colleges and at the national centre, educational research is also carried out by the National Centre for Social Research, by the

Centre for Development of Science Teaching, and by a number of other organizations.

Several educational research studies are carried out in collaboration with the World Bank, UNESCO, UNICEF, and other United Nations organizations. Examples of these are "Repetition and dropouts", "Ill-effects of endemic diseases", "Influence of nutrition on achievement", and "The motivation to literacy among adult illiterates". Bilateral aid from a number of friendly countries also supports educational research.

The goals of educational research are to help planners and policy makers, school administrators, teachers, and the public to improve the quantitative as well as the qualitative development of education.

8. Major Problems

The most important educational task in Egypt is the qualitative and quantitative development of the basic compulsory school (age group 6–14) so as to create educated and productive citizens and to suppress the flow of illiterates into the adult community. The country's attempt at least to match the world's technological progress is at present jeopardized by the extent of illiteracy. This problem has many dimensions, including resources, buildings, aids for teachers, curriculum, etc. Related to this problem is the changing shape of the education pyramid—narrowing at the base and broadening at the top. The reconsideration of the education pyramid means taking demography, employment, culture, resources and other factors into account.

Education suffers from the fact that the teacher has become little more than a mere transmitter of information and the student a passive recipient of it. The student should be developed into a positive, resourceful, self-reliant personality capable of effective and creative thinking. The student at any level should be educated in such a way that he or she is capable of self-renewal and self-education.

The educational problems in Egypt, as in any country, are continuously on show and one main defect is the consequent attempt to handle them piecemeal, that is, dealing separately with examinations, teacher–pupil relationships, books, buildings, etc. Educational reform must be regarded as a system within a larger system and with its own subsystems. What is lacking is a total approach with the immediate and long-range objectives and the individual and state objectives clearly thought out in advance.

Bibliography

Ain Shams College of Education with the World Bank 1979 *The Teacher for the Secondary School*, World Bank, Washington, DC
Ateek A A 1959 *Al-Azhar, Mosque and University.* Egyptian Bureau, London

Boktor A 1963 *The Development and the Expansion of Education in the United Arab Republic.* American University of Cairo Press, Cairo

Egypt, Ministry of Education 1980 *Development and Modernisation of Education in Egypt.* Ministry of Education, Cairo

Egypt, Ministry of Information 1980 *The Charter. State Information Service.* Ministry of Information, Cairo

Egypt, National Specialized Council *Reports, News and Publications on Education, 1974/82.* National Specialized Council, Cairo

Harby M K 1957 *Education in Egypt.* UNESCO Education Abstracts, Paris

Harby M K, Ibrahim M 1981 *A Description and Evaluation of Education in Egypt.* Institute of National Planning, Cairo

Hyde G D M 1978 *Education in Modern Egypt: Ideals and Realities.* Routledge and Kegan Paul, London

Jackson S H 1973 *Looking Ahead in Egyptian Education.* Institute of Education, Cairo

Al-Kabbani I 1946 *A Hundred Years of Education in Egypt.* Egyptian Bureau of Education, Washington DC

El-Koussy A A H 1953 Education in Egypt 1945-52. *Yearb. Educ.* Evans, London

El-Koussy A A H 1967 Recent trends and developments in primary and secondary education in the Arab world. *Int. Rev. Educ.* 13: 198–210

El-Koussy A A H 1971 Education in the Arab States of the Middle East. In: Adams M (ed.) 1971 *The Middle East: A Handbook.* Blond, London

Sanyal B C 1982 *University Education and the Labour Market in the Arab Republic of Egypt.* Pergamon, Oxford

UNESCO 1972 *Arab Republic of Egypt: An Outline of Strategy for the Reform and Development of Education.* UNESCO, Paris

UNESCO 1975 *Unedbas Mission to the ARE concerning the Reorganisation of Secondary Education.* UNESCO, Paris

World Bank 1982 *Annual Report.* World Bank, Washington, DC, p. 86

World Bank with the National Centre of Educational Research 1980 *Dropping out of Students from Primary Education.* World Bank, Washington, DC

A. A. H. El-Koussy

Eight-year Study

The concept of the Eight-year Study grew out of the desire of people associated with the Progressive Education Association to attempt a fundamental reconstruction of the American secondary school. Founded in 1919 by a group of parents and teachers associated with experimental schools, the organization had initially concentrated its efforts on implementing changes at the elementary level (Cremin 1961). The decision at the annual meeting in 1930 to focus on the high school in part reflected the increased domination of the group by professional educators, and a growing interest in the active dissemination of progressive ideals. The leaders of the study were also aware of the tremendous growth which had occurred in high-school attendance and

they were concerned that the curricula of nearly all American high schools were dominated by college preparatory courses, though only one in every six high-school students actually attended college. The progressives felt that by placing an undue emphasis on preparation for college, schools were failing to provide a significant educational experience for the vast majority of the students whose formal education ended in high school (Aikin 1942).

Members attending the 1930 annual meeting of the Progressive Education Association did not lack ideas for improving secondary education, but they were keenly aware that most high schools were unwilling to risk deviating from the subject-unit requirements dictated for college admission. Although the comprehensive American high school was intended to prepare students both for college and for life, past attempts to change the curriculum had been thwarted by the fear that modification might affect a few students' chances for college admission. In an attempt to alleviate this concern, the progressives directed that a Commission on the Relation of School and College be appointed to examine ways in which school and college work could better be coordinated and to seek an agreement from colleges and universities which would allow high schools the freedom to modify their programs without jeopardizing the possibility of college admission. The 26-member commission composed of school and college officials completed both tasks within two years, delivering a stinging indictment of the American high school in 1931, and reporting the following year that the necessary cooperation of nearly 300 colleges and universities had been secured. Beginning with the class entering college in 1936 and continuing for a period of five years, students from 30 selected high schools would be admitted to college based only on the recommendation of the high-school principal and a carefully compiled record of school life (Aikin 1942).

In the fall of 1933, representatives from the 30 high schools selected to participate in the project met with the Directing Committee to plan the eight years of work ahead. Naming the study from the length of time originally designated for the experiment, the schools examined ways in which each might alter their curriculum, organization, and procedures to better serve the needs of youth. Certain goals were common to all of the schools, including a commitment to help young people understand and appreciate the democratic way of life, and a desire to develop a greater unity and continuity in the curriculum. They wanted to improve the guidance of students and to implement concepts long associated with progressive education: cooperative planning by students and teachers; a curriculum reflecting the present concerns of youth as well as the skills and knowledge demanded by society; active student participation in the learning process; and attention to all aspects of the individual—physical, intellectual, emotional, and spiritual (Cremin 1961). The schools also believed that successful preparation for college did not depend upon the study of certain subjects for a specified length of time, and they recognized that proof of this assumption was vital to the success of the experiment (Aikin 1942).

The 30 public and private high schools chosen to participate in the Eight-year Study varied in size, location, finances, resources, and facilities, as well as in the social, economic, and academic background and ultimate destination of their students. As the experiment progressed, it was also apparent that each school differed in the type of administration and leadership available, and in the commitment of the teachers, parents, and community to change. These factors, as well as the decision to allow each school to proceed independently, led to considerable variation in the amount and type of modification which occurred. The account of the schools' experiences (Giles et al. 1942) reveals that some merely revised their subject matter content, or combined subjects such as biology and chemistry into a single broad field of science. Though all of the schools were characterized by some common developments, such as increased teacher participation in curriculum planning and the use of the community as a resource and topic of study, the less experimental schools adopted these changes within the framework of the subject-discipline design associated with traditional college preparatory work. More significant modifications occurred in those schools which reorganized instruction around the common problems of people in various cultural epochs, and in schools employing a core curriculum focusing on the needs of youth. The latter were designated "experimental schools" by the follow-up staff and appeared to have met the original goals of the Eight-year Study to the fullest extent.

Of the various committees, subcommittees, and consultants available to assist the 30 schools, none were more significant than the evaluation and follow-up staff under the direction of Ralph W. Tyler. The evaluation staff responded to the need of the schools to measure the achievement of objectives such as the inculcation of social attitudes and the development of effective modes of thinking. This cooperative venture not only produced new instruments in value, attitude, and skill areas not previously measured, but also led both teachers and staff to recognize that evaluation must be based upon a clear statement of objectives and should be a continuous and integral part of the curriculum planning process. To the follow-up staff fell the task of determining if the departure from the conventional pattern of college preparation had handicapped students' work in college. Matching 1,475 pairs of graduates from experimental and traditional schools on the basis of age, sex, race, scholastic aptitude scores, home and community background, interests, probable future, and college attended, the staff studied the graduates for a period ranging from one to four years. They concluded that graduates from the 30 schools had performed slightly better academically than matchees in college, and were rated higher in factors such as systematic and objective thinking, intellectual curiosity and drive, resourcefulness, vocational orientation, and concern for world affairs. Significantly, the largest differences in achievement were found among students from the most experimental schools in the Eight-year Study and their traditional matchees (Smith et al. 1942).

The four volumes reporting the work of the Eight-year Study (Aikin 1942, Chamberlin et al. 1942, Giles et al. 1942, Smith et al. 1942) published by the Progressive Education Association were almost immediately overshadowed by the war efforts. In the following decade, the entire progressive education movement was brought under attack, and the positive results of the Eight-year Study failed to have the desired long-term effect on either college entrance requirements or high-school curriculum. Nevertheless, this longitudinal experiment did have a significant impact on American education, for it spawned the field of evaluation, and it emphasized the integral relationship between goal setting, curriculum planning, and the evaluation process. As the United States continues to grapple with the question of how to provide a significant educational experience for all youth within the comprehensive high school, the account of the Eight-year Study may yet provide some insight into this persistent problem of secondary education.

Bibliography

Aikin W M 1942 *The Story of the Eight Year Study, with Conclusions and Recommendations.* Harper, New York
Chamberlin C, Chamberlin E, Drought N E, Scott W E 1942 *Did They Succeed in College? The Follow-up Study of the Graduates of the Thirty Schools.* Harper, New York
Cremin L A 1961 *The Transformation of the School: Progressivism in American Education.* Random House, New York
Giles H H, McCutchen S P, Zechiel A N 1942 *Exploring the Curriculum: The Work of the Thirty Schools from the Viewpoint of Curriculum Consultants.* Harper, New York
Smith E R, Tyler R W et al. 1942 *Appraising and Evaluating Student Progress.* Harper, New York

K. Strickland

El Salvador: System of Education

El Salvador is the smallest of the Central American countries with a total area of 21,041 square kilometers (8,124 square miles). The country has three distinct geographic regions: a hot, narrow Pacific coastal belt, a subtropical central region consisting of small valleys and plateaus, and a mountainous northern region. The hot coastal belt produces cotton and is characterized by a high concentration of land-holdings. The central region acts as a corridor that connects the areas of greatest settlement, including the San Salvador Metropolitan Area. Coffee is the dominant crop in this central region. The northern region is the least populated because the land is marginal and the terrain difficult.

Throughout most of the twentieth century, El Salvador has experienced rapid population growth. Between 1920 and 1978, the population more than quadrupled, increasing from 1.1 million to 4.4 million. In 1982, the population was estimated at almost 5 million. The rate of population growth steadily increased reaching a high of 3.4 percent in 1971, and then decreased to 3.1 percent in 1977. This decrease is the result of government efforts directed at reducing fertility through family-planning programs. Despite these efforts, however, the nation's population is expected to be at least 1.6 times its present size by the year 2000. With about 200 persons per square kilometer in 1979, the country already has a population density that ranks among the highest in the Americas. Thus, population growth is one of the country's fundamental long-term problems, one which will continue to contribute to social unrest, unemployment and underemployment, widespread urban and rural poverty, and the scarcity of basic social services.

The population has a homogenous composition and Spanish is the common language. With 60 percent of the population categorized as rural, the government has attempted to reinforce rural extension and training services to provide farmers and rural workers with modern production techniques. Efforts are also directed at strengthening industrial training at the skilled and semiskilled levels to meet the personnel demands of industry. Estimates placed annual personnel requirements through 1981 at about 76,000 workers, including 5,000 professionals and technicians, 14,000 office and sales workers, 18,000 agricultural workers, and 15,000 workers for the skilled and semiskilled ranks. The formal educational system is expected to provide professionals (21,100), office and sales personnel (8,700), and a relatively few industrial workers (2,400). Acute labor force shortages have been experienced among agricultural workers and skilled and semiskilled workers for industry.

Neither the formal nor the nonformal educational systems are capable of meeting these demands for new human resources. Nor is there sufficient capacity to provide needed training to upgrade the existing pool of workers. The government's response has been to place a high priority on the development of human resources through the educational system. However, despite a rapid expansion of educational services, about 40 percent of the total labor force

and 56 percent of the rural work force are illiterate. The challenge to education is monumental.

Agriculture accounts for about half of all employment in El Salvador. The dominant export crops are coffee followed by cotton and sugarcane. Until recently, the pace of industrial development was among the most active in Central America. This mostly involved small and medium-sized industries in such sectors as agroindustry, textiles, chemicals, construction, utilities, and transportation. Economic policies have been directed mainly toward import substitution and improvement of agricultural productivity, but economic growth has been slow as indicated by the 1.8 percent annual growth rate of gross domestic product (GDP) per capita between 1968 and 1978.

The agricultural sector is beset by complex problems stemming from the traditional concentration of landownership. The top 5 percent of landowners hold over two-thirds of the arable land, and about 80 percent of farmers hold less than two hectares. Govermental policies to deal with this situation are aimed at changing the structure of agricultural production in the medium term and diversifying the economy through industrial development in the long term. Land reform programs have been developed in recent years, but have not been fully implemented due to political opposition.

During this century, the political history of El Salvador has been marked by about five revolutions, which have interrupted the country's development as a democracy. In more recent years, the nation has experienced a period of political instability which started in 1979 and continues at the time of writing (1983). This period has been marked by civil strife, which periodically flares into civil war affecting all aspects of Salvadorean society. Educational development has been impeded as educational goals become secondary to higher economic priorities, and financial resources become increasingly scarce.

1. Goals of the Educational System

The foundation for the country's current educational goals was established in the First Education Development Plan (1968–72). That plan included the following goals: (a) to provide nine years of free basic education for every child and diversified programs for secondary students; (b) to strengthen the administration and supervision of education; (c) to provide free or low-cost learning materials and introduce educational television; (d) to reorganize teacher training; and (e) to improve educational opportunities for the rural population. The implementation of this plan met with limited success and the Second Education Development Plan (1973-77) sought mainly to continue the reform measures that the first plan had started.

The Third Education Plan (1978-82) had vestiges

of the first plan, as it sought to: (a) further strengthen the system, giving particular attention to redressing inequities between urban and rural schooling; (b) expand postsecondary technical education; and (c) continue expanding nonformal education and training programs for out-of-school youths and adults. The political difficulties that have beset the country since 1979 have hindered the fulfillment of these goals.

2. General Structure and Size of the Education Effort

Formal education consists of one year of preschool, nine years of basic education, three years of secondary education, and higher education with programs that extend from two to six years in universities and specialized postsecondary institutions.

Preschool serves children who are 5–6 years of age. This initial level is not yet well-developed, and only an estimated 10 percent of children in the eligible age group were covered in the period 1980–82, and of these most were urban children.

Basic education starts at age 7 and is organized in three cycles of three years each. The first two cycles (grades 1–6) are equivalent to primary education, while the third cycle (grades 7–9) is comparable to the lower-secondary level. A common curriculum is followed by the students at this level. In 1977, the total public and private school enrollment in basic education was 823,000, which represented 75 percent of the 7–15 age group. For the first and second cycles (grades 1–6), the enrollments were 690,000, representing 88 percent of the corresponding age group, while the enrollment for the third cycle was 133,000 or 42 percent of the age group for that level.

Enrollments in basic education are generally even between males and females through grade 4, but a slight imbalance develops by grade 6. In 1975, that imbalance favored the males (57 percent) against the females (43 percent). The imbalance in access and efficiency between urban and rural schools is more serious. In 1977, urban enrollment ratios for the 7–12 and 13–15 age groups were 115 percent (over age students included) and 94 percent respectively, compared with 70 and 8 percent in rural areas. The holding power of the first two cycles was poor with only 19 percent of those entering grade 1 in rural schools in 1977 completing the full six years, compared with 47 per cent in urban schools. The reason for this is that, although 64 percent of the primary schools are in rural areas, only 30 percent of those schools offer schooling beyond grade 5.

Secondary education (grades 10–12) is diversified (comprehensive) and offers programs in the following areas: academic, business administration, home economics, industrial arts, agriculture, hotel industry and tourism, navigation and fishery industry,

health services, and teacher training. The vast majority of these fourth-cycle schools are located in urban centers. In 1970, only 14 (2 percent) of the 863 secondary schools were in rural areas. This level of education had a total enrollment of 64,000 in 1977 and was more accessible to males (about 60 percent) than to females (about 40 percent); only 23 percent of the 16–18 age group were covered. The internal efficiency of the secondary level is weak. In a 1976 cohort study, only 34 percent reached grade 9 and 15 percent reached grade 12.

Higher education consists of two universities, one public and one private, and specialized postsecondary institutions, which mainly offer two-year programs. In 1977, higher education enrolled 30,000, representing 7 percent of the 19–24 age group, and of this total 92 percent were in university programs. It was estimated that the 1977 enrollment consisted of 70 percent males and 30 percent females. The efficiency of the universities is low, with dropout and repeater rates as high as 78 percent, while in the other postsecondary institutions the rates are about 30 percent. In 1975, the postsecondary institutions graduated a total of 383, while the universities produced less than 300 graduates. Enrollments at all levels between 1977 and 1982 are shown in Table 1.

Table 1
Total enrollments at all levels, including public and private schools, 1977–82 (in thousands)[a]

Level	1977	1978	1979	1980	1981	1982
Preschool	59	66	74	74	45	50
Basic education (cycles 1–3)	823	858	901	834	710	749
Secondary (cycle 4)	64	72	78	73	64	53
Higher education	30	32	33	13	25	42
Nonformal	62	69	85	42	34	42
Total	1,038	1,097	1,171	1,036	878	936

[a] Source: Ministry of Education 1981–82 *Annual Report*. San Salvador

As a result of the civil strife that has engulfed the country since 1979, the campus of the National University has been closed for an indefinite period. Some programs continue to operate off-campus and under private sponsorship, but the quality of university education has suffered a severe setback. This has placed a considerable strain on the private university (the Catholic University) and the other postsecondary institutions, whose facilities are incapable of absorbing the displaced students from the National University.

3. Administration and Finance

The Ministry of Education is responsible for all levels of education except the universities, which are individually autonomous. The Ministry's Office of Planning and Organization is responsible for planning, programming, budgeting, and coordinating all major activities, programs, and reforms. There are separate departments within the ministry that administer each of the educational levels; that is, basic education, the secondary level, the postsecondary level, and adult and continuing education. School supervision is organized through a network of zones with a number of supervisors assigned to each zone.

In 1977 educational expenditures amounted to ¢308 million (US $1 = 2.5 colones), or 4.3 percent of GDP. Of this amount, ¢279 million, or 90 percent, was provided by the central government and the balance by the private sector. The government devoted 27 percent of budget revenues to education. Most of the resources for financing education are from domestic sources. In 1977, foreign assistance to education amounted to ¢4.2 million, or 10 percent of capital expenditures on education.

Basic education and higher education receive the greatest share of financial support for the sector. In 1977, 64 percent of public recurrent expenditures were directed to basic education and 27 percent to higher education, while only 9 percent went to preschool and secondary education. In 1976, the recurrent cost per student in the first two cycles of basic education was ¢134, in the third cycle ¢153, in secondary education ¢347, in postsecondary ¢2,822, and in the universities ¢1,394. The low efficiency of the universities has been due in part to the secure source of revenues. By law, 2.5 percent of the government's general revenues must be allocated to universities. To achieve equity, more resources should be allocated to basic and secondary education, and less to higher education.

4. Supply of Personnel

As a result of the 1967 reform, all teacher training for basic and secondary education was assigned to one institution called *Ciudad Normal*. This institution also provides upgrading courses for teachers of basic education, school directors, and supervisors. Training for the teachers of the first two cycles (grades 1–6) is offered under three programs: (a) three years for those who have completed nine years of basic education; (b) one year for those who have completed grade 11; and (c) a summer course and three years of supervised teaching in rural schools for those who have completed secondary education. Teachers for the third cycle (grades 7–9) are trained under two programs: (a) two years for graduate primary teachers with no teaching experience in the third cycle; and (b) four summer courses for graduate

primary teachers teaching in the third cycle. Secondary teachers are selected from university graduates, graduates of *Ciudad Normal*, and upgraded primary teachers. Teachers for technical subjects are selected from graduates of secondary industrial schools. It is estimated that the system needs 700 new teachers annually, provided the proportion of teachers working two shifts increases to 54 percent in 1985 (from 19 percent in 1977).

5. Curriculum Development and Teaching Methodology

Curriculum development is centralized in the Ministry of Education, where the National Planning and Organization Office plays a key role. The process also involves the specialized departments of the ministry that are responsible for each level of the schooling system. The curriculum is, therefore, uniform for the entire country, but adaptation to local educational conditions is encouraged. The supervisory system ensures compliance with national curricular guidelines. The most popular classroom teaching method is the teacher-expository method, but it is generally recognized that more student participation in the learning process is needed.

Textbooks have to be purchased by students on the commercial market. Because of this, most rural students do not have textbooks. In an effort to improve the textbooks situation, the ministry established a textbook division in 1975, which is working to develop a textbook-production system. Eventually, this system is expected to provide basic textbooks for all basic-education students at very low cost.

6. Major Problems

The following are the main tasks to be tackled in education in the 1980s and 1990s:

(a) to improve educational opportunities for the rural population, thereby breaching the wide disparity in access and quality between urban centers and rural areas;

(b) to arrive at an equitable distribution of financial resources, which in the early 1980s favored basic education and the university;

(c) to improve internal efficiency at all levels but with an emphasis on the university level;

(d) to improve technical education to meet personnel needs;

(e) to improve the quality of the labor force by reducing illiteracy and raising the average level of education;

(f) to reduce the rate of population growth.

Overshadowing all of these problems is the unstable

political and economic situation in the country. As long as this situation continues, the problems will grow in magnitude and recovery will be more difficult.

Bibliography

Agencia para el Desarrollo Internacional 1975 *Estadísticas para el análisis del sector de la educación—El Salvador*, Agencia para el Desarrollo Internacional, San Salvador
Escamilla M L 1981 *Reformas educatives, Historia contemporánea de la educación formal en El Salvador*. Ministerio de Educación, San Salvador
Oficina de Planeamiento y Organización y División de Análisis Sectorial de la Agencia para el Desarrollo Internacional 1978 *Análisis sectorial de la educación en El Salvador—Documento de Trabajo*. Agencia para el Desarrollo Internacional, San Salvador
World Bank 1979 *Country Study: El Salvador, Demographic Issues and Prospects*. World Bank, Washington, DC

R. Ruiz-Esparza

Elderly, Education of

It is well-documented that the populations in most countries are ageing: in the United States, for example, 33 percent of the population is expected to be older than 45 years in the year 2000 compared to 28 percent in 1950. Whereas 8 percent of the population was over 65 years of age in 1950, by 2000 the percentage is expected to be 12 percent—that is about 30 million people out of a total of 262 million (Bureau of the Census 1977). However, the population of older people is heterogeneous. There is a marked individuality about ageing and chronological age is not always a sure measure of performance. There are also variations in previous education, health, housing, income, and family circumstances and it is likely that the population of people nearing the older age groups is similarly varied. With early retirement becoming increasingly common in industrialized countries both as a means of combating unemployment and hastening technological change, the proportion of people who need to cope with problems posed by retirement, expanding leisure time, and advancing age is likely to grow. Thus there has been increased recognition in recent years, particularly in the United States, that this section of the population, although difficult to define in precise terms, will have educational needs and interests for which existing educational provision may be inadequate.

1. Ageing and the Ability to Learn

There is a considerable body of research on ageing relevant to adult education and such topics as intelligence, short-term memory, disengagement (retirement), personality, and motivation have been dealt with at length in the literature of developmental psychology and social gerontology. Adult learning activity has attracted similar attention from researchers. In general, it is felt that physically active adults decline substantially less than sedentary adults and whilst vision, hearing, smell, touch, and the related ability of speech tend to be reduced, any observed decline in intellectual functioning is usually attributed to poor health, social isolation, economic plight, limited education, lowered motivation, and other variables not related to the ageing process. Recent research suggests that adults over 65 years of age can learn, given good health, if material is clearly presented and appeals to all learners, if each learner is given sufficient opportunity and time for practice, if material is organized to assist memorizing, and if different contexts for learning are provided such as lectures, seminars, tutorials, practical work, and so on (Osborn et al. 1982). Although much depends on an older person's willingness to learn and attitude to life, all indications are that mental exercise will lead to the recovery of functional loss caused by disuse and to the prolongation of capacity (Bromley 1980). Older people are capable of learning and evidence suggests that the elderly should be regarded as one of the community's resources and that they should have a continuing role as both givers and receivers in the adult education system (Withnall et al. 1980).

2. Educational Needs Specific to the Elderly

There is a marked division of opinion amongst providers of education for older people as to whether courses should be specially organized, for example, for people over 60, or whether over-60s should join in normal "all age" classes. What little research there is on this subject suggests that older people dislike segregation, but there are certain situations where age-segregated classes may be preferable (Withnall et al. 1980), as illustrated by the three categories that follow.

2.1 Subject Areas Referring to Role Needs

Apart from the widely observed need to prepare people for retirement, it has been shown that older people may have special educational needs which may often be forgotten. In the United Kingdom, for example, the Geriatric Nutrition Unit at Queen Elizabeth College, University of London, has carried out research into nutrition education with the aim of producing findings which will have both implications for other academics and practical relevance for the elderly. American educators have argued that sex is important to old people and that taboos against sex add to the loneliness, depression, and frustration of the elderly; hence there is a need for special sex education for older people. In both the United States and the United Kingdom, a number of institutes have begun courses in "death education" for elderly people which aim to approach the subject of death from both a practical and emotional standpoint (see *Death Education and Counseling*).

2.2 Subjects Requiring Special Teaching Methods

Because of the general decline in the physical abilities of some elderly people, those concerned with providing education for the elderly stress the need to adapt to circumstances. It has been found possible to provide art education for the elderly blind by nonvisual means; low-stress exercise programmes have been designed for the elderly in several countries; and reading programmes which were found to generate not only discussion of reading and books but also of life reminiscences and social problems have been successful with the elderly in the United States.

2.3 The Elderly in Isolated Units

Isolated units may include geriatric hospitals, where activities which seem popular are painting, modelling, music, cooking, local history, and games; or residential homes where reading programmes, described above, have been occasionally used in the United States with reasonable success. The needs of the housebound or those living in sheltered accommodation obviously merit special attention as participation in education is as much a matter of the supply of services as student inclination. At present, this is an area of disadvantage which many adult educators feel deserves priority in attention and resources.

Finally, it has been suggested that controversy over age-integrated and age-segregated models of provision is unnecessary and that both can profitably coexist in view of the great need for educational opportunities for older adults and their diversity (Marcus 1978).

3. Preparation for Retirement

Preretirement education can be defined as the acquisition of information, understanding, and appreciation which will assist in facilitating personal adjustment and self-fulfilment after retirement from the labour force at whatever age this occurs. There are a variety of forms which it may take including individual and group counselling, lectures and discussion groups, books and magazines dealing with retirement planning, and radio and television programmes. Many large companies conduct courses for their own employees and there are examples of organizations which include spouses of retirees in their programme schedules. In Europe, the involvement of pension insurance companies in preretirement activities is noteworthy as is the practice of using private institutions for educational purposes. One problem facing adult educators in this sphere is the timing and presentation of preretirement programmes; current

thinking suggests that preretirement education is too important to be left until later working life and that it should begin perhaps in the mid-40s when changes in family patterns occur and when there is a need for personal reappraisal and reorientation. Although it is obviously difficult to assess the effect that preretirement education will have on the quality of life in retirement, it can be expected that in different countries and communities, various community organizations, voluntary and statutory agencies, and industrial concerns will eventually recognize local need by expanding the provision of this special form of education.

4. University of the Third Age

The University of the Third Age was planned in France on the initiative of Pierre Vellas in 1972, accepted by the board of the University of Toulouse in 1973, and became operational that year. Broadly, its aims are to contribute to raising the standard of living of elderly people by health-promoting and sociocultural activities and by research; to improve the living conditions of elderly people through multidisciplinary research in law, economics, and related subjects, and by conferences, seminars, and the dissemination of information; to help private and public services and business through cooperative activities in training, information, and applied research. There is a monthly programme for about eight or nine months per year which anyone over retiring age can join for a modest fee. Classes include physical education, swimming, yoga, language classes, social and cultural topics, films and expeditions, all of which were initially based on the campus of the University of Social Sciences at Toulouse, although home study courses are available on radio and television. However, the University's prime task is to bring the elderly out of isolation into the stimulating atmosphere of a university campus where teachers and students are of different ages. Whilst the University undoubtedly provides a focal point for continuing education for the local elderly population, it has been criticized in that the present clientele are mainly drawn from the well-educated middle class. Nevertheless, the paradigm of the University has led to the development of similar projects elsewhere in France, Belgium, Canada, Switzerland, Poland, and the United Kindom and has provided a focus for further consideration of a range of philosophical and pedagogical issues among leading European gerontologists.

5. Elderhostel

There have been some initiatives to provide ease of access to higher education for the elderly, in the United States particularly, by legal provision for either free or reduced tuition. However, admitting older adults to the traditional university may pose problems of managing the campus environment and possibly reconsidering the potential role of faculty and support services. Thus an innovative attempt to use campus resources has been made through the elderhostel programme, originally organized at the University of New Hampshire in 1975.

The original concept of the elderhostel combined higher education opportunities on campus during the summer months with travel at low cost. It was inspired, indirectly, by the youth hostels and folk high schools, but was guided by the needs of older citizens for intellectual stimulation and physical adventure.

An original feature of the elderhostel is the network approach. Several colleges and universities participate in the programme. The participants move from campus to campus residing an average of one week on each campus. In 1975, only five institutions were involved. By 1981, 406 colleges and universities sponsored various courses for nearly 40,000 older adults. The 1983 programme projection estimated an enrolment of more than 60,000. Elderhostel is now a network embracing universities, folk high schools, and other institutions in the United States, Canada, the United Kingdom, Denmark, Sweden, Finland, and Norway. In terms of levels of previous education, a 1978 survey of elderhostellers showed the following breakdown: elementary school only, 2 percent; high school, 15 percent; some college, 29 percent; college degree, 24 percent; and graduate school, 30 percent (Gurewitsch 1980). This finding contradicts to some extent the original idea of elderhostel which was "to attract older people who had never had an opportunity to go to college and to create a meeting ground for perennial students and seniors who wouldn't or couldn't go to college in their youth".

Courses offered by each institution may vary. However, a typical programme includes liberal-arts courses, cultural offerings, and physical fitness programmes (see *Physical Education for Adults*). The participants live on campus in regular students' dormitories and take their meals in the student cafeteria. They use all the campus facilities such as libraries and tennis courts, and participate in concerts and picnics. Elderhostels are only open to people who are at least 60 years of age or married to someone who is.

6. Other Educational Initiatives

6.1 Statutory and Voluntary Provision

Although elderly people can join general adult education classes, much educational activity takes place within day centres, senior centres, and clubs whose aim is essentially to enable older people to live in their own homes but also to get out into the community as far as health will allow. They are mainly recreational centres for caring and sharing; they aim also to provide mental stimulus and act as pressure groups to remind the community of its responsibility towards the elderly. Although considerable variation exists with regard to the perception of these organizations as meeting places and community focal points among various agencies concerned with the elderly, they have been found to serve a broad cross section of older persons and they can provide an important structure for continuing self-realization through classes and lectures, creative, sedentary, or active recreational activities.

In the United States, a number of community colleges have mounted projects aimed to improve the quality of life of the elderly through innovative educational activities—those concerned with arts and crafts seem to prove the most popular. However, success depends on involving older people and their organizations in planning and operating activities, particularly with regard to transportation and the timing of classes.

6.2 The Mass Media

A notable development has been the provision of regular series or features for and about the elderly by the media, especially television. In many countries, the role of the elderly in society has become a major topic of discussion and some television networks have launched programmes aimed at retired people and those planning retirement featuring a number of aspects including regular political items of relevance to viewers, features on health, finance, leisure activities, safety, and so on. However, it can be argued that the priority need is to educate everyone on these matters and correct the broad image of ageing established through caricatures of the elderly on television.

Education for the retired is also provided through a growing number of retirement magazines and journals; obviously it is difficult to assess the impact of these but they mostly aim to offer help in retirement with practical problems and with suggestions for new leisure activities.

6.3 Self-help

Many people who are retired live outside an institutional framework and thus self-help groups form a means of avoiding social isolation. Examples include self-help keep-fit courses organized by and for senior citizens; self-managed educational courses including those of an intellectual nature; self-help groups with a specific type of membership such as the Institute for Retired Professionals at the School of Social Research in New York City which offers members, usually highly trained professionals from a variety of occupations, an opportunity to renew their education at university level. In practice, self-help may have its limitations; most self-help groups require professional assistance before becoming self-sufficient.

6.4 Assisting in the Educational Process

Information from the United States suggests that older people are increasingly being regarded as a useful resource in the educational system (Harris 1975), perhaps serving as volunteer teaching aides or resource persons in educational institutions or teaching in recreation, nutrition, and cultural programmes, thereby furthering their own educational experiences. In most countries, however, attitudes toward using people in the educational service appear generally restrictive.

7. Conclusion

To summarize, elderly people are able to learn and gain from learning even though some specific skills may wither. Their educational needs are as varied as is the population of the elderly, so that a range of provision is necessary together with a flexible approach to their problems on the part of educational gerontologists. Work in the area is only beginning and a great deal more needs to be done. In spite of the increasing efforts to respond to their needs only about 5 percent of elderly people participate in organized learning experiences (MacKeracher 1980). This limited take-up is due, as one writer indicates ". . . less to monolithic, biologically mediated decline than to a complex matrix of environmental and situation-specific variables" (Rebok 1981).

See also: Learning over Life Span: Implications for Educators; Learning Development over the Lifespan

Bibliography

Agruso Jr. V M 1978 *Learning in the Later Years: Principles of Educational Gerontology*. Academic Press, New York
Bromley D B 1980 Age and adult education. *Studies in Adult Educ.* 2(2)
Bureau of the Census 1977 *Statistical Abstract of the United States*, 98th edn. United States Government Printing Office, Washington, DC. Government Publication No. C3.134: 977
Gurewitsch E 1980 Elderhostel: A good idea is growing and growing. *Ageing*
Harris L 1975 *The Myth and Reality of Aging in America*. National Council on Aging, Washington, DC
Jones S (ed.) 1976 *Liberation of the Elders*. Speeches and papers from a seminar held at the University of Keele, 26–28 Mar 1976. Beth Johnson Foundation, Stoke-on-Trent
Kaplan M 1979 *Leisure, Lifestyle and Lifespan: Perspectives for Gerontology*, Saunders, Philadelphia, Pennsylvania
MacKeracher D 1980 Learning opportunities for older people. *Learning* 3(2)
Marcus L 1978 Ageing and education. In: Hobman D (ed.) 1978 *The Social Challenge of Ageing*. Croom Helm, London, pp. 117-48
Osborn M, Charnley A, Withnall A 1982 The psychology of adult learning and development. *Review of Existing Research in Adult and Continuing Education*, Vol. 11. National Institute of Adult Education, Leicester
Rebok W G 1981 Ageing and higher education: Prospects for intervention. *Educ. Gerontology* 6(2)
Tiberi D M, Boyack V L, Kerschner P A 1978 A comparative analysis of four pre-retirement models. *Educ. Gerontology* 3(4)
UNESCO 1982 *Education and Aging: Report to the World Assembly on Aging*. UNESCO, Paris
Weinstock R 1978 *The Graying of the Campus: A Report from EFL*. Educational Facilities Laboratories, New York
Withnall A, Charnley A, Osborn M 1980 The elderly. *Review of Existing Research in Adult and Continuing Education*, Vol. 2. National Institute of Adult Education, Leicester

A. M. E. Withnall; N. O. Kabwasa

Elective Subjects

Elective subjects is a term that designates those courses that students may select themselves or with the guidance of a professional educator. Electives, as they are often called, are distinguished from required courses: together elective subjects and required subjects constitute most of the course offerings that an educational institution provides. The purposes and varieties of elective subjects can best be understood through reference to their origins.

A primary contribution to the idea of elective subjects is the growth and diversification of knowledge; as knowledge grows it becomes analyzed, creating new categories or subjects. The rise and expansion of scientific knowledge in the German universities of the eighteenth-century Enlightenment "made the elective system virtually a necessity and directly affected the rise of the elective system in American colleges in the nineteenth century" (Butts 1947). Experimentation with electives could be found in the private "English" schools and within the academy movement initiated by Benjamin Franklin in the United States, both schools of the secondary level. One principal force behind the elective movement of this period was the pressure to include practical subjects of a commercial and vocational kind.

At the elementary-school level, the philosophy of naturalism that stemmed from Rousseau and Pestalozzi was coupled with notions of democracy and capitalistic individualism in nineteenth-century American educational systems; however, the idea was dominated by other emphases in most sectors. Seguel (1966) notes that it is more than a coincidence that elective subjects in the university and in the secondary school emerged at the same time as learned societies were established, during the second half of the nineteenth century. The vast increase in the number of possible subjects made the elective system a necessity. It was temporally and economically impossible to offer all subjects to each student.

Much of the work of the curriculum field, which evolved as a twentieth-century phenomenon (Schubert 1980) was devoted to the problem of dealing with the proliferation of courses. A number of different proposals emerged to deal with the problem and each carried a somewhat different notion of what was meant by elective subjects. Many curriculum theorists saw the need to be that of preventing both myopic specialization and haphazard selection of disconnected electives. One response to these problems is to specify a core of courses that are basic to a particular major area of study, to recommend sets of courses within which students may select areas of specialization, and also to provide a certain percentage of the program for students to be allowed to select freely from all courses available. This is a dominant form of curriculum design in the colleges and secondary schools of many nations today (see *Curriculum Design*).

Other curriculum theorists sought to resolve the course proliferation problem by departing from a subject orientation in varying degrees. Some advocated the joining of courses by combining subjects into broad fields. Another approach saw social problems as central themes that cut across disciplinary lines, enabling depth and breadth that had been missed in both required courses and free electives. In the 1950s, this style of curriculum was further refined and called a "core curriculum" (Faunce with Bossing 1958) (see *Core Curriculum*). At the elementary level, certain activities or projects became a central focus around which the curriculum was built, although these two examples represent opposite poles in terms of their curricular philosophy. An even greater deviation from the subject curriculum took experience of students (rather than activities, projects, texts, or course content) as the organizing center of the curriculum. This approach enabled learners, facilitated by teachers, to eclectically choose and create knowledge that added meaning and direction to their lives.

The point here is that the very idea of elective subjects is transformed away from one of taking course offerings imposed by an educational institution. It becomes, instead, centered in the student and community of learners who elect to study subjects that they decide will add meaning and direction to their lives (Schubert and Schubert 1981). This focus on reflection and choice is evident in the work of some curriculum writers known as reconceptualists (Pinar 1975).

While the above bear directly upon alternative interpretations of elective subjects in principle, recent curriculum practice has leaned toward increasing the variety and flexibility of course offerings, leading to minicourses, community-based learning experiences, alternative schools and paths within schools, free schools, and a vast array of elective offerings too numerous to mention here (Fantini

1976, Glatthorn 1975). It is also necessary to turn to literature on extracurricular offerings, for these too are electives that play an important role in the education of learners especially at the secondary-school level.

The literature on both alternatives and extracurricular activities provides a rich field of offerings that broadens the character of elective subjects. Conceptions range from an expanding array of courses, to methods of organizing them centered upon topics or student experiences, and to radically altered learning environments. The interest in providing a more productive repertoire of electives continues to be important today, as are new dimensions of the problem invoked by technological advance, the expansion of knowledge, and new conceptions of psychological and social development.

Bibliography

Butts R F 1947 *A Cultural History of Education: Reassessing our Educational Traditions*. McGraw-Hill, New York

Centro de Estudios Educativos (CEE) 1979 *El curriculo flexible*. CEE, Mexico

Fantini M D (ed.) 1976 *Alternative Education: A Source Book for Parents, Teachers, Students and Administrators*. Doubleday, Garden City, New York

Faunce R C, Bossing N L 1958 *Developing the Core Curriculum*, 2nd edn. Prentice Hall, Englewood Cliffs, New Jersey

Glatthorn A A 1975 *Alternatives in Education: Schools and Programs*. Dodd, Mead, New York

Pinar W F (ed.) 1975 *Curriculum Theorizing: The Reconceptualists*. McCutchan, Berkeley, California

Schubert W H 1980 *Curriculum Books: The First Eighty Years*. University Press of America, Lanham, Maryland

Schubert W H, Schubert A L 1981 Toward curricula that are of, by, and therefore for students. *J. Curric. Theorizing* 3: 239–51

Seguel M L 1966 *The Curriculum Field: Its Formative Years*. Teachers College Press, New York

W. H. Schubert; T. Miklos

Emotional Development

Emotion may be defined as a complex phenomenon, comprising at least three aspects: (a) the experience or conscious feeling of emotion; (b) the processes that occur in the brain and nervous system; and (c) the observable expressive patterns of emotion, particularly those on the face (Izard 1977). Each of these aspects has important implications for educators.

The first aspect refers to what transpires deep inside a person, hidden from the view or perceptions of others. The child feels something such as frustration, dread, revulsion, or affection. He or she may not be able to identify the cause for this feeling and may be unable to describe it in words; nevertheless, the feeling exists and it affects how the child will respond in certain situations that generate that feeling.

Emotions also involve activity in the brain and nervous system. When a person is under pressure or experiences stress, the limbic system becomes highly activated and learning is subsequently inhibited. As children seek to compensate for their inadequacies, whether real or imagined, they may exhibit behaviors that bring further pressure to bear and consequently continue the cycle of brain patterns that impede both the learning process and control of emotional behavior.

Finally, the third aspect of emotion refers to the intimate connection that prevails between inward feelings and outward expression. Ordinarily, emotional feelings manifest themselves in some form of observable external expression. Sackheim and Gur have reported that at least six emotions can be reliably recognized on the human face: happiness, surprise, fear, sadness, anger, and disgust (Bellak and Baker 1981).

1. Common Types of Emotions

Both the emotions themselves and their patterns of expression change with age and the child's overall development throughout infancy, childhood, youth, and adulthood. The most frequently expressed emotional reactions and expressions of feelings will generally settle into habits that become driving forces in a child's life.

Affection involves the expression of feelings which reflect concern, warmth, regard, caring, sympathy, and helpfulness. Young children are especially open about their feelings of affection toward others. As they reach preadolescence they show less physical affection but demonstrate their feelings through social interaction, confiding in one another, and participating in activities together.

Love is a feeling of deep personal attachment and commitment, a much stronger and more complex emotion than affection. Love may be openly expressed or communicated in subtle ways. Child psychologists appear to agree that children need to feel loved in order to have adequate emotional development.

Joy, happiness, and contentment are similar emotions. Joy is a feeling of gladness and delight; happiness is a sense of well-being that generates attitudes of good fortune and satisfaction. Contentment is a sense of satisfaction, peace of mind, and a feeling of being in tune with the universe.

Grief and sorrow are strong emotions that reflect distress at losing a loved person, animal, or object. Persons experiencing grief and sorrow feel somewhat helpless and they sense a great emptiness. Grief and sorrow are important in early childhood experiences that help build the foundation for future experiences.

Adults can help children with grief and sorrow when they are open and honest about a tragic event, yet are sensitive and understanding. Simple statements often help children feel free to ask questions and clarify mistaken or confusing ideas, especially in the case of death.

Fear is marked by such feelings as alarm, dread, anxious concern, fright, terror, and panic. Infants generally experience fears related to loud noises, strange persons and objects, unfamilar surroundings, pain, and sudden changes in lighting or temperature. As children grow and develop, experiencing life more fully, they come into contact with situations that bring about a broad range of feelings related to fear. Worry is a form of fear in which the child imagines that something dangerous or unpleasant will happen. Anxiety is an intense fear or worry that causes the child to feel helpless, uncomfortable, and nontrusting. Children who experience anxiety over a long period of time may become emotionally disturbed.

Anger is an emotion that children learn very early serves many purposes. It is an expression of intense displeasure, rage, or fury. While fear generally decreases in intensity with age, anger often increases both in forms or expression and intensity.

Jealousy is the thought or perception of possibly losing approval, affection, or love. This emotion can result in anger or resentment toward a loved one as well as toward one who gets attention from the loved one. Children are likely to experience deep feelings of jealousy around the age of 2 or 3 years while they are forming their independence. Another stage when children become jealous is at about age 10 to 12 when they begin to make the transition from childhood to adolescence.

2. Role of Emotions

Blaise Pascal was very perceptive when he wrote: "The heart has reasons the head knows not of" (Bartlett 1882 p. 363). Humans are feeling beings as well as thinking beings. Indeed, human emotions sometimes take control over reasoning. Primarily for this reason, the ancient Stoics advocated a life of *apathos*—emotion free—because the emotionless person does not suffer disappointment, sorrow, anger, or unhappiness; the Stoic was expected to rise above these mundane feelings. Unfortunately, neither does the Stoic experience joy, happiness, or pleasure—which may be one of the causes for the demise of Stoicism as a way of life.

Emotions play a vitally important role in ordering human experience. Without them life would be flat and devoid of excitement. Emotions often provide the stimulus or motivation to act in a certain way. They provide the inner force that attracts one person to another, or that repels one person from another. Emotions provide a sense of feeling with and for others (*Gemeinschaftsgefuhl*). They provide a sense of security, help persons cope with frustration, alert them to dangers, and prod them into action.

At the same time, emotions are also the cause of certain problems. Sometimes, for example, people say or do things they might later regret—primarily because they were acting on the basis of emotion rather than a reasoned response. Often when children do poorly in school, it is because they suffer the emotional trauma of problems at home or in their social life. Feelings of fear, anger, threat, or insecurity can often diminish a child's ability to respond in appropriate ways.

Emotions influence the child's view of the world and the role of the self in society. As children grow into adulthood they carry memories of their childhood with them. Emotional warmth, feelings of love and caring from others, and the appropriate expressions of both positive and negative feelings help children establish affectional relationships with others that reflect fulfillment and social skills.

Unfortunately, the systematic study of emotions in children has not kept pace with the vigorous studies of other aspects of human development, such as Piaget's work on intellectual development. It is possible to speculate that this omission may be due to the enormity of the task. That is, in the absence of the child's ability to articulate what he or she is feeling at a particular moment, the empirical scholar is left with little to report that is both observable and verifiable. It may also be the case that inasmuch as emotions are experienced at a precognitive level, they do not readily lend themselves to description according to the strict canons of scholarship.

3. Factors Influencing Emotions

3.1 Maturation

Rates of biological maturation vary from child to child and therefore influence their emotional development. As the brain and body mature, the child's functions become more sophisticated and differentiated. For example, as the memory improves and the ability to imagine and anticipate increases, children's emotional responses take on new dimensions. Children reactivate feelings of excitement and joy by repeating play activities that previously brought delight. Children who remember frightening experiences may show manifestations of fear when in similar situations.

The endocrine system helps to regulate bodily functions and plays a significant role in emotions. Soon after birth the adrenal glands decrease in size; they begin to increase rapidly up to about age 5, and then slow until about age 10 to 12. Rapid development of these glands occurs from about age 13 to 16. While the glands are active, surges of energy are brought on by the release of body fluids and the child is likely to show feelings through body movements as well as speech and mood states (Hurlock 1972).

3.2 Environment

A healthy "emotional climate" is a physical and psychological setting in which the child feels safe, develops trust in others, and builds relationships with a sense of confidence and trust. Opportunities to explore life and learn in an atmosphere of love and concern provide a sense of comfort and place the child at ease. Safe and healthy surroundings, adequate amounts of nutritious foods, and daily health habits add to the quality of life and, hence, to the child's sense of well-being.

Childhood experiences, both in the family and community, that are filled with genuine affection, happiness, and caring set the tone for healthy emotional development. Children feel free in expressing their feelings when appropriate limits are established and enforced. They learn to control, yet express, strong feelings, such as anger, disgust, and jealousy when adults provide guidance that reflects sensitivity to their individual needs.

The child's own perceptions of "how things are" influence personal feelings and the manner in which those feelings are expressed. The child who consistently sees himself or herself as esteemed and accepted by others will likely form a positive self-image and a sense of personal worth. In contrast, children who perceive others as consistently rejecting, neglecting, or ridiculing them may become less socially acceptable themselves, modeling the behaviors they most often experience and forming less than desirable self-images.

3.3 Cognition

Every emotion has a cognitive component, and every thought is influenced by emotional factors. Both emotion and thought are basic attributes, which in the human being are intimately meshed in a dialectical unity (Thomas and Chess 1980 p. 152). Differentiated psychological traits of older children and adults clearly reflect the interactive processes that involve emotion and thought. Feelings reinforce ideas, and ideas in turn reinforce feelings.

Emotions are categorized by adults in terms of feeling states which are linked with specific cognitive meanings. The identification of emotions requires a combination of subjective feelings and cognitive processes, supplemented by inferences from facial expressions, voice tone, and body gestures. In contrast to adults who can report a combination of subjective and objective data, the young infant's emotional inferences are limited by objective and observable data consisting of vocal, facial, and body movements that express what appear to be positive or negative mood states.

It is not possible to actually learn to control an emotion, per se. For example, a person who experiences fear cannot eliminate fear itself. Rather, what a person learns is how to cope with that fear by expressing appropriate behavior, whether it be by taking flight or by stating, "I am afraid." With maturation of the brain, nervous system, and muscles, the child increases the potential for a broad range of emotional reactions through various forms of learning—imitation and modeling, trial and error, conditioning, and insight.

3.4 Language and Communication Skills

Through the course of normal development children improve their language and communication skills. While early expressions are somewhat random and uncontrolled, infants soon learn a variety of ways to let their feelings be known. They gradually progress from such responses as laughing or crying to waving arms, jumping up and down, smiling, and simple words. As children develop verbal skills, they talk more about their feelings. Even so, throughout childhood body language along with speech is natural and prominent. Until children are about 7- or 8-years old, most are quite frank in letting others know how they feel. As children get older, they learn to control their feelings and to be more discreet about expressing them. Forms of verbal expression and use of body language to express feelings are also influenced by social and cultural patterns of behavior.

3.5 Socialization

Children's emotional responses, although spontaneous, are influenced by their social interactions. When there is someone present who is interested in how a child feels, emotions are usually freely expressed. Appropriate limits and exemplary models help children learn to express their feelings in ways that are socially acceptable. Children who are restricted or prevented from openly expressing themselves may repress or harbor feelings that eventually lead to serious emotional problems.

Emotional deprivation, the prolonged absence of sufficient stimulation from personal interactions and experiences of attachment and affection, inhibits the child's overall development. Children who are denied opportunities to experience love, joy, happiness, and contentment during infancy and in the early years have less opportunity for optimal physical, mental, and social development, resulting in possible delay of motor, language, and intellectual skills. When intimate social interactions are denied, the child has little basis on which to build a repertoire of positive emotional experiences that lead to healthy personality formation and a sense of self-esteem. Furthermore, the child tends to be self-centered and demanding, with a poorly developed self-concept formation.

Behavioral outcomes of prolonged emotional deprivation include listlessness, emaciation, undue quietness, general apathy, loss of appetite, and a variety of psychosomatic illnesses. Young children deprived of love and caring in their daily lives tend to exhibit manifestations of disturbed interpersonal relationships and inadequate social skills such as avoidance of others, aggression, and hostility.

3.6 Personality and Temperament

Personality characteristics vary with each individual in relation to time, place, and circumstances. It is therefore inappropriate to label a child on the basis of an emotional judgment that carries a global inference about one's personality, such as "she is an angry child," "he is a hostile boy," or "she is a happy baby." A school-age child may appear to be angry in the school setting when experiences are threatening, yet appear pleasant while playing with peers. A parent may be firm and forceful with a child in certain family circumstances, yet be gentle and warm in other instances.

Different infants exhibit different rates, ranges, and tempos of internal states that will, in turn, affect the outcome of interactions from individual to individual. These individual differences in infants, together with differing experiences and styles of mothering, contribute to the nature of the emotional interaction that occurs.

3.7 Motivation

Motivation, as a psychological construct, refers to the internal state of the individual which, under certain circumstances, appears to move the person toward a particular action or behavior. Emotion and motivation are bound together in human interaction. In a social context, the strength of the motivating force depends on how the child views the self and his or her needs in a given situation. Although perception may initiate the emoting process, the emotion that follows may, in turn, affect the perceptual process. With emotion there is usually an impulse to act. Feelings, essential to all human conduct and predominant factors in emotion, serve as underpinnings that not only bring about motivation to act but also influence the form that action will take.

4. The Brain and Nervous System

The early work of Papez and later the neuroscientist, Paul MacLean, advanced the concept that certain subcortical regions are involved with emotional behavior. MacLean emphasizes the role of the paleocortex and of the nuclei of the limbic system in relation to intense emotions and drives (Henry and Stephens 1977).

Evidence that the brain's right hemispheric complex is most closely related to the emotional response system and hence to the limbic structures is presented by Flor-Henry and co-workers who speculate that connections from the new association cortex in the right parietal and frontal regions to the limbic system determine affective responses. Sifneos draws a distinction between feelings and emotions: Experiencing emotion can be recognized by a person's behavior and its confirming neuroendocrine changes. Feelings, by contrast, involve subjective thoughts and fantasies and require neocortical activity (Henry and Stephens 1977).

The limbic system, comprising roughly one-fifth of the brain's area, surrounds the brainstem and is surrounded by the cerebrum. Extensive neural links with the brainstem help maintain a state of emotional balance. Connections with the cerebrum permit interplay between reason and emotion. The neocortex, the newest evolutionary part of the human brain which comprises almost five-sixths of the whole, functions less efficiently under pressure. Pressure of an emotional or psychological nature places greater stimulation on the limbic system and learning is subsequently inhibited (Henry and Stephens 1977).

Stress and pressure from various life experiences can therefore cause a person to function less effectively in the realm of rational thought. An example is the school-age child who is anxious about performing adequately on a given examination, resulting in the inability to think clearly and process the information needed to complete the task. As the child seeks to compensate for inadequacies, whether real or imagined, behaviors may be exhibited that bring further pressure to bear and therefore continue the cycle of brain patterns which impede the learning process.

Nerve pathways, interwoven throughout the limbic system, send electrochemical impulses that direct human drives and emotions. A small cluster of nerve cells called the hypothalamus serves as the center out of which arise feelings of pleasure, punishment, hunger, thirst, sexual arousal, aggression, and rage.

Certain physiological changes also accompany emotion. At times, these changes may be intensive and extensive, altering regulation of the bodily systems, including the respiratory, digestive, circulatory, and nervous systems and glands of internal and external secretion. In the case of fear and anger, for example, these physiological changes have been described as the body's mobilization of resources for "fight or flight" responses (Henry and Stephens 1977). First to react is the hypothalamus, which organizes a series of defenses to prepare the body for handling an emergency. Hypothalamic chemicals cause the pituitary to release a stress hormone through the bloodstream to the adrenal glands which, in turn, produce an adrenal chemical for converting fats and proteins into sugar. Adrenalin and noradrenaline cause the heart to pump faster, blood pressure to rise, and pupils of the eyes to dilate. The combined surge of hormones relaxes bronchial tubes for deeper breathing, increases blood sugar for greater energy, slows down digestive processes to conserve muscular energy, and shifts blood supplies for easier clotting in open wounds. In a matter of seconds the body is prepared to perform with strength and endurance far beyond its normal capacity.

5. Stages of Emotional Development

Overall, emotional development from infancy onward can be characterized by: (a) initial simple emotions becoming increasingly differentiated and elaborated, and (b) new, complex emotions coming into existence. Qualitative differences in the meaning of emotional terms must be considered at different developmental stages. For example, pride and guilt may begin to crystallize during the preschool years and are clearly different from pleasure or distress of the young infant. Emotions with highly developed cognitive components like empathy may not appear until middle childhood or adolescence.

Emotional development is primarily a result of maturation and learning, although manifestations of diffused emotional responses may appear soon after birth. Variations in the frequency, intensity, and duration of different emotions are generally a combination of heredity and maturation, environmental circumstances, and daily living experiences and personal health.

A brief summary of the child's emotional development from birth through adolescence has profound implications for educators. As the child progresses from one stage to the next, each subsequent stage is supported by a cumulative reservoir of past experiences, whether they be adequate and appropriate or lacking and inappropriate. The child's view of self and the world is greatly influenced by the emotional experiences that take place in each stage. These stages, for the most part, are consistent with Piaget's stages of cognitive development (see *Cognitive Development*).

5.1 Infancy (Birth to 2 Years)

During the infant stage, the mother serves as the child's main source of energy, power, possibility, and safety (Pearce 1977). The quality of the mother–infant relationship sets the tone for subsequent emotional development. Emotions are the child's language system during this period, for through the expression of feelings of distress or delight, the child is able to communicate needs and wishes as well as satisfaction or the lack of it. As the child makes a transition from the early parent–infant attachment to interest in other family members, expressions of emotions are manifested in behaviors toward others such as avoidance and approach.

5.2 Early Childhood (2 to 8 Years)

This is the stage during which the child becomes grounded in the experiences of everyday life within and beyond the immediate family. The child's world becomes the center of activity for exploring and discovering both human interactions and physical and material components of the environment. The child still needs the emotional support of the mother, but meaningful interactions expand to persons beyond her, with the father or other significant person serving as the pivotal opportunity to move beyond the mother and into the greater community. The child is very subjective, exhibiting the emotionally based egocentrism typical of this stage. Mastery of the body and emotions is a task during this time. The child's place is "here," the time is "now," and the center is "me." Emotional control begins to take shape, but the child remains open in expressing strong feelings. Mastery of language skills and increasing cognitive abilities help the child develop capabilities for socially acceptable ways of expressing emotions.

5.3 School-age Child (8 to 12 Years)

The child begins to rely on the self as the main source of possibility, energy and safety, yet remains emotionally grounded in the previous stages. This is a period of search for self-identity and use of the body and brain together as a resource for functioning on a concrete level. Emotions are expressed with greater control as the child seeks to function as a socially accepted human being, interacting with others and interdependent in relationships. The child assumes an objective interest in the world, experiencing delight from gathering facts and information, such as how many legs are on a caterpillar. Attachment to the world in a broader sense brings another shift in the child's emotional underpinnings.

5.4 Young Adolescent (12 to 16 Years)

The adolescent progresses to the application of abstract thought, no longer limited to concrete avenues of logic, trial and error, and cause and effect for discovery and learning. Still supported emotionally by the sense of self, the child now begins to rely more on abstract thought and internalizing feelings, capable of controlling emotions in order to interact appropriately as a social participant, accepted by peers and society in general. During this stage of transition from childhood into adolescence, hormonal changes occur and the individual becomes more sensitive to his or her own sexuality, with subtle outward behaviors as manifestations of inner feelings and concerns. By this time, the child is capable of reporting and describing personal feelings; even so, there is a tendency to withhold sharing real feelings.

5.5 Older Adolescent (16 to 20 Years)

Persons at this stage are inclined to want to practice their social and intellectual skills in ways that are personally gratifying to them. They are less interested in the study of how scholars think or feel and more interested in experiencing their own feelings and intellectual competencies. This is a stage of exploring more intimate relationships and new emotional attachments. The emotions are often expressed in artforms and cultural traditions. By this time the adolescent makes an attachment to the world in a broader sense, through private contemplation about the self and its relationship to others, to life itself, and to the universe.

6. Expressions of Emotions

Charles Darwin, for more than 40 years, gathered material on expressive movements and facial expressions of emotion in people around the world. His book, *Expressions of the Emotions in Man and Animals* (Darwin 1872), contained minutely detailed descriptions of the physiological and muscular changes involved in the expression of emotion. In his "Biographical Sketch of an Infant," published five years later, Darwin centered on the expression of emotion in infants as seen in one of his own children. Fear, he stated, is probably one of the earliest feelings that infants experience, shown by "their starting at any sudden sound when only a few weeks old, followed by crying." He observed expressions of "affection" before age 2 months, manifested by smiling at "those who took care of him." By 6 months the baby assumed a melancholy expression when his nurse pretended to cry; he showed signs of discomfort by age 13 months (Jackson and Jackson 1978).

Gerald Young and Theresa Décarie, at the University of Montreal, found that infant expressions usually affect many parts of the face—changes in the brow, eyes, mouth, cheeks, nose, jaw, chin, and throat as well as varied vocalizations. They observed three categories of expressions: (a) positive, or expressing pleasures (babbles, coos, laughs, squeals); (b) neutral or undifferentiated (attentive, detached, sober stares, and frowns, perplexed and surprised, sigh and yawn); and (c) negative, or expressing displeasure (disgust, fear, sadness) (Jackson and Jackson 1978).

As children progress in overall development, emotional behavior becomes increasingly directed and less chaotic. Crying and temper tantrums progress to physical aggression toward self and others, such as pulling hair, kicking, and hitting. Name calling and other verbal expressions accompany language acquisition.

The child generates emotions for the achievement of personal goals. For example, temper tantrums are often attempts to attract attention or exert power. One cannot always see the child's motive—only the manifestation of it. The temper tantrum may be the child's aim at obtaining power because of feelings of inferiority. If the child felt sure of his or her power, it would not be necessary to demonstrate it.

Emotions can be observed as expressions or indicators of movement toward or away from other persons. Disjunctive emotions separate a person from others; conjunctive emotions join a person to others.

Anger enables the child to oppose and dominate, or to hurt and to get even. Empathy, a conjunctive emotion, manifests itself as an expression of positive social concern in the child's ability to identify with the feelings of another person or persons and to express that concern in some meaningful way either verbally or nonverbally.

7. Theories of Emotional Attachment

Expressive patterns of emotions have their roots in early attachment experiences that infants have with their mothers or other primary caregivers (see *Mother–Child Relations*). Attachment, the emergent social relationship, and the attachment behaviors which function to maintain and modulate the flow of a social interaction, appear to begin taking shape during the first 6 months of life.

British psychoanalyst John Bowlby advanced the ethological theory of attachment, with emphasis on a long period of dependency with the identification of several kinds of infant behaviors. Known collectively as attachment behavior, these include crying, smiling, and vocalizing which attract the mother's attention. The active rooting, sucking, clinging, and embracing initiated by the infant produce and maintain proximity, as do crawling and walking. Cuddling and clinging represent immediate contact between infant and mother. Crying and fussing, orienting with looking, smiling, verbalizing, and cuddling serve as precursors of infant–mother attachment (Bowlby 1969).

Bowlby emphasized that attachment behaviors are controlled by a dynamic feedback system existing between the mother and child, resulting from an inborn biological propensity for the development of social bonds. Daniel Stern, Cornell University Medical Center, declares after extensive observations of infants and caregivers in homes, in laboratories, and in social settings, that the social interaction between the infant and mother is a biologically designed choreography that serves as a prototype for all later interpersonal exchanges (Stern 1977).

A baby's tendency to seek attachments may be increased by fear and also by illness and fatigue (Bowlby 1969). Attachments are most likely to be made to people who bring comfort to the baby, actively interact with the baby, and respond to the baby's cues (Ainsworth 1973). Attachment behavior also includes using the mother as a base from which to explore.

Attachment, from the beginning, must be viewed in terms of participating rather than in terms of two individuals sending discrete messages. Brazelton, in studying infant–mother reciprocity in face-to-face play situations by microkinesic analysis, found that reciprocity of behaving is fundamental to the human species and appears soon after birth. By 3 weeks of age, infants evidence behaviors which are different for objects than for human interactions. Infants engage the mother or caretaker in a rhythmical cyclical pattern of attention and nonattention (Brazelton et al. 1975).

Mary D. Ainsworth distinguished several stages in the development of attachment, according to ethological theory. First, the infant displays a variety of fixed-action patterns of behavior in signalling to and orienting toward other human beings indiscriminately. In the second stage, until about 6 or 7 months of age, infants continue to signal and orient but will respond differentially to the mother and one or two other persons. In a third stage from 7 months through about 2 years of age, infants take more and more initiative in maintaining proximity to the mother—clinging, following, and climbing into her lap (Ainsworth 1973).

In contrast to the ethological theory, in which the infant's attachment to the mother is seen as biologically determined, social-learning theory identifies attachment as a dependency relationship that is established by conditioning (crying by the hungry infant is reinforced by the mother's nurturant behavior) and through stimuli associated with the mother's presence (the infant acquires a drive to be close to the mother) (Jackson and Jackson 1978). In short, a "dependency drive" develops. The infant's "proximity behavior" has been conditioned to occur by the association of the closeness to the mother with rewards, such as food. The strength of attachment to the mother lies in her having more reinforcement control over the infant's "behavioral systems" than any other person in the environment.

See also: Human Development Theories; Social Learning Theory; Brain Development and Function

Bibliography

Ainsworth M 1973 The development of infant–mother attachment. In: Caldwell B M, Ricciuti H N (eds.) 1973 *Review of Child Development Research*. University of Chicago Press, Chicago, Illinois

Bartlett J 1882 *Familiar Quotations: Being an Attempt to Trace Their Sources Passages and Phrases in Common Use*. Little, Brown, Toronto, Ontario

Bellak L, Baker S S 1981 *Reading Faces*. Holt, Rinehart and Winston, New York

Bowlby J 1969 *Attachment and Loss*, Vol. 1: *Attachment*. Hogarth, London

Brazelton T, Tronick E, Wise S 1975 *Parent–Infant Interaction*. Associated Scientific Publishers, New York

Darwin C R 1872 *The Expression of the Emotions in Man and Animals*. Murray, London

Henry J P, Stephens P M 1977 *Stress, Health, and the Social Environment: A Sociobiologic Approach to Medicine*. Springer, Berlin

Hurlock E B 1972 *Child Development*, 5th edn. McGraw-Hill, New York

Izard C E (ed.) 1977 *Human Emotions*. Plenum, New York

Jackson J F, Jackson J H 1978 *Infant Culture*. Crowell, New York

Pearce J C 1977 *Magical Child: Rediscovering Nature's Plan for Our Children.* Bantam, Toronto, Ontario

Stern D 1977 *The First Relationship: Infant and Mother.* Harvard University Press, Cambridge, Massachusetts

Thomas A, Chess S 1980 *The Dynamics of Psychological Development.* Brunner/Mazel, New York

W. Draper

Employment and Education

The several purposes of education have received differing emphases over time. Both as a consequence and a cause of the development of human capital theory, the weight given to the economic dimension of education has grown. Education has widely come to be seen as an aid to the achievement of individuals' economic ambitions and/or national economic and social objectives as determined by the state. This has been the case in educational debates in both the less developed countries (LDCs) and those developed countries where large numbers of young people and members of particular racial and social groups are unemployed.

The relationships between education and employment are many and cannot all be covered in one entry. Here the stress is on the educational characteristics of individuals and the characteristics of the jobs they enter (or fail to enter). In the first section, the evidence from both developed countries and less developed countries of the close associations between age, educational background, occupational status, and earnings from employment is very briefly described. How school leavers become absorbed into the occupational labour force is the subject of the second section, which discusses some of the many theories of the labour market and the role played by the public sector. Much of the controversy between different theories of labour markets centres around interpretations of the demand side. In the third section some brief comments are made concerning the supply of educated labour (or the demand for schooling) and the attempts which have been made to explain and predict this supply. Finally, some aspects of youth and school-leaver unemployment are discussed. While much of the debate on the issues in this section has been conducted in the context of the less developed countries, the recent increased levels of youth unemployment in the United States and Western Europe make it increasingly relevant there.

1. Age, Education, Occupation, Earnings

Education, occupational status, and earnings from employment have been shown in a wide range of studies to be positively associated in countries adopting many different types of socioeconomic system and at different levels of economic development. Earnings functions and path analyses of the effect of individuals' background characteristics on occupational attainment and earnings have invariably indicated that while much of the variance remains unexplained, the largest single indicator is education. Jencks et al. (1979) for instance, utilizing a considerable amount of data for men aged between 25 and 64 years in the United States, concluded that the number of years of education is the best single predictor of the eventual occupational status of a labour force entrant. The results of similar (but less sophisticated) studies in a number of less developed countries show the same findings, generally even more strongly. Turning to earnings, Psacharopoulos (1975) has demonstrated that for the Organisation for Economic Co-operation and Development (OECD) countries, average annual earnings of secondary- and primary-school leavers show a differential of 40 percent, while higher-education graduates receive on average 77 percent more than secondary-school leavers. In the less developed countries, the differentials are much wider (Hinchliffe 1975).

Of interest to both individuals and the state is the relationship between the additional earnings associated with education and the cost of acquiring them. This is measured through rates of return arising from the resources used in education. International comparisons of rates of return demonstrate, in particular, two patterns: (a) returns are larger at lower levels of education, and (b) returns are larger in low-income than in high-income countries. In addition, as a result of the significant elements of public subsidy in educational provision, the net benefits to the individual are invariably greater than the social ones. This is particularly marked in low-income countries at the higher levels of education.

Empirical studies of the interrelationships between education and earnings have usually included a third variable, age. Age–earnings profiles demonstrate that for all educational levels, earnings rise with age up to a maximum and then level off. Further, the higher the educational level, the steeper the rise in earnings. The result, for both developed and less developed countries, is that while average earnings in wage employment vary significantly by educational level for all age groups, they do so most prominently in the older age group. Another general finding is that the distribution of earnings at each educational level is wider for older workers, particularly for those with higher education. Finally, increments of age and education also appear to have different effects depending on type of occupation, with both being larger for professional than for manual workers.

Earnings functions and rates of return on educational investment which have been calculated in the less developed countries have largely been restricted to observations of individuals in the formal wage sector. While this sector is the one entered by the majority of those with higher levels of education, the rural and urban informal sectors still contain most of the labour force, and even most recent school leavers, in many countries. Detailed studies of the relationship between education and earnings in these sectors are few. A recent review of 18 surveys in 13 countries relating the educational level of farmers to their productivity, however, has suggested that four years of schooling may be capable of increasing productivity by around 10 percent a year (Lockheed et al. 1980). Surveys of urban informal sector workers in, for instance, Nigeria and Colombia have similarly demonstrated a positive association between education and earnings. Such studies, however, have usually omitted consideration of other possible earnings-related factors.

Summarizing, the large amount of empirical investigation into the relationships between education, occupation, and earnings from employment which have been conducted since the 1960s in both high- and low-income countries have resulted in two major findings. The first of these is that the main criteria used by employers to recruit new entrants into the occupational structure are level and type of education. To formalize this, minimum educational entry requirements are generally set for each occupation. Second, there is a very close correlation between an individual's educational attainment and his or her level of lifetime earnings. Explanations of these observations, however, vary widely. Each is based on a different theory of the operation of labour markets.

2. Education and the Labour Market

Explanations of the interface between individuals with specific educational characteristics and the nature of the jobs they enter are each one part of more general theories of labour markets. In this section, the different interpretations of the empirical conclusions presented above are discussed.

Three major approaches may be identified. First there is an approach grounded on the argument that the educational system itself operates in such a way that it directly adds to an individual's cognitive abilities. These abilities range from basic numeracy and literacy at one end of the scale to a greater capacity for logical and analytical reasoning at the other. These increased abilities lead to higher individual earnings. A second approach also maintains that schools are effective in changing a person but that the important changes are not those of cognitive abilities. Class background is here seen as the major determinant of occupation and income and the educational system is said to operate in such a way that it develops different sets of productivity-related personality traits among children from different social classes. This both legitimizes the distribution of jobs, which simply perpetuates the existing structure of social class, and also increases the productivity of all classes in their ascribed occupations. Traits produced by schools in those individuals who will fill low-paying jobs include punctuality, obedience, and respect for authority, while those for high-status occupations include self-reliance and the ability to make decisions. Finally, there is a set of approaches which directly questions the view that through the development of either cognitive abilities or personality traits, schools increase the potential productivity of individuals. Rather, the educational system is said to act simply as a selection mechanism to sort out those who possess nonschool-related characteristics, such as intelligence and motivation, which are in some way connected to productivity. Schooling itself does not affect productivity.

These views of education are further discussed below in the context of the wider labour market theories to which they are related.

2.1 Neoclassical Theory

In orthodox neoclassical economics the theory of the labour market is based on the marginal productivity theory of demand, reflecting the profit-maximizing behaviour of employers, a supply theory based on the utility maximization of workers, and the notion of competitive equilibrium. Following on from the composition of demand for goods, individual firms derive a demand schedule for labour (relating amounts of labour demanded to different wages) and labour is employed up to the point where marginal productivity is equal to the industry wage. In early models, labour was regarded as homogeneous. With the development of human capital theory homogeneity is no longer assumed and labour demand has come to be interpreted in a set of markets each with a demand for specific productivity determining worker characteristics, with education and training being the most important. In response to these, individuals are assumed to compare the costs of acquiring the relevant characteristics with the increase in earnings which they can expect from them. As a result of these comparisons individuals invest in themselves and the aggregation of these decisions determines the supply of human capital. If the demand for productivity-determining characteristics exceeds the supply at a given wage rate, this will then rise and in turn supply will increase and demand fall. Conversely if supply exceeds demand, the wage will fall and employment increase. According to human capital theory, then, the labour market is capable of continually absorbing workers with ever higher levels of education provided that education-specific earnings are flexible downwards and the labour market is a single continuous one. This approach to the operation of labour markets may be termed the wage competition model.

Since the early 1970s a wide range of labour market theories has been developed at variance with the orthodox neoclassical/human capital school. The theories have emerged largely in response to a number of empirical observations of the United States labour market, which have been said to be at odds with the implications of orthodox theory. These include the persistence of poverty and income inequality, the failure of education and training programmes to raise the incomes of the poorest groups, continual upgrading of the qualifications required for jobs, continuing discrimination against sections of the labour force, and widespread worker alienation (Cain 1976). The interpretations of labour market functioning which have come to compete with orthodox theory may be divided into labour market segmentation and job competition models. Each of these contains variants and there is often a degree of overlapping between variants of all three theoretical approaches.

2.2 Alternative Theories

Segmentation models are discussed in detail elsewhere (see *Labour Market Theories and Education*). Essentially it is argued in these models that the labour market is characterized by a number of segments, each of which has different conditions of employment and recruits from among separate sections of the labour force. To some theorists the types and number of jobs in each segment are determined by technological requirements; to others segmentation occurs as the result of conscious actions by capitalists to divide the working class and reduce class consciousness. The latter view has two implications for education. First, educational expansion among those groups consigned to the secondary labour markets characterized by low pay, insecurity, and poor working conditions will not lead to increased earnings. Second, this view links up with the approach to education described above, which argues that the role of the educational system in capitalist society is to reproduce existing class relations by legitimating the stability of intergenerational occupational status and developing different sets of personality traits among different groups in society necessary for a hierarchical occupational structure. The technological interpretation of segmented labour markets has features which tend to run into this rather conspiratorial approach but also shares some of the arguments associated with the job competition model, which is concentrated on in the remainder of this section.

The third view of education described earlier argues that schooling merely acts as a screening device which helps employers to choose between people who have very different capabilities and compete for a small number of jobs. In this view, educational credentials are essentially signals which indicate the varying levels of "raw" intelligence, motivation, and so on, which affect future productivity or "trainability". These credentials may accurately predict future work performance but they do not directly add to it. Several attempts have been made to describe in detail the interrelations between schooling and the labour market based on this simple concept of screening. One of the most widely discussed is the job competition model associated with Thurow and Lucas (1972) and developed by them to counter the wage competition view of the United States labour market.

The job competition model is based on the uncertainty which surrounds the hiring of labour. Given the problems of accurately predicting the future performance of job applicants and the fact that most job-specific skills are learned on the job, the employer uses educational qualifications as a proxy for those characteristics which facilitate training. In the model, two sets of factors determine an individual's income. One set determines the job structure in the economy and the other an individual's relative position in the queue for jobs. Job structure is regarded as technologically determined and a central feature of the model is that productivity is seen as an attribute of jobs rather than of people. Consequently wages are based on the characteristics of jobs rather than the characteristics of people in them. Workers are distributed across job opportunities according to their position in the queue.

Potential workers come onto the labour market with a variety of background characteristics, the most important of which is amount of education. While these are insufficient to allow the worker to immediately perform in the production process, they do affect the cost of training, which is usually acquired formally or informally on the job. Potential workers are then ranked in a labour queue according to their expected training costs. Based on such a queue, jobs are distributed with employers offering high-productivity jobs to those at the head and working down. In contrast to the wage competition model, which sees the labour market as a market for matching demands and supplies of job skills, the job competition model sees it as a market for matching trainable individuals with training ladders.

Given the variations in skills required over the job structure, the amount of training will vary between jobs. Once a worker has landed a job and received the training to raise his or her productivity to that of the job, the time required for further training for a higher productivity job is likely to be less than that required for someone recruited from outside the firm. As a result, highly structured internal labour markets develop within the firm. As Blaug (1976) argues, it is the addition of the concept of internal labour markets to the simple screening effect of schooling which is used to counter those critics who argue that screening can account, at most, for education-related differentials in starting salaries but not for the often stronger correlation between schooling and earnings which continues through working life.

The theories of job competition and screening, in their various forms, have important implications for educational policy. As high-productivity jobs become scarce, competition to get to the head of the labour queue intensifies and the amount of education required increases. A leapfrogging process develops whereby the demand for education by individuals increases the more difficult it becomes for each education group to secure jobs. The effect of educational expansion is neither a fall in occupational wages nor an increase in jobs. What does result is that educational qualifications for jobs lower in the hierarchy rise and the more highly educated are then recruited to jobs that would have been filled in the past by the less educated. While the surplus of a particular educated labour group does not affect occupational wage levels, it does result in a lower average wage for the group. However, since the "bumping" process, once triggered, will extend right down the occupational ladder, wage differentials and hence the incentive to acquire further amounts of education may not decrease. However, if jobs are performed no differently by those with different levels of education, the social returns to this educational expansion are zero. If, on the other hand, all job entrants are not perfect substitutes in this sense and either levels of productivity within particular jobs can be affected by the individual or training costs do vary between individuals in line with their educational qualifications, the social returns to investment in education may be positive. In this case the returns result more from an occupation selection mechanism than from an increase in the quality of labour.

2.3 The Public Sector

The labour market theories into which the various views of education have been placed have been formulated essentially for analysing the labour markets of developed market economies. In the labour markets of the less developed countries there are two major differences. Employment in the formal wage sector is very much proportionately smaller and within this, the public sector has a more important place. It is this dominant role of the public sector in the less developed countries which has often been used in the argument that the job competition model is even more appropriate to use in these countries than the wage competition one. In virtually all less developed countries, the public sector is the largest single employer and for secondary-school leavers and above, the majority employer. Public sector employment is strongly sought not only for the level of wages offered—which while offering large differentials at the highest levels may be below those in the private sector—but also for the long-term security. Wage levels in the public sector are set administratively by commissions sitting every few years and the criteria adopted rarely allow supply factors much influence. The result tends to be inflexibility with respect to wage levels and differentials. In addition, in order to appear impartial and as a way of coping with the selection of recruits from a large number of potential applicants, emphasis tends to be predominantly placed on formal educational qualifications for recruitment. As a result of both these factors, the problem of surpluses of educated labour is not resolved by wage changes (as implied in the wage competition model), but is rather thrown back onto the educational system to solve by continuously expanding qualifications (as implied in the job competition model).

3. The Demand for Schooling

The job competition model and its variants offer rival interpretations of the demand side of the labour market to that offered by the human capital or wage competition school. They say little, however, that disagrees with the human capital interpretation of the supply side. Both wage and job competition models reject the earlier view of education as consumption and adopt the position that the demand for postcompulsory levels of education is related to the direct and indirect costs of that education and the earnings differentials associated with it. The notion that earnings forgone are perceived by potential students to be an important part of the private cost of education and that they make a careful assessment of future alternative earnings patterns before deciding whether or not to acquire more education is widely shared. According to Blaug (1976), the hypotheses resulting from this position come in two versions: first that total enrolments can be predicted by relating private costs to future expected benefits (i.e., by calculating expected rates of return) and second, more ambitious, that enrolments in specific fields of study can be predicted.

Despite the hypothesis that the demand for schooling can be predicted by private cost–benefit considerations being central to human capital theory and shared by many who criticize other aspects of the approach, Blaug has demonstrated that attempts to prove it have not been particularly successful. Early attempts made in the late 1960s to estimate the demand function for higher education in the United States tended to regress some measure of enrolments on household income and direct education costs while including neither forgone earnings nor measures of expected future earnings. In other words, the tests were more those of the consumption explanation. Later work turned away from total demand and towards the demand for specialized areas of study. Freeman's (1971) work on engineers and scientists is an example and one which appeared to bear out many of the predictions of human capital theory. A major drawback to this study, however, was the use made of starting salaries as a proxy for lifetime earnings, with the result that the hypothesis that students do take a life-cycle view of careers was not actually tested.

Problems of rigorously testing the demand for the schooling side of human capital theory in European countries have similarly been large, although more general explanations of the behaviour of demand for higher education along these lines have been plausible. For instance, the impressive rise in the age participation rates for higher education in the United Kingdom in the 1960s and their stability (and even fall) since the early 1970s have been plotted against changes in the availability of student grants, the fall in their value relative to the earnings of employed youth, and the fall in the ratio of graduates' starting salaries to the average wage. These types of explanations, however, remain at a rather general level. Turning to demand for specific subject areas, the rationing of higher education in Europe makes it almost impossible to test the extent to which subject choice is influenced by earnings. The major attempt to do this for the United Kingdom was unsuccessful (Klinov-Malul 1971).

While numerous surveys in both developed and less developed countries have concluded that the economic aspects of schooling are strongly considered by potential students and their families, the human capital hypothesis that it is possible to predict the strength of demand for schooling from variations in the ratio of private costs and expected returns has not been substantiated.

4. School-leaver Unemployment

Unemployment is one of the issues which has been given much attention since the early 1970s in the literature covering the less developed countries. Surveys of open unemployment (as opposed to underemployment) in these countries have generally shown that it is greater in urban than rural areas and that within urban areas it is more serious for females than males, for the 15-to-24 years age group than other age groups, and for the more educated, at least up to postsecondary education. In the early 1980s the world recession has also resulted in levels of unemployment in the developed countries higher than at any time since the peaks of the 1930s. Once again rates of unemployment are higher for females and for the 14-to-24 years age group. As overall unemployment has increased, its concentration among the young has intensified relative to other age groups. The relationship between unemployment and education in these countries, however, appears to be a straightforward negative one.

As an example of the nature of youth unemployment in the developed countries, Casson's (1979) study based on a labour force sample survey undertaken in European Economic Community (EEC) countries in 1973 and 1975 will be briefly described. Among the results of the survey were the following:

(a) Duration of search—while levels of unemployment are higher among the young, their duration of search is significantly shorter than for other age groups.

(b) First job seekers—the proportion of first job seekers among the unemployed is highest among young people and declines steadily with age: these proportions, however, vary considerably between countries, with around 40 percent of the unemployed under 18 years looking for their first job in the United Kingdom while in Italy the corresponding figure was 95 percent.

(c) Methods of job search—in those countries where public employment agencies are the major form of job search, young workers make below average use of them and rely more on direct enquiry; where employment agencies are less generally important there is little difference in frequency of use between the younger and older unemployed.

Turning to theories of youth unemployment, Casson argues that the statistical evidence supports the job search and school-leaver hypotheses. The job search hypothesis predicts that young people change jobs frequently, resign more commonly, and use informal procedures of job search. The school-leaver hypothesis is concerned mainly with unemployment during a recession. The predictions are that unemployment among school leavers will change in the same direction, but by a much greater amount than among the working population as a whole and that first job seekers constitute a high proportion of the young unemployed. The explanation behind these predictions is that other potential labour force entrants are much more flexible and find it easier to postpone entry to the labour market than do school leavers. As a recession deepens they withdraw whereas school leavers do not. Casson argues that the evidence does not support this explanation. On the one hand, the participation rate of adult women has continually increased, and on the other, the option of staying on at school has in general been taken. The results of a survey of employer attitudes towards younger and older recruits in the United Kingdom may be significant here. In all major respects apart from physical fitness, employers rated older recruits higher.

Turning to youth and school-leaver unemployment in the less developed countries, two features of labour supply dominate: the historically high growth of numbers and the increasing level of educational qualifications acquired by potential entrants. The annual average growth of the population between 1950 and 1970 in the less developed countries was 2.4 percent, three times that of today's developed countries in the nineteenth century. One result is that around 40 percent of the population is below the age of 15 years. The new labour force entrants are increasingly better educated as a result of rapid expansions in both primary and secondary enrolments since the 1960s. Not only, then, are new entrants more numerous than those retiring, they are better educated. Looked at in terms of jobs, while the required number of new jobs is increasing due to population growth, the quality of those jobs is also expected to increase. These combined pressures have been putting great stress on the labour markets, particularly in urban areas.

The most conspicuous feature of urban unemployment in less developed countries is that it is concentrated on the young with the ratio for the 15–24 years age group often being over two and three times that for the total labour force. Given the age profile of unemployment and the recent expansion of education, it is not surprising that the unemployed tend to be relatively well-educated. While there are countries which do not fit the overall pattern, the available evidence appears to show a positive relation between levels of urban open unemployment and education up to the end of secondary school followed by a reduced level of unemployment among tertiary-level leavers (Squire 1981). This pattern also appears to correspond with variations in the duration of job search, a measure which is arguably more useful for identifying employment "problems" than unemployment rates.

Disagreements over the appropriate analytical treatment of school-leaver unemployment have tended to be sharp. Recently there has been a shift away from those who lay the blame on the schools themselves and on the antimanual work aspirations which they are said to produce through inappropriate curricula and teaching methods, towards a greater emphasis on the effect of wage differentials. Wide differentials are said to provide a rationale for extensive periods of job search particularly in countries where labour market information is poor. In this interpretation of school-leaver unemployment, alterations in school practices may be desirable but cannot in themselves result in altering school-leaver aspirations and eliminating unemployment. Unemployment is, then, regarded as a period of job search with its duration depending on the relative strength of three factors: (a) the higher the level of education an individual receives, the wider the variance of possible wage offers and therefore the longer the likely period of job search; (b) the higher the level of education an individual receives, the higher the opportunity cost through earnings forgone while unemployed and therefore the shorter the likely period of job search; (c) the greater the amount of financial support from the individual's family, the longer the period of job search.

The period of job search is seen as resulting in greater labour market information and a reduction in aspirations to a more "realistic" level.

See also: Graduate Unemployment and Education; Youth Unemployment and Education; Earnings and Education

Bibliography

Blaug M 1973 *Education and the Employment Problem in Developing Countries.* International Labour Organization, Geneva

Blaug M 1976 The empirical status of human capital theory: A slightly jaundiced survey. *J. Econ. Lit.* 14: 827–55

Cain G G 1976 The challenge of segmented labor market theories to orthodox theory: A survey. *J. Econ. Lit.* 14: 1215–57

Casson M 1979 *Youth Unemployment.* Macmillan, London

Colclough C 1982 The impact of primary schooling on economic development: A review of the evidence. *World Dev.* 10: 167–85

Freeman R B 1971 *The Market for College-trained Manpower: A Study in the Economics of Career Choice.* Harvard University Press, Cambridge, Massachusetts

Hinchliffe K 1975 Education, individual earnings and earnings distribution. *J. Dev. Stud.* 11: 149–61

Jencks C, Bartlett S et al. 1979 *Who Gets Ahead? The Determinants of Economic Success in America.* Basic Books, New York

Klinov-Malul R 1971 Enrolments in higher education as related to earnings. *Br. J. Ind. Relat.* 9: 82–91

Lockheed M E, Jamison D T, Lau L J 1980 Farmer education and farm efficiency: A survey. *Econ. Dev. Cultural Change* 29: 37–76

Psacharopoulos G 1975 *Earnings and Education in OECD Countries.* Organisation for Economic Co-operation and Development, Paris

Squire L 1981 *Employment Policy in Developing Countries: A Survey of Issues and Evidence.* Oxford University Press, New York

Thurow L C, Lucas R E B 1972 *The American Distribution of Income: A Structural Problem.* Joint Economic Committee of the United States Congress, Washington, DC

Turnham D, Jaegar I 1970 *The Employment Problem in Less Developed Countries: A Review of Evidence.* Organisation for Economic Co-operation and Development, Paris

K. Hinchliffe

Employment Policy: The Role of Adult Education

In this article, adult education is understood in a broad sense, to include all organized learning activities intended to increase the skills of the adult population, technical, social, or political. Its relation to employment policy is reviewed in terms of its objectives, the sources of its provision, and its organization and finance. Finally, some specific issues are selected as significant for future developments. Illustrations are drawn largely, but not exclusively, from Europe and the United States.

Adult education has always had an implicit connection with employment policy in the very broad sense that it influences the overall skill level of the population. However, it is only relatively recently that explicit links have been developed between the two. Certainly adult education figured prominently in the British plans for rebuilding the country at the end of the First World War, but it was regarded then as a social policy separate from the task of reconstructing the economy and creating full employment. Even between the two World Wars, the potential of adult education for combating the problems of massive unemployment was left largely unexplored throughout the countries affected by the depression.

After the Second World War came massive growth in the world economy, full employment, and an explosion in postcompulsory education. This was perhaps most evident in the formal institutions of tertiary education, notably universities, catering for younger students coming straight from secondary school. But economic growth had two major consequences for adult education. First, it meant that resources were available for substantial expansion, even if in relative terms adult education benefited less than other sectors. Second, the surge of economic activity came up against bottlenecks caused by skill shortages, and this drew attention to the need for new education and training policies. The 1950s and 1960s thus witnessed the expansive phase of adult education. Its links with employment policy were evident, in different ways, in the active manpower policy pursued by Sweden; in the 1969 German Labour Promotion Act; and in the establishment of the Industrial Training Boards in the United Kingdom in 1964; all were intended to develop adult learning opportunities in order to smooth the path of sustained economic growth.

The 1970s and, more acutely, the 1980s, have seen the same links interpreted in a very different and essentially defensive fashion. Researchers and policy makers had already been interested in educational policies which encouraged alternation between work and education in a recurrent pattern (OECD/CERI 1973). A version of this pattern was now forced on many people by the massive surge in unemployment, the disappearance of the demand for many traditional skills, and the imposition of periods of involuntary leisure. Budgets for adult education as a consumption good dried up, to be replaced in part by expenditure on support for the unemployed, sometimes including an educational component. Adult education came to be seen as a buffer against unemployment as much as an instrument of positive employment policy (Stonier 1979).

1. Purposes

The goals of adult education seen in relation to employment policy are broadly threefold:

(a) To help supply the overall skills needed to sustain economic growth. The extent to which this is upheld as an objective depends on how clearly adult education is distinguished from vocational training, but in any case general skills are needed which are unrelated to a particular industry. At

a basic level, for example, many adults lack literacy and numeracy; they may be motivated more by a desire to participate socially than by the demands of a specific job, but a wider spread of these skills will help the functioning of the labour market and their own employment prospects (ACACE 1979).

(b) To counteract inequities in employment. This may take the form of helping groups with low economic participation rates to enter the labour market, or of countering the process of segmentation which locks workers into low-paying unskilled jobs and cumulates inequalities (Edwards et al. 1973). Immigrant workers are one such target group, helped in Sweden by the establishment of a right to 240 hours of language training (see *Second Language Programs for Adult Migrants*). Educational assistance to rural workers, especially in less developed countries, aims to redress the inequality between town and country, as well as to help balanced economic development (Coombs and Ahmed 1974). Nurturing confidence in women to enable them to enter the labour market even in male-dominated occupations is another such objective.

(c) Thirdly, adult education is a means whereby individuals can directly or indirectly further their own career development. In many instances this takes place informally, through seminars and conferences which may last only one day. In all countries, day and evening classes exist which provide opportunities for adults to acquire the skills and qualifications needed to progress occupationally.

Specific mention should be made of two broad groups within the general adult population.

(a) Young adults seeking an entry into the labour market. For these, adult education (as distinct both from initial education and from specifically designated vocational training) varies enormously in the closeness of its association with employment. Local Initiative Programs (LIPs) in Canada and the Youth Opportunity Schemes (YOPs) in the United Kingdom are examples of proliferating attempts to mix education with work experience.

(b) Adults approaching retirement, that is, preparing to leave the labour market. Demographic trends have made the elderly an increasingly significant group, and educational provision for those in retirement is growing (e.g., *Université de Troisième Age* in France). By definition the retired are marginal to a discussion of employment policy, but national policies of promoting earlier retirement, mainly as a way of reducing overall unemployment, clearly have major implications for adult education. Moreover, pre-retirement courses are becoming an integral part of company personnel practice.

2. Providers

All countries rely on a combination of providers, but vary in the extent to which they draw on different sources (Lowe 1975).

2.1 The Formal Education System

Many institutions within the formal education system put on courses for adults which have a more or less close connection with employment. Universities and other institutions of higher education tend to concentrate on professional categories such as teachers or medical personnel. The demand for certification and recertification has prompted a substantial growth in this area, notably in the United States—in some states, for example, doctors are required by law to undertake regular periods of refresher training. At other levels, technical colleges and community colleges obviously play a large role in supplying courses which meet employment needs. Typical of this is the Technical and Further Education (TAFE) sector in Australia. France and the Federal Republic of Germany are prominent examples of countries which rely heavily on the institutions of the formal education system.

2.2 Other Public Institutions

Establishments exist which provide education similar to that of the formal education system but which are separately administered. Most obviously, ministries of labour or employment run training centres as part of their industrial policy. In other instances the institutions are not directly under one ministry, or they function semi-independently of the state.

2.3 "In-house" Courses

Companies and public administrators put on many courses themselves for their employees. Naturally these tend to be tightly related to their own specific needs and therefore stand at one end of the education–training spectrum, but should not be ignored as a source of skills relevant to employment policy. Countries with a trade of strongly developed internal labour markets, such as Japan, are prominent in this respect.

2.4 Private Institutions

Partly as a consequence of the public sector's indifference to the needs of adults, there are many private establishments at various levels. Some are straight commercial operations, such as the agencies which proliferated in France following the 1971 law on educational leave. Others are non-profit-making organizations, particularly strongly represented in the United States.

2.5 Trade Unions

Trade Unions are an important source of adult education related to employment issues, and provide training for their representatives at all levels. In some countries this is carried out in public institutions (e.g., United States); in others (e.g., Federal Republic of Germany, Norway) the unions run an independent system.

3. Organization and Finance

As indicated above, there is a massive variety of provision and the organization and finance are correspondingly complex. Different ministries (education, labour, industry, health) are involved and different levels of government (national, regional, local). Perhaps the most that can be said is that there is everywhere a problem of coordinating the provision, whilst at the same time permitting diversity. In the United Kingdom, for example, education is for the most part the responsibility of local government whilst employment and workforce policies are operated centrally.

In many countries, formal rights to educational leave have been established, linked in varying degrees to employment considerations (von Moltke and Schneevoight 1979, OECD/CERI 1978). In France, a legal right to such leave has existed since 1971, but financial assistance for it is conditional upon approval by a joint labour/management committee of the enterprise. Laws also exist in several of the states in the Federal Republic of Germany, usually to the benefit of public employees. Australia provides an example of a different right: workers accumulate entitlement to long service leave (3 months after 10 years), which can be used for educational purposes at the individual's own discretion. In Italy, trade unions have been responsible for negotiating leave of 150 or more hours for workers in certain industries. The distribution of this leave is concentrated on groups lacking in basic educational qualifications. Several companies in the United States provide financial assistance for their employees to pay their way through college under so-called "tuition aid refund" schemes.

The link with employment policy is central to the consideration of the financing of adult education (Peston 1979). The costs are always difficult to quantify exactly, but cannot be properly estimated unless they are set against alternative uses of the resources (see *Financing Adult Education*; *Financing Vocational and Industrial Education*; *Financing Lifelong Education*). At times of high unemployment, the costs of adult education are low in that there is little output forgone. Financing people to participate in education may seem in any case to be a more positive use of resources than paying them the same amounts as unemployment benefit. The actual mechanisms for financing cover a combination of private fees and public subsidy. They may be oriented to the individual, the educational institution, the company, the industry, or the region. Specific forms which deserve mention are the payroll tax used in France and Sweden to finance their educational leave schemes, and the levy-grant system previously used in the United Kingdom to encourage industrial training by raising a levy from firms and paying it back in the form of assistance for training.

4. Some Topical Issues

Of many that exist, three crucial issues may be singled out:

(a) The implications of new patterns of education, work, and leisure—even should the world regain its economic momentum, it is unlikely that the old model of education–work–retirement will dominate to the same extent. Not only can a much more varied pattern of alternation between education and work be expected, but also greater leisure time (more or less voluntary) and far less rigid retirement ages can be expected. The relationship between the organization and financing of education, work, and leisure will therefore become far more complex.

(b) The content of adult education in its relation to employment—the analysis of learning needs and the extent to which they are determined by employees, companies, or public bodies will pose new problems. In particular, the impact of technological developments on skills in manufacturing and service industries is not a simple technical issue; the scope and character of jobs, and the extent to which they make use of human resources, are matters of social as well as economic choice, and this will be reflected in the content of education.

(c) Education and democracy—shifts in authority patterns at home and in the workplace will present new challenges. Moves towards greater economic and industrial democracy, and towards greater equality between the sexes have major learning implications; for the groups that currently hold power; for those that aspire to a greater share; and for those involved in teaching. Increased attention to the quality of paid and domestic labour can generate radically different learning requirements.

See also: Paid Educational Leave for Adults; Employment and Education

Bibliography

Advisory Council for Adult and Continuing Education (ACACE) 1979 *A Strategy for the Basic Education of Adults*. A report commissioned by the Secretary of State for Education and Science. ACACE, Leicester
Coombs P H, Ahmed M 1974 *Attacking Rural Poverty: How Non-formal Education Can Help*. Johns Hopkins Press, Baltimore, Maryland
Edwards R, Reich M, Gordon C 1973 *Labor Market Segmentation*. Conf. Harvard University, 1973. Heath, Lexington, Massachusetts
Lowe J 1975 *The Education of Adults: A World Perspective*. UNESCO, Paris
Organisation for Economic Co-operation and Development/Centre for Educational Research and Innovation (OECD/CERI) 1973 *Recurrent Education: A Strategy for Lifelong Learning*. OECD, Paris
Organisation for Economic Co-operation and Development/Centre for Educational Research and Innovation (OECD/CERI) 1976 *Developments in Educational Leave of Absence*. OECD, Paris
Organisation for Economic Co-operation and Development/Centre for Educational Research and Innovation (OECD/CERI) 1978 *Alternation Between Work and Education*. OECD, Paris
Peston M 1979 Recurrent education: Tackling the financial implications. In: Schuller T, Megarry J (eds.) 1979 *Recurrent Education and Lifelong Learning*. Kogan Page, London
Stonier T 1979 The third industrial revolution. *Effects of Modern Technology on Workers*. International Metalworkers Federation, Geneva
von Moltke K, Schneevoight J 1979 *Educational Leave of Absence*. Jossey-Bass, San Francisco, California

T. Schuller

Encounter Groups and T-Groups

In modern times, the psychological treatment of people in groups goes back to J. L. Moreno, a Viennese psychiatrist, who as early as 1910 began using spontaneous theater or dramatic re-enactments of personal and interpersonal conflicts, which he called psychodrama and sociodrama. However, the greatest interest in small-group therapy has stemmed from sensitivity training based originally on the Gestalt psychology of Lewin, who had discovered that people's attitudes and feelings might be changed through the process of group discussion. Shortly after the Second World War, what came to be called *T* (for training) groups of the National Training Laboratories in the United States, as well as similar experiences at the Tavistock Institute in the United Kingdom, first emphasized the important social dynamics developing from within the group. At the National Training Laboratories more emphasis came to be placed on what was happening to the individual, a process to which the term encounter was applied.

Encounter groups, for which the Esalen Institute in California is noted, reached their height in the 1960s and early 1970s. In the encounter approach, a group of people, usually previously more or less unknown to one another, meet over a period of weeks, or sometimes over a weekend. There are usually from 8 to 15 members, although sometimes the number can go as high as 20 or more. The idea of the encounter is to help the members become sensitive to the feelings of others, to search behind the facade that most people show to the world, and to find the true feelings and "hang-ups" behind the facade. It is then the goal to help the members realize how they appear to the world and to correct inappropriate ways of adaptation.

Techniques for conducting encounter groups vary greatly, with some of the underlying philosophy based on traditions from the Middle East and East Asia, such as from Japan, China, and India. In addition to verbal confrontation, both positive and negative, the process often emphasizes physical communication, as in touching, hugging, massaging, and even in taking turns being lifted and passed from hand to hand among other group members in order to develop trust in each other. Reliance is placed on many of the humanistic ideas of Carl Rogers and others, with the emphasis on the "here and now" as opposed to the psychoanalytic stress on one's past experiences. Group members are also encouraged to express their emotions instead of bottling them up, and they are encouraged to value all forms of communication.

The group leader serves as a guide rather than as a director. Since participants have usually come from relatively well-educated middle-class, verbal families, much of the impetus for the direction the group takes may come from members rather than the leader. Often the experience sought is one of personal growth and not as therapy for particular psychological problems. For this reason, the technique has sometimes been considered to be on the boundary between psychotherapy and another form of learning experience.

Members are frequently enthusiastic about the results of their encounters. However, a minority express very negative feelings and report psychological ill effects from the confrontations. Researchers have also found damage occurring from the overwhelming stress engendered, and even suicides have been reported as a result of the experience. Experts in the field consider it vital that the leader be knowledgeable and able to keep the interpersonal encounters within reasonable bounds. Sometimes it is also necessary to screen prospective participants in order to eliminate highly disturbed and overly hostile individuals.

Bibliography

Appley D G, Winder A E 1973 *T-Groups and Therapy Groups in a Changing Society*. Jossey-Bass, San Francisco, California

Harper R A 1975 *The New Psychotherapies*. Prentice-Hall, Englewood Cliffs, New Jersey

Marks I M, Bergin A E, Lang P J, Matarazzo H D, Patterson G R, Strup H H (eds.) 1972 *Psychotherapy and Behavior Change*. Aldine, Chicago, Illinois

Rogers C R 1970 *Carl Rogers on Encounter Groups*. Harper and Row, New York

S. M. Thomas

Energy Education

Energy education denotes the treatment of the topic of energy within the framework of the school programme. Throughout the present century energy has been a topic within the school curriculum in most countries. However, it is a concept of some difficulty for young people to grasp because it is not tangible and only reveals itself through transformation from one form to another. The difficulties in teaching about energy have only been given the attention they deserve in relatively recent years and it is only in those recent years that much thought has been given to the wider aspects of energy education now that shortages of energy sources have become apparent. This article considers some of the trends at the present time.

1. Energy Education in the Past

At one time energy education was the preserve of the physicists. They gave formal definitions of energy either in terms of capacity to do work or by relating it directly to work as force times distance. This in turn led to a mathematical treatment and a whole series of formulae, such as mgh or $\frac{1}{2}mv^2$, always learnt by heart by students. There was often confusion in the student's mind about "work done by" and "work done on", and the confusion was made even worse when what was learnt in mechanics was somehow different from that learnt in heat: was not energy in one case measured in calories, whilst in the other in quite different units, ergs or joules? These concepts were further complicated in the student's mind because the energy encountered in chemistry seemed to differ somehow from that met in physics.

2. The Beginning of the Change

Since the late 1950s there have been fundamental changes in science education, started by the great curriculum reforms at this time in the United States. There is now a much greater emphasis in teaching on school children gaining experience for themselves, on doing experiments, on "being a scientist for the day": an emphasis on the process of science. This has had its effect on energy education. First came a realization that it is through energy transformation— as energy is transferred from one form to another—

that the difficult concept of energy reveals itself. Then apparatus for the precise measurement of the mechanical equivalent of heat gave way to "energy conversion kits" by means of which school children themselves could turn energy from one form to another: for example, energy from a battery could drive a motor, which in turn could drive a flywheel, whereupon at the throw of a switch the energy stored in the flywheel could drive a motor in reverse as a generator, which in turn lit lamps. Yet a further change, relatively trivial in the academic world, but profound in the educational world, was the almost universal move to SI (*Système Internationale*) units: this certainly made energy teaching easier.

3. Science for All

Another profound change has been that science education in recent years has ceased to be the preserve of the academic few, but has become part of the education of all young people and, throughout the world) energy has become a topic within primary education. Again the approach is experimental as youngsters turn energy from one form to another, and UNESCO literature abounds with suggestions for simple experiments using simple apparatus at this level.

4. Useful Energy

The study of energy transformations at the secondary level leads to the idea of conservation of energy. If energy is always conserved, if it is always turned from one form to another and never lost, what is all this fuss about shortage of energy? Inevitably therefore, academic students at the secondary and tertiary levels must be introduced to basic ideas of thermodynamics and in particular to some appreciation of the Second Law of Thermodynamics, and all students need to have a feel for the fact that some forms of energy are more useful than others; some are "high grade" energy forms, some "low grade".

5. Science and Society

There is a further trend which is beginning to affect energy education. At one time science education was primarily concerned with "science for the enquiring mind" or perhaps "pure science" would be the better description. It was felt that this was fundamental, and applied science and technology could safely be left until a later step up the educational ladder. There is now much greater awareness throughout the world that "science for action" should also be a component of science education—and this inevitably has its influence on energy education. At one time students learned a formal definition of thermal conductivity and then how to measure it for good and bad con-

ductors; now they learn something about heat insulation in the home as well, and that is science for action.

However, there is now a realization that there should be another component to science education which might be called "science for citizens". School courses since the early 1950s have included reference to radioactivity, to the properties of alpha, beta, and gamma radiation, to the concept of half-life, but they have tended not to include nuclear power. But with decisions to be made in most countries about nuclear policy, it would seem essential to build up an educated population with some understanding of nuclear energy. This would go into the category of science for citizens.

Recent criteria established at UNESCO and other conferences concerned with science and technology education for development have all stressed the need to make education relevant to the needs of society. This must have profound effects on energy education. There is an increasing interest in science and society courses at all levels, and an awareness of the importance of energy in agriculture, in the production of minerals, and in industry is likely to pervade education in the 1980s. The quality of life and the quality of the environment will both depend in the future on energy; whether wise decisions are made about energy and whether limited resources are used in a sensible way will depend greatly on the way young people are educated for that future—and hence the importance of energy education.

Bibliography

Energy programs in the school: Awareness and involvement 1980 *Intercom* 98: 14–15

Kohl J 1981 Utilization of existing energy teaching materials. *J. Environ. Educ.* 12(3): 29–35

Krugger K C 1977 Some guidelines for energy programs. *Today's Educ.* 66(3): 60–62

Schlichting H J 1979 Energy and energy waste: A topic for science education, *Eur. J. Sci. Educ.* 1(2): 157–68

Social Studies Review 1980 19(2)

J. Lewis

English as a Foreign or Second Language for Adults

Two broad categories of adult students can be distinguished in terms of the settings within which English is taught.

Students of English as a foreign language (EFL) usually learn English in a country where the language has no special status, where the teacher or course materials are likely to be the only sources of English input, and where the students expect to use their newly acquired skills during travel abroad, to entertain English-speaking friends or business associates at home, or in reading material for academic or business purposes or cultural enrichment.

Students of English as a second language (ESL) learn English either in an English-speaking country or in countries such as India, Nigeria, Hong Kong, and Singapore, where English, though the mother tongue of few of the population, is widely used in education and public life. In these situations, input from the teacher or course materials is likely to be supplemented by the students' interactions with the wider community and the students mostly expect to use their English within that same community for a broad range of purposes such as further education, employment, or social, political, and cultural activities.

An important subcategory of the ESL group are those students whose primary language is a regional or social dialect of English which provides them with an effective means of communicating with a surrounding, but often small, group of speakers. These dialects are distinct in terms of the grammar, vocabulary, intonation, and pronunciation used. When faced with the need to widen their range of communication, such students usually elect to learn one of the standard varieties of English, for example, British, American, Canadian, Australian, West Indian, Indian, or West African. These various standard dialects, which share basically the same grammar and vocabulary, look very similar when written down and, even when spoken with their appropriate accents, are readily understood by all other speakers of standard English.

1. English Language Needs of Adult EFL/ESL Students

The amount of English which adult students need varies greatly from group to group and from individual to individual. At one end of the scale there are learners of English who can identify precisely the narrow range of functions which they will need to perform in and through English. The English they will require consists of a finite number of simple, consistently used, and predictably interpreted phrases to communicate situation-specific questions, answers, and commands. Deviation from the approved language forms is neither expected nor approved of. The English used by air-traffic controllers and the new English in preparation in 1982 for use by the merchant marine (SEASPEAK) (Glover et al. 1983) fall into this category.

At the other end of the scale, consider how much English, for example, non-English-speaking psychiatrists need to learn in order to requalify in an English-speaking country and practice their profession with English-using patients. Not only do they require a high degree of literacy to read the required texts and write the necessary examinations, reports, and case studies, they also need a well-developed interpretative sense of how different groups or individuals who are fluent in English choose to express human responses such as anger, outrage, depression, dissatisfaction, resignation, optimism, and pleasure. They also need an ability to interact orally with such patients in a highly flexible manner.

Most students of English have needs that fall somewhere between these two extremes. Learners who wish to make acceptable choices from a menu in English or to ask and, more importantly, follow directions on how to get from place A to place B obviously differ in their needs from students who wish to gain access to electronics information printed in English-medium journals and magazines. Recent immigrants or refugees, anxious to know how to go about obtaining and keeping employment have a different focus from students who want to study the literary preoccupations of a particular English-speaking community.

2. Programs

Programs for adults learning English generally fall into four major categories:

(a) *General purpose programs.* These programs contain a heterogeneous group of students who require a broad range of English language skills to allow them to function in an ESL setting. These programs are often held in local secondary schools and community colleges or are sponsored by church groups and community centers. Many offer a first opportunity for housebound immigrant women with young children or senior citizens to venture out into the wider community. The content of the programs is a combination of survival/orientation information and the basic English language skills which enable students to begin to interact with their new environment.

(b) *Pre-academic programs.* These programs are designed to prepare students for further study. These may be intensive English courses for foreign or immigrant students in English-speaking countries before such students enter regular postsecondary education or they may be adult basic education programs, held in schools, community centers, or even apartment buildings, in which students who have few, if any, literacy skills in their mother tongue seek both oral and written skills in English. Starting in the late 1970s, men and women emigrating from cultures with a largely oral tradition (such as the Hmong from Cambodia) or women from backgrounds where more importance has been accorded to the development of domestic and artistic skills rather than literacy, have provided ESL teachers with an interesting challenge in a field where, traditionally, the majority of students have been literate in their first language prior to embarking on second language studies.

(c) *Academic programs.* These programs are designed as support to postsecondary students as they concurrently pursue a course of study in an academic institution. Usually these programs aim to produce highly competent bilinguals who can function broadly in their second language and pursue further study or take up employment in that language. These programs may also combine several elements (language upgrading, cultural information, and teaching methods) in an overall course to train foreign nationals as teachers of English. The People's Republic of China, for example, contains many such programs at the moment, using experts mainly from the United States and the United Kingdom as teacher trainers. Universities or other institutions of advanced learning are the most common sponsors of these programs.

(d) *Specific purpose programs.* These programs, the most recent of the four, exist in both EFL and ESL settings—in oil fields in the Middle East, in industrial and technical centers in Europe and Japan, in hospitals, factories, and vocational training sites in the United Kingdom, Australia, the United States, and Canada to cite just a few examples. Teachers of English as a second or foreign language whose academic background may be in English literature or Hispanic studies are finding themselves in positions which require them to be experts in physics, computer engineering, medicine, urban planning. The companies that require their employees to use English in the course of their work usually sponsor such programs. However, increasingly, in organized labor settings, particularly where the addition of English language skills leads to promotion, labor movements are playing a larger part in the provision of these learning opportunities and, in some cases, English classes are seen as a negotiable benefit.

3. Techniques and Materials

The structures and vocabulary of English (such as the present continuous tense, words to describe time), the functions which are expressed (such as requesting information, persuading), and the topics and settings involved (such as making a dental appointment by telephone, writing a scientific report) all may be the starting point for the design of an EFL/ESL program. Since the 1940s, a linguistically graded curriculum, moving from simple to more complex forms and using a largely teacher-directed approach, has been, and in many places still remains, the most common method of organizing and presenting language input. Recently, functionally based and topic/setting-based curricula, which allow for the more immediate tailoring of courses to different student goals, have increased in popularity. Some caution is called for, however, in designing courses which are rigidly tied to the kind of terminal linguistic behavior that teachers or students identify as the target; it is often difficult to determine precisely what uses learners will find for their new language on com-

pletion of a course and, even if this can be done, the means to those ends may necessitate the practicing of language other than that identified as finally appropriate. Needs analysis then, is seen as a useful tool for motivating students and for preventing valuable class time being wasted on irrelevant material. The results obtained from such analyses require careful processing, however, before a program is finally drawn up.

As in many other fields of adult education, there is a move towards the establishment of a climate in the classroom that encourages student participation in the selection of goals, techniques, and materials, welcomes student feedback, and recognizes the equal status of students and teacher. Increased attention is being paid to group dynamics both within and outside the class setting, to the creation of a relaxed and nonthreatening teaching/learning atmosphere, to the contribution of subconscious learning, to the adult capacity to take an active role in the acquisition of new skills and knowledge, and to the need to consider learning styles in selecting teaching methods.

A heavy reliance on mimicry and memorization is now being supplemented with, and sometimes even replaced by, techniques which encourage learners to experiment in using what they know of their new language in a variety of real and simulated settings, using role-play, individual and group tasks, and problem-solving activities. Errors, once considered the bane of an EFL/ESL teacher's life and required to be nipped in the bud as soon as they appeared, are now viewed as a necessary and highly systematic part of the learning process, as students develop the inner criteria they need to evaluate their language usage against that of native and nonnative speakers/writers of English.

4. Current Concerns

4.1 The Complexity of English

Whereas in the past the basic unit of teaching and course design has largely been the sentence, a major focus for research in the 1980s is the analysis of how the English language operates in sentence or utterance sequences. What regular patterns can be identified as characterizing spoken and written interactions between a wide range of users who wish to use the language for a variety of purposes, across an almost infinite number of topics and settings? And what are the separate contributions of speakers and writers on the one hand, and hearers and readers on the other, to the complex business of negotiating meaning within these interactions? Native speakers are normally unaware of these strategies of negotiation, unless communication breaks down, and even then they may be left with no more than a vague uneasiness that the material is beyond their comprehension, or that the sender of the message is being unnecessarily obtuse. Since a breakdown in communication, however, is much more common between native and nonnative speakers or between nonnative speakers using English together, a careful specification of what is likely to cause difficulties and the strategies which can be used to overcome them is seen as a priority.

4.2 Program Evaluation

Another concern, given the range of program types presently in existence, is the need for systematic program evaluation which takes a close look at the many variables in terms of setting, teachers, students, methods, and materials and attempts to tease out from within that matrix the crucial elements which will ensure learner success.

In a further effort at informing the educational community, and indeed the public at large, individuals and groups within the profession are beginning to articulate the conditions necessary for quality programming, such as sufficiently trained staff, adequate funds for materials and equipment, provision for program development, and supervision.

4.3 English or Englishes?

In English as a foreign language, particularly where speech is concerned, it is clear that the English language will continue to develop regional varieties designed to serve local communication needs. Therefore, given the geographic spread of English and the variety of uses to which it is being put, the development of spoken Englishes, at least, seems inevitable.

An important implication of this is that the English spoken by native speakers of the language from major English-using countries may no longer be the most appropriate variety to teach new users of English in certain settings, at least initially.

4.4 ESL and Democracy

The teaching of English in second language settings is closely linked with issues of social justice and civil rights, such as equal access to education, jobs, and social services. Teachers currently keep a close eye on, and provide input to, legislative developments (and their fiscal implications) for changes which will affect the English language training opportunities for immigrant or minority adults, as well as their children.

4.5 Information Sharing

EFL/ESL programs are located throughout the world, often in places remote from major educational centers. The task of harnessing the activity generated within the profession and disseminating what results is monumental.

Organizations exist to promote communication both within and between nations: TESOL (Teachers of English to Speakers of Other Languages, based in the United States) and IATEFL (International As-

sociation of Teachers of English as a Foreign Language, based in the United Kingdom). Regional, national, and international conventions are held regularly, the largest of these being the annual TESOL Convention which attracts 3,000–5,000 people to each meeting.

Information centers (such as the Centre for Information on Language Teaching and Research, London; the Regional English Language Center, Singapore; the Center for Applied Linguistics, Washington, DC, and the ERIC service) perform an invaluable function as clearinghouses for data on language and language teaching. Journals, newsletters, and conference proceedings also supply welcome updates to both practitioners and researchers; these include *English Language Teaching Journal*, *TESOL Quarterly, Language Learning, Applied Linguistics, The ESP Journal, English Teaching Forum, TESOL Newsletter, NATESLA News, On TESOL.*
Publishing houses too, contribute many volumes each year to the growing list of texts for classroom use and teacher preparation.

See also: English: Teaching as a Foreign or Second Language; Foreign Language Education

Bibliography

Brown H D 1980 *Principles of Language Learning and Teaching.* Prentice-Hall, Englewood Cliffs, New Jersey
Glover A, Johnson E, Strevens P, Weeks F F 1983 *SEASPEAK Reference Manual.* Pergamon, Oxford
Kelly L G 1969 *Twenty-five Centuries of Language Teaching: An Inquiry into the Science, Art, and Development of Language Teaching Methodology, 500 BC–1969.* Newbury House, Rowley, Massachusetts
Oller J W Jr, Richards J C (eds.) 1973 *Focus on the Learner: Pragmatic Perspectives for the Language Teacher.* Newbury House, Rowley, Massachusetts
Procter P (ed.) 1978 *Longman Dictionary of Contemporary English.* Longman, London
Quirk R, Greenbaum S, Leech G, Svartvik J 1972 *A Grammar of Contemporary English.* Longman, London
Rivers W M, Temperley M S 1978 *A Practical Guide to the Teaching of English as a Second or Foreign Language.* Oxford University Press, New York
Stevick E W 1982 *Teaching and Learning Languages.* Cambridge University Press, Cambridge
Strevens P 1977 *New Orientations in the Teaching of English.* Oxford University Press, Oxford
Widdowson H G 1978 *Teaching Language as Communication.* Oxford University Press, Oxford

J. Handscombe; M. A. Clarke

English: Teaching as a Foreign or Second Language

English as a foreign language (EFL) is concerned with the teaching of English to speakers of other languages (TESOL). Sometimes the reference is to English as a second language (ESL), and this article attempts first to clarify the various acronyms of the field and their reference. The article continues with a discussion of the various domains of TESOL and closes with a brief look at the major trends in the field.

1. EFL, ESL, and TESOL

The original term for teaching English to those who did not know it and for the area of expertise associated with it, was English as a foreign language, known for short as EFL. On the whole, this continues to be the British usage in referring to overseas teaching of English. In the United States, the term ESL, English as a second language, became increasingly used, and today there are no less than three definitions of the term. American publishers increasingly avoided the term EFL in favor of ESL as they considered the term "foreign" to be pejorative and so to be avoided in the selling of textbooks. This usage is simply synonymous with EFL and begs the question of any difference between the two. The second usage of ESL refers to the learning of English in an English-speaking environment, such as by foreign students in England or in the United States. Finally, the third usage of ESL defines a second language as the nonhome but official language of a nation which must be learned by its citizens for full social, economic, and political participation in the life of that nation. Australian Aborigines, United States Chicanos, and British Gaelic speakers as well as immigrants all learn English as a second language according to this definition. All three usages are common, but the third is to be preferred because it is the relationship between the super- and sub-ordinate groups within a nation which gives second language learning its significant characteristics and which distinguishes it from learning a foreign language where attitudes are fairly neutral.

Exactly in order to avoid the dichotomy, EFL and ESL became united in TESOL, teaching English to speakers of other languages, which stands both for the field and for the international professional organization, which was founded in 1966. Unless a technical differentiation is intended, TESOL is the better cover term for the field.

2. The Domains of TESOL

The teaching of English to speakers of other languages, as a professional field, is a relative newcomer to language teaching compared to the teaching of Greek and Latin. Similar to those languages, the spread of English has also reflected social conditions such as emigration, colonialism, military power, and trade as well as advanced scientific knowledge, and in the case of English, advanced technology. The result necessarily has been a many-faceted picture of English teaching around the world.

Basically the field can be subdivided into four areas: EFL, ESL, bilingual education, and ESOD (English to speakers of other dialects) (Robinett 1972).

2.1 EFL (English as a Foreign Language)

The study of English began primarily as learning English as a cultural acquisition which would enable the learner to read the classics like Shakespeare and Milton in the original. The purpose, objectives, and methods of this type of English study are very similar to the study of French, German, and Italian as foreign languages.

Today, however, straight EFL overlaps with, and is superseded by, English as an LWC (language of wider communication), as the major lingua franca of the world. Until the First World War, French had been the major language of wider communication within Europe, but after the Second World War this role has been taken over worldwide by English. This fact is reflected in the considerable investment in English teaching—in curriculum, textbooks, and teacher training—held by Third World countries where English is not seen primarily as a cultural acquisition nor as a colonial legacy but practically as an instrumental means of international communication in an electronic world. It is also reflected in the popularity of the adult English classes sponsored by the British Council and the United States Binational Centers around the world. The Regional English Language Centre (RELC) in Singapore is another case in point.

As far as language attitudes are concerned, the study of EFL is the most neutral of the field. There are no external social, religious, or political pressures which enforce the study of English but rather it is a voluntary choice for instrumental or integrative purposes.

2.2 ESL (English as a Second Language)

In many parts of the world the study of English takes place because English is an official (or critically important public) language of that nation. This situation is almost always the result of earlier annexation or colonization. Actually, the situations vary widely from countries which are commonly thought of as monolingually English, such as Australia and the United States, to countries which are notedly multilingual such as Nigeria and India.

The purposes and motivations for maintaining English as the official language vary as the situation's social, economic, religious, and political factors vary. In Nigeria, for example, it has served both to neutralize ethnic group interests as well as to promote Pan-Africanism, and so a former colonial language remains tolerated as the official language among several national languages. In India, English remains preferred by many as the national language to the alternative of Hindi with its strong associations to a specific religious sect. In Singapore, English is a practical means of a multiethnic population for carrying on trade with the West. In the United States, English became unofficially (there exists no federal legislation on the matter) the official language for primarily practical concerns, until monolingualism became the idealized norm, although 16.3 percent of the population report a non-English mother tongue (Waggoner 1981). The United States is one of the few countries outside Britain in which nationalism has been an issue in English teaching.

The situations vary widely, and so do the attitudes toward the study of English that accompany them. All ESL situations share, by definition, an imposition of English on the learner and often this is perceived as a derogatory comment on the home culture with concomitant social strife. Spanish-speaking Puerto Rico is a good example of such tension. On the other hand, predominantly Spanish-speaking Gibraltar gladly welcomes English. The reasons for the various attitudes towards and the relative efficiency of learning ESL are ultimately to be found in the social settings (Saville-Troike 1976).

2.3 Bilingual Education

The domain of bilingual education within the field of TESOL refers to programs where equal emphasis is placed on learning the native language as well as English. Typically, the literature and discussions of bilingual education do not include elitist schooling which adds a component of EFL to the curriculum of private schools, but rather tend to include the concerns of minority-group children in public schooling where English is taught as a second language. An exception are the Canadian immersion programs where Anglophone children study in French and English, but another defining characteristic of bilingual education holds: the children study subject matter, such as history, through the medium of French, the target language (see *Immersion Education*).

Considerable conflict exists over the goals of bilingual education. In the United States, for example, the programs officially are denoted as transitional bilingual education and seen as a more efficient way of teaching the national language where the tacit goals are language shift through bilingualism and assimilation into mainstream culture. (Alaska is an exception.) Many Chicanos, Indians, and Puerto Ricans resent these goals and prefer to maintain their cultural identity of which language is an integral part. Their social goal is cultural pluralism with structural incorporation, that is, access to goods and services and to social institutions like education and justice. The goals of bilingual education, as they see it, are maintenance bilingual education programs, where the programs teach not only the native language but also the native culture. Bilingual programs in which the children speak the national language and which are voluntary tend to avoid such strife.

There is very little systematic knowledge of techniques and procedures for teaching children a second language at the elementary level which is coherently anchored in a theory of language acquisition. The elaboration of such a body of knowledge is an important priority for the future development of bilingual education (Paulston 1980) (see *Bilingual Education*).

2.4 English to Speakers of Other Dialects

The last domain of TESOL refers to ESOD (English to speakers of other dialects) or more commonly known as SESD (standard English as a second dialect). Standard English as a second dialect deals with teaching English to those whose home language is a distinct English dialect which differs markedly from standard English, such as the Maoris in New Zealand, the Native Americans in Alaska and Canada, Afro-Americans in the United States, creole speakers in the Caribbean, and so on. Even though the social settings differ widely, the educational problems remain markedly similar.

Since the early 1970s, Caribbean Creoles and black English have been the focus of intense scholarly interest and work which are reflected in the teaching of Standard English (Alleyne 1980). There were originally attempts to adopt foreign language teaching techniques, but such methods have not turned out very well, and most scholars believe with Allen that "A Second Dialect is not a Foreign Language" (1969). Some major issues have been: (a) applying linguistic descriptions to studies of interference in reading and writing and consequent implications for teaching; (b) teaching the legitimacy of the dialects as a linguistic system in its own right; (c) the identification of culture-specific speech acts and the legitimacy of the culture itself; (d) language attitudes; and (e) Labov's *The Study of Non-standard English* (1968).

Altogether, the domains of TESOL range over a wide variety of situations and needs. The particular situation of the learner needs always to be taken into account because the social, political, cultural, and economic factors tend to be of far more significance in influencing educational results than any language teaching methods per se.

3. Recent Trends

Foreign language teaching turns primarily to psychology for theory, models, and explanatory frameworks. With the recent concentration on student learning rather than on teaching, cognitive psychology has succeeded behavioral psychology as a more viable approach. Neurolinguistics is an area of study which has recently received much attention, but at this point it is premature to make any direct application to language teaching. In psycholinguistics, the amount of so-called second language acquisition research attests to the increasing emphasis and importance of empirical and quantificational research in language teaching.

In general, language teaching remains eclectic in its methods (Paulston and Bruder 1976, Rivers and Temperley 1978, Robinett 1978). The audiolingual method has been discredited but no one method has taken its place. Instead there is a plethora of methods among which may be mentioned community counseling–learning, notional–functional syllabi, rapid acquisition, the silent way, suggestopedia, and total physical response (see *Foreign Language Education*). These methods vary widely, and each has its supporters as well as detractors. Actually, as long as teachers and students have confidence that they are in fact learning, and all are happy in the process, methods probably do not make too much difference. Probably the most widespread method in TESOL in spite of all the scholarly criticism remains the grammar-translation approach, but the social incentives are so strong that students learn in spite of the methods.

By far the most important development in TESOL has been the emphasis on a communicative approach in language teaching (Coste 1976, Roulet 1972, Widdowson 1978). The one thing that everyone is certain about is the necessity to use language for communicative purposes in the classroom. Consequently, the concern for teaching linguistic competence has widened to include communicative competence, the socially appropriate use of language, and the methods reflect this shift from form to function.

One more development in TESOL deserves mention, namely the publication of *A Grammar of Contemporary English* (Quirk et al. 1972) and its shorter version *A Concise Grammar of Contemporary English* by Quirk and Greenbaum (1973). As reference grammars, they are not intended for EFL/ESL students, but they nevertheless provide a wealth of information for the English textbook writer, teacher, and serious student alike.

See also: Linguistics, Educational; Bilingual Education; Foreign Language Education; English as a Foreign or Second Language for Adults

Bibliography

Allen V F 1969 A second dialect is not a foreign language. In: Alatis J (ed.) 1969 *Linguistics and the Teaching of Standard English to Speakers of Other Languages or Dialects.* Georgetown University Press, Washington, DC

Alleyne M 1980 *Comparative Afro-American: An Historical-Comparative Study of English-Based Afro-American Dialects of the New World.* Karoma, Ann Arbor, Michigan

Coste D 1976 *Un Niveau seuil: Systèmes d'apprentissage des langues vivantes par les adultes.* Council of Europe, Strasbourg

Labov W 1968 *The Study of the Non-standard English of Negro and Puerto Rican Speakers in New York City.* ERIC, Center for Applied Linguistics, Washington, DC

Paulston C B 1980 *Bilingual Education: Theories and Issues.* Newbury House, Rowley, Massachusetts

Paulston C B, Bruder M N 1976 *Teaching English as a Second Language: Techniques and Procedures.* Winthrop, Cambridge, Massachusetts

Quirk R, Greenbaum S 1973 *A Concise Grammar of Contemporary English.* Harcourt Brace Jovanovich, New York

Quirk R, Greenbaum S, Leech G, Svartvik J 1972 *A Grammar of Contemporary English.* Harcourt Brace Jovanovich, New York

Rivers W M, Temperley M S 1978 *A Practical Guide to the Teaching of English as a Second or Foreign Language.* Oxford University Press, Oxford

Robinett B W 1972 The domains of TESOL. *TESOL Q.* 6: 197–207

Robinett B 1978 *Teaching English to Speakers of Other Languages: Substance and Technique.* McGraw-Hill, New York

Roulet E 1972 *Théories grammaticales, descriptions et enseignement des langues.* Nathan, Paris [1975 *Linguistic Theory, Linguistic Description and Language Teaching.* Longman, London]

Saville-Troike M 1976 *Foundations for Teaching English as a Second Language: Theory and Method for Multicultural Education.* Prentice-Hall, Englewood Cliffs, New Jersey

Waggoner D 1981 Statistics on language use. In: Ferguson C F, Heath S B (eds.) 1981 *Language in the USA.* Cambridge University Press, Cambridge, Massachusetts

Widdowson H G 1978 *Teaching Language as Communication.* Oxford University Press, Oxford

C. B. Paulston

Environmental Education for Adults

A basic premise of most environmental education is that problems caused by industrialization and technological development and underdevelopment are pressing and need urgent solutions. If this is correct, then it is critical that adults understand how the environment functions—at a sophisticated level for effective decision making, and at a general level for informed citizen participation in the discussion of issues. This article outlines some outcomes required from environmental education, and refers to nonformal and formal educational activities which need further development if environmental issues are to be dealt with effectively.

Environmental issues have a twofold place in adult education. First, they can present problems which need solutions developed by educated people. Second, they can be used as relevant and immediate examples in the teaching of much basic adult education such as literacy, health, welfare, and competence in civic, political, and community competence.

The demand for solutions can be best met when environmental education produces one or more of the following outcomes:

(a) The integration of environmental concern,

knowledge, and skill into all relevant areas of learning, that is many formal adult education programmes; considered on a worldwide basis this has probably progressed only in relation to health and hygiene to any significant extent.

(b) The development of environmentally literate and participative citizens; this is, possibly, the area in which the main thrust of adult environmental education should be made.

(c) The preparation of experts qualified to deal with specific environmental problems.

(d) The deepening of understanding for environmental matters by a large number of politicians, planners, civic leaders, and teachers at all school levels (Emmelin 1977).

The role of adult education in achieving the last two goals depends largely on the limits set to the term "adult education". The education of experts is normally considered the task of postsecondary institutions. It is, however, increasingly clear that this type of education will have to move into the adult education sector, in order to cope with environmental problems.

The United Nations Environment Programme distinguishes between the concept of "education" and "training" (UNEP 1978). Education serves to establish sensitivity to environmental problems, to raise the level of awareness, and to generate commitment. Training is for the development and mastering of skills, for the solution of practical problems, and for specialized action.

Although there is strong evidence that the media help to establish behaviour patterns and the acquisition of values directly detrimental to sound, environmental development, there are few systematic studies of the role of the media in relation to environmental education. Their effectiveness in environmental education is greatly diminished by their inattention to environmental skills training, their lack of educational goals for entertainment, and their delivery of persuasive content into the hands of the environmental exploiters (Sandman 1974).

They may be more effective in motivating people to become aware of issues than in actual teaching. Surveys of attitudes towards pollution control and specific environmental problems show a reasonable correlation between awareness of a given problem and the news coverage given to that problem. When, however surveys are followed by any form of testing of factual knowledge about a problem, it is evident that the educational role of the media has been rather limited. Their contribution to environmental education has been confined mainly to health and conservation issues.

As educators recognize that participation in concrete action directed towards a defined goal greatly enhances learning, much emphasis in environmental education has been placed on participation in the planning of an urban environment. In a number of major planning controversies, public participation and direct action have evolved from the education of citizens. In less spectacular cases, the educational importance of participation is possibly greater than actual input to the planning process.

The most sustained educational effort is supported by voluntary organizations and citizen groups with a high degree of permanence. Such organizations exist at a national level in many countries and deal with traditional wildlife conservation problems and, more recently, with pollution, environmental quality, and resource depletion.

To date, no systematic study seems to have been made of the educational importance of environmental action and citizen participation. It would seem an urgent priority in developing adult education programmes. A brief summary of such case studies that do exist is found in Holdgate et al. (1982).

Another target group for further environmental education is that of the decision makers. A United Nations review (1978) concludes that there is very little systematic knowledge in relation to the environmental education of decision makers (UNEP 1978). Certain experiments involving university institutes, responsible agencies, and voluntary organizations have been made with formal and informal education for these people, but much more is needed.

Formal adult education dealing with environmental problems is dominated by courses connected with a university or a college. One reason for this may be the pressure on these institutions to provide environmental education, especially when they have available appropriate subject experts. Other factors, such as declining student enrolment, have stimulated them to enter the area. If the argument is accepted that a research base is a prerequisite for sound environmental education, this would strengthen/consolidate the role of universities in environmental education. In several European institutions of higher education, the mixing of undergraduate teaching and adult education is also promoting community ties, which these institutions traditionally have lacked.

In developing nations, environmental education converges significantly with remedial adult education. It is an accepted pedagogic principle that literacy education, in order to be effective, must relate directly to people's daily lives, so the use of environmental education may serve as a vehicle for literacy education goals provided that the relevance of the environmental issues used is apparent to the people. Environmental education for adults has another important role to play in bringing about a cultural identity for many minority groups, and in cultural efforts at the postcolonial stage (UNESCO 1978).

There is a serious lack of organizations interested

in environmental education. Those that do exist in many countries are either too limited by finance or competence or have specialized in marketing vocationally oriented education. Institutions of higher education tend to have a distinct advantage because of their funding procedures.

The responsibility of government agencies to provide environmental education for adults has been largely neglected. Existing adult education organizations very often lack contact with competent environmental authorities. The establishment of liaison between various sectors of environmental protection, both official and voluntary, seems to be an urgent task. A related problem is the lack of leadership training and material development for adult education.

There is very little systematic research in the field of environmental education for adults outside the formal university system. An overview of the development during the period 1975 to 1980 is given by UNESCO (1980).

See also: Environmental Education Programs

Bibliography

Emmelin L 1977 Environmental education programmes for adults. In: UNESCO 1978 *Trends in Environmental Education.* UNESCO, Paris, pp. 177–90
Holdgate M W, Kassas M, White G F (eds.) 1982 *The World Environment 1972–1982: A Report.* Tycooly, Dublin
Sandman P 1974 Mass environmental education: Can the media do the job? In: Swan J A, Stapp W B (eds.) 1974 *Environmental Education: Strategies Toward a More Liveable Future.* Wiley, New York, pp. 207–47
United Nations Environment Programme, Kenya (UNEP) 1978 *Review of the Area Environmental Education and Training.* Report of the Executive Director, UNEP, Nairobi
UNESCO 1978 *Intergovernmental Conference on Environmental Education, Tbilisi, 14–26 October 1977, Final Report.* UNESCO, Paris
UNESCO 1980 *Environmental Education in the Light of the Tbilisi Conference.* Education on the Move No 3. UNESCO, Paris

L. Emmelin

Environmental Education Programs

Environmental education is characterized by its goal of providing education *for* the enhancement or preservation of the human environment. It is not sufficient to teach *about* the environment, or even to teach out of school *in* the environment. When the term became common in the early 1970s there was no consensus on its meaning, and many programmes described as "environmental education" did not attempt to produce appropriate behaviour and attitudes, a focus which is implicit in education *for* the environment. However, since the "Belgrade Charter" was adopted at an International Workshop in

Environmental Education in 1975, there has been an increasing international consensus that a focus on affective aims is necessary for environmental education. The text of the charter is available in *Connect*, a free UNESCO newsletter (1976 Vol. 1 No. 1).

Many approaches to environmental education within schools can meet the criteria in the Belgrade Charter. Some schools provide a special subject which may have a strong science bias, for example the environmental science syllabus of the Joint Matriculation Board in England and Wales, but others in the same country may require a broad interdisciplinary approach. The course in environmental studies of the University of London Schools Examination Department includes work drawn from geology and economics as well as biology, geography, and other disciplines. Other courses are described in Schoenfeld and Disinger (1977).

Some schools approach environmental education by individual teachers providing an environmental emphasis to their own subject—by the choice of example, homework exercise, and field trip. However, with independent activities in different subjects, students may react adversely to having "pollution pushed at us all the time". To avoid alienation by continual preaching in all subjects, some schools have produced carefully coordinated interdisciplinary curricular designed to build and reinforce appropriate value positions for their pupils (Carson 1978 Chap. 12).

The content of environmental education programmes must vary from continent to continent and from country to country. Human well-being is promoted by a large number of factors, ranging from the social aspects of cultural heritage that are embodied in the remains of the built environment of the ancient civilizations, to the supply of energy, and material for the next meal. Curriculum materials produced in one country necessarily respond to locally important questions and are thus even less transferable than curricula in the biological sciences. But despite the lack of common content there is an international sharing of experience, particularly through the information exchange programmes of UNESCO and the United Nations Environment Programme (UNEP). The shared programme descriptions stimulate ideas about approaches that will help in the notoriously difficult area of producing long-term behaviour changes through school programmes.

Unfortunately, much curriculum development consistent with education for the environment has been based on a naive belief that providing knowledge about an environmental issue will produce a "correct" behavioural response. Other teaching schemes have not assumed a direct link between knowledge and attitudes and have concentrated on attitude formation, while sharing the assumption that appropriate action will follow attitude inculcation.

Few of the authors of the environmental attitudes reports Lucas (1980) reviewed seemed aware that studies in social psychology have shown repeatedly that there is no strong link between measured attitudes to diffuse concepts, such as "quality of life", "ecological conservation", and subsequent behaviour. Indeed, studies of members of environmental organizations show that attitudes of concern sufficient to prompt joining the organization do not necessarily produce the personal behaviour the organization exists to promote. Studies of attitude formation and the curriculum of environmental education programmes are reviewed in Lucas (1980).

Although successful inculcation of general environmental attitudes is unlikely to produce the behaviours that will enhance or preserve the environment when issues arise, there is some prospect of success if personal attitudes are produced to narrow environmental issues. But unfortunately school-level environmental educators have insufficient time to produce specific attitudes to all the issues that will arise during their pupils' lives. More success might be obtained if the curriculum produced personal moral attitudes such as "I ought to consider the indirect consequences of my actions", taught effective information retrieval skills, and gave practice in applying this attitude in environmental contexts.

The difficulty of choosing specific targets for environmental education at school is reduced if there is a well-developed informal environmental education system accessible to adults, especially if it impinges upon most of the population. Mass media can be utilized in two ways. Firstly, by presenting planned instructional materials with specific learning goals, and secondly, by the production of entertainment material which also helps people think about relationships between humans and the environment in which they live. The Japan Broadcasting Corporation (NHK), for example, has been active in both modes, producing programs for schools which are repeated to encourage parents to watch with their children in an attempt to promote discussion within the family; and transmitting a regular entertainment program "Nature Album" which emphasizes the beauty, grandeur, and wonder of the Japanese environment (Ohno 1981).

Education for the environment cannot succeed if it is directed to school children alone, because they are not in a position to make many of the decisions needed to preserve the present environmental resources, but it might succeed if it deliberately attends to public education on a broader scale.

Bibliography

Carson S McB (ed.) 1978 *Environmental Education: Principles and Practice*. Arnold, London

Linke R D 1980 *Environmental Education in Australia*. Allen and Unwin, Sydney

Lucas A M 1980 Science and environmental education: Pious hopes, self praise and disciplinary chauvinism. *Stud. Sci. Educ.* 7: 1–26

Ohno R 1981 Use of the mass media in environmental education: Japan's experiences. *Environmental Education in Asia and the Pacific*. Bulletin of the UNESCO Regional Office for Education in Asia and the Pacific. 22: 294–99

Schoenfeld C, Disinger J (eds.) 1977 *Environmental Education in Action 1: Case Studies of Selected Public School and Public Action Programs*. ERIC Information Analysis Center for Science, Mathematics and Environmental Education, Ohio State University, Columbus, Ohio

A. M. Lucas

Environmental Influences on Classroom Management

Until the early 1960s it was not uncommon for individuals writing about life in classrooms to act as though schools were detached from the world around them. Classroom activities were treated as if they resulted exclusively from the intentions of teachers, school officials, and students. In recent years educators and researchers have begun to note that intentions are not always realized. Their efforts to explain this fact have led them to investigate the impact of environmental influences on classrooms.

Environmental influences can be divided into at least seven categories: technological, legal, political, economic, demographic, ecological, and cultural (Duke 1979b). These influences rarely operate in isolation from each other. Together they help to mold the expectations teachers and students bring to school, shape the nature of formal constraints on their conduct, and determine the resources to which they have access.

So consequential has the impact of environmental influences on schools become that researchers cannot fully understand an area such as classroom management without reference to them. Similarly, teachers cannot be trained to manage classrooms effectively without making them aware of these influences. An increasing amount of educational policy makers' time is devoted to the relationships between schools and external factors—government agencies, courts, communities, the economy.

Classroom management is defined as the provisions and procedures necessary to create and maintain an environment in which teaching and learning can occur (Duke 1979a). The remainder of this article consists of an analysis of some of the ways the seven environmental factors influence these provisions and procedures.

1. Technological Influences

As the numbers of students served by schools and the problems faced by educators have grown, more recommendations are heard that seek solutions from technology (applied science). While many teachers insist that teaching is more art than science, they nonetheless have come to rely heavily on technological developments.

Some technological influences on classroom management are so pervasive that it may be difficult for most teachers to realize they are taking place. These influences foster attitudes and predispositions which guide how teachers think about what they do. Consider, for example, the notion of progress. Spawned about two centuries ago and inspired by scientific theories and technological inventions, the belief in progress has become so ingrained in the thinking of many people—particularly in industrialized nations—that they cannot help expecting things to get better. Teachers may become disappointed when teaching and classroom management fail to grow easier from one year to the next. They frequently assume that, as they become more technically proficient and experienced, their jobs will be less taxing. What they may not realize, however, is that teaching is not completely analogous to production. Each cohort of students typically experiences a given grade or class only once. The uniqueness of being a second grader or taking algebra for each student suggests that expecting teaching to grow easier with each passing year can be unrealistic.

The way some teachers think about classroom management has also been subtly influenced by the "medical model." This model presumes that practitioners focus on diagnosing problems, prescribing treatments, and evaluating outcomes. Educational "specialists" are often needed to assist "general" practitioners with difficult classroom problems. The medical model sounds deceptively simple, but it implies a degree of clarity about desired outcomes that is less common in schools than hospitals. In addition, training teachers to look for problems may yield unexpected negative results. Individuals often find what they have been taught to see. The medical model can lead teachers to overemphasize problem management and ignore ways to define problems as opportunities. The proliferation of educational specialists has sometimes led to fragmentation of student instruction and coordination problems.

Another set of technological influences on classroom management takes the form of systematic, research-based strategies for dealing with student motivation and behavior problems. These strategies derive primarily from the work of behavioral and cognitive psychologists, sociologists, and psychoanalysts. Of all these approaches, behavior modification probably is the most widely used. Teachers are taught to apply the principles of systematic reinforcement and contingency management. Appropriate student behavior is reinforced, while inappropriate student behavior is modified through the use of token economies and other reward schemes

or aversive reinforcement. Considerable evidence exists that behavior modification techniques are successful in reducing classroom management problems, at least on a short-term basis (Meacham and Wiesen 1974).

A third form of technological influence comes in the form of time-saving and labor-saving equipment. Computers are a current example. In class, microcomputers can be used to individualize student learning, thus reducing the likelihood of student frustration over the pace of instruction (see *Individualized Instruction*). Teachers have more time to work intensively with particular students. At a school level, computers can be used for monitoring student attendance, grading, and other recordkeeping, thus reducing teachers' information processing tasks. Japan has probably made greater use of computers in schools than any other nation.

New equipment, of course, may bring classroom management problems as well as benefits. Expensive computers invite vandalism or theft and thus require security precautions. Critics contend that computers serve to further impersonalize learning, thereby harming certain students who need direct contact and caring.

Television illustrates the mixed impact of new technology. Used extensively throughout the world as an instructional device, television has meant that students in underdeveloped nations can have access to new ideas, no matter how far they live from urban centers. At the same time, television, in its commercial operations, has been accused of undermining traditional cultures and modeling aggressive and disrespectful behavior for impressionable youth.

A final type of technological influence comes in the form of changes in the learning environment. Architects and design specialists exert a direct impact on classroom management by determining how comfortable, well-lit, vandal-proof, and conducive to teaching are schools and classrooms (see *Instructional Spaces, Architecture of*). In the late 1960s and early 1970s, for example, open-space schools were built throughout the United States and Canada. Designed to facilitate team teaching and reduce building costs by minimizing interior partitions between rooms, these new facilities fostered a host of classroom management problems (see *Open Versus Formal Instruction*). Teachers often disliked working within clear view of neighbors and were bothered by peripheral noise. As a result, permanent walls were constructed in many of the open-space schools.

Of all these technological changes it can be said, in summary, that the persons most responsible for implementing and working with them—namely teachers—have rarely been involved in planning or developing them. Schooling in most countries is a big business, and technological changes represent potentially large economic gains for developers. New technology may not always be accompanied by the practitioner consultation, careful pilot testing, and impact analysis so vital to the ultimate success of innovations.

2. Legal Influences

Courts of law have tended to play a more active role in schools in industrialized nations than elsewhere. Elementary and secondary education in many underdeveloped countries is subject to highly centralized federal and state authority. Centralized decision making minimizes local variations in school policy, thereby reducing the occasions when litigation may be necessitated. A second reason why legal influences seem to be less potent in some nations is the acceptance of the principle of *in loco parentis* for educators. In other words, teachers are accorded the broad discretionary authority of a parent in their classes. Teachers in the United States, Canada, and Scandinavia have seen their status as "surrogate parents" challenged in recent years by plaintiffs representing the interests of particular students.

Legal influences in the United States take several forms. Through the courts, pressure is brought to bear on educators perceived to be trespassing on the constitutional rights of students. Professional malpractice—once the concern of physicians and engineers—has become an issue with which teachers must reckon. Finally, the increase of labor negotiations, collective bargaining, and contract law has made an impact on how teachers act.

Courts have dealt with student rights on a collective and individual basis. The concerns of minority students, for instance, have been addressed in the form of lawsuits against school districts for denying equal educational opportunity and tolerating discriminatory disciplinary policies. Teachers who regard suspension from class and school as a mechanism for maintaining control must be careful that minority students do not receive a disproportionate number of suspension notices. Suspending a student from school has been interpreted as an abridgment of his or her constitutional right to an education. "In-school suspension" has been developed as an alternative by many United States schools.

Some of the ways in which teachers can deny students equal educational opportunity have been explored in an ethnographic study of three years in the schooling of a group of black elementary-school students (Rist 1970). Routine classroom management decisions, such as where a student can sit and with whom a student can interact, were found to seriously affect students' chances of success in succeeding grades. To date, however, courts have focused more on equity issues at the level of school and local educational authority than classroom.

Where classroom teachers have been directly challenged is the area of freedom of expression and denial of due process rights. Teachers in the United States generally cannot prevent a student from expressing himself or herself verbally or symbolically, even if there is the chance problems will ensue. If a student must be suspended, he or she is entitled to due process, including a hearing at which charges are formally presented. The Supreme Court of the United States has made it clear that students do not "shed their rights at the school-house door."

Malpractice suits have tended to be brought against school systems rather than individual classroom teachers, but it is likely that teachers increasingly feel legally vulnerable. Vulnerability breeds caution. Teachers express fear that any oversight or mistake may be interpreted as negligence or malfeasance. Thus the mere threat of legal action may be sufficient to influence the classroom management behavior of many teachers.

Litigation concerning interpretations of teacher contracts is another way in which courts can influence classroom management. Courts, for example, have upheld the right of teacher unions to negotiate a variety of pertinent issues, including class size and supervisory responsibility. On the other hand, administrative decisions to require ineffective teachers to obtain more training and to remove teachers who are unable to control student behavior in class have also been supported.

3. Political Influences

While the formal study of the politics of education is a relatively recent phenomenon, the fact is that schools have been shaped by political influences since their inception. Political decisions having a direct bearing on the nature of classroom management include the designation of a school-leaving age, the determination of how schools will be financed, and the specification of societal expectations for schools and students. The role to be played by schools in youth development is by no means commonly agreed upon. The absence of a coordinated youth policy in the United States and Canada has meant that secondary schools act as the primary socialization agents for adolescents. Many other countries have not permitted schools to exercise such pervasive influence. Israel and the People's Republic of China, for example, require large numbers of youth to become involved in extrascholastic work experiences (Boocock 1974).

A political decision with important implications for classroom management involves the role schools are expected to play in social integration. By regarding schools as prime elements in the effort to break down racial barriers, United States policy makers have created a need for teachers to become more sensitive to cultural influences on behavior and more aware of the subtleties of their own expectations. Recently integrated schools frequently report increased classroom behavior problems and teacher dissatisfaction.

The decision to "mainstream" handicapped students in regular classrooms is another political decision with major implications for classroom management (see *Special Education*). As a result of Public Law 94–142 (1975), United States teachers must work with students who previously were taught in small classes by specially trained instructors. Often these students have difficulty maintaining attention and conforming to class rules. Subject to ridicule by other students, they frequently necessitate considerable teacher intervention to maintain order. Teachers are uncertain about applying the same rules governing behavior to handicapped students that they apply to other students.

The fact that teachers traditionally have not been influential in shaping the political policies that, in turn, shape their classrooms has led to greater politicization of the teaching profession. Teacher unions have become major political forces in many nations. Where they have succeeded in winning the right to collective bargaining, teachers have begun to negotiate conditions of work in their contracts. As indicated in the preceding section, such matters as maximum class size and the limits of supervisory responsibilities are often spelled out in detail. In trouble-plagued urban schools, United States teachers concerned about personal safety have won provisions for greater security. It is clear that classrooms are unlikely to be orderly and productive if teachers are anxious and fearful. Where teachers join administrators in shaping school rules and sanctions, they are also more likely to enforce disciplinary policies consistently.

Involvement of students and community members in making decisions concerning issues related to student behavior has also been shown to reduce the likelihood of major discipline problems (McPartland and McDill 1976). Bronfenbrenner (1970) found that students in the Soviet Union handled almost all of the behavior problems in their schools, with quite positive results. There generally has been less willingness in most other countries, however, to accord students extensive authority over disciplinary matters.

4. Economic Influences

The quality of schooling available to a particular group of students is a function, in large measure, of the fiscal resources the community is willing to allocate to education. Money buys talented teachers and administrators, learning materials, and facilities. Classroom management is not immune to the economic behavior of the citizenry or to fluctuations in the economy.

Recent evidence of this relationship comes from case studies of urban high schools in the United States during the aftermath of budget cuts (Duke et al. 1981, Duke and Meckel 1980b). Any reduction in school funds that is more than marginal must be effected by removal of staff members. As teachers are let go, average class size grows, increasing the workload for teachers. As workload increases, teachers find less time to spend with individual students. Students who have difficulty keeping up with their lessons grow more restless and frustrated, and classroom behavior problems increase. The more time teachers must devote to handling behavior problems, the less time they have for direct instruction. The less direct instruction students receive, the less likely they are to achieve what is expected of them. As student achievement declines, teacher workload increases once again. This entire process can be compared to a steadily decreasing spiral, where each change serves to accelerate the downward movement, causing classroom management to become more difficult.

The downward spiral is further influenced by the withdrawal of students whose parents can afford nonpublic education. Often these students are high achievers. Their departure serves to increase the concentration of lower-achieving students with whom public school teachers work and make teacher dissatisfaction more likely. Ultimately, budget cuts in public education—particularly where urban schools are concerned—threaten to widen the gap between advantaged and disadvantaged students (Duke and Cohen 1983).

An economic influence related to the present mood of fiscal restraint is the accountability movement. As inflation continues and taxpayer resistance mounts, demands grow for careful review of how public education funds are spent. Teachers often watch helplessly as externally supported programs, upon which they have come to rely, are curtailed because evidence of dramatic changes in student achievement is lacking. Paraprofessionals, teacher aides, and support staff are the first to lose their jobs. Teachers are also subjected to closer scrutiny, supervision, and evaluation. As a result, they tend to spend time primarily on those activities which lead to measurable outcomes. Schools come to resemble commercial enterprises driven by concern for efficiency more than service organizations devoted to the care and growth of youth.

In the United States, recent concern over the rising costs of public education has occasioned debate—long common in other nations—over which students are most deserving of formal secondary education. Students who are chronically absent, disruptive, or unmotivated are no longer assured places in secondary schools. The fear, however, is that the economy cannot provide meaningful employment for those who fail to complete high school. The ultimate cost to society of having to deal with nongraduates is difficult to estimate.

5. Demographic Influences

Classroom management is subject to a variety of demographic influences, ranging from fluctuations in the birth rate to changes in the types of students with whom teachers must work. For example, following the Second World War, the birth rate rose dramatically in many industrialized nations. Unprepared for the rapid growth in students, school systems lacked adequate facilities and appropriately trained teachers. It is conceivable that part of the purported increase in student behavior problems during the 1960s and early 1970s can be attributed directly to overcrowding and lack of skilled personnel.

If these factors contributed to behavior problems, it might be expected that the declining enrollments of the 1970s would bring a proportional reduction in problems. That this situation has not occurred universally, suggests that other influences may be at work. In the United States, for instance, the 1970s were characterized by increasing concentrations of nonwhite students in city schools, the arrival of large contingents of non-English-speaking immigrants from Southeast Asia and Latin America, and the mainstreaming of handicapped youngsters in regular classrooms. Teachers thus were faced with management problems arising from the special needs of different groups of students. Frequently these problems stemmed from the teachers' lack of familiarity with or sensitivity to the behavioral norms of youngsters from different cultures. Educational researchers began to note the impact of teachers' differential expectations on the behavior and academic achievement of students from different cultures (Brophy and Good 1974).

Another reason why behavior problems did not necessarily subside as school enrollments shrank may have been the fact that the average age of teachers rose during the 1970s. Due to seniority rules, older teachers were able to retain their jobs as positions were eliminated. These teachers may have been less likely to be aware of the needs of new groups of students and receptive to changing their behavior to accommodate these students.

The problem of controlling the behavior of contemporary students has been exacerbated by several major changes in the types of homes from which students come (see *Students' Social Background and Classroom Behaviour*). More students today come from one-parent homes than ever before, a fact that is reflected in the difficulty many teachers find enlisting parental support and meeting students' emotional needs. Students living with both parents are not immune from problems, since they may lack proper supervision as a result of both parents working. A third concern involves the growing number of students who are new to a school during a given year. As the populations of industrialized nations become more transient, the likelihood decreases that students will remain in the same school system until graduation. As a result, it is harder for teachers and school officials to monitor the growth and development of individual students and to provide them with "personalized" guidance.

Demographic changes not only seem to have influenced the behavior problems with which teachers must deal and the nature of their relationships with parents, but the way classroom resources are allocated. Teachers faced with heterogeneous groups of students are expected to respond to the special needs of each group—a task for which adequate materials, time, and expertise is often lacking. Where sufficient funds exist, paraprofessionals are often hired to assist teachers in working with special students.

6. Ecological Influences

Ecological influences include, among other things, the organizations that interact with schools on a regular basis. Among the organizations that can potentially exert an influence on classroom management are large corporations, local businesses, foundations, interest groups, lobbies, and agencies at various levels of government.

The increase in reports of student behavior problems may signal growing ecological influences on the schools. Since the Second World War, a variety of agencies—public and private—have specialized in providing services to troubled youth. As a result, in many industrialized nations teachers can often turn for assistance to child welfare workers, probation officials, juvenile justice specialists, psychiatric social workers, and pediatricians specializing in behavior problems, as well as school-based guidance personnel, school psychologists, peer counselors, and community liaisons. With so much expertise available, it is tempting for many teachers to regard referral as their primary strategy for maintaining control. The proliferation of specialists in youth problems may actually serve to reduce the likelihood that any one professional—typically the teacher—assumes overall responsibility for handling a particular student's problems.

The availability of outside resources and expertise may have yielded a second undesirable by-product. Increasing reliance on extraclassroom assistance can contribute to "learned helplessness" on the part of teachers. When resources diminish, as they do during times of reduced government spending, teachers find themselves without specialists to whom to refer troubled students and without the skills to handle behavior problems themselves. The disappearance of government-supported alternative schools, clinics, work–study programs, dropout centers, and counseling activities may force teachers to deal with more nonacademic matters in a regular classroom context.

7. Cultural Influences

Cultural influences on classroom management, though often among the most pervasive and potent, are difficult to identify. They involve phenomena such as norms, values, and beliefs about the young, authority, society, and learning. Classroom management is subject to cultural influence through the expectations that teachers and students bring to class.

Studies of white elementary-school teachers in the United States, for example, find that mischievous behavior is tacitly condoned for boys but not for girls, reflecting conventional sex-role stereotyping (see *Student Sex and Classroom Behavior*). White teachers also may behave toward nonwhite students in ways that encourage these individuals to feel they are not expected to achieve as much as white students. "Double standards" of this kind are deeply rooted in many cultures.

Attitudes toward competition and cooperation offer another illustration of cultural influence. While many teachers expect students to take pride in knowing more than their peers, some American Indian cultures value cooperation so greatly that students learn to avoid any situation—such as answering a question that a peer cannot answer—which might embarrass another. Scott (1975 p. 200) maintains that the high incidence of criminal behavior in American society (and presumably misconduct in American schools) is attributable, in part, to the high value the dominant culture places on competition and conflict.

How a teacher defines a particular student behavior cannot be separated from the culture in which the teacher has grown up, received training, and worked (see *Teachers' Social Backgrounds*). White teachers thus may misinterpret as insolence the fact that black students tend not to look directly at adults when being corrected. Decisions regarding which students are considered handicapped, gifted, or emotionally disturbed may have less to do with objective, universal criteria than with the idiosyncrasies of local communities. Teachers who transfer from suburban or rural assignments to urban schools often discover that their students are accustomed to different ways of communicating and acting.

One of the few expectations characterizing most societies is that teachers should be in control of their classrooms. How this control is to be achieved, however, varies widely. In some societies teachers establish control by teaching students how to behave responsibly. In other societies teachers operate on the assumption that students cannot be trusted. They rely on rules and punishments to maintain order.

8. Control Versus Authority

Classroom management does not occur in a vacuum. The preceding analysis illustrates that how classrooms are organized and operated can be influenced by a variety of factors besides teachers' professional training and official school policies. In recent years many of these factors have had the collective impact of pressing for greater teacher control over classrooms. Of interest, though, is the fact that the desire for more control has not been accompanied by a corresponding push for greater teacher authority. Teachers are caught in the awkward position of witnessing their authority diminish—the victim of more rules, laws, fiscal constraints, technological changes, demands for accountability, and community involvement in schools—at the same time that they are urged to exercise greater control over student behavior and achievement. Such a trend may be part of a broader effort to deprofessionalize teaching. Functionaries and civil servants, unlike professionals, are typically expected to maintain order without exercising authority.

As behavior problems in classrooms grow and pressure for greater control mounts, teachers frequently counter with demands for more parental involvement in schools and stronger support for school disciplinary policies at home. As a result of this kind of interaction, the environment in which classroom management occurs is increasingly characterized by confrontation and adversarial relations. In jeopardy is the traditional belief that teacher interests and parent interests are compatible.

See also: Instructional Spaces, Architecture of; Behaviour Problems in the Classroom; Teacher Expectations and Instruction; Management in the Classroom: Elementary Grades; Special Education

Bibliography

Boocock S S 1974 Youth in three cultures. *Sch. Rev.* 83: 93–111

Bronfenbrenner U 1970 *Two Worlds of Childhood: US and USSR.* Russell Sage Foundation, New York

Brophy J E, Good T L 1974 *Teacher–Student Relationships: Causes and Consequences.* Holt, Rinehart and Winston, New York

Dreikurs R, Grey L 1968 *A New Approach to Discipline: Logical Consequences.* Hawthorn, New York

Duke D L (ed.) 1979a *Classroom Management: Seventy-eighth Yearbook of the National Society for the Study of Education,* Pt. 2. University of Chicago Press, Chicago, Illinois

Duke D L 1979b Environmental influences on classroom management. In: Duke D L (ed.) 1979a

Duke D L, Cohen J S 1983 Do public schools have a future? *Urban Rev.* 15: 89–105

Duke D L, Meckel A M 1980a Disciplinary roles in American schools. *Br. J. Teach. Educ.* 6: 37–50

Duke D L, Meckel A M 1980b The slow death of a public high school. *Phi Delta Kappan* 61: 674–77

Duke D L, Cohen J S, Herman R 1981 Running faster to stay in place: Retrenchment in the New York City schools. *Phi Delta Kappan* 63: 13–17

King E J 1973 *Other Schools and Ours: Comparative Studies for Today,* 4th edn. Holt, Rinehart and Winston, Eastbourne

Lickona T (ed.) 1976 *Moral Development and Behavior: Theory, Research, and Social Issues*. Holt, Rinehart and Winston, New York

McPartland J M, McDill E L 1976 The unique role of schools in the causes of youthful crime. Report No. 216. Center for Social Organization of Schools, Johns Hopkins University, Baltimore, Maryland

Meacham M L, Wiesen A E 1974 *Changing Classroom Behavior*, 2nd edn. Intext Educational, New York

Rist R C 1970 Student social class and teacher expectations: The self-fulfilling prophecy in ghetto education. *Harvard Educ. Rev.* 40: 411–51

Scott J P 1975 *Aggression*, 2nd edn. University of Chicago Press, Chicago, Illinois

Skinner B F 1968 *The Technology of Teaching*. Appleton-Century-Crofts, New York

D. L. Duke

Epilepsy

Epilepsy is a term which derives from the Greek word meaning "to be seized". In modern medicine, epilepsy is considered to be a chronic brain syndrome of various etiology characterized by recurrent seizures with a variety of clinical and laboratory manifestations. The terms petit mal and grand mal cover two major classes of epileptic seizures.

Petit mal seizures are less severe than those of grand mal. The term petit mal designates ictal epileptic manifestations constituted exclusively by typical absences and by petit mal myoclonus, both of which belong in the framework of primary generalized epilepsy, that is, essential, genuine epilepsy. The electroencephalogram (EEG) is specific and essential to make the diagnosis.

Typical absences can be simple or complex and are characterized by a brief clouding or loss of consciousness (usually lasting from 2 to 15 seconds) which occurs and then ceases abruptly. A simple absence occurs when impairment of consciousness is the only detectable clinical sign whereas a complex absence has additional signs present—rhythmic flickering of the eyelids found in simple absences, bilateral muscular contractions which may reach the upper limbs, involuntary movements of the lips and tongue, urinary incontinence, a loss of postural tone, an increase in antigravitic postural tone producing backward extension of the head and conjugate upward deviation of the eyes and sometimes of the trunk, which may force the person to walk backwards to maintain balance.

Petit mal myoclonus is characterized by a brief and involuntary contraction (myoclonus) involving the agonist and antagonist muscles of several segments, usually the head, neck, and upper limbs, or the whole body. This type of myoclonus generally results in violent movements, usually in flexion due to the predominance of the involuntary muscle contraction or convulsion in the postural muscles.

Typical absences and petit mal myoclonus are both generally triggered either by hyperventilation or by intermittent light stimulation. They are characterized by the usual absence of neurological and psychological evidence of cerebral involvement during the interval between seizures; by their more frequent appearance in infants and adolescents, although they can occur at any age; and by the absence of any etiology suggesting, therefore, that they are derived essentially from a hereditary epileptic predisposition depending on genetic factors modulated by age, sex, and different hormonal factors. They may also be associated or followed in time by grand mal seizures. Both typical absences and petit mal myoclonus tend to respond well to anti-petit mal drugs such as diones, succinimides, benzodiazepine compounds, and sodium valproate.

In recent times, by extension and by mistake, the term petit mal has also been applied to some variant forms of minor attacks. For example, the "petit mal triad" was created: petit mal absences, petit mal myoclonus, and epileptic drop attacks. Epileptic drop attacks represent a form of atonic epilepsy in which the decrease or loss or postural tone is of brief duration, usually a fraction of a second. The attacks occur most often in children with chronic encephalopathy and some degree of mental retardation and, in particular, the Lennox–Gastaut syndrome, an encephalopathy of undetermined origin occurring in children (usually between ages 2 to 6), rarely in adolescents, and usually characterized by a degree of mental retardation, an abnormal EEG, and often abnormal computed tomography (CT Scan) and different epileptic attacks:

(a) tonic epileptic seizures usually lasting between 5 to 20 seconds and characterized by a clouding of consciousness, an autonomic discharge "en masse", and a symmetrical and bilateral tonic spasm causing the body to assume a position of partial opisthotonos with semiflexed arms elevated above the head;

(b) atonic epileptic seizures characterized by a decrease or abolition of postural tone for a brief period of 1 to 3 seconds;

(c) a typical absences characterized by EEG criteria different from those of typical petit mal seizure.

The term grand mal is generally synonymous with tonic–clonic epileptic seizure, lasting about a minute, and characterized by loss of consciousness, an "en masse" autonomic discharge, and symmetrical and bilateral convulsions generalized over the whole body—initially tonic and subsequently clonic. The clonic phase is the most convulsive one, characterized by violent alternate contractions and relaxations of the muscles.

A distinction is made between epileptic seizures generalized from the onset, secondarily generalized epileptic seizures, and secondary generalized epileptic seizures.

Epileptic seizures generalized from the onset start usually without warning. They can occur independently or in association with either typical absences or bilateral massive myoclonus belonging to genuine petit mal epilepsy. They have the same etiology.

Secondarily generalized epileptic seizures refer to a tonic–clonic epileptic seizure which may succeed a partial epileptic seizure, thus the term secondarily generalized. Clinically, the seizure may or may not be preceded by an aura (a preliminary warning that the convulsion may occur) or "signal symptom". Nausea, dizziness, flashes of light are frequent signal symptoms. They tend to be classified as elementary (motor, sensory) or autonomic and complex (purely psychological, psychosensory, psychomotor), depending on the localization of the starting point of the seizure. A secondarily generalized seizure can occur at any age. Its appearance requires a focal trigger zone to be at the origin of the epileptic discharge, even if the neurological examination is normal. The trigger zone is generally the consequence of a focal lesion which can be very discrete and, even with the most sophisticated tests, most difficult to identify. For these reasons further examinations are required. It can also be larger, whether a scar or a tumour, and easier to diagnose.

Secondary generalized epileptic seizures differ from secondarily generalized seizures. These seizures concern tonic–clonic seizures having the specific characteristics of appearing in association with tonic and atonic epileptic seizures and atypical absences. They occur in subjects displaying neurological or mental signs revealing a more or less diffused cerebral malfunction. Secondary generalized epileptic seizures appear most frequently in childhood although they may occur in adolescents, and only rarely in adults. They are the consequence of diffuse or multi-focal cerebral lesions visualized by EEG and CT scan.

Treatment for grand mal differs from that of petit mal. Grand mal and secondarily generalized seizures react better to barbiturates and hydantoines than to anti-petit mal drugs, with the exception of sodium valproate. Secondary generalized epileptic seizures react somewhat to classical anti-epileptics such as barbiturates and hydantoines and not at all to the anti-petit mal drugs.

Petit mal and grand mal seizures appear generally isolated. Petit mal seizures are usually more frequent than grand mal seizures. But the two, in some cases, may appear one after the other and result in what is called a *status epilepticus*.

Although some mentally retarded individuals may suffer from epileptic seizures, isolated seizures do not appear to be the cause of mental retardation. Mental retardation may be caused by brain lesions following a *status epilepticus*, or by brain lesions which initiate epilepsy in children. A long-term overdose of some anti-epileptic drugs in children may also have some detrimental effects.

Many anticonvulsive drugs are now available so that medical control of epileptic seizures is enhanced. With proper medication, and, in some cases, surgery, the severity of epileptic seizures which do occur can be markedly reduced. Unfortunately, negative attitudes and misinformation concerning epileptics persist among teachers, parents, and others. With proper medication, almost all epileptics can function normally in everyday life, and epileptic children and adolescents, can function normally in the classroom. However, teachers and others that an epileptic is likely to come into contact with need to be informed that that person is an epileptic, so that they can be aware of the possibility of seizures occurring and can assist in epilepsy management. Should a grand mal (primary or secondarily) seizure occur, actions will need to be taken to prevent physical damage (e.g., swallowing of the tongue, biting inside the mouth, striking parts of the body, etc.) which convulsions can cause, and medical assistance will need to be secured as quickly as possible. After a grand mal seizure, rest is needed. For an epileptic child without mental retardation, placement in the regular classroom is most appropriate with allowances made for rest, if needed. However, the major problems of the epileptic with today's medication is the one of attitudes which may be archaic and outmoded and result in discrimination against persons with epilepsy.

Bibliography

Broughton R J (ed.) 1982 Henri Gastaut and the Marseilles School's contribution to the neurosciences. *Electroenceph. Clin. Neurophysiol. Suppl. 35.* Elsevier Biomedical, Amsterdam

Bruya M A, Bolin R H 1976 Epilepsy: A controllable disease. *Am. J. Nursing* 76: 388–97

Gastaut H 1973 *Dictionary of Epilepsy.* World Health Organization, Geneva

Gastaut H, Tassinari C A (eds.) 1975 Epilepsies. In: Remond A (ed.) 1975 *Handbook of Electroencephalography and Clinical Neurophysiology.* Vol. 13, Part A. Elsevier, Amsterdam

Gastaut H, Jasper H, Bancaud J, Waltregny A (eds.) 1969 *The Physiopathogenesis of the Epilepsies.* Thomas, Springfield, Illinois

Geist H 1982 *The Etiology of Idiopathic Epilepsy.* Exposition Press, New York

Gibbs F A, Gibbs E L 1952 *Atlas of Electroencephalography,* Vol. 2. *Epilepsy.* Addison-Wesley, Reading, Massachusetts

International League Against Epilepsy 1970 Proposal for an international classification of epilepsies. *Epilepsia* 11: 117–19

Kram C 1963 Epilepsy in children and youth. In: Cruickshank W M (ed.) 1963 *Psychology of Exceptional Children and Youth.* Prentice-Hall, Englewood Cliffs, New Jersey

Lennox W G, Lennox M A 1960 *Epilepsy and Related Disorders.* Churchill, London
Livingston S 1954 *The Diagnosis and Treatment of Convulsive Disorders in Children.* Thomas, Springfield, Illinois
Penfield W, Jasper H 1954 *Epilepsy and the Functional Anatomy of the Human Brain.* Churchill, London

R. Naquet

Equality, Policies for Educational

. . . empirical data show that all Western industrial societies have been characterized since the end of World War II both by a steady decrease in Inequalities of Educational Opportunity and by an almost complete stability of Inequalities in Social Opportunity . . . . Indeed, the educational growth witnessed in all Western industrial societies since 1945 has been accompanied by an increase rather than a decrease in economic inequality, even though the educational system has become more equalitarian in the meanwhile. (Boudon 1974 pp. xii–xiii)

The subject of this article is policies for educational equality. Yet the quotation above illustrates that educational equality is generally not viewed as an end in itself. Rather, it is treated as one means of reducing economic and social inequality. Accordingly, some perspective on its place among other means and ends and among factors which promote or militate against them is a desirable preliminary.

1. Origins

What educational equality might mean in practice will be examined a little further on. At this point, the origins of concern with it need to be recalled. The concept has risen to sustained prominence only since the nineteenth century, policies to realize it have become general only in the twentieth century, and research and publication on the topic have risen to a flood only in the second half of the twentieth century. Its elaboration has coincided with or followed the increasing industrialization and bureaucratization of societies and the rise of various forms of elected representative government.

Six factors seem to explain it. The first is the perception that certain forms and degrees of inequality constitute a social problem. Inequality exists and persists in the distribution of wealth, incomes, social status, occupational status, and political power in all known major societies. Although the range of inequality in any aspect varies from society to society, no state has yet been able to abolish inequality. That states or societies might want to abolish it, or at least reduce it, implies the second factor, namely the idea and powerful appeal of egalitarianism. Expressions of it can be found in capitalistic polities, like that of the United States, in so-called social democratic welfare states like that of Sweden, and in socialistic ones like that of the Soviet Union.

Concomitant but not wholly consistent with the second is the third factor, the twin notions of meritocracy and social mobility: those who deserve to should be able to gain promotion through the various strata of a society to whatever position they desire. Merit is to be measured by impartial, objective criteria. Meritocracy concords with equality insofar as it supposes equal treatment for the equally deserving. It diverges from equality insofar as it implies the probability of unequal merit and, thus, unequal promotion (see *Meritocracy*).

Fourth are the associated notions that education improves the quality of a person, that an educated person is more productive economically and socially than one who is uneducated—and that a more educated person is more productive than a less educated person; and hence that an educated nation is likely to be a more productive and generally better nation. Education then is in both the public and the private interest (see *Human Capital and Education*). Fifth is the apparently consequent direct link created between education, on the one hand, and merit and eligibility for socioeconomic promotion, on the other. Education has been made a prime public and objective criterion for qualifying (and disqualifying) people for particular ranges of occupations and incomes. The means is a schedule of correspondence between scholastic attainment and eligibility for specific jobs or training for such jobs and their associated salaries, careers, and connections.

This link between education, employment, and incomes is clearly a phenomenon of a particular organization of employment and a particular organization of education—which is the sixth factor. It does not appear where independent household, individual, or even small enterprise employment are the only forms of livelihood. It presupposes instead relatively large-scale, bureaucratized employers selecting from among numerous would-be employees, and therefore actively attempting to distinguish inequalities of eligibility. The employers offer jobs on certain conditions, a major one of which is an educational qualification—particularly for young entrants to the employment market. Those who seek the jobs must of necessity satisfy the conditions. As societies have industrialized, so large-scale employers have increased and independent employment declined and wage-salary employment spread. An important consequence has been that educational qualifications have become more and more necessary to more and more people.

Correspondingly, the organization of education has shifted from being a concern solely of the family or household and perhaps of religious bodies to being a matter of the state. Education has become increasingly, almost exclusively, identified with a set of institutions called schools, universities, and the like. Most of them are now provided by the state from public funds, although in many countries significant private sectors flourish. They have enabled the establishment and elaboration of objective educational standards, credentials, and qualifications by which employers can distinguish between and select from numbers of applicants for employment. Further, since occupational status heavily influences social status as well, the credentials are doubly important. Hence access to qualifications has become an important political issue, for which policies need to be devised.

It will have been noted that education has been ranked only fourth and fifth among six factors. Even then, a sixth has followed, which again appears to explain, rather than be explained by, education. The inference is plainly that the concern for educational equality is a dependent phenomenon, deriving its importance less from educational, and more from economic and social considerations. A further inference may be that the educational system is itself subordinate to other forces in society and is less able to influence them than they it. Consequently, policies for educational equality may succeed in reducing educational inequality without—as the introductory quotation suggests—having the slightest effect on other inequalities.

That said, two points remain crucial. Both apply to all societies, which have moved away from inheritance as the major overt determinant of occupational and social status. The first is that, however unequal the society in economic or social terms, social mobility is considerable. Substantial proportions of people can move up the occupational, income, and social scales and similarly substantial proportions can move down. The observation may be truer of the currently industrializing countries than it is of the industrialized. The second point is that educational attainment is as yet the most important determinant of mobility. Without a good education, a person of low social status will find promoting himself (or particularly herself) extremely difficult. A person of higher social status correspondingly will have difficulty maintaining his or her position and will probably need to be protected by his or her family and peers. These difficulties will be more or less severe, according to the degree of meritocracy and bureaucratization in a society. In all cases, however, access to and the utilization of education remain issues of high concern for individuals intent on improving, or at least retaining, their status and that of their children. The aggregation of that intent creates the social demand for education, which in turn makes demands on social resources and so creates the need for policies. Policies in their turn are better oriented by clear values, concepts, and goals.

2. Educational Equality—Definitions

The values behind the idea of educational equality are clear enough. On the one hand, there are general notions of fairness and equity. On the other, there is the view that human rationality should as far as possible rectify the random inequities of nature and social history. As education can make such large differences in life chances and as it can be provided rationally, fairness seems to demand that (randomly) bright children born into (randomly) unfavouring environments should have the education to enable them to equal equally bright children born into favouring circumstances. Even more does fairness seem to require that such children should not be constrained by their unfavouring environment to do worse than less bright children born into favouring environments. This view is well-encapsulated in Section 26 of the United Nations Declaration of Human Rights which claims access to education for children, irrespective of the social class, economic conditions, and place of residence of their parents.

Fairness does not of course stop with the bright children. The less bright children also are the products of random distributions of genes and environments. For them, the sense of fairness demands that they should have such education as will enable them at least to maintain at a constant level their deficits vis-à-vis the brighter. Education should at least not widen the gaps between the bright and the less bright. At best, it might even enable some narrowing of the gap (Rawls 1971).

This illustration of values now highlights a cardinal and double difficulty with the concept of educational equality itself. If it is true that there are inequalities of "brightness"—the vague word is used deliberately—what can educational equality mean? For inequalities of brightness can be associated with inequalities of learning ability, talent, interest, motivation, energy, diligence, or manual dexterity. Should, indeed could, educational equality require the equalization of all these aspects?

At this point—and before proceeding to the second part of the difficulty—a debate needs to be noted. The preceding paragraph implies an assumption that at least part of brightness and other abilities is inborn or due to genetic inheritance. One school of thought would argue that, whatever the inheritance, its effects are negligible in relation to those of the environment. Social class, economic conditions, the education of parents, place of residence, the preferred peer group are all likely to provide the overwhelming influences on the development of brightness. A second school of thought, on the other hand, would point to the disparities of brightness not only within families, as between siblings born of the same parents, but even between identical or monozygotic twins, and even more between fraternal or dizygotic twins (see *Economic and Career Impacts of*

Education: Assessment by Means of Kin Studies). Here, environments are held virtually constant, yet considerable inequalities appear not only in educational attainments, but also in later occupations and incomes. On balance, ascribing only a residual importance to genetic inheritance seems implausible. Hence, the question remains of the possible role of education in compensating for genetic inequality (Husén 1974).

The second component of the double difficulty is that inequality is compounded by difference. Children observably vary in their personalities, temperaments, abilities, and interests. A plausible inference might be that a single form of education for all children would be excessively procrustean. Therefore, educational provision should be as varied as the pupils taking it. The drawback here is that the elements of educational diversity tend to become ordered or ranked in association with particular bands of occupation, income, and social status. The lower the latter, the more likely the former to be reserved for the less bright. Diversity is confused with inequality. That is, the inequalities of the larger society intrude upon and dominate educational choice and practice. All the same, the question remains whether educational equality might be feasibly delineated in terms of similar education for similar people, and different education for different people.

Only a little less difficult than the genetic question is the major component of environment, namely the social class of the family. Evidence from the industrialized countries and those with well-defined and established hierarchies suggest strongly that the higher the social class of a family, the more education it is likely to secure for its children and, conversely, the lower the social class, the less the education secured. In all classes, the actual amount of education taken by a particular child varies with its ability and scholastic performance—again at least partially reflecting the influence of the larger economy. However, there are significant differences. An upper-class child of only mediocre ability and performance is nevertheless likely to receive much more than average education. In contrast, children of lower classes often need to attain exceptionally high performance, before they go beyond even an average education. On the face of it, the phenomenon offends the value of fairness. That conclusion, however, assumes that the lower-class children of high ability are indeed interested in social and economic mobility, wish to achieve it through the normal avenue of educational credentials and would indeed take more education, if only they were not unfairly handicapped in some way. If this assumption is correct, what might be the handicaps?

There is certainly evidence from both industrialized and industrializing countries that biases within educational institutions do undermine the progress of children from less privileged social classes and rural areas. Educational personnel, their language, procedures, and norms may be strange and intimidating. It seems also to be the case that the milieu of the schools, largely reflecting that of the more privileged classes, is often uncongenial. Reciprocally, many teachers try to avoid and to escape from teaching in schools with large majorities of lower-class children. The consequence can be that such schools have staff, who are unwilling, unstable, and possibly below average in professional competence. Taken together, these factors would certainly constitute an unwarranted handicap on less privileged children who aimed at upward mobility.

There is, however, also evidence that the social milieu of the children in question has a part in shaping their horizons and aspirations. They may not wish to achieve mobility at all, or at least not on the usual terms. They may judge they can make their way by other means and be able to point to successful models in their parents or older siblings. They may be unwilling to risk alienation from their families and peers. Or they may set their ambitions at a level modestly above their present status but below their full potential. Their families—and they themselves—may prefer that they earn money earlier, rather than spend more time on education for possibly only slightly better paid employment and prospects. To the extent that these suggestions are accurate, the notions of handicap and unfairness are weakened. The issue is then whether such judgments are valid on their own terms, or the result of "false consciousness", misguided and damaging to their makers, or possibly defensive rationales against risking failure in attempts at social promotion.

Whichever explanation is the more applicable in a particular society at a particular time—and both are likely to be valid to some extent—the unequal use of education by people who are apparently equal in educational terms but unequal in social class has its sources not in schooling as such, but in the wider society. The variegation of values, cultures, stratifications, prejudices, and conflicts generates drives and inhibitions which affect education. If educational equality is viewed partly as a matter of equal use of educational resources by people who are equal in some appropriate standard, irrespective of social class and social ambition, then clearly educational policy will be insufficient on its own. However, it is possible that deliberately mixing social and ethnic groups in schools, in proportions approaching those in which they are found in a defined geographical area, may simultaneously promote social equality as well as equality in educational demand and use. If this were accepted, educational policy would certainly have a role in arranging for the mixing. Forms of community, neighbourhood, and comprehensive schools and arrangements to transport children of one socioeconomic area to schools in another ("busing") are attempts to do precisely that.

Connected with social class, and also with economic and political power, is another phenomenon. It can be observed in both industrialized and industrializing or developing countries, but is much more marked in the latter. Some schools, used in the main by the more affluent, better educated, and politically more influential groups, tend to attract higher levels of resources in terms of texts, equipment, other teaching resources and the quality and experience of teachers. The contrast extends to urban vis-à-vis rural schools, but remains even within the urban group. Indeed, the less favoured urban schools—whether they be the inner-city schools of the industrialized countries or the city-fringe slum schools of the developing countries—can be at a disadvantage even against rural schools. The inequalities of resources tend to be paralleled both with inequalities of internal efficiency—differences in the rates of attendance, repetition, desertion, graduation—and also with inequalities of attainment: the poorer schools do worse at standard tests and selection examinations.

There is, however, debate on the extent to which the correspondence reflects causal relationships between resources, processes, and outcomes. Some research in both industrialized and developing countries suggests that material resources such as money, buildings, laboratories, and books have little effect on internal efficiency or attainment, and neither do the formal qualifications and training of teachers. Inequalities in these aspects apparently do not necessarily give rise to inequalities in others. On the other hand, other research, again in both industrialized and developing countries, suggests that the commitment, quality, and leadership of teaching staff and the availability of at least basic, good quality texts do influence efficiency and attainment. Where the balance of probability might plausibly lie in this apparent conflict of evidence cannot be pursued here. Nevertheless, estimates of it should clearly be elements of policy (Rutter et al. 1979).

The two preceding paragraphs have introduced four further factors of educational inequality and have also shifted the focus from individual learners and social groups to inequalities between schools, or more generally between educational institutions. The first is the extension of the will for education to the willingness to use political power to secure good education for oneself or more commonly for one's protégés and allies. Again, this is a factor extrinsic to education itself. The second is inequalities in the distribution of resources between educational institutions. An additional dimension here is inequalities between different levels of educational institution, for example, between primary and secondary schools or between polytechnics and universities. In some countries, one secondary-school place may absorb resources equivalent to two primary-school places. Elsewhere, the ratio may be as high as 1:15. Disparities in ratios of the cost of university to the cost of primary-school places can range from 1:10 to 1:200. As the bulk of recurrent costs is absorbed by the salaries of personnel, the disparities are again largely due to economic inequality within a society, but they reflect on the scale and quality of educational provision.

The third factor is inequalities in the effectiveness of teachers. In part, these may arise from genetic variation among the teachers, in part from inequalities in the teachers' own education, in part from inequalities in the effectiveness of teacher trainers, and in part from inequalities of morale and commitment possibly induced by inequalities of resources, other forms of professional support and encouragement, and cooperation from the parents of students. The fourth factor is in part a product of the third and is the inequalities between schools on various indices of efficiency and effectiveness.

The discussion so far seems to have assumed implicitly that simple access to education is assured everywhere. The provision of sufficient primary schools and competent teachers to afford every child a place and adequate pedagogical attention and support has been taken for granted, as have enough secondary-school and tertiary-education places for those who want them. Implicit also has been the assumption that there are no barriers to access, either direct or indirect, and that the choice whether or not to take education is uncomplicated and free. Such is by no means universally the case, as even a glance at the UNESCO *Statistical Yearbooks* will show. To be sure, there are many countries, particularly but not exclusively among the industrialized, where such postulates would be safe. But there are also many countries, where the primary schools cannot cope with all the eligible children, where many children live too far from schools to be able to attend, and where what schools there are, are overcrowded, grossly underequipped, and unevenly distributed. In the very simplest sense of the term, access to education in the form of schooling is not equal.

Access is often made unequal also by both the direct and opportunity costs of schooling. Some governments feel constrained to charge fees even for primary education, so that, no matter how low the fees are, some households feel unable to afford them. Others are able to provide free tuition, but call upon the families to pay for textbooks, and writing materials—modest costs, indeed, but enough to exclude a proportion of households from participation. Some schools find it necessary to insist on uniform, sports charges, maintenance contributions, and the like, which also exclude the very poor families.

The opportunity costs include forgoing the assistance of children in the maintenance and livelihood of the family. Household, agricultural, pastoral, artisan, and industrial tasks within the family, as well as forms of casual, more or less permanent, wage labour can constitute indispensable contributions to family welfare and so reduce the opportunities (and increase the inequalities) for access to education for considerable proportions of children.

Much of the deficiency and maldistribution of educational provision, as well as much of the need for and inegalitarian impact of fees and charges, can be ascribed to the relative poverty of the societies concerned. A number of governments simply cannot afford to pay for a full system of education or to meet full costs of what provision is afforded. (Here of course is inequality on the international plane.) Additionally, there are historical and political contributions to the explanation. Possession by a colonial power and penetration by Christian missionaries had a large role in introducing scholastic education, in determining its patchy distribution, and in restricting and slowing its dissemination and universalization in most countries of Africa and Asia. For colonial governments, after all, equality could scarcely be a consideration, let alone a priority. Elsewhere, where colonial subjugation was either not experienced or terminated well before the twentieth century, other causes must be sought. Feudal or agrarian societies, for example, might have no interest in education, and their regimes might fear its spread. Examples could also be given of modernizing governments which, openly or surreptitiously, neglect or even discriminate against particular groups and areas, and favour others at the expense of the former. For equality or reduced inequality is not yet an objective common to all governments and societies, nor equally assiduously pursued by all who profess it. Educational inequality due solely to history or poverty is susceptible to mitigation by a steady application of policy and resources. When rooted in political and social values and interests, it is amenable only to political and social change, reformist or revolutionary. This observation again echoes the dependence of education upon the workings of the larger society.

An important aspect of provision is the ratio between different levels of education. Most developing countries provide many more primary-school places than secondary; all countries provide many more secondary places than tertiary. By that fact alone, of course, inequality is built into education, whatever the political philosophy of a society or its government. In poorer countries, that inequality may be exacerbated by the sacrifice of universal primary education to ensure some provision of the secondary and tertiary stages. However defended as necessary and temporary, such inequality cannot help but reinforce and prolong the other inequalities between those social groups who can use all the educational layers and those who cannot use even the first.

The fact of diminishing layers also requires selection between candidates. By definition, selection implies and requires inequality, whatever the criterion applied. There is in effect unequal provision, because there is an apparently inescapable and apparently universal belief in unequal abilities, expressed through unequal scholastic attainment. The discussion is thus taken back to its starting point about one of the major sources of educational inequality (see *Higher Education: Access*; *Selection Mechanisms for Entry to Higher Education*; *Selection Mechanisms for Entry to Secondary Education*).

However, in recent years, a partially countervailing belief has been emerging into higher prominence. It rejects the permanent validity of measurements of ability taken at particular moments early in life. Stated more positively, it is a belief in the "late developer", the person whose intellectual, cultural, or occupational interests are stimulated to grow at an age later than the conventional span of schooling. The social background and educational experience of a person may have stunted her or his capacities, while later social or occupational experiences may have brought them into play and demonstrated a need for guided development. This belief has been increasingly reinforced by the rates of technological and social changes since the late nineteenth century. Educational provision for adults at all stages of their lives and for all changes and adaptations in their livelihoods is a rising demand. It goes beyond the earlier provisions of adult education for occupational improvement or avocational interest. Indeed, it asserts itself as an element indispensable to the ability of a society to generate wider and greater well-being for its members and to keep abreast of advances in well-being elsewhere. Since adult education almost everywhere secures only very small proportions of the resources allocated to education, the "late developer" or "recurrent education" is in effect posing an issue of equality between generations: should there be more equality in provisions for children, adolescents, and young adults, on the one hand, and older adults on the other?

As a dozen or so aspects of educational inequality have been touched so far, a paragraph of review may be helpful, before proceeding to consider policy. The sources of inequality have been suggested to be:

(a) The genetic inheritance of individuals in terms of the variety of constellations of abilities, which are differently valued by societies and inequalities in specific abilities important for scholastic education.

(b) The social class of individuals in terms of perceptions of the values of education for life goals, actively securing education and assuring its quality, discouraging others from education, utilizing what education is made available, and succeeding in education.

(c) The political power of governments, social classes, and individuals in both providing and securing education.

(d) State and private resources for the provision of education.

(e) The allocation of resources between levels of education.

(f) Differences in the provision of educational institutions across geographical areas and social groups.

(g) Differences in the resources, efficiency, and attainments between educational institutions and groups of them.

(h) Differences between teachers in effectiveness.

(i) Direct and indirect costs to households in utilizing education.

(j) Selection for different levels of education.

(k) The allocation of resources between generations.

3. Equality of Opportunity

This array of inequalities is perplexing for any educational policy maker to confront. Certainly some of them seem within the practical grasp of governments truly intent on reducing whatever inequalities give rise to inequities. Others, however, arguably more important, seem to be such as no government or society can prevent. Indeed, a pessimist might argue that the inequalities which are manipulable are unlikely to be as important as those which are not. Not surprisingly, recourse has been had to the concept of "equality of educational opportunity". In brief, the suggestion is that a society's duty is merely to ensure that, as far as can be managed, educational facilities of equal quality should be equally available to every member of the eligible group. Thereafter, what use is made of educational opportunity is entirely up to the individual with the explicit or implicit concession that the utilization of opportunity will necessarily be unequal, because of differences of efficiency. As a first move towards educational equality, such a view is reasonable.

However, it is widely regarded as inherently flawed because it implicitly assumes that all eligible individuals are equally free and capable of being efficient in using or declining opportunity. If that were indeed the case, no objection could be advanced. Yet the summary list above suggests that most individuals are not wholly free and independent agents, equally capable of appraising and utilizing opportunities. On the contrary, most are heavily dependent on the resources of their households and wider social groups for information, orientation, guidance, and support—and households are widely unequal in all these matters. Equal opportunity offered in circumstances of inequalities of endowment and environment will perpetuate existing patterns not only of inequality, but of inequity as well, for equals on a given set of

criteria will be able to respond unequally to opportunity because of inequalities in environment. In parallel, the more powerful groups will be able to protect their less able members at the expense of the more able members of the less powerful groups. This school of thought would argue that, in order to respond equitably in educational terms to inequalities in people and their environments, a state should provide unequal educational opportunities: those at a disadvantage through genetic endowment, environment, or other accident should be offered and enabled to use greater educational opportunities, than those who are more privileged.

A separate point of objection is the meaning of equal opportunity in a situation of diversity in constellations of ability. On the one hand, a uniform education is bound to favour those whose constellations it fits closely and to discriminate in varying degrees against the rest. On the other, given an unequal society, where diversity of occupation overlaps to a large degree with inequality of status and income, diversity of education will inescapably come to correspond with social inequality. Indeed, by degrees it will grow to help predetermine eventual status. In doing so, it would come to offend against the value or principle of mobility. It would in effect overdetermine a child's future, before her or his range of potential could be fully assessed. Further, the very inequalities of society would constrain the better informed and more determined social groups to ensure that their offspring, whatever their abilities, avoid those programmes which seem oriented to what they would regard as lower-status futures.

A dilemma is presented which is insoluble, once again because a subordinate institution cannot easily operate on principles contradictory to those of the organisms on which it depends and for which it prepares its charges.

4. Issues of Policy

In moving to a discussion of policy for educational equality, an assumption has to be made about a society and its government. In part, it is that there is sufficient consensus in the society about the need for at least greater—if not absolute—equality to achieve greater equity among its members. In part, it is that there is sufficient agreement that education should be used as an instrument for equality and equity. The third part is that the government and its agents have the intent, sincerity, power, and capacity to implement whatever policies seem necessary, both in education and more widely, for greater equality and equity. If the assumption is invalid, the discussion is of course vain. At the same time, "sufficient consensus" does not require total consensus or the absence of all resistance from groups with interests vested in various forms of inequality and even of inequity. Indeed, part of policy will need to include measures to mitigate, buy off, circumvent, neutralize, or even crush such resistance.

Granted that assumption, a government has four major areas to consider: provision, access, utilization, and outcomes. Each of course has to be weighed against the resources available—material in terms of finance and equipment, human for the administrative and professional aspects. The availability of the resources themselves is of course a function of the trade-off between the various goals and priorities a government has. Although education is everywhere a major element of public expenditure, it has to compete against the claims of law and order, defence, economic development, and so on. Within education itself, however, the likely ordering of priority for resources coincides with the order of the list of areas above. For that is both a sequence of time and a ranking of importance. It is also a ranking of difficulty. The physical provision of educational personnel and facilities, for instance, is a prior and an easier matter than assuring that the outcomes of tuition and learning across schools or polytechnics are sufficiently equal.

4.1 Provision

The earlier discussion pointed out the need for a balance between two conventional requirements of provision. The first is the amount and quality of education which needs to be provided for every member of the society. The second is the pattern and volume of provision for successive stages of education to ensure that enough skills are formed to generate and sustain socioeconomic development. The poorer the society, the more acute will be this choice, for its consequences for social and economic inequality will be great. In an extreme case, the question could be at what sacrifice of quantity and quality should education for the many today be restricted to secure the education of the "necessary" few, in order to build a better future for the many of a succeeding generation? The wealthier the society, the less will choices of this nature need to be made.

The secondary choice follows, determining the phasing and speed of provision, so that all sections of the eligible population are eventually equally provided for. In the transition, however, inequality is necessarily involved. For allocating provision is in effect allocating privilege, however temporarily, and offering a form of "head start". The choice then is whether a fresh privilege should reinforce other privileges or be used to compensate for other disadvantages. In most countries, for instance, the already wealthier urban areas—and wealthier suburbs within them—or already privileged locations of accessible settlement have benefited first and most from educational provision. There are few instances where education has been used to pioneer the reduction of disadvantage.

After the physical provision follows the question of equality in quality. Where trained teachers are in short supply and very mobile, and where educational provision is being expanded rapidly, equalizing quality will be impossible and variation will be wide. At the same time, experience in the industrialized countries so far suggests that, although some reductions in inequalities of quality are feasible, some degree of variation will persist.

4.2 Access

Granted the educational personnel and facilities, do the eligible members of the society have sufficiently equal access to them? As with provision, this is a question of more acute importance to the developing countries, as the wealthier states can pay for measures to ensure virtually equal access. Are schools, for example, sited so that all their prospective pupils find it relatively equally feasible to enrol in and attend them? Or do inordinate distances, rivers, or mountains preclude some? Barriers to access are not restricted to geography. As already remarked, fees and charges of various kinds, even nominal payments for learning materials can debar many children even from primary education—as has been demonstrated by increases in primary-school enrolments, as soon as enrolment fees were abolished, in a number of countries. The need to pay for lodging and board can exclude a number of the officially eligible from secondary school.

Dependent on quantitative provision is the decision whether access to successive stages of education is to be determined by formal criteria of selection or can be left open for all comers. Linked with the provision of quality is the question whether such criteria should apply equally to all aspirants, or whether compensatory adjustments should be introduced to allow for variations in educational quality, which affect educational attainment. For instance, it is well-known in many countries that children from rural and poorer suburban schools do markedly worse on examinations for selection from primary to secondary schools. The reasons are thought to be a combination of social background and the quality of teaching, with the latter playing a very important part. Some governments judge that nothing can be done about the matter, except gradually to improve the quality of the less successful schools. Others, on the contrary, judge that the bias needs to be countered and operate systems to do so. Students from designated schools or districts can then be selected for secondary schools with lower attainments on the selection exams than students from better equipped districts. A natural consequence is that an apparent inequity is created: some students who are more qualified for secondary education have to give way to others less qualified than themselves. Governments have to choose which evil is the lesser. Similar provisions have been made in some countries to protect the access of particularly underprivileged social and ethnic groups. In at least one case, long-term political considerations entered to discriminate against students of privileged social backgrounds. In all such instances, as might be expected, there is public controversy, sometimes violent.

4.3 Utilization

Provision and access may be thought of as the "supply side" of education. The "demand side" is expressed in utilization: what use do people make of the education provided? As remarked earlier, utilization tends to be very unequal across social groups, within social groups, and also within households. Further, girls tend to utilize—or be allowed to utilize—education less than boys and the order of birth of a child also appears to influence what use she or he will make of education.

The reasons may be, as suggested, economic in three different senses. The direct and indirect or opportunity costs may be beyond a household's capacity to afford. Part of irregular attendance and premature leaving can be ascribed here. There may also be an assessment that the economic returns to education will be no greater than those offered by other ways of applying effort and time. There may be in addition more particular judgments that particular children are or are not capable of taking sufficient advantage from particular stages of education. More generally, among the lower-status groups, there may be overestimates of the magnitude of ability required for further education.

Other reasons may have cultural elements. In some societies or among some social groups, there may be a rejection of the school as an alien institution, which propagates values incompatible with those of the host society. At least part of the lagging participation of girls in a number of countries is explained by this. So, too, is part of the failure for school enrolments to grow, even among boys and even where schools and teachers are provided.

A contributory, perhaps underestimated, cause is simply the deficient dissemination of information on which appraisals of the benefits of education can be founded. More potent, and more intractable, particularly in strongly stratified societies, might be social prejudice. The more strongly the different strata stress their differences, and the more strongly particular levels of education are associated with particular social strata, the more reluctant or diffident will other strata be to utilize those levels and the more will the user strata discourage or repel the others.

What a given government does in any of these circumstances will clearly depend on its view of the importance of the particular programme of education in question. If the government is anxious that more general advantage should be taken of a particular provision, it can apply either coercion or inducements

to increase participation. A span of education might be declared compulsory and laws and resources applied to ensure that all those eligible do use it. Alternatively, participants in education may have not only their tuition fees paid, but receive in addition subsistence, lodging, and book and other allowances to relieve their households of at least the direct costs. Social differences in outlook and achievement may be evened out by special arrangements for socially mixed schools. Evidently, the degree and distribution of such support and inducement will be a function of the resources a government feels able to appropriate for such purposes at the expense of others. Evidently, too, wealthier societies will be able to afford more positive support than less wealthy—although, to be sure, the wealth of a society is no sure guide to its policies on support for compensatory or positively discriminatory educational measures.

4.4 Outcomes

So far as is known, no society intends that its educational system should produce wholly homogeneous graduates, even though some societies permit no pluralism in education, while others permit much. Indeed, the very fact that every society has differentiated branches and successive layers of education, each later stage accessible to fewer people, implies the acceptance of differentiation and inequality in abilities, knowledge, and skills. That said, it remains possible to interpret equality in terms of minimums or floors of competence: each graduate of a particular programme of education should have attained a defined minimum of skills and perhaps knowledge. For example, every young person who completes the 6-, 9-, or 12-year course of basic education available to all, might be expected to have developed at least self-sustaining skills and interest in reading, writing, and whatever numeracy is deemed essential not to be at a disadvantage in day-to-day commerce. Those who, for whatever reason, have difficulty in mastering even the minimum, could be accorded whatever pedagogical resources they need to bring themselves to the common level.

If equality is regarded as a floor, how might policy deal with the notion of excellence? More concretely, how might it allocate resources between assuring the floor and promoting excellence? By definition, excellence connotes inequality. Indeed, it could be said to praise inequality and urge it to even greater lengths. On the other hand, it has been argued that excellence is not, in practical terms, incompatible with equality because those who do not excel—by definition a majority—benefit from the excellence of the few. By raising the ceiling, so to speak, the excellent also raise the floor by pressing forward the boundaries of the possible. That is, the private inequality of individual achievement can be offset by greater well-being in the public domain. The task of policy then would be to multiply and diversify opportunities for excellence, while simultaneously safeguarding the minimums for all.

However persuasive the argument, the need for the safeguard requires emphasis. For the tendency in most societies has been to provide generously for excellence and much less adequately for the other tail of the distribution. (Ensuring that inequality on one dimension does not generate undue inequalities in other spheres may also be a matter for policy, but is wider than the remit of education.)

Equality of educational outcomes between individuals may be neither feasible nor even desirable. However, equality of outcomes between similar educational institutions is both. Absolute equality may be beyond human grasp, given the variations in the effectiveness of teachers, professors, and educational administrators such as principals. However, reducing inequalities, on whatever the dimensions measured, would appear a reasonable objective. A sharper conflict between equality and excellence can occur here. A number of experiments with "centres of excellence" have been attempted. They may indeed be pathfinders and provide stimulus for less excellent institutions. On the other hand, they also, perhaps necessarily, tend to deprive the less excellent of the wherewithal to develop excellence. For they attract not only disproportionate material resources, but also the more effective teachers and more able students.

4.5 Measures and Monitoring

A final comment is called for on an aspect common to all four areas of concern just discussed. Experience so far suggests that equality, or significant reductions in inequality, is not an easy objective to achieve. Nor, once achieved, is it easy to sustain. The social—some might claim, natural—forces remain powerful enough to reassert themselves, at any relaxing in efforts for equality. Accordingly, policies for educational equality generally provide for mechanisms and measures to monitor the progress, stagnation, or regression of equalization in each of the areas of provision, access, utilization, and outcomes.

See also: Reform Policies, Educational; Social Stratification and Education

Bibliography

Avalos B, Haddad W 1979 *A Review of Teacher Effectiveness Research in Africa, India, Latin America, Middle East, Malaysia, Philippines and Synthesis of Results.* International Development Research Center, Ottawa, Ontario. ERIC Document No. ED 190 551

Bardouille R 1982 The mobility patterns of the University of Zambia graduates: The case of the 1976 cohort of graduates. Mimeograph. University of Zambia Institute for African Studies, Lusaka

Boudon R 1973 *Education, Opportunity and Social Inequality: Changing Prospects in Western Society.* Wiley, New York

Bourdieu P, Passeron J-C 1977 *Reproduction in Education, Society and Culture.* Sage, London

Bourdieu P, Passeron J-C 1979 *The Inheritors: French Students and Their Relation to Culture.* University of Chicago Press, Chicago, Illinois

Blau P M, Duncan O D 1967 *The American Occupational Structure.* Wiley, New York

Carron G, Ta Ngoc Châu (eds.) 1980a *Regional Disparities in Educational Development,* Vol. 1: *A Controversial Issue.* International Institute for Educational Planning, Paris

Carron G, Ta Ngoc Châu (eds.) 1980b *Regional Disparities in Educational Development,* Vol. 2: *Diagnosis and Policies for Reduction.* International Institute for Educational Planning, Paris

Carron G, Ta Ngoc Châu (eds.) 1981 *Reduction of Regional Disparities: The Role of Educational Planning.* International Institute for Educational Planning, Paris

Cooksey B 1981 Social class and academic performance: A Cameroon case study. *Comp. Educ. Rev.* 25: 403–18

Dandekar V M 1955 *Report of Investigation into Wastage and Stagnation in Primary Education in Satara District.* Publication No. 32. Gokhale Institute of Politics and Economics, Poona

Dyer H S 1969 School factors and equal educational opportunity. In: Harvard Educational Review 1969 *Equal Educational Opportunity.* Harvard University Press, Cambridge, Massachusetts, pp. 41–59

Eckland B K 1967 Genetics and sociology: A reconsideration. *Am. Sociol. Rev.* 32: 173–94

Frankel C 1973 The new egalitarianism and the old. *Commentary* 56

Fry G W 1980 Education and success: A case study of the Thai public service. *Comp. Educ. Rev.* 24: 21–34

Fuller W P, Chantavanish A 1977 *A Study of Primary Schooling in Thailand: Factors Affecting Scholastic Achievement of Primary School Pupils.* Office of the National Education Commission, Bangkok

Halsey A H (ed.) 1961 *Ability and Educational Opportunity.* Organisation for Economic Co-operation and Development, Paris

Halsey A H, Floud I, Anderson C A (eds.) 1961 *Education, Economy and Society: A Reader in the Sociology of Education.* Macmillan, London

Halsey A H, Heath A F, Ridge J M 1980 *Origins and Destinations: Family Class and Education in Modern Britain.* Oxford University Press, London

Heyneman S P 1979 Why impoverished children do well in Ugandan schools. *Comp. Educ.* 15: 175–76

Heyneman S P 1982 Resource availability, equality and educational opportunity among nations. In: Anderson L, Windham D W (eds.) 1982 *Education and Development: Issues in the Analysis and Planning of Post-colonial Societies.* Heath, Lexington, Massachusetts

Heyneman S P, Currie J K 1979 *Schooling, Academic Performance and Occupational Attainment in a Non-industrialized Society.* University Press of America, Washington, DC

Heyneman S P, Jamison D T 1980 Student learning in Uganda: Text-book availability and other factors. *Comp. Educ. Rev.* 24: 206–20

Heyneman S P, Loxley W 1981 The effects of primary school quality on academic achievement across 29 high and low income countries. Paper presented to the Annual Meeting of the American Sociological Association, Toronto

Howard University Institute for the Study of Educational Policy 1978 *Equal Educational Opportunity: More Promise than Progress.* Howard University Press, Washington, DC

Husén T 1972 *Social Background and Educational Career: Research Perspectives on Equality of Educational Opportunity.* Centre for Educational Research and Innovation/Organisation for Economic Co-operation and Development, Paris

Husén T 1974 *Talent, Equality and Meritocracy: Availability and Utilization of Talent.* Martinus Nijhoff, The Hague

Husén T, Saha L J, Noonan R 1978 *Teacher Training and Student Achievement in Less Developed Countries.* Staff Working Paper No. 310. World Bank, Washington, DC

Jencks C 1979 *Who Gets Ahead? The Determinants of Economic Success in America.* Basic Books, New York

Jensen A R 1972 *Genetics and Education.* Methuen, London

Kyn O 1978 Education, sex and income inequality in Soviet type socialism. In: Griliches Z, Krelle W, Krupp H-J, Kyn O (eds.) 1978 *Income Distribution and Economic Inequality.* Wiley, New York, pp. 274–89

Lipset S M, Bendix R 1959 *Social Mobility in Industrial Society.* University of California Press, Berkeley, California

Lodge P, Blackstone T 1982 *Educational Policy and Educational Equality.* Robertson, Oxford

Mosteller R, Moynihan D P (eds.) 1972 *On Equality of Educational Opportunity.* Random House, New York

Nantiyal K C, Sharma Y D 1979 *Equalisation of Educational Opportunities for Scheduled Castes and Scheduled Tribes.* National Council for Educational Research and Training, New Delhi

Neave G R 1976 *Patterns of Equality: The Influence of New Structures in European Higher Education upon Equality of Educational Opportunity.* National Foundation for Educational Research, Slough

Rawls J 1971 *A Theory of Justice.* Harvard University Press, Cambridge, Massachusetts

Rutter M, Maughan B, Mortimore P, Ouston J, Smith A 1979 *Fifteen Thousand Hours: Secondary Schools and Their Effects on Children.* Open Books, London

Schiefelbein E, Farrell JP 1980 Education and occupational attainment in Chile: The effects of educational quality, attainment and achievement. Unpublished manuscript. World Bank Education Department, Washington, DC

Somerset H C A 1982 Examinations reform: The Kenyan experience. Mimeograph. Report prepared for the World Bank and Institute for Development Studies, Brighton

Taubman P 1976 The determinants of earnings: Genetics, family and other environments: A study of white male twins. *Am. Econ. Rev.* 66: 858–70

Taubman P, Behrman J, Wales T 1978 The role of genetics and environment in the distribution of earnings. In: Griliches Z, Krelle W, Krupp H-J, Kyn O (eds.) 1978 *Income Distribution and Economic Inequality.* Wiley, New York, pp. 220–39

Thurow L C 1975 *Generating Inequality.* Basic Books, New York

Tyler W 1977 *The Sociology of Educational Inequality.* Methuen, London

Unger J 1980 Severing the links between education and careers: The sobering experience of China's urban schools 1968–76. *IDS Bulletin* 11: 49–54

Wilson B R (ed.) 1975 *Education, Equality and Society.* Allen and Unwin, London

Yanowitch M, Fisher W 1973 *Social Stratification and Mobility in the USSR.* International Arts and Sciences Press, White Plains, New York

J. Oxenham

Equipment and Materials and Their Effects on Teaching

Equipment and materials constitute an important element of the physical environment for learning. It is often assumed that the physical environment of a school is important in student learning and this assumption is implicit in many programmes intended to improve the quality of schooling. A major review of research in this field suggests that the physical environment of the school does have effects upon patterns of behaviour of students and teachers and upon the attitudes of students even though substantial effects on achievement have not been consistently detected (Weinstein 1979).

1. Theoretical Perspectives

In the early 1970s, a review of research on the psychological and behavioural effects of the physical environment concluded that, even though there were studies which suggested environmental influences on behaviour, the mechanisms of those changes had not been elucidated and further theorizing was needed (Drew 1971). Since that review several new perspectives have helped to clarify issues in this area. These perspectives have concerned the types of dependent variables examined, the ways in which a physical environment might be described, and the mechanisms by which environmental influences might operate.

In terms of the outcomes considered to be influenced by the physical environment, an early distinction drawn between behavioural effects and psychological effects has continued (Drew 1971). Behavioural effects commonly can be considered in three categories: patterns of movement; other activity patterns (such as the use of materials); and patterns of attention and interaction. Psychological effects which are commonly examined include attitudes directly related to the physical environment (for example opinions about the pleasantness of the environment), more general attitudes (such as level of interest), and cognitive development. An important problem which needs further clarification is that of the relationship between behavioural and psychological effects of the physical environment. It is not clear to what extent changes in behaviour result from psychological effects, or vice versa.

It is now widely recognized that descriptions of the physical environment need to distinguish between the objective properties of the setting and the aesthetic properties of the setting. Several writers have argued for more systematic objective characterizations of the physical environment in terms of functional properties (Proshansky 1974). As an extension of this distinction it has been argued that an examination of the relationship between "the setting as it is" and the perceived setting "as it is experienced" constitutes an important part of research into the effects of environments on learning. Greater attention to the objective description of properties of the physical environment has also led to a more explicit consideration of materials and equipment as part of that environment in addition to more general design features. The distinction between the objective setting and the perceived setting has also served to emphasize the conceptual difference between the "physical environment" and the psychosocial "learning environment", and the importance of the study of the relationship between these two domains.

Consideration of the ways in which the physical environment influences student learning has led to two chains of influence being postulated. The first of these is the direct or pragmatic postulate that some features of the physical environment may simply impede certain activities. According to this view changes in the physical environment could change behaviour by removing impediments to activities which were considered desirable but not feasible. The second of the postulated chains of influence is that physical environments influence behaviour and attitudes through communicating a symbolic message or by being seen as "suggestive space". According to this postulate changes in the physical environment could cause changes in behaviour by suggesting possibilities which were not previously imagined. An extension of this argument might suggest that the influence of the physical environment on behaviour and attitudes might be transmitted through changes in the learning environment or classroom climate. Some of the research reviewed by Ainley (1981) suggests that this proposition is a plausible one and could prove to be a fruitful field of enquiry.

2. Research Studies in Schools

The expansion of most school systems during the 1960s and early 1970s was accompanied by major programmes of building and equipping schools. These programmes not only involved the construction of new schools which incorporated many architectural innovations, but frequently involved a reconsideration of the equipment and materials provided in schools. Accompanying this development was an arousal of interest in research into the influence of physical environments on learning. One particular area of interest was that of the relationship between "open-plan schools" (a design feature) and "open education" (a set of educational practices). Some research studies were concerned only with

architectural design but others involved consideration of the materials and equipment which constituted part of the physical environment. Weinstein (1979) reviewed a range of studies conducted in schools and concluded that, despite some inconsistencies and contradictory results, there was general support for the proposition that the abundance and quality of the materials and equipment in schools does influence the behaviour and attitudes of students and teachers. Evidence was drawn from both correlational and quasi-experimental studies. The correlational studies which were reviewed were concerned with a number of levels of schooling from day-care centres to college programmes and examined such effects as the involvement of students, levels of conflict, the rigidity of teacher restriction, sensitivity to individual requirements and patterns of movement, and use of materials. The review concluded that there was a noticeable influence of the physical environment on these types of variable at most levels of schooling. One experimental study was also reviewed. It reported changes in the behaviour of Year 2 and Year 3 students after an experimenter initiated intervention in the arrangement of equipment in an open-plan classroom (Weinstein 1977). After that change it was noted that students moved to areas which had been previously avoided (for example, the science room), a wider range of behaviours was exhibited (especially in the science and games areas), and changes occurred in the way materials were used.

Studies of open-plan schools have tended to produce conflicting results regarding the effect of these schools on students and teachers. Even though Weinstein was able to conclude that open-plan schools frequently lead to more interaction among teachers, greater feelings of autonomy, satisfaction, and ambition, and less time being consumed by routine procedures, it was considered that the evidence regarding effects on students was too fragmented to reach any firm conclusions. One of the problems of much research in this area appears to be the unspecific nature of the term "open plan". Studies employing more detailed descriptions of the physical environment seem more likely to produce consistent results.

3. Studies in Science Classrooms

The use of special materials and specially equipped rooms for the teaching of science has generated an interest in environmental influences on teaching and learning in that field. Ainley (1981) concluded that research in science education suggested that even though the provision of good facilities might not dramatically alter teaching patterns it did seem that well-equipped science rooms in combination with adequate apparatus would foster science teaching practices which involved students in a wide variety of stimulating activities. The review considered studies which looked at the limitations in science materials perceived by teachers to restrict their teaching, studies of curriculum implementation, studies which used teacher reports of their practices, and studies which used student reports of science lessons in relation to external indicators of their physical environment.

A number of the articles reviewed by Ainley contained evidence that teachers believed that insufficient laboratory facilities, overuse of those facilities, lack of assistants, and large classes impeded the use of laboratory work in science teaching. Most of the evidence came from responses to questions concerned with whether these types of activities were restricted by a lack of materials and equipment. Another group of articles were concerned with the ways in which science curricula have been implemented in schools. These studies suggested that new programmes based on integrated science and enquiry learning have sometimes not been able to be fully implemented in schools with poor equipment. In such schools the new programmes were either viewed with disfavour or the programmes were so transformed that they retained little of the original concept.

Further evidence of the effects of materials and equipment on learning was reported from studies in which teachers were asked to report on their use of particular teaching methods, with these reports being related to the types of science teaching facilities available to them. One such study was reported by Englehardt (1968) in which it was noted that the use of enquiry methods in teaching science was significantly associated with having classrooms equipped for dual use as laboratories, especially when teachers had adequate preparation time and sufficient materials. Those results were interpreted as not only resulting from removal of limitations but from the creation of an environment which suggested the desirability of new activities.

Student reports have also been used as a source of information about what happens in science classrooms with varying standards of equipment. Ainley (1978) used student reports of aspects of science lessons as part of a study of the association between the resources available and the quality of science education experienced by Year 9 students. The resources available were measured in terms of the availability of science rooms in proportion to the school population, the quality of those rooms in terms of equipment and fittings, the abundance of apparatus, and the number of laboratory assistants. It was reported that better facilities were associated with an enriched learning environment (greater involvement, better organization, and more stimulation through variety in the methods used) and more varied activities in science lessons (more experimental work, greater encouragement to explore, and less learning from textbooks).

Even though the results above derive from studies concerned with the effect of materials and equipment in one specialized area of teaching they are congruent with those reported from more general research studies in elementary and secondary schools, and in a general sense probably apply to other areas of the school curriculum.

4. Summary

In the current research literature there is little consistent evidence of a strong effect of the materials and equipment in schools on achievement. Such evidence may accumulate as the design of studies in this area develops further. However there is already available a substantial amount of evidence that the physical environment of a school or classroom can affect the behaviour of people and their attitudes to school and learning. This evidence is relevant to the provision of schooling not only because it is important to foster a variety of types of learning, and to attend to a wide range of goals in schools, but because the development of interests through participation in varied activities may have long-term effects on cognitive and affective development.

See also: Instructional Spaces, Architecture of; Open Versus Formal Instruction; Seating Arrangements in the Classroom

Bibliography

Ainley J G 1978 *The Australian Science Facilities Program: A Study of Its Influence on Science Education in Australian Schools.* Australian Council for Educational Research (ACER) Research Monograph No. 2. ACER, Hawthorn
Ainley J G 1981 The importance of facilities in science education. *Eur. J. Sci. Educ.* 3: 127–38
Drew C J 1971 Research on the psychological–behavioural effects of the physical environment. *Rev. Educ. Res.* 41: 447–65
Englehardt D F 1968 *Aspects of Spatial Influence on Science Teaching Methods* (Doctoral Dissertation, Harvard University) ERIC Document No. ED 024 214
Proshansky H M 1974 Theoretical issues in environmental psychology. *Sch. Rev.* 82: 541–55
Weinstein C S 1977 Modifying student behaviour in an open classroom through changes in the physical design. *Am. Educ. Res. J.* 14: 249–62
Weinstein C S 1979 The physical environment of the school: A review of the research. *Rev. Educ. Res.* 49: 577–610

J. G. Ainley

Eriksonian Theory of Human Development

Eric H. Erikson's theory of human or individual development represents much of the psychological hopes of a post-Second World War era. This theory, more than any other formulation of its time, defines human beings as products and shapers of their history. Erikson's psychoanalytic theory breaks with the traditional Freudian emphasis upon life's dangers and deviations by highlighting life's opportunities for success and a positive future within an individual's life synthesis. Human beings "are not only worse, but also better than they think they are" (Erikson 1959 p. 288). Human development, for Erikson, constitutes opportunities for growth; human problems serve as much to mark life's "victories" as to test difficulties. "There is little that cannot be remedied later", Erikson (1950 p. 145) proclaims, and "there is much that can be prevented from happening at all." In the first 25 years following the Second World War, Erikson's concept of psychological dialectics of the individual and society was hailed in psychoanalytic circles for the advancement of ego psychology and was also productively welcomed by educators, counselors, and the public in general. In the final quarter of this century, however, his teachings have been challenged for being outdated. His work unquestionably opened up new vistas, presenting the psychological and social sciences with findings yet to be verified and challenges still to be answered.

1. A Biographical Sketch

The theory's portrayal of human development and the theoretician's participation in his or her own history are intimately interconnected, Erikson teaches us (Erikson 1970, 1974). His observation applies aptly to his own life story.

Erik Homburger (Erikson) was born in Frankfurt, Germany, in 1902. His later salient work on issues of identity crises had its roots in his personal developmental history. It is interesting to note that he started life in a one-parent family. During his school years he lived with a strong, adoptive stepfather—a pediatrician. His youth was spent wandering around Europe until in his mid-20s, he became a Montessori teacher in Vienna. During his Vienna days he became associated with the Freudian circle, and from this entered into psychoanalytic training under Anna Freud's tutelage. During those Vienna years (1927–1933), he found his work and family commitments: he became a fully trained child analyst with several professional publications to his name and he also married Joan Mowat Serson, occupational therapist and later an author in her own right (Maier 1978 p. 276).

An invitation from Harvard Medical School in 1933 brought the Erikson family to the United States. Six years later, in 1939, the family not only adopted United States citizenship, but also the name Erikson as the family name (Erikson was his original father's family name). A wide range of clinical practice, teaching, and research projects brought Erikson appointments at Yale University (1936–1939), the University of California (1939–1951), and from 1951–1960 a combination of academic commitments at the Austen Riggs Center, Massachusetts Institute, University of Pittsburgh, and, in 1960, again at Harvard University (Division of Human Development). Since 1972, the year of his retirement as professor emeritus, Erik and Joan Erikson have lived in California, continuing their writing, lecturing, and consulting. In fact, in his early 80s Erik H. Erikson published an essay, emphasizing his psychosocial theory as cyclic and universal (Erikson 1982). Previously, developmental and historical relativity was interpreted along an intertwined chronological life progression. In his latest book he presented the life cycle in the form of unraveling from old age to infancy—from a never-ending wisdom at maturity descending to birth with its inherent trust in cosmic order. Moreover, Erikson's latest writing articulates his commitment to psychoanalytic inquiry, a perspective which guided him in his life's work; actually, he himself led psychoanalytic theory to a new stratum of thought.

Erikson's major published contributions are in three areas: (a) the human life cycle (1950, 1958, 1959, 1963, 1968), (b) identity formation (1962, 1974), and (c) the synthesis of psychological, historical, political, and ethnic phenomena into a psychohistorical analysis (1943, 1958, 1969, 1974, and Erikson 1973).

2. The Epigenesis of Life

Once a student of Sigmund and Anna Freud, he revolutionized his former teachers' teaching while remaining faithfully in their psychoanalytic camp. Erikson departs from Freudian concepts of the polarity of libidinal forces by proposing that development is as much anchored in a dialectic interplay between individuals and their society as in the interacting internal polarities. Erikson dethrones Oedipus rex. The oedipal child–father–mother triad loses part of its analytic significance because Erikson sees it as the young child's challenge for mastery as he or she joins communal institutions. He sees a similar phenomenon in the adolescent struggles over achieving cultural adaptation, an issue of "personal growth and communal change" (Erikson 1962, Maier 1978 p. 76). Most important, psychoanalytic concerns with the pitfalls and aberrations of development are replaced by a humanistic faith in the elasticity of human beings. In Erikson's words: "Children fall apart repeatedly, and unlike Humpty Dumpty, grow together again" (1950 p. 83).

Unconscious motivation is an accepted fact as evidenced by his clinical work and psychohistoric studies (Erikson 1943, 1950, 1958, 1963, 1969, 1975). His concepts on the cycles of human development, in contrast, establish essentially an ego theory, a theory of reality relationships for the management of daily living (Maier 1978 p.76).

Mutual regulation is central to Eriksonian theory. Erikson explores regulation between biological development and human orientation; between partners; between individuals and their social context; between parent and child; and the manifold mutualities which unite generation with generation, each generation and its culture, and each culture, in turn, with the cosmos (Maier 1978 p. 83). Humans are constantly faced with the promise and threat of synthesis. With Erikson, psychoanalytic theory has become an open system formulation.

Human development is epigenetic. Once born, the human organism continuously unfolds by a prescribed stage-like sequence of locomotive, sensory, and social capacities (Erikson 1950 p. 97). Each individual's culture specifies what that person is to do and to be and determines how she or he should be recognized within the culture as the individual progresses along universal developmental phases.

3. Selected Teachings

3.1 Human Development Within the Context of a Person's Psychohistorical Existence

The analysis of people's political and historic space and time is indigenous to Eriksonian thinking. He has provided a new turning point when, as an analyst, he focuses upon cultural and political issues, and particularly, assumes a strong philosophical bent. The lives of the Yurok (1943), psychohistorical studies of Martin Luther (1958), Mahatma Gandhi (1969) (for which he received a Pulitzer Prize), and Thomas Jefferson (1974) are presented in Erikson's poetic literary style. With the keen eyes of an artist and the inquisitive mind of an analyst, he paints a backdrop of historic issues with broad strokes and fills in a person's life experience in minute detail in order to join historical events and human adaptiveness as the "natural" synthesis of a person's course of life (Maier 1978 p. 75).

3.2 Identity Formation—The Crises of Adolescent Development

Erikson devoted more time and published accounts to the study of identity formation in adolescence than to any of the other seven developmental phases (1950, 1963, 1968, 1970). Prolonged adolescence (as was his own), is seen as a product of a time reflecting rapid social and technological change. It creates opportunities for incorporating the wide array of values, knowledge, and skill expectations at (biological) maturity; simultaneously, prolonged adolescence burdens the developing youth with a residue of emotional immaturity. The latter is aggravated by the inherent identity struggle of adolescence (1963 p. 12).

This identity struggle or crisis brings with it a developmental dilemma, namely, a shift from childhood desires to do and to be to the reality of becoming an actual part of a contemporary adult world. Simultaneously, the personal identity crisis is also a social issue because the youth's society lacks clarity in its expectations for rites of passage. Society and youth seek for moratoria (i.e., prolonged educational opportunities, alternative service years) to ward off too early adult commitment or potential voids in the availability of an expanding future and a more universal identity (Maier 1978 pp. 109–20). "A sense of identity" at the point of passage from adolescence to young adulthood, Erikson (1974 pp. 21–22) explains, "means a sense of being at one with yourself as one grows and develops; and it means a sense of affinity with a community's sense of being at one with its future as well as its history—or mythology."

3.3 A Human Developmental Progression

Erikson's epigenetic life cycle, an easy-to-grasp eight-stage developmental ladder, undoubtedly constitutes Erikson's major and best-known contribution (see below). His developmental chart depicts human beings in their capacity to grow, to overcome personal predicaments, and external obstacles. Sigmund Freud's original five psychosexual genetic stages are revolutionized into psychosocial open-system phases. The Freudian's treacherous psychosexual phases are envisaged for the opportunities they provide human beings to move beyond their present existence. In Shakespearian fashion, Erikson sets forth, from birth to old age, stages of human development. He is the first modern theorist who recognizes that human beings tend to continue to develop as adults.

In the Eriksonian development theory, infants first experience society through their body. Significant bodily experiences are babies' first social events which also then form psychological patterns for subsequent social experience. Erikson contends that inherent sex differences lead to basically different developmental experience, which in turn make the respective sex better prepared for a range of life tasks while less qualified for the other gender's modal tasks (Erikson 1950, 1959). This latter point was later challenged and brought Erikson into stark conflict with feminist concerns of the 1970s (see below) (Millet 1970, Reeves 1971, Smith 1973).

Throughout life, the individual is always a personality in the making, striving to incorporate dialectically irreconcilable opposites. Simultaneously, the ultimate solution of a particular phasal dilemma generates a struggle for the next one. Environmental life events both limit and free the individual. Society and its cultures preserve the unique qualities needed for their survival (Maier 1978 pp. 84–87). The growing human being "must at every step, derive a vitalizing sense of reality from the awareness that his or her individual way of mastering experience . . . is a successful variant of a group identity and is in accord with its space-time life plan" (Erikson 1963 p. 208).

Human development for Erikson is essentially affect development within a tridimensional progression. First, development always proceeds in the same order through a succession of interlinked phases, assuming that such a developmental predictiveness lends caregivers and the community "an almost somatic conviction that there is meaning to what they are doing" (Erikson 1950 p. 107). Second, development moves through a succession of mutualities, starting with caregiver and child, then mutuality between peers, and finally a mutuality between generations. Third, development progresses in phases, but phasal development is relative; previous developmental issues are differentially dealt with anew in each sequential phase.

4. The Eriksonian Life Cycle

Development is an evolutionary process—a universally experienced sequence of biological, psychological, social, and cultural events, including spontaneous recovery from periodic crisis-prone setbacks. Erikson identified eight phases in the life cycle.

4.1 Phase I: Acquiring a Sense of Basic Trust while Overcoming a Sense of Basic Mistrust—A Realization of Hope

After a life of prenatal rhythmic regularity, the achievement of basic trust and overcoming mistrust becomes the critical theme of the first developmental phase (approximately from birth to 18 months of age).

A sense of trust requires a feeling of physical comfort and a minimum amount of uncertainty and discomfort. Thus, bodily experiences provide the foundation for a psychological state of trust. Successful experience of having needs fulfilled increases favorable expectations and the infants' trust in their mistrust. The infant begins to learn to what degree hope is realizable. Trust produces inner comfort and interpersonal predictability of mutual adaptation by care receiver and caregiver, including the permissible degree of trust and mistrust implied to them by their caregivers' culture.

4.2 Phase II: Acquiring a Sense of Autonomy while Combating a Sense of Doubt and Shame—A Realization of Will

With the acquisition of trust and mistrust for the caring persons and their way of life, infants discover that they can pursue their own behavior while their continued dependence creates doubt and shame over their own capabilities. This conflict as to whether people should assert themselves or deny themselves the capacity for self-assertion furnishes the major dialectic phasal crisis between roughly 18 months to 3 years. Newly won motor and mental abilities, as well as the pleasure and pride over these freshly acquired capacities for body management and control, become major arenas for verification of autonomy. For toddlers, the skills needed to feed, walk, dress, toilet, and manipulate objects and people involves much of their own and their caregivers' energy and time. It is the "me do" stage. Mutual regulation—boundary maintenance—between child and caregiver becomes the theme of daily life. This child versus caregiver struggle eventually delineates how strongly and where the young "self" can appear buoyant and where the boundaries are to be drawn in order that the young child can assert herself or himself without shame.

4.3 Phase III: Acquiring a Sense of Initiative and Overcoming a Sense of Guilt—A Realization of Purpose

With the acquisition of a measure of conscious self-control and a clear capacity to imitate as instructed as well as to influence the environment, children move forward to new conquests in ever-widening social and spatial spheres. Children still in the preschool age discover they can imitate actions akin to those of the adults in their world. Incorporating their new prowess for reaching out with inquisitiveness, communicative language, and ever-expanding imagination, children can easily enjoy and fear the thought: "I am what I can imagine I will be" (Erikson 1950 p. 127). Children's conscience increasingly assumes the supporting and controlling functions of significant adults. In a truer sense, conscience is built out of the key adults' sociocultural heritage. Children are now fully on their way from an "attachment to their parents to the slow process of becoming a parent, a carrier of tradition" (Erikson 1963 p. 225). A struggle to move ahead, to be one's own parent, is constantly dialectically constrained by the accompanying sense of guilt for going too far and thereby defeating one's purpose.

Sex roles become markedly defined. Relationships to the parent of the same sex are strongly influenced by the parent of the opposite sex's expectations of attitude and behavior for persons of her or his opposite sex. Simultaneously, role expectations are also annunciated for girls by their mothers and for boys by their fathers. Children expand their social spheres beyond their family units and become aware of differential family standards. Whether children move on to the next phase with a thrust for initiative and subsequently outbalance their sense of guilt depends largely upon adults' response to their self-starting actions and apparently never-ending inquisitiveness.

4.4 Phase IV: Acquisition of a Sense of Industry and Fending Off a Sense of Inferiority—A Realization of Competence

Children's forward surging necessarily brings a wealth of experiences—many within the realm of their own age group. Their abundant energy is turned towards mastering the tasks within their spheres of activities. A perceived lack of progress in their chosen activities forebodes for the now school-age child a feeling of inferiority. Realization of competence through actual accomplishment—to be able "to do it" predictably is the life thread for this phase.

The world of peers and the institutions where peers can be found (school, playgrounds, street corners, or clubs) assume a position almost equal in importance to that of home life. Out-of-the-home experiences are of parallel importance to the home influence in determining whether elementary-school children incorporate into their life-style the urge to accomplish or whether they settle for a halfway measure and mediocrity. The latter may bring him or her too close to a sense of inferiority, and it remains that the child must both combat and accept this experience as a fact of life in order to move on with a sense of competence toward greater maturity.

4.5 Phase V: Acquiring a Sense of Identity while Overcoming a Sense of Identity Diffusion—A Realization of Fidelity

Identity development is closely linked with the acquisition of competence and a sense of being worthwhile. Once into adolescence in the ages between roughly 12 and 18, an identity struggle carries with it a sense of mastery of childhood issues and an increasing readiness to face the challenges of the adult community as a potential equal, withstanding the confusion of diffuse alternatives.

A struggle over one's identity, or an identity crisis, is neither a fatal event nor a pathological condition. It is instead an inescapable turning point for better or for worse. "Better" means confluence of the energies of adolescents and their particular segment of society; "worse" means a prolonged period of identity confusion for these young individuals and continued confusion for the manifold efforts invested by their communities (Maier 1978 p.111). Adolescents gradually establish a synthesis within this period of self-standardization in the search for identity as an adolescent, as members of a sexual and sociocultural age group, as members of a community, and as persons with a present and future (Erikson 1975 pp.18–19).

4.6 Phase VI: Acquiring a Sense of Intimacy and Solidarity, While Avoiding a Sense of Isolation—A Realization of Love

As young adults, individuals become full community members in Western society; their energies are thereupon invested in pursuits of career or love. Their major developmental theme establishes psychological readiness for intimate personal partnership and work commitments. Both in the world of work and in love, efforts are directed toward achieving mutuality and solidarity, a sense of shared identity. Intimacy assures mutual verification and shared membership while overcoming the dangers of isolation.

4.7 Phase VII: Acquiring a Sense of Generativity and Avoiding a Sense of Self-absorption—A Realization of Care

Full membership within a societal unit serves also as a prelude to concerns for the unit's maintenance and its perpetuation. An assured adulthood serves as the foundation for the care that the next generation requires. It is a period in the life cycle when individuals are apt to be productive in work or leisure to satisfy themselves, their partnership and, at times, people beyond their own immediate life spheres. Interestingly, it was the period when Erikson himself in his 40s and 50s, blossomed with his initial major works (Erikson 1950, 1959, 1963).

A sense of generativity includes parental and communal responsibility for society's efforts in supporting childcare, education, the arts and sciences, as well as the traditions which are to nurture the current and next generations' life span. Personal, ideational, and community life become one, to the extent that self-absorption no longer drains so much energy, thereby estranging the individual from his or her own community.

4.8 Phase VIII: Acquiring a Sense of Integrity and Avoiding a Sense of Despair—A Realization of Wisdom

Finally, as adults witness the development of a new generation, they simultaneously enjoy a fuller perspective of their own life history. They realize a generational wisdom, a sense of integrity, while overcoming a sense of despair over what was not meant to be. Substantive integrity rests upon an acceptance of the collective and the individual life cycle of human beings. Some individuals find in their last phase of their own life cycle a philosophical wisdom which extends beyond their own into future developmental cycles; they nurture the roots of a new cycle of life.

5. Implications for Child Rearing, Counseling, and Education

Eriksonian teachings have had profound effects upon the concepts in child caring, psychiatry, social work, and upon other forms of clinical work in the United States and in other parts of the Western world. Standard child development texts published in the 1960s and 1970s tend to incorporate fully his theory as part of the text's content or at least cite his life-cycle formulations. Erikson's propositions are well-reflected in United States government guidelines for day care and nursery programs. His catchy phrases highlighting his readily comprehendable concepts—such as developing basic trust, autonomy, or a sense of identity—have all become common household notions. His concepts and terminology have become ingrained in general psychological thought; psychiatrists, social workers, and clinical and educational psychologists have resolved much of their disenchantment with traditional psychoanalytic thinking by adopting Eriksonian theory as their own and reviewing their cases in Eriksonian terms.

6. *Eriksonian Theory Today*

Erikson's work has achieved a high prestige and popularity in both the academic and lay world. His work, however, has been acclaimed without the usual critical review and verification by empirical studies. A good number of his studies deal with persons and populations of various cultures. Yet, serious doubt exists whether his formulations are cross-culturally applicable. Whether they are or not remains unanswerable, for neither significant cross-cultural nor unicultural research has been carried out thus far (Roazen 1976).

Eriksonian and Freudian theoretical concepts remain in want of empirical verification at a time when validated theory is preferred. Erikson's theory seems presently to have lost much of its functional attractiveness along with the demise of psychoanalytic theory in general.

Eriksonian concepts have received their sharpest jolt from the feminist movement which poignantly challenges his analytic perceptions of women (Millett 1970, Reeves 1971, Smith 1973). Erikson was especially attacked as one of the leading psychoanalysts for his views on biological determinism, mystification of womanhood, upholding a sex-role hierarchy, and perpetuating the status quo (Smith 1973). Erikson, like most analysts of his time and before him, studied mankind as malekind, and his clinical and historical subjects in the literature are almost exclusively male. His writings belong to an era prior to feminine liberation. Although he himself has responded to these challenges and has tried to explain and justify his writings to the newly emerging position of women in these changing times, it has been almost impossible for him to meet the critical challenges (Maier 1978 pp. 127–30).

While Erikson's star may be fading in the last decades of this century, his contributions remain of substantive and historic significance. He bestowed a psychology of faith and hope for at least two generations of educators, clinicians, and people in general with a complete, internally consistent theory of human development and communal existence. Much of his teaching finds its continuation in new paradigms of psychological thought and in the pragmatics of everyday care, clinical inquiry, and educational wholeness.

Bibliography

Caplan P J 1979 Erikson's concept of inner space: A data based re-evaluation. *Am. J. Orthopsychiatry* 49: 100–08
Coles R 1970 *Erik H Erikson: The Growth of His Work*. Little, Brown, Boston, Massachusetts
Erikson E H 1937 Traumatische Konfigurationen im Spiel. *Imago* 23: 447–516
Erikson E H 1943 Observations on the Yurok: Childhood and world image. *Am. Archaelogical Ethnology* 35: 257–301
Erikson E H 1950 Growth and crisis of the "healthy personality." In: Senn M J E (ed.) 1950 *Symposium on the Healthy Personality*. Josiah Macy Jr Foundation, New York, pp. 91–146
Erikson E H 1958 *Young Man Luther: A Study in Psychoanalysis and History*. Norton, New York
Erikson E H 1959 Identity and the life cycle: Selected papers. *Psychol. Issues* 1: 1–171
Erikson E H 1962 Youth: Fidelity and diversity. *Daedalus* 91: 5–27
Erikson E H 1963 *Childhood and Society*, 2nd edn. Norton, New York
Erikson E H 1968 *Identity, Youth, and Crisis*. Norton, New York
Erikson E H 1969 *Gandhi's Truth. On the Origins of Militant Nonviolence*. Norton, New York
Erikson E H 1970 Autobiographic notes on the identity crisis. *Daedalus* 99: 730–59
Erikson E H 1974 *Dimensions of a New Identity: The 1973 Jefferson Lectures in the Humanities*. Norton, New York
Erikson E H 1975 *Life History and Historical Moment*. Norton, New York
Erikson E H 1978 (ed.) *Adulthood: Essays*. Norton, New York
Erikson E H 1982 *The Life Cycle Completed*. Norton, New York
Erikson K T (ed.) 1973 *In Search of Common Ground: Conversations with Erik H Erikson and Huey P Newton*. Norton, New York
Evans R I 1967 *Dialogue with Erik Erikson*. Harper and Row, New York
Maier H W 1978 *Three Theories of Child Development*, 3rd edn. Harper and Row, New York
Millett N E 1970 Inner space. In: Millett K (ed.) 1970 *Sexual Politics*. Doubleday, New York, pp. 210–20
Reeves N 1971 *Womankind Beyond the Stereotypes*. Aldine, Chicago, Illinois
Roazen P 1976 *Erik H Erikson: The Power and Limits of a Vision*. Free Press, New York
Smith J M 1973 Erik H Erikson's sex role theories: A rhetoric of hierarchical mystification. *Today's Speech* 21: 27–31
White R W 1960 Competence and the psychosexual stages of development. In: Jones M R (ed.) 1960 *Nebraska Symposium on Motivation*. Nebraska University Press, Lincoln, Nebraska, pp. 97–141
Whitman L E 1968 Adult developmental tasks as suggested by the writings of Erik H Erikson. Masters thesis, University of Washington

H. W. Maier

Error Analysis as a Curriculum Evaluation Method

Error analysis consists of analysing students' work—homework, school work, tests—to identify the major errors they are making, or to identify mislearning which is occurring. Error analysis is usually undertaken at two or three points in the curriculum development cycle. The first point is at the small–scale tryout stage of new curriculum materials (see *Curriculum Tryout*). The second point is at the larger-scale tryout stage; however, this stage is only undertaken in a few countries. The third point is at the quality-control stage when a probability sample of children is tested after the curriculum has been fully implemented in all schools.

The error analysis undertaken at the first point is more comprehensive than at the second and third points. The error analysis conducted for all three points consists of two analyses.

The first is to discover where an objective is being achieved by only a "few" students. "Few" must be operationally defined by the curriculum team. It is often defined as fewer than 40 percent of students.

At the small-scale tryout stage where perhaps only six classrooms are being used, the pattern of percentage correct for the first three items (one item measuring one objective) could be as shown in Table 1. It can be seen that the objective measured by Item 1 is well-achieved, by Item 2 is poorly achieved, and by Item 3 is well-achieved in some classes and poorly achieved in other classes.

What is "going wrong" with Item 2? At this point, the evaluator turns to the item analysis. This is also the analysis which is used for the larger-scale tryout

and quality-control stages. For all students the analysis may be as presented in Table 2 for a multiple-choice item with five possible responses.

Response C is considered to be the right answer or best answer. Responses A, B, D, and E are wrong answers but have been constructed such that they are errors which the students are likely to make. These responses are usually based on teachers' experience. Only 22.2 percent of the students obtained the correct answer. However, Response B was answered by 51.2 percent of all students and the discrimination index, which is typically a point biserial correlation, is positive. This indicates that the better students on the test as a whole are opting for Response B. Assuming that the item is a good item, then an error in learning has been discovered.

The next question is why or how has this error arisen? At the larger-scale tryout and quality-control points all that can be done is to examine the curriculum materials and hope that it is possible to identify what might be the cause. At the small-scale tryout stage the evaluators have usually collected other information of a qualitative nature from the teachers and students about problems they have had with the curriculum text or with the teaching—learning strategy used. By referring to the qualitative data it is usually possible to identify the cause. The two most frequent causes are that the level of language used is too difficult for the students or that the sequencing is inappropriate. The curriculum team is then in a position to revise the materials and/or the accompanying teacher guide.

The examples given above have used tests with multiple-choice format. However, it is also possible to use students' homework or classwork for such an analysis. There are certain types of achievement for which multiple–choice tests are inappropriate (Thorndike and Hagen 1969). The basic technique is to go through the set homework or school work of the group or sample of students in question and make a frequency count of the "errors" occurring. This yields information about the most frequent errors and again it is usually possible to identify "causes" in the small-scale tryout but not in the larger-scale tryout and quality-control stages.

Three other ways in which error analysis is used

Table 1
Percentage of correct responses in a sample of six schools

| | Schools | | | | | | |
	A	B	C	D	E	F	Average
Item 1	90	80	85	87	93	78	85.50
Item 2	20	30	27	19	15	22	22.16
Item 3	90	80	15	20	50	90	57.50

Table 2
Item analysis for Item 2

| | Omit | Responses | | | | |
		A	B	C[a]	D	E
Item 2:						
Percentage of students selecting	0.6	8.0	52.2	22.2	7.6	9.4
Discrimination	−0.04	−0.09	0.26	0.12	−0.12	−0.14

a The correct response

are worthy of brief mention. The first is the construction of distractors in multiple-choice items such that the wrong answer chosen by the student indicates to the teacher the likely error. Take for example the item

$$(-17) + (-14) = \text{A.} \quad -31$$

$$\text{B.} \quad +31$$

$$\text{C.} \quad -3$$

$$\text{D.} \quad +3$$

If a student answers B, the most likely error is that the student is confusing $(-) + (-)$ with $(-) \times (-)$. The second use links errors to the way in which teachers explain rules and principles. For example, it was found that some children in a particular target population were calculating $3 + (-7)$ as 10 and $(-6) + (-15)$ as 9. A small study then discovered that these errors were being made only in classes where teachers were attempting to teach the concept and operation of negation numbers using a number line—for example a line with unit intervals along it from -30 passing through zero to $+30$.

A third way (Lundgren 1976) in which error analysis is used is in the drawing of profiles of achievement of individual students as compared with what objectives they are meant to learn. Objectives are classified by theme and behaviour (in the taxonomic sense). Hence, there may be one category which involves the calculation of simple multiplication. If 12 items are involved in the testing of the objective, the profile indicates how many of the items are correctly answered. This, in turn, indicates to the teacher where remedial work is needed with an individual student.

See also: Profiles, Educational; Objectives, Educational, Taxonomies of; Error Analysis: Mathematics; Error Analysis: Foreign Language; Curriculum Evaluation; Curriculum Tryout

Bibliography

Johnstone A H 1981 Diagnostic testing in science. In: Lewy A, Nevo D (eds.) 1981 *Evaluation Roles in Education.* Gordon and Breach, New York

Klahr D (ed.) 1976 *Cognition and Instruction.* Erlbaum, Hillsdale, New Jersey

Lewy A (ed.) 1977 *Handbook of Curriculum Evaluation.* UNESCO, Paris

Lundgren U 1976 *Model Analysis of Pedagogical Processes.* Stockholm Institute of Education, CWK, Gleerup

Postlethwaite T N, Nasoetion N 1979 Planning the content of teacher upgrading programs: An approach in Indonesia. *Stud. Educ. Eval.* 5: 95–99

Thorndike R L, Hagen E 1969 *Measurement and Evaluation in Psychology and Education.* Wiley, New York

T. N. Postlethwaite

Error Analysis: Foreign Language

Correction of errors has always been a common practice in foreign language teaching. A systematic analysis of learners' errors was introduced in the wake of contrastive analysis (see *Contrastive Linguistic Analysis*). It was initially offered as a substitute for, or a complement to, contrastive analysis, when the latter failed in its original task of predicting learners' errors. The study of language learning problems was to begin with the investigation of the phenomenon, that is, negative transfer or interference (see *Foreign Language Teaching: Interference*), which was supposed to account for the problems, while contrastive analysis was assigned an explicatory role only. Variability in learner performance could not however be explained by means of error analysis alone, and the basic problems found in contrastive analysis, such as comparability of specific items and equivalence, still remained.

In error analysis, errors have often been given much too strong an emphasis at the cost of the communicative task of language, and therefore error analysis gradually gave way to the analysis of the learner's language as a whole. Static error analysis was replaced by research in which errors are seen to be essential ingredients in a dynamic process of language learning instead of malignant growths to be weeded out. A learner's deviant language is thus seen to be an unavoidable interim stage towards second language proficiency.

Traditional error analysis consists of five stages. In error recognition, an attempt is made to distinguish systematic competence errors from performance errors, that is, mistakes and lapses, easily corrected by the learner when pointed out (Corder 1981). Error recognition depends crucially on correct interpretation of the speaker's intentions. In the following stages, the errors are described according to a model and classified. In the explanation of the errors, three causes are usually distinguished: interlingual errors caused by interference from the mother tongue, intralingual errors caused by the target language system, and teaching-induced errors. At the final stage, the errors are compared with target language norms to assess their influence on the success of communication. The decisions about the nature of feedback to be provided to learners are crucially dependent on the systematicity of the errors.

More recent approaches to error analysis consider systematic errors to be markers of the learner's progress, and learner performance has come to be characterized as interlanguage, also described as transitional competence, approximative system, or idiosyncratic dialect (see *Foreign Language Learning: Interlanguage*). It is characterized as a distinct linguistic system resulting from the learner's attempts to achieve target language norms. Interlanguage is supposed to derive its features from five processes: language transfer, transfer of training, strategies of second language learning, strategies of second language communication, and overgeneralization of foreign language linguistic material (Selinker 1972). With many learners, progress in interlanguage development stops at the point at which some deviant features still remain in learners' performance. The true nature of such fossilization is unknown.

Strategies of second language learning have been exposed to intensive research, which has been mainly concerned with transfer and overgeneralization. A great deal of research which has been devoted to transfer has been unable to reveal its true nature. This would require a clearer picture of the processes involved in speech reception and production. Communication strategies mostly refer to procedures adopted by learners to overcome problems in second language communication; they include avoidance, paraphrasing, borrowing, and call for assistance. The research in the second language acquisition process has only recently begun, but in addition to certain features universal to all language acquisition, some phenomena characteristic of second language acquisition only have also been specified (Wode 1981).

One of the prominent aspects of learner performance is simplification, which seems to be due to several types of reduction processes at work in learner speech (Faerch and Kasper 1980). Similar simplification is also characteristic of foreigner talk, baby talk, caretaker speech, and teacher talk, but here simplification results from attempts to assist the interlocutor in the task of comprehension. The study of simplification has established a link between error analysis and the research in pidgins and creoles, in which phenomena similar to those occurring in second language acquisition can also be found (see *Foreign Language Learning: Interlanguage*).

Traditional error analysis works with naturalistic data drawn from various types of productions by language learners, above all translations and compositions. Free delivery of speech, various types of narration tasks, retelling of stories, cloze tests, multiple-choice tests, and direct observation of learner behaviour have also been used. Elicitation of errors has often proved necessary to expose learners to situations in which certain types of structures could be expected to occur (see *Contrastive Linguistic Analysis*).

The main problem in error analysis is the same as in contrastive analysis. The theory and methodology of linguistics is insufficient to explain the phenomena involved. A wider framework is needed involving psychological, sociological, neurological, and other related insights into cognitive mechanisms and information processing in the brain and the speech channel as a whole.

Bibliography

Arabski J 1979 *Errors as Indicators of the Development of Interlanguage*. Uniwersytet Slaski, Katowice

Corder S P 1981 *Error Analysis and Interlanguage*. Oxford University Press, London

Faerch C, Kasper G 1980 Processes and strategies in foreign language learning and communication. ISB-*Utrecht* 5: 47–118

Johansson S 1978 *Studies of Error Gravity: Native Reactions to Errors Produced by Swedish Learners of English*. Gothenburg Studies in English 44. University of Gothenburg, Gothenburg

Nickel G 1981 Aspects of error analysis (EA): Errare humanum est. *AILA* (International Association for Applied Linguistics, Spain) *Bull.* 29: 1–28

Palmberg R 1980 *A Select Bibliography of Error Analysis and Interlanguage Studies*. Åbo Akademi, Åbo

Richards J C 1974 *Error Analysis: Perspectives on Second Language Acquisition*. Longman, London

Richards J C 1978 *Understanding Second and Foreign Language Learning*. Newbury House, Rowley, Massachusetts

Selinker L 1972 Interlanguage. *IRAL* (*International Review of Applied Linguistics in Language Teaching*) 10: 209–31

Wode H 1981 *Learning a Second Language*. Narr, Tübingen

K. Sajavaara

Error Analysis: Mathematics

Error analysis in mathematics teaching strives to identify the nature of errors a learner may commit in dealing with a particular type of assignment. The results of such analysis may help the teacher to prescribe appropriate corrective teaching for the individual learner, and make recommendations to the curriculum developers for producing further instructional materials.

In practice, mathematics students are typically evaluated by counting the number of correct and incorrect responses. Those with only a few errors "know their mathematics," those with many errors do not. If a classroom test or homework is being evaluated, the results are often used to assign more homework to those who missed several problems. If an entire school is taking a standardized test, the results may be used to decide grade placement, promotion, scholarships, or perhaps the success of the school program. Error analysis differs from quantitative evaluation by attending to patterns of missed problems (and sometimes the associated written work). Its purpose is not to evaluate how much the student knows, but rather to describe what the student doesn't know. This description generally plays one of two roles: as an aid to classroom teaching, and as a method of research.

Although error analysis has been recommended to teachers for some time, it recently received a great deal of American attention with the publication of

Error Patterns in Computation (Ashlock 1976). Although it is often felt that error analysis should apply to all aspects of mathematics instruction, most attention is drawn to arithmetic algorithms where dramatic illustrations of its value occur. For example, a child using the standard American addition algorithm that computes $127 + 245 =$ _____ as

$$\begin{array}{r} 127 \\ +\ 245 \\ \hline 373 \end{array}$$

probably understands the algorithmic procedure and has simply made an error recalling $7 + 5 = 13$. On the other hand, if the student computes the sum as

$$\begin{array}{r} 127 \\ +\ 245 \\ \hline 3612 \end{array}$$

he/she probably doesn't know the correct algorithmic procedure and may lack certain place value concepts as well. In order to choose appropriate instruction it is necessary to understand the nature of the child's error.

The analysis of children's errors as a research tool has a long and honored history both within and without school mathematics. For example, many American researchers used error analysis to understand children's difficulties with arithmetic in the early part of this century. At about the same time, Piaget was studying children's errors on Binet's intelligence tests. More recently Gagné's work with learning hierarchies (which is often exemplified with mathematics topics) has encouraged mathematics educators to attend to the prerequisite skills which children need to be successful in mathematics—skills which are often shown by error analysis to be lacking. Error analysis has also played a role in recent studies investigating problem solving, word problems, applications, curriculum evaluation, and algebra difficulties (Radatz 1979).

Bibliography

Ashlock R B 1976 *Error Patterns in Computation: A Semiprogrammed Approach*, 2nd edn. Merrill, Columbus, Ohio
Radatz H 1979 Error analysis in mathematics education. *J. Res. Math. Educ.* 10: 163–72

J. D. Knifong

Essay Examinations

Since the time of Aristotle, educators have recognized the value of extended discourse for assessing students' understanding and for interpreting their academic and personal experiences. Oral examinations predominated for centuries, and continue today, as a test format preferred in educational contexts where intensive individual assessment is desirable and possible. Essay examinations, too, require students to express and elaborate their knowledge and viewpoints, but, unlike oral examinations, do not permit the examiner and examinee to interact and clarify the students' responses. Essay exams can represent both the accuracy and sophistication with which students use subject matter information and strategies; they can also document the clarity and coherence of students' manipulation of discourse structures (exposition, persuasion) and sentence-level conventions (syntax, punctuation).

Despite the rich cross-section of students' subject matter expertise and writing competence that essay exams can provide, they are often criticized as being unreliable and costly. Considering the extensive use of essay exams to inform educators about students' progress through and out of an educational system, there is remarkably little empirical research that addresses issues in essay examination methodology, particularly on techniques for improving their technical quality.

This article summarizes prevailing practices briefly, but will focus on methodological problems and potential solutions documented by empirical research. Many of the points derive from the expanding bodies of literature on test design, the comparability of essay exams and objective tests, and also the relatively recent research on methodological issues involved in the assessment of writing as a distinct communication skills domain.

1. Prevalence of Essay Examinations

Essay examinations are widely used in school systems throughout the world. They are given during school terms to monitor the development of subject matter and writing skill, at the end of courses and schooling levels to certify achievement, and as entrance exams to determine qualifications for admission to a higher level. In the recent past, however, the economic and methodological problems plaguing essay examination procedures have prompted some school systems to abandon the essay as a test format in favor of shorter, more economically scored objective tests. In the United States, for example, test publishers have conducted numerous studies in order to document the comparability of multiple-choice test results with scores from essay exams (see *Objective Tests*). For tests of writing, high correlations between objective test total scores and global essay scores were used as evidence to support the substitution of multiple-choice tests for essay exams. The dominance of this psychometric logic and methodology over the strong theoretical, but empirically unverified arguments of subject matter specialists resulted in the virtual elimination of essay examinations in large-scale assessment in the United States. In many other countries, multiple-choice tests have become widely used at both elementary- and secondary-school levels.

The prevalence of multiple-choice testing at all levels of schooling in the United States has been increasingly criticized. A recent report by the National Assessment of Educational Progress (NAEP) warned that students' ability to engage in disciplined thought and to express it in coherent, supported discourse is seriously deficient (NAEP 1981). The report attributes the problem to an overemphasis on low-level recognition responses to curriculum materials as well as in tests. Researchers are challenging the construct validity of multiple-choice questions for measuring subject matter and, especially, writing-skill development. They urge a return to essays and other constructed response test formats that will stimulate students to use higher-level reasoning processes as they formulate extended discourse, solve complex problems, or apply subject matter concepts and principles.

Increasingly, the concern of these researchers is supported by empirical research. In writing assessment, for example, studies are beginning to reveal weak relationships between subskill scores on multiple-choice tests and ratings of the quality with which students use those skills in their essays (Quellmalz et al. 1982). As researchers look to essays and other performance measures for valid and reliable representations of levels of competence, however, they question seriously many current essay examination practices.

2. Purposes of Essay Examinations

2.1 Functions

Essay tasks are intended to measure the quality or status of subject matter and writing ability. Since "quality" and "status" imply standards of judgment, the question arises "in comparison to what?" Evaluation literature frequently distinguishes between comparisons of individuals to each other (norm-referenced testing) and comparisons of individuals to standards of subject matter achievement (criterion- or domain-referenced testing). Norm-referenced tests permit identification of the best students within a particular pool; domain-referenced tests describe the level of subject matter mastery. Current evaluation thinking suggests that a well-constructed test can serve both functions. Students can be placed on a competence continuum that will permit monitoring and certifying of their level of development, and that will also allow comparing them normatively to the progress of other populations of students on the same skills continuum (see *Norm-referenced Assessment*; *Criterion-referenced Tests*; *Domain-referenced Tests*).

2.2 Goals

An important issue in the design of essay examinations is the rationale underlying selection of the skills to be assessed and taught. These skills presumably derive from information about the level of subject matter knowledge or writing skill required for students to function in their immediate and future school, work, and home environments. However, claims for the "ecological validity" of competencies and goals often lack empirical verification.

In some countries, the goal levels set for subject matter achievement or writing skill may vary for students of different ability or socioeconomic levels. Similarly, the skills required for entrance to advanced training may vary according to the population the trade school or university serves. In the United States, with its goal of universal schooling and literacy, many school systems have set minimum competency standards in the three basic skills areas of reading, writing, and mathematics (see *Minimum Competency Testing*). In some schools, these are survival-level skills that can be demonstrated in a single paragraph; in other schools (and other countries), the levels of performance and writing assignments are more ambitious. Subject matter goals, too, may vary from the simple recall of important facts, to the application of complex strategies and principles. Approaches to setting achievement standards have ranged from arbitrary decisions to careful analyses of future academic and job requirements. Seldom, however, have standards been empirically validated on actual criterion groups (Bush 1977).

Critical components of essay examination methodology are the precise definition of (a) the skills to be assessed; (b) the essay problem assignment; and (c) the scoring criteria. When schools use the same essay exam to assess both students' grasp of a specialized subject matter, and also their ability to use their knowledge to construct an organized essay, subject matter performance is often confounded with writing ability. A promising approach to this problem has been the use of test specifications to define important features of an exam's design, scoring, and interpretation (see Sect. 3).

3. Structure of Essay Assignments

3.1 Skill Specification

The most basic rule of measurement is that the skill to be measured must be sufficiently defined so that it can be assessed reliably. Essay exams have been repeatedly criticized for their lack of objectivity. To address this problem, the first step in formulating test specifications is to define the skill(s) assessed. Skill specification is generally considered to include definition of the content and behavior. In subject matter essay exams, the content would be facts, concepts, and principles (such as osmosis or taxation). The behavior would reference not just the observable behavior "write," but the procedures, strategies, and solution routines the student was to apply to the content. For example, "The student will write an essay comparing the economic causes of the revolutionary and civil wars." In tests of writing ability, the focus is not on content points covered, but on the discourse features of the requested essay, for example, whether the composition is a well-formed example of narrative or expository writing.

3.2 Components of the Writing Assignment

When assessments gather samples of students' written production, a series of issues arise regarding the structure of the assignments used to prompt the writing. The intent of test specifications is both to describe what is being assessed in relation to the problems or assignments previously set and the kind of response that is expected, and also to provide item-writing guidelines for generating additional homogeneous essay tasks. In subject matter essay exams, the specification would describe the range of ways the problem could be presented to students in the essay question. For example, how much and what kind of information about the topic is given to the student? Is the structure of the question sufficiently precise to elicit all desired concepts? Also, what level of interpretation is requested? Are students asked, for instance, to summarize, compare, analyze, or evaluate subject matter content? Does the assignment inform students of the scoring criteria (Ingenkamp 1977)?

In tests of writing ability, the structures of assignments have varied considerably. At one end of the continuum, essay tasks are described as "topics." As long as the topics are familiar, distinctions may not be made between terse prompts such as "Lost?" which could cue quite varied discourse structures, and "Convince the school board to change the dress code," which more clearly directs students' treatment of discourse mode, topic, and audience. Underlying the assumed comparability of vague, unstructured prompts is a view of writing as an undifferentiated construct—a skill that can be equally demonstrated in response to any one of a myriad writing tasks.

In contrast to this undifferentiated approach to designing writing assignments, a more detailed method has been developed. This is a result of studies of those factors in the writing task that cue students to produce essays that differ substantially in structure and style. Critics of the kinds of writing assignments typically presented in classroom and assessment tasks contend that most assignments do not present full rhetorical contexts that sufficiently inform students about the writing purpose, topic, audience, writers' role, and intended criteria for judging the essays (Britton et al. 1975). Recent research suggests that

different rhetorical purposes (to express, persuade, inform) place different cognitive demands on the writer and, consequently, students write differentially well when addressing different rhetorical aims and audiences (Quellmalz et al. 1982). Also, since the actual content or "topic" of the writing assignment is not the main issue in writing assessment, research is exploring ways of using pictures, other media, or reading passages to provide students with enough information about the topic so that they will be free to concentrate on structuring their essays. In some countries it is usual to deal with this problem by permitting a choice of topics.

A final, seldom studied, feature of essay assignments is the time allotted for planning, writing, and at least reviewing, if not revising, the essay. The amount of time scheduled for essay writing varies widely across countries and clearly can support or constrain students' chances to demonstrate their competence.

In sum, current test theory and research supports the advisability of structuring essay examination prompts that clearly specify the aim, topic, audience, writers' role, and evaluative criteria and that permit sufficient time for students to engage in all aspects of the writing process.

4. Scoring Criteria and Rating Scale Formats

The criteria used to judge essay examinations operationally define which features of content and test structure constitute a "good," or at least a "competent," response. To be credible, criteria should not reflect the preferences of only a few individuals, but should represent standards endorsed by a community of professionals knowledgeable about the subject matter. Moreover, these criteria should refer to those features of content and written expression amenable to instructional intervention. For example, the dimensions of "depth," "flavor," and "creativity" may enhance the quality of the essay, but a growing number of educators contend that it is neither logical nor fair to hold students accountable for subject matter or writing expertise that the schools cannot demonstrate that they can teach, and, therefore, should not test.

Criteria used to evaluate student content and written expression vary along a number of dimensions: (a) from qualitative value judgments to quantitative counts of information and text features; (b) from global reactions to analytic judgments; (c) from comprehensive attention to a range of concepts and text features to isolated focus on particular information or text features; (d) from vague guidelines to replicable precise definitions.

Generally, readers' reactions to students' essays involve three level of judgments: (a) subjective, global impressions of overall quality; (b) analytic judgments about component test features; (c) a holistic quality judgment combining subjective impressions with judgments about the quality of the combination of text elements. In general-impression scoring, a rater reads an essay once and assigns it a quality score. General-impression ratings are global, heavily qualitative, and based on vague guidelines that may not reference component text features nor their differential weighting or importance.

The most quantitative, detailed, and replicable scales are analytic rating scales where readers assign several scores for various features of the essay. Analytic scales vary considerably in the range of content, rhetorical, structural, and syntactic elements referenced and in the relative weights of these elements. For example, in an attempt to be comprehensive, the Diederich Expository Scale was derived from factor analyses of "good" essay elements cited by many raters. It presents nine subscales ranging from content ("ideas") to sentence-level mechanics ("spelling"). In contrast, other analytic text analysis schemes such as T-unit analyses or counts of cohesive ties focus on isolated components of the written piece. Some analytic scales rely heavily on several scores or "error counts" for readily spotted factual details or sentence-level mechanical essay features such as grammar and punctuation, yet give little attention to the relationships among concepts or features of the discourse structure, such as organization or elaboration. Holistic rating scales, where readers assign a single score, often combine characteristics of both general impression and analytic approaches. Holistic schemes vary widely in the range of text elements contributing to each score point and the specificity with which score levels are defined (Ingenkamp 1977, Quellmalz 1980).

Since the focus, specificity, and objectivity of criteria informing impressionistic, holistic, or analytic approaches may vary considerably, an examination program should weigh carefully the nature of the criteria selected and their underlying rationale. Otherwise, the program may find that the criteria do not mesh well with aims of the assessment and instructional program, and do not provide a useful status report and/or diagnostic feedback. For example, studies of alternative scoring schemes for evaluating writing competence have shown that seemingly compatible rating schemes may, upon application, result in quite different classifications of the same set of essays.

The need for explicit criteria is also apparent for scoring subject matter essay exams. Students commonly complain about the ambiguous subjective criteria used for subject matter essay exams in classroom assessments. Certainly, when the results of large-scale achievement exams have serious consequences for students (e.g., exit, selection, certification, or graduation), explicit, public, and rational scoring keys are imperative.

5. Rating Procedures

When large numbers of papers must be scored by a pool of readers, an assessment program must ensure that evaluation criteria are uniformly interpreted and applied. Such standardization involves both the formulation of explicit criteria and procedures for training raters. In the United States, rater training follows a fairly standard procedure. Following a brief introduction to the rating scale, readers begin to practice applying criteria to a set of papers representing the test sample. A trainer leads discussion of the features of each paper that result in the paper's classification to a particular grade. Training time varies according to the number of separate scores recorded for each paper and according to the clarity of the criteria. The rigor of the procedures used to decide if acceptable rater agreement levels have been attained at the end of training vary from a show of hands to pilot tests requiring independent scoring of essays. In many countries, subject matter examinations are scored by raters with subject matter expertise, but who receive little or no formal training. Failure to conduct any structured training or to check on prior agreement levels may increase the risk of unreliable scoring.

On exams of writing ability in the United States, training times reported for holistic and primary trait sessions have averaged 2 to 4 hours; analytic scales with five to eight subscales range from 4 to 8 hours. Trained raters can assign a holistic or primary trait score to a student's paper in from 30 seconds to $1\frac{1}{2}$ minutes, while the rating time required to assign five to eight separate analytic scores ranges from four to five minutes for multiparagraph essays and from two to four minutes for paragraphs.

Once independent scoring begins, some large-scale writing assessments attempt to maintain rater agreement, and prevent rater drift, by periodically conducting agreement checks on common papers. Discrepant ratings may be discussed with master readers, by the entire group, or may be referenced to written feedback sheets explaining the rationale for "expert scores" (Quellmalz 1980). An alternative procedure for resolving discrepancies is to adjudicate them with a third reading by a different rater.

In many assessment programs, the procedures for establishing and maintaining scoring standards vary dramatically, particularly for subject matter exams. There may be only one reader per paper. Readers may or may not receive a written scoring guide, and training on its use. In the United States, however, written examinations for admission to advanced university campuses or professional schools are read by two trained raters. In countries using essay exams for high-school or university admission, or for certification, an individual's score may vary; a problem attributable in part to imprecise criteria and less rigorous rating methodology (Spencer 1979).

6. *Reliability and Validity of Essay Examinations*

6.1 *Reliability*

The reliability of an examination program depends on the degree to which it eliminates measurement error. Four potential sources of error (or score fluctuation), identifed for examinations of writing ability, but applying as well to tests of subject matter skill, are: (a) the writer-within-subject individual differences; (b) the assignment variations in item or task content; (c) between-rater fluctuations; (d) within-rater instability.

To avoid within-subject error, achievement testing programs attempt to determine the reliability of students' performance by gathering performance on a pool of homogeneous items or assignments. Since essay writing requires at least 20 or 30 minutes, it is often logistically difficult to have students write many essays in an examination. Studies of the consistency of student performance across a series of essays often report low reliabilities for a single essay. However, analyses of the stability of student writing performance across several essays have also been confounded by the failure to limit essay task structure variability to differences in topic. Often the several essays differ in discourse mode as well and therefore do not represent homogeneous task or item requirements. Designing comparable essay assignments using the features discussed for specifying task structures is a promising method for reducing error variance due to the assignment. To reduce error associated with individual variability, most writing assessment experts recommend collecting essays on at least two parallel assignments. Similarly, the reliability of subject matter essay exams increases when scores on several essays are combined (Spencer 1979).

The most prevalent issue concerning reliability in essay examinations is that of interrater agreement. Statistical indices of agreement levels include coefficient alpha, generalizability coefficients, point biserial correlations, and simple percentages of agreement. In the United States, competency testing programs try to report agreement levels of at least 80 percent, and/or generalizability coefficients of at least 0.60. The most effective method of reducing interrater variability is to provide training on clearly specified criteria. To reduce error due to within-rater score fluctuations over time (rater drift) due to reader fatigue and/or carelessness, some form of interspersed check procedure seems helpful (Quellmalz 1980). Although a few studies report that readers tend to get more lenient or more harsh as rating progresses, few assessment programs routinely monitor this problem by comparing early and late scored essays.

With recent advances in computer technology, research is seeking ways to eliminate the cost and variability of human rating by devising programs for machine scoring of essays. However, computer scoring is still plagued by the computer's limitations to counting and pattern matching. To date, these matching and counting functions have been used mostly to count total numbers of words and words per sentence, types of punctuation, spelling errors, and to relate these frequencies to human ratings of overall essay quality. Counts of prepositions and "to be" verbs predict stylistic problems such as overuse of complex sentence structures or inactive verbs, while counts of cohesive ties relate to essay coherence. Page reports some success for use of the computer to score subject matter essays by having the computer count the frequency of key content terms. The basic programming problem, however, is to find commands that will recognize when commas or cohesive ties or subject matter facts are used appropriately. This current limitation and the logistical and economic problems of typing essays into the computer relegate computerized scoring for large-scale competency testing to the future (see *Computer Scoring of Essays*).

In order for a large-scale assessment to make generalizations about stability and level of students' competency, it is important that the design of the assignments, the number of assignments (items), and the scoring procedures show that irrelevant sources of score fluctuation have been controlled, and that the essay ratings represent reliable samples of students' writing competence.

6.2 *Validity*

The validity of an examination derives from evidence that the test accurately and dependably measures the specified skill(s). Evidence for the validity for an exam may take several forms. One form focuses on the test content (i.e., the items or essay assignments) and gathers judgments of subject matter experts that the items or essay tasks have content, face, or descriptive validity, that the experts judge the objectives or skills defined to be important and representative subject matter competencies, and that the items, problems, or writing assignments will elicit these skills.

Other forms of validity focus on test performance to examine (a) whether the scores are comparable to scores on other tests of the same skills (concurrent validity); (b) if the score levels predict future success (predictive validity); and (c) if the performance pattern appears to measure the underlying trait (construct validity).

In the United States, test specifications are often used to describe how the skill is defined and the rules for generating the items or assignments. The specifications serve as a reference for subject matter experts' judgments of the exam's content validity. Unfortunately, judgments of content validity for essay exams tend to refer to test objectives and assignments, and there is no consideration of the rating criteria. Equally unverified is whether experts judge that the essay assignments and criteria will distinguish among levels of skill development.

The most common methods of attempting to establish the validity of essay exams have been comparisons of scores to "related" measures. In the case of tests of writing ability, the "other" measures chosen as criterion variables are often reading tests, multiple-choice tests, or class grades (which themselves are often suspect). Several recent studies have found very low correlations between representations of writing-skill constructs. Even relating essay examination scores to grades on other essay exams may be technically questionable if the criteria for the two assignments differ. Recent research has documented how superficially similar rating scales can rank the same set of essays quite differently.

Studies of the predictive validity of essays face the same definitional problem of picking an appropriate criterion variable. Although many United States studies of the predictive validity of norm-referenced tests of writing ability found high correlations with future university success, it is unlikely that writing skills were as much the cause as other more general abilities.

The heart of a test's validity is whether it measures the underlying skill construct, that is, whether it taps the hypothesized mental store of information and strategies. Conventional factor analytic techniques used to establish construct validity are being replaced by facet analyses and multitrait–multimethod (MT-MM) analyses. A recent study using MT-MM to examine the factor structure underlying multiple-choice subscores and essay and paragraph ratings confirmed that essays provided more distinct information about hypothesized writing traits than did the objective test scores (Quellmalz et al. 1982). More studies using such techniques might elaborate our understanding of skill constructs.

7. Summary

The complexity of designing valid essay examination programs dramatically illustrates the more general problem educators face in integrating testing and instruction. Systematically conceptualized, designed, and validated tests require careful descriptions of objectives and their rationale, the structure of the assessment task, the scoring criteria and procedures, and evidence that the results are consistent, accurate, and predictive.

See also: Achievement Tests; Higher Education: Assessment of Students

Bibliography

Britton J, Burgess T, Martin N, McLeod A, Rosen H 1975 *The Development of Writing Abilities (11–18)*. Macmillan, London

Bush P 1977 Comparability of grading standards in public examinations in England and Wales: Methods and problems. In: Ottobre F M (ed.) 1977 *Criteria for Awarding School Leaving Certificates: An International Discussion*. Pergamon, Oxford, pp. 14–28

Coffman W E 1971 Essay exams. In: Thorndike R L (ed.) 1971 *Educational Measurement*, 2nd edn. American Council on Education, Washington, DC

Cooper C R, Odell L (eds.) 1977 *Evaluating Writing: Describing, Measuring, Judging*. State University of New York at Buffalo, Buffalo, New York

Ingenkamp K 1977 *Educational Assessment*. National Foundation for Educational Research, Slough

National Assessment of Educational Progress 1981 *Reading, Thinking, and Writing*. Educational Commission of the States, Denver, Colorado

Quellmalz E S 1980 *Problems in Stabilizing the Judgment Process*. University of California at Los Angeles Center for the Study of Evaluation (Technical Report No. 136), Los Angeles, California

Quellmalz E S, Capell F, Chou C 1982 Effects of discourse and response mode on the measurement of writing competence. *J. Educ. Meas.* 19(4): 241–58

Spencer B 1979 The assessment of English: What is needed? In: Dockrell W B (ed.) 1979 *National Surveys of Achievement*. Scottish Education Department, Edinburgh, pp. 84–96

E. S. Quellmalz

Estimation in Mathematics Education

In general usage, estimation is synonymous with judgment or opinion associated with value, worth, or significance. In more specific usage, estimation is the association of a quantity, amount, or size with the number of objects in a collection, the result of a numerical computation, the measure of an attribute of an object, the duration of an event, or the solution of a problem.

1. Advocates

In their suggestion of methods and activities for teaching estimation, advocates imply that teaching students to estimate will improve skills in computation and in problem solving (Schoen et al. 1981). A student who is capable of estimating and is willing to apply this capability to guess the solution of a problem can be expected to be more motivated to solve it (Polya 1965). The ability to estimate has been identified as one of the basic competencies recommended that everyone should have (Carpenter et al. 1976) and as necessary for employment (Dawes and Jesson 1979). Widespread use of computing technology places emphasis on estimation for verifying the reasonableness of computations and the need to formalize these techniques in reconsidering assumptions underlying mathematics instruction (Levin 1981).

Despite these claims, there is evidence that the

teaching of estimation has not become a major part of the mathematics curriculum. Furthermore, little research is found to support or refute the validity of methods and claims made for its inclusion in the curriculum.

2. Research

A review of research on estimation provides a few tentative generalizations: (a) estimation skills appear to be related to general intelligence and mathematics ability and less strongly related to computational skill and problem solving; (b) there appears to be little relationship between the ability to estimate lengths or areas and the ability to do computations rapidly; (c) there is limited evidence that teaching the rounding process improves the ability of fourth, fifth and sixth graders to make good estimates; and (d) estimation techniques can be taught. Also, there is contention that estimation requires greater understanding than precise calculations. There is conflicting evidence that estimation improves skill in solving verbal problems (Schoen et al. 1981).

3. Curriculum

Carpenter and others hypothesize that difficulties in estimation are caused by lack of prerequisite skills, including facility with mental arithmetic and ability to round numbers accurately (Carpenter et al. 1976). They recommend that estimation be integrated into the curriculum and applied whenever possible, noting that estimation encompasses a variety of mathematical skills, requires a genuine understanding of basic mathematical concepts, and takes years to learn.

A perusal of curriculum materials indicates that the main topic studied under the heading "estimation" is "rounding," and, more specifically, "rounding" numbers to some specific point. Johnson suggests a procedure to enable students to estimate at the lowest level by using the leading digit (e.g., $76 \times 15 = 70 \times 10 = 700$), then extending as the need is felt to rounding to the leading digit (e.g., $76 \times 15 = 80 \times 20 = 1600$), and finally to the use of "number sense" to obtain better estimates (e.g., 76×15: $70 \times 10 = 700$; $70 \times 5 = 350$; $700 + 350 = 1050$) (Johnson 1979).

4. Remarks

There is general agreement that developing skills in estimation should be a major objective of school mathematics and that estimation is essential for literate citizenship and more important than precise calculations for many common uses of mathematics. Yet it seems to be one of the most neglected skills in mathematics curricula. Furthermore, it is a difficult skill to measure, especially when assessing final results rather than processes. Criteria for good estimates seem ambiguous.

In the light of these factors, however, many researchers and educators share the hope of Trafton that "more will be learned in the next few years about how students develop estimation skills, how estimation can become integrated into the curriculum, and how instruction can more closely fit the psychology of the learner" (Trafton 1978 p. 213).

Bibliography

Carpenter T P, Colburn T G, Reys R E, Wilson J W 1976 Notes from national assessment: Estimation. *Arithmetic Teach.* 23: 296–302

Dawes W G, Jesson D J 1979 Is there a basis for specifying the mathematics requirements of the 16 year old entering employment? *Int. J. Maths Educ. Sci. Technol.* 10(3): 391–400

Johnson D A 1979 Teaching estimation and reasonableness of results. *Arithmetic Teach.* 27: 34–35

Levin J A 1981 Estimation techniques for arithmetic: Everyday math and mathematics instruction. *Educ. Stud. Math.* 12: 421–34

Polya G 1965 *Mathematical Discovery: On Understanding, Learning and Teaching Problem Solving*, Vol. 2. Wiley, New York, p. 105

Schoen H L, Friesen C D, Jarrett J A, Urbatsch T D 1981 Instruction in estimating solutions of whole number computations. *J. Res. Maths Educ.* 12: 165–78

Trafton P R 1978 Estimation and mental arithmetic: Important components of computation. *Developing Computational Skills*. National Council of Teachers of Mathematics, Reston, Virginia, pp. 196–213

E. G. Gibb

Ethical Considerations in Research

Concern with ethical considerations in educational research has grown in recent years, whereas in earlier years the emphasis was on technical standards. This concern can be viewed as relating to the subjects of study, to the customers for a particular investigation, to the scientific community, and finally to society in general. These sets of concerns are not independent but are interrelated, posing questions for researchers themselves and for all those concerned with research.

1. The Growth of Concern

Most books on educational research published in the 1970s (Butcher and Pont 1973, Kerlinger 1973, Taylor 1973), not only do not include a chapter or section on ethics but do not even include the term in their indexes. There is, however, a discussion of ethics as they apply to social research in general in a book published in 1979 (Barnes 1979), and a later book (Dockrell and Hamilton 1980) does have a chapter which includes ethics in its contents (Walker

1980), but even in this book the term does not appear in the index.

There has been, since the early 1970s, an increased awareness of ethical questions in research involving people. Earlier concern was with technical issues as manifested in such volumes as the *Technical Recommendations for Achievement Tests* (American Educational Research Association 1955) prepared by a committee of the American Educational Research Association and the National Council on Measurement Used in Education and a similar one, *Technical Recommendations for Psychological Tests and Diagnostic Techniques*, prepared by a committee of the American Psychological Association (American Psychological Association 1954). These two volumes were replaced by one prepared by a committee representative of the three organizations, on standards for educational and psychological tests (American Psychological Association 1966). More recently the emphasis has shifted. In 1973, a book on ethical principles in research with human participants (American Psychological Association 1973) was published as well as a substantial volume on standards for evaluation of educational programmes (Joint Committee on Standards 1981). This latter report continued the concern with technical matters but also included a section on propriety standards, which was largely ethical.

Technical standards are an important aspect of ethics in educational research. Whatever procedures are used must be valid, that is, they must provide accurate information relevant to the purposes for which they are used. Accuracy is relative. In most measurements, physical as well as educational, there is some error. Precise accuracy is not possible. The scales used in a maternity hospital for weighing newborn infants need to be more accurate than those used for measuring overweight middle-aged adults in a gymnasium. Each needs to be accurate enough for its purpose. Much of the 1966 volume issued by the American Psychological Association is devoted to this question of the validity of instruments and the rest to other related matters like the reliability of instruments, scales and norms used, instructions for scoring, and the general adequacy of the manuals.

The 1981 report of the Joint Committee on Standards for Educational Evaluations goes beyond this even in technical matters. Additional questions are raised with ethical implications.

2. Ethics in Relation to Subjects

The focus of the manual on ethical principles (American Psychological Association 1972) is exclusively on the subjects of an experiment. This is a major area of concern, but not the only one. The first question for the researcher in relation to his or her subjects is, do they understand fully what is being asked of them? The researcher must not minimize or indeed exaggerate the demands that are to be made in terms of time, effort, or stress on subjects.

It is easiest to be clear about the amount of time that will be required. It is sometimes difficult for a researcher to appreciate the stress that may be induced, for example, in school pupils by a test which proves to be too difficult for them. School children do not always understand the distinction between data which are being gathered anonymously for research purposes and assessments which are being made of them personally.

It may be easier for teachers to make this distinction. However, at the beginning of a study of the effects of different teaching styles, the extent to which their actual classroom practices will be monitored by an outsider may not be clear to the teachers involved. Whatever disclaimers may be made, the observer may appear to be a figure of some authority or at least in close contact with people in authority. The presence of a student in the classroom for a prescribed period may be quite acceptable. The presence of a researcher over a considerable period of time may be a source of considerable stress.

The mere presence of a researcher in a classroom or indeed in a school studying the use of corporal punishment may be a source of stress both to those who would wish to use corporal punishment but are constrained from doing so and to those who wish to see it eliminated but fear their discipline may not be tight enough. The researcher cannot be expected to anticipate the amount of stress in each case but can reasonably be expected to make clear precisely what is being expected and to ensure as far as possible that there is no misunderstanding about what will be involved.

The second area in which the researcher has obligations concerning the subjects of the study is the confidentiality of the information obtained. It is up to the researcher to ensure that the subjects know and agree what will be disclosed about them. Many research organizations have rules about the identification of schools or school districts, teachers, or pupils in published reports (as does the Scottish Council for Research in Education, for example). The application of this principle is easier in the traditional survey-type studies where information is disclosed only about categories of schools, teachers, or pupils. It is only in those rare circumstances where there are only a few cases in any one category that it is possible to identify individuals. However, with case studies which rely on providing substantial information about a limited number of subjects it may not be possible to disguise the individuals concerned. The use of a fictional name as in Elmstown (Hollingshead 1949) or Hightown Grammar (Lacey 1970) may not be sufficient to disguise the source of the information. It may be necessary in those cases to do as Richardson did in her Nailsea study (Richardson 1973), that is, to negotiate with all concerned before the publication of a report.

Whether an attempt is made to disguise individual persons or institutions by the use of a fictional name, or a number, or a letter, or whether their identity is fully disclosed, all concerned must have a chance to read the material before it is published. Should they also have the right to require the removal of any material about themselves to which they object even if this were to weaken the report to the point of rendering it valueless? What is the balance between the rights of the subjects in the study and of the community for whose benefit the study was carried out?

With unpublished materials a similar problem may arise. Information about an individual, whether he or she is explicitly identified or not, may be used as a basis of discussion for clarification or for explanation with colleagues or superiors. The individuals clearly have a right to know beforehand that this may happen to them. Do they equally have a right to exclude from such discussion any material about themselves which they find unacceptable?

The first concern outlined above was about the effects on the subjects. A second concern is about the benefits of research to them. A researcher must specify what return there will be to the subjects and not mislead them about the benefits of the investigation to themselves. It is not unusual for researchers to offer to provide the results of tests to participants in a study. If the test scores are to be meaningful to the participants it may be necessary to provide an interpretation which is not required for research purposes. For example, a test of academic achievement may be administered which provides only raw scores for experimental purposes. That information might be all that the researcher needs. Those scores, however, might be quite meaningless to teachers, pupils, or administrators unless they were related in some way to the objectives of the teaching or the performance of a reference group. If the subjects are to be offered benefits for themselves those benefits must be real.

A serious dilemma may arise when there is concern about the effect on subjects of knowledge of the object of the research. It may be important to know whether classrooms following a particular regime are more likely to induce persistence in their pupils than those adopting an alternative approach. It might be possible to devise an acceptable measure of persistence but what would the effect be on that measure of informing the children that this is what was being measured and not level of attainment? The same problem arises with classroom observation studies which are concerned with particular aspects of teacher behaviour. If teachers are told precisely what it is that the researchers are looking for, are they more likely to act in that way than if they were simply given general information? If the researcher believes

that full disclosure would affect the behaviour of the subjects, under what circumstances is he or she free to withhold relevant information and by doing so mislead? Is it ever legitimate to make false statements in order to disguise the true objective of an investigation?

It is incumbent on the researcher to be explicit in the definition of the role of both sets of participants in a study, researchers and subjects. In some cases the responsibility of each is clear enough. In others, for example in action research, it is sometimes not clear what the subjects can expect of the researchers by way of support for their activities. By contrast there are some research designs which require the researcher to take an authoritarian role and to ensure that certain actions are carried out. It should be clear to all participants what they can expect of each other. This does not mean that they need to follow a rigidly predefined path. Flexibility may be essential for the progress of the research. What is required is that at each stage the mutual expectations be explicit.

A final consideration with respect to the subjects is general cost effectiveness. Is the value that is to be gained from the investigation commensurate with what is being asked of the subjects? It is very rarely that educational research would involve actual psychological harm to children. However, parents sometimes raise this question when a new curriculum is being tried out in the schools. They are concerned that their children may be put at a disadvantage in comparison with others. It is a question which arises with experimental studies rather than with observation of variation in current practice. If a researcher introduces a change in practice he or she is depriving children of something they would otherwise have had, and providing a substitute. In what circumstances is the informed consent of parents required for such an experiment? Does a school have to get consent before trying a new reading scheme, a new form of grouping, a new teaching method? The existence of laboratory schools which parents choose to send their children to, provides one answer. However, it is not an alternative that is universally available (see *Laboratory Schools and Teacher Education*).

It is also important not to make an excessive demand on the time or resources of pupils or schools. Excessive in this context means not commensurate with any foreseeable benefit from the studies.

3. Ethics in Relation to Customers

A second set of concerns relates to the customers of research. In this context, customer refers to someone who has commissioned the research. At its simplest this can be summarized by saying that researchers should not promise more than they can deliver and that consequently they should deliver what they have promised. This principle applies whether the customer is looking for guidance about a specific course of action, or for better understanding of some theoretical issue. In this section the focus will be on customers whose interest is in research as a basis for action.

Ethical considerations in relation to customers refer primarily to communication. The first concern must be that the customer understand the limits of the information that will be made available. Research findings are rarely prescriptive. They never pre-empt careful consideration of the issues. It is unlikely that research will tell an administrator or teacher what to do. Usually it can only contribute to the examination of the options. The researcher therefore must be clear about what the data from a specific study can and cannot contribute to the thinking about a particular issue or set of issues.

The conclusions from research may range from a plausible hypothesis to a substantiated generalization. Whitehead's distinction in his paper on the rhythm of education (Whitehead 1932) may be applied to research (Dockrell and Hamilton 1980). He talks about the stage of romance which is when the researcher has an insight into the possible interpretation of a set of facts, the stage of precision where he or she attempts to specify the circumstances where the insight might apply, and finally the stage of generalization where the researcher can assert a particular principle or a particular set of relationships that will be of universal application. There is a risk that a research report which is at the stage of romance or indeed at the stage of attempted precision will be misconstrued as at the stage of generalization, even when the authors are careful to point out the limitations of their work as did Rutter and his colleagues (Rutter et al. 1979). The researchers must make clear to the customer what is the status of their conclusions.

It is in this area of relationships with customers that the traditional concern with technical questions is relevant. Researchers understand the meaning of statistical significance, that is, the probability of findings being other than accidental, but the customer may not. He or she may be presented with tables of relationships between groups and assume that the sample findings can be safely generalized to the population. Professional journals would insist on the inclusion of probability levels. They may, however, be excluded from unpublished reports to customers. Even some published reports have presented results which were not statistically significant in a way that might mislead a reader.

One of the conventional distinctions in discussion of educational research is between statistical significance and educational significance. Relationships which it is reasonable to assume actually exist in the population might be so small as to be irrelevant for practical purposes. A customer who is told that results are significant might assume that this means important and not merely probable. The importance of relationships is a matter of judgment and it is therefore the responsibility of the researcher to see that the customer understands the probable size of the differences as well as the likelihood of them being found in the parent population. A customer who thinks that a correlation of 0.5 is high might not do so if he or she appreciated the extent of the covariation that it indicated.

The measures used in research are frequently not direct measures of the variables which are of concern to the customers. Researchers might talk easily of achievement in mathematics or science, of intelligence or social class, always understanding that what is being referred to is a score on a particular measure. Whether that measure adequately represents what the customer means by the variable in his or her particular set of circumstances needs clarification. Scores on any test of attainment in, for example, physics, will cover only a sample of the skills and concepts which might legitimately be thought of as included in physics. As long as the sets used in the research coincide with those the customer had in mind for this purpose, no problems arise. It is up to the researcher to ensure that the customer understands the nature and content of the test and is consequently in a position to judge for himself or herself whether the measure is appropriate.

The problem is particularly acute in studies where surrogates are used. It is not easy, for example, to define social class and even where a definition is attempted it is the practice to use some surrogate like a scale of occupations. Surrogates may be satisfactory for research purposes but quite unsuitable for policy making. It is probably wisest to avoid using a general label like reading or physics or social class as far as possible and to be specific in saying what the scale assesses.

Where do the researchers' responsibilities end? Have they met their commitments when they present a set of results, or have they a responsibility to their customers to interpret their findings, to say what they mean in a particular context? The extent to which researchers can do this will vary from project to project, but it will be done by somebody and researchers do not absolve themselves from responsibility by saying that they have presented their results. Rather, their responsibility is to facilitate and participate in interpretation, ensuring that any conclusions are in accord with their understanding of the data.

If researchers do accept responsibility for interpreting and explaining their findings, they have the further responsibility of distinguishing between their findings and their extrapolations from them. It is legitimate to interpret results in the light of theory. It is important too to specify which of the researchers' opinions arise from the specific set of findings and which from theoretical or other considerations.

The researcher has a final responsibility to the

customer, that is, to ensure that he or she is understood. Researchers frequently use terms which have limited or extended meaning. That may be a convenient form of communication for people who share a particular background. It may be misleading to a customer who does not share the researcher's knowledge or assumptions. Many research organizations employ editors whose job it is to translate research findings into the language of the customers. Where researchers do not have this professional service available to them, they should be particularly alert to the needs and problems of their readers.

4. Ethics in Relation to Colleagues

The researchers' obligations to their colleagues are twofold. One is to them as scientists to ensure that they can make the fullest use of their researches and second, as members of the research community to ensure that what they say does not detract from the status of the community.

Research data are not private property. They are an individual contribution to a common wealth of knowledge and understanding. The first set of responsibilities are those most frequently specified and indeed frequently enforced by colleagues through the medium of reviewing research proposals for funding, articles for publication, and books once they have been published.

In technical reports which are addressed to the research community, far more detail about the way the data have been gathered and how the analyses have been made is called for than in a report to customers so that an adequate professional evaluation of findings may be made. Some research institutions prepare several reports on the same study, designed for different audiences. The report to colleagues should be sufficiently detailed for them to understand the limitations in the data and their analysis. The kind of interpretation and perhaps simplification which is involved in a popular report can be avoided and replaced with specific detail.

One common way of dealing with the question of analysis is to make data available for reanalysis. Social science archives are one way of doing this, though it may be appropriate for some kinds of data to be held in confidence and only made available in carefully controlled circumstances. This does not of course answer all the questions. It only makes available the data on file. It does not answer questions about how the data were gathered. It is important therefore to retain copies of tests, questionnaires, and other material.

In the case of ethnographic studies, the raw data may well be field notes including reports of interviews, descriptions of observations, and so on. In this case the raw data should be available for other scholars to read and interpret but so should a description of the circumstances in which the encounters took place.

Some researchers achieve fame or have it thrust upon them. It is in these circumstances that the researchers' responsibility to the research community is greatest. What is written will be seen as "research". When they are reported it will be "researcher says". They will be taken as representing the whole research community. The clearest responsibility is not to make statements which will bring research into disrepute. This does not mean that they must not participate or indeed provoke debate on important issues. If they do not make clear the significance of their findings for general issues who will? Researchers must not, however, overstate their cases—and must not assert the infallibility of research findings, particularly of their interpretation of their own findings.

5. Ethics in Relation to the Community

Finally, the researcher has responsibilities to the community as a whole. One of them is implicit in the last consideration of responsibility to colleagues. It may well be the responsibility of researchers to draw attention to the implications of their researches for policy. If they do not, they may be neglected or misinterpreted and the community as a whole may suffer. Important improvements that could have been made might not be made because of a researcher's reluctance to take part in social debate.

It is at this stage that researchers can be the voices of the voiceless. The customer in educational research is more likely to be an administrator with resources than teachers, parents, or pupils. The researcher can be the advocate of a different set of clients—the pupils who might suffer educationally from an apparently efficient set of arrangements or the teachers who might be forced into practices which have been evaluated from only one perspective and that one not their own.

There is a final consideration for the researchers. That is, whether it is appropriate to carry out a particular piece of research in specific social circumstances. A researcher like everyone else is responsible for the foreseeable consequences of his or her actions. In some societies simply to raise certain issues about racial or social differences might now or in the past have been a basis for the abridgement of human rights. The researcher has the obligation to ask questions fearlessly. He or she also has the obligation to be aware of the consequences of raising certain issues.

The relevance of a broad range of ethical questions to the conduct of research has been recognized in fields like medicine for many cultures. In physics, the development of nuclear weapons provided a jolt that led to soul searching and laid the old certainties open to question. As educational research has become less an academic pursuit and more directly a guide to educational practice, ethical issues have become more prominent and concern with them a topic of discussion among researchers.

See also: Teachers as Researchers

Bibliography

American Educational Research Association/National Council on Measurements Used in Education 1955 *Technical Recommendations for Achievement Tests*. National Educational Association, Washington, DC

American Psychological Association 1954 *Technical Recommendations for Psychological Tests and Diagnostic Techniques*. American Psychological Association, Washington, DC

American Psychological Association 1966 *Standards for Educational and Psychological Tests and Manuals*. American Psychological Association, Washington, DC

American Psychological Association 1973 *Ethical Principles in the Conduct of Research with Human Participants*. American Psychological Association, Washington, DC

Barnes J A 1979 *Who Should Know What? Social Science, Privacy and Ethics*. Penguin, Harmondsworth

Butcher H J, Pont H B (eds.) 1973 *Educational Research in Britain*, 3. University of London Press, London

Dockrell W B, Hamilton D (eds.) 1980 *Rethinking Educational Research*. Hodder and Stoughton, Dunton Green, Kent

Hollingshead A B 1949 *Elmstown's Youth: The Impact of Social Classes on Adolescents*. Wiley, New York

Joint Committee on Standards for Educational Evaluation 1981 *Standards for Evaluations of Educational Programmes, Projects, and Materials*. McGraw-Hill, New York

Kerlinger F N (ed.) 1973 *Review of Research in Education*, Vol. 3. Peacock, Itasca, Illinois

Lacey C 1970 *Hightown Grammar: The School as Social System*. Manchester University Press, Manchester

Richardson E 1973 *The Teacher, the School and the Task of Management*. Heinemann, London

Rutter M, Maughan B, Mortimore P, Ousten J, Smith A 1979 *Fifteen Thousand Hours: Secondary Schools and Their Effects on Children*. Open Books, London

Taylor W (ed.) 1973 *Research Perspectives in Education*. Routledge and Kegan Paul, London

Walker R 1980 The conduct of educational case studies: Ethics, theory and practice. In: Dockrell W B, Hamilton D (eds.) 1980, pp. 30–63

Whitehead A N 1932 *The Aims of Education, and Other Essays*. Williams and Norgate, London

W. B. Dockrell

Ethics of Evaluation Studies

Ethics are the rules or standards of right conduct or practice, especially the standards of a profession. What ethical standards have been proposed for the conduct of educational evaluation? What general principles underlie standards? Are these standards and principles sufficient to ensure an ethical practice?

These are the questions this article will address. The extent to which evaluation studies actually meet these ethical standards is not addressed here, except by implication.

The ethics of evaluation studies are a subset of ethics or morality in general but, of course, ethics applied to much narrower problems than those of general morality. "In the narrow sense, a morality is a system of a particular sort of constraints on conduct—ones whose central task is to protect the interests of persons other than the agent and which present themselves to an agent as checks on his natural inclinations or spontaneous tendencies to act" (Mackie 1977 p. 106).

Thus the task of an ethics of evaluation is to check the "natural inclinations" of evaluators that may injure the interests of another person, a task made all the more formidable by the fact that these inclinations may be unconscious, built into the very techniques and methods employed by the evaluator. Given the relative power of the evaluator over those evaluated, the ethics of evaluation are critical to the establishment of a responsible evaluation practice.

According to Sieber (1980 p. 52), "If there were a field of applied ethics for program evaluation, that field would study how to choose morally right actions and maximize the value of one's work in program evaluation. It would examine the kinds of dilemmas that arise in program evaluation; it would establish guidelines for anticipating and resolving certain ethical problems and encompass a subarea of scientific methodology for performing evaluation that satisfies both scientific and ethical requirements; and it would consider ways to promote ethical character in program evaluators."

There is yet another requirement for an ethics of evaluation: it must be rationally persuasive to evaluators. It seems reasonable to treat evaluators themselves as moral persons. "Thus to respect another as a moral person is to try to understand his aims and interests from his standpoint and try to present him with considerations that enable him to accept the constraints on his conduct" (Rawls 1971 p. 338).

Recently several codes of ethics and standards of practice have been proposed for educational evaluation in particular and for social science research in general. Many of these rules and standards are methodological directives but some are concerned with ethical behavior. For example, in the most elaborate and widely disseminated set of standards, there are four areas of concern—utility, accuracy, feasibility, and propriety. Under propriety the standards are formal obligations, conflict of interest, full and frank disclosure, the public's right to know, rights of human subjects, human interactions, balanced reporting, and fiscal responsibility. These standards relate mostly to privacy, protection of human subjects, and freedom of information. Generally the picture that emerges is that the evaluator should forge a written contract with the sponsor and adhere to that contract. He or she should beware of conflicts of interest in which the evaluator's personal interests are somehow involved. Openness, full disclosure, and release of information are the main ways of dealing with these problems. The limitations on full disclosure are the commonly understood rights of subjects. Ordinarily this means informed consent of the subjects must be obtained. There is also a call for respecting others who are engaged in the evaluation itself, a general admonition to decency.

Anderson and Ball (1978) have compiled a list of ethical responsibilities for the evaluator, as well as a list of ethical obligations for the commissioner of the evaluation. The evaluator is expected to acquaint the sponsor with the evaluator's orientation and values, develop a contract with the sponsor, fulfill the terms of the contract, adhere to privacy and informed consent standards, acquaint the sponsor with unsound program practices, present a balanced report, make the results available to legitimate audiences, allow for other professionals to examine the procedures and data, and publish rejoinders to misinterpretations of the evaluation results. The commissioner of the evaluation has obligations to cooperate in the various tasks of the evaluation. To the degree that they deal with ethics at all, other formal codes of ethics and standards suggest similar ethical principles and sets of problems. Mutual agreement of the evaluator and sponsor is emphasized in most codes.

Ethical issues also emerge from the use of particular techniques in designs, such as the use of control groups. For example, two ethical issues that are of concern in use of control groups are the potential for denying a valuable service to eligible clients who might not be chosen for the beneficial treatment and the equitable allocation of scarce resources to a large group of eligible recipients. Acceptance of the clients as equals is one proposed way of dealing with these problems, and multiple treatment groups is another.

A review of the literature suggests four basic ethical problems: (a) withholding the nature of the evaluation research from participants or involving them without their knowledge; (b) exposing participants to acts which would harm them or diminish their self-esteem; (c) invading the privacy of participants; and (d) withholding benefits from participants. These are all intrusions against the individual's person somehow, or infringements against personal rights.

What principles underlie these ethical concerns? The National Commission for the Protection of Human Subjects of Biomedical and Behavioral Research has identified three underlying principles—beneficence, respect, and justice. Beneficence means avoiding unnecessary harm and maximizing good outcomes. In the opinion of the commission this principle is served by the research or evaluation being valid, by evaluators being competent, by the participants being informed, by the results being disseminated, and by the consequences of the evaluation being weighed with others. The evaluation is supposed to be beneficial.

Respect means respecting the autonomy of others by reducing the power differential between the evaluator and participants, having participants volunteer, informing participants, and giving participants a choice in matters that affect them. Justice, in the commission's view, means equitable treatment and representation of subgroups within society. Justice is operationally defined by equitable design and measurement, and equitable access to data for reanalysis. These three principles constitute the rationale for ethical human research, including evaluation.

For the most part these ethical codes concentrate upon infringements to personal rights. The codes assume that there are inherent individual rights prior to the conduct of the evaluation, that the participants must be accorded these rights, and that the individual must voluntarily agree to participation. Almost all these codes of ethics require that the evaluator enter into a contractual agreement with the sponsor and adhere to the agreement as a matter of ethics. Not adhering to the agreement would be considered unfair. Those who are not a party to the agreement have certain personal rights, such as the rights to be informed about the study and the right to volunteer.

Fairness suggests that people are obligated to uphold their part of an agreement when they have voluntarily accepted the benefits of an arrangement or taken advantage of its opportunities to further their own interests. People are not to benefit from the efforts of others without doing their fair share.

Not just any agreement is considered binding, however. House and Care (1979) have asserted that a binding agreement must meet certain conditions. For example, a party cannot be coerced into signing the agreement. All parties must be rational, equally informed, and have a say in the agreement itself. Only under certain conditions can the agreement be considered an appropriate basis for the evaluation.

The fundamental ethical notion is that of a contractual ethics, the establishment of an implicit or explicit contract as the basis for conduct. This is consistent and, indeed, entailed by viewing society as a collection of individuals. "The essence of liberalism . . . is the vision of society as made up of independent, autonomous units who co-operate only when the terms of cooperation are such as make it further the ends of the parties" (Barry 1973 p. 166). Voluntary consent of the participants is essential to ethical conduct in this framework, and intrusions upon people without their consent is considered unethical and immoral. Individual autonomy is a primary principle within this conceptual framework, and autonomy is reflected in establishment of agreements, informing participants, and requesting consent. The ethics are essentially personal and contractual.

While these principles capture many of the concerns of those who have codified ethical principles for evaluation, other theorists have held that these notions of ethics are too restricted. Ideology plays an important role in how evaluation studies are conducted. In fact, Sjoberg contends that evaluation studies usually take for granted the structural constraints of the social system. Evaluations are used for effectiveness, efficiency, and accountability within the dominant bureaucratic hierarchies. The categories used by evaluators are those of the status quo, and the social indicators employed are allied to the political power structure. To the degree to which this is true, the formalized ethics of evaluation are limited to concerns which do not threaten the ideological statu quo. Many ethical problems are beyond the recognition of evaluators because they are excluded by the prevailing ideology. People are usually not aware of the limits of this ideological consensus until they step outside it.

For example, MacDonald has carried the principle of autonomy a step beyond the prevailing consensus. He has contended that evaluations usually serve the interests and purposes of bureaucratic sponsors or an academic reference group at the expense of those being evaluated. He has proposed that those being evaluated be shown the information collected from them and be given veto power over what is said about them in the evaluation report. Individual autonomy is carried to the extent that "people own the facts of their lives." This is a right not usually accorded to respondents. Within this framework knowledge of social action is the private property of practitioners, and truth is relative to the different interpretive frameworks by which social agents guide their conduct. This position is too extreme for most evaluators but is based upon an extension of an accepted principle. Another unusual ethical position is that evaluators should make themselves more vulnerable to those evaluated, thus redressing the balance of power between the two parties.

Underlying all these various notions of correct behavior in evaluation are contrasting conceptions of justice. The dominant implicit conception of justice is utilitarian, the idea being to maximize satisfaction in society. Any action which maximizes the total or average satisfaction is the right thing to do. Although such a notion seems remote from the practice of evaluation, indicators such as test scores are often taken as surrogate measures of satisfaction and the right thing to do is determine which educational programs maximize these scores. This thinking ultimately leads to a particular kind of evaluation study and technology, even though evaluators may not be fully cognizant of the underlying philosophical assumptions or ethical implications. For example, Schulze and Kneese have shown that the results of a cost–benefit analysis can vary dramatically depending upon which overall ethical system one adopts. They contrast utilitarian, egalitarian, elitist, and libertarian ethical views. As they note, the philosophical underpinnings of current cost–benefit analyses are utilitarian.

Contrasted to utilitarian justice are pluralist conceptions of justice which presume that there are multiple ultimate principles of justice. Such notions often translate into including the perceptions of various interest groups in the evaluation and distinguishing how different groups are served by the program. Pluralist/intuitionist conceptions of justice hold that there are several principles of justice and no overriding endpoint or measure of the general welfare. In practical terms, evaluations based on pluralist ideas treat interest groups as several in number and as having distinct interests from one another.

From different perspectives some theorists have argued that the interests of the disadvantaged and the lower classes are ordinarily neglected in an evaluation and that such interests should be represented or even given priority as an ethical matter. Such an obligation edges into the political and is quite different from an admonition to respect the rights of individuals. Current formal codes of ethics for evaluators restrict their content to individual rights within a contractual framework.

An expanded view of the ethics of evaluation would be based upon more principles than that of individual autonomy. Autonomy suggests that no-one should impose his or her will upon others by force or coercion or illegitimate means. No-one should be imposed upon against his or her will. Autonomy is intimately tied to the notion of choice and is manifested in the notion of individual rights and the social contract. Presumably a person's autonomy has not been violated if he or she chooses freely what to do.

However, autonomy alone is not sufficient as a moral basis for evaluation. Each person should have an equal right to advance his or her own interests for satisfaction. The fundamental notion of equality is that all persons should be taken as members of the same reference group and consequently should be treated the same. The satisfaction of each person's interests is worthy of equal consideration in the public determinations of wants. Individual rights are a protection against imposition by others but do not guarantee equal consideration. It is here particularly that social-class differences play a most significant but neglected role in evaluation. Often powerless groups are not entitled to consideration or representation of their interests in evaluation. Too often only the interests of the powerful are represented.

Of course, if each individual and group is allowed to advance its own interests, there are inevitable conflicts, and these conflicts must be settled impartially. An evaluation must be impartial, that is, in its procedures it must be fair to all interests. Sometimes impartiality is confused with objectivity, but it is possible to employ an objective procedure which is reproducible but biased against a particular social group. It is possible to have a test which discriminates in a systematic, reproducible but biased fashion against certain social groups. Impartiality is a moral principle that ensures fair consideration.

Impartiality is especially difficult when the evaluator must face a situation in which there are conflicting values. To what degree should the evaluator become involved with the participants? Eraut has suggested two moral principles in such a situation. First, people have a right to know what an evaluation is doing and why. Second, all those who might be considered as clients have a right to some stake in the evaluation. This position proposes the involvement of participants somewhat beyond the negotiation phase, even to the point of helping with data collection. However, even in such an expanded notion of participant involvement, the evaluator is not expected to side with one group or endorse a particular set of values.

There is one other principle worth considering as a moral basis for evaluation. On the basis of equality, autonomy, and impartiality a person could advance his or her own interests equally, not impose on others, and join others in settling conflicts impartially. Yet what about the losers in such a decision process? The winners have no responsibility for the losers, strictly speaking. Intuitively, a person is disturbed at such a situation. Reciprocity, treating others as you would like to be treated, adds an element of humanity. Reciprocity makes winners at least partially responsible for the losers. Reciprocity is not a primary value of liberalism because it suggests a sense of community which extends beyond the notion of separate individuals who cooperate with each other only to seek their own advantage. One of liberalism's deficiencies is this lack of caring and sense of belonging to a larger community.

Finally, there is the formidable problem of the application of these principles in the actual conduct of evaluation. Ethical principles are rather abstract notions, and it is not always obvious how such principles should be applied in a given situation. Concrete examples and guidelines are essential if a person is to model his or her behavior on such principles.

Even if a person endorsed all the ethical principles discussed here, their application would not be straightforward. Some of the most intractable ethical problems result from a conflict among principles, the necessity of trading off one against the other, rather than disagreement with the principles themselves. For example, both liberals and conservatives endorse the principles of autonomy and equality but weigh these principles differently in actual situations. The balancing of such principles against one another in concrete situations is the ultimate act of ethical evaluation.

See also: Ethical Considerations in Research; Evaluation Standards; Evaluator, Role of; Evaluation Models: Development

Bibliography

Anderson S B, Ball S 1978 *The Profession and Practice of Program Evaluation.* Jossey-Bass, San Francisco, California

Barry B 1973 *The Liberal Theory of Justice: A Critical Examination of the Principal Doctrines in 'A Theory of Justice' by John Rawls.* Clarendon Press, Oxford

Evaluation Research Society Standards Committee 1982 Evaluation Research Society standards for program evaluation. *New Directions for Program Evaluation* 15: 7–19

House E R 1980 *Evaluating with Validity.* Sage, Beverly Hills, California

House E R, Care N S 1979 Fair evaluation agreement. *Educ. Theory* 29: 159–69

Joint Committee on Standards for Educational Evaluations 1981 *Standards for Evaluations of Educational Programs, Projects, and Materials.* McGraw-Hill, New York

Mackie S L 1977 *Ethics.* Penguin, London

Rawls J 1971 *A Theory of Justice.* Harvard University Press, Cambridge, Massachusetts

Sieber J E 1980 Being ethical? Professional and personal decisions in program evaluation. *New Directions for Program Evaluation* 7: 51–61

E. R. House

Ethiopia: System of Education

The Ethiopian educational system may be studied in terms of five distinct historical periods, each characterized by unique sets of goals, problems, challenges, and achievements. The first is the period of religious education which began soon after the introduction of Christianity in the fourth century and was predominant for many centuries, though augmented by the Islamic and Falasha (Ethiopian Jewish) educational systems which usually served their own members. The second period began with the first decade of the twentieth century and introduced secular public education. It was followed by the third period beginning in 1936 under the Italian occupation, during which the preceding system was systematically destroyed. The fourth period (1941–73) saw efforts to revive and develop the nation's educational system by the restored government. The final period covers the time from the revolution of 1974 to the present. This article alludes only briefly to the earlier periods and focuses on the emergent, post-1974, era.

1. Background

The ancient east–central African nation of Ethiopia covers an area of 1,183,998 square kilometers (457,140 square miles). Although it is located between the equator and the Tropic of Cancer, the wide range of altitudes produces variations in climatic conditions which encourage agricultural and livestock developments. Some 85 to 90 percent of the people still live in rural communities, farming or raising cattle. The rugged terrain and deep valleys of the country have also contributed to the lack of effective communication among the inhabitants and has impeded the spread of social services.

There has never been a complete population census in Ethiopia. A 1981 estimate indicates a total population of 32 million people and a rate of increase of 2.5 percent per annum, which would double the population by the end of the century. An increasing percentage of the population will consist of children and young people as a result of the combined effect of rapid population growth and a relative decrease in child mortality. Current estimates indicate that the urban population is increasing by about 7 percent per annum; 5 percent of this growth is attributable to immigration of people from rural areas, indicating a rapid change in the rural–urban ratio of the population. The extension of education to all segments of society continues to be impeded by patterns of settlement of rural people, the absence of good transportation and communication systems, the political and administrative structure of government, and the different languages spoken by the various communities. Agropastoral activities are the main contributors to the gross domestic product. Agricultural production includes such cash crops as cotton, coffee, sugar, fruits, vegetables, oilseeds, and pulses. Other crops (produced primarily for domestic consumption) include teff (a type of millet specific to Ethiopia), wheat, maize, sorghum, and millet. The livestock potential of Ethiopia is very promising and is expected to play an even more significant role in the future.

Most of the modern sector of the economy is now under state control and management, including textile mills, mining, food processing, and production of beverages, tobacco, sugar, and footwear. National development programs for the construction of rural roads, housing, forestry settlement, and hydroelectric schemes are expected to accelerate the growth of the modern economic sector.

Economic activities in Ethiopia have been greatly enhanced by the 1974–76 nationalization and redistribution of all rural lands among the formerly landless populace, the reformation of urban land tenure, the nationalization of large industries, banks, and insurance and the improvement of labor conditions.

Ethiopia has probably undergone more convulsive social and political dislocations than any other African nation in this century. Fascist Italy under Mussolini invaded the country in 1935, and among the consequences was the systematic and ruthless destruction of the secular public-education system. In its place, the Italians established a few primary schools with prescribed and strongly pro-Italian curricula. When the national government was restored in 1941, rehabilitation of the educational structure proved difficult. Former teachers were dead or scattered. The Second World War was being waged in Europe, and recruitment of foreign teachers proved extremely difficult. In spite of many obstacles, the infrastructure of the educational system—from preprimary to college levels—was built within a decade. In the 1960s, the view of education as personnel training and development was balanced by the belief in education as a social service which must be assessible to all citizens on an equitable basis. A number of national commissions, established to study the educational situation, recommended steps intended to rectify the distorted nature of the system's curricula and accessibility and the quality of its alumni. No effective measures, however, were taken to address the problems identified by these studies.

In 1971, another commission, the Education Sector Review (ESR), was formed to examine the whole gamut of the educational establishment. This group, comprising outstanding Ethiopian and international educators and operating with the cooperation and financial assistance of a number of international and bilateral organizations, presented its report and recommendations to the Ministry of Education and the emperor in 1972. The report pointed out that the Ethiopian educational system was unacceptably narrow, elitist, expensive, inefficient, and discriminatory.

The report recommended that the whole system be restructured in such a way that, before the end of the twentieth century, 95 percent of all school children would complete basic education and then participate in some of the community practicums to be established in rural and urban centers under the auspices of the relevant government ministries. Provisions were also made for adults to participate in adult-literacy and basic-education programs. The commission urged that the government must also initiate economic and administrative reforms and must at the same time develop the people's confidence in these measures.

The ESR's findings were not made public by the government, and in any case its activities were overlooked during the ensuing period of civil unrest. A military mutiny in 1974 resulted in a fully fledged revolution which was followed by the abolition of the monarchy, suspension of the nation's constitution, and dissolution of parliament. A provisional military administrative council (PMAC) gradually assumed full control of the country.

The new socialist government decided to adopt much of the ESR study as policy. Thus, one might point out that an educational revolution was initiated before the national revolution swept the country.

The new government, adopting the ESR plan, gave it a new name and created the necessary conditions and institutions to make it possible to carry out the ideas originally suggested. A series of enabling legislation was proclaimed, of which the most important are the proclamations of December 14, 1975, which provide for the establishment of farmers' associations (*Yegeberoch Mahiber*) authorized to perform various civil functions. Significant among these is "the development and operation of schools, clinics, and social security for the old, sick, and disabled."

The associations' activities are coordinated by the appropriate government units at the subdistrict (*wereda*), district (*awraja*), provincial, and national levels. In the urban centers, urban-dwellers' associations (*Yekebele Mahiber*) were established with similar functions. There were several other enabling decrees.

The consequence of the emergence of these new institutions is the revolutionizing of the concept of education in the country to make it Ethiopian in its inspiration and in its relevance to the environment and requirements of the country.

2. Goals of the Educational System

The major goals of Ethiopian education have shifted from time to time depending on how needs were perceived by those in power. By the beginning of the 1970s, the emphasis and orientation had shifted from selective high-level personnel training to mass education, which meant that the goals of the earlier period were maintained while efforts were made to provide education for the entire population—rural and urban. The 1971–72 ESR gave this aim further impetus.

The post-1974 government launched an imaginative and far-reaching program which calls for the rapid expansion of mass literacy and basic education so that the entire population will be better able to participate in the overall development of the country. It is intended that this be achieved through the rapid expansion of primary schools and the provision of polytechnical education for about nine million children from grades 1 to 8; through the development of parallel nonformal and continuing education for all citizens who are not engaged in full-time education; by strengthening the scientific and technical areas of the general polytechnic system of education and the establishment of new facilities for specific technical education and training; and by creating a new management and organizational structure for the administration of education which reflects the broad divisions of labor in general polytechnic education, mass education, technical education and training, and higher education and which permits an appropriate decentralization of responsibilities.

Primary and adult basic education are provided in a number of the major national languages of Ethiopia,

thereby providing for the cultural and vocational relevancy of education to the people.

So far, attempts to translate these goals into functioning programs have enjoyed local, national, and international support.

3. General Structure and Size of the Educational Effort

The present educational system provides three years of preschool education (beginning at the age of 4), six years of primary education (grades 1–6, beginning at the age of 7), two years of junior-secondary school (grades 7–8), and four years of senior-secondary school (grades 9–12). In addition, specialized instruction is provided in technical/vocational schools, which recruit students from grade 8 for two to four years of training, and in primary-teacher training, which recruits from grade 12 for a one-year training period.

The number of school-age children and youths is estimated at 10 million. Enrollment ratios of the preschool group are negligible. Some 30 percent of the primary, 10 percent of the secondary, and 2 percent of higher education levels are involved. Figures 1 and 2 present the enrollments in primary and secondary schools from 1940 to 1980. Post-secondary enrollment figures are nonexistent for the 1974–77 period due to political turmoil or cessation of classroom activities to enable teachers and students to participate in development campaigns.

At the tertiary level are the Addis Ababa University system with several campuses in several centers, Asmara University, a number of junior colleges, and four colleges of the armed forces. Except for the latter group, all postsecondary educational activities are coordinated by the new Higher Education Commission. These institutions award cer-

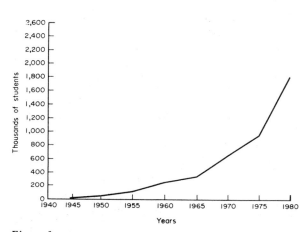

Figure 1
Primary-school enrollment 1940–80

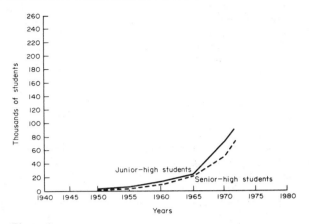

Figure 2
Secondary-school enrollment 1940–80

tificates, diplomas, first degrees, and recently graduate degrees.

University admission is highly competitive and is based on achieving high scores in the Ethiopian School Leaving Examinations; this tends to favor those who come from the urban-based (and hence better equipped) secondary schools which are concentrated in the major centers around the country.

Except in some instances, public education in Ethiopia has always been free for those fortunate enough to have access to it. Historically, the metropolitan centers of Addis Ababa and Asmara (together with their immediate environs) and, to a lesser extent, the Harar and Wollega regions have provided more educational opportunities than elsewhere in the country. Gross imbalances of access to education at all levels continued to adversely affect the majority of the rural people, as well as females. This inequitable pattern persists, but measures are being taken to eliminate the discriminatory patterns of the past. The system of adult and nonformal education is extending opportunities for adult literacy, basic education, and skill training to citizens of postschool age.

Under the new government a national literacy campaign was initiated in 1979 and has produced impressive results. Through the combined efforts of the formal and nonformal institutions, Ethiopia expects to attain universal literacy within the 1980s.

Basic adult education programs have been initiated to provide Ethiopian adults with the fundamental information—attitudes, skills, and knowledge—required by all citizens who wish to participate fully in their society and which is consonant with the political views of that society. A multipurpose system of Community Skill Training Centers (CSTCs) is being established in each subdistrict to provide training in improved craftsmanship, healthy living, sanitation, nutrition, civic responsibilities, and similar skills to

help people live better lives. These programs are locally controlled and administered with some technical and material assistance from the regional or national government. The results achieved so far inspire hope that they are the ideal response to the needs of a long-neglected rural majority.

4. Administrative and Supervisory Structure and Operation

The structure of administration and supervision of the Ethiopian school system is evolving. Until 1974, educational administration was highly centralized. Although Ministry of Education representatives served at various government levels throughout the country, most major policy decisions and directions were issued from the Ministry of Education's headquarters in Addis Ababa. A number of steps were taken after 1974 in an attempt to reverse this unhealthy concentration of power in the hands of remote and distant administrators.

The proclamation for administration and control of the schools by the people (No. 103, 1976) provides for local administration and control of schools. Members of local education and school committees are drawn from representatives of popular organizations; the latter also include a teacher representative, the principal of the particular school, and a student representative of at least 16 years of age.

These arrangements have some flaws, given the present educational level and lack of experience of many of the communities, but the intentions are noble and the goals worth striving for. In the long run, they strengthen pride in and responsibility for the institution.

By making mass participation possible in the educational system, the new organizational structure has removed many obstacles to development and has directly linked popular organizations with general development programs.

5. Finance

In the post-1941 period, public education in Ethiopia was financed by taxes on rural land. Postprimary and urban-based primary schools were financed by the central treasury. Since rural per capita income was stagnant at this time (about US$4 per annum), income from rural lands was limited. This retarded the development of education in rural areas. A new education tax on urban property and income was initiated in the early 1970s, but this did little to alleviate the needs and pressures in rural areas.

The combined effort from government and nongovernment sources amounted to about 20 percent of the nation's total annual expenditure. In terms of the gross domestic product (GDP), this represents approximately 2 percent per annum, which is very low in comparison to expenditures by other developing nations, or in terms of Ethiopia's real needs. The estimated total expenditure from all sources for the 1970–71 period was US$70 million (Ethiopian Ministry of Education 1972 pp. IV–28).

Data for the 1970s indicate that the distribution of expenditures by all agencies among the different levels of education was: nonformal education 12 percent, primary 41 percent, secondary 23 percent, and tertiary 24 percent. Systematic educational finance data for the post-1974 period are nonexistent, but the trend seems to suggest that basic adult and primary education will receive a larger share of the education budget (without much increase in the total budgetary commitment), perhaps even at the expense of post-primary education.

In the current period, local popular organizations are providing means and materials for the establishment and operation of schools. There is as yet no well-established accounting system to indicate the magnitude of their impact. The religious organizations also continue to operate at reduced levels. The central government's education budget is further enhanced through the use of such unconventional means and sources as using secondary and college students as unsalaried teachers during the long vacations and obtaining similar service from military personnel and regular teachers who do not demand, or receive, additional pay.

A considerable amount of aid for postprimary and tertiary education has come from the World Bank, United Nations agencies, and developed countries in North America and Europe in the form of loans for specific projects, general grants, and scholarships for overseas training.

6. Supplying Personnel

A shortage of qualified teachers, always a problem in the Ethiopian educational system, continues to impede plans for expansion. In 1980, the Ministry of Education reported (*Ethiopian Herald*, July 26) that there were 30,600 elementary, 4,640 junior-secondary, and 4,350 senior-secondary school teachers: a combined total of 39,590 teachers in grades 1 to 12. With the addition of some 600 college teachers, there is a grand total of 40,190. The statistics do not indicate whether teachers in nongovernment schools are included, but in any case their number is relatively small. About 5,000 new teachers graduate annually from the nation's teacher-training institutions. There are nine of these at present and more are being developed. The present teaching force is reaching some 30 percent of the school-age population; if the expected plan of achieving universal literacy within a decade is to be realized, at least 120,000 more teachers are needed over the plan period.

The usual requirement for prospective primary-school teachers seeking admission to training institutes is completion of grade 12; the actual training period lasts for one year. Secondary-school teachers are trained at the School of Pedagogical Science of Addis Ababa University and at the Agricultural College of Alemaya. Graduates from these two institutions receive a bachelor's degree and are assigned to senior-secondary schools. There are at least three other colleges that prepare teachers for junior secondary and technical schools.

In order to cut the timespan and improve the quality of teacher preparation, several unorthodox measures have recently been initiated. One of these involves establishing at least one pedagogical center in each of the 106 districts to serve as a focal point for the training of teachers using formal and informal means such as inservice programs, seminars, and workshops.

Problems, however, still remain. There are many schools that are operating on two- or three-shift systems, due primarily to lack of qualified teachers and classroom space. This shortens students' learning time, overworks school personnel, and reduces the efficiency of the learning process.

Further, though by 1974 some 75 percent of university teachers were highly qualified Ethiopians and some colleges were almost entirely staffed by Ethiopian faculties, after 1974, many of these leading administrators and faculty left the country and now hold positions all over the world. Consequently, when the nation's colleges resumed operation after the 1974–77 interruption that enabled students and staff to participate in development campaigns, the authorities of necessity resorted to employing as teachers foreign personnel, staff from the civil service, and college graduates with a first degree. As a result, the quality of instruction and scholarship declined. This issue can best be addressed by re-creating an atmosphere that encourages (a) the normal functioning of university personnel and (b) an aggressive graduate-training program which attracts bright and motivated young people at both Ethiopian and foreign schools and provides them with inducements to seek teaching–research careers in their own country.

7. Curriculum Development and Teaching Methodology

Before 1974, the development and distribution of teaching–learning materials was performed by the Ministry–Education in Addis Ababa. After 1974, appraisal was made of the work, occupations, and hence of the educational needs of the Ethiopian people. As a consequence, efforts are being made to render education relevant to their needs through comprehensive changes in the curriculum, with the realization that for the vast majority of the people the main preoccupations are shortage of food due to lack of fertilizer, modern agricultural technology, or drought; shortage of timber for fuel; difficulty of access to safe and reliable water; lack of basic health services; absence of adequate communications; lack of proper housing and sanitation; and lack of suitable technology to increase productivity (UNDP and UNESCO 1980 p. 3). The curricula are being made to reflect these realities.

Temporary, transitional measures are being adopted while plans are implemented to decentralize curriculum development and administration policies. The department of curriculum and supervision of the Ministry of Education in Addis Ababa organizes panels of experts in each subject area; these specialists are required to research and develop textbooks, teachers' guides, workbooks, and related materials for all grades 1 to 12.

These materials are sent to representative schools in different parts of the country for examination, evaluation, and comment by teachers and school administrators. Revisions are made in the light of these reactions from the field, and the materials are produced as standard texts. The trend, however, is towards the localization of curriculum-development responsibilities.

By means of such a decentralized approach it is intended that the educational activities of the respective communities respond to the immediate needs of each community without neglecting the need for educational modernization. The key elements are relating education to productive work, doing while learning, and self-sufficiency through the teaching of science and technology. The core curricula, consisting of science, mathematics, productive technology, agriculture, and the social sciences, are provided within the school proper and at work places so that there are continued linkages and interactions between the worlds of work and learning.

Educational materials are being prepared in at least four minority languages in addition to Amharic, Ethiopia's national language. There are plans to use additional minority languages in basic adult education. Directly or indirectly the national radio system also broadcasts education-related programs in some of the local languages.

Lectures constitute the predominant pedagogical method in the Ethiopian school system. This method, a carry-over from ancient methods practiced by religious institutions, encourages learning by rote without the student necessarily understanding the material covered. Attempts are now being made to alter this approach by requiring learners to relate the information they acquired to the daily resolution of immediate problems of working and making a living.

There are numerous problems awaiting solutions in the areas of curricula and teaching methods, both in the grade school and postsecondary educational systems. Perhaps the major one is a lack of resources: of trained personnel and supporting equipment and of facilities and funds to constantly research, test,

evaluate, and adapt new and improved teaching methods and instructional materials.

Higher education is a very expensive undertaking for a poor country like Ethiopia, but it is extremely doubtful whether such a poor country can do without the trained human resources that the colleges produce. Attempts to do justice to the traditionally neglected majority of the people could all too easily result in neglecting or starving the teaching and research activities of the university system. If this should happen, not only will the university suffer lasting damage but the lower grades of the public schools, whose faculty and staff are trained in the universities, will suffer as well.

8. Systems of Examination, Promotion, and Certification

As a rule, promotion from one grade to the next is decided on the basis of school or classroom tests which are usually administered twice a year but sometimes more often. At the completion of grades 6 and 8, all students take centrally developed and administered nationwide examinations involving the core courses that have been covered so far. On the basis of this, some students are promoted to the next grade and some are allowed to repeat if space is available.

All students who wish may take the Ethiopian School Leaving Certificate Examination (ESLCE) at the completion of grade 12. The examinations are administered nationwide on the same days and are centrally developed and evaluated by the Ministry of Education. During the first two decades of the postwar era, successful matriculants were automatically accepted by colleges. This is not possible any longer. Due to shortage of places only about 20 percent are admitted to the colleges.

Many educators and students believe that the certification functions of the examination should be separate from the university-admission function, since nonadmission to college marks the majority of students as "failures," thus prejudicing their chances of employment or further education through other channels in other localities, including study abroad.

9. Educational Research

Educational research conducted during the first two decades after the restoration of the national government in 1941 was largely related to the production of teaching materials and educational policy and administration. A modest amount of research was carried out regarding Ethiopian history, ethnography, and culture after the regional colleges and the state university were established. Since 1970, the Ministry of Education has been carrying out some policy- and curricula-oriented research, but not enough to meet needs. The Ministry of Education carries out some research and the national university has performed some quality research and publication work through the Research Center of the School of Pedagogical Science. There are also regularly published journals and periodicals.

10. Major Problems

In the 1980s and 1990s, it is likely that postsecondary education and particularly university education will suffer due to increased attention paid to basic and primary education. The university will suffer from both inadequate resources and from lack of the freedom necessary for faculty and students to conduct research and disseminate the results.

In summary, Ethiopian education may be adversely affected by a scarcity of money and of trained, experienced, and professional faculty and staff and by a fragile political system and untested political institutions.

Bibliography

Amare G 1979 Social functions of African education. In: *Africa and the World*. Oxford University Press, Addis Ababa, pp. 193–204
Ethiopian Herald 26 July 1980
Ethiopian Ministry of Education 1972 *Education: Challenge to the Nation, Report of the Education Sector Review*. Ministry of Education, Addis Ababa
Ethiopian Ministry of Education 1980 *The National Literacy Campaign in Ethiopia*. Ministry of Education, Addis Ababa
Ethiopian Ministry of Education 1981 *Notes on the Education System in Ethiopia*. Ministry of Education, Addis Ababa
Habte Aklilu 1977 The public service role of the university. In: Thompson K W, Fogel B R, Danner H E 1977 *Higher Education and Social Change: Promising Experiments in Developing Countries*. Praeger, New York, pp. 56–85
Kalewold I 1970 *Traditional Ethiopian Church Education*. Teachers College Press, New York
Jemberie A S 1978 *A Brief Description of Educational Development in Ethiopia with Special Reference to its Planning Requirements*. UNESCO, Paris
United Nations Development Programme (UNDP) and UNESCO 1980 *Ethiopia: Basic Education Programme: Project Findings and Recommendations*, Serial No. FMR/ED/OPS/80/220[UNDP]. UNESCO, Paris
Wagaw T G 1978 Appraisal of adult literacy programs in Ethiopia. *J. Read.* 21(6): 504–8
Wagaw T G 1979 *Education in Ethiopia: Prospect and Retrospect*. University of Michigan Press, Ann Arbor, Michigan
Wodajo M 1967 The state of educational finance in Ethiopia: A short survey. *Ethiop. J. Educ.* 1: 18–26
World Bank 1981 *Accelerated Development in Sub-Saharan Africa: An Agenda for Action*. World Bank, Washington, DC

T. G. Wagaw

Ethnographic Research Methods

Some educational researchers have recently advocated the adoption of the ethnographic methods employed by cultural and social anthropologists in their field studies of social groups and communities. These methods are considered to be particularly appropriate for empirical research on the relatively bounded system of a school or classroom but they also have their place in the study of the role of the family, social organizations, or ethnic communities in education. Ethnographic research consists essentially of a description of events that occur within the life of a group, with special regard to the social structures and the behaviour of the individuals with respect to their group membership, and an interpretation of the meaning of these for the culture of the group. Thus ethnography is used both to record primary data and to interpret its meaning. It is naturalistic enquiry as opposed to controlled, and a qualitative, as opposed to quantitative, method. In ethnography the researcher participates in some part of the normal life of the group and uses what he or she learns from that participation to produce the research findings. It is consequently often treated as being equivalent to participant observation (see *Participant Observation*), in contrast with nonparticipant observation in which the observer as an outsider records the overt behaviour of the subjects, but it involves more than that. Participation in a group provides investigators with an understanding of the culture and the interactions between the members that is different from that which can be obtained from merely observing or conducting a questionnaire survey or an analysis of documents. The investigators' involvement in the normal activities of the group may be treated as a case of partial acculturation in which they acquire an insider's knowledge of the group through their direct experience with it. These experiences provide them with tacit knowledge which helps them to understand the significance to the group members of their own behaviour and that of others and enables them to integrate their observations about that behaviour with information obtained from other sources such as interviews with informants and documentary material.

1. The Development of Ethnographic Methods

Field research was employed by anthropologists and sociologists in the nineteenth and early twentieth centuries, but the first to stress the need for a systematic approach to its conduct was the Polish–British scholar Malinowski, who emphasized the need for ethnographers to employ controls in their assembly of data in a manner that he described as analogous, although by no means similar, to those of the natural scientists. Malinowski laid down the requirement that observers should tabulate the data on which their conclusions are based, including verbatim statements, and should indicate whether they are derived from direct or indirect sources, a method that he called "concrete statistical documentation" (see the introductory chapter on methodology in Malinowski 1922). He stressed the need for the investigator to establish "trustworthiness" in respect of the study. Malinowski described the goal of ethnographic studies as "to grasp the native's point of view, his relation to life, to realise his view of his world" (p. 25). In order to achieve this, the investigator should learn the language of the community being studied, reside for a protracted period in the community—preferably out of contact with "white" people, and use both observation and informed interviews with selected informants from within the community as sources of data.

The field methods laid down by Malinowski have, to a greater or lesser degree, been adapted for studies of segments of modern, urbanized societies which have provided a model for the application of the methods to educational research. For example, studies have been carried out of the unemployed in Austria, industrial organizations (Tavistock Institute), urban areas in the United States (Middletown, Yankee City), hobos, gangs, and dance musicians, to name just a few. These studies each raised their own peculiar problems of research strategy, but what they all have in common is their method of research in which the investigator becomes closely involved over a prolonged period in the everyday life of the members of a designated group or community in order to understand its culture. This contact enables the researchers not only to obtain an intimate and a broad knowledge of the group but also to test and refine hypotheses about the phenomena being studied.

Ethnographic methods of research came to education fairly late in the piece. The team of sociologists from the University of Chicago who studied medical students (Becker et al. 1961) were probably the pioneers in the field of education, while Smith and Geoffrey (1968) were the first to base a study of classroom processes on anthropological field studies using a method which they described as microethnography. They stated that their "primary intent was to describe the silent language of a culture, a classroom in a slum school, so that those who have not lived in it will appreciate its subtleties and complexities" (p. 2). Smith observed the classroom every day for one semester and kept copious field notes, which he used as a basis for his daily discussions with the class teacher, Geoffrey, with the purpose of clarifying the intentions and motives behind the teacher's behaviour in order to move towards a conceptualization in abstract terms of the teaching process. Both of the investigators were participants in the classroom, although one was more of an observer and the other more of an initiator and an informant.

A word should be added about the terms used in describing ethnographic studies in education. Smith and Geoffrey seem to have simply meant an intensive field study by their term microethnography, while Erickson (1975) confines it more narrowly to studies that use extensive observation and recording to establish the interactional structures in the classroom, a usage which Mehan (1978) prefers to call constitutive ethnography. For the purposes of this present article, the term ethnography is interpreted liberally to include case studies, the concept preferred by the ethnographers in the United Kingdom. The intensive study of a bounded community is a clear example of a simple case study, even though there are many individuals who make up that community (see *Case Study Methods*).

2. The Scientific Status of the Ethnographic Method

The use of ethnographic methods involves some important questions relating to the tactics, ethics, and validity of the study.

2.1 The Social Role of the Investigator

The description of the investigator as a participant in the life of the group implies that he or she has some role in it which is recognized by the group. Sometimes this role is simply that of participant observer, a role which does not usually exist in most formal group structures, but one which does have a meaning in many classrooms where outsiders come to observe the class on occasions for one purpose or another. Thus, Louis Smith was introduced to both the children and the teachers as someone from the university who was interested in children's learning, a role which is understood and accepted in modern classrooms. In other cases the investigator fills a normal role in the group other than that of a researcher. For example, a study of an orthodox Jewish school was conducted while the researcher concerned was a regular classroom teacher in the school, a situation that represents participant observation in the fullest sense of the word. Another example would be a student who studies his or her college or professors on the basis of his or her normal personal experience with them. The role of participant observer has some advantages as a viewing point over that of the participant who plays the additional role of observer. The former is expected by the group to share, probe, ask questions, take notes, and so on because this is consistent with his or her role as an observer whereas the latter has tactical and ethical problems in doing so because of his or her obligations as a participant. On the other hand there is a danger that a participant observer can become so much absorbed into the group after a time that his or her status as an observer may be compromised.

The group member who also acts as an investigator may do so overtly or covertly, or as a mixture of both where it is known to some members of the group that he or she is observing for research purposes but not to others. Covert observation raises serious ethical issues as does semicovert, but, on the other hand, overt observation by a person who has another role in the group can place him or her in an anomalous position with regard to the carrying out of a normal group role. Furthermore, colleagues are likely to respond to him or her as an observer in a biased fashion because of their other involvement with him or her. A distinction is often made between obtrusive and unobtrusive methods of research according to whether the subjects of the research are aware that they are being studied. A participant observer, by definition, plays an obtrusive role and this fact may influence the behaviour of the group whereas the observer participant may or may not be obtrusive as a researcher.

2.2 The Inside–Outside View

One of the main advantages of the ethnographic method is that, in the course of becoming involved in the group, the investigator becomes acculturated to it. This means that he or she develops personal knowledge about the rules of the group and begins to perceive the same meanings in events as do the members of the group. The investigator learns what behaviour is expected when, where, and in response to what situations. This process of acculturation is sometimes described as transition from the status of a "stranger" to that of "a friend", that is, a person who knows the "silent language" of the group and is in intimate communication with its members. It is, however, significant that a scholar who is studying the subculture of a school in his or her own society is unlikely to be as complete a stranger at the beginning as an anthropologist studying a traditional society.

Nevertheless, being an insider has its drawbacks as a method of studying a group. First, as already indicated, there are constraints imposed by propriety and ethics on an insider revealing to others the secrets of the group (see *Ethical Considerations in Research*). There may, of course, be the same constraints on an outsider but, at least, the group can usually control his or her access to information by barring entry.

Second, the insider may not always have even as much access to information as an outsider. He or she may have personal knowledge of only a segment of the group's life, sometimes without being aware of the limitation. He or she may even be denied access to the other segments: for example, a teacher may not be permitted to study the classroom of a colleague. In contrast, a stranger who is accepted as an observer

may be deliberately informed and invited to observe just because he or she is a stranger. Futhermore, an outsider is more likely to be able to take steps to obtain a representative sampling of people, occasions, and settings in the group and thus can help to offset the suspicion of biased observation. A third drawback that may arise as a result of being an insider is that highly salient data may be overlooked just because it is so familiar. Strangers will notice events that stand out as a result of their contrast with the expectations that they have brought with them from their own cultural background and may therefore be better placed to infer their meaning and significance for other events in the group. Some element of surprise aids awareness. A further problem is the one mentioned earlier of the subjects' reactivity to being studied, particularly when the observer is a full participant in the group. Whether or not the observation is obtrusive, it is reactive observation; that is, the observer affects the behaviour of the people being studied and consequently will have to take into account his or her own influence when assessing the group. As Everhart puts it "the fieldworker, rather than appearing to be one of many in the audience observing the drama on stage, is himself on stage, interacting with the other actors in 'his' setting and playing a role in the resolution of the production" (1977 p. 14). In order to take into account their own contributions and to assess what the situation would be if it were not for the fact that their presence is influencing the group, investigators need a great deal of self-awareness and a thorough understanding of the group processes. This necessity for playing the dual roles of participant and detached observer can impose a severe strain on the ethnographic investigator and calls for continual monitoring of the effect the investigator has on others.

2.3 Subjectivity, Reliability, and Validity

The fact that investigators have a role in the group not only requires them to be aware of their own influence but also may give them an emotional stake in a particular research outcome. For example, if the observer is also a teacher, there may be a tendency for observation to be slanted towards a justification of the style of teaching normally used. Since ethnographic researchers use themselves as the instrument through which they observe the group, the method lends itself to extreme subjectivity; that is, the interpretation may be idiosyncratic to the observer with all of the associated limitations, eccentricities, and biases and is not matched by the interpretation of other observers. This raises questions concerning the reliability of the observations and the validity of the conclusions. The difficulty is that the observations are not easily subject to public scrutiny. Observations and interpretations are by their very nature subjective but they still can be made susceptible to reliability checks and it is still possible for the investigation to follow rules that can increase the validity of the conclusions.

Reliability, that is accuracy, of the observations can be enhanced by following the prescription laid down by Malinowski of recording wherever possible the concrete data in the form of a "synoptic chart" on which the inferences are to be based, including verbatim utterances and opinions. Modern audio-visual methods of recording events so that they can be examined at leisure offer ethnographers unprecedented possibilities today of attaining accuracy, but there are still sampling problems in the selection of the data and limitations to accuracy due to bias and lack of opportunity, as well as tactical and ethical considerations in making the recordings.

The reliability of the observations is assisted by the long period of exposure to the data in ethnographic research which provides opportunities for investigators to cross check their observations over time and to reconcile inconsistencies. Cross checks may also be made by triangulation (see *Triangulation*), a procedure in which multiple sources are used to obtain evidence on the same phenomenon. Thus, the observations may be supplemented by interviews, feedback to the members of the group for their comment, and documentary evidence such as school notices, correspondence, minutes, and other archives. An additional source of reliability is to have more than one observer as, for example, in the study by Smith and Geoffrey (1968), a situation which is relatively rare in traditional anthropological studies. In the typical case, the multiple observers may be members of a team who are exposed to the same events and are then able to cross check each other's data.

Validity is a quality of the conclusions and the processes through which these were reached, but its exact meaning is dependent on the particular criterion of truth that is adopted. In ethnographic research the most appropriate criterion is credibility although even that term is subject to fuzziness in meaning. Here the concern will be only with the steps that ethnographic research workers can take to improve the credibility of their analyses. Credibility is dependent on the apparent accuracy of the data and all the steps described above that are intended to increase reliability are relevant. Much depends on the way in which the study is communicated to the scientific audience. A report in which the investigator describes the precautions that have been taken to ensure the accuracy of the observations has more credibility than one in which the reader is merely asked to take the data and findings "on faith". The report should contain indications that the investigator is aware of the need to convince the audience of the validity of the study. The interpretations made from the data are more credible when the researcher describes the evidence on which they are based and also any efforts made to test for evidence that would tend to disconfirm any tentative conclusions. One of the procedures that is often taken in ethnographic studies to confirm the validity of interpretations is to feed them back for comment to selected members of the group or to other persons who know the group (see *Participant Verification Procedures*). In the case of literate participants such as are found in educational research, the research workers may submit to the members drafts of sections of their reports as well as oral accounts of their impressions. If necessary, the interpretations can be "negotiated" with the participants so that the final product is more likely to represent the situation as they see it, but there is always a danger in this procedure that the participants may exercise distortion and cover-up for their own reasons or that the researcher finds it impossible to obtain consensus. Different members of the group may hold different perceptions of the events, for example, teachers and students, or boys and girls. Some researchers have attempted to overcome these problems by setting up small groups of about four participants to engage in discussions towards establishing their shared meanings by acting as "checks, balances, and prompts" for each other, but in practice there are distinct limitations to the possible application of this procedure.

2.4 The Role of Theory, Hypotheses, and Generalizations

Malinowski specifically recommends that a field worker should commence with "foreshadowed problems" arising from his or her knowledge of theory, but should not have "preconceived ideas" in which he or she aims to prove certain hypotheses. The ethnographic method is qualitative and holistic, making use of the investigator's intuition, empathy, and general ability to learn another culture. The investigator is more concerned with discovery than with verification and this requires preparedness to formulate, test, and, if necessary, discard a series of hunches. As investigators develop hypotheses in the course of pursuing a foreshadowed problem they should be alert for data which refute, support, or cast doubts on their hypotheses and should be prepared to alter them in accordance with increased acquaintance with the phenomena. Research workers as they puzzle over the meaning of the behaviour of the group, and perhaps seek help from informants, are likely to obtain illumination through a sudden shaft of understanding. Thus there is a continual dialogue between an orientation towards discovery and one towards verification. Gradually a theoretical basis for the understanding of the group processes may emerge through the process often described as grounded theory, that is, grounded in the research process itself. Theory that emerges from exposure to the data is more likely to fit the requirements than theory that is preconceived on an abstract basis. Also the actual data are more likely to produce categories that are appropriate for describing the particular case. The main problem that arises from grounded theory derived from a case study is that of making generalizations beyond the particular case viewed at a particular time. A straight out description of concrete happenings has some value as an addition to the corpus of information that is available to the investigator and to other interested people—including members of the group itself. However, its value is greatly enhanced when the case can be "located as an instance of a more general class of events" (Smith 1978 p. 335). To achieve this, the investigator treats the case in point as either a representative of, or a departure from, a particular type. Sometimes the actual group or groups that are studied have been chosen initially as representatives of a designated type of case and this facilitates generalizations based on it but they should still be treated with reserve.

2.5 Ethnography as a Case Study Method

The problem of the relationship between the One and the Many, a perennial one in philosophy, arises in different guises in the social sciences—idiographic versus nomothetic treatments of data, -emic versus -etic approaches to comparative studies, and the case study versus the sample survey research design (see *Case Study Methods*; *Survey Research Methods*). In order to generalize from an individual case study of behaviour in one group to behaviour in others it is necessary to reach sufficient understanding about the significance of the events in relation to the context in which they occur in order to extend interpretations to other contexts and other groups. In the process of generalizing it is necessary to violate somewhat the full integrity of any one group by describing events in some language that extends beyond the bounds of the culture of that group. The ethnographers are partially acculturated to the group that they are studying, but they are also familiar with other groups with which they compare their experience of the group. To maintain the analogy, an ethnographer is multicultural with respect to the object of study. When an investigator attempts to understand one group, he or she is aided by knowledge of other ones and his or her impressions are partially consolidated with the others. Thus, generalizations are built up through the investigator being able to mediate between one group and others; an ethnographic account of a school, then, derives its value largely from the fact that the investigator—and also the readers—are familiar with other schools, and with schools in general. Diesing refers to this as "pluralism" which he describes as follows: "one might say the method is relativistic in its treatment of individual cases and becomes gradually absolutistic as it moves toward broader generalizations" (1971 pp. 297–98).

In ethnographic studies no generalization can be treated as final, only as a working hypothesis for further studies which may again be ethnographic, or

may consist of a survey by means of interviews, questionnaires, or tests. The ethnographic method gains credibility when it combines both subjective and objective methods but it need not be regarded as deriving its value only as a preliminary and exploratory procedure prior to the use of more conventional semiobjective techniques. It can make its own legitimate independent contribution at any stage of a research including the confirmation of hypotheses that have emerged out of other sources provided that the basic principles on which its credibility rests are observed.

See also: Naturalistic and Rationalistic Enquiry; Observation Techniques

Bibliography

Becker G S, Geer B, Hughes E, Strauss A 1961 *Boys in White: Student Culture in Medical School.* University of Chicago Press, Chicago, Illinois
Diesing P 1971 *Patterns of Discovery in the Social Sciences.* Aldine-Atherton, Chicago, Illinois
Erickson F 1975 Gatekeeping and the melting pot: Interaction in counseling encounters. *Harvard Educ. Rev.* 45: 44–70
Everhart R B 1977 Between stranger and friend: Some consequences of "long term" fieldwork in schools. *Am. Educ. Res. J.* 14: 1–15
Malinowski B 1922 *Argonauts of the Western Pacific: An Account of Native Enterprise and Adventure in the Archipelagoes of Melanesian New Guinea.* Routledge, London
Mehan H 1978 Structuring school structure. *Harvard Educ. Rev.* 48: 32–64
Roberts J I, Akinsanya S K (eds.) 1976 *Educational Patterns and Cultural Configuration: The Anthropology of Education.* McKay, New York
Smith L M 1978 An evolving logic of participant observation, educational ethnography, and other case studies. In: Shulman L S (ed.) 1978 *Review of Research in Education*, Vol. 6. Peacock, Ithaca, Illinois, pp. 316–77
Smith L M, Geoffrey W 1968 *The Complexities of an Urban Classroom: An Analysis Toward a General Theory of Teaching.* Holt, Rinehart and Winston, New York
Spradley J P, McCurdy D W 1972 *The Cultural Experience: Ethnography in Complex Society.* SRA, Chicago, Illinois
Wilson S 1977 The use of ethnographic techniques in educational research. *Rev. Educ. Res.* 47: 245–65

R. Taft

European Institute of Education and Social Policy

The European Institute of Education and Social Policy was set up in 1975—under the original title of the Institute of Education of the European Cultural Foundation (Amsterdam)—in cooperation with the Commission of the European Community (Brussels) and the International Council for Educational Development (New York). With headquarters in Paris and an office in Brussels, the Institute undertakes comparative studies and other activities relating to policy issues in postcompulsory and higher education, and the relationship of both to the world of work. In so doing, it forges a link between educational research and policy makers, thereby promoting closer cooperation in these fields at European level. Its present name, the European Institute of Education and Social Policy, was introduced in the course of 1982 in order to reflect the greater emphasis in the Institute's activities on problems relating to employment, unemployment, and social policy.

Although an integral part of the European Cultural Foundation, the Institute enjoys full academic autonomy. Its activities are guided by a 15-member council of distinguished academics from both Western and Eastern Europe, as well as representatives of international organizations. The Institute employs a staff of some 15 people (including 8 to 10 full-time researchers), supplemented by a European network of national correspondents and consultants.

1. Activities and Publications

The work of the Institute focuses on three main areas. First, research into the problems of higher education: the bulk of the Institute's work in this field has been concerned with quantitative developments, new policies and their implementation, structural and qualitative changes, questions of student mobility in Europe, and the access of foreign students to higher education. Second, research into the relationship between education and employment and problems of social policy: research and surveys have been undertaken on linked work and training schemes, the transition from school to work, policies for reducing unemployment among young people, and education and work in poorer or underdeveloped regions, part-time work, and various aspects of unemployment. Third, encouragement of European cooperation in education: here, the Institute's most important undertaking is the scheme it has been running since 1978 for the Commission of the European Community. This scheme takes the form of grant assistance for the development of joint study programmes, the aim of which is to strengthen interuniversity cooperation within the Community by means of courses provided jointly by two or more establishments of higher education from different countries. Since the Institute became responsible for the scheme, the steadily growing reputation of the latter has been reflected in the rapid increase in the number of participating institutions, which trebled from 100 to 300 in the period between 1978 and 1981.

In 1981, the Institute also took over management of the European Commission's scheme for short study visits, the purpose of which is to promote cooperation by providing higher education staff members (whether in teaching, research, or administration) with an opportunity of enhancing their knowledge of higher education systems elsewhere in the European Community.

In addition, Institute staff act as the secretariat to several independent associations concerned with furthering European cooperation in specific fields (such as engineer or teacher training). Since 1981, the Institute has also provided the secretariat for the Liaison Committee of the Rectors' Conferences in member countries of the European Economic Community.

The publications of the Institute can be divided into two main groups. The first of these are the occasional papers, which generally consist of short essays or original contributions. They are either based on research undertaken by the Institute itself or written independently by researchers or others associated with Institute activities. The second group, reports, constitute the results of the research performed by the Institute. They are published either by the Institute or (in book form) by commercial publishers.

The official journal of the Institute is the academic quarterly, the *European Journal of Education*. This constitutes a regular collection of articles devoted to research, development, and policies, principally in upper-secondary and higher education, placing special emphasis on the national and international problems associated with these issues in Europe.

2. Finance

The 1981 budget of the Institute was approximately US$650,000. An annual grant of some 500,000 guilders (about US$200,000) from the European Cultural Foundation is supplemented by income which the Institute receives from its research and administrative work undertaken on a contractual basis for national or international organizations (e.g., the European Commission), other foundations, and national or regional authorities. Further information can be obtained from the headquarters of the Institute at Université de Paris IX—Dauphine, 1 place du Maréchal de Lattre de Tassigny, 75116 Paris, France, or the Belgian office at 51 rue de la Concorde, 1050 Brussels, Belgium.

L. Cerych

Evaluating Teaching: Criteria

Efforts to improve the quality of teaching in the schools depend for their effectiveness on the availability of accurate, detailed, and objective evaluations of teaching. This article presents an overview of the state of the art of teacher evaluation in the early 1980s and is organized around three distinct criteria which may be used in such evaluations. It is addressed to professional educators and others concerned with the problem. No attempt is made to present both sides of controversial issues or to fully document every assertion made. The reader interested in these matters should consult some (or all) of the references listed.

The focus is on the evaluation of teaching rather than on the evaluation of teachers; more specifically, it is on interactive teaching, on what is called the teaching act itself. A discussion of teacher evaluation would need to address a broader range of problems which arise from the need to isolate the contribution of the teacher's abilities (and other characteristics) to the quality of the teaching from the many other factors that affect it.

1. Definitions

1.1 Criterion

The term "criterion" is used here in sharp distinction from the term "standard." A criterion is an aspect or dimension of the quality to be evaluated, which is to be assessed and then compared with an arbitrary standard or level of this quality as a basis for evaluating it. The concern of this article is with criteria rather than standards.

Evaluation of teaching may be based on one of three distinct types of criteria: (a) the outcomes of the teaching; (b) the learning behaviors or experiences of pupils that the teaching provides; and (c) the behavior of the teacher while teaching.

By far the largest part of all evaluation of teaching made by supervisors employs the third criterion, teacher behavior. Informal evaluations are based on impressions formed from casual observations of teacher behavior; formal evaluations are based on observations using some kind of a teacher rating scale. Teachers, on the other hand, tend to evaluate their own teaching on the basis of observations of how their pupils behave in class. The first type of criterion—outcomes—is the one favored by the public and its legislative and policy-making representatives, who seem to feel that it is reasonable to judge teaching by its results just as they do most other activities.

The purpose of teaching is, of course, to produce pupil learning; it seems perfectly logical, therefore, to evaluate teaching on the basis of outcomes. But since the function of the teacher in the production of learning is to provide pupils with experiences likely to result in learning, it also seems logical to evaluate teaching on the basis of the experiences it provides—that is, on the basis of pupil behavior in the classroom. And yet, since the means by which the teacher affects pupil behaviors and (through them) learning outcomes are the behaviors the teacher exhibits, it seems equally logical to base evaluations of teaching on teacher behavior.

1.2 Teaching

The formulation of an authoritative definition of teaching is much too large a task to be undertaken here. But it is necessary to formulate a working definition, one which can guide efforts to evaluate teaching. Depending on the type of criterion to be used, one of three approaches to this problem may be used (see *Teaching: Definitions*).

For present purposes a merely formal definition, one which specifies the types of tasks a teacher must perform, without saying how they are to be performed, will suffice. It is useful to think of teaching as involving the simultaneous performance of three tasks: (a) maintaining the classroom learning environment; (b) providing learning experiences appropriate to the changing needs of individual pupils; and (c) implementing those experiences in which the teacher is an active participant.

For convenience, performance of the first task is referred to as "environmental maintenance," the second as "managing learning," and the third as "instructing."

Performance of the first two tasks requires the teacher in the classroom to make hundreds of decisions each day; and each decision must be made almost instantaneously, because a failure to make a decision in time to implement it is in itself a decision—a decision not to make a decision. The quality of these decisions is, of course, the principal determiner of the quality of the teaching. The effects of all of the knowledge and skill a teacher possesses depend almost entirely on their being deployed appropriately, on their being used at the right time and with the right pupil; in short, on the interactive decisions the teacher makes.

However, it is unrealistic to expect a teacher to base interactive decisions directly on any knowledge of research, theory, subject matter, or anything else: there just isn't enough time to recall such knowledge. Effective teaching involves a two-stage decision process. In the pre-active phase of teaching the teacher must draw on his or her own knowledge base, knowledge of pedagogy and of subject matter, of the pupils and community, of the resources available, to decide upon a plan, strategy, or model of teaching to be followed during the interactive phase of teaching. Out of this must come a set of rules that will guide the teacher's interactive decisions. In the classroom the teacher must decide what to do next according to the strategy or model he or she has decided to follow, not by any direct appeal to the knowledge base. Because the knowledge base is used in choosing the strategy or model rather than in implementing it, the choice can be rational. Because it is made outside the classroom there is time to reflect, to consult the literature, or even a colleague (see *Teachers' Interactive Decision Making*; *Teachers' Planning*).

1.3 Evaluation

The problem of defining evaluation is almost as large as that of defining teaching and, like it, lies outside the scope of this entry. But again it is necessary for present purposes to develop only a working definition of evaluation as it applies to human performance. Assessment of teaching, regardless of which type of criterion is being assessed, is but one instance of the assessment of human performance—that is, of the assessment of purposive human behavior in the execution of some task. Successful performance assessment involves three phases or steps, all of which are essential.

(a) *The standard task or set of tasks*. The first step in the assessment of human performance is the definition of the task or tasks the candidate for evaluation is to perform. The task must be specified in such a way that three requirements are met. First, the task must be of such a nature that the candidate has to demonstrate possession of the ability or the quality being evaluated in order to perform the task successfully. Second, the task must be specified so that it is possible to discriminate appropriate elements in a performance from inappropriate ones as a basis for scoring the performance. And, finally, the task or tasks set for all candidates must be either identical or equivalent, so that differences in the quality of performances will not arise because of differences in tasks.

(b) *The documentary record*. Those elements in the behavior or performance of a candidate on which the score will be based must be recorded in scorable and permanent form. Such a record is essential for objective and accurate scoring; it constitutes the only tangible basis for checking the scoring, for defending its fairness, objectivity, and validity. And how valid the score is depends almost entirely on how detailed, objective, and accurate the record is.

(c) *The scoring key*. Finally, there must be a procedure for deriving a criterion score from the record which will yield valid scores that are equal when based on records of equal quality, no matter who does the scoring.

Among these three critical phases or steps in performance assessment, the second—the documentary record—is the one most often neglected in the evaluation of teaching. This is probably due to the fact that most assessment theory is derived from experience with paper-and-pencil tests. When a candidate takes such a test, the record is automatically produced as the candidate answers the questions.

A well-constructed multiple-choice test represents the state of the art of performance assessment—or, more correctly, of its technology. In such a test the three steps are accomplished in the following manner:

(a) *The standard tasks*. The items on an objective test define the set tasks to be performed. The items are exactly the same for everyone who takes the same form of the test; they are equivalent for candidates who take alternative forms.

(b) *The documentary record*. The candidate records his own performance; as he or she answers the items and marks the answer sheet the candidate creates an accurate record of the outcomes of his or her peformance. The record is perfectly objective, since no other person is involved in its creation.

(c) *The scoring key*. The use of a machine-scorable answer sheet makes it possible for a machine to be programmed to recognize appropriate responses and so ensure that the same score is assigned to equivalent performances, without regard to other characteristics that may distinguish different candidates.

The validity and reliability of assessments based on objective test scores depend, then, on the nature of the tasks or problems presented and on the nature of the scoring key; neither is affected by the wisdom, skill, or sophistication of the scorer or of any other human being, once the instrument has been built.

When the focus of assessment is on the process used by the candidate rather than on the results obtained from its use, it is not usually possible for the candidate to create the record. Someone else must observe the performance and record the process used in a quantifiable form.

This person presents a grave threat to objectivity, one that is quite different from any threat to objectivity in a paper-and-pencil test: a threat to the objectivity (and accuracy) of the record itself rather than to the objectivity of the procedure used to score it. When different observers record the performance of different candidates, there may be differences between records of different candidates which have nothing to do with differences between their performances, but which reflect differences in the perceptions of the two observers instead. The validity of process assessments therefore depends at least as much on the accuracy and objectivity of the records as on those of the scoring key.

These definitions of criteria, teaching, and evaluation will provide the basis for the rest of this article. The next section will be devoted to a consideration of the first step in the process of teacher evaluation, that of defining the task to be set.

2. Defining Tasks for Evaluating Teaching

It might appear on first thought that the nature of the task defined for a teacher whose teaching is to be evaluated would depend on the nature of the criterion on which the evaluation is to be based. If the evaluation is to be based on certain behaviors of the teacher, such as explaining clearly or asking higher order questions, would it not be most efficient simply to ask the teacher to conduct a discussion and ask a number of higher order questions during it? If the evaluation is to be based on the teacher's ability to provide certain pupil experiences, such as getting pupils to interact with one another during a class discussion, why not ask the teacher to demonstrate that he or she can do these things? Or if the evaluation is to be based on the ability to teach pupils new spelling words, why not ask the teacher to teach the words on a list?

The answer is, of course, that none of these tasks requires the teacher to *teach*. In the instance in which the task specified a teacher behavior, only the ability to exhibit that behavior on demand was required. In the instance in which the task specified pupil behaviors to be elicited, the same objection applies. At best, these tasks call for the use of certain skills which are used in the process of teaching but are by no means equivalent to it: they do not provide samples of teaching behavior on which an assessment of teaching can be based. The third example requires the teacher to achieve an outcome which falls far short of those a teacher must achieve.

2.1 Eliciting a Relevant Behavior Sample

In order to elicit a sample of teaching behavior, the task the candidate is to perform must be defined in terms of outcomes, not process; and the outcomes must be ones that teachers are expected to accomplish in the practice of their profession. Limited or artificial goals like the teaching of 10 spelling words may elicit instructional behavior, but they do not require the candidate to bear the full range of responsibilities or deal with the full complexities of teaching.

Nor can a true sample of teaching behavior be obtained by having the candidate "teach" a group of pupils especially assembled for the purpose. A teacher teaching his or her own class works toward a very different set of objectives than one "teaching" some other group of pupils for whom the teacher has no long-term responsibility. In the latter situation the teacher is responsible only for helping the pupils increase their score on whatever test the evaluator uses to assess the outcomes the teacher produces; in the former situation, the teacher is responsible for helping the pupils to grow toward all of the goals of education in that school system. What one gets in the artificial situation is a sample of coaching rather than of teaching behavior.

It seems clear, then, that the task specified must be the one the teacher performs every day.

2.2 Laying a Basis for Scoring

When the criterion used is based on outcomes, specifying the task in this way also ensures that the second requirement—that the specification provide a basis for scoring the records—is met. Changes in pupils toward the goals of the system are seen as indicators of good teaching; changes in the opposite direction, or absence of change, are seen as indicators of poor teaching.

When the criterion is based on in-class behaviors of teachers or pupils, the basis for scoring records is less obvious; but it rests ultimately upon knowledge of what the teacher is trying to accomplish, knowledge available when the task is specified in this way.

2.3 Defining Equivalent Tasks

The final requirement, ensuring equivalence of tasks assigned to different teachers, is by far the most difficult of the three requirements to satisfy, mainly because the characteristics of pupils as individuals and of classes as groups have so much to do with the nature of the task the teacher faces. No two classes are identical, even within the same school, subject, and grade; much less when they come from different schools and grades.

There is a theoretical solution to this problem: to assign pupils to classes by a random process. This would ensure that the classes differed only by chance; it would also provide a standard error to serve as a yardstick to use to detect nonrandom differences in the performances of different teachers.

But such randomization is, of course, impossible. Restricted randomization—randomization within schools, grades, and subjects is not impossible; but it is and will remain impractical unless and until the administrators responsible for assigning pupils to classes decide that valid assessments of teaching are worth the small extra effort such assignments would entail.

Creating a situation in which valid assessments of teaching based on outcomes criteria are feasible is, then, difficult if not impossible. The requirement that the task specification elicit genuine samples of teaching behavior can be met by basing the evaluation on the performance of a teacher with a class that he or she teaches regularly. The requirement that the task specification provide a valid basis for scoring can also be met in this way. But the problem of providing identical or equivalent tasks for different teachers has no practical solution. All that can be done is to make some sort of adjustment to compensate for this nonequivalence as part of the scoring procedure.

3. Assessing Teaching on the Basis of Learning Outcomes

When learning outcomes are to be used as the criterion of teaching quality, the elements on the documentary record take the form of scores earned by the teacher's pupils on measures of the knowledge, abilities, and other characteristics that pupils are supposed to acquire as the result of teaching; the major problem in scoring the record is that of isolating and assessing the parts of these measurements that are attributable to the teaching that is being evaluated (see *Teaching, Effects of*).

3.1 Obtaining Records of Learning Outcomes

Because the records in this case consist of pupils' scores on tests and self-report questionnaires, there are no technical problems in obtaining them beyond those involved in any testing program. It will be presumed that any system that proposes to evaluate the teaching in its schools will have in place a testing program designed to measure students' achievement of the major objectives of the system. If this is not so, then the setting up of such a program must be the first step in the assessment process.

This particular use of the systemwide testing program requires that the tests be administered at both the beginning and end of the school year in which the evaluation is to take place, so that changes during the year can be assessed. It is strongly recommended that such a program be supplemented by the administration of measures of other outcomes of teaching besides those adopted as school objectives, in order to detect any side effects or unintended outcomes. Sometimes goals identified as important are achieved at the expense of other equally important goals, especially when teachers know that their teaching is to be evaluated in terms of achievement of the former. Quality teaching cannot be assessed without some heed being paid to the full range of outcomes it produces. Failure to do so can reduce the quality of teaching instead of enhancing it.

3.2 Scoring Records of Learning Outcomes

There are two major problems which must be solved before a defensible criterion of the quality of teaching can be derived from a set of pretest and posttest scores of the pupils who have been taught. One is the problem of isolating the portion of changes in pupil scores that is attributable to the teaching from the portion that is not—the part that would have happened anyhow. The other problem is the problem of weighting the various kinds of changes shown in the record in arriving at a composite measure of outcomes that may be used as a criterion of the overall quality of teaching performance.

The second problem is not the sort of problem that can be dealt with in a methodological discussion; its solution depends on such value considerations as the philosophy of the school and of the community. It will therefore be assumed in the discussion to follow that this difficult problem has somehow been resolved so that there exists a single posttest score Y which measures the status of each pupil with respect to the goals of education in that school at the end of the period during which the teaching takes place. It is the problem of deriving from this score a measure of the effectiveness of the teaching that has occurred which will be dealt with here.

The problem may be restated as one of assessing the effect on Y of all factors other than the teaching, and then somehow adjusting the value of Y to remove these effects. These "contextual" factors manifest themselves at pretest time in two ways: in their effect upon the status of the individual pupil and in their effect on the status of the class as a group.

Suppose that the pretest battery is equivalent to the posttest battery and that the score it yields is X. Then it follows that all pre-existing factors of any kind that affect X will also affect Y in the same way. Thus a pupil's score on X will measure the past effects on that pupil of all such factors, known and unknown; and the mean score of the class on X will measure the past effects of such factors on the class as a group. If a value of Y differs significantly from the corresponding value of X, the difference will be attributed to the teaching that took place between X and Y.

In the past, a variety of different statistical procedures have been used to adjust the mean posttest score $\bar{Y}$ of a teacher's class to allow for the factors measured by the mean pretest $\bar{X}$. The earliest (and simplest) procedure was to use the "mean raw gain" $\bar{Y} - \bar{X}$ as a measure of the effects of teaching. Unfortunately, there is an artifactual negative correlation between this gain score and the pretest mean $\bar{X}$; this means that the lower the mean pretest score of the class, the less effective the teaching will appear. Since this is precisely the error which the adjustment is supposed to prevent, the adjustment fails in its purpose.

The use of mean raw gains was replaced by the use of "residual gains." In this procedure, class mean values $\bar{Y}$ were regressed on class mean values $\bar{X}$, and the regression line obtained was used to predict the value of $\bar{Y}$ that would be expected if there were no variations in the quality of teaching between classes. The difference between the actual mean value of $\bar{Y}$ in a class and its predicted value was taken as a measure of the quality of teaching in that class. Mitzel and Gross (1958) pointed out that the use of the between-class regression in this manner actually removes some of the differences between classes that the technique is supposed to measure, and recommended the use of the analysis of covariance to estimate the regression. The measure so obtained is called the "adjusted mean gain." But unless the pupils have been assigned to the classes at random, this procedure also tends to overcorrect. In other words, the effect of the teaching in a class which scores low on the pretest is underestimated while that in a class which scores high is overestimated (Campbell and Erlbacher 1971).

None of these procedures yields an unbiased estimate of the effects of teaching, then. Moreover, none of them estimates the effects of teaching on individual pupils. In each instance the effects measured are those on the class mean; what varies is the method used to compensate for differences in the means of different classes. None of the methods is successful.

There is an alternative procedure (which so far as

is known has not been described in print before) that seems to be free from this defect. This procedure uses information that the other procedures ignore, information that is highly relevant to the quality of teaching. This information is contained in the correlation between pupils' pretest and posttest scores within the same class.

This information is used to set up a separate regression equation within each class for predicting a pupil's score at the end of the year from the pupil's score at the beginning. Outcomes of teaching in different classes can then be estimated, not just for the average pupil in each class but for a pupil with any specified pretest score in each class.

Suppose that the regression equations for the classes of three teachers are as follows:

Teacher A: $Z = 16 + 0.8X$
Teacher B: $Z = 20 + 0.7X$
Teacher C: $Z = 26 + 0.6X$

Then the posttest score of a pupil whose pretest score is 35 would be expected to be 44 in class A, 44.5 in class B, or 47 in class C; such a pupil would learn most in class C. But the posttest score of a pupil whose pretest score is 65 would be expected to be 68 in class A, 65.5 in class B, or 65 in class C; such a pupil would do best in class A.

The value of Z for a pupil with a specified pretest score would seem to be a particulary simple and direct measure of the learning outcomes in that class; and so it is. However, it should not be interpreted as a measure of the quality of the teaching because there is a possibility that if the same teacher had taught in the same way in a different class, the results might have been different.

The correlation between the Z value in a class and $\bar{X}$, the mean pretest score of the class, provides a measure of the degree to which the average ability of a class is related to how much the specified pupil learns (regardless of who teaches the class). And the regression equation for predicting Z from $\bar{X}$ provides an estimate Z' of this quantity in any given class, such as class A. If Z, the pupil's posttest score when Teacher A teaches the class, is higher than Z', this indicates better than average teaching in that class. This difference is the measure of the learning outcomes attributable to the quality of teaching in that class.

There is no need to restrict the number of pretest scores used to one; characteristics of pupils or of classes that are not expected to change as the result of teaching, but which may affect pupil learning—such as socioeconomic status or sex—can be controlled in this way when randomization is not feasible.

This seems to be the only way, short of random assignment of pupils to classes, to ensure any kind of equivalence in the tasks performed by different teachers.

Unless there is good reason for using some other

value it seems logical to assess teaching quality in terms of its effects on a pupil whose pretest score is equal to the mean in the grade and subject taught.

Some readers may conclude from this that the development of a criterion for evaluating teaching in terms of learning outcomes involves some rather elaborate statistical gymnastics. So it does. Most of them would be unnecessary if obtaining valid assessments of teaching were considered important enough to justify taking the trouble to assign pupils randomly to classes. It has been shown that these statistical manipulations do control those contextual factors that can be measured before the teaching begins; but there may be others, unknown to the evaluator. These remain uncontrolled.

4. Assessing Teaching on the Basis of Teaching Behavior

In practice, most of the evaluation of teaching that goes on in today's schools is process based, that is, based on the behavior of the teacher in the classroom. Process assessments use records of how the teacher teaches rather than of the effect that the teaching has on pupils.

There are two advantages in using teacher behavior as the criterion for evaluating teaching: the evaluations obtained are diagnostic and they are timely. If the quality of a teaching performance is low, it is possible to examine the record to ascertain what the teacher is doing—or failing to do—that makes his or her score so low. And this can be done promptly—as soon as the evaluation is complete. When pupil learning outcomes are used as the criterion for evaluating teaching, it is only some months after the teaching took place that the record on which the evaluation is based becomes available. And when the record does become available it contains no description of the teaching behavior being evaluated, no clue as to what the teacher should do differently in order to get a higher score the next time.

The principal drawback in process-based teacher evaluation is that the evaluations lack the validity intrinsic to outcomes-based evaluations. The validity of process assessments depends on the amount of reliable knowledge of the nature of effective teaching behavior available, on how accurately it is possible to distinguish in a record of teaching behaviors those which indicate competent effective teaching from those which do not. At present the amount that is known about the nature of effective teaching is woefully inadequate, and process records must be and are scored mainly to reflect someone's best judgment rather than verified research findings.

4.1 The Teacher Rating Scale

The device used in almost all formal evaluations of teaching since the early twentieth century has been the teacher rating scale. A teacher rating scale essentially consists of a list of dimensions or aspects of teacher behavior (or other teacher characteristics) to be assessed, and provision for recording the assessments, usually by entering a number or marking a point on a graphic scale (most commonly in a range from one to five or ten) for each item to be rated.

The person who makes the assessment is called the rater. The rater is instructed (a) to observe a sample of the teaching behavior of a candidate; (b) to form the best judgment he or she can of the degree to which the observed behavior exemplifies each characteristic on the list; (c) to record (or mark) the number (or point) on the scale which most accurately reflects that judgment, and (d) to form some sort of a composite of the ratings on all of the listed characteristics (usually a simple total or mean) which is used as an overall assessment of the quality of the teaching observed. The individual ratings remain as an aid to diagnosis.

Hundreds of such devices have been used since 1915, when the publication of a 45-item rating scale in an early yearbook of the National Society for the Study of Education gave this new procedure wide visibility (Boyce 1915). The quality of any one rating scale depends mainly on three characteristics: which aspects of teaching (or characteristics of teachers) it lists; how clearly each one is defined; and how accurate the raters' perceptions are of each of them (see *Research on Teaching, Evolution of*).

Much thought and research has been devoted to the selection of the dimensions of teaching that should be included as items in a rating scale in order to maximize its validity. What indicators of the quality of teaching are visible in the behavior of teachers (and of their pupils) during the process of teaching? Since these instruments are designed primarily for use in evaluating teachers, they often include ratings of other characteristics (such as knowledge of subject matter) than ones that have to do with how the teacher performs in the classroom, as well as ratings based on behaviors of pupils (e.g., the level of pupil involvement or the amount of disorderly behavior).

Until around 1950, it was generally assumed that how well a teacher taught was mainly a matter of personality characteristics of the teacher. It was assumed that there were certain abilities and traits which characterized effective teachers; and teacher rating scales were intended to indicate which of these characteristics a teacher possessed, and to what degree, rather than to describe how the teacher behaved in the classroom while teaching.

During this period a considerable amount of research was conducted whose purpose was to identify the "characteristics of effective teachers" so that rating scales could be designed which would measure these characteristics (Charters and Waples 1929). The data on which this research was based consisted entirely of the opinions of teacher educators, school administrators, and others who might be expected to possess insight into the nature of effective teaching and the characteristics of effective teachers.

Early in this period an attempt was made by Barr to validate some of the rating scales then in use by comparing ratings of teachers with the outcomes they produced. As Barr pointed out, the ultimate criterion of the quality of teaching is its effect on pupils, not its effect on expert observers. The findings of the study were negative, indicating that the average correlation between the overall rating a teacher received and the amount of gains showed by that teacher's pupils was close to zero. Only three raters were involved in the study—not a large enough sample to produce definitive conclusions—but the results were suggestive and (as it turned out) prophetic.

During the next decade or two, at least six other investigators tried to verify this finding in as many different studies. Their results were unanimous in reaching the same conclusion. In every instance, the correlation between supervisors' ratings of teacher effectiveness and measured pupil gains in their classrooms was near zero (Medley and Mitzel 1963 pp. 257–58). It is somewhat curious that so few researchers have attempted to look at this lack of correlation, or to explain it empirically. By default it appears necessary to conclude that, whatever the average rating scale measures, it does not measure how effective teaching is. If by the quality of teaching is meant how well it achieves its ultimate purpose of facilitating those changes in pupil achievement that schooling is supposed to produce, such evidence as exists unanimously concludes that rating scales do not measure the quality of teaching at all.

The lack of validity of these devices (designed to codify the judgments of the raters as to how closely the characteristics of the teacher rated corresponded to those that experts believed were associated with teaching quality) also suggests that these experts' idea of what an effective teacher is like were erroneous. Since different raters tended to agree rather well, they must have been agreeing about the wrong things.

Some time between 1950 and 1960 scholars interested in research in teacher effectiveness began to abandon the assumption that how well a teacher teaches depends on his or her personality, and to assume instead that it depends on how the teacher behaves while teaching. The first tangible outcome of this change in viewpoint was another rating scale, all 25 items on which were defined in terms of classroom behavior (Ryans 1960). This instrument was a kind of hybrid which purported to describe only teacher characteristics manifest in the classroom. Wisely enough, Ryans postponed doing any research to indicate which characteristics were related to teacher effectiveness, and how they might be weighted in achieving a composite measure of the quality of teaching, until some time that is still in the future.

A few years later, teacher educators became interested in an approach to the preparation of teachers called competency-based teacher education (see *Competency-based Teacher Education*), which assumed that the quality of teaching was mainly determined by the competencies the teacher possessed; and rating scales began to contain competencies rather than behaviors or other teacher characteristics.

The teacher rating scale has few or none of the properties essential for valid performance assessment. No standard task to be performed by the teacher is defined, no record of behavior is made, and the procedure used to assign numbers to the various elements of the performance rated is completely subjective. The observer is required to perform two difficult tasks simultaneously: to observe the performance in considerable detail while making the difficult discriminations needed to assess the contribution of each detail to one of 25 or more different dimensions of performance.

Raters are rarely given adequate training in performing these feats; nor are they selected with any particular care. Just about every supervisor and principal in any school uses one rating scale or another. It is possible that among all of these raters there are some who are naturally gifted with a knack for judging the quality of teaching; their ratings are probably valid enough. But no-one knows who they are; the ratings made by others who lack this talent are used interchangeably with ratings made by these few gifted raters. As has been noted, the average validity of all these ratings is near zero.

Factor analyses of ratings generally suggest the operation of what is called the "halo" effect. What most raters seem to do is to form a strong general impression of the competence of the teacher which has more to do with the rating of the teacher's performance on any given item than any specific behavior that the teacher may exhibit. If the general impression is related to the overall quality of the performance observed, then the composite rating of that sample of teaching is related to its quality and the rating has validity. Most of the time the impression is unrelated and the rating has no validity.

For reasons such as these it is strongly recommended that educators follow the example set by the process–product researchers and discard the teacher rating scale in favor of the systematic observation system.

4.2 The Systematic Observation System

The usefulness of the rating scale in the evaluation of teaching is limited primarily by the fact that it attempts to bypass entirely one of the three essential phases of the assessment process: the creation of the record of performance. Until fairly recently, no alternative procedure for assessing teacher performance was available; but this is no longer true.

An alternative is the structured observation system, a form of instrument developed for use in process–product research. Process–product research is a form of research which seeks to establish correlations between measurements of classroom behavior (process) and measures of pupil learning (product) in the same classrooms (see *Process-oriented and Product-oriented Programs*), and to learn something about the nature of effective teaching from these correlations. A large number of different observation systems have been developed (including among many others *Flanders Interaction Analysis Categories* (FIAC), OSCAR *(Observation Schedule and Record)*, and the *Reciprocal Category System*), many of which have been collected and reprinted by Simon and Boyer (1967, 1969, 1970).

The observer using an instrument of this kind is expected to record classroom behavior in quantifiable form, but not to judge or evaluate it in any way. The observer's record is scored much as a paper-and-pencil test is; that is, by applying an objective scoring key to it, one which yields a weighted composite score based on the events in the record. The judgments of experts are incorporated into the scoring key rather than being applied to individual samples of behavior, as they are when ratings are obtained. The scoring of a record becomes a clerical task, one which can be performed by a computer.

Objectivity is, of course, a matter of degree, and records made by different observers using different observation schedules vary somewhat in objectivity. But even the least objective record yields a much more objective score than the most objective rating scale.

Observation systems tend to take one of three forms referred to as sign systems, category systems, or multiple-coding systems.

A sign system is the simplest to construct and to use. In form it is a list of discrete events, each one of which has been included because its occurrence in a classroom is believed to indicate either the presence or the absence of a competency, behavior dimension, or other element of teaching that the instrument is supposed to measure.

The time an observer using a sign system spends in a classroom is divided into several brief periods of equal length—usually between three and five minutes long. The observer's task is to record which of the signs in the system occur during these three to five minutes, but not how often. Any sign not recorded as having happened is assumed not to have happened. During a single visit to a classroom, the record may show that any given sign did not occur at all, that it occurred in every three-minute interval, or that it occurred in one, two, or more of them. Thus the approximate frequency of occurrence of the event is indicated.

The fact that the observer need not record each sign each time it occurs makes it possible to include many more items on the list than would otherwise be possible, without making the task so difficult that the reliability of the records would be reduced and the task of learning to use the system would become too difficult.

One of the advantages of the sign system is the ease with which it can be revised. Signs can be added or deleted without noticeable effect on other items. Signs related to a great variety of aspects of classroom behavior can be mixed together—verbal and nonverbal, pupil and teacher behaviors, or whatever.

A category system is quite different from a sign system in a number of ways. For one thing, it requires that every event in a specified domain of events be recorded each time it occurs. For another thing, only events in a single domain can be included. Most category systems deal with the domain of verbal interaction and require that each utterance made by the teacher or a pupil—and nothing else—must be recorded.

The observer's task is to record the frequency of occurrence of verbalizations in each of the set of categories which defines the system. The set of categories must be finite in number; the categories must be mutually exclusive, so that any one verbal event is classifiable in one and only one category. The categories must also be all-inclusive; that is, there must be a category into which any verbal event can be classified.

The most widely used of all existing category systems, without a doubt, is that devised by Flanders, called the *Flanders Interaction Analysis Categories* (FIAC).

Instead of recording individual events, it requires the observer to code the interaction observed in each three-second interval during a visit. The system consists of just 10 categories, seven of which cover teacher utterances, two of which apply to pupil utterances, and one which covers silence or confusion. These 10 categories have been in continuous and extensive use since before the 1960s.

Most category systems are built around some set of assumptions about, or model of, teaching which determines how the domain of behaviors is subdivided into categories. This makes subdividing existing categories just about the only way in which a category system can be revised without destroying it.

However, it is often possible to devise scoring keys for an existing instrument that extract information about dimensions of teaching behavior other than the one the instrument was designed to measure, a possibility to be borne in mind during the search for an existing instrument which can be used to evaluate teaching.

A multiple coding system may be thought of as a scheme for coding classroom events on two or more different category systems simultaneously. Most multiple coding systems are time based; that is, call for a record of what happened during a brief interval or

at a particular point in time, and disregard events that occur at other times. Thus only a sample of what occurs is recorded, but the loss of information incurred is offset by the greater detail recorded about events in the sample.

One of the most widely used multiple coding systems is the one developed by Jane Stallings at the Stanford Research Institute (Stallings 1977). Each interaction observed is coded on four sets of categories: *Who*, *To Whom*, *What*, and *How*. The *Who* categories have to do with who initiates the event; the *To Whom* with the passive participant; the *What* categories with the type of event (command, open-ended question, instruction, etc); and the *How* categories are descriptive (happy, touch, academic, etc.).

Because several categories are available on each of four separate dimensions, the number of possible combinations is very large. This means that a very large number of different events can be distinguished in a record. This richness of detail simulates what would be available in a detailed narrative record of what happened; but records made on this system are precoded so that a computer can easily be programmed to "read" a record to extract almost any data one might wish to see from it in the quantitative form.

The evaluator interested in using an observation system must either choose one (or more) of the systems already in existence or construct a new one. The former course will be preferred by many. Most of the systems that have received widespread use in research studies will be found to be the end products of several years of development and revision, as a consequence of which they tend to be substantially more reliable and (for the purposes for which they have been used) valid than any newly constructed device is likely to be.

The principal problem the evaluator will encounter in following this strategy arises from the fact that most existing systems were developed by research workers to measure variables they wished to study rather than to assess the quality of teaching. As a result, it becomes difficult to find one suitable for the present use. In examining one of these systems it is best to look not at the scores it yields or the dimensions it measures, but at the events that can be distinguished in the records from which the scores are derived.

It is useful to think of an observation system primarily as a device for obtaining an accurate record of a sample of classroom events. Once such a record has been obtained it may be scored in many different ways for many different purposes. The user need not be able to use the scoring keys developed by the originator of the system in order to capitalize on the intrinsic quality of the system: the application of a new scoring key to a record after it has been obtained does not affect the quality or accuracy of the record in any way. The decision whether to use a system or not should be based, then, on whether the record contains the information needed—on what events are recorded—not on whether useful scoring keys are available. A multiple coding system like that described by Stallings, for instance, yields records with much more information than Stallings and her associates were able to use. A careful study of the instrument will make it clear whether this information can be adapted to the evaluation of teaching.

If a decision is made to develop a new system, a valid and reliable homemade sign system can be developed far more easily and rapidly than any other kind. It is much easier to set down and compile a list of indicators of teaching quality than it is to construct a set of mutually exclusive, all-inclusive categories whose relative frequencies will indicate teaching quality. There are almost no restrictions on the type of indicators that can be included, and (as was noted earlier) it is much simpler to add or delete signs than to revise a set of categories in a trial-and-error process.

The first set of signs adopted should represent the best judgment of the constructors about how good teaching looks, about what behavioral cues are the most valid on which to judge teaching quality. The instrument should then be tried out and its effectiveness in discriminating good and poor teaching should be studied item by item. The results may call for a reappraisal of the original concept of good teaching and the deletion, addition, and redefinition of some of the signs on the list. A second version of the instrument should then be tried out and revised in the same way, and the process repeated as necessary until a satisfactory instrument is obtained.

This process forces one to define what good teaching is in behavioral terms specific enough so that observers can use them, and gives immediate—and merciless—feedback which provides an experience so valuable in itself as to almost justify the effort for what can be learned from it, without regard to the value of the instrument that is produced.

4.3 Obtaining the Records

Because the observer's function is merely to observe and code, not to evaluate, when a systematic observation system is used, it is not necessary—and probably not desirable—to use expert teachers or researchers or highly trained professionals as observers. When rating scales were used to evaluate teaching, the professional expertise of the rater was critically important, since the validity of the ratings depended on the quality of the rater's judgments. When a systematic observation system is used, however, how much professional expertise the observer possesses does not matter. The validity of the scores obtained is unaffected by any characteristic of the observer except skill in using the system.

It is recommended that only paraprofessional personnel be trained and used as observers—personnel who have no other responsibility in the institution that employs them than to make visits to classrooms and code behaviors. They do not need to know anything about how the codes they make are to be scored or used; indeed, the less they know, the more objective their codings are likely to be.

Professional personnel should be used as professionals: they should be expert not in obtaining but in interpreting behavior codings and scores derived from them.

When codings of teaching behavior are being collected for use in teacher evaluation, the most efficient strategy is (a) to make as many visits per classroom as possible, (b) to have only one observer code behavior in a classroom at any one time, and (c) to have a different observer code behavior on each visit to the same teacher.

Increasing the number of visits increases the reliability of the assessments much more rapidly than increasing the length of a visit or the number of coders per visit; using a different observer on each visit may lower the reliability of the measurements, but it will do so by reducing the effect of the biases that individual observers may develop. If the budget will cover only four visits per teacher, then four observers should be trained and each one should visit every teacher who is to be evaluated.

It has been suggested that instead of sending observers into the classroom, technicians or camera operators should be sent to record the behaviors on audiotapes, videotapes, or film which can then be evaluated more thoroughly and exhaustively than the transient behaviors in the classroom can. This strategy is relatively costly: even if an hour of videotape costs no more to obtain than an hour recorded on an observation system, the data collection costs would be equal in both cases. But the videotapes would still have to be viewed by trained observers and coded on the observation system before they could be scored. This would double the cost—unless the observers took advantage of the permanence of the videotapes to replay them one or more times to increase the accuracy of their coding, in which case the cost per hour of behavior coded could treble or quadruple.

For most categories of teaching behavior used in observational instruments, there is in reality no advantage to be gained from coding and recoding the behavior recorded on a single videotape until the record is as accurate as possible, or in having two or more observers visit a class together to insure the accuracy of the coding of that particular sample of behavior. The additional information gained about the behavior of the teacher is minuscule in either case, particularly when compared with the gain that would accrue if a different sample of the teacher's behavior had been coded each time. Moreover, since a visit from a camera operator is much more intrusive than one from a human observer, and since the observer can see much more of what is going on when he or she is physically present than when he or she watches a tape of it, the validity of codings made live is almost certainly greater, except in those cases where the complexity of the behavioral unit to be coded is so great that live coding is out of the question.

4.4 Scoring the Records

The central problem involved in scoring a record of teacher performance is that of assessing the appropriateness of the teacher behaviors that are observed and coded during the performance. The traditional approach to this problem has been to employ an observer who is an expert judge of teaching, one who is (presumably) able to decide what portion of the decisions the teacher makes are correct ones in the context in which they are made, as a basis for rating the performance.

It seems clear that in order to be able to do this, the expert must have at least as full and complete an understanding of the context in which the teacher works as the teacher has (or should have). The rater must know as much as the teacher does about the pupils, about their personal characteristics, the interpersonal relationships among them, their previous experiences in this class and out of it; the rater must also know the teacher's intentions and the resources available for carrying them out, which include the teacher's own personal strengths and weaknesses as well as the materials, media, and so on available; and the rater must also understand any other factors that enter into, or should enter into the teacher's decisions. All of this special knowledge is necessary in addition to the general knowledge of professional practice which the rater brings to the situation.

It is difficult to see how a rater who visits a teacher's class for less than an hour could possibly have all this knowledge; but without it, how is it possible for the rater to second-guess the teacher, to say that the teacher should have done something else, that some other decision would have been better than the one the teacher made?

In the definition of teaching presented earlier in this article, a distinction was made between preactive and interactive decisions which is relevant here. What the classroom observer sees are, of course, the interactive decisions the teacher makes. So long as the assessment is based on them alone there is no adequate method by which the quality of the teacher's preactive decisions can be judged, because the data on which these decisions are based are not available to the observer. It might be possible to assess a teacher's preactive decisions by the use of some combination of questionnaires and interviews which make the bases of the teacher's decisions visible. (Much more needs to be done along this line

than is done at present; but these are matters that fall outside the scope of this discussion.)

As the definition of teaching indicates, one product of preactive decision making is (or ought to be) a set of decision rules which the teacher plans to follow during the interactive phase of teaching. This set of rules, defined by the teacher, provides the best basis for deciding whether any given action of the teacher is appropriate or inappropriate. Effective teaching depends first on making correct decisions about what to do in the classroom; and, second, on implementing those decisions. It is the second aspect that the observations are designed to assess, not the first.

Without knowing what rules the teacher has decided to follow during the period of observation it would seem impossible for anyone, however expert, to discriminate appropriate actions from inappropriate ones. Even if the observer knew the rules, the task would be extremely difficult. But the observer need not know anything about these rules in order to make an accurate record of what happens. This knowledge becomes relevant later, when an attempt is made to score the record.

Use of structured observations (rather than ratings) requires unequivocal a priori decisions about the weight to be assigned to each item in a record. Keys can be (and should be) revised from time to time: but between times these weights constitute the definition of effective teaching with which the evaluator must live. Process–product researchers have faced this problem in their efforts to derive empirical weights for scoring performances; in doing so, they have evolved two strategies. One is direct, the other is indirect.

An example of the use of the direct strategy is provided by a precedent-setting experiment in helping teachers to become more effective teachers of reading in small groups (Anderson et al. 1979). These researchers correlated events in behavior records with outcomes one by one to identify those that were associated with greater learning gains, and translated the results into prescriptions for better teaching. The decision whether an event was appropriate (which would be part of the prescription) was made directly—on the basis of that item's correlation with outcomes.

The indirect strategy first groups items into separate clusters on scoring keys that are internally consistent and which measure different aspects or dimensions of teaching behavior, and then intercorrelates these clusters or dimensions with outcomes (Soar pp. 97–119 in Peterson and Walberg 1979). Individual events are selected on the basis of their relationship to the cluster rather than directly to outcomes.

The main advantage claimed for the indirect approach is that cluster scores are more reliable and interpretable than scores on single items, and that they provide a smaller number of variables to consider in specifying decision rules and in communicating diagnostic information to teachers. The direct approach may be defended as less susceptible to distortion by the biases and preconceptions of the evaluator.

Sets of decision rules defined by teachers have been referred to by terms such as "teaching strategies" and "models of teaching." The most elaborate development of this idea has been the work of Joyce and Weil (1980), who propose that teacher education be organized around the selection and implementation of a set of models, at least one of which is appropriate to any situation a teacher encounters. Evaluation of teachers trained in this way would require the use of a different scoring key (if not a different observation system) for each model; whenever a teacher's performance was to be evaluated the teacher would declare which model he or she would use so it could be evaluated properly.

Very few teachers are trained in this way at present, because the profession has not yet developed definitions of alternative models, strategies, or sets of decision rules which are generally accepted and which form part of the teacher education curriculum. Most present-day teachers have been trained to use a single, general purpose set of decision rules—often called a "teaching style"—and use this style with only minor changes (usually unplanned) in all teaching situations. They are better prepared for the task of maintaining the general learning environment than for the task of managing learning experiences.

This seems to work fairly well for the teachers; the best of them are adept at making those decisions that relate to maintaining the learning environment. Pupils learn to work within the limits that the teacher sets on their behavior more rapidly because the limits are stable and consistent. But managing learning activities is a different matter; it seems obvious that appropriate decisions in this area would lead the teacher to change the rules from time to time and from pupil to pupil. For some purposes it is best to praise pupils whenever they do well; for others, it may be best to withhold praise and provide neutral feedback only; for still others, it may be best to withhold feedback, too, and encourage pupils to evaluate their own performances.

The fact that such adaptations are relatively rare, that teachers today do not vary the models or strategies they use to any measurable degree, probably explains the recent emergence of a number of reliable findings from process–product research. Classroom observations made in such studies are made at random times, and variations in teacher behavior from visit to visit are treated as errors of measurement. And yet some highly stable differences in teacher behavior are found which correlate significantly with learning outcomes (Medley pp. 11–27 and Rosenshine pp. 28–56 in Peterson and Walberg 1979).

These findings support the notion that there exists a single general teaching style which is characteristic of the most effective teachers in the schools today. The teachers whose pupils are making the greatest gains in basic skills as measured on standardized achievement tests seem to behave in this way whenever they are observed, regardless of variations in the immediate goals set that day or hour. It makes sense, then, to seek an evaluation instrument which will measure how closely the behavior of a teacher conforms to this pattern, and in what ways it deviates from it. This pattern may provide the basis for choosing or constructing an observation instrument and developing a key for scoring it. But it is important to remember that this is only an interim solution.

5. Assessing Teaching on the Basis of Pupil Behavior

In many ways this is the most attractive of the three types of criteria available for evaluating teaching. By not basing the evaluation on how the teacher behaves it lessens the pressure on the teacher to display atypical behavior while being evaluated. By basing it on what happens while the teaching is in progress, it provides results promptly enough so that they can be used immediately. And its validity is much less dependent on the teacher's own decision rules.

In the past, pupil behavior has been used in teacher evaluation in combination with teacher behavior; most rating scales include ratings of pupil involvement and the like along with those of teacher characteristics; and so do many observation systems. But it seems worthwhile to separate pupil behaviors (which are outcomes) from teacher behaviors (which are means). It might appear logical to say that only those pupil behaviors which are known to relate positively (or negatively) to learning outcomes should be used in teacher evaluation; but most educators and parents as well have some definite and strong convictions about the kinds of experience pupils should have in school. It is widely agreed, for example, that pupils should enjoy school; and this has nothing to do with how much pupils learn. Children spend many hours in school, and society is reluctant to have them be miserable for so large a part of their lives.

One attempt to move toward this use of pupil behavior is the work done in the later phase of the Beginning Teacher Evaluation Study. This has defined a construct called academic learning time (ALT), and hypothesized that how much a pupil learns in school is a direct function of the amount of ALT the pupil gets in school (see *Time and School Learning*). Academic learning time is "time a student spends engaged in an academic task that he/she can perform with success. The more ALT a student accumulates, the more the student is learning" (Fisher et al. 1980 p. 8). The proposal is that pupil behavior be substituted for learning outcomes as a criterion for evaluating teaching. More conservatively it may be regarded as a measure of how well the teaching is succeeding in providing pupils with experiences most likely to result in learning. The means used by these investigators to measure ALT may leave something to be desired, but they represent an important methodological innovation.

6. Concluding Remarks

It is not any part of the responsibility of the author of such a piece as this to tell those who happen to read it what to do. For this reason, no attempt has been made to define the criteria for evaluating teaching in a substantive way; no attempt has been made to say which teacher behaviors are appropriate or inappropriate, which learning outcomes are important and which are not, or what kinds of experiences pupils should be having. The group or individual concerned with evaluating teachers must define these things in accordance with the purposes of the evaluation. If research in teaching had established strong relationships between learning outcomes and pupil learning activities in the classroom, or between those learning activities and teaching behavior, then these definitions would need to be specified in terms of the relative importance of outcomes.

But these relationships have not yet been established; indeed, very little is known about them. This makes it necessary for the evaluator to define good teaching at whatever level he or she proposes to assess it: in terms of process (how the teacher behaves), of function (how the teacher gets pupils to behave), or of effectiveness (the changes the teacher brings about). Defining good teaching in terms of outcomes and then proceeding to evaluate it in terms of process makes no sense unless the evaluator is prepared to make some strong assumptions about the relationships between the two. And these assumptions should be explicit and visible. Certainly the evaluator has a right to his or her own opinions about these relationships—about how a teacher should act in order to be most effective, for example—and to base his or her evaluation procedures squarely upon these opinions.

But there is also an obligation to the pupils, the teacher, and society to make it clear how much or how little evidence there is that these assumptions are true, because if they are not true, the ministrations of the evaluator may be worthless. Worse yet, they may do harm: harm to the pupil who is deprived of the opportunity to learn which is his or her right; harm to the teacher whose effectiveness is eroded; harm to society by wasting some of its resources.

This obligation implies a second: the obligation constantly to review and test these assumptions not only against the literature on teaching but also by follow-up and evaluation of the evaluator's own efforts. A complete evaluation system must collect data of all three types, and must monitor the impact of one upon the other. If changes in teacher behaviors indicated by the evaluation are implemented but no change takes place in the experiences of pupils as a result, the definition of effective teacher behavior which led to the changes needs to be reexamined and revised. Evaluations based on pupil behaviors must also be tested against the outcomes that result from them. When such monitoring becomes a part of all of the teacher evaluation systems operating in the schools and in the teacher education colleges of the world, then progress will be steady and inevitable not just toward a solution of the problem of evaluating teaching, but toward the better teaching that the world so desperately needs.

See also: Affective Characteristics of Student Teachers; Teaching, Technical Skills of

Bibliography

Anderson L M, Evertson C M, Brophy J E 1979 An experimental study of effective teaching in first grade reading groups. *Elem. Sch. J.* 79: 193–223

Borich G D, Fenton K S 1977 *The Appraisal of Teaching: Concepts and Processes*. Addison-Wesley, Reading, Massachusetts

Boyce A C 1915 *Methods of Measuring Teachers' Efficiency. Fourteenth Yearbook of the National Society for Study of Education*, Part 2. Public School Publishing, Bloomington, Illinois

Campbell D T, Erlbacher A 1970 How regression artifacts in quasi-experimental evaluations can mistakenly make compensatory education look harmful. In: Hellmuth J (ed.) 1970 *The Disadvantaged Child*, Vol. 3: *Compensatory Education: A National Debate*. Brunner/Mazel, New York

Charters W W, Waples D 1929 *The Commonwealth Teacher-training Study*. University of Chicago Press, Chicago, Illinois

Fisher C W, Berliner D C, Filby N N, Marliave R, Cahen L S, Dishaw M M 1980 Teaching behaviors, academic learning time, and student achievement: An overview. In: Denham C, Lieberman A (eds.) 1980 *Time to Learn*. National Institute of Education, Washington, DC

Gage N L (ed.) 1963 *Handbook of Research on Teaching: A Project of the American Educational Research Association*. Rand McNally, Chicago, Illinois

Joyce B, Weil M 1980 *Models of Teaching*, 2nd edn. Prentice-Hall, Englewood Cliffs, New Jersey

Medley D M, Mitzel H E 1963 Measuring classroom behavior by systematic observation. In: Gage N L (ed.) 1963

Mitzel H E, Gross C F 1958 The development of pupil growth criteria in studies of teacher effectiveness. *Educ. Res. Bull.* 37: 178–87, 205–15

Peterson P L, Walberg H J (eds.) 1979 *Research on Teaching: Concepts, Findings, and Implications*. McCutchan, Berkeley, California

Ryans D G 1960 *Characteristics of Teachers: Their Description, Comparison, and Appraisal: A Research Study*. American Council on Education, Washington, DC

Simon A, Boyer E G (eds.) 1967, 1969, 1970 *Mirrors for Behavior: An Anthology of Classroom Observation*

Instruments. Research for Better Schools, Philadelphia, Pennsylvania

Stallings J A 1977 *Learning to Look: A Handbook on Classroom Observation and Teaching Models.* Wadsworth, Belmont, California

Travers R M W (ed.) 1973 *Second Handbook of Research on Teaching: A Project of the American Educational Research Association.* Rand McNally, Chicago, Illinois

D. M. Medley

Evaluation, Assessment, and Measurement

These three topics are treated in numerous articles scattered throughout the Encyclopedia. They are, however, interpreted separately and differently. The purpose of this article is to draw as clear a distinction as possible between the different terms and to provide some guidance as to where to look for a treatment of a particular problem or issue.

In the United States during the 1970s, and now increasingly in other parts of the English-speaking world, evaluation is being used with less and less regard to its original meaning. In the minds of many educational practitioners the words evaluation, testing, and measurement appear to be used interchangeably.

In this Encyclopedia an attempt has been made to maintain the semantic distinctions that are embedded, for example, in the writings of Ralph Tyler who may be appropriately regarded as the founding father of educational evaluation (Tyler 1950). What evaluation, assessment, and measurement have in common is testing. Each frequently (but not always) makes use of tests; but none of them is synonymous with testing, and the types of tests required for each of the three processes may be different. Keeping the ultimate objective, whether evaluation, assessment, or measurement, in mind will help the practitioner determine the type of test that will optimally serve his or her purpose. The three areas of application are considered in reverse order.

1. Measurement

The regular dictionary definition of "assigning a numerical quantity to . . ." will serve in most educational applications. While instruments such as rulers and stopwatches can be used to determine height, speed, and so on, many intellectual capacities or other quantities of educational interest must be measured indirectly. Thus tests are typically used to measure such dimensions as level of intelligence, the ability to apply a given principle in a variety of situations, the proportion of material learned or forgotten.

Measurement is rarely carried out for its own sake. It may be included in an assessment or evaluation (see below), but is more to be regarded as a basic research procedure. Because of this, a complete miniscience of psychological measurement, psychometrics, has developed to describe the different approaches to "mental" measurement and some of their properties. A number of basic psychometric concepts are relevant for users of tests for evaluation or assessment (see *Item Analysis*; *Objective Tests*; *Reliability of Test Results*; *Validity*; *Guessing, Correction for*; *Confidence Marking*).

In many applications, raw scores on tests are unsatisfactory as measures (because of their nonlinear nature, and the uncertainty as to the meaning of zero and perfect scores) so the reader will find several references to the topic of scaling (see *Scaling Methods*). There are also more general treatments of measurement theory (see *Generalizability Theory*; *Latent Trait Measurement Models*; *Item Response Theory*; *Rasch Measurement Models*).

2. Assessment

As far as possible the term assessment should be reserved for application to people. It covers activities included in grading (formal and nonformal), examining, certifying, and so on. Student achievement on a particular course may be assessed. An applicant's attitude for a particular job may be assessed. A teacher's competence may be assessed. Note that the large monitoring program within the United States, the National Assessment of Educational Progress (NAEP), is not an assessment within this definition. Although individual students are given tests, no interest is attached to their individual results. Data are aggregated before analysis, interpretation, and reporting (e.g., "Performance levels of 17-year-olds are declining," or "The gap in standards between the South Eastern states and the Far West is decreasing"). NAEP is an example of evaluation rather than assessment.

Throughout the world, most educational systems find it appropriate to record student achievement in some way, whether with a number, a letter code, or a comment such as "satisfactory" or "needs improvement." Such assessments are based on the informal synthesis of a wide variety of evidence, and although they often include test results, they rarely have much in common with scientific measurement. These procedures are increasingly being labeled "student evaluation" in the United States, perhaps because of the legitimacy accorded educational evaluation by the United States Congress when it passed the Elementary and Secondary Education Act in 1965. However, neither the purposes served by grading students, nor the procedures used, match the compilation of evidence regarding program quality that Congress had in mind (see *Achievement Tests*; *Examinations, External*; *Minimum Competency Testing*; *Adaptive Testing*).

3. Evaluation

In general, it would seem preferable to reserve the term educational evaluation for application to abstract entities such as programs, curricula, and organizational variables. Its use implies a general weighing of the value or worth of something, and, as Scriven pointed out in an important article (1967), it usually involves making comparison to other programs, curricula, or organizational schemes.

Just as assessment may be characterized as a routine activity in which most educators will be involved, evaluation is an activity primarily for those engaged in research and development. Its potential importance in the improvement of educational systems has been accorded almost universal recognition, but fierce controversy surrounds the issue of evaluation methods (see *Evaluation Models: Development*; *Program Evaluation*; *Formative and Summative Evaluation*; *Evaluator, Role of*; *Adversary Evaluation*; *Decision-oriented Evaluation*; *Curriculum Evaluation*; *Goal-free Evaluation*; *Illuminative Evaluation*; *Intrinsic Evaluation*; *Judicial Evaluation*; *Naturalistic Evaluation*; *Responsive Evaluation*; *Transactional Evaluation*; *Tyler Evaluation Model*).

Bibliography

Scriven M 1967 The methodology of evaluation. In: Tyler R W, Gagné R M, Scriven M (eds.) 1967 *Perspectives of Curriculum Evaluation*. Rand McNally, Chicago, Illinois
Tyler R W 1950 *Basic Principles of Curriculum and Instruction*. University of Chicago Press, Chicago, Illinois

B. H. Choppin

Evaluation for Utilization

The Joint Committee on Standards for Educational Evaluation in the United States (1981) identified four primary criteria by which evaluations should be judged: utility, feasibility, propriety, and accuracy. Evaluators differ in the emphasis they place on these criteria. Evaluators who place priority on the utility criterion believe that evaluations should be judged first and foremost by how they are used. It does not matter how technically rigorous an evaluation is if it is not useful—and actually used.

Placing priority on the utility of evaluations has profound implications for every aspect of the evaluation process. In recent years, a comprehensive framework for utilization-focused evaluation has emerged that is based on giving highest priority to the utility criterion in the new standards for evaluation. Eleven premises of that framework are presented below.

1. Basic Premises of Utilization-focused Evaluation

The first premise is that concern for utilization should be the driving force in an evaluation. At every point where a decision about the evaluation is being made, whether the decision concerns the focus of study, design, methods, measurement, analysis, or reporting, the evaluator asks: "How would that affect the utilization of this evaluation?"

The second premise is that concern for utilization is ongoing and continuous from the very beginning of the evaluation. Utilization is not something one becomes interested in at the end of an evaluation. By the end of the evaluation, the potential for utilization has been largely determined. From the moment decision makers and evaluators begin conceptualizing the evaluation, decisions are being made which will affect utilization in major ways.

The third premise is that evaluations should be user oriented. This means that the evaluation is aimed at the interests and information needs of specific identifiable people, not vague passive audiences. Therefore, the first step in utilization-focused evaluation is identification and organization of specific decision makers and information users. The evaluator must determine who the potential users are, and aim the evaluation at those users.

A fourth premise is that, once identified, these interested decision makers and information users should be personally and actively involved in making decisions about the evaluation. Working actively with people who have a stake in the outcomes of an evaluation (the "stakeholders") is aimed at increasing the potential for utilization by building a genuine commitment to and understanding of the evaluation over the course of the evaluation process. Such an approach recognizes the importance of the "personal factor" (Patton 1978) in evaluation utilization. People who are personally interested and involved in an evaluation are more likely to use evaluation findings. The best way to be sure that an evaluation is targeted at the personal concerns of stakeholders is to involve them actively at every stage of the evaluation.

A fifth premise is that there are multiple and varied interests around any evaluation. Teachers, administrators, parents, public officials, students, and community leaders all have an interest in evaluation, but the degree and nature of their interests will vary. The process of identifying and organizing stakeholders to participate in an evaluation process should be done in a way that is sensitive to and respectful of these varied and multiple interests. At the same time, it must be recognized that resource, time, and staff limitations will make it impossible for any single evaluation to answer all possible questions, or to give full attention to all possible issues. Identified decision makers and information users, representing various constituencies, should come together at the beginning of the evaluation to decide which issues and questions will be given priority in the evaluation in order to maximize the utility of the evaluation. The process of focusing the content of the evaluation should not be done by evaluators acting alone, or in isolation from users.

A sixth premise is that careful selection of stakeholders for active participation in the evaluation process will permit high quality participation, and high quality participation is the goal, not high quantity participation. The quantity of group interaction time is often inversely related to the quality of the process. Thus, evaluators conducting utilization-focused evaluations must be skilled group facilitators and have a large repertoire of techniques available for working actively with stakeholders in the evaluation (Patton 1981).

A seventh premise is that high quality involvement of stakeholders will result in high quality evaluations. Many evaluators assume that methodological rigor will inevitably be sacrificed if nonscientists collaborate in making methods decisions. This need not be the case. Decision makers want data that are useful and accurate (Weiss and Bucuvalas 1980). Skilled evaluators can help nonscientists understand methodological issues so that they can judge for themselves the trade-offs involved in choosing among the strengths and weaknesses of design options and methods alternatives. Such involvement in collaborative deliberations on methodological issues can significantly increase stakeholders' understanding of the evaluation, while giving evaluators a better understanding of stakeholder priorities and situational constraints on the feasibility of alternative approaches. These shared decisions can thus enhance both utilization potential and methodological rigor.

An eighth premise is that evaluators committed to enhancing utilization have a responsibility to train decision makers and information users in evaluation processes and the uses of information. By training stakeholders in evaluation methods and processes, the evaluator is looking to both short-term and long-term utilization. Making decision makers more sophisticated about evaluation can contribute to greater use of evaluation data and evaluation processes over time.

A ninth premise is that there are a variety of ways in which evaluation processes and findings are used (see *Evaluation Studies, Impact of*). Evaluations can directly influence major, specific decisions. Evaluations can be used to make minor adjustments in programs. Decision makers can, and do, use evaluations to reduce uncertainty, enlarge their options, increase control over program activities, and increase their sophistication about program processes. Sometimes evaluations have more of a conceptual impact, that is, they influence how stakeholders think about a program, rather than an instrumental impact, that

is, evaluation utilization manifested in concrete actions and explicit decisions. A broad view of utilization reveals multiple layers of impact over varying amounts of time. All of these kinds of utilization are important and legitimate from a utilization-focused evaluation perspective. This view of utilization also broadens the notion of evaluation impact to include use of the entire evaluation process as a stakeholder learning experience, not just use of the findings in a final report.

A tenth premise is that attention to utilization involves financial and staff time costs that are far from trivial. The benefits of these costs are manifested in greater utilization. These costs should be made explicit in evaluation proposals and budgets so that utilization efforts are not neglected for lack of resources.

An eleventh premise is that a variety of factors affect utilization. These factors include community variables, organizational characteristics, the nature of the evaluation, evaluator credibility, political considerations, and resource constraints (Alkin et al. 1979). In conducting a utilization-focused evaluation, the evaluator attempts to be sensitive to and aware of how these various factors affect the potential for utilization. An analysis of the factors that may affect the usefulness of an evaluation should be undertaken jointly with stakeholders early in the evaluation process. These factors, and their actual effects on utilization, are then monitored throughout the utilization-focused evaluation process.

2. Taking Utilization Seriously

Different evaluators working from different frameworks operate with different premises (see *Evaluation Models: Development*). The premises reviewed above are not shared by all evaluators, not even by all evaluators who place a high priority on utilization. Taken together, however, these premises constitute a fairly comprehensive framework for the practice of a particular approach to educational evaluations, a "utilization-focused approach" (Patton 1978). From this point of view, it is as important to deal with potential threats to utility in an evaluation as it is to deal with threats to validity. Taking utilization seriously means not leaving utilization processes to chance, or to the end of the evaluation. Utilization considerations are built into the evaluation at every step along the way.

Bibliography

Alkin M C, Daillak R, White P 1979 *Using Evaluations: Does Evaluation Make a Difference?* Sage, Beverly Hills, California

Braskamp L A, Brown R D 1980 *Utilization of Evaluative Information.* Jossey-Bass, San Francisco, California

Dickey B 1981 Utilization of evaluations of small scale educational projects. *Educ. Eval. Policy Anal.* 2(6): 65–77

Guba E G, Lincoln Y S 1981 *Effective Evaluation: Improving the Usefulness of Evaluation Results Through Responsive and Naturalistic Approaches.* Jossey-Bass, San Francisco, California

Joint Committee on Standards for Educational Evaluation 1981 *Standards for Evaluation of Educational Programs, Projects, and Materials.* McGraw-Hill, New York

Leviton L, Hughes E 1981 Research on the utilization of evaluations: A review and synthesis. *Eval. Rev.* 5: 525–48

Patton M Q 1978 *Utilization-Focused Evaluation.* Sage, Beverly Hills, California

Patton M Q 1981 *Creative Evaluation.* Sage, Beverly Hills, California

Weiss C, Bucuvalas M 1980 Truth test and utility test: Decisionmakers' frames of reference for social science research. *Am. Sociol. Rev.* 45: 302–13

M. Q. Patton

Evaluation in Adult Education

The heterogeneity of adult education provision and of its student population renders measurement difficult, but the maturity of its participants facilitates investigation in depth and the use of qualitative methodologies. The planning of an evaluation gives rise to significant questions of value and purpose; the interests of groups involved may conflict. In this article the need for evaluation in adult education, the principal agents, work done, and methods used since the early 1960s are briefly reviewed, with some indications of possible further development.

1. Distinctive Features of Evaluation in Adult Education

It must be stressed that "evaluation" is a term of historically recent currency in adult education, although the need to investigate its effectiveness has long been felt. Many analyses, records of experience, and enquiries carried out in the recent past and recognized as research may now be categorized as evaluation, although that claim is not made by their authors. Systematic evaluations undertaken so far in the field of adult education have not been numerous, nor large in scale. Several reasons can be identified for this and will illuminate the peculiarities of adult education.

Firstly, until recently adult education has not received large allocations of public funds, and has therefore been under less pressure to demonstrate results. Secondly, it has been provided by a wide range of statutory, vocational, and voluntary bodies, many of which will not have had the motive or the resources for evaluation. Thirdly, it is and has always been an activity widely dispersed into local centres, for the most part using premises built for other uses.

It has therefore lacked visibility, and not been seen as an obvious target for critical review. Fourthly, the majority of participants were not seeking credit or qualification; the providers did not therefore need to establish their efficiency in this regard.

Beyond these structural considerations, however, there is a historical–ethical one which is perhaps more fundamental. From its early origins, the providers and practitioners of adult education have considered their activities to be worthwhile beyond question. This belief rested on the assumption that education was a primary "good" in itself, and or the liberal principle that all individuals should have access to it. Furthermore, the day-to-day and face-to-face experience of adult educators convinced them of the validity of their ethos. From this perspective, evaluation would be seen as superfluous, and also as unrealistic because of the intangible mysteries of human development.

The increasing significance attached to adult education marks a qualitative shift from the assumptions on which institutional education for young people has been based, assumptions relating to needs, motivation, maturity, and experience. Correspondingly, the areas of provision, the organizational structures, and the objectives are distinct from those of youth education. In working with adults, the opportunities for evaluation in depth are greatly enhanced, while simple models developed for use in schools cannot be applied. In the school situation, groups or classes homogeneous in respect of age, sex, educational background, and even "intelligence" are available, a situation ready-made for controlled experiment. In adult education few classes are so homogeneous. The enhanced possibilities arise from the capacity of the adult to reflect and report on his/her own experience. In the process of evaluation, adult learners will be subjects rather than objects.

It may be relatively easy to measure the extent to which simple objectives have been realized: but those formulated for adult education courses are likely to employ such phrases as "the enrichment of experience", "facilitation of personal development", "growth of insight and empathy", or "interpersonal skills". The problems of ascertaining whether such objectives have been met are considerable. The literatures of academic and clinical psychology, especially the American literatures, are replete with rigorous tests of subjective changes gained by observing the behavioural correlates. Such tests however have not usually convinced teachers of literature, history, or religious studies. Where such tests are used for evaluation, their claims to validity and generalizability are commonly contested (see *Validity*).

2. The Felt Needs

Beyond the need recognized by all providers and sponsors of adult education to ensure that money spent is yielding a proportionate return, that objectives are being realized to some degree, and that target populations are being reached, there are the needs felt by administrators and practitioners. The former may wish to know whether local citizens are sufficiently informed of what is on offer; whether programmes are appropriate for towns and districts of differing social composition; whether preset curricula are well-chosen for ostensible purposes. Practitioners may feel the need to discover whether the assembled students have the attainments, motivation, and social characteristics envisaged; whether the teaching methods adopted are effective; whether there is evidence of personal development transcending the aims of cognitive learning; whether location, family, and vocational circumstance, or personal history favour or inhibit the class members' participation in study. It is characteristic of adult education that the desire for knowledge of results is manifested across the range, from the microlevel of the classroom to the directors of international programmes.

3. The Agents of Evaluation: Some Examples

Some of the largest and most sophisticated programme evaluations have been undertaken by the international agencies, notably the World Bank and the World Health Organization, who work under the pressing need to justify their expenditures to the contributing member states. The relative failure of much financial and technical aid has led to an awareness of the centrality of adult education as an instrument for social development (Cuca and Pierce 1977).

At the national level, an example of a multifaceted evaluation of a large programme of education for system and behaviour change is to be found in Nordlie (1981). All of the educational research institutes of the Scandinavian countries have published valuable investigations of the outcomes of legislation directed towards equalization of access to adult education and increased take-up by disadvantaged groups (Höghielm and Rubenson 1980) (see *Program Evaluation*). Because there are so few captive audiences in adult education—it is a sector where participants vote with their feet—providers have always needed to discover the social characteristics, motivation, and responses of the participants. Early researchers of great value in this regard were Johnstone and Rivera (1965) in the United States, and Trenaman (1967) in the United Kingdom. A much cited investigation at the microlevel, identifying goal-oriented, activity-oriented, and learning-oriented students, was that of Houle (1963).

In the United Kingdom, examples of state-sponsored evaluations of publicly financed programmes have been Charnley and Jones (1979) on adult literacy teaching and the report of a joint team from Nottingham University and the National Institute of Adult Education on the training of part-time teachers of adults (Graham et al. 1982). These were in one sense typical in that accurate quantification was known to be impossible from the outset in both cases; each of the researches assembled and analysed a large sample of qualitative material making it possible for convincing conclusions to be reached.

Local authorities and municipalities have similarly sought to inform themselves about citizen participation in education, usually for administrative purposes. The associated reports, where for instance an authority is reorienting its provision towards community education, may be of considerable interest (see *Community Education and Community Development*). Although not published, they may be available on request.

In the United Kingdom, much pioneering work has been initiated and evaluated by university adult educators. This has generally been on a small scale, the findings having doubtful significance beyond the local circumstance. In the United States where larger resources have been available, larger enquiries have been possible. These have mainly focused upon existing provision and clientele. It should be remembered however that in the United States alone many hundreds of doctoral and master's theses and dissertations in the field of adult education have been completed, and that similar work is rapidly aggregating in the United Kingdom, Australia, and elsewhere. These individual researches exhibit a wide diversity of sophisticated methodologies.

4. Methods

For reasons mentioned above, the methods used in the evaluation of adult education programmes have tended towards qualitative, anthropological, phenomenological, or illuminative models (see *Illuminative Evaluation*) rather than positive ones (but see Skager 1978). Some researches have involved extensive in-depth semistructured or non-directive interviewing. Survey methods are essential for monitoring and analysing the response of populations to programme provision, and have generally been adopted for large-scale enquiries.

Because all participants in adult education are mature citizens, often sharply aware of civil rights, ethical issues in evaluation are likely to be more salient and more complex than in the investigation of school education. Challenges may be formulated as open questions such as: In whose interest is this evaluation being undertaken? What prior consultation has there been with subjects/students/teachers? Will the policies and the practice of administrators be excluded from investigation? Will all the data be made public? Who will edit the report? To whom will the research be credited? For example, research in hand indicates that industrial training is evaluated almost entirely in terms of its effect on productivity. It hardly needs saying that it might be judged by the learner on a quite different basis (see *Evaluator, Role of*; *Ethics of Evaluation Studies*; *Program Evaluation*). Programme planning and the choice of methods need to be undertaken with such questions in mind.

5. The Main Areas of Evaluation

The main topics of some 400 books and other items reporting evaluations in adult education, or considered by their authors to be significant for evaluation, have been categorized. They were mainly English language texts, with American, British, and Canadian work predominating, but a smaller number of items from Scandinavia, the Netherlands, France, and the Federal Republic of Germany were also listed. The following conclusions emerged.

In order of frequency, the main areas of concern subjected to evaluation between 1960 and 1980 have been: distance teaching; medical, nursing, and health education; programmes and policy making; basic education and literacy; teaching method; and counselling.

Notable trends during the period appear to have been: a sharp increase in the evaluation of counselling; increases in the evaluation of vocationally oriented courses, those for the disadvantaged and for industrial workers; and a fall in the evaluation of basic adult education.

Liberal adult education, political education, provision for trades unions and cooperatives—all areas of traditional concern—have been little subject to evaluation throughout.

In respect of the above list of subject areas, the following explanatory hypotheses may be offered. There has been an emphasis on distance teaching because: (a) its methods are of historically recent development, not resting on traditional sanctions; (b) large investments have been made in the necessary capital and operational provision; and (c) the learning process is not visible to the providers.

In respect of medical and health education, (a) its vital import calls for a constant review of its effectiveness; (b) health-related behaviour, for example, smoking, drinking, sexual activity, has proved to be resistant to change.

Educational counselling is an expensive provision requiring special justification, which in principle may be obtained from (a) a systematic consideration of evidence of its life-determining function; and (b) the wastage involved in the dropping out of students in whose prior education large sums have been invested.

There has been a low level of activity in the evaluation of liberal adult education, despite the high regard in which it is generally held by adult educators, because (a) its practitioners have felt that its outcomes, for example, the response to poems or pictures, will always elude rational attempts to regis-

ter and measure them; (b) its courses are rarely linked to marketable qualifications; and (c) its values are felt to be intrinsic and self-validating for teacher and learner.

It should be recognized that 400 evaluation-related publications represent no more than the visible manifestations of a large, almost universal, process. Enquiry has shown that the prevalence of systematic self-determined individual learning is greater than had been supposed. This is a situation that calls for self-evaluation of the chosen learning systems and methods. The work of Allen Tough (1971) has greatly extended knowledge in this field and has related the research findings to practice and policy.

6. Recent Trends

Adult education is increasingly called upon to contribute to the resolution of social problems. Examples are (a) programmes of vocational preparation to help unemployed persons to compete more effectively for notified vacancies; and (b) programmes for, or concerned with, ethnic minorities. Both of these disadvantaged groups are increasing in Western societies. Educational measures cannot alone resolve the associated problems; it is predictable that apparent failures will call for an evaluation of programmes.

More positively, a further increase in the provision of part-time, modular, and inservice courses for adults can be foreseen. Researches into this field have revealed a student population exhibiting every variety of circumstance, motivation, social character, and personal history. The need for ongoing evaluation programmes designed to illuminate the complex interrelations of institutional requirements, personal needs, technological change, and vocational choice will become increasingly evident.

The surest prediction is that programme sponsors will continue to be concerned with the difficulty of securing a proportionate response from those sections of the community whose educational attainments are low, and may be presumed to be in greatest need. No general solution to this seemingly intractable problem has been found. Every innovatory problem in this field of action calls for systematic evaluation.

It is less well-recognized that there are extensive unresearched educational programmes for those at the higher end of the scale of privilege, the elites who occupy the seats of power and influence. Examples are to be found in staff college programmes for top civil servants, senior officers of the forces and police services, and the executives of international companies. It is in the public interest to know what teaching in law and economics, for instance, is provided for the generals who so often find themselves called upon to reinforce the civil authority, or even to take over the government of a country; or what training in social studies is available for justices of the high courts. It is to be hoped that the need for formal evaluation in this area will be recognized in the near future.

Adult educators are rapidly made aware of the extent to which the learner's thinking is influenced, or even determined, by the mass media and their content, including all that is communicated by visual images. Attempts to characterize these and to determine their effects on informal learning are in progress in most Western countries.

By way of conclusion, a cautionary word may be in order. Evaluation in other fields of provision has refuted some large claims and disappointed expectations. In Europe overall, the reorganization of secondary education has not succeeded in redistributing life chances to the hoped-for extent. There are as yet few indications that adult education can respond to the challenging requirements of lifelong education, now accepted in principle by most countries around the world. It may be hoped that evaluation *will* highlight the central importance of the organizational flexibility, the community links, and the humane values that have always characterized the best practice of adult education.

See also: Evaluation in Adult Education: Developing Countries

Bibliography

Charnley A H, Jones H A 1979 *The Concept of Success in Adult Literacy.* Huntington, Cambridge

Cuca R, Pierce C S 1977 *Experiments in Family Planning: Lessons from the Developing World.* Johns Hopkins University Press for the World Bank, Baltimore, Maryland

Gelpi E 1979 Suggestions for an evaluation of experiences. In: Gelpi E 1979 *A Future for Lifelong Education.* Department of Adult and Higher Education, University of Manchester, Manchester, pp. 97–109

Graham T B, Daines J M, Sullivan T, Harris P, Baum F E 1982 *The Training of Part-time Teachers of Adults.* University of Nottingham and National Institute of Adult Education, Nottingham

Hall B, Tandon R, Grossi F V, Conchelos G, Kassam Y, MacCall B 1981 Participatory research: Developments and issues. *Convergence* 14(3)

Höghielm R, Rubenson K (eds.) 1980 *Adult Education for Social Change: Research on the Swedish Allocation Policy.* Stockholm Institute of Education, Stockholm, Sweden

Houle C 1963 *The Inquiring Mind.* University of Wisconsin Press, Madison, Wisconsin

Jenkins D R 1976 *Curriculum Evaluation.* Open University Press, Milton Keynes

Johnstone J W C, Rivera R J 1965 *Volunteers for Learning: A Study of the Educational Pursuits of American Adults.* Aldine, Chicago, Illinois

Nordlie P G 1981 *Monitoring and Evaluating Equal Opportunity Progress in the Army.* United States Commission on Civil Rights, Washington, DC

Parlett M R, Hamilton D 1972 *Evaluation as Illumination: A New Approach to the Study of Innovatory Programs.*

Centre for Research in Educational Sciences, University of Edinburgh, Edinburgh

Ruddock R 1981 *Evaluation: A Consideration of Principles and Methods.* Department of Adult and Higher Education, University of Manchester, Manchester

Skager R W 1978 *Lifelong Education and Evaluation Practice: A Study on the Development of a Framework for Designing Evaluation Systems at the School Stage in the Perspective of Lifelong Education.* UNESCO Institute for Education and Pergamon Press, Oxford

Tough A M 1971 *The Adult's Learning Projects: A Fresh Approach to Theory and Practice in Adult Learning.* Ontario Institute for Studies in Education, Toronto, Ontario

Trenaman J M 1967 *Communication and Comprehension: The Report of an Investigation, by Statistical Methods, of the Effective Communication of Educative Material and an Assessment of the Factors Making for such Communication, with Special Reference to Broadcasting.* Longman, London

R. Ruddock

Evaluation in Adult Education: Developing Countries

This article will trace the involvement of multinational and bilateral funding and assistance organizations in evaluation activities in adult and nonformal education. It will concentrate on activities in developing countries. No attempt will be made to catalog all evaluation efforts, but rather to identify trends and suggest selected references. Evaluation activities in industrialized countries, such as those funded in the United States by the National Institute of Education, are not included as these are well covered in other standard references.

1. Early Evaluation Efforts in Adult Education

A case can be made that the adult education field, broadly defined, has pioneered many of the approaches now advocated by specialists in program and project evaluation.

In the 1920s and 1930s, agricultural extension specialists in the United States carried out a wide range of studies on the effect of various extension practices. Such studies indicated that farmers were most likely to change practices when they saw a demonstration of a technique on a farm similar to their own. Publications, radio programs, and face-to-face visits of extension workers reinforced efforts to change farming practice. These various techniques in themselves often missed the mark because the change agent lacked an understanding of what the farmer already knew, thought, felt, and did. Agricultural education specialists early practiced what would now be called formative evaluation when they tested extension publications in order to see which words farmers knew, used, could read with ease, and which words were used only by agricultural specialists.

In the 1950s and 1960s, a number of international projects began to build on some of the earlier agricultural extension concepts. UNESCO's Regional Center for Fundamental Education in Latin America (CREFAL), established in Patzcuaro, Mexico, built into its training program various experiences involving the collection of information on the rural population to be served by adult education activities. Such approaches later would be called needs assessment and would be considered as important contributions to formative evaluation (see *Needs Assessment in Adult Education*; *Formative and Summative Evaluation*).

Also in the 1950s, the Organization of American States (OAS) established the Latin American Fundamental Education Press, a program involving the preparation and testing of a series of adult education booklets designed for adults of limited reading ability in Latin America. This series included booklets in health, agriculture, civics, recreation, and other topics considered at the time important in Latin American development. The series was pretested in a number of Latin American countries by surveying reading interests in rural and urban areas; working with a sample of adults in various socioeconomic settings to see what they could read, understand, and remember of the booklets being prepared; and evaluating the effect of various formats (e.g., illustrations and captions with text) on interest and comprehension (Spaulding and Nannetti in Richards 1959).

During the same period, the Inter-American Institute for Agricultural Sciences, with its headquarters in Costa Rica, embarked on a series of activities, in cooperation with the OAS, involving research and training in agricultural communications. Again, the emphasis was on needs assessment, and formative and summative evaluation. These early efforts led to the establishment of a formal department of agricultural communications at La Molina Agricultural University in Peru, which has taken regional leadership in training and research in this area.

UNESCO's work in adult education, literacy, and reading materials for the new literate during the 1950s and 1960s stressed various kinds of evaluative approaches, described as topic testing, pretesting, posttesting, study of the environment, and so on. In 1957, UNESCO held a regional seminar on reading materials for new literates in Rangoon, Burma, which entailed the collection of information on village needs, writing and pretesting of reading materials, and evaluation of the impact of such materials. A regional meeting was held in Pakistan, which outlined evaluation and research needs in the area of reading materials and literacy programs (Richards 1959). During the 1950s, UNESCO, the Ford Foundation, and other international agencies assisted a number of national programs involved in the creation and evaluation of adult education literature. Among these were the East African Literature Bureau, the Burma Translation Society, the Bureau of Ghanaian Languages, and the Marbial Valley Project in Haiti. In 1962, the East African Literature Bureau, with headquarters in Nairobi, was the host of a UNESCO-sponsored regional workshop on the preparation of reading materials for new literates which included authors, editors, publishers, and artists from both English- and French-speaking African countries. Participants formed teams and worked in village areas to identify needs as felt by villagers and community development experts. They then designed reading materials which were tried out in villages, revised, and duplicated.

2. The UNESCO Experimental World Literacy Program

In the mid-1960s, UNESCO proposed massive support for an experimental world literacy program, designed to combine social and economic skills training with traditional communication skills training. The United Nations Development Program (UNDP) was the usual source of support for such projects within the United Nations system. The UNDP was approached to help finance the effort, but was distinctly cool to the idea. Although economists had begun to treat formal education as investment rather than consumption, there was not yet much acceptance of the case for investment in literacy and adult education. The UNDP finally agreed, however, to finance several experimental projects, on the condition that UNESCO would bring into each project an evaluative system designed to show how each project affected the behavior of individuals and communities involved in the functional literacy programs (Spaulding 1966).

Ultimately, 11 experimental projects were funded under the experimental effort, most of them becoming operational in the late 1960s and terminating in the 1970s. Despite the efforts to design comparable evaluative procedures in each project beforehand, the local context of each project was such that few comparable data were collected. Most governments wanted a national literacy effort rather than a pilot experimental project. Some projects separated evaluation from program development, and the evaluator (usually a social scientist) maintained a distance from the operational staff. Other projects considered evaluation to be a formative activity, with the evaluator collecting data to be shared with program developers in order to help improve the project as it progressed.

In the 1970s, UNESCO established an evaluation unit in Paris which labored without success for some months in an attempt to integrate diverse data from the 11 literacy projects into some kind of comparable reporting design. Finally an international committee of evaluation was established. Two educators were invited to examine and summarize the findings of each project and to report on trends that were evident between and among projects. The result was a joint UNDP/UNESCO report which was generally well-received by the scholarly community, but was considered controversial within UNESCO (Spaulding and Gillette 1976).

The report looked at the political problems that plagued the various projects; the administrative and organizational problems; the staffing problems; the cost of the projects; the nature and effectiveness of the teaching materials and methods used; and the apparent effect on people and communities. Essentially, the report highlighted the complexity of any attempt to make major changes in an adult population through any one adult education or literacy effort; the need to adjust any such program to local conditions; the need to get high-level policy support to ensure success of any program; and the need to integrate such efforts into broader development plans.

3. Current Evaluation Activities

During the 1970s and early 1980s, the governing bodies of most international organizations called for more evaluative efforts. Both UNDP and UNESCO established offices of evaluation which, in turn, undertook to jointly evaluate a number of educational projects. UNESCO published guidelines on project evaluation to help short-term consultant teams brought in to do mid-term project evaluations (UNESCO 1979) and a manual on how to do structured evaluations of literacy programs (Couvert 1979). The United States Agency for International Development (USAID) established, in October 1979, a major division for project evaluation which has produced a remarkable series of reports on various USAID-assisted projects in rural education, rural development, and related fields, most with adult education components (i.e., Giovanni et al. 1981).

The United States Agency for International Development (USAID) has also supported a variety of evaluation efforts through contracts with universities and consulting agencies, including the Stanford University Institute for Communications Research and Academy for Educational Development, the Center for International Education at the University of Massachusetts, Michigan State University, World Education, and the Institute for Development Anthropology.

Major studies financed by USAID and others include a three-year effort by Florida State University to evaluate the extensive work of *Acción Popular Cultural* (ACPO) in Colombia. The ACPO, over the years, has evolved a radiophonic education effort which includes publications, volunteer monitors in many villages, and a variety of adult education activities which are supported by the communications infrastructure. The complexity of developing and managing such a program and attracting continuing interest of participants has been highlighted in this study (Bernal et al. 1978, Morgan et al. 1980).

The USAID also initiated in the early 1980s a major demonstration of the uses of satellites to improve communication in rural and community development. This effort will have a major evaluation component. Liberia is the location of the first of several country projects, each of which emphasizes the role of communication in adult education. This effort is consistent with an increasing concern of a number of funding agencies for the integration of adult education services into comprehensive community development efforts (Coombs 1980).

The World Bank has an office which undertakes evaluations of projects funded by the various regional bureaus of the Bank, but most of these "audits" are for internal use only and are not made public. At the end of the 1970s, however, the Bank began to encourage borrowing nations to build into each project it funds a continuous evaluation system which will provide information useful for improving project performance as it progresses as well as cumulative information to help in the ultimate summative evaluation of the effort. One of the more elaborate of such built-in feedback evaluation mechanisms, to cost several million dollars over a seven-year period, was developed in Papua New Guinea in 1980 as part of a primary education reform loan (which also included a small adult education component). The Bank also undertakes a variety of efficiency, dropout, rate of return, labor market, and other studies which all contribute to educational decision making and thus fit within the context of evaluation efforts. The Bank, in the mid-1970s, assisted the Saudi Arabian government in a major evaluation of their adult education and literacy efforts, with the help of faculty from the International and Development Education Program of the University of Pittsburgh, the University of Linköping in Sweden, Ain Shaims University in Cairo, World Education, and other groups.

The Canadian International Development Agency (CIDA) has participated in a variety of evaluation efforts, often in cooperation with the International Council for Adult Education in Toronto and the International Development Research Center in Ottawa (see *International Council for Adult Education*). The Swedish International Development Authority has similarly funded a variety of adult education projects with an evaluative component, including one to train adult educators in Portugal undertaken by the University of Linköping (Erasmie and Norbeck 1978). The Overseas Development Authority in the United Kingdom has funded a number of such overseas projects, especially through the University of Reading, which has a long-standing interest in agricultural and rural development (Bowers 1977).

Finally, a joint UNESCO–UNICEF program of studies has issued an extensive series of reports which includes evaluative material on a variety of nonformal projects and programs for children, youth, and women. And the UNESCO Regional Office in Asia is host to the Asian Program for Educational Innovation and Development (APEID) which has supported a number of institutions involved in evaluative studies of educational innovation in the region.

4. Institutional Evaluation Policies

Most international evaluation efforts in nonformal and adult education have been initiated by multinational and bilateral funding and assistance organizations. There is, however, little agreement among and between agencies and governments as to what evaluation is about.

Some in the agencies see evaluation as an exercise whereby experts are sent for a few days or weeks to look at a project in progress to decide whether or not it is meeting its objectives and whether or not any changes are needed in the project plan. Governing boards of international and funding organizations see evaluation as a means of providing data to help them set priorities on what should be funded in the future. National governments, project administrators, and groups involved in projects, however, are more attracted to the idea of evaluation as an information system which can help provide data for ongoing improvement in project management and design.

The picture is further complicated by the internal structures of international and funding organizations. If the evaluation unit of the organization is not placed at a high enough level in the organization and given sufficient resources, autonomy, and authority to do its work, its work will be limited and its information will be little used in policy making and operational decision making.

Perhaps more importantly, evaluation efforts, to be effective in improving performance, must be built into program and project activities with the idea of helping answer participants' questions. External evaluations done by evaluation specialists may serve a function, but until evaluation is a state of mind shared by all participants in a program, evaluation will not be fully effective. For this reason, a major function of any in-house evaluation unit should be to help operational units within the organization in the design of their own self-evaluation efforts.

5. The Future

Since the early 1960s project and program personnel have been sensitized both in international agencies and in national governments to the need for evalu-

ative data on project and program activities. Increasing worldwide interest in nonformal and adult education will be accompanied by increasing interest in evaluation efforts designed to provide information for the constant improvement of projects and programs. Evaluation models will increasingly stress participation of the target audiences of nonformal and adult education efforts. Such participatory evaluation in itself will be a powerful adult education medium, consistent with current priorities on the development of community-based nonformal education efforts reflecting the needs and interests of local communities.

See also: Evaluation in Adult Education; Integrated Rural Development: Specialized Training Programs

Bibliography

Bernal H, Masoner P, Masoner L 1978 *Acción Cultural Popular: Pioneer Radiophonic Education Program of Latin America, 1947–1977.* International Division, Acción Cultural Popular, Bogotá, Columbia

Bohla H S 1979 *Evaluating Functional Literacy.* Hulton, Amersham

Bowers J 1977 Functional adult education for rural people: Communications action research and feedback. *Convergence* 10(3): 34–43

Clark N, McCaffery J 1979 *Demystifying Evaluation.* World Education, New York

Coombs P H 1980 *Meeting the Basic Needs of the Rural Poor: The Integrated Community-based Approach.* Pergamon, New York

Couvert R 1979 *The Evaluation of Literacy Programmes: A Practical Guide.* UNESCO, Paris

Erasmie T, Norbeck N 1978 *Annual Report 1977/78: The Portugal Project.* School of Education, Linköping University, Linköping

Farmer J A, Papagiannis G 1975 *Program Evaluation.* World Education, New York

Giovanni R S, Armstrong L T, Jansen W H 1981 *Thailand: Rural Non-formal Education: The Mobile Trade Training Schools.* United States Agency for International Development, Washington, DC

Guba E, Lincoln Y S 1981 *Effective Evaluation.* Jossey-Bass, San Francisco, California

Institute for Development Anthropology 1981 *Development Anthropology Network* 1(1): 8

Kinsey D C 1981 Participatory evaluation in adult and nonformal education. *Adult Education* 31(3): 155–68

Morgan R M, Muhlmann L, Masoner P 1980 *Evaluación de sistemas de comunicación educativa.* Acción Cultural Popular, Bogotá, Colombia

Nonformal Education Information Center 1981 *NFE Core Bibliographies.* Institute for International Studies in Education, Michigan State University, East Lansing, Michigan

Richards C G 1959 *The Provision of Popular Reading Materials.* UNESCO, Paris

Spaulding S 1966 The UNESCO world literacy program: A new strategy that may work. *Adult Education* 16(2): 70–84

Spaulding S 1974 Life-long education: A modest model for planning and research. *Comp. Educ.* 10: 101–13

Spaulding S, Gillette A 1976 *The Experimental World Literacy Programme: A Critical Assessment.* UNESCO, Paris

UNESCO 1979 *Evaluation of Technical Cooperation Projects in Education.* Document ED-79/23/159, Paris

Werdelin I 1977 *Evaluation.* Manual of Educational Planning 9, School of Education, Linköping University, Linköping

S. Spaulding

Evaluation in Vocational and Industrial Education

The main theme of this entry is that vocational educators need an expanded view of the potential contributions of evaluation practices and that they should begin to look more broadly at their conception of evaluation and the consequences of present practice, so that future action might be based upon more alternatives. This entry attempts to show how the analysis of evaluation in vocational education can be invigorated by the application of a wide range of approaches. Vocational education evaluation is spoken of not simply as a technical activity or a search for knowledge, but also as an ethical and a political activity.

1. Evaluation as an Ethical and a Political Activity

Evaluation can be seen as an ethical activity since value judgments are made which influence peoples' lives. The questions addressed by evaluators are not simply questions about how to conduct evaluations, but also ethical questions of how social life is to be conducted. Ultimately, such questions emerge if evaluators are pushed for reasons which support their value judgments in any kind of evaluation.

Evaluation is also a political process—political in the sense of the intelligent management of social affairs. What is included in the evaluation report is important; what is not reported can be just as important. Misrepresenting reality may obscure alternatives, mask the evaluators' responsibility, encourage apathy, and perpetuate or justify inequities and misconceptions.

2. Justifying Practice

There seems to be a great concern in the recent literature about the lack of use of the results of evaluation. There are several possible reasons for nonuse:

(a) evaluation practice may be seen as a threat and of little significance to practice;

(b) educators may be expressing uncertainty and skepticism regarding the purposes of evaluation and the intentions of the evaluator;

(c) the evaluator may be seen as an external agent exercising excessive power over the educational process;

(d) educators may fear that it will jeopardize professional or personal status; or

(e) the possibility that evaluators are merely particularizing the obvious, an activity seen as a waste of time since no insights are gained.

Any of these reasons pose a threat to the potential contributions of evaluation. To reduce the threat it would appear that there is need to develop closer relationships between purposes and practices.

Careful thought about the goals of vocational education and the purposes of evaluation is required. Reflection on practice mandates an examination of practice as it actually occurs. It would be premature to make recommendations regarding the improvement of practice if an assessment of current practice had not occurred as a prior step.

It is assumed that vocational education practices are based upon some normative structure and that they are dependent upon a historical and cultural context. Practices carried out contain, therefore, a set of beliefs and values held by the practitioners. An argument can be made that, given the historical and cultural dependency of practice, vocational educators are captives of this dependency. It can also be argued that, given the structural constraints on individuals within any given cultural context, it is imperative to take a highly critical look at practice.

3. Evolving Evaluation Models

Changes in vocational evaluation have often been made in response to objections that have been raised against past evaluation practices. In the 1930s and 1940s evaluation was done by many who made private judgments about students' progress, courses taught, or programs operated. Judgments were private in the sense that reasons were not given and the criteria used to make the judgment were not made explicit. Evaluation was not always done in an objective, systematic way. Instead, the credibility of the evaluation process rested on the reputation of the evaluator.

Those who did the evaluation would make some observations of what was occurring and then, based upon their experiences, would make judgments about the appropriateness or adequacy of current practice (Steinmetz 1975). Since the criteria used for evaluation were not necessarily explicit, the observations were not usually well-documented, and the results were difficult to substantiate. This process is still used but it has been influenced by the adoption of experimental and statistical methods.

4. The Prevailing Conception of Evaluation

Many vocational educators of the 1950s and 1960s viewed evaluation as the systematic collection of data on identified variables. Data were collected which seemed important for making decisions regarding satisfactory operation of a program.

In adopting experimental methods, the evaluator takes reality to mean that which is observable, measurable, and objective. Many vocational educators recognize that the techniques of experimental design are useful in collecting information to be used in making judgments about the results of an educational activity. They are also aware that evaluation can be used for justifying a vocational activity and may also be for the purpose of establishing an activity. This is often referred to as summative and formative evaluation. More recently, a popular form of evaluation has been the application of management theory to the problems of vocational instruction. It is assumed that the information collected will be used for making some judgment about value. The evaluator's role is to provide the appropriate information so managers in charge of programs can make informed decisions. Evaluation is a service, thus, to decision makers with the goal of improving the educational activity.

4.1 Assumptions Underlying Evaluation for Decision Making

The present trend has been to use experimental methods in a framework of management theory. Both experimental methods and management theory are based upon an empirical view of inquiry. In an empirical view, human behaviors are believed to be based upon some estimated regularities. The social world is viewed as an aggregation of variables which can be studied independently and in combinations.

The cause-and-effect relationships among variables is conceived as useful in predicting future outcomes. Observations and/or quantifications of variables occur in order to construct theories and test hypotheses.

An empirical view of inquiry is based upon several interrelated assumptions. Evaluation based on this view has taken the form of developing procedures which make explicit as many of the evaluators' activities as possible. It uses means/ends reasoning and is mainly interested in efficiency and effectiveness. The view of change that is used in this conception of evaluation is described by referring to adjustments which are necessary. It ordinarily assumes that the basic institutions of education are fundamentally sound. The problems of education are seen as defects which can be remedied by appropriate action.

4.2 Critique of the Empirical Approach

The empirical approach can be criticized on several grounds. Only four will be addressed: (a) value-free position, (b) limited conception of reality, science, and evaluation, (c) complexity and interrelatedness of reality are denied, (d) limited to addressing technical questions.

To be accurate it must be acknowledged that evaluation models used in vocational education are not necessarily neutral. It is clear that certainty and control are implicit interests in assumptions underlying a management view. Management theory has an interest in maintaining administrative and technical control. This has social consequences. Using such a value-laden conception of inquiry, the evaluation model tends to limit the problems to be addressed and tends to uphold the existing framework for vocational education. Evaluation based upon the empirical view often tends to ignore complex value issues. For example, "what is a vocationally educated person?" or conceptual issues such as "education vs. training" are often avoided.

The view of reality underlying the empirical view assumes a quest for order that sometimes ignores the means of dealing with competing views that influence educational processes. It tends to ignore what can contradict and, nevertheless, improve what presently exists. Consideration is given to being "scientific" with a preferred view of inquiry. There is a lack of appreciation of the need for internal criticism in the field. It is such criticism which often leads to corrective action. Conflict among members with various views provides a means for intellectual growth.

Even though evaluation procedures have been developed to redress the limitations of previous methods there is a tendency, nevertheless, to use a form of thought which is formal. Evaluation may be very incomplete when limited to the linear progression of stating goals and assessing them. In the realm of human activity, becoming informed does not function so smoothly. By assuming that it does, the potential exists for missing many things which are, or should be, occurring in the process.

There are few arguments to deny the ethical and political complexities of vocational education. Evaluation often occurs as a partisan, political process involving an assessment of the distribution of benefits. If evaluation is limited by administratively determined problems then the evaluation process is also limited.

Any legitimation of vocational education must include a consideration of its ultimate ends, the institutions which presently exist, as well as the effects which other systems (e.g., political and economic) have on it. Evaluation as a service to administration often supports the bureaucratic structure of the institution. Giving answers to questions about "what ought to be done" requires the identification of the many complexities involved. Failure to evaluate the institution ultimately tends to support the status quo.

5. A Critical Theory of Society

The models of evaluation, thus, suffer from misinterpretation, fragmentation, and empiricism. In the late 1960s, however, there arose some lively debates in what has been called the "new sociology of education." The orientation used insights from a concept known as critical theory. The concept emerged from the workings of the Frankfurt School in Germany. Jürgen Habermas's work in critical theory has received increasing attention.

5.1 Habermas and Human Interest

Habermas has identified different types of scientific activity, each of which he has used to address educational questions. His argument is based on the idea that all knowledge is grounded in human interest. He distinguishes three models of inquiry according to each interest.

There are, according to Habermas, three functional cognitive interests which are based upon the three areas of human activity. Each cognitive interest results in a particular approach to inquiry.

(a) A technical cognitive interest in control underlying empirical analytical science.

(b) A practical cognitive interest in consensus underlying interpretative science.

(c) A critical cognitive interest in emancipation or liberation underlying critical science.

Habermas's conception of interest evolved from his rejection of Kant's transcendental consciousness and his attraction to Hegel's early works. Hegel defended the thesis that knowledge is a result of peoples' interaction with one another. Learning, he claimed, is a continuous process which is equally individual and social. This learning process required three patterns of mediation. Hegel labels these patterns "work," "language," and "communicative interactions."

Using the analysis of Hegel, Habermas considers "interest" as follows: the process of social evolution takes place in three main areas of human activity—production, socialization, and system maintenance and development. In production, nature is appropriated by society for the satisfaction of human needs. Work is the activity of people involved in the producing dimension of life. It is through work that people enter into direct interchange with their environment. This production process takes place by means of purpose-guided action. It is instrumental action to meet the needs and wants of people. There is a desire to exercise control. Instrumental action is governed by technical rules. For example, what are the best means to achieve predetermined ends?

Socialization is the interaction of human beings with society through communicative activity. Language provides the medium through which people reflect about their environment. There is an interest in developing intersubjective understanding and establishing a sense of community.

Habermas's third dimension is that of changes in the society's power to maintain itself. It is society's steering and growth capacity. Power is the dimension which focuses upon the struggles for recognition among contending human beings.

Each area of work, language, and power yields a system of principles underlying development which determine what is defined as progress in each area. The three related areas of interest are technical, communicative, and emancipatory interests.

The three related areas of interest produce different kinds of knowledge, information, interpretation, and critique. The different kinds of knowledge provide a distinction to differentiate approaches to inquiry.

5.2 Assumptions Underlying Critical Theory

Critical reflection on technical control is the central task of Habermas's perspective. He perceives that when the technical interests dominate human communicative interest, the result is a degradation and belittling of human beings. Empirical analytical science is viewed as irrationally fixated on instrumental action and economic reality. His theory attempts to show how society can and should be altered or reestablished by reflection and rational reconstruction. Balance between technical and communicative interest is, according to Habermas, the key to effective functioning and to maximizing human life.

Knowledge plays an important role in creating the balance between technical and communicative interest according to Habermas. Undistorted knowledge is advanced as the means people can use to free themselves from the technical rationality which dominates society. Knowledge is utilized to free individuals from oppressing forces so that the development of the individual's full potential can be realized.

6. Critical Theory and Evaluation Practice

In attempting to apply critical theory to evaluation there are several interrelated ideas which purport to guide practice. Evaluation which denies the complexity of educating limits the problems which can be addressed. Any evaluation which does not acknowledge the complexity is unrealistic since the model of the environment is distorted. This distortion would tend to reduce the richness of the concepts formed. Deformed concepts tend to lead to deformed problems and solutions.

If complexity is to be accommodated, differing points of view must be assessed before the evaluation is made. When evaluation is viewed in this way it reinforces the ethical responsibility of evaluators by allowing diversity of judgments in regard to the options available and is not simply conformity to the evaluator's own perceptions.

In a more critical approach to evaluation, solutions would be evaluated considering the constraints in the context in which the decision must be made. The evaluator would be aware that circumstances are never ideal and that judgments must be made regarding actions to be taken that will most likely promote and will least likely hinder the preferred goal.

7. The Critical Evaluator

Evaluation involves the way in which the evaluators choose to address their tasks. Evaluators can facilitate good performance by asking questions such as: what are the consequences to all of those affected? What are the consequences today and in the future? Whose interests are being served? What are the consequences to the individual and to the society as a whole?

Education is not a finished process after the student graduates from compulsory school or vocational school. Evaluating success makes sense only if success also remains unfinished. It should not be the description of the status quo which is important to evaluation, but how evaluation knowledge is used as a means to facilitate, and indeed create, desirable change. Evaluation serves as a corrective activity which should not make claims about finality. Creative evaluators look on the world as having the potential for change. They often look to their practice as a means to that change.

8. Evaluation in Vocational Education

The intention here has not been to outline a comprehensive model for evaluation. Rather the intention has been to take a metatheoretical view of current practices and to consider what purposes evaluation might serve in vocational education. The suggestion is that vocational evaluators should accept the complexity of vocational education and seek to illuminate the normative positions within this complexity. It seems more likely that evaluation procedures can facilitate the complicated process of making choices and value judgments if the questions of value are openly and reflectively acknowledged and examined. At the more general level, evaluation will necessarily address the existence of social norms and power structures which organize and institutionalize social norms. There is no reason to assume that the social organization and norms that are a part of the vocational–educational structure cannot be examined as a part of any complete evaluation process. Beliefs, values, and social arrangements are part of the reality of vocational education and are a medium by which vocational education is carried out. This does not deny the usefulness of what is ordinarily

reported in evaluation, but it does suggest that "objective" knowledge of programs may not be enough. Self-conscious reflection on beliefs and values can help ensure adequate choice because it is based on an understanding of our social situation and possibilities available.

See also: Evaluator, Role of; Evaluation, Assessment, and Measurement; Evaluation in Adult Education; Vocational and Industrial Education: Quality Standards

Bibliography

Bernstein R 1976 *The Restructuring of Social and Political Theory*. Harcourt, Brace, Jovanovich, New York

Bronowski J 1978 *The Origins of Knowledge and Imagination*. Yale University Press, New Haven, Connecticut

Giroux H 1980 Critical theory and rationality in citizenship education. *Curric. Inq.* 10: 329–66

Habermas J 1971 *Knowledge and Human Interest*. Beacon Press, Boston, Massachusetts

Habermas J 1979 *Communication and the Evolution of Society*. Beacon Press, Boston, Massachusetts

Held D 1980 *Introduction to Critical Theory: Horkheimer to Habermas*. University of California Press, Berkeley, California

McCarthy T A 1978 *The Critical Theory of Jürgen Habermas*. MIT Press, Cambridge, Massachusetts

Peters R S 1976 *Ethics and Education*. Allen and Unwin, London

Schroder H M 1977 Die Bedeut Samkeit von Komplexite. In: Mandl H, Huber G (eds.) 1977 *Kognitive Komplexität: Bedeutung, Weiterentwicklung, Anwendung*. Verlag für Psychologie, Göttingen

Scriven M 1974 *Speaking of Educational Evaluation: Trends in Education*. McGraw-Hill, New York

Steinmetz A 1975 The ideology of educational evaluation. *Educ. Tech.* 6: 51–58

D. L. Coomer

Evaluation Models: Development

Evaluation models either describe what evaluators do or prescribe what they should do. Generally, evaluators are concerned with determining the value or current status of objects or states of affairs. The term "model" is used in two general ways. (a) A prescriptive model, the most common type, is a set of rules, prescriptions, prohibitions, and guiding frameworks which specify what a good or proper evaluation is and how evaluation should be carried out. Such models serve as exemplars. (b) A descriptive model is a set of statements and generalizations which describes, predicts, or explains evaluation activities. Such models are designed to offer an empirical theory.

The importance of studying evaluation models is shown in a number of ways. For example, understanding the various evaluation models provides insights and a framework for conducting evaluations in a more defensible way. Prescriptive models provide consistent frameworks and strategies for performing evaluations, and descriptive models present a range of validated possibilities for conducting evaluation. Further insights for practice are gained from the dynamics of model development itself.

Before examining differences among model types, it is appropriate to present some areas of common concern. Most often, educational evaluation models direct their attention to evaluating teaching, learning, and curriculum efficacy. But some evaluation models also consider those activities, practices, and policies designed to facilitate teaching, learning, and curriculum efficacy. For example, evaluation might focus on the decision-making process which manages education. Hence, evaluation models are often concerned with the financing, the administration, and in general, the sociopolitical organization of education.

The scope and depth of issues and problems which fall under the rubric of educational evaluation are surprisingly extensive. For example, the evaluation might be primarily directed towards problems of statistical inference and empirical generalization, but might also involve problems of how one can and how one should arrange the decision-making structures of a community. The topics range from specific and important problems in epistemology and scientific inquiry to specific and important problems in a political and ethical theory.

The wide disparity of topics and issues included in evaluation models is attributable to two factors. First, evaluation is still an emerging field seeking to bring definition and description both to its activities and to the way these activities might be conducted. Second, individual model builders have restricted the purposes or goals for developing their models.

There are a number of things that will not be explicitly examined within this article—primarily because they do not precisely come within the domain of evaluation models as currently conceived. Since evaluation models have tended to focus on program evaluation, this article will not be concerned with evaluation of students or teachers (assessment). Nor will it consider personnel evaluations (appraisal).

Similarly, some theories or models relate to the various tools or components of evaluation. For example, evaluation often requires the use of measurement procedures, statistical analyses, financial analyses, and so on. Modeling activities related to these kinds of matters are also not to be included within the discussion of curriculum/program/system evaluation.

Before turning, however, to an examination of the further distinctions between prescriptive and descriptive models and to a closer view of the variety of prescriptive models in particular, it is appropriate to examine the logical thought progression of the rationales which underlie the development of evaluation models.

1. Principles Underlying Evaluation Models

In this section the set of principles which underlie the dominant evaluation models will be analyzed.

When considering whether a program is a good or worthwhile one, it seems reasonable to determine whether it achieved its intended objectives. One of the earliest and most dominant prescriptive views of evaluation has this determination as its ultimate purpose. It is often called the Tylerian approach.

For those using this approach, the important questions ask how the objectives are to be determined, classified, behaviorally defined, and measured. In large studies, such as the National Assessment Project, the sampling of the various objectives becomes an important issue. Other important areas include the consideration of short-term and long-term objectives and the use of traditional and non-traditional forms of measurement.

One example of a situation where being guided by considerations of this type would provide useful information is the characterization of the status of student learning in the population. This approach also prescribes activities which appear to be central to any evaluation activity: (a) formulating the objectives clearly and finding reliable measures for them, and (b) using learning achievement information to judge the program.

In summary, the Tylerian view suggests the following as a basic principle: principle (a)—*the evaluation should judge that a program is good if, and only if, its objectives are achieved.*

There are limitations, however, to this basic principle. Suppose it is found that the program's objectives are not achieved? Does it follow that the program is not a good one? On the other hand, if it is found that the program's objectives are achieved, does it follow that it is a good one? Not necessarily. In the former case, it may turn out, for example, that the program is generally effective, but it did poorly because the student population was atypical. Perhaps the program was never implemented properly. In the latter case, it may turn out that something else caused the student achievement.

Thus, whether a program is a good one or worthwhile depends not only on the achievement of its objectives, but also on the degree to which such achievements are caused directly by the program. In the 1950s and the early 1960s, the causal efficacy of a program was assumed but never tested.

The recognition that the evaluation of a program should determine its causal efficacy gave rise to a cluster of evaluation approaches which took as their sole purpose, or the ultimate purpose, the determination of causation. Those who view evaluation in this way generally prescribed randomized controlled experiments as the method, or the ideal method, of establishing causation. Some prescribed quasi-experimental or "causal modeling" procedures.

A principle, then, derived from the "evaluation as an experiment" point of view is the following: principle (b)—*the evaluation should judge that a program is good if, and only if, it causes the achievement of its objectives.*

Both of these principles (practices to the exclusivity of other concerns) soon came under criticism. It was argued that the evaluation activity is typically comparative. Seldom is it shown that a program achieved all of its objectives or that a program was completely efficacious in causing the achievements. Thus, it was recommended that principles (a) and (b) be replaced by: principle (c)—*the evaluation should judge that program X is better than program Y if, all other things being equal, programs X and Y meet all of the intended objectives while program X meets others as well*; and principle (d)—*the evaluation should judge that program X is better than program Y if, all other things being equal, program X is causally more effective with respect to the objectives than program Y.*

Among those who accept principle (d) there is a dispute about whether an evaluation should provide a causal explanation of how the program produces the achievements or whether it is sufficient to show that the program *does* produce the outcomes. Prominent evaluation theorists have long maintained the former position, thereby prescribing the extensive use of randomized controlled experiments whenever possible. Others have defended the latter position, thereby recommending less structure in the experiment. Both sides agree, however, on the relevance of causal efficacy.

When one program is achieving some of the objectives while another program is achieving others, principle (c) does not apply—because weighing of the two programs is required. In order to accomplish a relative weighing of programs, it seems the objectives or the ends of the programs themselves must be evaluated. If the objectives of a program are trivial or worthless, then it seems unimportant that the program can achieve its objectives. This position recommends adding the following: principle (e)—*the evaluation should judge that program X is better than program Y if, all other things being equal, program X's objectives are better or more valuable than program Y's.*

Different positions are held, however, concerning who should make the various judgments about "better" and "more valuable" and how they should be done. In essence, each of these viewpoints represents a different corollary of principle (e), with authors disagreeing about who determines intrinsic value (see Sect. 3). Scriven has argued that the evaluator should make the judgments; Stake has at one time argued that the evaluator should collect data relevant to the values of all the various groups in the community and then make the overall judgment. Because Scriven and Stake recommend that the evaluator make this

judgment, their models are often called judgmental models. Some writers doubt whether a single evaluator can fairly present the views of all sides. They have argued that each side of the dispute must have its own "advocate" and these advocates must present the arguments to a jury or a judge. Here the evaluation model is likened to judicial (or legal) proceedings (see *Judicial Evaluation*). Stufflebeam argued that the evaluator should collect data relevant to the values or criteria of the decision maker who has "charge" of the evaluation; others argued that the evaluator should collect and provide information to each of the various audiences so that they may judge (Cronbach et al. 1980).

It has also been argued that evaluating a program only in terms of its intended objectives is likely to be quite misleading. For the program is also likely to have unintended consequences and such unintended consequences should be used in evaluating the impact of the program. Thus, it has been argued that evaluation should look at the unspecified outcomes, and that the evaluation should be "goal free." Of course, the unintended consequences can be good or worthwhile as well as being bad. But the "side effects" may be so bad that they outweigh the good the program is bringing about. Such a view recommends the following principle: principle (f)—*the evaluation should judge that program X is better than program Y if, all other things being equal, program X's total consequences are on balance better than program Y's total consequences.*

In order for evaluators to follow principle (f), they must discover or identify the unintended consequences. Furthermore, they must have procedures for weighing the various consequences of the two programs. These are two sizable and difficult tasks.

Another comparative principle is often recommended for evaluating programs: principle (g)—*the evaluation should judge that program X is better than program Y if, all other things being equal, program X is less costly than program Y.*

Often, however, an expensive program may bring about very valuable learnings while an inexpensive program may only bring about somewhat less valuable learnings. In such situations, financial considerations must be weighed against the value of achieving certain educational outcomes. Principles (f) and (g) evolve naturally into the following: principle (h)—*the evaluation should judge that program X is better than program Y if, after considering both the financial aspects and the total consequences on balance of the two programs, program X outweighs program Y.*

With the elucidation of principle (h), and with the growing concern for large state-funded and federally funded programs, many evaluation theorists have attempted to deal with a new level of complexity. For often, in order to apply (h), the party making the judgments would not only have to consider the total consequences and costs of achieving the intended educational objectives A; he or she would also have to weigh the importance of objectives A against the importance of different educational objectives B. For example, it might be necessary to evaluate "new mathematics" versus "old mathematics," or the new mathematics program versus a new writing program. In some situations it might be necessary to evaluate an educational program versus a noneducational program, for example, a new reading program versus a new health-care program. Communities and legislatures often face such choices.

Evaluators concerned about the choices that are faced by the various audiences or potential users of the report dictate yet another principle: principle (i)—*the evaluation should judge programs based upon information needs of particular audiences.*

Although most evaluation theorists have said that their models are intended to influence and assist audiences, for the most part the nature and the role of these audiences has been given little or no special emphasis.

Early attention to audiences as a major determinant in the way that evaluation should be conducted focused on decision makers. Such theorists generally believed that evaluations should be performed in the service of individuals or groups responsible for making decisions, and should provide information which is useful to them. It was held that useful information is that which satisfies predetermined criteria evolved through the initial interaction of the evaluator and the decision maker (see *Decision-oriented Evaluation*). The incorporation of the decision makers' perceptions and values determines in large part the questions to be asked and the range of possible answers.

A further extension of the principle that evaluations should be relevant to the audience is to be found in those who advocate a broader role for the evaluator (see *Evaluator, Role of*). This role acknowledges the various ways an evaluator can be useful to a potential user, whether or not that user is an immediate decision maker. This point of view recognizes that all "uses" of evaluation need not eventuate in immediate decisions and that decision making is incremental (Patton 1978, Alkin et al. 1979). It is recommended that evaluators seek out potential users and engage the users in active and continuing interaction. It is held that an important result of this interaction is reflected in changes in the users' perceptions and understanding (see next section and *Evaluation for Utilization*).

In this section, the development of evaluation principles has been discussed. Also it has been shown that these principles provide insight into the proper purposes of evaluation activities and the methods for achieving those purposes, and it has been indicated that the prevalent evaluation models are guided by individual principles or combinations of these principles. Consideration of the underlying principles of evaluation provides a way of understanding evaluation models and the relationships between them.

2. Prescriptive Evaluation Models

A prescriptive evaluation model prescribes which evaluation activities are good or bad, right or wrong, adequate or inadequate, rational or irrational, just or unjust. It implicitly claims that evaluation activities should be conducted in certain ways; it talks about the evaluator's obligations, responsibilities, and duties. A model is prescriptive because it gives advice, recommendations, warnings, and guidance about doing evaluations. The recommendations appear as recipes, flow diagrams, maxims, priority rules, strategies, and general guidelines. Often, a prescriptive model points out problems, pitfalls, demands, and restrictions in doing an evaluation. In developing an evaluation model, a theorist is implicitly (or explicitly) specifying which standards, criteria, principles, and guidelines are the proper or appropriate ones to regulate the activities of an evaluator.

Almost everyone who has written about educational evaluation has, one way or another, made prescriptions. Some have spent more time systemizing their standards, criteria, and principles. A few have tried to defend or justify their prescriptions.

All prescriptive evaluation models have three aspects: empirical (methodology), valuational (values), and purposive (uses). The empirical aspect is concerned with describing or explaining various properties of an educational phenomenon which the model builder perceives as important. The valuational aspect is concerned with ascribing or determining the value of the object, given that it has such properties. Third, the purposive aspect pertains to the evaluation purposes or functions. An examination of the various prescriptive evaluation models shows that all have these three aspects stated or implied, but controversy and disagreement arise about each aspect.

"Methodology," "values," and "uses" are considered to be the major bases for categorizing the various evaluation models. These concepts emerged in the generation and discussion of evaluation principles. All evaluations involve some kind of methodology for description and explanation; all necessitate the valuing of data acquired; and all evaluations are conducted with some use in mind. Thus, the distinction between evaluation models based upon these three dimensions is not one based on exclusivity—for example, that one model only believes in the use of methodology and others do not. Rather, the category system is based upon relative emphasis within the various models. It might then be possible to ask this question: when evaluators must make concessions, what do they most easily give up and what do they most tenaciously defend?

A number of evaluation model builders are strong advocates of a particular methodology or methodological approach which dominates the way in which they think about evaluation. There are a variety of "types" within this category. Some perceive evaluation as nearly synonymous with experimental research methods. Others advocate an emphasis on the richness of qualitative data as the sine qua non of evaluation. As noted above, many insist that proper measurement is the essence of quality evaluation—failure to measure well nearly abrogates the evaluation findings. A slight variation of this theme may be found among those whose erstwhile belief is that only the use of criterion-referenced testing procedures can lead to appropriate evaluation. Other major positions to be found within this general category include those whose concern for causal modeling, quasi-experimental procedures, and so forth dominate their approach to evaluation.

Another group of evaluation model builders are best categorized as having values as their primary concern. We have alluded to several of them in the discussion of principle (e) in the previous section. When looking at the issue of making judgments, it was noted that some model builders recommend that the evaluator make the valuational judgment. In some instances the evaluator is to benefit from data collected from a variety of relevant groups; in other instances the evaluator's personal background, knowledge, and experience serves to ground the valuing process.

The final category, use, includes those evaluation model builders who advocate that the primary emphasis within evaluation must be the concerns of decision makers and other users. Thus, even though they recognize the necessity for employing diverse methodology and for valuing data, they would make compromises on these dimensions in order to produce valid data relevant for decision/user audiences. (Note that their definition of "valid" would differ from those in the methodology category.) As previously indicated, early emphasis within this category revolved around decision makers and the explication of questions of concern to this group. A more recent thrust within the category has focused on users and recognized the dynamic relationship between evaluators and users—a relationship in which decision concerns have been replaced by interaction attuned to decisions in a more incremental sense (e.g. knowledge acquisition, and attitude change). Though it might be said that some evaluation model builders who view "evaluation" as nearly synonymous with "research" are governed to a large extent by *their* intended use and user audience (the research community), this article has generally tended to classify these individuals within the methodology category (see *Evaluation for Utilization*).

3. General Features of Prescriptive Evaluation Models and Their Justification

In the previous sections some principles underlying evaluation models and a way of categorizing the models were discussed. Implicit within this discussion has been the meaning of "model" as exemplified by current work. It is important to note the way that the term "evaluation model" has been used. A consideration of Michael Scriven's work best illustrates the point in question. Scriven was among the first to clearly articulate and argue for principles (c), (d), (e), and (f) (in Sect. 1). Such principles in the aggregate are often taken to constitute the essence of Scriven's evaluation model. As Scriven has often said, evaluation consists simply of the gathering and combining of performance data with a weighted set of criterial scales to yield either comparative or numerical ratings, and in the justification of (a) the data-gathering instruments, (b) the weighings, and (c) the selection of criteria. Sometimes, however, Scriven's "model" of evaluation is depicted simply as his views on goal-free evaluation. At issue is whether an individual's "model" of evaluation consists of a particular writing or, more generally, of an individual's full body of writing over time. This confusion is, of course, further complicated by the fact that many model builder's views (and thus perceptions) change over time. (This point will be discussed more fully in Sect. 5.) In this article, an attempt has been made to refer to "models" as the largest coherent set of ideas put forward by a particular model builder at a particular time. Thus, authors' models would be differentiated if they changed over time (e.g. "early Cronbach" and "recent Cronbach").

Items referred to as "models" also differ with respect to yet another dimension—their level of specificity and detailed prescription. Here it is possible to contrast a single idea (conceptualized but not fully described) portrayed as a model (Scriven's goal-free evaluation) against a step-by-step kit intended as a detailed recipe for the beginning evaluator.

General issues concerning the justification of prescriptive models will now be discussed, and the valuational and empirical aspects of evaluation models will be examined. Similar remarks pertain to the purposive aspect. The following distinctions will be helpful in examining the valuational aspect of evaluation models: (a) extrinsic value: properties which render a program instrumental as a means to something desirable or good; (b) intrinsic value: properties which are desirable or good as an end in themselves. Intrinsic value is presupposed by extrinsic value. (c) "Value" refers to what is valued, judged to have value, thought to be good, or desired. The expression "one's values" refers to what a person thinks to be good. Many people assume that nothing has objective value, that "value" means only being valued and "good" means being thought to be good.

But there is a related sense: (d) "value" refers to what *has* value or is valuable, or good, as opposed to what is regarded as good or valuable. What certain people regard or think is good or desirable is, of course, a question empirical science can answer. Whether anything has *objective* value is a question which belongs primarily to moral or political philosophy.

In general, the cluster of models within the decision maker/user category view the evaluator (the evaluation group) as an advisor to the decision-making body, or an educator of the affected audiences, in much the same way as lawyers interact with their clients. These models make the assumption that intrinsic value refers to what some decision maker, manager, or group thinks of or regards as valuable. Many of these evaluation models assume that the society's legal and political structures are in compliance with a justifiable democratic theory. Hence, they are anxious to forbid the evaluator from preempting the legitimate roles of such people in their decision making. It is plausible that evaluation should not take on a decision-making role. However, it is possible that evaluation models within this cluster might provide for the role of critic of the system and its structure (Benn and Mortimore 1976).

Some models have an air of impartiality because they recommend that it be determined what all parties or all sides think is good, or each person thinks is good. But such models offer few or no principles for selecting the appropriate reference groups. House (1978) has tried to develop criteria for group selection by using the work of a social political philosopher, John Rawls. House argues that the least advantaged group of society should always be a reference group. Overall, model builders have yet to clarify and defend their sociopolitical assumptions and commitments.

The empirical aspects of evaluation models also require validation. Many evaluation theorists see themselves as social scientists and urge that their work have the objectivity appropriate to such sciences. This is particularly true for those within the methodology category. Many of the global prescriptions within these models are defended by appeals to the philosophy of science. For example, the requirement for "operational" and for "behavioral" definitions were defended on the grounds that that is the way proper science is conducted. Another issue illustrating proper science methodology involves causation. A large number of evaluation theorists hold that the causal efficacy of the program must be shown in the evaluation. They hold that randomized, controlled experiments are the best way to establish causation. But what is causation? Are there causal laws in the social sciences? Indeed, these are questions pertaining to the philosophy of social science, and whose answers are still controversial.

In the previous discussion, the controversies related to the nature of social science principles have been considered as a justification of evaluation models. Beyond the validation of models using these principles, a related concern associated with the social sciences is the extent to which evaluation models may draw upon presumed models from other disciplines. For example, many current educational evaluation models focus on problems and issues in management and organizational theory. Whatever the value of such inquiries, it is debatable whether these areas have achieved status as a science.

There is, therefore, much disagreement among the evaluation models as to the kind and level of precision and objectivity appropriate to the evaluation tasks being carried out. There is the realization that the imposition of unrealistic standards and criteria can only retard model development and limit the value of models in practice.

4. Descriptive Educational Evaluation Models

A descriptive model is a "theory." An evaluation theory (a descriptive model) is a general set of empirical statements containing generalizations (or laws) for describing, predicting, or explaining evaluation activities. Since the early 1970s, there has been no single global study which was directed towards the development of a comprehensive theory of evaluation. Most of the research has been directed at particular aspects of evaluation.

A good example of research on evaluation directed at particular aspects is provided by the recent studies of evaluation utilization. While these studies constitute attempts at evaluation theory building, they are limited by their focus and their points of view. Determination of factors influencing the use of evaluation findings provide the first steps in what might ultimately be a well-confirmed theory (Alkin et al. 1979). In all but one instance, these researchers have used case studies of educational evaluations to produce their generalizations. Thus, their theory formulations are directly grounded in field data.

Findings from the evaluation utilization research provide the evidence upon which ultimate elements of an evaluation theory might be constructed. For example, Patton's findings suggest the likely importance of the "personal factor" in a complete theory of those factors which influence evaluation use. Again, several researchers suggest that a single database may not be useful to all audiences of the evaluation. However, even if well-confirmed theoretical formulations are developed, a theory of evaluation utilization would be only a part of a possible comprehensive theory of evaluation. For as was noted earlier, evaluation oriented towards utilization is but one of many dimensions of evaluation.

Other attempts at building descriptive models have drawn on general social science studies. The implication is that the generalizations produced by social scientists pertaining to institutions in general apply to educational institutions in particular. Most notable are the attempts to describe and explain the educational decision-making process in this way (Cronbach et al. 1980). These researchers use social science generalizations to ground their theoretical formulations.

Although the development of descriptive evaluation models is in but a preliminary stage, its importance should not be underemphasized. Not only is theory useful in the understanding of evaluation activities but, more importantly, descriptive evaluation models should undergird prescriptive models. Descriptive models provide the limitations and possibilities for the prescriptive models.

5. *Evaluation Model Development*

Since the early 1970s, evaluation theorists have been increasingly aware of the need for systematization and the defense of their purposes and methods for carrying out educational evaluations. This has led to an increasing amount of literature on the articulation and the contrast and comparison of various evaluation models. Some attention has also been given to understanding the process of evaluation model development itself.

Much of the work on articulation and systematization has resulted in the development and refinement of category systems of the various evaluation prescriptive models. These categorizations have generally been in terms of the model's ultimate purposes and related procedures and methods. Such category systems serve model development by identifying hidden commonalities and related possibilities or tasks among the models. The category systems developed by Worthen and Sanders (1973) and House (1978) are illustrative of this work.

As in jurisprudence, such systematization and codification do not seek an absolute and final category system. Rather, such efforts are part of the dialectical process of developing new models and methods which will fulfill more of the pressing needs and demands for evaluations in our society.

Empirical studies investigating the comparative merit of various descriptive evaluation models have been few. Such studies might contribute both to an understanding of how the prescriptive models actually work (an alternative basis for generating data for descriptive theory) and provide grounds for preferring one prescriptive model over another.

A few works have examined the process of evaluation model development. Given that a model builder is at least trying to develop a coherent and realistic set of prescriptions for evaluation, evidence suggests that theorists' views of the key problems and their prescriptions change dynamically over time. Often these changes are brought about by renewed reflection on a person's own writings. Surprisingly enough, it seems that even the most articulate writers

formulate only some of the more salient points of their models. Often key assumptions and presuppositions remain hidden in the background. These matters have been investigated by Alkin and Ellett (1979).

Bibliography

Alkin M C, Ellett F S Jr 1979 An inquiry into the nature of evaluation theorizing. *Stud. Educ. Eval.* 5: 151–56
Alkin M C, Daillak R, White P 1979 *Using Evaluations: Does Evaluation Make a Difference?* Sage, Beverly Hills, California
Benn S I, Mortimore G W (eds.) 1976 *Rationality and the Social Sciences: Contributions to the Philosophy and Methodology of the Social Sciences.* Routledge and Kegan Paul, London
Cronbach L J et al. 1980 *Toward Reform of Program Evaluation: Aims, Methods, and Institutional Arrangements.* Jossey-Bass, San Francisco, California
Glass G V, Ellett F S Jr 1980 Evaluation research. *Ann. Rev. Psychol.* 31: 211-28
House E R 1978 Assumptions underlying evaluation models. *Educ. Res.* AERA 7(3): 4–12
Patton M Q 1978 *Utilization-focused Evaluation.* Sage, Beverly Hills, California
Raizen S A, Rossi P H (eds.) 1981 *Program Evaluation in Education: When? How? To What Ends?* National Academy Press, Washington, DC
Worthen B R, Sanders J R 1973 *Educational Evaluation: Theory and Practice.* Wadsworth, Belmont, California

M. C. Alkin; F. S. Ellett Jr.

Evaluation Standards

Evaluation standards are generally agreed upon principles of what makes good evaluation. Prior to 1981 there was no compilation of such principles in education to guide the evaluation of educational programs, projects, and materials. In 1981, a Joint Committee on Standards for Educational Evaluation, appointed by 12 professional organizations in the United States[1], published the *Standards for Evaluations of Educational Programs, Projects, and Materials* (1981) thus adding to an existing body of literature on standards for various professions. Although there have been other recent efforts directed toward setting standards for evaluation

1 The following professional organizations in the United States appointed members to the Joint Committee that developed the *Standards*: American Association of School Administrators, American Educational Research Association, American Federation of Teachers, American Personnel and Guidance Association, American Psychological Association, Association for Supervision and Curriculum Development, Council for American Private Education, Education Commission of the States, National Association of Elementary School Principals, National Council on Measurement in Education, National Education Association, and National School Boards Association.

(Ridings 1982), this article is limited to the 1981 Joint Committee *Standards*.

The project to develop the *Standards* began in 1975, was directed by Dr. Daniel L. Stufflebeam, and was conducted at the Evaluation Center of Western Michigan University in the United States.

The 1981 Joint Committee *Standards* were written, reviewed, and field tested by more than 200 educators and evaluators mainly in the United States over a five-year development period. Those who participated in the development came from all levels and roles of American education. Their collective wisdom about principles of good evaluation practice are reflected in the presentation of each standard.

The *Standards* are divided into four categories that address the qualities of good evaluation practice: utility, feasibility, propriety, and technical soundness. Each standard is presented with an overview that provides definitions and a rationale for the standard, list of guidelines, pitfalls, and caveats for the standard that reflect suggestions, cautions, and warnings collected from past experience of evaluators and educators, and an illustrative case that describes an evaluation practice that could have been guided by the particular standard. A list of the 30 standards may be found in Table 1.

1. The Need for Standards

The body of literature on evaluation of educational programs, projects, and materials has grown substantially since 1965. This literature provides scores of evaluation "models," various perspectives about how to conceptualize evaluation, often confusing jargon and differing definitions of frequently used terms, numerous practical tips, and a collection of reports that reflect both good and bad evaluation practice. This literature is more than any one individual could hope to master. There has been a need to collect and organize the wisdom contained in a widely scattered body of literature on the evaluation of educational programs, projects, and materials.

There has also been a good amount of experience with evaluation that people involved in education had accumulated. Much of this experience, embodied in many practical tips that had been learned through trial and error, has never appeared in print. Practices of experienced evaluators and educators had not been shared to any great extent. There has been a need for learning about evaluation from the collection and publication of practical suggestions, cautions, and warnings of the professional education community.

A third reason for the development of professional standards in evaluation has been a growing concern for accountability of those who evaluate educational practices. Evaluations of programs, projects, and materials can influence tremendously the decisions and thinking of those who are in responsible positions

Table 1
Standards for evaluations of educational programs, projects, and materials

(a) *Utility standards*
    (i)   Audience identification
    (ii)   Evaluator credibility
    (iii)   Information scope and selection
    (iv)   Valuational interpretation
    (v)   Report clarity
    (vi)   Report dissemination
    (vii)   Report timeliness
    (viii)   Evaluation impact

(b) *Feasibility standards*
    (i)   Practical procedures
    (ii)   Political viability
    (iii)   Cost effectiveness

(c) *Propriety standards*
    (i)   Formal obligation
    (ii)   Conflict of interest
    (iii)   Full and frank disclosure
    (iv)   Public's right to know
    (v)   Rights of human subjects
    (vi)   Human interactions
    (vii)   Balanced reporting
    (viii)   Fiscal responsibility

(d) *Accuracy standards*
    (i)   Object identification
    (ii)   Context analysis
    (iii)   Described purposes and procedures
    (iv)   Defensible information sources
    (v)   Valid measurement
    (vi)   Reliable measurement
    (vii)   Systematic data control
    (viii)   Analysis of quantitative information
    (ix)   Analysis of qualitative information
    (x)   Justified conclusions
    (xi)   Objective reporting

in education. They can also use up scarce resources and require substantial amounts of time to complete. Trust in evaluations is frequently placed blindly by audiences who are not in a position to assess their merits. Moreover, those conducting an evaluation can find themselves seeking recourse when arbitrary decisions detract from or misapply what in their judgment is good evaluation practice. By having an authoritative statement of what constitutes good evaluation practice, both clients and evaluators can have a common point of reference.

2. Utility of the Standards

In the introduction to the *Standards*, the Joint Committee stated that development of sound standards could provide the following benefits:

> . . . a common language to facilitate communication and collaboration in evaluation; a set of general rules for dealing with a variety of specific evaluation problems;

a conceptual framework by which to study the often-confusing world of evaluation; a set of working definitions to guide research and development on the evaluation process; a public statement of the state of the art in educational evaluation; a basis for self-regulation and accountability by professional evaluators; and an aid to developing public credibility for the educational evaluation field. (Joint Committee 1981 p. 5)

The Joint Committee also noted in the introduction that ". . . evaluation is an inevitable part of any human undertaking. . . and. . . sound evaluation can promote the understanding and improvement of education, while faulty evaluation can impair it" (Joint Committee 1981 p. 5). Toward the end of promoting sound evaluations, the standards were indexed with a functional table of contents, addressing the practical evaluation functions of:

(a) administering evaluations;

(b) analyzing information;

(c) budgeting for evaluation;

(d) deciding whether to evaluate;

(e) defining the evaluation problem;

(f) designing evaluations;

(g) collecting information;

(h) contracting for evaluations;

(i) reporting evaluation;

(j) staffing for evaluation.

Under each functional heading is a list of standards that contain suggestions, cautions, and warnings that are relevant to the particular function.

The uses of the *Standards* include guidance in planning evaluations, a widely accepted basis for critiquing evaluations, an organized syllabus for preservice and inservice education in evaluation, and a management device for monitoring or auditing formal evaluations that have been commissioned.

As a guide to planning evaluations, the *Standards* provide a number of practical suggestions aimed at improving the practice of evaluation. A trained evaluator should be able to find in the *Standards* at least a few suggestions that had not been previously considered when an evaluation is planned. There are insights throughout the *Standards* that could only have been compiled from a large number of writers. One person could never hope to possess the wide range of experiences of the contributors to this document.

As a widely accepted basis for critiquing evaluations, the *Standards* are the end product of writing and reviews by national panels, field testing in at least 20 different settings and uses, and testimony received in several hearings. The content of this document went through five drafts, each time refining, editing, and polishing the substance of previous drafts. What has resulted is a document that reflects the conventional wisdom of present-day educational evaluation. The *Standards* can be used as a check of whether an evaluation has included elements that are generally accepted to be characteristic of good evaluation practice. Used in a formative role, the *Standards* may be used by evaluators to improve evaluation practices. Used in a summative role, the *Standards* may be used by consumers of evaluation findings to assess the merit or worth of an evaluation.

As an organized syllabus for preservice and inservice education in evaluation, the *Standards* represent a topical outline of essential knowledge for practicing evaluators. They also present a list of issues that educators might want to pursue as part of their professional development. Discussion topics include writing and report dissemination in our schools, studying the cost effectiveness of school program evaluations, protecting the rights of people involved in an evaluation, and the need for compiling factual and complete descriptions of school programs that are to be evaluated.

3. Limitations of the Standards

The *Standards* do not provide a cookbook of mechanical steps to follow in conducting an evaluation of a program, project, or set of materials. The principles reflected in the *Standards* are a compilation of commonly agreed upon characteristics of good evaluation practice. In the final analysis, choices must be made by the evaluator for each standard, and there are trade-offs across standards that also must be made. Furthermore, there are many issues in educational evaluation that remain to be resolved, and most issues are not discussed in the *Standards*.

The Joint Committee recognized that the *Standards* will change as experience in using them is gained and as educators learn more about the practice of evaluation. Thus, they noted that the 1981 edition is viewed as a first approximation that must be used, reviewed, and revised as appropriate in subsequent years. The Joint Committee has established a set of Principles and Bylaws which allow for an ongoing standard setting process.

Finally, it must be recognized that the development of the *Standards* was done by educators in the United States who have a cultural perspective about evaluation which may differ from educators in other countries. Care must be taken to determine the appropriateness of each standard given the cultural context of evaluations in international settings.

Bibliography

Evaluation News 1981 2: 140–187 (issue devoted to an examination of the *Standards for Evaluations of Educational Programs, Projects, and Materials*)

Joint Committee on Standards for Educational Evaluation 1981 *Standards for Evaluations of Educational Programs, Projects, and Materials*. McGraw-Hill, New York

Ridings J M 1982 *Standard Setting: The Crucial Issues: A Case Study of Accounting and Auditing*. Evaluation Center, Western Michigan University, Kalamazoo, Michigan

Ridings J M, Stufflebeam D L 1981 The project to develop standards for educational evaluation: Its past and future. *Stud. Educ. Eval.* 7: 3–16

Stufflebeam D L 1980a *A Report on the Forthcoming Publication: Standards for Evaluations of Educational Programs, Projects, and Materials*. Evaluation Center, Western Michigan University, Kalamazoo, Michigan

Stufflebeam D L 1980b *Standards for Evaluations of Educational Programs, Projects, and Materials: The Light at the Tunnel's End*. Evaluation Center, Western Michigan University, Kalamazoo, Michigan

J. R. Sanders

Evaluation Studies, Impact of

Evaluation studies collect, analyze, and report information about programs or policies. Evaluation typically is designed to produce information that will aid decision making. Therefore, beneficial impact, in the form of better decisions about programs or policies, is expected from evaluation.

Evaluation impact may be defined broadly as an evaluation's discernible influence upon the activities or attitudes of individuals or groups. Impacts resulting from information, such as findings or recommendations generated in an evaluation, are the most commonly discussed evaluation impacts. Apart from their informational results, however, the processes of evaluation can also influence activities and attitudes to yield an equally important category of impacts.

Use must be distinguished from impact. The term "evaluation use" is often reserved to mean the purposive application of evaluation information or evaluation processes to achieve desired ends. Some evaluation impacts result from and are the intended ends of evaluation use; other impacts may be quite unintended.

1. Impacts of Evaluation Information

Evaluation information can dramatically sway program or policy decisions. More commonly, however, evaluation information is only one of several sources considered by decision makers, and evaluation information's influence on program or policy actions is partial rather than total. Evaluation can, of course, be said to have had influence, hence impact, in cases where it acts as a contributing factor.

Evaluation information can receive serious attention, yet be overruled by other considerations. In such situations, evaluation information will have influenced decision-making activity (to the extent that the information was given a serious hearing), and may even have influenced individual decision makers' choices, yet the program or policy in question may show no overt mark of evaluation influence.

Evaluation information's influence may also be masked, but in a different way, when evaluation results show that a current policy, program, or practice is succeeding. If there is little controversy surrounding a current practice, then positive evaluation results may receive little notice, even though negative findings might have generated great concern. Thus, if evaluation is viewed as corrective feedback, to nudge programs onto a proper course, then impact could be expected to be visible only for programs in difficulty. It would not be possible to conclude that the feedback system, that is, evaluation, had lost its influence simply because of a finding that successful programs had shown no sign of evaluation impact.

Evaluation information's influences upon attitudes or beliefs—sometimes called the conceptual influences of evaluation—are among the most complex impacts. While actions and attitudes may be left unchanged by agreeable evaluation results, beliefs may be strengthened by supportive evaluation results. Partisans in a policy debate, for example, may take great comfort from evaluation data favorable to their position, even if they recognize that the other side will not be swayed by the data. Evaluation's results may be a comfort even in the absence of external debate: a decision maker may welcome information that validates a previous decision.

Significantly, evaluation information can alter attitudes or beliefs without altering actions. For example, evaluation results could persuade school decision makers that preschool programs are worthwhile, without causing them to establish such programs in the schools. "Purely conceptual" impacts of this kind may later result in action.

2. Impacts of the Processes of Evaluation

Evaluation processes can have important impacts quite apart from those resulting from evaluation information. Some of these additional impacts are prosaic (although occasionally overlooked). For example, evaluations consume educational resources. Money is spent directly on evaluation studies, and time is demanded from educators as well as often from students.

Other more subtle impacts include evaluation's influences upon communication within school organizations. The manner and form of the evaluation's conduct have a variety of impacts. Many evaluations focus attention on "goals" and "objectives," thus perhaps altering the terms in which educational work is conceptualized. Some evaluations bring together groups of practitioners to discuss program strategies, encouraging collegiality where there may have been isolationism. Such effects are difficult to prove. Evaluation's effects on some attitudes can be measurable, however. The prospect of evaluation frequently causes staff to become anxious. Prior to evaluative reviews, programs often take steps to comply more fully with regulatory guidelines, and they may attempt to correct deficiencies that would otherwise draw evaluative criticism.

The evaluation process may have political or symbolic impacts as well. Policy making may be deferred until after an ongoing evaluation is completed. The mere fact that a program is evaluated may help to legitimize the program. To the public or to legislators, evaluation may signal program management's cost-consciousness, responsibility, or accountability (Alkin 1975).

3. Measuring Evaluation Impact

Measures of evaluation impact are complicated by four principal difficulties: the lack of observability of many impacts, the presence of contributing influences besides evaluation, problems with diffusion of evaluation information, and the manifold nature of impact itself.

Choice, decision making, and attitude formation are mental activities which leave traces that vary in accessibility. When these activities occur in a group context, for example, there may be documentary evidence to indicate the role played by evaluation. Judgments by single individuals, however, are less likely to be well-documented. Indeed, those individual judgments that ratify the status quo (e.g., a manager's decision to continue current activities) may leave virtually no documentary traces. With documentary evidence so often slim, measures of evaluation impact have come to rely heavily upon decision makers' self-reports. In addition, impact is often inferred, or at least suspected, when actions in line with evaluation conclusions occur soon after relevant evaluation information is received by decision makers.

These measurement approaches are quite susceptible to error. The presence of multiple contributing influences upon actions or beliefs make it difficult to infer evaluation's influence in any particular situation. Decision makers' and program participants' assessments may be the best available guide to evaluation's impact, but even these respondents may have difficulty judging evaluation's relative contribution.

As the time span between evaluation and a subsequent impact increases, measurement difficulties multiply. As time elapses, many other potential influences will have had the opportunity to affect events. In addition, evaluation information may diffuse into the general knowledge base underlying the program or policy system, and participants in the system may be affected by evaluation information without ever knowing its source.

Finally, unitary measures of impact are elusive, since it is possible for many different types and degrees of impact to occur, even from the same evaluation. Information and process impacts at levels throughout the educational system must be explored in order to assess fully evaluation's impact.

4. Studies of Evaluation Impact

Empirical studies of evaluation impact burgeoned in the 1970s, in large part because it seemed that evaluation was not influencing educational practice in a significant way. Most studies examined information impacts in particular programs, for example, investigating the local school impacts of evaluation information in programs funded through Title I of the United States Elementary and Secondary Education Act (David 1981).

The ensuing research has suggested that evaluation studies have had mixed effects upon education. Most studies have found that uses are made of evaluation information, thus refuting the most pessimistic assertions of earlier observers. However, the impacts of evaluation appear to have been modest. Few dramatic changes in programs or policies can be directly attributed to evaluation. Instead, evaluation information is most often mentioned, when mentioned at all, as one of several convergent factors leading to a decision. For example, program managers may cite positive evaluation results as evidence of program effectiveness. Negative evaluation findings, however, seldom stimulate change directly, but if they persist, and if they are substantiated by other indicators, may lend weight to program or policy reassessments.

A complete and balanced picture of evaluation's impacts upon education is difficult to assemble, however. Because of measurement difficulties, research on impact has relied primarily upon interview surveys and case studies. Consequently, the samples that have been investigated have been relatively small and, to an extent, questionably representative of evaluation studies as a whole. Furthermore, process-related evaluation impacts have received relatively little attention, and little is confidently known about them.

5. Factors Explaining Evaluation Impact

Evaluation impact research was stimulated in part by perceptions that evaluation was not having adequate impact. Not surprisingly, therefore, attention was also devoted to explaining why evaluations had greater or lesser impact in specific cases. Explanations for information impacts again garnered the greatest attention. Several themes have emerged from recent studies (Leviton and Hughes 1981, Weiss 1977).

The nature of decision making in organizations appears to have had important implications for evaluation. Formal program or policy decision making—in the sense of a conscious choice at a given point in time between discrete decision alternatives—seems to be less common than was previously thought. More frequently, program or policy activities seem to result from an accretion of actions and small unheralded choices on the part of many different individuals within an organization. The individuals involved may not perceive themselves as being engaged in "decision making," particularly not with regard to macroscopic policies or program directions. They tend to base their actions on quite circumscribed grounds—routines, standard procedures, and immediately relevant considerations—and they may see evaluation's global pronouncements as largely irrelevant to their day-to-day work.

When formal decision making does occur, it is likely to deviate significantly from posited decision-making models. Rather than engaging in an exhaustive search for and assessment of decision options, decision makers are likely to consider a limited number of alternatives and may examine only a small amount of data pertinent to each, focusing on a few particularly critical criteria that a satisfactory choice must fulfill (Simon 1957). Political and bureaucratic needs are often among these critical concerns. Evaluations almost always focus on a different set of concerns, namely, a program or policy's tangible outcomes for a service population. Moreover, evaluations very often seek to avoid the controversy associated with discussions of political and bureaucratic issues. Consequently, evaluation usually provides only part of the data that decision makers desire. When all the critical criteria are taken into account, decision makers may reasonably arrive at judgments that seem at odds with evaluation information.

Evaluation's impact can be moderated by common organizational circumstances. There are also other factors that can affect evaluation information's impact, many of which can be more directly controlled by evaluators, or at least accommodated in constructive ways. These include evaluation's relevance and credibility; the manner in which information is shared between evaluators and users; the information processing styles of administrators; and the degree to which potential information users become actively interested in evaluation (Leviton and Hughes 1981). One unifying point here is that there are important personal and psychological components to information use. Evaluations which attend to these components are more likely to have their findings used.

Evaluation information that is relevant to administrators' or policy makers' self-perceived information needs is more likely to be considered in decision making. The timeliness with which evaluation information is delivered is an aspect of relevance, but research suggests it must be considered in proper perspective: poor timing can preclude the use of evaluation information in particular decisions, but because information's useful lifespan can extend for months or years, even tardily delivered information can ultimately have impact.

If information is disbelieved, it is naturally less likely to have impact. Administrators and policy makers appear to judge information's credibility through a variety of means. Evaluation information usually is compared with information from other sources that appear credible; information from first-hand experience or trusted advisors frequently seems to be considered more valid than evaluation information.

Evaluation information is judged in part by judging the messenger, the evaluator: thus, evaluator credibility is important to information credibility and impact (Alkin et al. 1979). Methodological quality has been less convincingly associated with impact, because poor quality is not always detected. In highly politicized situations, however, methods have often come under close scrutiny, and methodological defects have impeded credibility and impact (perhaps appropriately so).

Effective information sharing between evaluators and users appears to facilitate impact in several ways. At the outset of the evaluation, better targeting to the interests and information needs of users can produce more useful information. At the conclusion of the evaluation, careful dissemination of evaluation results, with appropriate follow-up, helps deliver accurate understandable information to those persons who need and can use the information. Also, much has been said about the need to make evaluation presentations in a style that communicates effectively. One way to assure needed effectiveness is to match the preferences and characteristics of information users. Clarity of report language is, of course, critical. Presentations may have to be carefully adapted, since many potential information users are not technically trained in social research procedures. Indeed, managers often prefer regularly held discussions with evaluators, concisely written reports, and qualitative rather than quantitative data.

There is strong evidence that personal commitment and advocacy can affect evaluation information impact. When some administrator or policy maker takes a special interest in evaluation, evaluation is more likely to have impact. An interested user can draw others' attention to evaluation findings and can push for organizational changes suggested by evaluation. It has been suggested that evaluators should seek out and cultivate such potential users (Patton 1978).

See also: Evaluator, Role of

Bibliography

Alkin M C 1975 Evaluation: Who needs it? Who cares? *Stud. Educ. Eval.* 1(3): 201–12

Alkin M C, Daillak R H, White P 1979 *Using Evaluations: Does Evaluation Make a Difference?* Sage, Beverly Hills, California

David J L 1981 Local uses of Title I evaluations. *Educ. Eval. Policy Anal.* 3(1): 27–39

Leviton L C, Hughes E F X 1981 Research on the utilization of evaluations: A review and synthesis. *Eval. Rev.* 5: 525–48

Patton M Q 1978 *Utilization-focused Evaluation.* Sage, Beverly Hills, California

Simon H A 1957 *Administrative Behavior.* Macmillan, New York

Weiss C H 1977 *Using Social Research in Public Policy Making.* Lexington Books, Lexington, Massachusetts

M. C. Alkin; R. H. Daillak

Evaluator, Role of

The role of an evaluator depends on the way evaluation is being perceived, the purposes it is expected to serve, and the "things" which are the objects of the evaluation. Thus, the role of the evaluator can be understood through a consideration of three aspects: (a) the definition of evaluation, (b) the functions of evaluation, and (c) the objects of evaluation.

1. The Definition of Evaluation

Many definitions of evaluation can be found in the literature. They can be summarized here in three major groups. The first group includes the goal-based definitions of evaluation following the definition suggested by Ralph Tyler who defined evaluation as "the process of determining to what extent the educational objectives are actually being realized" (Tyler 1950 p. 69). The second group includes the nonjudgmental descriptive definitions of evaluation. They perceive evaluation as providing information for decision making (e.g., Stufflebeam et al. 1971), or as a systematic examination of educational or social programs (Cronbach et al. 1980). A third group of definitions—the judgmental definitions—point to the judgmental nature of evaluation and define it as the assessment of merit or worth (Scriven 1967, House 1980, Joint Committee 1981) or as a combination of both description and judgment (Guba and Lincoln 1981).

Those various definitions present a very broad view of evaluation which would include assessment, measurement, and testing as parts of evaluation and as terms having a narrower meaning than the term evaluation. Obviously, the various definitions of evaluations imply different perceptions for the nature of the role of the evaluator. The goal-based definitions of evaluation suggest for the role of the evalu-

ator the nature of a controller, a comptroller, or an audit, who direct their efforts to determine the extent that institutional goals are being achieved and approved plans are being carried out. The nonjudgmental descriptive definitions of evaluation suggest an evaluator with the nature of an intelligence officer, a public scientist, or an educator whose roles are to inform their audiences regarding issues and concerns at stake and deepen the audience understanding of those issues and concerns. The judgmental definitions of evaluation call for an evaluator with the nature of a judge, a referee, or an art critic.

2. The Functions of Evaluation

Evaluations are initiated for many purposes and functions, sometimes conflicting ones. Scriven (1967) coined the terms "formative evaluation" and "summative evaluation" referring to two major functions of evaluation (see *Formative and Summative Evaluation*). In its formative function, evaluation is used for the improvement and development of an ongoing activity (or program, person, product, etc.). In its summative function, evaluation is used for accountability, certification, or selection.

A third function of evaluation, which has been less often treated by evaluation literature (Cronbach et al. 1980), should also be considered. This is the psychological or sociopolitical function of evaluation. In many cases it is apparent that evaluation is not serving any formative purposes nor is it being used for accountability or other summative purposes. However, it is being used to increase awareness of special activities, motivate desired behavior of evaluees, or promote public relations. Regardless of personal feelings about the use (or misuse) of evaluation for this purpose, it cannot be ignored.

Another somewhat "unpopular" function of evaluation is its use for the exercise of authority. In a formal organization it is the privilege of the superior to evaluate his or her subordinates and not vice versa. In many cases a person in a management position might evaluate someone to demonstrate his or her authority over that person. This may be referred to as the "administrative" function of evaluation.

To summarize, evaluation can serve many functions: (a) the formative function—for improvement, (b) the summative function—for selection, certification, or accountability, (c) the psychological or sociopolitical function—for motivation, to increase awareness, and (d) the administrative function—to exercise authority. An evaluator may be called in to serve any one of those functions and his/her role will be shaped accordingly.

3. The Objects of Evaluation

Students and teachers have always been popular objects of evaluation in education. Almost all of the measurement and evaluation literature in education up to the mid-1960s dealt with the evaluation of students' learning. Up to that time it was very difficult to find any substantial guidance regarding the evaluation of other objects such as educational projects, programs, curricular materials, or educational institutions, although data on students' achievements have often been used to make decisions regarding curricula, educational projects, or educational institutions. Various developments in the educational system of the United States (e.g., the Elementary and Secondary Education Act of 1965) led to a significant shift of focus regarding the objects of educational evaluation from students to projects, programs, and instructional materials, which have since then been most common in the writings of the major authors in the evaluation literature in education. Sometimes distinctions were made between the assessment of students and school personnel and the evaluation of educational projects, programs, or curricula. Such distinctions were followed by suggested procedures for the conduct of assessment or evaluation of various objects.

From a review of the contemporary evaluation literature it seems to be evident that almost everything can be an object of evaluation (e.g. Lewy and Nevo 1981) and evaluation should not be limited to the evaluation of students or school personnel. Typical evaluation objects suggested by evaluation literature and evaluation practice in education are as follows: (a) students, (b) school personnel (teachers and administrators), (c) curricula and instructional materials, (d) educational programs and projects, and (e) educational institutions and organizations. Teachers and school psychologists are typical examples of student evaluators. Teachers and school administrators are usually evaluated by their superiors or in some cases by professional evaluators. The evaluation of curricula and instructional materials has become since the early 1960s a prominent specialization among evaluation specialists. Another widely spread specialization among evaluators is program and project evaluation (Stufflebeam et al. 1971, Cronbach et al. 1980, Guba and Lincoln 1981). The evaluation of educational institutions has been demonstrated for a long period by various evaluation practices used for the accreditation of secondary schools, colleges, and universities in the United States.

4. Many Roles for the Evaluator

The perception (definition) of evaluation, its functions, and its objects are three independent dimensions which determine the role of the evaluator, although some perceptions of evaluation might be more appropriate than others to serve a certain function of evaluation. For example, the nonjudgmental descriptive approach might be more appropriate for the conduct of formative evaluation rather than the judgmental approach, although both approaches are legitimate for formative as well as for summative evaluation. Considering three types of definitions (goal-based, descriptive, and judgmental), four functions of evaluation (formative, summative, psychological, and administrative), and five kinds of evaluation objects (students, school personnel, curricula, projects, and institutions) will result in a three-dimensional classification of a wide range of up to 60 different roles of an evaluator. He or she may be a goal-based formative evaluator of students, whose role is to determine the extent that students are achieving the educational objectives to help them improve their performance at school. He or she can be a nonjudgmental formative curriculum evaluator assisting a curriculum project to improve its instructional materials, or a nonjudgmental summative evaluator gathering information about several instructional packages to help a school district choose the one most appropriate for its needs. Both of them can be part of a judgmental teacher evaluation team whose function is to motivate teachers by letting them know that their work at school is being evaluated. They can also be a goal-based evaluation team of secondary schools in a developing country hired by the central ministry of education to demonstrate its authority over the local schools. These are only some examples of the wide variety of roles an evaluator has to assume according to his or her perception of evaluation, the function the evaluation is expected to serve, and the object of the evaluation.

According to their roles, evaluators are expected to choose methods of inquiry appropriate for answering particular evaluation questions. However, their work cannot be limited to the technical activities of data collection and analysis. Although there seems to be no agreement among evaluation experts regarding the "best" process to follow when conducting an evaluation, most of them would agree that all evaluations should include a certain amount of interaction between evaluators and their audiences at the outset of the evaluation, to identify evaluation needs, and at its conclusion, to communicate its findings.

The status of evaluators within the administrative structure of the organizations in which they function, defining their authority and responsibility, should also be determined according to their roles. The evaluation literature suggests a distinction between an internal evaluator and an external evaluator. Internal evaluators of a project are usually employed by the project and report directly to its management. Obviously, their objectivity as well as their external credibility might be lower than those of external evaluators who are not employed directly by the evaluated project and who will enjoy a higher degree of independence. At the same time, the internal evaluator is usually less perceived as a threat to the project and has a better chance to develop rapport with its team. To a certain degree both types of evaluators may serve similar functions. The external independent expert can serve not only the summative function of evaluating the project, but also provide invaluable feedback to the project team to improve its ongoing activities. The internal evaluator, who is a member of the project team, can not only serve the formative function of evaluation for the project, but also provide valuable information to demonstrate the merit of the project to funding agencies or other external audiences. However, it seems to be clear that an internal evaluator will be preferred when a formative evaluation is considered, and an external evaluator will be preferred when a summative evaluation is required. A combination of both types for one single object is strongly recommended whenever feasible.

See also: Evaluation, Assessment, and Measurement; Evaluation Models: Development; Ethics of Evaluation Studies; Evaluation Studies, Impact of

Bibliography

Cronbach L J, Ambron S R, Dornbusch S M, Hess R D, Hornik R C, Phillips D C, Walker D E, Weiner S S 1980 *Toward Reform of Program Evaluation.* Jossey-Bass, San Francisco, California
Guba E G, Lincoln Y S 1981 *Effective Evaluation.* Jossey-Bass, San Francisco, California
House E R 1980 *Evaluating with Validity.* Sage, Beverly Hills, California
Joint Committee on Standards for Educational Evaluation 1981 *Standards for Evaluations of Educational Programs, Projects and Materials.* McGraw-Hill, New York
Lewy A, Nevo D (eds.) 1981 *Evaluation Roles in Education.* Gordon and Breach, New York
Scriven M 1967 The methodology of evaluation. In: Stake R E (ed.) 1967 *Curriculum Evaluation.* American Educational Research Association (AERA) Monograph Series on Evaluation, No. 1. Rand McNally, Chicago, Illinois
Stufflebeam D L, Foley W J, Gephart W J, Guba E G, Hammon R L, Merriman H O, Provus M M 1971 *Educational Evaluation and Decision-making.* Peacock, Itasca, Illinois
Tyler R W 1950 *Basic Principles of Curriculum and Instruction.* University of Chicago Press, Chicago, Illinois

D. Nevo

Examinations, External

Inevitably an article of this length on a topic as wide ranging as external examinations can only deal with general issues in a relatively superficial fashion. In particular, the wealth of illustrations required to illuminate these issues is impracticable and it is essential, therefore, that readers check the relevance and the validity of the comments made by reference to examinations with which they are familiar.

Reference to a dictionary will show the word "external" to mean amongst other things "outside", whilst an examination is a "test" or "enquiry". External examinations are thus tests or enquiries conducted by outsiders, that is to say, by people who are not directly connected with those being tested. This definition, incidentally, says nothing about who is to be tested, how they are to be tested, or for what purposes. Ironically, in view of recent developments, the original impetus to create external examinations was an egalitarian one stemming as it did from a desire to remove nepotism and patronage as a basis for selection, often into government service, and to extend the range and numbers of those from whom the selection took place. External examinations were also designed to smooth out disadvantages arising from uneven distribution of resources whether physical, human, or financial. The examinations (mainly oral) conducted by the Imperial Chinese Civil Service and those for selection for grammar schools in the United Kingdom—the 11+ (largely written)—provide two good illustrations of this intention.

Over time, the operation of external examinations has been characterized by certain features. First, there is the scale of their operation. This is in general substantial, not least because of the trends towards ever larger entries, particularly in the period 1950 to 1980. The examinations are in consequence mainly organized today by large agencies whose revenue comes from the fees of those who take them. The bureaucratic and commercial implications of this particularly in relation to timing and to the range of assessment techniques used are significant.

These agencies fall into a number of different categories, although the distinctions between them are often blurred in reality. Many are directly controlled by government, either central or local as, for example, the *baccalauréat* in France and the *Abitur* in Germany. Alternatively, the examinations can be conducted through agencies approved or underwritten by the government as, for example, the boards administering the General Certificate of Education (GCE) and the Certificate of Secondary Education (CSE) examinations in the United Kingdom. These latter have, incidentally, provided a particularly influential model around the world as a result of the United Kingdom's colonial past; note, for example, the West African Examinations Council (WAEC), the Caribbean Examinations Council (CXC), and the Malaysian Examinations Syndicate (MES). Occasionally, as in Sweden, the government itself is directly involved in the process of examining. Here the National Board of Education (NBE) develops tests which are used as the monitor for teacher assessment of students in schools.

Other agencies are non-profit-making educational corporations such as the Educational Testing Service (ETS) and the Psychological Corporation in the United States. Such bodies act as agents for clients of all kinds in the field of specific examination construction as well as undertaking substantial research and development into testing in general. Then there are the directly commercial testing agencies. These tend to be much more significant in areas such as North America where there is no system of public examinations in schools of the kind that exists at present in Europe and in much of the developing world. Many of these testing agencies as, for example, Harcourt, Brace and World (USA) and the National Foundation for Educational Research/Nelson (UK) now form part of large publishing conglomerates. The tests produced by such agencies are naturally designed to sell but they are usually subject to rigorous standards and the constructors lay great stress upon providing users with information for interpretation (see *Standardized Tests*). Finally, there are the professional bodies which, as part of the process of maintaining standards, may set their own entrance examinations or more commonly examinations which lead to additional qualifications as the individual moves up the professional ladder. The Institute of Bankers in the United Kingdom provides an illustration of such a body.

A second general feature has been the marked emphasis placed upon the use of the results of external examinations for the purpose of selection. There are, of course, a whole variety of possible purposes to which such results can be put. These may be briefly summarized as diagnosis, evaluation, guidance, grading, prediction, and selection. The evidence produced from examinations, whatever their nature, necessitates the making of comparisons if they are to be put to use but those comparisons may take one of two basic forms. An individual's performance can either be measured against the performance of a group, for example an age group or a class or another school, or it can be measured against some predetermined standard of mastery. Testing which does the former is called norm-referenced (see *Norm-referenced Assessment*), whilst testing which does the latter is called criterion-referenced (see *Criterion-referenced Tests*). The design models necessary to facilitate these two approaches are markedly different, notably in their capacity to discriminate; in the former, discrimination is essential, indeed central, whilst in the latter it is unnecessary. Failure to distinguish between the possible and the actual usage of the results of external examinations has undoubtedly led to an overemphasis upon a discriminating design model and has made them in consequence unhelpful for diagnostic and evaluative use. The effect of this upon attitudes to external examinations and to assessment in general has been extremely significant.

A third feature has been the relatively limited range of what is actually assessed in external examinations. This is the result both of their origins and of the scale of their operations. The original egalitarian thrust was in reality extremely limited, extending as it did the opportunities hitherto limited to the privileged and wealthy to the slightly less privileged and slightly less wealthy, or in class terms from the aristocracy to the middle class. The range of opportunities opened up by external examinations was also restricted and the major emphasis was placed upon academic competencies and/or subject-based achievement. This emphasis still continues today. The result is an academic cocoon which envelopes most external examinations and ensures that they concern themselves either with testing achievement in relation to specific subjects or specific areas of the curriculum or with the testing of those aptitudes deemed appropriate for success in higher education. More often than not the parameters of what is to be tested are marked out by the examining agencies by means of prescribed syllabi. In general, countries which have retained external examinations at the terminal school-leaving age, as in the United Kingdom, have concentrated upon testing subject achievement. Those which have no such examinations as, for example, the United States, have in general made use of aptitude tests of which the Scholastic Aptitude Test (SAT) developed by ETS provides a good example.

Two notable exceptions to the academic domination of external examinations are to be found in the areas of industrial and trade testing and commercial examinations (particularly office skills). It is, however, significant that an institution such as the City and Guilds of London Institute (CGLI) which was founded in 1878 is still regarded as a world leader in the field of industrial examinations. This owes nearly as much to the relative scarcity of expertise in this area as it does to the quality of the CGLI's examinations.

The scale of operations carried out by the majority of the agencies currently conducting external examinations is extensive and this has been used by them as a reason for severely curtailing their range of testing techniques and for restricting the timing of their examinations. Written terminal tests remain the norm and oral and practical testing and assessment spread over time continue to be little used except in relatively small-scale experiments. Moreover, since knowledge is both easier and cheaper to test than concepts, skills, personal characteristics, and attitudes, most external examinations emphasize the former and neglect the latter. They are also slow to respond to change and to encourage innovation.

Consideration of the three features which have been expanded in the preceding paragraphs permits an operational rather than a dictionary definition of external examinations to be made. It suggests that a very large majority of present-day external examinations are norm-referenced, terminal, written tests designed for those in full-time education. They tend to be unsympathetic to group work and to interdisciplinary curricula and are primarily concerned with the measurement of knowledge and/or aptitudes which are deemed relevant to further academic studies.

Support for such a definition which some might regard as unfair and overstated is to be found in the arguments which are frequently put forward in defence of external examinations. These state that such examinations motivate student learning; they check whether or not the stated aims of specific courses of study have been realized; they give the community at large a reliable yardstick against which to measure the effectiveness of knowledge; they raise the status of subjects in schools; they provide a key qualification for school leavers which is of value to a wide range of employers; and they identify those likely to benefit from further full-time education.

The picture presented in this account has made, directly and indirectly, major criticisms of external examinations. If these are justified then the development of substantial opposition to the continuance of external examinations might be expected. This is indeed the case, particularly in developed countries in Europe, North America, and Australasia where alternatives mainly in the shape of teacher-moderated assessment are being explored and introduced.

Future directions are, however, far from clear. On the one hand there is growing concern throughout the world about the effectiveness of the educational system in general and of the comprehensive school in particular. This has caused governments to look more closely at possible approaches to monitoring the effectiveness of the system. One such approach could be a closely supervised system of external examinations either nationally controlled or nationally underwritten. There have been a number of recent developments in this direction. In the United States there is the National Assessment of Educational Progress (NAEP) programme with its marked impact upon the development of statewide minimum competency programmes (see *Minimum Competency Testing*). In the United Kingdom there has been the establishment of the Assessment of Performance Unit (APU) and a programme of public examination reform carefully orchestrated by the government. The Australians have considered the possibilities of establishing something similar to the APU but have not pursued it, whilst in Sweden a government sponsored research study into a possible programme of national assessment is currently under way (see *Standards, National: Monitoring*).

On the other hand there are a number of factors, worldwide in their impact, although particularly relevant for developed countries, which argue for the abolition of external examinations and their replacement by more broadly based forms of assessment. Such assessment would make use in particular of those who by definition are excluded from implementing external examinations—the teachers of those being assessed. The two major factors here are the continued development of the comprehensive school and the growth of youth unemployment which is unlikely ever to go away. The first of these has questioned the external examination system designed to test the academic and hence the minority, whilst the latter by removing the "meal-ticket" value of the external certificate has started to erode, for the first time, public confidence in the system.

It is not easy to forecast in which direction the future will lie and indeed different countries will almost certainly need to make different decisions. There would appear to be four major possibilities and they are not mutually exclusive. The first would be the continuance of the present limited model with the likelihood of its remaining useful for fewer and fewer and becoming in consequence more formal and academic in its design and approach. A second possibility would be the creation of a more open and extended system. The development of CSE in the United Kingdom in the 1960s and of the CXC Basic in the Caribbean in the 1980s provide two illustrations of this approach which might also involve the development of profile reporting. The third possibility would be the creation of rather different kinds of examining agencies which placed their major emphasis upon the encouragement of locally based curricula. Australia provides some interesting exemplars here in the Victorian Institute of Secondary Education (VISE), the Australian Commonwealth Territory (ACT) Schools Authority, and the Queensland Review of School Based Assessment (ROSBA) programme. Fourthly and finally, external examinations could be abolished. A decision to this effect would require the development of alternative approaches with particular reference to admission to higher education and a massive programme of inservice training for teachers. In many countries, particularly in the developing world, it is doubtful whether the necessary political will or societal support would be forthcoming for such action. What seems certain, however, is that external examinations as they are at present constructed and operated are in need of careful reconsideration. If this is not undertaken, criticism will grow and abolition will become both more attractive and more realistic.

H. G. MacIntosh

Exemplar Approach

The application of examples in the teaching–learning process as a tool for imparting knowledge is one of the major characteristics of the exemplar approach.

The basic ideas underlying the exemplar approach can be formulated as follows. Formative learning which encourages the independence of the learner and thus contributes to the development of understanding, abilities, and attitudes does not take place by a reproductive mastery of single items or of disjointed units of knowledge. Only by actively working on several selected representative or exemplary instances of a particular body of knowledge can learning lead to such outcomes. It is necessary to identify those characteristics of a particular concept which are essential, fundamental, typical and structural, and utilize these concepts for dealing with concrete problems. It is possible to deal with structurally identical or similar problems, and even solve them with the help of general ("categorical") insights and abilities derived from thoroughly examining characteristic examples (Klafki 1964, 1975).

1. Historical View

Historical precedents of the "principle of example" can be found in the *Encyklios Paideia* of Hellenism and in the *Studia Humanitalis* of Cicero (Derbolav 1957). It also appears in the pedagogical and philosophical writings of Comenius, Wolff, Kant, and Husserl and above all in Pestalozzi's theory of elementary education and in its offshoot, the reform pedagogy (Buck 1971). As a systematic approach to the teaching–learning process it was developed and first put to test between the years 1950 to 1970 in the Federal Republic of Germany. Martin Wagenschein adapted this idea to teaching mathematics and natural sciences (Wagenschein 1977, 1980). Bruner's conception of "generic learning" and "discovery learning" and his suggestion of concentrating curricula on "the structure of the disciplines" and developing spiral curricula (see *Spiral Curriculum*) are also associated with the notion of the exemplar approach (Bruner 1960). Outside the realm of the school, Oskar Negt, in his critical blueprint for the social–political education of workers represents an original variant of this principle (Negt 1975). Since the 1970s, interest in the exemplar approach has diminished.

2. Definitions and Problems

The exemplar approach is based on the conception that learning within and outside the school should enhance both independent thinking and critically justified action and should impart the ability of continued independent learning. The teaching process is not regarded as a mere transmission of accumulated knowledge and predetermined sets of contents, but rather as a support to the pupil's active learning or as a "Socratic teaching" (Wagenschein 1977). In this respect, the exemplar approach opposes the traditional curricula of past and present, which are overloaded with materials to be mastered by the learners.

Independent learning is, however, possible only if the teaching–learning process is clearly related to the cognitive, aesthetic, motivational, and moral stages of the learner, and if it is suitable to the learner's interest, style of thinking, and learning habits. Additionally, the learning must not focus on readily provided sets of rules, principles, or structures to be memorized, but it should rather lead the learner to discover rules and afterwards, step by step, through logical analysis of changing situations, the learner should be able to extend the applicability of these rules. Wagenschein thus speaks of "generic teaching and learning," whilst Bruner demands "learning by discovery." Both support a kind of spiral curriculum which takes into consideration the intellectual capabilities of the learner and his/her ability to process information of a certain type.

The exemplar approach also resists the erroneous interpretation of the academic orientation toward learning. It rejects attempts to build the school curriculum in a way which constitutes a watered-down reflection of the entire systematic structure of a particular discipline. Rather it supports a curriculum which helps the learner to become familiar, step by step, with the nature of scientific questions, methods, and hypotheses through selected examples, and through knowledge of and competence in everyday matters.

The central curricular problem consists of classifying which fundamental questions, basic ideas, or concepts, and which rudimentary methods should be mastered by pupils at various ages and stages of development, in order to develop an appropriate critical understanding of themselves and of the world, and in order to acquire skills needed to deal with situations within the scope of their experience and practice.

The solution of this problem necessitates "categorical" research in the field of general and disciplinary didactics, since the concrete manifestations of the exemplar approach vary from discipline to discipline.

Thus, for example, the application of the example principle to the study of natural sciences differs from its application to the study of sociohistorical studies. Moreover, even within the context of a single discipline the principles may change as various sections of that particular discipline are dealt with.

Bibliography

Bruner J S 1960 *The Process of Education*. Harvard University Press, Cambridge, Massachusetts
Buck G 1971 Beispiel, Exempel, exemplarisch. In: Ritter J (ed.) 1971 *Historisches Wörterbuch der Philosophie*, Vol. 1. Schwabelo, Stuttgart, pp. 818–23
Derbolav J 1957 Das "Exemplarische" im Bildungsraum des Gymnasiums: *Versuch einer Pädagogischen Ortbestimmung des exemplarischen Lehrens*. Schwann, Düsseldorf

Klafki W 1964 *Das pädagogische Problem des Elementaren und die Theorie der Kategorialen Bildung*. Beltz, Weinheim

Klafki W 1975 Kategoriale Bildung. In: Klafki W (ed.) 1975 *Studien zur Bildungstheorie und Didaktik*, 2nd edn. Beltz, Weinheim, pp. 25–45

Negt O 1975 *Soziologische Phantasie und exemplarisches Lernen. Zur Theorie und Praxis der Arbeiterbildung*, 6th edn. Eurpäischera, Frankfurt

Wagenschein M 1977 *Verstehen Lehren: Genetisch, sokratisch, exemplarisch*, 6th edn. Beltz, Weinheim

Wagenschein M 1980 *Naturphänomene sehen und verstehen: Genetische Lehrgänge*. Klett, Stuttgart

W. Klafki

Existential Theory of Human Development

There are numerous ways to analyze the currents of existential thinking. As a system of philosophy or a school of thought, existentialism is a revolt against traditional metaphysics. As a theory of human development, it is an approach to highlight the existence of being, the process of becoming. Since a person, in the becoming state, always exists in a constantly dynamic phase, "his life may be regarded as a journey on which he finds ever newer experiences and gains greater insights" (Kingston 1961 p. xii).

Existentialism represents a protest against the rationalism of traditional philosophy, against misleading notions of the bourgeois culture, and the dehumanizing values of industrial civilization. Since alienation, loneliness, and self-estrangement constitute threats to human personality in the modern world, existential thought has viewed as its cardinal concerns a quest for subjective truth, a reaction against the "negation of Being," and a perennial search for freedom. From the ancient Greek philosopher, Socrates, to the twentieth century French philosopher, Jean Paul Sartre, thinkers have dealt with this tragic sense of ontological reality—the human situation within a comic context.

1. Existentialism Defined

Various definitions of existentialism have been proposed by different authors. Blackham (1952 p. 150) has described existentialism as a philosophy of being, "a philosophy of attestation and acceptance, and a refusal of the attempt to rationalize and to think Being." The peculiarity of existentialism, according to Blackham (1952 pp. 151–52), is that "it deals with the separation of man from himself and from the world, which raises the questions of philosophy, not by attempting to establish some universal form of justification which will enable man to readjust himself but by permanently enlarging and lining the separation itself as primordial and constitutive for personal existence."

Harris and Levey (1975 p. 911) define existentialism as "any of several philosophic systems, all centered on the individual and his relationship to the universe or to God." Tiryakian (1962 p. 77) defines it as "an attempt to reaffirm the importance of the individual by a rigorous and in many respects radically new analysis of the nature of man."

In the opinion presented here, existentialism is a humanistic perspective on the individual situation, a philosophy of existence, of being, of authenticity, and of universal freedom. It is a quest, beyond despair, for creative identity.

2. Basic Tenets

The main tenets of existentialism involve a kind of subjective and direct approach upholding the emergence of the person in a rather impersonal environment.

The first important tenet is that the essence of humans is their existence. A synthesis of immanency and transcendency, guided by a primordial sense of ontological wonder and subjective knowledge, constitutes existence. Sartre (1956) wrote that freedom is existence, and in it existence precedes essence.

The cardinal concept of subjectivity essentially concerns a person's openness and uniqueness, their encounter with the "thou," the transcendent. To Sartre, consciousness of freedom relates to "nothingness." This perspective on existence is inspired by a stance which is against positivism, scientism, and a logico-rational approach to reality.

Other tenets of existentialism relate to human suffering, despair, alienation, and anguish. The events that led to the First World War, followed by Auschwitz, Nagasaki, Hiroshima, and Bangladesh, generated a disillusionment which can lead to detachment and enlightenment. According to existential thought, people are able to appreciate human fortitude only through extreme situations. Sorrow, disappointment, and death enable humans to achieve authentic life. Existential writings—plays, poems, novels—seek to offer experiences of nausea and extremity (Scott 1978).

3. A Perspective Toward Human Development

Human development is seen by existentialists as independent of external forces, guided by the creative forces of the integral self. In other words, development is a self-directed synthesis of self-destined energy, potential, aspirations, and needs. From the existential perspective, the individual has freedom of choice, which implies a capacity to change. It is a freedom that helps with the self-emerging process. Identity and security attained at the cost of freedom constitute bad faith. Likewise, to question the dynamism of the personality is an act of bad faith. Thus, human personality is conceptualized as a transcendental reality that emerges through inner creative forces, with natural growth viewed as an integrative process marked by authenticity. Development consists of a uniquely subjective style by which the individual relates to others and to the processes of being and becoming.

4. Educational Implications

The implications of existentialist formulations for child-rearing, education, and counseling practices are many. Since existentialists behold human life as unique and emerging, a child is to be recognized as a full person and not simply as an incomplete adult. The practices by which the child is socialized varies from one culture to another. If the emphasis in the culture is on mundane security and on the value of worldly essence, then the individual may experience neurotic growth through the conflict between these unsuitable values and the person's inner forces of creativity that continue to aspire for unique emergence and subjective expression. The extent to which a child is accepted or rejected, succeeds or fails, and develops satisfactorily or is retarded depends on the experiences and processes which explain the meaning of things (persons, objects, situations) in relation to the child's being.

Educational standards and practices that manipulate the child's behaviors in an arbitrary manner violate the principle of free choice. From the existential point of view, many teaching practices, testing procedures, and bureaucratic systems of classifying children may be questioned. Existential critics of these practices say that overstructured public and parochial school systems enslave rather than liberate young souls. Such educational institutions serve a political rather than a truly educational purpose, promoting the manufacture of efficient robots rather than inspired, enlightened, and creative individuals. As a result, various contemporary educational theories are radicalizing the institutionalized structures of learning. Teachers who have learned to provide existential encounters for their students enable the learners "to create meanings in a cosmos devoid of objective meaning, to find reasons for being in a society with fewer and fewer open doors" (Greene 1967 p. 4).

If the purpose of education is to build character, to optimize potential and creativity, and to enhance the quality of life through knowledge, then from an existentialist perspective bureaucratization needs to be replaced by humanization. That the existential goal is not being achieved today is illustrated by such evidence as that produced in a study of students' values indicating that American students predominantly seek to learn survival skills rather than to develop a social conscience, a situation contrary to an existentialist view of satisfactory development (*Chronicle of Higher Education* 1982). This crisis in education is not confined to the West but is observed in Eastern cultures as well (Mohan 1972).

In the realm of counseling, existential intervention is conceptualized as "a conscious attitudinal perspective toward rebuilding the impaired self" (Mohan 1979). The existential influences on counseling practices, though not yet fully acknowledged nor duly assessed, have been far-reaching. Some form of existential intervention is employed by such a range of practitioners as those using gestalt therapy, "antipsychiatry," rational–emotive psychotherapy, psychodrama, transactional analysis, communication and cognitive approaches, encounter groups, and reality therapy.

The existential view of development is not without its critics, many of whom view the theory and its practices as representing a neurotic, narcissistic philosophy of pain and anguish. In contrast, existentialism's protagonists see it as the only hope for human survival.

Bibliography

Blackham H J 1952 *Six Existentialist Thinkers.* Routledge and Kegan Paul, London

Chronicle of Higher Education 1982 April p. 10

Greene M 1967 *Existential Encounters for Teachers.* Random House, New York

Harris W H, Levey J S (eds.) 1975 *The New Columbia Encyclopedia.* Columbia University Press, New York

Kaufmann W A (ed.) 1959 *Existentialism from Dostoevsky to Sartre.* Meridian, New York

Kingston F T 1961 *French Existentialism: A Christian Critique.* University of Toronto Press, Toronto, Ontario

Mohan B 1972 *India's Social Problems.* Indian International Publications, Allahabad

Mohan B 1979 Conceptualization of existential intervention. *Psychol: Q. J. Hum. Behav.* 16(3): 39–45

Sartre J P 1956 *Being and Nothingness: An Essay on Phenomenological Ontology.* Barnes H E (trans.) Philosophical Library, New York

Scott N A 1978 *Mirrors of Man in Existentialism.* Collins, New York

Tiryakian E A 1962 *Sociologism and Existentialism: Two Perspectives on the Individual and Society.* Prentice-Hall, Englewood Cliffs, New Jersey

B. Mohan; B. M. Daste

Expectancy Tables

An expectancy table is a tabular device designed to report, in probabilistic terms, the relationship between two or more variables. This may be taken to mean that the relationship between the variables is expressed as a table of expected probabilities of possible values (outcomes) of one of the variables, usually called the criterion, for the sets of observed combinations of values on the other variables, usually called the predictors. In other words, the table provides the conditional distribution of criterion values for different combinations of values of the predictors.

Although many formats have been used for expectancy tables, most of these have, in one way or another, specified the relationships between the variables in terms of cross-tabulations, as in contingency tables. Indeed the usual starting point in the construction of an expectancy table is a scatter plot with a superimposed grid or, equivalently, a contingency table (frequency table). In education, the units of analysis of expectancy tables are persons, and the variables appearing in the tables represent characteristics of the persons or conditions or treatments applied to the persons. The numbers of persons or cases falling in the cells of the cross-tabulations provide the primitive database of an expectancy table, but in practice most expectancy tables report the probabilistic relationship between the variables in terms of relative frequencies, conditional probabilities (proportions), or percentages (see *Contingency Tables*).

1. Constructing an Expectancy Table

When constructing an expectancy table, the choice of criterion from the set of variables being used must be guided by substantive considerations. As a rule, only one variable from the set is chosen to be the criterion, but the criterion may itself be a composite of two or more variables.

It is common to identify expectancy tables according to the numbers of their predictors. As examples, tables with one predictor are called single-entry expectancy tables, and tables with two predictors are called double-entry expectancy tables. Because of the problems of interpreting tables with more than two predictors, few such tables have been constructed.

In order to illustrate the concepts introduced in the forgoing discussion, two examples are presented here of expectancy tables. Table 1 is a single-entry expectancy table which reports the predictive relationship between scores on a mathematics aptitude test (the predictor) and scores on a mathematics achievement test (the criterion). The purpose of this table was to provide information which could be used to counsel and select future applicants to a university mathematics course, by providing them with measures of their likely chances of scoring satisfactorily in the course, based on their scores on the aptitude test. For this purpose, the variables were categorized as shown in Table 1; both tests allowing a maximum score of 100. Because the table was to be used in a predictive sense, the table's cell entries were expressed as conditional probabilities (raw frequencies shown in parentheses), which were computed by dividing each cell frequency by the total frequency of the row containing the cell. According to Table 1, the expected probability that a future applicant to the mathematics course will obtain a score on the achievement test in the score interval 60–79, given that the applicant's score on the aptitude test falls in the interval 40–59, is 0.39. Also, if the applicant's aptitude score falls in the interval 60–79, the expectancy table states that the probability that the applicant's achievement score will be greater than 59 is 0.78 (0.40 + 0.38).

Table 2 represents a more detailed breakdown of the data on which Table 1 was based. It is a double-entry expectancy table involving two predictors—the aptitude test score reported in Table 1 and a predictor indicating the sex of the applicants. The purpose of this expectancy table was to allow finer predictions for each of the sexes. Table 2 clearly shows that, in general, female applicants have better chances of obtaining higher achievement scores than males, for the same aptitude scores. Consequently selection decisions based on Table 2 would be more favourable to the female applicants than the male applicants, whereas the male applicants would generally be expected to do better if decisions for them were based on Table 1 instead. Table 2 shows that by introducing a second predictor, namely the sex of the applicants, improved information about chances of success in the course can be gained for each applicant.

The above examples suggest how expectancy tables could be employed to predict performance; information which could subsequently be used to select applicants to courses. Typically an applicant could be selected if the applicant's scores on the

Table 1
Example of a single-entry expectancy table

Aptitude test score	Achievement test score			
	20–39	40–59	60–79	80–100
80–100		0.01 (2)	0.29 (50)	0.70 (120)
60–79	0.02 (5)	0.20 (50)	0.40 (100)	0.38 (93)
40–59	0.11 (29)	0.39 (100)	0.39 (100)	0.11 (30)
20–39	0.48 (85)	0.43 (85)	0.06 (10)	0.03 (5)

Table 2
Example of a double-entry expectancy table

	Achievements test score	Aptitude test score			
		20–39	40–49	60–79	80–100
Female applicants	80–100	0.05	0.18	0.45	0.76
	60–79	0.11	0.48	0.39	0.24
	40–59	0.51	0.30	0.16	
	20–39	0.33	0.04		
Male applicants	80–100		0.04	0.29	0.63
	60–79		0.28	0.42	0.35
	40–59	0.35	0.49	0.25	0.02
	20–39	0.65	0.19	0.04	

predictors were greater or equal to cutting scores corresponding to an appropriately chosen level of achievement on the achievement test. It is important to understand that the validity of decisions based on expectancy tables such as Tables 1 and 2 are group dependent, and that tables should be used only with individuals or groups who are sufficiently similar to the group on which the expectancy table was based.

Perhaps one of the most important applications of expectancy tables is in test research and development, where the tables can provide a simple framework in which to report validity studies. Instead of presenting validity data in terms of correlational and regression statistics, which the nonstatistician may find difficult to understand or apply, these data often have been presented just as effectively, for most practical purposes, in tabular form as in expectancy tables. In many instances, one advantage of an expectancy table is that it can provide a picture of validity relationships rather than just a set of summary numbers.

There is no easy answer to the question of whether one, two, or more predictors should be used in an expectancy table. By and large the number of predictors is an arbitrary decision that must be rationalized on substantive grounds, and the question of ease of interpretation should be kept in mind. However, only one criterion is employed in an application of an expectancy table.

The problem of how to categorize the predictors and criterion variables is an important consideration when designing an expectancy table. Should a variable be expressed in terms of points, a dichotomy, or three or more mutually exclusive and exhaustive categories? Often the nature of a variable determines its categorization. Thus variables which are measured at the nominal level, such as the sex of individuals, come already categorized. However variables which are measured at higher measurement levels may not suggest obvious categorizations. In these cases there is no simple answer; the purpose of the table from the points of view of the constructor and user should provide the necessary guidelines. In general, the variables should be categorized in a way that is readily understood and usable by the user of the table. The point form of the variables is advantageous when computing cell entries in the expectancy table on the basis of regression analysis. However, the categorized form can often provide a more meaningful indication of the effectiveness of prediction. The use of few categories may simplify the reporting process, but it may also lead to loss of information through the aggregation of the data. The dichotomous form is useful when decisions are based on cutting scores.

As a rule, variables should not be overcategorized when there are few subjects, because the reliability of the data in an individual cell is proportional to the number of cases that fall in that cell.

The measurement units of the predictors and criterion is another important consideration. Should variables be left in their original form or expressed in terms of relative standing in the defined group? The relative standing may be expressed in terms of quantities such as percentiles and stanines. Use of the original units is recommended when the expectancy table is to apply to a single group, such as the students in a particular school or university. However, if useful comparisons are to be made between groups it is necessary to convert original units to percentages or other standardized values.

2. Technical Issues in the Construction of Expectancy Tables

Methods for constructing expectancy tables may be concrete in that they make no distributional assumptions about the variables or the relationship between variables, or they may be theoretical in that they do make distributional assumptions.

Concrete methods utilize only the observed frequencies in the cells and margins of the contingency table to construct the expectancy table. Conditional probabilities, corresponding to cells, are computed directly from the cell frequencies and the marginal frequencies. Tables 1 and 2 are examples. The advantage of a concrete approach is its mathematical simplicity: it does not entail making complex transformations of the data to accommodate statistical assumptions. It is suited to decision making without concern for distributional assumptions. It also avoids the introduction of underlying model assumptions, which may be erroneous or unrealistic. Its major disadvantage is that without some kind of summary index, such as the correlation coefficient, which depends on statistical assumptions, it is difficult to evaluate the expectancy table or to compare it with other tables.

In contrast, the theoretical approach permits greater flexibility in the design of tables. Assumptions about the nature of the data may be varied, and different statistical techniques may be employed, in order to construct expectancy tables that serve particular purposes. Statistical techniques which have been used include those that involve the normal distribution, including regression and correlational methods and, more recently, techniques based on Bayesian statistics (Novick and Jackson 1974) (see *Bayesian Statistics*).

Some advantages of theoretical methods include (a) the facility to "smooth" cell entries so that cell entries display regular progressions, free of idiosyncratic fluctuations, (b) the facility to derive results for extrapolated regions where data are very scanty, and (c) the facility to adjust variables so as to take into account restriction of range.

Of these, perhaps the one of greatest importance is the use of smoothing of data techniques. Two reasons are frequently put forward for smoothing the entries in expectancy tables: (a) some cell samples may be small and (b) the relationships between predictors and criterion may not be monotonic, because of reversals in the cell data. Reversals may occur because of sampling fluctuations. Consequently, some have suggested that before expectancy tables are used, the tables should be smoothed by statistical means rather than left in their unsmoothed form. For example, in a counselling situation, it can be argued that it would be unsound to make recommendations that capitalized on sampling reversals in the data. Recent research (e.g. Perrin and Whitney 1976) on smoothing methods has examined methods that are based on (a) linear and multiple regression procedures, (b) isotonic regression procedures, (c) iterative maximum likelihood procedures, and (d) noniterative minimum chi-squared procedures.

In summary, expectancy tables are simple statistical devices useful for summarizing and reporting predictive data. The information conveyed by expectancy tables enables users to see at a glance the probabilistic relationship between criterion and predictors in terms of the pattern of cell entries.

Bibliography

Novick M R, Jackson P H 1974 *Statistical Methods for Educational and Psychological Research*. McGraw-Hill, New York

Owen D B, Li L 1980 The use of cutting scores in selection procedures. *J. Educ. Stat.* 5(2): 157–68

Perrin D W, Whitney D R 1976 Methods for smoothing expectancy tables applied to the prediction of success in college. *J. Educ. Meas.* 13: 223–31

Schrader W B 1967 A taxonomy of expectancy tables. In: Payne D A, McMorris R F (eds.) 1967 *Educational and Psychological Measurement: Contributions to Theory and Practice*. Blaisdell, Waltham, Massachusetts, pp. 209–15

G. Morgan

Expected Rates of Return

The expected earnings and other returns expected from education over the life cycle when related to costs, as they are in expected rates of return, are of great interest primarily because of their strong influence on student and family decisions about the types and amount of education students seek to acquire. But if, in addition, expected net returns are a reasonably accurate predictor of actual net returns, then the expected rate of return is also a convenient, albeit somewhat incomplete, guide to educational budget and policy decisions designed to achieve social efficiency. In this case if individuals and educational institutions respond by investing more where the private and social expected rates of return are relatively high, the growth of per capita income is facilitated, as well as the growth of productivity and economic growth and development in the society in general.

The expected rate of return is a type of cost–benefit calculation that relates earnings that students expect to receive as the result of their education to educational costs. Specifically, it is that percentage rate of return that discounts the stream of earnings expected by the student (or by others) over his or her life cycle back to its present value and equates them to the total educational costs compounded forward to the date of graduation.

It is particularly useful for two reasons. First, it permits comparison of the relative return to widely different forms of investment, either in education or in physical capital or financial assets. Second, the rate of return is a widely understood concept, facilitating communication with the financial community and widely diverse fields within and outside of education. However, it also has its limitations. The major one is that the benefits from education that enter into the calculation are normally limited to earnings, thereby excluding nonmonetary private returns and social benefit externalities. Since the latter nonmonetary returns should in principle be included, and are omitted only because they are hard to measure, the result is that the total expected returns to education will tend to be understated. The reader should see, however, summaries of the progress made in recent research in beginning to measure these nonmonetary private and social benefits under other entries in this Encyclopedia (see *Consumption Benefits of Education; Externalities in Education; Option Value in Education; Spillovers in Education*).

The remainder of this article will consider more specifically the relatively high degree of correspondence between expected and actual earnings and the basic methods of calculating expected rates of return. It will also consider the differences that exist among the expected rates of return to investment in different types of education (e.g., by occupational field, by degree level, and by type of institution) as well as differences in expected rates of return by race, sex, and among those few countries where studies thus far here have been done (United States, United Kingdom, Philippines, and Egypt). It will be suggested that the evidence that exists indicates that student and family expectations are not so myopic as might be supposed.

Consideration of the way in which student and family expectations actually are formed has implications for the debate between adaptive and rational expectations, as well as for educational policies that attempt to deal with problems of motivation, such as among black male high-school underachievers. In sum, the study of expected rates of return, as distinguished from manpower planning approaches, has considerable significance for the socially efficient operation of the relatively decentralized educational systems characteristic of most nations.

1. Measurement of Expected Rates of Return

To measure expected rates of return requires first that information be obtained from the student and perhaps also from the family on the earnings he or she expects to receive at future times over his or her life cycle. This data then can be used to estimate an entire age–earnings profile, similar to those shown in Fig. 1, for the level of education the student attains. Before turning to the two main methods used for calculating expected rates of return it is important to consider some data for several countries on the earnings that students expect to receive at graduation and later in their life cycles in relation to actual earnings, since those enter in a major way into the calculation.

1.1 Expected Earnings and Actual Earnings

The earnings students in the United States expect to receive when they complete their formal schooling are compared with the earnings they expect to receive 25 years after completion of their bachelor's degree in Table 1. Students were asked to estimate their

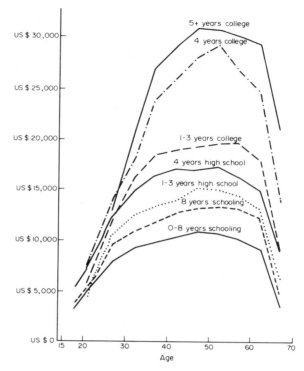

Figure 1
Age–earnings profiles of white males in March 1979[a]

a Source: US Bureau of the Census 1980 *Money Income of Families and Persons in the United States.* Current Population Reports, Series P60, No. 123

expected earnings in the absence of inflation (as for the expected rates of return reported for United States students below), based on a nationwide survey of 5,346 college students described in McMahon (1974 pp. 43–8, 167–79) and analyzed further in McMahon and Geske (1982 Chap. 7).

It is clear that both male and female students receiving bachelor's degrees in 1975 (at the top of Table 1) expect somewhat lower starting salaries than those who planned to finish master's degrees in 1976 or Ph.D.s in 1978. But all groups of students expect a higher rate of growth of earnings later in their life cycle upon completion of college training. Their mean expected salary 25 years hence not only reveals expected age–earnings profiles that are more peaked at each higher degree level, typical of the age–earnings patterns found the world around. But their expectations also compare very closely to the actual earnings patterns for college graduates shown in the United States census data toward the top of Fig. 1. This pattern of growth of actual earnings of college

Table 1
Expected starting and future salaries and growth in earnings[a]

	Mean expected starting salary[b]	Mean expected salary in 25 years	Ratio of earnings in 25 years to starting salary	Average annual expected real rate of growth in earnings[c]
		Bachelor's degree		
Male	$10,087	$18,005	1.78	3.56
	(2,792)	(6,768)		
White	10,084	18,038		3.58
	(2,824)	(6,690)		
Black	10,119	17,680		3.39
	(2,493)	(7,603)		
Female	8,457	14,192	1.67	3.08
	(2,479)	(5,600)		
White	8,367	14,054		3.08
	(2,534)	(5,702)		
Black	8,899	14,866		3.04
	(2,152)	(5,070)		
		Master's degree		
Male	10,346	20,367	1.97	4.84
	(2,864)	(9,188)		
White	10,278	19,235		4.35
	(2,794)	(7,416)		
Black	10,500	22,955	5.93	
	(3,024)	(11,942)		
Female	9,000	16,304	1.81	4.05
	(2,566)	(6,643)		
White	8,780	14,876		3.47
	(2,507)	(5,127)		
Black	9,346	18,548		4.92
	(2,631)	(8,023)		
		Doctor's degree		
Male	11,244	28,296	2.51	8.92
	(5,181)	(22,581)		
White	10,623	27,112		9.13
	(4,685)	(25,104)		
Black	12,884	31,422		8.46
	(6,073)	(13,668)		
Female	10,776	21,848	2.02	6.04
	(4,529)	(16,062)		
White	9,808	19,231		5.68
	(4,029)	(16,555)		
Black	12,523	26,568		6.59
	(4,944)	(14,311)		

a Source: McMahon and Wagner (1981, pp. 276–7)   b Standard deviations are shown in parentheses below each entry   c Annual real growth rate calculated from mean expected salary point estimates. Percentage increase from starting salary to future salary divided by number of intervening years: bachelor's 22 years; master's 20 years; doctor's 17 years

graduates in the United States has been sustained over a long period of time as reported in Table 2.

Similar patterns have been found in several other countries. There is a close correspondence of earnings expected at graduation with the actual earnings of those who have been in the labor force in the United Kingdom, as well as in the United States, as shown in Table 3. If the time is expanded to encompass the first five years after graduation, a reasonably close correspondence between expected and actual starting salaries have been found for the Philippines and Egypt as well. These data are from

Table 2
Ratio of mean income of college to high-school graduates[a]

All workers								Year								
Ages	Midpoint	1967	1968	1969	1970	1971	1972	1973	1974	1975	1976	1977	1978	1979	1980	1981
Graduation	22															
25–34	30	1.33	1.32	1.33	1.33	1.27	1.22	1.19	1.15	1.19	1.26	1.21	1.24	1.22	1.27	1.32
35–44	40	1.53	1.47	1.58	1.54	1.55	1.55	1.52	1.55	1.56	1.55	1.48	1.47	1.52	1.48	1.42

a Source: Various issues of *Current Population Reports*. Series P-60, US Bureau of the Census

Table 3
Expected and actual earnings

	At graduation Y_0	After 5 years Y_5	After 25 years Y_{25}	Ratio Y_5/Y_0	Y_{25}/Y_0
United States (dollars)					
Males' expectations[a]	10,087		18,005		1.78
Females' expectations[a]	8,457		14,192		1.67
Actual starting salaries[b]	10,119	11,510	17,405	1.14	1.72
United Kingdom (pounds)					
Males' expectations[c]	2,100	3,371	5,199	1.60	2.47
Males' actual[d]	2,399		5,856		2.44
Females' expectations[c]	1,835	2,587	3,391	1.41	1.84
Females' actual[d]	2,161	2,894	3,193	1.34	1.47
Philippines (pesos)					
Males' expectations[e]	9,912	14,892		1.50	
Females' expectations[e]	6,756	16,380		2.42	
Actual earnings[f]	n.a.	7,992			

	At graduation Y_0	Y_{10}	Y_{10}/Y_0
Egypt (Egyptian pounds)			
Males' expectations[g]	564	1,512	2.7
Males' actual[h]	252	654	2.6
Females' expectations[g]	432	1,104	2.6
Females' actual[h]	264	481	1.8

Sources: a Table 1   b McMahon and Wagner (1981 p. 280 Col. 3)   c Williams and Gordon (1981 p. 202)   d Williams and Gordon (1981 pp. 225–26 Col. 1) Y_0 and Y_{25} found by interpolation for ages 20–24 and age 47   e Psacharopoulos and Sanyal (1981b p. 459), converted to annual basis   f Psacharopoulos and Sanyal (1981b p. 451 for salaries and p. 460 for Y_{10})   g Psacharopoulos and Sanyal (1981a p. 4)   h Psacharopoulos and Sanyal (1981a p. 23), annual basis

the only four studies of expected earnings and expected rates of return that have been made thus far. The United Kingdom data (and the United Kingdom expected rates of return discussed below) are from a sample of 2,944 high-school students who were planning higher education, as analyzed by Williams and Gordon (1981 pp. 202, 225–26). The Philippines data are from a nationwide sample of 9,105 college students collected by the International Institute for Educational Planning (IIEP) and analyzed by Psacharopoulos and Sanyal (1981b p. 451). Egyptian data are from a sample of 1,935 college students and 1,712 other college graduates, also collected by the International Institute for Educational Planning with the Supreme Council of Universities, and analyzed by Psacharopoulos and Sanyal (1981a p. 4).

The accuracy of students' expectations in the United Kingdom about earnings 25 years hence is also remarkable; males expect earnings to grow 2.47 fold, whereas the General Household Survey shows that actual earnings of graduates have grown 2.44 fold, for example. Expectations of earnings 5 and 10 years after graduation in both the Philippines and Egypt are overly optimistic (see Table 3). But

expected inflation was not fully removed in these cases, and even at that, the rate of increase in expected earnings as shown in the last columns of Table 3 are not all that much greater than the percentage increases in actual earnings. Female expectations are somewhat optimistic in all countries including the United States in relation to the age–earnings profiles actually experienced. But opportunities have been improving for women in some nations (Ferber and McMahon 1979) and continuation of these improvements may be expected by students.

1.2 Method of Calculation of Expected Rates of Return

There are two basic methods for calculating the expected rates of return. The first uses the standard formula, widely understood in educational and in all other branches of finance for calculating a pure internal rate of return, whereas the second uses the first derivative of an expected-earnings function estimated by regression methods. Both involve using a smaller number of points to approximate the expected age–earnings profiles illustrated in Fig. 2 as $E_1(t)$, earnings expected at each age from graduation up to retirement. $E_0(t)$ measures forgone earnings prior to graduation, and $E_0(t)$ after graduation represents the earnings that could have been expected in the absence of the increment to education. For the expected rates of return, the two points of earnings expected at graduation (Y_0) and earnings expected 25 years hence near the peak of the age–earnings profile (Y_{25}) are used to determine the level of each age–earnings profile. Each profile is assumed to be the same shape as those observed in Fig. 1 to determine the values for all other years to calculate the "net earnings differential." Williams and Gordon (1981) use similar points (specifically Y_0, Y_5, and Y_{25}) for the United Kingdom, but assume that earnings rise linearly between these points to peak at Y_{25}, and then level off until retirement at age 65 to compute expected lifetime earnings. This then is used as the dependent variable in an expected earnings function.

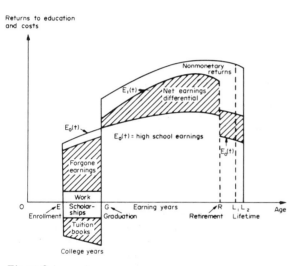

Figure 2
Investment in higher education and private returns over the life cycle[a]

a Source: McMahon and Wagner (1982)

The pure expected rate of return, r^*, is given by solving the following formula iteratively on the computer, using individual micro data for each student:

$$\sum_{t=E}^{G} [E_0(t) + C(t)](1 + r^*)^t \qquad (1)$$

$$= \sum_{t=G}^{R} [E_1(t) - E_0(t)](1 + r^*)^{-t}$$

where the terms, as illustrated in Fig. 2, are $E_1(t) - E_0(t)$ = the expected net earnings differential

attributable to the next higher level of education; $E_0(t)$ = the forgone earnings, or indirect costs; $C(t)$ = direct costs consisting of tuition and fees (if any), books, and special fees; r^* = the expected rate of return; t = age; $E, \ldots, G$ = beginning of education to graduation, for the level of education being evaluated; and R = retirement.

The "short-cut method" suggested and used, when appropriate, by Psacharopoulous (1980a) and by Psacharopoulous and Sanyal (1981a, 1981b) focuses on the net earnings differential at graduation, Eqn. (2a), or at the overtaking age 8 years after graduation, Eqn. (2b):

$$r^* = \frac{E_1 - E_0(G)}{\sum_{t=0}^{5} [E_0(t) + C(t)]}, \qquad (2a)$$

or

$$r^* = \frac{E_1(G + 8) - E_0(G + 8)}{\sum_{t=0}^{5} [E_0(t) + C(t)]} \qquad (2b)$$

This short cut has the strong advantage of being easy to calculate for approximate comparisons. But the authors recognize that Eqn. (2a) especially must be used with caution because the focus on initial earnings does not take into account the growth of earnings thereafter, and therefore underestimates pure rates of return. Starting salaries can even be below the earnings of high-school graduates whose steady growth of earnings on the job while others are in college precedes less growth later. Notice the close proximity in Fig. 1, for example, of earnings of 22-year-olds with high-school diplomas to those facing low starting salaries after college, compared to the potential for growth later. Starting salaries can be very erratic, especially in recessions, and can involve initial periods of unemployment, in relation to salaries at the overtaking age eight years later (see *Student Labor Market Expectations*).

The second method in use for calculating expected rates of return is to estimate an earnings function of the type originally developed by Mincer (1974), or with variants that measure the school-leaving age differently as used by Williams and Gordon (1981 p. 218):

$$\ln E = \beta_1 s + \beta_2 s^2 + \beta_3 st + \beta_4 t + \beta_5 t^2 \qquad (3)$$
$$+ \beta_6 A + u$$

where: $\ln E$ = log of annual expected earnings; s = number of years of schooling; t = number of years of experience on the job; A = ability test scores to control for differences in ability; and u = disturbances. The partial derivative of this function, $\delta \ln E / \delta s$, is then the expected rate of return to the last year of school—when t represents the overtaking age and therefore is set equal to approximately eight years of experience.

2. Differences in Expected Rates of Return

Using the first, more elaborate formula, expected rates of return vary widely by occupational field and degree level as shown in Table 4. The rates shown are expected social rates, including the full institutional cost specific to each student at each type of institution, which are more relevant to policy decisions and more practical for international comparisons.

2.1 Expected Rates of Return by Occupation and Degree Level

The lower expected rate of return at each higher degree level reading horizontally across Table 4 is a

Table 4
Expected and realized social rates of return, US white male students, by occupation and degree objective[a]

| Occupation | Degree level[b] | | | | All degree levels | |
	Associate	Bachelor's	Master's	Doctor's/ professional	Average expected	Realized
Health		16.1 (1.5)		11.1 (1.0)	12.7	7.2
Doctor, dentist				12.2 (0.8)	12.2	11.7
Health technician		9.1 (2.5)			9.4	
Pharmacist		20.1 (1.1)		3.9 (4.8)	15.2	12.4
Lawyer				15.5 (2.1)	15.5	14.1
Engineering–Technical	36.4 (8.0)	24.4 (2.2)	8.5 (0.7)	7.2 (0.8)	19.0	12.6
Architect		23.6 (2.3)	10.5 (1.6)		17.2	8.5
Engineer		18.9 (2.0)	10.0 (0.6)	7.4 (0.4)	14.1	11.0
Electrical technician	41.3 (4.1)	43.8 (1.0)			40.8	24.6
Business	22.1 (1.4)	17.1 (0.9)	10.4 (0.7)		15.9	11.3
Accountant	23.0 (1.1)	17.8 (1.5)	10.7 (1.2)		17.3	9.0
Manufacturing manager		16.0 (0.8)	10.8 (0.9)		13.2	15.2
Sales, retailing		16.6 (1.1)			15.5	12.4
Other Professional		7.6 (1.6)	7.8 (1.0)	1.4 (1.6)	6.5	3.7
Clergyman				−2.1 (3.6)	−2.8	−17.5
Natural scientist			7.4 (3.0)	3.2 (3.1)	9.4	7.7
Social scientist				−4.8 (4.5)	−4.1	8.0
Education		10.3 (1.6)	0.0 (1.6)	3.1 (2.0)	3.8	−2.8
Elementary and secondary teacher		10.3 (1.6)	−0.8 (1.6)	2.0 (3.0)	3.3	−3.8
College professor				5.2 (1.2)	7.6	5.5

a Source: McMahon and Geske (1982 Chap. 7)   b Standard errors, computed as $s/\sqrt{n}$, are shown below each mean pattern typically found. It is caused primarily by higher forgone earnings costs at each successively higher degree level. Rising forgone earnings costs lower the rates of return, even though expected earnings are higher at each level, as was shown in Table 1. In another example of the effects of variation in costs on expected rates of return, the economies of scale in educational institutions in less developed countries (LDCs) (Psacharopoulos 1980b) and unemployment among the young and less skilled both operate to reduce direct and forgone earnings costs. If the later ages in the life cycle of expected earnings are taken into account, the effect of these lower out-of-pocket and opportunity costs is to raise expected rates of return, and hence to encourage expansion of investment in junior college and other postsecondary education.

The expected rates of return are averaged across all degree levels within each occupational field of study in column 5 of Table 4. They then can be compared with the actual rates of return as given by United States census data in column 6, and with expected rates of return by occupation in Egypt (and elsewhere) as in Table 5. The students' expected

Table 5
Expected rates of return by field of study in Egypt, 1978[a]

Occupational field of study	Expected rate of return (%)
Medicine	17.2
Physical sciences	14.9
Architecture	20.3
Agronomy	15.3
Commerce	13.3
Veterinary medicine	13.0
Fine arts	12.2
Social sciences	11.8
Economics and politics	11.0
Overall	15.0

a Source: Psacharopoulos and Sanyal (1981a)

rates of return first can be seen to be quite accurate estimates of the actual rates of return for each degree field. The highest expected and actual rate of return fields are medicine, engineering, and business administration, with expected and actual rates of return that are all in the 12 to 15 percent range. The lowest expected rate of return fields are elementary education and the ministry (as well as music, which is not shown), falling in the low −17 to +3.3 percent range. There is evidence from studies using 1960 census data by Eckhaus et al. (1974 pp. 352–57) that similar patterns of differences in rates of return have tended to persist over relatively long periods of time. Since other studies find that students' choices

are heavily influenced by differences in expected private monetary rates of return (Freeman 1971, Ferber and McMahon 1979, McMahon 1984), this persistence of different rates of return is most likely to be due in part to the limitations on entry imposed by some fields (e.g., medicine), combined with the relative ease of entry in other fields (e.g., primary and secondary education). It is also possible that there are larger expected psychic and social benefits in some fields, such as music and the ministry. If so, the true expected rates of return are understated in these fields in Tables 4 and 5, explaining persistence of some differences in the expected purely monetary rates.

The expected rates of return for Egypt shown in Table 5 reveal a very similar pattern. Again, medicine, architecture, and the physical sciences (the latter may include some of what is called engineering in the United States) are at the high end, in the 15 to 20 percent range. The relevance of education to agriculture and business administration are reflected in the medium to high expected rates of return for agronomy and commerce. At the lower end are several fields that may contain a number of prospective teachers, whereas in the United States expected monetary returns are lower.

2.2 Expected Rates of Return by Sex and by Type of Institution

When expected rates of return are compared internationally, as in Table 6, a remarkable similarity emerges among male students, especially at the bachelor's level. Females in all of the countries shown receive significantly lower earnings (e.g., 74 percent of male earnings in Egypt, 66 percent in the United Kingdom) which also lowers forgone earnings. The higher rates of return expected by females in the United States may be partly due to the increasing entry of women into more advanced degree programs, followed by employment in the high-earnings fields such as medicine, business administration, engineering, and law, as mentioned above.

Relatively little is known about how expected rates of return differ by type of institution. The only study that incorporates the specifics of private and total cost differences among institutions to calculate private and social expected rates of return is for the United States, and appears in McMahon and Geske (1982 Chap. 7 Tables 4 and 5). The conclusions reached there suggest first, that the terminal undergraduate degrees at the public comprehensive colleges and junior colleges where many undergraduate programs tend to be more vocationally oriented are very cost-effective. Expected private rates of return, for example, at the bachelor's degree level are never below 15 percent in any ability quartile, and average 21 percent across all ability quartiles. At the same time, the four-year liberal arts college and the public and private research universities are most cost-effec-

Table 6
Expected social rates of return for several countries by sex and degree level (%)

	US[a] (1976)	England[b] (1977)	Philippines[c] (1977)	Egypt[d] (1978)
Upper secondary				
Male		2.16		
Female		11.7		
Higher education				
Males: Bachelor's	15.2	13.0	15.8	15.4
Master's	14.9	9.9	12.6	
Ph.D.	16.6		32.0	
Females: Bachelor's	37.2	9.9		14.5
Master's	30.4			
Ph.D.	21.6			

a Ferber and McMahon (1979 p. 416–17), using Eqn. (1) above   b Williams and Gordon (1981 p. 219), using a variant of Eqn. (3)   c Psacharopoulos and Sanyal (1981b pp. 468–69). This one column reports actual rates of return for all students, since the expected rates "must be downward biased as they are based on initial earnings" only. It uses Eqn. (2b)   d Psacharopoulos and Sanyal (1981a p. 12), using Eqn. (2a)

tive for those planning graduate work. At the master's and Ph.D. or professional-school levels, both the expected private and social rates of return for those planning advanced degrees are higher in these types of institutions.

These expected (and actual) rates of return are a much more comprehensive measure for use in comparisons than either the costs of education, or expected returns, taken alone. High-cost programs can be viable candidates for expansion if the expected returns are also high, and vice versa. There are now a number of excellent studies that document the wide variation in costs among institutions: Bowen (1980) develops the differences among higher educational institutions in the United States, Verry and Davies (1976) analyze the economies of scale by degree program and by institution in the United Kingdom, and Psacharopoulos (1980b) develops the major economies of scale in higher education to be found in international comparisons among many less developed countries. There is also a new but rapidly growing literature on educational cost differentials at the primary and secondary level (Chambers 1979 pp. 97–110, McMahon and Melton 1977).

3. The Formation of Expectations

Whether student expectations are formed by a cognitive process, as is emphasized by the rational expectations hypothesis, or as the result of experience, as stressed by adaptive expectations, together with the realism of the resulting expectations, is of significance to educational and other policies designed to aid educational choices and to make labor markets work better. Although average student expectations may

be reasonably close to actual job market outcomes as suggested above, there are changes in the job markets that may not be accurately anticipated, overly myopic expectations held by students coming from disadvantaged backgrounds, wider degrees of uncertainty in recession periods, and wider degrees of uncertainty among females, all of which affect behavior.

Economists have generally assumed in the past in theoretical and econometric models that income (and price) expectations are formed by an adaptive process. Friedman's permanent income hypothesis, for example, assumes that expected future income can be estimated by applying a distributed lag to immediate past incomes using geometrically declining weights. This gives the heaviest weight in the formation of expectations about the future to the most recent past experiences. Students of course do not normally have full-time earnings experience on which to base their expectations about the future growth of earnings but they observe what has happened within their families, to friends in their neighborhoods and school peer groups, to recent graduates, and to older friends of their families and teachers who may sometimes serve as role models. The rational expectations hypothesis has challenged this adaptive process, assuming instead that expectations are formed through a cognitive understanding of how the economy works and what the implications of policy changes are for job markets. Rational expectations are assumed to be subject only to random errors, and to become the basis for deliberate decisions. The dispute between these extremes cannot be settled here, but a more moderate view would suggest that there is some adaptive learning by the student of patterns and of what to expect, as well as some cognitive extrapolation of changes.

Empirical work over 30 years on the formation of expectations leads Katona (1980) to conclude that behavior is guided most commonly by repeated and rewarded past experience. This conditions expectations about the future and is consistent with a major stream of learning theory in psychology. He suggests that expectations about change add a "feeling tone that spreads over very many people and influences action . . . (whereas) the cognitive (rational expectations) content of expectations may be vague and may differ from person to person" (p. 33). Some adaptive effects are direct: high levels of unemployment among teenagers in 1981–83, for example, lowered opportunity costs and thereby raised the expected rate of return to education, maintaining enrollment in the junior colleges in these years in spite of the effects of falling birth rates. However, some job market changes may be cognitively perceived. The American College Testing Program in Iowa City and the College Entrance Examination Board in Princeton provide information to college and high-school counselors on both college costs and on starting salaries in many occupations in the United States (McMahon and Wagner 1981 Table 2). Data on the shape of age–earnings profiles as shown in Table 1 are now available from surveys and census data in many countries.

At the high-school level, Benson (McMahon and Geske 1982 Chap. 3) reports that both neighborhood experiences and the education or socioeconomic status of parents are significant influences on the students' use of time for study and hence presumably on their expectations about the future value of education.

3.1 Are Students Myopic?

It is only recently that student expectations have been studied empirically, and found to be fairly accurate with respect to the growth of earnings that students expect following further education. This was shown in Tables 1 and 2, as well as the earnings growth expected in engineering and other fields in addition to the traditional fields of law and medicine as shown in Table 4. There are significant empirical implications of the fact that students do not appear to be overly myopic, focusing only on starting salaries and on immediate job openings, but anticipate search time after graduation and regard cyclical declines in fields such as engineering as temporary (see *Student Labor Market Expectations*). The controversial thesis of overinvestment in college education, for example, as advanced by Freeman (1975) depends on a myopic preoccupation with starting salaries by students, ignoring the lower opportunity costs of education during the worldwide recessions in 1974-75 and 1980-81 as well as the growth of earnings later in the life cycle.

A model stressing investment by the family, rather than only by the "independent student," stresses that the family's financial resources and the family's expectations as a group help to finance the high-school and college years of most students, and encourage the student's expectations to be less myopic (McMahon 1984).

3.2 The Uncertainty of Expected Earnings

Although analytically uncertainty can either increase investment in human capital as a hedge, or reduce it (Levhari and Weiss 1974, p. 956), there has been little empirical study of students' uncertainty about their future prospects. Table 7 suggests that females have a higher degree of uncertainty about their expected future earnings 25 years hence than do males as one might expect. Schultz (1971 p. 182) has postulated that those with lower ability may be more uncertain about their future prospects. But if anything Table 7 suggests that the higher ability males and females who have the higher American College Testing (ACT) test scores are the ones that are more uncertain about their expected earnings.

Table 7

Uncertainty about future earnings by sex and ability[a]
(1 = very uncertain, to 0 = very certain)

Ability level	Males		Females	
(ACT test scores)	Mean	(n)	Mean	(n)
All ability levels	0.46	1009	0.55	1668
22-highest	0.49	538	0.59	725
18–21	0.46	195	0.54	407
16–17	0.43	85	0.53	164
lowest-15	0.42	191	0.49	372

a Source: Questionnaires and survey as shown in McMahon (1974 Appendix A)

No studies have yet been made of changes in the degree of student uncertainty, or shifts in the dispersion of student expectations over time, although Katona (1980 p. 33) suggests that these changes are relevant to other types of household saving and investment decisions.

In conclusion, expected rates of return appear to be more accurate than might be expected by occupational field, degree level, type of institution, sex, and length of the investment planning horizon. In the absence of accurate means of forecasting manpower needs, they provide a decentralized system with incomplete but useful guides to educational choices conducive to individual and social growth.

See also: Cost–Benefit Analysis in Education; Human Capital and Education

Bibliography

Bowen H 1980 *The Costs of Higher Education: How Much Do Colleges and Universities Spend per Student and How Much Should They Spend?* Jossey-Bass, San Francisco, California

Chambers J 1979 Educational cost differentials. In: Committee of the National Academy of Education 1979 *Economic Dimensions of Education.* National Academy of Education, Washington, DC, pp. 97–116

Eckhaus R S, El Safty A, Norman V D 1974 An appraisal of the calculation of rates of return to higher education. In: Gordon M S (ed.) 1974 *Higher Education and the Labor Market.* McGraw-Hill, New York, pp. 233–71

Ferber M E, McMahon W W 1979 Women's expected earnings and their investment in higher education. *J. Hum. Resour.* 14: 405–20

Freeman R B 1971 *The Market for College-trained Manpower: A Study of the Economics of Career Choice.* Harvard University Press, Cambridge, Massachusetts

Freeman R B 1975 Overinvestment in college training? *J. Hum. Resour.* 10: 287–311

Katona G 1980 How expectations are really formed. *Challenge* 23(5): 32–35

Levhari D, Weiss Y 1974 The effect of risk on the investment in human capital. *Am. Econ. Rev.* 64: 950–63

McMahon W W 1974 *Investment in Higher Education.* Heath, Lexington, Massachusetts

McMahon W W 1984 Why families invest in education. In: Sudman S, Spaeth M (eds.) 1984 *The Collection and Analysis of Consumer Behavior Data: In Memory of Robert Ferber.* University of Illinois Press, Urbana, Illinois

McMahon W W, Geske T (eds.) 1982 *Financing Education: Overcoming Inefficiency and Inequity.* University of Illinois Press, Urbana, Illinois

McMahon W W, Melton C 1977 A cost of living index for Illinois counties and school districts. In: *Perspectives on Illinois School Finance.* United States Office of Education State Aid Equalization Study. Illinois Office of Education, Springfield, Illinois, pp. 74–113

McMahon W W, Wagner A P 1981 Expected returns to investment in higher education. *J. Hum. Resour.* 14: 274–85

McMahon W W, Wagner A P 1982 The monetary returns to education as partial social efficiency criteria. In: McMahon W W, Geske T (eds.) 1982 p. 153

Mincer J 1974 *Schooling, Experience, and Earnings.* National Bureau of Economic Research, New York

Psacharopoulos G 1980a Returns to education: An updated international comparison. In: King T (ed.) 1980 *Education and Income: A Background Study for World Development.* Staff Paper No. 402, World Bank, Washington, DC

Psacharopoulos G 1980b *Higher Education in Developing Countries: A Cost-Benefit Analysis.* Staff Paper No. 440. World Bank, Washington, DC

Psacharopoulos G, Sanyal B 1981a *Student Expectations and Graduate Market Performance in Egypt.* UNESCO-International Institute for Educational Planning, Paris

Psacharopoulos G, Sanyal B 1981b Student expectations and labour market performance: The case of the Philippines. *Higher Educ.* 10: 449–72

Psacharopoulos G, Soumelis C 1979 A quantitative analysis of the demand for higher education. *Higher Educ.* 8: 159–77

Schultz T W 1971 *Investment in Human Capital: The Role of Education and Research.* Free Press, New York

Verry D, Davies B 1976 *University Costs and Outputs.* Elsevier, Amsterdam

Williams G, Gordon A 1981 Perceived earnings functions and ex ante rates of return to post compulsory education in England. *Higher Educ.* 10: 199–227

W. W. McMahon

Expenditure on Education: International Statistics

Evidence on international differences in educational expenditure is limited generally to data on public expenditures. The developed nations of Europe and the Americas spend significantly more than the developing nations of Africa and Asia, although differences have begun to narrow slightly. For the world as a whole, per capita public education spending in 1978 was US$146, or 5.6 percent of world gross national product (GNP).

1. Data Availability

The most complete set of statistics on international educational expenditures is compiled and published by UNESCO. Their *Statistical Yearbook*, published annually, provides data on educational expenditures of approximately 200 nations and territories, based upon official replies to UNESCO questionnaires and special surveys. These data refer solely to public expenditure on education—that is, government-financed expenditures for public education plus subsidies for private education. Private expenditures on education are not published by UNESCO because few nations gather such information. It is possible to compare private consumption expenditures allocated to education for member nations of the Organisation for Economic Co-operation and Development (OECD).

2. Public Expenditures on Education

Tables 1 and 2 summarize statistics on public expenditures on education for specific regions and countries. Table 1 groups nations by continents as well as development status in offering comparative expenditure data for 1965 and 1978. Spending totals are presented both as a percent of GNP and on a per capita basis expressed in United States dollars. According to these data, total world spending on education increased significantly from 1965 to 1978, measured either as a percent of world GNP or in absolute dollars per capita. However, both the level of and increase in spending differ across regions of the world. The level of spending in both years is far greater on the continents of America and Europe

Table 1

Public expenditures on education 1965 and 1978[a]

	Percent of GNP		Per inhabitant (in US$)	
	1965	1978	1965	1978
World	4.8	5.6	38	146
Africa	3.4	4.8	6	29
America (North and South)	5.1	6.0	94	291
Asia	3.5	5.0	7	55
Europe (including the Soviet Union)	5.0	5.7	63	271
Northern America[b]	5.4	6.6	187	622
Latin America[b]	3.0	4.0	13	60
Developed nations[c]	5.1	5.9	86	366
Developing nations[c]	2.9	4.1	5	26

a Source: UNESCO *Statistical Yearbook 1981* Table 2.12   b Northern America includes Bermuda, Canada, Greenland, St. Pierre and Miquelon, and the United States. Latin America includes the rest of America   c Developed nations include all European countries, the Soviet Union, the United States, Canada, Japan, Israel, Australia, and New Zealand. Developing nations are the rest of the world excluding South Africa, People's Republic of China, Democratic People's Republic of Korea, Laos, and Vietnam

than Africa or Asia. Measured in terms of changes in spending between 1965 and 1978, the ranking of regions is just reversed: the largest increases in education spending occurred in developing nations on the continents of Africa and Asia. While these differential changes from 1965 to 1978 have tended to reduce differences in educational expenditures, the spending gap between rich and poor nations is still very wide.

Educational expenditures for selected countries

Table 2

Public expenditures on education by selected countries 1977[a]

	Percent of GNP	Percent of total government spending	Per inhabitant (in US$)
Argentina	2.4	10.7	49
Australia	6.5	16.2	455
Bahamas (1978)	9.8	22.9	228
Brazil	3.6	NA[b]	51
Canada	8.3	18.9	694
Colombia (1978)	2.3	19.9	20
Egypt	4.7	NA	27
Federal Republic of Germany	4.7	9.9	373
France	5.5	NA	397
Haiti	1.3	NA	3
India	2.9	9.9	5
Indonesia (1976)	2.0	8.7	7
Israel	7.7	7.0	317
Italy (1978)	4.6	9.8	212
Japan	5.5	16.5	339
Mexico	4.8	11.7	54
Netherlands	8.4	NA	646
Nigeria	3.8	12.5	22
Soviet Union	7.4	12.3	155
Spain (1976)	2.1	16.8	63
Sweden	8.4	12.7	797
Switzerland	5.2	18.9	520
United Kingdom (1976)	6.3	14.3	254
United States	6.3	17.7	558

a Source: UNESCO *Statistical Yearbook 1981* Table 4.1 and 1977 population and exchange rate data   b NA = not available appear in Table 2. Data refer to 1977. Three types of data are offered: expenditures on education as a percent of GNP; expenditures on education as a percent of total goverment expenditures; and expenditures per capita in United States dollars. As a percent of GNP, Haiti spends the least on education among all nations and the Bahamas spends the most. In absolute dollar amounts, Haiti spends the least per capita, while Sweden spends the most. Generally the developed nations of Europe and North America spend more dollars on education and devote a larger fraction of their GNP to it than do African, Asian, or South American countries. Education spending accounts for between 10 and 20 percent of all government spending. Countries that spend relatively more on education generally devote a larger share of their total spending to it, but the correlation is by no means exact.

2.1 The Distribution of Expenditures

Table 3 offers statistics on various types of education expenditures for selected countries in 1977. The first column shows the percent of total public education spending devoted to current expenditures, which include spending on administration, emoluments of teachers and staff, school books and teaching materials, scholarships, and maintenance of buildings.

All other expenditures are classified as capital spending. Roughly 80 to 90 percent of all spending is classified as current, with developed nations reporting the higher percentage figures.

Another way to classify spending is by level of education. UNESCO provides current expenditure data for five levels of education — preprimary, first level (primary), second level (secondary), third level (postsecondary or higher), and all other types. The vast majority of public spending is for first, second, or third level. Table 3 reports the percentages of current expenditures devoted to primary education and higher education. In general developing nations spend relatively more at the primary level than do developed nations, while developed nations spend relatively more on higher education, although once again the correlation is not exact.

3. Private Expenditures on Education

Much less is known about international differences in private spending on education. However, this limitation may not be too severe since the vast majority of education spending is government financed. The United States publishes detailed information on its sources of education spending. For 1977 total expenditures from all sources amounted to $140.4

Table 3
Distribution of public expenditures on education by selected countries 1977[a]

	Percent allocated to current expenditures	Percent of current expenditures allocated to primary education	Percent of current expenditures allocated to higher education
Argentina	86.1	39.9	20.6
Australia	87.0	NA[b]	26.6
Bahamas (1978)	84.3	NA	NA
Brazil (1978)	NA	34.2	30.4
Canada	92.2	NA	26.8
Colombia (1978)	76.6	51.4	19.7
Egypt	81.5	NA	32.8
Federal Republic of Germany	85.2	17.9	15.4
France	NA	17.5	13.6
Haiti (1978)	NA	61.0	7.6
India (1975)	NA	21.2	22.0
Israel	87.5	33.7	26.8
Italy (1978)	89.4	30.2	10.1
Japan	NA	38.9	11.1
Mexico	NA	40.5	28.8
Netherlands	85.0	19.7	28.0
Nigeria (1978)	71.5	42.6	35.3
Soviet Union	83.4	36.0	13.6
Spain (1976)	87.3	61.2	15.1
Sweden	89.9	37.7	11.0
Switzerland	85.2	NA	16.5
United Kingdom (1976)	90.9	24.4	19.9
United States	91.1	NA	30.1

a Source: UNESCO. *Statistical Yearbook 1981*. Tables 4.1 and 4.3   b NA = not available billion, or 7.4 percent of GNP. According to Table 2 public education spending in the United States was 6.3 percent of GNP, so by inference, private spending on education represented a relatively modest 1.1 percent. As evidence below will suggest, most nations devote far fewer private resources to education.

The OECD publishes private consumption expenditures for selected developed nations. Table 4 reproduces these figures for 1977. Column one presents private per capita consumption expenditures on education in United States dollars for selected OECD nations. Per capita spending varies from a high of $139 in Canada and $107 in the United States to a low of $9 in Italy, the Netherlands, and Sweden.

Table 4
Private consumption expenditures on education by selected countries 1977[a]

	Per inhabitant (in US$)	Percent of total consumption expenditures allocated to education
Australia	20	0.46
Belgium	11	0.21
Canada	139	2.86
Denmark	40	0.77
France	14	0.31
Greece	33	1.80
Italy	9	0.36
Netherlands	9	0.21
Norway	24	0.50
Spain	54	2.36
Sweden	9	0.17
United Kingdom	57	2.17
United States	107	1.94

a Source: *National Accounts of OECD Countries: Vol. 2 — Detailed Tables, 1962–1979* Table 5

The second column shows the percentage of total consumption spending allocated to spending on education in the various nations. In general, consumers in countries with high private education spending devote a larger fraction of their budget to education: Canadian consumers devote the largest fraction to education and Swedish consumers the smallest. Among European nations, Spain and the United Kingdom report the highest private consumption expenditures on education.

Bibliography

Organisation for Economic Co-operation and Development (OECD) 1981 *National Accounts of OECD Countries, Vol. 2: Detailed Tables, 1962-1979.* OECD, Paris

UNESCO 1981 *Statistical Yearbook.* UNESCO, Paris
United States Department of Education 1980 *Digest of Education Statistics.* United States Department of Education, Washington, DC

J. W. Graham

Experience-based Curriculum

Experiential learning is usually defined as "learning in which the learner is directly in touch with the realities being studied. Experiential learning typically involves not merely observing the phenomenon being studied but also doing something with it, such as testing the dynamics of the reality to learn more about it, or applying the theory learned to deliver some desired result" (Keeton and Tate 1978a).

However, others define it more broadly as the living through of events and assert that, at least for the purposes of building an experiential taxonomy, "There is no taxonomic difference between an experience in which one is physically involved or one in which there is vicarious involvement" (Steinaker and Bell 1979 p. 9). Steinaker and Bell's generic experiential taxonomy includes five levels: exposure, participation, identification, internalization, and dissemination.

The concept of experiential learning is related to other older terms in education such as discovery learning, lifelong learning, fieldwork, school–community education, and clinical experience. There has been a recent resurgence of interest in experience-based learning by educational institutions, although learning by doing, master–protégé, as well as other types of apprenticeship arrangements, are of ancient and historic vintage. A modern counterpart for this historic orientation occurs in the lifelong learning movement encouraged by UNESCO for both developed and developing countries. In their view, lifelong learning "includes formal, nonformal, and informal learning extended throughout the life span of an individual and . . . includes learning that occurs in the home, school, community and workplace and through mass media [becoming] a continuous quest for a higher and better quality of life" (Dave 1975 p. 42).

Today, experience-based curricula or programs exist at the elementary, secondary, collegiate, and graduate levels. They may be either alternatives to formal instruction, supplementary to or integrated with classroom instruction.

At the elementary level, experiential learning is often encouraged in classrooms taught by teachers familiar either with the cognitive development theories of Jean Piaget or with John Dewey's emphasis on discovery of the "backward and forward connection between what we do to things and what we suffer from things in consequence" (Dewey 1964 p. 140). In those classrooms, the role of the teacher is "to provide a variety of concrete materials for the children to manipulate, to allow and encourage them to work with and learn from one another, and to assist them in their efforts to assimilate information from their environment by asking them questions which will help them to think about and interpret their experiences" (Bank et al. 1981 p. 133). Mathematics and science materials for such classrooms have been developed by the Nuffield Foundation (1967), among others, and are used in infant schools in England and Wales.

At the secondary level, experiential learning programs have focused on a number of subject areas. Foremost among them are work experience and training programs, career exploration programs, and community service programs. During the 1970s, at least four different models for experience-based career education programs were developed for use in United States high schools. Additional areas in which local experiential learning programs have been created are writing, outdoor education, consumer education, and health care (see *Outdoor Education*; *Consumer Education*; *Health Education Programs*). Special secondary-school populations served by experiential programs include the handicapped, the gifted, and migrant children (see *Gifted and Talented, Education of*).

James Coleman's contrast between an information assimilation instructional pattern whose medium is symbolic language—written, spoken, visual, or graphic—and an experiential learning pattern whose medium is the reality of natural, constructed, social, and cultural environments encouraged reform-minded educators in the 1970s to assert that the two interactional patterns are not conflicting but complementary (Coleman 1976). However, some educators resist experiential education partly because of unresolved issues of how to maintain academic quality, how to assess achievement of outcomes, and how to plan relationships among purposes, procedures, and outcomes without adequate research-based knowledge.

Evaluation studies, rather than research studies, have been the dominant mode of inquiry about secondary schools' experience-based programs. Shortcomings of those studies include lack of an adequate conceptual framework, an absence of a comparison group to identify program effects, and they focus on short-term rather than long-term impacts.

A coordinated approach to research on experiential education at the secondary level has been suggested by Owens et al. (1979). Among their suggestions are:

(a) derive specific postulates that could help explain existing findings about experiential programs and direct future research and planning from theories about social learning, attribution, maturation, personal/social development;

(b) identify instruments that can detect significant gains for particular populations and for particular outcomes; develop new instruments to fill the gaps;

(c) synthesize study findings, differentiating by relevant participants' characteristics such as age, sex, achievement level, socioeconomic status.

In higher education, two areas of paramount concern related to experiential education are: (a) how to assess students' previously acquired life or work experiences, and (b) how to organize sponsored work experience or clinical programs within collegiate or graduate studies.

Both of these concerns have been stimulated by an increasingly heterogeneous student population of older adults. Some are returning to undergraduate or graduate work with extensive experience. Others are seeking professional advancement, credentials, or skills for career shifts.

Colleges and universities therefore have had to develop standardized procedures for placing such students in appropriate courses, for modifying existing programs to fit the special needs of skilled students, and for granting course credit for work or life experience. This has become an especially pressing need for those higher-education institutions which grant external or professional degrees or operate continuing education programs. Among the procedures they use to assess prior work experience are portfolio evaluations, testimony and references, structured interviews, and oral examinations.

The justification of experiential learning programs within the university setting has been traced by Maehl (1982) to scholarly empirical inquiries into archeology and history emanating from nineteenth-century German universities.

> The tools of this new knowledge were essentially experiential. Rhetoric was replaced by research. Direct experiences with original artifacts and documentary sources, field and laboratory methods were reserved for those elite students who were permitted to participate in original research, whose "home" in the German university was the graduate seminar. (p. 33)

Among the experiential courses currently offered at the graduate level and integrated with regular degree programs are internships, practica, directed field work, supervised clinical work, practice teaching, and studio art. In assessing these offerings, some argue that generic characteristics for experiential courses should be the same as those for didactic courses: rigor, that is, possessing academic quality controls and standards; appropriateness, that is, integral to overall program goals; and balance, that is, only one of several approaches to the study of the discipline or profession (Jacobs 1982).

Theory development, research on the effects of crediting prior experience, and the systematic development of experiential formats has lagged behind the practical needs of educational institutions to respond quickly to student needs. Kolb (1976) has described a four-stage learning cycle which uses (a) concrete experience as the basis for (b) observation and reflection, which in turn assist in the (c) formulation of concepts and generalizations, they, in turn, leading to (d) testing of concepts in new situations, which is then followed by additional concrete experience. Other work on styles of learning and teaching suggest that experiential learning programs may have special benefits for certain students, for specific disciplines, for particular types of learning outcomes, and under particular conditions. "Given the utility of experiential methods in classroom as well as nonclassroom learning, in independent study as well as in group endeavors, the outcomes of a research effort in this field are likely to enrich and be applicable to the whole of higher education" (Keeton and Tate 1978b p. 99).

See also: Experiential Learning for Adults

Bibliography

Bank A, Henerson M, Eu L 1981 *A Practical Guide to Program Planning: A Teaching Models Approach.* Teachers College Press, New York
Coleman J S 1976 Differences between experiential and classroom learning In: Keeton M T (ed.) 1976 *Experiential Learning: Rationale, Characteristics and Assessment.* Jossey-Bass, San Francisco, California
Dave R H (ed.) 1975 *Reflections on Lifelong Education and the Schools.* UIE Monograph 3. UNESCO Institute for Education, Hamburg
Dewey J 1964 *Democracy and Education: An Introduction to the Philosophy of Education.* Macmillan, New York
Jacobs F 1982 Experiential programs in practice: Lessons to be learned. In: Jacobs F, Allen R J (eds.) 1982 *Expanding the Missions of Graduate and Professional Education.* Jossey-Bass, San Francisco, California
Keeton M T, Tate P J 1978a The boom in experiential learning. In: Keeton M T, Tate P J (eds.) 1978 *Learning by Experience: What, Why, How.* Jossey-Bass, San Francisco, California
Keeton M T, Tate P J 1978b What next in experiential learning? In: Keeton M T, Tate P J (eds.) 1978 *Learning by Experience: What, Why, How.* Jossey-Bass, San Francisco, California
Kolb D A 1976 *Learning Style Inventory: Self-scoring Test and Interpretation Booklet.* McBer, New York
Maehl W H Jr 1982 The graduate tradition and experiential learning. In: Jacobs F, Allen R J (eds.) 1982 *Expanding the Missions of Graduate and Professional Education.* Jossey-Bass, San Francisco, California
Nuffield Foundation 1967 *I Do and I Understand; Beginnings; The Duck Pond; Apparatus; Animals and Plants and Others.* Wiley, New York
Owens T R, Owen S K, Druian G 1979 *Experiential Learning Programs: Synthesis of Findings and Proposed Framework for Future Evaluations.* Northwest Regional Laboratory Education and Work Program, Portland, Oregon
Steinaker N A, Bell M R 1979 *The Experiential Taxonomy: A New Approach to Teaching and Learning.* Academic Press, New York

A. Bank

Experiential Learning for Adults

While all learning is an experience, the concept of experiential learning as a subject for educational research began only in the early 1930s in the United States. In its simplest form the term "experiential learning" connotes learning from experience or learning by doing. Interest in this form of learning has expanded in recent years, largely as a reaction to the more passive, traditional methods of education. These latter methods are primarily concerned with transferring already assimilated knowledge from the teacher to the student through books and specialized language.

1. Historical Background

In noncomplex societies living and learning are naturally combined, typically in a family setting and with different adults assuming the role of teachers for succeeding generations. With increasing industrialization, educational systems for providing more specialized knowledge and skills are required. Practical education tends to be supervised by craft guilds, industry, and the workplace while universities assume responsibility for research, technical and professional training, and classical studies. This pattern was particularly evident in Western Europe, with a gradual replacement of older more experience-based systems by formal educational institutions.

The experiential learning "movement" began in the mid-nineteenth century as a means of redressing the balance between formal abstract learning and practical experience. "Laboratory sciences," "applied studies," and "clinical experiences" were introduced into academe at this time. Early in the twentieth century "cooperative education" (various forms of off-campus experiences) were initiated as radically innovative complements to classroom learning. In 1939 John Dewey made an incisive contribution to the developing movement in *Experience and Education.* In this short work Dewey urged that all sources of experience be added to traditional forms of education and suggested an "intellectual" method for affirming such learning.

2. The Experiential Learning Model

Our lives consist of thousands of trivial and significant experiences daily. For these experiences to become learning, or for change to occur in awareness and behavior, selected experiences are singled out, reflected and acted upon. "Experiential learning means the learning that occurs when changes in judgments, feelings, knowledge or skills result for a particular person from living through an event or events" (Chickering 1977). While the subject of experiential learning may have once implied an either/or dichotomy with traditional methods, researchers are beginning to view them as parts of a whole.

A model which illustrates this process (Kolb and Fry 1975) depicts learning as a four-stage cycle with each stage requiring different abilities and skills on the part of the learner. As illustrated in Fig. 1, stage (a) is a concrete personal experience which is followed by (b) observation and reflection of that experience. These reflections are connected to and reworked into (c) abstract concepts and generalizations which are (d) then tested in new situations. In turn these lead to new experiences for a repetition of the cycle. In order for learning or change to take place, the four stages of the cycle must be integrated; for example, an experience which is not reflected upon or is not tested in actual practice, is lost as potential learning.

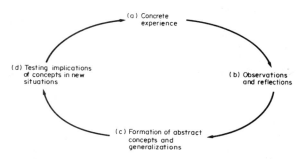

Figure 1
The experiential learning model

The process may take place over a span of time, within formal and informal learning environments, intra- or inter-personally, and/or through actual or vicarious experience. One of Kolb's findings suggests that individuals have preferred styles of learning which affect their choices and patterns of learning; for example, some people learn best through experiences while others prefer a more conceptual mode. The traditional (conceptual) method in teaching and learning is described by the model as beginning at stage three. The selection of one predominant mode over another depends on what is being learned, the context in which the learning takes place, and the skills and abilities of the teacher and learner. Whichever mode is selected as a starting point, successful learning depends on realizing each of the stages.

3. Approaches to the Study of Experiential Learning

Two main themes can be identified in current research in the field of experiential learning, based on the definition of experience and the context in which it is being examined; pragmatic–institutional and individual–existential. Several approaches are distinguishable within each theme, each with distinct implications for the design, facilitation, and evaluation of learning.

3.1 Theme One: Pragmatic–Institutional

This theme focuses on the participation of the learner in acquiring or mastering concrete skills based on a sequence of learning events specified in advance. While this kind of learning takes place naturally in everyday life, the literature appears to be limited to that which occurs within credit-granting institutions. The following approaches are elaborations of this theme.

(a) *Learning by doing*—learning as a result of direct experience is the commonly accepted definition of experiential learning. In developing countries this term is interchangeable with experience-based education or training (see *Experience-based Curriculum*). Examples are most forms of apprenticeship, agricultural and industrial training programs, modular instructional programs, athletic and wilderness training.

(b) *Sponsored or cooperative education*—the primary focus in the area of "guided," "sponsored," or "cooperative education" is learning which is undertaken within the structure of a college or university program in an off-campus setting. Close liaison between faculty and field supervisor is considered important for the purpose of designing and measuring learning goals. Programs of this type include preprofessional training practicums and internships, career exploration, service–learning internships, field research, cross-cultural and overseas experiences. Problematic for the institution is the articulation of appropriate learning objectives and the establishment of procedures for measuring skills and competencies gained (Chickering 1977).

(c) *Credit for life experience*—many of the new students enrolling in academic programs have acquired learning through a range of life activities, jobs, and/or community involvement. A large number of these learners tend to be female, from minority groups, and/or working class, who are disadvantaged by seeking work in a society which requires academic qualifications for better paying jobs. One way to help these learners is to validate their prior experience and offer commensurate credit. Traditional intelligence tests and standard assessment procedures have not been found adequate for these learners. The Council for Advancement of Experiential Learning was formed in the United States in 1973 to conduct research in this area.

3.2 Theme Two: Individual–Existential

This field of inquiry values personal experience as an important source of knowledge and places the learner at the center of the learning process. "Truth" is relative to each learner in his or her particular social context and "teachers" perform supportive or facilitative roles. The whole person (mind, body, and emotions) is involved in the process of discovery on a variety of dimensions. Four different approaches (overlapping in some respects) have developed from this value base (Rogers 1969).

(a) *Learning how to learn*—living in a society undergoing rapid social change requires continued education and re-education. According to Tough (1971) 80 percent of the population is continually engaged in a series of learning projects of which only 20 percent are occurring in formal classes. Kidd (1973) helped our understanding of how this majority learns and undertook groundbreaking work in revaluing experiential learning on an international institutional level. Knowles (1975) has directly addressed the issue of facilitating self-directed learning for diverse types of learners. Elaboration of the concept of lifelong learning has been an important aspect of research in this area.

(b) *Personal learning from everyday experience*—another focus views experiential learning as moving from concerns with outer-directed world experiences to inner-directed personal ones. "Experiential learning involves becoming aware of the qualities, patterns and consequences of one's own experiences as one experiences it" (Torbert 1972). This author posits four levels of experiences as a basis for learning: (i) the world outside; (ii) a person's behavior; (iii) a person's internal cognitive–emotional–sensory structure; (iv) a person's consciousness or intentional life aims. Compatible with Kolb's experiential learning cycle, each of these levels requires reflection, conceptualization, and testing in new situations for learning to occur. Examples of this type of learning are experiential therapies, for example, Jungian and Gestalt, meditation, dream analysis, and journal writing (Torbert 1972, More 1974).

(c) *Experiential social group processes*—a natural extension of learning from personal experience has been the development of a wide range of social skill training activities frequently referred to as laboratory or human relations training. In T-groups (T for training), the experience of the members in a relatively unstructured environment becomes data for personal and social learning. Experiential learning groups ranging from management training to personal growth have spawned numerous educational innovations. Well-known centers for training leadership in this area have been the National Training Laboratories (US) and Tavistock (England) (Cooper and Alderfer 1978, Torbert 1972).

(d) *Experiential learning in the classroom*—the group process movement has enriched classroom learning with a host of new activities. Role plays, games and simulations, value exercises, and socio- and psycho-drama engage learners in concrete experiences which, when processed, lead to cognitive as well as attitudinal and behavioral change. Other activities include the use of audiovisual methods, art, drama, music, dance, and play. Critical in using these methods is the provision of adequate time for reflection and conceptualization (Coleman 1976).

(e) *Experiential learning for social and political action*—the national and international implications of helping individuals and groups learn from their own experience ("name their world") has been explored by Freire (1970) in his work in Africa and South America. In a postcolonial era, survival for poor countries depends on valuing the knowledge, skills, and experiences of their indigenous people, as contrasted with education imposed by the dominant culture. Popular education programs develop skills based on collective experience in the hope that people will act upon and change oppressive social structures.

4. Areas for Future Research

Research opportunities will accelerate as learning programs in the 1980s move from academic institutions into living and work places. Interest in learning will progress beyond the concerns of individual students to those of communities and organizations who want to develop their capacities to change and grow. Research into age, stage, and gender differences of the developing adult is already having important implications for the design of learning programs. Attention will likely be focused on understanding more about the reflective process and the social nature of learning. Literacy education will increasingly be based on the life experiences of learners. The problem of assessment will demand further research as institutions and learners face the continuing challenge of awarding credentials to the endless variety of experiences which constitute learning.

The study and application of experiential learning will command increasing attention in formal and informal educational settings as adults throughout the world demand greater access to learning which is relevant, effective, and engaging.

See also: Prior Life Experience in Higher Education

Bibliography

Chickering A W 1977 *Experience and Learning: An Introduction to Experiential Learning*. Change Magazine Press, New Rochelle, New York

Coleman J S 1976 Differences between experiential and classroom learning. In: Keeton M T (ed.) 1976 *Experiential Learning: Rationale, Characteristics, and Assessment*. Jossey-Bass, San Francisco, California

Cooper C L, Alderfer C P (eds.) 1978 *Advances in Experiential Social Processes*. Wiley, New York

Dewey J 1963 *Experience and Education*. Collier, New York

Freire P 1970 *Pedagogy of the Oppressed*. Seabury, New York

Kidd J R 1973 *How Adults Learn*. Association Press, New York

Knowles M S 1975 *Self-directed Learning: A Guide for Learners and Teachers*. Association Press, New York

Kolb D A 1984 *Experiential Learning: Experience as the Source of Learning and Development*. Prentice-Hall, Englewood Cliffs, New Jersey

Kolb D, Fry R 1975 Towards an applied theory of experiential learning. In: Cooper C L (ed.) 1975 *Theories of Group Processes*. Wiley, New York

More W S 1974 *Emotions and Adult Learning*. Saxon House, Farnborough

Rogers C R 1969 *Freedom to Learn: A View of What Education Might Become*. Merrill, Colombus, Ohio

Torbert W R 1972 *Learning from Experience: Toward Consciousness*. Columbia University Press, New York

Tough A M 1971 *The Adult's Learning Projects: A Fresh Approach to Theory and Practice in Adult Learning*. Ontario Institute for Studies in Education (OISE), Toronto, Ontario

L. Melamed

Experimental Curriculum

Experimental curriculum, broadly conceived, refers to the attempt to provide a course offering that is different from those currently provided. In addition, the term experimental implies that the offering in question involves formal or informal hypotheses and draws attention to probable consequences. Experimental curricula sometimes use an experimental research design to assess results, but this is not always the case.

The variety of different interpretations of experimental curriculum can be explained in part by the fact that conceptions of curriculum itself vary (Eisner and Vallance 1974, Schubert 1980). For example, if curriculum is defined as a written course of study or document, then experimental curriculum would refer to the extant variation of implementation and outcomes that accrues from a change of policy. If, however, curriculum is defined as all of the experiences which the students have under the auspices of a school, experimental curriculum could pertain to any intervention that had impact upon learning experiences for which the school could be held responsible.

There is great varation as to the breadth or scope of a curricular experiment. It may range from a national policy alteration, to the adoption of a new curriculum by a school district (see *Curriculum Adoption*), or even to the attempt by an individual teacher to try something novel. It may be an attempt to experiment with an entire program, or to do so with a salient feature that runs through a program but does not alter the whole directly, or it may even refer to one relatively minor aspect of a program.

A curriculum experiment may focus upon any one or several of the following topics that perennially appear under the curriculum rubric: purposes, learning experiences or content, scope and sequence, methodology or instruction, learning environments, and evaluation or accountability practices (see *Accountability in Education*).

The variety of types of experimental curricula can be exemplified by a brief sampling drawn from the history of curriculum in this century (see *Curriculum History: An Overview*). John Dewey designed his Laboratory School at the University of Chicago (1896–1904) as an experiment in the sense that it set out to actualize the theory that a school curriculum could become a community that fostered both social and individual growth (see *Curriculum Planning: Community Participation*). Beginning in 1932, the Progressive Education Association designed an experiment to compare students from traditional and progressive curricula of the Deweyan genre, known as the Eight-year Study (see *Eight-year Study*). The unique nature of this project points to two very different orientations to experimental curricula. One form of experimentation consisted of the use of instruments developed to quantitatively and qualitatively portray outcomes of experimental and control groups. However, a second form of experimentation consisted of a deliberation among personnel from the 30 experimental schools about what was worthwhile to teach and learn. In this orientation, experimentation took the form of an encounter among teachers, students, administrators, and consultants who seriously reflected together and revised practices on a continuous basis. This kind of curriculum experimentation is reflected in the teacher-as-researcher movement in England and Wales (Stenhouse 1975). It interprets science as problem solving and interprets curriculum itself as an interaction among commonplaces that Schwab has labeled teacher, learner, subject matter, and milieu (Schwab 1978). Herein lies a practical notion of curriculum experimentation in which hypotheses are tested informally in the consequences of action.

Much more formal is the outgrowth of the dominant form of evaluation research which carefully specifies treatment, verifies its implementation, and tests preordained objectives against outcomes by the use of sophisticated statistical tools or ethnographic observations. Massive national curriculum reforms such as the post-Sputnik projects (Atkin and House 1981) in science and mathematics and antipoverty programs such as Head Start in the United States are often criticized on the grounds that the implementation of specified treatment is not verified (see *Head Start Program*).

Thus, it is both large- and small-scale efforts of considerable variety that have historically been regarded as experimental curricula. They range from national movements to innovative action taken in a specific classroom situation.

See also: Curriculum Tryout

Bibliography

Atkin J M, House E 1981 The federal role in curriculum development, 1950–1980. *Educ. Eval. Policy Anal.* 3(5): 5–36
Eisner E W, Vallance E (eds.) 1974 *Conflicting Conceptions of Curriculum.* McCutchan, Berkeley, California
Schubert W H 1980 *Curriculum Books: The First Eighty Years.* University Press of America, Lanham, Maryland
Schwab J J 1978 *Science, Curriculum, and Liberal Education: Selected Essays.* University of Chicago Press, Chicago, Illinois
Stenhouse L 1975 *Introduction to Curriculum Research and Development.* Heinemann, London

W. H. Schubert

Experimental Design

Experimental design attempts to ensure valid causal inferences from randomized experiments conducted within practical constraints of available resources and time. This design process must first consider whether an experiment is, in fact, feasible. If so, the design process continues and attempts are made to anticipate possible threats to the validity of conclusions and to eliminate or minimize those threats. It should be noted that there is another, more narrow, methodological literature often labeled "experimental design" which is concerned with the associated statistical design and analysis. Important concepts in this statistical literature are included as one component in the broader framework considered here.

1. The Experiment

A "true" or randomized experiment is defined as an inquiry in which experimental units have been randomly assigned to different experimental treatments. A sense of the versatility of the experiment is offered by consideration of each of the elements in this definition. An "inquiry" might be a research study to improve theoretical understanding or an evaluation seeking a pragmatic comparison of different instructional programs. Such inquiries can be conducted either in laboratory settings or in real "field" settings. The experimental "unit" is usually the focus of the inquiry. Thus, in studies of variables influencing the behavior and achievement of individual students, the unit would be the student, while the class would be the appropriate unit in studies of class-level variables on average class outcomes. In other words, an experiment can be used to understand phenomena at any level of the educational hierarchy. The experimental "treatments" may be different levels of a single theoretical construct or variable, for example "degree of structure in instruction," or they may be several instructional programs which differ on many dimensions. Often, one of the treatments is a "control" treatment, that is, a group with no implemented treatment at all. Finally, the random assignment of subjects ("subjects" will be used for "units" hereafter for concreteness) to treatments will result in experimental groups associated with each of the treatments.

An experiment can also be defined as an inquiry in which there are one or more active treatment variables or factors. An active variable is one which has been manipulated in the inquiry, where "manipulation" consists of the random assignment of subjects to different levels of the variable. This definition illustrates that a study may have more than one treatment variable, each variable having multiple treatment levels. For example, an investigator may wish to consider simultaneously the variable "degree of structure" having the three levels of low, medium, and high structure and a second variable "feedback to student" with two levels of "daily feedback" and "no feedback." The subjects would be randomly assigned to each of the resulting six treatment combinations of low structure/daily feedback, and so on. The simultaneous consideration of multiple treatment variables allows the identification and description of interactions between the variables.

The goal of an experiment is causal inference. "Causation," in this context, is defined in a commonsense fashion; if a treatment variable is manipulated or changed while holding constant all other possible determinants of the outcome of interest, and there is a subsequent change in the outcome, then it is said that there is a causal relationship between the manipulated variable and the outcome. There is no implication that the manipulated variable is the only cause of the outcome, only that it is one of probably many causes. It should be noted that use of the concept of causation is sometimes challenged, with some arguing that the concept is "prescientific."

There should be little difficulty, however, with the relatively narrow definition used here, a definition which is compatible with utilitarian inquiry seeking understanding of those variables which can be manipulated in the attempt to improve society.

Typical outcomes or dependent variables of interest in educational inquiry which focuses on the individual student include academic achievement, attitudes, traits, self-perceptions, and job performance. The analysis of outcome data for individuals almost always describes the treatment effect on the central tendency (often the mean) of the outcome; it is also usually of interest to determine any effects on the variability and the shape of the distribution of the outcome variable. When the unit is some aggregate like the class or the school, the investigator will be interested in within-aggregate characteristics like the mean or variability of an individual-level outcome or the correlation between several variables within each class or school. The study of the aggregates may also consider various global outcomes like measures of group or organizational harmony and efficiency.

The experiment, when it is feasible, is a particularly efficacious mode of inquiry for causal inference. This is due to the random assignment of subjects to treatments. Generally, outcome differences across different treatment groups can be the result of two factors—differences in the attributes of the subjects in the different groups and the differential effects of the various treatments. Random assignment creates treatment groups which are initially comparable (in a probabilistic sense) on all subject attributes; it can then be concluded in an experiment that any final outcome differences are due to the treatment effects alone, assuming that other possible threats to validity to be discussed below have been controlled.

2. Threats to Validity

The design of an experiment should ensure adequate validity or truthfulness of conclusions. Cook and Campbell (1979), restructuring somewhat the classical discussion of Campbell and Stanley (1963), have identified four different validities which may be pertinent. These are associated with different aspects of the general experimental goal of concluding that a causal relationship between treatment and outcome constructs does or does not exist in specified populations of units, settings, and times. This conclusion will typically be based on the observed relationship between experimental operationalizations of the constructs of interest for a sample of units, settings, and times. The different validities, then, refer to the following component questions leading to the general conclusion (validity type given in parentheses): (a) Does an empirical relationship between the operationalized variables exist in the population (statistical conclusion validity)? (b) If the relationship exists, is it causal (internal validity)? (c) Can the relationship

between the operationalized variables be generalized to the treatment and outcome constructs of interest (construct validity of cause and effect)? (d) Can the sample relationship be generalized to or across the populations of units, settings, and times of interest (external validity)?

Design can be viewed, in part, as the process of anticipating different possible threats to the validity of conclusions and seeking study procedures which will eliminate or minimize those threats. Some of the many common threats which have been discussed in detail by Campbell and Stanley (1963), Cook and Campbell (1979), and others will now be briefly considered (see *Validity*).

2.1 Statistical Conclusion Validity

The statistical conclusion about the presence or absence of a relationship in the population is often based on statistical hypothesis testing. Statistical conclusion validity results, then, from the use of the appropriate test procedure with acceptable error probabilities. The probability of a false rejection of the null hypothesis of no relationship in the population, that is, the significance level, must be set before the test is conducted, with values of 0.01 or 0.05 usually being considered acceptable. A second error probability is the probability of failing to reject the null hypothesis when it is false. Alternatively, the power of the test defined as the probability of correctly rejecting a false null hypothesis can be considered. For a given significance level and effect size (i.e., strength of relationship), it is possible to determine the sample size required to produce an acceptable power.

The "fail to reject" decision from a test can sometimes be taken further. If the test has adequate power (say 0.90) for the "threshold" effect size defining an effect of practical importance, then a "fail to reject" outcome results in confidence that a practically important relationship does not exist in the population. That is, adequate power allows a decision to "accept," for all practical purposes, the null hypothesis.

Inadequate power is one of the most common threats to statistical conclusion validity when the researcher wishes to be able to detect an effect of practical importance. If the power for the threshold effect size is low, then it is, of course, incorrect to interpret "fail to reject" as implying there is no relationship of practical importance. There are many possible reasons for low power; these reasons and some approaches for ensuring adequate power are discussed in Sect. 4. Another threat is the use of an inappropriate statistical procedure. For example, if important assumptions of the procedure being used are violated by the study data, then the actual error rates may be different from the nominal rates set for the study. Statistical analysis procedures will be discussed briefly in Sect. 5 (see *Hypothesis Testing*)

2.2 Internal Validity

The threats to validity of a conclusion that final outcome differences in a study are due to the treatment effect would consist of any other reasonable explanations for the outcome differences. For example, as indicated in Sect. 1, the primary purpose of random assignment of subjects to treatments is to control the "selection" threat to internal validity, that is, the threat that final outcome differences may simply reflect initial group attribute differences. Randomization also controls some other threats to internal validity. First, once the selection threat is controlled, then a series of threats based on interaction with selection are also controlled. For example, different maturation rates for initially different groups (i.e., the selection × maturation interaction) are not a threat in an experiment. Also, since initial selection is not based on a prescore (e.g., to create "highs" and "lows"), statistical regression to the mean is not a problem.

Cook and Campbell (1979) point out, however, that random assignment may often aggravate other threats to internal validity. Treatment-related attrition and atypical behavior on the part of subjects are two threats which are often due to the differences in desirability typically found across different treatments in an experiment. Subject attrition which is related to the treatment variable may mean the initially comparable groups are no longer comparable at the end of the study; the resulting group attribute differences then represent an alternative explanation for any final outcome differences. Atypical behavior might include either "compensatory rivalry" (the "underdog" trying harder) or "resentful demoralization" on the part of subjects in the less desirable treatments or control groups (see *Hawthorne Effect*; *John Henry Effect*)

2.3 Construct Validity of Causes and Effects

It is important that the treatment and outcome constructs of interest are adequately fitted by the operational manipulations and measures actually used. Construct validity is questioned when there is a "possibility that the operations which are meant to represent a particular cause or effect construct can be construed in terms of more than one construct" (Cook and Campbell 1979 p. 59). Consider a possible study of the effect of "degree of structure" which randomly assigns students to different treatments based on varying structure. If other instructional variables, such as amount of time devoted to helping individuals or amount of diagnostic testing, are also inadvertently varied across the treatments, there will be a question about the "real" reason for any final outcome differences. Threats to construct validity would consist of any reasons for an operation either underrepresenting all of the aspects of a construct or overrepresenting a construct by including irrelevant aspects. For example, since it can be argued that a construct is seldom precisely represented by a single operation, a "mono-operation bias" may result unless multiple operations are used to define both treatment and outcome.

2.4 External Validity

External validity refers to the validity of the generalization of study results to explicit or implicit target populations of subjects, settings, and times. The validity of such generalizations depends, of course, on the degree to which the samples of persons, settings, and times used in the study are representative of the populations of interest. Formal random sampling procedures (e.g., simple random, stratified random, and cluster sampling) and the associated statistical inferential procedures are available and, if used, allow precise statements about the probability of any degree of nonrepresentativeness due to chance (see *Sampling*).

For many research and evaluation studies, however, the assessment of external validity is not so formal and precise (e.g., Bracht and Glass 1968). Often, sampling is not directly from the ultimate target population of interest, but rather from some subpopulation which is accessible to the investigator. This distinction between accessible and target populations means that external validity must then be concerned with the validity of two inferential leaps, one from the sample to the accessible population, and the other from the accessible population to the target population. If the sample is the result of a formal random sampling procedure, then precise statements can be made about the validity of the first inferential leap. Sample size is a critical factor here, as with statistical conclusion validity, with larger sample sizes resulting in an increased confidence in sample representativeness. The validity of the second inference, generalizing from the accessible population to the target population, also depends on representativeness. However, this is not ensured by the use of a formal sampling procedure, but must be demonstrated by adequate similarity between the two populations on all characteristics which might be important contextual variables for the relationship of interest.

A judgment of external validity is also required when a researcher wishes to generalize across different populations or subpopulations. For example, a goal may be to demonstrate that a certain treatment effect is found in both boys and girls and across several grade levels. Of course, such a generalization also implies the researcher must be able to generalize separately to each of the individual subpopulations.

External validity is threatened when there is a combination of two factors: (a) a question about representativeness of the sample, and (b) a possibility of interaction between treatment and subjects, settings, or times. The first factor is present when representativeness has not been ensured through use of an appropriate sampling procedure and/or demonstrated through empirical comparisons. The second factor, interaction, refers to the possibility that the effect of a treatment may vary across the different persons, settings, and times comprising the target population. Thus, any treatment effect found in some ill-defined portion of the target population may not be the same as the effect of interest in the total population. Since in most cases, adequate theory or empirical evidence which convincingly argues against such interaction does not exist, a serious question about representativeness is all that is needed to conclude that external validity has not been demonstrated.

3. The Decision to Use an Experiment

The decision concerning which mode of inquiry to use for a planned causal study involves three questions. (a) Which of the available modes of inquiry, including the experimental, are feasible? (b) What can be achieved with each of the feasible modes under the constraints of allowed resources and time? (c) Which mode is best for the purposes of the inquiry? Consider, first, two of the possible alternative approaches for a quantitative causal inquiry. One alternative is a quasiexperimental approach (Cook and Campbell 1979) in which t..ere is a treatment intervention but no assumption of random assignment of subjects to treatments. One variation of this approach is the "nonequivalent group" design in which treatments are introduced to existing groups. Another variation is the "interrupted time series" design involving assessment of a treatment effect with a series of measures before and after introduction of the treatment. Second, when there is no treatment intervention, that is, in correlational or naturalistic studies, path analysis allows an investigator to determine whether a hypothesized causal model is consistent with observed empirical correlations (see *Structural Equation Models*).

The question of the feasibility of an experiment for the planned inquiry depends in large part on the feasibility of random assignment of the subjects to different treatments. First, many individual attribute variables such as sex, race, age, IQ, personality traits, and so on cannot be experimentally manipulated. Researchers in sociology of education, for example, are often interested in the effects of individual and family attributes, and must use techniques like path analysis in their search for causal models. Also, high levels of variables like pain, fear, and stress could not be included in experiments for obvious ethical reasons, and controversial programs concerning, say, sex education or training in political protest, may not be allowed in some communities for political reasons. Thus, the experiment is not, by definition, an option

when manipulation of the treatment variable is not technically, ethically, or politically feasible.

Another aspect of feasibility is whether it is possible in practice to obtain permission to randomly assign subjects. In laboratory settings, this is usually not difficult, since only the agreement of each volunteer subject is necessary, and volunteers understand before the experiment that assignment to different treatments will be involved. In field settings, however, the same task is often much more difficult. When it is desired to study individuals, such as students or teachers, in their "everyday" work or study environment, it is necessary to obtain permission from both administrative "gatekeepers" of the environment of interest and the subjects themselves. Gatekeepers may often be reluctant to grant such permission because of their concern about possible inconvenience and disruption of work, or their doubts about the value of the treatments being studied. If the gatekeepers do perceive a proposed treatment as being valuable, they may object to the random assignment of some teachers and students to control groups or less desirable treatments. Finally, even if the gatekeepers do permit access to the teachers and students, the potential subjects themselves may choose not to participate for the same reasons given above.

An experiment, if feasible, is usually superior to the alternatives for controlling certain critical threats to internal validity (i.e., the validity of causal inference). This is, of course, an important consideration when conducting a causal inquiry. Random assignment in an experiment does not guarantee correct causal conclusions, but it usually does result in fewer assumptions being required for a causal inference. For example, "selection" is a critical threat for the nonequivalent group design because of the use of intact groups. The investigator must therefore attempt to explicitly model all of the important group differences to allow the necessary statistical adjustments, and there is usually some question about the assumption that the causal modeling is appropriate. Selection (or, in causal modeling terminology, misspecification) is also a serious threat to causal inferences from path analysis in correlational studies. "History" is a potential threat in the interrupted time series design, and it is necessary to assume (with adequate empirical support) that the introduction of the treatment did not coincide with some other event which could have been the real reason for change in the outcome. Both of these threats, selection and history, are controlled by the random assignment in an experiment.

The degree of intervention associated with the different modes of inquiry ranges from the strong intervention of the experiment to the weak or nonexistent intervention in a correlational study. This variation may have important implications. There may be situations, especially in field settings, where overt intervention may distort or change the setting and the behavior of subjects from those of interest (as with, for example, the resentful demoralization or compensatory rivalry mentioned in Sect. 2). Also, since a greater degree of intervention may often take more time to plan and implement and may therefore cost more, the choice of inquiry mode may be partially constrained by available resources and time. Thus, it may be said that the experiment is superior for causal inquiry, other things being equal, but of course the "other things" in the qualification are often not equal.

Since the difficulty of obtaining permission for random assignment often depends on the setting, it is perhaps best to consider the laboratory versus field decision simultaneously with the inquiry mode decision. The dominant factor in selecting the setting is often external validity. If (a) the target setting for the inquiry is a real field setting, (b) the setting is viewed as important in influencing the phenomena of interest, and (c) it is not feasible to design a laboratory setting to adequately simulate the field setting, then a field setting is clearly needed for acceptable external validity. For example, the basic premise in research on "contextual effects" in the school setting is that context is an important determinant of individual teacher or student behavior; such research would thus usually require field research in school settings. On the other hand, many instructional treatments are designed for efficiently teaching specific topics to small groups of students and often might best be studied in laboratory settings.

The laboratory versus field decision also has other implications. For example, the greater control of irrelevant factors which is allowed in the laboratory setting would provide, for the same sample size, greater statistical power than would be found in the relatively "noisy" field setting, thus improving statistical conclusion validity. The tighter control on the implementation of treatments in the laboratory would also contribute to construct validity. Finally, the arrangement for and implementation of studies in field settings, especially when there are multiple widespread sites, will often be more time consuming and costly than a laboratory study.

The interaction of the laboratory versus field decision with the inquiry mode decision can be illustrated with a situation where both the laboratory and the field settings may be viable options for an inquiry. Depending on the circumstances, the choice may be difficult. Assume, for example, the gatekeepers for the field setting of interest will allow a treatment intervention but not random assignment. The investigator is then faced with the choice between a laboratory experiment or a field quasiexperiment. Some of the factors involved in such a choice would include the extent to which the laboratory setting simulates the target setting, the comparability of intact groups available in the field setting, the potential for sys-

tematic attrition and atypical behavior in each of the settings, the resources and time required to conduct the inquiry in each setting, and the relative importance of the different validities for the study.

In summary, there is no suggestion here that an experimental approach, assuming it is feasible, should always be used. Rather, the choice of the optimal approach should involve an estimation of the validities of conclusions which could be obtained under each of the feasible alternatives. The different inquiry modes and settings typically offer different strengths and weaknesses, and the final choice will be the setting/mode combination which best fits the purpose of the inquiry.

4. Design of the Experiment

The "decision to use an experiment" and the "design of the experiment" may at first appear to be two separate steps in the conduct of an inquiry. As indicated in the previous section, however, the choice of a mode of inquiry implies at least a partial design for each of several approaches to predict the relative strengths and weaknesses of each. The current section, then, is concerned with the continuation and refinement of the design process already underway, assuming that an experiment is to be used.

Design is concerned with anticipating and eliminating or minimizing important threats to validity within the constraints of available resources and time. It is not possible here to discuss design considerations associated with all of the many possible validity threats, but the process can be illustrated with several of the more common design concerns. First, different approaches to ensuring adequate statistical power will be discussed. Relatively more space is devoted to this topic, not because it is logically more important than other topics, but because it has proven to be more amenable to quantification and elaboration and has been considered extensively in the literature. Next, the internal validity threat of treatment-related attrition of subjects will be discussed. Finally, the importance of detailed descriptive information for validity will be emphasized.

4.1 Power

Consider a simple experiment with two treatments. The treatment effect size is defined here as the difference in the outcome means for the two populations associated with the treatments. As indicated in Sect. 2, the investigator can define a threshold value of the effect size which represents a difference of practical or scientific importance. Once the level of significance is specified, there are two remaining parameters which influence the power of the hypothesis test (in this case, a t-test) to detect an effect equal to the threshold value. One is the sample size, n; an increase in n, other things being equal, results in an increase in power. The second is the error variability, often represented with the standard error of estimate. For the simple two-group t-test, this is just the estimated standard deviation of the outcome variable, Y, for each of the two populations. It can also be understood by reference to the analysis model which underlies the test of interest, a model which expresses Y as a function of one or more independent variables. (The model for the t-test consists simply of a single "dummy" variable representing the active treatment variable.) The error variability, then, is the variability of Y which is not explained by the independent variables in the model. Since error variability can also be viewed as background noise in which the treatment effect is embedded, increasing error variability makes it more difficult to detect the effect, that is, it decreases the power.

The most direct route to ensuring adequate power for a test is simply to determine and use the sample size required for a power of, say, 0.90 to detect the threshold effect size. This is easily accomplished with available tables (e.g., Cohen 1977) and adequate resources. An estimate of the anticipated size of the standard error of estimate is required, but otherwise the determination is straightforward. Unfortunately, the required sample size for an analysis model consisting of just the active treatment variable(s) can often be larger than study resources will allow. Also, even if the required n would be allowed by the study budget, most investigators would still be interested in improving the efficiency of the inquiry to achieve the same power with smaller n and less cost.

The key to improving the efficiency of a test lies in the control of and reduction of the error variability. There are two general approaches to this goal. Consider, first, the different contributors to error for an analysis model containing just the active treatment variables. The error variability is due to measurement error in Y, the inherent variability associated with the target populations of subjects and settings, and variability due to extraneous study factors such as undesired variation in treatment implementation or the occurrence of atypical events during the study. Two obvious ways to improve efficiency, then, would be to improve the reliability of the Y measure and to minimize extraneous factors operating in the study. Also, the investigator may choose to use subject and/ or setting subpopulations which are more homogeneous than the target populations. The increase in power associated with this last approach, however, would be accompanied by a threat to external validity of the study.

The second basic approach to error reduction attacks the problem of population heterogeneity, not by using a more homogeneous subpopulation, but by expanding the analysis model to include one or more attribute variables which are related to the outcome variable. The addition of such "control" variables to the model already containing the active treatment variables will result in an increase of the Y variability which is explained by the model and a corresponding decrease in the unexplained or error variability. Randomized block designs and analysis of covariance (ANCOVA) designs are two main variations on this theme which have been developed in the experimental statistical design literature (e.g., Kirk 1968, Myers 1979, Neter and Wasserman 1974, Winer 1971) (see *Analysis of Variance and Covariance*).

The randomized block design can be illustrated with a simple experiment involving one active treatment variable with *k* levels. If there is large variability of ability in the population of students of interest and a strong relationship between Y and ability, then the investigator may elect to block on ability. The sample of students would be ranked on ability and grouped into homogeneous blocks of size *k* based on this ranking. Then, the *k* students in each block would be randomly assigned, one to each of the *k* treatment levels. Randomization within the blocks is often referred to as a restriction in randomization. The associated analysis model consists of two independent variables, the treatment variable and the categorical blocking variable, with the addition of the blocking variable resulting in the desired reduction in error variability.

A blocking variable is most effective when subjects within blocks are very homogeneous and there is great heterogeneity between blocks. Since the blocking variable is a categorical variable, it can be formed in many different ways. In addition to using a ranking on a single interval variable (as in the example above), blocks can also be created by combining several interval, ordinal, or nominal variables. Another way to create blocks is to expose each subject to each of the *k* treatments, considering each individual subject to be a block. This repeated measures design may be said to permit each subject to "act as his/her own control," and can provide very efficient tests; it should only be used, however, when there is confidence that there is no "carry-over" effect from treatment to treatment.

Analysis of covariance is similar to a randomized block design in that it reduces error variability and increases power by adding one or more control variables (called covariates or concomitant variables) to the analysis model. It is also different, however, in several important aspects. Analysis of covariance does not involve any initial restriction on randomization like that in randomized block designs. That is, subjects are randomly assigned to the different treatment levels without regard to covariate values. Also, ANCOVA assumes the covariate is an interval rather than categorical variable; thus, it is necessary to properly specify the functional nature of the relationship between Y and the covariate (i.e., whether it is linear or nonlinear). It is assumed that the covariates are measured before implementation of the treatments or, if not, that they have not been affected by the treatments. In addition to increasing power, ANCOVA also allows an adjustment of outcome differences to compensate for any initial group differences resulting from the random assignment.

When a potential control variable is an interval variable, the investigator may chose to use it either as a covariate or to create a blocking variable. Since (a) analogous randomized block and ANCOVA designs provide roughly the same power for typical Y—control variable correlations, (b) both designs in their classical form have similar assumptions (e.g., that there is no interaction between the treatment and control variables), and (c) both can be modified to handle violations of these assumptions (see Sect. 5), it makes little difference for these considerations which design is used. One possible basis for a choice between the two would lie in the assumed measurement level of the control variable. If the investigator does not wish to be concerned about the nature of the functional relationship between the outcome and control variables, the randomized block design would be chosen. On the other hand, use of an ANCOVA will allow an explicit description of the Y–covariate relationship, a description which may be of interest in its own right when nonlinear relationships are discovered. A second basis of choice is that the decision to use the randomized block design must be made before the start of the study because of the required restriction in randomization. In contrast, the decision to use an ANCOVA can be made at any time during or after the study, as long as appropriate covariate measures are available.

In summary, there are many approaches to the improvement of the power of a test. The goal usually is to provide acceptable power for detecting the threshold effect size. However, it should be noted that even when this goal cannot be realized because of limited resources and a small sample size, continuation of the inquiry is still legitimate as long as the limitations are recognized. In this situation, the investigator is gambling that the real effect size is sufficiently greater than the threshold value so that there is a good chance of detecting it. Also, it must be recognized that the "fail to reject" conclusion in this case offers little information about whether an effect of practical importance really exists.

Finally, the above discussion assumes that hypothesis testing is the inferential mode being used to make decisions about the presence or absence of a relationship in the population. Interval estimation can also be used with (or instead of) hypothesis testing to describe the treatment effects. All of the above discussion also applies to interval estimation, except the criterion is, instead of adequate power, the desired maximum width of the confidence intervals on treatment contrasts (see *Analysis of Variance and Covariance*).

4.2 Treatment-related Attrition

Even when initial comparability of treatment groups has been achieved through random assignment, the presence of treatment-related attrition of the subjects can result in groups which are no longer comparable at the end of the study, a nonequivalence which may be the real reason for any outcome differences. One important facet of the attack on this problem is the avoidance of any unnecessary burden, inconvenience, or frustration for subjects which may result in their leaving the study. For example, efforts to work within the schedule of each subject or to provide necessary transportation may pay off in reduced attrition. It is more difficult to avoid differences in the desirability of different treatments in a study, differences which are probably the major reason for treatment-related attrition. This may be especially true for control groups which do not have the benefit of any treatment at all. One possible way to improve the retention of subjects in control groups and less desirable treatment groups is to promise that these subjects may have the superior treatment at some later date.

When some attrition does occur in a study, it is important to gather the necessary information to determine if it is related to the treatments. Thus, each subject leaving the study could be asked, in a nonthreatening way, for the reason. Also, the extent to which attrition is treatment-related can be described quantitatively. The attrition rate and various subject attribute variables can be tested as a function of the treatment variable during and at the end of the study.

The investigator should plan a back-up analysis when there is a possibility that treatment-related attrition will occur. The logical backup for an experiment consists of the various analyses associated with the nonequivalent group design for quasi-experimental inquiry. Since these analyses depend on adequate quantitative modeling of the ways in which the groups differ, the investigator anticipating attrition should always attempt to collect relevant subject attribute data before the study starts. Even if there is some question about the precise nature of final group differences in the presence of treatment-related attrition, it is still sometimes possible to draw conclusions if the general direction of those differences is known. Consider, for example, a simple treatment group versus control group comparison; if (a) it is clear that there has been systematic attrition and that the final control group is generally more able and motivated than the treatment group, and (b) the mean achievement for the treatment group is still higher than that for the control group, then there is little question about the superiority of the treatment group even though the exact degree of superiority cannot be determined.

4.3 Description for Validity

Detailed descriptions of subjects, treatments, and settings are a critical element in establishing the validity of conclusions from a study. The description of subject attributes provides a basis for establishing external validity, making covariate adjustments to improve power, determining if any attrition is treatment related, and conducting quasiexperimental analyses if necessary. Detailed description of each treatment as implemented is important for construct validity. It is of little value to know precisely the size of a treatment effect without knowing precisely what treatment was responsible for the effect. And, of course, it is not uncommon for a treatment as implemented to be very different from the treatment as planned. Description of the setting is valuable for external validity, with pertinent aspects including physical dimensions such as lighting and noise level and organizational characteristics like school discipline policy and grading procedures. Finally, the interaction of subjects with the treatments should be described in the search for unanticipated treatment effects. Such process description will also often provide important clues when the treatments are not working as expected.

In summary, the design of an experiment may include the considerations briefly discussed here plus many others. Design is further complicated by the possibility that attempts to minimize one threat to validity may simultaneously aggravate another threat. For example, the use of extensive observation and measurement to provide the detailed description suggested above may, because of associated distraction of the subjects, drastically alter the setting from the one of interest. Clearly, the optimal design of an inquiry can be a complex and subjective task, a process not easily represented by mechanical formulas or guidelines.

5. Statistical Analysis of Data

The appropriate analysis model for an experiment can often be found in the traditional analysis of variance (ANOVA) and analysis of covariance (ANCOVA) literature (e.g., Kirk 1968, Myers 1979, Winer 1971). There are many models and associated considerations of potential interest; only some can be mentioned here. For example, completely randomized ANOVA models like one-way ANOVA (for a single treatment variable) or a k-way factorial design (for k treatment variables) may be used when it is not necessary to include control variables. When control variables are required to ensure adequate power, many variations of the randomized block design and ANCOVA are available. Block designs may include multiple blocking variables, and when the numbers of treatment variables and levels increase, there are incomplete block and fractional replication

designs which provide efficient tests with blocks of reasonable size. ANCOVA models can also be elaborated by including multiple treatment variables and multiple covariates.

The simplicity of computations for these models will depend on the pattern of cell sizes in the design. All fixed effects ANOVA and ANCOVA models are special cases of the general linear model (e.g., Neter and Wasserman 1974). In general, it is not feasible to compute general linear model results by hand. However, the computational procedure simplifies drastically for ANOVA designs with only one factor or factorial designs with equal or unequal but proportional cell sizes, producing the simple computational equations found in standard ANOVA texts. On the other hand, when a factorial ANOVA/ANCOVA design has unequal and disproportionate cell sizes, the factors of the resulting "nonorthogonal" design are correlated, and the general computerized procedure for the linear model must be used for an exact solution.

It is not uncommon to find that the assumptions associated with standard analyses are violated for the study data at hand. Fortunately, there is evidence that significance tests are relatively robust to the violation of some assumptions. For example, moderate violations of the homogeneity of variance and normality assumptions in the presence of approximately equal cell sizes can usually be tolerated. In contrast, other violations may be more critical, requiring adjustments or use of a different analysis technique. Thus, drastic violations of the homogeneity and normality assumptions may require the consideration of transformations of the outcome variable or the use of an alternative analysis like generalized least squares or a nonparametric procedure. As another example, there may be evidence of the existence of an interaction between a treatment variable and a control variable, a violation of an important assumption in both the standard randomized block design with a cell size of one and the ANCOVA design. Interaction terms must then be added to the analysis model, using either a generalized randomized block design with cell size larger than one or a general linear model representation of ANCOVA. It should be noted that this last model no longer produces an ANCOVA in the conventional sense, but is identical to the aptitude–treatment–interaction (ATI) model mentioned briefly below. It may also be found in ANCOVA that the relationship between Y and the covariate is nonlinear, another violation of the standard analysis. Again, a general linear model with added polynomial terms would allow adequate fit of the model to study data.

There are some designs of interest in educational research and evaluation which are not fitted precisely by standard ANOVA/ANCOVA models. For example, ATI research attempts to identify and describe interactions between active instructional treatment variables and student aptitudes. An ATI analysis model would typically consist of a categorical treatment variable, one or more interval aptitude variables, and the necessary interaction terms. Another nonstandard design is one with interval treatment variables such as amount of study time allowed in class or the number of homework problems required. A general linear model with any required polynomial or interaction variables would allow the estimation of a multidimensional "response surface" describing the treatment effects.

Finally, there are sometimes multiple outcomes of interest in a study. Often, the investigator will simply conduct multiple analyses, one for each of the outcome variables. If the number of outcomes is relatively large, however, the investigator will be confronted with an inflation of error rate due to the many tests and a cumbersome and complex description based on numerous results. In this situation, the multivariate general linear model (e.g., Timm 1975) may be used. Multivariate global hypotheses and simultaneous inference procedures provide the necessary control of error rates and confidence levels, while the associated generalized discriminant analysis may provide a more parsimonious description of the effect in terms of derived optimal variates.

See also: Statistical Analysis in Educational Research; Multivariate Analysis

Bibliography

Bracht G, Glass G 1968 The external validity of experiments. *Am. Educ. Res. J.* 5: 437–74
Campbell D T, Stanley J C 1963 *Experimental and Quasi-experimental Designs for Research.* Rand McNally, Chicago, Illinois
Cohen J 1977 *Statistical Power Analysis for the Behavioral Sciences*, rev. edn. Academic Press, New York
Cook T D, Campbell D T 1979 *Quasi-experimentation: Design and Analysis Issues for Field Settings.* Rand McNally, Chicago, Illinois
Kerlinger F N 1973 *Foundations of Behavioral Research*, 2nd. edn. Holt, Rinehart and Winston, New York
Kirk R E 1968 *Experimental Design: Procedures for the Behavioral Sciences.* Brooks/Cole, Belmont, California
Myers J L 1979 *Fundamentals of Experimental Design*, 3rd edn. Allyn and Bacon, Boston, Massachusetts
Neter J, Wasserman W 1974 *Applied Linear Statistical Models: Regression, Analysis of Variance, and Experimental Designs.* Irwin, Homewood, Illinois
Phillips D C 1981 Toward an evaluation of the experiment in educational contexts. *Educ. Res.* AERA 10: 13–20
Timm N H 1975 *Multivariate Analysis with Applications in Education and Psychology.* Brooks/Cole, Monterey, California
Winer B 1971 *Statistical Principles in Experimental Design.* McGraw-Hill, New York

R. Tate

Externalities in Education

The external benefits of education are those benefits to society that are above and beyond the private benefits realized by the individual decision maker, that is, the student and the family. They are above and beyond both private monetary benefits, in the form of increased earnings due to education, and the private nonmonetary consumption benefits, both of which are captured by the decision maker and taken into account by him or her as the decision is made.

External benefits to others include, for example, those satisfactions of living in a society with functioning democratic institutions and their related freedoms, lower crime rates, more books, more newspapers, and more literature. The economy and the markets on which it depends function better when there is mathematical literacy, adaptability, and understanding. The increased earnings from education generate not only private benefits but also social benefits in the form of public goods paid for by these increased earnings, and also savings in public welfare costs. As a final illustration, research discoveries which depend on an educational base benefit persons other than the researcher, including future generations, in very substantial ways.

The survey of research on the external benefits and external costs of education which follows distinguishes these from the private monetary benefits of education and from the private (nonmonetary) consumption benefits of education, both of which are covered in separate entries (see *Consumption Benefits of Education*; *Benefits of Education*). It also will not cover the spillover effects of education, even though spillovers are one type of externality, because they are covered in a separate entry that focuses on geographical spillovers between decision-making jurisdictions (see *Spillovers in Education*). There are some external costs of education (e.g., smarter criminals) that are included in this survey, but they are frequently offset (e.g., smarter criminals but much lower crime rates), and hence relatively less important.

1. Research on Externalities in Education

There has been a remarkable amount of new research that seeks to measure specific types of external benefits of education. Much needs to be done however before more comprehensive measures of the value of these external benefits is available. It is a huge task, making use of shadow pricing and techniques for imputation that seek to estimate both the direct effects (e.g., better health) and then imputing the value of the benefits and/or the savings in costs (e.g., reduced medical costs), going beyond the taxonomy that has characterized the earlier stages of inquiry. It is the observation of external benefits, however, including observation by the reader, and not necessarily their measurement, that is crucial from an epistemological point of view to establish their existence.

Nevertheless, measurement does help. Great care is required, first, to avoid double counting. What appears to be an external benefit may sometimes be a private benefit for the student or the family. Purely distributional effects also must be eliminated—if some nonstudents gain at the expense of others, the net external benefits may be negligible.

A second caution when it comes to measurement is that the worst errors appear to be errors of omission. Some writers merely ignore external benefits. If their existence is admitted, and they are appraised to be positive and substantial, it then follows on purely efficiency grounds that there must be public tax support for education and/or other market corrections if economic efficiency within the system is to be attained. That is, unaided private decision makers who cannot capture external benefits will cause the quantity and quality of education produced to be too small, and Pareto optimality will not be attained.

The basic voting model which allows voters to observe these external benefits and to respond by voting public support to secure them was developed by Howard R. Bowen (1943), who has continued to be a leader in the identification and analysis of external benefits in education (Bowen 1971, 1977, 1980). Weisbrod (1962, 1964) has also pioneered in this field. There has since been a vast amount of new research seeking to measure specific benefits, the main lines of which are surveyed below under the main headings of benefits to society as a whole, and benefits within the neighborhood and workplace. The benefits of education per se to other family members are omitted here because the family rather than the student, especially at younger ages, is regarded as the basic decision unit. From this point of view they are not externalities, but private consumption benefits of education. Equity considerations also are not covered here. Equity is the other major basis for public support of both public and private education—for example, the provision of greater equality of educational opportunity for students coming from lower income families or students that are disadvantaged in other ways. Equity in educational finance is also discussed in a separate entry, and goes beyond purely efficiency considerations with which this entry is concerned (see *School Finance*).

2. External Benefits to Society at Large from Education

(a) *Necessary for effective democracy and democratic institutions.* Viewing education as the key to the preservation of democratic freedoms in government and other institutions, Thomas Jefferson felt that education should be the primary responsibility of the state, and sought to have governmental constitutions amended to that effect.

(b) *Important for efficient markets and the adaptation to technical change.* Schultz (1975 p. 843) refers to this as "the ability to deal successfully with economic disequilibria, which is enhanced by education, and . . . is one of the major benefits of education accruing to people in a modernizing economy." Some of these benefits of course are realized privately, but as markets function more honestly and respond to new technologies effectively others share in the benefits.

(c) *Lower crime rates and reduced penal system expense.* Spiegleman (1968) presents evidence that juveniles involved with education are less prone to commit juvenile crime. Webb (1977) finds a limited educational background among adult prison inmates, estimating the cost to society of deficiencies in their education at US$19.8 billion (1982 dollars) annually. Ehrlich (1975) finds a strong positive relation between inequalities in schooling, relative density of the poverty end of the family income distribution, and specific crimes against property. He stresses the inequalities in the distribution of schooling and training rather than their mean levels as related to the incidence of property and violent crimes. Finally, Phillips et al. (1972) show that labor market status, which is heavily influenced by education, is a sufficient factor to explain rising youth crime rates.

(d) *Lower welfare, medicaid, unemployment compensation, and public health costs.* Garfinkle and Haveman (1977 p. 53) find a strong negative relation between education of the head of the household and poverty status, with its associated welfare and medicaid costs. The value of the external benefits of education have not been estimated, however, in relation to the specific reduced costs for aid to dependent children, public housing, or medicaid. With respect to the effect of education on better health, a strong connection has been extensively documented by Lefocowitz (1973), Lando (1975), Orcutt et al. (1977), and Grossman (1982).

(e) *Reduced imperfections in capital markets.* Students with little collateral have limited capacity to borrow from banks to finance their own education without governmental guarantees of student loans and some interest rate subsidy. This rationale was developed by Hartman (1973) and is widely accepted—even by Freeman (1973) who has argued vigorously that there is "overeducation," partly by discounting the value of all other external benefits (Hartman 1973 pp. 322–27). There are some private benefits to the students involved here, but also some benefits to others in the form of reduced tax costs for education.

(f) *Public service in community and state agencies.* Every community and state has wide ranges of voluntary boards and commissions that benefit from the service of educated public spirited citizens. These include united fund campaigns, community development commissions, jury duty, family service agencies, hospital volunteers, community symphony boards, and many more. It seems most reasonable that many individuals display some altruism in their behavior, including charitable giving, which is being studied by Burton Weisbrod and others at the University of Wisconsin. Not all of this is purely self-serving; the services rendered and gifts in fact do benefit others. Political scientists have found that high-school and college graduates are more likely to participate in these kinds of community service activities, as well as political activities. Political activities can be purely self-serving of special interests, and in this case are not external benefits. McMahon (1984) has found that students do not weigh community service possibilities significantly in making their educational investment decisions, suggesting that they do not view them as private benefits.

(g) *Complementarities in production: Noneducational benefits*. Primary schools provide baby-sitting services to working mothers as a by-product of their educational activities, which Weisbrod (1962) has valued at US\$5 billion per year reexpressed in 1982 dollars. Drivers' education benefits not only the drivers, but also others who gain from a lower accident rate. Poor children and farmers benefit from school lunch programs, and community groups such as the Boy Scouts benefit from the low-cost use of school facilities.

3. Neighborhood and Employment-related Benefits

There has been less research on imputing a value for many of these:

(a) Neighborhood children display more socially acceptable behavior norms and offer better peer-group experiences (Weisbrod 1962).

(b) School closings cause adverse neighborhood effects, on which there has been research in specific localities.

(c) Leadership in charting new courses for society can have positive effects such as environmental improvements cited by Bowen (1977), as well as other neighborhood effects such as the draft riots in the late 1960s.

(d) In the workplace, Berg and Freedman (1977) argue that "overeducation" can lead to frustration in mundane tasks. Others more recently have suggested that as these tasks are "robotized," the worker can shift to tasks where education is more productive (e.g., programming the robots). Weisbrod (1962) suggests that there are also offsetting external benefits in the workplace in that the productivity, flexibility, and adaptability of each member of the group enhances the productivity of other members.

See also: Option Value in Education

Bibliography

Berg I E, Freedman M 1977 The American workplace: Illusions and realities. *Change* (November): 24–30
Bowen H R 1943 The interpretation of voting in the allocation of economic resources. *Q. J. Econ.* 58: 27–48. Revised in: Bowen H R 1948 *Toward Social Economy*. Rinehart, New York, Chap. 18
Bowen H R 1971 Appendix on the social benefits of higher education, In: Orwig M D (ed.) 1971 *Financing Higher Education: Alternatives for the Federal Government*, American College Testing Program, Iowa City, Iowa, pp. 168–70
Bowen H R 1977 *Investment in Learning: The Individual and Social Value of American Higher Education*. Jossey-Bass, San Francisco, California
Bowen H R 1980 *The Costs of Higher Education: How Much do Colleges Spend Per Student and How Much Should They Spend?* Jossey-Bass, San Francisco, California
Ehrlich I 1975 On the relation between education and crime. In: Juster F T (ed.) 1975 *Education, Income, and Human Behavior*. McGraw-Hill, New York
Freeman R B 1973 On mythical effects of public subsidization of higher education: In: Solmon L C, Taubman P J (eds.) 1973 *Does College Matter?* Academic Press, New York
Garfinkel I, Haveman R H 1977 *Earnings Capacity, Poverty, and Inequality*. Academic Press, New York
Grossman M 1982 Determinants of children's health. National Center for Health Services Research Report, PHS 81-3309 and NTIS P380-163603, Washington, DC
Hartman R W 1973 The rationale for federal support for higher education. In: Solmon L C, Taubman P J (eds.) 1973 *Does College Matter? Some Evidence on the Impacts of Higher Education*. Academic Press, New York, pp. 271–93
Lando M E 1975 The interaction between health and education. *Soc. Security Bull.* 38: 16–22
Lefocowitz M J 1973 Poverty and health: A reexamination. *Inquiry* 10(1): 3-13
McMahon W W 1982 Efficiency and equity criteria for educational budgeting and finance. In: McMahon W W, Geske T G (eds.) 1982 *Financing Education: Overcoming Inefficiency and Inequity*. University of Illinois Press, Urbana, Illinois, pp. 1–35
McMahon W W 1984 Why families invest in education. In: Sudman S, Spaeth M (eds.) 1984 *The Collection of Analysis of Economic and Consumer Behavior Data*. University of Illinois Press, Urbana, Illinois, Chap. 4
Orcutt G H, Franklin S D, Mendelsohn R, Smith J D 1977 Does your probability of death depend on your environment? A microanalytic study. *Am. Econ. Rev. Papers Proc.* 67: 260–64
Phillips L, Votey H L, Maxwell D 1972 Crime, youth, and the labor market. *J. Polit. Econ.* 80: 491–504
Schultz T W 1975 The value of the ability to deal with disequilibria. *J. Econ. Lit.* 13: 827–46

Spiegleman R G 1968 A benefit/cost model to evaluate educational programs. *Soc.-Econ. Plann. Sci.* 1: 443–60

Webb L D 1977 Savings to society by investing in adult education. In: *Economic and Social Perspectives on Adult Illiteracy*. State of Florida, State Department of Education, Tallahassee, Florida, pp. 52–73

Weisbrod B A 1962 Education and investment in human capital. *J. Polit. Econ.* 70 (Suppl.): 106–23

Weisbrod B A 1964 *External Benefits of Public Education: An Economic Analysis*. Research Report No. 105, Industrial Relations Section, Department of Economics, Princeton University, New Jersey, pp. 1–143

W. W. McMahon